"Human mobility, migration, dislocation and displacement present a challenge to established notions of language in use. In this book Suresh Canagarajah has met the challenge, doing justice to the multilingual realities of lives led on the move: he has assembled a stellar array of scholars who together present exciting new understandings and re-examinations of language in contexts of mobility. This wide-ranging, compelling volume could not be more timely."
James Simpson, University of Leeds, UK

"Ever since the cultural turn and the mobility turn in the social sciences, the study of language in migration studies has assumed new urgency. This Handbook is the place where I turn for stimulating and informed accounts of research. Beyond that, the contributions provide vital insights that, like its subject matter, transcend national borders and disciplinary boundaries."
Thomas Faist, Bielefeld University, Germany

"A terrific selection of articles by cutting edge scholars, useful for teachers, researchers and theorists across disciplines looking for an overview on language and migration. An excellent introduction to the field for both novices and experts."
Anne Whiteside, San Francisco State University, USA

The Routledge Handbook of Migration and Language

The Routledge Handbook of Migration and Language is the first comprehensive survey of this area, exploring language and human mobility in today's globalised world. This key reference brings together a range of interdisciplinary and multidisciplinary perspectives, drawing on subjects such as migration studies, geography, philosophy, sociology and anthropology. Featuring over 30 chapters written by leading experts from around the world, this book:

- Examines how basic constructs such as community, place, language, diversity, identity, nation-state, and social stratification are being retheorized in the context of human mobility;
- Analyses the impact of the 'mobility turn' on language use, including the parallel 'multilingual turn' and translanguaging;
- Discusses the migration of skilled and unskilled workers, different forms of displacement, and new superdiverse and diaspora communities;
- Explores new research orientations and methodologies, such as mobile and participatory research, multi-sited ethnography, and the mixing of research methods;
- Investigation of the place of language in citizenship, educational policies, employment and social services.

The Routledge Handbook of Migration and Language is essential reading for those with an interest in migration studies, language policy, sociolinguistic research and development studies.

Suresh Canagarajah is Edwin Erle Sparks Professor and Director of the Migration Studies Project in the Departments of Applied Linguistics and English at Pennsylvania State University, USA.

Editorial Advisory Board
Adrian Bailey, Hong Kong Baptist University, Hong Kong
Michael Baynham, Leeds University, UK
Adrian Blackledge, University of Birmingham, UK
Ingrid Piller, Monash University, Australia
Mastin Prinsloo, University of Cape Town, South Africa
Vai Ramanathan, University of California, Davis, USA

Routledge Handbooks in Applied Linguistics

Routledge Handbooks in Applied Linguistics provide comprehensive overviews of the key topics in applied linguistics. All entries for the handbooks are specially commissioned and written by leading scholars in the field. Clear, accessible and carefully edited *Routledge Handbooks in Applied Linguistics* are the ideal resource for both advanced undergraduates and postgraduate students.

For a full list of titles in this series, please visit www.routledge.com/Routledge-Handbooks-in-Applied-Linguistics/book-series/RHAL

The Routledge Handbook of Migration and Language
Edited by Suresh Canagarajah

The Routledge Handbook of Pragmatics
Edited by Anne Barron, Yueguo Gu and Gerard Steen

The Routledge Handbook of English Language Teaching
Edited by Graham Hall

The Routledge Handbook of Language Learning and Technology
Edited by Fiona Farr and Liam Murray

The Routledge Handbook of Language and Identity
Edited by Siân Preece

The Routledge Handbook of English for Academic Purposes
Edited by Ken Hyland and Philip Shaw

The Routledge Handbook of Language and Digital Communication
Edited by Alexandra Georgakopoulou and Tereza Spilioti

The Routledge Handbook of Literacy Studies
Edited by Jennifer Rowsell and Kate Pahl

The Routledge Handbook of Interpreting
Edited by Holly Mikkelson and Renée Jourdenais

The Routledge Handbook of Hispanic Applied Linguistics
Edited by Manel Lacorte

The Routledge Handbook of Educational Linguistics
Edited by Martha Bigelow and Johanna Ennser-Kananen

The Routledge Handbook of Migration and Language

Edited by Suresh Canagarajah

LONDON AND NEW YORK

First published 2017
by Routledge
2 Park Square, Milton Park, Abingdon, Oxon OX14 4RN

and by Routledge
711 Third Avenue, New York, NY 10017

Routledge is an imprint of the Taylor & Francis Group, an informa business

© 2017 selection and editorial matter, Suresh Canagarajah; individual chapters, the contributors

The right of the editor to be identified as the author of the editorial material, and of the authors for their individual chapters, has been asserted in accordance with sections 77 and 78 of the Copyright, Designs and Patents Act 1988.

All rights reserved. No part of this book may be reprinted or reproduced or utilised in any form or by any electronic, mechanical, or other means, now known or hereafter invented, including photocopying and recording, or in any information storage or retrieval system, without permission in writing from the publishers.

Trademark notice: Product or corporate names may be trademarks or registered trademarks, and are used only for identification and explanation without intent to infringe.

British Library Cataloguing-in-Publication Data
A catalogue record for this book is available from the British Library

Library of Congress Cataloging-in-Publication Data
A catalog record for this book has been requested

ISBN: 978-1-138-80198-1 (hbk)
ISBN: 978-1-315-75451-2 (ebk)

Typeset in Times New Roman
by Apex CoVantage, LLC
Printed and bound by CPI Group (UK) Ltd, Croydon, CR0 4YY

We dedicate this handbook to the millions
Excluded from nation-state borders and citizenship rights,
Inhabiting nebulous social spaces and uncertain futures,
Seeking homes away from environmental catastrophe,
discrimination, violence, and surveillance.

Contents

List of figures   *xii*
List of tables   *xiii*
Acknowledgements   *xiv*
List of contributors   *xv*

Introduction: the nexus of migration and language: the emergence of a disciplinary space   1
Suresh Canagarajah

PART I
Concepts   29

1. Translanguaging in mobility   31
   Adrian Blackledge and Angela Creese

2. Nation-state, transnationalism, and language   47
   Joseph Sung-Yul Park and Lionel Wee

3. Superdiversity and language   63
   Gabriele Budach and Ingrid de Saint-Georges

4. Neoliberalism, language, and migration   79
   Kori Allan and Bonnie McElhinny

5. Space, place, and language   102
   Christina Higgins

6. New orientations to identity in mobility   117
   Zhu Hua

7. Social class in migration, identity, and language research   133
   David Block

8 National and ethnic minorities: language rights and recognition 149
   Stephen May

PART II
Contexts **169**

9 Regional flows and language resources 171
   Ellen Hurst

10 Displacement and language 187
   Kathleen Heugh

11 Migration trajectories: implications for language proficiencies
    and identities 207
    Alla V. Tovares and Nkonko M. Kamwangamalu

12 Slavery, indentured work, and language 228
    Rajend Mesthrie

13 Settler migration and settler varieties 243
    Daniel Schreier, Nicole Eberle, and Danae M. Perez

14 Trade migration and language 258
    Huamei Han

15 Migrations, religions, and social flux 275
    Paul Badenhorst and Sinfree Makoni

16 Language in skilled migration 296
    Loy Lising

17 Rethinking (un)skilled migrants: whose skills, what skills, for what,
    and for whom? 312
    Cécile B. Vigouroux

18 Diaspora and language 330
    Jonathan Rosa and Sunny Trivedi

PART III
Methods **347**

19 Complexity, mobility, migration 349
    Jan Blommaert, Massimiliano Spotti, and Jef Van der Aa

20 Spatiotemporal scales and the study of mobility 364
   Mastin Prinsloo

21 Narrative in the study of migrants 381
   Anna De Fina and Amelia Tseng

22 Multisited ethnography and language in the study of migration 397
   Hilary Parsons Dick and Lynnette Arnold

23 Traveling texts, translocal/transnational literacies, and transcontextual analysis 413
   Catherine Kell

24 Intersections of necessity and desire in migration research: queering the migration story 431
   Mike Baynham

PART IV
Policies **449**

25 Citizenship, immigration laws, and language 451
   Kamran Khan and Tim McNamara

26 A rhizomatic account of heritage language 468
   E. K. Tan

27 Language-in-education policies and mobile citizens 486
   Beatriz P. Lorente

28 Mobility and English language policies and practices in higher education 502
   Jennifer Jenkins

29 Mobility, language, and schooling 519
   Margaret R. Hawkins and Anneliese Cannon

30 Communication practices and policies in workplace mobility 540
   Marta Kirilova and Jo Angouri

31 Language-mediated services for migrants: monolingualist institutional regimes and translinguistic user practices 558
   Maria Sabaté Dalmau, Maria Rosa Garrido Sardà, and Eva Codó

Index *577*

Figures

12.1	Multi-generational scenario of creole genesis	233
12.2	Comparison of six diagnostic features of seven varieties of overseas Bhojpuri-Hindi	239
29.1	The ecology of schooling	521
31.1	Written translinguistic user practices	569

Tables

12.1	Major languages of the North Indian immigrants in South Africa 1860–1911	237
12.2	Proportion of linguistic features shared by South African Bhojpuri-Hindi (SB) and different sets of antecedent Indian varieties	237
12.3	Regional variation in basic verb endings in the three dialects of Bhojpuri-Hindi in KwaZulu-Natal	238
28.1	Top ten destinations for international students	504

Acknowledgements

I thank the authors of the chapters for their patience in working through many drafts during the review, revision, and copyediting process.

In addition to the authors who reviewed each other's chapters, I thank additional invited scholars who reviewed the chapters pertaining to their expertise. The chapters were reviewed by the following: Jo Angouri, Adrian Bailey, Mike Banyam, Gary Barkhuizen, Rakesh Bhatt, Adrian Blackledge, David Block, Xiao Lan Curdt-Christiansen, Peter De Costa, Anna De Fina, Nelson Flores, Huamei Han, Margaret Hawkins, Kathleen Heugh, Christina Higgins, Marnie Holborow, Ellen Hurst, Dong Jie, Nkonko Kamwangamalu, Andy Kirkpatrick, Ryuko Kubota, Jerry Won Lee, Rebecca Lorimer Leonard, Loy Lising, Dorte Lønsmann, Sibusisiwe Makoni (nee Dube), Sinfree Makoni, Glenn Martinez, Stephen May, Tommaso Milani, Elizabeth Miller, Kathy Mortimer, Cynthia Nelson, Emi Otsuji, Joseph Park, John Pill, Ingrid Piller, Mastin Prinsloo, Vaidehi Ramanathan, Ben Rampton, Thomas Ricento, Thor Sawin, Edgar Schneider, Elana Shohamy, Massimiliano Spotti, Alla Tovares, Bonnie Urciuoli, Stephanie Vandrick, Lionel Wee, Li Wei, Rachel Wicaksono, Mary Shephard Wong, and Stanton Wortham.

My thanks also go to the editorial advisory board members for their help in shaping the organization and content of the handbook and in reviewing many of the chapters. Finally, I thank Helen Tredget and Nadia Seemungal of Routledge for their patience through this mammoth publishing project!

Suresh Canagarajah
Happy Valley, Pennsylvania.
USA.
November 8th, 2016.

Contributors

Kori Allan is SSHRC Postdoctoral Fellow at the University of Newcastle, Australia. She is also an affiliated researcher of 'Social Science for the C21st', led by Lisa Adkins at the University of Tampere and the University of Turku in Finland.

Jo Angouri is Associate Professor at the University of Warwick, UK. Her research expertise is in sociolinguistics, pragmatics, and discourse analysis, and her work concerns both online and face-to-face interaction. She has published work on language and identity as well as teamwork and leadership in professional settings. She has is currently working on a monograph tentatively called *Intercultural Communication at Work* (Routledge).

Lynnette Arnold received her PhD in sociocultural linguistics at the University of California, Santa Barbara. She currently serves as Lecturer in Linguistic Anthropology in the Department of Anthropology at the University of Massachusetts Amherst. Her research in sociocultural linguistics takes a multisited approach to the examination of language and mobility in transnational Latin American communities, with a focus on families from El Salvador.

Paul Badenhorst is a PhD candidate in Curriculum & Instruction and Comparative & International Education at Pennsylvania State University. His research approach includes exploring the dialogic intersection of structural positions of 'belonging' and post-structural interruptions of 'becoming' with regard to identity performativities. His passions include brewing 막걸리 – Korean rice wine – and pondering the significance of (re)presentations of the human face.

Mike Baynham is Professor of TESOL at the School of Education at the University of Leeds. His research interests include oral narrative. He is currently developing a research interest in Lesbian, Gay Bisexual, Transgender, and Queer (LGBTQ) issues in Adult ESOL and is co-investigator on the ESRC Seminar Series "Queering ESOL@ towards a cultural politics of LGBT issues in the Adult ESOL classroom" (2013–2015). He was also a consultant on the British Council Nexus Project "Exploring LGBT Lives in Adult ESOL" (2013–2014).

Adrian Blackledge is Professor of Bilingualism and Director of the MOSAIC Centre for Research on Multilingualism at the University of Birmingham, UK. He is the author of numerous articles and books based on his research on multilingualism in education and wider society. His latest books include *Heteroglossia as Practice and Pedagogy* (2014), *The Routledge Handbook of Multilingualism* (2012), and *Multilingualism. A Critical Perspective* (2010).

Contributors

David Block is ICREA Research Professor in Sociolinguistics at the University of Lleida (Spain). He has published on a variety of topics in applied linguistics and is currently examining issues around class, social movements, multiculturalism, and bi/multilingualism, drawing on scholarship in political economy, sociology, anthropology, and geography.

Jan Blommaert is Professor of Language, Culture, and Globalization; Director of the Babylon Center at Tilburg University, the Netherlands; and Professor of African Linguistics and Sociolinguistics at Ghent University, Belgium.

Gabriele Budach is an Associate Professor at the University of Luxembourg. Her research expertise is in sociolinguistics, multilingual education, social semiotics and multimodality. She has published work on multilingualism and social meaning making in education with a particular focus on the role of materiality and objects.

Anneliese Cannon works in language and literacy and teacher education at Westminster College in Salt Lake City, Utah. Her research interests include arts-based education and teaching and learning, mobility, and education in Western Europe and the United States, and arts-based qualitative research methods.

Eva Codó is Associate Professor of English Language and Linguistics at Universitat Autònoma de Barcelona. Her research, mostly ethnographic, centers on the critical study of multilingualism in various kinds of state and non-state institutions.

Angela Creese is Professor of Educational Linguistics at the School of Education, University of Birmingham, and is the principal investigator of the AHRC large grant "Translation and Translanguaging: Investigating Linguistic and Cultural Transformations in Superdiverse Wards in Four UK Cities." Her research interests are in linguistic ethnography, language ecologies, multilingualism in society, and multilingual classroom pedagogy.

Anna De Fina is Professor of Italian Language and Linguistics in the Italian Department and Affiliated Faculty with the Linguistics Department at Georgetown University. Her interests and publications focus on identity, narrative, migration, and diversity. Her books include *Identity in Narrative: A Study of Immigrant Discourse* (2003), *Analyzing Narratives* (co-authored with Alexandra Georgakopoulou), and the *Handbook of Narrative Analysis* (co-edited with Alexandra Georgakopoulou, 2015).

Ingrid de Saint-Georges is Associate Professor in Education/Sociolinguistics at the University of Luxembourg. She investigates communication, professional development, and learning. Her recently co-edited volumes include: *Multilingualism and Mobility in Europe: Policies and Practices* (2014) and *Multilingualism and Multimodality: Current Challenges for Educational Studies* (2013).

Hilary Parsons Dick is an Associate Professor of International Studies at Arcadia University. She received her Ph.D. in Anthropology from the University of Pennsylvania. She recently completed a tenure as a Wenner-Gren Hunt Fellow, during which she finished her book Words of Passage: National Belonging, Ethical Practice, and the Imagined Lives of Mexican Migrants (under contract, The University of Texas Press). She investigates Mexico-U.S.

migration from the perspectives of discourse analysis; the political economies of language; and gender, class, and ethno-racial relations.

Nicole Eberle is a graduate teaching and research assistant at the English Department of the University of Zurich. She received an MA in English Linguistics from the University of Zurich, and is currently working on her PhD on Bermudian English. She has been published in *English World-Wide*, and her research interests include language variation and change, and dialect contact, with a regional focus on the Caribbean.

Maria Rosa Garrido Sardà is a postdoctoral researcher at the Institute of Multilingualism, University of Fribourg (Switzerland). She holds a PhD in English Studies from the Universitat Autònoma de Barcelona (Catalonia, Spain).

Huamei Han is Associate Professor in the Faculty of Education at Simon Frasier University. Her research centers on language learning, multilingualism, and socioeconomic inclusion of linguistically marginalized individuals and groups in globalization, who often are also marginalized along the lines of race, class, religion, and gender.

Margaret R. Hawkins is Professor in the Department of Curriculum and Instruction at the University of Wisconsin–Madison. Her research focuses on languages and literacies in classroom, home, and community-based settings. Her published work examines classroom ecologies, families and schools, language teacher education, global digital partnerships for youth, and responses of new destination communities to mobile populations.

Kathleen Heugh is Associate Professor in Applied Linguistics at the University of South Australia. She is a socio-applied linguist whose research has mostly focused on multilingual policies and education practices in sub-Saharan Africa. This includes fieldwork in remote, post-conflict settings. She uses multilingual and translanguaging pedagogies in her teaching at the University of South Australia.

Christina Higgins is Associate Professor in Second Language Studies at the University of Hawaii at Manoa. She is interested in multilingual practices, globalization, and identity, drawing on discourse analytic, ethnographic, and qualitative approaches to study various facets of the global spread of English, Swahili variation, and multilingual identities. Much of this work is synthesized in her book *English as a Local Language: Post-colonial Identities and Multilingual Practices* (2009).

Zhu Hua is Professor of Applied Linguistics and Communication and Head of Department at Birkbeck College, University of London, UK. Her main research interests are intercultural pragmatics, language and intercultural communication, and child language development. Her most recent books include *Exploring Intercultural Communication: Language in Action* (2014), *Research Methods in Intercultural Communication* (2016), and *Crossing Boundaries* (2016).

Ellen Hurst works as a senior lecturer in the Humanities Education Development Unit at the University of Cape Town where she teaches academic literacies, discourses, and genres. Her research interests are concerned with multilingualism and style in African languages, with a special focus on youth and urban varieties, language and migration, language and globalisation, and language and higher education.

Contributors

Jennifer Jenkins holds the Chair of Global Englishes at Southampton University. She has conducted research into English as a Lingua Franca since the 1980s (most recently, into English as a Multilingua Franca in academic settings) and has published copiously in this field as well as authoring a university coursebook on Global Englishes.

Nkonko M. Kamwangamalu is Professor at Howard University, Washington, DC. He is co-editor of *Current Issues in Language Planning*, author of *The Language Planning Situation in South Africa*, author of *Language Policy and Economics* (forthcoming), and author of articles on language planning, multilingualism, code-switching, and African linguistics.

Catherine Kell is Associate Professor in Language and Literacy Education in the School of Education at the University of Cape Town, South Africa. She works in digital literacies and has published on the sociolinguistics of mobility. She co-edited a Special Issue of *Social Semiotics* in 2015 on *Language and Objects in Trans-Contextual Analysis*.

Kamran Khan is an ESRC research associate at the University of Leicester, working on the 'The UK Citizenship Process: Exploring Immigrants' Experiences' project. He completed his PhD at the University of Birmingham (UK) and University of Melbourne (Australia).

Marta Kirilova is a research associate at the Center for Internationalisation and Parallel Language Use and the Department of Nordic Studies and Linguistics at the University of Copenhagen. Her current research interests include linguistic and cultural norms in gatekeeping institutional settings.

Loy Lising is honorary associate at the Department of Linguistics, Macquarie University, Australia. She was previously the program coordinator for the Master of Crosscultural Communication program at University of Sydney. Loy's research interests lie in the nexus of multilingualism, skilled migration, and intercultural communication.

Beatriz P. Lorente is a lecturer at the Department of English of the University of Basel and a postdoctoral fellow at the Institute of Multilingualism of the University of Fribourg. Her research interests are in language and globalization, language and migration, and language policy.

Bonnie McElhinny is Associate Professor of Anthropology and Women and Gender Studies at the University of Toronto. Recent publications include *Words, Worlds, Material Girls: Language and Gender in a Global Economy* (2008) and *Filipino Lives in Canada: Spectres of Invisibility* (2012).

Tim McNamara is Professor in Applied Linguistics at the University of Melbourne. His work on language and identity has focused on poststructuralist approaches to identity and subjectivity, and the writings on language of the French philosopher Jacques Derrida. He is the author of *Language Testing* (2000) and co-author (with Carsten Roever) of *Language Testing: The Social Dimension* (2006). He is currently working on a book titled *Language and Subjectivity* and (with Ute Knoch) a new book, *Rasch Measurement in Second Language Assessment*.

Sinfree Makoni is a pan-Africanist. He was educated in Ghana and Edinburgh. He has lived and taught in a number of universities in southern Africa. He is currently Associate Professor at the Department of Applied Linguistics and the program in African Studies at Pennsylvania State University.

Stephen May is Professor of Education in Te Puna Wananga (School of Maori Education) in the Faculty of Education and Social Work, University of Auckland, New Zealand. He has written widely on language rights, language policy, and language education and has, to date, published fifteen books and over ninety academic articles and book chapters in these areas.

Rajend Mesthrie is Professor of Linguistics at the University of Cape Town, where he holds a National Research Foundation (NRF) chair on Migration, Language, and Social Change. Among his publications are *Language in South Africa* (2002), *World Englishes* (with Rakesh Bhatt, 2008), *A Dictionary of South African Indian English* (2010) and the more "popular" book, *Eish, But Is It English: Celebrating the South African Variety* (with the journalist Jeanne Hromnik 2011). He is a current co-editor of the Cambridge University Press journal *English Today*.

Joseph Sung-Yul Park is Associate Professor in the Department of English Language and Literature at the National University of Singapore. He is a sociolinguist working in the areas of linguistic anthropology and interactional linguistics, and his current research focuses on various aspects of language and globalization, including linguistic identity and migration.

Danae M. Perez is a postdoctoral research and teaching associate at the University of Zurich. In her research she focuses on the linguistic, social, and cultural processes triggered by the contact between communities of different linguistic and ethnic origins.

Mastin Prinsloo is Emeritus Professor in the School of Education at the University of Cape Town (UCT). His recent research has been around language, literacy, and diversity. His co-edited books include *Language, Literacy and Diversity: Moving Words* (2015); *Educating for Language and Literacy Diversity: Mobile Selves* (2014); *Literacy Studies* (5 vols., 2013); *The Future of Literacy Studies* (2009); *Literacies, Local and Global* (2008) and *The Social Uses of Literacy* (1996). He has most recently published research articles in *TESOL Quarterly*; *Journal of Multilingual and Multicultural Development*; and in *Language and Education*.

Jonathan Rosa is Assistant Professor in the Graduate School of Education and Center for Comparative Studies in Race and Ethnicity at Stanford University. His research combines sociocultural and linguistic anthropology to theorize the co-naturalization of language and race.

Maria Sabaté Dalmau is a lecturer in the English and Linguistics Department at the University of Lleida (Catalonia, Spain), where she conducts research on multilingualism and migration and transnationalism from a critical sociolinguistic perspective, within the research group Circle of Applied Linguistics.

Daniel Schreier is Professor for English Linguistics at the University of Zurich. His research focus lies in variationist sociolinguistics and contact-induced language change, with a focus on English in the South Atlantic Ocean, and he has published in journals such as *Language Variation and Change, Journal of Sociolinguistics, Diachronica, American Speech, English*

World-Wide, and *Language in Society*. He is co-editor of *English World-Wide: A Journal of Varieties of English*.

Massimiliano Spotti is a lecturer in Sociolinguistics at the Department of Culture Studies at Tilburg University, the Netherlands and Deputy Director of Babylon, Centre for the Study of Superdiversity at the same institution. His research deals with the institutional responses to the (linguistic and cultural) complexity brought to bear in online and offline phenomena by superdiversity with a specific focus on asylum seeking.

E. K. Tan is Associate Professor of Comparative Literature and Cultural Studies in Cultural Analysis and Theory at Stony Brook University. He is the author of *Rethinking Chineseness: Translational Sinophone Identities in the Nanyang Literary World* (2013).

Alla V. Tovares is Associate Professor at Howard University, Washington, DC. She is the co-author of *How to Write about the Media Today* (2010). Her articles have appeared in *Text and Talk, Narrative Inquiry, Journal of Language and Social Psychology*, and *World Englishes*.

Sunny Trivedi is a graduate student in the Department of Anthropology at Purdue University. His research interests include ethnoracial category-making, language ideologies, diasporic formations, and (im)migrant socialization.

Amelia Tseng is lecturer and director of Bilingual Education in the School of Education and Affiliated Faculty in the Center for Latin American and Latino Studies at the American University. Her research focuses on language, identity, and mobility in multilingual immigrant communities and has been recognized through awards from the National Science Foundation, Georgetown University, and the Society for Applied Anthropology.

Jef Van der Aa is a postdoctoral researcher at the Department of Cultural Studies, Tilburg University. He is currently active in linguistic and psychological anthropology with a special focus on migrant and refugee youth narratives. He was also the 2011–2012 Daytal L. Kendall Library Fellow at the American Philosophical Society, researching the oeuvre of Dell Hymes.

Cécile B. Vigouroux is Associate Professor of Sociolinguistics at Simon Fraser University. She has widely published on different aspects of language and transnational African migrations to South Africa. Her current research is on the intersection of language and economy.

Lionel Wee is Professor in the Department of English Language and Literature at the National University of Singapore. His research focuses on language policy, new varieties of English, and general issues in sociolinguistics and pragmatics. He is also interested in general sociological issues, where he works on the sociology of emotions, urbanization, and consumption.

Introduction
The nexus of migration and language
The emergence of a disciplinary space

Suresh Canagarajah

This handbook explores the interface between language and human mobility, which is gaining considerable geopolitical significance and generating scholarly inquiry. While language and semiotic resources are becoming important in mediating, regulating, and shaping migrant processes, mobility is also motivating a lot of rethinking on the understanding of language uses and forms. As scholars from the humanities and social sciences undertaking migration studies are beginning to address the role of language, applied linguists are borrowing from constructs in migration studies to understand communicative practices in mobile contexts. Such work is taking place in different academic and social spaces as it relates to particular themes and issues of interest to diverse scholars. This handbook endeavors to home in on the language/mobility nexus so that interdisciplinary scholars can take stock of the emergent scholarship for critical reflection and further development.

Published under a series in applied linguistics (i.e., Routledge Handbooks in Applied Linguistics), this volume's disciplinary scope is somewhat bounded. The handbook brings together scholars in the field of applied linguistics (including cognate fields like sociolinguistics, anthropological linguistics, literacy, language policy and planning, and language teaching) to review the way language/migration nexus shapes their work. The handbook doesn't feature scholars from other fields in the humanities and social sciences (such as comparative literature, geography, sociology, or anthropology) who are engaged in studying mobility, though their work has significantly influenced the scholarship and theorization of applied linguists represented here. The purpose of the handbook then is to critically reflect on how applied linguists study the language/migration nexus in order to sharpen their tools, methods, and theoretical frames. Scholars in other fields will find the linguistic constructs presented in the handbook useful to conduct their own work. Additionally, the handbook introduces scholars from the cognate fields within applied linguistics to the work in their own discipline, as applied linguists in diverse parts of the world studying this nexus don't necessarily enjoy a shared scholarly identity or disciplinary space.

Migration and language

Why has the language/migration nexus emerged as significant? Scholars are talking about a "mobility turn" or "mobilities paradigm" in diverse disciplines (Urry 2000; Buscher, Urry, and Witchger 2011; Faist 2013). Though it is not a new experience, migration has attracted considerable recent attention due to new social, technological, and geopolitical developments. These developments have intensified the space/time compression (Harvey 2005) we see in contemporary social life. Texts, languages, and semiotic resources are crossing boundaries easily as diverse temporal and geographical zones are brought closer. People too are shuttling across borders more frequently, thanks to these developments. As the mobility of things and ideas as well as people intensifies in relation to these changes, territorialized (i.e., spatially rooted and circumscribed) ways of conducting social ties, identities, and community life are receiving less significance. Transcending localized, physically fixed, and placed definitions, we are aware of fluid, changing, and socially constructed ways in which these features are defined. Distant and virtual forces shape identities, communities, and social ties. In this context, language and semiotic resources become important for how these social constructs and experiences are defined and practiced. For example, my identity as a Sri Lankan Tamil, my ties with people belonging to this group, and our collective identity are primarily established and experienced through communicative media (i.e., via telephone, email, Skype, and FaceTime). This is because we live in different lands nowadays, having fled Sri Lanka during its ethnic conflict, losing the luxury of constant and direct physical contact. Even family life is transnational and semiotic. My siblings and I conduct our family life through digital media, as we live in different time zones and national borders in the UK, United States, Australia, and Sri Lanka. Language thus gains significance as a resource that mediates, shapes, and builds such relationships. It is not that language didn't play this role before in history. It is simply that its role is more salient now, in the context of the facilities that enable us to compress the space/time diffusion.

This compression has also given importance to "simultaneity" (Levitt and Glick Schiller 2004: 1003). Beyond crossing boundaries, we are able to collapse boundaries, and bring to bear diverse ties, identities, and communities on a single interaction or relationship. These relationships of "layered simultaneity" (Blommaert 2005: 237) also gain a semiotic dimension, enabled primarily by language and communication. From this perspective, one enjoys multiple identities and community memberships, which might gain salience differently in mobile interactions, further challenging territorialized, essentialized, and primordial ways of defining such social relationships. We are also able to conduct social ties and activities in diverse locations at the same time, drawing from multiple identities simultaneously, transcending our physical location.

Such developments are contributing to relationships and affiliations that are diversified and changing, built on hybrid and fluid semiotic resources. Social scientists have coined a new term, *superdiversity* (Vertovec 2007), to describe the more fluid forms of community being established by migrant communities in European urban spaces. People from diverse national and ethnic groups that settle in an urban space are able to form new communities with mixed features from their languages becoming a new shared repertoire to conduct their social life in the new habitation. These superdiverse communities are more layered and mixed compared to the separated ethnic enclaves that characterized previous waves of migrant settlement. Other terms such as *diaspora* are also being used in more expansive ways to index the experience of newer and more diverse migrant groups spread beyond their traditional homelands (Hall 1997). *Cosmopolitanism* is being adopted to index the dispositions that facilitate cultural and linguistic engagement between diverse communities in contexts of mobility (Vertovec and Cohen 2002).

Migration and language have also received new impetus in the contemporary neoliberal economy built on production and marketing relationships that value mobile workers, capital, and products, facilitated by cross-border flows. To facilitate these flows, language has become an important form of human capital. Communicative repertoires are critical for enabling and managing such production and marketing. An important dimension of this form of economy is labor migration (Kuznetsov 2006). Talented people from diverse countries are encouraged to move across borders by industries in developed communities to contribute to their technological innovation. Language and communication become important for this domain as well, as workers from different nationalities collaborate in shared workplaces and production and marketing networks. Furthermore, the primary means of production in the neoliberal economy has shifted to tertiarization (Heller and Duchene 2012). Departing from the earlier focus on obtaining raw materials for industrialization, and the secondary stage of synthetic production, the focus of current production is on symbolic work. Tertiarization involves work on innovation, branding, client service, and marketing, all providing an important role for language and communication, in globally expansive economic relationships. Consider that in earlier forms of industrialization talk was censored and punished on the factory floor (Boutet 2012). What was expected then was physical labor for efficient material production. Now talk is encouraged as workers are expected to think outside the box to innovate and brand products in creative ways for the global multilingual market. For all these reasons, language repertoires have become an important form of human capital in neoliberal forms of mobility.

While language is important for mobility, mobility has also changed our understanding of language. Here again, it is not that the forms and functions of language being theorized are new. Mobility has simply made visible new communicative practices. Scholars are attempting to document, analyze, and theorize these practices with new terms and constructs. While I will discuss these new realizations later, it is good to introduce here the many new terms being coined and the debates regarding their relevance. Paralleling the "mobility turn," applied linguists now talk of a "multilingual turn" (May 2014). To index the more intense forms of contact that transcend labeled, territorialized, and separated languages, and the synergy of new meanings and grammars being generated through this mobility of codes, some scholars have adopted the term *translanguaging* (see Blackledge and Creese, this volume). Other labels such as *plurilingualism* (García 2009), *metrolingualism* (Pennycook and Otsuji 2015), and *transidiomaticity* (Jacquemet 2005) have also been coined by applied linguists, befitting their purposes and contexts, for roughly the same idea. As people borrow language features from diverse communities to index new identities and affiliations in mobility, even when they don't have full or advanced competence in the borrowed language, Rampton (2008) has coined terms such as *crossing* and *styling* to refer to this activity. Blommaert (2010) has coined the term *truncated multilingualism* for a competence that involves adopting bits and pieces of diverse languages for communicative functions in diverse migrant spaces.

We have to be cautious of claiming any kind of novelty to what is being indexed by these neologisms in this disciplinary space (see Pavlenko forthcoming for a critique). Though some scholars have treated sedentariness as traditional and mobility as modern (Zelinsky 1971), others have demonstrated that mobility is not a new human experience. There have been different, but equally complex, forms of mobility, transnationalism, and globalization in the past (Hoerder 2002; Faist, Fauser, and Reisenauer 2013: chap. 3; Han this volume), including in premodern times (Anthony 1990, 2007; Cameron 2013). Similarly, languages have always been in contact, generating synergies of new meaning and grammar (see examples from before modernity and colonization in Pollock 2006; Canagarajah 2013: chap. 3). As Faist et al. (2013) argue, recent social and technological changes have simply intensified mobility, contact, and diversity rather than initiating them. However, this new visibility has changed the discourse in productive ways. In the place of territorialized, bounded, and static ways of talking about language and social practices, we are now adopting constructs that index their mobile, hybrid, and constructed nature. It is the discourse that is new, not the migration experience. Attempts to move inquiry beyond static, primordialist, and territorialized perspectives do require a creative and meaningful language. While acknowledging that mobility and translanguaging are not new human experiences, I see a need to construct new terms and models to correct the previously reductive discourses in scholarship and inquiry.

Rather than romanticize mobility as novel, what needs to be examined is the changing configurations of boundaries and flows in different social formations through history. There have always been policies and institutions that regulated flows to serve the interests of different social groups. There have never been unrestricted possibilities or unqualified scope for mobility. Therefore, Faist (2013) paradoxically states that mobility is a form of boundary management. Boundaries have always channeled mobility in particular ways for different groups of people. Consider, for example, the capitalist formation accompanying modernity. Capitalism found mobility useful for the economic and social world it was constructing, facilitating greater mobility for the middle class, relative to the restrictions of feudalism. The previous feudal order thrived on a more stable noble/vassal relationship, with caste-like reification of social hierarchies reproduced through generations, in privately owned land. Mobility unleashed the potential for knowledge and entrepreneurship by freeing many from the static and permanent feudal relationships and the bounded places they were locked in. However, precisely because of this social fluidity, mobility had to be regulated. Mechanisms had to be set up to protect capital, property, and ownership. Nation-states and citizenship territorialized subjects and identities. As I will argue later, the ideologies and discourses promoted by modernity were motivated by controlled mobility. Similarly, though the late-modern formation characterized by contemporary neoliberalism might appear to provide more scope for mobility across borders, it comes with its own boundaries to channel the flows in specific ways, giving access to certain people to certain spaces, as I will discuss in detail later.

Migration and mobility

Before we discuss the ways migration studies and applied linguistics have influenced each other to generate new theoretical constructs and analytical methods, a word about the connection between migration and mobility. The title of this handbook references migration rather than mobility. This is because the handbook focuses specifically on human mobility. Mobility as a general term includes the movement of many other resources and objects beyond human agents. The circulation of capital, products, information, and knowledge are part of the general term of mobility. A handbook on mobility, therefore, would feature different topics and scholarship than those represented in this one. This handbook places the spotlight on human mobility. Though the contributors to this handbook do discuss the ways diverse factors participate and are implicated in human mobility, they are not focusing on them for their own sake. As they consider the geographical movement of people, the contributors are interested in examining how applied linguistics can be informed by broader paradigms of spatiotemporal mobility.

There are other distinctions we need to be aware of in the way the term *migration* is used in order to appreciate the scope of the term *mobility*. In policy and public discourse, the privileged who enjoy the resources and access for travel are considered mobile, and the less privileged are referred to as migrants. The mobile are welcome everywhere and have the resources to shuttle across borders as they please; migrants seek opportunities and refuge elsewhere. Reflecting on the biases behind this distinction, Faist (2013: 1640) observes:

> In the welfare-competition state, the movement of persons is dichotomized in public debate into mobility and migration, with mobility connoting euphemistic expectations of gain for individuals and states, and migration calling for social integration, control and the maintenance of national identity.

It is important to problematize the distinction between these terms, and examine questions of inequality in mobility in this handbook.

We have to also distinguish between vertical and horizontal mobility. This handbook is primarily concerned with horizontal (that is, geographical and spatial) mobility. Note, however, that mobility has also been used as synonymous with social (i.e., class and, thus, vertical) mobility in some scholarly contexts (see, for example, Graff 1991). Furthermore, vertical mobility has been implicated in horizontal mobility. There are social discourses that associate the desire for or possibility of geographical mobility as a sign of social/class mobility. Being sedentary or rooted is associated with lack of resources, being conservative, or the refusal to better one's prospects. Reflecting this bias, Bauman notes: "Local in a globalized world is a sign of social deprivation and degradation" (Bauman 1998: 2–3). This distinction too must be problematized. Geographical mobility doesn't always lead to social mobility. Many types of geographical mobility (including labor, climate-induced or conflict-driven displacement, and political exile) result in people ending up in worse economic and social status than what they enjoyed before migration. Though focused on horizontal mobility, this handbook examines the unequal chances for different migrant groups in vertical mobility (see Block, this volume).

Finally, both mobility and migration are volitional in connotation. The terms assume agency on the part of those moving outside their usual habitations. Traditionally, push/pull factors have been adopted to explain such human movement (Anthony 2007). While some factors, such as lack of opportunities for social or economic betterment serve as push factors, the possibility of advancement in the new places of habitation serve as pull factors. However, there are many migrant groups that have moved involuntarily in history. In consideration of these groups that experienced only push factors, usually of the most life-threatening kind, some scholars have preferred less volitionist terms such as "population circulation" (see Schachner 2010; Cameron 2013). Though the handbook uses the term *migration*, several contributions explore involuntary displacement to provide a balanced perspective.

Theoretical shifts

The greater visibility of mobility, and attendant social and communicative changes, has generated epistemological shifts that have affected social sciences and linguistics alike. Treating "mobility as method," we must approach mobility as not just a topic to be discussed under existing paradigms, but explore how it shapes the way we study and interpret social and communicative practices. In framing it thus, I follow Mezzadra and Neilson (2013), who coin "border as method" to explore borders not only as a research object but also as an epistemic framework, with illuminating outcomes. I now outline these theoretical shifts in applied linguistics before identifying the analytical constructs and methods emerging for the study of language and communication. Though inspired by mobility, these constructs are beginning to have an impact on all aspects of language studies beyond the theme of migration.

The dominant discourses of modernity promoted paradigms that assumed territorialization, structure, and stability. They were influenced by such geopolitical developments as nation-state formation, private property, and colonization which had an interest in fixing communities and individuals in particular locations and identities despite (or because of) the increasing mobility unleashed by technological changes. As a specific example of the discourses of modernity, consider the "Herderian triad" (Bauman and Briggs 2000). This ideology made an equation between language, community, and place. In effect, German language identifies the German people who are placed in the nation-state of Germany. The language represents the spirit of the people which emerges from the soil of the land. Those who speak this language from elsewhere are therefore interlopers, as they cannot represent the spirit of the land that informs the language and its people. As we can see, this ideology territorializes language. Language is also turned into a static system that cannot move to other places or locations without losing its essential character. Many effects follow – and are still with us. People are located in specific lands/places with the language that naturally belongs to them. A person migrating from Turkey in childhood and speaking German as her most proficient language would perhaps still be considered an interloper in the language, unable to represent the original or pure spirit and values of the Germans in their language, thus considered a "non-native speaker." As we can see, the Herderian triad accounts for ideological constructs such as native speakerism, language ownership, essentialized/unitary identities, and exclusive/bounded community memberships.

Mobility disturbs many of the assumptions behind the Herderian triad. As people move across borders, they are taking their languages with them and also appropriating new semiotic resources for their identities and communication. With such changes, we must also go beyond considering each person as an owner of a single language. It is possible for speakers to claim intimate and proficient relationship with multiple languages simultaneously. We should be open to considering how diverse languages might represent hybrid, changing, and situated identities for individuals. We should also grapple with changing configurations of community relationships and affiliations for individuals. More importantly, people's social ties extend beyond local communities and physical boundaries to occupy *transnational social fields* (i.e., spaces that transcend nation-states; Faist et al. 2013). As the locus of social ties beyond national borders or physical places, these spaces might be imagined, socially constructed, and semiotically mediated. In other words, language plays an important role in establishing and enabling transnational social fields.

As people's relationship with territorialization changes, place itself is getting diversified. Scholars have begun to study the dynamic relationship between place and space. Though variously defined (see Higgins, this volume), virtual *space* sediments into geographical *place* through ongoing human activity; however, there are social *spaces* people construct to establish alternate and oppositional communities, countering the dominant groups and traditional norms of a *place*. These distinctions help us also move beyond territorialized constructs and consider home making, community formation, and place making as ongoing activities in mobility, often mediated and regulated by language. These considerations also allow us to redefine the language implications for identity and community. We treat these constructs as mediated and constructed by language, not independent of them, allowing for changing, mobile, and situated representations of identity and community.

Just as people's relationships with languages change with mobility, our understanding of language is also changing. This is because not only people, but language is also mobile, whether accompanied by people or not. Mobility has challenged the static, objective, and bounded ways in which we perceived social or communicative activities. Structuralism, arguably the legacy of linguistics to many other fields such as sociology and anthropology, motivated scholars to treat language as a sui generis system that explained its own coherence in the way it was tightly structured, without the need to consider other domains such as society, culture, history, or geography. In adopting this framework, language was turned into a static, abstract, and autonomous system suitable for objective analysis. This tendency has also led to perceiving each labeled language as having its own system, separated from others. Similar shifts occurred in other fields in relation to their objects of inquiry, such as social structure or cultural systems, which were treated as autonomous and stable.

In the context of mobility, scholars are considering languages unbound – that is, they are endeavoring to understand the flows across time and space of semiotic resources, unfettered from an imposed structure. In order to do so, they treat these resources (of which verbal resources are also a part) as floating signifiers. They can be appropriated by people in a specific time and place for their meaning-making purposes. They become sedimented into grammars, and index values and norms over time, through a history of social use. Such a perspective would resist the territorialization of labeled languages as belonging to one place or community, with static norms and meanings deriving from a preconstructed structure. This shift is behind Blommaert's claim that we should perceive communication as shaped by "mobile resources" and not "immobile languages" (2010: 49). From this perspective, we shouldn't treat labeled languages as the starting point for the analysis of social and communicative practices. We should consider how diverse verbal resources (unrestricted by their labels) are taken up by people to establish meanings and negotiate relationships. The metaphor of resources also adds a functional perspective to the study of language. Communicative activity is the framework within which language forms should be analyzed. Norms and meanings emerge in relation to the functions people perform in situated interactions. This effort to go beyond labeled, autonomous, and separate languages, and consider the synergy between verbal resources in meaning-making activity, is behind the shift to translanguaging.

As we treat communicative activities as facilitated by mobile resources, we are also paying more attention to the way language works in tandem with diverse semiotic resources, social networks, and material conditions to produce meaning. Beyond questioning labeled languages as autonomous, we are now ready to consider language itself as embedded in social and material features, thus questioning the autonomy of language as a meaning-making system. In addition to including diverse semiotic resources in our consideration of meaning, we are also treating meaning as multimodal and multisensory, by including affective, imaginative, aesthetic, and material considerations in our analysis. It is in this way that we are able to explain the communicative success of "truncated multilingualism" and "styling." Since verbal resources are aligned with other social and material affordances to make meaning, a full and advanced competence in a single language is not required. Migrants are able to use the available verbal resources strategically, in relation to the diverse and social ecological affordances in their context, for effective communication that might deviate from the norms of native speakers or grammar books.

These orientations on language as a mobile resource are moving us away from the structuralist tradition that treated language as an autonomous and perhaps superior system for meaning-making. We are learning a lot from models that resist structuring to understand meaning-making practices. Many of these models have been better articulated in fields beyond linguistics, such as the social sciences or philosophy. Influenced by practice-based orientations (De Certeau 1984), we are treating communication as an activity. Such a functionalist orientation enables us to consider how norms and meanings emerge in relation to the situated and social functions people perform over space and time. In adopting this perspective, we are also open to considering meanings and norms as shaped by an "assemblage" of diverse resources. Drawing from this construct articulated by Deleuze and Guattari (1987) and Latour (2005), we now consider diverse social networks, ecological resources, and material objects as going into the construction of meaning in dynamic ways. We benefit from a "flat ontology" (Marston, Jones, and Woodward 2005), to guard against prioritizing specific factors, such as cognition or language, as more important than others for meaning-making activity. We consider all the factors that contribute to the emergence or construction of meaning without preconstructed boundaries, exclusions, or hierarchies. We distinguish the assemblages that gain changing significance in situated activities and are open to the different affordances and resources that contribute to meaning. From these perspectives, we are also reconsidering the place of material resources in social and communicative life. Posthumanist thinking and object-oriented ontologies have made us aware of the agency of things and objects (Barad 2007; Braidotti 2013), and the way they shape cognition and communication. We cannot treat material resources as inactive or merely instrumental for human communicative interests. Things have a life of their own, and significantly influence human thinking and communicative activity.

As we thus treat verbal and semiotic resources as mobile and situate them in spatial and temporal contexts, removed from their autonomy in predefined and abstract structures, applied linguists are searching for theoretical paradigms beyond structuralism. Many scholars are persuaded to adopt a spatial paradigm as better attuned to mobility. Influenced by the thinking of geographers (like Massey 2005; Thrift 2007), the spatial orientation to communication would involve the following assumptions:

- Acknowledge space as agentive, shaping social activities in significant ways;
- Treat space as diverse, dynamic, and changing, involving reconfigurations of space and place;
- Consider communication as an activity embedded fully in the environment, situated in space/time conditions;
- Understand communicative activities as fully material, treating diverse objects, artifacts, and physical nature as shaping meaning;
- Take into consideration all the affordances and constraints in the context (i.e., diverse semiotic resources, social networks, and material conditions) as equally shaping the communicative activity.

As we treat space as the starting point of our analysis of communicative activities, or orientate to space as the locus and frame of our inquiry into meaning, this shift enables us to problematize other constructs such as language, community, nation-state, and human cognition. It helps scholars consider the emergence of these constructs they traditionally took for granted or defined before the analysis (see Glick Schiller and Caglar 2011b who adopt a similar approach towards urban migration). Constructs such as identities, community, and meaning can be considered for the manner in which they are put together through diverse material, social, and ecological factors, or emerge as an assemblage through diverse semiotic resources.

Spatiality enables us to counteract the dominant "metaphysics of presence" (Buscher et al. 2011: 5), which treats only those phenomena that are immediate, local, and physical as worthy of analysis. Those that are not immediately available to the senses are not treated as shaping talk or texts in this approach. The metaphysics of presence is also informed by the modernist bias towards empirical and positivist inquiry. However, as we grapple seriously with simultaneity, we are aware that factors in other times and places influence meaning-making and social activities. We cannot discount the influence of factors that are invisible, distant, or non-present on identity, meaning, and communication. Spatiality brings a sensitivity to the ways diverse spatial and temporal scales impinge on texts and talk.

Such a shift involves moving from grammar as the primary meaning-making system to a consideration of *spatial repertoires* (as they are beginning to be conceptualized by many scholars; see Fast 2012; Otsuji and Pennycook 2015; Canagarajah forthcoming b). They are different from grammars in the sense that they involve diverse semiotic resources. They are spatial in the sense that the resources are defined by and embedded in the space/time contingencies in which activities occur. They are different from genres, as genres have been traditionally defined in terms of largely verbal resources and are somewhat fixed and predefined. We can understand the notion of spatial repertoires as an alternative to grammatical structure for explaining the competence of language users. Communicative activities require certain objects, words, discourse conventions, physical movements, gestures, body postures, and participant frameworks for interactional success. Though interlocutors don't need the ability to form complete grammatical sentences, they must know how words align with objects, people, and contexts to be meaningful. We have to think of spatial repertoires as a heuristic or a template to guide interactions, rather than as fixed rules. They are situated, ecological, negotiated, and emergent. Participants must know how to adopt reciprocal strategies with interlocutors in contexts of spatial variation.

Spatial repertoires put the focus on practices and strategies rather than on norms, patterns, and structures for communicative success. Mobility requires a qualitatively different orientation to meaning-making and competence in order to explain the paradoxical features of fixity and fluidity, stability and change, order and emergence in communication. It requires a focus on the processes, practices, flows, links, and assemblages involved in meaning-making, beyond a focus on meaning as a product or pre-established norms. While we focused on the *what* earlier, we are now more concerned about the *how*. We now realize that how meanings are negotiated, established, and achieved is key to communication and social life. The earlier focus on meanings and identities in a product-oriented manner was informed by a static, territorialized, and homogeneous treatment of communication and language. The current shift is informed by the move toward *non-representational* thinking in many fields (Thrift 2007). While representational thinking focused on the *what* as the objective of inquiry, non-representational thinking focuses on the *how* (among other differences). The former lends itself to essentializing meanings and identities. As we become sensitive to diversity, fluidity, and complexity in mobility, the focus is more on the practices and processes, and affective and material factors, which explain the way meanings and identities are constructed. It is significant that scholars are now treating social and communicative constructs not as nouns (to index meanings and products), but as verbs, as in grammaring, translanguaging, place making, homing, and meaning-making.

As we have seen, mobility has provided more complexity to communicative activity, compelling us to develop new theoretical orientations to the analysis of language. We have had to develop new constructs for inquiry, analysis, and interpretation. The constructs I have introduced in this brief narrative, such as simultaneity, spatiality, transnational social fields, non-representational thinking, assemblage, and translanguaging, will inform the chapters in the handbook and become fleshed out in the discussions.

Research and analytical methods

These shifts in theoretical orientations have generated new questions about the scope and focus of analysis in communicative interactions. There are two fundamental challenges for research and inquiry as applied linguists move forward. They can be explained as follows:

1   *Scope of analysis*: What is the scale, scope, or boundary of the interaction that should be analyzed? In short, what is a relevant unit of analysis for communicative interactions? This decision becomes problematic when we consider diverse spatial and temporal scales as mediating interactions, compounded by the simultaneity that introduces layers of meanings, identities, and investments from different times and places in the same interaction. Where do we draw the line on a text, talk, or interaction that is a valid object or artifact for analysis?
2   *Focus of analysis*: What verbal and semiotic features should be included in our analysis? Now that we are open to considering communication as translingual, multimodal, material, and spatial, an infinite number of features can become meaning-making resources. However, certain resources might be more salient than others in specific interactions.

To understand the significance of these questions, let us consider how we addressed these concerns traditionally and how they are called into question in a mobile orientation to semiotic resources and interactions.

To consider the first question, recall that scholars in applied linguistics and many other fields often treated the nation-state as the default and implicit boundary for communicative and social interactions. This bias is referred to as "methodological nationalism" (Wimmer and Glick Schiller 2002). The possibility of transnational social fields suggests that our social ties and interactions exceed the nation-state and adopt liminal spaces as their locus. From this perspective, methodological nationalism might turn out to be an irrelevant and reductive framing for certain interactions. A similar framing is the community – treated often as an ethnic group that shares certain norms and values about language and communication. In applied linguistics, scholars operationalized this framing as a *speech* or *discourse community*. Some have critiqued this framing as the "ethnic lens" (Glick Schiller and Simsek-Caglar 2011b: 65). Pratt (1987) has argued that these assumptions of shared group norms are a "linguistic utopia" that ignore that all social spaces are contact zones where people with diverse norms engage in communicative activities.

While the nation-state or the community framed the unit of analysis at the macro level, we defined the object of analysis at the micro level in a slightly different way. Applied linguists have treated the verbal resources of two or more individuals in a face-to-face interaction as the relevant micro unit of analysis. Meanings should be recoverable from the language used in the immediate interaction. Any interpretive resource brought from outside the immediate interaction was secondary. They were admitted only when the resources in the immediate/local verbal interaction were inadequate to explain what was going on. Similarly, in literacy, the bounded text and the physical activity of writing by an author or collaborators, or the reading activity of an individual or group, were considered the scope of analysis. Individuals who are not present in the face-to-face conversational interaction or literacy event were not considered relevant. Other non-human influences on language or the expanded spatiotemporal flows of words and texts did not actively influence interpretation. This analytical orientation was influenced by the "metaphysics of presence" that valued immediately available sensory data as permissible evidence for knowledge claims.

However, as we discussed, there are many shaping and constraining influences on the conversational interaction or text from outside the immediate participants and interaction. Consider the non-present human agents who might also be part of the communicative interaction. Blommaert, Spotti, and Van der Aa (this volume) discuss a refugee interviewee in their study in Belgium being influenced by a family member who was overhearing their interview via Skype (through a laptop that was always in her hands during the interviews). When the researchers accidentally discovered this distant and invisible "participant," they realized that the meanings and content of the interview were shaped by this family member as well. In the context of time/space compression and the resulting simultaneity, our inquiry now has to be open to influences from participants outside the immediate physical context of interaction. The participants in a study could themselves be relating their meanings and identities to other places and times beyond the situated interaction.

Many resources and factors presumed to be lying outside the focus on the verbal data were relegated traditionally to "context." The construct "context" enabled us to draw the line on what we considered "talk," "text," or "interaction" that merited close analysis. From an expanded spatiotemporal perspective on communicative interactions, we run into problems in separating context from text. Traditionally, for reasons explained earlier, we treated the immediate physical and temporal environment of a face-to-face interaction as belonging to the text; all other spatiotemporal influences and factors were relegated to context. Two dominant metaphors have been adopted to characterize the text/context relationship. The classic metaphors of figure and background are implicit in many studies. The figure (i.e., text) receives primary focus. The background only brings it into relief, and perhaps contributes secondary and contingent meanings from the context. A slightly different metaphor that was applied in certain other studies is that of the context as container. From this perspective, the context shapes the meaning of the text which is contained. This application can be a bit deterministic, with what is considered context controlling the possible choices of interpretation.

Though both metaphors acknowledge some influence from the context on talk/text, they are characterized by certain limitations:

- The influence of context is one-sided. Not much attention is given to the possibility that language and/or speakers can renegotiate, reconstruct, and recontextualize the interaction in dynamic ways throughout the talk or interaction. In fact, language or text can constitute its own context. Furthermore, interlocutors can reframe how social and material context are made relevant to their talk or texts as they interact.
- Context is treated as somewhat static. This probably comes from the bias that material environment lacks agency. The work of posthumanist theorists makes us realize that the material/physical environment is changing, dynamic, and agentive. Material life also shapes human interactions, considerably qualifying human agency. From this perspective, objects and the environment can mediate and shape language and cognition in complex ways.

- Context is monolithic. Its multiplicity or diversity is not acknowledged. The notion of layered simultaneity acquaints us to the fact that there are multiple scales of influence, from places and times of different distance and proximity. The contexts or factors that mediate and shape multilingual interaction can belong to different scales of consideration, nested or overlapping with one another. For example, a classroom interaction is regulated by the institution (school); shaped by policies of the larger state, regional, or national educational administration; and nested within global educational systems. We have to determine which contextual scale becomes relevant at what point. It is not also acknowledged that context is relative. What is global or local (or immediate or distant) in an interaction might differ for each participant, and also change as the interaction proceeds. This distinction becomes especially problematic when we consider that the local and global interpolate each other (see Wortham and Reyes 2015 for a discussion).
- Context is treated usually as geographical, without adequate attention to temporal influences. Features of the setting, such as place, community, or nation-state, are acknowledged, accommodating related notions such as culture or social structure. But the influences from time are not given attention beyond the generalized notion of "historical context." Time would explain the mobility of people and semiotic resources through diverse scales (i.e., present but also past and future) often all scales coming together in layered simultaneity.
- What is included in context is largely impressionistic and arbitrary, rarely treated as an empirical question that needs to be ascertained. Context is assumed before the data collection or analysis without being problematized. Researchers rarely keep the relevant spatiotemporal frames for analysis open throughout the diverse stages of the study, sensitive to how context may itself be changing at different stages of the interaction as well as their study.
- Finally, the binary distinction of context/text is misleading and irrelevant when we consider that communicative practices involve diverse resources across many levels of time and space with different horizontal and hierarchical influences. The binary collapses this amalgamation of influences into two, with one given more importance than the other in our analysis. The spatial orientation would consider how meaning is an emergence of diverse resources across different scales of space and time. From this perspective, the contexts of interaction are very expansive. They can involve unlimited time and space considerations shaping the focused interaction.

The way we have traditionally circumscribed our unit of analysis, by making an arbitrary context/text distinction, also shapes our understanding of what semiotic features we take into consideration as meaning-making resources. Our focus of analysis is the verbal resource from a single language we consider as enjoying meaning-making potential in the interaction. Everything else is relegated to insignificant context. The spatial orientation would complicate our focus of analysis. As in Latour's (1987) telling metaphor, there is an "Ariadne's thread" of diverse networked resources from ever-expanding spatiotemporal scales that shape talk. Applied linguists are already pushing back against the "lingual bias" in our field (Block 2014) that treats verbal resources as the only or superior medium of communication.

Note that even in studies of multilingual interactions the focus of analysis is still one language at a time. In studies in second language acquisition, interactions in other languages are treated as side sequence to resolve problems in the language being learned (see Firth and Wagner 2007 for a critique). In studies of English as a lingua franca (ELF), the use of languages other than English was traditionally ignored in favor of describing the corpus of English used by multilingual speakers (Seidlhofer 2004). Other verbal resources were not analyzed for the possible synergy with English or the new indexicalities of meaning beyond labeled languages. Similarly, the less obvious cognitive or affective influence of diverse languages on the use of English by multilinguals as they shuttle between languages was also not treated as ascertainable or relevant. If we accommodate language contact and the new meanings produced out of this synergy, along the orientation to translanguaging, we should include the meshing of codes from diverse separately labeled languages and consider deviation from established norms as part of the indexicalities of meaning.

Studies in mainstream applied linguistics also treat non-verbal resources in limited ways. In some analytical traditions, para-verbal resources have been excluded as tainting the analysis. For example, ELF has prioritized words (see Pitzl 2010: 92 for her justification on focusing on words and accommodating non-verbal resources in limited exceptional cases). Though laughter and silence have been addressed in some studies, they have been largely treated as para-verbal cues that point to the more important language work in the interaction (see Matsumoto 2015 for a critique). Silence can indicate lack of uptake of the previous utterance, for example. But it has rarely been considered as a semiotic resource in its own right for producing meaning that complements or enriches the verbal (see Glenn 2004 and Matsumoto 2015 for such a demonstration). Similarly, laughter has been treated as a face-saving strategy for filling silence or marking lack of uptake, without considering how it might contribute to additional meanings (see Matsumoto 2015 for a corrective).

To move further, features of the body (such as gaze, gesture, posture, proximity, and positioning) have also not been given adequate significance in multilingual interactions (see Goodwin 2000 for a notable exception). Despite a small group of scholars in applied linguistics focusing on gesture as complementary to talk (see Smotrova and Lantolf 2013 and Matsumoto 2015 for emergent work in classroom contexts), a majority of studies have largely treated gesture as a compensatory strategy, but not as a meaning-making resource in its own right. It has also not been considered as complementary to verbal resources, conveying meaning beyond words, as a separate channel of communication. Other features of the body should also be considered more closely for the way they function as semiotic resources, conveying meanings that parallel, constrain, or enrich verbal communication. Interactions in multilingual and migrant professional settings suggest that because of workplace contingencies (i.e., noise, speed of production, wearing masks) a lot of effective and efficient communication occurs without words or with minimal language use (see Kleifgen 2013). Not including them in the focus of analysis would mean losing significant information on the meaning of these interactions.

Much of the work on non-verbal resources gets addressed under the field of multimodality. However, the spatial orientation expands multimodal analysis. Multimodality has hitherto addressed certain predefined modes and features scholars have considered as "communicative," such as gestures, sound, images, and visuals (see Kress 2000; Stein 2000). Spatial orientation goes beyond to include all material and social affordances, such as objects, artifacts, and social networks as equally communicative (Rickert 2013; Pigg 2014). In fact, anything can become communicative, based on the indexicality achieved in situated interactions over time. There is also a tendency in multimodal analysis to systematize communicative modes for their norms and patterns in meaning-making (see Kress 2010 for an attempt); but spatiality adopts a more open orientation to modes as an assemblage. In this sense, multimodality still makes a distinction between context/text, distinguishing communicative modes from non-communicative contexts; but spatiality considers all the environmental/spatial resources as potentially entextualized in complex and subtle ways into the emergence of meanings. Furthermore, multimodality considers communicative modes and resources as already endowed with certain meanings, while spatiality considers how modes that are not necessarily considered communicative (such as machines or artifacts in a workplace) might index meanings in situated social activity (see Canagarajah forthcoming a, for an analysis). Finally, multimodal scholars adopt an agentive orientation to consider how people use multimodal resources for their communicative intentions; however, spatiality considers the way the alignment between people and modes shape meanings. There is greater acceptance of the shaping influence of things and other semiotic resources on human cognition and verbal facility in the spatial orientation.

It is salutary that scholars in applied linguistics do address strategies of communication beyond meanings and identities. This move towards *procedural* (rather than *propositional*) competence (see Byram 2008) is a gesture towards non-representational thinking. It is possible to presume that a focus on communicative strategies would bring a broader social and material orientation to interactions, giving greater significance to diverse semiotic resources. However, communicative strategies are largely analyzed in relation to the negotiation of verbal meanings in many fields in applied linguistics (see Bjorkman 2014 for a recent state of the art on how strategies are studied in ELF). That is, interlocutors are observed for the strategies they adopt to anticipate or repair communicative breakdown in words. Also, the strategies they adopt are deployed verbally. How they might use the body, objects, or other resources in the setting to repair breakdown is not considered as part of the analysis or their communicative competence. (In fact, competence and meaning are defined in terms of grammatical control.) More importantly, how communicative strategies might enrich or complement verbal meaning by bringing other social and material resources into communication is not explored.

To appreciate the scope of resources that can be included in a spatial orientation, consider the treatment of *alignment*, a construct that is used in different applied linguistic models to address procedural competence. As it is used in conversation analysis (see Steenstig 2013), it refers to the strategies interlocutors adopt (such as back channeling cues) to indicate focus on the interaction and uptake of words. However, alignment could also be indexed by proximity, gaze, or positioning. It can also mean how resources in the communicative ecology (such as objects and artifacts) are marshaled to complement meaning. The latter possibilities are addressed in the sociocognitive model (Atkinson, Churchill, Nishino, and Okada 2007: 171), which is salutary for exploring the "mind-world-body" connection. However, a limitation of the sociocognitive orienation is that the resources taken into consideration are situated in the here-and-now (adhering to the metaphysics of presence). Also, the alignment is eventually studied for its effects on cognitive and grammatical control one language at a time. Other models, such as the communities of practice (Wenger 1998), study alignment in relation to resources and social networks that are distant in time and space. From this perspective, alignment can mean how one positions oneself in relation to social networks, objects, and semiotic resources that are not immediately present in an interaction to perform an activity. However, there is a strong sense of human agency in this orientation, treating the strategies as adopted by individuals and groups. Spatial orientation would posit that alignment can accommodate diverse objects in the material and social environment to be strategically configured to generate meanings that are beyond cognitive control and that are not fully under the competence of the individual. Alignment in the latter sense is an adaptation to diverse semiotic resources that requires bodily and affective dimensions beyond the cognitive for meaning and identity construction. To move away from the cognitive bias in terms such as *alignment* and *competence*, some scholars in the spatial orientation adopt the terms *emplacement* (Pigg 2014) or *ambience* (Rickert 2013). These terms connote that meanings emerge with greater shaping influence from bodily alignment and material resources. From this perspective, human agents may have to contend with the constraining influence of material factors to strategically work with available resources to negotiate possible meanings. As it is evident, the spatial orientation on mobility compels a qualified view of human agency, verbal facility, and cognitive mastery in meaning-making activity (see Canagarajah forthcoming a, for a fuller discussion).

Methodological ways forward

Though expanding the scope and focus of analyses is important, we have to recognize that there are ways in which the scale and resources are delimited in each interaction. Sometimes, interlocutors cue how they want the interaction to be framed. Certain semiotic resources might become more salient than the others for a variety of reasons. Furthermore, a "flat ontology" doesn't fully contend with the fact there are power inequalities, which might place certain scales and semiotic resources as more important than the others in certain interactions. Hierarchies and boundaries are obdurate social facts. Therefore we have to turn to the question of which contexts of consideration and which semiotic resources should be included in a given analysis. I review a few approaches applied linguists have come up with in response to this question, as we continue to engage with these methodological challenges.

Scalar analysis is becoming useful for applied linguists to address the emerging analytical questions (see Prinsloo, this volume). This is a construct applied linguists have recently borrowed from anthropology and political science. Scales enable us to consider how participants and analysts frame texts or interactions. Scales remind us of Goffman's (1983) notion of *frames*. But scalar analysis enables us to address frames in more layered and complex ways. Furthermore, scales enable us to address non-visible and non-immediate features that Goffman left out because of his prioritization of the local in his treatment (see Lempert 2012 for a critique). Though there are significant debates on the definitions and operationalization of scales (see Canagarajah and De Costa 2016 for a review), we can orientate to scalar analysis as follows:

Scales are both spatial and temporal. More importantly, they help us consider how they are dynamically implicated in each other. Bakhtin's (1986) metaphor of chronotopes reminds us that spatiotemporal scales have to be addressed as connected and interrelated.

Scales are layered. There are not only many scales, thus opening up "context" to diversity, they are also relative to each other. For example, scales can accommodate nested or ladder relationships, providing possibilities to consider communication as shaped by layered influences. Though nesting and ladder are somewhat linear and hierarchical (i.e., one scale is more global or determinative than the other), some treat scales as rhizomatic to avoid those implications. Rhizome suggests that scales might influence talk in non-linear, unpredictable, and non-synchronous ways. We can thus invoke frames of different levels or magnitude for the way they relate to meanings and communicative outcomes. Scales enable us to move beyond the traditional binary of macro and micro or global and local, considering them as relative and interpolating each other in fluid ways.

Scales are semiotic. They are not objectively out there, thus existing before analysis or interactions. They are constructed by institutions and people to understand or explain social interactions. They are mediated, negotiated, and established through semiotic activity.

Scales are changing. As scales are constructed and negotiated, social institutions and actors are actively involved in rescaling interactions.

Scales also help us address the distinction made between agency and structure in more complex ways. Agency is often assumed to thrive in the local scales, while the global is associated with more deterministic structures in traditional understandings of context. However, the nested and ladder orientation to scales help us understand how translocal scales shape the local. Similarly, the rhizomatic orientation to scale helps us understand how new structural arrangements may emerge from different spaces between the local and the global, reconfiguring each in unpredictable ways. More importantly, material environment is itself agentive and can rescale interactions, going beyond the notion of context as passive or human actors as fully agentive.

The distinction of scales as a *category of analysis* and *category of practice* can help us triangulate data and perspectives to home in on the appropriate unit and focus of analysis. Scales as a category of analysis is the frames that researchers adopt to study an interaction. Scales as a category of practice is the way participants frame and rescale their interactions. Though these uses of scales have been debated as conflicting (see Lempert 2012), they can also be productively brought together. While the scaling activity of participants provides an emic perspective on the interaction, we have to be open to the possibility that researchers can also adopt different scales as relevant, based on the questions they pose or problems they are trying to address. That is, the story researchers want to tell and the objectives they want to accomplish by analyzing communicative interactions would determine which scales become relevant and which semiotic resources are significant for that scale of consideration. Of course, they have to triangulate the data and analysis with the participants' own categories of practice, and evidence from extended and close fieldwork. Furthermore, the participants' perspective can be limited. The spatial orientation would suggest that the participants themselves are not always aware of all the environmental resources shaping and constraining their talk. Besides the reality of ideologically influenced misrecognition, we have to also contend with the limitations of human agency and cognitive control. Therefore certain non-visible scales of institutional or translocal relationships that shape our interaction should be accommodated in the analysis.

Other approaches have also been adopted to figure out the appropriate unit and focus of analysis in mobility. Blommaert, Spotti, and Van der Aa (this volume) suggest that the expanded fieldwork of ethnography would help researchers understand which scales and features become relevant for an interaction. Multisited and longitudinal studies that are sensitive to all variables in a communicative situation might help researchers to problematize the unit of analysis without predefining what is relevant for a given interaction. As they thus empirically determine the scales that are relevant, they would also attune themselves to the semiotic resources that play an important role in each scale in meaning-making activity. Blommaert et al. also mention that critical moments in an interaction (or a study) can make relevant certain unexpected semiotic features or scales that researchers hadn't considered before. The narrative mentioned earlier on how they accidentally discovered the online and virtual presence of the relative of their participant constituted a critical moment. Thereafter, they had to accommodate this distant and invisible member's presence in their interviews to understand the interactions appropriately.

Wortham and Reyes (2015) propose a "discourse analysis beyond the speech event" that would situate meaning-making activities in an expanded spatiotemporal scale and problematize the indexicality of semiotic resources. They outline a hermeneutic process whereby semiotic resources can be tracked across time and space for the ways they acquire and change meanings, beyond the immediate face-to-face encounter. In this way, they develop a method for tracing emergent and achieved indexicality across time and space, beyond the traditional demarcations of physically circumscribed context or predefined meanings and norms. Though Wortham and Reyes discuss the construction of verbal meanings in diverse media (spoken, written, digital), they don't apply their model to extra-verbal resources (such as objects, images, or gestures). It is not impossible to imagine ways in which we can adopt their analytical method to diverse semiotic resources beyond those accommodated typically in verbal or multimodal analysis.

As we thus expand our focus and unit of analyses, we are also challenged to come up with new methods for observing interactions and collecting data. There are of course many challenges here that require creative resolutions. For example, though we know that meanings and interactions might be realized or enacted in diverse spatial and temporal scales simultaneously, researchers are physically limited to being in only one place at a time. Besides, there are resource limitations that might prevent researchers from studying interactions in multiple locations or employing collaborators in diverse places. A study of mobility requires observing flows, processes, and changes in diverse places and times simultaneously. Creative methods are being devised to overcome these challenges. The following are some examples of methodological innovations coming into prominence, which would be discussed in greater detail in the chapters in the handbook:

Multisited ethnography: As a corrective to traditional ethnography in which scholars studied cultural practices in a single location by becoming saturated into the practices of a community over a long period of time, scholars are spending shorter but more intensive periods of observations in multiple locations to study the continuities or connections in communicative practices. Though there is an attempt to develop an insider and emic perspective, there is also the realization that meaning or activity transcends the immediate context (see further Dick and Arnold, this volume).

Mobile methods: Within this label introduced by Buscher et al. (2011), research methods involve following participants, artifacts, or semiotic resources through multiple locations and times. In these methods, the researchers are themselves mobile, considering the liminal *spaces* of mobility (beyond the physical *place* or location) as their research setting. The authors review some illustrative approaches such as: following people, either directly by shadowing them or covertly "stalking" them (Buscher et al. 2011: 8); participating in people's movement through a walk-along or ride-along to experience the contexts and activities of subjects; obtaining time-space diaries from subjects to plot people's movements; exploring virtual mobility through blogs, emails, listservs, and tweets to capture the flow of texts and their meanings; and using mobile positioning devices which involve cell phones or other tracking devices to plot people's movements, networks, and frequencies. Obviously, there would be challenges in obtaining institutional approval and participant consent for some of these methods.

Participatory research: Many scholars are treating subjects themselves as co-researchers to gather information on their flows and movements, in addition to unveiling attitudes and experiences that researchers can't always have access to. These methods turn out to be full-bodied, providing access to participants' affect and imagination, beyond impersonal facts and figures. For example, researchers are gathering useful information from creative literature or dramatic performances written by migrants, which sometimes provide fictional representations that still provide significant insights into migrant experiences. Drama, autobiographies, and novels are useful texts for relevant data (as Baynham shows in his chapter in this volume). Along the same lines, narratives have emerged as significant tools for exploring experiences, attitudes, and relationships, often elicited by researchers themselves through sensitive but strategic interview questions (see DeFina and Tseng, this volume).

Mixed methods: A modest proposal is to adopt mixed methods to capture simultaneity. Boccagni (2012) proposes this as an approach to sample demographic movements through survey and quantitative methods, while zeroing in on specific locations for a qualitative study of migrant experiences.

Disciplinary implications

As we can see, migration and mobility have generated new orientations to language and social inquiry. They have helped scholars question some of the territorialized, bounded, static, and representational thinking in applied linguistics as in other fields in humanities and social sciences. The expansion of the scope and focus of analysis have resulted also in greater interdisciplinarity. There is a lot of borrowing and sharing of theoretical constructs and research methods in applied linguistics, humanities, and the social sciences. As we have seen in the preceding discussion, applied linguists has been borrowing theories and methods from diverse other disciplines to strengthen their inquiry. We have reviewed constructs from geography (i.e., Massey, Thrift), philosophy (Deleuze and Guattari, Bardotti), sociology (Latour, Urry), anthropology (Glick Schiller), and physics (Barad) in the preceding pages. However, other disciplines have not always benefited from the scholarship of applied linguistics. The latter is often treated as a service discipline to teach languages to migrant families, students, and workers, rather than valued for making intellectual contributions of its own. In this section, I want to articulate some ways in which migration studies can benefit from the scholarship of applied linguists.

First we have to acknowledge that applied linguistics has itself a lot of work left for redefining and retheorizing basic constructs in its field. After a period of positivistic/empirical inquiry when scholars moved in a settled trajectory towards final answers on key questions, adopting the structuralist and experimentalist orientation, there is now a realization that we might have to start all over again in the context of mobility. The observations of Kramsch on foreign language pedagogy are relevant to many other areas in applied linguistics:

> There has never been a greater tension between what is taught in the classroom and what the students will need in the real world once they have left the classroom. In the last decades, that world has changed to such an extent that language teachers are no longer sure of what they are supposed to teach nor what real world situations they are supposed to prepare their students for.
>
> *(Kramsch 2014: 296)*

Beyond pedagogy, her statement points to basic questions in proficiency and competence remaining unresolved. As we have discussed here, when meaning-making practices involve negotiating diverse semiotic resources in different spatiotemporal scales, we have to ask what it means to be proficient in a language. Is it relevant to define competence one language at a time, when people are shuttling between languages and, in fact, treating verbal resources as floating signifiers that can be taken over for their communicative functions with desired indexicalities? Can we separate grammatical knowledge from the competence to use diverse other semiotic resources in achieving our communicative objectives? Is a language proficiency developed in terms of grammatical/verbal resources for separately labeled languages appropriate when communicative unpredictability is the norm, with interactions always involving interlocutors with diverse codes in mobility? Is it possible to define competence in terms of propositional knowledge when mobile spaces always present a diverse mix of participants with no norms or values shared for communication (thus requiring procedural knowledge)? As people are compelled to keep expanding their resources constantly, with new genres and changing communicative norms, we have to ask whether we can ever define a threshold level for assessing proficiency when one can stop learning or consider him/herself competent. There are similar questions for other domains in applied linguistics, such as language policy, testing, and literacy, which have been based on territorialized language norms and identities, with reductive notions of language as an autonomous and static system. We have to explore these questions in relation to diverse contexts, disciplinary insights, and emergent paradigms in ongoing inquiry.

As language has become important in mobile contexts for shaping identities, communities, and social practices, applied linguistics too has much to offer other disciplines. In recognition of this, many scholars in diverse fields are already using linguistic constructs in their disciplinary inquiry. Scholars in fields such as migration studies, geography, sociology, and anthropology are addressing language in their work. However, because they don't have familiarity with linguistics, their work is sometimes superficial or questionable. Though a formal training in applied linguistics is too much to ask for, an understanding of work relevant to their research questions might be convenient to obtain – as in this handbook. Next, I give examples of recent work in migration studies that can benefit from greater engagement with applied linguistics.

Consider the study of highly skilled migration. As mobile professionals are becoming key to innovation and productivity in the neoliberal economy, there has been considerable research interest on how language proficiency correlates with employment success in a new country. These studies have been conducted by those in geography and social sciences adopting quantitative and statistical approaches. These demographic studies show a positive correlation between those who are proficient in the dominant language of the host country and their economic success (see Dustmann 1994; Chiswick and Miller 1995, 2002, 2007; Dustmann and van Soest 2002; Dustmann and Fabbri 2003; Bleakley and Chin 2004). Many of these studies show that those who are proficient in English tend to be better employed, considering English as the global professional language. They also suggest that those who are from countries which provide an important place for English in their education or society (such as former British colonies, India or Singapore) are more successful, while those from countries which have lacked English exposure (i.e., West Asian or East European countries) tend to be less so. Williams and Balaz (2008: 29), reviewing many studies of this nature, summarize the rationale behind this body of research thus:

> The classic human-capital perspective suggests that immigrants tend to adapt to their host countries via accumulating human capital. A critical element of human capital is fluency in the host country's language, which mediates their integration into that country's labor market.

These demographic and quantitative studies, however, overlook significant complicating information that applied linguists are aware of. They don't explore what languages are actually involved in professional communication (i.e., though subjects might be proficient in English, is that the only language they are using in their workplace?); the attitudes of the migrants towards the languages they use (i.e., though subjects might be proficient in English, do they value it over their other repertoires?); and the other forms of social capital that languages may or may not provide access to (i.e., is English the critical factor in professional success, or is it the social connections and professional status subjects may enjoy through English?). This tradition of migration studies has to be qualified by knowledge from interactional sociolinguistics and ethnographies on attitudes and practices in workplace communication (see for example Kubota 2013; Canagarajah 2016; Kirilova and Angouri, this volume; Lising, this volume). Such studies point to the following. To begin with, languages cannot be essentialized. For example, English is not a monolithic or homogeneous language. The Englishes spoken by Indians and Nigerians are very different from the varieties that are privileged by native speakers in the UK or United States. Besides, there are strong biases against the varieties spoken by postcolonial subjects in native speaker communities. Therefore, treating the proficiency of the speaker and the norms of the host community as equal is misleading. Furthermore, applied linguists who study language negotiations and social practice in situated interactions would question the equation of formal proficiency (judged in terms of standardized tests such as TOEFL or IELTS) with actual communicative practices and outcomes in workplaces. The communicative practice in situated social interactions can have little relevance to the grammatical norms in tests. Workplace communication studies show many diverse possibilities (see Kubota 2013; Canagarajah 2016); that is, transnational and multilingual workers may not use the privileged languages or norms in their interaction; they typically use truncated multilingualism (i.e., bits and pieces of diverse languages successfully); and verbal resources may matter less where material and physical resources (artifacts, gestures, etc.) might be more important. Therefore, an understanding of the diversity of communicative practices from applied linguistics would fruitfully complicate demographic studies and correlationist claims in migration studies, leading to more triangulated data and nuanced interpretations.

The social scientific research cited earlier also tends to shape policy and pedagogy. Based on the assumption that a proficiency in host country language is important for professional relationships, policies on workplace employment in many countries emphasize a formal proficiency in English. There are policies of English Only or monolingualism in many workplaces that penalize nonnative varieties or other languages in professional communication (see Kirilova and Angouri, this volume; Lising, this volume). Employment policies in many countries (such as Canada, Australia, the UK, and New Zealand) mandate a high score on the IELTS (International English Language Testing System) for qualification or selection. Immigration to such countries on work visas also emphasize a high score on such tests. Under pressure to perform well in these requirements, there is a global scramble to learn English (Piller and Cho 2013). There is a belief that English is the linguistic capital everyone needs for success in the neoliberal economy, leading to the commodification of English and marketization of testing instruments such as TOELF and IELTS. However, applied linguistics studies on workplace interactions (as reviewed earlier and presented in the chapters in this volume) and interviews with migrant professionals (see Kubota 2013; Canagarajah 2016) show that workplace communication is much more multilingual, multimodal, and polysemiotic, differing from the normative and formal requirements of these tests and policies. Multilingualism can account for efficiency and productivity, countering the policy perspective that shared codes and universal norms lead to such outcomes (as reviewed critically by Grin 2001). More importantly, beyond language norms, we are finding that dispositions of tolerance, lifelong learning, and collaboration are more critical for social and employment success as migrants are able to engage with diversity and expand their repertoires for a diverse workplace and society. Therefore, a greater familiarity with the qualitative and situated interactional studies of applied linguists will help formulate more relevant pedagogies and policies for professional migration.

To consider another line of inquiry in migration studies, the tradition of studies on social adjustment of migrant students in host country schools adopts the construct linguistic distance/similarity to explain their success. These studies project how students who come with a language background that is similar to the language of schooling in the host community are more successful (see Beenstock, Chiswick, and Repetto 2003; Chiswick and Miller 2005). From this perspective, German students from Germany would be considered more successful in the United States, as English and German belong to the same family of languages, unlike Tamil students whose language family is Dravidian. However, claims about difficulty of acquisition based on language distance have been debunked in applied linguistics (Li Wei 2000). It is quite possible for similar languages to generate challenges in keeping them apart during learning. It has also been argued that projections of language similarity or distance are subjective and impressionistic. Furthermore, the pedagogical implications are based on the linguistic interference hypothesis, which ignores additive and dynamic orientations to acquisition that posit languages enabling each other and leading to more complex competencies (see García 2009). Projecting interference and difficulty based on language structure is unduly deterministic.

Another area of migration studies which might benefit from applied linguistic scholarship is scalar analysis on how cities, economies, communities, and institutions are being rescaled in the context of mobility (see collection of studies in Glick Schiller and Simsek-Caglar 2011a). For example, small American or European towns are integrated into global capital flows with the influx of migrants. So far, geographers, anthropologists, and political scientists have adopted broad social and material factors (such as new social relationships, institutions, and artifacts – see Swyngedouw 1997; Uitermark 2002; Glick Schiller and Simsek-Caglar 2011a) to demonstrate rescaling. However, applied linguists are able to demonstrate how fine-grained semiotic resources are adopted by subjects for rescaling purposes (Clonan-Roy, Rhodes, and Wortham 2016; Dong and Blommaert 2016). Features such as contextualization cues (lexical, syntactic, and phonological switches), semiotic processes (such as narratives, language ideologies, social positioning), and framing devices (such as participant structures) may help social scientists attend to the ways scaling processes take place at the micro-social level. They can provide fine-grained evidence at the level of micro-analysis of talk on how subjects orientate to particular scalar dimensions in their interactions. For example, Lempert (2012) demonstrates the rescaling practices of his subjects by drawing from linguistic cues as well as physical postures, material resources, and institutional changes, exemplifying the value of applied linguistic tools for social scientists.

Though there is evidence that researchers in migration studies are beginning to borrow from work in applied linguistics (see Valentine, Sporton, and Bang Nielsen 2008; Fast 2012; Bailey, Mupakati, and Magunha 2014), more sharing and collaboration will facilitate interdisciplinary synergies – which we hope this handbook generates. The separation of scholarly fields is itself a result of the territorialization and boundary making designs of modernity, which mobility problematizes. Those attuned to mobility have advocated "border thinking" (Mignolo 2000) or "nomadic theory" (Braidotti 2013) that engages the liminal spaces between disciplines and paradigms for knowledge making.

Cautions and qualifications

As we continue explorations on this productive disciplinary space at the nexus of language and mobility, we have to be also cautious of exaggerating the mobility turn. How wise it is to adopt mobility as the dominant construct to perceive social and communicative life? Faist asks, "Is mobility really a human universal, as anthropologists tell us?" (Faist 2013: 1644). We have to first recognize that a desire to be "placed" (i.e., establishing homes, valuing rootedness, and inhabiting sovereign geopolitical spaces) is equally human. Rather than treating mobility and sedentariness as dichotomies, we should consider them as relational and interconnected. Even as people are mobile, they are constructing new homes. Migrants construct new in-groups and diaspora communities that celebrate heritage languages and cultures (though not without changes to the way they have been traditionally defined). Migrants are also constructing new homes, neighborhoods, and communities constituting diverse people and languages, going beyond their traditional identities and affiliations. These examples show that place, home, and community are compelling needs for everyone. What is different from previous paradigms is that these spaces and habitations are not treated as essentialized, homogeneous, bounded, or primordial. In other words, these spaces are socially and linguistically constructed in mobility. They are also relational, constructed relative to other social groups. They exist side by side with other communities and feature diversity. Therefore, such homes and spaces are constructed from *within* mobility, contact, and diversity – not outside. Consider the Arabic neighborhoods in many European cities that feature a mix of Middle Eastern communities, with different ethnicities, religious practices, languages, and sects, but still consider themselves cohesive and placed.

It is also important to theorize forms of immobility as we study mobility. There are new forms of border making that are coming up to prevent and surveil certain groups in mobility. The discourses of securitization and policies of surveillance are gaining more ground in Europe and other Western countries. The surge of refugees from conflict zones is not only an unpleasant form of mobility that is less studied or theorized in scholarly circles; it is also generating new policies that restrict movement. Discourses of citizenship and nationalism are also counteracting the treatment of mobility as desirable. One might say that intensified forms of mobility are generating intensified resistance in the form of increased policies and regulations for border control, boundary making, and sovereign spaces. Furthermore, we shouldn't ignore differential material access for mobility. There are people who don't have the resources or possibilities for geographical or social mobility.

However, all this doesn't mean that people occupy a static and homogeneous social space. The mobility paradigm helps us to consider how all of us are implicated in mobility, even those who don't move. All of us inhabit spaces marked by and shaped by mobility, though some may experience relative immobility. For example, even though some long-standing local residents in my American university town have not traveled much, their lives are shaped by diversity and contact as they live side by side with students and faculty members who are international. They are starting businesses that cater to mobile citizens, develop languages and cultural values from elsewhere, and inhabit a place marked by diversity around them. On the other hand, many of my compatriots in Sri Lanka who don't have the resources to flee elsewhere as refugees still receive remittances from their relatives abroad, implicating their lives in mobility. Therefore, we have to examine the different causes and consequences of relative immobility for some in an economy and geopolitics based on migration. However, both mobile and relatively immobile people live in spaces marked by transnational relations and contact zones. In that sense, mobility does shape everyone's life, whether physically migrating or not.

We have to also interrogate the current neoliberal dispensation, in which mobility has been treated as a new and desirable norm for everyone. There is a tendency to consider mobility as more progressive, and sedentariness as backward and traditional. Neoliberal discourses also treat mobility as an economically and socially equalizing global process. These assumptions are bolstered by neoliberal ideologies which treat open competition in the free market, sometimes transcending nation-state boundaries, as ensuring opportunities for everyone. Therefore, Faist asks "whether mobility is a new norm, that is, whether nomadism is replacing sedentarism as one of the dominant principles of social order" (Faist 2013: 1644). As we consider this question, we have to grapple with the fact that mobility is unequal and reproduces inequality. For example, in labor migration, while educated professionals are considered "wanted and welcome," less skilled workers are "wanted but not welcome" (Zolberg 1987). While both groups of workers participate in mobility, they receive differential treatment and economic rewards. We have to also understand how certain social groups pay a higher cost for mobility. It is well known that mobility in this way is gendered. There are cases of men migrating for work, letting women alone in the home country to manage the family. In reverse, there are occupations such as maids and nurses where women are more mobile and their caregiving disposition is abused for labor. They then receive less time and opportunity to care for their own families. Their children too pay the price for this mobile work opportunity.

In the hands of neoliberalism, mobility is becoming exploitative for the profit-making interests of a few (see collection of critical articles in Glick Schiller and Faist 2010). Mobility is regulated by neoliberal establishments for their own profit. From this perspective, certain trajectories and channels of migration are preferred (i.e., certain types of work in certain locations) while others are dispreferred (i.e., the movement of refugees to Europe). The global flow of talent and resources, with a translocal network of production and marketing, is playing into neoliberal hands to be orchestrated by those with resources to control these flows. As production places are moved from place to place in search of cheap labor and resources, local communities are losing their share of material benefits. We also know that local communities find their ecological and cultural resources exploited or destroyed in the name of production. Mobility can thus be a threat to local communities and ecologies. Consider also the way local communities find their relationships rescaled and integrated into translocal production and economic networks, in the face of mobile companies and networks, losing their sovereignty.

From these perspectives, it is important to approach language and mobility from nuanced, balanced, and critical perspectives as we collaborate across disciplines to study this important human experience. As mobility becomes increasingly discoursed this productive disciplinary space should lead to more inclusive scholarly constructs and policy proposals.

Organization

This handbook is structured into four parts. Part I examines how basic constructs such as community, place, language, diversity, identity, nation-state, and social stratification are being retheorized in the context of human mobility. The authors examine the limitations of traditional assumptions as they explore the implications of new theoretical realizations for the way we study familiar applied linguistic concerns such as competence, pedagogy, and policy.

Part II considers diverse trajectories and flows of human mobility in relation to language. The authors explore South/South mobility as much as the better discussed South/North mobility; less skilled and indentured workers as much as skilled professionals; displacement in many forms to balance agentive mobility; new linkages in the form of diaspora communities; and different trajectories such as chain, step, circular, and return migration.

Part III samples emergent research methods for studying language and mobility. Contributors examine ways of conducting ethnography in multiple sites, redefining the relationship between context/text in more complex ways, adopting expressive literature and arts to study the role of affect and desire in mobility, utilizing narratives and scalar analysis for studying mobility, and charting the trajectories of traveling texts in literacy.

Part IV deals with policy implications as they pertain to language and mobility. Contributors examine policies in schools, workplaces, service agencies, and governmental and nongovernmental institutions. The section also examines the implications of mobility for education and pedagogy in diverse levels of learning.

The handbook brings together international applied linguists with affiliations in diverse universities around the world and homes in different academic departments. The contributors come from institutions in Australia, Belgium, Canada, China, Denmark, Germany, the Netherlands, New Zealand, the Philippines, Singapore, South Africa, Spain, and Switzerland, in addition to the UK and United States. They boast of social backgrounds and research experience around the world. Given this diversity, there is the need to introduce their scholarship to each other. An important function of this handbook is that it becomes a "who's who" in the study of language and migration in applied linguistics. The authors have adopted a language and style that makes the chapters accessible to graduate students and advanced scholars in cognate fields in applied linguistics and those engaged in exploring language and mobility in diverse disciplines.

References

Anthony, D. W. (1990). Migration in archaeology. *American Anthropologist* 92(4): 895–914.
Anthony, D. W. (2007). *The Horse, the Wheel, and Language: How Bronze-Age Riders from the Eurasian Steppes Shaped the Modern World*. Princeton, NJ: Princeton University Press.
Atkinson, D., Churchill, E., Nishino, T. and Okada, H. (2007). Alignment and interaction in a sociocognitive approach in second language acquisition. *Modern Language Journal* 91: 169–188.
Bailey, A., Mupakati, L. and Magunha, F. (2014). Misplaced: Language, remitting and development practice among Zimbabwean migrants. *Globalisation, Societies and Education* [online]. doi:10.1080/14767724.2014.937404
Bakhtin, M. M. (1986). *Speech Genres and Other Late Essays* [Translated by V.W. McGee]. Austin: University of Texas Press.
Barad, K. (2007). *Meeting the Universe Halfway: Quantum Physics and the Entanglement of Matter and Meaning*. Durham: Duke University Press.
Bauman, R. and Briggs, C. L. (2000). Language philosophy as language ideology: John Locke and Johann Gottfried Herder. In P. V. Kroskrity (ed.), *Regimes of Language: Ideologies, Polities, and Identities* (pp. 139–204). Oxford: James Currey.
Bauman, Z. (1998). *Globalization: The Human Consequences*. New York: Columbia University Press.
Beenstock, M., Chiswick, B. R. and Repetto, G. L. (2003). The effect of linguistic distance and country of origin on immigrant language skills: Application to Israel. *International Migration* 39(3): 33–60.
Bjorkman, B. (2014). An analysis of polyadic English as a Lingua Franca (ELF) speech: A communicative strategies framework. *Journal of Pragmatics* 66: 122–138.

Bleakley, H. and Chin, A. (2004). Language skills and earnings: Evidence from childhood immigrants. *Review of Economics and Statistics* 84(2): 481–496.

Block, D. (2014). Moving beyond "lingualism": Multilingual embodiment and multimodality in SLA. In S. May (ed.), *The Multilingual Turn: Implications for SLA, TESOL, and Bilingual Education* (pp. 54–77). New York: Routledge.

Blommaert, J. (2005). *Discourse: A Critical Introduction*. Cambridge: Cambridge University Press.

Blommaert, J. (2010). *The Sociolinguistics of Globalization*. Cambridge: Cambridge University Press.

Boccagni, P. (2012). Even a transnational social field must have its boundaries: Methodological options, potentials and dilemmas for researching transnationalism. In C. Vargas-Silva (ed.), *Handbook of Research Methods in Migration* (pp. 295–318). Cheltenham: Edward Elgar.

Boutet, J. (2012). Language workers: Emblematic figures of late capitalism. In A. Duchene and M. Heller (eds.), *Language in Late Capitalism* (pp. 207–229). New York: Routledge.

Braidotti, R. (2013). *The Posthuman*. Cambridge: Polity.

Buscher, M., Urry, J. and Witchger, K., eds. (2011). Introduction: Mobile methods. In *Mobile Methods* (pp. 1–19). London: Routledge.

Byram, M. (2008). *From Intercultural Education to Education for Intercultural Citizenship*. Clevedon: Multilingual Matters.

Cameron, C. (2013). How people moved among ancient societies: Broadening the view. *American Anthropologist* 115(2): 218–231.

Canagarajah, A. S. (2013). *Translingual Practice: Global Englishes and Cosmopolitan Relations*. London: Routledge.

Canagarajah, A. S. (2016). *Translingual Practices and Neoliberal Policies: Attitudes and Strategies of African Skilled Migrants in Anglophone Workplaces*. Berlin: Springer.

Canagarajah, A. S. (forthcoming a). The unit and focus of analysis in Lingua Franca English interactions: In search of a method. *International Journal of Bilingual Education and Bilingualism*.

Canagarajah, A. S. (forthcoming b). English as a spatial resource: Explaining the claimed competence of Chinese STEM professionals. In *World Englishes*.

Canagarajah, A. S. and DeCosta, P. (2016). Introduction: Scales analysis, and its uses and prospects in educational linguistics. *Linguistics and Education* 34: 1–10.

Chiswick, B. R. and Miller, P. W. (1995). The endogeneity between language and earnings. *Journal of Labour Economics* 13(2): 246–288.

Chiswick, B. R. and Miller, P. W. (2002). Immigrant earnings: Language skills, linguistic concentrations and the business cycle. *Journal of Population Economics* 15(1): 31–57.

Chiswick, B. R. and Miller, P. W. (2005). Linguistic distance: A quantitative measure of the distance between English and other languages. *Journal of Multilingual and Multicultural Development* 26: 1–11.

Chiswick, B. R. and Miller, P. W. (2007). *The International Transferability of Immigrants' Human Capital Skills*. IZA Discussion Papers 2670, Institute for the Study of Labor (IZA). Retrieved from ftp://repec.iza.org/RePEc/Discussionpaper/dp2670.pdf [Accessed 24 February 2011].

Clonan-Roy, K., Rhodes, C. and Wortham, S. (2016). Moral panic about sexual promiscuity: Heterogeneous scales in the identification of one middle-school Latina girl. *Linguistics and Education* 34: 11–21.

De Certeau, M. (1984). *The Practice of Everyday Life* [Translated by S. Rendall]. Berkeley: University of California Press.

Deleuze, G. and Guattari, F. (1987). *A Thousand Plateaus*. Minneapolis: University of Minnesota Press.

Dong, J. and Blommaert, J. (2016). Global informal learning environments and the making of Chinese middle class. *Linguistics and Education* 34: 33–46.

Dustmann, C. (1994). Speaking fluency, writing fluency and earnings of migrants. *Journal of Population Economics* 7: 133–156.

Dustmann, C. and Fabbri, F. (2003). Language proficiency and labour market performance of immigrants in the UK. *Economic Journal* 113: 695–717.

Dustmann, C. and van Soest, A. (2002). Language and the earnings of immigrants. *Industrial and Labor Relations Review* 55(3): 473–492.

Faist, T. (2013). The mobility turn: A new paradigm for the social sciences? *Ethnic and Racial Studies* 36(11): 1637–1646.

Faist, T., Fauser, M. and Reisenauer, E. (2013). *Transnational Migration*. Cambridge: Polity.

Fast, H. (2012). *Language-use as Spatial Experience: Migrants' Non-fluent Participation in Stabilisations of Linguistic Practice*. Master's thesis, Department of Geography, Utrecht University, Utrecht.

Firth, A. and Wagner, J. (2007). Second/foreign language learning as a social accomplishment: Elaborations on a reconceptualized SLA. *Modern Language Journal* 91: 798–817.

García, O. (2009). *Bilingual Education in the 21st Century: A Global Perspective*. Oxford: Wiley-Blackwell.

Glenn, C. (2004). *Unspoken: A Rhetoric of Silence*. Carbondale: Southern Illinois University Press.

Glick Schiller, N. and Simsek-Caglar, A., eds. (2011a). *Locating Migration: Rescaling Cities and Migrants*. Ithaca: Cornell University Press.

Glick Schiller, N. and Simsek-Caglar, A. (2011b). Locality and globality: Building a comparative analytical framework in migration and urban studies. In N. Glick Schiller and A. Simsek-Caglar (eds.), *Locating Migration: Rescaling Cities and Migrants* (pp. 60–84). Ithaca: Cornell University Press.

Glick Schiller, N. and Faist, T. (2010). *Migration, Development and Transnationalization: A Critical Stance*. New York: Berghahn Books.

Goffman, E. (1983). The interaction order. *American Sociological Review* 48: 1–17.

Goodwin, C. (2000). Action and embodiment within situated human interaction. *Journal of Pragmatics* 32: 1489–1522.

Graff, H. (1991). *The Literacy Myth: Cultural Integration and Social Structure in the Nineteenth Century*. New York: Transaction.

Grin, F. (2001). English as an economic value: Facts and fallacies. *World Englishes* 20(1): 65–78.

Hall, S. (1997). Old and new identities, old and new ethnicities. In A. D. King (ed.), *Culture, Globalization, and the World System* (pp. 41–68). Minneapolis: University of Minnesota Press.

Harvey, D. (2005). *A Brief History of Neoliberalism*. Oxford: Oxford University Press.

Heller, M. and Duchene, A. (2012). Pride and profit: Changing discourses of language, capital, and nation-state. In A. Duchene and M. Heller (eds.), *Language in Late Capitalism* (pp. 1–22). New York: Routledge.

Hoerder, D. (2002). *Cultures in Contact: World Migrations in the Second Millennium*. Durham, NC: Duke University Press.

Jacquemet, M. (2005). Transidiomatic practices: Language and power in the age of globalization. *Language and Communication* 25(3): 255–277.

Kleifgen, J. (2013). *Communicative Practices at Work: Multimodality and Learning in a High-Tech Firm*. Bristol: Multilingual Matters.

Kramsch, C. (2014). Teaching foreign languages in an era of globalization: Introduction. *Modern Language Journal* 98(1): 296–311.

Kress, G. (2000). Multimodality: Challenges to thinking about language. *TESOL Quarterly* 34(2): 337–340.

Kress, G. (2010). *Multimodality: A Social Semiotic Approach to Contemporary Communication*. New York: Routledge.

Kubota, R. (2013). "Language is only a tool": Japanese expatriates working in China and implications for language teaching. *Multilingual Education* 3(4): 1–20.

Kuznetsov, Y., ed. (2006). *Diaspora Networks and the International Migration of Skills*. Washington, DC: World Bank.

Latour, B. (1987). *Science in Action: How to Follow Scientists and Engineers through Society*. Cambridge, MA: Harvard University Press.

Latour, B. (2005). *Reassembling the Social: An Introduction to Actor-network-theory*. Oxford: Oxford University Press.

Lempert, M. (2012). Interaction rescaled: How monastic debate became a diasporic pedagogy. *Anthropology & Education Quarterly* 43(2): 138–156.

Levitt, P. and Glick Schiller, N. (2004). Conceptualizing simultaneity: A transnational social field perspective on society. *Annual Review of Sociology* 33: 129–156.

Li Wei (2000). Dimensions of bilingualism. In Li Wei (ed.), *The Bilingual Reader* (pp. 2–21). London: Routledge.

Marston, S., Jones, J. and Woodward, K. (2005). Human geography without scale. *Transactions of the Institute of British Geographers* 30(4): 16–432.

Massey, D. (2005). *For Space*. London: Sage.

Matsumoto, Y. (2015). *Multimodal Communicative Strategies for Resolving Miscommunication in Multilingual Writing Classrooms*. Dissertation submitted to Penn State University.

May, S., ed. (2014). *The Multilingual Turn: Implications for SLA, TESOL, and Bilingual Education*. New York: Routledge.

Mezzadra, S. and Neilson, B. (2013). *Border as Method, or, the Multiplication of Labor*. Durham: Duke University Press.

Mignolo, W.D. (2000). *Local Histories/Global Designs: Coloniality, Subaltern Knowledges, and Border Thinking*. Princeton: Princeton University Press.

Pavlenko, A. (forthcoming). Superdiversity and why it isn't: Reflections on terminological innovation and academic branding. In *Sloganizations in Language Education Discourse*.

Pennycook, A. and Otsuji, E. (2015). *Metrolingualism: Language in the City*. Abingdon: Routledge.

Pigg, S. (2014). Emplacing mobile composing habits: A study of academic writing in networked social spaces. *College English* 66(2): 250–275.

Piller, I. and Cho, J. (2013). Neoliberalism as language policy. *Language in Society* 42: 23–44.

Pitzl, M.-L. (2010). *English as a Lingua Franca in International Business*. Saarbrucken: Verlag.

Pollock, S. (2006). *The Language of the Gods in the World of Men: Sanskrit, Culture, and Power in Premodern India*. Los Angeles: University of California Press.

Pratt, M.L. (1987). Linguistic utopias. In N. Fabb, D. Attridge, A. Durant and C. MacCabe (eds.), *The Linguistics of Writing: Arguments between Language and Literature* (pp. 48–66). Manchester: Manchester University Press.

Rampton, B. (2008). *Language in Late Modernity: Interaction in an Urban School*. Cambridge: Cambridge University Press.

Rickert, T. (2013). *Ambient Rhetoric*. Pittsburgh: University of Pittsburgh Press.

Schachner, G. (2010). *Population Circulation and the Transformation of Ancient Zuni Communities*. Tucson: University of Arizona Press.

Seidlhofer, B. (2004). Research perspectives on teaching English as a Lingua Franca. *Annual Review of Applied Linguistics* 24: 209–239.

Smotrova, T. and Lantolf, J.P. (2013). The function of gesture in lexically focused L2 instructional conversations. *Modern Language Journal* 97(2): 397–416.

Steenstig, J. (2013). Conversation analysis and affiliation and alignment. In C. Chapelle (ed.), *Encylopedia of Applied Linguistics* [Online]. Wiley-Blackwell. doi:10.1002/9781405198431.wbeal0196

Stein, P. (2000). Rethinking resources: Multimodal pedagogies in the ESL classroom. *TESOL Quarterly* 34(2): 333–336.

Swyngedouw, E. (1997). Neither global nor local: Glocalization and the politics of scale. In K.R. Cox (ed.), *Spaces of Globalization: Reasserting the Power of the Local* (pp. 137–177). New York: Guilford Press.

Thrift, N. (2007). *Non-representational Theory: Space, Politics, Affect*. London: Routledge.

Uitermark, J. (2002). Re-scaling, "Scale fragmentation" and the regulation of antagonistic relationships. *Progress in Human Geography* 26(6): 743–765.

Urry, J. (2000). *Sociology beyond Societies: Mobilities for the Twenty-First Century*. London: Routledge.

Valentine, G., Sporton, D. and Bang Nielsen, K. (2008). Language use on the move: Sites of encounter, identity, and belonging. *Transactions of the Institute of British Geographers* 33: 376–387.

Vertovec, S. (2007). Super-diversity and its implications. *Ethnic and Racial Studies* 30(6): 1024–1054.

Vertovec, S. and Cohen, R., eds. (2002). *Conceiving Cosmopolitanism*. Oxford: Oxford University Press.
Wenger, E. (1998). *Communities of Practice*. Cambridge: Cambridge University Press.
Williams, A. M. and Balaz, V. (2008). *International Migration and Knowledge*. London and New York: Routledge.
Wimmer, A. and Glick Schiller, N. (2002). Methodological nationalism and beyond: Nation-state building, migration, and the social sciences. *Global Networks* 2(4): 301–334.
Wortham, S. and Reyes, A. (2015). *Discourse Analysis beyond the Speech Event*. Abingdon: Routledge.
Zelinsky, W. (1971). The hypothesis of mobility transition. *Geographical Review* 61(2): 219–249.
Zolberg, A.R. (1987). "Wanted but not welcome": Alien labor in western development. In William Alonso (ed.), *Population in an Interacting World* (pp. 36–73). Cambridge, MA: Harvard University Press.

Part I
Concepts

1
Translanguaging in mobility

Adrian Blackledge and Angela Creese

Introduction

In order to understand social life in the 21st century we need to understand mobility, and understanding mobility requires attention to the movement of linguistic and other semiotic resources. In this chapter we ask what we mean by 'mobility', and consider mobility as movement in and of geographical and historical locations. To give us purchase on the movement of people and linguistic and semiotic resources in time and space, we develop an understanding of translanguaging which views mobility in relation to trajectories of human emergence or ideological becoming. We can make such processes visible through attention to communicative repertoire and voice.

Overview

In this section we provide an overview of key concepts in relation to language, migration, and mobility. Globalization has compelled scholars to see sociolinguistic phenomena and processes as characterized by mobility. Blommaert (2010) argues that mobility is a central theoretical concern in the sociolinguistics of resources, as it describes the dislocation of language and language events from the fixed position in time and space attributed to them by a more traditional linguistics. An approach to language which concerns itself with mobility views human action in terms of temporal and spatial trajectories. A sociolinguistics of mobility focuses not on language-in-place but on language-in-motion, with various spatiotemporal frames interacting with one another. Furthermore, a sociolinguistics of mobility "is a sociolinguistics of speech, of actual language resources deployed in real sociocultural, historical, and political contexts" (Blommaert 2010: 5). Blommaert (2014) argues that adopting mobility as a central concept in a sociolinguistics of globalization has three major methodological effects: (1) it creates a degree of unpredictability in what we observe; (2) we can only solve this unpredictability by close ethnographic observation of the minutiae of what happens in communication; and (3) it keeps in mind the limitations of current methodological and theoretical vocabulary. In contexts of mobility, people appear to take any linguistic and communicative resources available to them and blend them into complex linguistic and semiotic forms (Blommaert 2014). Old and established terms such as 'code-switching', and even 'multilingualism', exhaust the limits of their descriptive and explanatory adequacy in the face of such highly complex sets of resources. Taking mobility as a principle of sociolinguistic research requires us to challenge traditional notions of the static and unitary nature of language.

Changes in economic and technological infrastructure have affected what we understand by mobility (Blommaert 2010). People and their attributes move around, and they do so in new and unpredictable patterns of complexity we now call superdiversity (Kroon, Dong and Blommaert 2015). Whereas migration, especially migration to Europe, was previously viewed in terms of apparently homogeneous groups moving from one country to another, recent patterns have brought a change in the nature and profile of migration to Western societies. We are now seeing that the extreme linguistic diversification of neighbourhoods generates complex multilingual repertoires layering the same social space. In a globalizing world we need to consider language as a complex of mobile resources, shaped and developed both *because* of mobility, by people moving around, and *for* mobility, to enable people to move around. We will consider the implications of mobility for communicative practices.

A sociolinguistic system is a complex system characterized by internal and external forces of perpetual change, operating simultaneously and in unpredictable mutual relationships (Blommaert 2014). Canagarajah and Liyanage (2012) have noted that even so-called monolinguals shuttle between codes, registers, and discourses, and can therefore hardly be described as monolingual. Just as the traditional distinction between languages is no longer sustainable, so the distinction between 'monolingual', 'bilingual', and 'multilingual' speakers may no longer be sustainable. Blommaert (2012) argues for a recognition that the contemporary semiotics of culture and identity need to be captured in terms of complexity rather than in terms of *multiplicity* or *plurality*. Indeed he argues that

> a vocabulary including 'multi-lingual', 'multi-cultural', or 'pluri-', 'inter-', 'cross-', and 'trans-' notions all suggest an a priori existence of separable units (language, culture, identity), and they suggest that the *encounter of such separable units produces peculiar new units*: 'multilingual' repertoires, 'mixed' or 'hybrid' identities and so forth.
>
> *(2012)*

Blommaert argues that a perspective which focuses on 'code-switching' is emblematic of this view. Bailey (2012) engages with the limitations of an approach to linguistic analysis which emphasizes code-switching, arguing that a focus on linguistic features that are officially authorized codes or languages (e.g., 'English' or 'Spanish'), can contribute to neglect of the diversity of socially indexical resources *within* languages. Bailey points out that if the starting point is social meanings, rather than the code or language in use, it is not crucial to ask whether a speaker is switching languages, alternating between a dialect and a national standard, register shifting, or speaking monolingually in a variety that highlights language contact. Language, whether monolingual or multilingual, carries social meanings through phonological, lexical, grammatical, and discourse level forms: "these forms index various aspects of individuals' and communities' social histories, circumstances, and identities" (Bailey 2012: 506).

We will review recent concepts and terms in relation to the mobility of communicative practices. Recently, a number of terms have emerged, as scholars have sought to describe and analyze linguistic practices in which meaning is made using signs flexibly. These include, among others: flexible bilingualism (Creese and Blackledge 2010); codemeshing

(Canagarajah 2011); polylingual languaging (Jørgensen, Karrebaek, Madsen, and Møller 2011); contemporary urban vernaculars (Rampton 2011); metrolingualism (Otsuji and Pennycook 2011); translingual practice (Canagarajah 2013); heteroglossia (Bailey 2012; Blackledge and Creese 2014); and translanguaging (García 2009; Creese and Blackledge 2011). The shared perspective represented in the use of these various terms considers that meaning-making is not confined to the use of 'languages' as discrete, enumerable, bounded sets of linguistic resources.

Canagarajah (2013) adopts the term 'translingual practice' to capture the common underlying processes and orientations of the mobility and complexity of communicative modes. In doing so he argues that communication transcends individual languages and involves diverse semiotic resources. He points out that languages in contact mutually influence each other, and so labelling them as separate entities is an ideological act. Multilingual speakers deploy repertoires rather than languages in communication, and do not have separate competences for separately labelled languages. Language is only one semiotic resource among many, and all semiotic resources work together to make meaning. Separating out 'language' from other semiotic resources distorts our understanding of communicative practice. Canagarajah (2013) points out that further research is needed to understand the complexity of communicative strategies that make up translingual practice, and to explore the implications for meaning construction, language acquisition, and social relations.

García uses the term 'translanguaging' to refer to the flexible use of linguistic resources by bilinguals as they make sense of their worlds. She proposes that in educational contexts translanguaging as pedagogy has the potential to liberate the voices of language minoritized students. For García (2009) a translanguaging approach to teaching and learning is not about code-switching, but rather about an arrangement that normalizes bilingualism without diglossic functional separation. She draws from Baker (2011: 288), who defines translanguaging as the process of "making meaning, shaping experiences, gaining understanding and knowledge through the use of two languages." In the classroom, translanguaging approaches draw on all the linguistic resources of the child to maximize understanding and achievement. Thus, both or all languages are used in a dynamic and functionally integrated manner to organize and mediate understanding, speaking, literacy, and learning (Lewis, Jones, and Baker 2012). García argues that bilingual families and communities must translanguage in order to construct meaning. She further proposes that what makes translanguaging different from other fluid languaging practices is that it is transformative, with the potential to remove the hierarchy of languaging practices that deem some more valuable than others. Translanguaging, she argues, is about a new languaging reality, a new way of being, acting and languaging in a different social, cultural and political context, allowing fluid discourses to flow, and giving voice to new social realities (García 2009). Li Wei (2011: 1223) makes a similar argument, that the act of translanguaging "is transformative in nature; it creates a social space for the multilingual language user by bringing together different dimensions of their personal history, experience and environment." Hornberger and Link (2012) apply such translanguaging constructs in educational contexts, proposing that educators recognise, value, and build on the multiple, mobile communicative repertoires of students and their families.

Thus translanguaging leads us away from a focus on 'languages' as distinct codes to a focus on the agency of individuals engaged in using, creating and interpreting signs for communication. Lewis et al. (2012) argue that the distinction between code-switching and translanguaging is ideological, in that code-switching has associations with language separation, while translanguaging approves the flexibility of learning through two or more languages.

García and Li Wei (2014) argue that the term translanguaging offers a way of analysing the complex practices of speakers' lives between different societal and semiotic contexts as they interact with a complex array of speakers. García and Li Wei (2014) extend the notion of translanguaging as an approach which views language practices in multilingual contexts not as autonomous language systems, but as one linguistic repertoire with features that have been societally constructed as belonging to separate languages. For García and Li Wei, the 'trans' prefix in 'translanguaging' refers to (1) a trans-system and trans-spaces, in which fluid practices go between and beyond socially constructed language systems, structures and practices; (2) the transformative nature of translanguaging, as new configurations of language practices are generated, and orders of discourses shift and different voices come to the forefront; and (3) the transdisciplinary consequences of languaging analysis, providing a means of understanding not only language practices but also human sociality, human cognition and learning, social relations and social structures. Translanguaging does not refer merely to two separate languages nor to a synthesis of different language practices, or to a hybrid mixture. Rather, translanguaging refers to new language practices that make visible the complexity of language exchanges among people with different histories. García (2009) sees translanguaging practices not as marked or unusual, but rather taken as the normal mode of communication that characterizes communities throughout the world. Thus translanguaging is commonplace and everyday.

Translanguaging also perceives the language system differently. García and Li Wei (2014) view translanguaging as not only going between different linguistic structures, systems, and modalities, but going beyond them. Going beyond language refers to transforming the present, to intervening by reinscribing our human, historical commonality in the act of languaging. Translanguaging "signals a trans-semiotic system with many meaning-making signs, primarily linguistic ones that combine to make up a person's semiotic repertoire" (2014: 42). García and Li Wei conclude that translanguaging enables us to imagine new ways of being so that we can begin to act differently upon the world. A translanguaging repertoire incorporates biographies and learning trajectories; it includes aspects of communication not always thought of as 'language', including gesture, dress, humour, posture, and so on; it is a record of mobility and experience; it includes constraints, gaps, and silences as well as potentialities; and it is responsive to the places in which, and the people with whom, semiotic resources may be deployed. As such it is responsive to the mobility of linguistic and other semiotic resources in time and space. In order to engage with semiotic resources in time and space we will consider the notion of chronotope (literally 'timespace').

Mobility implies not merely movement of people from one country to another to make a new life, but the mobility of linguistic and other semiotic resources in time and space. In considering language practices we need to account for both time and space – history and location. Human life is categorized by movement, whether through time or through space: we are always in motion (Pennycook 2010). In no other time has the coming together of time and space become more significant than in our own technological, global society (Wang 2009). Bakhtin (1981) borrowed the metaphor of the 'chronotope' from Einstein's theory of relativity to describe the connectedness of temporal and spatial relationships. In the literary chronotope, "time, as it were, thickens, takes on flesh, becomes artistically visible; likewise, space becomes charged and responsive to the movements of time, plot, and history" (Bakhtin 1981: 84). Analysis of chronotopes enables us to view synchronous social life historically. Chronotopes can be seen as "invokable chunks of history organizing the indexical order of discourse" (Blommaert 2015). Busch (2015: 14) summarises Bakhtin's notion of chronotope as "the co-presence of different spaces and times in speech," and argues that it can be transferred to the linguistic repertoire, as we not only position ourselves in relation to what is immediately present, but we also implicitly position ourselves in relation to other spaces and times from which we take our bearings. Chronotopes, therefore, "encroach on the here-and-now."

Pennycook (2012) argues for a focus on mobility as part of an inquiry into questions of movement in relation to time and space, and the ways in which places are produced by the flows and movements through them. Attention to mobility, he proposes, is essential for an understanding not only of the contemporary world but also of how our contemporary conditions came to be. Pennycook points out that place and locality are not so much defined by physical aspects of context as by the flows of people and languages through the landscape. We should therefore situate our investigations about language in questions of place and movement. Accordingly, Liebscher and Dailey-O'Cain (2013) distinguish between 'place' and 'space'. Places have a physicality, and when people regularly carry out particular practices in particular places, those practices become emplaced in, or fundamentally associated with, those places. Thus a place can be a country, a city, a building, or a room. Space, on the other hand, does not have a geographic location or a material form. A space is constructed through the process of interaction between human beings who occupy it and make reference to it.

In developing our understanding of language in use, we need to consider the mobility of linguistic and other semiotic resources in time and space. In order to do so we will attend to the notion of *repertoire*. Blommaert (2013) proposes that the collective resources available to anyone at any point in time constitute a repertoire. In his definition repertoires are biographically emerging complexes of indexically ordered, and therefore functionally organized, resources. Repertoires include linguistic, semiotic, and sociocultural resources used in communication. Rymes (2014) adopts the term 'communicative repertoire' to refer to the collection of ways individuals use language and other means of communication to function effectively in the multiple communities in which they participate. Repertoire can include not only multiple languages, dialects, and registers in the institutionally defined sense, but also gesture, dress, posture, and even knowledge of communicative routines, familiarity with types of food or drink, and mass media references including phrases, dance moves, and recognizable intonation patterns that circulate via actors, musicians, and other superstars. A repertoire perspective recognizes that it is not possible to link types of communication with person-types. In fact, the more widely circulated a communicative element is, the more highly diverse the interactions with it. Rymes argues that not only do we change languages and ways of speaking from activity to activity, we use bits and pieces of languages and ways of speaking to shift the way we talk within a single conversation or even within a single sentence. People's communicative repertoires are expanding by necessity. But this growing embrace of multiple languages may also provide us with a means of finding connection across difference and developing more participatory sources of knowledge and validation. In everyday encounters with diversity, individuals stretch their repertoires to find points of overlap.

Blommaert and Backus (2011) point out that repertoires in a superdiverse world are records of mobility: of movement of people, language resources, social arenas, technologies of learning, and learning environments. A relevant concept of repertoires needs to account for these patterns of mobility, for these patterns construct and constitute contemporary late-modern subjects. Repertoires enable us to document in great detail the trajectories followed by people throughout their lives: the opportunities, constraints, and inequalities they were facing; the learning environments they had access to (and those they did not have access to);

their movement across physical and social space; their potential for voice in particular social arenas. Repertoires are indexical biographies, and analyzing repertoires amounts to analyzing the social and cultural itineraries followed by people, how they manoeuvered and navigated them, and how they placed themselves into the various social arenas they inhabited or visited in their lives. Busch (2015) also takes a biographical orientation to repertoire. She understands repertoire not as something that an individual possesses but as something formed and deployed in intersubjective processes located on the border between the self and the other. She focuses on the biographical dimension of the linguistic repertoire to reconstruct how the repertoire develops and changes throughout life. Busch (2015) moves away from the idea that the repertoire is a set of competences, a kind of toolbox, from which we select the 'right' language, the 'right code' for each context or situation. The range of choices available to a speaking subject is not limited only by grammatical rules and knowledge of social conventions. Instead, particular languages or ways of speaking can have such strong emotional or linguistic-ideological connotations that they are unavailable or only partly available at particular moments.

Pennycook and Otsuji (2015) understand repertoire as available resources at a point in time and space, including, for example, songs, snippets of diverse languages and the wider semiotic surrounds. They propose that by taking this approach we can start to envisage an interaction between the resources brought to the table by individual trajectories (with all the social, historical, political, economic, and cultural effects this may entail) and the resources at play in a particular place. Pennycook and Otsuji (2015) expand the notion of repertoire in relation to the more extensive dynamics between language and urban space ('spatial repertoires'), which links the repertoires formed through individual life trajectories to the particular places in which these linguistic resources are deployed. Spatial repertoires draw on individual as well as other available resources, while individual repertoires contribute to and draw from spatial repertoires. Pennycook and Otsuji focus on understanding practices in place, those sedimented or momentary language practices in particular places at particular times.

Blommaert (2010) points out that a sociolinguistics of globalization should not just look at the world and its languages, but also to the world and its registers, genres, repertoires, and styles, if it wants to have any empirical grounding. He argues that even notions such as repertoire have an intrinsic historical dimension. While we can observe repertoires only in their synchronic deployment, we know that what is there in the way of resources and skills was there prior to synchronic deployment, and we know that these resources and skills got there because of personal biographies and the histories of social systems. Abandoning a structural notion of language compels us to replace it with an ethnographic concept such as *voice*, which embodies the experiential and practical dimensions of language, and which refers to the ways in which people deploy their resources in communicative practice.

Issues and ongoing debates

In this section we argue that in developing our understanding of language in use we need to consider the mobility of linguistic and other semiotic resources in time and space, but also the mobility of linguistic and other semiotic resources in trajectories of emergence and becoming. Pennycook (2010: 140) proposes that we should understand space and language not only in terms of location but also in terms of emergence, subjects in process "performed rather than preformed – and thus becoming." Bakhtin conceptualized language as a medium through which we participate in a historical flow of social relationships, struggles, and meanings (Bailey 2012: 501). When we engage with the words of others in a "contact zone" (Bakhtin 1981: 345), we selectively assimilate these words. This process of assimilation is "the ideological becoming of a human being" (1981: 341). In the process of assimilation, the unique speech experience of each individual is shaped and developed in continuous and constant interaction with others' individual utterances (Bakhtin 1986: 89). The discourse of the other no longer performs as information, directions, rules, and so on, "but strives rather to determine the very bases of our ideological interrelations with the world, the very basis of our behaviour" (1981: 342). That is, we become what we are, and never stop becoming what we are, by engaging in social relations with others. In his research on adolescents in England, Rampton summarised ideological becoming as "the dialogical processes by which people come to align with some voices, discourses and ways of being, and to distance themselves from others" (2014: 276). Our speech is filled with the words of others, which we re-accent and rework. Wortham (2001: 147) points out that to become a self one must speak, and "in speaking one must use words that have been used by others." In ethnographic research in a South African township, Blommaert and Velghe (2014: 150) speak of the process of "learning voice" for a young woman in a marginalized community as she draws on the repertoires of others to achieve her social goals. As we acquire new knowledge we also acquire attitudes and beliefs constituted in discourses with which we come into contact (Malinowski and Kramsch 2014). These notions of voice, emergence, and becoming have great potential in conceptualizing new forms of linguistic diversity associated with the increased mobility of linguistic resources.

The process of ideological becoming is ever-present and ongoing. It is therefore empirically challenging, as analysis of discrete speech events offers limited purchase on change. Wortham and Reyes (2015) argue that in order to understand long-term processes such as ideological becoming we must uncover how people, signs, knowledge, and dispositions travel from one event to another and facilitate behaviour in subsequent events. For this reason Wortham and Reyes propose analysis of the pathways on which linguistic forms, utterances, cultural models, individuals, and groups travel across events. Blommaert (2013) argues that we are at any point of time always 'experts' in language as well as 'apprentices', depending on the specific forms of language we need to use. Wang (2009) suggests that in a global society emergence is made possible by encounters in which historical encounters – including both life history and social history – intersect with, or on some occasions are intensified by, intercultural encounters. Rather than pre-existing in people's minds and then merely being referred to in interaction, people's selves – and, through these, the social spaces that result from the convergence of several selves being positioned in the same way – emerge or 'come into being' in the first place through the part of the social realm that is most basic in interaction (Liebscher and Dailey-O'Cain (2013).

In order to illustrate these emerging concerns, we present an empirical example from ongoing research. The example is an audio recording of an interaction between a customer and market traders on a butcher's stall in Birmingham, England, recorded in November 2014. The research was conducted as part of a four-year project funded by the Arts and Humanities Research Council, 'Translation and Translanguaging: Investigating Linguistic and Cultural Transformations in Superdiverse Wards in Four UK Cities'.[1] The aim of the project was to investigate how people communicate when they bring different histories, biographies, and trajectories to interaction.

In this part of the research Adrian Blackledge and bilingual researcher Rachel Hu were observing communicative interactions at a butcher's stall in Birmingham Bull Ring market, owned by a Chinese couple, Kang Chen (KC) and Meiyen Chew (MYC). Kang Chen said he was originally from Changle in Fujian, in the south of China. He had relatives in the UK, and had arrived in 2001. Meiyen Chew was from Furong, Malaysia.

In the example here, an African Caribbean woman (FC), a regular customer known to the stall-holders, is buying chicken from an English assistant butcher, Bradley (BJ), and has complained that the chicken pieces are 'too skinny':[2]

1	BJ	they are the skinny ones blame the chicken not me they are on a diet
2	KC	skinny one's good fat one no good hehe skinny one more taste
3	FC	come on I have to go home early
4	BJ	all right stop shouting
5	KC	haha no no no one's happy today hello how are you? I am just so so
6	FC	not too bad
7	KC	hehe not too bad only so so (.) come on then another one OK just put it in the till twenty pounds skin off yea that's it
8	BJ	[to FC:] twenty pounds (.) [to KC:] yeah her roof broken all the water inside [to FC:] you choose yourself you never like the one I choose
9	FC	come on I've only got half an hour
10	KC	put it in the bag put it in the bag
11		[to MYC:] 她不喜欢因为鸡太瘦了！ < she doesn't like it because it's too skinny >
12	MYC	她要肥的，汁多的，像火鸡的那种。她今天听上去不开心，好像　说是她家屋顶漏了。 < she wants the fat juicy one she wants those like turkeys (3) she doesn't sound happy today it sounds like her roof is leaking >
13	KC	什么？ < what? >
14	MYC	她家屋顶漏了 < her roof is leaking >。
15	KC	我们家的也漏，不过是楼顶的棉花把水吸走了。 < ours the same it's leaking but it was absorbed by the cotton wool there >
16	KC	[to BJ:] very angry today
17	BJ	her roof's broken (2) all the water inside
18	KC	all the water inside [to FC:] you you you want some carry bag? you need some carry bag going home put all your money inside make sure it's get wet hahahaha put all money inside yea
19	FC	[laughs] (xxxx)
20	KC	it's all right just turn on the heater that might get rid of the water [to BJ:] it's all right twenty-five
21	BJ	twenty-five is all right
22	FC	I shall love you and leave you
23	BJ	yes go for your chat and then love and leave them too
24	FC	(xxxx) happy day I am a young girl
25	BJ	oh happy birthday
26	FC	eighty-seven
27	KC	hello [wolf whistles] hello pretty lady you all right? hahaha
28	BJ	you going to the pub tonight then?

29	FC	no I don't drink
30	BJ	you can still have a lager shandy (.) lemonade
31	FC	water
32	BJ	yeah water cheap cheap I'll take you out if you want! hehe
33	FC	(xxxx) never mind (.) I don't smoke I don't like (xxxx) when he comes in ah just (xxxx)
34	BJ	I'll ask them to get it out of the tap even cheaper (3) you sure?
35	KC	you sure? it's still half an hour
36	BJ	yes fix your roof
37	FC	(xxxxx)
38	BJ	put on the heater (2) tell him don't ask him just tell him hehe
39	FC	(xxxx) all fish in my house
40	BJ	haha got everything?
41	FC	thank you bye bye see you next week
42	BJ	yes you will [FC leaves]
43	KC	[to BJ:] haha haha I only got half an hour
44	BJ	hehe I need to rush only got half an hour
45	MYC	什么事这么好笑？ < what's so funny? >
46	KC	hahaha fucking Jesus
47	BJ	I'm in a rush (.) half hour later
48	KC	I early go home early go home

In this interaction, the customer and Bradley initially engage in what appears to be mock irritation, as they negotiate over the quality of the chickens on offer. Bradley tries to make light of the woman's complaint, joking 'blame the chicken, not me, they are on a diet' (line 1). Kang Chen joins in with the topic, saying that skinny chickens have more taste than fat ones. When the woman displays mock (or possibly real, or perhaps both mock and real) irritation (line 5), Kang Chen metacomments 'no one's happy today.' As if to restart the sales interaction he says 'hello, how are you, I am just so so,' also introducing humour with the slightly off-key greeting. At this point (line 11) Kang Chen speaks to Meiyen Chew in Mandarin, seeking the private realm as a context in which he can (meta)comment on the woman's mood. Meiyen Chew tells him that the customer's roof is leaking, and Bradley corroborates this. Kang Chen's response, as we often saw, is to respond with a joke, loudly offering the woman a plastic carrier bag in which to keep her money dry at home. The woman seems amused, and Kang Chen offers her a discount on her purchase ('it's all right twenty five'). When the woman announces that it is her eighty-seventh birthday, Kang Chen performs a highly stylized mock flirtation, wolf-whistling and saying 'hello pretty lady you all right?' Bradley joins in with the mock flirtation, offering to take the woman out for the evening to celebrate. Rachel's field note of her observation of these events reads as follows:

> all three of them were saying happy birthday to her, when she announced proudly that she's eighty-seven today. 'I'm still a young girl!' the woman took a step back, sticking her hip out and putting one hand on it as if posing for a photographer. KC wolf-whistled at her: 'hello, young lady!' and the four of them laughed loudly, chatting among themselves that they should take her out tonight for a celebration.

The customer is clearly a willing participant in the joke. What we can see in the field note, but not hear in the audio-recording, is the corporeal dimension of the convivial interaction, as the eighty-seven-year-old woman makes a stylized performance of a much younger woman. All of the participants appear to enjoy the deployment of this stereotype as a resource for humour and convivial entertainment. The woman takes her leave, saying she will see them next week. However, as soon as the customer leaves the stall both Kang Chen and Bradley represent her in stylized, evaluative metacommentary, parodying her voice, and making fun of her stated wish to get home in half an hour (lines 41–46).

Here several voices move not only across 'languages', but across genres and registers. Kang Chen and Meiyen Chew speak to each other in Mandarin in the main. The African Caribbean woman's accent is both Jamaican and 'Brummy' (indexing the city of Birmingham); Bradley's accent is decidedly Brummy; Kang Chen has a broad Fuzhounese accent when speaking English; and Meiyen Chew speaks English with an accent at once Chinese and Malaysian. But neither languages nor accents are the key dimensions of this interaction. Resources in play in the translanguaging event include convivial humour, market banter, metacommentary, stereotypes, performance, non-verbal signs, stylization, reported speech (voicing), narrative, and more besides. In considering this interaction we make visible dimensions of the ideological becoming of Kang Chen and (perhaps to a lesser extent) Meiyen Chew, as they explicitly appropriate the words of others, implicitly try out voices, and engage in evaluative metacommentary on other people's words. In these ways they engage in dialogical processes by which they come to align with some voices, discourses, and ways of being, and distance themselves from others (Rampton 2014: 276). In these ongoing processes they find a voice. Kang Chen repeats the words of the customer ('not too bad'; 'still half an hour'), and of Bradley ('all the water inside'; 'you sure?'). Kang Chen's deployment of 'just so so' and 'only so so' is a recontextualisation of this customer's usual response to the greeting 'how are you?' The customer came to the stall every Tuesday morning, and 'so so' was her typical response to being asked how she was doing. Kang Chen takes her words and tries them out, prompting her to respond in typical fashion, and when she doesn't do so (line 6) he both echoes her words in the present ('not too bad') and her words in the past ('only so so').

Kang Chen has learned the norms of market discourse, and is able to deploy humorous banter. In line 2 he quickly picks up Bradley's joke and adds to it. As we saw on many other occasions, the two men bounce off each other like a comedy duo, picking up each other's cues and elaborating on each other's jokes. Normally Bradley is the straight man, and Kang Chen the clown. As soon as the eighty-seven-year old woman leaves the stall they both more or less collapse with laughter. Meiyen Chew doesn't get the joke, asking Kang Chen, 'What's so funny?' But for Kang Chen and Bradley it does not need explanation. Instead they jointly and simultaneously make a stylized representation of the customer, each of them mocking the fact that although she had said she had no time to chat, she nevertheless lingered at the stall. Each of them takes her words and recontextualises them, making a verbal evaluation of her words such that they are half hers and half theirs. Kang Chen takes the voice of the customer and creatively re-accents it, parodies it, and evaluates the customer's verbal performance by creating an artistic representation of that performance. Like Bakhtin's sly and ill-disposed polemicist (1981: 340), he takes his customers' words and reframes them as comical. His parodistic voice clashes with the represented voice of the customer, and in the process he finds his voice.

Implications

What, then, are the implications of the ways in which repertoires are deployed as people encounter each other in superdiverse public spaces? One thing that becomes clear is that the most important question is not about which language is mainly in use, but rather about what signs are in use and action, and what these signs point to. A translanguaging analysis enables us to better understand how people communicate. There may be much to learn from adopting a translanguaging lens through which to examine language practices, to ensure that we bring into play, both in practice and in pedagogy, voices which index students' localities, social histories, circumstances, and identities. This interaction was one of many we observed which included movement across languages, but in which languages were by no means the most significant dimension of the translanguaging event. The translanguaging repertoire in play was a repertoire which incorporated biographies and learning trajectories; it included aspects of communication not always thought of as 'language', including performance, humour, mock flirtation, wolf whistling, and so on. The translanguaging event was a record of mobility and experience; it was responsive to the marketplace in which, and the people with whom, it occurred. In this and many other examples of translanguaging events we observed in Birmingham Bull Ring Indoor Market, spaces for communication were opened up, and people made meanings in whatever way possible. The market was a place where this could happen. This was a place where communicative resources could be tried out in translanguaging spaces. The market was a space where people made fun of each other, teased each other, and sometimes became irritated with each other. Fundamentally it was a space for buying and selling. And translanguaging was a means by which this was successfully and convivially managed.

Our empirical research leads us to conclude that emergence and becoming are never finished. However we assimilate the words of others, re-accent them, add our evaluative tone, creatively develop them, make them our own – still the becoming goes on. During our time observing in the market we took brief glimpses of many people in the often-crowded hall. Some of them we saw from week to week as they visited the Chinese butcher to buy chickens' feet, blood curd, or pigs' hearts. Most of them, however, we would never see again. Each of them was on their own journey of becoming, assimilating voices, developing a changing ideological view of the world. We were fortunate that we were allowed to observe the traders at the Chinese butchers' stall repeatedly and frequently. They gave us an insight into their journey, into their ideological becoming, that could not have been provided by other means. We observed speech events that were connected on pathways and trajectories that allowed us to make visible how they travelled from one to another and shaped not only subsequent events, but also ways of being. We were able to analyse discourse beyond the individual speech event and "capture the heterogeneity of relevant resources and study the contingent emergence of social actions" (Wortham and Reyes 2015: 182). We saw and heard in the butchers' interactions in the market their humour, mickey taking, teasing, sales patter, clowning around, complaining, mocking, and much more. We saw and heard them engage in complex language exchanges with people who brought different histories and backgrounds to the interaction. We saw and heard communication that went beyond 'languages', as people made meaning by whatever means possible. We also saw that communicative practices were not universally successful, as exchanges and encounters were situated in unequal structures of power. We saw that the journey for Kang Chen and Meiyen Chew was not just about movement from one temporal frame and geographical location to another; not just another timespace. It was also about a biographical trajectory of learning through encounters with others, with their voices, and with their signs. It was about emergence and becoming, and about finding a voice.

Future directions

We should expand the study of language/mobility nexus beyond the traditional settings such as schools, reviewed earlier, to other everyday encounters. Markets are places where we encounter difference. More than any other city spaces, they define human engagement with difference, with different people, different clothes, different goods, and different ways of speaking (Pennycook and Otsuji 2015). The marketplace has historically been the centre of all that is unofficial, it remains with the people. In the marketplace "a special kind of speech was heard, almost a language of its own" (Bakhtin 1994: 213). Markets offer "an ideal setting to explore the relationship between economy and society, especially when we consider the ways that these markets reflect, but also shape, the nature and meaning of social and cultural diversity" (Hiebert, Rath and Vertovec 2015: 16). They entail encounters between people, frequently across lines of social and cultural difference. For some people street markets are the primary means by which they encounter people from other backgrounds. Hiebert et al. (2015) propose that the "spatial concentration of diversity" (p. 17) in a marketplace inevitably contributes to cosmopolitan attitudes and identities. They argue that diversity shapes markets, and markets shape diversity. Markets also contribute to the configuration of social life. They reflect the basic sociocultural and socio-economic diversity of local areas, bringing together people into a public arena who might otherwise remain apart. This happens, say Hiebert et al., in settings that are both relatively controlled through 'rules of engagement' and also highly adaptive and dynamic. Markets offer particularly rich seams for social research because they "exemplify the global process of space-time compression, juxtaposing people with backgrounds from distant places and distinct cultures together in the same place" (Hiebert et al. 2015: 17).

Duruz, Luckman, and Bishop (2011: 599) describe food markets as "significant spaces of intercultural exchange, everyday belonging, and citizenship." They suggest that markets offer a particularly beguiling research landscape, representing cosmopolitanism in microcosm, with diversity a hallmark of their everyday interactions. Markets, they propose, are not purely economic settings, but are also distinctive cultural sites where different ethnic groups come into contact through everyday activity, and where complex, fluid relations may be found and encouraged.

Watson (2009a: 1577) argues that markets represent a much neglected public space and site of social connections and interaction in cities. In her review of existing studies, she finds that markets have been subject to surprisingly limited analysis to date. Watson (2009b) argues that the sociocultural context of markets warrants textured investigation to make sense of when, where, and how encounters across difference occur productively or antagonistically, or somewhere in between. In her study she explores the potentiality of markets as public space where multiple forms of sociality are enacted. Watson conducted research in eight UK markets (Watson 2006, 2009a), focusing on a multiplicity of lived encounters and connections, and found that markets represented a significant public and social space as a site for vibrant social encounters, for social inclusion and the care of others, for 'rubbing along' and for mediating differences. Watson shows that the social encounters and connections found in markets provide the possibility for the inclusion of marginalised groups and for the comingling of differences (2009b). Her research in the market sites revealed their significance as social space across four dimensions: 'rubbing along'; social inclusion;

theatricality/performance; and mediating differences. Markets are found almost anywhere. As such they offer opportunity for research which provides important implications for our understanding of how people get along even when they may traverse perceived 'difference' in order to do so.

In the same AHRC-funded research project in which we observed the fine grain of commercial transactions in the market, we also conducted detailed linguistic ethnographic observations in the heritage sector, in community sport, and in legal settings. The concepts set out in this chapter were no less relevant in these settings than in the markets. For example, in a major public library, a meeting place for people with different histories and heritages, translation and translanguaging were often deployed as communicative means which transformed interactions between people whose trajectories were different from each other. In interactions in the library everyday translation and translanguaging were emblematic of a positive orientation to superdiversity, as linguistic, cultural, ethnic, and national differences were acknowledged, and deployed as resources for communication. The public library was a convivial place where a multitude of histories, trajectories, and expressions converged in overlapping and intersecting localities, and this practice of conviviality constituted a means to safeguard and preserve a positive orientation to superdiversity as a heritage for the future (Blackledge, Creese, and Hu 2016). The implications of translanguaging and mobility extend to other public spaces in the superdiverse city. The study of mobility and diversity should expand to such settings beyond the school or educational contexts where it has largely focused so far.

Summary

We began this chapter by saying that in order to understand social life in the 21st century we need to understand mobility. We also proposed that understanding mobility requires attention to the movement of linguistic and other semiotic resources. In the course of the chapter we have asked what we mean by 'mobility', and we considered mobility as movement in and of geographical and historical locations. We have also suggested that we should develop an understanding of translanguaging which views mobility in relation to trajectories of human emergence, or ideological becoming, or, put more simply, as a dimension of communicative repertoire and voice. We said that in order to develop our understanding of language in use we need to consider the mobility of linguistic and other semiotic resources in time and space, and in mobile trajectories of emergence and becoming. We further proposed that in order to do so we need to attend to notions of repertoire and voice.

Related topics

Superdiversity and language
New orientations to identity in mobility
Complexity, mobility, migration

Further reading

Bakhtin, M.M. (1981). *The Dialogic Imagination. Four Essays.* Ed. M. Holquist. Austin: University of Texas Press.

In this text Bakhtin sets out his theoretical position on language as dialogue.

Bakhtin, M. M. (1994). *The Bakhtin Reader: Selected Writings of Bakhtin, Medvedev, Voloshinov.* Ed. P. Morris. London: Arnold.

Morris provides an accessible, annotated introduction to Bakhtin, and includes extracts from the seminal work.

Blommaert, J. (2010). *The Sociolinguistics of Globalization.* Cambridge: Cambridge University Press.

Blommaert formulates the consequences of globalization for the study of language in society.

García, O. and Li Wei (2014). *Translanguaging. Language, Bilingualism, and Education.* London: Palgrave.

This book sets out clearly and briefly new theoretical and practical approaches to translanguaging.

Pennycook, A. and Otsuji, E. (2015). *Metrolingualism. Language in the City.* London: Routledge.

Through detailed empirical research the authors explore the dynamic interrelationship between language practices and urban space.

Notes

1 AHRC: Translation and translanguaging: Investigating linguistic and cultural transformations in superdiverse wards in four UK cities. Angela Creese (Principal Investigator), Mike Baynham, Adrian Blackledge, Jessica Bradley, John Callaghan, Lisa Goodson, Ian Grosvenor, Amal Hallak, Jolana Hanusova, Rachel Hu, Agnieska Knas, Bharat Malkani, Li Wei, Jenny Phillimore, Daria Pytel, Mike Robinson, Frances Rock, James Simpson, Caroline Tagg, Janice Thompson, Kiran Trehan, Piotr Wegorowski, and Zhu Hua.

2 Transcription conventions:

(xxxx)	unclear speech
!	animated tone or exclamation
(.)	a brief interval within an utterance
(2)	a brief interval within an utterance, in seconds
[word]	paralinguistic features and situational descriptions
< >	English translation of speech in Mandarin

References

Bailey, B. (2012). Heteroglossia. In M. Martin-Jones, A. Blackledge and A. Creese (eds.), *The Routledge Handbook of Multilingualism* (pp. 499–507). London: Routledge.

Baker, C. (2011). *Foundations of Bilingual Education and Bilingualism* (5th ed.). Clevedon: Multilingual Matters.

Bakhtin, M. M. (1981). *The Dialogic Imagination. Four Essays.* M. Holquist (ed.). Austin: University of Texas Press.

Bakhtin, M. M. (1986). *Speech Genres and Other Late Essays.* M. Holquist and C. Emerson (eds.). Austin: University of Texas Press.

Bakhtin, M. M. (1994). *The Bakhtin Reader: Selected Writings of Bakhtin, Medvedev, Voloshinov.* P. Morris (ed.). London: Arnold.

Blackledge, A. and Creese, A. (2010). *Multilingualism, a Critical Perspective.* London: Continuum.

Blackledge, A. and Creese, A. (2014). Heteroglossia as practice and pedagogy. In A. Blackledge and A. Creese (eds.), *Heteroglossia as Practice and Pedagogy* (pp. 1–20). London: Springer.

Blackledge, A., Creese, A. and Hu, R. (2016). *Protean Heritage, Everyday Superdiversity.* Working Papers in Translanguaging and Translation.

Blommaert, J. (2010). *The Sociolinguistics of Globalization.* Cambridge: Cambridge University Press.

Blommaert, J. (2012). *Chronicles of Complexity. Ethnography, Superdiversity, and Linguistic Landscapes.* Tilburg Papers in Culture Studies 29.

Blommaert, J. (2013). *Language and the Study of Diversity*. Working Papers in Urban Language & Literacies 113.

Blommaert, J. (2014). *From Mobility to Complexity in Sociolinguistic Theory and Method*. Working Papers in Urban Language & Literacies 135.

Blommaert, J. (2015) Chronotopes, scales and complexity in the study of language in society. *Annual Review of Anthropology* 44: 105–116.

Blommaert, J. and Backus, A. (2011). *Repertoires Revisited: Knowing Language in Superdiversity*. Working Papers in Urban Language & Literacies 67.

Blommaert, J. and Velghe, F. (2014). Learning a supervernacular: Textspeak in a South African township. In A. Blackledge and A. Creese (eds.), *Heteroglossia as Practice and Pedagogy* (pp. 137–154). London: Springer.

Busch, B. (2015). Expanding the notion of the linguistic repertoire: On the concept of Spracherleben – the lived experience of language. *Applied Linguistics*. First published online July 23, 2015, doi:10.1093/applin/amv030.

Canagarajah, S. (2011) Codemeshing in academic writing: Identifying teachable strategies of translanguaging. *Modern Language Journal* 95: 401–417.

Canagarajah, S. (2013). *Translingual Practice. Global Englishes and Cosmopolitan Relations*. London: Routledge.

Canagarajah, S. and Liyanage, I. (2012). Lessons from pre-colonial multilingualism. In M. Martin-Jones, A. Blackledge and A. Creese (eds.), *The Routledge Handbook of Multilingualism* (pp. 49–65). London: Routledge.

Creese, A. and Blackledge, A. (2011). Separate and flexible bilingualism in complementary schools: Multiple language practices in interrelationship. *Journal of Pragmatics* 43(5): 1157–1450.

Duruz, J., Luckman, S. and Bishop, P. (2011). Bazaar encounters: Food, markets, belonging and citizenship in the cosmopolitan city. *Journal of Media & Cultural Studies* 25(5): 599–604.

García, O. (2009). *Bilingual Education in the 21st Century*. Oxford: Wiley Blackwell.

García, O. and Li Wei (2014). *Translanguaging. Language, Bilingualism, and Education*. London: Palgrave.

Hiebert, D., Rath, J. and Vertovec, S. (2015). Urban markets and diversity: Towards a research agenda. *Ethnic and Racial Studies* 38(1): 5–2.

Hornberger, N.H. and Link, H. (2012) Translanguaging and transnational literacies in multilingual classrooms: A biliteracy lens. *International Journal of Bilingual Education and Bilingualism* 15: 261–278.

Jørgensen, J.N., Karrebaek, M.S., Madsen, L.M. and Møller, J.S. (2011) Polylanguaging in superdiversity. *Diversities* 13(2): 23–38.

Kroon, S., Dong, J. and Blommaert, J. (2015). Truly moving texts. In C. Stroud and M. Prinsloo (eds.), *Language, Literacy and Diversity: Moving Words* (pp. 1–15). Abingdon: Routledge.

Lewis, G., Jones, B. and Baker, C. (2012). Translanguaging: Developing its conceptualisation and contextualisation. *Educational Research and Evaluation* 18(7): 655–670.

Liebscher, G. and Dailey-O'Cain, J. (2013). *Language, Space and Identity in Migration*. London: Palgrave Macmillan.

Li Wei (2011). Moment analysis and translanguaging space: Discursive construction of identities by multilingual Chinese youth in Britain. *Journal of Pragmatics* 43(5): 1222–1235.

Malinowski, D. and Kramsch, C. (2014). The ambiguous world of heteroglossic computer-mediated language learning. In A. Blackledge and A. Creese (eds.), *Heteroglossia as Practice and Pedagogy* (pp. 155–178). London: Springer.

Otsuji, E. and Pennycook, A. (2011). Social inclusion and metrolingual practices. *International Journal of Bilingual Education and Bilingualism* 14(4): 413–426.

Pennycook, A. (2010). *Language as a Local Practice*. London: Routledge.

Pennycook, A. (2012). *Language and Mobility. Unexpected Places*. Bristol: Multilingual Matters.

Pennycook, A. and Otsuji, E. (2015). *Metrolingualism. Language in the City*. London: Routledge.

Rampton, B. (2011). From "Multi-ethnic adolescent heteroglossia" to "Contemporary urban vernaculars". *Language & Communication* 31(4): 276–294.

Rampton, B. (2014). Conviviality and phatic communication? In J. Blommaert and P. Varis (eds.), *The Importance of Unimportant Language*, Special issue of *Multilingual Margins*.

Rymes, B. (2014). *Communicating beyond Language. Everyday Encounters with Diversity*. London: Routledge.

Wang, H. (2009). Chronotopes of encounter and emergence. *Journal of Curriculum Theorizing* 25(1): 1–5.

Watson, S. (2006). *City Publics. The (Dis)enchantments of Urban Encounters*. London: Routledge

Watson, S. (2009a). Brief encounters of an unpredictable kind: Everyday multiculturalism in two London street markets. In A. Wise and S. Velayutham (eds.), *Everyday Multiculturalism* (pp. 125–140). London: Palgrave.

Watson, S. (2009b). The magic of the marketplace: Sociality in a neglected public space. *Urban Studies* 46(8): 1577–1591.

Wortham, S. (2001). *Narratives in Action. A Strategy for Research and Analysis*. New York: Teachers College Press.

Wortham, S. and Reyes, A. (2015). *Discourse Analysis beyond the Speech Event*. London: Routledge.

2
Nation-state, transnationalism, and language

Joseph Sung-Yul Park and Lionel Wee

Introduction

The greater prominence of transnationalism in our globalizing world is often seen as undermining the nation-state. If the modern nation-state was premised on the nexus of territory, ethnicity, and language, the growing cross-border flows of people, products, and ideas may imply a challenge to that nexus, as it can be seen as leading to a weakening of essentialist ties between language and national identity. One key topic in the research on language and migration has been the extent to which this idea of the weakening nation-state holds true. On the one hand, scholars have revealed how globalization and the new economy have facilitated the delinking of language and national identity through the promotion of global languages and the commodification of language. On the other hand, studies also pointed out how essentialist ties between language and national identity continue to be invoked as a model in the context of transnationalism, for instance, in constructions of authenticity or language policies that regiment the linguistic resources of transmigrants. These discussions show that the relationship between language, nation-state, and transnationalism is one of great complexity, shaped and mediated by multiple ideologies of language that may sometimes appear contradictory and conflicting. Evolving geopolitical conditions and discourses suggest that research on migration and language needs to pay attention to the complex ways in which such ideologies intersect with the material conditions that shape the understanding of nationhood and the process of transnationalism.

Overview

Language and the nation-state

Since the late 18th century, the notion of a state with jurisdiction over a particular territory and its citizens has become a powerful point of reference for people's understanding of the world and their own identities (Gellner 1983; Hobsbawm 1990; Anderson 1991). Whereas subjects of a political entity such as a multiethnic empire did not necessarily see themselves as sharing a common identity and fate, citizens of newly emerging sovereign states considered themselves as having equal rights, sharing a common culture and history, and jointly occupying a non-transferable territory. This convergence between the political entity of the *state* (a system of government with sovereignty over a definite population and territory) and the cultural entity of the *nation* (a group of people sharing common characteristics of ethnicity, customs, or historical memory, etc.) resulted in the nation-state, which served as the mechanism by which the novel concept of nationalism came to have a powerful grip on people's imagination. The nation-state can thus be understood as a demarcated sovereign territory that is occupied by and comes under political governance by representation of a single cultural group. As Smith (1995: 86) puts it,

> We may term a state a "nation-state" only if and when a single ethnic and cultural population inhabits the boundaries of a state, and the boundaries of that state are coextensive with the boundaries of that ethnic and cultural population.

Language played an important role in the establishment of nation-states. This single ethnic and cultural population is often assumed to speak a single language, which serves as the national language, official or otherwise, of the nation-state, commonly considered to be the carrier of the ethnic/national culture, transmitting historical memories, collective values, and the inherited wisdom of ancestors to current and future generations, as well as serving as the basis for unified government of the state. For instance, the German language played an important role in the formation of German nationalism. Figures such as Johann Gottfried Herder were influential in establishing the belief that language is the tie that binds a nation together, which was a particularly important argument in the case of German nationalism, due to the lack of a single German state that could be used to easily define the German 'people'. In fact, it was the existence of a distinct language that served as the justification for the creation of a unified German state (Hobsbawm 1990). On the other hand, in the case of France, French as the national language was seen as representing the modernist ideals of equality that the French Revolution and the resultant French nation-state stood for. Even though France had already been unified as a state by the Kingdom of France for centuries, promotion of French was crucial for disseminating the new understanding of the state as nation, transforming its subjects into French 'people', despite the fact that in 1789 less than half of the population of France actually spoke French (Grillo 1989; Hobsbawm 1990).

These examples show how the link between territory, ethnicity, and language that serves as the foundation for the nation-state is a social construction and an idealization; by representing the nation-state as a clearly bounded and internally united homogeneous entity, these ideologies justify and naturalize the existence of the nation-state. At the same time, they show that such links are crucial assumptions that must be sustained in an essentialist manner (that is, the connection between them must be understood as natural and timeless) through enormous work of erasure (Irvine and Gal 2000). Even apparently homogeneous nation-states such as South Korea and Japan are able to maintain this narrative of national homogeneity only by ignoring the presence of other ethnic groups that exist within their respective societies. This is indeed the work of nationalism. Nationalism refers to any social and political movement that aims to foster unity and solidarity, bringing together members of a single ethnic group or members from multiple ethnic groups so as to imbue in them the sense that they are or have the potential to constitute a nation (Smith 2010). Nationalism, in this sense, is an ideologically driven movement that attempts to downplay or even erase various (linguistic, ethnic, cultural, social, or political) differences in favor of emphasizing the shared destiny of members.

What this means is that nationalism cannot be taken for granted as a stable feature of any society. It has to instead be constantly maintained and revitalized in the face of multiple kinds of diversity, via various social mechanisms – including regular observance of events such as National Day or Independence Day, performance of the national anthem at key sporting events, recitation of the national pledge and raising of the national flag in schools, or even careful cultivation of a siege mentality by demonizing outsiders/foreigners as 'them' whom 'we' need to be wary of. Again, the promotion of a national language, which is shared and disseminated through the educational system and media, is one of such social mechanisms, which contributes to the formation of an 'imagined community' that is the unified nation (Anderson 1991).

Transnationalism and the challenges to the nation-state

The project of sustaining the nation-state, already highly challenging, arguably becomes even more complicated in the context of globalization. The increasing prominence of actors such as international agencies and transnational corporations diminishes the role that nation-states play in international politics and the global economy (Muehlmann and Duchêne 2007; Pujolar 2007). The growing reflexivity introduced by globalization leads to the appropriation of nationalist discourses by ethnic minorities, also problematizing the nexus of nation and state (Heller 2011). But a more fundamental complication comes from the phenomenon of transnationalism. Transnationalism refers to the connections across national borders that are facilitated by the cross-boundary flows of people, products, and ideas (Basch, Glick Schiller, and Szanton Blanc 1994). For instance, if migrants in the past were typically expected to be uprooted from their 'home country' to settle and integrate themselves into new societies, the greater mobility and connectivity that globalization offers means that they are more properly understood as 'transmigrants' whose 'daily lives depend on multiple and constant interconnections across international borders and whose public identities are configured in relationship to more than one nation-state' (Glick Schiller, Basch, and Szanton Blanc 1995: 48).

Viewed in this way, then, transnationalism is not just relevant for migrants who physically move from one place to another, but is also a phenomenon that characterizes the lives of people who are not necessarily on the move themselves. For example, what defines diasporic populations as transnational is not the historical fact of their origins elsewhere, but their 'imagining and planting roots, in a place or multiple places, while sharing or contesting memories of having arrived from elsewhere' (Daswani 2013: 37). Likewise, developments in information and communication technologies, which allow individuals to keep in touch with each other without necessarily having to travel to each other's locations, are extremely powerful in forming cross-border ties in the form of virtual speech communities formed via email, Skype, Twitter, and Facebook, among others.

Transnationalism, then, presents an interesting complication for the nation-state because it problematizes the essentialist ties between territory, language, and national identity that form the very foundation of the nation-state. The imagination of multiple belongings and flexible sense of moorings mean that the need to rely on the territorial boundedness and security of the nation-state is, arguably, lessened. For example, it has been suggested that one of the effects of transnationalism is the production of a 'deterritorialized culture' (Mir, Mathew, and Mir 2000: 28). Even though members of the same ethnic or national group may share a language, as they find themselves living in different societies spread across the globe, this shared ethnic/national identity may slowly become detached from any sense of physical territory. Physical location is an inescapable fact of existence, of course, and since the state is defined primarily in terms of territorial sovereignty (Berking 2004: 52), all individuals may accept and recognize, with varying degrees of permanence, their membership in a particular state. However, these same individuals may not be willing to go further and construe themselves as members of a nation that is bounded by the limits of the state's territory, that is, as members of a nation-state. In other words, while the state itself may still remain valued as a necessary institutional arrangement, it may, qua nation-state, no longer be looked upon as relevant for articulating a richer set of values and ideals, particularly those associated with fidelity to specific national identities (Brooks and Wee 2014: 38–39).

While this scenario nonetheless remains optimistic about the continued value and relevance of the state (in contrast to the more pessimistic diagnosis concerning the nation-state, cf. Ohmae 1996), more fundamental challenges may also be possible. This is because citizens who treat the state primarily as an institution that serves their various needs but who do not regard it as an institution to which they feel any strong sense of loyalty or belonging may – from the viewpoint of the state – simply abandon the state for some other in times of difficulty. In this regard, Ong (1999) has described as 'flexible citizenship' the practice of choosing one's citizenship with the intention of maximizing economic opportunities and advantages rather than (as would be expected under a more traditional notion of citizenship) making the choice on the basis of community identification, loyalty, and shared political rights. This means that the notion of citizenship and its mooring in the nation-state not only becomes more fluid, but also gets inserted in dimensions of power and control in more complicated ways. For instance, the ability to exercise flexible citizenship, or put differently, the degree to which citizenship is flexible, may be different for the economically poor as opposed to the mobile elites, since citizenship as a formal status cannot be unilaterally claimed by individuals but must be awarded by the state. In such cases, the cultural basis of the nation-state plays a less significant role, with the conditions for citizenship becoming less dependent on senses of loyalty and belonging that used to characterize membership in the nation-state. Indeed we see an increasing number of states that employ economic criteria when selecting potential new citizens (we return to this point later). As Turner (2011: 935, italics added) points out:

> Of course new migrants are economically poor and exploited, but the membership – or rather quasi-membership – of minority communities within the host society is typically perceived as the key issue. New theories of citizenship have stressed the issue of ethno-cultural marginality in such notions as 'flexible citizenship', 'post-national citizenship' or 'semi-citizenship' in order to capture this grey world of minorities. *The modern state continues to operate as a territorial sovereign power, but the global labour market assumes porous political and legal boundaries.*

Transnationalism, then, in many ways heralds an age of post-nationalism in which the state may still remain relevant but the nation-state less transparently so. Given the centrality of language for the nation-state, this also leads to various questions regarding the role of language in this process. Are the essentialist ties between language and national identity necessarily being weakened? Or do such essentialist views of language continue to shape the way we understand ourselves and our sense of belonging? If so, how? These questions have been a major issue for applied linguists and sociolinguists investigating the intersection of migration and language. In the following section, we detail some of the issues and debates that have emerged through this discussion.

Issues and ongoing debates

Scholars have argued that globalization and the concomitant flow of people, goods, and ideas across borders have facilitated the delinking of language and national identity. But at the same time, studies have also pointed out how essentialist ties between language and national identity continue to be invoked as a model in the context of transnationalism, for instance in constructions of authenticity or language policies that regiment the linguistic resources of transmigrants. What these debates highlight is the complexity of the relationship between language, nation-state, and transnationalism. Ideologies of language that mediate the role of the nation-state in transnationalism are always multiple and diverse, and need to be analyzed for the contradictions and tensions they engender.

The cross-border connectivity facilitated by the movement of people and ties mediated by information and communication technology give rise to what Jacquemet (2000, 2005) refers to as transidiomatic language, or transidiomaticity, where language resources are recombined, mixed, or hybridized. Arguing that globalization has raised fundamental problems for assumptions about the coherence of language systems and their stable relationships to identifiable language communities, Jacquemet (2005: 261) suggests that one significant consequence is:

> the intersection between mobile people and mobile texts – an intersection no longer located in a definable territory, but in the deterritorialized world of late modern communication. An increasing number of people around the globe learn to interact with historically and culturally distant communicative environments through new technologies (including the asynchronous channels of e-mail and voice-mail, the abridged idioms of cellular digital messaging, and the multi-media capabilities of web pages) and use newly acquired techno-linguistic skills (control of English, translation capabilities, knowledge of interactional routines in mediated environments). In so doing, they gain, or increase, their social worth. They achieve power, in other words, by learning how to interact in a deterritorialized world.

At the same time, though, as we noted earlier, individuals, however mobile, still need to be physically located somewhere, which mitigates any claims about deterritorialization. Also, depending on who these individuals are and where they are located or attempting to be located, there will always be localized constraints that they need to negotiate – which therefore means that any discussion about power will also need to be carefully qualified. These points have been raised by Maryns and Blommaert (2001: 63–64, italics in original) in their discussion of the narratives produced by asylum seekers:

> Asylum-seekers' narratives can almost by definition be characterized in terms of what Jacquemet (2000) calls *deterritorialized* and *transidiomatic* language ... Both terms have a language-ideological load and point to connections between linguistic resources and aspects of ownership rights and authority. They presuppose that a number of 'global' processes have called into question the assumed fixity of languages and localities – the latter seen as a conglomerate of spatial, temporal and sociocultural features. At the same time, such processes have been met with (paradoxical) tendencies toward hegemonization and 'centering' of language and linguistic practices, generating emphases on purity and ownership right as part of the political imagination of 'groupness'. Phenomena of deterritorialization and transidiomaticity therefore open up a space of struggle over the value and function of codes and varieties in language.

Even though asylum seekers have been deterritorialized, the narratives that they produce in order to convince the host society's authorities that they deserve to be granted asylum, as well as the kinds of language practices that they subsequently engage in as they – to varying degrees – integrate into the host society, are all reflections of attempts at reterritorializing or emplacing language in specific locations. Such attempts at reterritorialization are of course not straightforward, and often, as Maryns and Blommaert point out, lead to struggles over the legitimacy of differences in language use. Migrants' use of language will tend to be influenced by their own varied sociolinguistic trajectories, whether in the form of distinctive accents, lexical innovations, idiomatic morphosyntax, or pragmatics. The relevance of the nation-state here is that such differences are often evaluated in relation to local ideological frameworks which are still centered around the hegemonic positioning of the local national language, leading to social discrimination against migrants on the supposed grounds that their version of the language lacks legitimacy.

We can see a good example of this in the case of Rinkeby Swedish. The Rinkeby district of Stockholm, which started out as cheap housing for both native Swedes and migrants, became a predominantly 'immigrant ghetto' (Hoge 1998) as the former moved out and left the housing units to be increasingly occupied by the latter. As Hoge (1998) points out:

> Mazhar Goker, 35, came to Rinkeby from Turkey in 1972, and his family were the only immigrants on the block. Today, he said, there are no native Swedes left.
> "When I first came here, we were exotic creatures, and people liked to look at us and feel our hair," he recalled. "Now they take detours not to see us."

And though the immigrants living in Rinkeby actually come from a variety of backgrounds (including Greek, Somali, Iraqi, Hungarian, and Spanish), ideologies about immigrant language in Sweden have led to a derogatory characterization of 'their' version of Swedish as 'Rinkeby Swedish'. Wee (2011: 9) observes:

> Speakers can also be marginalized because they are seen as non-legitimate speakers of a variety that 'rightly' belongs to a native group. Thus, in Sweden, immigrants – despite their ethnic heterogeneity – are stereotypically characterized as speaking Rinkeby Swedish. This is a pan-immigrant variety that is considered by both native Swedes and the immigrants themselves to be inauthentic, improper Swedish in relation to the 'authentic/proper' variety spoken by 'real' Swedes (Stroud 2004).

What the Rinkeby Swedish example shows us is that migrants often struggle to find legitimacy for their language use from members of the host society, which uses the nation-state as the reference point for community. The converse is also possible – where the host society may struggle to find legitimacy for its own language among migrants.

Consider Heller's (1999) account of the French Canadian high school of Champlain, which is officially committed to presenting itself as a monolingual space for preserving Canadian French. This official commitment exists in tension with the language practices of students as well as teachers, who negotiate a mix of English, Parisian French and Canadian French in their quotidian activities. Much of the reason for this tension is due to the recent arrival of migrants from former French colonies, who have chosen to make Canada their home in part because of a shared French background. The linguistic differences between Parisian French and Canadian French are indexical of the fact that these migrants do not have a heritage-based interest in Canadian French, preferring to prioritize Parisian French and English as languages worth learning because of their presumed global value. The school of Champlain, then, is caught in a sociolinguistic bind. On the one hand, it wants to retain its original mission of providing an educational space where the heritage language of Canadian French might be privileged. But on the other hand, the more recent arrivals do not share this heritage commitment, and if the school wants to be seen as educationally relevant and to continue enrolling healthy student numbers, it has to find a way of accommodating other languages such as Parisian French and English without being seen as having abandoned the heritage/preservationist ideals that led to its founding in the first place. Here, then, patterns of migration into Canada, the language curricula of a local high school, and perceptions of what language resources might be globally valued all intersect, bringing together different groups (longtime residents, newly arrived migrants, language teachers, students) and their respective assumptions about what roles various languages might play in their (current and projected) social trajectories.

The preceding discussion shows how the conditions brought about through transnationalism complexify the relationship between language and nation-state. Ideologies of language and identity that posit an essentialist connection between language and national identity are juxtaposed with ideologies that view the connection between language and identity as flexible and malleable. At the same time, the divergent interests and social positions of different groups and their varying conditions for mobility lead to competing ideologies that must be negotiated through local social interaction and institutional processes. And while it might be argued that similar processes would have taken place in earlier times and thus this complex relationship between language and the nation-state is not necessarily new, what is significant here is how the reflexivity and awareness of life elsewhere brought about by globalization and the transnational connections that such sensitivity facilitates (Dick 2010) open up a new terrain for such contestation of ideologies to take place.

This complexity, then, necessarily has multiple implications for language use in social context, raising various problems that we must consider in terms of policy, research, and pedagogical practice. In the following section, we provide a detailed discussion of those implications by focusing on three specific domains that are relevant to scholars of language: language and citizenship, heritage language education, and language in the new economy.

Implications

Language and citizenship

One important implication of transnationalism for the nation-state is that it raises questions regarding how to situate multilingualism in relation to citizenship. Migration, as we have seen, leads to increased linguistic diversity, and such diversity inevitably results in different valuations of the codes and varieties, which can, if left unchecked, in turn, lead to social discrimination and even a sense of segregation or ghettoization. There are therefore major language policy decisions that need to be made if a sense of community is to be cultivated that can maintain national unity while respecting diversity (Wright 2004). But such decisions are rarely made rationally and free from the influence of essentialist language ideologies. Especially, it is important that essentialist language ideologies be critically scrutinized, for these often become the basis of intolerance. Consider, for instance, the seemingly reasonable demand that the nation-state might make – with the likely backing of many citizens – that newly arrived migrants ought to learn the national language if they wish to take up permanent residence or citizenship. In 2002, this demand was concretized in Sweden in the form of a language test for citizenship, on the grounds that it would enhance integration. However, as Milani (2008: 30, italics added) points out:

> the public claims advanced in 2002 about the necessity of introducing a language test for naturalization are not simply about objective measurement or assessment of immigrants' language skills, but are the tangible manifestation of a competing language ideology – one could call it an ideology of language testing – *that attempts to defy multilingualism and multiculturalism by tying proficiency in one language to knowledge of one culture* as the compulsory prerequisite for the granting of rights of membership in Swedish society and the Swedish nation as an imagined community.

The idea of language testing, although superficially innocuous, is therefore based on the rather more dangerous precept that there is one specific language that embodies the national culture and community. Following on from this precept, formal admission into this national community, that is, the awarding of citizenship status, is dependent on the applicant demonstrating appropriate competence in this language. More importantly, under this view, competence in other languages or even 'having an accent' – which is a natural consequence of the migrants' transnationalism – is seen as suspect; it is interpreted as a refusal to integrate into the nation-state, which leads to the idea that migrants must prove their willingness to integrate by passing the language test (see also Piller 2001). Of course, such beliefs are usually justified on the grounds that acquisition of the national language is essential for the migrant community's inclusion into the host society. But in the context of transnationalism, any argument for learning the national language (whether via testing or otherwise) cannot reasonably ignore the fact that the national language itself inevitably will undergo various changes as a result of being learned and transmitted by speakers coming from other linguistic backgrounds. This argument also cannot ignore the need for speakers from other cultural and linguistic backgrounds to be given the space and respect that such diversity deserves (May 2014). In times of increasing multilingualism and multiculturalism often discussed under the name of superdiversity (Vertovec 2006), it becomes particularly crucial to interrogate the assumptions about transidiomatic practices that mediate our understandings of language and citizenship.

Heritage language education

Heritage language education in globalization can be a contested site. Many of the migrants may be keen to preserve their own heritage through education while also seeking socioeconomic advancement. Also, it is often in the interest of the state to allow sufficient space for different ethnic groups to preserve their distinct identities while also ensuring that a sense of national solidarity is cultivated. Yet, these are not easy tasks because of various problems, including the need to share curriculum time with national language instruction as well as other subjects that are considered to have more 'practical' value, such as mathematics and science. But a more fundamental problem lies in the contesting ideologies that attribute different indexical properties to different varieties.

A good illustration of this comes from Blackledge and Creese's (2008) study of Bengali schools in Birmingham. Blackledge and Creese show that there are significant controversies and disagreements within the migrant community as to what language properly represents their heritage. While community members are in general agreement that knowledge of

Bengali is necessary for the maintenance of Bangladeshi roots (2008: 539–540), educators prefer to teach the standard variety. For these educators, a more regional variety is considered inappropriate or even unacceptable (2008: 542). Speakers of a regional variety, such as Sylheti, are characterized as members of a 'scheduled' or 'untouchable' caste, despite the fact that boundaries between standard Bengali and Sylheti are by no means clear, as Blackledge and Creese (2008: 544) point out:

> Whilst some speakers in our study considered 'Sylheti' to be quite different from 'Bengali', others regarded the two sets of resources as indistinguishable . . . Those who argued that the 'languages' were completely different from each other were speakers of the prestige language, unwilling to allow the lower status language to contaminate their linguistic resources. Those who argued that the 'languages' were almost the same as each other were speakers of Sylheti, which was held to index the lower status, less educated group.

Moreover, there was also opposition from the students themselves about whether any form of Bengali is even necessary for their Bengali identity. For them, Bengali plays no necessary role in constituting their ethnic identity.

Examples like this show that heritage language education in the context of transnationalism raises fundamental questions about the nature of language and heritage. While it is easy to suggest, in diasporic contexts, that heritage language education must closely align with dominant practices of the 'homeland', it is also important to recognize that such perspectives use the model of the nation-state as point of reference, in which standardized, national languages serve as the key basis for national and ethnic identity. However, the transidiomatic practices of the younger generations of migrants challenge such perspective on language and heritage. As Canagarajah (2013: 152) notes,

> They are able to address their personal interests of socioeconomic mobility by constructing hybrid identities, without abandoning affiliation with their heritage language and ethnic community. They are able to be mobile without abandoning inherited identities and community solidarity. They accomplish this feat by constructing ideologies of language and ethnicity that are flexible enough to let them shuttle across spatiotemporal contexts and communities easily.

From a pedagogical perspective, then, it is important to recognize how transnationalism offers both challenges and opportunities for heritage language education. On the one hand, transnationalism problematizes the framework of heritage based on the model of the nation-state, pressing educators and communities to seek new ways to situate the relevance of heritage language learning. On the other hand, changing conceptualizations of heritage identity and heritage language serve as alternative spaces for diasporic communities to articulate their social position. Building a relevant model for heritage language education in the context of transnationalism would not be possible without sensitivity to this tension.

Language in the new economy

A prominent aspect of globalization is the new conditions of the global economy. In this new economy, production is increasingly carried out on a global scale, with outsourcing and offshoring becoming more commonplace, and transnational corporations playing a greater role in the global capitalist system. As mentioned earlier, this is another way in which the role of the nation-state is undermined (Pujolar 2007). However, this does not mean that the nation-state model becomes irrelevant in the work of transnational corporations. Indeed, transnational corporations may actively adopt essentialist language ideologies of the nation-state to rationalize the conditions of multinational and multicultural work. That is, essentialized notions of the relationship between language and identity do not simply disappear but instead 'are reintegrated into a new system of valuation, working in tandem with newer conceptions of self' (Park 2013: 557).

For instance, managerial imperatives such as 'diversity management', in which the diversity of the workforce is embraced as a crucial resource for profit, in fact serve as social mechanisms of control in the workplace, by the way they refer back to the essentialist views of language and identity. That is, even though cultural and linguistic differences of transnational workers are often prized as resources in the multinational corporation, not all forms of difference are equally valued, with employees from particular nation-states (e.g., native English speakers from Western countries) seen as having communicative skills appropriate for the global workplace. Subtle pressure is then exerted on employees from other backgrounds (e.g., Korean employees) to converge towards dominant linguistic and communicative practices, a convergence that is legitimized by ideological assumptions that treat cultural difference as ahistorical and essential. Park (2013: 17) thus argues that:

> This also explains why older discourses of identity that reify national difference do not disappear in the age of commodification of language and identity; they serve as important resources for explaining, rationalizing, and reframing issues of inequality as something innocent, something that can be transformed into a justification for the dominant social order of the workplace.

These issues highlight the continuing relevance of the nation-state model for transnational work. The fact that employees of transnational corporations work across linguistic and cultural boundaries of the nation-state does not mean that they are free from its underlying assumptions, as they are constantly identified as belonging to certain nationalities and evaluated in ideological terms linked with such identities.

This reminds us that the conditions of the new economy are always mediated by ideological processes. We can see such effects not only within transnational corporations, but within the working of the nation-state as well. Carver and Mottier (1998: 14) point out that citizenship is a category that involves 'gradations of esteem', where different kinds of rights, responsibilities, and privileges accrue to different sub-categories of citizens. In the context of neoliberalism, 'gradations of esteem' may manifest themselves as 'graduated sovereignty' (Ong 2006: 78) where the more productive and skilled citizens are, the more likely they are to enjoy some form of sovereignty from the state. This is particularly the case with the issue of citizenship granted to migrants. According to Ong (2006: 78–79), 'administrative strategies are informed by . . . "explicit calculations" about human life in terms of its growth and productivity' and, especially in 'Asian tiger states' (such as Singapore, Malaysia, Thailand), 'low-skilled workers enjoy fewer civil rights and less welfare protection than higher-skilled workers in science parks and high-tech centers.' Thus, while high-paid transnational professionals enjoy more flexible choices in acquiring citizenship in other countries, lower class migrant workers often struggle to claim even basic human rights, let alone rights as citizens (see, however, Ricento 2015, for cases where even immigrant professionals may have difficulty in having their rights or credentials recognized in the host country; also see discussion later in this chapter). As we have seen, ideological evaluations of linguistic competence clearly play a role in such 'explicit calculations'. For this reason, research into the specific ways in which essentialist ideologies of the nation-state are incorporated into practices of differentiation and discrimination in the new economy is an important contribution scholars of language can make.

Future directions

One important issue for research that emerges from the foregoing discussion is how the changing role of the nation-state under transnationalism must be understood in relation to the multiple connections, trajectories, and pathways that define the transnational experience. We must recognize that the rubric of transnationalism does not always sufficiently distinguish between different kinds of migrants and different migration trajectories. As Faist (2000: 37) points out, relevant causes that impact on a person's decision to migrate

> may be related to improving and securing: wealth (e.g. income), status (e.g. prestigious job), comfort (e.g. better working and living conditions), stimulation (e.g. experience, adventure, and pleasure), autonomy (e.g. high degree of personal freedom), affiliation (e.g. joining friends or family), exit from oppression of all kinds, meaningful life (e.g. improving society), better life for one's children, and morality (e.g. leading a virtuous life for religious reasons). In this view the potential migrant could not only be a worker, a member of a household or a kinship group, but also a voter, a member of ethnic, linguistic, religious, and political groups, a member of a persecuted minority, or a devotee of arts or sports.

Unless these differences are consistently borne in mind in any discussion of transnationalism, we are in danger of losing sight of the fundamental fact that people are mobile for very different reasons and face very different constraints and priorities. Paying greater attention to the multiple pathways of transnationalism and the different ways in which the ideologies of the nation-state affect different migrants, then, can be a rich site for future research.

In particular, a focus on social class can be a useful approach to such investigations. Block (2013) shows how social class has been a long-neglected concept in applied linguistics. The influence of the poststructuralist perspectives on language over the past few decades has meant that the intersection of language and society has mostly been explored through the discursive construction of identity. However, this has also meant an inattention to the material conditions of life that serve as a necessary basis for identity, in particular the way in which social class in the capitalist system leads to multiple forms of inequality. Social class and the nation-state, both of which are deeply intertwined with the historical structure of modern capitalism, take on new meanings and relations in transnationalism. Global connectivity and mobility often serves as a new way of reproducing and rationalizing class interests; and nation-states find new ways of articulating their significance in the transnational experience of citizens. An analytic focus on how these changing conditions intersect with relations of class can thus offer a productive direction for research on language, transnationalism, and the nation-state.

For instance, as we observed earlier, migrant workers and migrant professionals face drastically different constraints in their attempts to fit into the host society, and policies – including policies that relate to migrant language education – have to be constructed with this in mind. As a simple example, consider the plight of Javier Lopez (Bowe, Bowe, and

Streeter 2000: 230), an illegal migrant from Mexico, who sorts chicken parts in a poultry factory in North Carolina:

> The large majority of the workers here are illegal Hispanics, like me. There's also some legal Hispanics, some Haitian and black gringos. But most of us are illegal Hispanics. The bosses know we're illegal, and it's illegal for them to hire us, but we're the cheapest, so they don't care. We probably wouldn't work such a bad job if we had documents. And they always yell at us Hispanics. With the others they are more flexible, more lenient. The others come late sometimes, they talk on the phone. And they can get away with it. The black gringos that work here have more flexibility, they speak English. The blacks talk back, and they can argue because they speak English.

Since the language of negotiation with 'the bosses' in the poultry factory is English, those competent in English, such as the 'black gringos', are able to argue for greater autonomy and somewhat better working conditions. In contrast, Spanish, the language that Lopez is competent in, is not accorded any value in the workplace. This makes it difficult, if not impossible, for Lopez and other co-ethnics to negotiate for better working conditions, the issue of their illegal and undocumented status notwithstanding.

The migrant professional's relationship to the host society can be significantly different (Wee 2014). For one, the relationship is more that of equals, between professional colleagues, all of whom – whether migrants or members of the host society – are well educated, relatively affluent and successful. We are speaking here of migrants whose professional qualifications are recognized and valued in the host society. This is not always the case, of course, since a physician from Colombia, for example, may not find his/her professional background valued in Canada due to resistance from local/national professional societies (Ricento 2015: 138). In contrast, Indian and Chinese engineers are highly valued as 'skilled foreigners' in Silicon Valley (Shin and Choi 2015: 3). Thus, whether or not particular migrants are treated as 'skilled foreigners' depends largely on the needs and receptiveness of the host society. That being said, given their greater mobility, migrant professionals typically have a high degree of individual autonomy in deciding whether and how long to stay in the host society. More importantly, their linguistic repertoire is more likely to be understood as 'an index of their cosmopolitan flair' (Park and Wee 2012: 153), due to greater room they are allowed to negotiate the value of their competence.

Such differences in the position of various groups of transmigrants may be considered a reflection of the difference in relative power the speakers have. But the general lesson here could be that we need more complex sensitivity toward the intersection of class, mobility, and transnationalism, as the interaction of such conditions within the context of the nation-state does not always lead to predictable outcomes. This would push us to engage more deeply into the structural conditions that give rise to multiple inequalities and understand how the tensions that transnationalism introduces into the nation-state become relevant here. For instance, ideological interpretations of the convertibility of the value of the linguistic capital of different groups of migrants (Park and Wee 2012) are constrained by the different positions the migrants occupy in the structure of global capitalist production. That is, the trajectory of migration for both groups, which condition how their linguistic competence is evaluated, is ultimately shaped by the changing systems of capitalist production, the specific position different groups of transmigrants occupy within those systems, and how nation-states cope with such changes. Tracing the ways in which shifting ideologies of language and identity are negotiated through transmigrants' everyday experience, then, can be a useful site for investigating the structural bases of inequalities that are reproduced in the space of the nation-state.

At the same time, future research should be able to better account for the fact that highly mobile migrants – whether lower-class workers or professionals – all have to be prepared to constantly renegotiate changing local perceptions and valuations of their language resources. Here, language competence has to be reconceptualized so that its 'truncated' and 'fragmented' nature (Blommaert, Collins, and Slembrouck 2005) can be better appreciated, instead of being considered evidence of language deficiencies. But such a reconceptualization cannot only be applied to the language of migrants as though the language of the host society was somehow privileged: in a very fundamental sense, all forms of language competence are truncated because what gets construed as competence is always mediated by the dominant language ideologies of the local settings – particularly that of the nation-state.

How language ideologies of completeness and truncatedness differentially exert their effects on official policies and unofficial language attitudes, then, becomes a major area of research interest. For instance, there has been much criticism of the perspective of linguistic cosmopolitanism, in which acquisition of global languages such as English are assumed to facilitate democratic communication and mutual understanding on the global stage. May (2014), for instance, critiques this idea as not sufficiently addressing the class-based nature of cosmopolitanism, and suggests that language policies of nation-states must be informed by a better understanding of the truncated nature of linguistic competence. Also, while nation-states sometimes rely on the assumption of 'untrammelled monolingualism' (May 2014: 374) to insist that immigrants, as well as linguistic minorities, should move away from their own languages for their social integration and economic benefit, the view of language competence as fragmented and adaptive would suggest that there is in fact no contradiction between maintenance of the home language and acquisition of the standard national variety. There can indeed be a complementarity across varieties and domains so that speakers are not necessarily faced with an either/or option, especially one where they are expected or urged to relinquish their competence in private/minority/lesser-valued languages (see also May, this volume).

Future directions for applied linguistic research, then, are twofold. One, there is a need to more properly account for the multiplicity of transnational experiences and how they relate to the differential value attributed to the linguistic resources transmigrants bring with them. Linking such multiplicity with the structural aspects of the global economy allows us to trace the shifting conceptions of language and identity that are reconfiguring the ideological bases of the nation-state. Two, there is a need to actively integrate analysis of transnational experience with a more sophisticated notion of linguistic competence as fragmented or truncated. Such a framework, once systematically articulated, can then be applied to better understand how migrants' motivations for movement meet with resistance or find facilitation in different host societies. Taken together, we believe that such a research program can contribute significant insights into how competing language ideologies mediate our understanding of nationhood, citizenship, and mobility, and the complex consequences these have for transmigrants' experience.

Summary

In this chapter, we offered a critical review of the relationship between language, nation-state, and transnationalism, and its implications for the research on migration and language. We began with an overview of the concepts of nation-state and transnationalism, how they both become crucial issues and sites of tension in the context of globalization. Next, we reviewed the issues surrounding the debate on whether and how transnationalism undermines the place of the nation-state, considering some of the key studies within applied linguistics and sociolinguistics that explore the changing role of the nation-state in transnationalism. We then discussed the implications of those studies for policy, research, and pedagogy by considering three specific domains where the intersection of language, nation-state, and transnationalism introduces new tensions and questions – language and citizenship, heritage language education, and language in the new economy. As suggestions for future research, we highlighted the need to consider the multiplicity of transnational experiences through the lens of social class, and to adopt a perspective on language that views fragmentation and truncatedness as central to the nature of language use.

Related topics

Translanguaging in mobility
National and ethnic minorities
Traveling texts, translocal/transnational literacies, and transcontextual analysis
New orientations to identity in mobility
Language in skilled migration
Diaspora and language
Citizenship, immigration laws, and language
A rhizomatic account of heritage language
Language-mediated services for migrants

Further reading

Basch, L., Glick Schiller, N. and Szanton Blanc, C. (1994). *Nations Unbound: Transnational Projects, Postcolonial Predicaments, and Deterritorialized Nation-States*. Langhorne: Gordon and Breach.

As a foundational study of transnationalism, Basch, Glick Schiller, and Szanton Blanc problematize the perspective on migrants as 'uprooted' people who sever ties with their homeland, and instead highlight the transnational connections they make with multiple places. The ethnographic studies they offer illustrate how the experiences of transmigrants undermine the assumptions of the nation-state by foregrounding the multiple and liminal modes of belonging that transgress ethnolinguistic boundaries.

Heller, M. (2011). *Paths to Post-Nationalism*. Oxford: Oxford University Press.

Heller critically examines common assumptions about language, culture, identity, nation, and state, showing how these are problematic in the light of globalization processes, the rise of neoliberal ideology, and the new economy. She argues that the conditions of late modernity are producing significant challenges to established and, indeed, cherished assumptions about how we go about legitimizing our sense of self.

Kelly-Holmes, H. and Mautner, G., eds. (2010). *Language and the Market*. Houndmills, Basingstoke: Palgrave Macmillan.

This collection of papers investigates the relationship between language and the market in the context of globalization. Divided into a number of themes (employment, commercial multilingualism, revitalization, ideologies, and corporate discourses), the volume provides a number of useful case studies that include call centres, rap music, and mission statements. Together, the contributions illustrate the multiple ways in which conditions of the new economy introduce challenges to the language ideologies of the nation-state.

Pennycook, A. (2012). *Language and Mobility: Unexpected Places*. Clevedon: Multilingual Matters.

This book provides a highly readable and thought-provoking discussion about how our expectations about language, culture, and identity are tied to particular places. By highlighting the issue of mobility and how this often results in language surfacing in 'unexpected places', Pennycook forces us to rethink and re-evaluate the bases of these expectations.

Schneider, B. (2014). *Salsa, Language and Transnationalism*. Clevedon: Multilingual Matters.

Focusing on salsa dance and salsa communities in Germany and Australia, Schneider's book is a detailed ethnographic study of how salsa dancers in these countries attempt to balance cosmopolitanism and consumerism with their national identities, especially when, as a form of Latin culture, salsa is an activity that belongs to 'others' rather than Germans or Australians. Schneider's discussion gives interesting insights into the various discourses and cultural practices surrounding dance, transnationalism, and multilingualism.

References

Anderson, B. (1991). *Imagined Communities: Reflections on the Origin and Spread of Nationalism*. Revised ed. London: Verso.

Basch, L., Glick Schiller, N. and Szanton Blanc, C. (1994). *Nations Unbound: Transnational Projects, Postcolonial Predicaments, and Deterritorialized Nation-States*. Langhorne: Gordon and Breach.

Berking, H. (2004). "Ethnicity is everywhere": On globalization and the transformation of cultural identity. In U. Schuerkens (ed.), *Global Forces and Local Life-worlds* (pp. 51–66). London: Sage.

Blackledge, A. and Creese, A. 2008. Contesting "language" as "heritage": Negotiation of identities in late modernity. *Applied Linguistics* 29: 533–554.

Block, D. (2013). *Social Class in Applied Linguistics*. New York: Routledge.

Blommaert, J., Collins, J. and Slembrouck, S. (2005). Spaces of multilingualism. *Language & Communication* 25: 197–216.

Bowe, J., Bowe, M. and Streeter, S., eds. (2000). Poultry factory worker, translated from the Spanish by Sonia Bowe-Gutman. *Gig: Americans Talk about Their Jobs* (pp. 227–232). New York: Random House.

Brooks, A. and Wee, L. (2014). *Consumption, Cities and States: Comparing Singapore with Asian and Western Cities*. London: Anthem Press.

Canagarajah, S. (2013). Reconstructing heritage language: Resolving dilemmas in language maintenance for Sri Lankan Tamil migrants. *International Journal of the Sociology of Language* 222: 131–155.

Carver, T. and Mottier, V. (1998). Introduction. In T. Carver and V. Mottier (eds.), *Politics of Sexuality: Identity, Gender, Citizenship* (pp. 1–12). London: Routledge.

Daswani, G. (2013). The anthropology of transnationalism and diaspora. In Quayson, Ato and Daswani, Girish (eds.), *A Companion to Diaspora and Transnationalism* (pp. 29–53). Malden: Blackwell.

Dick, H.P. (2010). Imagined lives and modernist chronotopes in Mexican nonmigrant discourse. *American Ethnologist* 37(2): 275–290.

Faist, T. (2000). *The Volume and Dynamics of International Migration and Transnational Social Spaces*. Oxford: Oxford Scholarship Online.

Gellner, E. (1983). *Nations and Nationalism: New Perspectives on the Past*. Oxford: Blackwell.

Glick Schiller, N., Basch, L. and Szanton Blanc, C. (1995). From immigrant to transmigrant: Theorizing transnational migration. *Anthropological Quarterly* 68(1): 48–63.

Grillo, R. D. (1989). *Dominant Languages: Language and Hierarchy in Britain and France*. Cambridge: Cambridge University Press.

Heller, M. (1999). *Linguistic Minorities and Modernity: A Sociolinguistic Ethnography*. New York and London: Longman.

Heller, M. (2011). *Paths to Post-Nationalism*. Oxford: Oxford University Press.

Hobsbawm, E.J. (1990). *Nations and Nationalism since 1780*. Cambridge: Cambridge University Press.

Hoge, W. (1998). A Swedish dilemma: The immigrant ghetto. *New York Times* 6 October 1998.
Irvine, J. T. and Gal, S. (2000). Language ideology and linguistic differentiation. In Kroskrity, Paul V. (ed.), *Regimes of Language: Ideologies, Polities, and Identities* (pp. 35–83). Santa Fe: School of American Research Press.
Jacquemet, M. (2000). Beyond the speech community. Paper presented at the 7th International Pragmatics Conference, Budapest, July 2000.
Jacquemet, M. (2005). Transidiomatic practices: Language and power in the age of globalization. *Language & Communication* 25: 257–277.
Maryns, K. and Blommaert, J. (2001). Stylistic and thematic shifting as a narrative resource: Assessing asylum seekers' repertoires. *Multilingua* 20(1): 61–84.
May, S. (2014). Contesting public monolingualism and diglossia: Rethinking political theory and language policy for a multilingual world. *Language Policy* 13: 371–393.
Milani, T. (2008). Language testing and citizenship: A language ideological debate in Sweden. *Language in Society* 37: 27–59.
Mir, A., Mathew, B. and Mir, R. (2000). The codes of migration: Contours of the global software labor market. *Cultural Dynamics* 12: 5–33.
Muehlmann, S. and Duchêne, A. (2007). Beyond the nation-state: International agencies as new sites of discourses on bilingualism. In Monica Heller (ed.), *Bilingualism: A Social Approach* (pp. 96–110). London: Palgrave Macmillan.
Ohmae, K. (1996). *The End of the Nation-State: The Rise of the Regional Economies*. New York: Touchstone Press.
Ong, A. H. (1999). *Flexible Citizenship: The Cultural Logics of Transnationality*. Durham: Duke University Press.
Ong, A. H. (2006). *Neoliberalism as Exception*. Durham: Duke University Press.
Park, J. S. (2013). Metadiscursive regimes of diversity in a multinational corporation. *Language in Society* 42: 1–21.
Park, J. S. and Wee, L. (2012). *Markets of English: Linguistic Capital and Language Policy in a Globalizing World*. New York: Routledge.
Piller, I. (2001). Naturalization language testing and its basis in ideologies of national identity and citizenship. *International Journal of Bilingualism* 5(3): 259–277.
Pujolar, J. (2007). Bilingualism and the nation-state in the post-national era. In Monica Heller (ed.), *Bilingualism: A Social Approach* (pp. 71–95). London: Palgrave Macmillan.
Ricento, T. (2015). Refugees in Canada: On the loss of social capital. In B. Spolsky, O. Inbar-Lourie and M. Tannenbaum (eds.), *Challenges for Language Education and Policy: Making Space for People* (pp. 135–147). London: Routledge.
Shin, G. and Choi, J. N. (2015). *Global Talent: Skilled Labor as Social Capital in Korea*. Stanford: Stanford University Press.
Smith, A. D. (1995). *Nations and Nationalism in a Global Era*. Cambridge: Polity Press.
Smith, A. D. (2010). *Nationalism* (2nd ed.). Cambridge: Polity.
Stroud, C. (2004). Rinkeby Swedish and semilingualism in language ideological debates: A Bourdieuean perspective. *Journal of Sociolinguistics* 8: 196–214.
Turner, B. S. (2011). Judith N. Shklar and American citizenship. *Citizenship Studies* 15(6–7): 933–943.
Vertovec, S. (2006). *The Emergence of Super-Diversity in Britain*. Centre on Migration, Policy and Society, Working Paper 25.
Wee, L. (2012). Migrant workers and language competencies: Focus on organizations. Paper presented at the workshop on "Language Practices, Migration and Labour: Ethnographing Economies in Urban Diversities", Cape Town, 9–10 October 2012.
Wee, L. (2014). Evolution of Singlish in late modernity: Beyond phase 5? In Sarah Bushfeld, Thomas Hoffman, Magnus Huber and Alexander Kautzsch (eds.), *The Evolution of Englishes* (pp. 126–141). Amsterdam: John Benjamins.
Wright, S. (2004). *Language Policy and Language Planning: From Nationalism to Globalisation*. London: Palgrave.

3
Superdiversity and language

Gabriele Budach and Ingrid de Saint-Georges

Introduction/definitions

Since the term 'superdiversity' has caught the attention of researchers in sociolinguistics and linguistic anthropology, it has enjoyed a quick and broad appeal. Scholars have adopted the 'superdiversity lens', considering it a useful and generative concept to approach contemporary conditions of cultural and linguistic contact. To understand the appeal of the term 'superdiversity', it is useful to grasp where it comes from, the conditions leading to its emergence and what it originally meant. The term 'superdiversity' was first introduced by the social anthropologist Steven Vertovec (2007) with the aim to understand and analytically penetrate the changes in the composition of immigrant groups in the UK that can be seen to have started emerging in the late 1980s and 1990s. From a geopolitical and communicational perspective, this period was characterized by two major changes. The first relates to the development of a globalized economy and socioeconomic changes in a post-Soviet era, forming new patterns of mobility. While prior to the 1980s migrants tended to settle in one host community and had only sporadic links with the home community, at the end of the 1990s, migrants began to experience more complex migration trajectories, moving to more places but also keeping ties with their different places of dwelling, which led to new forms of transnationalism. The second change relates to the progressive development of digital technologies (the internet, cable TV, mobile devices) affording the migrants to keep stronger links with home and to remain active on two or more national stages simultaneously, and those staying immobile to engage in more transnational relations than before. All these changes begin to upset significantly our established understanding of 'migrant communities' and their relation to the 'host community'. While in the pre-1990s governments could cultivate the illusion that migrants formed rather homogeneous groups (coming from a limited number of countries, and sharing more or less similar economic, social, cultural, religious, or linguistic backgrounds), after the 1990s, this perception became increasingly problematic, challenging also the discourses and policies of 'multiculturalism'. With the term 'superdiversity' thus, Vertovec (2007) meant to capture that with more individuals migrating, and with migrant trajectories developing in more complex patterns (e.g., people traversing and moving to more places), our contemporary world shows a 'diversification of diversity' (Hollinger 1995). It is not just society that is becoming more diverse but also the composition of the immigrant groups themselves which has become more differentiated in terms of social stratification, internal organization, legal statuses, plurality of affiliations, rights, and restrictions (Vertovec 2007: 1048). With these changing patterns and social conditions, Vertovec considers that there are important stakes in understanding and appraising the nature and extent of this diversity, if policy makers and practitioners want to provide more just structures and policies to respond to this complexity of a new scale and different quality in civil society (Vertovec 2007: 1050).

Following up on the pioneering work from Vertovec, the term 'superdiversity' has subsequently been picked up in disciplines as varied as sociology, business, studies, anthropology, education, social work, geography, law, management, media studies, and linguistics (Vertovec 2013). This appeal has surged, on the one hand, from the fact that the term touches something of the zeitgeist. In a globalized world, there is hardly any domain or geographical area not concerned by diversity as it results from migratory movements. On the other hand, the term also manages to crystallize incredibly complex phenomena under a very simple term that has caught on across disciplines. This deceiving simplicity, Vertovec notes, has led to the term being used with a variety of meanings, not all intended initially by him (Vertovec 2013). Thus, 'superdiversity' as a research term sometimes means 'very much diversity'; in other contexts it means 'more ethnicity' or, to move beyond ethnicity as a category of analysis. Yet, in other contexts, it is used to refer to more scattered geographical distribution of migrants, variegated forms of networking and mixed cultural identities.

Some researchers have also heralded superdiversity as a new paradigm. They talk about a 'superdiversity turn' in their disciplines and how it generates the need for new methodological approaches. The notion also has its detractors who question 'what it really means and who profits from the term' (Westermann 2014). In any case, the concept has become so transversal that it seems difficult to ignore or dismiss without closer examination. The purpose of this chapter is therefore to provide such an examination, looking more critically at how the idea of 'superdiversity' has caught up in the field of language studies, particularly sociolinguistics and applied linguistics, and what it brings, does, reveals – or obscures – in this context.

Overview

That the agenda developed by Vertovec in social anthropology appeals to applied and sociolinguists may not come as a surprise. After all, particularly sociolinguistics have had a long term interest in 'analyzing and interpreting (linguistic) diversity' (Parkin and Arnaut 2014). Issues linked to migration, mobility, or language contact have moreover been at the core of the sociolinguistic project since its early endeavors (Gumperz and Hymes 1972). In fact, the notion of 'superdiversity' as Arnaut and Spotti (2014: 1) argue, fits with a certain naturalness with post-structuralist views on diversity and identity adopted by many linguistic anthropologists or sociolinguists – a perspective that considers for example that identities and speech communities, far from being static and immutable, are to the contrary complex, hybrid, unstable and changing; much as the 'ethnic communities' considered by Vertovec.

In sociolinguistics, the term first appears in a paper by Creese and Blackledge (2010) titled 'Towards a Sociolinguistics of Superdiversity'. In this text, the authors suggest that studies in superdiversity would benefit from including a gaze on the linguistic (p. 549). They propose to investigate language practices where they become a 'site of negotiations over linguistic resources' (p. 549) as this could offer a lens into the kind of social complexity brought about by superdiversity. What becomes interesting in the study of such complex language practice is thus to investigate how people articulate belonging to different social worlds and communities simultaneously. Creese and Blackledge invite scholars to look at situations where multilingual speakers cross over from one language to another, borrowing from more than one repertoire and transforming these repertoires as they use them, and to consider the 'histories, geographies, and indexical orders' which shape those crossing practices (2010: 570). To investigate them, the authors make use of two existing concepts in sociolinguistics. One is the concept of 'translanguaging' (García 2009: 140; García and Li Wei 2014). Engaging critically with the notion of separate 'national', 'autonomous' languages, they recommend to examine the different linguistic features and semiotic resources that speakers borrow from and to see how they mix and play with them in order to enhance their communicative potential as they see fit. The second concept is (second order) 'indexicality' (Silverstein 2003), which refers to social meanings, evoked by language users, that lie beyond the referential meaning of language (or first order indexicality). For example, beyond the content of what they say, the features speakers use (e.g., intonation, accent, tempo, idiomatic expressions) might be revealing of their age, gender, social class, ethnicity, religion, race, sexual orientation, and so forth. For Creese and Blackledge (2010), thus, the study of translanguaging and indexicality is suggested as a means to locate and disentangle more complex patterns and social configurations, akin to the 'superdiverse' social fabric that Vertovec describes.

Blommaert and Rampton (2011) broaden this research program in a text on 'Language and Superdiversity', now widely cited among superdiversity researchers. The text is an articulation of different layers of ideas.

Epistemologically, the article proposes that the superdiversity lens allows tying together a number of previously disparate threads in sociolinguistics. It functions a bit like a 'meta-term', and under its roof different strands of research can be housed that have contributed over the years to de-reifying traditional notions such as language, community, or communication. For example, there is a strong focus on language in *urban spaces*, considered as laboratories for the study of complexity and heterogeneity in social organization that has contributed to the final demise of a view of language as a stable, bounded entity. Urban sociolinguists have introduced terms such as 'polylanguaging' (Jørgensen 2008), 'crossing' (Rampton 1995), or 'translanguaging' (García 2009) to take issue with the naturalness of (imagined) boundaries of language, community, and communication. Others have repurposed the concept of *heteroglossia* (Blackledge and Creese 2012, drawing on Bakhtin 1981) that points to the inherent diversity existing in each act of communication, always assembled out of multiple layers of internally differentiated voices, genres, styles, discourses, and social norms. Related to *communication*, social semioticians and their multimodal approaches to discourse have probably made the greatest dent on viewing communication as predominantly 'language-centered'. They propose instead to reconnect to the idea that language is only one of the multiple modes people can co-opt to make meaning, act, and communicate (Kress, Jewitt, Ogborn, and Tsatsarelis 2001), thus placing again here too diversity and multiplicity of semiotic practices at the heart of communication. As for *community*, Blommaert and Rampton (2011) echo Vertovec's critique to the term 'ethnic communities' and project it onto 'speech community' or 'ethnolinguistic group' as key concepts in sociolinguistic studies. They contend that these concepts are too static and bounded to be useful and invite instead to consider the myriad ways in which

> 'people take on different linguistic forms as they align and disaffiliate with different groups at different moments and stages' and to 'investigate how (people) (try to) opt

in and opt out, how they perform or play with linguistic signs of group belonging, and how they develop particular trajectories of group identification throughout their lives'.
(Blommaert and Rampton 2011: 5)

On a first level, thus, the text aims to articulate a contribution to superdiversity scholarship from sociolinguistics. The authors argue that notions such *language, community*, and *communication* cannot be usefully understood as homogenous and predictably patterned entities, even less so in times of increased physical mobility, virtual connectedness and social semiotic complexity. While, in essence, such a critique is not new and has been voiced since the 1970s and 1980s in linguistic anthropology and postcolonial studies, the 'superdiversity' lens is said to bring these conceptual developments into focus even more sharply. As Arnaut and Spotti (2014: 3) put it:

> To some extent, this 'new kind of sociolinguistics' is heir to a 'linguistics of contact' (Pratt 1987) which has been steadily moving away from the idea of languages and speakers as discernable units towards that of sociolinguistic resources and repertoires. Overall, this implies a double shift (a) away from unitary, localized and quantifiable speech communities to transnational ones, both 'real' and 'virtual' (Rampton 2000; Pennycook 2012; Leppänen 2012a), and (b) away from presupposed fully-fluent native speakers' competence to a sociolinguistics that looks at the individual whose competences consist rather of a plurality of 'registers' (Agha 2004), 'styles' (Rampton 2011b) and genres (Blommaert and Rampton 2011: 6) that constitute 'super-diverse repertoires' (Blommaert and Backus 2013).

From a conceptual standpoint, the text (and the scholarship that later builds on it) moreover seem to suggest that research on 'superdiversity' in sociolinguistics can best be understood as crystallizing around four intertwined notions: *mobility, complexity, unpredictability*, and *governmentality.*

The focus on the first notion – mobility – leads researchers to highlight that if we take into account the trajectory of real people across time, space, and borders, then simplistic, stationary, static and predictable perspectives about human lives and interactions are no longer possible. Examining interactions thus cannot be limited to looking at what happens in the here-and-now between interactants but must include taking into account their histories, geographies, the discourse formations that influence their contributions, and the dissipative nature of the organization of all these dimensions. Mobility does not only affect individuals' trajectories; it also reorganizes the social fabric. Under conditions of social diversity, 'older diversities superimpose upon newer diversity,' leading to 'their mutual re-articulation in the process' (Parkin and Arnaut 2014: 2):

> Everywhere around the world, the interaction of 'the' autochthonous population with different generations and groups of migrants, engenders the cultural differentiation of the former. In South Africa the collapse of the racial boundaries has in itself given rise to new configurations which Nuttall (2009: 20) calls 'entanglements'.

These entanglements and re-articulations, Parkin and Arnaut argue (2014: 2), redefine drastically the very possibility for population to 'self-recognize' themselves as simple, unitary wholes. They thus require ways to analytically unpack complexities that do not lay open to superficial gaze. This leads Arnaut and Spotti (2014: 3) to propose *simultaneity* as an analytical lens to do justice to these new complexities:

> the metaphor of simultaneity combines the idea of (a) *superimposition, nesting, and palimpsest* – of earlier and later 'generations' of migrants in particular neighbourhoods, [...] with the idea of (b) *intersection* and *entanglement* – for instance the combination of different codes or idioms carrying different national class-based or ethnic indexicalities into one 'urban vernacular' (Rampton 2011a).

What makes the new situation *complex* surges thus from three sources for them: (1) the *multiple embeddness of migrants*, who engage in a variety of differentiated social fields and networks of relations; (2) *intersectionality*, or the idea that in any historically specific contexts, a complex nexus of economic, political, cultural, psychic, subjective, and experiential axes come together; and (3) *scalarity*, or the fact that each social level presents its own forms of coherence but which have sometimes contradictory dynamics (Arnaut and Spotti 2014: 3).

When we combine mobility and complexity, another term emerges: 'unpredictability'. *Unpredictability* arises from (1) the complex trajectories of people that, emerging from unscripted configurations of experience, produce unexpected meanings; and (2) unprecedented forms of social organization, unconventional alliances among people with different backgrounds who would not easily fit the definition of a 'speech community'. This leads to (3) the perception of a misfit of existing descriptive categories and vocabulary which seem unsuitable to capture the kinds of complexities to be discovered in 'superdiversity'.

If one begins to acknowledge the full 'breadth of 'differences' that constitute 'diversity' (Arnaut 2012: 6), then new challenges are also posed to '*governmentality*'. First, old ways of thinking about 'multiculturalism' or 'diversity management' appear more and more inadequate as the nation-states find themselves in a position where they cannot easily hide or tame the diversification of diversity. Here the question becomes how does the nation-state deal with – and regiment – diversity, complexity, and unpredictability in this new world order when easy simplification does not work anymore; second, the very idea of 'the nation/state/society [as] the natural social and political form of the modern world' (Wimmer and Glick Schiller 2002: 302) is also put into question. Authors in the superdiversity paradigm are prompt to observe that, with new technologies in particular, we have entered a 'post-panopticon state' (Arnaut 2012: 6). The idea of the state as the all-seeing and all-controlling 'panoptical state' (Foucault 1975) is progressively being challenged by new forms of governmentalities from below. As Arnaut (2012: 8–9) argues, these are to be found particularly in cities and cyberspaces, and can take the form of 'auto-governing' groups or 'counter-governmentality' (Appadurai in Arnaut 2012). They arise when the wider public appropriates the internet – a panoptical technology originally developed for the US military – and transforms it into an ever-differentiating structure for communication, learning, and socialization. In the post-panopticon society, it is said that 'the machinery of surveillance is now always potentially in the service of the crowd as much as the executive' (Boyne 2000: 301, in Arnaut 2012: 9).

Finally, from a methodological standpoint, Blommaert and Rampton's (2011) research program emphasizes the need for researchers interested in superdiversity to move away from the study of larger (community) patterns, shifting to a focus on individual practice and repertoires. To unravel complexities linked to superdiversity, the authors recommend ethnography that enables to observe instances in which the re-integration of multiple variables (such as age, gender, ethnicity, religion, sexual orientation, or being a gamer or a vegan) becomes palpable. Such instances can be discovered more accurately in the varying practices of individuals and in their engagement with multiple communities across time and space, rather than by seeking out broader generalizations about the behavior of presumably homogenous groups. Consequently, the program proposes to investigate 'the linguistic signs of group belonging' as a key unit of analysis and to focus on the trajectory of individual across national, linguistic, and cultural borders. The focus on trajectories moreover includes a need for long-term, multisited research that investigates connection and connectivity between contexts.

Issues and ongoing debates

Beyond the research agenda unraveled by Blommaert and Rampton (2011), there is an increasing number of case studies which take up their ideas on superdiversity and seek to illustrate or tease out some of the points we just developed. In this section, we would like to discuss a selection of them, focusing more specifically on how they address two important questions in our view:

- What is being learned about social complexity by studying the complex language/semiotic practice that these studies investigate?
- How and for whom does "unpredictability" emerge as an issue/analytical or interpretational challenge in these studies?

Our focus will be on a number of sites, social spheres, activities, and players, including (1) practices controlled by the state (e.g., language citizenship testing, interviews with asylum seekers), (2) civil society (schools and neighborhoods), (3) virtual spaces on the internet (e.g., webpages, blogs and YouTube). We conclude the section by discussing some debates relating to the term.

Practices controlled by the state

A first area which has been extensively covered by the literature on superdiversity is the domain of language and citizenship testing – an increasingly fortified arena of state control in European nation-states, and a domain in which the reign of the all-seeing eye of the state remains uncontested, despite ongoing social complexification. Citizenship testing is one of the ways nation-states have developed to 'regiment' diversity: that is to control, monitor and, ultimately, reduce incoming migration and social complexity. The literature shows that in a number of countries (Extra, Spotti, and Van Avermaet 2009), systems of deterritorialized language practices are put into place – language tests have to be taken by the applicants over the phone in their country of origin. Through this apparatus, the homogenizing ideology of the nation-state with respect to language and culture becomes reinforced. Unpredictability of the encountered 'other' is deliberately ignored. Those who do not fit the required standard simply will not pass the test. On the other hand, as Spotti (2011) states, the selection that is achieved retains a certain element of predictability (which may or may not have been intended by those who designed the test) as the test usually plays out in favor of people with higher literacy skills and better access to the test sites.

Another topic investigated from a 'superdiversity' angle are interviews between government officials and asylum seekers to determine their status. Jacquemet (2015) explains how in these interviews unpredictability arises when the asylum seekers' migrational trajectories and interactional moves are at odds with what is expected from the government officials and the legal system of the host country. For example, while the officer might have the 'referential meaning' that a migrant from Algeria should speak Arabic, but not Berber or Tamazight, the history of migration of the asylum seeker might well mean that he has incorporated these repertoires. Conflict over meaning also arises from culturally different interpretation of kinship relations (such as who counts as a cousin or a brother in different cultures). These differences can lead to an interpretation that disqualifies the narrative of the claimant as incoherent and the claimant himself as not trustworthy, a judgment on which his request for asylum may then be denied. However, the research also shows that, occasionally, interpreters act as cultural mediators and that they are able to clarify the ambiguity and mend the conflict. Here, a focus on 'what is unpredictable' and how to go about 'expected unpredictability' is indeed, an interesting and important perspective to explore.

Diversity in schools and neighborhoods

A second area in which state control retains a tangible influence is (state) schools. It is a truism that school curricula tend to ignore or, at least, streamline the diversity in classrooms (Duarte and Gogolin 2013), and there is little will or serious engagement of most 'self-declared-monolingual' nation-states to change this orientation in the near future. Evaluation, in most cases, remains based on the standard of the 'monolingual competent speaker', and recalling the inappropriateness of such principles does not seem to induce much change. The study by Kapia (2013) is a laudable exception which actually attempts to challenge this logic in concrete, empirical ways. She suggests that when assessing the narrative competence of speakers in 'superdiverse' environments, monolingual norms should be used only to assess macro structural elements which are acquired at the same rate by first and second language learners (and which can be transferred by the learners across languages, such as the knowledge about literacy or textual genres), but that schools should refrain from evaluating micro structure elements (such as morpho-syntactic structures or forms of verbal morphology) that second language learners take longer to acquire.

Since such claims and the search for more equitable treatment and evaluation of multilingual students are not new (Menken 2008), 'superdiversity' does not seem to offer much of a new perspective on the diversity in schools. However, the term has been adopted by some scholars whose work on inclusive pedagogy stood out, even before the advent of superdiversity. Such an example is multilingual bookmaking (Busch 2012), which offers children with complex backgrounds a space to explore and express 'the unknown and unpredictable' in their trajectories, and to lay it open to themselves, to their teachers, to fellow students, parents, and researchers.

Other researchers have focused on a more specific domain in education: complementary schools that are run and supported by migrant communities. Creese and Blackledge (2010) have investigated the diaspora of Bangladeshi community in Birmingham, UK, and followed individuals from the first and second generation from school to home. Their study highlights that the language practices of the learners in complementary schools reveal complex and intersecting indexical orders. In their data for example the learners resorted sometimes to Bangla (the national language of Bangladesh representing heritage and prestige in school and community) or to Sulheti (a spoken, informal language, representing poverty and a low level of education) in their speech. But they also noticed that these meanings were not consistent across space, time, and interactional frames, but varied. New meanings emerged, for instance as stylization of Sulheti is used by UK-born second-generation girls to exclude newcomers from Bangladesh. Thereby stylization indexes a social boundary even among people who have a shared repertoire. In the work of Creese and Blackledge, 'indexicality' and stylization are used as an analytical tool to show how meanings can be intersecting and how the same linguistic form – emphasized in a differently nuanced tone – can mean either social inclusion or exclusion. This example points to the inner differentiation of the local Bangladeshi community articulated along the lines of generational belonging and migrant status (newcomer or UK-born), rather than to multiple belongings of the same individual.

Beyond school, investigations have also focused on 'superdiversity' in neighborhoods – an area of reduced state control compared to some of the previous scenarios. To capture new forms of demographic and social complexity in mixed neighborhoods, the term 'conviviality' is often employed. For Padilla, Azevedo, and Olmos-Alcaraz (2015), the term provides a framework to understand how interculturality is lived and experienced at the local level. The notion focuses on how (new) relational patterns among groups are emerging and how interactions between residents of different origins and backgrounds unfold, in which notions such as race, ethnicity, and gender are being renegotiated. Conviviality thereby requires studies of interaction around a thematic focus that touches on issues of social peace and solidarity, hinting to alternative policies that can usefully replace 'multiculturalism'.

In sociolinguistics, the notion of conviviality has been adopted by Blommaert (2014a). Focusing on multilingual signs in a multiethnic neighborhood in Ghent, Belgium, Blommaert reconstructs the increasing heterogeneity of the local Chinese-speaking community for which he finds evidence in the complexification of the linguistic repertoire of local Chinese speakers. These Chinese speakers adapt to the changes arising from new waves of immigrants by learning varieties of the Chinese newcomers, namely Mandarin and simplified characters, in addition to their already existing repertoire of Cantonese and traditional ideography. With a linguistic landscaping approach, Blommaert's analysis concentrates on written artifacts, such as shop signs or billboards, which are contextualized with socio-economic and demographic data. Yet, the absence of any ethnographic data accounting for interactions of and with the producers of this data leaves the task of interpretation solely to the researcher who, on the basis of singular instances makes assumptions about a trajectory of learning and factors presumably significant in the structuration of an individual's linguistic repertoire. Furthermore, the reliance on concepts such as 'orthographic norm' and 'error' which are used to describe the written artifact leaves the reader pondering: whose normativity is at stake?

Digital practices

The third area in which researchers have used the 'superdiversity gaze' is the domain of new technologies of communication Androutsopoulos, J. and Juffermans, K. (2014). New technologies allow for the complexification of participation patterns, and the diversification of language/semiotic practices, with more or less short- or long-term socially structuring effects.

One set of studies focusing on 'superdiversity' in this domain relates to the *global diaspora* (Heyd 2014 for Nigeria; McLaughlin 2014 for Senegal; Sharma 2014 for Nepal). These studies observe communities where people share an interest in political and sociocultural events in the home country but where the participants are spread globally – often across various continents. While one could expect that such global communities make room for showing the diversification of individual linguistic repertoires, acquired in the context of migration, one observes that, on the contrary, a homogenization of language used in the platforms appears to be taking place. The repertoire in use often echoes the languages and language varieties common in the home country. While linguistic homogenization seems to reflect a normative stance of the sociolinguistic situation 'back home', we note that geographic diversification tends to be rather downplayed or hidden. This may not be surprising if the goal of such an endeavor is to build a globally interconnected diaspora. A similar case of linguistic homogenization, but related to immigration into one country (Luxembourg), is reported by Belling and De Bres (2014), who describe the linguistic homogenization of a consumer platform where participants converge towards the Luxemburgish language (instead of the other official languages of the country – German or French, English as a lingua franca, or languages of migration such as Portuguese, Italian or others, who would also be possible in that context) due to pressures of the local sociolinguistic economy.

Studies by Dong (2012) and Staehr (2014) provide examples for how affinity circles are formed around a particular interest in lifestyle (e.g., in Saab cars [Dong 2012]) or globally circulating semiotic resources of youth culture (e.g., the illuminati [Staehr 2014]) that shape new communities of practice in on- and offline encounters.

Yet others examine multiply authored, multimodal performances (e.g., buffalaxing; Leppänen and Häkkinen 2014) and investigate experimental semiotic practices in which authors alter existing material (mostly music videos) by recombining semiotic modes in unconventional ways, challenging to conventional interpretations. For instance, sounds related to one language (e.g., Hindi) are mapped on and written down in English words which create distorting effects readable as a critique of the visual content presented or, to a certain extent, a self-mockery of the 'second' authors. Here, the unconventional assemblage and play with rules of semiotic composition for sound, writing, and visual image (e.g., traditional dance performance) clearly stretches conventional stereotypical depictions of gender, race, and ethnicity.

Careful examination of these cases shows that the engagement with linguistic/semiotic practice in these studies contribute to understand particular aspects of communicative practice in on- and offline environments. Yet, we learn relatively little about the 'diversification of diversity' and how the complexification of social patterns is reflected in concrete linguistic practice. What emerges rather clearly, however, are the homogenizing tendencies and a presumably self-selected reduction of linguistic variety to communicative patterns that are shared, predictably, by a specific community of practice, be it local or translocal. In addition, it seems that, rather than revealing the 'unpredictable or unknown', multiple linguistic resources are drawn on by the interlocutors (and interpreted by the analyst) in ways that we would call predictable. Maybe it is this kind of disjuncture between the claimed object of inquiry and the empirical facts that has led to much debates and discussion to be prompted by superdiversity research in sociolinguistics and applied language studies. We review some of them in the next section.

Debates and controversies

For many researchers, including the ones who have imported the notion of 'superdiversity' as part of the analytical toolkit of researchers of linguistic and semiotic practices, 'superdiversity' is still seen 'as a zone of academic development with an explorative, tentative and unfinished character' (Blommaert 2014b: 15). Further conceptual and empirical consolidation is to be expected with the forthcoming publication of several monographs on this topic (Rampton, Blommaert, Arnaut, and Spotti 2015; Arnaut, Blommaert, Rampton, and Spotti forthcoming; Arnaut, Karrebaek, and Spotti forthcoming; Meissner and Vertovec forthcoming). These will aim to consolidate the institutionalization of 'superdiversity' research and, most likely engage with the criticisms raised so far by the detractors of the term. Some of these critiques relate to the term 'superdiversity' and its scope and meaning. Others engage with the project of developing a new – more fine-grained – language of description in view of capturing complex phenomena more adequately and serving as an analytical toolkit that can enable a 'new way of seeing'. Yet others relate to the kind of purchase the term 'superdiversity' has for the political agenda of engaging policy makers in a new thinking for diversity management.

With regards to the term 'superdiversity', ambiguity has been detected on several levels. Makoni (2012) notes that 'super' in 'superdiversity' can be understood as referring to both 'hyper' (as in highly layered and socially stratified local neighborhoods) and 'trans' (where it pinpoints to translocal practices such as in internet communication across contexts and territories). If the term covers both dimensions, we could ask to what extent it provides an increased analytical purchase, and whether the relationship between 'locally complex' and 'translocal' would need to be clarified more explicitly.

Some scholars have raised concerns about 'superdiversity' as a Eurocentric perspective – seen as hardly meaningful in postcolonial contexts and settler societies that have been composed of highly diverse, socially complex populations for generations, if not centuries. Makoni (2012) notes that the term 'superdiversity' is a white European invention, similar to the terms 'migration' and 'nomadism' which are used selectively to refer to specific phenomena of mobility in specific (pre- and postcolonial) time periods. 'Superdiversity' therefore resonates with the position of a privileged elite of white researchers, guilty of a certain 'social romanticism' risking to obscure the social conditions enforcing mobility, at least on the African continent, and covering up issues of great social division and injustice. It also has been criticised as aligned with a neoliberal rhetoric praising the 'supersize' and 'big' society (Reyes 2014).

Yet other researchers have critiqued 'superdiversity' and refuted the notion because of its limited focus and lack of historicity. Building on antecedents in sociolinguistic research that we described earlier, superdiversity research puts strong emphasis on the 'urban', viewed as the birthplace of new forms of 'superdiverse' linguistic practice. It also adopts a critical position towards the nation-state and its ideologies which mostly emerged in Europe and where exported globally through colonialism. Given this epistemological anchoring, superdiversity turns a blind eye to (1) multilingual mixed language practices in historical periods preceding colonialism and the existence of nation-states in the modern understanding, notably in parts of the world outside of Europe; (2) the contact of the colonizers with indigenous populations and the mixed language practices arising from this encounter; and (3) up to this date, the specific situation of indigenous languages in postcolonial contexts (for example, language revitalization efforts of indigenous languages). Concerning multilingual practices in precolonial times, scholarship from South East India (Khubchandani in Canagarajah 2013) notes that mixing languages was the norm and not an exception throughout that period. Languages tended to be associated with territories rather than ethnic groups or nations and people were expected to be mobile and to use multilingual repertoires that they mobilized according to situational needs. Negotiating meaning between interlocutors through the purposeful assembling of diverse individual repertoires was the order of the day – a situation very different from more contemporary expectations that everyone should be able to converse fully competently in the language of the nation-state. Another set of mixed language practices emerged from the encounter of colonizer and colonized. It is in so-called auto-ethnographic texts (Pratt 1991) such as the 1,200-page manuscript written in Quechua and ungrammatical expressive Spanish by the indigenous Andean scribe Felipe Guaman Poma de Ayala (1613) that the use of mixed language embodied both the appropriation and subversion of the voice of the oppressor – a mockery quite different from the one described by Rampton (1995) for inner London youth – but surely not less powerful or rebellious. While rebellion in both cases has different addressees and happen in different socio-historical contexts, it could be fruitful to contrast the cases to uncover, for each of them, what appropriation is about.

As for the issue of indigenous languages in postcolonial contexts, Moore et al. (2013) stress that displacement – today often associated with the trajectories of migrants – has been afflicted on indigenous people without them necessarily having to move at all. Reporting on language revitalization efforts in Warm Springs Reservation in Oregon, where pre-colonial community multilingualism included the languages of Sahaptins, Wascos, and Paiutes, these researchers highlight how language courses are offered today on just one language, which reduces and homogenizes the initial multilingualism. However, on closer examination, it becomes clear that what matters most to the indigenous teachers and learners is neither the learning of a monolingual norm, nor the ideal of the fully competent speakers that underlies many Western language teaching practices, but rather the transmission of indigenous ritual knowledge and appropriate ways of performing it.

Learning about indigenous contexts adds an important dimension to existing superdiversity research. It helps refocus the role of the individual (and individual repertoires) – somewhat overemphasized in current sociolinguistic superdiversity scholarship – and the collective (and collective interests and rights) that some see disregarded and banalized by readings that interpret languages as primarily individual attributes or fashion statements (e.g., Maher 2005, on metroethnicity).

Beyond those critiques, another area of indeterminacy requires clarification. While in some contexts 'superdiversity' scholars identify specific 'superdiverse' phenomena (e.g., globalized youth culture or forms of internet communication, Varis and Wang 2011; Blommaert 2013), in others they highlight 'superdiversity' rather as a theoretical perspective – an emerging discourse (Arnaut 2012), or even a new ontology (Parkin 2012) – which has no specific objects, but rather depicts a researcher's stance that pays heightened attention to issues of complexity (Blommaert and Rampton 2011) and the growing awareness of such complexity among researchers and laypersons (Blommaert and Varis 2011). This leads us to another ongoing discussion among 'superdiversity' scholars, which is about developing a more fine-grained language for describing complexity. While there have been attempts to suggest such new vocabulary (e.g., 'supervernacular' see Blommaert 2011), the conceptual work is still ongoing and the vocabulary to make explicit the changes observed in 'superdiverse' language and semiotic practice does not yet exist (van der Aa and Blommaert 2015).

The question thus remains how meaningful a theory or ontology can be if it is not coupled with methodological strategies that can be operationalized in concrete research, particularly in an empirical science which is said to derive important meaning from generating observational, qualitative data. This is by no means to say that the existing tools would be adequate. However, if one considered them insufficient, the question remains what new tools could or should look like.

Implications

To recap, what surges from the review conducted in the previous sections is that 'superdiversity' as a lens has the merit of allowing sociolinguists to pursue the long tradition of asking questions such as: what are sites of engagements (Scollon 1997) where migrants and host community members meet? How can we conceptualize migrant/non-migrant social spaces and their strategies of negotiating meaning in different languages and across different social settings? What vocabulary is best suited to talk about language use and social relationships in these sites? How can we capture and comprehend interactions in these sites of engagement through suitable methodologies? In addition, we could add: What are the consequences of participation for individuals? And what are consequences for society when contact zones multiply? The research review makes clear that it is complex frames of understanding we are in need of, rather than overly simplifying ones, frames that are able to show resolvable tensions and contradictions as well as irresolvable paradoxes of sharing lives together.

In terms of implication for research, the analyses we have reviewed leave us however with a number of conceptual and methodological questions: For example, are multilingual language practice and social complexification intrinsically linked, and where and how can we actually observe social complexity through forms of linguistic/semiotic practice? Heyd (2014) combines methodologies such as mapping (by locating participants across the globe), corpus analysis, and qualitative analysis of life trajectory narratives. This seems a promising avenue to pursue for the future. However, at the moment, studies we examined leave singular instances of practice and larger patterns of social complexity rather unrelated. An exception is the study by Juffermans, Blommaert, Kroon, and Li (2014), which looks at Facebook discussions among young people of Chinese descent in the Netherlands and their views on language policy decisions in mainland China. The analysis is interesting as it reveals lived and imagined trajectories of language learning of these young people, including different varieties of Chinese. Here, the notion of trajectory, recommended as a research focus (Blommaert and Rampton 2011) is taken more seriously, shedding light also on hopes, fears, and the predicted worth of linguistic resources for their lives and in different scenarios.

While well-established analytical concepts such as 'language ideologies' and 'indexicality' are used very fruitfully in the aforementioned studies, the perspective of 'simultaneity' (see Arnaut and Spotti 2014) seems still largely underexplored. Here is certainly scope and potential for development to make an analytical purchase of 'superdiversity' research more visible. A further research agenda therefore would be to go beyond paying mere lip service to this question of the 'diversification of diversity' and delve even deeper into understanding both superimposition and nesting of earlier and later 'generations' of migrants as well as the 'entanglement' and cross-sectional transaction between migrants and host community members and the cultural frictions, tensions, or new convivialities resulting from them. How to go about studying those dimensions empirically still remains to be imagined, however.

In addition, most studies keep a focus on the 'linguistic sign of group belonging' – continuing to prioritize language over other modes of representation (such as images, music, or dance) which poses certain limits to exploring semiotic practice as a vector for understanding social complexity.

Finally, despite all critical efforts to reframe 'community' conceptually, either as a 'community of practice' (Lave and Wenger 1991) or a social (physical or virtual) network of people, it needs to be noted that 'community' remains a key concept to which individuals adhere. Therefore, it seems important to investigate what new forms and meanings 'community' takes on, how people live and talk about them, and what these understandings of community mean for us as researchers whose work remains committed to people and community institutions as social players and research partners (Li Wei 2014).

As for policy and pedagogy, while the majority of case studies investigate multiple language practices as an illustration of social complexification in various areas of civil society, only few of them go as far as formulating recommendations that could be relevant for policy makers and practitioners. Since a social agenda is not explicitly proposed in most of the studies, it still needs to be spelled out how a linguistic focus on 'superdiversity' can inform policy in meaningful ways.

Future directions

In a discussion of superdiversity and 'civil integration', Vertovec asked what 'meaningful [communicative] interchanges look like, how they are formed, maintained or broken, and how the state or other agencies might promote them' (2007: 27). Surely, sociolinguistics and applied language research have an important contribution to make to this agenda. At present, however, we recognize that we ultimately lack the temporal perspective to assess whether the 'superdiverse' approach is the best way to do that. We also do not know whether this term will make a dent in the history of the field or serve as just another temporary stepping stone in the history of conceptualizing 'linguistics of contact' (Pratt 1991), especially given that some of the most engaged researchers of 'superdiversity' themselves acknowledge some of the past 'shadows of superdiversity' (Rampton et al. 2015), and propose to view the term as a temporary placeholder ready to be replaced whenever more relevant categories come to light.

With or without the term 'superdiversity', the phenomena that it seeks to address seem real and deserving our attention, and we do believe that language sciences can contribute to the more global agenda of imagining 'more just structures and policies' to respond to the 'diversification of diversity' of the new migration flows for which Vertovec first imagined the term (Vertovec 2007: 1050). From a research perspective, we believe that contributing to this agenda will require opening up to interdisciplinary dialogue, engaging for example with social policy studies, social geography, moral philosophy, education, or gender and race studies. These have started to examine topics such as the 'ethics of living together' (Jensen 2011) and the 'art of living in parallel' (Chimienti and Van Liempt 2011) or the question of 'white privilege' (McIntosh 1989) or multilingual pedagogies (García 2009). We believe language and discourse accompany these different dimensions and we find important to investigate what role language plays at these different levels to sustain or undermine practices of conviviality and to draw barriers of inclusion/exclusion. We also find that if we pursue these lines of research, we will need to interrogate even more than ever the very positions from which we write and speak, and the contact zones which exist in our own academic institutions and academic lives which at present do not seem to show the same diversification of diversity as do other pockets of social life.

Summary

Since the term 'superdiversity' first caught the attention of researchers in sociolinguistics and linguistic anthropology, it has enjoyed a quick and broad appeal. The chapter reviews where the term comes from and what it originally meant. It also examines more critically some of the conceptual, methodological, and political challenges raised by the use of this term for language studies and for conceptualizing the complexity of what happens in the 'contact zones' between migrants and host communities.

Related topics

> Translanguaging in mobility
> National and ethnic minorities
> Multisited ethnography and language in the study of migration
> Citizenship, immigration laws, and language

Further reading

Arnaut, K. and Spotti, M. (2014). Superdiversity discourse, *Working Papers in Urban Language & Literacies*, Paper 122, 1–11.

The article presents a dense and well-developed synthesis of superdiversity research and its epistemological underpinnings. It situates superdiversity as an academic discourse and links it with previous research on language in society. It is thought-provoking in outlining an agenda for future research and analytical perspectives on issues of complexity.

Blommaert, J. and Rampton, B. (2011). *Diversities, 13*(3). Retrieved from http://www.unesco.org/shs/diversities/vol13/issue2/art1

This collection of papers makes an important early contribution to studies on superdiversity from a perspective of language in society. Widely cited among superdiversity researchers, it is a good starting point to identify important lines of inquiry embedded in a sociolinguistic, ethnographic tradition.

Duarte, J. and Gogolin, I., eds. (2013). *Linguistic Superdiversity in Urban Areas: Research Approaches*. Amsterdam: John Benjamins.

Papers in this edited volume engage with the concept of superdiversity from a range of disciplinary and methodological perspectives exploring linguistic diversity and the challenges it poses for policies and practices of managing diversity in place.

Makoni, S. (2012). A critique of language, languaging and supervernacular. *Uma crítica à noção de língua, linguagem e supervernáculo. Muitas Vozes, Ponta Grossa, 1*(2), 189–199.

The texts engages with superdiversity from a critical perspective. The author interrogates central terms used in superdiversity research (e.g., supervernacular), scrutinizing their implications with respect to historicity, geographical reach, and epistemological foundation.

Vertovec, S. (2007). Super-diversity and its implications. *Ethnic and Racial Studies, 30*(6), 1024–1054.

This text marks the beginning of research on superdiversity in social anthropology. Cited by scholars across disciplines, it identifies and explains the phenomenon of 'superdiversity' for the first time linking it to policies, social practices and discourses in the UK.

References

Androutsopoulos, J. and Juffermans, K. (2014) Digital language practices in superdiversity (Double special issue). *Discourse, Context and Media* 4–5.

Arnaut, K. (2012) Super-diversity: Elements of an emerging perspective. *Diversities* 14(2): 1–16.

Arnaut, K., Blommaert, J., Rampton, B. and Spotti, M., eds. (forthcoming). *Language and Superdiversity*. New York: Taylor and Francis.

Arnaut, K., Karrebaek, M.S. and Spotti, M. (forthcoming). *Engaging with Superdiversity*. Bristol: Multilingual Matters.

Arnaut, K. and Spotti, M. (2014). *Superdiversity Discourse*. Working Papers in Urban Language & Literacies, Paper 122, 1–11.

Bakhtin, M. (1981) *The Dialogic Imagination: Four Essays*. Austin: University of Texas Press.

Belling, L. and De Bres, J. (2014). Digital superdiversity in Luxembourg: The role of Luxembourgish in a multilingual Facebook group. *Discourse, Context and Media* 4–5: 74–86.

Blackledge, A. and Creese, A., eds. (2012). *Heteroglossia as Practice and Pedagogy*. Heidelberg, New York and London: Springer.

Blommaert, J. (2011). *Supervernaculars and their Dialects*. Tilburg Papers in Culture Studies, Paper 9.

Blommaert, J. (2013). *Etnography, superdiversity and linguistic landscapes: Chronicles of complexity*. Bristol: Multilingual Matters.

Blommaert, J. (2014a). Infrastructures of superdiversity: Conviviality and language in an Antwerp neighborhood. *European Journal of Cultural Studies* 17(4): 431–451.

Blommaert, J. (2014b). *Superdiversity Old and New*. Tilburg Papers in Culture Studies, Paper 105, 1–17.

Blommaert, J. and Rampton, B. (2011) Language and superdiversity. *Diversities* 13(3). Retrieved from http://www.unesco.org/shs/diversities/vol13/issue2/art1.

Blommaert, J. and Varis, P. (2011). *"Enough Is Enough": The Heuristics of Authenticity in Superdiversity*. Tilburg Papers in Culture Studies, Paper 2.

Boyne, R. (2000) Post-Panopticism. *Economy and Society* 29(2): 285–307.

Busch, B. (2012). Building on heteroglossia and heterogeneity: The experience of a multilingual classroom. In A. Blackledge and A. Creese (eds.), *Heteroglossia as Practice and Pedagogy* (pp. 21–40). London: Springer.

Canagarajah, S. (2013) *Translingual Practice. Global Englishes and Cosmopolitain Relations*. London: Routledge.

Chimienti, M. and Van Liempt, I. (2011). "Super diversity" or the art of living in parallel worlds? Paper presented at the Conference: Ethnography, Diversity, and Urban Space, St. Anne's College, Oxford University.

Creese, A. and Blackledge, A. (2010) Towards a sociolinguistics of superdiversity. *Zeitschrift für Erziehungswissenschaft* 13(4): 549–572.

De Bres, J. and Belling, L. (2014) Free Your Stuff Luxembourg! Language policies, practices and ideologies in a multilingual Facebook group. *Language Policy* 3(4).

Dong, J. (2012) Mobility, voice, and symbolic restratification: An ethnography of "elite migrants" in urban China. *Diversities* 14(2): 35–48.

Duarte, J. and Gogolin, I., eds. (2013) *Linguistic Superdiversity in Urban Areas: Research Approaches*. Amsterdam: John Benjamins.

Extra, G., Spotti, M. and Van Avermaet, P., eds. (2009) *Language Testing, Migration and Citizenship: Cross-National Perspectives* (pp. 65–85). London: Continuum.

Foucault, M. (1975) *Surveiller et punir. Naissance de la prison*. Paris: Gallimard.

García, O. (2009) Education, multilingualism, and translanguaging in the 21st century. In T. Skutnabb-Kangas, R. Phillipson, A.K. Mohanty and M. Panda (eds.), *Social Justice through Multilingual Education* (pp. 140–158). Bristol: Multilingual Matters.

García, O. and Li Wei (2014). *Translanguaging: Language, Bilingualism and Education*. London: Palgrave Macmillan.

Gumperz, J.J. and Hymes, D., eds. (1972). *Directions in Sociolinguistics: The Ethnography of Communication* (pp. 35–71). London: Blackwell.

Heyd, T. (2014). Doing race and ethnicity in a digital community: Lexical labels and narratives of belonging in a Nigerian web forum. *Discourse, Context and Media* 4–5: 38–47.

Hollinger, D. (1995) *Postethnic America: Beyond Multiculturalism*. New York: Basic Books.

Jacquemet, M. (2015). Asylum and superdiversity: The search for denotational accuracy during asylum hearings. *Language & Communication* 1–10. Retrieved from http://dx.doi.org/10.1016/j.langcom.2014.10.016.

Jensen, O. (2011). "Our house, in the middle of our street . . .": Dynamics of housing and belonging in a multi-ethnic neighbourhood in south-east England. Paper presented at the Conference: Ethnography, Diversity, and Urban Space, St. Anne's College, Oxford University.

Jørgensen, J.N. (2008) Poly-Lingual languaging around and among children and adolescents. *International Journal of Multilingualism* 5(3): 161–176.

Juffermans, K., Blommaert, J., Kroon, S. and Li, J. (2014). Dutch–Chinese repertoires and language ausbau in superdiversity: A view from digital media. *Discourse, Context and Media* 4–5: 48–61.

Kapia, E. (2013). Assessing narrative development in bilingual first language acquisition: What can we learn from Monolingual norms? In J. Duarte and I. Gogolin (eds.), *Linguistic Superdiversity in Urban Areas: Research Approaches* (pp. 179–190). Amsterdam and Philadelphia: John Benjamins.

Khubchandani, L.M. (1997) *Revisualizing Boundaries: A Plurilingual Ethos*. New Delhi: Sage.

Kress, G., Jewitt, C., Ogborn, J. and Tsatsarelis, C. (2001) *Multimodal Teaching and Learning: The Rhetorics of the Science Classroom*. London: Continuum.

Lave, J. and Wenger, E. (1991) *Situated Learning: Legitimate Peripheral Participation*. Cambridge and New York: Cambridge University Press.

Leppänen, S. and Häkkinen, A. (2014) Buffalaxed superdiversity: Representations of the other on YouTube. *Diversities* 14(2): 17–33.

Li Wei (2014). Researching multilingualism and superdiversity: Grassroots actions and responsibilities double special issue. Multilingua 33: 5–6.

Maher, J. (2005). Metroethnicity, language, and the principle of cool. *International Journal of Sociolinguistics*,175/176: 83–102.

Makoni, S. (2012) A critique of language, languaging and supervernacular. Uma crítica à noção de língua, linguagem e supervernáculo. *Muitas Vozes, Ponta Grossa* 1(2): 189–199.

McIntosh, P. (1989) White privilege: Unpacking the invisible knapsack. In *Beyond Heroes and Holidays: Practical Guide to K-12 Anti-racist, Multicultural Education and Staff Development* (pp. 79–82). Wellesley, MA: Network of Educators on the Americas.

McLaughlin, F. (2014). Senegalese digital repertoires in superdiversity: A case study from Seneweb. *Discourse, Context and Media* 4–5: 29–37.

Meissner, F. and Vertovec, S., eds. (forthcoming). *Comparing Super-Diversity*. London: Routledge.

Menken, K. (2008). *English Learners Left Behind: Standardized Testing as Language Policy*. Tonawanda, NY: Multilingual Matters.

Moore, Robert. (2012) "Taking up speech in an endangered language: Bilingual discourse in a heritage language classroom." *Working Papers in Educational Linguistics* 27(2): 57–78.

Padilla, B., Azevedo, J. and Olmos-Alcaraz, A. (2015) Superdiversity and conviviality: Exploring frameworks for doing ethnography in Southern European intercultural cities. *Ethnic and Racial Studies* 38(4): 621–635.

Parkin, D. (2012) From multilingual classification to translingual ontology: Concluding commentary. *Diversities* 14(2): 71–83.

Parkin, D. and Arnaut, K. (2014). *Super-Diversity & Sociolinguistics – A Digest*. Tilburg Papers in Culture Studies, Paper 95, 1–6.

Pratt, M.-L. (1991). *Arts of the Contact Zone*. Modern Language Association, 33–40.

Rampton, B. (1995) *Crossing: Language and Ethnicity among Adolescents*. London: Longman.

Rampton, B., Blommaert, J., Arnaut, K. and Spotti, M. (2015). *Superdiversity and Sociolinguistics*. Working Papers in Urban Language & Literacies, Paper 152, 1–13.

Reyes, A. (2014) Super-new-big. *American Anthropologist* 116(2): 366–378.

Scollon, R. (1997) Handbills, tissues, and condoms: A site of engagement for the construction of identity in public discourse. *Journal of Sociolinguistics* 1(1): 39–61.

Sharma, B.K. (2014). On high horses: Transnational Nepalis and language ideologies on YouTube. *Discourse, Context and Media* 4–5: 19–28.

Silverstein, M. (2003) Indexical order and the dialectics of sociolinguistic life. *Language and Communication* 23: 193–229.

Spotti, M. (2011). Ideologies of success for superdiverse citizens: The Dutch testing regime for integration and the online private sector. *Diversities* 13(2): 39–52.

Staehr, A. (2014). The appropriation of transcultural flows among Copenhagen youth – The case of Illuminati. *Discourse, Context and Media* 4–5: 101–115.

Varis, Piia, and Xuan Wang. (2011) "Superdiversity on the Internet: A case from China." *Diversities* 13(2): 71–83.

Van der Aa, Jef, and Jan Blommaert. (2015) "Ethnographic monitoring and the study of complexity." *Tilburg Papers in Culture Studies* 123.

Vertovec, S. (2007) Super-diversity and its implications. *Ethnic and Racial Studies* 30(6): 1024–1054.

Vertovec, S. (December 2013). *Reading "Super-diversity"*. Blog entry. Retrieved from http: http://www.mmg.mpg.de/online-media/blogs/2013/reading-super-diversity/.

Westermann, R. (August 2014). *Review of the #superdiversity conference, 2014*. Blog "Migration Systems". Retrieved from https://www.migrationsystems.org/superdiversity-conference-2014/.

Wimmer, A. and Glick Schiller, N. (2003). Methodological nationalism, the social sciences and the study of migration: An essay in historical epistemology. *International Migration Review* 37(3): 576–610.

4
Neoliberalism, language, and migration

Kori Allan and Bonnie McElhinny

Introduction

"Neoliberalism" is used in applied linguistics and sociolinguistics both too little and at moments too extensively. Several recent works (e.g., Block, Gray, and Holborow 2012; Park and Lo 2012) have noted the need for more attention to current political and economic developments in applied linguistics, especially neoliberalism, to make research more politically relevant and effective. Others, however, note that the overly wide use of neoliberalism may assume the spread of market forces in ways that neoliberal theorists can only aspire to (Fairclough 1992). In addition, neoliberalism, globalization, and late capitalism are sometimes used interchangeably. This chapter speaks to these concerns. We begin with an overview of the history of the rise of neoliberal thought, various theories of neoliberalism, and the unevenness of neoliberalism in various contexts. This overview provides some background for our general survey of work done on neoliberalism within sociolinguistics, linguistic anthropology, and applied linguistics, allowing us to ask which questions get taken up in this literature and which do not, and how linguistic research is articulated with other disciplinary accounts of neoliberalism. Studies of migration have often, perhaps even more than other areas of sociolinguistics and applied linguistics, been attentive to economic trends that shape movement (Kerswill 2006). In the final portion of the chapter, we consider what is distinctive about linguistic issues in the context of migration in the current moment, drawing on two detailed case studies of neoliberalism, language, and migration (Canada and the Philippines) to exemplify the application of some of the theoretical insights and debates as a model for future research in these areas.

Overview of neoliberalism

What we call *neoliberalism* began with the ideas of Friedrich von Hayek and Milton Friedman who promoted a political economic theory in the mid-20th century, which proposes the market is the best device for ensuring individual freedom and for mobilizing human behaviour for the benefit of all. While *liberalism* and *neoliberalism* are both premised upon individuals' freedom, liberalism articulates a distinction between non-economic and economic actions, while neoliberalism interpellates individuals as entrepreneurial actors in every sphere of life. Furthermore, unlike neoclassical economics, neoliberals do not conceive of the market or rational economic behaviour as natural; rather they are constructed through cultural norms or state regulation (Brown 2005).

Neoliberalism, globalization, and *late capitalism* are often conflated in applied linguistics research (see Block et al. 2012: 7 for a slightly different critique). Such conflations raise questions about the analytical purchase of the term neoliberalism. We give neoliberalism a narrower definition than globalization or late capitalism, for all aspects of the latter are not neoliberal. For instance, papers in the *Handbook of Language and Globalization* (Coupland 2010) offer both critical and celebratory accounts of globalization, only some of which specifically analyze neoliberalism. Similarly, while *late capitalism* is a temporal marker to describe transformations in capitalism, *neoliberalism* can be traced to particular networks, theories, and projects. Regardless of the terms used, there is agreement that a new kind of capitalism emerged in the Global North in the 1970s, which involved two kinds of shifts. The first entailed a shift from Fordist to post-Fordist labour regimes. The second involved a shift from Keynesian to neoliberal political economic theory regarding the appropriate relationship between government and economy (Ortner 2011).

Often, when *neoliberalism* is invoked in applied linguistics and sociolinguistics, the reference is to initiatives that dismantle impediments to the "free market," including the Keynesian welfare state. According to Keynesian economic theory, states should actively intervene in the economy to maximize stability for the collective welfare of citizens. Welfare state supports also attempted to socialize the risks of insecure capitalist markets. For instance, Keynesian fiscal and monetary policies were used to ensure full employment, while standards for social wages were introduced through welfare systems (health care, education, unemployment insurance, etc.). In advanced capitalist countries, the welfare state delivered high rates of economic growth in the 1950s and 1960s. By the end of the 1960s growth slowed, and the crisis of capital accumulation in the 1970s led to rising unemployment and accelerating inflation (Harvey 2005: 14). These conditions enabled neoliberalism to move from being a theory to a set of transformations of the welfare state in the Global North and structural adjustments in the Global South. In the Global North, neoliberal governments attempted to dismantle or roll back the commitments of the welfare state, included privatizing public enterprises, reducing taxes, breaking labour unions, encouraging entrepreneurial initiative, and inducing a strong inflow of foreign investment. For instance, in 1979 the US Federal Reserve changed monetary policy from ensuring full employment to fighting inflation. This resulted in a recession that broke unions and drove debtor countries such as Mexico into insolvency, beginning the era of structural adjustment in the Global South, through which the International Monetary Fund (IMF) and the World Bank enforced free market fundamentalism in return for debt rescheduling. By 1991, seventy-five of the world's poorest countries received adjustment loans (Harvey 2005). At this time, socialism was also "rolled back." In China, economic reforms that began "socialism with Chinese characteristics" (see Harvey 2005; Yang 2007) wedded neoliberal and Keynesian economic policies, centralized state planning, and authoritarian rule.

Deregulation and tax breaks for investment encouraged the movement of capital to the Global South, leading to de-industrialization in the unionized Global North and the development of export processing zones in the Global South. The creation of flexibility in the labour market resulted in lower wages and increasing job insecurity in the Global North. Deregulation also resulted in the "financialization of everything" (Harvey 2005). The draconian impact of structural adjustment policies often led to increased internal and especially external *labour migration* as people sought better lives. In addition, middle-class families seek to address the anxieties of newly uncertain financial positions with *educational migration* (discussed further later). Often, also, there are changes in the provision of support services for migrants, with government programs being cut, or morphing into public-private partnerships, or being shouldered by non-governmental organizations (NGO) or religious or other sectors.

By the 1990s it became clear that recurrent failures of the market called for responses outside the narrow repertoire of deregulation and privatization. This led to new forms of neoliberalism, called *roll-out neoliberalism* (Tickell and Peck 2003) or a "Third Way," which focus on certain consequences of economic liberalization, such as crime and poverty, through incarceration, surveillance, and a range of microregulatory interventions (see Wacquant 2012). In other nations, resistance to the consequences of structural adjustment led to changes in government, to leaders who pledged to talk back to international agencies. This happened earlier in South America, and more recently in Greece (see Canale 2015 for a thoughtful analysis of the ways that the meaning of English as a Foreign Language (EFL) changes when the Uruguayan government shifted to the left, and Theodossopoulos 2014 for an analysis of anti-austerity narratives in Greece).

Issues and ongoing debates

Different theoretical approaches to neoliberalism

The two main theoretical paradigms that have predominated in studies of neoliberalism are Marxist and Foucauldian. An exemplar of the Marxist approach is Harvey (2005), which argues that neoliberalism is a political project to restore class power for a new imperialist capitalist class (e.g., financiers and CEOs). Harvey (2005) argues that there are inherent contradictions between neoliberal theory and the pragmatics of neoliberal policy and programs. For instance, the spread of neoliberalism relies on undemocratic institutions such as the IMF and it is often sustained by authoritarianism. While many scholars have emphasized the, necessity of authoritarianism for neoliberalism to take hold (Klein 2007), others have labeled an increase in authoritarianism post-9/11 as indicative of the emergence of law-and-order security states, in which policing rather than the free market is the primary mechanism for governance (Hyatt 2011). Also, state power has often been used to bail out companies or avert financial failures before but most significantly after the financial crisis of 2008 (see Holborow 2015 on Ireland). These contradictions are important for Harvey because they suggest that the problem is not that neoliberalism is not yet realized, but that it may not be realizable, and indeed is contested. For social scientists, including linguists, this means that the task is not simply to spot evidence of neoliberalism – a move which may grant the ideology of neoliberalism too much power (see also critiques by Fairclough 1992 and Holborow 2015) but to map precisely these forms of unevenness and contradiction.

A Foucauldian approach treats neoliberalism as a mode of government (i.e., theorized as governmentality) that encompasses but is not limited to the state and which produces particular kinds of subjects (Brown 2005; Foucault 1991). As a rationality of government, neoliberalism problematizes the Keynesian welfare state as rigid, bureaucratic and encouraging dependency. Neoliberal government "recommend(s) the reform of individual and institutional conduct so that it becomes more competitive and efficient . . . by the extension of market rationality to all spheres" (Dean 1999: 210). For example, governmental technologies enacted through unemployment and welfare contractual obligations aim to transform passive citizens into active job seekers. Governmental scholars, however, also stress that neoliberalism is found within a field of contestation. Rose (1999), for instance, uses the term *advanced liberalism* to encompass various ways of governing in contemporary liberal democracies, including neoliberalism, neoconservativism, and more.

Marxist approaches to neoliberalism as a hegemonic global top-down programme leave unanswered questions of *how* economies and institutions are neoliberalized in practice (Wacquant 2012). A focus on governmentality addresses precisely these questions. However, the latter perspective has been critiqued for its functionalist explanation of subject formation. It is also often unclear what makes a technology of conduct "neoliberal" (Wacquant 2012). Song (2009) finds Foucauldian studies of neoliberal government useful for examining *how* institutions and techniques of government aim to create entrepreneurial subjects and extend market logic, while Marxist perspectives are helpful for analyzing "the consequences of (neo)liberal governing in the capitalist labor market" (p. 12; see also Bjornson 2007; Allan 2013; Bell 2013). Both Marxist and Foucauldian approaches have been criticized for not taking into account how neoliberalism impacts, and is resisted by, different communities (Kingfisher and Maskovsky 2008). Brenner, Peck and Theodore (2010) argue that neoliberalism is *variegated*; that is, "*simultaneously* patterned, interconnected, locally specific, contested and unstable" (p. 184). For instance, Muehlebach (2012) argues that neoliberal reforms in Italy articulated with Catholicism and socialist solidarity to facilitate moral action through volunteering, which was viewed as valuable precisely because it was not commodified. Other approaches, especially those adopting an ethnographic approach, include understanding neoliberalism as a cultural formation (Kingfisher 2002; Kingfisher and Maskovsky 2008) or as a social ethos (Song 2009).

Theoretical debates about neoliberalism within sociolinguistics and applied linguistics are sometimes debates between scholars adhering to different perspectives (cf. Holborow, Block, Gray and McGill's use of Marxist theory to critique the more Foucauldian perspectives of Fairclough and Pennycook). Pennycook (2010) meanwhile, argues that the "dystopic" focus on economistic discourse occludes other forms of agency and social practices. Heller and Duchêne (2016) draw on more ethnographically oriented approaches, including Bourdieu, to counter certain aspects of Marxist critique.

There are at least three key clusters of debates in studies of language and neoliberalism, on the themes of *legitimation, materiality*, and *value*. In ongoing work, we explore these in more detail. Here, we briefly note the questions, and a few key texts. Building on the call in the late 1970s and 1980s to further understand how *legitimation* of inequity occurs, as well as to challenge overly reductionist accounts of the manipulation of people by ruling class interests, a significant site for work in linguistic anthropology, critical discourse analysis and postcolonial sociolinguistics through the 1990s built on work by Foucault, Gramsci, Volosinov, Williams and Said to understand discourse and ideology. Influential texts include Fairclough (1992), Schieffelin, Woolard, and Kroskrity (1998), Kroskrity (2000), and Blommaert et al. (2003). Cavanaugh and Shankar (2014) critique a language ideological approach, offering a focus on materialism (see also Shankar and Cavanaugh 2012) as an alternative, though it is important to note that not all materialist approaches focus on inequity. Strikingly, the question of base and superstructure, as well as other questions about *materiality*, which seemed to have been laid to rest twenty-five years ago with invocations of Williams's and Gramsci's work, is again a significant question for debate. Recent work by sociolinguists drawing explicitly on Marxist thought (Block et al. 2012; McGill 2013; Holborow 2015) returns to a base/superstructure distinction; compare Gal (2012) on the independence of linguistic ideologies, and Heller (2010) and Heller and Duchêne (2016) for more ethnographic perspectives. Questions about how to understand the *value* of language are evident in discussions of what counts as commodification. Certain scholars (Cameron 2002; Tan and Rubdy 2008; Heller 2010; Heller and Duchêne 2012) argue that language is increasingly commodified, while Block et al. (2012) and McGill (2013) disagree that language can be commodified. These debates could be helpfully informed by Italian Marxism (see McGill 2013) and technoscience approaches to understanding economy and commodity (Murphy 2013) that suggest examining the economization rather than the commodification of language might be helpful. See also Park (2015) for an argument that the Marxist critiques are focusing too much on the product of labour, and not on labour processes themselves. These theoretical debates on legitimization, value, and materiality play themselves out in research in which applied linguists and linguistic anthropologists have begun to consider the ways that neoliberalization, globalization, and late capitalism are leading to new ways of understanding language, as well as to the creation of new forms of labour, personhood, citizenship, and education.

Neoliberalism and political economy in sociolinguistics and applied linguistics

Labour and personhood

While older studies of language and work tended to emphasize talk in medical, legal, therapeutic, and educational professions in ways which largely neglected other work sites, new research examines a wider range of occupations in the interests of studying tertiarization. Nonetheless language in the primary and secondary sectors (resource extraction/agriculture, and the processing of these products in factories and warehouses), in both the Global North and especially the Global South, remains a largely neglected topic in applied linguistics, a gap which perhaps shares the ideologies of institutions which do not perceive linguistic practice and form as part of their work. Call centres have received particular attention in studies by sociolinguists, linguistic anthropologists, and applied linguists, including in England (Cameron 2000), Francophone Canada (Roy 2003), India (Mirchandani 2012), and the Philippines (Salonga 2010). Heller (2010) insightfully argues that call centres get such attention because they are symbols of the transition from industrial, white, masculine, working-class, first-world work to feminized, racialized, "offshore" production. Domestic work is a counterpart in the realm of reproduction. Domestic work in affluent countries in Asia, Europe, and North America is often provided by migrants, and thus studies of paid caregiving have received particular attention because of the ways they highlight the interaction of the negative impact of structural adjustment policies in the Global South with the privatization of health, elder care, and child care in the Global North (see e.g., England and Stiell 1997; Lorente 2007). (Other chapters in this volume provide some detailed overviews of how language and migration are linked to various kinds of work – see Lising, this volume, for example.)

A wealth of scholarship in the Asia Pacific (especially Japan, Korea, Hong Kong, and Singapore), Europe, and North America examines the role of language in workplaces, particularly in "white collar" tertiary sectors. From a Foucauldian governmentality perspective, Fogde (2007) examines how a neoliberal discourse of *employability* shifts the responsibility from the state to the individual through concepts of lifelong learning and flexibility. More culturally oriented research also examines how workers are imagined as *flexible* and adaptable both in their bodies and in the ways they fit into corporate culture (Martin 1994). Such notions place the onus on individuals to deal with the loss of jobs in ways that obscure such trends as corporate downsizing and casualization. McElhinny (2012, forthcoming) argues that sociolinguistic approaches for challenging essentialist notions of identity since the 1990s can be complicit with ideologies of flexibilization in late capitalist economies, for they suggest that flexible personhood is desirable and indeed already achieved.

The *flexible* worker is also often re-imagined as a "bundle of skills," which are commodifiable as aspects of personhood with exchange value on the labour market (Urciuoli 2008). A putative lack of skills can be used to blame workers rather than structural conditions for unemployment or underemployment. Workers and migrants are often responsible for acquiring language skills, viewed as enhancing one's competitiveness and economic value in the global economy (Inoue 2007; Wee 2008; Park 2011; Urciuoli and LaDousa 2013; Bae 2014; Said-Sirhan 2014). In the context of increasing unemployment and job insecurity, new technologies of assessment, such as standardized language tests, were introduced to evaluate Korean workers' English skills (Park 2011; Gao and Park 2015; Jang 2015a, 2015b), often fuelling attempts to migrate elsewhere to develop such skills. Learning English is also seen as key to Singapore's attempt to be seen not for what it produces; it now markets itself for how it uses information as well as arts-based activities (Rubdy 2005). However, scholarship shows how the ideology of language as an acquirable and commodifiable skill exists in tension with an ideology of language as tied to essentialized ethnic or national difference, illustrating the limits of neoliberal self-improvement (Heller 2010; Duchene and Heller 2012; Park and Lo 2012; Park 2014). Entrepreneurial aspirations to acquire language skills thus often backfire, as particular varieties of English acquired in one context may not be valued in another (Park and Wee 2012; Bernstein et al. 2015; Jang 2015a).

Acquiring specific skills or knowledge is often not, however, as important as indexing a particular kind of self (Inoue 2007; Park 2011; Park and Lo 2012; Allan 2013; Bell 2013; Bae 2014). Urciuoli (2008) demonstrates how soft skills constitute ways of fashioning subjectivity in line with corporate values and which function to reproduce a self-monitoring workforce. A neoliberal view of personhood as responsible, autonomous, self-sufficient, and entrepreneurial leads, simultaneously, to a celebration of choice and self-realization through the market. The artist Jay Z was recently quoted as saying, "I am not a businessman, I am a business, man!" This comment neatly encapsulates the changes that neoliberalism might require in personhood – from a version where work is a portion of one's life to a new form of subjectivity linked to a neoliberal theory of human capital in which one's entire being is viewed as a business – a Me, Inc. (Gershon 2011). The entrepreneurial vision of human capital, including Gary Becker's, is premised upon making investments according to cost/benefit calculations in regard to profit and satisfaction. However, with financialization, Feher (2009) argues that the primary goal of accumulating human capital is to continually appreciate: to accumulate assets with potential future value. In a financialized neoliberal economy, one is thus a portfolio manager of the self, of one's stock value.

Linguistic anthropological and sociolinguistic studies in a variety of different sites have attempted to consider how and where neoliberal changes of personhood are actively engineered. This is evident in the attempt to engineer work sensibilities among welfare recipients in New Zealand (Kingfisher 2002), in the emergence of new words for talking about self-responsibility in Japan (Inoue 2007), and in host-caller exchanges on a Moscow talk show (Matza 2009). Language and self are managed in the restructuring of socialist states as well, from workers' interactions in the transition from a Maoist planned economy to a Dengist market economy (Yang 2007) to resume workshops for workers in the Slovak Republic (Larson 2008). In interviews and resumes, job seekers need to communicate a particularly kind of self that embodies employer values while seeming authentic (see Fogde 2007 on Sweden; Roberts and Cooke 2009 on the UK; Allan 2013 on Canada). Cameron

(2002) argues that styles of speaking considered to comprise "effective communication," regardless of the language used, are presented as global even though they express the values of the educated American middle class. Research on language, migration, and neoliberalism, however, has tended to focus on mobile groups (often middle class) rather than on immobile groups (Bae 2014), which perhaps makes neoliberalism and the proliferation of entrepreneurial forms of personhood seem more ubiquitous than they are. Strikingly, the use of management-based ideologies are now evident in domains that were earlier shaped by nationalist discourses (Urla 2012).

Recent scholarship on labour and personhood has also started to examine how modes of neoliberal government and neoliberalized economies reproduce particular forms of affect (McElhinny 2010). In applied linguistics, Park (2014) analyzes linguistic insecurity as a lens for understanding how, under neoliberalism, workplaces do not deliver the realization of selves, but rather anxiety (see also Yang 2007; Bae 2014; Hall 2014; Hiramoto and Park 2014). Fears of being left behind often compel job seekers to increase their value in the job market through continuous self-development (Yang 2015). More research on how existential precarity may be linked to insecurity and precarious work could further illuminate the affective effects of neoliberalism.

Both neoliberal ideologies and perspectives critical of them (including Marxism) may over-emphasize the economic aspects of life. However, approaches which critique overly economic approaches by focusing only on other "desires" (Pennycook 2010) may overlook the ways in which desire, leisure, and love are also shaped in complex ways by economic circumstances. We also note that while much work focuses on the effects of neoliberalism in terms of market productivity, the market also requires consumers. The disciplined self, required for work, may be at odds with the indulgent self required for consumption; however, the enterprising self also seeks to achieve freedom and fulfill the self through lifestyle consumption (Rose 1999), in ways that trouble the separation between production and consumption (see Yang 2015). More work is needed on these questions. Gray's (2012) analysis of textbooks for teaching English in the global market shows a dramatic increase in the use of celebrities since the 1970s, to market the cosmopolitan and successful lifestyles to which learners are told they can aspire to with the use of English. A focus on consumer-based identities thus obscures structural barriers to achievement, but also eclipses class-based forms of solidarity by creating consumer-based ones. It may also explain some sites where there is resistance to neoliberal arguments for learning English – compare religious concerns about the cultural values associated with English language instruction that have led to resistance to English in some countries in the Middle East.

One of the sharpest changes in the corporate world in the last fifteen years is that many successful corporations now produce brands rather than products. Brands advertise a lifestyle, an experience, and penetrate into domains previously untouched by commercialism (Klein 2000). While some scholars celebrate new forms of ludic identity produced by transnational flows (Maher 2010; Pennycook 2010), others are more cautious of the roles that corporations play, and the ways they benefit, from "lifestyle identities" (Machin and van Leeuwen 2010). For some recent ethnographic approaches on the meanings of brands and identity see Bucholtz (2007), Zhang (2007), and Shankar (2015).

Citizenship: integration, training, and education

Research on national language policy highlights how social inclusion agendas, which have emerged with the neoliberalized shift away from the welfare state, tend to focus on employment and language as the key to citizens and migrants' integration (Harris, Leung, and Rampton 2002; Piller and Takahashi 2011). The need for labour migrants in wealthy countries in the period after World War II led to the development of varieties of multilingual and multicultural policies in a number of nations (cf. Canada, Netherlands, Sweden, and the UK). However, in the face of increased migration from Eastern Europe with the fall of the Iron Curtain; the expansion of the European Union; continuing migration from sites of European, American, Japanese, and other colonies; migration away from poverty-stricken and war-torn countries; the anti-Islamic sentiment engendered by acts of terrorism and the War on Terror; and in the face of claims of family members of workers recruited earlier, key European politicians on the right and the left have argued that multiculturalism has failed (Blackledge 2009), and that countries need to focus more on *integration* (see also Pujolar 2015). Strikingly, the word *assimilation* is largely avoided, as a notion associated with earlier, coercive practices. Immigrants and prospective citizens are increasingly asked to take language tests, as well as tests on knowledge about the country they want to enter, a requirement which has been critiqued on pragmatic and political terms by a number of scholars (Milani 2008; Hogan-Brun, Mar-Molinero, and Stevenson 2009; McNamara 2009; Shohamy 2009; van Avermaet 2009; Piller 2001). For parallel developments in Australia, see Cox 2010; see McElhinny under review for further discussion). Like the tests for English (mentioned later), these tests participate in neoliberal audit culture, where more readily quantified, technical processes are valued. They are also seen as neutral and transparent, and they constitute a savings for states which are rolling back the provision of certain social services. Often, also, immigrants now have to pay for these tests, whereas in the past such support tended to be provided by nation-states accepting migrants (see Bjornson 2007; Extra and Spotti 2009; Slade 2010; Allan 2016; Flubacher et al. 2016; Yeung 2016). The tests chosen, and the immigrants who are required to take them (since policies don't require all to do so), create zones of exception that construct often racialized hierarchies of citizenship.

Services for migrants, including language services, have been devolved/offloaded to civil society, trade unions, or NGOs, in keeping with neoliberal rationality in Spain (Pujolar 2007; Codó 2013; Codó and Garrido 2014) and Canada (Da Silva and Heller 2009; Allan 2014). Longergan (2015) shows how a series of austerity cuts to English as a Second or other language classes in the UK are underpinned by a neoliberal model of citizenship: only migrants who take full responsibility for learning English with minimal government assistance are worthy of becoming citizens. As a result of devolution and in combination with discourses of active inclusion, volunteerism for the un(der)employed has also proliferated (see Codó and Garrido 2014 on Spain). Motobayashi (2015) documents a new volunteer program for language instruction for long-standing Japanese migrant communities in South America, which are now being construed as providing key bridges to these markets in ways which also re-constitute what counts as Japanese and who counts as a speaker. However, national belonging can also be fraught in resistance to neoliberalism (Theodossopoulos 2014).

Educational practices are always closely linked to national and economic needs – though sometimes these can be at odds (see e.g., papers analyzing the contradictions that can arise between decolonization and globalization in Lin and Martin 2005, or between national pride and economic profit (Duchêne and Heller 2012)). Education in North America and Western Europe has been restructured to service the economy through the production of human capital (Gray and Block 2012; Holborow 2012). Education may also be used to create labour desired by employers (Da Silva and Heller 2009; Urciuoli 2010) and to export labour in some nations (Lorente 2012).

One of the questions most frequently debated in the emerging literature on language and globalization may be how best to understand the effects of cultural and linguistic imperialism, especially of English (Canagarajah 1999; Pennycook 2007). English is increasingly promoted as natural, neutral (especially when there are other significant and competing languages in a nation), and technical. The European Union's Bologna Process, adopted in 1999, aimed to ensure the transnational transferability of higher education by, in part, promoting and commodifying English (see Singh and Han 2008; Wodak and Fairclough 2010); for papers looking at EFL in a wide-ranging group of nations, see Bernstein et al. (2015). Piller and Cho (2013) examine how English has increasingly become the medium of instruction (MoI) in South Korean higher education after the Asian financial crisis of 1997–1998. With the neoliberal socioeconomic transformations that followed, the core value of "competitiveness" structured the assessment of higher education. University rankings, which positively evaluate an institution's internationalization, favor English (Piller and Cho 2013). Their analysis highlights the social cost of competitiveness, including the rise of suicide rates in South Korea. Kubota (2011) argues linguistic instrumentalism (see Wee 2008) contributes to the proliferation of the language teaching and testing industry in Japan and is linked to the neoliberal discourse of human capital and employability, though rather than economic returns, language learning often measures one's effort to be employable in the neoliberal economy rather than one's proficiency. Block (2002: 121) argues that McCommunication – "the framing of communication as a rational activity devoted to the transfer of information between and among individuals as efficient, calculable, predictable and controllable" – also underlies much Second Language Acquisition (SLA) research and task-based language teaching. Language teachers are also increasingly contract knowledge workers who are flexible and replaceable (Bernstein et al. 2015).

Papers on India (Annamalai 2005), Hong Kong (Lin 2005), Iran (Riazi 2005), Malaysia (Martin 2005), Mexico (Sayer 2015), Singapore (Rubdy 2005), South Africa (Probyn 2005), South Korea (Jang 2015a, 2015b), Turkey (Reagan and Schreffler 2005) and Uruguay (Canale 2015) all show how education is generally being retooled to teach English in more places, and/or at earlier ages, or in ways that are seen as more authentic and "native-like" with discourses of national need and social justice complicatedly intertwined with discourses of competitiveness. Many educators in sites where English has been mandated as a language of instruction, but where neither instructors nor students may have ready access to English, are concerned it fosters imitative rather than creative learning (see Annamalai 2005 on India; Brock-Utne 2005 on Tanzania and South Africa; Probyn 2005 on South Africa). In applied linguistics, the dominance of English is often ascribed to imperialism (e.g., Phillipson 2008; Majhanovich 2014; Hsu 2015) or globalization or is construed as the embodiment of neoliberal ideology. In such accounts, language acquires a static character, ascribing English an overly functionalist role (Holborow 2012; Park and Wee 2012). English can, in fact, have many meanings. Martin (2005) cites the former prime minister of Malaysia saying that true nationalism means doing everything possible for the country, even learning English (p. 93). Because the apartheid regime in South Africa required instruction in minority languages, access to English, a lingua franca of the resistance, is associated with equity, redress, and access, and is often preferred to Afrikaans (Probyn 2005). Rubdy (2005) notes that though the new economy requires creative workers, this may be at odds with the Singaporean regime's desire to mute political dissent. Since *creativity* is also a keyword of the neoliberal economy, it's worth exploring in detail which notions of creativity challenge and which are complicit with neoliberalism.

Transnational educational migration has "become an important strategy for acquiring valuable linguistic resources in the globalized neoliberal economy" (Hiramoto and Park

2014: 146) after the Asian financial crisis and the subsequent neoliberal economic reform. Bae (2014) examines how middle-class Korean families aim to develop their pre-university children as global elites through *jogi yuhak* ("early study abroad"). Enrolling students in schools in multilingual Singapore or the Philippines is often used as a strategic way of gaining access to English universities in the West (Gao and Park 2015; Jang 2015b). Neoliberal reforms also shape programs at Western universities which have experienced funding cuts due to roll-back neoliberal measures and can charge international students higher tuition rates than domestic students. The University of Toronto, for example, has a new program which admits select international students (at the moment, largely from East Asia) to a five-year degree which focuses in the first year on English language instruction and acclimatization to Canadian educational culture. Another strategy for learning English is recruiting domestics who are fluent in English to provide early childhood socialization (cf. employers of Filipinas in Taiwan and Singapore; Lan 2003; Lorente 2007).

Implications: case studies of migration in two sites

Earlier studies of migration examined other moments of crisis and consolidation in global capitalism. Kerswill (2006) provides a useful overview of some of these moments, though his review does not focus on what causes migration so much as what the impact of migration on language use is. In two case studies, we look at whether, when, and how migration might differ in light of neoliberal economic restructuring.

We note that such accounts require at least five features: (1) a historical perspective on government policy and practices with respect to migration; (2) analysis of government policy and official government institutions; (3) analysis of when and how other non-governmental institutions support immigration or emigration; (4) attention to how migration is linked to government policies that address finance, security, and definitions of labour shortage/excesses; and (5) language policies. Canada is a settler colonial site with two official languages (English and French), which relies on the recruitment of migrants to fuel its economy, including in recent years significant numbers from the Philippines. The Philippines has, since its colonization by the Spain and United States, long been a site for the recruitment of labour by other nations. Together, these two case studies allow us to address a frequent criticism of studies of migration, that is that they tend to study receiving countries more than sending countries (cf. Juffermans and Lorente 2015). However, recent research is beginning to show that even the binary models are inadequate, since there are few studies of South-South migration, or cases where people migrate from or to "semi-peripheral" sites (sometimes as way stations to other forms of migration, and sometimes not), as when Chinese workers move within China to sites where they can practice English with foreigners (Gao and Park 2015); when students from South Korea study in Singapore or the Philippines, sometimes before going to Canada, the US or Australia (Gao and Park 2015; Jang 2015b); or when Singapore recruits skilled English speakers from elsewhere in Asia (cf. de Costa 2015). Such sites need much more sociolinguistic attention.

Canada

Canada's official policy, Multiculturalism in a Bilingual Framework, erases the colonization of indigenous peoples and constructs the unmarked dominant core culture of the nation as Anglophone and Francophone (Mackey 2002; Thobani 2007; Haque 2012). Language is thus a terrain through which belonging to the Canadian nation is often construed. The province of Québec aims to recruit Francophones, many of whom come from former French colonies which are largely Islamic/North African, resulting in tensions over the "reasonable accommodation" of Muslims in a secularized Catholic Québec. This case study, however, focuses on English Canada and especially on Toronto, since it is Canada's largest immigrant-receiving city, with forty-six percent of its population being foreign-born (Stasiulis, Hughes, and Amery 2011).

Although Canada's early immigration policies were explicitly racist (Thobani 2007), in 1967, race and nationality were eliminated as justifiable means of exclusion, and a points system was introduced to evaluate economic class applicants. A separate family class was also established. These different classes of migrants were granted unequal access to citizenship. Unlike family class immigrants, male breadwinners who came through the economic immigration stream were eligible for social programs to help them become fully employed under the post-war welfare state. For example, the National Language Training Program (NLTP) provided full-time language training with a living allowance to increase immigrants' opportunities for employment (Arat-Koc 1999: 46).

With economic and welfare state restructuring in the 1980s and 1990s, the government further prioritized economic class over family class immigrants, construing the latter, along with refugees, as costly to the nation's social programs, though immigration services were also "rolled back" for economic class immigrants. For instance, in 1992, NLTP was replaced by language training programs that did not offer a living allowance. The selection criteria for economic class immigrants was modified to further emphasize language competency, education, and work experience, for the government aimed to recruit highly skilled (mostly professional) immigrants who possessed the human capital and skills needed to be flexible and self-sufficient entrepreneurs in Canada's tertiary economy (Thobani 2007; Allan 2014).

Nonetheless, foreign-trained professional immigrants have experienced high levels of un(der)employment, declining wages, and increasing poverty since the 1980s (Satzewich and Liodakis 2013). The foreign experience and credentials of racialized professional immigrants from Asia, Africa, and Eastern Europe are largely discounted in the Canadian labour market (Satzewich and Liodakis 2013). The growing poverty of skilled immigrants is also related to growing labour market inequality, reduced social services, and the increasing costs of retraining (Shields 2003). A broad coalition of civic leaders formed the Toronto City Summit Alliance (TCSA) in 2002 to address the gaps left by the retreating arms of the welfare state. To be more competitive and to recruit investors in the global economy, urban regions like Toronto often try to attract highly skilled workers by providing enhanced quality of life (Harvey 2001). The "added value" of skilled immigrants' international contacts and multilingualism was also seen as an untapped resource. TCSA thus argued that Toronto needed to ensure immigrants obtained jobs commensurate with their education and skills. While the TCSA represents a shift away from roll-back neoliberalism, it remained dedicated to entrepreneurial investment. TCSA's agenda, however, was not reducible to neoliberalism, for the quality of life focus included investment in redistributive programs, such as subsidized housing.

The TCSA helped establish the Toronto Region Immigrant Employment Council (TRIEC) in 2003, a public-private partnership that addressed the underemployment of skilled immigrants in line with a neoliberal model of social inclusion. Through public-private partnerships, the federal government subsequently provided funding for Enhanced Language Training and Bridge-to-Work (ELT) programs to address the characterization of the "underemployment problem" as, in large part, a language problem, namely the lack of appropriate language skills in English or French. Discrimination and the insecure nature of the labour market thereby became cast as apolitical technical problems that needed to be addressed through individual skills training. Rather than teach language skills, in everyday practice ELT teachers primarily taught soft skills, such as communication skills, which simultaneously prescribed the right attitudes worker-subjects were urged to adopt to increase their "employability" (Allan 2013). These programs largely did not lead to job placements, but rather they encouraged immigrants to entrepreneurially invest in the self through skills upgrading. ELT students, however, often critiqued the government for not providing substantive employment supports.

Unlike TRIEC's approach, the current federal government aims to download more of the costs of integration onto individual immigrants. For example, minimum language levels have been introduced for all economic streams of immigration, and applicants are required to take standardized language proficiency exams. For skilled workers, language is viewed as the key to social inclusion. The government has also controversially increased the number of temporary labour migrants who have limited access to social and welfare supports. Security measures have always been entangled with neoliberal modes of government, particularly since 9/11 when anti-terrorism acts institutionalized suspicion of Muslim immigrants and refugees as security threats (Thobani 2007). The government now emphasizes these more, however, in campaigns against immigration fraud and its reliance on temporary work permits.

This case study illustrates various forms of neoliberalization, from the roll-back policies of the 1990s to the roll-out policies of the 2000s. This account also draws on both Foucauldian and Marxist perspectives to examine how neoliberal technologies of government attempt to regulate migrants, in line with supply-side economic development. Immigrants' critiques of policies which do not help them find jobs do not necessarily fall outside of neoliberal frames, when they argue racism is impeding the proper working of the job market; they may instead ask them to be more fully realized; where they are insistent on the value of all humans, they provide a more significant challenge. This case study also demonstrates how neoliberal rationalities are often contested, incomplete or partial on the ground. Finally, it illustrates how states paired heightened surveillance for less desirable populations with neoliberal government at a distance for desirable migrants, viewed as capable of governing themselves, further illustrating the unevenness of neoliberalization as well as an increase in authoritarian government.

Philippines

The Philippines was colonized by Spain from 1521 to 1898, and by the United States from 1898 to 1946, with a brief period of occupation by Japan during World War II. Universal education in Spanish was established relatively late (in 1863), and by the end of its imperial rule approximately sixty percent of the population spoke at least some Spanish. A keystone of American imperialism was public education in English (Tupas 2008). English is often used in business, government, the legal system, medicine, the sciences, some media, and as a medium of instruction. The United States permitted Filipino migration to the United States, even at a period when other Asian migration had been barred, because Filipinos were considered US "nationals." In the early 20th century, a number of elite Filipinos were recruited under a *pensionada* scheme for education in US institutions; much larger numbers worked as labourers on plantations in Hawaii (also newly acquired as an imperial possession) or as agricultural and other workers on the west coast of the United States. In the 1950s and 1960s, even before racialized immigration quotas had been fully reformed in the United States and Canada, professional Filipina/os who were nurses, doctors, laboratory technicians, and office workers were recruited to overcome the labour shortages, because of their fluency in English and education in American, or sometimes American-influenced institutions (see McElhinny, Davidson, Catungal, Tungohan, and Coloma 2012 for an overview, and Gumperz 1982 for an analysis of miscommunications arising in a medical setting between a Filipino physician and American patients). The 1987 constitution specifies Filipino and English as the two official languages of the Philippines.

Migration policies which emerged in the period associated with neoliberalism were driven in part by the implementation of structural adjustment policies required by the World Bank and the International Monetary Fund in the 1980s, which were said to achieve greater efficiency through trade liberalization, privatization, and de-regulation (Bello, Docena, de Guzman, and Malig 2004); the Marcos government developed a labour export policy (Bakan and Stasiulius 1997, 2005) to address debt repayment problems and unemployment. Conditions of underdevelopment and poverty and political unrest in the Philippines, experienced by worker-citizens as unemployment, underemployment, lack of educational and occupational opportunities, and low standards of living (Eviota 1992), have led to the Philippines becoming critically economically reliant on remittances. Overseas workers are celebrated as heroes by the federal government (Rafael 2000) and putatively supported, but also monitored, by a number of government supported overseas employment agencies. Migration has steadily increased since the 1970s (http://www.worldometers.info/world-population/philippines-population/, accessed January 27, 2015), with ten percent of the whole population overseas (Bello et al. 2004: 3). This wave of migration has a gendered face, with many Filipinas working as domestics or child or elder care workers in other countries in Asia (especially Taiwan, Hong Kong, and Singapore), in the Middle East, in Europe, and in North America. Indeed, Canada has set up controversial foreign domestic worker and live-in caregiver migrant streams that are now overwhelmingly staffed by Filipinas; Parrenas (2001) calls Filipinas the "servants of globalization" (p. 2). Filipinas' linguistic ability in English has long been seen as key to their employability and is indeed a requirement for migration to certain nations (England and Stiell 1997; Lorente 2007), but increasingly Filipinas are also required to learn other languages. Lorente (2012) describes the 2007 founding of the Language Skills Institute by the federal government to help train workers for the range of destinations of overseas workers, with instruction in Spanish, Mandarin, Korean, Nihono, Italian, and Russian, noting English is no longer sufficient to sustain the "competitiveness" of foreign domestic workers as "supermaids" (p. 198). Somewhat weakly, the federal government also noted, in response to critiques of its own powerlessness to protect Filipinos abroad, that increased linguistic abilities would also ensure women's safety.

Increasingly, also, the Philippines, along with India, is a site for other industries that require fluency in English. Most notably, these include call centres, though copy-editing and English language instruction (especially for other Asians) are also noteworthy (Salonga 2010). In 2000, there were only two call centers in the Philippines; by 2010, there were over 1,000 (Salonga 2010: 80). Scholars working on call centres describe the impact of this *virtual migration*, noting that workers in industries which require them to work during the hours when customers in the UK and North America are awake, and who are trained in certain forms of social and cultural knowledge (current events, holidays, sports, celebrities), have bodies which are geographically and temporally at home, but their body, sense, time, and performances are also linked to another nation (Mirchandani 2012, see also Salonga 2010: 180). While for some this places them out of sync with families and friends, for others it offers an opportunity to perform gendered and classed cosmopolitan selves that they find empowering (Salonga 2010).

The Philippines case study illustrates how neoliberalized structural adjustment exacerbates poor economic conditions and an increase of migration from poor countries as well as how language training is key to the promotion of workers, including low skilled "supermaids." In both case studies, migration trajectories and discourses of integration are linked to debates about colonialism and postcolonialism. Together, these two case studies illustrate how the implications of neoliberalism for language learning and mobility cannot be prescribed outside of understanding local context, as well as the range of historical and ethnographic tools, and simultaneous awareness of macro and micro contexts, which must be incorporated into sociolinguistic analyses to both identify neoliberalism and fully document its contestation.

Future directions

Applied linguistics can make significant contributions to richer understandings of late capitalism with more robust and historicized accounts of emigration and immigration in various sites which attends to contestations between neoliberalism and other forms of governance. It is critical not simply to undertake studies which try to spot neoliberalism, since such studies may over-emphasize neoliberalism, but rather contextualize moments where neoliberal ideologies and practices arise alongside other policies. Our case study analysis of how neoliberalism often combines with racialized and colonialized histories also underscores the need for context-specific historical analysis. Future studies also need to be attentive to the possible emergence of post-neoliberal forms of governance. The economic crisis of 2008 challenged the political and ideological legitimacy of neoliberalism, prompting many to ask: what comes next? Peck, Nik, and Brenner (2009) point out that its uneven spatial development is central not only to understanding neoliberalism, but also efforts to move beyond it. Because neoliberalism as enabling the free market was never an accurate portrayal of neoliberal governance in practice, and in the absence of a robust ideological counterweight to neoliberalism, a revisionist fourth way may result post-crisis (Peck et al. 2009). Being attentive to how neoliberalism is reworked in new hybrid or uneven ways is thus particularly important for analyzing post-crisis shifts in governance. As many of the aforementioned studies show, the capillaries of neoliberal governance are being both re-entrenched in austerity policies and actively challenged, as the case of Greece illustrates. We need more studies that are attentive to authoritarianism to determine whether we are witnessing a shift to increasingly more authoritarian modes of government or a continuation of the contradictions of neoliberalism. There should be more studies in countries where leaders have been elected because of pledges to fight the state transformations required by structural adjustment. See for instance Canale's (2015) study of the re-signification of the meaning of English-language learning with the advent of a centre-left administration in Uruguay; while still seen as valuable, English is valued alongside other regional languages and cultures, and is re-defined not simply as having "practical," economic value, but seen as one valuable tool in political struggles over what it means to be human and construct utopian futures, in knowledge production and in empowerment of people in struggles for equity.

Gershon (2011) argues that pointing out the unevenness and local forms of neoliberalism, while important, is insufficient. Rather, scholars need to highlight moral epistemological difference, rejecting neoliberal efforts to neutralize difference. Some of the most profound criticisms of neoliberalism have come from those groups too often construed as "immobile" (i.e., indigenous groups), as they articulate an alternative ethic for understanding "sustainability" and "diversity" (Simpson 2011). Indeed, on the ways gaps have been created between those considered as indigenous and those considered as migrants see Bauder (2011); these literatures are often construed as distinct in linguistics as well (though see Haque 2012). Thinking about common ground within the critiques evident in each of these literatures will be an important intervention.

In applied linguistics, some of the richest accounts of contestations of neoliberalism have been documented in nuanced ethnographic studies of classrooms as well as critical analyses of policy documents. These serve as models for analysis needed in other national sites, as well as examples of policy and pedagogical interventions. Lopez (2015) also shows that there are spaces for critical interventions in English literacy and civics education programs for migrants in Queens, New York. While students reproduced neoliberal discourses of personal responsibility, they simultaneously contested the premise of neoliberal discourses by highlighting the structural and systemic barriers they face. Hsu (2015) argues that we need to make visible the colonial conditions of global English in order to de-naturalize linguistic instrumentalism. Ramirez and Hyslop-Margison (2015) propose the use of a Critical Reading Sheet (CRS) as a pedagogical tool for examining the semiotics of the discourse of "crisis" that justifies neoliberal austerity. See also Davis and Phyak (2015) for an engaged language policy and practices (ELP) approach to raising awareness of inequitable neoliberal ideologies in indigenous/minority education, as well as means of challenging educational inequality through community engagement, drawing on examples of engaged ethnographic projects that support indigenous languages in Nepal and multilingual educational policy in Hawaii.

In addition to more case studies on various national sites, we have highlighted other forms of research which we believe remains to be done. There should be more studies of language in primary and secondary labour spheres. The financialization of the economy is regularly noted, but studies of language in the finance industries themselves remain rare. Gao and Park (2015) call for more attention, in applied linguistics, to how language learning is shaped in spatial terms under neoliberalism, arguing that an analysis of space in relation to language learning and mobility further allows scholars to explore the "material constraints and inequalities of language learning" (p. 94).

The focus on language tests (for English, or for migrants) has led to a number of pragmatic efforts to make better and more effective and more valid instruments. However, more promising in challenging neoliberalism are debates about why there is a focus on language, and on testing, analyses which need to be tailored to the historical moments and political crises that testing is meant to solve. Shohamy asks, "How essential is knowledge of a specific language in an era of globalization, diversity, common markets, transnationalism, multilingualism, strong diasporas and flexible boundaries?" (2009: 49). For examples of ground-breaking work on these questions, see papers in Hogan-Brun et al. (2009) and Slade et al. (2010), as well as Piller (2001) and Milani (2008).

Summary

Neoliberalism has facilitated particular kinds of mobility and migration, particularly for entrepreneurial subjects willing to dedicate themselves to self-development through language learning. Temporary migration and mobility, in particular, is tied to aspirations to learn language skills valued in the global economy and competitive workplaces. These migration strategies often do not provide immigrants with social mobility nor does having the "right" language skills necessarily lead to successful "integration," in the case of permanent migration. Nevertheless, language requirements often measured through standardized testing, shape access to both employment and nation-states, in ways which often re-inscribe racial and colonial hierarchies.

Whether or not one believes that language is increasingly central to late capitalism, it is certainly the case that language is a key terrain on which neoliberal polices are often justified, one often seen as less controversial than policies stated more directly in terms of economic, ethnic, racial, or even national rationales. Language policies are often promoted as neutral, or technical, and language practices are deemed readily measured and quantified.

Related topics

Nation-state, transnationalism and language
Superdiversity and language
Language in skilled migration
Rethinking (un)skilled migrants: whose skills, what skills, for what, and for whom?
Citizenship, immigration laws, and language
Communication practices and policies in workplace mobility

Further reading

Bernstein, K., Hellmich, E., Katznelson, N., Shin, J. and Vinall, K. (2015). Guest Editors of "Critical Perspectives on Neoliberalism in Second/Foreign Language Education". *L2 Journal* (an open-access, on-line journal), 7(3).

This special issue includes papers, many of which are on English language education, on the impact of neoliberalism, and challenges to it, in classrooms and policy debates in China, Mexico, Nepal, the Philippines, Puerto Rico, South Korea, Uruguay, and the United States.

Block, David, Gray, J. and Holborow, M. (2012). *Neoliberalism and Applied Linguistics.* London: Routledge.

The three authors contribute a shared introduction and then individual chapters on debates about ideology and class, neoliberal keywords, celebrity in textbooks, and changing forms of teacher education, each of which elaborates on Marxist critiques of neoliberalism.

Duchêne, A. and Heller, M. eds., (2012). *Language in Late Capitalism: Pride and Profit.* New York: Routledge.

Collection on the changing significance of language and nation in a range of sites (European Union policy, sports arenas, linguistic minority businesses, tourism, education, the military, Silicon Valley) in Asia, Europe, Canada, and the United States.

Holborrow, M. (2015). *Language and Neoliberalism.* London: Routledge.

This book offers a wide-ranging theoretical overview of works on neoliberalism as they interact with the history of sociolinguistic works on language and political economy, as well as some detailed case studies, largely drawn from educational and linguistic practice in Ireland.

Urciuoli, B. (2008). Skills and selves in the new workplace. *American Ethnologist, 35*(2), 211–228.

This influential article examines how, in the neoliberal imaginary of capitalism, workers' value is measured by their skills, which are commensurable and commodifiable.

References

Allan, K. (2013). Skilling the self: The communicability of immigrants as flexible labour. In Alexandre Duchêne, Melissa Moyer, and Celia Roberts (eds.), *In Language, Migration and Social (In)equality. A Critical Sociolinguistic Perspective on Institutions and Work* (pp. 56–80). Bristol: Multilingual Matters.

Allan, K. (2014). *Learning How to "Skill" the Self: Citizenship and Immigrant Integration in Toronto, Canada*. PhD thesis, University of Toronto.

Allan, K. (2016). Going beyond Language: Soft Skill-ing cultural difference and immigrant integration in Toronto, Canada. In Mi-Cha Flubacher and Shirley Yeung (eds.), Special issue: Discourses of Integration: Language, Skills, and the Politics of Difference. *Multilingua* 35(6): 617–648.

Annamalai, E. (2005). Nation-building in a globalized world: Language choice and education in India. In Angel Lin and Peter Martin (eds.), *Decolonisation, Globalization: Language-in-Education Policy and Practice* (pp. 20–38). Bristol: Multilingual Matters.

Arat-Koc, S. (1999). Neoliberalism, state restructuring and immigration: Changes in Canadian policies in the 1990s. *Journal of Canadian Studies* 34(2): 31–56.

Bae, S. (2014). Anxiety, insecurity and complexity of transnational educational migration among Korean middle class families. *Journal of Asian Pacific Communication* 24(2): 152–172.

Bakan, A. and Stasiulis, D. (1997). *Not One of the Family: Foreign Domestic Workers in Canada*. Toronto: University of Toronto Press.

Bakan, A. and Stasiulis. (2005). *Negotiating Citizenship: Migrant Women in Canada and the Global System*. Toronto: University of Toronto Press.

Bauder, H. (2011). Closing the immigration-Aboriginal parallax gap. *Geoforum* 42(5): 517–519.

Bell, L. (2013). *Diamonds as Development: Why Natural Resource Exploitation Fails to Improve the Human Condition*. PhD thesis, University of Toronto.

Bello, W., Docena, H., de Guzman, M. and Malig, M. (2004). *The Anti-Development State: The Political Economy of Permanent Crisis in the Philippines*. Manila: University of the Philippines, Diliman.

Bernstein, K.A., Hellmich, E.A., Katznelson N., Shin, J. and Vinall, K. (2015). Introduction to Special Issue: Critical Perspectives on Neoliberalism in Second/Foreign Language Education. *L2 Journal* 7(3): 3–14.

Bjornson, M. (2007). Speaking of citizenship: Language ideologies in Dutch citizenship regimes. *Focaal: European Journal of Anthropology* 49: 65–80.

Blackledge, A. (2009). Being English, speaking English: Extension to English language testing legislation and the future of multicultural Britain. In Gabrielle Hogan-Brun, Clare Mar-Molinero and Patrick Stevenson (eds.), *Discourses on Language and Integration: Critical Perspectives on Language Testing Regimes in Europe* (pp. 83–108). Amsterdam and Philadelphia: John Benjamins Pub. Co.

Block, D. (2002). "McCommunication": A problem in the frame for SLA. In David Block and Deborah Cameron (eds.), *Globalization and Language Teaching* (pp. 117–133). London and New York: Routledge.

Block, D., Gray, J. and Holborow, M. (2012). *Neoliberalism and Applied Linguistics*. London: Routledge.

Blommaert, J., Collins, J., Heller, M., Rampton, B., Slembrouck, S. and Verschueren, J. (2003). Introduction to special issue on Ethnography, Discourse and Hegemony. *Pragmatics* 13(1): 1–10.

Brenner, N., Peck, J. and Theodore, N. (2010). Variegated neoliberalization: Geographies, modalities, pathways. *Global Networks* 10(2): 182–222.

Brock-Utne, B. (2005). Language-in-education policies and practices in Africa with a special focus on Tanzania and South Africa – Insights from research in progress. In Angel Lin and Peter Martin (eds.), *Decolonisation, Globalization: Language-in-Education Policy and Practice* (pp. 173–193). Bristol: Multilingual Matters.

Brown, W. (2005). *Edgework: Critical Essays on Knowledge and Politics*. Princeton and Oxford: Princeton University Press.

Bucholtz, M. (2007). Shop talk: Branding, consumption and gender in American middle-class youth interaction. In Bonnie McElhinny (ed.), *Words, Worlds, Material Girls: Language, Gender and Global Economies* (pp. 371–402). Berlin: Mouton de Gruyter.

Cameron, D. (2000). *Good to Talk?: Living and Working in a Communication Culture*. London: Sage.

Cameron, D. (2002). Globalization and the teaching of "communication skills". In David Block and Deborah Cameron (eds.), *Globalization and Language Teaching* (pp. 67–82). London and New York: Routledge.

Canagarajah, S. (1999). *Resisting Linguistic Imperialism in English Teaching*. Oxford: Oxford University Press.

Canale, G. (2015). Mapping Conceptual Change: The Ideological Struggle for the Meaning of EFL in Uruguayan Education. In Katie Bernstein, Emily Hellmich, Noah Katznelson, Jaran Shin and Kimberly Vinall (eds.), Special Issue: Critical Perspectives on Neoliberalism in Second/Foreign Language Education. *L2 Journal* 7(3): 15–39.

Cavanaugh, Jillian R. and Shankar, S. (2014). Producing authenticity in global capitalism: Language, materiality, and value. *American Anthropologist* 116(1): 51–64.

Codò, E. (2013). Trade unions and NGOs under neoliberalism: Between regimenting migrants and subverting the state. In A. Duchêne, M. Moyer and C. Roberts (eds.), *Language, Migration and Social Inequalities* (pp. 25–55). Bristol: Multilingual Matters.

Codò, E. and Garrido, M.R. (2014). Shifting discourses of migrant incorporation at a time of crisis: Understanding the articulation of language and labour in the Catalan non-governmental sector. *International Journal of Multilingualism* 11(4): 1–20.

Coupland, N. ed. (2016). *Theoretical Debates in Sociolinguistics*. Cambridge: Cambridge University Press.

Cox, L. (2010). The value of values? Debating identity, citizenship and multiculturalism in contemporary Australia." In Christina Slade and Martina Möllering (eds.), *From Migrant to Citizen: Testing Language, Testing Culture* (pp. 77–101). Basingstoke and New York: Palgrave Macmillan.

Da Silva, E. and Heller, M. (2009). From protector to producer: The role of the state in the discursive shift from minority rights to economic development. *Language Policy* 8: 95–116.

Davis, K.A. and Phyak, P. (2015). In the Face of Neoliberal Adversity: Engaging Language Education Policy and Practices. Special Issue: Critical Perspectives on Neoliberalism in Second/Foreign Language Education. *L2 Journal* 7(3): 146–166.

Dean, M. (1999). *Governmentality: Power and Rule in Modern Society*. London: Sage.

De Costa, P. (2015). From black box to black hole: Unpacking the designer student immigration apparatus in Singapore. Paper presented at The Sociolinguistics of Globalization: (De)centring and (de)standardization, University of Hong Kong, 3–6 June 2015.

Duchêne, A. and Heller, M., eds. (2012). *Language in Late Capitalism: Pride and Profit*. New York: Routledge.

England, K. and Stiell, B. (1997). "They think you're as stupid as your English is": Constructing foreign domestic workers in Toronto. *Environment & Planning A* 29(2): 195–215.

Eviota, E. (1992). *The Political Economy of Gender: Women and the Sexual Division of Labour in the Philippines*. London: Zed.

Extra, G. and Spotti, M. (2009). Language, migration and citizenship: A case study on testing regimes in the Netherlands. In Gabrielle Hogan-Brun, Clare Mar-Molinero and Patrick Stevenson (eds.), *Discourses on Language and Integration: Critical Perspectives on Language Testing Regimes in Europe* (pp. 61–82). Amsterdam and Philadelphia: John Benjamins Pub. Co.

Fairclough, N. (1992). *Discourse and Social Change*. Cambridge: Polity Press.

Feher, M. (2009). Self-appreciation; or, the aspirations of human capital. *Public Culture* 21(1): 21–41.

Flubacher, M.-C., Coray, R. and Duchêne, A. (2016). Language, integration and investment: The regulation of diversity in the context of unemployment. In Mi-Cha Flubacher and Shirley Yeung (eds.), Special issue: Discourses of Integration: Language, Skills, and the Politics of Difference. *Multilingua* 35(6): 675–696.

Fogde, M. (2007). The making of an employable individual. In Birgitta Höijer (ed.), *Ideological Horizons in Media and Citizen Discourses: Theoretical and Methodological Approaches* (pp. 131–146). Göteborg: Nordicom.

Foucault, M. (1991). Governmentality. In Graham Burchell, Colin Gordon and Peter Miller (eds.), *The Foucault Effect: Studies in Governmentality* (pp. 87–104). Chicago: University of Chicago Press.

Gal, S. (2012). Sociolinguistic regimes and the management of "Diversity". In Alexandre Duchêne and Monica Heller (eds.), *Language in Late Capitalism: Pride and Profit* (pp. 230–261). New York: Routledge.

Gao, S. and Park, J.S.-Y. (2015). "Space and Language Learning under the Neoliberal Economy." In Katie Bernstein, Emily Hellmich, Noah Katznelson, Jaran Shin, and Kimberly Vinall, eds. Special Issue: Critical Perspectives on Neoliberalism in Second/Foreign Language Education. *L2 Journal* 7(3): 78–96.

Gershon, I. (2011). Neoliberal agency. *Current Anthropology* 52(4): 537–555.
Gray, J. (2012). Neoliberalism, Celebrity and 'Aspirational Content' in English Language Teaching Textbooks for the Global Market. In David Block, John Gray and Marnie Holborow (eds.), *Neoliberalism and Applied Linguistics* (pp. 86–113). London: Routledge.
Gray, J. and Block, D. (2012). The Marketization of Language Teacher Education and Neoliberalism: Characteristics, Consequences and Future Prospects. In David Block, John Gray and Marnie Holborow (eds.), *Neoliberalism and Applied Linguistics* (pp. 114–143). London: Routledge.
Gumperz, J. (1982). Face and inference in courtroom testimony. In John Gumperz (ed.), *Language and Social Identity* (pp. 133–145). Berkeley: University of California Press.
Hall, K. (2014). Hypersubjectivity: Language, anxiety, and indexical dissonance in globalization. *Journal of Asian Pacific Communication* 24(2): 261–273.
Harris, R., Leung, C. and Rampton, B. (2002). Globalization, diaspora and language education in England. In David Block and Deborah Cameron (eds.), *Globalization and Language Teaching* (pp. 29–46). London and New York: Routledge.
Haque, E. (2012). *Multiculturalism within a Bilingual Framework: Language, Race, and Belonging in Canada*. Toronto: University of Toronto Press.
Harvey, D. (2001). *Spaces of Capitalism: Towards a Critical Geography*. New York: Routledge.
———. (2005). *A Brief History of Neoliberalism*. Oxford: Oxford University Press.
Heller, M. (2010). The commodification of language. *Annual Review of Anthropology* 39: 101–114.
Heller, M. and Duchêne, A. (2012). Pride and profit: Changing discourses of language, capital and nation-state. In Alexandre Duchêne and Monica Heller (eds.), *Language in Late Capitalism: Pride and Profit* (pp. 1–21). New York: Routledge.
Heller, M. and Duchêne, A. (2016). Treating Language as an Economic Resource: Discourse, Data and Debate. In Nik Coupland (ed.), *Theoretical Debates in Sociolinguistics* (pp.139–156). Cambridge: Cambridge University Press.
Hiramoto, M. and Park, J.S.-Y. (2014). Anxiety, insecurity, and border crossing: Language contact in a globalizing world. *Journal of Asian Pacific Communication* 24(2): 141–151.
Hogan-Brun, G., Mar-Molinero, C. and Stevenson, P., eds. (2009). *Discourses on Language and Integration: Critical Perspectives on Language Testing Regimes in Europe*. Amsterdam and Philadelphia: John Benjamins.
Holborow, Marnie. (2012). Neoliberal Keywords and the Contradictions of an Ideology. In David Block, John Gray and Marnie Holborow (eds.), *Neoliberalism and Applied Linguistics* (pp. 33–555). London: Routledge.
Holborow, M. (2015). *Language and Neoliberalism*. London: Routledge.
Hyatt, Susan B. (2011). What was neoliberalism and what comes next?: The transformation of citizenship in the law-and-order state. In Davide Peró, Cris Shore and Susan Wright (eds.), *Policy Worlds: Anthropology and the Anatomy of Contemporary Power* (pp. 205–223). Oxford and New York: Berghahn Press.
Inoue, M. (2007). Language and gender in an age of neoliberalism. *Gender and Language* 1(1): 79–91.
Jang, I. C. (2015a). Language learning as a struggle for distinction in today's corporate recruitment culture: An ethnographic study of English study abroad practices among South Korean undergraduates. In Katie Bernstein, Emily Hellmich, Noah Katznelson, Jaran Shin, and Kimberly Vinall (eds.), Special Issue on Critical Perspectives on Neoliberalism in Second/Foreign Language Education. *L2 Journal* 7(3): 57–77.
Jang, I. C. (2015b). Stratification of English-speaking Interlocutors in educational migration: A discursive strategy of South Korean undergraduates studying English overseas. Paper presented at The Sociolinguistics of Globalization: (De)centring and (de)standardization, University of Hong Kong, 3–6 June 2015.
Juffermans, K. and Lorente, B. (2015). Language and the black box of migration: Asian and African perspectives, Paper presented at The Sociolinguistics of Globalization: (De)centring and (de)standardization. University of Hong Kong, 3–6 June 2015.
Kerswill, P. (2006). Migration and language. In Klaus Mattheier, Ammon Ulrich and Peter Trudgill (eds.), *Sociolinguistics/Soziolinguistik: An International Handbook of the Science of Language and Society* (pp. 2271–2284, 2nd ed., Vol. 3). Berlin: De Gruyter.

Kingfisher, C., ed. (2002). *Western Welfare in Decline Globalization and Women's Poverty*. Philadelphia: University of Pennsylvania Press.

Kingfisher, C. and Maskovsky, J. (2008). Introduction: The limits of neoliberalism. *Critique of Anthropology* 28(2): 115–126.

Klein, N. (2000). *No Logo: Taking Aim at the Brand Bullies*. Toronto: Vintage.

———. (2007). *The Shock Doctrine: The Rise of Disaster Capitalism*. Toronto: Vintage Canada.

Kroskrity, P., ed. (2000). *Regimes of Language: Ideologies, Polities, and Identities*. Santa Fe, NM: School of American Research Press.

Kubota, R. (2011). Questioning linguistic instrumentalism: English, neoliberalism, and language tests in Japan. *Linguistics and Education* 22: 248–260.

Lan, P.C. (2003). "They have more money, but I speak better English!": Transnational encounters between Filipina domestics and Taiwanese employers. *Identities: Global Studies in Culture and Power* 10(2): 133–161.

Larson, J. (2008). Ambiguous transparency: Resume fetishism in a Slovak workshop. *Ethnos* 73(2): 189–216.

Lin, A. (2005). Critical, transdisciplinary perspectives on language-in-education policy and practice in post-colonial contexts: The case of Hong Kong. In Angel Lin and Peter Martin (eds.), *Decolonisation, Globalization: Language-in-Education Policy and Practice* (pp. 38–54). Clevedon: Multilingual Matters.

Lin, A. and Martin, P. (eds.) (2005). *Decolonisation, Globalization: Language-in-Education Policy and Practice*. Clevedon: Multilingual Matters.

Longergan, G. (2015). Migrant women and social reproduction under austerity. *Feminist Review* 109: 124–145.

Lopez, D. (2015). Neoliberal Discourses and the Local Policy Implementation of an English Literacy and Civics Education Program. In Katie Bernstein, Emily Hellmich, Noah Katznelson, Jaran Shin, and Kimberly Vinall, eds. Special Issue: Critical Perspectives on Neoliberalism in Second/Foreign Language Education. *L2 Journal* 7(3): 97–122.

Lorente, B. P. (2012). The making of "Workers of the World": Language and the labor brokerage state. In Alexandre Duchêne and Monica Heller (eds.), *Language in Late Capitalism: Pride and Profit* (pp. 183–206). New York: Routledge.

Lorente, B. P. (2007). *Mapping English Linguistic Capital: The Case of Filipino Domestic Workers in Singapore*. PhD thesis, National University of Singapore.

Machin, D. and van Leeuwen, T. (2010). Global media and the regime of lifestyle. In Nikolas Coupland (ed.), *The Handbook of Language and Globalization* (pp. 624–643). Oxford: Wiley-Blackwell.

Mackey, E. (2002). *The House of Difference: Cultural Politics and National Identity in Canada*. Toronto: University of Toronto Press.

Maher, J. (2010). Metroethnicities and metrolanguages. In Nikolas Coupland (ed.), *The Handbook of Language and Globalization* (pp. 572–591). Oxford: Wiley-Blackwell.

Majhanovich, S. (2014). Neoliberalism, globalization, language policy and practice issues in the Asia-Pacific region. *Asia Pacific Journal of Education* 34(2): 168–183.

Martin, E. (1994). *Flexible Bodies: Tracking Immunity in American Culture from the Days of Polio to the Age of AIDS*. Boston: Beacon Press.

Martin, P. (2005)."Safe" language practices in two rural schools in Malaysia: Tensions between policy and practice. In Angel Lin and Peter Martin (eds.), *Decolonisation, Globalization: Language-in-Education Policy and Practice* (pp. 74–97). Bristol: Multilingual Matters.

Matza, T. (2009). Moscow's echo: Technologies of the self, publics, and politics on the Russian talk show. *Cultural Anthropology* 24(3): 489–522.

McElhinny, B. (2010). The audacity of affect: Gender, race and history in linguistic accounts of legitimacy and belonging. *Annual Review of Anthropology* 39: 309–328.

McElhinny, B. (2012). Silicon Valley sociolinguistics? Analyzing language, gender and *Communities of Practice* in the new knowledge economy. In Alexandre Duchêne and Monica Heller (eds.), *Language in Late Capitalism: Pride and Profit* (pp. 230–261). New York: Routledge.

McElhinny, B. (forthcoming). Language and political economy. In Nancy Bonvillain (ed.), *Handbook of Linguistic Anthropology*. London: Routledge.

McElhinny, B. (under review). "Who counts?: Accountability, assessment and language testing regimes for migrants in late capitalism." In Mi-Cha Flubacher and Shirley Yeung (eds.), Special Issue: Discourses of Integration: Language, Skills, and the Politics of Difference. *Multilingua*.

McElhinny, B., Davidson, L., Catungal, J. P., Tungohan, E. and Coloma, R. (2012). Introduction: Spectres of (in)visibility. In Roland Coloma, Bonnie McElhinny, Ethel Tungohan, J. P. Catungal and Lisa Davidson (eds.), *Filipino Lives in Canada: Disturbing Invisibility* (pp. 5–45). Toronto: University of Toronto Press.

McGill, K. (2013). Political economy and language: A review of some recent literature. *Journal of Linguistic Anthropology* 23(2): 84–101.

McNamara, T. (2009). Language tests and social policy: A commentary. In Gabrielle Hogan-Brun, Clare Mar-Molinero and Patrick Stevenson (eds.), *Discourses on Language and Integration: Critical Perspectives on Language Testing Regimes in Europe* (pp. 153–164). Amsterdam and Philadelphia: John Benjamins.

Milani, Tommaso M. (2008). Language testing and citizenship: A language ideological debate in Sweden. *Language in Society* 37(1): 27–59.

Mirchandani, K. (2012). *Phone Clones: Authenticity Work in the Transnational Service Economy*. Ithaca: Cornell University Press.

Motobayashi, K. (2015). *Nihongo-Japanese in the Politic of the Japanese State*. PhD thesis, University of Toronto.

Muehlebach, A. (2012). *The Moral Neoliberal: Welfare and Citizenship in Italy*. Chicago and London: University of Chicago Press.

Murphy, M. (2013). Economization of life: Calculative infrastructures of population and economy. In Peg Rawes (eds.), *Relational Ecologies: Subjectivity, Sex, Nature and Architecture* (pp. 139–155). London: Routledge.

Ortner, S. (2011). On neoliberalism. *Anthropology of this Century* 1 [Online]. Available from http://aotcpress.com/articles/neoliberalism/.

Park, J.S.-Y. (2011). The promise of English: Linguistic capital and the neoliberal worker in the South Korean job market. *International Journal of Bilingual Education and Bilingualism* 14(4): 443–455.

Park, J.S.-Y. (2014). "You say *ouch* and I say *aya*": Linguistic insecurity in a narrative of transnational work. *Journal of Asian Pacific Communication* 24(2): 241–260.

Park, J.S.-Y. (2015). Language as commodity, language as doing. Paper presented at The Sociolinguistics of Globalization: (De)centring and (de)standardization, University of Hong Kong, 3–6 June 2015.

Park, J.S.-Y. and Lo, A. (2012). Transnational South Korea as a site for a sociolinguistics of globalization: Markets, timescales, neoliberalism. *Journal of Sociolinguistics* 16(2): 147–164.

Park, J.S.-Y. and Wee, L. (2012). *Markets of English: Linguistic Capital and Language Policy in a Globalizing World*. New York and London: Routledge.

Parrenas, R. S. (2001). *Servants of Globalization: Women, Migration and Domestic Work*. Stanford: Stanford University Press.

Peck, J., Nik, T. and Brenner, N. (2009). Postneoliberalism and its malcontents. *Antipode* 41(S1): 94–116.

Pennycook, A. (2007). *Global Englishes and Transcultural Flows*. London: Routledge.

Pennycook, A. (2010). Popular cultures, popular languages, and global identities. In Nikolas Coupland, (ed.), *The Handbook of Language and Globalization* (pp. 592–607). Oxford: Wiley-Blackwell.

Phillipson, R. (2008). The linguistic Imperialism of neoliberal empire. *Critical Inquiry in Language Studies* 5(1): 1–43.

Piller, I. (2001). Naturalization language testing and its basis in ideologies of nationality and citizenship. *International Journal of Bilingualism* 5(3): 259–277.

Piller, I. and Cho, J. (2013). Neoliberalism as language policy. *Language in Society* 42: 23–44.

Piller, I. and Takahashi, K. (2011). Linguistic diversity and social inclusion. *International Journal of Bilingual Education and Bilingualism* 14(4): 371–381.

Probyn, M. (2005). Language and the struggle to learn: The intersection of classroom realities, language policy, and neocolonial and globalisation discourses in South African Schools. In Angel Lin and Peter Martin (eds.), *Decolonisation, Globalization: Language-in-Education Policy and Practice* (pp. 153–172). Bristol: Multilingual Matters.

Pujolar, J. (2007). African women in Catalan language courses: Struggles over class, gender, and ethnicity in advanced liberalism. In Bonnie McElhinny (ed.), *Words, Worlds, Material Girls: Language, Gender, Globalization* (pp. 305–348). Berlin: Mouton de Gruyter.

Pujolar, J. (2015). Language, immigration and the nation-state. In Nancy Bonvillain (ed.), *Handbook of Linguistic Anthropology*. London: Routledge.

Rafael, V. (2000). *White Love and Other Events in Filipino History*. Durham: Duke University Press.

Ramirez, A. and Hyslop-Margison, E. (2015). Neoliberalism, Universities, and the Discourse of Crisis. Special Issue: Critical Perspectives on Neoliberalism in Second/Foreign Language Education. *L2 Journal* 7(3): 167–183.

Reagan, T. and Schreffler, S. (2005). Higher education language policy and the challenge of linguistic imperialism: A Turkish case study. In Angel Lin and Peter Martin (eds.), *Decolonisation, Globalization: Language-in-Education Policy and Practice* (pp. 115–130). Bristol: Multilingual Matters.

Riazi, A. (2005). The four language stages in the history of Iran. In Angel Lin and Peter Martin (eds.), *Decolonisation, Globalization: Language-in-Education Policy and Practice* (pp. 98–114). Bristol: Multilingual Matters.

Roberts, C. and Cooke, M. (2009). Authenticity in the adult ESOL classroom and beyond. *TESOL Quarterly* 43(4): 620–642.

Rose, N. (1999). *Powers of Freedom: Reframing Political Thought*. Cambridge: Cambridge University Press.

Roy, S. (2003). Bilingualism and standardization in a Canadian call center: Challenges for a linguistic minority community. In R. Bayley and S. Schecter (eds.), *Language Socialization in Multilingual Societies* (pp. 269–287). Clevedon: Multilingual Matters.

Rubdy, R. (2005). Remaking Singapore for the new age: Official ideology and the realities of practice in language-in-education. In Angel Lin and Peter Martin (eds.), *Decolonisation, Globalization: Language-in-Education Policy and Practice* (pp. 55–73). Bristol: Multilingual Matters.

Said-Sirhan, Y. (2014). Linguistic insecurity and reproduction of the Malay community's peripherality in Singapore. *Journal of Asian Pacific Communication* 24(2): 221–240.

Salonga, A. O. (2010). *Language and Situated Agency: An Exploration of the Dominant Linguistic and Communication Practices in the Philippine Offshore Call Centers*. PhD thesis, National University of Singapore.

Satzewich, V. and Liodakis, N. (2013). *"Race" and Ethnicity in Canada: A Critical Introduction* (3rd ed.). Oxford: Oxford University Press.

Sayer, P. (2015). "More and Earlier": Neoliberalism and Primary English Education in Mexican Public Schools. Special Issue: Critical Perspectives on Neoliberalism in Second/Foreign Language Education. *L2 Journal* 7(3): 40–56.

Schieffelin, B., Woolard, K. and Kroskrity, P., eds. (1998). *Language Ideologies: Practice and Theory*. Oxford: Oxford University Press.

Shankar, S. (2015). *Advertising Diversity: Producing Language and Ethnicity in American Advertising*. Durham, NC: Duke.

Shankar, S. and Cavanaugh, J. (2012). Language and materiality in global capitalism. *Annual Review of Anthropology* 41: 355–369.

Shields, J. (2003). *No Safe Haven: Markets, Welfare, and Migrants*. CERIS Working Paper 22. Joint Centre of Excellence for Research on Immigration and Settlement, Toronto.

Shohamy, E. (2009). Language tests for immigrants: Why language? Why tests? Why citizenship? In Gabrielle Hogan-Brun, Clare Mar-Molinero and Patrick Stevenson (eds.), *Discourses on Language and Integration: Critical Perspectives on Language Testing Regimes in Europe* (pp. 45–60). Amsterdam and Philadelphia: John Benjamins.

Simpson, L. (2011). *Dancing on Our Turtle's Back: Stories of Nishaabeg Re-creation, Resurgence and a New Emergence*. Winnipeg: Arbeiter Ring.

Singh, M. and Han, J. (2008). The commoditization of English and the Bologna process: Global products and services, exchange mechanisms and trans-national labour. In Peter K. W. Tan and Rani Rubdy (eds.), *Language as Commodity: Global Structures, Local Marketplaces* (pp. 204–224). London and New York: Continuum.

Slade, C. (2010). Shifting landscapes of citizenship. In Christina Slade and Martina Möllering (eds.), *From Migrant to Citizen: Testing Language, Testing Culture* (pp. 3–23). Basingstoke and New York: Palgrave Macmillan.

Slade, C. and Möllering, M., eds. (2010). *From Migrant to Citizen: Testing Language, Testing Culture*. Basingstoke and New York: Palgrave Macmillan.

Song, J. (2009). *South Koreans in the Debt Crisis: The Creation of a Neoliberal Welfare Society*. Durham and London: Duke University Press.

Stasiulis, D., Hughes, C. and Amery, Z. (2011). From government to multilevel governance of immigrant settlement in Ontario's city-regions. In Erin Tolley and Robert Young (eds.), *Immigrant Settlement Policy in Canadian Municipalities* (pp. 73–147). Montreal and Kingston: McGill-Queens University Press.

Tan, P.K.W. and Rubdy, R, eds. (2008). *Language as Commodity: Global Structures, Local Marketplaces*. London and New York: Continuum.

Theodossopoulos, D. (2014). The ambivalence of anti-austerity indignation in Greece: Resistance, hegemony and complicity. *History and Anthropology* 25(4): 488–506.

Thobani, S. (2007). *Exalted Subjects: Studies in the Making of Race and Nation in Canada*. Toronto: University of Toronto Press.

Tickell, A. and Peck, J. (2003). Making global rules: Globalisation or neoliberalisation? In J. Peck and H. Yeuon (eds.), *Remaking the Global Economy: Economic-Geographical Perspectives* (pp. 163–181). London: Sage.

Tupas, T.R. (2008). Anatomies of linguistic commodification: The case of English in the Philippines vis-à-vis other languages in the multilingual marketplace. In Peter K., W. Ran and Rani Rubdy (eds.), *Language as a Commodity: Global Structures, Local Marketplaces* (pp. 89–105). London: Continuum.

Urciuoli, B. (2008). Skills and selves in the new workplace. *American Ethnologist* 35(2): 211–228.

Urciuoli, B. (2010). Neoliberal Education: Preparing the Student for the New Workplace. In Carol J. Greenhouse (ed.), *Ethnographies of Neoliberalism* (pp.162–176). Philadelphia: University of Pennsylvania Press.

Urciuoli, B. and LaDousa, C. (2013). Language management/labour. *Annual Review of Anthropology* 42: 175–190.

Urla, J. (2012). Total quality language revival. In Alexandre Duchêne and Monica Heller (eds.), *Language in Late Capitalism: Pride and Profit* (pp. 73–92). New York: Routledge.

Van Avermaet, P. (2009). Fortress Europe: Language policy regimes for immigration and citizenship. In Gabrielle Hogan-Brun, Clare Mar-Molinero and Patrick Stevenson (eds.), *Discourses on Language and Integration: Critical Perspectives on Language Testing Regimes in Europe* (pp. 15–44). Amsterdam and Philadelphia: John Benjamins Pub. Co.

Wacquant, L. (2012). Three steps to a historical anthropology of actually existing neoliberalism. *Social Anthropology* 20(1): 66–79.

Wee, L. (2008). Linguistic instrumentalism in Singapore. In P.K. Tan and R. Rubdy (eds.), *Language as Commodity: Global Structures, Local Market Places* (pp. 31–43). London: Continuum.

Wodak, R. and Fairclough, N. (2010). Recontextualizing European higher education policies: The cases of Austria and Romania. *Critical Discourse Studies* 7(1): 19–40.

Yang, J. (2007). "Re-employment Stars": Language, Gender and Neoliberal Restructuring in China. In Bonnie McElhinny (ed.), *Words, Worlds, Material Girls: Language, Gender and Global Economies* (pp. 73–102). Berlin: Mouton de Gruyter.

Yang, S. (2015). *The Korean Internet Freak Community and Its Cultural Politics, 2002–2011*. PhD thesis, University of Toronto.

Yeung, S. (2016). From cultural distance to skills deficits: "Expatriates", "Migrants" and Swiss integration policy. In Mi-Cha Flubacher and Shirley Yeung (eds.), Special Issue: Discourses of Integration: Language, Skills, and the Politics of Difference. *Multilingua* 35(6): 723–746.

Zhang, Q. (2007). Cosmopolitanism and linguistic capital in China: Language, gender and the transition to a globalized market economy in Beijing. In Bonnie McElhinny (eds.), *Words, Worlds, Material Girls: Language, Gender and Global Economies* (pp. 403–423). Berlin: Mouton de Gruyter.

5
Space, place, and language

Christina Higgins

Introduction

This chapter discusses *the spatial turn* that emerged in the humanities and the social sciences in the 1970s and discusses what it can offer to the study of language, migration, and mobility. The main purpose of this chapter is to examine recent work in applied linguistics that has engaged with the view of language practices as spatial practices and to consider how this view reframes lines of inquiry in language and migration. Scholars from other disciplines who have contributed to the spatial turn have argued for an understanding of space as dynamic and socially constructed. Accordingly, much of this work treats as its target the processes involved in *spatialization* rather than the more static notion of *space* in order to examine the human activities and materialist processes through which spaces are made and remade. The spatial turn is often traced to the writings of Henri Lefebvre (1974, 1991) and Michel de Certeau (1984), whose seminal work challenged the premise that space is a container for language and instead asserted that space is the ongoing construction of human activity and practices. This view has many implications for the study of language and migration, for it calls into question the static view of spaces as inherently associated with languages and draws attention to the need to study how spaces – including nation-states, but also spaces of language instruction and language use – are produced through the intersection of human activity, including the imagining of spaces as belonging to particular ethnicities, religions, genders, and languages. Lefebvre (1974) theorized space as a triad of physical, social, and imagined spaces, and argued that since imagined space is where we conceive and analyze social events and the physical environment, all three spaces are ultimately inseparable. An important consequence of this triadic view is that a physical space is never really an objective space since it is always conceived by and for people. Hence, all spaces are ultimately political realms, and power is constantly embedded in their representation and in how people experience them. In De Certeau's well-known essay, "Walking the City" (1984), he presents a vision of urban space as one that is produced through an embodied experience of moving through city streets, and constructed through people's narratives about their day-to-day lives in urban spaces. For De Certeau, pedestrians create a city as they walk through it, giving new meanings to places and thoroughfares which are different than those originally assigned to them by urban planners and city officials.

A proliferation of scholarship took up these ideas in the 1980s and 1990s that brought together new lines of thinking in fields such as urban planning, geography, and philosophy to address questions of power in relation to the social construction of space. A shared concern driving the spatial turn was that time was seen as the primary organizing principle of history, and that social and political problems were presented largely as chronological developments in response to historical events and activities. In making space just as relevant as time, concepts like "undeveloped" nations could then be critically reexamined. In the field of geography, for example, Doreen Massey (1994) developed the concept of *power geometry* to draw attention to the uneven effects of globalization across the globe and the spatially disparate economic growth rather than the time-oriented result of some nations 'evolving' at faster rates than others. She argues that "we recognise space as the product of interrelations; as constituted through interactions, from the immensity of the global to the intimately tiny" and she identifies space as "the existence of multiplicity in the sense of contemporaneous plurality" (1994: 9). Similarly, from the fields of urban planning and geography, Edward Soja (1996) developed the concept of *Thirdspace* to emphasize the spatiality of human history and to draw attention to the ways that material places intersect with imagined and representational spaces to produce a collective experience of *spatiality*, including spaces of privilege and exclusion. *Thirdspace* builds off of the triadic understanding of space laid out by Lefebvre: *First space* is the rational mapping of spaces, relating to physical boundaries; *second space* refers to people's conceptualizations of physical spaces; and *Thirdspace* refers to people's experiences in spaces, which includes their experiences with both physical and imagined understandings of space.

None of these scholars explicitly addressed the thorny issue of defining space and place in relation to language. In most applied linguistics research, it must be acknowledged that *place* and *space* are usually conflated. Alternatively, *place* is often treated as the discursively constructed instantiation of *space*, a conceptualization that aligns with the urban planning concept of place-making, or the idea that physical spaces are transformed through the human actions of planning into places. The reverse conceptualization is found in Michel De Certeau's writing (1984: 117), however. He uses *place* to refer to "the order (of whatever kind) in accord with which elements are distributed in relationships of coexistence." Places are thus the result of physical configurations and institutional orders. For example, any city is a *place* because of its traffic signals, grids of streets, and street signs guiding the actions of drivers, cyclists, and pedestrians. On the other hand, for De Certeau, *space* describes the geography of the activities in a place, which are constantly in flux. In Honolulu, for example, city streets can be closed off because of construction or for festivals, and a myriad of unsanctioned activities also take place on these same city streets, including panhandling, sleeping (there is a sizeable homeless population), collecting money to support local schools' sporting events, and selling newspapers. Hence, "space is a practiced place" (De Certeau 1984: 117), and just because places have been established, their material aspects do not determine people's behavior. With this perspective, it is possible to see how places can change over time without any obvious adaptations to their physical qualities. *Space* is arguably a more meaningful concept since it refers to the ever-changing nexus of activities that happen in any place. A dynamic view of space allows us to examine how migrants, transnationals, and other highly mobile populations experience space, and how they use their language resources in their practiced places.

In the pages that follow, I discuss how De Certeau's idea of space as practiced place plays a central role in the experiences of mobile people. Space both shapes and is shaped by multilinguals' language practices, and hence, spaces should be seen as sites where power relations and inequities are made visible, but also where they can be transformed. The chapter also discusses how a spatial approach helps to make sense of why primordialist associations conventionally attributed to languages often do not hold, and why normative linguistic understandings of languages as distinct and compartmentalizable codes are problematic for many migrants and transnationals. As other contributions in this handbook explain in more detail, straightforward linkages between nation-states, ethnicities, and languages are at odds with the experiences of mobile populations whose movements across time and space have altered their identifications with nationality, ethnicity, and language.

Overview

This section provides a brief overview of how space and place have been treated in sociolinguistic and applied linguistics research that examines mobility (and lack thereof) as a key factor in understanding space and place. This section examines whether and to what degree dialectology, variationist sociolinguistics, and linguistic landscape research have engaged with the ideas discussed earlier that treat space as practiced place and which view language as a semiotic system that is spatially organized. The purpose of this section is to historicize scholarly understandings of language and space in order to better make sense of the metadiscourse circulating about language and space which migrants, transnationals, and people with long generational ties to places encounter in their daily lives. Though a growing amount of current research treats space as the dynamic outcome of intersecting flows of human activities, more static perspectives toward space are also in operation at the ideological level, which in turn have the potential to restrict migrants' and mobile people's experiences and affiliations.

Variationist sociolinguistic frameworks

Regional dialectology was arguably the first linguistic approach to take an explicitly spatial orientation to language. In great contrast with the views about space and spatiality discussed earlier, this work represented the "first wave" of sociolinguistics (Eckert 2012) since it treated place as the explanation for language variation. Field workers interviewed local speakers and mapped out dialect areas by identifying the boundaries for vocabulary and sound changes. The resulting dialect cartographies provide a clear example of the conflation of space and place along linguistic lines. Places where dialects are spoken, such as the Northern Cities dialect in the U.S., are the spaces identified as unique or distinct by linguists. The *Atlas of North American English* (Labov, Ash, and Boberg 2005) represents recent work in this area. This project has benefited from computerized databases and software programs that provide sociolinguists with the ability to examine dialectal variation and other social correlates such as class, gender, and age.

Similar views are found in the "second wave" of variationist sociolinguistics, which considers social formulations shaped by space and place as explanatory principles behind language variation. For example, Milroy (1980) used social network theory in her study of three working-class communities in Belfast to understand variation in vernacular phonological variables. She gave speakers a network strength score based on their social ties with other people in their neighborhood, the workplace, and in recreational activities. Speakers who maintained vernacular variants had high network scores and generally carried out their lives in a tightly knit set of social spaces; they lived near the people they worked with, and they socialized together as well. In contrast, those with low network scores who had weak ties across their social spaces exhibited more variation and adopted phonological innovation from other social networks. Social network theory has also been applied to endangered and minority language varieties in contact with more widespread or dominant varieties, where groups with weak ties are presumed to be susceptible to language shift because of the overt prestige of majority languages. Li Wei's (1994) study of Chinese families in England illustrates this outcome, as he found that the speakers who had the weakest ties to the host community, or who were the least "integrated," maintained Chinese the most. However, additional studies found that language shift was underway even in communities with strong, dense social networks. Rasinger (2013) showed that the tight-knit community of Bangladeshis in London generally devalued Bengali, even in the domain of the home, because of the prestige accorded to English. The community had dense networks whose members interacted socially more with each other than with members of other ethnic groups, but language shift was underway due to priorities placed on economic mobility.

While second wave sociolinguistic research engaged with the role of space in shaping language, this perspective identified patterns in language use as "incidental fallout from social space" (Eckert 2012: 94). More recent work in the "third wave" reverses this by treating social and geographic spaces, and identities associated with place, as the outcome of human activity and language practices. Hence, language choices are not due to their geographic or class-based positionality, but instead are the means by which they construct their personas in different social spaces. Johnstone's (2013) research on Pittsburghese provides a clear example of third wave research. Though this dialect is characterized by variables that have historically been used among the Polish working class in the city, Pittsburghese has shifted from marking ethnicity and socio-economic class to representing Pittsburgh as a place. Johnstone shows how this *enregisterment*, or "processes through which a linguistic repertoire becomes differentiable within a language as a socially recognisable register of forms" (Agha 2003: 231), has been achieved through the commodification of the language on T-shirts, dolls, and other local products, the recurring association of the dialect with local institutions such as the Pittsburgh Steelers, and the re-entextualization of the dialect in the media. Though the dialect can be understood more as an imagined one than a way of speaking that necessarily relates to the population of Pittsburgh, the point is that Pittsburgh as a place is created in and through the metonymic relationships between language, class, and place in discourses about the city (Johnstone 2013).

In variationist work on regional dialects in England, Britain (2013) has shown that linguistic changes can best be explained by studying the effects of mobility, including urbanization, counterurbanization, migration, commuting, and geographical patterns of consumption, to name a few. Similarly, in her analysis of speech variation among adolescents in the East End of London, Fox (2015) explains changes in the Cockney dialect of English with reference to new flows of Bangladeshi migrants to the community and new configurations of the local economy. This perspective has great implications for people whose lives have been affected by mobility, as it directs researchers to examine not just where people are from, but more importantly, what sort of spaces and interactions with others they experience in their daily lives.

Though these researchers do not invoke the theories of space articulated by Lefebvre, De Certeau, Massey, and Soja, their research resonates with these ideas. Rather than viewing the language practices of migrants and other border crossers as the result of their movements, they examine social spaces and trajectories as a foundation for understanding language.

Linguistic Landscape approaches

A much more recent approach to language, place and space, Linguistic Landscape (LL) research explores the ways that languages function in public spaces. Though LL research certainly began with first and second wave views of space and place (Landry and Bourhis 1997), a growing number of LL researchers analyze the use of language in public space as an ongoing construction that is embedded in particular social and political histories. This work builds on Scollon and Scollon's (2003) comprehensive geosemiotic analysis of language in the material world. In their cutting edge book, they echo De Certeau's ideas in their theory of nexus analysis, which places human actions at the center of investigation. Language is interpreted with a materialist perspective and is theorized as the nexus of human activity at the interstices of visual semiotics of spaces, the interaction order within spaces, and place semiotics. The Scollons (2003) provide a detailed framework for examining place semiotics through *inscription systems*, mainly focusing on font selection and durability of signs; *code preference*, which refers to the prominence of languages on signs and the information each language conveys; and finally *emplacement*, or the meanings signs acquire due to their placement in the material world. The Scollons' (2003) book was the first major publication to articulate the interrelatedness of language and space and to provide a detailed framework that treated activities as a starting point for analyzing language-in-space. Though it was published over a decade ago, it remains highly contemporary in research on language, space, and place.

Over the past decade, languages of migrant groups has not been the focus of most LL research, which remains dominated by studies that examine global linguae francae like English in cities such as Bangkok (e.g., Huebner 2006) or which explore the geosemiotic positioning of autochthonous minority languages such as Sámi (e.g., Pietikäinen 2014). Blommaert (2013) is an exception to this trend, and his book-length examination of signs in Berchem and Antwerp, Belgium, expands the methodological approaches usually taken in LL research by outlining how researchers can study the linguistic landscape to interpret social change through the lens of language in public spaces. A key contribution is his materialist analysis of context through a historical study of the linguistic landscape and the layers of social and spatial arrangements it indexes. For Blommaert, signs turn spaces into specific locations filled with expectations as to codes of conduct, semiotic practices, and interpretation. He uses the term *enskillment* to refer to the process by which a historicized space also turns humans into historicized actors-in-space. People become enskilled by space (e.g., looking both ways while crossing the street), but also in their interactions in spaces that are layered with the movements of people and superdiversity (Vertovec 2007). While signs on second- and third-generation Turkish-owned stores in Berchem are in "immaculate Dutch," those on shops run by Polish entrepreneurs, who are more recent arrivals, are in "ecumenical Dutch" (Blommaert 2013: 66), and are more multilingual in nature with this L2 variety of Dutch appearing alongside Polish and languages such as Arabic and Russian. In shops operated by Indian migrants, there is professionally produced English and Dutch signage, but there are also temporary signs printed on computer paper in Polish that cater to the recent numbers of Polish migrants who are in Berchem working as construction workers. Blommaert refers to this mutual co-existence of people in shared social space as *convivial* superdiversity, for the use of one another's languages and lingua franca Dutch in public space is in part responsible for producing relationships of mutual dependency. The point Blommaert makes is that the linguistic landscape can act as a chronicle of sociolinguistic complexity that not only documents the infrastructure of a superdiverse landscape but reveals the multiple histories that coalesce into a synchronized space. Rather than seeing landscapes as measures of linguistic and cultural vitality, Blommaert pushes LL research to ethnographically investigate the historical layering of the LL and the ways that changes in society show up in uneven and power-laden ways.

As a final point in discussions of LL research, I include the important contributions on *metrolingualism* by Alastair Pennycook and Emi Otsuji (2015), for whom *metrolingual multitasking* refers to the way that languages, everyday practices, and social space are intertwined. Though they do not always frame their work as LL research, *metrolingualism* has much in common with Blommaert's views since they assert that "the layers of LL need to be understood not so much in terms of static physical emplacements, but rather as the mobilization of history through everyday practices" (2015: 155) Building off of Massey, Soja, and Lefebvre, they examine the "creative linguistic conditions across space and borders of culture, history and politics, as a way to move beyond current terms such as multilingualism and multiculturalism" (Otsuji and Pennycook 2010: 244). In line with third wave sociolinguistics and views on space as the dynamic and ongoing production of social relations, they replace the place-based view of *speech community* and the individual-based notion of *communicative repertoires* with the spatially informed concept of *spatial repertoires*, or how mobile resources are used in tasks and practices to produce language in spatial arrangements. In their ethnographic studies of multilingual practices in Tokyo and Sydney, they demonstrate how multilingual residents of these cities operate in the spaces of restaurant kitchens and produce markets. Placing tasks such as buying mangoes at fruit stands at the center of analysis, they take up Thrift's (2008) *associational* view of space in order to grasp how individuals, objects, and language form the communicative activity within spaces. An example from an encounter with a Greek customer in a store owned by a Chinese Lao and Thai couple in Sydney illustrates these ideas (Pennycook and Otsuji 2015: 92):

(G: Greek regular customer, S: Song, R: Researcher)
Greek: bold, English: plain (translation in parentheses)

1   G: She know Greco. Greco forget.
2   S: Yeah, **yashou yashou**. (hello hello.)
3   R: You can speak Greek!
4   G: **Yassou, kala, afharistro**. (hello, good, thank you.)
5   S: **Yassou**. (hello).
           [laughter]
6   G: See you tomorrow!
7   S: Yeah, see you!

Pennycook and Otsuji explain that the shop owner Song's spatial repertoire has formed in her shop-space in and through the material actions of selling goods to customers while creating a convivial and sociable atmosphere for them. Her spatial repertoires change according to her customers, their language backgrounds, and the activities they are involved in at the shop.

A key question such spatial repertoires raise is how they come to be in the first place. The answer invokes the work of cultural anthropologist Arjun Appadurai (1990, 1996) and his writing on global cultural flows, or *scapes*. As migration and transborder movements become a central part of life affecting a larger number of people, scapes help us to take a deeper look at how identity and language is formed in relation to mobile, spatial relationships. Scapes thus replace place as the locus for language processes. In the example in Song's shop in

Sydney, the *ethnoscape*, or flows of people across borders and into new spaces, intersects with the *financescape*, or flows of money and commerce, thereby producing dynamic spaces in which people use language, form relationships, and create spatial repertoires.

Just as scapes intersect to produce convivial interactions such as that between Song and her Greek customer, other social spaces are produced by policing the spaces and disallowing certain groups, and their languages, access. These tensions have much in common with *territorialization* and *deterritorialization* (Deleuze and Guattari 1977), processes through which territory is constituted, and this constitution is in turn the organization of the individuals in it. For migrants and other mobile populations, these terms help to express the ideologies underpinning discourses about heritage and ethnolinguistic identity. In the next section, I examine the multiple tensions that have been examined in applied linguistics that arise as a result of people's fluid and fixed understandings of language and space. First, I consider relations between newer migrants and long-time residents of communities and the process of territorialization. I then turn to explore how transnationals and other mobile populations engage with processes of deterritorialization as they negotiate their ethnolinguistic identities.

Issues and ongoing debates

Territorialization

If current trends of intranational and international migration continue, the character of places will depend much on how language emerges in public spaces and how convivial people are in their tolerance of one another's languages and cultural ways of being. Of course, it is expected that power struggles and claims built on territorialization will be a part of these ongoing transformations. As Blommaert (2013: 6) writes, "The spaces are always someone's space, and they are filled with norms, expectations, conceptions of what counts as proper and normal (indexical) language use and what does not count as such." Counterexamples to conviviality are not hard to come by. In the U.S., for example, in 2012, Frederick, Maryland, became the first county in the state to adopt an ordinance making English the official language after a boom in immigration by Spanish-speaking newcomers. The rise in Latinos brought bilingual signage in fast food restaurants, the opening of Spanish-medium churches, and an overall increased visibility of Latino language and culture in public spheres. The ordinance now requires all non-emergency dealings with the county government to be transacted in English and is seen by many supporters as a way to discourage illegal immigrants from settling in Frederick. While the ordinance remains in place, many residents reject the logic behind it. For example, in response to news reports of the ordinance, one online post challenged the historical claim between the place of Frederick and English: "First, deport all the REAL illegal immigrants – the descendants of the English who invaded North America in the early 1600s. Then pass a law that the official language of Frederick County is the REAL oldest language – Susquehannock (perhaps also that of the Tutelo and Saponi tribes)" (Constable 2012: n.p.). The reactions to the changing nature of space due to migration are important to explore. Tensions are sure to follow the in-migration of newcomers to regions that are not used to linguistic and cultural diversity.

Other examples of non-convivial spaces in which migrated people co-exist are described by Pennycook and Otsuji, who find that diversity is both celebrated and used a resource for degrees of discrimination. In metrolingual spaces, occasions of racial essentializing or downright discrimination are part of the range of practices involved in multilingual and multicultural spaces. Otsuji and Pennycook (2010) describe this as the spectrum of *fixity* and *fluidity*, where fixity describes the deployment of fixed categories tied to language and identity, and fluidity refers to the ways that spatial repertoires are under constant formation depending on the semiotic resources and the material practices of actors. More recently arrived migrants have fewer *rights to the city* (Lefebvre 1968), as evidenced in anti-immigrant slogans such as "we grew here, you flew here" heard in Sydney in 2005 towards Middle Eastern migrants (Pennycook and Otsuji 2015: 101). These sentiments are ultimately (unofficial) acts of policing space and contesting different groups' rights to space. Similarly, in Dar es Salaam, Tanzania, I have recently observed public tensions on the city streets between the majority Black population and new generations of Chinese migrants, including Chinese street vendors who are now competing for customers for relatively low-income sales such as Swahili-medium newspapers, an industry that has historically been dominated by underemployed Black youth. Despite long ties between Tanzania and China dating to the period of independence in the 1960s, animosity has been building as Chinese residents vie for a greater range of economic markets, including those occupied by low income entrepreneurs. More recently, a news article (*Raia Wema*, April 22, 2015) described claims by Tanzanians that a Chinese supermarket barred Black Tanzanians from entering because the shop owners were unable to communicate in a language other than Chinese. Such events echo the tensions documented in Los Angeles among Black customers and Korean shopkeepers who ran a convenience store (Bailey 2000), where the customers expected the shopkeepers to engage in extended conversations, and the shopkeepers preferred to limit their interactions to the consumer tasks. As a result, the customers felt the shopkeepers were disrespectful due to their apparent lack of interest in getting to know them, and the Korean shopkeepers felt the customers breached the norms of the assumed customer–service provider relationship. More complex than racial tension, the interactional awkwardness was due to different norms and expectations of what counts as proper and normal language use in the space of the convenience store.

Deterritorialization

In applied linguistics work, deterritorialization, or the delinking of place with language, culture, and human activity associated with place, is very much dependent on whether speakers have a *primordialist* view of language and ethnolinguistic identity (Pieterse 1997), which treats language as an immutable characteristic of a group with reference to ethnicity, religion, or nationality. In contrast, an *instrumentalist* approach treats language as utilitarian. If a language helps speakers to succeed socio-economically through business networks, then it is treated as valuable. From an instrumentalist perspective, language is only a surface feature of ethnicity and hence can be abandoned if the situation calls for it without any harm done to one's identity. The deterritorialization of ethnolinguistic identities can be a central characteristic of diasporic populations, where tensions can arise due to different place-bound affiliations, sometimes even across generations in a single household. Parents may insist on a nation-of-origin orientation to language and culture, but their children can respond quite differently, affiliating with their local context instead. Zhu Hua (2010) gives examples of very different attitudes expressed towards forms of Chinese language and culture in an ethnically Chinese family in England comprised of first-generation parents and their second-generation children. In one illustration, one of the children, Jeff, challenges his parents' use of Chinese reference terms by questioning the need to refer to a visitor he doesn't know as his uncle, instead preferring to refer to him as "Liu guy" in English. What follows is a lesson about what the parents consider to be appropriate Chinese language use, which includes referring to an elder as *lao* ('old'), which Jeff finds disrespectful based on his English-based connotations of the word. In terms of space and place, it is important that his parents remind him about times when they visited China and the address terms used there in their efforts to teach him 'appropriate' Chinese, thereby attempting to instill a translocal value system. Jeff ultimately rejects his parents' efforts, and Zhu Hua sees this act of constructing his own social and cultural identity as an instance in which changes to the family's sense of norms and place-based affiliations are made visible.

Though members of the diaspora are by definition distanced from their country of origin, ideologies about language from their homeland can lead to language shift in the diaspora. This has been the case in Canagarajah's (2008) research on the Tamil diaspora in Canada, the United States, and England, where he found rapid language shift to English not even spanning the course of one generation. Still, some interviewees commented on how many parents and grandparents were simply not interested in passing on Tamil to their children as an explanation for the lack of Tamil maintenance. However, more than disinterest, the language shift to English is explained by time-space linkages to language ideologies in the Tamil diaspora, which are ultimately rooted to Sri Lanka. The prestige accorded to English in Sri Lanka has had carryover effects in the diaspora, particularly among those whose families did not have access to English before migrating. As one interviewee explained, "Sometimes the parents what they are lacks in their life, they are trying to achieve through their children" (Canagarajah 2008: 160).

Despite physical relocation, nation-based ideologies are also often found among more privileged, transnational populations, such as South Korean families who move to pursue *jogi yuhak* or "early (English) study abroad" (ESA) for their children. As Song (2012) has documented, many of these families are motivated by the cultural capital that proficiency in English promises to provide for their children in South Korea, where English plays a pivotal role in children's success in an increasingly competitive educational market. While living in the United States, many families remain oriented to South Korea as the context for which English is learned, going so far as to enroll their children in schools where there are not many ESL students in order to give their children the most "native-like" experience possible. In addition, these families avoid other Koreans, preferring that their children interact with Caucasian children. Hence, the very idea of study "abroad" is refashioned to fit a Korean stereotype of the "best" English, including ideologies of race that circulate in South Korea about which speakers provide English learners with the premium input. In the end, then, although they are physically located in the United States, Korean ESA families deterritorialize English in the American context and reterritoralize it to suit Korea-based indexicalities.

It is important to acknowledge that deterritorialized visions of language and place can also challenge what nation-based identities mean in the first place. For example, flows of Korean adoptees returning to live in Korea have led to more diverse perspectives on the typically homogenous view of Korean ethnic identity (Higgins and Stoker 2011). When ethnic Koreans who were adopted by foreigners return to the country of their birth later in life, they do not fit in linguistically or culturally, and their learner varieties of Korean are often questioned since they do in fact appear Korean. While many adoptee-returnees experience discrimination and marginalization as a result, others have pushed back and claimed a space to belong, going so far as to rally to change citizenship laws for adoptee returnees, who are now eligible for Korean passports. Rather than becoming authentically Korean from a nation-state orientation, Korean adoptee-returnees are asserting their hybrid identities in more complex ways through self-ascribed labels such as "an overseas Korean," and "an adoptee who is a member of society" (2011: 407–408), ways of describing oneself that simultaneously index dislocation and legitimacy in the same context.

Reterritorialization describes how ethnic identities can be reestablished in the face of physical dislocation. In their research on diasporic Filipinos in Norway, Lanza and Svendsen (2007) found that social networks were key to language maintenance, but that the theory needed to expand to include Appadurai's notion of scapes to account for the boundless nature of social networks through technology and media. Filipinos who maintained their languages also maintained their economic ties to the Philippines and regularly interacted with friends and family by telephone, text, email, and the internet. As they explain (2007: 279), "through globalization, social relations are no longer territorially restricted." Similar globalized networks through digitally based communities have been studied by Lam (2014), who examined how Kaiyee, a young adult from China who had lived in the United States for two years, used instant messaging and web-based blogs to navigate three distinct communities, with each demanding a different communicative repertoire. First, she used Mandarin, Cantonese, and English in instant messaging to interact with peers from her school and the local Chinese community. Second, in an online game that she regularly played, she used features of African American English and hip hop references with other Asian Americans spread across the United States. Finally, she maintained a transnational network of her friends and relatives from China, with whom she blended Shanghainese and Mandarin in conversations referencing Shanghai, including discussion of her possible future return after she finished schooling in the United States. Kaiyee's use of her communicative repertoire offers a clear case of how spatially oriented language can be, and how scapes function in producing distinct linguistic practices across local and transnational geographies.

Implications

In this section, I consider the implications of the spatial turn in the contexts of schooling, a realm of life which tends to resist deterritorialization, at least in terms of ideologies about language and place in curriculum designed for language learners. Nevertheless, learners and teachers do sometimes challenge the primordialist linkages between language and place, as studies of these language classrooms have revealed. It may be especially important to examine what spatial associations language is given in educational contexts for heritage learners who are navigating the complex layers of language, place, and identity for themselves.

Though space is not often foregrounded in educational research on migrants, several key studies have examined the links between language, culture, and ideologies of place in heritage language classrooms, where migrant and second-generation learners study side by side. A key finding is that such classrooms often act as vacuum-sealed versions of the home country. For example, Blackledge and Creese (2012) provide rich examples of how one-to-one linkages between language, ethnicity, and place were presented but also challenged by learners in complementary schools in four English cities. The schools offered Gujarati, Turkish, Chinese, and Bengali to second-generation students and were run on the weekends and/or after school. The authors describe the form of instruction as "nationalism at a distance" (2012: 84), characterized by instruction about festivals, traditional rituals, and cultural artifacts, all directed at creating an identity for the heritage learners that was based on a sense of loss and sentiment about the home country despite relocation. In the classroom interactions, however, the students often mocked the cultural practices being taught, such as Turkish folk dances, by exaggerating the movements and fusing hip hop dance styles into their performance. Though the students were clearly undermining their teachers, the point to be made is that the heritage learners were not necessarily disengaged with the material, but instead were reterritorializing it and layering on top of it their own, more familiar cultural practices.

In the context of Spanish language learning in the United States, a range of responses are found regarding the 'location' of Spanish. Some heritage learners themselves territorialize Spanish as a language located in other countries, rather than in local Spanish-speaking communities. In their study of postsecondary heritage learners, Coryell, Clark, and Pomerantz (2010) found that though the learners were often able to use Spanish alongside English to communicate in their local communities in the U.S., they chose to study Spanish because they felt that the acquisition of "proper Spanish," a variety delimited to countries in which only Spanish was spoken, was part of an idealized identity for which they all strived. On the other hand, in a study of the perceptions of Spanish textbooks in a university-level Spanish class, DeFeo (2015) found that heritage learners embraced their "borderlands" identities rather than identifying with the language of Spain or Mexico. They took issue with the representation of Spanish as a language for travel and Spanish culture as located in other countries, and they found the textbooks to be inauthentic in reference to their own experiences.

Li Wei (2011, 2014) sees the complementary/heritage language classroom as a space created by and for language learning practices where location-based visions of language and ethnicity can be supplanted with new configurations of translingual and transcultural repertoires. He argues that the classroom can be a *translanguaging space*, a concept that treats the activities of learning and teaching at the center and allows for teachers and students to use all aspects of their linguistic repertoires to participate in those activities. In his (2014) discussion of a Mandarin complementary school in England in which Cantonese-English-speaking children were enrolled, he presents the case of a boy asking how to write the Cantonese form of "excuse me." The boy is told (erroneously) that such expressions cannot be written in Cantonese, and he is then given other options for how to write a Mandarin expression, which is more formal in nature. This then leads to a flurry of translingual activity, including the use of Cantonese and English to learn about Mandarin, metalinguistic discussions of written and spoken language, and metalinguistic questions about the pragmatic differences between Mandarin and Cantonese. As a result of the discussion, the students became more aware of the status differences between Mandarin and Cantonese, something that is echoed in a larger scale outside the classroom, where Mandarin is quickly taking over the spaces where Cantonese used to dominate, including the Chinese media and cultural activities such as the Chinese New Year celebrations. Li Wei (2014: 173) explains that contrary to widely circulating beliefs that languages need to be kept separate, "the complementary school classroom for multilingual minority ethnic children is a translanguaging space where the conventional configurations, categories, structures and power relations are challenged and where new meanings, values and subjectivities are developed." This translanguaging space does more than affirm use of students' home languages and allow them to co-exist. Instead, translanguaging "creates a social space for the multilingual language user by bringing together different dimensions of their personal history, experience and environment, their attitude, belief and ideology, their cognitive and physical capacity into one coordinated and meaningful performance, and making it into a lived experience" (Li Wei 2011: 1223).

Similar perspectives are offered in the context of adult ESOL courses, where Baynham and Simpson (2010) theorize the identity positions that are routinely made available to English speakers of other languages (ESOL) learners in England in courses meant to prepare them to pass exams required for citizenship within the National Qualifications Framework (NQF). In their analysis of one NQF classroom, they analyze the spatial arrangements involved in the construction of the ESOL learners as located in a liminal space with reference to English society. Their "classroom" was actually in the main hall of a community center at a university, which meant that people passed through with regular frequency as they attempted to maintain their focus on learning English. In addition, the discourse of levels of English and language learning ("moving up") were represented in spatial terms among both teachers and students and formed the basis of their language learner identities as they aspired to pass the exam. Baynham and Simpson write (2010: 438):

> It is hard not to see a Foucauldian disciplining and regulation of the self at work, as learners are literally transformed in the words of their teachers and themselves into Entry 1s, 2s, and 3s, embarking implicitly on a vertical trajectory that can in theory lead them upwards and onwards.

While the preparation to pass the NQF citizenship exam raises questions about the value of the relatively basic forms of English the learners were acquiring, the larger point is that classrooms such as these offer students a "space of becoming" (Baynham and Simpson 2010: 438) that is deeply interconnected to governmental policies about migration and citizenship.

Future directions

An approach to language that foregrounds spatial practices and analyzes them within their historical and political contexts is essential for understanding the ways that migrants and other dislocated/relocated people navigate their new environments. Promising lines of research on language, space, place, and migration include place-making among migrants and diasporic affiliations that transcend place. As previous work has shown (Lanza and Svendsen 2007), it will be important to consider networks from a spatial perspective, including people's virtual communities. Greater attention can be placed on understanding how the superdiversity produced through migration complexifies space through layers of space and place relations as well. This work can be even more meaningful if deeper engagements are made with current scholarship in geography, urban planning, and anthropology that treats human activity and interconnectedness as the starting point for locating migration and understanding reconfigurations of space (Soja 1996; Glick Schiller and Simsek-Caglar 2010).

In the context of language education, a deeply contextualized analysis of space is needed for research on how official policies affect language learning and socioeconomic mobility. Researchers can explore how the spaces of pedagogy are shaped by policy with attention to the curriculum and the institutional identities performed by teachers and learners. More work also needs to be done that examines learners' critical responses to the ways that languages, cultures, and people are positioned in language learning spaces. Research that builds on De Certeau's and Lefebvre's activity-orientation to place will be of special importance in the area of heritage language education.

Summary

This chapter has examined the ways that space, place, and language are being retheorized in light of the spatial turn, with attention to the increasing mobility of populations around the world. Spatial orientations to language were discussed with reference to variationist work in sociolinguistics, linguistic landscape research, and scapes, and the impact of these ideas was considered in the context of language education. As migration and border crossing continues to become a norm for much of the world, spatial perspectives can play a growing role in understanding changing language practices and in developing pedagogical practices that benefit translocal, multilingual speakers.

Related topics

Nation-state, transnationalism, and language
Displacement and language
Diaspora and language
Spatiotemporal scales and the study of mobility
A rhizomatic account of heritage language

Further reading

Blommaert, J. (2013). *Ethnography, Superdiversity and Linguistic Landscapes: Chronicles of Complexity*, Bristol: Multilingual Matters.

Using an innovative approach to linguistic landscape research, this book demonstrates how multilingual signs in Antwerp, Belgium, can be read as chronicles that document and analyze the complex histories of a place.

Kell, C. (2015). Ariadne's thread: Literacy, scale and meaning-making across space and time. In C. Stroud and M. Prinsloo (eds.), *Language, Literacy and Diversity: Moving Words*, London and New York: Routledge, pp. 72–92.

In this chapter, Kell examines how people "make things happen" by projecting meaning-making across space and time. Through studies of literacy practices in New Zealand and South Africa, she traces text trajectories in conjunction with their material consequences and uses this to expand scalar forms of analysis.

Pennycook, A. and Otsuji, E. (2015). *Metrolingualism: Language in the City*, London and New York: Routledge.

This book outlines the notion of metrolingualism and draws on vivid examples from Tokyo and Sydney to show how language and the city are intricately involved in a constant exchange between flows of people, history, material objects, and linguistic resources.

Scollon, R. and Scollon, S.W. (2003). *Discourses in Place: Language in the Material World*. New York: Routledge.

This groundbreaking book outlines the framework of *geosemiotics*, an integrative view toward language in the material world that combines visual semiotics, the interaction order, and place semiotics which can be used to analyze place as lived experience in a space.

References

Agha, A. (2003). The social life of cultural value. *Language & Communication* 23(3): 231–273.
Appadurai, A. (1990). Disjuncture and difference in the global cultural economy. *Theory, Culture and Society* 7(2): 295–310.
Appadurai, A. (1996). *Modernity at Large: Cultural Dimensions of Globalization*. Minneapolis: University of Minnesota Press.
Bailey, B. (2000). Communicative behavior and conflict between African-American customers and Korean immigrant retailers in Los Angeles. *Discourse & Society* 11(1): 86–108.
Baynham, M. and Simpson, J. (2010). Onwards and upwards: Space, placement, and liminality in adult ESOL classes. *TESOL Quarterly* 44(3): 420–440.

Blackledge, A. and Creese, A. (2012). Negotiation of identities across times and spaces. In S. Gardner and M. Martin-Jones (eds.), *Multilingualism, Discourse, and Ethnography* (pp. 82–94). London: Routledge.

Blommaert, J. (2010). *The Sociolinguistics of Globalization*. Cambridge: Cambridge University Press.

Britain, D. (2010). Supralocal regional dialect levelling. In C. Llamas and D. Watt (eds.), *Language and Identities* (pp. 193–204). Edinburgh: Edinburgh University Press.

Britain, D. (2013). Space, diffusion and mobility. In J. Chambers and N. Schilling (eds.), *Handbook of Language Variation and Change* (2nd ed.). Oxford: Wiley-Blackwell.

Canagarajah, A. S. (2008). Language shift and the family: Questions from the Sri Lankan Tamil diaspora. *Journal of Sociolinguistics* 12(2): 143–176.

Constable, P. (2012). In Frederick, English language law sows conflict amid Hispanic immigrant boom. *Washingtonpost.com*. (Feb 25, 2012).

Coryell, J. E., Clark, M. C. and Pomerantz, A. (2010). Cultural fantasy narratives and heritage language learning: A case study of adult heritage learners of Spanish. *Modern Language Journal* 94(3): 453–469.

De Certeau, M. (1984). *The Practice of Everyday Life* [Translated by S. Rendall]. Berkeley: University of California Press.

DeFeo, D. J. (2015). Spanish is foreign: Heritage speakers' interpretations of the introductory Spanish language curriculum. *International Multilingual Research Journal* 9(2): 108–124.

Deleuze, G. and Guattari, F. (1977). *Anti-Oedipus: Capitalism and Schizophrenia*. New York: Viking.

Eckert, P. (2012). Three waves of variation study: The emergence of meaning in the study of sociolinguistic variation. *Annual Review of Anthropology* 41: 87–100.

Fox, S. (2015). *The New Cockney: New Ethnicities and Adolescent Speech in the Traditional East End of London*. London: Palgrave Macmillan.

Glick Schiller, N. and Simsek-Caglar, A. (2010). *Locating Migration: Rescaling Cities and Migrants*. Ithaca and New York: Cornell University Press.

Higgins, C. and Stoker, K. (2011). Language learning as a site for belonging: A narrative analysis of Korean adoptee-returnees. *International Journal of Bilingual Education and Bilingualism* 14(4): 399–412.

Huebner, T. (2006). Bangkok's linguistic landscapes: Environmental print, codemixing and language change. *International Journal of Multilingualism* 3(1): 31–51.

Johnstone, B. (2013). *Speaking Pittsburghese: The Story of a Dialect*. Oxford: Oxford University Press.

Labov, W., Ash, S. and Boberg, C. (2005). *The Atlas of North American English: Phonetics, Phonology and Sound Change*. Berlin: Walter de Gruyter.

Lam, W.S.E. (2014). Literacy and capital in immigrant youths' online networks across countries. *Learning, Media and Technology* 39(4): 488–506.

Landry, R. and Bourhis, R. Y. (1997). Linguistic landscape and ethnolinguistic vitality: An empirical study. *Journal of Language and Social Psychology* 16(1): 23–49.

Lanza, E. and Svendsen, B. A. (2007). Tell me who your friends are and I might be able to tell you what language (s) you speak: Social network analysis, multilingualism, and identity. *International Journal of Bilingualism* 11(3): 275–300.

Lefebvre, H. (1968). *Le droit à la ville*. Paris: Editions Anthropos.

Lefebvre, H. (1974). La production de l'espace. *L Homme et la société* 31(1): 15–32.

Lefebvre, H. (1991). *The Production of Space* [Translated by D. Nicholson-Smith]. Oxford: Blackwell.

Li, W. (1994). *Three Generations, Two Languages, One Family: Language Choice and Language Shift in a Chinese Community in Britain*. Clevedon: Multilingual Matters.

Li, W. (2011). Moment analysis and translanguaging space: Discursive construction of identities by multilingual Chinese youth in Britain. *Journal of Pragmatics* 43(5): 1222–1235.

Li, W. (2014). Translanguaging knowledge and identity in complementary classrooms for multilingual minority ethnic children. *Classroom Discourse* 5(2): 158–175.

Massey, D. (1994). *Place, Space and Gender*. Minneapolis: University of Minnesota.

Milroy, L. (1980). *Language and Social Networks*. Oxford: Blackwell.
Otsuji, E. and Pennycook, A. (2010). Metrolingualism: Fixity, fluidity and language in flux. *International Journal of Multilingualism* 7(3): 240–254.
Pieterse, J.N. (1997). Deconstructing/reconstructing ethnicity. *Nations and Nationalism* 3(3): 365–395.
Pietikäinen, S. (2014). Spatial interaction in Sámiland: Regulative and transitory chronotopes in the dynamic multilingual landscape of an indigenous Sámi village. *International Journal of Bilingualism* 18(5): 478–490.
Rasinger, S.M. (2013). Language shift and vitality perceptions amongst London's second-generation Bangladeshis. *Journal of Multilingual and Multicultural Development* 34(1): 46–60.
Soja, E.W. (1996). *Thirdspace: Journeys to Los Angeles and other Real-and-imagined Places*. Oxford: Blackwell.
Song, J. (2012). Imagined communities and language socialization practices in transnational space: A case Study of two Korean "study abroad" families in the United States. *Modern Language Journal* 96(4): 507–524.
Thrift, N. (2008). *Non-representational Theory: Space, Politics, Affect*. London and New York: Routledge.
Vertovec, S. (2007). Super-diversity and its implications. *Ethnic and Racial Studies* 30(6): 1024–1054.
Zhu, Hua (2010). Language socialization and interculturality: Address terms in intergenerational talk in Chinese diasporic families. *Language and Intercultural Communication* 10(3): 189–205.

6
New orientations to identities in mobility

Zhu Hua

Introduction

Identities are a plural concept with rich, and sometimes contradictory, meanings. As defined by Tracy (2002: 17–18), identities are "best thought of as stable features of persons that exist prior to any particular situation, and are dynamic and situated accomplishments, enacted through talk, changing from one occasion to the next. . . . Identities are social categories and are personal and unique."

Identities entail the juxtapositions between the self and the other, the personal and the social nature, stability and situated accomplishment, and product and process, all of which are well reflected in the trajectories of identity research. With the recognition that self cannot exist without "the other" (e.g., Hegel 1807/1977), the social nature of identities has gradually moved to centre stage in a number of disciplines, of which applied linguistics is one. There has been extensive sociolinguistic research exploring the social and collective nature of identities as embodied in a range of social, and relatively stable, variables and group categories such as social class, gender, ethnicity, and religion (e.g., language and ethnicity in Fought 2006; language and gender and religion in Edwards 2009). Recent years have seen a paradigm shift with many studies following a social constructivist perspective and conceptualising identity as a discursive performance, constructed and negotiated through interactions (e.g., Antaki and Widdicombe 1998; De Fina, Schiffrin, and Bamberg 2006). What emerged from these studies is that identities are multiple and multi-layered. There are master, interactional, relational, and personal identities (Tracy 2002); imposed, assumed and negotiable identities (Pavlenko and Blackledge 2003); audible, visible and readable identities (Zhu Hua 2014); self-oriented identities or those prescribed by others (Zhu Hua 2014); and hierarchy of identities (Omoniyi 2006). At the same time, identities require "management" from participants who can do a number of things with group memberships. They can ascribe membership to others, claim memberships of groups to which they do not normally belong (e.g., "crossing," Rampton 1995, "passing," Bucholtz 1995), or resist membership assigned by others (Day 1998).

In the last few years, there has been a new focus on *identities in mobility*, which places identities in the context of border crossing, transnational or translocal space. Such a new focus reveals the unprecedented level of complexity of identities and addresses a number of key questions in identity research: that is, to what extent one's membership, affiliation, and sense of belonging are affected by the process of change; how people take on the challenges of developing and creating new identities; and how different aspects of identities interact with each other. The new focus on identities in mobility also feeds into the wider debate on the notions of diaspora, transnational communities, and more recently, translocal communities (see Quayson and Daswani 2013), as researchers find terms such as migrants or minorities increasingly unsatisfactory.

This chapter is a review of the main pursuits and contributions among studies on identities in mobility. It addresses contemporary and seminal works carried out in the broad disciplinary area of applied linguistics and several other related areas such as anthropology, cultural studies, and international education. It focuses on three inter-related themes: complexity, doing/becoming identities, and intersectionality. For the purpose of consistency with the cited articles, this chapter refers to those on the move as *migrants* or *transnationals* without orienting to the rubric of the nation-state often implied in the term of migrants.

Overview

Complexity

Studies of identities in mobility demonstrate the complexity of identities in an unprecedented way. There are numerous studies, and consequently a wealth of terms, which attempt to capture the impact of mobility on identity, in particular, how those involved deal with different sets of cultural values and social practices of home and the host. In some early literature in the 1990s, the term "marginality" was often used to describe feelings of confusion, loss of direction, and internal conflict experienced by those who found themselves lodged between opposing host and heritage cultural values (Schaetti 1998). However, marginality could also entail opportunities and empowerment. Bennett (1993, 2008) differentiated encapsulated marginals from constructive marginals: the former being trapped by marginality, feeling alienated, detached, frustrated with ambiguity, and lost in the margins between cultures and consequently fail to meet the competing requirement of each; the latter feeling comfortable in negotiating and constructing cultural margins and in fact being empowered by a sense of agency as they choose which values and perspectives to act upon. Schaetti (1998) further expanded the notion of constructive marginality by proposing the term of liminality. According to her, liminality constitutes a psychological space between cultures, imbued with great promise and "emerging possibility," as one lives "between the ending of what was and the beginning of what will be" (p. 35). Liminality "informs the both/and identity, the dancing in-between, the life lived ongoing on the threshold with a foot in each of multiple cultural traditions" (p. 36).

Hybridity is another term often invoked in describing the extent of mixture in one's identities. Originated in biology, the term is used in postcolonial and cultural studies (e.g., Bhabha 1994) to describe the mix and plurality of identity that results from the phenomenon of "togetherness-in-difference," borrowing Ang's term (2001), in the context of an increasingly mobility and growing destabilisation of the cultural make-up of the nation-state. Ang (2001: 16) argues that "as a concept, hybridity belongs to the space of the frontier, the border, the contact zone. As such, hybridity always implies a blurring or at least a problematizing of boundaries, and as a result, an unsettling of identity." The "boundary blurring" effect on identity in mobility is echoed in a number of studies. For example, as a result of transnational connections and being exposed to social practices of more than one system, there is often a sense of "double belonging," as manifested through everyday practices among migrants. They are often reported to share narratives of events and display material goods that come from both home and host countries as well as assess and critique the social practices in one country by referencing what they have experience in another place (Lam and Warriner 2012). Another manifestation of hybridity is the "hyphenated" nature of identities, a term used controversially at the turn of the 20th century (e.g., Higham 1955) and then later reclaimed to describe multiple identities of second or third generations of (e.g., Indo-Trinidadian communities, in Raghunandan 2012). Hybridity, double belonging, or hyphenatedness do not imply that there is a "harmonious fusion or synthesis of multiple identities" (Ang 2001: 195) or a simple blend of disparate cultural elements (Frello 2015: 197). Instead, they need to be conceptualised as displacement and therefore enable researchers to focus on "contestations of established power hierarchies, narratives and identities" (Frello 2015). Recent years have seen some critique about the "celebratory" undertone in describing linguistic and cultural hybridity (phrased as "happy hybridity" in Otsuji and Pennycook 2010). Lorente and Tupas (2013) remind us of the hidden economic agendas underneath some discourse of hybridity.

The notions of marginality and hybridity are developed on the assumption that identities are territorial and therefore their construction involves dualistic positioning and comparative perspectives between here and there. However, the here and there division is challenged by increasing connectivity and changing migration patterns among transnationals on several fronts. Digital technology and communication tools have made it possible for people to remain connected on the move and to cross borders virtually at the click of a mouse or swipe of a finger, and to build new communities as illustrated by several available transnational digital case studies (e.g., Lam 2008, 2013, 2014; Li and Juffermans 2011). In addition, flexible citizenship and reverse, circular, and serial movement are on the increase (Duff 2015). Some migrants maintain active patterns of returning to their home countries and then moving back to the host countries. In some cases, migrants reach back to past times or places of origin through the practice of "heritaging" (e.g., Blommaert 2013; De Fina and Perrino 2013) and "traditionalisation" (e.g., Bauman 1992; Bucholtz and Hall 2005) whereby they construct practices or objects under the concern as authentic or invented tradition, borrowing Hobsbawm's term (1983). De Fina (2013) shows how big corporations use heritaging, that is, emphasising common cultural background and authentic customs and values, to commercialise their products and to sell to audiences.

Central to the practice of heritaging or traditionalisation is the desirability of authenticity. In this sense, authenticity is no longer an analyst's notion of what counts as pure and real, but a strategic position taken up by those who are involved. Shenk (2007) demonstrates that authenticity is not only a "negotiated accomplishment replete with ideology, social action, and identity" (p. 214), but also highly representational and arbitrary. She reports how bilingual Mexican American students deploy "authenticating discourse" to construct themselves or others as more or less authentic. Yet what counts as Mexicanness among the students is represented, arbitrarily, by purity of bloodline, nationality, and Spanish linguistic fluency. For example, one of Shenk's participants, Lalo, claims to be a pure-blooded Mexican by tracing his bloodline to "the Aztecs," which ideologically represent an archetype of Mexicanness for many Mexican Americans. However, it emerged later that Lalo's parents were actually born in the Mexican states of Zacatecas and Jalisco, not part of the Aztec Empire at all. In another study, (Lee 2009), the authentic logic which emerged in her subjects is aptly summarised as the title of the paper, "She's Hungarious So She's Mexican but She's Most

Likely Indian." Hungarious is a made-up word by the girls who may have confused the term Hungarian with "Honduras." For them, hungarious is a type of Mexican.

Authenticity is a matter of degree. Blommaert and Varis (2011) use "enoughness" to describe the heuristics of authenticity. "One has to 'have' enough of the emblematic features in order to be ratified as an authentic member of an identity category" (p. 146). The issue is: one can have "not enough of X; or too much of x" (Blommaert and Varis 2011). Cutler (2003) describes that in her study some white hip hoppers who are not considered as a core member of the hip hop community have to play the game of enoughness very carefully. In order to gain enoughness, the peripheral white hip hoppers use more overt speech styles associated with African American English (AAE) than core white hip hoppers. But at the same time, they also need to respect ethnolinguistic differences: sounding too black might actually make one less "real" because one is trying to be something one is not. Although Cutler's works does not concern identities in mobility directly, it illustrates the intricacies of identity work people do in order to become a member of the desired community.

In a special issue, De Fina and Perrino (2013: 512) question the practice of describing identities in mobility in terms of binary dichotomies such as "the national and the transnational, the rooted and the routed, the territorial and the deterritorialized" (borrowing the terms from Jackson, Crang, and Dwyer 2004: 2), due to a variety of virtual and physical connections that allow them to be "here" and "there" at the same time. To add to the list, other frequently used but equally problematic dichotomies in the literature include: minority vs. majority, immigrant vs. local, outsider vs. insider. These dichotomies very often come with the logic that there is an antagonistic relationship between the two: the former is (expected to be) victimised by the latter. However, as Tsagarousianou (2004) argues, it is important to focus on the ability of those on the move to "construct and negotiate their identities, everyday life and transnational activities in ways that often overcome the ethnic identity versus assimilation dilemma" as well as "various creative possibilities" in both local and transnational contexts" (p. 58).

Therefore, complexity of identities is not confined to marginality and hybridity, but lies in the need to resist the temptation to reification through the use of binary contrasts, to normalise contradictories and ambivalence in transnationals' identification and to see identities as situated and temporal as well as in its historicity. Jenkins's take on ethnicity (2008: p. 14) illustrates well how contradictory and dialectical identities such as ethnicity can be. Specifically, she states:

- Ethnicity is a matter of cultural differentiation . . . [and] always involves a dialectical interplay between similarity and difference.
- Ethnicity is centrally a matter of shared meanings . . . produced and reproduced during interaction.
- Ethnicity is no more fixed or unchanging than the way of life of which it is an aspect, or the situations in which it is produced and reproduced.
- Ethnicity, as an identification, is collective and individual, externalized in social interaction and the categorization of others, and internalized in personal self-identification.

The complexity embedded in identities in mobility as discussed earlier is unprecedented in its scale, multiplicity, and inherent contradictions. The ever-increasing connectivities among people on the move have made it a prerequisite to see this level of complexity as the norm rather than an exception. As Blommaert (2013: 619) states, "complexity is not the absence of order, it is the presence of a complex, non-categorical and non-linear form of order." We shall continue to examine different, but interrelated, aspects of complexity of identities in the next two sections: the section "From being to becoming and doing" focuses on how identities have become a matter of becoming and doing; the section "Intersectionality" looks into how different identities intersect with each other.

From being to becoming and doing

As mentioned in the introduction, studies of identity in recent years have argued that identities are not fixed. They are dynamic and emerge through interactions and discourse practices. The "identities in mobility" perspective follows this line of argument and offers new insights, in particular, to the questions of whether or to what extent "fixed" identities such as ethnicity which have been traditionally associated with nationalities and therefore fixed can be transported (Zimmerman 1998), imposed, assumed, or negotiable (Pavlenko and Blackledge 2003) during the process of migration, in the context of increasing connectivities with home and the local as well as superdiversity in every corner of the world. It also contributes to the current research on identity by further developing established analytical notions and proposing new ones.

According to Harris and Rampton (2003), there are two broad conceptualisations about ethnicity: "roOts" vs. "roUtes." While the former takes the view of "ethnicity-as-a-fixed-and-formative-inheritance," the latter believes that ethnicity depends on one's "strategic" emphasis and choice. The strategic emphasis and choices include "embracing and cultivating their ethno-cultural/linguistic legacy," "trying to downplay and drop it as a category that is relevant to them," "drawing attention to the different ethnicities of other people," "taking on someone else's ethnicity," or "creating a new one and developing hybrid and new ethnicities" (p. 5). They also state that developing new hybrid ethnicities is clearly a very complicated process and often provokes intense argument about "authenticity, entitlement and expropriation," a point outlined in the previous section. There are a number of ways of resisting identities ascribed by others. Day (1998) uses the interactional examples in two Swedish factories with a large number of migrant workers. The examples illustrate how an ethnic group membership was ascribed and resisted sequentially through dismissing its relevance, minimising the supposed differences, reconstituting essential features of the group so that one can be excluded, or turning the table by ethnifying the ethnifier. A number of recently published edited volumes showcase a variety of approaches and mechanisms for doing and becoming identities, for example, Dervin and Risager's collection on interculturality (2015); De Fina and Perrino's special issue in *Applied Linguistics* (2013) and the 2015 issue of *Annual Review of Applied Linguistics* themed on identity.

Imagination plays a key role in making and doing identities. In his study of nationalism, Anderson (1983/1991) proposes the notion of "imagined communities" to describe how nations as political communities came to be imagined and live in the minds of each member "who will never know most of their fellow members, meet them, or even hear them" (1991: 6). In the case of diasporas, Cohen (2008) argues that there are "imagined" homelands where the members of the diasporas have never been before and "imagined" transnational communities which "unite segments of people that live in territorially separated locations" (p. 13). The very notion of imagination also affects language choices of those on the move. The Continental African immigrants and refugees in a high school in Ontario in Ibrahim's study (1999) imagined themselves as "Black American" and thus chose to speak "Black stylised English" which they accessed through rap and hip hop. The differing multilingual experiences, reported in Zhu Hua and Li Wei (2016b), with regard to learning, maintaining and using languages, as evident in three transnational families from China living in Britain are tied to the families' and individuals' sense of belonging and imagination. The notion of imagination is also relevant to language classrooms where "language learners' actual and desired memberships in imagined communities affect their learning trajectories, influencing their agency, motivation, investment, and resistance in the learning of English" (Pavlenko and Norton 2007: 669).

Diverse identification practice challenges the myths of "homogenous" communities. Transnational communities are often labelled as Chinese, Polish, or Somali communities using their countries of origins or ethnicity, as if they are homogeneous entities. However, within communities, there are internal differences and complexities. Through investigating the use of address terms and "talk about social, cultural, and linguistic practice" in intergenerational talk in Chinese transnational families, Zhu Hua (2010) reveals that there are intergenerational differences in their sociocultural affiliation. The explicit and inexplicit discussion about appropriateness of linguistic, social and cultural practices serve as a direct means of socialising younger generations into the identities which parent generation holds on to. But new identities also emerge through agency of younger generation. Li Wei and Zhu Hua (2013) demonstrate how new identities are developed. A group of "Chinese" students in London universities with diverse linguistic and migrant backgrounds have opted to create a new, multilingual, transnational identity for themselves. They take control over positioning themselves flexibly, and develop new modes of communication through translanguaging practices and new language ideologies. While fully aware of differences among themselves, they are able to construct a transnational identity, free from the physical boundaries of the countries of origin, and focus on the here-and-now.

When identity becomes identification and doing, and is achieved through "strategic emphasis" (Harris and Rampton 2003) or "strategic positioning" (De Fina and Perrino 2013), the underlying assumption is that participants are rational: they set goals, determine actions, and mobilise resources to achieve the goal. While it is questionable how applicable and generalisable this rational model is, a number of studies have confirmed the employment of "strategic essentialism" (a term proposed by Spivak 1985/1996) in migrants' attempt to temporarily "essentialise" themselves in order to achieve certain goals. Eide (2010) discusses the media experience of individuals with a minority background in Norway. Some of them have to emphasise their ethnicity in order to obtain media attention. One of her subjects, Hamid, reported that as an elected leader of an organisation, he has tried to contact the press to voice a certain political initiative which has nothing to do with ethnicity, minority, or religion. His effort was ignored until he presented himself as the first such leader from an ethnic minority background. In a discussion as part of the research project of "Translation and Translanguaging: Investigating Linguistic and Cultural Transformations in Superdiverse Wards in Four UK Cities," one key participant talked about her experience of applying for a casting role as an actress. As someone with a Polish background and an Eastern European appearance, she often gets a call from her agent when they are looking for a Polish or Russian nurse or cleaning lady. While she does not like it, she has to live with it and work around it, since they seem to be the only roles she gets. Once she figures out the inner working of the "typecast," she begins to introduce herself as a "Polish actress" half-jokingly when she meets other members of a cast (Zhu Hua, Li Wei and Lyons, 2016a).

Seeing identity as something with which participants can do a number of things requires an understanding that identification is a process of negotiation (Canagarajah 2007, 2015;

Zhu Hua 2014, 2015b). The negotiation is about differences and similarities, alignment between self-oriented identities and other-ascribed identities, power relations and voice. Zhu Hua (2014) illustrates the process through a model of (mis)alignment: alignment occurs when self-oriented identity matches the identity ascribed by others. However, when they do not match, there is a misalignment and participants can negotiate whether and to what extent they would accept identities assigned by others. In a conversation among a group of international students from VOICE corpus analysed in Zhu Hua (2015b), an Argentinian speaker resisted the Spanish identity assigned by another speaker by saying "yeah but actually we're not Spanish" with a clear emphasis on "not Spanish." The first person plural pronoun "we" in his utterance was likely to refer to other Argentinian participants in the conversation and hence serves as an inclusive marker for Argentinian participants, but an exclusive marker for other non-Argentinian participants. In the rest of the conversation, his resistance was rejected by the first speaker who insisted on legitimacy of assuming one's ethnicity on the basis of the "language" they speak, as well as sympathised with or echoed to various degrees by other conversation participants. Although there was laughter between utterances, the conversation characterised with overlapping and latched utterances, collaborative completion of turns, fast turn-taking came through as an emotionally charged event.

Research on identities in mobility also contributes to the current research on identities by building on or triggering renewed interest in established analytical tools and concepts and developing new ones. The following are some examples.

Membership categorisation device (MCD, Sacks 1972) explains how people order objects of the world into categories such as family, Londoner, Mexican, student, and so forth, according to some *conventional expectations* about what constitutes normative behaviour of a category (category-bound activities). MCD has proved to be conducive to the analysis of how some identities are made relevant or salient by speakers through drawing inferences on the choices of and changes in categories. Using MCD as its main analytical concept, Zhu Hua (2015a) examines intergenerational interactions among Chinese immigrant communities in the UK and demonstrates that assumed "cultural" memberships of speakers (be it Chinese, English, or Sino-British) are not relevant to interactions all the time. Instead, their relevance is contingent on the interplay of self-orientation and ascription-by-others. Other examples of the application of MCD can be found in Antaki and Widdicombe (1998) and Nguyen and Kasper (2009).

Participants in interactions rely on *indexicality* or indexical cues to evoke the relevance of particular category-bound features and activities associated with identities. Examples of indexical cues include accent, code-switching, address terms, and cultural-specific terms, among other things. The link between linguistic form and identity is indirect in the first place but gradually becomes direct over time when these forms are used as strategic social actions (Ochs 1992, 1993, 1996). Silverstein (2003) further develops a model which argues for multiple levels or "orders" of indexicality. Blommaert (2007) provides an example of how orders of indexicality, along with the notion of polycentricity (i.e., multiple concurrent linguistic norms within a community), enable analysts to "connect microscopic instances of communicative practice to larger-scale political and sociological patterns and structures" (p. 127).

Stance, as defined by Du Bois (2007: 163), is "a public act by a social actor, achieved through overt means, of evaluating an object, positioning the self, and aligning with other subjects in respect of any salient dimension of the stance field." It is closely related to the notion of indexicality, as language along with other semiotic resources indexes one's affective, epistemic or evaluative interactional stance. Bucholtz (2009) illustrates how the notions of stance and indexicality can be applied to interpret how Mexican immigrant youth take stance and index their gender, ethnicity, age, or region through "fleeting" interactional moves. Baynham (2015) uses stance to analyse a narrative of a Moroccan talking about his early stages of migration in the UK in the 1970s.

Similar to stance, the notion of *positioning* is often used in identity research to differentiate how interactants make their choices of or orient to a particular kind of identity. Harré and van Langenhove (1999) propose several kinds of positioning: first and second positioning, performative and accountative positioning, moral and personal positioning, self and other positioning, and tacit and intentional positioning. Further contrasts have been proposed lately: formulaic and narrative positioning (Dailey-O'Cain and Liebscher 2006), direct vs. indirect positioning (Bucholtz and Hall 2005) and explicit vs. implicit positioning (Liebscher and Dailey-O'Cain 2013). Liebscher and Dailey-O'Cain (2013) provide examples of how German migrants in Canada make use of multilingual tools as well as non-linguistic resources to position selves and others as German language experts, attriters (those who have lost their first languages), balanced bilinguals, or language learners.

In recent years, new constructs have been incorporated into studies on identities in mobility. For example, Goebel (2013, 2014) uses the notion of *enregisterment*, defined by Agha (2007: 55) as a process "whereby diverse behavioural signs (whether linguistic, non-linguistic, or both) are functionally reanalysed as cultural models of action," to analyse social and language/semiotics dynamics. Goebel studies show how a group of Indonesians do togetherness in a transnational setting located in Japan and how language, identity and social relationships play out in two areas in Indonesia characterised by linguistic and cultural diversity amid flow of population. Wortham and Rhodes (2012) explore how narratives of Mexican immigrants in an American town emerge and move across different *scales*, which, as an analytical notion, transcend the "micro-macro dialectic," and become an important resource for their social identification.

Intersectionality

Anthias (2012: 102) argues that "transnational migration studies need to be framed within a contextual, dynamic and processual analysis that recognises the interconnectedness of different identities and hierarchical structures relating to, for example, gender, ethnicity, 'race' and class at different levels in society." The heuristic device that equips researchers with the required analytical sensitivity is, as she proposes, the idea of intersectionality. The concept of intersectionality originated from feminist scholarship during the 1970s and 1980s (e.g., Crenshaw 1989) in their attempt to counter the trend in gender studies which often depart from "white middle-class heterosexual women's experiences" (Lundström 2014: 16) and therefore fail to contest social inequality and power structure dividing women as well as between men and women (for a review, see Choo and Ferree 2010). By investigating multiple positions such as race, gender, class, sexuality, age, nationality, religion, and so forth together and in an nonadditive way, intersectionality thus "complicates one-dimensional racial locations, gendered relations or class positions, and rejects the idea that categories can be neatly added to each other" (Lundström 2014: 16). Choo and Ferree (2010) further analyse three foci of intersectionality in practice, which are termed as group-, process-, and system-centred. They argue that intersectionality moves "multiply marginalised" groups and their perspectives from the periphery to the centre (group-centred focus). Seeing intersectionality as a process does not just add groups into the mix, but highlights the transformative effect of intersectional relations at multiple levels (process-centred focus); viewing intersectionality as shaping the entire social system, not confined to a specific institution, enables researchers to interpret social inequality in its situated and historical contexts (system-centred).

Recently, some studies on identities in mobility have adopted an intersectionality approach and draw attention to the interaction of race, ethnicity, gender, class, or sexuality in the process of identification. In Lundström's multi-site ethnographic study of Swedish migrant women in the United States, Singapore, and Spain, she examines the intersection of whiteness and gender in mobility and "how western privilege has to be re-located and re-negotiated in relation to local formations of race, class, gender, sexuality and age in different geopolitical spaces" (2014, p. 170). It offers a complex view of how transnational, national, and regional racial logics of whiteness interplay with each other: Swedish women, who represented a modern colonial version of European whiteness, can pass as the local in the United States, but not in Spain; in Singapore, their natural, suntan-like whiteness is demoted due to the destabilisation of a British colonial version of racial hierarchies and the locals' paradoxical desire to appear visually white. In addition to these regional variations, Swedish women are often confronted with "lingering gender inequality" both in their (former) homes and in the host country. In Singapore, Swedish women and Filipino and Indonesian migrant women often come together as "mistresses" and "maids" in the former's domestic space, a contact zone of inequality and privilege. Tiers clearly exist in the transnational workforce and global restructuring (Parreñas 2001: 31). For the Swedish women, who often take a career break and are relocated to Singapore as housewives, hiring domestic workers serves as a "cushion" for them in the new form of power structure where they put on hold their career, financial independence, gender equality, and social equality.

Block (2015a) discusses that a "class-based" intersectional approach can be useful in highlighting the ways that "individuals are declassed and then reclassed in host societies" (p. 15). An example of such an approach can be found in Block and Corona (2014), which explores the experience of adolescent Latinos in Barcelona in terms of their social class, and racialised, ethnicised, and gendered positioning. All of them have the experience of being the object of racial profiling as they stand out with their South American appearance. They were frequently regarded as "danger" on the street. One informant originally from the Dominican Republic reported that he felt compelled to wear baggy clothes as a rapper, because he was Black and it is what "adolescent males with his physical experience were expected to do" in the local discourse (p. 37).

Intersectionality opens up a new line of investigation in researching identities in mobility. When used alongside the existing approaches in a balanced and coherent manner, intersectionality gives voices to "concerns about inequality based on misrecognition and misrepresentation (racism, sexism, homophobia, national hatred, etc.) and inequality based on the unequal distribution of economic resources" (Block and Corona 2014: 39). It has the potential to develop exciting areas in research on identity in mobility in the future.

Issues and ongoing debates

Within the research on identities on a whole, there has been a general shift away from an essentialist position on identity which sees identity as stable, fixed and pre-determined towards a dynamic, emergent account of identity which regards identity as a process rather than an end product. Although there has not been a full-scale replacement of essentialist views (Lytra, 2016), the emergent account has become a default position in applied linguistics (Block 2015b). The question, however, remains: how far can we go when we talk about agency, fluidity, and flexibility which come with social constructivism? Ultimately, this is a question about the relationship between structure and agency (for a review, see Block 2015a). As critiqued by May (2001) and Dervin (2012), in some studies following social constructivism approach, agency of participants in doing identity has been taken to an extreme to imply that all choices become possible and identity has become a "free-floating" concept. The previously discussed issues of authenticity and enoughness surface frequently in studies of identities in mobility and remind us that while negotiation is the key to identification, there are limits to it due to social structure, power relationships, and unequal access to resources. The ultimate test for becoming and doing identities can be found in Chun (2013), in which the author presents a case of a young Chinese American YouTube star constructing an "ironic blackness" identity through embodying speech style typically regarded as "black" in the United States and making fun of hegemonic images of black and Asian masculinity. The viewers' interpretations, as revealed in quotations, metalinguistic remarks and declaration of love in the comments, are mixed: some viewers problematised the star's linguistic essentialism or inauthenticity and denied his blackness, while some viewers aligned with his experience of acting black.

Similar to authenticity, the issue of legitimacy is closely linked to political struggle over identity and belonging in terms of who is in and out and who is here first. Frello (2015) analyses how the legitimacy of blended identities of two migrants living in Denmark was positioned differently by the programme hosts and their co-debaters on Danish television. Abraham Topcagic was introduced as a "typically Bosnian" in a debate about the Bosnian war alongside a "Serb" and a "Croat" participant. His mixed family background was brought up in the introduction as a basis for legitimacy and his (supposedly well-informed) insights. In contrast, Slavko Labovic, originally from Serbia and having spent most of his life in Denmark, was "squarely" treated as a "Serb" by the host in a debate about the Kosovo War. His attempt to utilise his co-Danishness in front of a Danish audience was rejected by other participants, due to the fact that he was speaking the politically unacceptable discourse of Serbian nationalism. The author further argues that "the legitimacy of hybridity could not be claimed. It could only be given" (p. 204). The author may be pessimistic when talking about the non-negotiability of legitimacy, but in the case of Labovic and many others, they are not in any position to negotiate.

Implications

The unprecedented complexity of identities in global migration era calls for a different approach to identities in practice. In a paper with an intriguing title, "You Can't Put Me in a Box: Super-diversity and the End of Identity Politics in Britain," published by the Institute for Public Policy Research, a UK leading think tank, Simon Fanshawe and Dhananjayan Sriskandarajah (2010) made a case for reframing the "tick-box approach to identity" underpinning many policies towards promoting equality. The authors argue that while the identity politics and social movements since the 1960s have given voice to women or minorities who were marginalised, it is time to consider changes to this orthodox approach to identity and to think about new ways of political mobilisation. Putting people into a box or labelling them according to one of the boxes (gender, race, disability, sexuality, faith and belief, and age), which characterises the current practice, are too simplistic and too blunt to lead to any effective remedies.

In the last few years, there are some imaginative grass-roots campaigns aimed at questioning the bias in people's thinking about race and ethnicity. "I, Too, Am Harvard" is such an example. Originated in Harvard University, the campaign uses a collection of photos of black students from Harvard University holding messages about their experience of being black and being misrepresented. The examples of messages include "Having an opinion does not make me an angry black woman"; "Can you read?"; or "You don't sound black. You sound smart." The campaign quickly spread to other universities including the University of Oxford, University of Cambridge, and McGill University and turned into an international campaign challenging stereotypes against visible minorities. Another example is the Drop-the-I-word campaign which started in the United States in 2010. The campaign has led to the discontinued use of the adjective "illegal" in many countries when referring to immigrants who cross borders without authorisation. The argument behind the campaign is that although the act is illegal, the person involved is not.

Future directions

Inequality agenda

The issues of authenticity and legitimacy, practices of "fitting into a box," "strategic essentialism," and "heritaging" and intersubjective, contradictory, and dialectical aspects of identities discussed earlier invite further investigations into the tension between structure and agency; the power struggle between insiders and outsiders; and most importantly, the social, political and economic inequality in identification. As researchers, our task is to go beyond decoding the process of identification and to ask the questions of "why?," "what consequences?," and "who bear the consequences?"

Superdiversity agenda

We have seen some impact of superdiversity on identities in mobility. The connectivities that take place virtually, physically, or through imagination among people on the move challenge the validity of binary dichotomies we use every day, such as minority vs. majority, immigrant vs. local, homeland vs. host. With superdiversity permeating every corner of the world, how does it continue to impact the way people go about identities or identification?

Summary

To conclude, research on identities in mobility contributes to identity research by testing out many claims on identity in the context of change, contact, and connectivity. It offers an opportunity to examine to what extent one's membership, affiliation, and sense of belonging to their place or culture of origin and new place of settlement are affected by the process of border crossing and how new identities and dynamics develop through the process. What has emerged through new orientations to identities in mobility is an unprecedented complexity, an emphasis on identification rather than identity, and intersection of multiple identities such as race, ethnicity, gender, class, or sexuality. There is a greater need to resist the temptation to reification embedded in existing labels and binary contrasts, to normalise contradictories and ambivalence in identification, and to see identities as situated and temporal accomplishment as well as in its historicity.

Related topics

Nation-state, transnationalism and language
Multisited ethnography and language in the study of migration
Complexity, mobility, migration
Citizenship, immigration laws, and language

Further reading

Annual Review of Applied Linguistics. (2015, Volume 35).

This volume contains a number of review articles on identities including social class by Block, translanguaging and identity in educational setting by Creese and Blackledge, identity and a model of investment by Davin and Norton, and transnationalism and multilingualism by Duff.

De Fina, A. and Perrino, S., eds. (2013). "Transnational identities". A special issue of *Applied Linguistics*, *34*(5), 509–622.

A collection of empirical research articles on the construction of transnational identities in different geographical areas and via different media.

Dervin, F. and Risager, K., eds. (2015). *Researching Identity and Interculturality*. New York: Routledge.

A collection of chapters offering a multi-disciplinary overview on researching identity.

Preece, S., ed. (2016). *Handbook of Language and Identity*. New York: Routledge.

A handbook providing a clear and comprehensive survey of the field of language and identity from an applied linguistics perspective.

References

Agha, S. (2007). *Language and Social Relations*. Cambridge: Cambridge University Press.
Anderson, B. (1983/1991). *Imagined Communities: Reflections on the Origins and Spread of Nationalism*. London: Verso.
Ang, I. (2001). *On Not Speaking Chinese. Living between Asia and the West*. London: Routledge.
Antaki, C. and Widdicombe, S., eds. (1998). *Identities in Talk*. London: Sage.
Anthias, F. (2012). Transnational mobilities, migration research and intersectionality. Towards a translocational frame. *Nordic Journal of Migration Research* 2(2): 102–110.
Bauman, R. (1992). Contextualization, tradition, and the dialogue of genres: Icelandic legends of the *kraftaskáld*. In A. Duranti and C. Goodwin (eds.), *Rethinking Context: Language as an Interactive Phenomenon* (pp. 125–145). Cambridge: Cambridge University Press.
Baynham, M. (2015). Identity brought about or along? Narrative as a privileged site for researching intercultural identities. In F. Dervin and K. Risager (eds.), *Researching Identity and Interculturality* (pp. 67–88). London: Routledge.
Bennett, J.M. (1993). Cultural marginality: Identity issues in intercultural training. In R.M. Paige (ed.), *Education for the Intercultural Experience* (pp. 109–135). Yarmouth, ME: Intercultural Press.
Bennett, J.M. (2008). On becoming a global soul: A path to engagement during study abroad. In V. Savicki (ed.), *Developing Intercultural Competence and Transformation* (pp. 13–31). Sterling, VA: Stylus.
Bhabha, H.K. (1994) *The Location of Culture*. London: Routledge.
Block, D. (2015a). The structure and agency dilemma in identity and intercultural communication research. In C. Jenks, J. Lou and Aditi Bhatia (eds.), *The Discourse of Culture and Identity in National and Transnational Contexts* (pp. 6–27). New York: Routledge.
Block, D. (2015b). Social class in applied linguistics. *Annual Review of Applied Linguistics* 35: 1–19.

Block, D. and Corona, V. (2014). Exploring class-based intersectionality. *Language, Culture and Curriculum* 27: 27–42.

Blommaert, J. (2007). Sociolinguistics and discourse analysis: Orders of indexicality and polycentricity. *Journal of Multicultural Discourses* 2(2): 115–130.

Blommaert, J. (2013). Complexity, accent, and conviviality: Concluding comments. *Applied Linguistics* 34(5): 613–622.

Blommaert, J. and Varis, P. (2011). *Enough Is Enough: The Heuristics of Authenticity in Superdiversity*. Working Papers in Urban Language and Literacies, Paper 76 (London, Albany, Ghent, Tilburg).

Bucholtz, M. (1995). From mulatta to mestiza: Language and the reshaping of ethnic identity. In K. Hall and M. Bucholtz (eds.), *Gender Articulated: Language the Socially Constructed Self* (pp. 351–374). New York: Routledge.

Bucholtz, M. (2009). From stance to style: Gender, interaction, and indexicality in Mexican immigrant youth slang. In A. Jaffe (ed.), *Stance: Sociolinguistic Perspectives* (pp. 146–170). Oxford: Oxford University Press.

Bucholtz, M. and Hall, K. (2005). Identity and interaction: A sociocultural linguistic approach. *Discourse Studies* 7: 585–614.

Canagarajah, S. (2007). Lingua Franca English, multilingual communities, and language acquisition. *Modern Language Journal* 91: 923–939.

Canagarajah, S. (2015). Agency and power in intercultural communication: Negotiating English in translocal spaces. In C. Jenks, J. Lou and A. Bhatia (eds.), *The Discourse of Culture and Identity in National and Transnational Contexts* (pp. 82–104). New York: Routledge.

Choo, H.Y. and Ferree, M.M. (2010). Practicing intersectionality in sociological research: A critical analysis of inclusions and institutions in the study of inequalities. *Sociological Theory* 28(2): 129–149.

Chun, E. (2013). Ironic blackness as masculine cool: Asian American language and authenticity on YouTube. *Applied Linguistics* 34(5): 592–612.

Cohen, R. (2008). *Global Diasporas* (2nd ed.). London: Routledge.

Crenshaw, K. (1989). Demarginalizing the intersection of race and sex: A black feminist critique of antidiscrimination doctrine, feminist theory, and antiracist politics. *University of Chicago Legal Forum* 140: 139–167.

Cutler, C. (2003). "Keeping it real": White hip-hoppers' discourses of language, race, and authenticity. *Journal of Linguistic Anthropology* 13(2): 211–233.

Dailey-O'Cain, J. and Liebscher, G. (2006). Language learners' use of discourse markers as evidence for a mixed code. *International Journal of Bilingualism* 10(1): 89–109.

Day, D. (1998). Being ascribed, and resisting. Membership of an ethnic group. In C. Antaki and S. Widdicombe (eds.), *Identities in Talk* (pp. 151–170). London: Sage.

De Fina, A. (2013). Top-down and bottom-up strategies of identity construction in ethnic media. *Applied Linguistics* 34(5): 554–573.

De Fina, A. and Perrino, S. (2013). Transnational identities. *Applied Linguistics* 34(5): 509–515.

De Fina, A., Schiffrin, D. and Bamberg, M., eds. (2006). *Discourse and Identity*. Cambridge: Cambridge University Press.

Dervin, F. (2012). Cultural identity, representation and othering. In J. Jackson (ed.), *The Routledge Handbook of Language and Intercultural Communication* (pp. 181–194). Cambridge: Cambridge University Press.

Dervin, F. and Risager, K., eds. (2015). *Researching Identity and Interculturality*. New York: Routledge.

Du Bois, J. (2007). The stance triangle. In R. Englebretson (ed.), *Stance Taking in Discourse: Subjectivity, Evaluation, Interaction* (pp. 139–192). Amsterdam: John Benjamins.

Duff, P. (2015). Transnationalism, multilingualism, and identity. *Annual Review of Applied Linguistics* 35: 57–80.

Edwards, J. (2009) *Language and Identity*. Cambridge: Cambridge University Press.

Eide, E. (2010) "Strategic essentialism and ethnification. Hand in glove?" *Nordicom Review* 31(2): 63–78.
Fanshawe, S. and Sriskandarajah, D. (2010). "You Can't Put Me in a Box. Super-diversity and the End of Identity Politics in Britain." London: ippr.
Fought, C. (2006). *Language and Ethnicity.* Cambridge: Cambridge University Press.
Frello, B. (2015). On legitimate and illegitimate blendings. Towards an analytics of hybridity. In F. Dervin and K. Risager (eds.), *Researching Identity and Interculturality* (pp. 193–210). New York: Routledge.
Goebel, Z. (2013). *Indonesians Doing Togetherness in Japan.* Tilburg Papers in Culture Studies, Paper 67 (Tilburg University).
Goebel, Z. (2014). *Language, Migration, and Identity: Neighborhood Talk in Indonesia.* Cambridge: Cambridge University Press.
Harré, R. and van Langenhove, L. (1999). Introducing positioning theory. In R. Harré and L. van Langenhove (eds.), *Positioning Theory* (pp. 14–31). London: Sage.
Harris, R. and Rampton, B. (2003). *The Language, Ethnicity and Race Reader.* London: Routledge.
Hegel, G.W.F. (1807/1977). *Phenomenology of Spirit* [Translated by A.V. Miller]. Oxford: Clarendon Press.
Higham, J. (1955). *Strangers in the Land: Patterns of American Nativism,* 1860–1925. New Brunswick, NJ: Rutgers University.
Hobsbawm, E.J. (1983). Inventing traditions. In E.J. Hobsbawm and T.O. Ranger (eds.), *The Invention of Tradition* (pp. 1–14). Cambridge: Cambridge University Press.
Ibrahim, A. (1999) "Becoming black: Rap and hip-hop, race, gender, identity, and the politics of ESL learning." *TESOL Quarterly* 33(3): 349–369.
Jackson, P., Crang, P. and Dwyer, C. (2004). Introduction: The spaces of transnationality. In P. Jackson, P. Crang and C. Dwyer (eds.), *Transnational Spaces* (pp. 1–23). London: Routledge.
Jenkins, R. (2008). *Rethinking Ethnicity. Arguments and Explorations* (2nd ed.). London: Sage.
Lam, W.S.E. (2008). Language socialization in online communities. In P. Duff and N.H. Hornberger (eds.), *Encyclopedia of Language and Education: Vol. 8. Language Socialization* (pp. 301–311). New York: Springer.
Lam, W.S.E. (2013). Multilingual practices in transnational digital contexts. *TESOL Quarterly* 47(4): 820–825.
Lam, W.S.E. (2014). Literacy and capital in immigrant youths' online networks across countries. *Learning, Media and Technology* 39(4): 488–506.
Lam, W.S.E. and Warriner, D.S. (2012). Transnationalism and literacy: Investigating the mobility of people, languages, texts, and practices in contexts of migration. A review of research. *Reading Research Quarterly* 47(2): 191–215.
Lee, J.-E.J. (2009). "She's hungarious so she's Mexican but she's most likely Indian": Negotiating ethnic labels in a California junior high school. *Pragmatics* 19(1): 39–63.
Li, J. and Juffermans, K. (2011). *Multilingual Europe 2.0: Dutch-Chinese Youth Identities in the Era of Superdiversity.* Working Papers in Urban Language and Literacies 71. Retrieved from http://www.kcl.ac.uk/innovation/groups/ldc/publications/workingpapers/download.aspx.
Li Wei and Zhu Hua (2013). Diaspora: Multilingual and intercultural communication across time and space. *AILA Review* 26: 42–56.
Li Wei and Zhu Hua (2013). Diaspora: Multilingual and intercultural communication across time and space. AILA Review 26: 42–56.
Liebscher, G. and Dailey-O'Cain, J. (2013). *Language, Space and Identity in Migration.* London: Palgrave Macmillan.
Lorente, B.P. and Tupas, T.R.F. (2013). (Un)emancipatory hybridity: Selling English in an unequal world. In R. Rubdy and L. Alsagoff (eds.), *The Global-local Interface and Hybridity: Exploring Language and Identity* (pp. 66–82). Clevedon: Multilingual Matters.
Lundström, C. (2014). *White Migrations: Gender Whiteness and Privilege in Transnational Migration.* Basingstoke: Palgrave Macmillan.

Lytra, V. (2016). Language and ethnic identity. In S. Preece (ed.), *Handbook of Language and Identity* (pp. 131–145), New York: Routledge.

May, S. (2001). *Language and Minority Rights*. London: Longman.

Nguyen, H.T. and Kasper, G., eds. (2009). *Talk-in-Interaction: Multilingual Perspectives*. Hawai'i: University of Hawai'i National Foreign Language Resource Center.

Ochs, E. (1992). Indexing gender. In A. Duranti and C. Goodwin (eds.), *Rethinking Context: Language as an Interactive Phenomenon* (pp. 335–358). Cambridge: Cambridge University Press.

Ochs, E. (1993). Constructing social identity: A language socialization perspective. *Research on Language and Social Interaction* 26: 287–306.

Ochs, E. (1996). Linguistic resources for socializing humanity. In J. Gumperz and S. Levinson (eds.), *Rethinking Linguistic Relativity* (pp. 407–437). Cambridge: Cambridge University Press.

Omoniyi, T. (2006). Hierarchy of identities. In T. Omoniyi and G. White (eds.), *Sociolinguistics of Identity* (pp. 11–33). London: Continuum.

Otsuji, E. and Pennycook, A. (2010). Metrolingualism: Fixity, fluidity and language in flux. *International Journal of Multilingualism* 7: 240–254.

Parreñas, R.S. (2001). Migrant Filipina domestic workers and the international division of reproductive labor. *Gender and Society* 14(4): 560–580.

Pavlenko, A. and Blackledge, A. (2003). Introduction: New theoretical approaches to the study of negotiation of identities in multilingual contexts. In A. Pavlenko and A. Blackledge (eds.), *Negotiation of Identities in Multilingual Contexts* (pp. 1–33). Clevedon: Multilingual Matters.

Pavlenko, A. and Norton, B. (2007). Imagined communities, identity, and English language learning. In J. Cummins and C. Davison (eds.), *International Handbook of English Language Teaching* (pp. 669–680). New York: Springer.

Quayson, A. and Daswani, G. (2013). Introduction – Diaspora and transnationalism. Scapes, scales and scopes. In A. Quayson and G. Daswani (eds.), *A Companion to Diaspora and Transnationalism* (pp. 1–26). Oxford: Wiley Blackwell.

Raghunandan, K. (2012). *Hyphenated Identities: Negotiating "Indianness" and Being Indo-Trinidadian*. CRGS, no. 6, ed. Gabrielle Hosein and Lisa Outar, pp. 1–19.

Rampton, B. (1995). *Crossing: Language and Ethnicity among Adolescents*. New York: Longman.

Sacks, H. (1972). On the analyzability of stories by children. In J. Gumperz and D. Hymes (eds.), *Directions in Sociolinguistics* (pp. 325–345). New York: Holt, Rinehart & Winston.

Schaetti, B.F. (1998). *Global Nomad Identity: Hypothesizing a Developmental Model*. Unpublished doctoral dissertation, The Graduate College of the Union Institute, Seattle, WA.

Shenk, P.S. (2007). "I'm Mexican, remember?" Constructing ethnic identities via authenticating discourse. *Journal of Sociolinguistics* 11(2): 194–220.

Silverstein, M. (2003). Indexical order and the dialectics of sociolinguistic life. *Language and Communication* 23: 193–229.

Spivak, G.C. (1985/1996). Subaltern studies. Deconstructing historiography. In D. Landry and G. MacLean (ed.), *The Spivak Reader* (pp. 203–236). London: Routledge.

Tracy, K. (2002). *Everyday Talk: Building and Reflecting Identities*. New York and London: Guilford Press.

Tsagarousianou, R. (2004). Rethinking the concept of diaspora: Mobility, connectivity and communication in a globalized world. *Westminster Papers in Communication and Culture* 1(1): 52–65.

Wortham, S. and Rhodes, C. (2012). The production of relevant scales: Social identification of migrants during rapid demographic change in one American town. *Applied Linguistics Review* 3(1): 75–99.

Zhu Hua (2010). Language socialisation and interculturality: Address terms in intergenerational talk in Chinese diasporic families. *Language and Intercultural Communication* 10(3): 189–205.

Zhu Hua (2014). *Exploring Intercultural Communication: Language in Action*. London: Routledge.

Zhu Hua (2015a). Interculturality: Reconceptualising cultural memberships and identities. In F. Dervin and K. Risager (eds.), *Researching Identity and Interculturality: Towards a More Reflexive and Critical Methodology* (pp. 109–124). London: Routledge.

Zhu Hua (2015b). Negotiation as the way of engagement in intercultural and lingua franca communication: Frames of reference and Interculturality. *Journal of English as Lingua Franca* 4(1): 63–90.

Zhu Hua, Li Wei, & Lyons, A. (2016a). Playful subversiveness and creativity: Doing a/n (Polish) artist in London. Working Papers in Translanguaging and Translation (WP 16). Accessible at http://www.birmingham.ac.uk/generic/tlang/documents/playful-subversiveness-and-creativity.pdf.

Zhu Hua & Li Wei (2016b). Transnational experience, aspiration and family language policy. *Journal of Multilingual and Multicultural Development* 37(7): 655–666.

Zimmerman, Don H. (1998). Identity, context and interaction. In C. Antaki and S. Widdicombe (eds.), *Identities in Talk* (pp. 87–106). London: Sage.

7
Social class in migration, identity, and language research

David Block

Introduction

Writing over a decade ago, Jim Collins made the point that despite opinions to the contrary, the United States is 'a highly class differentiated society, with large social and economic differences between the owning and managing elites and the working-class majority, and a widening gap between the incomes and education of middle class and working-class households' (Collins 2006: 3). He goes on to argue that within this class-differentiated society, 'immigrant populations are sharply differentiated with, for example, wealthy entrepreneurs, middle class professionals, and low-wage service workers found among most groups,' leading him to conclude that 'class is a significant structural feature in the contemporary United States, and it is a significant "category of difference" in immigrant communities' (Collins 2006: 3). In effect, what Collins is saying is that those who study immigration, and in particularly those applied linguists who study the interrelationship between migration, identity and language (MIL), need to adopt class as a key construct in their work. He does so in the context of ongoing academic research in North America examining how bi/multilingualism often has been and often continues to be framed in a negative manner in the United States (Urciuoli 1996; Lippi-Green 1997/2011) and how bi/multilinguals themselves are often subjected to what Charles Taylor (1994: 25) calls the 'misrecognition', that is, they 'suffer real damage, real distortion . . . [when] the people or society around them mirror back to them a confining or demeaning or contemptible picture of themselves'. A call for more attention to social class in research on MIL is in no way an attempt to undervalue research on misrecognition. However, it does mean questioning how much this research may achieve if the goal is to provide a complete picture of the migrant experience in terms of all of the variables impacting on it or to challenge inequality in societies, which may be seen as being as much about economics as cultural issues (if not more).

In this sense, Collins's view is a mild critique of researchers who have focused exclusively on migrants in terms of their identities and their language and cultural practices, but not with reference to their material existences in unequal societies. The aim of this chapter is to develop this critique in more detail with a view to proposing a way forward. Class matters in migration and identity research because migrants, like everyone else in society, live their lives within class-based hierarchies. Where migrants are different is in the duality of their class-based existence: they embody class-inflected subjectivities in their home contexts and they do so in their new host environment. Interestingly, however, there is no guarantee that they will maintain a class position from one context to the other and, indeed as we will see later in this chapter, *declassing* (losing one's class position) and *reclassing* (resituating oneself in a new class configuration) are common occurrences (Block 2006, 2014).

I begin this chapter with a lengthy discussion of key frameworks and constructs relevant to the topic of migration, transnationalism, and social class in applied linguistics. I then discuss, briefly, the state of research which focuses on migration and MIL from a political economic perspective which includes social class as a key construct. From here I move to discuss what I see as key issues around research focusing on social class, before considering the implications of working in such a way. I close with a brief note about future directions.

Overview

Migration and transnationalism

In recent years social scientists have come to the realisation that mobility and migration are essential constructs in any informed understanding of societies and how individuals and collectives live in them (Sheller and Urry 2006; Grieco and Urry 2012; Faist 2013). Mobilities (in plural) come in many shapes and sizes, but here it is human mobilities that are of interest. Human mobilities may be understood in two general senses: (1) as the relative ability of people to move freely and easily, focusing on the availability and/or disposition of people to move or to be moved (e.g., by government institutions or companies), and (2) as the reality of people moving across geographical, political, economic, social, cultural, and linguistic borders.

Human mobilities are also known as migration, the study of which has evolved considerably over the past thirty years. In particular, from the 1990s onwards, prominent migration scholars began to advocate and adopt approaches to research which framed the phenomenon as a complex global force. Thomas Faist (2000) encapsulated this trend well with his multi-level migration systems theory, according to which migration is framed as a series of overlapping and interacting systems working across scales of human activity, from the macro to the meso to the micro. An integral part of this multi-level approach to migration is the understanding that migrant experiences today develop and unfold in ways which differ from what would have been the case, for example, 100 years ago.

'Transnationalism' is a term that has been introduced with a view to capturing how migrant individuals and collectives live their lives under increasingly complex conditions in increasingly complex societies. The term was defined some years ago by Basch, Glick Schiller, and Blanc-Szantson (1994: 6) as "the processes by which immigrants form and sustain multi-stranded social relations that link together their societies of origin and settlement." More recently, it has been described as the "sustained linkages and ongoing exchanges among non-state actors based across national borders – businesses, non-government organizations, and individuals sharing the same interests" (Vertovec 2009: 3). Importantly, as Jordan and Düvell (2003: 76–77) note, transnationalism

> defies notions of assimilation and acculturation to the national 'core', and goes beyond the ethnic pluralism of multicultural membership . . .[,] suggest[ing] that dual or multiple

forms of nationality and citizenship might better reflect and recognize the realities of these socio-economic systems.

(Jordan and Düvell 2003: 76–77)

A transnational approach involves several core notions, elements and positions. Among other things, it tends to focus on 'transnationalism from below', or grassroots, emergent social relations, as opposed to policy level and institution-driven 'transnationalism from above'. It aims to document, monitor, and explain the processes by which migrants live the aforementioned 'multiple forms of nationality and citizenship' (Jordan and Düvell 2003: 77) and how they 'build social fields which link their country of origin and their country of settlement' (Faist, Fauser, and Reisenauer 2013: 12). The individuals involved are not just 'migrants' – they are 'transmigrants' who 'build such social fields by maintaining a wide range of affective and instrumental societal practices spanning borders' (Faist et al. 2013: 12). Though not cited explicitly by Faist et al. (2013), another key element in a transnational approach should be an acknowledgement and engagement with the ways in which political economic developments generate changes in movements across borders and therefore the kind of transnationalism that takes place (Glick Schiller 2010; Portes 2010). For example, since the economic crisis of 2007/2008 began, southern European countries such as Greece, Italy, Portugal, and Spain have experienced great changes as regards their incoming and outgoing migration patterns. Indeed, in a relatively short period of time (some twenty years), they have moved from being countries of rapid and intense immigration, from the early 1990s onwards as the economic boom took shape, to being countries of emigration, as both recently arrived immigrants and long-term citizens leave due to considerably worsened short- and long-term life prospects (especially high employment, which is particularly pronounced among young people). However, it is worth noting that in earlier emigration periods, in the 1950s, '60s and '70s, which again were the result of economic disequilibrium between northern and southern Europe during the post–World War II boom, those leaving these counties tended to be less qualified citizens in terms of education and skills. In recent times this trend has changed, in that citizens of these countries across a range of education and skill levels are departing and indeed, with reference to well-educated and highly qualified émigrés, there is reason to frame what is going on as a 'brain drain'.

Differences among emigrants in terms of education and skills point to the increasing complexification of migratory flows and the difficulty faced by those who cling to crude, rough-and-ready classifications such as 'Greek migrant', 'Italian migrant', 'Spanish migrant' and so on. And there are ultimately class differences which index the growing inequalities in countries around the world, even as these inequalities are, in effect, exported elsewhere. But of course education and skills are but a small part of what constitutes class as a key construct in any understanding of contemporary societies and individuals and collectives within them. In the next section, I take on class as construct.

Social class

Marx (e.g., 1990 [1867]) is a common starting point for a discussion of class, even if he never actually provided a clear-cut definition of the key construct in his work (Block 2014). Nevertheless, it is possible to glean what he meant by class from his discussions of the relationship between individuals and the means of production in England and other industrialising European countries in the 19th century, and how from these relations there arose very different class-based ways of life and class-based consciousnesses. Scholars writing about class after

Marx, from the 1880s onwards, bore witness to the increasing complexification of societies, with Emile Durkheim (1984 [1893]) first, and later Max Weber (1968 [1922]) being the sociologists who most thoroughly reconfigured understandings of class in the light of changes taking place. Weber's work is of particular interest as he introduced the notions of status and status situation as a way of making sense of inequality and stratification in industrialized societies, not only in terms of material conditions (economics), but also in terms of more abstract, socially constructed cultural phenomena. The latter include practices and activities such as the consumption of particular goods and engagement in particular pastimes, both related to differentiable lifestyles which are valued unequally in societies in terms of what Weber (1968) called 'prestige' and what Pierre Bourdieu (1984) later called 'distinction'.

For his part, Bourdieu is an interesting unifying figure in the history of class-based scholarship: while like Marx, he saw inequality in class terms as a matter of material states and processes (see his 'economic capital'), like Weber he framed inequality as emergent in the practices and cultural activity of individuals in fields, or domains of social activity (see his 'cultural capital', as legitimized knowledge and know-how, and 'social capital', as social relations facilitating paths to success in individual life trajectories). As I note elsewhere (Block 2012, 2014, 2015, 2016), over the past several decades there has been a dominant tendency in sociology to conceptualise and discuss class in a broadly Bourdieusian manner (e.g., Crompton 2008; Bennett et al. 2009; Savage et al. 2013), allowing for a conflation of generally Marxist and generally Weberian views. This Bourdieusian view is by no means free of deficiencies. For example, David Harvey has written of his 'profound objections to Bourdieu's characterisation of personal endowments . . . as a form of capital' (Harvey 2014: 186), arguing that while 'capital undoubtedly uses . . . signs of distinction in its sales practices and pitches, . . . that does not mean that distinction is a form of capital' (Harvey 2014: 187). Rather, Harvey argues, distinction is about the symbolic orders emerging from and intertwined with the ongoing development of capitalism and the economic inequalities which come with this development. It therefore need not bear the label of 'capital', even if it is obviously part and parcel of the sociocultural construction of class and inequality in contemporary societies.

These and other reservations about aspects of Bourdieu's work notwithstanding, his view of class, as I noted earlier, has become central to any discussion of the phenomenon. With this state of play in mind, I have, in recent years, attempted to frame class for my own purposes by drawing on the foundational work of Marx and Weber and the more recent contributions of Bourdieu (1984) and Savage et al. (2013). I have put together a *constellation of interrelated dimensions* model to capture the long list of dimensions that index class: in different ways in different contexts, cultures, and societies. This model consists of five general categories which are then subdivided into dimensions as follows:

Economic resources

- Property: land and housing;
- Property: other material possessions, such as electronic goods, clothing, books, art, etc.;
- Income: salary and wages;
- Accumulated wealth: savings and investments.

Sociocultural resources

- Occupation: manual labour, unskilled service jobs, low-level information-based jobs, professional labour, etc.;

- Education: level of formal education attained and the corresponding cultural capital acquired;
- Technological know-how: familiarity and ability to use evolving technologies;
- Social contacts and networking: people regularly associated with as friends and acquaintances in class terms (the extent to which middle-class people tend to socialize with middle-class people, working-class people with working-class people, and so on);
- Societal and community status and prestige: embodied, achieved, and ascribed.

Behaviour

- Consumption patterns: choice of shops, buying brands or not, ecological/organic consumption, etc.;
- Symbolic behaviour (e.g., how one moves one's body, the clothes one wears, the way one speaks, how one eats);
- Pastimes: golf, skiing, cockfighting, online for participation.

Life conditions

- Political life: one's relative position in hierarchies of power in society;
- Quality of life: in terms of physical and psychological comfort and health;
- Type of neighbourhood: a working-class neighbourhood, a middle-class neighbourhood, an area in the process of gentrification.

Spatial conditions

- Mobility: physical movement, from highly local to global;
- Proximity to other people during a range of day-to-day activities;
- Dimensions and size of space occupied: layout of dwelling or place of work, size of bedroom; size of office, etc.;
- Type of dwelling: trailer, house (detached/semidetached), flat (studio, small, large), etc.

Adopting this broad view of class is not without its problems and 'handle with care' seems to be a good caveat to insert at this point. I say this not least because the model itself is under a constant state of revision (compare this version to one appearing in Block 2012) as my cumulative reading about class in different contexts across time leads me to add, delete, and reorder the various dimensions listed under the five headings (and the five headings are, of course, subject to revision). In addition, there is a degree of conceptual and categorical slippage in the conflation of more material aspects with more cultural, status-oriented ones, and the relative acceptability of combining what in effect are Marxist and Weberian perspectives. This issue of Marx/Weber commensurability vs. incommensurability has been the subject of a great deal of debate for some time (e.g., Giddens 1973; Wright 1985), although space does not allow a thorough treatment here (see Block 2014 for a discussion). It reminds us of the complexity of class as something of a moving target which evolves as societies themselves evolve.

Social class in migration research

However it is understood, class has had a chequered history in migration research, past and present (Wu and Liu 2014), and there has not been a sustained strand of research on migration situated firmly within a political economy frame, where political economy is understood to be the study of the relationships between the individual and society, on the one hand, and the market and the state, on the other, as well as how social institutions, activities, and the economy are interconnected (Block 2017). Nor has there been a clear line of research, philosophically grounded in the work of Marx, Weber, Bourdieu, and other scholars who have focused on class, which frames social relations related to migrant experiences in societies in terms of this construct. For scholars such as Glick Schiller (2010) and Wu and Liu (2014), the turn to transnationalism as the focal point of research is at least partially to blame, as migration has come to be understood almost entirely in sociocultural terms while a more political economy–based angle has been left out of the equation. Migration research has, therefore, tended to marginalise issues such as 'the differences and tensions between co-ethnic employers and migrant workers in terms of value system, resource access, social behaviours and uneven distribution of income and profits, which have been reinforced by the uneven effects of globalization' (Wu and Liu 2014: 1392).

Of course, there have been exceptions to this trend over the years (e.g., Castles and Kosack 1973; Piore 1979; Portes and Zhou 1993; de Genova 2005; Wills et al. 2010). For example, in *Immigrant Workers and Class Structure in Western Europe*, Castles and Kosack focused on four wealthy industrialized Western European societies (Germany, France, Switzerland, and the UK) which by the late 1960s had received a substantial number of immigrants from southern European (e.g., Greece, Italy, Portugal, and Spain) and non-European countries. Among the latter group were immigrants from ex-colonial national states (e.g., migrants from South Asia and the Caribbean going to the UK; migrants from North Africa going to France) as well as countries like Turkey. This wave of immigration came on the back of the economic boom in Western Europe, which began to take shape in the 1950s, generating labour shortages in key sectors of the economy. While some of these new arrivals competed with the local working class for skilled and semi-skilled manual jobs in factories and in construction, a good proportion took unskilled poorly paid manual jobs, such as cleaning and serving, which local workers would no longer do.

Migrants faced discrimination on several fronts. First, they had to deal with employers who refused to hire anyone who was not local (and white). And when they were hired, newly arrived migrants found that they were expected to do the jobs that local workers refused to do. In addition, even when migrant workers were deemed to be performing well, they were often denied promotion and pay raises simply because they were migrants. Discrimination also meant that migrants were more often than not excluded from trade unions, which faced the difficult balancing act between catering to the indigenous white working class and extending class solidarity to newly arrived migrants. To make matters worse, migrants were especially vulnerable to threats by employers, who could fire them and thus jeopardize their access to housing or even their permanence in their host countries. For these and other reasons, migrants lived in a constant state of tension provoked by their extreme vulnerability, which turned them into what in effect was a version of Marx's (1990) 'reserve army', more willing to take lower wages and put up with poor work conditions than indigenous workers.

Wills et al.'s (2010) *Global Cities at Work: New Migrant Divisions of Labour* is a more recent publication focusing on the 'invisible' migrant workforce which carries out the low-level service work, from cleaning to caring to serving, in London and other global cities. The authors discuss the dramatic demographic changes which have taken place in globalised environments around the world, in particular in a city like London, where the figures for the foreign-born population had risen to over thirty percent by the beginning of the 21st century. There are important resonances between the earlier work of Castles and Kosack (as well as that of Piore 1979; Portes and Zhou 1993; de Genova 2005) and Wills et al., not least the ways that newly arrived migrants are inserted into local labour markets and how particular job sectors become racialised. As a result of this rapid influx of newcomers, the authors note how

> London's labour market is now exhibiting clear signs both of occupational polarisation – with a growing proportion of both very highly paid and very poorly paid jobs – and of bifurcation at the bottom end, with high levels of economic inactivity sitting alongside a growth in the proportion of those in low-paid work, many of whom have seen their real wages *fall* in recent years.
>
> *(Wills et al. 2010: 37)*

Workforces thus become categorised in national and racial terms as employers' hiring practices are mediated by an elaborate web of theories about different groups of workers based on their attributed and sometimes self-embraced nationality and racial phenotypes. Thus migrants may be classified as not being up to the task of doing certain jobs while they may be deemed to be harder working than the local population, thus resulting in discrimination against the latter when workers are hired.

These two examples provide us with a flavour of what a political economic perspective on migration can provide. Migrants are presented not only in terms of their nationality, their race, their ethnicity and culture, or in terms of how they are situated in established gendered hierarchies, but also in terms of the material conditions of their lives and how they are inserted into existing class systems both in their countries of origin and their current host countries. This is an intersectional approach to both class and identity, in that it shows us how any exploration of individual or collective identity must necessarily include attention to how multiple dimensions interrelate. The result of such an approach is a richer representation of the migrant experience and narratives which are more explanatory of why migrants live the lives that they live. However, as I noted earlier, such an approach has been a minority strand in migration studies at best, even if the way forward to more publications in this line can be found in recent publications such as Parella, Petroff, and Solé (2013), writing about the upward occupational mobility of immigrant women in Spain, and Rutten and Verstappen (2014), writing about the experiences of middle-class Indian youth in London.

Social class and MIL research

If an approach to migration from a political economic perspective has been on the whole lacking in sociology, it has been virtually non-existent in applied linguistics.

There is, to be sure, a fairly well-established strand in the field which focuses on MIL issues (e.g., Norton 2000, 2013; Kanno 2003; Block 2006; Byrd-Clark 2007; Bigelow 2010), although, as I note elsewhere (Block 2014), none of this literature is undergirded by an explicit and well-developed political economy frame with a specific focus on social class. And even in collections which at least mention political economy or are purportedly immersed in it (e.g., Duchêne, Moyer, and Roberts 2013; Pietikainen and Kelly-Holmes 2013), there is usually very little explicit focus on class. In what follows, I will examine three specifically migrant-focused examples which somewhat buck this trend, albeit in a very modest way.

Bonny Norton's (2000, 2013) ground-breaking *Identity and Language Learning* contains a somewhat indirect incorporation of class into the analysis and interpretation of the language-mediated lives of migrants. I say this because while class does manage to get a look-in, it is not theorised to any degree anywhere in the book. Norton focused on a cohort of five immigrant women in Canada over a period of fifteen months in 1990–1991, examining the interrelationship between identity and power in the women's access to and use of English in classroom and naturalistic settings. In two cases, she invoked class, more specifically what we might call *declassing* and *reclassing*, as key mediating factors in the relative access that her informants had to English-speaking networks. While *declassing* refers to changes in one's life conditions and reference points, specifically the loss of the economic power and prestige and status which previously marked one's class position, *reclassing* is about the reconfiguration and realignment of class position in society due to changes in one's life conditions (Block 2014). The first case which shows this class movement in action is that of Katarina, a Polish woman in her mid-thirties, who had recently immigrated with her husband. Katarina had an MA in Biology and claimed proficiency in Czech, Slovak, Russian, and German. However, she and he husband spoke no English upon their arrival in Canada, and this meant that they were divested of their professional identities and self-images. Katarina was all too aware of her situation and the role of her lack of English language competence in it, and she was eager to work her way out of it, learning English while taking jobs well below her level of qualifications. The second case in which declassing figured in Norton's analysis was that of Felicia, a Peruvian woman in her mid-forties, who had moved to Canada with her husband and three children. Like Katarina, Felicia felt aggrieved with regard to the move to Canada, lamenting what she and her family had given up not only in economic and comfort terms, but also in terms of their relative status in society and overall quality of life. Especially hard hit was her husband, whom Felicia presented as a successful businessman who had provided the family with a high standard of living in Peru, but who in Canada was hardly able to find a job. Felicia concluded that Canada was not a good country for wealthy and educated people like herself, but that it was good for what she called 'some kinds of immigrants', whom she defined as 'people who lived in countries under communism . . . or people who never had anything in their countries' (Norton 2000: 56).

Some twelve years after Norton's study, I carried out research on Spanish-speaking Latinos in London, and in my data analysis I situated class more centrally, even if on my current standards I did not go far enough. In the lengthiest account of this research (Block 2006), I noted how Carlos, a well-educated Colombian who was married to a British woman proficient in both English and Spanish, lived his personal life as a middle-class, transnational, cosmopolitan Spanish speaker. This despite the fact that his job was in the relatively low-skilled service sector (he was a porter in a large building in central London), thus making him a classic example of the kind of *declassing* and *reclassing* that comes with migration discussed earlier. With reference to the workplace, I note how Carlos was never completely at ease with his work colleagues, all white working-class Londoners, even if he did acquire basic survival strategies, among other things learning how to engage in teasing banter in English. In addition, working intersectionally, I show how Carlos's physical appearance (in British census terms, he was 'mixed race': his father was black and his mother was *Indígena*), his national identity (Colombian) and his middle-class interests and pastimes (which included reading, going to the cinema and relatively frequent weekend trips to European cities, all of which he could afford because he and his wife owned property which they rented), created a degree of dissonance and tension among his colleagues. The latter alternated between positioning him either as the dark immigrant from a dangerous country associated with drugs and violence, or as the embodiment of middle-class values and interests which were, on the whole, anathema to them. In the end, Carlos was never going to fit in and indeed he never did, leaving for a better job in a hospital a year after my contacts with him.

Elsewhere, Stephanie Vandrick has focused on a very different type of migrant experience, that of what she initially called 'privileged international students' (Vandrick 1995) and later referred to as 'students of the new global elite' (Vandrick 2011). In both cases, we are in the realm of young adults who 'are comfortable with privilege and know they will return to their countries and step into positions of power, wealth, and influence' (Vandrick 1995: 375). However, the use of 'new' in Vandrick's more recent work seems to be an attempt to capture the way that since the 1990s privileged students have become that much more privileged and that beyond being more cosmopolitan than the majority of their fellow students (privileged international students always have been), they are *extremely more cosmopolitan*. Thus,

> they have lived, studied, and vacationed in various places throughout the world; they may carry passports or permanent visas from more than one country; their parents may have homes and businesses in more than one country; they may speak several languages; they have often been educated at Western high schools – frequently boarding schools – and colleges.
>
> *(Vandrick 2011: 160)*

Ultimately, these students will take their places as full-fledged members of what scholars such as Sklair (2001) and Carrol (2010) have called the 'transnational capitalist classes', that is, the movers and shakers of 21st-century capitalism.

What can we glean from this brief review of three example studies in which the authors have introduced class to some degree in their attempts to make sense of MIL experiences? Two things come to mind. First, I would say that the three studies show that there is something to be gained by taking such an approach, both in terms of refined theoretical understandings of MIL *and* the educational policies and practices which might derive from research. Second, such work needs to be more firmly embedded in general work in political economy and sociology, which focuses on the intersection between migration on the one hand, and inequality, stratification and class on the other. Nevertheless, these are just two general points. There are, to be sure, bigger issues remaining around class and how it intersects with various phenomena related to migration, such as multiculturalism and multilingualism in contemporary societies. I turn to a consideration of some of these issues in the next section.

Issues and ongoing debates

As I suggested above, situating class as central in research on migration in general, and MIL research in particular, is not an entirely unproblematic enterprise. Indeed, there are a number of issues which are in need of consideration before proceeding. First, we must understand that any version of class, such as the one I presented earlier, is as I have noted necessarily partial and incomplete, as it is always possible to think of new dimensions to add to the list. Class-centred research is therefore always organised around a provisional category in need of constant revision. Second, there is the need to examine how the different dimensions of class outlined above tend to co-occur in individuals, or 'crystallize' (Grusky and Ku 2008). Thus being from a wealthy background is usually closely related to (i.e., it crystallizes around) other upscale dimensions such as political power, high status and prestige in society, a spacious home in a good neighbourhood, high income and accumulated wealth, ownership of multiple dwellings and material possessions, membership in legitimized and respected social groupings (social networking), and good health (quality of life). Meanwhile, being from a poor background is usually closely related to the opposite: low political power, low status and prestige in society, a small home in a rough neighbourhood, and so on. In order to exemplify this contrast applied to migrants, we need only go back to Vandrick's (2011) research to see how her informants embody the former values for key class dimensions, while the informants in Wills et al. (2010) are carriers of the latter values.

A third issue to consider is intersectionality, defined earlier, which reminds that any exploration of individual or collective identity must necessarily include attention to how multiple dimensions – such as race, ethnicity, gender, nationality, sexuality, religion, disability, and so on – interrelate and shape each other. Intersectionality arose out of black feminist scholarship from the mid-1970s onwards (e.g., Combahee River Collective 1977; hooks 1981; Crenshaw 1989), and much intersectional work has focused on the confluence of race (and ethnicity) and gender in the lives of individuals (but see hooks 2000 for an interesting triangulated discussion of race, gender, *and* class). However, it is also possible to research identity by starting with social class and examining how it intersects with (and is intersected by) the aforementioned identity dimensions (Block and Corona 2014, 2016).

Related to intersectionality, there is question of emphasis, and here we come to a distinction to be made between class and the identity dimensions cited earlier. As Nancy Fraser (1995) noted two decades ago, in the second half of the 20th century a culture-based view of identity and society came to the fore in many parts of the world and this led to the rise of 'identity politics' as the focal point of debate and as central to understanding how people lived together in increasingly more complex societies. Fraser juxtaposes the emphasis on 'recognition' with an interest in redistribution (understood as the structuring and allocation of material resources in an equitable fashion) and she notes how the former has come to take precedence over the latter in public debates and in in the social sciences and humanities. Fraser does not propose the abandonment of recognition claims, but she does argue for the need to explore how these recognition claims intersect with material inequalities arising from capitalism – both globally and locally – and vice versa.

Dealt with separately or in an intersected way, recognition and redistribution can be treated in two very different ways. On the one hand, they can be subjected to 'affirmative' action, which provides 'remedies aimed at inequitable outcomes of social arrangements without disturbing the underlying framework that generates them' (Fraser 2008: 28). With recognition, this is what happens when diversity and difference are supported, promoted and provided legal guarantees in more self-consciously multicultural societies. An example of affirmative action applied to redistribution would be what happens when social democracy is practiced, for example when tax money is used to finance the provision of resources and services to citizens. In neither case is anything done to deal with underlying conditions which lead to misrecognition or the existence of economic inequality. Thus, for Fraser, affirmation can never be enough if we wish to do something about the roots of injustice and inequality in society. For this to happen, 'transformative' action is necessary. Such action provides 'remedies aimed at correcting inequitable outcomes precisely by restructuring the underlying generative framework' (Fraser 2008: 28). Transformative recognition would mean problematizing and undermining group differentiations, such as gay vs. straight, male vs. female, black vs. white and so on. Meanwhile, transformative redistribution would mean a deep restructuring of the political economy of a nation-state, that is, the arrival of socialism.

In general, migration and MIL research has tended to adopt a purely recognition-oriented agenda, although in the case of research which intersects social class with migrant subjectivities, race, ethnicity, gender, and nationality (see Block and Corona 2014, 2016; see more on this later), the emphasis is as much on redistribution as it is on recognition. In such research, a more robust account of how inequality emerges and occurs is needed, on the way to proposing transformative strategies (although we must be reminded that one publication does not a revolution make!). Indeed, there is the additional issue of the impact that a class-centred approach to MIL research might have, a topic to which I turn in the next section.

Implications

Working from political economy and focusing on social class as central to understandings of being in contemporary societies together have serious consequences for how research on MIL is framed. First of all, it means working in an interdisciplinary manner, drawing on research and scholarship in political economy and social class on the one hand, and applied linguistics research on MIL on the other. There is, therefore, an attempt to link a long list of political economic phenomena, such as aggregate economic activity, resource allocation, capital accumulation and income inequality, with notions that have for some time formed part of the lexicon of applied linguists, such as mobility, migration, space, sociocultural activity, and communication. Interdisciplinary research, if done thoroughly and with rigour, is not easy and requires reading a good number of sources outside one's area of inquiry.

Working from political economy and focusing on social class also means reconsidering how we position ourselves with regard to ontology and epistemology: ontology refers to what we consider to be the nature of being and existence, our 'actual reality' and what it is we are studying, researching and writing about, while epistemology refers to what we consider to be the origin, nature, and limits of human knowledge, and how we come to 'know it'. Political economy and social class research are based on realist philosophies, which are in conflict with poststructuralist approaches which have become dominant in MIL research. As Patsy Duff notes,

> Poststructuralism is an approach to research that questions fixed categories or structures, oppositional binaries, closed systems, and stable truths and embraces seeming contradictions. . . . Poststructural researchers examine how such categories are discursively and socially constructed, taken up, resisted (the site of struggle), and so on.
> *(Duff 2012: 412)*

Postructuralism is usually positioned as being in direct opposition to positivism, which *is* about 'fixed categories or structures, oppositional binaries, closed systems, and stable truths', and above all control of variables and prediction. In his elaboration of a critical realist approach to the social sciences, Roy Bhaskar takes on part of the poststructuralist agenda when he writes that the social sciences are about 'the direct study of phenomena that only ever manifest themselves in open systems [in which] invariant empirical regularities do not obtain' (Bhaskar 1998: 45) and which are 'characterised by both a plurality and multiplicity of causes' (Bhaskar 1998: 87). His critical realist approach thus eschews accurate prediction as a goal, not least because social phenomena cannot be accessed at the level at which they are generated, in isolation from the effects which they cause, as is the case with some physical phenomena. However, embedded in what Bhaskar writes is the notion that there are deep-down causal mechanisms at work in the social world which exist independent of our ability to know and understand them. Indeed, Bhaskar criticises poststructuralists for committing what he calls the 'epistemic fallacy', which takes social constructivism to the extreme of conflating representations of social reality, as social constructed or discursively constructed, with social reality *itself*, thereby reducing ontology to epistemology. As Bhaskar

(1989: 17–18) puts it, 'statements about being cannot be reduced to or analysed in terms of statements about knowledge . . . [and] ontological questions cannot always be transposed into epistemological terms.' The way forward, according to Bhaskar, is to adopt his critical realist perspective, according to which:

> there is no inconsistency between being an ontological realist . . . believing that there is a real world which consists in structures, generative mechanisms, all sorts of complex things and totalities which exist and act independently of the scientist, which the scientist can come to have knowledge of . . . [and] saying that that knowledge is itself socially produced; it is a geo-historically specific social process, so it is continually in transformation.
>
> *(Bhaskar 2002: 211)*

Scholars in political economy and social class research adopt a view of the world which is consistent with Bhaskar's critical realism, and in this sense they may be considered, at a minimum, default critical realists. My reason for introducing critical realism into the discussion at this point is my belief that a key implication of developing MIL research in an interdisciplinary manner (in this case bringing political economy and social class into our discussion of MIL) is the need to be cognizant of the epistemological and ontological frames within which source authors are working. It is simply not enough to cherry-pick a few ideas; researchers need to engage more deeply with the disciplines they are intersecting with, even if in doing so they are led into a kind of epistemological and ontological dissonance that causes them to change their way of understanding the world and how it works.

Future directions

The future MIL research that emerges from everything discussed thus far in this chapter will be based on the idea that migration is a complex phenomenon which is more transnational in nature than it is international or even national. Migrants themselves will be understood in terms of race, ethnicity, nationality, gender, sexuality, religion, and other dimensions, as well as varieties of intersectional combinations of these dimensions. An interdisciplinary approach to the topic will mean drawing on political economy and research on social class to develop a fuller social understanding of migration processes and the lives of migrants. Class will be understood as a complex multidimensional phenomenon constituted and indexed by a long list of economic, sociocultural, behavioural, and spatial and life conditions. The result will be research which starts with political economy and class as the central construct and work outward to the aforementioned identity dimensions.

Victor Corona and I have attempted to do just this in recent years (e.g., Block and Corona 2014, 2016), as we have drawn on Corona's research focusing on the life experiences of male Latino adolescents in Barcelona (Corona 2012). The parents of these boys immigrated to Barcelona during the economic boom in Spain, which lasted from the mid-1990s until the economic crisis of 2007/2008 began to take its toll. Lacking in economic resources (property, wealth) and sociocultural resources (education, skills, technological know-how, social contacts, societal status), many took jobs in the low-level services sectors, such as cleaning, deliveries, and home care, as well as in construction, and their adolescent children were on the way to similar work when the economic crisis began. Corona's research does not cover the crisis and its aftermath, but it does provide an excellent snapshot of the ways in which his informants lived their lives and were constructed (by others) in terms of race, ethnicity, nationality, and gender. My role in our ongoing collaboration has been to inject a more political economic and class-based analysis which starts from social class and then works into race, ethnicity, nationality, and gender. One interesting aspect of this approach is that it allows us to see how the coping strategies adopted by Corona's informants serve to reproduce the lower class positions of their parents and how any kind of upward mobility becomes virtually impossible. This is the case because these boys, like the 'lads' in Paul Willis's (1977) oft-cited study of working-class adolescent masculinities in 1970s Britain, do not take school seriously, abandoning their studies at the earliest opportunity (i.e., at the age of 16). Meanwhile, they engage in behaviour and embody semiotic forms which convey hard working-class masculinities. Intertwined with the latter is the adoption of new forms of Spanish as the normal means of communication (Corona, Nussbaum, and Unamuno 2013) and a rejection of Catalan, marked as the official language of Catalan institutions (from education to politics) and seen as a sell-out to middle-class values (Corona 2012). Meanwhile, in society at large, the boys are racialised, as having what is known in mainstream society as 'a South American appearance', which in turn indexes relative poverty, a position at the bottom of the Catalan economic ladder and society, possible illegal and/or violent behaviour, and ultimately a kind of erasure from mainstream polity. In effect, the MIL narrative which emerges is a class-based one embedded in the political economy of contemporary Catalonia.

Summary

The example in the previous section brings to an end this chapter, in which I have attempted to develop in more detail Collins's (2006) critique of the lack of class (and political economy) in most MIL research. After dealing with some theoretical background on migration, transnationalism and social class, I have examined how class has been a key construct in some migration and MIL research, although as I note, in both areas of inquiry, class has generally suffered a form of conceptual erasure (Block 2014). This is the case not least because researchers have tended to focus exclusively on issues around recognition (Fraser 1995) and have marginalised a more political economic perspective on society which prioritises redistribution. My remedy for what I see as a gap in MIL research is for researchers to take on board a political economy agenda in their work and to seek out ways in which class intersects with race, ethnicity, gender, nationality, and other identity dimensions in the lives of their informants. Of course, taking this step means taking on board the problematics of class-based research and I have discussed a few salient issues in this chapter in need of resolution. It also means situating class as a core and central baseline aspect of being and belonging in contemporary societies, an epistemological position which may be anathema to many readers of this chapter. As I suggested earlier, moving in this direction is not a matter of conducting blitzkrieg raids on political economy (or sociology, anthropology, or geography, for that matter) to pick up an idea or two; rather, interdisciplinary inquiry is serious business which requires more than a light engagement with what in all likelihood are new ideas and above all, conceptual frameworks. There are also deeper philosophical issues to consider, around ontology and epistemology, which I discuss here. And out of this consideration comes a very important question: can one be a poststructuralist and still carry out research framed in the critical realism, de facto or otherwise, which is so foundational to current work in political economy? My response is that one cannot have it both ways, which means that taking on board what I propose in this chapter may require a fair amount of soul-searching on the part of interested MIL researchers.

Related topics

New orientations to identity in mobility
Neoliberalism, language, and migration
Rethinking (un)skilled migrants
Language-mediated services for migrants

Further reading

De Geneva, N. (2005). *Working the Boundaries: Race, Space, and "Illegality" in Mexican Chicago*. Durham, NC: Duke University Press.

This book is not about language issues per se, but English/Spanish bilingualism is an integral part of De Geneva's portrayal of 'Mexican Chicago' as an exemplary case of how race and class intersect in the discursive construction of Mexicans as an 'undesirable' immigrant population in the United States.

Dubord, E.M. (2014). *Language, Immigration and Labor. Negotiating Work in the U.S.-Mexico Borderlands*. London: Palgrave Macmillan.

This monograph charts how newly arrived Mexican migrants in the southwest United States enter increasingly unstable labour markets. It manages to link macro-level ideologies with unfolding events on the ground, while showing how language practices are intermeshed with the construction of inequality.

Duchêne, A., Moyer, M. and Roberts, C., eds. (2013). *Language Migration and Social Inequalities: A Critical Sociolinguistic Perspective on Institutions and Work*. London: Routledge.

The contributions to this collection focus on the experiences of migrants, showing how inequality is constructed in the increasingly precarious institutional and workplace settings in which their lives unfold.

References

Basch, L., Glick Schiller, N. and Blanc-Szantson, C. (1994). *Nations Unbound: Transnational Projects, Postcolonial Predicaments, and Deterritorialized Nation-states*. London: Routledge.
Bennett, T., Savage, M., Silva, E., Warde, A., Gayo-Cal, M. and Wright, D. (2009). *Culture, Class, Distinction*. London: Routledge.
Bhaskar, R. (1989). *Reclaiming Reality*. London: Verso.
Bhaskar, R. (1998). *The Possibility of Naturalism* (3rd ed.). London: Routledge.
Bhaskar, R. (2002). *From Science to Emancipation: Alienation and the Actuality of Enlightenment*. London: Sage.
Bigelow, M. (2010). *Mogadishu on the Mississippi: Language, Racialized Identity, and Education in a New Land*. Oxford: Wiley-Blackwell.
Block, D. (2006). *Multilingual Identities in a Global City: London stories*. London: Palgrave.
Block, D. (2012). Class and second language acquisition research. *Language Teaching Research* 16(2): 188–205.
Block, D. (2014). *Social Class in Applied Linguistics*. London: Routledge.
Block, D. (2015). Identity and social class: Issues arising in applied linguistics research. *Annual Review of Applied Linguistics* 35: 1–19.
Block, D. (2016). Social class in language and identity research. In Preece, S. (ed.), *The Routledge Handbook of Language and Identity* (pp. 241–254). London: Routledge.
Block, D. (2017). Political economy in applied linguistics research. *Language Teaching* 49.
Block, D. and Corona, V. (2014). Exploring class-based intersectionality. *Language, Culture and Curriculum* 27(1): 27–42.

Block, D. and Corona, V. (2016). Intersectionality in language and identity research. In Preece, S. (ed.), *The Routledge Handbook of Language and Identity* (pp. 507–522). London: Routledge.
Bourdieu, P. (1984). *Distinction*. London: Routledge.
Byrd-Clark, J. (2007). *Multilingualism, Citizenship, and Identity: Voices of Youth and Symbolic Investments in an Urban, Globalized World*. London: Continuum.
Carroll, W.K. (2010). *The Making of a Transnational Capitalist Class: Corporate Power in the 21st Century*. London: Zed Books.
Castles, S. and Kosack, G. (1973). *Immigrant Workers and Class Structure in Western Europe*. Oxford: Oxford University Press.
Collins, J. (2006). *Where's Class in Second Language Learning?* Working papers in Urban Language & Literacies, 41, King's College London.
Combahee River Collective. (1977). *The Combahee River Collective Statement*. Retrieved from http://www.sfu.ca/iirp/documents/Combahee%201979.pdf.
Corona, V. (2012). *Globalización, identidades y escuela: lo latino en Barcelona* [Globalization, Identities and School: Latinity in Barcelona]. PhD thesis, Universitat Autònoma de Barcelona.
Corona, V., Nussbaum, L. and Unamuno, V. (2013). The emergence of new linguistic repertoires among Barcelona's youth of Latin American origin. *International Journal of Bilingual Education and Bilingualism* 16(2): 182–194.
Crenshaw, K. (1989). Demarginalizing the intersection of race and sex: A black feminist critique of antidiscrimination doctrine, feminist theory, and antiracist politics. *University of Chicago Legal Forum* 139–167.
Crompton, R. (2008). *Class and Stratification* (3rd ed.). Cambridge: Polity.
de Genova, N. (2005). *Working the Boundaries: Race, Space, and "Illegality" in Mexican Chicago*. Durham, NC: Duke University Press.
Duchêne, A., Moyer, M. and Roberts, C., eds. (2013). *Language in Late Capitalism: Pride and Profit*. London: Routledge.
Duff, P. (2012). Issues of identity. In Gass, S. and Mackey, A. (eds.), *The Routledge Handbook of Second Language Acquisition* (pp. 410–426). London: Routledge.
Durkheim, E. (1984 [1893]). *The Division of Labor in Society*. New York: Free Press.
Faist, T. (2000). *The Volume and Dynamics of International Migration*. Oxford: Oxford University Press.
Faist, T. (2013). The mobility turn: A new paradigm for the social sciences? *Ethnic and Racial Studies* 36(11): 1637–1646.
Faist, T., Fauser, M. and Reisenauer, E., eds. (2013). *Transnational Migration*. Cambridge: Polity.
Fraser, N. (1995). From redistribution to recognition? Dilemmas of justice in a "post-socialist" age. *New Left Review* 212: 68–93.
Fraser, N. (2008). *Adding Insult to Injury: Nancy Fraser Debates Her Critics?* [Edited by K. Olsen]. London: Verso.
Giddens, A. (1973). *The class structure of advanced societies*. London: Hutchinson.
Glick Schiller, N. (2010). Global perspective on migration and development. In Glick Schiller, N. and Faist, T. (eds.), *Migration, Development and Transnationalism* (pp. 22–62). Oxford: Berghahn Books.
Grieco, M. and Urry, J., eds. (2012). *Mobilities: New Perspectives on Transport and Society*. London: Ashgate.
Grusky, D. and Ku, M. (2008). Gloom, doom, and inequality. In Grusky, D. (ed.), *Social Stratification: Class, Race, and Gender in Sociological Perspective* (pp. 2–28). Boulder, CO: Westview Press.
Harvey, D. (2014). *Seventeen Contradictions and the End of Capitalism*. London: Profile Books.
hooks, b. (1981). *Ain't I a Woman: Black Women and Feminism*. Boston: South End Press.
hooks, b. (2000). *Where We Stand: Class Matters*. London: Routledge.
Jordan, B. and Düvell, F. (2003). *Migration: The Boundaries of Equality and Justice*. Cambridge: Polity.
Kanno, Y. (2003). *Negotiating Bilingual and Bicultural Identities: Japanese Returnees Betwixt Two Worlds*. Mahwah, NJ: Lawrence Erlbaum.

Lippi-Green, R. (1997/2011). *English with an Accent. Language, Ideology and Discrimination in the United States*. London: Routledge.
Marx, K. (1990 [1867]). *Capital: A Critique of Political Economy* (Vol. 1). Harmondsworth: Penguin.
Norton, B. (2000). *Identity and Language Learning: Gender, Ethnicity and Educational Change*. Harlow: Longman/Pearson Education.
Norton, B. (2013). *Identity and Language Learning: Extending the Conversation*. Bristol: Multilingual Matters.
Parella, S., Petroff, A. and Solé, C. (2013). The upward occupational mobility of immigrant women in Spain. *Journal of Ethnic and Migration Studies* 39(9): 1365–1382.
Pietikäinen, S. and Kelly-Holmes, H., eds. (2013). *Multilingualism and the Periphery*. Oxford: Oxford University Press.
Piore, M. (1979). *Birds of Passage: Migrant Labor and Industrial Societies*. Cambridge: Cambridge University Press.
Portes, A. (2010). Migration and social change: Some conceptual reflections. *Journal of Ethnic and Migration Studies* 36(10): 1537–1563.
Portes, A. and Zhou, M. (1993). The new second generation: Segmented assimilation and its variants. *Annals of the American Academy of Political and Social Sciences* 530: 74–96.
Rutten, M. and Verstappen, S. (2014). Middling migration: Contradictory mobility experiences of Indian youth in London. *Journal of Ethnic and Migration Studies* 40(8): 1217–1235.
Savage, M., Devine, F., Cunningham, N., Taylor, M., Li, Y., Hjellbrekke, J., Le Roux, B., Friedman, S. and Miles, A. (2013). A new model of social class? Findings from the BBC's Great British Class Survey experiment. *Sociology* 47: 219–250.
Sheller, M. and Urry, J. (2006). The new mobilities paradigm. *Environment and Planning* 38(2): 207–226.
Sklair, L. (2001). *The Transnational Capitalist Class*. Oxford: Wiley-Blackwell.
Taylor, C. (1994). The politics of recognition. In Gutman, A. (ed.), *Multiculturalism: Examining the Politics of Recognition* (pp. 25–73). Princeton: Princeton University Press.
Urciuoli, B. (1996). *Exposing Prejudice*. Boulder: Westview Press.
Vandrick, S. (1995). Privileged ESL University students. *TESOL Quarterly* 29: 375–381.
Vandrick, S. (2011). Students of the new global elite. *TESOL Quarterly* 45: 160–169.
Vertovec, S. (2009). *Transnationalism*. London: Routledge.
Weber, M. (1968 [1922]). *Economy and Society, Volumes 1 & 2*. Berkeley, CA: University of California Press.
Willis, P. (1977). *Learning to Labour: How Working Class Kids Get Working Class Jobs*. London: Saxon House.
Wills, J., Datta, K., Evans, Y., Herbert, J., May, J. and McIlwaine, C. (2010). *Global Cities at Work: New Migrant Divisions of Labour*. London: Pluto Press.
Wright, E.O. (1985). *Classes*. London: Verso.
Wu, B. and Liu, H. (2014). Bringing class back in: Class consciousness and solidarity among Chinese migrant workers in Italy and the UK. *Ethnic and Racial Studies* 37(8): 1391–1408.

8
National and ethnic minorities
Language rights and recognition

Stephen May

Introduction

In an increasingly globalized world, marked by transmigration, transnationalism, and the apparent porosity of national borders, debates over what constitutes (ongoing) citizenship in modern nation-states have become increasingly contested. What rights and responsibilities ensue for national citizens in this late modern, globalized age? How should nation-states respond to rapidly changing demographic patterns that reflect the rise of what Vertovec (2007) has termed "superdiversity" – the rapid ethnic and linguistic diversification of constituent national populations via migration and transmigration, particularly in major urban areas? What distinct entitlements (if any) might be accorded existing minority populations in these territories – that is, those groups who have long been associated historically with a particular territory but who, as a result of colonization, confederation, or conquest (or some combination of all three), now find themselves socially and politically marginalized? These broad groups are most often described as "national minorities" (Kymlicka 1995) and include within them the distinct subset of indigenous peoples (Xanthaki 2007; May 2012a). And what of ethnic minorities – those who have migrated to a new country and/or have been the subject of forced relocation? Do their histories of recent migration afford them any rights or recognition beyond the usual national imperatives of cultural and linguistic assimilation?

When these questions are asked, it becomes immediately apparent that issues of language use also often come to the fore. In particular:

1   Whether speaking the national language – that is, the majority or dominant language of the state – is, or should be, a *requirement* of national citizenship and a demonstration of both political and social integration by its members (especially for those who speak other languages as a first language).
2   Whether this requirement should be at the *expense* of, or in *addition* to, the maintenance of other languages – minority, or non-dominant languages, in effect – within the state. Or to put it another way, whether public monolingualism in the national language should

be enforced upon an often-multilingual population or whether some degree of public as well as private multilingualism can be supported.

Nation-states the world over have been remarkably consistent in their responses to these questions. More often than not, they opt for public monolingualism in an official or "national" language – requiring its use in all public/civic communication and thus within key formal language domains, such as education, law, and administration. In these contexts, public monolingualism in the national language is simply taken for granted by its citizens. For those remaining states with more than one officially recognized language, the predilection towards an (at most) highly delimited form of public multilingualism nonetheless remains strong. The majority of these latter states do not officially recognize more than two or three languages – certainly, the endorsement of widespread formal multilingualism remains extremely rare.[1] And even where there is an ostensibly multilingual national language(s) policy, the actuality is that one language variety (at most, two or three) still dominates in terms of its widespread use in the public domain.[2]

Following from this, citizenship in modern nation-states is also invariably linked to at least some knowledge of, and facility in, the requisite national language(s) as a key indicator or proxy of one's wider civic and national commitment (Wright 2000; Bauman and Briggs 2003; May 2008, 2012a). Those who (still) lack facility in a national language, most often ethnic minorities, are regularly chastised, and sometimes punished, by states for their "willful" failure to "integrate." For example, in the United States over the last fifteen years we have seen the widespread circumscription and subsequent dismantling of Spanish-English bilingual education programs for Latino students. The basis for this opposition has been a view that the mere recognition, let alone incorporation, of Spanish as an educational language undermines a wider commitment to learning English as the (de facto) national language of the United States and thus also to a related widespread monolingual conception of US citizenship (Schmidt 2000; Crawford 2008; May 2012a, chap. 6). Meanwhile, across Europe, multiculturalism as public policy is in apparent full retreat, as European states increasingly assert that minority groups "integrate" or accept dominant social, cultural linguistic and religious mores as the price of ongoing citizenship (Modood 2013). In relation to language, this has been demonstrated explicitly by increasingly harsh language testing regimes, which privilege national languages, and which increasingly constitute the price of citizenship in European nation-states (McNamara and Roever 2006; Extra, Spotti, and Avermaet 2009).

In this chapter, I will explore whether modern nation-states can or should formally accommodate the language varieties spoken by national and ethnic minorities within their borders and, if so, in what contexts and/or to what extent? This requires that we first address the imperative of linguistic and cultural homogeneity that underpins the current nation-state system. Second, we need to determine the differing positioning of national and ethnic minorities within these states, and related debates about any linguistic entitlements that might ensue for them. Third, we need to address how the emergence of linguistic superdiversity (i.e., the layering of newly mobile languages over previously existing languages in communities) and the increasingly hybrid language use that is its consequence, necessarily complexifies any attribution of rights or entitlements for particular language minority speech communities. This includes addressing directly how the increasingly complex and fluid multilingual repertoires of today's national and global citizens brings into question the notion of (distinct) speech communities in the first place and thus whether any language rights can be usefully accorded beyond an individual level.

Overview

Linguistic homogeneity and the nation-state system

The apparently inextricable coupling of national citizenship and national language(s) is a relatively recent historical phenomenon – the product, in turn, of the nationalism of the last few centuries and the modern nation-state system to which it gave rise (see also Park and Wee, this volume). This age of nationalism arose out of the specific historical and social developments of modernization and its concomitants – industrialization, political democracy, and universal literacy – in 18th- and 19th-century Europe. Prior to this, the feudal, dynastic, and largely agrarian societies of the day had little notion of national sentiment – those feelings of collective "national" belonging – that characterizes the modern nation (Gellner 1983; Anderson 1991).

The important distinctions between premodern and modern nations can be summarized as follows. First, modern nations tend to be equated directly with their political representation in the nation-state and its formal administrative territory. In other words, modern nations are seen as "mass" nations, based on the notion of universal enfranchisement, and with the specific goal of administrative and political representation in the form of the nation-state (Smith 1995). Second, and relatedly, the term "nation" in its modern sense embodies two interrelated meanings – the "nation" as the people living *within* a nation-state, and the "nation" as *the* nation-state (Billig 1995). Accordingly, the modern nation is viewed as both a "historical culture-community" and a "legal-political" one (Smith 1995), with the latter invariably taking precedence over the former. These two dimensions, and their coalescence in the institutionalized nation-state, are again products of the ideology of political nationalism. Thus, nationalism legitimates the construction of a particular sense of national identity for those historical culture-communities that are said to inhabit their own nation-state. This involves the exercise of *internal* political and legal jurisdiction over its citizens and the construction (or attempted construction) of a homogeneous national culture in which political and ethnic boundaries are seen to coincide (Gellner 1983).

Third, the link between the modern nation, and its institutional embodiment in the nation-state, is further predicated on the rise of a bureaucratic state organization, a capitalist economy, and a "high" literate and scientific culture; the latter based, usually, on a single and distinctive vernacular language. In contrast, previous cultural communities tended to be localized, largely illiterate, and culturally and linguistically heterogeneous (Anderson 1991; Hutchinson 1994). Indeed, as Gellner (1983) argues, in his influential account of the rise of nationalism, prior to industrialization, political forms of organization required neither the demarcation of clear territorial boundaries nor the fostering of internal integration and homogeneity. Feudal elites, for example, controlled wide territories but exercised little centralized control. Empires, larger in scale again, demanded political loyalty from their diverse people groups and acceptance of one's place in the social/political hierarchy but made little, if any, demands for cultural and linguistic homogeneity (Grillo 1998). As long as due honor was given to Caesar and taxes were paid, all was well.

In contrast, the modern industrialized society – with its literate, mobile, and occupationally specialized division of labor – required cultural and linguistic continuity and, where possible, cultural and linguistic homogeneity in order to function effectively. To this end, the development of a standardized, context-free, and unitary (national) language becomes crucial, with this in turn facilitating and reflecting the development of a "high" literate and, crucially, a perceived *common* culture. As Gellner asserts: "whereas in the past the connection [between state and culture] was thin, fortuitous, varied, loose and often minimal . . . now it [became] unavoidable. That is what nationalism is all about" (1983: 38). The result was the emergence of the current nation-state model in which cultural and political, as well as linguistic, boundaries are seen to conveniently converge. Nationalism has flourished, Gellner concludes, because "well-defined . . . and unified cultures" (1983: 55), as he puts it, offer a path to modernity, a basis of political legitimacy, and a means of shared cultural and linguistic identity.

The pre-eminence of national languages in this history of nationalism, and in the related construction of national identities, is also highlighted by Benedict Anderson:

> What the eye is to the lover – that particular, ordinary eye he or she is born with – language – whatever language history has made his or her mother tongue – is to the patriot. Through that language, encountered at mother's knee and parted only at the grave, pasts are restored, fellowships are imagined, and futures dreamed.
>
> *(1991: 154)*

Anderson is not suggesting here that national languages are somehow primordial. Rather, he is attempting to explain why national languages, which *are* clearly constructed out of the politics of nationalism, nonetheless can invoke such passion and commitment from their speakers. In this sense, a key aspect of language is "its capacity for generating imagined communities, building in effect *particular solidarities*" (1991: 133; emphasis in original). The sociolinguist Monica Heller makes a similar point when she discusses the interrelationship between language and ethnic identity in a French immersion school in Toronto, Canada:

> Language use is . . . involved in the formation of ethnic identity in two ways. First, it constrains access to participation in activities and to formation of social relationships. *Thus at a basic level language use is central to the formation of group boundaries.* Second, as children spend more and more time together they share experience, and language is a central means of making sense out of that shared experience.
>
> *(1987: 199; my emphasis)*

Language, as a communally shared good, then, serves an important boundary-marking function (Tabouret-Keller 1997; Bucholtz and Hall 2004; Fought 2006). This also helps to explain why, despite their historical recency, national languages, and related notions of cultural and linguistic homogeneity, have continued to be so closely associated with the idea of, and sociopolitical obligations attendant upon, national citizenship. Political nationalism may only be a few centuries old, but the notion of a "common" national culture and an allied unifying *state-sanctioned* and *public* national language (more rarely, a number of languages) is now seen as a sine qua non of the modern nation-state system.

Where, then, does this leave minority language speakers within modern nation-states? The usual response, historically, has been to exclude their language varieties from the public realm – delegitimizing them, in the process, as languages of little (if any) real value or worth (Wright 2000; May 2012a). This state-led "ideology of contempt" (Grillo 1989) towards other language varieties constructs them as having little linguistic, social, or utilitarian value – as relics or vestiges of antediluvian, premodern forms of communalism, in effect. Such language varieties might perhaps be tolerated in an ongoing way (only) in the private/familial domain but certainly not as public languages and/or languages of wider communication. Not surprisingly perhaps, speakers of these socially and politically *minoritized* language varieties have thus inevitably shifted over time to the dominant language(s), given the latter's apparent association with modernization, civic inclusion, and social mobility. As Nancy Dorian summarizes it: "it is the concept of the nation-state coupled with its official standard language... that has in modern times posed the keenest threat to both the identities and the languages of small [minority] communities" (1998: 18). Florian Coulmas observes, even more succinctly, that "the nation-state [system] is the natural enemy of minorities" (1998: 67).

Issues and ongoing debates

Language rights in international law

The privileging of state-sanctioned, national languages, an allied predilection for cultural and linguistic homogeneity, and the consequent public delimiting of the use of other minoritized language varieties in the public domain, have also been reinforced by developments in international law, particularly post–World War II. These developments, most clearly encapsulated in the (1948) United Nations Universal Declaration of Human Rights (UDHR), focus on individual rather than group-based human rights as the basis for human rights. Following from this, language rights in international law post–World War II have been viewed primarily as *individual* rights for the protection of ongoing language use in the private domain rather than a group/communal language right to language use and support in the public realm.

The sociolinguist Heinz Kloss (1971, 1977) captures this distinction in his use of the terms "tolerance-oriented language rights" and "promotion-oriented language rights." For Kloss, tolerance-oriented rights ensure the right to preserve one's language in the private, non-governmental sphere of national life. These rights may be narrowly or broadly defined. They include the right of individuals to use their first language (L1) at home and in public, freedom of assembly and organization, the right to establish private cultural, economic, and social institutions wherein the L1 may be used, and the right to foster one's L1 in private schools. The key principle of such rights is that the state does "not interfere with efforts on the parts of the minority to make use of [their language] in the private domain" (Kloss 1977: 2).

In contrast, promotion-oriented rights regulate the extent to which language rights are recognized within the public domain, or civic realm of the nation-state. As such, they involve "public authorities [in] trying to promote a minority [language] by having it used in public institutions – legislative, administrative and educational, including the public schools" (1977: 2). Again, such rights may be narrowly or widely applied. At their narrowest, promotion-oriented rights might simply involve the publishing of public documents in minority languages. At their broadest, promotion-oriented rights could involve recognition of a minority language in all formal domains within the nation-state, thus allowing the minority language group "to care for its internal affairs through its own public organs, which amounts to the [state] allowing self government for the minority group" (1977: 24). The latter position would require, for example, the provision of state-funded minority language education *as of right*.

The key challenge for any recognition of promotion-oriented language rights in international law – particularly for minoritized language speakers – is that it also necessarily entails a *communal* right to language, something which the UDHR specifically disavows. In effect, those who identify as speaking a minoritized or non-dominant language – even when this has been long associated with a particular territory – have no *automatic* right to the support of their language varieties in the public domain. This antipathy to promotion-oriented language rights, particularly for minority/minoritized groups, was the result of an emerging widespread conviction at the time of the formulation of the UDHR that minority group rights were somehow incompatible with national and international peace and stability. As Claude has observed of these developments:

> The doctrine of human rights has been put forward as a substitute for the concept of minority rights, with the strong implication that minorities whose members enjoy individual equality of treatment cannot legitimately demand facilities for the maintenance of their ethnic particularism.
> *(1955: 211)*

Language rights are especially prone here to ongoing associations with the (unnecessary) promotion of ethnic particularism (see Park and Wee, this volume) at the perceived expense of wider social and political cohesion. As the prominent sociolinguist Joshua Fishman ably summarizes this view:

> Unlike "human rights" which strike Western and Westernized intellectuals as fostering wider participation in general societal benefits and interactions, "language rights" still are widely interpreted as "regressive" since they would, most probably, prolong the existence of ethnolinguistic differences. The value of such differences and the right to value such differences have not yet generally been recognized by the modern Western sense of justice.
> *(1991: 72)*

As a result, minority language rights were largely subsumed within the broader definition of human rights adopted by the UDHR. Individualized human rights were thought, in themselves, to provide sufficient protection for minorities, including (and, perhaps especially) for linguistic minorities.

National minorities

This generalist position on human rights remains prominent some seventy years on. However, more recent developments in international law, particularly in the post–Cold War era, have begun to modify this position somewhat (Preece 1998). This is particularly so for those who have come to be termed "national minorities" in international law. As the political theorist Will Kymlicka (1995) describes it, national minorities are those who have been long associated with a particular territory but who, for reasons of conquest, confederation, or colonization (or some combination of all three), now find themselves as a sociopolitical minority within their respective nation-states. These groups include, for example, the Welsh in Britain, Catalans and Basques in Spain, Bretons in France, Québécois in Canada, and some Latino groups (e.g., Puerto Ricans) in the United States, to name but a few. They also include indigenous peoples, who are emerging in international law as a distinct subset of national minorities more broadly (May and Aikman 2003; Xanthaki 2007; May 2013).

A number of key legal instruments have thus since allowed for *prospective* promotion-oriented language rights for those identified as national minorities, including, by extension, the right to L1 education. One of the first examples of this is the United Nations Declaration on the Rights of Persons Belonging to National or Ethnic or Religious Minorities, adopted in December 1992. This UN Declaration, contra the premises underpinning the UDHR, recognizes that the promotion and protection of the rights of persons belonging to minorities actually contributes to the political and social *stability* of the states in which they live (Preamble):

> Persons belonging to national or ethnic, religious and linguistic minorities . . . have the right to enjoy their own culture, to profess and practise their own religion, and to use their own language, in private *and in public*, freely and without interference or any form of discrimination.
>
> *(Article 2.1; my emphasis)*

Significantly, the formulation recognizes that minority language varieties may be spoken in the public as well as the private domain, without fear of discrimination. That said, the 1992 UN Declaration remains a recommendation and not a binding covenant – in the end, it is up to individual nation-states to decide if they wish to comply with its precepts. In a similar vein, the actual article which deals with minority language education (Article 4.3) qualifies the more general positive intent of Article 2.1 considerably: "States *should* take *appropriate* measures so that, *wherever possible*, persons belonging to minorities have *adequate* opportunities to learn their mother tongue *or* to have instruction in their mother tongue" (see Skutnabb-Kangas 2000: 533–535 for an extended discussion).

Another significant example of the recognition of an emerging promotion-oriented language right for national minorities can be found in the (2007) United Nations Declaration on the Rights of Indigenous Peoples (UNDRIP). The UNDRIP was formulated over a twenty-five-year period. This included the development over more than ten years of the (1993) Draft Declaration by the Working Group on Indigenous Populations (WGIP), in turn a part of the United Nation's Sub-commission on the Prevention of Discrimination and Protection of Minorities. The merits of the Draft Declaration were subsequently debated for nearly fifteen years, with many UN member states raising substantive and repeated objections to its promotion of greater self-determination for indigenous peoples (see Xanthaki 2007 for a useful overview). Despite these objections, UNDRIP retained its strong assertion of indigenous rights, *including* specific promotion-oriented language and education rights. Article 14.1 states, for example, that "Indigenous peoples have the right to establish and control their educational systems and institutions providing education in their own languages, in a manner appropriate to their cultural methods of teaching and learning." Nonetheless, individual nation-states are still able to decide the degree to which they actively support these principles and whether and to what extent they subsequently implement them in practice for their indigenous peoples.

A third example is the 1992 European Charter for Regional or Minority Languages. It provides a sliding scale of educational provision for national and regional minority languages (but not immigrant languages) which ranges from a minimal entitlement for smaller groups – preschool provision only, for example – through to more generous rights for larger minority groups such as primary and secondary language education. Again, however, nation-states have discretion in what they provide, on the basis of both local considerations and the size of the group concerned. European nation-states also retain considerable scope and flexibility over which articles of the Charter they actually choose to accept in the first place. In this respect, they are only required to accede to thirty-five out of sixty-eight articles, although three of the thirty-five articles must refer to education (Grin 2003).

A similar pattern can be detected in the 1994 Framework Convention for the Protection of National Minorities, which was adopted by the Council of Europe in November 1994 and came into force in February 1998. The Framework Convention allows for a wide range of tolerance-based rights towards national minorities, including language and education rights.

It also asserts at a more general level that contributing states should "promote the conditions necessary for persons belonging to national minorities to maintain and develop their culture, and to preserve the essential elements of their identity, namely their religion, language, traditions and cultural heritage" (Article 2.1). That said, the specific provisions for language and education remain sufficiently qualified for most states to avoid them if they so choose (see e.g., Nic Craith 2006; Trenz 2007).

Developments in international law for national minorities are at once both encouraging and disappointing. The principle of separate minority recognition in language and education is legally enshrined at least as a minimal tolerance-oriented right – that is, when restricted to the private domain. However the more promotion-oriented rights for national minorities that have been canvassed over the last twenty to thirty years still remain largely dependent on the largesse of individual nation-states in their interpretation of international (and national) law.

Ethnic minorities

But what of ethnic minorities? Ethnic minorities, in common parlance, comprise voluntary migrants and (involuntary) refugees living in a new national context – the result of increasingly complex processes of migration, transmigration, and forced relocation in this late modern world. These groups may retain elements of their culture, language, and traditions – sometimes over the course of a number of generations – in the new host society. However, their general aim is to integrate into the host society and to be(come) accepted as full members of it. As such, ethnic minorities can be distinguished from national minorities/indigenous peoples because their ethnic and cultural distinctiveness is manifested primarily in the private domain and is not inconsistent with their institutional integration into the nation-state (Kymlicka 1995).

This does not mean, however, that ethnic minorities are quiescent or accede to processes of assimilation into the dominant national language(s) and culture of their new nation-states. Far from it – as the politics of multiculturalism over the last fifty years (and despite recent retrenchments; see later) clearly attest (Kymlicka 2007; May 2009; Modood 2013). Rather, ethnic minorities are increasingly arguing for a more *plural* and *inclusive* conception of national identity and culture, which recognizes their contribution to and influence on the historical and contemporary development of the host nation-state. In the process, the boundaries of nationhood – what it is that constitutes the national community – is opened up for debate. Of central concern in this debate are the questions of who is (and who is not) to be included in the national collectivity, and on what (and whose) terms are the criteria for inclusion to be based. For our purposes, it also raises the key question of what to do with their language varieties and whether ethnic minorities might also have access to some public recognition and support of their language varieties (à la promotion-oriented language rights).

This is important because, unlike national minorities/indigenous peoples, ethnic minorities continue, largely, to be ignored as rights holders – both by individual nation-states and in supranational/international legal instruments – when it comes to promotion-oriented language (and education) rights. We saw this, for example, in the specific exclusion of ethnic minorities from the remit of the 1992 European Charter for Regional or Minority Languages, discussed earlier. These tendencies have resulted in national and ethnic minorities continuing to be treated quite separately in relation to language and education rights, despite their coterminous presence in modern nation-states. This dichotomization between national and ethnic minorities has been further entrenched with the general retreat post-9/11 from multiculturalism as public policy across both North America and Europe (May 2009; Modood 2013).

The retreat from multiculturalism as public policy notwithstanding, key proponents of multiculturalism still offer a useful way forward in (potentially) addressing the language and education rights of ethnic minorities. To this end, Kymlicka (1995, 2001, 2007) provides a useful further distinction between the rights attributable to national and ethnic minorities. Kymlicka argues that in addition to the civil rights available to all individuals, two additional forms of group-specific rights should be recognized in liberal democracies: (1) self-government rights and (2) polyethnic rights[3] (1995: 26–33). Self-government rights acknowledge that the nation-state is not the sole preserve of the majority (national) group and that legitimate national minorities have the right to equivalent inclusion and representation in the civic realm. We have seen the nascent development of this view in international law, as discussed in the previous section. Where national minorities have also been recognized within existing nation-states, multinational and/or multilingual federalism has been the most common process of political accommodation that has been adopted. An obvious example here is the degree of autonomy given to French-speaking Québec as part of a federal (and predominantly Anglophone) Canada. The establishment of seventeen regional "autonomías," including Catalonia and the Basque Country, in the post-Franco multinational Spanish state is another clear example. Self-government rights, then, typically involve the devolution of political power to members of a national minority who are usually, but not always, located in a particular historical territory. The key in providing for such rights is their *permanent* status. They are not seen as a temporary measure or remedy that may one day be revoked.

Polyethnic rights also challenge the hegemonic construction of the nation-state but for a different clientele and to different ends. Polyethnic rights are intended to help ethnic minorities to continue to express their cultural, linguistic, and/or religious heritage, principally in the private domain, without it hampering their success within the economic and political institutions of the dominant national society. One might add here that these rights are also available so that an undue burden of cultural and linguistic loss and/or change is not placed upon such groups (Kymlicka 2001; May 2012a). Like self-government rights, polyethnic rights are thus also seen as permanent, since they seek to protect rather than eliminate cultural and linguistic differences. However, their principal purpose is to promote integration *into* the larger society (and to contribute to and modify that society as a result) rather than to foster self-governing status among such groups.

What Kymlicka's formulation of polyethnic rights allows for, then, is a notion of cultural and linguistic reciprocity that ethnic minorities are themselves increasingly advocating in the potential (re)formulation of national identity, citizenship, and public participation in modern nation-states. Or to put it another way, the notion of polyethnic rights reconstructs integration as a *reciprocal* process rather than the far more common unidirectional expectation that ethnic minority groups simply accommodate to the majoritarian national culture and language(s). Following from this, I have argued at length elsewhere (May 2012a) that Kymlicka's notion of polyethnic rights also allows for the possibility of ethnic minorities gaining access to promotion-oriented language and education rights *under certain circumstances*. Two further concepts are important here – that of "reasonableness" and "where numbers warrant" (May 2010b, 2011a, 2011b).

Reasonableness refers to the expectation that *significant* ethnic minorities within a given state have a *reasonable* expectation to some form of state recognition of, and support for, their historically associated language(s) and cultures (de Varennes 1996; Carens 2000). In other words, while it would be unreasonable for nation-states to be required, for example, to fund language and education services for all minorities, it is increasingly accepted that, where a language is spoken by a significant number within the nation-state, it would also be unreasonable not to provide some level of state services and activity in that language. The question of what constitutes a "significant" ethnic minority group is also necessarily subject to interpretation, depending on the context, rather than a strict numerical criterion. However, the associated notion of "where numbers warrant" has increasingly been deployed to address this issue – that is, language rights may be granted only when there are deemed to be a *sufficient* number of particular language speakers in a given context to warrant active language protection and the related use of such languages in the public domain. Finland adopts this principle with respect to first language Swedish speakers living there. Swedish speakers can use their language in the public domain in those local municipalities where there are a sufficient number of Swedish speakers (currently, at least eight percent) for these municipalities to be deemed officially bilingual. Canada similarly applies the principle of where numbers warrant in relation to French speakers outside of Québec, via the 1982 Canadian Charter of Rights and Freedoms. That said, in both contexts, these language rights are seldom extended to other language speakers. In Canada, for example, the provision of immersion education programs for languages other than French is minimal. Indeed, in Ontario, it is illegal to use languages other than English or French as a medium of instruction in schools (Haque 2012; Cummins 2014).

We need to turn to India, with over 200 language varieties spoken across thirty states and five Union territories, to find perhaps the best example of this principle in operation. On the one hand, we have seen in India the long-standing promotion of English, and more recently Hindi, as the state's elite, pan-Indian, languages. On the other hand, there are eighteen languages recognized in India as "principal medium languages," which, in addition to English and Hindi, include sixteen official state languages. The division of India's states along largely linguistic grounds means that local linguistic communities have control over their public schools and other educational institutions. This, in turn, ensures that the primary language of the area is used as a medium of instruction in state schools (see Pattanayak 1990; Daswani 2001). As a result, regional majority language schools account for eighty-eight percent of all elementary schools in India (Khubchandani 2008). But not only that, the Constitution of India (Article 350A) directs every state, and every local authority within that state, to provide "adequate" educational facilities for instruction in the first language of linguistic minorities, at least at the elementary school level. As a result, over eighty minority languages are employed as medium of instruction in elementary schools throughout India.

While these just-cited examples still tend to prioritize existing national minorities, it is my argument that there is nothing *in principle* against extending these notions to significant ethnic minority groups within given state contexts. In New Zealand, for example, Maori-medium education is provided on the basis of the (national minority) rights of Maori as New Zealand's indigenous peoples (May 2004a, 2004b). To date, no comparable language education provision has been accorded any other ethnic minority groups in New Zealand. However, in recent years, this has increasingly been brought into question, particularly in relation to New Zealand's Pacific migrants, now known as Pasifika.[4] Pasifika currently constitute seven percent of the New Zealand population, of whom nearly half are Samoan. Concomitantly, of the over 100,000 speakers of Pasifika languages in New Zealand, over two-thirds are Samoan speakers (Statistics New Zealand 2014). On this basis, it has been argued that New Zealand should provide bilingual Pasifika education options, particularly for the predominant Samoan community, on the grounds of both reasonableness and where numbers warrant (May 2010a). While this has yet to eventuate as a nationally supported educational policy, it does provide the template for one, both in New Zealand and elsewhere.

Indeed, a recent report by the Royal Society of New Zealand (2013) has argued that New Zealand's still predominantly monolingual education system is increasingly at odds with the rapid growth in linguistic superdiversity that New Zealand is currently experiencing.

Addressing the problem of "groupism"

Linguistic superdiversity, and the growth in migration and transmigration upon which it is based, thus bring into even sharper relief the increasing disjuncture between still predominant monolingual state language and education policies, and the burgeoning ethnic and linguistic diversification of constituent national populations. However, recent work in linguistic superdiversity also highlights the increasingly fluid (ethnic) identities, and increasingly complex (multilingual) language practices, attendant upon these developments (see, for example, Blommaert 2010, 2013; Pennycook 2010; May 2014a; Pennycook and Otsuji 2015). This raises, in turn, the question of the degree to which groups, including speech communities, can be defined with any certainty in the first place.

The problem of group identities (and related group boundaries) has long been raised in anthropology, particularly since Frederik Barth's (1969) seminal essay on ethnic group boundaries. It is evident in a parallel sociological consensus on the arbitrary constructedness of ethnic groups – a process Rogers Brubaker (2002) has dismissively described as "groupism" – and a related rejection of the apparent fixity of such identities. Barth, for example, argued that ethnic groups could not be defined on the basis of their particular cultural (and linguistic) characteristics, what he termed the "cultural stuff" of ethnicity. Rather, ethnic groups are situationally defined in relationship to their social interactions with other groups, and the boundaries established and maintained between them as a result of these interactions. In other words, cultural attributes, such as language use, only become significant as markers of ethnic identity when a group deems them to be *necessary*, or socially effective, for such purposes. Thus, particular cultural attributes, such as a group's language(s), may vary in salience, may be constructed or reconstructed, and may even be discarded by an ethnic group, depending on the particular sociohistorical circumstances of their interactions with other groups, and the need to maintain effectively the boundaries between them. In short, there is no inevitable link between particular languages and particular ethnic group identities.

Given Kymlicka's grounding in political theory, his formulation of group-based rights for national and ethnic minorities does not address this anthropological and sociological critique of groupism directly (see Carens 2000; May 2012a for further discussion; see also later). Nonetheless, he attempts to address the problems of group-based rights from a different direction – by dismantling the apparent dichotomization between individual and group rights that has been a feature of the human rights and international law since World War II. In particular, Kymlicka rejects the assumption that group-differentiated rights are "collective" rights that, ipso facto, stand in opposition to "individual" rights. Group-differentiated rights are not necessarily "collective" in the sense that they privilege the group over the individual – they can in fact be accorded to individual members of a group, or to the group as a whole, or to a federal state/province within which the group forms a majority. For example, the group-differentiated right of Francophones in Canada to use French in federal courts is an *individual* right that may be exercised at any time. The right of Francophones to have their children educated in French-medium schools, outside of Québec, is an individual right also but one, as we have seen, that is subject to the proviso "where numbers warrant." Meanwhile, the right of the Québécois to preserve and promote their distinct culture in the province of Québec highlights how a minority group in a federal system may exercise group-differentiated rights in a territory where they form the majority. In short, there is no simple relationship between group-differentiated rights accorded on the basis of cultural membership and their subsequent application. As Kymlicka concludes, "most [group-based] rights are not about the primacy of communities over individuals. Rather, they are based on the idea that justice between groups requires that the members of different groups be accorded different rights" (1995: 47).

Second, Kymlicka rejects the related criticism that the recognition of group-differentiated rights might end up being illiberal – forcing individuals to accede to particular cultural and linguistic norms that they no longer wish to maintain. Kymlicka addresses this problem by drawing a key distinction between what he terms "internal restrictions" and "external protections" (1995: 35–44; 2001: 22–23). Internal restrictions involve *intra-group* relations where the ethnic or national minority group seeks to restrict the individual liberty of its members on the basis of maintaining group solidarity, creating in the process "internal minorities" (Kymlicka 2007). These rights, when excessive, may be regarded as illiberal.

In contrast, external protections relate to *inter-group* relations where an ethnic or national minority seeks to protect its cultural and linguistic identity – or, more accurately, its ongoing access to and maintenance of *multiple* identities, rather than subsumption to a dominant ethnolinguistic identity – by limiting the impact of the decisions of the larger society. External protections are thus intended to ensure that individual members are able to maintain a distinctive way of life *if they so choose* and are not prevented from doing so by the decisions of members outside of their community (see Kymlicka 1995: 204n11). This too has its dangers, although not in relation to individual oppression in this case but rather the possible unfairness that might result between groups. The ex-apartheid system in South Africa provides a clear example of the latter scenario. However, as Kymlicka argues, external protections need not result in injustice:

> Granting special representation rights, land claims, *or language rights* to a minority need not, and often does not, put it in a position to dominate other groups. On the contrary . . . such rights can be seen as putting the various groups on a more equal footing, by reducing the extent to which the smaller group is vulnerable to the larger.
> *(1995: 36–37; my emphasis)*

Kymlicka argues that, on this basis, one can endorse certain external protections – such as promotion-oriented language rights – where they promote fairness between groups, while still contesting internal restrictions which unduly limit individual rights. Indeed, Kymlicka concludes that "most demands for group-specific rights made by ethnic and national groups in Western democracies are for external protections" (1995: 42). It is this pattern that has been increasingly recognized by national and international law with respect to the promotion-oriented language rights of national and ethnic minorities (McGoldrick 2005; Kymlicka 2007).

Future directions

The challenges of superdiversity

Be that as it may, and returning to the difficulties of defining clearly what constitutes minority groups in the first instance, linguistic superdiversity presents another key challenge to prospective language rights for national and ethnic minorities. If group identities in this late-modern era of globalization and transmigration are increasingly fluid and complex, so too, inevitably, are their (multilingual) language repertoires. Indeed, exploring these complex interconnections has become a prominent feature of recent influential work in critical sociolinguistics in what has come to be termed "the multilingual turn" (May 2014a; see also Makoni and Pennycook 2007, 2012; Blommaert 2010, 2013; Pennycook 2010; Blommaert and Backus 2013; Pennycook and Otsuji 2015).

This recent work highlights the complex, fluid multilingual repertoires of individuals in their local (usually, urban and superdiverse) contexts and how these differ significantly from more narrow conceptions of "languages" (read: standardized language varieties) in the public domain or civic realm. Such repertoires have been described by Makoni and Pennycook (2012: 447) as "lingua franca multilingualism," where "languages are so deeply intertwined and fused into each other that the level of fluidity renders it difficult to determine any boundaries that may indicate that there are different languages involved." Other comparable terms include Rampton's (2011) "contemporary urban vernaculars"; Canagarajah's (2011) "codemeshing"; Creese, Blackledge, et al.'s (2011) "flexible bilingualism"; Pennycook's (2010) "metrolingualism"; García's (2009) "translanguaging"; and Jørgensen's (2008) "polylingual languaging," to name but a few.

The terminological proliferation notwithstanding, the increasing focus on superdiverse linguistic contexts is welcome. It has usefully foregrounded multilingualism, rather than monolingualism, as the new norm of applied linguistic and sociolinguistic analysis. It has increasingly challenged bounded, unitary, and reified conceptions of "languages" and related notions of "native speaker" and "mother tongue," arguing instead for the more complex, fluid understandings of "voice" (Makoni and Pennycook 2007, 2012), "language as social practice" (Heller 2007), and a related "sociolinguistics of mobile resources" (Blommaert 2010). And, following from both, it has highlighted the need for more nuanced ethnographic understandings of the complex multilingual repertoires of speakers in urban environments, along with their locatedness, scale (Blommaert 2010), flow, and circulation (Heller 2011) in a globalized world. As Makoni and Pennycook (2012) summarize it in their recent discussion of the notion of "metrolingualism," the aim of this new, critical, urban applied linguistics is to describe "the ways in which people of different and mixed backgrounds use, play with and negotiate identities through language" (p. 449).

The implications for language rights appear, it seems, equally clear. Such are the now acknowledged complexities of intralanguage (within group) use that they negate the efficacy (or even relevance) of interlanguage (between group) rights and recognition. The argument here is that narrow, reified conceptions of language will always fail to match the actual complexities and fluidity of individual multilingualism. On this basis, even if language rights are extended to minority language speakers, this does not necessarily lead to their greater social and political participation, or the diminishing of inequalities, because of the ongoing mismatch between formal language recognition and individual language use (see, for example, Wee 2010; Makoni 2012). These critical sociolinguistic accounts acknowledge that such language use has been inevitably shaped by wider sociohistorical/sociopolitical factors, including discrimination and exclusion. However, language rights are still rejected in these accounts as a viable alternative for one of two related reasons, sometimes both. Given the internalization over time of negative attitudes to a minority language variety, many of its speakers may no longer view a historically associated language as being particularly useful and may thus actively prefer to shift to a majority language. This foregrounds the need to guarantee language choice and exit for minority language speakers (à la Kymlicka's notion of internal restrictions, discussed earlier). The second reason is that the transfer of a minority language from the private to the public domain inevitably raises questions about what constitutes the agreed norms and form of the language in question. If, as is likely, the language has been used in widely differing ways by individuals, there may be little agreement within a given language or speech community about this.

This recent "multilingual turn" in sociolinguistics has considerable merit – not least in recognizing, albeit belatedly, multilingualism as a core area of study and a related attention to the micro sociolinguistic complexity "on the ground" in superdiverse urban contexts. But the analysis also misses a key point. Put simply, it fails to recognize the *recursive* influence of the public recognition of minority languages on individual language use. That is, if particular language varieties are, via promotion-oriented language rights, *recognized* and *used* in public language domains, this, in turn, will inevitably reshape (often negative, internalized) perceptions over time concerning the status and use of the language varieties in question. Failing to recognize the importance of promotion-oriented language rights in this regard, results, ironically, in critical sociolinguistic accounts endorsing a post-hoc validation of established boundaries of public/private domain language use(s), particularly, for minority language speakers in modern nation-states (May 2014b). Ironically, what this position also continues to reinforce, rather than to dismantle, are the associated linguistic "hierarchies of prestige" (Liddicoat 2013) that underpin these contexts in the first place. As Blommaert has earlier argued, a sociolinguistic approach that fails to take cognizance of these wider sociopolitical and sociohistorical factors takes no account of human agency, political intervention, power, and authority in the formation of particular (national) language ideologies. Nor, by definition, is it able to identify the establishment and maintenance of majority languages as a specific "form of practice, historically contingent and socially embedded" (1999: 7).

Indeed, as I have argued recently elsewhere (May 2012b, 2014c), this new preoccupation with urban (oral) multilingual repertoires, and a related rejection of language boundaries, is itself problematic. It still reinforces, ironically, a highly modernist dichotomization of the global and the local, and the urban and rural, in relation to language varieties and their use(s). In this brave new world, multilingual urban repertoires are constructed as dynamic and cosmopolitan, while supposedly local, often rural, language varieties are dismissed as static and ossified. This is an unnecessary, as well as a historically inaccurate, bifurcation (see May 2014c for further discussion). Meanwhile, the foregrounding of transmigration and globalization, important though they are, also leads to the at times overstated assumption that the nation-state model is somehow in permanent decline (cf. Park and Wee, this volume). And yet, nation-states – for all their limitations, not least those discussed in this chapter – still remain the *primary* social, political, *and linguistic* frame of reference for our everyday *public* lives. What is needed, then, is not the unreflexive, de rigueur, dismissal of the nation-state model in this increasingly globalized world but rather the urgent requirement to rethink it in more linguistically plural and inclusive ways.

The current turn towards multilingualism also fails to address adequately the relationship between the actual language uses of multilingual speakers and their access to standardized language varieties, particularly in written form. The latter, as we know, are particularly important for the development of (bi)literacy and educational (and wider social) mobility and it is surely better to look to "proximal" language varieties for this purpose rather than to reject all standardized varieties tout court (May 2012b). To this end, the recognition of individual (private) multilingualism, a welcome development in itself, is not *necessarily* antipathetic to a concomitant recognition of public (communal) multilingualism, despite the necessary attenuation of the complexities of actual multilingual use, in so doing (see also Busch 2012). Language diversity on the ground will always deconstruct standardized conceptions of languages, to be sure. But this should not, ipso facto, preclude the possibility of the public recognition of, and support for, minority languages along the lines discussed in this chapter.

Implications

The issues canvassed in this chapter thus lead me to the conclusion that all linguistic minorities should have granted, *at the very least*, tolerance-oriented language rights under established human rights principles. Moreover, there are clear principles in international law which provide both precedent and support for the granting of promotion-oriented language and education rights to national minority groups. But it has also been my argument here that such promotion-oriented language rights could (and should) be extended to ethnic minorities on the basis of the notion of "where numbers warrant." In combination, these principles provide the basis for the further expansion of promotion-oriented rights for linguistic minorities. While ensuring that individuals can "exit" the linguistic groups in question, if they so choose, these language rights allow for the alternative promotion of linguistic complementarity rather than the language replacement ideology that has so dominated nation-states until now. Moreover, the recognition of multilingualism can finally move beyond the individual level and the private domain. Instead, multilingualism can be recognized as a collective (albeit inevitably variegated) right and resource in the public domain, or civic realm, as well. In this late modern age of globalization and rapidly increasing diversity, such developments seem not only entirely appropriate but also overdue, not least for those national and ethnic minorities who have for far too long been denied them.

Related topics

Nation-state, transnationalism, and language
Displacement and language
Regional flows and language resources
Mobility, language, and schooling

Further reading

Kloss, H. (1971). The language rights of immigrant groups. *International Migration Review*, 5, 250–268.

Highlights the distinction between tolerance-oriented and promotion-oriented language rights. While migration patterns have changed significantly since this article was written, the distinction remains an important/useful one, even in today's context of complex processes of migration and transmigration.

Kymlicka, W. (1995). *Multicultural Citizenship: A Liberal Theory of Minority Rights*. Oxford: Clarendon Press.

This book challenges the (until then) consensus in liberal political theory that individual rights should predominate in questions of justice and citizenship and that the recognition of group rights is intrinsically problematic. Addresses language rights as part of a wider discussion of these group-differentiated rights.

Kymlicka, W. (2001). *Politics in the Vernacular: Nationalism, Multiculturalism, and Citizenship*. Oxford: Oxford University Press.

A collection of essays that extends Kymlicka's arguments for group-differentiated rights, and related public policies of multiculturalism. The contributions include a prominent focus on both language and education rights for minorities and the implications of such rights in an increasingly globalized world.

May, S. (2011). Language rights: The "Cinderella" human right. *Journal of Human Rights*, *10*(3), 265–289.

This article critically examines why language rights are under-represented and/or problematized as a key human right, particularly in the post–World War II era. It traces recent developments in both political theory and international law which are contesting/countering this dismissal of language rights.

May, S. (2012). *Language and Minority Rights: Ethnicity, Nationalism and the Politics of Language* (2nd ed.). New York: Routledge.

A major interdisciplinary analysis of language, identity, and education alongside a defense of group-differentiated language rights. The key argument is that the causes of many of the language-based conflicts in the world today lie with the nation-state and its preoccupation with establishing a "common" language and culture via mass education. The solution proffered is to rethink nation-states in more culturally and linguistically plural ways while avoiding, at the same time, essentializing the language-identity link.

Notes

1 The 1996 post-apartheid South African Constitution is one such example. Along with its ongoing official recognition of English and Afrikaans, the new South African Constitution recognized a further nine African languages, and subsequently also South African Sign Language, bringing the total to twelve official languages.
2 Returning to the South African example, and despite its language policy of official multilingualism, subsequent developments have seen the rapid default/de facto emergence of English language dominance in the public domain, particularly within education (Heugh 2008).
3 Kymlicka also discusses a third category of "special representation rights" for groups that face some systemic disadvantage in the political process which limits their view from being effectively represented. However, this fall beyond the scope of this current discussion.
4 The Pasifika population in New Zealand are a key pan-ethnic migrant group, comprising peoples from the principal Pacific islands of Samoa, Tonga, Cook Islands, Niue, Tokelau, Tuvalu, and Fiji, who began migrating to New Zealand in significant numbers from the 1960s onwards.

References

Anderson, B. (1991). *Imagined Communities* (Rev. ed.). London: Verso.
Barth, F. (1969). *Ethnic Groups and Boundaries*. Boston, MA: Little, Brown.
Bauman, R. and Briggs, C. (2003). *Voices of Modernity: Language Ideologies and the Politics of Inequality*. Cambridge: Cambridge University Press.
Billig, M. (1995). *Banal Nationalism*. London: Sage.
Blommaert, J., ed. (1999). *Language Ideological Debates*. Berlin, Germany: Mouton de Gruyter.
Blommaert, J. (2010). *The Sociolinguistics of Globalization*. New York: Cambridge University Press.
Blommaert, J. (2013). *Ethnography, Superdiversity and Linguistic Landscapes*. Bristol: Multilingual Matters.
Blommaert, J. and Backus, A. (2013). Superdiverse repertoires and the individual. In I. de Saint-Georges and J.-J. Weber (eds.), *Multilingualism and Modality: Current Challenges for Educational Studies* (pp. 11–32). New York: Springer.
Brubaker, R. (2002). Ethnicity without groups. *Archives Européennes de Sociologie* 53(2): 163–189.
Bucholtz, M. and Hall, K. (2004). Language and identity. In A. Duranti (ed.), *A Companion to Linguistic Anthropology* (pp. 369–394). Malden, MA: Blackwell.
Busch, B. (2012). The linguistic repertoire revisited. *Applied Linguistics* 33(5): 503–533.
Canagarajah, A.S. (2011). Codemeshing in academic writing: Identifying teachable strategies of translanguaging. *Modern Language Journal* 95: 401–417.

Carens, J. (2000). *Culture, Citizenship and Community*. Oxford: Oxford University Press.
Claude, I. (1955). *National Minorities: An International Problem*. Cambridge, MA: Harvard University Press.
Coulmas, F. (1998). Language rights: Interests of states, language groups and the individual. *Language Sciences* 20: 63–72.
Crawford, J. (2008). *Advocating for English Learners: Selected Essays*. Clevedon: Multilingual Matters.
Creese, A., Blackledge, A., Barac, T., Bhatt, A., Hamid, S., Li Wei, . . . Yagcioglu, D. (2011). Separate and flexible bilingualism in complementary schools: Multiple language practices in interrelationship. *Journal of Pragmatics* 43(5): 1196–1208.
Cummins, J. (2014). To what extent are Canadian second language policies evidence-based? Reflections on the intersections of research and policy. *Frontiers in Psychology* 5. doi:10.3389/fpsyg.2014.00358
Daswani, C., ed. (2001). *Language Education in Multilingual India*. New Delhi: UNESCO.
de Varennes, F. (1996). *Language, Minorities and Human Rights*. The Hague: Kluwer Law International.
Dorian, N. (1998). Western language ideologies and small-language prospects. In L. Grenoble and L. Whaley (eds.), *Endangered Languages: Language Loss and Community Response* (pp. 3–21). Cambridge: Cambridge University Press.
Extra, G., Spotti, M. and Van Avermaet, P., eds. (2009). *Language Testing, Migration and Citizenship*. London: Continuum.
Fishman, J. (1991). *Reversing Language Shift*. Clevedon: Multilingual Matters.
Fought, C. (2006). *Language and Ethnicity*. Cambridge: Cambridge University Press.
García, O. (2009). *Bilingual Education in the 21st Century: A Global Perspective*. Malden, MA: Blackwell.
Gellner, E. (1983). *Nations and Nationalism*. Oxford: Basil Blackwell.
Grillo, R. (1989). *Dominant Languages: Language and Hierarchy in Britain and France*. Cambridge: Cambridge University Press.
Grillo, R. (1998). *Pluralism and the Politics of Difference: State, Culture, and Ethnicity in Comparative Perspective*. Oxford: Oxford University Press.
Grin, F. (2003). *Language Policy Evaluation and the European Charter for Regional or Minority Languages*. Basingstoke: Palgrave Macmillan.
Haque, E. (2012). *Multiculturalism within a Bilingual Framework*. Toronto: University of Toronto Press.
Heller, M. (1987). The role of language in the formation of ethnic identity. In J. Phinney and M. Rotheram (eds.), *Children's Ethnic Socialisation: Pluralism and Development* (pp. 180–200). Newbury Park, CA: Sage.
Heller, M. (2007). Bilingualism as ideology and practice. In M. Heller (ed.), *Bilingualism: A Social Approach* (pp. 1–22). Basingstoke: Palgrave Macmillan.
Heller, M. (2011). *Paths to Post-nationalism: A Critical Ethnography of Language and Identity*. Oxford: Oxford University Press.
Heugh, K. (2008). Language policy in Southern Africa. In S. May and N. Hornberger (eds.), *Encyclopedia of Language and Education*, 2nd ed., vol. 1: *Language Policy and Political Issues in Education* (pp. 355–367). New York: Springer.
Hutchinson, J. (1994). *Modern Nationalism*. London: Fontana.
Jørgensen, J. (2008). Poly-lingual languaging around and among children and adolescents. *International Journal of Multilingualism* 5(3): 161–176.
Khubchandani, L. (2008). Language policy and education in the Indian subcontinent. In S. May and N. Hornberger (eds.), *Encyclopedia of Language and Education*, 2nd ed., vol. 1: *Language Policy and Political Issues in Education* (pp. 369–381). New York: Springer.
Kloss, H. (1971). The language rights of immigrant groups. *International Migration Review* 5: 250–268.
Kloss, H. (1977). *The American Bilingual Tradition*. Rowley: Newbury House.
Kymlicka, W. (1995). *Multicultural Citizenship: A Liberal Theory of Minority Rights*. Oxford: Clarendon Press.

Kymlicka, W. (2001). *Politics in the Vernacular: Nationalism, Multiculturalism, and Citizenship.* Oxford: Oxford University Press.

Kymlicka, W. (2007). *Multicultural Odysseys: Navigating the New International Politics of Diversity.* Oxford: Oxford University Press.

Liddicoat, A. (2013). *Language-in-education Policies: The Discursive Construction of Intercultural Relations.* Bristol: Multilingual Matters.

Makoni, S. (2012). Language and human rights discourses: Lessons from the African experience. *Journal of Multicultural Discourses* 7(1): 1–20.

Makoni, S. and Pennycook, A. (2007). Disinventing and reconstituting languages. In S. Makoni and A. Pennycook (eds.), *Disinventing and Reconstituting Languages* (pp. 1–41). Clevedon: Multilingual Matters.

Makoni, S. and Pennycook, A. (2012). Disinventing multilingualism: From monological multilingualism to multilingual francas. In M. Martin-Jones, A. Blackledge and A. Creese (eds.), *The Routledge Handbook of Multilingualism* (pp. 439–453). New York: Routledge.

May, S. (2004a). Medium of instruction policy in New Zealand. In J. Tollefson and A. Tsui (eds.), *Medium of Instruction Policies: Which Agenda? Whose Agenda?* (pp. 21–41). Mahwah, NJ: Lawrence Erlbaum Associates.

May, S. (2004b). Accommodating multiculturalism and biculturalism in Aotearoa/New Zealand: Implications for language policy. In P. Spoonley, C. McPherson and D. Pearson (eds.), *Tangata, Tangata. The Changing Ethnic Contours of Aotearoa/New Zealand* (pp. 247–264). Southbank, Australia: Thomson/Dunmore Press.

May, S. (2008). Language education, pluralism and citizenship. In S. May and N. Hornberger (eds.), *Encyclopedia of Language and Education*, 2nd ed., vol. 1: *Language Policy and Political Issues in Education* (pp. 15–29). New York: Springer.

May, S. (2009). Critical multiculturalism and education. In J. Banks (ed.), *Routledge International Companion to Multicultural Education* (pp. 33–48). New York: Routledge.

May, S. (2010a). Aotearoa/New Zealand. In J. Fishman and O. García (eds.), *Handbook of Language and Ethnicity* (pp. 501–517). New York: Oxford University Press.

May, S. (2010b). Derechos lingüísticos como derechos humanos [Language rights as human rights]. *Revista de Antropología Social* 19: 131–159.

May, S. (2011a). Language rights: The "Cinderella" human right. *Journal of Human Rights* 10(3): 265–289.

May, S. (2011b). Language rights: The forgotten dimension of human rights. In T. Cushman (ed.), *Handbook of Human Rights* (pp. 311–323). New York: Routledge.

May, S. (2012a). *Language and Minority Rights: Ethnicity, Nationalism and the Politics of Language* (2nd ed.). New York: Routledge.

May, S. (2012b). Contesting hegemonic and monolithic constructions of language rights "discourse". *Journal of Multicultural Discourses* 7(1): 21–27.

May, S. (2013). Indigenous immersion education: International developments. *Journal of Immersion and Content-Based Education* 1(1): 34–69.

May, S., ed. (2014a). *The Multilingual Turn: Implications for SLA, TESOL and Bilingual Education.* New York: Routledge.

May, S. (2014b). Contesting public monolingualism and diglossia: Rethinking political theory and language policy for a multilingual world. *Language Policy* 13: 371–393.

May, S. (2014c). Contesting metronormativity: Exploring indigenous language dynamism across the urban–rural divide. *Journal of Language, Identity and Education* 13(4): 229–235.

May, S. and Aikman, S. (Eds.). (2003). Indigenous education: New possibilities, ongoing restraints. *Comparative Education* 39(2): 139–145.

McGoldrick, D. (2005). Multiculturalism and its discontents. *Human Rights Law Review* 5(1): 27–56.

McNamara, T. and Roever, C. (2006). *Language Testing: The Social Dimension.* Malden, MA: Wiley-Blackwell.

Modood, T. (2013). *Multiculturalism* (2nd ed.). Cambridge: Polity Press.

Nic Craith, M. (2006). *Europe and the Politics of Language: Citizens, Migrants, and Outsiders.* London: Palgrave Macmillan.
Pattanayak, D., ed. (1990). *Multilingualism in India.* Clevedon: Multilingual Matters.
Pennycook, A. (2010). *Language as a Local Practice.* New York: Routledge.
Pennycook, A. and Otsuji, E. (2015). *Metrolingualism: Language and the City.* New York: Routledge.
Preece, J. (1998). *National Minorities and the European Nation-states System.* Oxford: Clarendon Press.
Rampton, B. (2011). From "multi-ethnic adolescent heteroglossia" to "contemporary urban vernaculars". *Language & Communication* 31: 276–294.
Royal Society of New Zealand. (2013). *Languages in Aotearoa New Zealand.* March 2013. Wellington, NZ: Author.
Schmidt, R. Sr. (2000). *Language Policy and Identity Politics in the United States.* Philadelphia, PA.: Temple University Press.
Skutnabb-Kangas, T. (2000). *Linguistic Genocide in Education – Or Worldwide Diversity and Human Rights?* Mahwah, NJ: Lawrence Erlbaum.
Smith, A. (1995). *Nations and Nationalism in a Global Era.* London: Polity Press.
Statistics New Zealand. (2014). *2013 Quick Stats – About Culture and Identity.* Retrieved from http://www.stats.govt.nz/Census/2013-census/profile-and-summary-reports/quickstats-culture-identity.aspx.
Tabouret-Keller, A. (1997). Language and identity. In F. Coulmas (ed.), *The Handbook of Sociolinguistics* (pp. 315–326). Oxford: Blackwell.
Trenz, H. (2007). Reconciling diversity and unity: Language minorities and European integration. *Ethnicities* 7(2): 157–185.
Vertovec, S. (2007). Super-diversity and its implications. *Ethnic and Racial Studies* 30(6): 1024–1054.
Wee, L. (2010). *Language without Rights.* Oxford: Oxford University Press.
Wright, S. (2000). *Community and Communication: The Role of Language in Nation State Building and European Integration.* Clevedon: Multilingual Matters.
Xanthaki, A. (2007). *Indigenous Rights and United Nations Standards.* Cambridge: Cambridge University Press.

Part II
Contexts

9
Regional flows and language resources

Ellen Hurst

Introduction and definitions

This chapter discusses regional flows and the dynamics of language resources within those flows. First it outlines the scholarship on language as resource, particularly in terms of migration, and defines the terms to be used in the chapter. Second it gives an overview of regional flows of people and the role of language within that, outlining current literature on language as a resource in migration. Next the chapter considers the issue of the changing value of resources in different contexts and what implications this has for regional flows. It draws mainly on research conducted in South Africa, looking at both the value of English as a resource and the value of African languages.

The chapter describes how the value of language (value in the Bourdieusian sense of economic and/or cultural capital) changes within various regional flows – and how language resources are conferred value at a local level. The chapter demonstrates through the lived experiences of people that language resources carried between regions do not maintain a neutral or static value but that value is always negotiated within local contexts, and that in many migration scenarios this can result in language resource attrition.

Language as resource

The concept of 'language as resource' can be understood in a number of different ways. The first relates to the economy. Heller (2010) considers the ways that the globalized new economy positions language a resource and a commodity. She highlights the consequences for language of the expansion of capitalism and the creation of new markets and products, particularly the following effects: an increase in the number of people involved in the global market (and therefore an increase in linguistic difference); an increase in the forms of communication (e.g., technology); a tension between standardization and 'authenticity', where authenticity links to specificity of local linguistic varieties; and a shift towards language not just as part of the work process, but to become a work product (as an essential part of the information economy). She then goes on to discuss the production, distribution, and attribution of value to linguistic resources and how that value is measured. English in the current global setting is attributed value as a resource in the global economy. Mufwene (2010) traces the current status of English back to "settlement colonization" and "exploitation colonization," processes of mass migration and English language mobility that have led to its current status as a world language. In addition, its current status is also in large part due to the global domination of the capitalist economic system; as Mufwene (2010: 31) explains:

> The players or partners involved in the relevant world-wide networks of interconnectedness and interdependence do not hold equal economic powers; it is the more powerful who control which populations and commodities (including languages) are transported more freely, and in which directions.

Language can in Heller's (2010) sense translate into economic capital if it is actually the product of "language industries" – industries which either sell information or rely heavily on information to sell a final product, or even where language itself is the final product such as in language learning – or if it translates into economic success for the person who holds the linguistic capital. In much recent research on the language resources of migrants, there appears to be a correlation between proficiency in the dominant language of the host country and economic success for the migrant (cf. Chiswick and Miller 2002; Dustmann and van Soest 2002; Bleakley and Chin 2004), although Canagarajah (2013: 3) suggests that these studies often lack crucial contextualizing information.

In Bourdieu's (1988) work, on the other hand, individuals have access to various forms of capital (cultural, economic, social, and symbolic capital), and individuals will be able to operate successfully in fields that value the types of capital that they hold. He acknowledges both cultural and linguistic capital. Cultural capital is a "species of power" which is possessed by individuals and "commands access to the specific profits that are at stake in [a given] field" (Bourdieu and Wacquant 1992: 97). Bourdieu (1988) posits that linguistic capital is a subcategory of cultural capital, and different linguistic capital may be deployed in social contexts for the specific profits at stake (not necessarily economic), so in this way language can be seen as a cultural resource. However, not having the 'right' kinds of capital or having restricted access to types of valued cultural and linguistic capital can adversely impact on the success of someone in a given field. Liebowitz (2005: 661) highlights how simple language proficiency is not necessarily the only requirement for linguistic capital, and suggests that "The way the dominant language is taught and acquired interacts with various sociocultural and economic factors."

A number of current authors make an argument for multilinguality as a resource, such as Bamgbose (2000) and Agnihotri (2010). They separately suggest that colonial languages should not dominate other languages, as multilinguality itself constitutes a resource for (both social and economic) advancement. This is in keeping with a theoretical shift in sociolinguistics away from the idea of homogenized language units and monolingualism as the norm (a monolingual orientation is described by Canagarajah (2013: 1) as the belief that "for communication to be successful we should employ a common language with shared norms"), towards valuing what Coupland and Jaworski (2009) have described as an emphasis on the concept of *social practice*. This includes the proposal that multilingualism and multilinguality is the new linguistic order – although the terminology of multilingualism has been critiqued as promoting the idea of mere multiple monolingualisms, leading to more recent work on concepts such as polylanguaging, translanguaging and translingual practice (Canagarajah 2013).

This leads to another sense in which language can be described as 'resource': 'language resources' refers to the idea that people hold a range of resources, or a 'repertoire' made up of different languages, dialects, sociolects, registers, and so forth, rather than a set of monolingual competencies. The concept of linguistic repertoire is useful for theories of migration and language, and describes a fluid set of linguistic resources, from which speakers choose in order to convey meaning (Gumperz 1964: 138). According to Gumperz (1964: 140), multilingualism and alternation strategies (such as code-switching) between both languages and dialects "form a behavioural whole, regardless of grammatical distinctness, and must be considered constituent varieties of the same verbal repertoire." This removes the distinction between individual discrete languages in the speech of an individual – instead, an individual can choose from whatever linguistic practices they are familiar with. Building on this, Blommaert (2010: 170) describes a "polyglot repertoire," which is "not tied to any form of 'national' space, and neither to a national, stable regime of language. It is tied to an individual's life and it follows the peculiar biographical trajectory of the speaker." Blommaert (2010: 103) argues that "No one knows all of a language. That counts for our so-called mother tongues and, of course, also for the other 'languages' we acquire in our life time." People may acquire language resources through migration and globalization processes. Blommaert develops the idea of a "truncated repertoire," and applies this in the case of migrants:

> the super-diversity that arises from globalization processes results in communities of people whose repertoires are structured as such: as truncated complexes of resources often derived from a variety of languages, and with considerable differences in the level of development of particular resources. Parts of these multilingual repertoires will be fairly well developed, while others exist only at a very basic level.
>
> *(Blommaert 2010: 106)*

Blommaert (2010: 106) suggests that these truncated repertoires oblige speakers to engage in "collaborative communicative work," and that this results in "something that has a very unfinished character: partial realizations of genres with partially 'correct' bits of language." By highlighting 'correct' in this phrase, he indicates that there is no 'correct' language as such, but that migrants language may be received as 'incorrect' by native speakers. However, this notion of truncated repertoires has been critiqued as implying that multilingual speakers are deficient (Canagarajah 2013: 10). This has led Canagarajah to an emphasis on translingual practice in which speakers develop fuller communicative competence through drawing on all their available language resources, particularly in migration scenarios.

This chapter uses both senses of language resource described earlier – in the sense of the resources (dialects, sociolects, registers, 'languages') of an individual, as well as in the sense of how these resources can be used as an economic and cultural resource, or can be employed for economic and social profit or advancement.

Regional flows

This chapter follows the terminology outlined in the World Migration Report (2013: 36) as follows:

> The report adopts the terminology used in development discourse to categorize countries according to their economic status . . . broadly speaking, 'North' refers to high-income countries and 'South' to low- and middle-income countries, as classified by the World Bank.

'North' here broadly refers to countries with 'developed' economies in the northern hemisphere, particularly in the continents of Europe and North America, as well as East Asia (the term 'developed' is used with caution as it positions the capitalist economic system as the aspirational norm, cf. Escobar 1995). The 'South' on the other hand broadly refers to South America, Africa, the Middle East, and southern Asia. So the terms North-South migration, South-North migration, and South-South migration are used loosely to refer to people moving between different economic regions. The authors of the World Migration Report caution however that these labels have their limitations, with 'North' and 'South' encompassing a wide range of different migrant situations and categories, and with "different definitions of 'North' and 'South' producing varying results regarding the magnitude and characteristics of migration." Nevertheless, they suggest that the division is useful for looking at migration and development in a "more holistic way" (World Migration Report 2013: 36).

The term 'rural-urban migration', similarly, is a binary distinction contested by authors such as Bekker (2006) who argues that areas categorized as 'rural' in South Africa, for example, increasingly contain urban-like characteristics particularly in terms of economic activity, and his observation is equally relevant in other contexts in which technological and economic change has led to changes in labour patterns and configurations of human settlements. This results in "Conceptual uneasiness with these opposed categories – commercial vs subsistence; agribusiness vs smallholder; urban vs rural" (Bekker 2006: 4).

The terms 'region' and 'regional' are used with little consensus in migration literature. Here I use them to refer to the different zones that people move between, for example, regional flows within a country (internal migration) or continent, as well as flows between international regions, that is, the Global North and the Global South.

The emphasis in the past four decades when reporting migration in policy debates, research and popular media has been on migratory flows from poor to rich countries, from South to North – those movements of people which involve the search for economic improvement, and happen between countries seen as unequal in terms of their ability to provide employment and security for their citizens (World Migration Report 2013: 36). On the other hand, according to the World Migration Report (2013: 36):

> South-South migrants are economically important, due to the magnitude of numbers and the potential scale of remittances, but their life experiences are a largely understudied area. This "blind spot" for policymakers largely reflects the lack of reliable data on migrants who move from one developing country to another.

The focus on South-North flows can contribute to negative discourses regarding migrants, representing them as an economic and cultural threat to wealthy countries. South-North flows are prominent within global migration, but are not the only large migratory flows that are taking place. In fact, the largest migratory flows are those migrants moving within the same regions, for example, North-North migration and South-South migration –

> It is clear from the data that a more inclusive approach to migration and development is needed. According to Gallup sources, only 40 per cent of migrants move from South to North. At least one third of migrants move from South to South (although the figure could be higher if more accurate data were available), and just over a fifth of migrants (22%) migrate from North to North. A small but growing percentage of migrants (5%)

migrate from North to South. These figures can vary somewhat, depending on which definition of "North" and "South" is used.

(World Migration Report 2013: 25)

It is also not the poorest people who move – people need resources to migrate, and often those who are able to migrate are educationally and financially the best resourced (cf. Amin and Mattoo 2007). There are also people flowing back to their home countries or engaged in ongoing migration journeys as part of their economic and life strategies (return or circular migration). Traditional theories of migration conceptualized migration as "a change in the spatial organization of one's life in an enduring way" (Blommaert 2010: 6). Migration was seen as a permanent one-directional movement of a person from one nation to another. This view of migration has persisted in much popular media. However, theorists have come to understand migration as an ongoing process of flows, and have focused on descriptions of the mobility, trajectories, and practices that make up this flow (cf. Vertovec 2009). Migration happens for a variety of 'push' and 'pull' reasons, and can be circular, temporary, long-term, or short-term (Zimmerman 2014). Even what might be considered permanent migration is often accompanied by ongoing social, economic, and emotional connections between migrants and their home countries (Levitt, DeWind and Vertovec 2003). More recent migration theory and sociolinguistics theory has become aware of these fluid and impermanent aspects of migration, hence the use of the term 'flows' in this chapter.

Overview

Regional flows and the role of language resources

Regional flows have characterized the distribution of languages and language families over the globe. First we have a 'peopling' of the world and the 'out of Africa' theory – 'colonisation' of the planet in the biologists' sense. As a corollary, we can also trace migration patterns of humans through the contemporary distribution of language resources, such as the large Semitic and Indo-European language families. Second we have 'political' colonization – processes such as the spread of empires and the control of overseas territories, which led to movements of humans and their languages, such as during the slave trade, as well as the export of language resources through, for example, mission schools and colonial education systems. Globally, we see language continua and chains resulting from these processes of migration, which historically took place through the terrestrial movements of people. Since the entrenchment of the worldwide system of nation-states, alongside the concurrent advances in technologies that have allowed for different forms of travel, as well as a near-instantaneous global economy and forms of communication (Castells 2001), migration patterns and their language effects have complexified.

In terms of regional flows, the migration of people between ex-colonial powers and ex-colonies has a language dimension. English provides a clear example where migrants from ex-British colonies such as India, Zambia, Malawi, and Zimbabwe have historically favoured migration not only to Britain but to other English-speaking countries such as Canada and the US (cf. Docquier and Marfouk 2004). Thus there is some evidence that language "organizes and facilitates mobility" (Park 2014: 84), leading to what Park (2014: 84) calls "cartographies of language" – "acts of understanding space through the mediation of metalinguistic conceptions of language and communication."

This chapter focuses on relatively recent migratory movements – particularly those described by the sociolinguistic literature of the 21st century. Recent literature on language and migration has started to expand our understanding of how language travels across borders such as internal, national, and international; of what happens to speakers and their languages when they travel; and of the impacts on language identities, and the identities of speakers when language travels. In much recent sociolinguistics work that draws on migration theory, there is an argument that languages are valued differently in different contexts, for example the (economic) value placed on the linguistic resources of a speaker of an African language in her home country may not be retained in a migration context. Blommaert (2010) describes a sociolinguistics of mobile resources which takes into account the ways that "people manage or fail to make sense across contexts; their linguistic and communicative resources are mobile or lack such semiotic mobility, and this is a problem not just of difference, but of inequality" (Blommaert 2010: 3). In other words, languages are not equal in terms of their value in a migration context. However, viewed as resources, a speakers' repertoire may retain different kinds of value depending on context, and multilingualism in this way may add collective value.

Much of the recent (21st-century) literature on language and migration has emerged from the Global North, and it should be noted that the contexts of European cities are markedly different from those in the Global South. European and North American cities have experienced large influxes of migrants from culturally or ethnically (and linguistically) distinct countries, for example, in the cases of Denmark (Jørgensen, Karrebaek, Madsen, and Møller 2011) and Britain (Creese and Blackledge 2010). Blommaert and Rampton (2011) have drawn on Vertovec's (2006) concept from migration theory, "superdiversity," while authors such as Otsuji and Pennycook (2010) have focused on "metrolingualism," to explain some of the complexities of language in modern Northern urban centres. Superdiversity refers to the period since the 1980s characterized by small waves of migration from a wide range of places and as a result

> a tremendous increase in the categories of migrants, not only in terms of nationality, ethnicity, language and religion, but also in terms of motives, patterns and itineraries of migration, processes of insertion into the labour and housing markets of the host societies, and so on.
>
> *(Blommaert and Rampton 2011: 2)*

This has, according to superdiversity theorists, resulted in a diversification of languages and a resultant change in the character of urban centres – shifting from a perceived (although never achieved) monolingualism mapped onto a national identity, towards multilingualism characterised by an increased ethnic diversity.

Metrolingualism, on the other hand, "is a product typically of modern, urban interaction" (Otsuji and Pennycook 2010: 245) which refers to "creative linguistic conditions across space and borders of culture, history and politics" (Otsuji and Pennycook 2010: 244) arising in contexts of "movement, migration and mixing," although Otsuji and Pennycook (2010: 246) caution that the kinds of mixed language use that metrolingualism is intended to refer to has many earlier precedents such as the multilingualism of precolonial communities before the categorization processes of European modernity were imposed. Drawing on the notion of 'metrosexuality', metrolingualism additionally invokes "the queering of ortholinguistic practices across time and space that may include urban and rural contexts, elite or minority communities, local or global implications." As a concept, similarly to superdiversity, metrolingualism has emerged from a particular moment in time and space – the early 21st century in the Global North – and as such reflects the relevant concerns and discourses. In the case of both superdiversity and metrolingualism, the concepts have since been taken up by researchers in the Global South with varying success (Beyer 2014; Heugh 2014; McLaughlin 2014).

In the exploitation colonies of the Global South, Mufwene (2010: 41) suggests that the norm has historically been and remained "societal and individual multilingualism, with relatively clear geographical and ethnographic divisions of labor in the usage of indigenous vernaculars, indigenous varieties of lingua franca, and European languages," where European languages are "emblems of socioeconomic achievement and status" (Mufwene 2010: 39). In other words, superdiversity has been present in the Global South for a long time, and is not a replacement for a monolingual project (although it should be reiterated that the nation-state projects of the global 'north', and colonization of some territories, for example Australia, both directly and indirectly destroyed pre-existing indigenous multilingualism).

Because of the colonial forms of their political formation, the majority of nation-states in Africa, for example, were mapped onto regions containing many indigenous languages. This has led to the linguistic situation in countries such as Cameroon, which has as many as 230 languages, with French and English operating as official languages. The patterns of migration in the 20th and 21st centuries in much of the Global South have been characterized by large rural to urban migrations and the influx of multiple local languages, coupled with the often official role of colonial European languages. Kerswill (2006) writes that in Europe, urbanization may have resulted in dialect leveling and koineised (mixed, levelled and sometimes simplified) new dialects. However,

> In the developing world, rural–urban mass migration is a phenomenon of the latter part of the 20th century, with Sub-Saharan Africa the latest region to be affected . . . In West Africa, the dominant sociolinguistic effect appears to be an increase in individual multilingualism and the spread of lingua francas.

The effects of this largely rural-urban migration on language are therefore quite different from the effects of international migration to urban centres described by scholars in the Global North, and the emergence of urban vernaculars in African urban centres may be one manifestation of recent migration patterns (McLaughlin 2009; Nassenstein and Hollington 2015). The linguistic resources drawn on in African urban vernaculars are primarily local resources: local languages (such as African languages and colonial European languages) and varieties (such as registers and dialects).

In terms of how multilinguality operates as a resource in migration, a number of recent authors have examined the dynamics of language resources in migrations from the Global South to the Global North. For example, Victoria (forthcoming) conducts an ethnography with immigrants to Canada from Congo, Haiti, India, Bangladesh, Jordan, and the Philippines, and highlights how "they creatively mobilised previously acquired pragmatic strategies and resources from their L1 to suit the demands of the ongoing interaction in English." Bailey, Mupakati, and Magunha (forthcoming) examine the lives of Zimbabweans in Yorkshire in the UK, and show that as a result of the new transnational spatial relations arising from migration, their emerging language practice involves multilingualism and cross-cultural communicative competency. On the other hand, valued resources may be devalued; Garrido and Codó (forthcoming) examined the labour and social trajectories of educated African migrants in Barcelona and discovered that their language capital, particularly English language, was devalued in the employment context, and that the agencies that placed them drew on "tabula-rasa discourses that delanguage and, more generally, deskill migrants." The next section will develop these ideas further.

Issues and ongoing debates

The value of resources

To highlight the issues and ongoing debates, this section will use a number of examples from research conducted in South Africa, which will highlight how language resources are not accorded the same value in different regions/contexts. This will be demonstrated at the international level with an example of highly skilled migrants whose migration journeys take them both South-North and North-South; at the continental level with an example of migration within the African continent; and at the internal level with an example that relates to rural-urban migration. The section describes how the value of language resources (value in the Bourdieusian sense of economic and/or cultural capital) changes within particular regional flows, and therefore how language resources are accorded value at a local level. The research examples are primarily based on qualitative interview and narrative data to draw out the lived experiences of migrants. Through these lived experiences of people, the section demonstrates how the value of language resources carried between regions is often renegotiated within local contexts. Migration may result in simultaneous gain and loss of language resources, as migrants adapt to new linguistic contexts resulting in increased multilinguality or language resources, but also may ultimately experience attrition of devalued language resource.

International scale

In terms of an example of a North-South flow, the shifting value of resources at the international scale is demonstrated by two research projects conducted in 2010 and 2013 with African academics and postgraduate students who were working or studying in South Africa but originated from other African countries; most had spent some time in the Global North as skilled or educational migrants during their migration trajectories (Hurst 2014; forthcoming a). Many of the academics who were interviewed had substantial English language resources prior to their initial migration. All but one of the academics were from African countries where English is the official language (due to the colonial history of much of Africa), so English was their first, if not home language, and they also had high levels of education prior to migration – education was one of the main resources they needed in order to migrate and obtain academic work, or undertake further studies abroad. As a result they were highly skilled in an academic English register. They also tended to migrate to countries where their language resources would be most valued – other English-speaking countries, often those with colonial links to their home countries. This meant that their language resources enabled migration and they experienced little need to obtain new language resources in the host country. Yet these highly skilled migrants encountered many difficulties with the 'accentedness' of their English both in the Global North, and in South Africa. When asked whether they faced any tensions between the variety of English they spoke and the variety spoken in the host communities they had encountered, a number of the academics explained that their students complained about their accent, finding them 'not easy to follow', and an 'issue' which led to students claiming they were unable to understand their teaching. In contrast, the academics themselves described how they had become flexible when listening to other accents, because they were 'forced to' in a migrant context (Hurst, forthcoming a). They also described negative effects on obtaining funding and promotions as a result of their English resources.

Mufwene (2010: 46) cautions that the burden is typically on speakers of languages that are seen as deviations from the metropolitan norms, to " 'improve' their intelligibility – not the other way around." While the respondents in this research held significant academic English language resources, their specific proficiency was being evaluated within local contexts, and their accent was seen to deviate from the norm. Thus, while English itself enables mobility in relation to particular migration flows, a particular variety of, for example, Zambian or Zimbabwean English can still constrain at a local level in a host country. Ultimately this could impact on a migrant's career and economic prospects (for example, in the case of these academics, student evaluations form part of the measure for promotion).

Another outcome of many of the migration trajectories described by these participants was language loss – migrants described both first- and second-generation loss of first language resources as a result of their migration. In many cases, the children of these academics did not speak the African languages of their parents; and in some cases, the academics themselves felt they had lost the ability to speak their mother tongue/home language with any great proficiency. This was due to the central role of English language in both the academy and their migration journeys, as well as a lack of opportunity to speak their home languages outside their home country (home languages may not be shared with other migrants from their home country, particularly in the case of languages spoken only in small communities).

Continental scale

In terms of flows within a continental region, the next example is drawn from recent sub-Saharan Africa migrant flows, specifically those from Zimbabwe to South Africa (South-South). In this case there are significant 'push' factors that led to an increased flow of migrants, particularly during the hyperinflation of Zimbabwean currency in 2008–2009. In 2008, during a series of what were labeled 'xenophobic' attacks in South Africa – a spate of violence against migrants from other parts of Sub-Saharan Africa who were seen as a threat to employment and security – reports emerged that foreigners were being identified partly by whether or not they could correctly pronounce words and phrases in Zulu (Orman 2012). Ndebele, a major Zimbabwean language, is closely related to Zulu, while Shona, another major Zimbabwean language, is not. According to Ndlovu (2010), during the xenophobic attacks, attackers asked suspected migrants to pronounce the Zulu word for 'elbow' (*idolo*). Siziba (2013) suggests this resulted in Ndebele speakers passing the shibboleth test while Shona speakers either did not know the Zulu word or were unable to correctly pronounce it, resulting in an attack on their person. Thus, while Ndebele language resources retained cultural value across a political border (because of historical links with Zulu, Swati, and Xhosa – the Nguni cluster of languages), Shona language resources lost cultural value, and any local (Zulu) resources gained by Shona speakers were devalued through accent. The value of these migrants' multilingual resources changed when the economic climate shifted, and as a result the social climate towards migrants shifted and one specific local accent and language became prioritized (this led to economic as well as social effects as foreign-owned businesses were targeted).

Orman (2012: n.p.) argues that "In the case of African migrants to South Africa, mobility is often seen to entail a reductive reordering and re-evaluation of their linguistic repertoires which serve to both index and be partly constitutive of their unequal social status." He highlights the current intolerance and hostility towards outsiders particularly from other parts of Africa, and that language is indexical of otherness. He suggests that migrants encounter difficulty in being 'heard' and making themselves understood, something that constitutes a critical component of the communicative process. Many African migrants in South Africa rely on English to communicate, but their particular English resources may not protect them from stigmatization, because as Orman (2012: n.p.) states:

> In most cases the Englishes spoken by Nigerians and other African migrants differ saliently from those forms of English which function as elite or high-prestige varieties in the South African context. In some cases, they may only differ perceptibly in terms of accent but this is still nevertheless sufficient to index a meaningful otherness and therefore become a potential catalyst for differential or unequal treatment.

So even though these migrants have the language resources needed for mobility and social and economic activity in another environment, they are at risk from subtle linguistic differences within a complex decolonizing country. The result is, as Orman suggests, a 'reductive reordering', and possibly, in the event of long-term migration, attrition of devalued language resources.

National scale

As a result of the emphasis on the Global North in much migration and language literature, and the monolingual orientation of European nation-states, there has been little theory developed regarding the ways in which language flows between regions *within* multilingual countries, for example rural-urban migration. When we focus on local migration in contexts in the Global South, we uncover patterns, strategies, and effects that can extend our understanding of the dynamics of language and migration, and the shifting value of resources at a national level.

Rural areas are often excluded from and decentred by the dominant economic system, which can manifest in particular attitudes towards rural forms of language. In South Africa, a strong rural-urban dichotomy can be traced back to the colonial/apartheid system of racial classification which resulted in language-based 'homelands' – rural territories designated for Black African people (as designated by apartheid racial and ethnic classifications) to live in on a principle of 'separate development' (Mda 2010). In these 'homelands', primary education took place in African languages; but the homelands were underfunded and lacked the resources that were invested in the urban centres. The urban areas were predominantly reserved for White people and dominated by English and Afrikaans. Thus questions of rurality and urbanity (and ultimately, citizenship of the republic) were tied to race classifications (Mda 2010). Since the end of apartheid, there has been a huge influx of people from the old homelands (now incorporated into the nine provinces of South Africa) towards the urban centres, resulting in the rapid growth of peri-urban 'townships' (large residential areas characterized by government housing and informal housing). Many recent and long-term internal migrants staying in the townships retain family and ancestral links with the rural areas, travelling regularly from the city for occasions such as initiations and funerals.

Within these migratory flows, different languages and registers of languages are privileged according to the context of use; in the cities, rural people and their speech may be mocked by urbanites as slow or backwards in comparison to urban vernaculars, which are seen as modern. For example, research highlights that particular forms of African languages – the urban varieties – are valued and considered 'city-smart' by young people in South Africa's townships while the rural forms are considered old-fashioned (Hurst, 2017). This leads to derogatory terms for rural people relating to them being 'slow' or 'backwards' like their speech, for example in South African Tsotsitaal, *Cowza,* from English 'cow', means 'someone from rural areas' (Bogopa 1996: 126). Brookes (2014: 63) explains,

> If a young man does not display sufficient communicative skill to hold the attention of his peers, they describe him as boring and label him a *bari* "a stupid," which is the label township dwellers give to people from rural areas who are considered backward and tribal.

Yet the 'deep' rural forms of African languages retain value in the rural areas and among older and more 'traditional' township residents, and when young people go back to rural areas for visits, their urban forms are not valued, and are seen as 'disrespectful'; and young urbanites lament their 'loss' of rural forms which would have value in this context (Hurst 2008).

Migration flows between urban and rural areas clearly lead to changes in the cultural value of language resources. Furthermore, when people arrive in the urban centres as part of their migration trajectories (often with the aim of economic improvement), language differences may also have economic implications. Deumert, Inder, and Maitra (2005) investigated the language dynamics of rural-urban internal migrants in Cape Town, and found that "inadequate knowledge of dominant urban languages (English and Afrikaans) limits opportunities for employment and access to public services" (Deumert, Inder, and Maitra 2005: 303). This highlights some of the dynamics of language mobility internally within a particular country, particularly the dominance of the centres and how this reflects economic power. In the South African context the privileging of the English language in particular, but also Afrikaans, over African languages, reflects a legacy of European and later Afrikaner economic power in a country which was plagued by segregation in the form of apartheid until the late 20th century. This privileging played out particularly through preferential employment policies and separate education which placed English and Afrikaans in dominant positions to African languages and afforded them economic power.

Added to this, English resources are currently highly valued at the bigger (global) scale (reflected in the current global demand for English language education), and this cements their value at the national scale in many of Britain's ex-colonies, in formal domains such as education, business, and politics. Again using South Africa as an example, the country has a complex language history due to factors such as the influx of missionaries and colonialism, alongside various long- and short-term continental and internal migrations. As a result of its complex language history, South Africa has adopted an unusual language policy which recognizes eleven official languages. Yet English is the dominant language used in most public and formal domains, and the medium of higher levels of education (from grade 4, ages eight to nine and upwards). Hurst (2016) highlights the language difficulties that students who speak an African language as their first or home language encounter in various transitions, including the internal migrations they have undertaken. The students surveyed were from a range of backgrounds – rural, suburban, urban, and township, as well as from a range of economic backgrounds and schooling experiences. Students from the rural areas in particular talk about their lack of exposure to languages other than their home languages as they were growing up. Although the majority of high schools in South Africa have an English medium of instruction policy, in practice many teachers continue to use African languages in the classroom. This may be for a variety of reasons – for example, the need for teachers to explain concepts in students' home languages for clarity, or the English proficiency of the teachers themselves may be a limitation. This unofficial medium of instruction practice was sometimes blamed by students for their poor performance when they arrived at the English medium university. Being taught in African languages at school is seen as a 'disadvantage', particularly in terms of economic prospects. English, on the other hand, is seen as the global language which provides access to employment (Hurst, forthcoming b). The result of these pressures is that young people find themselves losing their home languages (Hurst 2016, forthcoming b). This is experienced as a cultural or social loss, and real social effects are experienced as a result of this loss – young people who only speak English due to their education are called 'coconuts' (an offensive slang term meaning "black on the outside, white on the inside"); one student described how she was told she was not a 'real Xhosa woman' because she had lost her home language. So while English may be seen as adding economic value, it can result in the attrition of language resources that hold cultural value.

Thus English is the language that is privileged in official domains in the urban centres, and African languages become a disadvantage, devalued, and a constraint on mobility. The language resources of students from rural areas are still valued in the metropolis in informal domains where they are an important cultural resource (for example, Xhosa speakers from the Xhosa ex-homeland the Transkei, which now forms part of the Eastern Cape Province, find their language resources particularly valuable in the large Xhosa-speaking townships on the periphery of the city of Cape Town where large numbers of Eastern Cape migrants reside), but in terms of educational and economic mobility they are devalued. English on the other hand enables mobility and confers status – if a student does well in English, she may be accepted to enter one of the English-medium universities in a metropolis, and she is more likely to succeed if her English were learned in a strictly English-medium school, which are predominantly found in urban centres or more wealthy suburbs. As a result, families adopt strategies to enable their children to move into urban contexts, strategies that can be more or less successful depending on structural factors. One strategy is rural-urban migration, which is used as a family strategy to prepare a child for education and employment. Part of this migration strategy is the expectation that schools in urban areas will use English, so language itself is one of the direct drivers of this regional flow. The linking of the metropolis with a better education is therefore tied to a rural-urban duality, and its accompanying language dimension – the cities were reserves of the European languages, while African languages were relegated to the rural homelands. The legacy of this legislation still informs people's spatial and linguistic experiences today, and constrains regional flows.

Implications

Language resource devaluation is happening at all levels of regional flows in the examples given in this chapter – international, continental, and national. Migrants' language resources may lose value economically, but also in terms of cultural capital, through the negotiation of what is valued within local contexts, and this has an effect on people's lived experiences, relationships, identities, and life trajectories.

Research is beginning to show how multilingualism and home languages can constitute resources that can be retained and leveraged for economic and social gain, which suggests that policies reflecting a "strongly modernist, nationalist framework" (Orman 2012: n.p.) and promoting monolingualism need to be reviewed. In continents and national contexts where monolingualism has never been an established norm, these issues are even more pertinent; and education and language policy models based on the norms of the Global North need to be urgently interrogated (cf. Makoni and Pennycook 2005, for an argument relating to the 'disinvention' of languages). Policies need to be considered that promote multilingualism rather than nationalistic monolingualism or even multiple (ethnic) monolingualisms; the dismantling of categories of ethnic difference based on language or skin colour would be a welcome rejection of those very categorization processes that caused division and violence throughout Africa during the colonial period and beyond, and today result in outbreaks of xenophobic violence such as those seen in South Africa in recent years.

At a national scale, English dominates the South African language landscape and its use in domains such as education is usually defended on economic grounds. Yet the result is widespread inequality (of other languages, dialects, etc.), and a resultant disadvantage for the majority of South Africans for whom English is not a first language. Ongoing academic and policy discussions continue to grapple with this issue (cf. Busch, Busch, and Press 2014). Monolingual projects are particularly contested in contexts such as many sub-Saharan African countries where the status and roles of colonial languages are under political and popular scrutiny, but where the multilingual terrain particularly in the urban centres allows for no easy decisions about alternative official languages. Unfortunately the historical and ongoing emphasis on colonial European languages at the expense of other languages due to their current global status is a short-term view, which can result in language loss at a personal and national level.

Future directions

Some specific focused research or theoretical questions relating to this topic that could be developed further in future research include the following:

- Under what conditions is language maintained in migration contexts? What are the effects of maintenance, and on the other hand, what are the effects of short- and long-term language attrition (first and second generation) on migration trajectories?
- What are the tensions between economic value and social value in terms of maintenance? In cases where economic value takes precedence in the short term, does social value reassert itself in the revival of the relevant language resources?
- What differences are there between the Global North and the Global South in terms of the language implications of different phases of urbanization and migration? How has nationalism and colonialism played out in language policy and reality?

Summary

There are various understandings of the term 'language resources', for example, the conceptualization of language as an economic and cultural resource, as well as the resources held by an individual, constituted by languages, dialects, registers, sociolects, and so on. Language resources are involved in the regional flows of migrants between the Global North and South, within continents, and within national flows such as rural-urban migration. Language resources can confer mobility as well as constrain it, and the value of migrants' language resources are always renegotiated within the local contexts of their migration trajectories. Many renegotiations result in the devaluing of resources that were previously valued in the migrants' home contexts – both in economic terms (migrants may no longer be able to use their languages as capital, or to enable capital through employment) and in cultural terms (resources are no longer able to be leveraged as cultural capital) – and this can lead to "reductive reordering" or ultimately, language loss among first- or second-generation migrants. These considerations are equally applicable at a national level as a feature of rural-urban migration flows, as they are at an international level as part of South-North, North-South, South-South, and North-North flows. Thus, by conducting research on internal migrations in historically multilingual contexts such as those found in much of sub-Saharan Africa, we can increase our understanding of the effects of regional flows on language resources.

Related topics

Translanguaging in mobility
Nation-state, transnationalism, and language
Space, place, and language
Migration trajectories

Further reading

Blommaert, J. (2010). *The Sociolinguistics of Globalization*. Cambridge: Cambridge University Press.

This book describes a sociolinguistics of mobile resources and provides examples of migrant repertoires.

Bourdieu, P. (1986). The forms of capital. In J. Richardson (ed.), *Handbook of Theory and Research for the Sociology of Education*. New York: Greenwood, pp. 241–258.

Bourdieu describes three forms of capital – economic, cultural, and social – and focuses on their accumulation and the perpetuation of social inequality.

Coupland, Nikolas. (2010). *The Handbook of Language and Globalization*. Oxford: Wiley-Blackwell.

This book contains some important chapters relating to language resources, such as Heller's chapter "Language as a Resource in the New Globalized Economy".

Mignolo, W. (2005). *The Idea of Latin America*. Malden: Blackwell.

In this manifesto, Walter Mignolo sets out the fundamentals of decolonial thinking and challenges the continued dominance of 19th-century European thought.

Singleton, D., Fishman, J., Aronin, L. and O Laoire, M., eds. (2013). *Current Multilingualism: A New Linguistic Dispensation*. Berlin: De Gruyter.

This volume looks at contemporary multilingualism, focusing particularly on the themes of education, sociolinguistics, and language policy.

References

Agnihotri, R. (2010). Multilinguality and the teaching of English in India. *EFL Journal* 1(1): 1–13.
Amin, M. and Mattoo, A. (2007). *Migration from Zambia: Ensuring Temporariness through Cooperation*. World Bank Policy Research Working Paper 4145.
Bailey, A.J., Mupakati, L. and Magunha, F.M. (forthcoming). Misplaced: Language, remitting and development practice among Zimbabwean migrants. *Globalisation Societies and Education*.
Bamgbose, A. (2000). *Language and Exclusion: The Consequence of Language Policies in Africa*. Hamburg: Lit Verlag.
Bekker, S. (2006). Migration from South Africa's rural sending areas: Changing intentions and changing destinations. In Gallo-Mosala, S. (ed.), *Migration to South Africa within International Migration Trends*. Cape Town: The Scalabrini Centre. Available at http://www.simonbekker.com/simonsdocs/Scalabrini%20paper%20internal%20migration.doc.

Beyer, K. (2014). Urban language research in South Africa: Achievements and challenges. *Southern African Linguistics and Applied Language Studies* 32(2): 247–254.

Bleakley, H. and Chin, A. (2004). Language skills and earnings: Evidence from childhood immigrants. *Review of Economics and Statistics* 84(2): 481–496.

Blommaert, J. (2010). *The Sociolinguistics of Globalization*. Cambridge: Cambridge University Press.

Blommaert, J. and Rampton, B. (2011) Language and superdiversity. *Diversities* 13(2): 1–21.

Bogopa, D. (1996). *The Language and Culture of the Youth in the "Nicaragua" Section of Tsakane in Gauteng*. MA thesis, University of Durban-Westville.

Bourdieu, P. (1988). *Homo Academicus* [Translated by P. Collier]. Stanford, CA: Stanford University Press.

Bourdieu, P. and Wacquant, L. (1992). *An Invitation to Reflexive Sociology*. London: University of Chicago Press.

Brookes, H. (2014) Gesture in the communicative ecology of a South African township. In Seyfeddinipur, M. and Gullberg, M. (eds.), *From Gesture in Conversation to Visible Action as Utterance: Essays in Honor of Adam Kendon* (pp. 59–73). Amsterdam: John Benjamins.

Busch, B., Busch, L. and Press, K. (2014). *Interviews with Neville Alexander: The Power of Languages against the Language of Power*. Durban: UKZN Press.

Canagarajah, S. (2013) *Translingual Practice: Global Englishes and Cosmopolitan Relations*. New York: Routledge.

Castells, M. (2001) The new global economy. In Muller, J., Cloete, N. and Badat, S. (eds.), *Challenges of Globalisation: South African Debates with Manuel Castells* (pp. 2–21). Cape Town: Juta.

Chiswick, B. and Miller, P. (2002). Immigrant earnings: Language skills, linguistic concentrations and the business cycle. *Journal of Population Economics* 15(1): 31–57.

Coupland, N. and Jaworski, A. (2009) Social worlds through language. In Coupland, N. and Jaworski, A. (eds.), *The New Sociolinguistics Reader* (pp. 1–21). Basingstoke: Palgrave Macmillan.

Creese, A. and Blackledge, A. (2010) Towards a sociolinguistics of superdiversity. *Zeitschrift Für Erziehungswissenschaft* 13(4): 549–572.

Deumert, A., Inder, B. and Maitra, P. (2005) Language, informal networks and social protection: Evidence from a sample of migrants in Cape Town, South Africa. *Global Social Policy* 5(3): 303–328.

Docquier, F. and Marfouk, A. (2004) *Measuring the International Mobility of Skilled Workers (1990–2000)*. Policy Research Working Paper 3381, The World Bank, Washington, DC.

Dustmann, C. and van Soest, A. (2002) Language and the earnings of immigrants. *Journal of Industrial and Labor Relations Review* 55(3): 473–492.

Escobar, A. (1995). *Encountering Development: The Making and Unmaking of the Third World*. Princeton: Princeton University Press.

Garrido, M.R. and Codó, E. (forthcoming). Deskilling and delanguaging African migrants in Barcelona: Pathways of labour market incorporation and the value of "global" English. *Globalisation Societies and Education*.

Gumperz, J. (1964). Linguistic and social interaction in two communities. *American Anthropologist* 66: 137–154.

Heller, M. (2010). Language as a resource in the new globalized economy. In Coupland, N. (ed.), *Handbook of Language and Globalization* (pp. 349–365). London: Blackwell.

Heugh, K. (2014). Multilingualism, the "African lingua franca" and the "new linguistic dispensation". Paper presented at The Cape Town Language and Development Conference: Looking Beyond 2015.

Heugh, K. T. (2010). The structure and entrenchment of disadvantage in South Africa. In Snyder, I. and Nieuwenhuysen, J. (eds.), Closing the Gap in Education?: Improving Outcomes in Southern World Societies (pp. 95–110). Clayton: Monash University.

Hurst, E. (2008). *Style, Structure and Function in Cape Town Tsotsitaal*. PhD Thesis, University of Cape Town.

Hurst, E. (2014) English and the academy for African skilled migrants: The impact of English as an "academic lingua franca". In Malcolm Tight and Nina Madaad (eds.), *Academic Mobility* (pp. 153–173) International Perspectives on Higher Education Research 11. Bingley: Emerald Press.

Hurst, E. (2016). Navigating language and education: The "colonial wound" in South Africa. *Language and Education* (online publication date 29 October 2015).

Hurst, E. (forthcoming a) Local villages and global networks: The language and migration experiences of African skilled migrant academics. *Globalisation Societies and Education* (online publication date 14 November 2014).

Hurst, E. (2017). Rural/urban dichotomies and youth language. In Ebonguè, A. and Hurst, E. (eds.), *Sociolinguistics in African Contexts*. Springer.

Hurst, E. (forthcoming b) Hierarchies and coloniality: Students' language ideologies and attitudes in Cape Town. Submitted to *Southern African Journal of African Languages*.

Jørgensen, J.N., Karrebaek, M., Madsen, L.M. and Møller, J.S. (2011). Polylanguaging in superdiversity. *Diversities* 13(2): 23–37.

Kerswill, P. (2006) Migration and language. In Mattheier, K. Ammon, U. and Trudgill, P. (eds.), *Sociolinguistics/Soziolinguistik. An International Handbook of the Science of Language and Society* (Vol. 3, pp. 2271–2285). Berlin: De Gruyter Mouton.

Levitt, P., DeWind, J. and Vertovec, S. (2003). International perspectives on transnational migration: An introduction. *International Migration Review* 37(3): 565–575.

Liebowitz, B. (2005). Learning in an additional language in a multilingual society: A South African case study on university-level writing. *TESOL Quarterly* 39(4): 661–681.

Makoni, S. and Pennycook, A. (2005). Disinventing and (re)constituting languages. *Critical Inquiry in Language Studies* 2(3): 137–156.

McLaughlin, F., ed. (2009). *The Languages of Urban Africa*. London: Continuum.

McLaughlin, F. (2014). Senegalese digital repertoires in superdiversity: A case study from Seneweb. *Discourse, Context & Media* 4–5: 29–37.

Mufwene, S. (2010) Globalization, global English, and world English(es): Myths and facts. In Coupland, N. (ed.), *The Handbook of Language and Globalization* (pp. 31–55). Chichester: Blackwell.

Nassenstein, N. and Hollington, A., eds. (2015) *Youth Language Practices in Africa and beyond*. Berlin: De Gruyter Mouton.

Ndlovu, T. (2010) Where is my home? Rethinking person, family, ethnicity and home under increased transnational migration by Zimbabweans. *African Identities* 8(2): 117–130.

Orman, J. (2012) Language and "new" African migration to South Africa: An overview and some reflections on theoretical implications for policy and planning. *Language Policy* 11(4): 301–322.

Otsuji, E. and Pennycook, A. (2010). Metrolingualism: Fixity, fluidity and language in flux. *International Journal of Multilingualism* 7(3): 240–254.

Park, J. (2014). Cartographies of language: Making sense of mobility among Korean transmigrants in Singapore. *Language & Communication* 39: 83–91.

Siziba, G. (2013). *Language and the Politics of Identity in South Africa: The Case of Zimbabwean (Shona and Ndebele speaking) Migrants in Johannesburg*. PhD thesis, Stellenbosch University.

Vertovec, S. (2006). *The Emergence of Super-Diversity in Britain*. Centre on Migration, Policy and Society, Working Paper 25.

Vertovec, S. (2009). *Transnationalism*. Abingdon: Routledge.

Victoria, M. (forthcoming). English: Its role as the language of comity in an employment programme for Canadian immigrants. *Globalisation Societies and Education*.

World Migration Report. (2013). *Migrant Well-being and Development*. International Organisation for Migration.

Zimmermann, K. (2014). *Circular Migration: Why Restricting Labor Mobility Can Be Counterproductive*. IZA World of Labor 1.

10
Displacement and language

Kathleen Heugh

Introduction

Displacement, as discussed in this chapter, is a fairly recently recognised phenomenon within studies of migration, where people flee from their local environment to another location inside their own country, rather than to another country as refugees. The phenomenon occurs as a result of involuntary departure usually because of conflict, rapid onset disaster, or climate change. These conditions cause not only spatial dislocation, but also a range of associated disruptions in the linguistic ecology, epistemology, and cosmology of affected people. These in turn result in psycho-social ruptures for individuals and communities (e.g., Dunn 2014). By far the majority of people affected by dislocation are marginalised communities and the locations to which they flee are often remote borderlands. Here the circumstances of vulnerability may be overlooked by national governments, international agencies, and researchers. The focus in this chapter is to draw attention to the paucity of research, including both migration studies and linguistics (sociolinguistics and educational linguistics) in regards to people who have been displaced inside their countries or in the porous border regions of adjoining countries. It is also to point towards the need for cautious research among communities that have suffered ongoing cycles of displacement, and how such research may contribute to ethical understandings of the relationship among conflict and or disaster, marginality, vulnerability, and the role of language(s), well-being (Polzer and Hammond 2008), and (dis)citizenship (see also Ramanathan 2013).

The discussion of displacement here differs in at least four ways from literature that addresses similar or related issues for vulnerable or marginalised communities. First, although numerous authors have drawn attention to the disruptive consequences of colonisation for communities and the linguistic ecologies and education systems of Latin and North America, Africa, Asia, Australia, and the Pacific (e.g., Hamel 1997; Bamgbose 2000; Heugh 2006; Watson 2009; Ouane and Glanz 2011; Sercombe and Tupas 2014), few studies address the consequences of displacement in recently emerging migration theory. Second, although there is a substantial literature that discusses linguistic diversity and colonial or postcolonial marginalization of language communities, this often suggests a flattened dichotomy between endogenous language communities and exogenous (colonial) languages. In other words, there has been insufficient discussion of the longue durée of pre-colonial as well as colonial and postcolonial layers of hierarchical marginalisation. These layers result in multi-scaled differences and degrees of (in)visibility between more powerful and less powerful indigenous language communities. Mohanty (2010) draws attention to the 'double divide' between powerful regional and local language communities and tribal communities that are subjected to ongoing historical marginalization in India. This 'double divide' is equally palpable in Africa (e.g., Heugh 2014a) where there are significant differences between the linguistic capital held by speakers of regionally powerful languages such as Amharic, Hausa, Wolof, and isiZulu, compared with the systemically minoritised language communities, such as the speakers of San and Khoe languages in Southern Africa. It is these communities that are most susceptible to displacement. Third, there is already a well-established literature on the causes of language displacement, shift, loss, and endangerment (e.g., Brenzinger 1997, 2015; Ostler 2011), and language revitalization (e.g., Grenoble and Whaley 2006). These are usually addressed through the lenses of historical linguistics, sociolinguistics, and/or anthropological linguistics. The purpose here is to breach linguistics and to explore an interdisciplinary approach that includes displacement as a sub-branch of migration studies (itself including perspectives from psychology, sociology, and anthropology) alongside linguistics. Fourth, there appears to be an intersection of the dispersal of displaced people caught within layers of marginality to geopolitical peripheries and borderland theory (Anzaldúa 1987; Martinez 1994) in which people experience ongoing stigma and "dis-citizenship," to borrow from Ramanathan (2013). They have to undergo language shift or expand their linguistic repertoires in order to survive. Fifth, what is missing from the literature is an attempt to understand displacement as this articulates with an interrelatedness of community language, epistemology, cosmology, and well-being.

The purpose here is to begin a discussion of displacement and language that goes beyond postcolonial analyses of disrupted linguistic ecologies. It is to attempt to unveil the linguistic consequences of historical and systemic layers of marginality and invisibility of displaced minority communities that live in borderlands, out of sight and mostly out of mind.[1]

Overview

Whereas people who are forced to seek refuge outside of their countries are known as 'refugees', the term 'displacement' has recently gained currency in the literature of migration studies that distinguishes between those displaced within their own countries and those obliged to seek refuge outside of their countries (e.g., UNICEF 1996; UN 1998; Brookings-Bern Project on Internal Displacement 2008; Polzer and Hammond 2008; Yoder 2008; Phuong 2010; Jacques 2012; Dunn 2014; IMDC 2014a, 2014b). While the attention of this chapter is primarily directed towards internally displaced persons (IDPs) rather than refugees, there are ambiguous historical circumstances of shifting and porous geopolitical borders; therefore, these distinctions are not always clear or constant. Since IDPs have been recognised as experiencing extreme circumstances of marginalisation and human rights abuse, and since many of these occur in remote borderland settings, the discussion here includes displacement of people who are obliged to follow porous routes that criss-cross remote political boundary lines. For all intents and purposes, such people exist as IDPs rather than as refugees who are documented and who have recourse to internationally agreed provisions.

Although displacement of people has been an ongoing feature of human existence for as long as historical information exists, attention towards the plight of people within the geopolitical borders of their own countries has been largely left in the hands of nation-state authorities. Whereas people who are displaced from their own to other countries have since 1950 fallen under the remit of the United Nations High Commissioner for Refugees (UNHCR), IDPs have existed under the radar of international monitoring organisations, and have often passed undocumented in their own countries. Lack of information about internal displacement has meant that IDPs have fallen outside of legal provisions and policies of international agencies, including UNHCR, leaving IDPs particularly vulnerable to poor provision of human rights' protection and public services in their own countries. In cases of ongoing cycles of displacement, including conflict, there is likely to be political and economic instability that leave displaced people living in conditions of long-term vulnerability (UN 1998). Vulnerability includes poverty; susceptibility to ill-health; limited or dysfunctional provision of health care and education; inadequate access to administrative services; inadequate provision of and information about safety and security; and circumstances which bring about cultural and linguistic discrimination and possible loss of language, culture, epistemologies, and ways of being. By the early 1990s it became clear that there needed to be internationally recognised instruments to protect IDPs. The *Guiding Principles on Internal Displacement* (UN 1998) was the first international document circulated to governments, UN-affiliated bodies and non-governmental organisations (NGOs) for the first time. This document serves as the starting point for a growing set of reports, documents, and legal instruments that focus attention on the scale and nature of, and international responses to displacement.

Internal displacement, currently estimated at sixty million people, arises from several causes. The most prevalent cause is socio-political or faith-based conflict, usually accompanied by violence and human rights violations. The 20th and early 21st centuries, for example, have witnessed appalling examples of ethnic, faith-based, or political cleansing and genocide across Africa, Asia, Europe, Latin America, and the Middle East. In each case, there has been large-scale human dislocation, with only one-third of displaced people able to seek refuge elsewhere (IMDC 2014a).

The second most frequent cause of displacement is 'rapid-onset' disaster (e.g., tropical cyclones, floods, droughts, earthquakes, and tsunamis). A third, often related, cause of forced relocation arises from environmental change resulting, for example, in desertification, famine, and plague. A fourth, less documented cause arises from political and economic interests in natural resources (e.g., resulting in deforestation of equatorial forests alongside the Amazon and Congo Rivers) or mineral resources (resulting in mining-induced displacement) located in areas inhabited by (tribal or minority) communities with limited political or socio-economic power (IMDC 2014b). A fifth cause is attributed to environmental interests where communities are displaced, ostensibly in order to protect the natural habitat of indigenous flora and fauna. In many cases, two or more of these causes overlap (IMDC 2014b).

Whereas there is a substantial body of literature and published research concerned with refugees (e.g., as evident in three prominent journals: *Journal of Refugee Studies*, Oxford; *Refugee Survey Quarterly*, Oxford; and *Journal of Immigration & Refugee Studies*, Taylor & Francis), this is not the case with IDPs. The reason is that IDPs are usually located in remote settings, often out of sight and because conflict both exacerbates vulnerability and restricts humanitarian aid and research access for reasons of safety and security. This means that the relationship between displacement and language is not well understood beyond the circumstances of those most affected and a limited number of NGO workers whose experience and knowledge of linguistic concerns have limited passage into UNICEF or UNESCO documents on education, and less so into academic literature. The role of language as the conduit to information required for life-sustaining and safety mechanisms, and humanitarian support, has therefore been under-represented in the newly emerging body of IDP literature. It has similarly received limited attention in literature which addresses resettlement and reintegration of vulnerable communities.

Significant aspects of vulnerability include various forms of systemic human rights abuse, including physical and mental brutality in the form of abductions, rape, forced marriage, human trafficking, and child soldiering; torture, mutilation, and genocide; and an ongoing environment of fear and instability. Such circumstances require emergency responses from humanitarian aid workers whose training lies beyond sociolinguistics and education. The likelihood that aid workers are able to communicate in IDP languages, particularly in areas of linguistic diversity, is slim. The role of language in relation to how information is transmitted and received as trustworthy or duplicitous, enabling or disabling, inclusive or exclusive, empowering or sub-alterning, and permitting or foreclosing of voice, is either not fully understood or not attended to by international agencies delivering emergency relief or engaging with reconstruction. It is also a context which remains under-researched by sociolinguists, despite the unprecedented scale of human displacement during recent years.

In this chapter, I hope to draw attention to issues of language in relation to well-being, epistemology, and cosmology (belief) and communities who are displaced. These issues will be discussed in relation to three examples of contexts in which remote communities experience multiple or overlapping causes for displacement, and where these have consequences for language(s) that have been little understood or that remain largely invisible in mainstream discussions. These examples have been selected for several reasons. First, sub-Saharan Africa has been identified as the region most likely to experience increasing internal dislocation for multiple overlapping reasons for several decades to come. These include conflict, rapid-onset disaster, environmental change, and deforestation and mining, which are expected to result in the highest incidence of IDPs in the world over the next several decades (IDMC 2014a, 2014b). Second, it is also possible to demonstrate the residual, cyclical, and long-term nature of displacement in relation to some implications for language in these settings. Third, the author is also able to draw on ethnographic field data that may bring some immediacy to the discussion.

While these examples have been selected to illustrate extreme experiences of displacement, they are in no way intended to eclipse experiences of displacement elsewhere. Cases of displacement that have caused large-scale human suffering have characterized much of the 20th century and first two decades of the 21st century, for example as evidenced by minority communities in the post-Yugoslav states (e.g., Pupavac 2006), Colombia (e.g., Olarte and Wall 2012), Georgia (e.g., Dunn 2014), Mexico and Central America (IMDC 2015a), and notably large-scale displacement of communities in Syria and Iraq (IMDC 2015b).

The first example, ongoing overlapping cycles of displacement of minority indigenous San communities of Southern Africa over hundreds of years, illustrates the longue durée of displacement. These circumstances include forced migration, political and economic conflict, and interests of 'conservation', diamond mining, and fracking. The second example, that of pastoral communities in the Afar and Somali Regions of Ethiopia, illustrates the consequences of settlement programmes, climate change, and desertification, and overlaps with trafficking of young women, border conflict, opportunistic lawlessness, and differences of belief/faith. The third example draws attention to systemic human conflict (armed insurgencies of rebel groups and government forces) in borderlands of Northern Uganda, South Sudan, and the Democratic Republic of Congo, along with human trafficking and genocide. In each case, the consequence of displacement, whether as a result of conflict and/or competing interests, affect livelihood and well-being, and are amplified by clashing systems of belief/faith.

Whereas migration studies literature on displacement distinguishes between different causes of displacement, the field data discussed here suggests that marginalised communities in borderlands are subjected to a repeated or successive mix of socio-political, conflictual, and environmental factors that cause displacement over long periods of time. The mix of factors contributes to physical displacement and also psycho-socio vulnerabilities that compound poverty, hunger, lack of personal safety, and marginalization (see also Martinez 1994; Polzer and Hammond 2008; Dunn 2014). Field data reported later in this chapter suggest that in settings of marginality and diversity, displacement also has consequences in which local knowledge systems (epistemologies) residing within local languages/repertoires of language and evolving from specific contexts may rupture or atrophy when people have to move to places that are environmentally alien. At the same time, and conversely, communities on the fringes, more used to mobility, may also acquire socio-cultural and linguistic resources of survival, reinvention, and the establishment of new sets of sociolinguistic identities and affinities (see also discussion of community occupation of public space in Bogota, Colombia, in Olarte and Wall 2012).

In the following examples, changes in language practices of IDPs are often conflated in development literature in ways that 'voice' and 'agency' of affected people are assumed to have disappeared, and issues of voice and language are reduced, misunderstood, or positioned through Northern or Western perspectives (e.g., Dunn 2014). Nevertheless, informants express their view of and association with repertoires of language, culture, and epistemologies (e.g., Heugh 2014b) through a variety of media, including, for example, art, dance, trance, and use of new technologies. It is also the case that informants express particular agency towards literacy and languages in education and in new local economic enterprises of resettlement (e.g., Heugh and Mulumba 2014). In each case, language regimes radiate outwards from the administrative centre. These regimes articulate awkwardly with communicative practices of marginalised communities responsive to the sociolinguistic ecology of borderlands. Although neither national government authorities nor various UN agencies have much pragmatic traction regarding how language practices and policies are reinterpreted in these settings, there are NGO and missionary agents with specific interests and these have implications for languages.

Issues and ongoing debates

As indicated earlier, whereas international agencies have been monitoring the mobility of refugees, there have been serious gaps of information regarding the circumstances of internal displacement and resettlement (UNICEF 1996, 2009; UNESCO 2011). It was only in 1998 that the Norwegian Refugee Council (NRC) established the International Displacement Monitoring Centre (IMDC) to collect reliable data. Statistical data and forecasts on conflict- and/or disaster-related displacement: (IMDC 2014a, 2014b) indicate an increase of the incidence of displacement and that humanitarian and associated socio-political, educational, and economic concerns, signal international crises (e.g., UNESCO 2011). Instruments for gauging medium- to long-term human impact have not yet taken into account the implications for language practices beyond a rudimentary acknowledgement of linguistic diversity.

IMDC (2014a: 9) indicates that the number of people affected by conflict-induced displacement rose from 19.3 million in 1998 to 33.3 million in 2013. The number of people affected by natural disaster or hazard-induced displacement has averaged twenty-seven million per year between 2008 and 2013, affecting people in 161 countries (IMDC 2014b: 15, 11). Together sixty million people were identified as displaced as a result of conflict and/or natural disaster by the end of 2013.

The regions most affected by armed conflict induced displacement are sub-Saharan Africa, North Africa, and the Middle East, with sixty-three percent of displacements in 2013 from Syria, Colombia, Nigeria, the Democratic Republic of the Congo (DRC), Sudan, and South Sudan (IMDC 2014a: 9). Currently IMDC (2015b) reports that the numbers of refugees are 1.5 million in Nigeria, 2.85 million in DRC, 4 million in Iraq, and at least 7.8 million in Syria. Between 2008 and 2013, eighty-one percent of disaster or natural hazard displacement occurred in Asian countries. Africa is the second most frequent site of natural disaster. Because of projected population growth statistics, IMDC (2014b: 25) anticipates that the number of people affected by disaster in Africa will rise and outstrip other regions within a few decades. In many cases there is a coincidence of armed conflict and natural disaster (IMDC 2014b: 44). Nigeria, Sudan, and South Sudan are examples where rapid-onset disaster-related and conflict-related displacement coincide. Colombia is an example where displacement occurs for multiple reasons over several decades, that is, ongoing political and civil conflict, natural disaster, mining-induced displacement, drug cartel intimidation, and crime (see also Olarte and Wall 2012), while conflict-induced displacement is increasing in Mexico, Central America, and the Middle East (IMDC 2015a).

Conflict-induced displacement exerts particular psychological trauma, with long-term consequences for people forced to flee their homes (e.g., Dunn 2014), experience genocide, and endure abduction and enslavement for purposes of sexual abuse or child soldiering. Such abuses have been and/or are prevalent in country-level and regional conflicts, for example in the former Yugoslavia, Rwanda, Liberia, Sierra Leone, the Central African Republic (CAR), DRC, South Sudan, Somalia, Uganda, and Nigeria over the last several decades. Global media have drawn attention to the ravages of rebel groups (insurgents) as related to Al-Qaeda in Afghanistan and Pakistan; Islamic State in Syria and Iraq; the Lord's Resistance Army in Northern Uganda, Central African Republic and South Sudan; Boko Haram in Nigeria; and Al-Shabaab in Kenya. However, the extent and long-term effects of displacement are little understood. Resettlement may only be possible several years or decades after displacement. In contrast, people affected by rapid-onset disaster are usually temporarily displaced and resettlement occurs within months or a couple of years. The international community steps in fairly quickly with various kinds of support to assist the administrative authorities in disaster-affected contexts. Conflict and disaster thus affects IDPs in different ways and over different scales of time. Limited national and international access to IDPs in situations of conflict result in inadequate monitoring of human rights. Since few sociolinguists have had access to displaced people in these circumstances, little attention has been given to the inter-relationship among language, literacy, linguistic practices and education, health care, safety and security, and economic livelihoods, or in relation to competing socio-political, environmental, and economic interests.

Language has received limited attention in reports that relate to children affected by war. The first notable document to address educational and other concerns for children caught in conflict, Graça Machel's report on the 'Impact of Armed Conflict on Children' (UNICEF 1996), mentions language only in passing. Machel's follow-up 10-Year Strategic Review, 'Children and Conflict in a Changing World' (UNICEF 2009) mentions language six times. Once this is in relation to 'language barriers', and once to recommend that rights of children should be published in the official languages of the UN. Yet, these languages are not the ones that are used by the children who are most likely to be affected by displacement.

The most substantive document to address the implications for language across a spectrum of circumstances affecting displaced persons is *Protecting Internally Displaced Persons: A Manual for Law and Policymakers* (Brookings-Bern Project on Internal Displacement 2008). This document builds on the 'Guiding Principles on Internally Displaced Persons' (UN 1998), and spells out principles and legal requirements regarding the treatment and provisions for IDPs by internal governments, NGOs, and UN-related bodies. The manual draws attention to the need for vulnerable people to have access to information, health care, safety, shelter, food, and education in a language that they understand. It also draws attention to the consequences of increased vulnerability and exploitation of people, particularly women and girls, arising from language barriers.

Although attention to matters of language is greater in the Law and Policymakers' Manual than in other documents, this document is relatively recent, and it is by no means clear the extent to which its recommendations are being adhered to in situations of conflict. As indicated earlier, access to IDPs may be limited to emergency medical attention, UN-administered food depots, and the erection of internally displaced people's camps (IDPCs), where communities to which IDPs have fled are unable to absorb or accommodate newcomers. Concerns for safety and security of aid workers in situations of conflict limit possibilities for external agencies to respond adequately to the linguistic needs of minority communities, or to monitor and collect data on wider political, educational, linguistic, or cultural issues. However, the implications of and for languages in these situations, which are often ones in which linguistic diversity coexists with hierarchical scales that compound vulnerability, deserve careful attention that is mindful of potentially harmful consequences for IDPs (Polzer and Hammond 2008).

Issues relating to displacement and language: three examples from sub-Saharan Africa

As suggested earlier, sub-Saharan Africa is expected to experience a significant increase in rapid-onset and conflict-related displacement. Also, as indicated earlier, displacement occurs along a continuum of co-occurring factors which may be overlooked when international agencies focus on the immediacy of shelter and food provision. The discussion now turns to three different contextual examples of displacement with sociolinguistic implications.

Long-term displacements of San and Khoe peoples of Southern Africa

The San, often referred to as Bushmen, and Khoe peoples are minority indigenous peoples of Southern Africa (present-day Angola, Botswana, Namibia, and South Africa), pre-dating the large-scale southern migration of people using Niger-Congo languages from Central Africa between 2,500 and 3,000 years ago. Whereas the languages of the Khoe and San are often discussed in literature relating to language loss or death over a 300-year period of contact with European settlers from the mid-17th century (e.g., Traill 2002), displacement of communities such as these has been endemic over longer scales of time and space. While there are consequences for languages and language practices, these may be inseparable from epistemology (including knowledge of art, medicine, sustainable livelihoods) and cosmology (including belief and practices of song, dance, trance), in ways that cross both material and metaphysical borders and world experiences (see also Deacon and Dowson 1996; Crawhall 2004).

Migration and settlement of more economically and political powerful African and European communities have resulted in various stages and forms of displacement. First, lands over which mobile communities traversed in pursuit of their hunting and gathering livelihoods have been systematically appropriated. This occurred through the occupation of land by African and then European settler pastoralists and farmers (Crawhall 2004). This was followed by 18th- and 19th-century European demarcation of geopolitical borders, with restrictions placed on the mobility of people. The 20th century brought the designation of wildlife conservation areas (parks) and eco-tourism in precisely the areas where San and Khoe communities traditionally practised sustainable hunting. Communities were forcibly moved from the Kalahari Gemsbok Park on the South African side of the border with Botswana in 1930. Several decades later, on the Botswanan side, Baswara San were forcibly removed from hunting-rich areas on the basis that they are variously accused of poaching and because they need to be closer to where their children can attend school. However, provision of schooling is both culturally and linguistically inappropriate and carries more risks than opportunities (Pamo 2011; Sekere 2011; Bolaane 2014). It is also the case that large multinational companies have diamond mining interests in the area and more recently, the government has issued permits for fracking operations in areas traditionally associated with the Baswara habitat (Hitchcock 1998; IRIN 2009; Vidal 2014). In each of these cases epistemology (knowledge) and cosmology (belief) have been rooted in the physical space over which communities regularly travelled. Communities have epistemological and cosmological reasons and needs for their mobility (e.g., Deacon and Dowson 1996); and knowledge, experience, expertise, and belief are embedded in their practices of language in both the physical and metaphysical world. These linguistic practices include speech; trance communication with ancestors, shamans and healers; rock and other forms of art; and reading and interpreting signs and tracks of insects and animals. Displacement involving restricted mobility and forced relocation therefore has consequences in which connections among knowledge, belief, and the use of language to communicate undergo rupture.

The second form of displacement has occurred as a result of conflict (war). Owing to knowledge of tracking, San trackers living in the border areas between Northern Namibia (then South West Africa), Botswana and Angola, were co-opted into the South African Defence Force during military operations in the region in the late 1980s. After Namibian independence and the retreat of the South African military, approximately 4,000 people from two linguistic groups, the !Xun (San) and the Khwe (Khoe), were obliged to seek refuge inside South Africa because some of their members had been coerced into serving as trackers. They had effectively lost their status as citizens of Namibia or Angola. They were brought to a temporary army camp in a dusty and arid part of the Northern Cape, an alien environment, and encircled by army camp fencing, where they remained for the next fourteen years. Here they were completely dislocated from the places in which their knowledge of the land, food sources, medicinal knowledge of plants, water sources, and connections with their ancestors and their spiritual world was situated and connected. Local communities objected to their presence, the government was reluctant to offer South African citizenship, and the displaced communities have suffered extreme ruptures of identity and well-being.

As suggested, the consequences of displacement for mobile communities such as the San and Khoe reach much further than physical relocation. Crawhall (2004) argues that settlement of farmers has resulted in cultural genocide through, among other things, the destruction of the biodiversity of the Kalahari (now desert) in which hunter-gatherer and farming communities currently try to survive. Before the occupation and fencing off of land by farmers,

> Up to a million springbok used to migrate across the desert, pouring uric acid over the plant life and leaving fertile droppings ... [that] stimulated plant growth. ... The elders remember a time when [what has now become] the desert was bursting with food in summertime.
>
> *(Crawhall 2004: 250)*

Fencing and farming have interrupted and decimated wildlife populations and resulted in desertification of the Kalahari. The significance for this in relation to language is that once the biodiversity had been destroyed, the epistemological substance of San and Khoe languages also disappeared. Once people were physically removed from the places (often particular water sources) associated with their ancestors, they could no longer use their practices of dance, song, and trance to communicate with the ancestors for healing advice or for bringing rain. The purposes for which their languages were needed, including the passing on of knowledge and expertise, evaporated (see Crawhall 2004: 251ff). The loss of the functional uses of San and Khoe languages partly explain language loss. However, there is at least one additional reason that Crawhall in his two decades of research has found, and which this author similarly found in 1997. Although linguists (e.g., Mesthrie 2000) indicate that there are no longer speakers of the Khoe language Gri in the Northern Cape, both Heugh (1998) and Crawhall (2004) have found speakers of Gri. Heugh, accompanied by Northern Cape Government officials, found at least 200 speakers of Gri who lived on the outskirts of a town, Douglas, in 1997. The speakers of the community had taken what appeared to be a pragmatic choice of assuming the identity of 'Other Coloured' during the apartheid regime, because they would be entitled to some form of minimal social security provisions if they did so. This would not have been possible if they had identified as speakers of either a San or Khoe language. So, the speakers of Gri shifted to Afrikaans in order to close the ethnolinguistic gap between themselves and 'Coloured' speakers of Afrikaans.

However, the speakers of Gri acknowledged to this author that the language shift had consequences for their health and well-being. First, they indicated concern that farming and urban settlement had an impact on the disappearance of herbs with medicinal properties from the veld. Second, the last Gri-speaking doctor in Douglas had died and with him went knowledge of how to prepare and administer traditional herbal medicines (Heugh 1998). Crawhall (2004) found that informants from other communities of people who speak Nama (another Khoe language) and San languages were similarly worried about the connection between the loss of linguistic knowledge and loss of traditional healing knowledge (identification, gathering, preparation, and use of herbs from the veld). The inability to pass on what is known as *veldkennis* or knowledge of the veld, particularly in regard to how to gather and prepare indigenous plants for medicinal purposes, appears to have serious consequences for community well-being in the cosmology of several Khoe and San communities.

There is a further dimension to language loss or language displacement (Brenzinger 1997). Because of the socio-political and ethnolinguistic hierarchies of apartheid (1948–1994), and because speakers of Gri believed that they had become outsiders in the very place into which others had migrated and assumed ownership, they had been dispossessed of their land. Language, specifically the use of clicks, became a marker of stigma, marginality, and shame. The youth are too ashamed to learn the language:

> *Die jong mense sê dat ons taal klink na klippe aanmekaar kap.*
> [The youth say that our language sounds like stones that are being hit together.]
>
> *(Gri informant in Douglas, Northern Cape,*
> *July 1997, recorded in Heugh 1998)*

The sense of shame is deeply felt by young members of the community who believe that upward social mobility lies through Afrikaans and then English. Contact with speakers of African languages in Botswana has similarly resulted in stigma and shame. Chebanne (2008) indicates that the Baswara San have been stigmatised as ignorant 'foragers' and social outcasts. Stigma and shame resonates with other vulnerable and marginalised communities existing in the shadows of borderlands (e.g., Martinez 1994). These matters are not simply matters of language loss or physical displacement; they go far deeper into the psyches of human beings and their place in the world of socio-political hierarchies of marginality and exclusion.

Displacement of pastoral peoples of Eastern Africa

The second discussion draws attention to the displacement of pastoral, nomadic people of Eastern Africa, particularly in the Somali, Afar, and Oromo Regions of Ethiopia. Pastoralists historically have traversed wide stretches of arid and semi-arid lands across Africa, and have been the largest contributors to the supply of meat for the populations of their countries (Oxfam 2008). They developed their own sustainable systems of water protection and management of grazing lands. Encroachment on and shrinking of pastoral lands now occurs as a result of controversial international development agency policies of settlement and bore-hole drilling, and powerful settler communities. Settlement policies have led to unanticipated consequences of over-grazing, resulting in desertification, loss of animal stock through pasture shortage, increasing poverty, and marginalisation (e.g., Oxfam 2008). Displacement in such circumstances arises from a shrinkage of mobility and access to land use. These exacerbate competition for grazing and water resources, which leads to conflict and further displacement (PFE, IIRR, and DF 2010).

Border conflict contributes additional pressure on pastoral communities. Ethiopia's ongoing sabre-rattling on its northern and eastern borders with Eritrea and Somalia; Kenya's disputes with Somalia; and the unstable borderlands of Northern Uganda and South Sudan are accompanied by cross-border raids of bandits involved in stock-theft and human traffickers involved in abductions of women and girls. Unstable borders feature militant insurgencies and human rights abuse, as discussed in the third example in this section. So, pastoralists may be displaced towards the geo-political margins of a country because of encroaching occupation of former grazing lands by other more powerful stakeholders. Once restricted to marginal or borderland areas, they become more vulnerable to the circumstances of unstable and volatile incursions. It is in such conditions that school enrolment, retention and achievement come under threat. It is also in such conditions that the provision of education that is sensitive to the rhythms of pastoral life and inclusive of pastoralist knowledge, experiences, systems of belief and faith, and languages are necessary (Heugh 2014b).

Ethnographic data from the Afar and Somali Regions of Ethiopia reveal layers of marginalisation experienced through and compounded by displacement. Restricted mobility increases pressure on the grazing lands to deliver not only stock grazing but firewood fuel for domestic use and this results in desertification. Wood as a potentially renewable source of energy is no longer renewable under conditions of restricted mobility or displacement from traditional pasture lands. As it becomes increasingly scarce, girls and women who are responsible for sourcing this have to walk longer distances to find supplies. The further they travel from their hamlets, the more vulnerable they become to bandits and raiding parties in search of young women to take back across the borders for enslavement, for example, in Yemen, Saudi Arabia, and Somalia (Heugh 2014b). The Regional Governments of Afar and

Somali have provided few alternative basic education (ABE) primary schools in pastoral areas. Secondary schools are only available in one or two major towns, and unsurprisingly, only five percent of pastoralist children attend secondary school (PACT Ethiopia 2008). For most children, the ABE schools are impossible to reach by foot, and it is too dangerous for girls to try to reach school even if there is time both to collect firewood and attend school. Where girls can attend the minimum of three years of primary school, it is likely that this would be spasmodic attendance and all the more reason for education to be provided in the local languages which are known and used by students in their communities. Education in languages not well known or used in the immediate community has little relevance, and there is no evidence that such provision supports retention or access to secondary education in such settings (Skutnabb-Kangas and Heugh 2012).

Restricted mobility, unsafe borders, and environmental changes force some Afar pastoralists closer to the towns along the trade route through Afar, and between Djibouti, Ethiopia's only access to a seaport, and Addis Ababa. Yet this also brings danger of abductions along the Djibouti route. Although education policy since 1994 requires primary schools to teach through the medium of a regional language, this has not been the case in Afar Region where primary and secondary education in the towns is conducted in Amharic, a language associated with the Coptic Christians and the politically dominant Amhara community of the federal capital, Addis Ababa, and Amhara Region. In Afar, where Islam predominates, the insistence on Amharic medium education in primary school is interpreted as discriminatory along lines of language and faith. The reluctance of either the regional or federal governments to provide mobile schools and/or more ABE primary schools close to pastoral hamlets exacerbates inequality. Federal and regional government insist that pastoralists send their children to urban boarding schools and position pastoralists as unco-operative if they resist. However, pastoralist community spokespersons are reluctant to leave children, especially girls, in boarding schools in towns where parents fear that their children will experience discrimination, alienation from pastoral traditions and epistemology, and possible abduction (Heugh 2014b). The only way that pastoralists can send their children to school with some protection is if they relocate to towns and thus jeopardise their livelihoods. However, since children are taught Islamic literacy in hamlets and villages by community members, there is reason to suggest that the federal and regional governments could foster informal education systems in ways that include a wider primary school curriculum. The needs of pastoral communities in the Afar, Somali, and Oromo Regions could be met through a sustainable system of mobile schools that would draw on the linguistic and faith-based resources within pastoral communities.

The following excerpt shows that pastoralists are not unco-operative; they do wish for their children to participate in school, and they do not wish to exclude girls. However, it also demonstrates a claim to linguistic citizenship by arguing for Afar medium of instruction followed by English medium. The omission of Amharic indicates resistance towards the federal government, its language policy, and Coptic Christianity:

> Girls should go to Grade 8 or beyond. We used to think foolishly that ladies should not get education – now we know that first ladies must get education . . . in Afar for Grades 1–4. . . . From Grade 5 it should be English
> *(chairperson, Dudub Hamlet, Afar Region, 2006)*[2]

Sustainable education here points to the need for Afar medium of instruction, Islamic literacy to increase access for faith-related well-being and to reading and writing, the inclusion of local epistemologies, English as a subject, and flexible school hours to suit the conditions of hot, arid areas and the rhythms of pastoral life (e.g., Heugh 2014b). Increased participation in primary education is more likely to ensure meaningful access to secondary education. Viable opportunities for participation in school education offer viable alternatives to early marriage for pastoral daughters, and opportunities for inclusive engagement and participatory citizenship for local, regional, and global purposes.

Ethnographic data collected in this context demonstrates that marginalised pastoral communities voice clear objectives for the education of their children. These are particularly evident in views regarding the provision of language(s) in education. In this case it is Afar and English, although some community members also recognise the pragmatic usefulness of Amharic for regional and national purposes of communication.

Internal displacement and conflict

The third discussion relates to the impact of armed conflict on displaced persons and their language practices. Specifically, attention is drawn to the impact of three decades (1979–2009) of conflict on communities of North West Uganda that border South Sudan and the DRC. Violence in the North West Nile districts of Uganda began with inter-ethnic violence towards the Kakwa-speaking minority of Koboko District bordering the DRC after the expulsion of Idi Amin, a dictatorial prime minister of Uganda originally from this district. This conflict was followed by the 1987 emergence of the Lord's Resistance Army (LRA), a militant insurgency group in Gulu District and associated with Joseph Kony, involving amputations, genocide, abductions, boy-soldiering, rape of girls and women, and maiming. The LRA has displaced nearly two million people across Northern Uganda, and another 400,000 in neighbouring South Sudan, DRC, and the CAR. Emergency IDP camps established by the Ugandan government had poor hygiene, were disease-ridden, and had few if any schools. Local schools, if they were able to continue to function, could not absorb displaced children. Even if children could be absorbed, they encountered linguistic mismatches between themselves, other students and teachers. Since 2008, approximately eighty percent of displaced Ugandans have returned home, but after twenty to thirty years of dislocation, the socio-political and economic fabric of communities has been destroyed. For example, the majority of people in the Acholi-speaking areas of Gulu, Amuru, and Nwoya districts were relocated from rural areas to IDP camps near apparently safe towns. Returning after at least twenty years in IDP Camps' reliance on UN food depots, and almost zero school education, decimated family units no longer have the knowledge of how to till the land or to grow crops, or how to engage in other sustainable economic activities. Development agencies and NGOs provided assistance to communities worst affected by the insurgencies for the first four to five years after the LRA was forced to leave Uganda. Short-lived interventions within a post-traumatic and disordered society, on the scale evident across Northern Uganda, have not been sustainable. Reconstruction in post-conflict settings requires long-term sustainable solutions, local participation and agency, and in the languages used by the communities (Heugh and Mulumba 2014).

Displacement for many people from Arua, Koboko, Yumbe, Moyo, and Adjumani Districts largely meant crossing porous borders into DRC or South Sudan from 1979 onwards and attempts to merge with communities across the borders. Linguistic diversity is a significant feature of the North West Nile, DRC, and South Sudan, and mobility of people in these areas requires multilingual repertoires. In addition to languages shared across the borders of Uganda and South Sudan, that is, Kakwa, Ma'di, and Acholi (Lwo), many people have acquired Kiswahili, Juba (South Sudanese) Arabic, and languages of neighbouring countries. Displacement across the borders has not been one-directional from Uganda. Instability and ongoing conflict in South Sudan and DRC has resulted in movement of people into Northern Uganda depending on insurgent operations. Borders in this area are porous, and there has been a lack of government-enforced attempts to seal these from any of the three neighbouring countries while insurgents have had the upper hand. Although in some areas IDPs have been returning home since 2004, it is only subsequent to the expulsion of most LRA groups from Uganda in 2008 that co-ordinated steps towards resettlement and reconstruction have been possible. Nevertheless, fresh outbreaks of conflict in South Sudan are destabilising the area again.

Although UN-related documents that respond to displacement acknowledge that information and services should be provided in local languages, guidelines were not available or had not been put into effect in Northern Uganda between 1979 and 2009. New district administrative centres established to manage local government, including health and education, coincided with the implementation of a new primary school curriculum policy in which the first three years are to be taught through the local language. Since the education system had disintegrated in the North West Nile, this has had to be re-developed. In many areas, primary and secondary schools built before the conflict remain even if in disrepair. Teacher development centres have had to be established in order to support teachers, many of whom have not taught for years, and who need to adjust to the new curriculum, and specifically to teach through the local language which may not match a language of the teacher's repertoire. There is a paucity of written materials for teaching, particularly in local languages and the National Curriculum Development Centre (NCDC) of the Ministry of Education and Sports (MoES) in Kampala has neither the capacity nor the budgetary resources to develop written materials and teacher guides.

The Literacy and Basic Adult Education (LABE) NGO has worked with rural communities in a way that is inclusive of multiple stakeholders and that builds sustainability. In 2009 LABE began a mother-tongue education project in the local languages of five (now six) North West Districts most severely affected by the conflict. The project supports national and local/district government efforts to re-establish primary school education in post-conflict areas in conjunction with the implementation of the new curriculum and in the five languages of these districts.

LABE's collaborative approach includes village and district-level stakeholders in ways that encourage agency and participation. Each village has identified 'parent educators' to act as liaisons between the school and village, and to encourage reciprocal investment between primary school education and adult basic education initiatives in local languages. LABE has also supported the establishment of local language boards for each of the Kakwa, Lugbara, Aringa, Ma'di, and Acholi languages and it has assisted in orthographic development training where necessary. LABE has also facilitated the writing of storybooks based on local knowledge, which are used by children and adult literacy learners. District officials, and the NCDC and the MoES in Kampala acknowledge that this intervention has been exceptional. LABE's experience in providing teacher development support in local languages is now being used by NCDC as a guide for the rest of the country (Heugh and Mulumba 2014).

The Ugandan example also demonstrates that language policies decided at the federal level may be too crude for highly diverse and marginal settings. After three decades of displacement, people have not returned to their villages linguistically unchanged. In many cases, although they may have fled mainly speaking one or two languages, they have returned with wider repertoires. Thus the restriction to one local language medium of education in each district does not match altered (or changing) linguistic realities. For a minority of people who observe Islam in this corner of a predominantly Christian country, there is a further complication. This is the need to accommodate Islamic literacy. It would be sensible if the local and national education systems were to acknowledge the need for Islamic literacy, where appropriate, and to incorporate this into regular school and community practices.

A further complication arises from teacher-deployment practices, where the federal government has not matched teachers' linguistic profiles with those of school communities and the new early primary curriculum. Finally, the Summer Institute of Linguistics (SIL) is assisting language boards in various districts to develop orthographies that will contribute towards the writing of literature and educational material. Yoder (2008) offers a detailed discussion of the societal conditions in which this kind of work has taken place in South Sudan, and how SIL has addressed the challenges there. In North West Uganda, the approach taken by SIL linguists has been to emphasise differences among closely related spoken language varieties. This approach includes the introduction of difficult to use diacritics, and an increased number of vowels in a variety of Acholi. These are questionable practices on pragmatic and theoretical grounds. In a post-conflict situation, capacity-building and sustainability are particularly crucial, so this kind of intervention may carry risks. First, it is more likely to encourage communities to believe that their languages are too difficult for reading, writing, and printing (see also Yoder 2008). Second, an emphasis on ethnolinguistic division may exacerbate conflict rather than reconciliation in a post-conflict setting.

Implications

Displacement as discussed here results in fractured systems and vulnerable communities in which language is intimately connected with physical and mental well-being. Whereas literature on migration makes passing mention of the need for communication in local languages, there is little evidence that the international community understands how mobile and marginalised people make use of language and its relationship with knowledge, cultural practices, livelihoods, and faith. Development agency reports and documents translated into the various official languages of the UN are of little practical and direct value to affected people. What matters to IDPs is their access to information in languages that they understand so that they can access services that will help them to survive. What matters once resettlement is possible, is that counselling, repair, rebuilding, and reconstruction can be effective and sustainable through participation and agency. Participation and agency are only possible in languages and practices known and used. These are not the languages of the UN. Displacement alters the linguistic ecology of each community, and reconstruction of communities is likely to benefit from a nuanced understanding of how the linguistic ecology has changes and contemporary community needs.

Although there is substantial research on the long-term effects of trauma on refugees and asylum seekers, this has not been the case for IDPs. In large part this is because such research would require personnel who understand the linguistic and cultural practices of IDPs well enough to be able to navigate highly fraught circumstances. The linguistic phenomena of one setting will differ from the next, and so inflexible language policies, even where these are inclusive of diversity, are unhelpful. Where minority indigenous people have lived on the margins of society, such as the Khoe and San of Southern Africa, the Pygmies of Cameroon, or indigenous peoples of Australia, language is not simply spoken, written, or signed. The linguistic repertoire may include various forms of signs (knowledge of human and animal signs), art (rock paintings), song, dance, trance, and dream. The consequence of displacement, marginalization, and stigma is so severe that even where some individuals express narratives of resistance, there is evidence that pressure to disguise or obscure linguistic and cultural identities brings about linguistic, epistemological, and cosmological loss on scales and in dimensions between the physical and other worlds that have not yet been fully understood by linguistic anthropologists. Pastoral peoples of East Africa may well be associated with a particular language; however, mobility and reliance on selling livestock in markets require expanded repertoires. Such repertoires, however, may not coincide with the language regime of the federal system. For complex socio-economic, cultural, and faith-based reasons, including displacement, pastoralists are likely to be in an antagonistic relationship with administrative agencies of national or federal centres. Resistance towards the scripts of the centre is demonstrated in this chapter by pastoralists in Afar who claim the right to use their language and English in the education of their children, rather than Amharic, the national working language of Ethiopia. In situations of conflict or post-conflict, language poses risks and opportunities. Mobility increases the likelihood of expanded repertoires as people relocate in order to find places of refuge in other parts of a country or in remote border regions of neighbouring countries. Expanding one's linguistic repertoire is necessary for survival, and in situations in which formal education collapses, and the expanded repertoire facilitates access to informal knowledge and expertise of new locations. This may increase opportunities for trade and local enterprises in border regions in times of resettlement. However, (restricted) placement in IDP camps for protracted periods, such as experienced by Acholi speakers in Gulu district in Northern Uganda, may limit opportunities for expanding repertoires of language and knowledge. In the absence of opportunities to continue livelihood enterprises, people and communities also lose earlier held knowledge and expertise. The language of resettlement, counselling, and education in post-conflict contexts such as this may very well need to be in Acholi because this is the language of the Gulu camps. However, for communities resettled in Koboko, Yumbe, Adjumani, and Arua, and who fled across borders and who have returned as speakers of several languages, it does not make sense to restrict education and services to one district language. Instead, multilingual services and education make more practical sense.

Future directions

Language policies in South Africa and Botswana have thus far failed to address the particular needs of the most marginalised of their respective linguistic communities, the Khoe and San people who have experienced various forms of ongoing discriminatory practices, including displacement. South Africa's human rights-based constitution has not ensured equality of linguistic and cultural citizenship for Khoe and San communities. The government of Botswana has used opportunistic measures to displace people and to provide inappropriate educational and other services. The linguistic realities of vulnerable communities in these countries indicate that in addition to language loss or death, centuries of knowledge of the environment, sustainable livelihoods, belief systems intimately connected with well-being, all of which are embedded in language, will soon be lost.

The language policy of Ethiopia, although geared towards equal treatment of regional languages and communities, is not implemented in relation to educational provision for pastoral communities in Afar and Somali regions where Islam is observed. First, the mobility of pastoral communities is restricted through the resettlement of outsiders on pastoral lands. Second, resettlement exacerbates over-grazing and desertification and this increases poverty and increases risks of human trafficking. Third, restricted provision of education for pastoral children of Islamic faith in a predominantly Coptic Christian country has overtones of faith-based and/or ethnic discrimination. Together these increase alienation and disaffection from the state. A partial solution would be to tap into community practices and resources of teaching and learning Islamic literacy in mobile schools and to assist communities to expand these practices in ways that suit pastoral lifestyles, provide early primary education for children, and facilitate access to upper primary and secondary education.

Decades of debates about the use of local languages in primary education of Uganda finally resulted in a policy in which local languages are to be used as medium of instruction for the first three years of primary school from 2007. Government, however, was unable to implement this policy while an NGO, LABE, has done this in 240 schools in post-conflict North West Uganda. LABE demonstrates how to build community agency, multi-party stakeholder capacity, and how to bring children back into schools and to remain in schools after decades of conflict. The success of the LABE intervention owes much to the development of agency and partnerships in which the district officials, community leaders, parents, and schools are jointly invested in rebuilding the school system and providing adult basic education in the villages and schools. Its success is also attributed to LABE's involvement in developing orthographies, dictionaries, storybooks, and learning materials in the local languages. As these were being developed, so too were the expertise and capacity of community members, local experts, teacher development officers, and district education officials. What the Ugandan example also points towards are possible risks. The first is that the language education policy decided upon in Kampala does not quite fit the linguistic reality of each setting. Displacement from one district to another or across borders has increased linguistic diversity and repertoire for people who were not placed in IDP camps. Policy makers therefore may need to consider how policies might be sufficiently decentralised or adjustable to accommodate changing linguistic circumstances. The isolation of people in IDP camps may have precluded expansion of linguistic repertoires. Policy implementation would therefore need flexibility. Then NGO interventions, such as that of LABE, may be positive. Others, with methodologies and practices that foster difference, such as SIL's approach to orthographic development, may inadvertently have impractical linguistic outcomes and also exacerbate ethnic difference in a volatile post-conflict situation.

These examples indicate that the linguistic practices of displaced people in marginal settings need to be understood in relation to other dimensions of the well-being of human beings. Language policies and regimes conceived of in national or federal centres, even where ostensibly well-intentioned, are not likely to articulate closely with the needs of IDPs in borderland contexts. There is reason to argue for decentralised approaches that engage local agents and communities. Linguists and those who have an interest in language (education) policy and practices may find that displacement, in difficult-to-reach areas,[3] is one that is under-researched. It is also one in which researchers need to tread carefully and to anticipate the consequences of possible errors of judgement.

Summary

There was a forty-year gap between the 1950s recognition of refugees and asylum seekers and the 1990s recognition of internally displaced persons (IDPs) by international development agencies. With sixty million IDPs identified by 2013, and large-scale conflict since 2014, displacement is a global crisis. Refugees who are able to escape the conflict-ridden countries draw international attention, including research on the linguistic implications of migration. However, this is seldom the case with IDPs. Partly this is because most displaced people are located in inaccessible areas. This chapter considers displaced people in three marginal contexts. The first is in relation to small endangered and marginalised San and Khoe communities of Southern Africa. The second is in relation to pastoral people in Ethiopia who experience restricted mobility, desertification, impoverishment, and linguistic and faith-based discrimination. The third is in relation to post-conflict North West Uganda where socio-political and educational reconstruction occurs in the context of a changing linguistic landscape.

In each example, displaced, peripheral communities receive limited access to services and resources while they experience extreme vulnerability and marginalisation. Short-term emergency relief or aid brought by international development agencies are not yet responsive to the roles and functions of community language practices in such contexts. National governments and smaller agencies may bring educational and linguistic resources and expertise, but they may also bring theoretical and pedagogic practices that may exacerbate marginalisation and trauma. There is, however, some evidence to suggest that locally developed responses that tap into local languages and epistemologies may increase the prospects of sustainable literacy, language 'development' and educational practices.

Related topics

Place, space, and language
National and ethnic minorities
New orientations to identity in mobility
Migration trajectories
Multisited ethnography and language in the study of migration
Regional flows and language resources

Further reading

Bolaane, M. (2014). San cross-border cultural heritage and identity in Botswana, Namibia and South Africa. *African Study Monographs 35*(1), 41–64.

This paper offers contemporary insights of displacement for San communities in Southern Africa.

Brookings-Bern Project on Internal Displacement. (2008). *Protecting Internally Displaced Persons: A Manual for Law and Policymakers*. Washington, DC: Brookings Institution-Bern Project on Internal Displacement (For the UN Secretary-General on the Human Rights of Internally Displaced Persons). Retrieved 14 April 2015, from http://www.refworld.org/pdfid/4900944a2.pdf.

This document differentiates the needs of refugees from those of internally displaced persons. However, there are no reliable checks and balances to ensure that the recommendations of this document are put in place.

Crawhall, N.T. (2004). *!Ui-Taa Language Shift in Gordonia and Postmasburg Districts, South Africa*, unpublished PhD Dissertation, University of Cape Town.

Crawhall's study is unique in tracing the history of language shift in Southern Africa, and particularly in uncovering traces of language practices thought to have become extinct.

Heugh, K. and Mulumba, B.M. (2014). *Implementing Local Languages Medium Education in the Early Primary Curriculum of Ugandan Schools: A Literacy and Adult Basic Education (LABE) Intervention in Six Districts in North and North West Uganda*, Kampala: LABE. Retrieved 16 December 2015, from http://labeuganda.org/reports/LABE%20MTE%20Evaluation%202013%20Final%20 SEPS%20jan.pdf.

This study draws attention to how language interests in fragile, border communities can bring about educational and socio-economic change and empowerment at the micro-level and meso-level.

UNESCO. (2011). *Education for All Global Monitoring Report 2011: The Hidden Crisis: Armed Conflict and Education*, UNESCO, Paris. Retrieved 30 January 2015, from http://unesdoc.unesco.org/images/0019/001907/190743e.pdf.

This document foreshadows one of the most significant challenges for the 21st century, which is the increased incidence of displacement and the consequential challenges which this brings to the adequate provision of education for displaced and refugee communities, in their own countries and in receiving countries.

Notes

1 See, for example, 'Bombed, Displaced, Starving: Rains about to Cut Off People of Blue Nile and South Kordofan from International Aid, Even If Sudan Allows It In'. https://www.aegistrust.org/bombed-displaced-starving-rains-cut-people-blue-nile-south-kordofan-international-aid-even-sudan-allows/
2 Cited in Heugh (2014b: 130).
3 A notable exception is the occupation of central parklands in Bogota by indigenous IDPs (Olarte and Wall 2012).

References

Anzaldúa, G. (1987). *Borderlands/La Frontera: The New Mestiza*. San Francisco: Spinsters/Aunt Lute.
Bamgbose, A. (2000). *Language and exclusion: The consequences of language policies in Africa*. Münster: Lit Verlag.
Bolaane, M. (2014). San cross-border cultural heritage and identity in Botswana, Namibia and South Africa. *African Study Monographs* 35(1): 41–64.
Brenzinger, M. (1997). Language contact and language displacement. In F. Coulmas (ed.), *The Handbook of Sociolinguistics* (pp. 273–284). Oxford: Blackwell.
Brenzinger, M., ed. (2015). *Language Diversity Endangered*. Berlin and Boston: De Gruyter Mouton.
Brookings-Bern Project on Internal Displacement. (2008). *Protecting Internally Displaced Persons: A Manual for Law and Policymakers*. Washington, DC: Brookings Institution-University of Bern Project on Internal Displacement (For the UN Secretary-General on the Human Rights of Internally Displaced Persons). Retrieved 14 April 2015, from http://www.refworld.org/pdfid/4900944a2.pdf.
Chebanne, A. (2008). The language ecology of marginalised ethno-linguistic groups in Southern Africa. In A. Creese, P. Martin and N.H. Hornberger (eds.), *Encyclopedia of Language and Education,* 2nd Edition, Volume 9: *Ecology of Language* (pp. 1–13). New York: Springer Science+Business Media LLC.
Crawhall, N.T. (2004). *!Ui-Taa Language Shift in Gordonia and Postmasburg Districts, South Africa*. Unpublished PhD dissertation, University of Cape Town.
Deacon, J. and Dowson, T., eds. (1996). *Voices from the Past. Xam Bushmen and the Bleek and Lloyd Collection*. Johannesburg: Witwatersrand University Press.
Dunn, E.C. (2014). Humanitarianism, displacement, and the politics of nothing in postwar Georgia. *Slavic Review* 73(2): 287–306.
Grenoble, L.A. and Whaley, L.J. (2006). *Saving Languages: An Introduction to Language Revitalization*. Cambridge: Cambridge University Press.
Hamel, R.E. (1997). Language conflict and language shift: A sociolinguistic framework for linguistic human rights'. *International Journal of the Sociology of Language* 127(1): 105–134.
Heugh, K. (1998). *Considerations for and Background to the Draft Language Policy for the Northern Cape*. PRAESA, University of Cape Town, Cape Town (Unpublished Report for the Northern Cape Government).
Heugh, K. (2006). Language education policies in Africa. *Encyclopaedia of language and linguistics* (2nd ed., Vol. 6, pp. 414–423). Amsterdam: Elsevier Science.

Heugh, K. (2014a). Turbulence and dilemma: Implications of diversity and multilingualism in Australian education. *International Journal of Multilingualism 11*(3): 347–363.

Heugh, K. (2014b). Shades, voice and mobility: Remote communities resist and reclaim linguistic and educational practices in Ethiopia. In M. Prinsloo and C. Stroud (eds.), *Educating for Language and Literacy Diversity: Mobile Selves* (pp. 116–134). Houndsmills, Basingstoke: Palgrave Macmillan.

Heugh, K. and Mulumba, B. M. (2014). *Implementing Local Languages Medium Education in the Early Primary Curriculum of Ugandan Schools: A Literacy and Adult Basic Education (LABE) Intervention in Six Districts in North and North West Uganda.* LABE, Kampala. Retrieved 16 December 2015, from http://labeuganda.org/reports/LABE%20MTE%20Evaluation%202013%20Final%20SEPS%20jan.pdf.

Hitchcock, R.K. (1998). Resource rights and resettlement among the San of Botswana. *Cultural Survival Quarterly (CSQ) 22*(4). Retrieved 14 April 2015, from http://www.culturalsurvival.org/publications/cultural-survival-quarterly/botswana/resource-rights-and-resettlement-among-san-botswan.

IMDC. (2014a). *Global Overview. People Displaced by Conflict and Violence.* IMDC (Internal Displacement Monitoring Centre) and NRC (Norwegian Refugee Council), Geneva. Retrieved 30 January 2015, from http://www.internal-displacement.org/assets/publications/2014/201405-global-overview-2014-en.pdf.

IMDC. (2014b). *Global Estimates 2014. People Displaced by Disasters.* IMDC (Internal Displacement Monitoring Centre and Norwegian Refugee Council), Geneva. Retrieved 30 January 2015, from http://reliefweb.int/sites/reliefweb.int/files/resources/201409-global-estimates.pdf.

IMDC. (2015a). *New Humanitarian Frontiers. Addressing Criminal Violence in Mexico and Central America.* Retrieved 3 December 2015, from http://www.internal-displacement.org/assets/publications/2015/201510-am-central-americas-violence-en.pdf.

IMDC. (2015b). *Global Figures.* Retrieved 13 December 2015, from http://www.internal-displacement.org/global-figures.

IRIN. (2009). *Botswana: San Controversy Rekindled.* IRIN Humanitarian News and Analysis. Retrieved 16 April 2015, from http://www.irinnews.org/report/86309/botswana-san-controversy-rekindled.

Jacques, M. (2012). *Armed Conflict and Displacement: The Protection of Refugees and Displaced Persons under International Humanitarian Law.* Cambridge Studies in International and Comparative Law, Cambridge: Cambridge University Press.

Martinez, O. (1994). *Border People: Life and Society in the US-Mexico Borderland.* Tuscon: University of Arizona Press.

Mesthrie, R. (2000). South Africa: A sociolinguistic overview. In R. Mesthrie (ed.), *Language in South Africa* (pp. 11–26). Cambridge: Cambridge University Press.

Mohanty, A. (2010). Languages, inequality and marginalization: Implications of the double divide in Indian multilingualism. *International Journal of the Sociology of Language 205*: 131–154. doi:10.1515/ijsl.2010.042

Olarte, O. C. and Wall, I. R. (2012). The occupation of public space in Bogotá: Internal displacement and the city. *Social & Legal Studies 21*(2): 321–339.

Ostler, N. (2011). Language maintenance, shift and endangerment. In R. Mesthrie and W. Wolfram (eds.), *Cambridge Handbook of Sociolinguistics* (pp. 315–334). Cambridge: Cambridge University Press.

Ouane, A. and Glanz, C. (eds). (2011). *Optimising Learning, Education and Publishing in Africa: The Language Factor – A Review and Analysis of Theory and Practice in Mother-Tongue and Bilingual Education in Sub-Saharan Africa.* Hamburg: UNESCO Institute for Lifelong Learning.

Oxfam. (2008). *Survival of the Fittest Pastoralism and Climate Change in East Africa.* Oxfam Briefing Paper 116. Retrieved 15 April 2015, from https://www.oxfam.org/sites/www.oxfam.org/files/bp116-pastoralism-climate-change-eafrica-0808.pdf.

PACT Ethiopia. (2008). *Education for Pastoralists: Flexible Approaches, Workable Models.* USAID and PACT Ethiopia. Retrieved 25 April 2015, from http://pdf.usaid.gov/pdf_docs/PNADN691.pdf.

Pamo, B. (2011). San language development for education in South Africa: The South African San Institute and the San Language Committees. *Diaspora, Indigenous, and Minority Education: Studies of Migration, Integration, Equity, and Cultural Survival* 5(2): 112–118.

PFE, IIRR and DF. (2010). *Pastoralism and Land: Land Tenure, Administration and Use in Pastoral Areas of Ethiopia*. Pastoralist Forum Ethiopia, Addis Ababa, International Institute of Rural Reconstruction, Nairobi, and Development Fund, Norway. Retrieved 17 April 2015, from http://www.pfe-ethiopia.org/pub_files/pastoralism%20&%20Land%20full%20Book.pdf.

Phuong, C. (2010). *The International Protection of Internally Displaced Persons*. Cambridge Studies in International and Comparative Law, Cambridge: Cambridge University Press.

Polzer, T. and Hammond, L. (2008). Invisible Displacement. *Journal of Refugee Studies* 21(4): 417–431.

Pupavac, V. (2006). Language rights in conflict and the denial of language as communication. *International Journal of Human Rights* 10(1): 61–78.

Ramanathan, V., ed. (2013). Language policies and (dis)citizenship: Rights, access, pedagogies. In Ramanathan, C. (ed.), *Language Policies and (Dis)Citizenship: Rights, Access, Pedagogies* (pp. 1–16). Bristol: Multilingual Matters.

Sekere, B. (2011). Secondary education for San Students in Botswana: A new Xade case study. *Diaspora, Indigenous, and Minority Education: Studies of Migration, Integration, Equity, and Cultural Survival* 5(2): 76–87.

Sercombe, P. and Tupas, R., eds. (2014). *Language, Education and Nation-building Assimilation and Shift in Southeast Asia*. New York: Palgrave Macmillan.

Skutnabb-Kangas, T. and Heugh, K., eds. (2012). *Multilingual Education and Sustainable Development Work: From Periphery to Center*. New York and London: Routledge.

Traill, A. (2002). The Khoesan languages. In R. Mesthrie (ed.), *Language in South Africa* (pp. 27–49). Cambridge and Cape Town: Cambridge University Press.

UN. (1998). *Guiding Principles on Internal Displacement*. Office of the High Commissioner for Human Rights (OHCHR). Retrieved 30 January 2015, from http://daccess-dds-ny.un.org/doc/UNDOC/GEN/G98/104/93/PDF/G9810493.pdf?OpenElement.

UNESCO. (2011). *Education for All Global Monitoring Report 2011, The Hidden Crisis: Armed Conflict and Education*. UNESCO, Paris. Retrieved 30 January 2015, from http://unesdoc.unesco.org/images/0019/001907/190743e.pdf.

UNICEF. (1996). *Impact of Armed Conflict on Children, Report of Graça Machel*. Retrieved 24 January 2015, from http://www.unicef.org/graca/a51-306_en.pdf.

UNICEF. (2009). *Children and Conflict in a Changing World, Machel Study 10-Year Strategic Review*. Retrieved 24 January 2015, from http://www.unicef.org/publications/files/Machel_Study_10_Year_Strategic_Review_EN_030909.pdf.

Vidal, J. (2014). Botswana Bushmen: "If you deny us the right to hunt, you are killing us". *Guardian*. Retrieved 15 April, from http://www.theguardian.com/environment/2014/apr/18/kalahari-bushmen-hunting-ban-prince-charles.

Watson, I. (2009). *Aboriginality and the Violence of Colonialism*. Borderlands, 8.1. Retrieved 9 December 2015, from http://www.borderlands.net.au/vol8no1_2009/iwatson_aboriginality.pdf.

Yoder, J. B. (2008). Minority language development and literacy among internally displaced persons (IDPs), refugees, and wartime communities. *Canadian Modern Language Review* 65(1): 147–170.

11
Migration trajectories
Implications for language proficiencies and identities

Alla V. Tovares and Nkonko M. Kamwangamalu

Introduction/definitions

"Migration" can be defined as "the movement from one place to another" (Deumert 2013: 57) or, as Boyle, Halfacree, and Robinson (1998: 34) put it, "a move within or across the boundary of an areal unit." Boyle and his colleagues refer to the move within an areal unit as "internal migration" (e.g., *rural-urban* migration), and to the move across an areal unit as "external" (e.g., *south-north*) (Kamwangamalu 2013: 35). Migration, whether *rural-urban, south-north*, or such other categories as *south-south, north-north, north-south, return migration, circular migration, chain migration*, and *step migration* to be discussed in this chapter, redefines an individual's linguistic repertoire – ways of speaking that were useful and highly valued in one place can be meaningless in another (Deumert 2013). The ways individuals use their linguistic repertoires in a migration or non-migration context are informed and shaped by such questions as (1) who am I? (Bernstein 1986: 495), (2) how am I perceived by others in the community of which I am a member?, and (3) how would I actually want to be perceived? (Kamwangamalu 1992: 33). Question (1) concerns individual (self)identity, how the individual perceives himself/herself, while questions (2) and (3) have to do with individual's social identities – the relationship between the individual and society. Individual and social identities are interconnected, and so will be treated as such in the discussion that follows. Identity is a moving target; that is, identity is never static or enduring but is "endlessly created anew according to very various social constraints . . . and social contexts" (Tabouret-Keller 1997: 316). Thus, individuals' ways of speaking – their linguistic acts – are what Le Page and Tabouret-Keller (1985) refer to as "acts of identity": "people create their linguistic systems so as to resemble those of the groups with which from time to time they wish to identify" (Le Page 1986: 23). It follows that "as the product of situated social action, identities may shift and recombine to meet new circumstances" (Bucholtz and Hall 2004: 376). An individual's identities, or "*practical [linguistic] accomplishments*" (emphasis added) in the sense of Jenkins (1994: 218), may shift in the context of migration or any social context for that matter because, as already noted, identity is "open-ended, fluid, and constantly . . . constructed and reconstructed as individuals move from one social situation to another" (Zegeye 2001: 1). That is to say, when people migrate, they rarely, if ever, move across or arrive to uninhabited places; instead, their journeys, as well as their destinations, inevitably involve encounters, brief or extended, with other people, their linguistic practices and repertoires. These encounters, in turn, shape and determine the identities that migrants wish to project in the host community as they are preoccupied with such identity-related questions as those highlighted in (1)–(3). As Blommaert and Dong (2010: 368) put it, "The movement of people across space is therefore never a move across empty spaces," with pre-determined, non-negotiable identities. Moreover, as these researchers go on to suggest, spaces are not only horizontal, they are vertical: each space has a dynamic and layered hierarchy of linguistic varieties "filled with norms, expectations, conceptions of what counts as proper and normal (indexical) language use and what does not" (Blommaert and Dong 2010: 368). Furthermore, trajectories of migration not only involve movement in space, but in time as well; thus, time scales are also important in exploring the relationships between migration and language. That is, how long it takes migrants to reach their destination and how long they stay in one place influence linguistic repertoires and identities of migrants and of those people who come in contact with them. It follows that an exploration of migration trajectories, the movement in time and space, is an investigation of the trajectories of human contact and the influence of this contact, linguistic and otherwise, on the parties involved. In this chapter, we focus on the relationship between different migration trajectories and identities and linguistic repertoires and resources. First, we consider the types of migration trajectories mentioned earlier, namely, return migration, circular migration, rural-urban migration, peri-urban, south-north, north-south, south-south, north-north, chain migration, and step migration. The aim here is to explore how these migration trajectories impact identities and language proficiencies. Next, we discuss the impact of migration trajectories on migrants' linguistic repertoires and identities in the host destination. We conclude with a discussion of new challenges and directions in the study of migration trajectories and their broader socio-linguistic implications in the age of superdiversity (Blommaert 2013).

Overview

Rural-urban, peri-urban, south-north, north-south, north-north, and south-south migration

Typically, *rural-urban migration* refers to the movement from agricultural rural places to industrialized urban areas. As with any category, rural-urban migration is a complex notion that includes sub-categorization and refinement. For instance, a move from a village to a small town or a small urban center ("peri-urban center") is identified as peri-urban migration (CODESRIA, Nov. 5, 2004). Additionally, as Dong and Blommaert (2009: 4) find in their research on migration in China, people are also moving from smaller towns to larger cities, that is from peri-urban to urban areas. Conway (1980: 7) views "the transition of individuals or family members through the rural-to-urban residence" as a continuum. While rural-(peri)urban migration trajectory refers to the movement from a periphery to a center, both south-north, north-south, and south-south migration trajectories refer not to directional or geographical configurations per se, but rather to social and political ones (Portes and Dewind 2007). Namely, the trajectory that takes migrants from a developing country to a developed country is known as *south-north migration*; the movement from a developed to a developing country is known as *north-south migration*; one from a developed country to another developed country is known as *north-north migration*; and that between developing countries is understood as *south-south migration*. Both south-north and south-south migrations are considered the most prevalent and extensive (Ratha and Shaw 2007). According to the United Nations estimates, in 2010 there were about seventy-three million international south-south and seventy-four million international south-north migrants by origin and destination (United Nations 2012).

Migration, whether rural-urban, south-north, south-south, or north-north, is not merely a move from one place to another, but it is a move that individuals make in search of a better socioeconomic life for themselves and family members they have left behind. At the same time, each migration trajectory has its peculiarities. For instance, rural-urban migrations typically involve people with lower levels of education, most of whom may not have completed high school, let alone college-level education. South-north migrations, however, tend to involve highly educated individuals (Borland 2006; Cavallaro 2010). Also, rural-urban migrants tend to return to or visit regularly with their villages of origin, whereas this is hardly the case for south-north migration, especially due to the financial costs involved. As Deumert (2013: 55) notes with respect to local migrations in South Africa, moving from the village to the city does not imply a decisive move from one place to another; it is not a one-off movement from village to town, but rather "a series of interlocking, shuffling movements between the two places, . . . the opening up of a new place/home without abandoning the previous place/home." Like rural-urban migrants, south-south migrants retain close connections with their homelands. It is estimated that almost eighty percent of south-south migration takes place "between countries with contiguous borders, and most appears to occur between countries with relatively small differences in income" (Ratha and Shaw 2007: v). For example, Maphosa (2009: 10) notes that migrants from Zimbabwe "neither settle permanently in South Africa nor cut ties with their country of origin but maintain close ties through, among other things, frequent visits, sending remittances and communication." Maphosa (2009: 29) also reports that language plays an important role in the ability of some migrants from Zimbabwe to blend in and avoid arrests and deportations. Specifically, "migrants from Matabeleland have an advantage over migrants from other areas because they easily master South Africa languages such as Zulu which have a similarity to Ndebele, Venda and Sotho, which are spoken in some parts of Matabeleland."

South-north migrants, however, tend to reside for a longer period of time in the destination country. They generally maintain, through long-distance communication, a link between themselves and relatives in their country of origin. However, over time this link is tested by the financial costs involved, and is gradually eroded and eventually broken, especially for distant relatives. It follows that, in this context, continuity with the place of origin is not always guaranteed. South-north migrants' goal is to resolve what Canagarajah (2013) calls the dilemma of mobility and identity. For such migrants, the encounters with a new culture, a new language, and language practices in the host country tend to result in complex linguistic repertoires and entangled identities, involving the preoccupation with such questions as those raised earlier in questions (1)–(3). For instance, in his research on identity, migration, and happiness, Bartram (2011: 11), using the World Values Survey and focusing primarily on British south-north immigration, finds that immigrants are typically less happy than natives "in part because they are living in a situation where they find it difficult to have a feeling of belonging in the national context." Bartram goes on to suggest that because governments engage in "impression management" for the benefit of the ruling majority by putting pressure on immigrants to assimilate culturally and linguistically rather than engaging in genuine efforts of fostering shared valued and integration policies, ethnic and religious minorities feel more alienated than integrated in a new country.

It is worth noting that, depending on socio-political and economic factors, one area or one country could experience different types of migration at different times in history. For instance, in the last hundred years Ukraine, a former Soviet Union Republic, has experienced various migration patterns, including rural-urban, south-south and south-north, and most recently internal displacement (for a discussion on language and displacement, see Heugh, this volume). As noted earlier, rural-urban migration trajectory has been traditionally linked to industrialization when fast-developing industries in the city offer more employment opportunities to rural dwellers. For instance, rapid industrialization contributed to the massive rural-urban migration in early 20th-century Ukraine, especially during the years of its membership in the Soviet Union. Such a move inevitably affected the linguistic practices and repertoires of the migrants: the increased use of the Russian language and partial loss of Ukrainian, Russian-Ukrainian bilingualism, and the rise of a mixed Russian-Ukrainian variety called *surzhyk*. All of these developments are often viewed, at least in part, as results of the migration of rural Ukrainians to the cities (see Lewis 1971; Bilaniuk 2005; Masenko 2009; Ivanova 2013). At the same time, to gain a more nuanced understanding of the linguistic changes in Ukraine that were precipitated by rural-urban migration, it is important to situate this issue within the larger sociopolitical context of the former Soviet Union. Lewis (1971: 154) reports that from its inception the Soviet Union was engaged in "switching of populations" – a planned, state-sanctioned long-distance migration of peoples, either forced (e.g., deportations of the Volga Germans and the Crimean Tatars, resettlements of Ukrainians and Poles) or voluntary (e.g., the development of Kazakhstan, Siberia, and the Soviet Far East). Such actions and policies were part of both economic (to move labor resources) and political reasons (to achieve the "blending" of the peoples from various linguistic, ethnic, and other backdrops that would result in the formation of a new integrated Soviet identity). As a result, urban heterogeneous communities were created where Russian was the lingua franca of the people with diverse ethnic and linguistic backgrounds. Thus, it is not surprising that when rural Ukrainians moved to the cities in Ukraine and especially to the cities in other parts of the former Soviet Union, their linguistic repertoires and identities were altered. More specifically, they increased their use of the Russian language, which led to a partial loss of Ukrainian, Russian-Ukrainian bilingualism, and the rise of *surzhyk*.

In 1991, with the collapse of the former Soviet Union, the borders opened and that resulted in a significant migration flow from the country, both north-south and south-south. Of interest, different migration trajectories in Ukraine are gender-linked. While sixty percent of Ukrainian men who migrate tend to go to Russia (south-south migration), Ukrainian women typically migrate to the developed Western European countries, hence south-north migrations, where they work in home and service sectors, with Italy receiving around forty percent of all women who emigrate from Ukraine (Montefusco 2008). Montefusco (2010) calls such migrant women "pioneers" because they typically migrate alone, leaving loved ones behind, but sending remittances home. This type of migration is often viewed as maternal sacrifice: women sacrifice their personal lives for the well-being of their children (Vianello 2009; Tolstokorova 2010, 2012). Because of the increasing number of migrating women – not only in Ukraine but also around the globe – the topic of "feminization" of migration and its effects on women and their families has been discussed in academia and public discourse (e.g., Schmalzbauer 2008). For instance, as Tolstokorova (2012) argues, the immersion into Western societies where gender relations are more egalitarian, in addition to economic independence, leads to the transformation of the identities of Ukrainian women-migrants: their social status increases and their understanding of gender roles alters. At the same time, the public discourse of "lost childhood" or "Euro orphans" puts blame on Ukrainian migrant women by reinforcing normative gender roles of mothers as providers of daily care and love for their children, and in so doing questioning and delegitimizing the identities of women migrants (Rubchak 2011; Fedyuk 2015).

The annexation of the Crimean peninsula, a Ukrainian territory, in March 2014 by the Russian Federation and the armed conflict between Ukrainian military and pro-Russian groups in the East have led to a different type of migration in Ukraine: internal displacement. The United Nations (*Guiding Principles on Internal Displacement*, United Nations, 1998, E/CN.4/1998/53/Add.2) defines internal displacement as a situation where people have to flee or leave their homes "as a result of or in order to avoid the effects of armed conflict, situations of generalized violence, violations of human rights or natural or human-made disasters, and who have not crossed an internationally recognized state border" (for more information, see Heugh, this volume). The Internal Displacement Monitoring Centre (IDMC) reported that as of July 2015 there were over 1.3 million internally displaced people (IDP) in Ukraine. Because many of the IDPs are Russian speakers (Russian is a predominant language in the Crimea and the East), how their linguistic practices would influence and will be influenced by the receiving population (many of the receiving communities are in western Ukraine where Ukrainian is predominantly used in public and private spheres) merits further investigation.

We note a similar situation of internal migration or displacement in the war-torn Democratic Republic of Congo (DRC). According to *Forced Migration Review*, internal displacement has plagued the Congo for the past twenty years, peaking at 3.4 million people in 2003 (http://www.fmreview.org/DRCongo). The most affected areas include the east and south of the country, although displacement is also evident elsewhere. In the east the populations are constantly on the move, fleeing the armed conflict between various rebel groups over control of mineral resources. In the south, especially the Katanga Province, in the 1990s the local populations exerted ethnic cleansing of Luba speakers, again over control of resources, forcing them to return to the Kasai Province, where their ancestors originated. Linguistically, internal migration arguably had little impact on the migrants in the east of DRC, especially since Swahili is the lingua franca there. However, migrants in the south of the country had to learn the language of their ancestors, Ciluba, a language they had forsaken for Swahili, the lingua franca in the Katanga province.

Globalization and migration

Migration trajectories are influenced not only by political and socio-economic factors in a particular country or countries, but by the process of globalization as well. For instance, Dong and Blommaert (2009: 2) show that "rural-urban migration has taken place on a massive scale within China's borders in the last twenty years. It happens in the context of rapid economic and social changes both from inside China, and of China's integration in globalisation processes." Globalization, an evolving, complex and multi-faceted phenomenon, is linked to "the phenomenal expansion of transnational, global mobility and in the massively increased intensity of commercial and cultural exchanges and exploitation" (Coupland 2013: 5). Globalization has influenced not only rural-urban migration, but also – and to a greater extent – south-north migration. For instance, the 2006 United Nations report indicates that in 2005 one-third of all international migrants were south-north migrants: they moved from less developed countries to more developed countries (United Nations cited in Hugo 2006: 108). Moreover, as Hugo (2006: 116) suggests, "increased international mobility of highly skilled workers is an integral feature of contemporary globalization process, making developed and rapidly-developing countries, such as Singapore, compete for the migrants," especially for those who combine "English language communication skills and expert skills and experience relevant to the local needs" (Hugo 2006: 119). In this regard, English, as a global lingua franca, becomes a valued commodity on a (linguistic) market place that people use to project a "marketable" transnational professional identity. (English as a valuable and valued resource is also discussed in the "Issues and ongoing debates" section of this chapter.)

Despite these highlighted differences, both rural-urban and south-north migrants engage in what Deumert (2013, after Bank 2011: 15–17) calls processes of *place-making* and *people-making*. For rural-urban migrants, the former refers to a process whereby migrants use such semiotic resources as mixed language varieties (e.g., *Tsotsitaal* in South Africa, *Sheng* in Kenya, and *surzhyk* in Ukraine) to establish an identity or identities that are valued in the new environment. Thus, they also project particular social personae, that is, engage in *people-making*, or we wish to say *new identity-making*, without necessarily discarding the old one, the rural (Deumert 2013: 70). While *Sheng, surzhyk,* and *Tsotsitaal* are all classified as dynamic mixed languages or mixed codes (but see Mesthrie and Hurst (2013) for a different view on *Tsotsitaal*) that have emerged primarily as a result of rural-urban migration, only *Tsotsitaal* (Afrikaans-based mixed variety) and *Sheng* (Swahili-based mixed variety) are linked to and index what could be identified as *covert* (Labov 1972; Trudgill 1974) prestige. As Glaser (2000: 4) notes, in the 1940s and 1950s Tsotsitaal was part of a young urban masculine identity, especially a gang member identity, with "fighting skill, independence, street wisdom, feats of daring, law-breaking, clothing style . . . and success with women" as other attributes of such an identity. With time, *Tsotsitaal* has become less of a gang "argot" and now "signifies a cosmopolitanism internal to township life, one produced in and through the otherwise violent histories of migrant labor and forced relocation through which individuals from diverse language worlds came to live with each other" (Morris 2010: 105). In other words, *Tsotsitaal* indexes "the high life of the city – the urban, the cool, the hip, and the sophisticated" (Childs 1996 cited in Slabbert and Myers-Scotton 1997). *Sheng* has undergone a somewhat similar process: from an urban variety associated with poor sections of Nairobi (Kang'ethe-Iraki 2004), it has evolved to symbolize young people in general, especially young men. As one of the participants in our larger study,[1] a student at Moi University in Kenya whom we call Alvin, observes, "Use it to identify yourself as being a youth."

Like Tsotsitaal, *Sheng* is a linguistic resource young people use to project modern, trendy, urban identities (see Nassenstein and Hollington (2015) for a discussion on youth language practices in Africa). It is worth noting that *Sheng*, as well as *surzhyk* and *Tsotsitaal,* are not a monolithic variety but rather a set of unstable evolving varieties (see Kioko 2015 for a discussion). It is a hybrid language speakers use to index hybrid identities, or in Bosire's (2006: 192) articulation, Sheng is "a way to break away from the old fraternities that put particular ethnic communities in particular neighborhoods/'estates' and give them a global urban ethnicity, the urbanite: sophisticated, street smart, new generation, tough." Moreover, because of

> the rate of rural-urban migration in Kenya today, a sizable percentage of children are born and socialized in multi-ethnic urban settings where daily interactions and communication are devoid of mother tongues. Therefore, most urban-socialized children and youths lack knowledge of their mother tongue(s) and are thus increasingly identifying with Sheng as a first language.
>
> *(Kioko 2015: 130)*

At the same time, as Makewa, Miwita and Ocharo (2014) and other researchers note, some educators in Kenya view *Sheng* as a threat to both standard English and kiSwahili, that is, they exhibit what can be identified as "purist" ideology toward language. Such purist ideology is even more prevalent in Ukraine, where prominent academics publicly voice their resentment toward *surzhyk* as "a language illness of the postcolonial country" (Masenko 2009) and write books with titles like *Anti-zurzhyk* (Serbens'ka 1994: 6–7), in which this mixed variety is described as "a crippled language [that] makes a person stupid." In addition to strong resentment from Ukrainian academics and activists, unlike *Tsotsitaal* and *Sheng*, *surzhyk*, although not a monolithic linguistic phenomenon (Bilaniuk 2004), has not become associated with urban masculinity or stylish urban youth culture; instead, it still retains some degree of rural connotation and is often used to create comedic characters, such as Verka Serduchka, a *surzhyk*-speaking middle-aged woman played by a male actor Danylko (Yekelchyk 2010). Having discussed rural-urban migration and south-north migration trajectories and their impact on identity construction in migrant communities, we now turn to the next migration trajectory, return migration. Next, we focus on circular migration trajectory, and this will be followed by a discussion of chain migration and step migration. We argue that, regardless of the category of migration trajectory involved, each migration trajectory has an impact, though to varying degrees, on migrants' social identities and proficiency in both the migrant community language as well as the language of the host community.

Return migration

While migration, especially international migration, is typically viewed as a one-time and one-way movement, the reverse trajectory – the return migration – has a long history as well. For instance, Gmelch (1980: 135) notes that as early as the 19th-century, Ravenstein, in his list of migration laws derived from the migration patterns in the UK, includes a reference to return migration. "Each main current of migration," writes Ravenstein (1885: 187), "produces a compensating counter-current." At the same time, while most scholarly and government publications agree that return migration involves a reverse trajectory, there seems to be a variety of understanding of how long the emigrants have to stay during their return for it to be considered a return migration. Gmelch (1980), for instance, views return migration as a return of migrants to their homeland to resettle for good, but does not view migrants' return home for holidays or for a prolonged visit without an intention to stay permanently as such. The Organisation for Economic Co-operation and Development (OECD) stipulates that migrants who intend to stay in their home country for at least a year are considered return migrants. In its Xpeditions Human Migration Guide (2005) for educators, the National Geographic Society conflates return migration with *circular migration*, to be discussed later, by referring to return migration as "the voluntary movements of immigrants back to their place of origin. This is also known as circular migration." In this study, however, we distinguish between return migration and circular migration. The former, we suggest, essentially entails the return of migrants with an intention to resettle; while the latter, to which we will return in the next section, involves periodic returns. We also recognize that migration categories as theoretical constructs can only to a certain degree capture the complexity of migration as a dynamic and multifaceted phenomenon. For instance, in her research on Luso descendants (Portuguese immigrants in France), Koven (1998, 2013) further problematizes the notion of return migration by referring to Luso immigrants who build houses in Portugal, travel there annually for an extended period of time, maintain their use of Portuguese, but who also perpetually delay their permanent relocation to Portugal as return migrants. In other words,

Luso immigrants in France are in the state of the continual "just about" return migration. Economist Christian Dustmann (1997, 2003) indicates that the length of migrants' stay in a host country is often determined by the buying power they would have in their home country using the capital accumulated in the host country.

Migrants' intent to return to their homeland is intimately connected to their linguistic repertoires and identities and vice versa. For instance, Koven (1998, 2013) reports that because Portuguese immigrants in France have always viewed their stay as temporary, they and their children have maintained the Portuguese language and traditions, even though with passing years the permanent return to Portugal has become "indefinitely deferred" (Koven 1998: 414). In contrast, some children of undocumented Mexican immigrants in the United States, a south-north migration, who at any moment could return or be forced to return to their birth country, are often English monolinguals with some rudimentary knowledge of Spanish. This indexes their orientation toward and identification with the United States, its language and culture. As reported by Lara (2013), those English-speaking youngsters who voluntarily or because of the deportation return to Mexico struggle to adjust in part because of their limited Spanish-language proficiency and lack of cultural knowledge. In this regard, the idea of a sociolinguistic center, somewhat reminiscent of the deictic center as considered in pragmatics, is important in the exploration of the language practices and identities of migrants. As Koven (2013: 325) shows in her research on Luso immigrants, the diasporic model of such spatiotemporal orientation is "to an imagined Portuguese homeland as their sociolinguistic 'center,'" while in a transnational model in which the orientation is polycentric "Portugal is no longer the evaluative center." Speakers' language practices and identities are reflective and co-constructive of such orientations, often in one interaction. For instance, through the lens of the diasporic model, the use of French by Luso descendants is viewed as "an intentional, immoral abandonment of one's 'real' identity and homeland" (Koven 2013: 328). As one of Koven's (2013: 328) participants noted, Luso immigrants who live or are even born in France "have no [moral] right to deny [their Portuguese] language" and culture. At the same time, the transnational model views the use of French as an inevitable result of living in France for a long period of time. Thus, different identities can be enacted by the use of the same language: the use of French by Luso immigrants could be viewed as either an abandonment of one's "true" Portuguese identity or as merely indexing an identity of a person who lives and works in France.

The issues connected to the relationship between language and identity are also experienced by the return migrants in Puerto Rico. A great number of those who moved to Puerto Rico are return migrants and their children (Duany 2003). As Duany's (2003: 430) research on migration and identities of Puerto Ricans shows, "second-generation migrants who return to the Island – often dubbed pejoratively Nuyoricans[2] – may speak English better than Spanish and still define themselves simply as Puerto Ricans." Similarly, Zentella's (1990, 1997) research shows that Puerto Ricans returning to the island from the mainland United States, second generation especially, may identify with their home community (Puerto Rico) while being more proficient in the language of the host community (mainland United States). Furthermore, Duany (2003: 431) suggests that since 1917, when US citizenship was extended to the inhabitants of Puerto Rico, some (not all) Puerto Ricans are involved in *el vaivén* (literally translated as *coming and going*). Namely, they are involved in what can be identified as a type of circular migration between the island and the mainland. At the same time, Duany (2003) indicates that it would be restrictive to view Puerto Ricans as circular migrants who are just constantly moving between Puerto Rico and the United States. Rather the author, following Zentella (1990, 1997), views Puerto Rican identities both on the mainland and the island as hybrid and fluid.

Circular, step, and chain migration

As the discussion of the return migration demonstrates, it is not always easy to differentiate between circular and return migration. Typically, circular migration refers to the movement and trajectory "between an origin and destination involving more than one migration" and return and entails "migrants sharing work, family, and other aspects of their lives between two or more locations" (Hugo 2013: 2). Hugo distinguishes circular migration from return migration, which involves a singular return after a prolonged absence, and from commuting, which entails a daily return to a single place of residence. The European Commission (2007: 10), with a special focus on migration between the European Union and third countries, defines circular migration as "a form of migration that is managed in a way allowing some degree of legal mobility back and forth between two countries." Circular migration is more frequently linked to other types of migration trajectories, especially to rural-urban and south-south, which involve constant shuttling between locations. As Vertovec (2007: 5), following Chapman (1979), Elkan (1967) and Cordell, Gregory and Piché (1996), states, "circular migration represents an age-old pattern of mobility, whether rural-urban or cross-border." For instance, in her longitudinal study of migration in a city of Harare, Zimbabwe, Potts (2010: 1) suggests that circular migration in Zimbabwe is strengthening and revitalizing and views "circularity as one element in rural-urban migration patterns." Posel and Marx (2013) show that in South Africa temporary individual labor migration was prevalent during apartheid and is still predominant in the post-apartheid years. As a type of migration trajectory, circular migration has an impact on identities and language practices and proficiencies of migrants. As Potts (2010) shows, many rural-urban circular migrants maintain their membership, and claim their identities, in two communities. At the same time, as Posel and Marx (2013: 820) find in their study of two informal settlements in the Durban metropolitan area of South Africa, identifying with the "original" household "is not synonymous with their [migrants'] intended return migration to that household." This shows fluidity between different migrant trajectories, such as circular migration and permanent (re)settlement. Posel and Marx (2013), as well as other researchers (e.g., Peil, Ekpenyong, and Oyeneye 1988; Bekker 2001; Falkingham, Chepngeno-Langat, and Evandrou 2012), indicate that the duration of migration and the distance from the "original" household are two primary factors that weaken migrants' aspirations to return: the longer the migrants stay in their host communities and the farther the distance to the "original" household, the more likely are the "temporary" migrants to become "permanent" settlers. Posel and Marx (2013) identified marriage as an indication of a more permanent stay: migrants who are cohabitating tend to identify with dual households (home and host) while married migrants tend to identify just with one household. In a related vein, Castles and Ozkul (2014) bring attention to the social and human dimension of circular migration. The authors argue that while many government programs, especially in host communities, presume that "individuals take their decisions alone and only for economic benefits (Castles and Ozkul 2014: 31), migrants' decisions – and identities – are inextricably connected to their families and surroundings. Hugo (2013) finds that while circular migration may enhance migrants' skills and experience and improve their and their families' income, the periodic separation may have negative effects on personal and familial relationships of migrants.

Similar to circular migration, step migration is also linked to personal and family relations and identities of migrants. It refers to a migration pattern that consists of a series of extreme or less extreme locational changes. For example, if a person moves from a farm to a small town, then to a larger town and finally a city, it is an example of less extreme step migration.

In this case, it seems that step migration, as an incremental process, may not have as much effect on language proficiency, maintenance, and identity as may chain migration, a point to which we will return in the next section. In other cases, however, step migration may involve extreme locational changes. Current as of migration crisis in Europe is an example of step migration that involves extreme locational changes in which individuals and families fleeing conflict in the Middle East migrate from one intermediary country to another, such as from Turkey to Greece, in hopes of reaching Germany or Sweden, their target countries. Schapendonk's (2012) study of African migration trajectories to Europe refers to such cases as *fragmented migration to the north*. It is explained that as a result of restrictive migration policies in the European Union (EU), most of the conventional roads to the EU are blocked. Therefore, sub-Saharan African migrants undertake fragmented and risky journeys to "the North." Migration trajectories in this case are not only about mobility, but even more so about periods of rest, re-orientation and (un)expected and (un)intended temporary or long-term settlements. Schapendonk offers the following account by Sony, a twenty-two-year-old Cameroonian migrant, of his migration trajectories:

> In my country there is no future . . . Everybody knows it and many people go out. They just go! I did the same, just go! I went to Nigeria to look for work . . . At that time, I did not think of Europe, Nigeria was promising, the economy was booming, so you go there and you search for a place . . . I had a good life there. But then you hear about Nigerians leaving for Europe, you hear about success and so on. One day, three of my [Nigerian] friends created the plan to go, and I wanted the same . . . Now [in Morocco] I want to reach Spain. I will stay there for one year. Then I will go to Paris or London, and if there is a chance, I will go to New York or Washington!
>
> *(Schapendonk 2012: 32)*

It seems that step migration trajectories, especially if they involve extreme locational changes and lengthy stays in a host destination, might impact migrants' identities and language proficiency in the host destination.

While both circular and step migration trajectories may involve groups of individuals, the collective nature of migration is most prominent in chain migration. MacDonald and MacDonald (1964: 82) define chain migration as "that movement in which prospective migrants learn of opportunities, are provided with transportation, and have initial accommodation and employment arranged by means of primary social relationships with previous migrants." It is a process where relatives who have previously migrated to a new country sponsor family to migrate to the same country. It entails a tendency by foreigners from a certain city or region to migrate to the same areas as others from their city or region. There is evidence of this in several cities around the world. The emergence of such language islands (Kloss 1966) as "Little India," "Chinatown," "Little Italies," and so on, with reference to a geographical concentration of Indians, Chinese, and Italians in some areas of the United States, is a typical example of chain migration. Chain migration is closely connected to family reunification and government regulations concerning family reunification (e.g., Massey et al. 1994; Pflegerl 2002; Croes and Hooimeijer 2010). This, in turn, raises the issue of definition of a family and family identity. For instance, in Europe family reunification is restricted to spouses and children, while the United States includes a broader circle of relatives (Croes and Hooimeijer 2010). Croes and Hooimeijer (2010: 122), in their study of Aruba chain migration, note that because "the opportunities for family reunification depend upon the social and economic position of the pioneer migrant in the Aruba labour market," it is more difficult for women to bring their spouses and children to the host country. In other words, to bring a spouse or a child, a migrant has to have "a valid work permit for more than three years, to have a stable job providing sufficient income, and to have acquired appropriate housing" (Croes and Hooimeijer 2010: 122). Women, who are often recruited to work in the private sector with unstable, low-paid jobs, have a hard time meeting such requirements. Thus gender identities, which are linked to employment identities and opportunities, play the role in chain migration. At the same time, as discussed earlier, with more and more women as pioneer migrants supporting their families rather than migrants who join their husbands, women may be using migration as a step to achieve independence as individuals (Raghuram 2004) or "those women who participate in migration are less firmly tied to family structures in their home country" (Croes and Hooimeijer 2010: 133).

Issues and ongoing debates

Migration, language maintenance and shift, and identity

One of the issues being debated in the literature on migration trajectories concerns the fate of the languages that migrants bring along into the host communities (Tuominen 1999; Borland 2006; Beykont 2010; Cavallaro 2010). In this section we would like to briefly address that issue, with a focus on language maintenance, shift, and identity in migrant communities. Borland (2006) proposes two sets of factors as playing a crucial role in language shift in migrant communities, namely, *facilitating* and *motivating factors*. Facilitating factors are aspects of the socio-political context that allow for language maintenance, among them, supportive government policies and frequent contacts with the migrants' homeland. Motivating factors refer to a conscious individual decision and commitment to maintain and transmit the home language to the next generation. These factors are captured in what Giles, Bourhis, and Taylor (1977) term the *ethnolinguistic vitality* of a group or community. The authors define *ethnolinguistic vitality* as that "which makes a group likely to behave as a distinct and active collective entity in inter-group situations" (Giles et al. 1977: 308). They go on to explain that the ethnolinguistic vitality of a group is measured in terms of the status of its language relative to other languages in a polity, the demographic strength of the group, and institutional support. We argue that in south-north migrations the absence of facilitating and motivating factors coupled with utility-maximization (i.e., greatest benefit of language shift) (Tuominen 1999) and colingualism (Schell 2008) – the tendency by bilinguals to communicate in a shared second language (L2) even if they share a common first language (L1) – accelerates language shift rather than maintenance. However, the presence of facilitating and motivating factors in rural-urban migrations leads to a different outcome: maintenance of the migrant language (Kamwangamalu 2013) or emergence of such mixed linguistic varieties as *Tsotsitaal, Sheng*, and *surzhyk*, as discussed earlier. Of all the migration trajectories discussed in this paper, it is clear that return and chain migration, which appear to be sustained by both facilitating and motivating factors, play a positive role in migrant language maintenance and related identities.

For example, Beykont (2010: 96) reports that in Australia, the largest concentration of Turkish immigrants resides in the state of Victoria, many in proximity to other Turkish speakers. This geographical concentration of Turkish speakers, aided by ethnic media (Turkish radio, newspapers, TV programs) and endogamy, enables youngsters to hear Turkish in the neighborhood, and thus contributes to Turkish proficiency and maintenance in the host country. Likewise, in his study of the Chechen migrants in Jordan, Al-Khatib (2001: 168) lists the following among the factors contributing to proficiency in and maintenance of the

Chechen language in that host country: (1) the existence of linguistic and cultural islands, whereby the Chechens live in tightly knit communities; (2) the use of the Chechen language in the home and in the community; (3) the positive attitudes of the Chechens towards their language and the high value placed on it in relation to their ethnic identity; (4) resistance to exogamy (i.e., interethnic marriage); and (5) the roles of religion (Islam) and religious beliefs, which have strengthened the role of language as a symbol of group unity. In the absence of many such factors, there is the high potential for language loss and attendant shift to the language of the host country, as Cavallaro (2010) discusses in his study of language shift in Sicilian-Italian migrant communities in Australia. The study shows that Italian is being replaced by English as a result of linguistic fragmentation (the members of the Italian community in Australia speak a wide range of Italian dialects or a mixture of these); the high rate of exogamy; and the lack of exposure to Italian in the home because of preference for English (Cavallaro 2010: 115, 147). With respect to the latter factor, research shows that socioeconomic pressure in the host country works against the maintenance and intergenerational transmission of immigrant languages: A majority language must be learned to function successfully and move up in the host community (Slavik 2001). As pointed out by Ladefoged,

> what do you tell a parent who encourages his/her child to move away from their ancestral land and/or from their language in search of better economic opportunities? How does one advise such migrants to maintain their ethnic languages when they move to a place where they probably will no longer be in regular contact with their homeland?
> *(Ladefoged cited in Mufwene 2010: 918)*

It seems that the language used in a given social situation, as Stevens (1992: 174) observes, depends on the sociolinguistic attributes attached to the users of that language. For example, in a study of language shift in second-generation Albanian immigrants in Greece, Gogonas (2009) notes that there was a tendency on the part of Albanian pupils to "hide" their knowledge of Albanian due to stigmatization of their ethnic group in Greece: Albanian immigrants in Greece are generally described as inherently criminal, primitive, invaders, traditional enemies, cunning, and untrustworthy. Accordingly, to avoid being associated with a stigmatized group and language, Albanian pupils downplay their knowledge of Albanian and use Greek instead (Gogonas 2009: 104). Put differently, the Albanian pupils are aware of the stigmatized nature of what Blommaert (2005: 251) refers to as *ascriptive identity*, that is, "an identity attributed to someone by others," usually to define and impose a social category; therefore, they distance themselves from both the group and the language and embrace the Greek language instead, especially since it is perceived as the language of upward social mobility. Laitin (1993) remarks that the choices that such immigrants make to integrate into the host community can be explained from the perspective of what he calls "a competitive assimilation game": despite the loyalty they might have for their home language, working-class or unemployed immigrants have a strategic incentive to assimilate the language of their new home to be able to compete for middle-class jobs (Laitin 1993: 59). Thus, says Laitin, destination language fluency and earnings are positively correlated. This is especially true in case of forced migration due to civil wars; for example, as discussed in Mugaddam's (2005) study of language attitude and shift in migrant communities in Khartoum, Sudan, who fled the civil war in the south of the country in the mid-1980s. In this case, migrants hardly have had opportunities to maintain contact with their region of origin. Consequently, the younger generations of migrants in particular have integrative motivation to assimilate the language of the host region. Mugaddam's study shows that migrant parents encourage their children to learn Arabic, the lingua franca in Khartoum, and English for their instrumental value at the expense of ethnic languages apparently because the latter play no role in the children's socio-economic life. This also shows that ethnic or cultural identities often do not correspond with linguistic identities and practices.

Implications

The migration trajectories discussed in this chapter, particularly south-north migration, have implications for policy and pedagogical practices in the host country. The relevant question here is how can a host country integrate migrants and their languages into the wider society. What policies should be developed to achieve integration? A related question is whether migrant languages should be offered a place in the curriculum. It seems that the fate of migrant languages in the host country rests on a number of variables: the previously discussed ethnolinguistic vitality of the migrant group (Giles et al. 1977), the presence or lack thereof of motivating and facilitating factors (Borland 2006), and the value that both the migrants themselves (and the host country) associate with migrant languages, that is, whether they consider the community language as a core value (Smolicz 1984). The ethnolinguistic size of the migrant group and the status of a migrant language in the country of origin may work in favor of institutional support for the language in the host country. Consider the Chinese language in the United States. Chinese receives institutional support in the United States because there is a sizeable population of Chinese migrants in this country. Also, Chinese has a higher status as the official language of the People's Republic of China. The international status of China as an economic powerhouse adds value to the Chinese language not only at home but also abroad. However, smaller languages may not attract the attention that Chinese does to receive institutional support in the host country, as Kamwangamalu (2013) has demonstrated in a study of African migrants in the Washington, DC, metropolitan area. Consequently, speakers of smaller migrant languages tend to abandon their home language and assimilate the mainstream language, English in this case, the language of upward social mobility. But even for such larger migrant communities as the Chinese in the United States or elsewhere, migrations, irrespective of the trajectory types, appear to always come with a price. For example, Delargy (2007: 134) notes that the second or third generation of Chinese Americans often speak fluent English but have limited skills in their heritage language, and experience attendant intergenerational difficulties to communicate effectively with grandparents and in some case even parents, because of language differences. A related example is provided by Cavallaro (2010) in his study of language shift in Italian migrant communities in Australia, as discussed in the preceding section. Again, the study shows that despite a supportive infrastructure (large community, institutional support, etc.), younger Italian migrants in that country have limited skills in Italian and prefer to communicate through the medium of English rather than of their heritage language, Italian. It seems that unless migrant communities, large or small, view their heritage language as a core value (Smolicz 1984), the ethnolinguistic size of the group and institutional support by the host country may not be enough to stop the shift from the community language to the mainstream language, especially for the younger generations of migrants. As Hatoss (2006) pointedly remarks,

> Language policies do not necessarily bring the desired effects on the linguistic environment of migrant communities. For contemporary language communities . . . , it is

> essential that they take initiatives for the maintenance and development of the cultural and linguistic heritage.
>
> *(Hatoss 2006: 302)*

McDermott (2012) suggests some initiatives, including community festivals, arts projects, grass roots community initiatives, and so on, to showcase the migrant community's culture, literature and language, music, dance, and so forth. These initiatives, complemented by institutional educational programs offering tuition in the migrant community language, might help stem the tides of language shift to the mainstream language. For example, Smolicz and Secombe's (2003) study of programs for Cambodian immigrants in Australia, cited by McDermott (2008: 495), "found that the provision of tuition within the mainstream classroom in a community language achieved both high levels of bilingualism as well as high academic success in other subjects."

Future directions

The rapid development of mobile communication technologies and major geopolitical changes that began in 1990s have not only contributed to the expansion and complexity of mobility and migration (Arnaut and Spotti forthcoming), but they have also led to new ways of thinking about these phenomena. As an example, in the context of globalization, step migration, which traditionally refers to smaller "local" moves, may also refer to international migration. In this regard, Block (2010: 490) observes that some people may migrate several times transnationally, a "two-step" or "multi-step" migration, "thus making issues around national and ethnolinguistic identity, as well as migration type difficult to qualify." Block illustrates this point by referring to Wallace's study of migrant children in London in which one such child-migrant was born in Germany to Sri Lankan parents and at the age of thirteen migrated to London alone (his parents joined him later) and who "speaks Tamil with his mother, but German with the rest of his family" (Wallace cited in Block 2010: 490). Block goes on to suggest that as researchers we are preoccupied with categorization, including migrant categorization, often at the exclusion of the perspectives of those whose lives we try to understand. Moreover, there is a tendency to emphasize the novelty of the phenomena under study, with the recent notion of "superdiversity" (Vertovec 2007; Blommaert and Rampton 2011) being one of them. As Heugh (2013: 6) observes, "Considerations and theorization of diversity are therefore not new," as deliberations on social division and difference go back to Plato's *Republic* and Thomas More's *Utopia*. At the same time, as Reyes (2014: 368) notes, superdiversity as a theoretical notion is based on the premise of "what is understood as an empirical change in migrants, which has caused 'us' [researchers] to identify them as newly unpredictable and the societal conditions they alter as superdiverse." In other words, as Reyes (2014: 368) reminds us, it is important to ask, "Who, in fact, perceives the world as superdiverse? Who experiences it as superdiverse? If it is superdiverse now, how was it diverse to some 'regular' degree before?" Additionally, as Arnaut and Spotti (forthcoming) observe, the notion of superdiversity with its focus on diversity may obscure inequality, and, as we suggest, its focus on individual actors and individual identities may mask collectivities and shared group identities. In a similar vein, Makoni (2014: 82) states that the notion of superdiversity generates a strong sense of social romanticism, "creating an illusion of equality in a highly asymmetrical world", and suggests that as researchers we need to uncover power differences as well as to distinguish between those migrants who travel willingly and those who are forced to do so by circumstances.

Perhaps, similar to Herring's (2013) conceptualization of discourse in new media as *familiar, reconfigured*, and *emergent*, research in the area of language and migration can explore a range of connections between the old and new phenomena, between the old and new theories and methodologies, adopting a "moving forward while looking back" approach. While migration and diversity have been around for centuries, "What appear to be new," argues Heugh (2013), "are exponential changes in speed, scale and complexity" and "an increasing multi-directional mobility of individuals and communities" (6). Thus, as researchers in the 21st century, we are faced with the fluidity of and interconnection between categories of individuals and communities. "Communities cohere, diverge and reconverge along ever reconfiguring lines of gender, age, class, language, education, aspiration and digital and social network connectivity" (Heugh 2013: 7). In her research on language practices of Sudanese and Afghan immigrants in South Australia, Heugh finds that maintaining ancestral language is not an obstacle to integration. "There is evidence of both language maintenance and expansion of linguistic, cultural and other repertoires of identity, and there is also evidence of agency, participation and citizenship" (Heugh 2013: 28). Blackledge and Creese (2014: 1) suggest that multilingualism is the norm in the conditions where "large numbers of people migrate across myriad borders, and as advances in digital technology make available a multitude of linguistic resources at the touch of a button or a screen, so communication is in flux and development." In sum, what appears to be new is that migration, diversity, and multilingualism are becoming the norm worldwide and the role of the researchers is to explore the complexity of migration trajectories and the fluidity of migrant identities, their linguistic practices, and their resources.

Summary

In this chapter we have explored the relationship between different migrant trajectories and individual identities and linguistic repertoires. Drawing on prior studies on language and migration (e.g., Barkhuizen and Kamwangamalu 2013; Deumert 2013) and using examples from Africa, North America, Europe, and other parts of the world, we have demonstrated how individuals (re)negotiate their linguistic identities and proficiencies when they migrate to new places or return to old ones. Following Lewis (1982), Boyle et al. (1998), Kerswill (2006) and others, this work suggests that migrant trajectories and their implications for language proficiency, identity, and maintenance or shift can be better understood if they are not separated from other important parameters, such as time, motivation, and socio-cultural factors. While in rural-urban internal migrations language shift is not typical, in some instances internal rural-urban migration results in some migrants adopting a mixed vernacular variety, such as *Tsotsitaal* in South Africa, *Sheng* in Kenya, and *surzhyk* in Ukraine, with different types of values, identities, and proficiencies attached to each variety. We have also discussed how return migrants, children especially, may identify with their home community while being more proficient in the language of the host community, as in the case of Puerto Ricans returning from the mainland United States (Zentella 1990, 1997). We concluded with a discussion of new challenges and directions in the study of migrant trajectories and their broader socio-linguistic implications in the age of globalization and superdiversity (Blommaert 2013).

Related topics

> National and ethnic minorities: language rights and recognition
> Space, place, and language
> Regional flows and language resources

Further reading

Beguy, D., Bocquier, P. and Zulu, E. M. (2010). Circular migration patterns and determinants in Nairobi slum settlements. *Demographic Research*, *23*(20), 549–586.

The authors measure migration flows and determinants in two slum settlements in Nairobi City between 2003 and 2007, with a focus on circular migration patterns. They conclude that migration is more intense during early adulthood, and that mobility is more intense among women compared to men.

Greenwood, M.J. (1997). Internal migration in developed countries. In M. R. Rosensweig and O. Stark (eds.), *Handbook of Population and Family Economics*. Amsterdam, Netherlands: Elsevier Science, pp. 647–720.

This study examines the literature on the causes and consequences of internal migration in developed countries. It considers return migration as well as such questions as who migrates, where to, when, and what consequences result.

Kerswill, P. (2006). Migration and language. In K. Mattheier, U. Ammon and P. Trudgill (eds.), *Sociolinguistics/Soziolinguistik: An International Handbook of the Science of Language and Society* (2nd ed., Vol. 3, pp. 2271–2285). Berlin, Germany: Walter De Gruyter.

This article links relocation to migration to show how language shift, second language acquisition, and multilingualism are mostly affected by the extent of relocation than other language barriers.

Poertner, E., Junginger, M. and Muller-Boker, U. (2011). Migration in far west Nepal: intergenerational linkages between internal and international migration of rural-to-urban migrants. *Critical Asian Studies*, *43*(1), 23–47.

This article draws on Bourdieu's "Theory of Practice" to address linkages between internal and international migration practices in Nepal. It sees migration as a social practice or strategy that social agents apply to increase or transfer capitals and ultimately secure or improve their social position.

Schapendonk, J. (2012). Turbulent trajectories: African migrants on their way to the European Union. *Societies*, *2*, 27–41.

This study discusses the dynamic motivations and shifting migration trajectories taken by African migrants on their way to Europe in search of a better life. It offers moving accounts by the migrants, whom the author groups into the following categories: stranded migrants, stuck migrants, and more or less settled migrants.

Notes

1 A larger research project (#59530-MA-PIR) centers on everyday linguistic practices, code-switching in particular, of young educated Africans and is funded by the US Army.
2 The term, also spelled as a "Neoricans," refers to the individuals of Puerto Rican descent who have spent a lot of time on the mainland United States and who may speak English better than Spanish, engage in English-Spanish code-switching, or mix the two languages.

References

Al-Khatib, M.A. (2001). Language shift among the Armenian of Jordan. *International Journal of the Sociology of Language* 152: 153–177.

Arnaut, K. and Spotti, M. (forthcoming). Superdiversity discourse. In K. Tracey (ed.), *The international Encyclopedia of Language and Social Interaction*. Wiley-Blackwell.

Bank, L.J. (2011). *Home Spaces, Street Styles: Contesting Power and Identity in a South African City*. Johannesburg: Wits University Press.

Barkhuizen, G. and Kamwangamalu, N.M. (2013). Introduction. *International Journal of the Sociology of Language* 222: 1–3.

Bartram, D. (2011). Identity, migration and happiness. *Sociologie Româneasca?* 9(1): 7–13.

Bekker, S. (2001). Diminishing returns: Circulatory migration linking Cape Town to the Eastern Cape. *SA Journal of Demography* 8(1): 1–8.

Bernstein, B. (1986). A sociolinguistic approach to socialization; with some reference to educability. In J. Gumpez and D. Hymes (eds.), *Directions in Sociolinguistics* (pp. 465–497). New York: Basil Blackwell.

Beykont, Z.F. (2010). "We should keep what makes us different": Youth reflections on Turkish maintenance in Australia. *International Journal of the Sociology of Language* 206: 93–107.

Bilaniuk, L. (2004). A typology of surzhyk: Mixed Ukrainian-Russian language. *International Journal of Bilingualism* 8(4): 409–425.

Bilaniuk, L. (2005). *Contested Tongues: Language Politics and Cultural Correction in Ukraine*. Ithaca: Cornell University Press.

Blackledge, A. and Creese, A., eds. (2014). *Heteroglossia as Practice and Pedagogy*. Heidelberg: Springer.

Block, D. (2010). Problems portraying migrants in applied linguistics research. *Language Teaching* 43(4): 480–493.

Blommaert, J. (2005). *Discourse: A Critical Introduction*. Cambridge: Cambridge University Press.

Blommaert, J. (2013). *Ethnography, Superdiversity and Linguistic Landscapes: Chronicles of Complexity*. Bristol: Multilingual Matters.

Blommaert, J. and Dong, J. (2010). Language and movement in space. In N. Coupland (ed.), *The Handbook of Language and Globalization* (pp. 366–385). Malden: Wiley-Blackwell.

Blommaert, J. and Rampton, B. (2011). Language and superdiversity. *Diversities* 13(2): 1–22.

Borland, H. (2006). Intergenerational language transmission in an established Australian migrant community: What makes the difference. *International Journal of the Sociology of Language* 180: 23–41.

Bosire, M. (2006). Hybrid languages: The case of Sheng. In O.F. Arasanyin and M.A. Pemberton (eds.), *Selected Proceedings of the 36th Annual Conference on African Linguistics* (pp. 185–193). Somerville, MA: Cascadilla Proceedings Project.

Boyle, P., Halfacree, K. and Robinson, V. (1998). *Exploring Contemporary Migration*. London: Longman Harlow.

Bucholtz, M. and Hall, K. (2004). Language and identity. In A. Duranti (ed.), *A Companion to Linguistic Anthropology* (pp. 369–393). Oxford: Blackwell.

Canagarajah, S. (2013). Reconstructing heritage language: Resolving dilemmas in language maintenance for Sri Lankan Tamil migrants. *International Journal of the Sociology of Language* 222: 131–155.

Castles, S. and Ozkul, D. (2014). Circular migration: Triple win, or a new label for temporary migration? In G. Battistella (ed.), *Global and Asian Perspectives on International Migration* (pp. 27–49). Cham: Springer International.

Cavallaro, F. (2010). From trilingualism to monolingualism? Sicilian-Italian in Australia. *International Journal of the Sociology of Language* 206: 109–134.

Chapman, M. (1979). The cross-cultural study of circulation. *Current Anthropology* 20(1): 111–114.

Childs, G.T. (1996). The status of Isicamtho, an Nguni-based urban variety of Soweto. In A.K. Spears and D. Winford (eds.) *The Structure and Status of Pidgins and Creoles* (pp. 341–370). Amsterdam: Benjamins.

CODESRIA (2004). Urban governance in Africa. http://www.codesria.org/spip.php?article60 [Accessed August 10, 2015].

Conway, D. (1980). Step-wise migration: Toward a clarification of the mechanism. *International Migration Review* 14(1): 3–14.

Cordell, D.D., Gregory, J.W. and Piché, V. (1996). *Hoe and Wage: A Social History of a Circular Migration System in West Africa*. Boulder: Westview Press.

Coupland, N. (2013). Introduction: Sociolinguistics in the global era. In N. Coupland (ed.), *The Handbook of Language and Globalization* (pp. 1–27). Malden: Wiley-Blackwell.

Croes, H. and Hooimeijer, P. (2010). Gender and chain migration: The case of Aruba. *Population, Space and Place* 16: 121–134.

Delargy, M. (2007). Language, culture and identity: The Chinese community in Northern Ireland. In M.N. Craith (ed.), *Language Power and Identity Politics* (pp. 123–145). Basingstoke: Palgrave Macmillan.

Deumert, A. (2013). Xhosa in town (revisited)—Space, place and language. *International Journal of the Sociology of Language* 222: 51–75.

Dong, J. and Blommaert, J. (2009). Space, scale and accent: Constructing migrant identity in Beijing. *Multilingua* 28(1): 1–24.

Duany, J. (2003). Nation, migration, identity: The case of Puerto Ricans. *Latino Studies* 1: 424–444.

Dustmann, C. (1997). Return migration, uncertainty and precautionary savings. *Journal of Development Economics* 52: 295–316.

Dustmann, C. (2003). Return migration, wage differentials, and the optimal migration duration. *European Economic Review* 47: 353–369.

Elkan, W. (1967). Circular migration and the growth of towns in East Africa. *International Labour Review* 96(6): 581–589.

The European Commission. (2007). *Circular Migration and Mobility Partnerships between the European Union and Third Countries* [Online]. Retrieved from http://europa.eu/rapid/press-release_MEMO-07-197_en.htm [Accessed 7 March 2015].

Falkingham, J., Chepngeno-Langat, G. and Evandrou, M. (2012). Outward migration from large cities: Are older migrants in Nairobi "returning"? *Population, Space and Place* 18: 327–343.

Fedyuk, O. (2015). Growing up with migration: Shifting roles and responsibilities of families of Ukrainian care workers in Italy. In M. Kontos and G. Bonifacio (eds.), *Migrant Domestic Workers and Family Life: International Perspectives* (pp. 109–129). London: Palgrave Macmillan.

Giles, H., Bourhis, R.Y. and Taylor, D.M. (1977). Towards a theory of language in ethnic group relations. In H. Giles (ed.), *Language, Ethnicity and Inter-group Relations* (pp. 307–348). London: Academic.

Glaser, C. (2000). *Bo Tsotsi: The Youth Gangs of Soweto, 1935–1976.* Cape Town: David Philip.

Gmelch, G. (1980). Return migration. *Annual Review of Anthropology* 9: 135–159.

Gogonas, N. (2009). Language shift in second generation Albanian immigrants in Greece. *Journal of Multilingual and Multicultural Development* 30(2): 95–110.

Hatoss, A. (2006). Community-level approaches in language planning: The case of Hungarian in Australia. *Current Issues in Language Planning* 7(2/3): 287–306.

Herring, S. (2013). Discourse in web 2.0: Familiar, reconfigured, and emergent. In D. Tannen and A.M. Trester (eds.), *Discourse 2.0: Language and New Media* (pp. 1–25). Washington, DC: Georgetown University Press.

Heugh, K. (2013). Mobility, migration and sustainability: Re-figuring languages in diversity. *International Journal of the Sociology of Language* 222: 5–32.

Hugo, G. (2006). Globalization and changes in Australian international migration. *Journal of Population Research* 23(2): 107–132.

Hugo, G. (2013). *What We Know about Circular Migration and Enhanced Mobility.* Washington, DC: Migration Policy Institute.

Ivanova, O. (2013). Bilingualism in Ukraine: Defining attitudes to Ukrainian and Russian through geographical and generational variations in language practices. *Sociolinguistic Studies* 7(3): 249–272.

Jenkins, R. (1994). Rethinking ethnicity: Identity, categorization and power. *Ethnic and Racial Studies* 17(2): 197–223.

Kamwangamalu, N.M. (1992). Multilingualism and social identity in Singapore. *Journal of Asia-Pacific Communication* 3: 33–47.

Kamwangamalu, N.M. (2013). Rural-urban and south-north migration and language shift. *International Journal of the Sociology of Language* 222: 33–49.

Kang'ethe-Iraki, F. (2004). Cognitive efficiency: The Sheng phenomenon in Kenya. *Pragmatics* 14(1): 55–68.

Kerswill, P. (2006). Migration and language. In K. Mattheier, U. Ammon and P. Trudgill (eds.), *Sociolinguistics/Soziolinguistik: An International Handbook of the Science of Language and Society* (2nd ed., Vol. 3, pp. 2271–2285). Berlin, Germany: Walter De Gruyter.

Kioko, E.M. (2015). Regional varieties and ethnic registers of Sheng. In N. Nassenstein and A. Hollington (eds.), *Youth Language Practices in Africa and beyond* (pp. 119–148). Berlin and Boston: Walter de Gruyter.

Kloss, H. (1966). German-American language maintenance efforts. In J.A. Fishman, V. Nahirny, J. Hofman and R. Hayden (eds.), *Language Loyalty in the United States* (pp. 206–252). The Hague: Mouton.

Koven, M. (1998). Two languages in the self/the self in two languages: French-Portuguese bilinguals' verbal enactments and experiences of self in narrative discourse. *Ethos* 26(4): 410–455.

Koven, M. (2013). Speaking French in Portugal: An analysis of contested personhood in narratives about return migration and language use. *Journal of Sociolinguistics* 17(3): 324–354.

Labov, W. (1972). *Sociolinguistic Patterns*. Philadelphia: University of Pennsylvania Press.

Ladefoged, P. (1992). Another view of endangered languages. *Language* 68(4): 808–811.

Laitin, D. (1993). Migration and language shift in urban India. *International Journal of the Sociology of Language* 103: 57–72.

Lara, T. (2013). *DREAMers in Mexico: Former Migrants Struggle in Their Home Country*. POLITIC365 [Online]. Retrieved from http://politic365.com/2013/04/15/dreamers-in-mexico-former-immigrants-struggle-in-their-home-country/ [Accessed August 10, 2015].

Le Page, R.B. (1986). Acts of identity. *English Today* 8: 21–24.

Le Page, R. and Tabouret-Keller, A. (1985). *Acts of Identity: Creole-based Approaches to Ethnicity and Language*. Cambridge: Cambridge University Press.

Lewis, G. (1971). Migration and language in the U.S.S.R. *International Migration Review* 5(2): 147–179.

Lewis, G. (1982). *Human Migration: A Geographical Perspective*. London: Canberra.

MacDonald, J.S. and MacDonald, L.D. (1964). Chain migration ethnic neighborhood formation and social networks. *Milbank Memorial Fund Quarterly* 42(1): 82–97.

Makewa, L., Miwita, M. and Ocharo, G. (2014). Student and educator perceptions of prevalence of use, attitude and views about *Sheng* speakers. *International Journal of Academic Research in Business and Social Sciences* 4(6): 265–278.

Makoni, S. (2014). "The Lord is my shock absorber": A sociohistorical integrationist approach to mid-twentieth-century literacy practices in Ghana. In A. Blackledge and A. Creese (eds.), *Heteroglossia as Practice and Pedagogy* (pp. 75–97). Heidelberg: Springer.

Maphosa, F. (2009). *Rural Livelihoods in Zimbabwe: Impact of Remittances from South Africa*. Dakar: CODESRIA.

Masenko, L. (2009). Language situation in Ukraine: Sociolinguistic analysis. In J. Besters-Dilger (ed.), *Language Policy and Language Situation in Ukraine* (pp. 101–137). Frankfurt am Main: Peter Lang.

Massey, D.S., Arango, J., Hugo, G., Kouaouci, A., Pellegrino, A. and Taylor, J.E. (1994). An evaluation of international migration theory: The North American case. *Population and Development Review* 20(4): 699–751.

McDermott, P. (2008). Acquisition, loss or multilingualism? Educational planning for speakers of migrant community languages in Northern Ireland. *Current Issues in Language Planning* 9(4): 483–500.

McDermott, P. (2012). Cohesion, sharing and integration? Migrant languages and cultural spaces in Northern Ireland's urban environment. *Current Issues in Language Planning* 13(3): 187–205.

Mesthrie, R. and Hurst, E. (2013). Slang registers, code-switching and restructured urban varieties in South Africa: An analytic overview of tsotsitaals with special reference to the Cape Town variety. *Journal of Pidgin and Creole Languages* 28(1): 103–130.

Montefusco, C. (2008). Ukrainian migration to Italy. *Journal of Immigrant and Refugee Studies* 6(3): 344–355.

Montefusco, C. (2010). *Final Report: Capacity Building Action towards Ukrainian Local Institutions for the Empowerment of Migratory and Social-Educational Policies on Behalf of Children, Women, and Local Communities* [Online] Rome: IOM. Retrieved from www.childrenleftbehind.eu/wp-content/uploads/2011/11/Final-Report-ITA-UKR-project-IOM-Italy.pdf [Accessed 15 August 2015].

Morris, R.C. (2010). Style, Tsotsi-style, and Tsotsitaal: The histories, aesthetics, and politics of a South African figure. *Social Text* 28(2 103): 85–112.

Mufwene, S.S. (2010). The role of mother-tongue schooling in eradicating poverty: A response to language and poverty. *Language* 86(4): 910–932.

Mugaddam, A.R.H. (2005). *Language Attitudes and Language Shift among Ethnic Migrants in Khartoum (Sudan)* [Online]. Retrieved from http://www.afrikanistik online.de/archiv/2005/181/index_html?searchterm=mugad [Accessed July 30, 2015].

Nassenstein, N. and Hollington, A., eds. (2015). *Youth Language Practices in Africa and beyond.* Berlin and Boston: Walter de Gruyter.

National Geographic Society. (2005). *Xpeditions: Human Migrations Guide* [Online]. Retrieved from http://www.nationalgeographic.com/xpeditions/lessons/09/g68/migrationguidestudent.pdf [Accessed 16 March 2015].

Peil, M., Ekpenyong, S.K. and Oyeneye, O.Y. (1988). Going home: Migration careers of Southern Nigerians. *International Migration Review* 22(4): 563–585.

Pflegerl, J. (2002). Family and migration. Research developments in Europe: A general overview. *Österreichisches Institut für Familienforschung, ÖIF, Austrian Institute for Family Studies* 21: 1–35.

Portes, A. and Dewind, J., eds. (2007). *Rethinking Migration: New Theoretical and Empirical Perspectives.* New York: Berghahn Books.

Posel, D. and Marx, C. (2013). Circular migration: A view from destination household in two urban informal settlements in South Africa. *Journal of Development Studies* 49(6): 819–831.

Potts, D. (2010). *Circular Migration in Zimbabwe and Contemporary Sub-Saharan Africa.* James Currey.

Raghuram, P. (2004). The difference that skills make: Gender, family migration strategies and regulated labour markets. *Journal of Ethnic and Migration Studies* 30(4): 303–321.

Ratha, D. and Shaw, W. (2007). South-South migration and remittances. *World Bank Working, Paper* 102 [Online]. Retrieved from http://siteresources.worldbank.org/INTPROSPECTS/Resources/334934-1110315015165/SouthSouthMigrationandRemittances.pdf [Accessed April 16, 2015].

Ravenstein, E.G. (1885). The laws of migration. *Journal of the Statistical Society* 48: 167–235.

Reyes, A. (2014). Linguistic anthropology in 2013: Super-new-big. *American Anthropologist* 116(2): 366–378.

Rubchak, M.J. (2011). *Mapping Difference: The Many Faces of Women in Contemporary Ukraine.* New York and Oxford: Berghahn.

Schapendonk, J. (2012). Turbulent trajectories: African migrants on their way to the European Union. *Societies* 2: 27–41.

Schell, M. (2008). Colinguals among bilinguals. *World Englishes* 27(1): 117–130.

Schmalzbauer, L. (2008). Family divided: The class formation of Honduran transnational families. *Global Networks* 8(3): 329–346.

Serbens'ka, O. (1994). *Anti-Surzhyk.* L'viv: Svit.

Slabbert, S. and Myers-Scotton, C. (1997). The structure of Tsotsitaal and Iscamtho: Code-switching and in-group identity in South African townships. *Linguistics* 34: 317–342.

Slavik, H. (2001). Language maintenance and language shift among Maltese migrants in Ontario and British Columbia. *International Journal of the Sociology of Language* 152: 131–152.

Smolicz, J.J. (1984). Minority languages and the core values of cultures: Changing policies and ethnic responses in Australia. *Journal of Multilingual and Multicultural Development* 5: 23–41.

Smolicz, J. and Secombe, M. (2003). Assimilation or pluralism? Changing policies for minority languages education in Australia. *Language Policy* 2(1): 3–25.

Stevens, G. (1992). The social and demographic context of language use in the United States. *American Sociological Review* 57: 171–185.
Tabouret-Keller, A. (1997). Language and identity. In F. Coulmas (ed.), *The Handbook of Sociolinguistics* (pp. 315–326). Oxford: Blackwell.
Tolstokorova, A. (2010). Where have all the mothers gone? The gendered effect of labour migration and transnationalism on the institution of parenthood in Ukraine. *Anthropology of East Europe Review (AEER)* 28(1): 184–214.
Tolstokorova, A. (2012). "Mommy washes windows in Rome": Gender aspects of transnational parenthood in Ukraine. *Zhurnal Issledovaii Sotsialnoi Politiki (Journal of Social Policy Studies)* 10(3): 393–408.
Trudgill, P. (1974). *The Social Differentiation of English in Norwich.* London: Cambridge University Press.
Tuominen, A. (1999). Who decides the home language? A look at multilingual families. *International Journal of the Sociology of Language* 140: 59–76.
United Nations. (2006). *World Population Monitoring, Focusing on International Migration and Development. Commission on Population and Development.* Thirty-Ninth Session, 3–7 April, Report of the Secretary-General. New York: Population Division, Department of Economic and Social Affairs.
United Nations. (2012). *Migrants by Origin and Destination: The Role of South-South Migration Population Facts.* Department of Economic and Social Affairs, Population Division: June 2012 (3).
Vertovec, S. (2007). *Circular Migration: The Way Forward in Global Policy?* IMI Working papers, No. 4 (Oxford: International Migration Institute, University of Oxford) [Online]. Retrieved from http://www.imi.ox.ac.uk/pdfs/wp/wp-04-07.pdf [Accessed 8 March 2015].
Vianello, F.A. (2009). *Migrano Sole: Legami Transnazionali tra Ucraina e Italia.* Milan: Franco Angeli.
Wallace, C. (2008). Literacy and identity: A view from the bridge in two multicultural London schools. *Journal of Language, Identity and Education* 7(1): 61–80.
Yekelchyk, S. (2010). What is Ukrainian about Ukraine's pop culture?: The strange case of Verka Serduchka. *Canadian-American Slavic Studies* 44: 217–232.
Zegeye, A., ed. (2001). *Social Identities in the New South Africa.* Cape Town: Kwela.
Zentella, A.C. (1990). Return migration, language, and identity: Puerto Rican bilinguals in dos worlds/two mundos. *International Journal of the Sociology of Language* 84: 81–100.
Zentella, A.C. (1997). *Growing up Bilingual: Puerto Rican Children in New York.* Malden, MA: Blackwell.

12
Slavery, indentured work, and language

Rajend Mesthrie

Introduction

Among the large-scale dislocations in the modern world that have had tangible sociolinguistic consequences, two stand out particularly: the forced migration associated with slavery, and the semi-forced migrations associated with the system known as indenture. The first section of this chapter will deal with the slave trade and its consequences for language maintenance and new language formation. To keep a tight focus, the section will concentrate on slavery from out of Africa into the 'New World' as controlled by Europeans from the 15th century on. The resulting field of pidgin and creole linguistics remains one of the major branches of contact linguistics and sociolinguistics. The chapter will examine slavery in the light of migration and summarise current linguistic thinking about the origins and development of pidgins and creoles. This is a complex field in which it is rare to find major scholars in agreement over conceptualizations of contact and its outcomes. The main theories that will be outlined are the Life Cycle theory (Robert A. Hall Jr.), the Bioprogramme (Derek Bickerton), Gradualism (John Singler, Philip Baker, Jacques Arends), Genetic Parallelism (Salikoko Mufwene), Anti-exceptionalism (Michel DeGraff), and its opposite, Exceptionalism (as espoused by John McWhorter). For all the internal disagreements, pidgin and creole linguistics affords us with the best tools for understanding language contact among large groups of migrants. The second major section of the chapter will survey the semi-forced movements of indentured labourers from South Asia into European colonies in different parts of the world, often into the very terrains from which slaves had been freed in the early 19th century. This time language maintenance was possible, and South Asian languages survived in new forms that showed robust traces of migration, social realignments, and language and dialect contact. Chief focus will fall on comparative research on Bhojpuri, the major language of the indentured Indian diaspora. The chapter will conclude with a brief reflection on lessons for applied linguistic research and practice.

Overview on slavery

Slavery is as old as recorded history, it being documented in the history of ancient Mesopotamia, Egypt, Greece, Rome, and other territories. The practices of one of these societies has given sociolinguistics a key term: 'vernacular', which today denotes the most colloquial style of a local variety. Etymologically based on Latin *verna* 'home-born female slave', the adjective *vernaculus* meant 'domestic' or 'national' (rather than 'foreign'). The modern sociolinguistic emphasis on variation, social networks, identity, and style lead us to expect sociolinguistic differentiation where there are power and social asymmetries within a broad community. The next section will provide a background to the power asymmetries of slavery in the modern world, with especial focus on European colonisation.

The slave trade: The two defining features of the modern era (stretching from medieval European times to the advent of globalisation, which we may take roughly as the year 1550 onwards, were European colonisation and its handmaiden, slavery. European trade, conquest, and/or colonisation affected almost all territories outside Europe. In places where there was no indigenous population (e.g., the islands of Mauritius and St. Helena), or where the indigenous population was largely devastated by initial colonial contact (e.g., in the Caribbean) or resisted forced labour (e.g., the Cape Colony), slaves were imported from Africa and Asia. Slavery was thus essential in developing and sustaining new colonies established on the economic system of the plantation. Mesthrie, Swann, Deumert, and Leap (2009: 274–275) drew attention to the historian's notion of triangular trade (or a sale triangle), which I summarise here. Ships from European ports like Liverpool, Amsterdam, and Bourdeaux sailed for West Africa, carrying goods for exchange (liquor, firearms, cotton goods, and trinkets). Trading took place at posts known as slave factories along the Gulf of Guinea (then known as *the Slave Coast*), to which people captured in the interior parts of Africa were forcibly brought.

> The majority of slaves originated from west Africa in the area bounded by the Senegal river in the north and Angola in the south. They came from a variety of ethnic and linguistic backgrounds, including those of the Wolof, Malinke, Fulani, Akan, Yoruba, Ibo, Hausa and Mandinka. Slaves experienced the horrors of being captured in their homes or while travelling, of being marched on the long journey to the coast in chains, and often having to wait a ship at collection posts for many months.
> *(Mesthrie et al. 2009: 274–275)*

The middle passage was an even more perilous journey of three months or more to the New World colonies of the southern United States, South America, and the West Indies. Conditions on-board ship could hardly have been worse. There was overcrowding as slaves were packed in the hulls to save space, and frequently chained to avoid insurrection or suicide. Provisions of food, sanitation, and ventilation were grossly inadequate. Estimates are that about twenty percent of slaves did not survive the long journey. On arrival in places like Chesapeake, Carolina, and Georgia slaves would recover only to undertake even more uncertain journeys after being sold to often distant plantations. The third leg of the triangular trade would involve the ship returning to Europe, with New World products for sale: sugar, tea, tobacco, indigo, coffee, rare plants, and so forth. As Mesthrie et al. (2009: 275) point out, one of these items was molasses, used to distil rum, which was used as one means of purchasing slaves on the next trip. In the new setting slaves were employed in heavy manual labour on mines, in ports, and above all, in plantations. Occasionally they were employed in various trades or in domestic service.

We can only conjecture at the sociolinguistic trauma that accompanied the social and physical traumas of slavery. Gillian Sankoff (1979: 24) writes of the "catastrophic break in linguistic tradition," since slavery usually precluded a return to one's home continent. She writes further:

> It is difficult to conceive of another situation where people arrived with such a variety of native languages, where they were so cut off from their native language groups;

where the size of no language group was enough to ensure its survival; where no second language was shared by enough people to serve as a useful vehicle of intercommunication; and where the legitimate [= official – RM] language was inaccessible to almost everyone.

Issues and ongoing debates

Linguistic outcomes of slavery

The linguistic diversity of slaves, coming from large and demographically diverse sections of the African continent, meant that no single home language of the immigrant slaves could emerge as a lingua franca: instead it is assumed by many (but not all) scholars that pidgins and creoles arose out of this diversity. In other words, the relatively rapid need for communication precluded the ordinary slow process of second language acquisition, in which speakers could use and maintain their home languages in appropriate social contexts, while gradually acquiring a necessary second language. At the same time in slavery such a 'target' language was neither socially nor educationally accessible, given segregation and lack of schooling for slave children. This applied equally to the slave forts of Africa, the slave ships, or the New World plantations. Such conditions where maintenance of home languages and shift to an established new language were equally difficult would favour the growth of a pidgin as a means of basic communication. In their very earliest stages, pidgins and second languages follow similar stages: a one-word stage, a two-word stage, a stage of basic main clause usage before the gradual emergence of elements like tense and aspect, negation, number marking, and so forth. What distinguishes the two is the availability of a target. Under second-language acquisition, the initial basic outputs of speakers are in time modified in the direction of the target language, via accessibility of speakers and opportunities to communicate with them. Situations that engender a pidgin are more "off track," as the initial, basic outputs are modified by the need for more complex communication, *without* significant access to the target language. Pidginization is thus untargeted: languages don't *become* pidgins, rather pidgins arise as new systems for basic communication when no other alternative exists. Under certain social conditions a pidgin develops into a complex new system that linguists label a creole. Mühlhausler (1986: 5) summarises matters succinctly:

> Pidgins are examples of partially targeted or non-targeted second-language learning, developing from simpler to more complex systems as communicative requirements become more demanding. Pidgin languages by definition have no native speakers, they are social rather than individual solutions, and hence are characterised by norms of acceptability.

Some norms of acceptability from Tok Pisin, a major language of Papua New Guinea, originally based on a rudimentary pidgin form of English, are illustrated briefly:

Reduplication: The repetition of a root to express emphasis or intensity (e.g., *tok* 'to talk' vs. *toktok* 'to chatter');
Causatives: The formation of causatives by compounding with 'make' (e.g., *save* 'to know' vs. *meksave* 'to inform'; Mühlhausler 1986: 126);
New structural items: Use of *belong* to denote characteristic or quality of noun, that is, as a preposition, rather than a verb (e.g., *man belong toktok* 'talkative person').

By contrast, a creole is not a simple language, but a complex communicative system that developed and stabilised with the rise of a new community. Creolisation is the process that turns a relatively basic pidgin into a creole. Note that the term is used differently in linguistics compared to its sociological-anthropological uses, where it refers to intense and sustained forms of culture contact. Most linguists stress the independence of creole languages from their lexifiers and their substrates. 'Lexifier' denotes the language that supplies much of the vocabulary in the Creole, frequently the European language of power or 'superstrate'. The term 'substrate' refers to languages originally spoken by the slave population, which receded in importance, given the diversity of language backgrounds and power relations. For a long while a 'life-cycle' theory associated with Hall (1966) was influential, which implicitly maintained that all creoles developed from a previous pidgin. Whereas a pidgin is a second or auxiliary language, a creole becomes the first language of a community. In this sense a pidgin and creole are prototypically different. The life-cycle theory incorporated the idea of further development or decreolisation if and when a creole language came into substantial contact with its lexifier. Decreolisation results in a gradual restructuring in the direction of the superstrate language.

For the majority of slave-holding plantations the life-cycle theory remains a hypothesis, albeit a plausible one. The reason for this is that in most plantations, especially those of the Caribbean, intensive research into early phases of plantation history has so far failed to uncover decisive evidence for the existence of a pidgin. Thomason and Kaufman (1988) hence introduced the concept of "abrupt creolization," for the rise of a creole language within a generation, without the existence of a well-defined pidgin stage. Their formulation laid stress on creolisation as a process in which the lexicon and syntax of the new language were largely derived from different source languages: the lexicon in Caribbean creoles came chiefly from a European language and the syntax mainly from West African substrates.

Widespread belief in the lack of sufficient input from the superstrate language to warrant the growth of a second language variety of it led creolists to focus on creolisation as a special (or 'exceptional') process. Two positions emerged which can be characterised as a 'substrata versus universals' polarisation, though as we shall see other processes of language learning and development are also relevant. The substrate position holds that despite the relatively small number of words that survived from the slaves' languages, the influence of their languages loomed large at the less visible – but more important – level of semantic and, especially, syntactic organisation. An example of West African substrata in the lexicon of Bahamian Creole English involves the suffix 'boy' or 'girl' used to differentiate gender. Thus pairs like *boy-chil'* 'boy-child, son' vs. *gyal-chil'* 'girl-child, daughter' show the semantic influence of West African languages like Bambara and Yoruba (Holm 1988: 87).

An extreme position is that a creole language could be characterised as a relexified African language: that is, having the syntax of an African language with the actual words being replaced by words from the superstrate European language. However, few creolists would accept as stark an account as Lefebvre's (1986) of Haitian Creole being largely the Ghanaian language Fongbe, relexified by French vocabulary.

The other end of the debate, that creoles are entirely manifestations of linguistic universals, has proved equally controversial. Bickerton's influence over the field has been enormous and is therefore worth recapping, even though it no longer holds centre stage. His theory of the "bioprogramme" stresses the difference between pidgin and creole. In a memorable formulation (Bickerton 1977: 49) he argued that pidginisation was second-language learning with restricted input, while creolisation was first-language learning with restricted input. A child growing up in the socially fraught and linguistically complex environment of the plantation faced a problem of language acquisition in that no language was sufficiently available to ensure its learnability and transmission in its pre-existing form. Under such conditions the pidgin that was the only widespread code would have been expanded by the children and refashioned into a 'full' language or creole. In this process the human capacity for language and universal principles would have 'taken over'. Because it drew its inspiration from Chomsky's notion of Universal Grammar, Bickerton's theory of the Bioprogramme was initially widely accepted. However, major criticisms soon emerged. The theory rested largely on twelve features that Bickerton claimed to be common across creole languages, but uncommon in the substrates. He argued that such features were motivated by principles of Universal Grammar, in the absence of input from particular languages. Of these twelve features two are exemplified here: the use of adjectives as verbs and active forms of verbs in passive use.

> *Adjectives as verbs*: Use of an adjective in verb-like ways, without a preceding verb 'to be' (e.g. *i wiiri* 'he is tired' [literally 'he tired']) versus use of a preverbal marker *a* for the continuative (the same as with verbs) '*i a wiirii* 'he is getting tired' – Guyanese Creole from Bickerton (1981: 68).
> *Active forms of verbs in passive use*: For example, *Di trii plaan* 'The tree was planted' (lit. 'The tree plant(ed)', where *plant* is the active form of the verb) – (Jamaican Creole from Bickerton 1981: 72).

However, subsequent research showed that many of the twelve features could indeed be attributed to African language carryovers. In fact both structures illustrated are plausibly analysable in this way. Moreover, research to a large extent inspired by the bioprogramme hypothesis showed a large cleavage between Atlantic creoles (in which African languages were a crucial historical ingredient) and Pacific creoles (where they were not). Instead, 'gradualists' stressed a slower unfolding of the language that would be labelled 'creole', rather than what Singler (personal communication June 2010) has criticised as an "instantaneous" (or unigenerational) view of creolisation. Arends (1989) argued on demographic and linguistic grounds that this was the case for Sranan, a Creole language of Suriname. Roberts's (2004) research in Hawaii – one of the main centres of Bickerton's empirical work – showed a more complex sociolinguistic history than the 'plantation children lacking sufficient input' theory allowed for. On the basis of detailed sociohistorical documentation she demonstrates that Hawaiian Creole English arose not with the first native-born generation, but the second. Moreover, it arose in Hawaiian urban centres rather than on plantations. A gradualist position was put forward forcefully by Baker (in Baker and Corne 1982) who marked out decisive periods in the formation of a pidgin and creole in relation to relative demographics. He referred to these milestones as 'events': *Event 1* was when the number of imported slaves equalled the number of colonists; *Event 2* was when the locally born black population equalled that of the colonists; *Event 3* was when the importation of slaves ceased. These have repercussions for language maintenance, acquisition, shift, and creolisation. After Event 1 it would become harder for slaves to acquire the colonial language; Event 2 would favour the growth of a systemically different Creole rather than a partially restructured version of the colonial language; Event 3 affects the prominence of the African input, especially the robustness of substrate influence on the developing Creole. Singler (1986) points out a milestone missed in Baker's original typology when the locally born black population equals that of the foreign-born black population.

The language experiences of different generation of slave migrants and their descendants would show overlaps that gradually yielded different repertoires. Becker and Veenstra (2003) characterise these differences as follows (where G is short for "Generation"):

G1 (foreign-born immigrants)	L1 ancestral language(s)
	L2 pidgin
G2 (first generation locally born)	L1 ancestral language(s)
	L1 pidgin/creole
G3 (second generation locally born)	L1 creole
	(L2 ancestral language(s))

Figure 12.1 Multi-generational scenario of creole genesis (based on Becker and Veenstra 2003: 234–235; Veenstra 2008)

Becker and Veenstra's term "pidgin/creole" in G2 (the second generation) represents an intermediate stage between pidgin expansion and creole formation. Figure 12.1 thus depicts a gradualist view of creolisation. Studying pidgins and creoles and showing their significance in language contact studies, historical linguistics, and sociolinguistics was an act of affirmation. Linguists were heedful of the covert value of creoles and their role in societal development as full systems capable of taking on greater educational and public roles.

To round off this survey of major positions in the field of creolistics, it is necessary to consider three views which might be labelled 'anti-exceptionalist'. These views critique the fundamental belief that creole studies deal with special cases of language contact, whose structural outcomes set them apart from other languages. This belief was particularly foregrounded in Thomason and Kaufman's (1988) characterisation of 'normal' and 'abnormal' transmission. The former involved transmission of the lexicon and grammar of the same language intact from one generation to the next. In the latter these two components emanated from different languages – as in creolisation and bilingual mixed languages. The terms 'normal' and 'abnormal' were unfortunate (types I and II would have done), and spurred positions that stressed the opposite. Mufwene (2001) drew on population genetics to propose that all language learning (L1, L2, and pidgin/creole development) was subject to the same principles, with the specifics of the total pool of variants determining the outcome. Among his important arguments are that (1) creoles developed by the same restructuring processes that mark the evolution of non-creole languages; (2) contact is an important factor in *all* such developments; and (3) external ecological factors play a role in all matters of language growth, change, and vitality/endangerment (Mufwene 2001: 1). De Graff (2003) studied Haitian Creole in relation to the history of French dialects and was led to claim that the same processes of variation and change can be traced in both. This claim is starting to be critically evaluated. The third moderately anti-exceptionalist position tries to link creolisation more closely with second language acquisition (SLA). Building on earlier work by Andersen (1981) and Klein and Perdue (1997), Siegel (2008) proposes that simplification and transfer are common to both phenomena. He concedes that certain types of transfer (e.g., of word order) are mostly short-lived, unless there is extremely limited contact with the superstrate. This appears to be the crucial difference between pidgin and SLA – that the degree and nature of contact with superstrate speakers influences the pathways of language development differently.

A stringent critic of anti-exceptionalism is McWhorter (e.g., 2015) who has argued extensively that pidgins and creoles are indeed different from L2 varieties and from older non-contact induced 'historical' L1s. He draws attention to the features of Palenquero, a Spanish creole of Colombia which he argues is different from the colloquial varieties of Spanish in South America: "What most robustly differentiates Palenquero from colloquial Latin American Spanishes is not feature selection from Kikongo or Spanish, but degree of simplification of both Spanish and Kikongo grammar." McWhorter's insistence that creoles are simpler grammars than that of other languages (in terms of morphological marking especially) does not sit well with most linguists, who assume that languages cannot easily be ranked in terms of complexity, feature by feature. A related recent comprehensive study by Kortmann and Lunkenheimer (2012) makes no such assumptions about complexity, but does give typological support for English creoles as a special sub-group. The authors surveyed seventy-four varieties of English around the world, according to their use of 235 selected non-standard features. They analysed the resulting data according to geographical regions and variety type (i.e., whether it was traditionally conceived of as an L1, L2, pidgin, or creole). The results show a statistical difference in the feature pools of creoles, L1 'colonial', and second language varieties that does not give much support for the anti-exceptionalist positions. Rather, pidgins and creoles of the type surveyed in this chapter are reminders of the fraught, fragile, and often hostile world of communication in colonial, slave-trading, and slave-holding contexts. Creoles show the resilience and the efflorescence of the human capacity for communication, as well as the social bonds of the new communities that developed them. And it is necessary to stress that their special characteristics are of a formal, not functional nature. Creoles function efficiently in a range of registers as do all L1s, and have the same capacity for development in technical registers as any other language.

Overview on indenture

The term *indenture* refers to the fixed contracts binding an employee to work for a particular employer for a set period. It had its heyday in the colonial era. Indentured certificates issued to labourers were so-called because of their serrated edges, indicating that an original had been broken up into two copies, one each for the employer and the employee. Indenture frequently involved the employment of migrants. It was not always a voluntary affair or motivated entirely by push factors, and it is no coincidence that it was established as a major labour practice soon after international humanitarian efforts resulted in the emancipation of slaves (from 1834 on in the British Empire). For many colonial plantations this would have spelt bankruptcy, but for the planters' plans to again move potential labourers from one part of the world to another. Between 1834 and 1837 English, Scottish, German, and Irish labourers were introduced into the West Indies, primarily Jamaica (Lal 2006: 46), but this attempt was not a success owing to the failure of Europeans to acclimatise to field work under tropical conditions. The most successful solution from the planters' point of view was to induce large numbers of Asians to leave places like 19th-century Philippines, China, and India to work on plantations abroad. The British historian Sir Hugh Tinker (1974) characterised this migratory labour practice as a new system of slavery in his book-length treatment of Indian indenture in the Caribbean. The remainder of this section will focus on the sociolinguistic consequences of migrations out of India, which have spawned a tradition of comparative research within sociohistorical contact-linguistics second only to creole studies.

Migrations under the British system of indenture to new colonies took place in very large numbers out of the British 'presidencies' of the time between the 1830s and 1940s. These were from north-east and central India, with Calcutta (now Kolkata) as the port of departure, South India with Madras (now Chennai) as the port, and to a lesser extent, mid-west India with Bombay (now Mumbai) as the port. Indian young adult males and smaller proportions of women and children were shipped to the receiving colonies. Carter (1996: 32) records that these journeys took anything from six weeks (for Madras to Mauritius) to twenty (for Calcutta to the West Indies). Among the major 'receiving colonies' of indentured Indian labour were Mauritius (1834–1917), Guyana (1839–1916), Trinidad (1845–1917), Natal (1860–1911), Suriname (1873–1915), and Fiji (1879–1946). Taking the perspective of new recruits awaiting the next ship at Calcutta, Lal (2006: 50) summarises the position as follows:

> The prospect of a new life fostered a new sense of subaltern companionship and togetherness, cutting across the barriers of religion, caste and place of origin. Taboos about food, caste relationships or marriage that had been such an integral part of life in village India began to fracture and lose relevance, aided by the attitude of the authorities, who viewed the recruits not as people worthy of individual humanity and dignity, but as a mass of 'coolies', units of labour to be worked for profit. Nonetheless, fragmentation was one part of the equation. The other, equally important, was reconstitution, by which new ideas, values and associations were being forged along the way, more out of necessity rather than by choice, which would over time lay the foundations of a new, more egalitarian, more pragmatic, and less protocol-driven culture in the colonies. As the emigrants waited anxiously in the crowded depots for their ships to leave, they got a foretaste of things to come in the distant and strange lands for which they were destined, and from which most would never return.

Issues and ongoing debates

To keep the discussion tight this section will focus on the migrations from north India to the colony of Natal (now KwaZulu-Natal province in South Africa). The key point is that migrations from north and north-east India emanated from a vast area, largely out of what are today's Bihar, Uttar Pradesh, Jharkhand, and Uttarakhand. Languages of the Indo Aryan family (like Bhojpuri, Magahi, Maithili, Awadhi, and eastern forms of Hindi) are spoken here as well languages of the Austronesian family (like Santali and Mundari). Speakers of the latter were called 'hill coolies' in the British records and feature mainly in the earliest migrations to Mauritius and British Guyana. The Indian languages at the extremities of what we might consider, for present purposes, the migratory belt are not mutually intelligible: thus Bengali in the east and Panjabi in the north-west are not mutually intelligible. However, overall there is mutual intelligibility in terms of communication between adjacent areas of the speech continuum. Two sources of information have proved invaluable in studies of the indentured diaspora. The first is the extensive records of ships' lists, which documented details of every migrant in terms of name, place of origin, age, caste, and less relevant details for linguistic purposes, like identifying marks. Using these documents scholars have been able to reconstruct a fairly detailed picture of the ethos of migration – see Lal (1983) for Fiji, and Bhana (1991) for South Africa. However, the records do not specify the languages spoken by migrants. To ascertain what these were we can match the place of origin of an individual with the dominant language of the area, provided the records of the time enable us to make those links with confidence. Fortunately for studies of the diaspora, the most detailed survey ever of Indian languages (the *Linguistic Survey of India*, edited by Sir George Grierson 1903–1928), with a rich record of village speech, folk tales, and songs, was being undertaken at roughly the time of the great migrations. For Bhojpuri-Hindi diaspora studies it is doubly fortunate that George Grierson, the leader of the survey, was based in Bihar as a civil servant and later magistrate, and was an eyewitness to the process of indentured migrations (Grierson 1883), an author of detailed grammars of the Bihar area (1883–1887), and a self-avowed aficionado of the people and culture (1885).

Transplanted Bhojpuri-Hindi as a high-contact language

Using the detailed samples of speech of the relevant districts in the *Linguistic Survey of India* (vol. 5, part 2; vol. 6) Mesthrie (1991) documented processes of grammatical and sociolinguistic continuity as well as change in the years between the end of indenture (1911 for Natal) and the time of his fieldwork (1982–1983) with mainly second- and third-generation offspring of migrants in Natal. Mesthrie shows that out of the large number of input dialects, a new distinctly South African variety arose that was usually called 'Hindi', though alternate names like *Kalkatyā bāt* ('Calcutta language') also survived. Both terms are misnomers: the first reflecting the label of the prestige variety of North India, Hindi, which was not the vernacular form of a majority of migrants, and which was not the variety spoken in Natal (except by a few priests and others and mostly on formal occasions). The second term implies affiliation with Calcutta, which is not accurate since not many migrants came from Calcutta itself. However both linguonyms are informative in reflecting the prestige of Hindi as an overarching and aspirational language for North Indians and the recognition of the importance of Calcutta as a symbol of a new identity – the port to which people from all over north India had been transported and where they were housed in depots pending the arrival of the next ship. Mesthrie (1991) proposed the term South African Bhojpuri (or Bhojpuri-Hindi) instead, showing that this was a koine, or blend of mutually intelligible languages. This koine is a recognisably North Indian variety that does not accord with any single antecedent Indian dialect. Labels used by linguists for the overseas varieties reflect this flux: Mauritian Bhojpuri, Guyanese Bhojpuri, Trinidad Bhojpuri, South African Bhojpuri, Sarnami Hindi (of Suriname), and Fiji Hindi. These labels are used in the ensuing tables, although the label Bhojpuri-Hindi is also used when emphasising that all these overseas varieties are a slice of the north Indian continuum.

We can imagine a high degree of contact-induced variation in the first generation, both internally within the North Indian diaspora as well as with contacts with new languages of the colony (Zulu and English). There was also contact with other languages from India that would have been unfamiliar to the North Indian speakers (Dravidian languages like Tamil and Telugu, as well as Indo-Aryan Gujarati from the west). That the Bhojpuri-Hindi that developed was indeed a high contact language (see Trudgill 2009) is demonstrated later. Using Grierson's classification one would need to further break the label Bhojpuri down into eastern and western dialects. Table 12.1 matches the places of origin of South African Bhojpuri-Hindi speakers with the major language and dialect areas spoken there, using Grierson (1903, 1904) as a guide.

As a point of comparison the respective figures for Fiji, calculated by Siegel (1987: 141), are (reading downwards in Table 12.2) 39.3 percent, 37.1 percent, 15.2 percent, and 5.8 percent.

Table 12.2 shows the give and take between these languages and dialects in the South African koine. These features are important ones that give the South African variety a flavour

Table 12.1 Major languages of the North Indian immigrants in South Africa 1860–1911 (from Mesthrie (1992: 25))

Districts in which Bhojpuri and other 'Bihari' dialects predominated	46%
Districts in which Awadhi and Eastern Hindi dialects predominated	36%
Districts in which western forms of Hindi predominated	10%
Districts with other languages (e.g., Bengali, Rajasthani, Panjabi and indeterminate)	8%

Table 12.2 Proportion of linguistic features shared by South African Bhojpuri-Hindi (SB) and different sets of antecedent Indian varieties

Features present in South African Bhojpuri-Hindi:	SB	Standard Hindi	Western Hindi	Eastern Hindi	Bihari
and all other North Indian varieties [16 features]	+	+	+	+	+
and all but Standard Hindi [3 features]	+	−	+	+	+
and Eastern Hindi and Bihari [6 features]	+	−	−	+	+
and Bihari (only) [6 features]	+	−	−	−	+
and Eastern Hindi (only) [2 features]	+	−	−	+	−
and Standard Hindi (only) [1 feature]	+	+	−	−	−
and western and eastern Hindi [1 feature]	+	−	+	+	−
and all but Bihari [1 feature]	+	+	+	+	−
and standard and western Hindi [2 features]	+	+	+	−	−
Total number of shared features	(38)	20	23	29	31

that does not accord with any one dialect or dialect cluster in India. Nevertheless, they do show that the Bihari and Eastern Hindi varieties have a stronger influence than Standard and western Hindi. (The details of the features itemised in Table 12.2, as well as other complications like features lost or new features based on South African languages, can be found in Mesthrie 1991: 57–62).

There is a missing temporal dimension in this comparison. In the earlier years of indenture recruitment concentrated on more easterly parts closer to the port of Calcutta. In time recruiters had to expand their activities increasingly into the interior of North India. For the colony of Natal this was coincidentally matched by areal employment patterns, with the bulk of the early migrants being employed in the (easterly) coastlands, where they set up sugar, tea, coffee, and tobacco plantations. Initial resistance to Indian immigration in the interior of Natal soon gave way as planters there realised the value of their labour. By the time they relented, recruitment patterns in India had changed as more people were recruited from the interior regions of India, with a greater concentration of speakers of Awadhi and allied varieties. Bhojpuri-Hindi in Natal appears to be unique among the overseas varieties in that three related dialects gelled in this way. The first is the Coastlands dialect showing a greater Bhojpuri input; the second an Uplands variety showing a greater Awadhi input; and the third an intermediate Natal Midlands variety. Table 12.3 shows some of the (variable) differentiating features.

Table 12.3 Regional variation in basic verb endings in the three dialects of Bhojpuri-Hindi in KwaZulu-Natal

	Coastlands	Midlands	Uplands
Future 1 sg.	-ab	-b ~ -egā	-egā
Future 2 sg.	-be	-be ~ -egā	-egā
Future 3 sg.	-ī	-ī	-ī ~ -egā
Past trans. 3 sg.	-lak ~ -las	-is	is ~ -ā
Past intrans. 3 sg.	-l	-l ~ -a	-l ~ -a ~-is
Past trans. 3 pl.	(as for sg.)	(as for sg.)	-n
2nd person copula	hawe	he	he

[KEY: ~ denotes variation between two or more verb forms; a macron or bar above a vowel denotes a long vowel.]

We now turn to an international comparison of the transplanted varieties of Bhojpuri-Hindi starting with Mauritius and ending with Fiji. Figure 12.2 gives an indication of the presence or absence of six diagnostic features in the seven varieties compared. Varieties are arranged according to the timelines of migration, specifically the time of the earliest migrations to each colony. For reasons discussed above the South African varieties were split into Uplands and Coastal varieties according to time of first migrations.

A plus or minus in Figure 12.2 reflects the presence or absence of the grammatical form in each row in each territory. The pluses also reflect the forms associated more with eastern languages and dialects in North India (Bhojpuri and Magahi), while the minuses reflect more westerly forms (like Awadhi and Eastern Hindi). All varieties in Figure 12.2 differ in small ways from each other, and from all other varieties of their Indian precedents. However, the geographical and temporal tracks of the recruitment give a strong indication that the diaspora leaves its linguistic footprints in orderly ways, at least for the chosen features. The oldest diaspora in Mauritius has the most easterly Bhojpuri character (with six pluses), the youngest, Fiji, has the most westerly (Awadhi or Eastern Hindi) character (with no pluses). The geographical and temporal line of recruitment accounts for the varieties in between. An even finer pattern is discernible for South Africa. As explained earlier, the recruitment to Natal can be split into a coastal period (1860 onwards) and a later interior (Uplands) Natal period (from about 1880 onwards). The Uplands variety of Natal according to Figure 12.2 accords more with Sarnami and Fiji Hindi, two varieties that were formed from the 1870s onwards (sharing four of the six features with each). On the other hand, the Coastal variety of Natal shares only two features with this group. It shares four features with Trinidad formed from 1945 onwards and Mauritius (formed from 1834 onwards). Figure 12.2 thus vividly tracks (1) the recruitment patterns in India (starting in the north east and moving westerly inland); (2) the shipping patterns (first to Mauritius, last to Fiji); and (3) a further nicety of recruitment patterns in Natal (first to the coast, later to the Uplands).

To complete the picture of language contact and its outcomes, we need to consider the influence of local languages and early as well as late attrition. Certain important social distinctions of 19th-century North India became less significant in the context of plantation life. These pertained to a gradual weakening of caste distinctions and greater gender equality (Kuper 1955; Desai and Vahed 2007). Linguistic results include loss of suffixes differentiating masculine and feminine gender in verb paradigms, and loss of special pronouns denoting hierarchical relations between speakers ('respect' vs. 'familiarity'). The influence of other languages of South Africa (especially English and Zulu) is mostly in the lexicon.

	MB 1834–	GB 1839–	TB 1845–	CSB 1860–	SH 1873–	USB 1875–	FH 1879–
Present habitual -*lā* or – *e* + aux (vs. *tā* + aux)	+	+	+	+	+	+	–
Present continuous -*at* +aux (vs. -*tā* +aux)	+	+	+	+	+	+	–
Future -*b* or -*i* (vs. -*ega*)	+	+	+	+	±	–	–
Past transitive -*l* (vs. *ā* or -*is*)	+	+	+	+	±	–	–
Classifier *go* (vs *ṭho*)	+	+	+	–	±	–	–
Aux/copular *ba* (vs *hai*)	+	–	+	–	±	–	–

Figure 12.2 Comparison of six diagnostic features of seven varieties of overseas Bhojpuri-Hindi

[Key: MB – Mauritian Bhojpuri; GB – Guyanese Bhojpuri; TB – Trinidad Bhojpuri; CSB – Coastal South African Bhojpuri; SH – Sarnami Hindi; USB – Uplands South African Bhojpuri; FH – Fiji Hindi; ± denotes the use of both variants within a territory. Based on Domingue (1973); Gambhir (1981); Mesthrie (1991); Mohan (1978); Siegel (1987).]

Third-generation speakers of Bhojpuri show the incorporation of the English modal *must* into a hybrid pattern *mas kar ke* ('must – do – having') followed by the main verb, denoting internal compulsion ('to feel the urge, to want compulsively'). It is necessary to point out that many of the transplanted varieties of Bhojpuri-Hindi are in decline today, with the varieties in Guyana, Trinidad, and South Africa facing endangerment. In these territories a process of language shift has gradually taken place with Creole and English replacing Bhojpuri in the first two, and English (and to some extent Afrikaans) doing so in South Africa.

Implications

This chapter has focused on the linguistic outcomes of two high-profile forced and semi-forced labour migration patterns. It would, however, be a false inference that slavery implies creolisation, and indenture implies koineisation, with later language shift. What matters are the demographics, social, and power relations and availability of the dominant language of the new society. Kihm and Rouge (2103) outline a context in which creolisation did not go hand in hand with slavery. Portugal and Spain were two European countries, which – exceptionally – took in large numbers of slaves from West Africa in the 15th century. They fulfilled functions rather like migrants in today's modern world – essential low-grade urban jobs as well as working in the countryside. Despite de facto segregation of slaves and their descendants, we do not anticipate this as being a creole-engendering scenario, since large numbers of speakers of the target language (Portuguese) were present. And there were social and occasional sexual relations between migrants and locals. Kihm and Rouge (2013) describe what they call a Basic Variety (after Klein and Perdue 1997) that evolved among slaves, which was presented (and perhaps caricatured) in stage performances of the time. It would appear that this second language (which was not particularly close to the L1 of the wider society) stabilised into a first language in ensuing generations. This would have been a recognisable social dialect/ethnolect within the society. We would expect under such circumstances that a wide range of variation would ensue, with speakers veering to more mainstream ends of a continuum in certain contexts and more in-group forms in others. This range of variation has been documented for South African Indian English (Mesthrie 1992) and for Singapore English (Chew 1995), both varieties characteristic of multilingual migrant labour. In the Portuguese case, the ex-slave population was more or less slowly absorbed into the mainstream, together with its social dialect.

To show that koineisation is not a *necessary* effect of migration and indenture, we turn briefly to Tamil in South Africa – a sister language to Bhojpuri-Hindi, insofar as speakers of this language emigrated at the same time and under the same conditions. However, Tamil speakers originated in a smaller area (present-day Tamil Nadu) than the vast plains of North India for Bhojpuri-Hindi. Of the four main dialect areas identified for Tamil, an analysis of the ships' lists suggests that the majority (eighty-five percent) came from the Northern dialect area (Mesthrie 2007), with less than fifteen percent from the remaining three dialect areas. Mesthrie analysed the diagnostic features of the different dialects and concluded that koineisation had not occurred in South African Tamil. Rather, a simple demographic majority accounted for its overwhelming Northern dialect character (according to a large extent with the features of the North Arcot dialect).

Future directions

While the days of slavery and indenture as planned and politically sanctioned systems are over, the robustness of the sociolinguistic and language contact work on these topics are of enduring value. In the global era migration continues to contribute to the superdiversity of societies. The crisis of state management and mismanagement as well as parlous economics has recently seen migration out of Asia and Africa into Europe, America, and elsewhere on a scale that foregrounds important issues concerning the sociolinguistics of linguae francae and the linguistics of unequal contact. Research areas such as these have everything to gain from the fields of pidgin and creole linguistics and the koineisation studies cited in this chapter.

I conclude with a few general observations relating to the enormous disparity between the need for accommodation in everyday communication among new groups of migrants and the standard and official languages of their former and adopted homelands. Such accommodation spawns new varieties of existing languages or even new languages altogether. Creolists and contact linguists have demonstrated the rule-governed nature of these new codes, even if they are not always accorded prestige by outsiders. As such they can be developed into languages serving a wider range of roles than the ones for which they developed (face-to-face communication and community solidarity). However, educators and applied linguists also need to take into account more pragmatic considerations relating to speakers' aspirations for their children in deciding what would work best in the educational realm. Frequently it is the power of the dominant languages that wins out here. However, a truly just society has to work out means for empowering its citizens, including its oppressed and exploited migrants, without devaluing their hard-won cultural and linguistic resources.

Related topics

>National and ethnic minorities
>Displacement and language
>Social class in migration, identity, and language research

Further reading

Kouwenberg, S. and Singler, J., eds. (2008). *The Handbook of Pidgin and Creole Studies*. Oxford: Blackwell.

A comprehensive overview by specialists in this field.

Mesthrie, R. (1991). *Language in Indenture: A Sociolinguistic History of Bhojpuri-Hindi in South Africa*. Johannesburg: Witwatersrand University Press (International edition: Routledge, 1992).

A detailed study of the historical context of indentured migration out of India, with special reference to the Bhojpuri koine of South Africa.

Michaelis, S., Maurer, P., Haspelmath, M. and Huber, M., eds. (2013). *The Survey of Pidgin and Creole Languages* (4 vols). Oxford: Oxford University Press.

A four-volume work describing seventy-four individual varieties of pidgins and creoles.

References

Andersen, R. (1981). Two perspectives on pidginization as second language acquisition. In R. W. Andersen (ed.), *New Dimensions in Second Language Acquisition Research* (pp. 165–195). Rowley, MA: Newbury House.

Arends, J. (1989). *Syntactic development in Sranan: Creolization as a gradual process*. Unpublished PhD thesis. Catholic University of Nijmegen.

Baker, P. and Corne, C. (1982). *Isle de France Creole: Affinities and Origins*. Ann Arbor: Karoma.

Becker, A. and Veenstra, T. (2003). The survival of inflectional morphology in French-related creoles: The role of SLA processes. *Studies in Second Language Acquisition* 25: 283–306.

Bhana, S. (1991). *Indentured Indian Emigrants to Natal 1860–1902 – A Study Based on Ships' Lists*. Delhi: Promilla.

Bickerton, D. (1977). Pidginization and creolization: Language acquisition and language universals. In Albert Valdman (ed.), *Pidgin and Creole Linguistics* (pp. 49–69). Bloomington: Indiana University Press.

Bickerton, D. (1981). *Roots of Language*. Ann Arbor: Karoma.

Carter, M. (1996). *Voices from Indenture: Experiences of Indian Migrants in the British Empire*. London: Leicester University Press.

Chew, P.G.L. (1995). Lectal power in Singapore English. *World Englishes* 14(2): 163–180.

De Graff, M. (2003). Against Creole exceptionalism. *Language* 79(2): 391–410.

Desai, A. and Vahed, G. (2007). *Inside Indenture: A South African Story*. Durban: Madiba.

Domingue, N.C. (1971). *Bhojpuri and Creole in Mauritius: A Study of Linguistic Interference and its Consequences in Regard to Synchronic Variation and Language Change*. PhD thesis, University of Texas.

Gambhir, S. K. (1981). *The East Indian Speech Community in Guyana: A Sociolinguistic Study with Special Reference to Koine Formation*. PhD thesis, University of Pennsylvania.

Grierson, Sir George A. (1883). *Report on Colonial Emigration from the Bengal Presidency*. Calcutta: Government Printer.

Grierson, Sir George A. (1883–7). *Seven Grammars of the Dialects and Sub-Dialects of the Bihari Language*. Calcutta: Bengal Secretariat Press.

Grierson, Sir George A. (1885). *Bihar Peasant Life* (Repr. New Delhi: Cosmo 1975).

Grierson, Sir George A. (1903–1928). *Linguistic Survey of India*. Calcutta: Government of India. 11 vols. (1903. Vol. V Part 2 *Bihari and Oriya Languages*. 1904. Vol. VI *Eastern Hindi*).

Hall, Robert A. Jr. (1966). *Pidgin and Creole Languages*. Ithaca: Cornell University Press.

Holm, J. (1988). *Pidgins and Creoles: Volume I, Theory and Structure*. Cambridge: Cambridge University Press.

Kihm, A. and Rouge, J.-L. (2013). *Lingua de Preto*, the basic variety at the root of the West African Portuguese creoles: A contribution to the theory of pidgin/creole formation as second language acquisition. *Journal of Pidgin Creole Languages* 28(2): 203–298.

Klein, W. and Perdue, C. (1997). The basic variety (or couldn't natural languages be much simpler?). *Second Language Research* 13(4): 301–347.

Kortmann, B. and Lunkenheimer, K. eds. (2012). *The Mouton World Atlas of Variation in English*. Berlin: De Gruyter Mouton.

Kuper, H. (1955). Changes in caste of the South African Indians. *Race Relations Journal* 22: 18–26.

Lal, Brij V. (1983). Girmityas: The origins of the Fiji Indians. *Journal of Pacific History* (Special issue).

Lal, Brij V. (2006). The Indenture System. In Brij V. Lal (ed.), *The Encyclopedia of the Indian Diaspora* (pp. 46–53). Singapore: Editions Didier Millet.

Lefebvre, C. (1986). Relexification in creole genesis revisited: the case of Haitian Creole. In Pieter Muysken and Norval Smith (eds.), *Substrata versus Universals in Creole Genesis* (pp. 279–301). Amsterdam: Benjamins.

McWhorter, J. (2015). It's not over: Why it matters whether there is such a thing as a creole (Guest column). *Journal of Pidgin & Creole Languages* 28(2): 409–423.

Mesthrie, R. (1991). *Language in Indenture: A Sociolinguistic History of Bhojpuri-Hindi in South Africa*. Johannesburg: Witwatersrand University Press.

Mesthrie, R. (1992). *English in Language Shift: The History, Structure and Sociolinguistics of South African Indian English*. Cambridge: Cambridge University Press.

Mesthrie, R. (2007). The origins of colloquial South African Tamil. *Oriental Anthropologist* 7(1): 17–38.

Mesthrie, R., Swann, J., Deumert, A. and Leap, W. (2009). *Introducing Sociolinguistics*. Edinburgh: Edinburgh University Press.

Mohan, P. (1978). *Trinidad Bhojpuri: A Morphological Study*. PhD thesis, University of Michigan.

Mufwene, S. (2001). *The Ecology of Language Evolution*. Cambridge: Cambridge University Press.

Mühlhäusler, P. (1986). *Pidgin and Creole Linguistics*. Oxford: Basil Blackwell.

Roberts, S. (2004). *The Emergence of Hawai'i Creole in the Early Twentieth Century: The Sociohistorical Context of Creole Genesis*. PhD dissertation, Stanford University.

Sankoff, G. (1979). The genesis of a language. In K. Hill (ed.), *The Genesis of Language* (pp. 23–47). Ann Arbor: Karoma.

Siegel, J. (1987). *Language Contact in a Plantation Environment – A Sociolinguistic History of Fiji*. Cambridge: Cambridge University Press.

Siegel, J. (2008). Pidgins/Creoles and second language acquisition. In John Singler and Sylvia Kouwenberg (eds.), *The Handbook of Pidgin and Creole Languages* (pp. 189–218). New York: Blackwell.

Singler, J. V. (1986). Short note. *Journal of Pidgin and Creole Languages* 1(1): 141–145.

Thomason, Sarah G. and Kaufman, T. (1988). *Language Contact, Genetic Linguistics and Creolization*. Berkeley: University of California Press.

Tinker, H. (1974). *A New System of Slavery: The Export of Indian Labour Overseas 1830–1920*. Oxford: Oxford University Press.

Trudgill, P. (2009). Sociolinguistic typology and complexification. In G. Sampson, D. Gil and P. Trudgill (eds.) *Language Complexity as an Evolving Variable* (pp. 98–109). Oxford: Oxford University Press.

Veenstra, T. (2008). Creole genesis – The impact of the Language Bioprogramme hypothesis. In Silvia Kouwenberg and John Victor Singler (eds.), *The Handbook of Pidgin and Creole Studies* (pp. 219–241). Chichester: Wiley-Blackwell.

13
Settler migration and settler varieties

Daniel Schreier, Nicole Eberle, and Danae M. Perez

Introduction and definitions

This chapter surveys a particularly influential group in the dynamic scenario of language change induced by migratory movements: the 'settler varieties'. We first define our understanding of the term and discuss some terminological issues involved. Subsequently, we outline the implications of colonial settlers for language spread, language contact, and language change, as well as new forms of settler migration in postcolonial contexts. This is followed by a short survey of the sociolinguistics of relocation-diffusion and migration patterns and an outline of some of the major issues and debates (the emergence of new varieties, dialect contact and koineization, dialect loss) in light of recent theoretical advances (such as Schneider's 2003, 2007 dynamic model of World Englishes, that hinges fundamentally on the settler strand). We prominently focus on language shift processes, in particular the concept of ethnolinguistic vitality that is crucial in the maintenance/loss of settler varieties.

The term 'settler varieties' (SV) is used here with reference to the vernaculars spoken typically by European colonizing groups who migrate for political, economic, or religious reasons to geographically distant, often overseas, territories. These vernaculars are spoken natively by the original colonial populations or the first locally born generations, and the migration movements very often (though not necessarily) involve concerted settlement plans or indentured laborship. Thus, the SVs hold a special position in the field of migration and language change, as they represent distinct social and regional varieties and are characterized by linguistic diffuseness and social heterogeneity. Their coexistence in new locales is nearly always unprecedented, giving rise to unique "feature pools" (Mufwene 2001: 3–6) out of which new (post)colonial varieties emerge. It is for this reason that dialectologists have researched SVs in places such as New Zealand (Trudgill 1986; Gordon et al. 2004), South Africa (Mesthrie 1993), or Fiji (Siegel 1985), with particular interest in sociolinguistic processes such as mixing, leveling, or simplification that operate during settler migration and contribute to the formation of 'new' contact-derived dialects (or koines; Siegel 1985). The heterogeneous nature of such settings is evident in that there are relatively few scenarios of exclusive or 'pure' dialect contact (the Falkland Islands probably coming closest, Sudbury 2000, 2001; note also dialectologists' interest in so-called *Sprachinseln*, or 'language islands' embedded into heteroglossic environments; see later). There is nearly always contact with indigenous languages (leading to language contact) or other transplanted dialects spoken by coexisting settler populations (English, French, and Dutch in South Africa, for instance).

During language contact, the SVs very often represent the socially superior variety in terms of social status of their speakers, because they are spoken by the colonial power and an emerging local elite, along with members of the local community who are in frequent exchange via bartering or trade (acting as brokers). Even though they are spoken by a minority, at least when there are conditions of language contact, they play a major role in linguistic ecology (in the sense of Mufwene 2001) and are crucial in shaping the outcome of diffuse contact scenarios. While the importance of classical migration effects, such as face-to-face interaction, has arguably decreased somewhat as a consequence of recent internationalization and globalization patterns (Blommaert 2010; see discussion in this chapter), the overall contribution of SVs as a historical legacy in former colonies remains considerable. Hence, careful scrutiny is necessary to identify the conditioning factors that play a role in the development and evolution of (post)colonial Englishes (as a corollary of second language acquisition, substrate influence and socio-cultural motivations, see later in this chapter).

Overview

Sociolinguists and dialectologists have a long tradition of studying the impact of migratory movements, for instance in gravity models where migration flows are regarded as a function of the size of populations at origin and destination and the distance between them (Chambers and Trudgill 1998). A first and crucial question raised is how and to what extent settler varieties are extraterritorially spread through wider migration patterns. It is paramount to identify the SVs exported and to collect as much information as possible on sociolinguistic factors such as social stratification (maintenance, reshuffling, or collapse of social class differences), network theory (what is the nucleus of newly forming colonies and how and by whom are new networks established) and communities of practice (what is the effect of language as social practice in new settings).

There is general consensus that "relocation-diffusion" (Britain 2002) is a complex phenomenon that includes social, psychological, and economic criteria. A general distinction, borrowed from economic sciences, is made between pull versus push factors: why do migrants leave their ancestral territories and what is their motivation? Do they leave of their own free will or due to force? Is the transport of settlers and their vernaculars the product of a concerted settlement policy or the result of random, individualistic, and *ad hoc* decisions? The foundations of new colonies around the world, for instance Argentina, South Africa, or Hong Kong, to name but three, are very often meticulously planned in advance. Thomason (2001: 17–21) suggests a typology of contact settings (such as 'the movement of one group into another group's territory', 'immigration of small groups or scattered individuals', 'importing a labor force, or cultural contacts through long-term neighborhood'); Mufwene in particular has argued that social differences induced by migration patterns determine the regularity and contact patterns, the power stratification, as well as the amount of integration versus segregation between the parties involved. He makes a threefold distinction, first outlining effects in "trade colonization" settings (Mufwene 2005: 23), where contacts are superficial and spurious, so that there is no negative impact on the target language and enrichment of SVs via lexical borrowings. Second, in "settlement colonization" settings (Mufwene 2005: 24), colonizers teach their SV (often a standardized form) to an emerging elite class or translators, missionaries, and brokers, as a scholastic variety and serving as an official language of administration or higher education. Here, a European language is selected as lingua franca for wider communication, at the expense of other colonial and indigenous varieties, though this does not necessarily lead to language endangerment and attrition. Third, there are "exploitation colonies" (Mufwene 2005: 27), exemplified by the scramble for Africa, where the aim was to get maximal economic profit with a minimum of colonial involvement (which, however, often had long-term consequences; see later discussion). From a general perspective then, colonization always involves fixed allotments and pre-specified numbers of settlers, sometimes even from different regions. If a population move into previously inhabited areas is planned, however, also soldiers and military personnel need to be drafted and sent, and a necessary infrastructure needs to be set up. If agriculture is a purpose for the colony, then farmers need to be sent along with equipment. This can be exemplified by the case of the Antipodes, where

> New Zealand's founding stock was drawn predominantly from village life in the Old World, and the village outlook which they brought with them was sustained and reinforced by the colony's geography.
>
> *(Arnold 1994: 118)*

Settlers were enticed to leave and promised all sorts of economic benefits (free passage, financial support, land grants, etc.). Recruiting agencies and local administrative bodies were set up to administer their transport and oversee their enterprises in the New World.

Forced migration, as a result of famine, wars, persecution, or ecological disasters, differs in that migration patterns are planned on a smaller scale, often at family level. Migration happens in clusters, the main motivation being the move to a place where one has family or trustworthy social connections to facilitate integration. To give just one example: as a result of the Irish potato famine in the 1840s, more than a million Irish migrants moved to North America, above all cities such as Boston (37,000 in 1847 alone) or New York (where the Irish-born population outnumbered Dublin's in 1850, Hickey 2010). The conditions in which they arrived were disorganized and led to massive tensions with the local populations, particularly the working classes, who became fierce competitors for low-paying blue-collar jobs. Many of the new arrivals were taken advantage of and exploited (being promised cheap and affordable housing, jobs, or sold forged tickets for onward journeys, etc.), only to lose whatever little money they brought along and find themselves in dire straits. As a result, the Irish population dispersed and marginalized in the wider society, losing the social impact it may have had due to its numeric power, and Hickey (2004) argues that this may have been one of the reasons why Irish English was not as influential in this setting as it might have been.

A second question is the directionality of settlers' voyages. The New Zealand scenario is a clear indication that only a minority of the colonists traveled there directly. Rather, most of the passages were interrupted. Carmichael (1993: 516) notes that "by 1854, the European population totaled 32,500[,] 12,000 in Auckland, a garrison town with probably over half its European population . . . having come from Australia." The strong similarities between Australian and New Zealand English (discussed in Gordon et al. 2004) may therefore be explained by the fact that "many settlers had a period of Australian experience behind them, and an intricate network of interrelationships [that] gave a significant Australasian dimension to colonial New Zealand" (Arnold 1994: 120). Hong Kong is also interesting as, in addition to the English-speaking settlers, hundreds of thousands of Chinese chose to leave Mainland China and went to live in Hong Kong (leaving their motherland for a 'foreign' colony), which adds to the complexity of the language contact situation and blurs the line between settler and indigenous strands (see later discussion).

The third criterion to be taken into consideration is social, namely the degree of contact(s) between settlers of different groups and other populations. Were the migrants integrated into the general population or isolated? Some groups actively seek contact and integration within the wider community, without giving up their cultural heritage (Greeks in Sydney, for instance). Their open attitudes often give rise to emerging bilingualism and a sense of bipolar identity by group members (see Schneider's model, discussed later). A segregationist settler group, in contrast, "fearing extinction, . . . minimises contact with the outside world, through segregation and by limiting outmarriage" (Coleman 1997: 1471; quoted in Kerswill 2006), and is therefore likely to maintain their own vernacular to the extent of becoming a *Sprachinsel* (Schreier 2009): regionally confined varieties spoken by relatively small(er) and endocentric speech communities that typically reside in a relatively large and sparsely populated geographical area (Born and Jakob 1990). A general distinction is made between *Aussensprachinseln* (i.e., 'language islands' in a heteroglossic environment, such as the German-speaking communities of Colônia Tirol in Brazil or Carlos Pfannl in Paraguay, cf. Rein 1977) and *Binnensprachinseln* (where speakers of a certain dialect are embedded in a heterodialectal community, for example, the Scottish community in Corby, Northamptonshire, a steel town in the English Midlands, Dyer 2002; cf. also the case of Paraguay). Despite such different levels of integration, all migrants reorient themselves and engage in "custom shedding" (to varying degrees), for example in New Zealand, where Belich (1996: 330) reports that

> for European settlers migration was a chance to select cultural baggage – to discard as well as take. Highly overt class differences[,] . . . excessive deference towards the upper classes and customs that publicly implied subordination were leading candidates for the discard pile.

This arguably led to a diminishing of former social class differences and more egalitarian societal structures.

In conclusion, the development of SVs depends on macro-social and economic factors: the 'action plan', interest and commitment of colonial bodies; the attitudes of settler groups to the new settings, local inhabitants and their languages; the waves and directionality of migration patterns (single vs. successive); and the readiness with which they are welcomed and received.

Issues and debates

Given the colonial baggage and historical dimension of the transportation of SVs, the linguistic, sociolinguistic, and sociopolitical factors involved make this an extraordinarily complex field of inquiry. As a consequence, we focus on three issues here: (1) the formation and maintenance of settler varieties; (2) the emergence of postcolonial varieties along two strands (settler and indigenous) and evolutionary identity-driven patterns; and (3) the manifestation of ethnolinguistic vitality that will determine the process of language maintenance or shift.

As regards our first issue, formation and maintenance, the task of modeling the interaction of SVs (leading inter alia to new-dialect formation) or assessing their stability rests on several indicators: overall speaker numbers (absolute and relative), strength of ethnic identity, economic base, or range of domains of use. The analysis of SVs in interaction has to integrate two related issues: first, what happens to the original input varieties when its speakers start interacting with each other in the new contexts? Second, how are local varieties formed as a result of interaction between SVs and local languages (for instance in language contact situations, leading to pidginization or creolization)?

With regard to the first question, more than thirty years of research (Siegel 1985; Trudgill 1986, 2004) have shown that a number of processes are at work when SVs interact. The principal mechanisms involve modifications in the speech of the founding settlers themselves (generation 0, which migrates to the colony). At first, there is considerable accommodation due to face-to-face interaction between individual speakers. This leads to the adoption of structures from other vernaculars and the loss of own features (particularly stigmatized and marked ones, see later). Following an initial mixing stage of variants, there is a continuing decrease in variation among speakers (Siegel 1985). The leveling of dialect differences favors variants that are in a majority in the dialect mix, unmarked as opposed to marked, acquired early by children, and socially neutral as opposed to strongly stigmatized by belonging to a particular social or geographical grouping (whether standard or non-standard; see Schreier 2008 for a discussion). This goes hand in hand with simplification: an advance of regularity, fewer categories (such as gender, case) and, for example, fewer person/number inflections than in the original dialects. When several variants survive, then each form is reassigned to serve new functions in the wider community. So-called reallocation operates when former regional differences are re-interpreted as social markers, for instance. The TRAP vowel in words such as *dance* or *grass* indicates regional differences in England, but has been refunctionalized in Australia so that it now is an index of social class membership (Britain and Trudgill 1999).

Migration waves and the timing of arrival are crucial as well, the idea being that earlier arrivals have more influence in shaping the outcome of dialect contact (see the discussion of founder effects later in this chapter). For example, Hickey (2004) argues that input of Irish Gaelic on Irish English depends both on the social organization of the community at the new location and the period at which this input was prevalent: in Newfoundland, Irish English influence was considerable compared to most settings in North America, where it was rather small as the large numbers of (southern) Irish immigrants arrived after the formative period of English. Indeed, one of the most engaging debates in recent years revolved around the question whether the emergence of new dialects due to contact of SVs is a socially or linguistically driven process (see Trudgill 2004).

As for theories on the emergence of localized varieties, a more recent and very influential model is Schneider's Dynamic Model of the evolution of postcolonial Englishes (2003, 2007). Rather than focusing on individual varieties and "regard[ing] these varieties as individual entities" (2003: 241), Schneider highlights common processes (2007: 5, cf. also Kirkpatrick 2007: 34) that underlie the emergence and formation of new English dialects in colonial and postcolonial as well as migration settings, where settler communities get in contact with indigenous communities. He argues that a "uniform developmental process, shaped by consistent sociolinguistic and language-contact conditions, has operated in the individual instances of relocating and re-rooting the English language in another territory" (2007: 5). While he applies the model mainly to colonial and postcolonial settings, it is, however, not this nature of the setting that is of crucial importance, but rather the different types of contact situations that are a reflection of sociocultural embedding, historical development and "the expansion and relocation of the use of a single language to new territories where a characteristic type of language contact situation evolves" (Schneider 2003: 235).

Three important aspects form the backdrop of Schneider's argument. The first aspect (which also plays a role in the emergence of new varieties of English in language contact scenarios more generally), are the patterns of feature selection and the linguistic input that are characteristic for the contact situations he discusses. There is coexistence of features and structures from English input dialects spoken by the settler communities and from indigenous language(s) as well. Mufwene (2001) proposes the concept of the "feature pool" from which features are selected in a "competition-and-selection process" (Schneider 2007: 21). Such "a mixture of features is typically determined largely in the early phase of contact, while things are still in flux, so [that] a 'founder effect' (Mufwene 1996, 2001) can be expected to play a role" (Schneider 2003: 240–241), and so that diffusion occurs. Second, drawing once more on the notion of the feature pool, Schneider argues that the parties involved define and redefine their social, cultural, and linguistic identities. Features selected from the pool carry all sorts of identities about speaker groups (regional origins, position in social hierarchy, etc.), which are renegotiated and redefined in the process of identity formation. These redefinitions influence linguistic processes; indeed, for Schneider they are at the core of his argument: "central to the model . . . is the notion of social identity and its construction and reconstruction by symbolic linguistic means" (2007: 26, 29).

The third aspect, certainly the most important one in this context, is that Schneider's model hinges fundamentally on two perspectives, or strands: that of the colonizers, or settlers (STL), and that of the colonized, or indigenous (IDG) (2003: 240). These perspectives are both competing, yet approximating as new varieties emerge. In an early stage, they are separated along settler and indigenous population lines; after some time, very often as a product of nativization, they become more closely intertwined due to accommodation, perhaps also bilingualism, and may merge as new-dialect formation progresses. While we will largely focus on the STL strand here, the processes of approximation and accommodation mentioned earlier, both on a cultural and linguistic level, are effective in both directions and all parties involved, leading to dialect convergence and, finally, "the emergence of an overarching language community with a set of shared norms" (Schneider 2003: 243, 2007: 31). Importantly, the intertwining of both strands does account for the five-step model, detailing the evolutionary process of these new varieties as a "cyclic series of characteristic phases determined by extralinguistic conditions" (Schneider 2007: 5). Paramount for each phase are the socio-political background, identity constructions, the sociolinguistic conditions as well as linguistic effects, starting with the foundation phase and going on to the exonormative stabilization, nativization, endonormative stabilization, and differentiation phases (2007, chap. 3).

During the first phase, foundation, a homogenization process can be witnessed in the STL strand, "by such processes as levelling, 'focusing', simplification, and the occurrence of phonetically or grammatically intermediate 'interdialect' forms in the spoken vernacular" (Schneider 2003: 244). In contrast, the IDG strand develops some degree of bilingualism, as speakers start to interact with speakers of the STL strand (Schneider 2003: 244). During the second phase, exonormative stabilization, changes in the linguistic setting develop further, but the variety that is spoken still shows a high degree of similarity in comparison to the variety that was imported (Kirkpatrick 2007: 32). During this phase, a "slow movement of the STL variety towards the local variety and the beginning of the expansion of the IDG variety" can be seen (Kirkpatrick 2007: 32). In the third phase, nativization, the intertwining of strands begins (Schneider 2007: 41), which then, in turn, "results in the heaviest effects on the restructuring of the English language itself" (Schneider 2003: 247; cf. also Kirkpatrick 2007: 32). By phase four, endonormative stabilization, "processes of linguistic change and nativization have produced a new language variety which is recognizably distinct in certain respects from the language form that was transported originally, and which has stabilized linguistically" (Schneider 2007: 51). This variety is gradually accepted as the norm (cf. Kirkpatrick 2007: 32); hence, norm orientation within the speech community has changed from an exonormative orientation towards an endonormative one. In the last phase, finally, differentiation, the new variety has evolved and "reflects local identity and culture" (Kirkpatrick 2007: 32). At this stage, variability comes into play, with the development of regional, social, and ethnic varieties: "As a consequence of external stability, there is now room for internal differentiation" (Schneider 2007: 53), and "this is not the end point of linguistic evolution but rather a turning point from which something new springs: the stage of dialect birth" (Schneider 2007: 53–54).

Not all settlements, however, manage to establish their language so that a new colonial dialect emerges. It is important to consider that the variety is usually in contact (Mufwene would say: in competition) with other languages, either colonial or indigenous ones. As outlined earlier, a range of factors determines whether the SV will be maintained or marginalized as the settler community's main means of communication. Rather than establishing a *Sprachinsel* ('language island'), SVs are often exposed to considerable sociolinguistic forces that induce the speakers to shift away from their heritage (or community) language to the locally dominant language. The study of such processes began with Haugen's (1972) seminal work on the fate of Norwegian in the United States, with a principal focus on the socio-historical condition in which languages coexist. Giles, Bourhis, and Taylor (1977) then proposed the first conceptual framework to determine the *ethnolinguistic vitality* of languages in contact. They defined three factors as crucial: institutional support, demography, and status. Institutional support includes the social and political conditions in which a language is used, ranging from governmental decisions on schooling and legal services to language use in the media. Institutional support – or the lack of it – is important since it frames the usage of a language (or its ban) in society from a top-down perspective. The demographic factor considers the number of speakers and the constellation of families and communities, since a larger number of individuals and families using the heritage language will enhance its vitality among future generations. Status, finally, refers to the social status of a language and the values attached to it: the higher the social prestige of a language, the more likely is it that its speakers will opt for using and others for learning it. Ideally, the classification of a language's ethnolinguistic vitality as either high or low will predict how likely the language is to persist or disappear.

Giles et al.'s (1977) conceptual tool proves highly useful with regard to settings in which languages came into contact before mass media and, above all, the internet were established. It has been applied with great success to case studies around the world. As a case in point, we would like to present the representative case of English attrition in Paraguay, as it highlights the contribution of all three factors. The community has a peculiar social history. At the turn of the 20th century, a group of more than 600 Anglophone settlers sought to set up a society based on socialist ideas in eastern Paraguay. Their utopian project failed, however, and today the fourth- and fifth-generation descendants speak Guarani as their first and Spanish as their second language. This case is exceptional in that it seems to be the only case in the history of English in which a considerable group of English-speaking settlers shifted from their prestigious first or native language to a local indigenous language. A close look at the process of language shift among Anglo-Paraguayans reveals that all three variables were decisive in the process of language shift: a complete lack of institutional support failed to impose English in schools and religious services; the demographic development soon resulted in a large number of interethnic, that is multilingual marriages, and the social status of English in this setting was rather low. These conditions lowered the ethnolinguistic vitality of English and favored the shift toward the local indigenous language (i.e. Guarani; see Perez 2016).

However, even though the concept of ethnolinguistic vitality proved viable in a number of language contact scenarios, studies on language vitality and shift should nowadays also consider factors such as globalization and interpersonal (and international) networks. Landry and Allard (1994) propose to add language behavior, including networks of linguistic contacts as well as a person's individual aptitude, as relevant factors in the determination of ethnolinguistic vitality. Especially in light of globalization and the importance of the virtual world, these realities are highly dynamic and must be analyzed carefully.

Implications

The preceding discussion has laid the groundwork for implications in various fields, not all of which are easy to map out in a short overview chapter. Before looking at some selected ones in more detail, we need to address an issue that has loomed large, yet so far not received the attention it should have: the impact of globalization and international expansion. The theoretical foundation of these processes has received much attention after Blommaert's groundbreaking (2010) publication. We would like to point out that the mobility of people, and hence also the linguistic consequences of migration, by default include the mobility of linguistic and sociolinguistics resources: "People whose language repertoires are studied, even if they are migrants, are 'fixed', so to speak, in space and time" (Blommaert 2010: 4). The sociolinguistics of globalization field hinges on the processes of globalization proper, geopolitical globalization, geocultural globalization and mobility, all of which have to be considered in the task of establishing a "kind of sociolinguistics [. . .] in which we de-synchronize and historicize sociolinguistic phenomena" (p. 145).

This is of great relevance here. When assessing the contribution of migratory movements on language change, we need to address the question whether modifications in migratory patterns over time lead to differential change processes. For instance, we have discussed the sociolinguistic consequences of settlement types (settlement vs. exploitation) and shown that such histories (among other factors) influence the directionality of contact between varieties. At the same time, the commitment to colonial affairs (and therefore the impact of SVs in local contact ecologies) has changed fundamentally over the last 100 years. Given the geopolitical situation today, the main colonial powers have shifted in contrast to the 17th, 18th, and 19th centuries, especially with regard to claims and taking possession of new territories. The language of the former British Empire still has much influence, of course, though no longer as a consequence of direct settlement and colonization (particularly in countries where it is used as a foreign language). Also, there has been a reversal of migration, out of the formerly colonized areas back into the motherland, very often to urban centers that have a long history (at times back to the Middle Ages) of receiving in-migration. As a result, SVs, transported to new settings and transformed there via all sorts of contact processes, are brought back to the homeland by their speakers; crucially, they have undergone considerable changes and are returned in altered form (pidgins, creoles, established koine varieties, second-language varieties, etc.). Consequently, SVs are detached from the original community as a result of transplantation to extraterritorial settings, where they are structurally und functionally reconfigured before returning as the vernacular of re-migrating members of the speech community – "the Empire speaks back," so to say. This involves new and perhaps even more complex (re)directionalities of feature adoption, both in host and migrant communities (cf. Kerswill 2006).

To quote Blommaert again, transfer processes of this kind entail the following shift in focus:

> From a view in which language is narrowly tied to a community, a time and a place ... and in which language is primarily seen as having local functions to a view in which language exists in and for mobility across space and time.
>
> *(2010: 181)*

Multicultural London provides a pertinent case in point here. According to Baker and Eversley (2000), thirty-three percent of primary school children do not have English as a first or home language, ten languages have more than 40,000 speakers in London, and forty more than 1,000 speakers. Whereas the capital of the UK has always attracted newcomers (just as New York did in the United States), the multilingual and multicultural character of London is the result of massive in-migration since World War II. According to Kerswill, Cheshire, Fox and Torgersen (2013), who carried out sociolinguistic research in the two communities of Hackney and Havering, the departure of locals due to suburbanization has been matched by the arrival of migrants from former colonies. Hackney, a former stronghold of traditional white working-class London English now hosts an unprecedented number of varieties in everyday life: creole-influenced varieties, ex-colonial Englishes, learner varieties (English as a second language), traditional local London vernacular, and also more standard-type varieties encountered in school (Standard English, teachers' varieties). Monolingual English speakers are regularly exposed to all these varieties.

One sociolinguistic outcome is the process of multiethnolectalization (for an in-depth discussion, see, among others, Svendsen and Røyneland 2008, Quist 2008). Multiethnolects are described as new varieties, or, with reference to Mufwene, as pools of variants, shared by more than one ethnic group in a (typically urban) area. Features from migrants' varieties are reshuffled and cross-selected in the general sociolinguistic repertoire of the community and its speakers. They are shared by members of minority and majority groups alike. Language here, in Blommaert's (2010: 181) terms, "exists in and for mobility across space and time." A multiethnolect is non-ethnic in affiliation and remarkably neutral in terms of indexicality, at least in the community in which it is spoken, whereas outside its own community it may sound "ethnic." It is arguably vernacularized, spreading quickly throughout the wider speech community (mostly adolescents) and picked up in other social networks elsewhere.

The phenomenon is widespread and has been described in various European cities: Copenhagen, Stockholm, Oslo, Gothenburg, Malmö, Amsterdam, Berlin, Mannheim, and London (discussion in Dorleijn and Jacomine 2013). Kerswill, Cheshire, Fox, and Torgersen (2013) show that adolescents in Hackney now use several innovative grammatical and discourse features that take their origins in contact with varieties spoken by migrant communities. Among others, they list the following features: indefinite pronoun *man* ("it's her personality *man's* looking at"); *still* as a discourse marker ("I got the right moves innit but I ain't telling you though *still*"); a new quotative expression *this is + speaker* ("*this is me* 'I'm from east London'"; discussion in Kerswill et al. 2013: 272–282). Migration, therefore, is likely to have a permanent effect on the dialect landscape of urban areas; the coexistence of migrant varieties and former SVs leads to the emergence of new vernaculars that are locally emblematic, shedding their ethnic indexical value of individual speaker groups and instead represent the mixed community. As a result, the concept of ethnolinguistic vitality has to be critically reassessed in these contact settings. The balance between institutional support, demography, and status is reconfigured and demography emerges as the single most dominant factor (there is no institutional support whatsoever and the multiethnolect, at least in its initial stages, carries negative prestige throughout the wider community).

Notwithstanding, alternative scenarios may develop and migration does not necessarily lead to the formation of new varieties. For one, it is certainly possible that migration may have no or very little effect on SVs. The move of Amish communities to Pennsylvania led to the creation of *Sprachinseln* ('language islands'). When communities are segregated (or segregate themselves, a line that is not always easy to draw), then there necessarily are few contacts, and this favors the maintenance of SVs and often gives them an allegedly conservative character (as seen in the debate of the concept of "colonial lag"; Hundt 2009, Schreier 2009). Also, of course, we must not forget the opposite scenario, namely that there is loss of varieties due to re-adaptation or more or less complete accommodation to local vernaculars. As discussed earlier, Australian English could have become an influential SV in the local context of rural Paraguay, yet became obsolete for reasons linked to its rather diminished ethnolinguistic vitality (Perez 2016). Today, there is no endemic variety of Paraguayan English; the potential traces of this SV have almost completely disappeared.

On a more general note, if migration continues and intensifies, then the communities on the move, dispersed far and away from their home countries, will become prime research sites (see Vertovec's concept of "superdiversity" [Vertovec 2007], as taken up and discussed by Blommaert 2010; see later). The diaspora represents a hotspot for the investigation of SVs, and it can be defined as follows:

> A diaspora is a minority ethnic group of migrant origin which maintains sentimental or material links with its land of origin, either because of social exclusion, internal cohesion or geo-political factors. It is never assimilated into the whole society but in time develops a diasporic consciousness which carries out a collective sharing of space with others.
>
> *(Esman 1996: 316)*

To give a pertinent sociolinguistic example, Rathore-Nigsch (2013) shows in her case study of the so-called twice migrants (Indian migrants in Uganda who were forced to move to the English Midlands in the 1970s) that accommodation and shift processes can occur remarkably quickly, at times within one generation. These migrants represent a particularly complex community in the SV canon. At the end of the 19th century, their ancestors moved from various settings (Gujarat, Punjab, Goa, etc.) in northwestern India to East Africa, following the European colonizers into the interior. The British had a strong interest in these settlers; they were highly valued for their entrepreneurial skills and spoke English, thus ideally representing brokers with the local population (see earlier). Even though no more than two percent of the total population had Indian origins, they were most significant economically. They were in regular contact with the British population (hence exposed to SVs), yet already spoke a transformed former SV due to the fact that English was available to the local elite in India via officialized usage in education. In East Africa, the Indians had little contact with the African populations and mostly lived under segregated conditions, which would have favored the maintenance of their native variety of Indian English (see Hundt and Sharma 2014). After political independence and Idi Amin's Africanization program of local economies, there were discriminatory measures against Indians and a dramatic large-scale exodus of Indians from Kenya and Tanzania followed, culminating in the expulsion of all Indians by

Amin from Uganda in August 1972 (Rathore-Nigsch 2013). Many of them fled to England, and tens of thousands arrived in the East Midlands to make a new start. Rather than maintaining their variety (as an emerging ethnolect in the sociolinguistic landscape of cities like Leicester), Rathore-Nigsch showed in her detailed study of sociolinguistic variables that a rapid shift was taking place. Whereas the first immigrant group still showed a strong affiliation with IndE (variable rhoticity, occurrence of linking /r/ vs. lack of intrusive /r/, widespread use of taps and trills rather than approximants), the second generation, born locally in the 1970s, showed extensive contact to East Midlands English: non-rhoticity was nearly categorical, there was occurrence of both linking /r/ and intrusive /r/ and a use of approximants rather than taps or trills. In other words, though there was no process of language shift as in Paraguay, the traces of this particular SV had rapidly disappeared due to near-complete accommodation of local features in face-to-face accommodation, within one generation.

To summarize, SVs are highly relevant for contact-induced language change, both in individual speakers (which we have not considered in due detail here) and collective groups and sub-groups. They may themselves act as targets when new varieties emerge, in combination with what Schneider (2007) would call the IDG strand, or undergo shift and disappear under social conditions that diminish their ethnolinguistic vitality. Possible explanations for the different outcomes need to be assessed case by case, and a number of social and sociolinguistic criteria have to be taken into account (demography, population stability, function of language in the repertoires of speakers and communities, indexicality, and language as social practice).

Future directions

There is no doubt that the function, importance, and perhaps also the regional presence of SVs are very much different than two centuries ago; they have changed so much that one might go as far as to question whether SVs can still be compared. We would take issue with Blommaert here; the massive changes in social or political affairs make it difficult to "de-synchronize and historicize sociolinguistic phenomena" (2010: 145), at least in what regards the SVs. While their legacy is now omnipresent in the form of global languages, which continue to influence the sociolinguistic landscape on international levels, the export of varieties to new settings (as in the colonization of the British Empire, South Africa, Australia, etc.) is no longer common these days. As a result, contact scenarios that involve traditional strands, as theorized by Schneider (2003, 2007), are rarely found.

So what future developments can be expected? While migration continues to be a pressing global phenomenon, the export of varieties to new permanently established settings (dependencies, colonies, nation-states), as was common in the 17th, 18th, and 19th centuries, has given way to concerted population movements into preexisting political entities. We feel confident to predict that, as a result of mass poverty, natural disasters, political changes, and other issues, such migration will continue and perhaps, as is currently the case in the Mediterranean, even increase in the decades to come. Internationalization and globalization will continue and intensify, which is in line with Blommaert. At the same time, we need to recognize that the role of SVs has changed fundamentally, a point emphasized by Mair (2013): from one of the most important source varieties in the emergence of endemic local varieties to a host variety into which offspring varieties are embedded. Just as urbanization continues (the population of Istanbul, for instance, increased from 2.2 million inhabitants in 1980 to almost fourteen million today, the one of London from six million to almost ten million in the same period), multiethnolectalization processes are likely to continue in large urban centers around the world. They will be accompanied by enduring patterns of language and dialect contact, the precise outcome of which needs to be determined for each case separately. At the same time, while re-migration is taking place in many cases (cf. multiethnicities in London and elsewhere), substantial numbers of British people still migrate to other places, for example Australia or South Africa. As these tend to be professionals with skills, the settler strand is constantly replenished. This is likely to have linguistic-ecological consequences, for example, further dialect contact and the possibility for renewed dialect leveling. In other words, while re-migration is taking place and perhaps intensifying, so is migration, at least in certain contexts. The complex nature of various strands thus increases, and this certainly offers exciting research perspectives.

Some caution is required when it comes to the role of English SVs in the disappearance of dialects and of course the mechanisms of language shift and death. Blommaert's claim that "where English occurs, indigenous (and especially minority) languages are threatened, first with attrition and eventually with language death" (2010: 182) may have some validity when it comes to the global prestige of English, but not in terms of colonial languages exported into new territories, which hardly occurs. Postcolonial attraction will lead to long-lasting contact of all sorts of varieties, which will all have effects on each other and transform their role, features, and status in the respective communities.

Summary

In the context of sociolinguistic consequences of migration, SVs, defined here as the natively spoken vernaculars of early colonial populations and the first (locally born) generations, have always obtained a prominent position. As a result of relocation-diffusion, they served as target languages to speakers of indigenous (substrate) languages around the globe, functioned as one of the most visible signs of colonial involvement, and gave rise to the emergence of structurally nativized local varieties.

The contact scenarios, of which they were an important part, saw all kinds of contact between speakers and their vernaculars, which triggered change mechanisms such as mixing, leveling, and so forth. They gave rise to important issues and debates (Mufwene's feature pool, Schneider's Dynamic Model, ethnolinguistic vitality, to name but three), which foreground their importance for theoretical concerns. At the same time, their overall contribution has changed considerably. In the heyday of colonization (between the 17th and the 19th centuries), when new territories were settled and incorporated into the Empire, the SVs were transplanted varieties that coexisted in new and unprecedented combinations of regional and social lects. They merged into new varieties (in the form of koines or second-language varieties, for instance) and were highly emblematic; they were considered both as a link to the mother country (for those employed in the colony) and as the language of the suppressor. This changed during the course of the 20th century, and changes in migration patterns (permanent colonization is now rare) in the form of repatriation or return of populations from former colonies have led to a redirection of SV diffusion. It is now common for these varieties to be also transported back to the home country, typically in modified form so that they are noticeably distinct where they are spoken alongside other vernaculars, very often in large urban settings, and thus influence the local feature pool. The emergence of multiethnolects throughout Europe is a consequence of such re-migration and arguably the most visible sign of how the nature and impact of SVs has changed. We would predict that this trend intensifies. One needs to bear in mind that this is not the usual outcome. It may turn out to be challenging theoretically to attempt finding general parameters whether the varieties survive or disappear, due to accommodation and shift. The importance of these questions for sociolinguists and contact linguistics is immense.

Further reading

Blommaert, J. (2010). *The Sociolinguistics of Globalization*. Cambridge: Cambridge University Press.

A standard reference on sociolinguistic consequences of globalization.

Gordon, E., Campbell, L., Hay, J., Maclagan, M., Sudbury, A. and Trudgill, P. (2004). *New Zealand English: Its Origins and Evolution*. Cambridge: Cambridge University Press.

A concise and theoretically relevant discussion of the origins and development of New Zealand English.

Schneider, E. W. (2007). *Postcolonial English: Varieties around the World*. Cambridge: Cambridge University Press.

Perhaps the most influential current model to account for the development of postcolonial Englishes, with reference to identity formation.

Schreier, P.T., Schneider, E. and Williams, J.P., eds. (2010). *The Lesser-Known Varieties of English: An Introduction*. Cambridge: Cambridge University Press (Studies in English Language Series).

An introduction to lesser-known varieties of English around the world, with detailed settlement accounts and sociohistorical overviews.

References

Arnold, R. (1994). *New Zealand's Burning – The Settler's World in the Mid 1880s*. Wellington: Victoria University Press.

Baker, P. and Eversley, J., eds. (2000). *Multilingual Capital: The Languages of London's Schoolchildren and Their Relevance to Economic, Social and Educational Policies*. London: Battlebridge.

Belich, J. (1996). *Making Peoples: A History of the New Zealanders from Polynesian Settlement to the End of the Nineteenth Century*. Auckland: Penguin.

Blommaert, J. (2010). *The Sociolinguistics of Globalization*. Cambridge: Cambridge University Press.

Born, J. and Jakob, G. (1990). *Deutschsprachige Gruppen am Rande und außerhalb des geschlossenen deutschen Sprachgebiets: eine bibliographische Dokumentation von Literatur zum Thema "Sprache" aus der Zeit nach 1945* (2nd ed.). Mannheim, Germany: Institut für deutsche Sprache.

Britain, D. (2002). Space and spatial diffusion. In Chambers, Jack, Peter Trudgill and Natalie Schilling-Estes (eds.), *The Handbook of Variation and Change* (pp. 603–637). Oxford: Blackwell.

Britain, D. and Trudgill, P. (1999). Migration, new dialect formation and sociolinguistic refunctionalisation: *Reallocation* as an outcome of dialect contact. *Transactions of the Philological Society* 97: 245–56.

Carmichael, G.A. (1993). A history of population movement between New Zealand and Australia. *International Migration* 31: 513–560.

Chambers, J.K. and Trudgill, P. (1998). *Dialectology* (2nd ed.). Cambridge: Cambridge University Press.

Coleman, D.A. (1997). The origins of multi-cultural societies and the problems of their management under democracy. *Proceedings of the 23rd International Population Conference* 3: 1457–1496.

Dorleijn, M. and Nortier, J. (2013). Multiethnolects: Kebabnorsk, Perkerdansk, Verlan, Kanakensprache, Straattaal, etc. In Bakker, Peter and Yaron Matras (eds.), *Contact Languages: A Comprehensive Guide* (pp. 229–272). Berlin: de Gruyter.

Dyer, J. (2002). "We all speak the same round here": Dialect levelling in a Scottish-English community. *Journal of Sociolinguistics* 6: 99–116.

Esman, M.J. (1996). Diasporas and international relations. In Hutchins, J. and Smith, A. (eds.), *Ethnicity* (pp. 316–320). New York: Oxford University Press.

Giles, H., Bourhis, R. Y. and Taylor, D. M. (1977). Towards a theory of language in ethnic group relations. In Howard Giles (ed.), *Language, Ethnicity, and Intergroup Relations* (pp. 307–348). New York: Academic Press.
Gordon, E., Campbell, L., Hay, J., Maclagan, M., Sudbury, A. and Trudgill, P. (2004). *New Zealand English: Its Origins and Evolution*. Cambridge: Cambridge University Press.
Haugen, E. (1972). *The Ecology of Language*. Stanford: Stanford University Press.
Hickey, R. (2004). Introduction. In Raymond Hickey (ed.), *Legacies of Colonial English: A Study of Transported Dialects* (pp. 1–30). Cambridge: Cambridge University Press.
Hickey, R. (2010). The Englishes of Ireland. Emergence and Transportation. In Andy Kirkpatrick (ed.), *The Routledge Handbook of World Englishes* (pp. 76–95). London: Routledge.
Hundt, M. (2009). Colonial lag, colonial innovation, or simply language change? In Rohdenburg, Günter and Julia Schlüter (eds.), *One Language, Two Grammars: Morphosyntactic Differences between British and American English* (pp. 13–37). Cambridge: Cambridge University Press.
Hundt, M. and Sharma, D., eds. (2014). *English in the Indian Diaspora*. Amsterdam: Benjamins.
Kerswill, P. (2006). Migration and language. In Mattheier, Klaus, Ulrich Ammon and Peter Trudgill (eds.), *Sociolinguistics/Soziolinguistik: An International Handbook of the Science of Language and Society* (2nd ed., pp. 2271–2285). Berlin: de Gruyter.
Kerswill, P., Cheshire, J., Fox, S. and Torgersen, E. (2013). The role of children and adolescents in language change. In Schreier, Daniel and Marianne Hundt (eds.), *English as a Contact Language* (pp. 258–282). Cambridge: Cambridge University Press.
Kirkpatrick, A. (2007). *World Englishes: Implications for International Communication and English Language Teaching*. Cambridge: Cambridge University Press.
Landry, R. and Allard, R. (1994). Subjective ethnolinguistic vitality: A comparison of two measures. *International Journal of the Sociology of Language* 108: 117–144.
Mair, C. (2013). The mobile system of Englishes: Accounting for the transnational importance of mobile and mediated vernaculars. *English World-Wide* 34.3: 253–278.
Mesthrie, R. (1993). Koineization in the Bhojpuri-Hindi Diaspora – with special reference to South Africa. *International Journal of the Sociology of Language* 99: 25–44.
Mufwene, S. S. (1996). The founder principle in creole genesis. *Diachronica* 13: 83–134.
Mufwene, S. S. (2001). *The Ecology of Language Evolution*. Cambridge: Cambridge University Press.
Mufwene, S. S. (2005). *Créoles, écologie sociale, évolution linguistique*. Paris: L'Harmattan.
Perez. Danae M. 2016. English and Language Shift in Paraguay's New Australia. *World Englishes* 35.1: 160–176.
Quist, P. (2008). Sociolinguistic approaches to multiethnolect: Language variety and stylistic practice. *International Journal of Bilingualism* 12: 43–61.
Rathore-Nigsch, C. (2013). *Dialect Variation and Change in the Diaspora: A Sociophonetic Study of the East African Indian Community in Leicester, UK*. PhD dissertation, University of Zurich.
Rein, K. (1977). *Religiöse Minderheiten als Sprachgemeinschaftsmodelle: deutsche Sprachinseln täuferischen Ursprungs in den Vereinigten Staaten von Amerika* (Zeitschrift für Dialektologie und Linguistik, Beihefte 15). Wiesbaden: Steiner Verlag.
Schneider, E. W. (2003). The dynamics of New Englishes: From identity construction to dialect birth. *Language* 79: 233–81.
Schneider, E. W. (2007). *Postcolonial English: Varieties Around the World*. Cambridge: Cambridge University Press.
Schreier, D. (2008). *St Helenian English: Origins, Evolution and Variation*. Amsterdam and Philadelphia: John Benjamins.
Schreier, D. (2009). Language in isolation, and its implications for variation and change. *Blackwell Language and Linguistics Compass* 3: 682–699.
Siegel, J. (1985). Koines and Koineisation. *Language in Society* 14: 357–378.
Sudbury, A. (2000). *Dialect Contact and Koinéisation in the Falkland Islands: Development of a Southern Hemisphere Variety*. PhD dissertation, University of Essex.

Sudbury, A. (2001). Falkland Islands English: A southern hemisphere variety? *English World-Wide* 22: 55–80.
Svendsen, B.A. and Røyneland, U. (2008). Multiethnolectal facts and functions in Oslo, Norway. *International Journal of Bilingualism* 12: 63–83.
Thomason, S.G. (2001). *Language Contact: An Introduction*. Edinburgh: Edinburgh University Press.
Trudgill, P. (1986). *Dialects in Contact*. Oxford: Blackwell.
Trudgill, P. (2004). *New Dialect Formation: The Inevitability of Colonial Englishes*. Edinburgh: Edinburgh University Press.
Vertovec, S. (2007). Super-diversity and its implications. *Ethnic and Racial Studies* 29.6: 1024–1054.

14
Trade migration and language[1]

Huamei Han

Introduction

Trade migration as a category and a form of migration in contemporary societies and scholarly discourses is an unusual term. This is largely because trade, migration, and employment are often seen as related but separate. International trade treaties and tariffs are negotiated by ministers under the auspice of the World Trade Organization (WTO), and international trade seems to be carried out largely by governments and multinational corporations (MNC), both of which seem to have little to do with migration. However, I have met many migrant traders from Africa who have resided in China for five to fifteen years, and Chinese traders running shops in Africa for ten or fifteen years. Besides these "stationed traders," I have also met many more transient traders from all over the world who go to China regularly or irregularly to buy goods, including many from Africa, or who originated in Africa but reside in North America and Western, Northern and Southern Europe as first-generation immigrants or their descendants. I met these stationed and transient traders when doing fieldwork researching *grassroots multilingualism* (Han 2013) in the context of "trade *and* migration," as I had called it. This project includes working with African traders in China since 2009, with Chinese traders in South Africa and Namibia since 2010, with visits to several other southern and western African countries over the years, and focusing on the stationed traders' interactions with locals and internal migrant traders as well as international traders. While visas, work permits, or residency have presented a major challenge, in addition to trade on their own, with or without running a shop, a logistic company, or a trading company, stationed traders in Guangzhou often act as market guides cum interpreters or agents for transient African traders, which makes them the core of the African trade community in Guangzhou. The stationed Chinese traders in Namibia and South Africa are mainly engaged in running the so-called China shops.

Traders like them in fact comprise an inherent and vital component of the economic life in the post-communist transitional economies in Eastern Europe and Southeast Asia (e.g., Nyiri 2003, 2013), in Africa (Haugen and Carling 2005; McNamee 2012; Vigouroux 2013), and in Asia and Latin America (Mathews 2011; Green 2012; Mathews, Ribeiro and Vega 2012). They are in Europe (e.g., MacGaffey and Bazenguissa-Ganga 2000) and North America (Stoller 2002) too, but in far smaller numbers and generally much more hidden.

Drawing on various historical studies in cross-cultural and long-distance trade and trade diaspora, as well as contemporary sources and my ongoing fieldwork in China and Africa, and complemented by my work with skilled immigrants in Canada, I loosely define *trade migration* as one category of migration, and the activities and processes people engage in when crossing primarily national borders, which involves seeking new goods or new markets. These trade and trade migration are "private," or initiated and facilitated by individuals and families, in contrast to "public" (or official) trade sponsored by states, MNCs and other large corporations – but the two have interacted and intertwined in complicated ways.

There are a few caveats here in relation to terminology. First, scholars frame trade migration and migrant traders differently: some focus on "trade," others on "migration," and still others call them "traders" or "merchants." I will follow the original usages when citing others' work, but I myself will use "trade migration" and "migrant traders." Second, prominent economic historian Philip Curtin uses *cross-cultural trade* to refer to "exchange across cultural lines" or trade with "people with a different way of life" (1984: 1); others call it *long-distance trade* and emphasize the complementary nature of the goods being exchanged (e.g., Meillassoux 1971). But in discussing contemporary trade migration, I choose to emphasize *national borders*. Even though a relatively recent creation in human history, nation-states constitute the dominant mode of organizing the world in which we live today (Billig 1995; Hüsken and Klute 2010), and they have material consequences for most of the world's population in the current globalization (Haugen 2012; Han 2013). In addition to national borders, our definition must accommodate other consequential borders (e.g., for the domestic borders that internal migrants in Guangzhou, China, crossed, see Han 2013; Lan 2014; for internal borders within some African countries, see Mechlinski 2010).

Third, given the fact that the purposes of migration are often multiple and subject to change due to various complicated circumstances before and after embarking on the journey, I define trade migration as activities and processes *involving* the search for new products (e.g., African traders in China) or new markets (e.g., Chinese traders in Africa). This definition recognizes the fact that in various settings many actors are involved in a multitude of tasks in order to move goods across borders, which will become clear in subsequent discussion of various trading communities worldwide over time. Fourth, private traders are often called *small traders* (e.g., Mathews, Ribeiro, and Vega 2012): while for most cases it is true that the *initial* capital seems very small when compared to public trade in core countries, it is not necessarily that small for the specific contexts of trade, and may yield remarkable profits, which have attracted many more to get involved. Additionally, a small number of individuals and families with substantial capital are involved in wholesale trade; historically and contemporarily, the size of their capital may be comparable to or even exceed that of some national economies. I use "traders" and recognize that those who run shops, including shop owners, shopkeepers, and apprentices as the core group, while there are a small number of wealthy wholesalers in each trade community, and the number of independent traders who have not accumulated enough capital and experience to open their own shops is dependent on specific trade communities. For instance, there are many such independent small traders of African descent in Guangzhou, but significantly fewer among Chinese traders in Oshikango; however, the earliest cohort of Chinese traders who arrived in Oshikango in the mid-1990s started as street vendors before accumulating capital to rent shops, and about a dozen became wealthy wholesalers and some built Chinatowns.

The goals of this chapter are twofold. First, I describe and argue that trade migration started in prehistoric times, continued through and survived European colonialism, and has expanded ever more widely and quickly in the current era of capitalist globalization but with new players. The current expansion has occurred despite the fact that there is no dedicated migration category for long-term (e.g., over a year) stationed traders in the current visa permit and residency scheme in most countries around the world. This has forced many migrant traders try to fit into other migration categories, which not only renders them bureaucratically ambiguous or even invisible, but also risks producing "illegality," intentionally or not (e.g., Stoller 2002). Second, I identify linguistic *consequences* or *products* traditionally associated with trade migration; and I then focus on "grassroots multilingualism" that has emerged from the context of trade migration but is primarily concerned with linguistic and socioeconomic *practices, ideologies*, and *processes*, to further explore and develop it as a useful applied and sociolinguistic concept that is associated with, but also goes beyond, trade migration. I argue that multilingualism is an inherent and important dimension of trade migration, which provides a strategic entry point for studying multilingualism as well as social processes. However, traditional theoretical linguistic studies focusing on linguistic products are biased toward standard or national languages, and have largely ignored and stereotyped mixed languages or linguae francae, and prioritized studying creoles emerged out of slavery in the Atlantics. The precarious and relatively transient nature of trading communities thus means that they are rarely studied because they rarely leave linguistic footprints in the form of languages as stabilized linguistic systems.

I will first provide an overview of the topic by recovering some historical roots and linkages of trade migration that are not readily observable, but are nonetheless instrumental for us to understand trade migration today. I will emphasize patterns over time and across regions; but to keep a relatively tight focus, I will include only brief examples focusing on trade migrations in and from Africa and China. I will then turn to discuss issues in jargon, pidgin, and lingua franca research before describing and further conceptualizing "grassroots multilingualism" with data from my ongoing fieldwork in China and Namibia. After briefly addressing relevant issues of and for debates and implications for policy and research, I will discuss future directions for researching trade migration and language.

Overview

Based on my fieldwork and historical and contemporary resources, transient traders are characterized by their movement: they reside at one base – often their home countries, but not always – and travel regularly or irregularly to one or several other countries to source goods during an extended period of time, and may switch to another set of destination countries when markets and other circumstances change (Clark 2010). On the contrary, stationed traders spend years on end residing in the host country and may even build families there; but again, when economic and life circumstances change, many move on, or move back (Clark 2010; Howard 2012). But stationed traders are highly mobile in sourcing goods within their host and surrounding countries and regions, and are not necessarily settled or resident traders in the sense that many of them often do not have residency, not to mention citizenship status, in the countries where they operate. Both transient and stationed traders may interact with local traders and residents, but usually stationed traders' interactions are more frequent, prolonged, and intense than transient traders. Both groups may engage in *cross-border* (e.g., Pophiwa 2010) and/or *long-distance trade,* which can be *overland* or *riverine*, while *maritime* trade usually involves even longer distance and travel (Curtin 1984; Wang 1992, 1998; Howard 2012). Compared to various categories of immigrants, traders and trade communities are more transient, which means that their footprint in terms of *linguistic products* is often more transient too.

The preceding characteristics of trade migration and traders were similar to those found in cross-cultural trade in history, which has been the most important external stimuli to societal change, discounting the immeasurable and less benign impact of wars (Curtin 1984). According to Curtin, "Trade communities of merchants living among aliens in associated networks are to be found on every continent and back through time to the very beginning of urban life," and are one of the most widespread and most important human institutions (1984: 3). Indeed, long-distance trade pre-dated the formation of the Sumerian city-states in Mesopotamia as early as 5300 BC (Howard 2012), and the history of cross-cultural trade shows remarkable similarities not only among different regions of the world, but also from the past to present. Below I summarize some patterns from prehistoric time through the end of World War II, and I argue that private trade survived European colonialism, and trade migration has continued in globalization with many new players.

Historical patterns of trade migration

First, cross-cultural trade, particularly long-distance trade, has always entailed high financial investment but potentially lucrative gains, as well as physical risks for those who traveled. In ancient times, long-distance trade required the domestication of animals for transportation and later the development in sailing capabilities needed for long-distance travel, communication in verbal and written forms, established trade routes, specialized and experienced transportation personnel, and considerable capital with slow turnover. But there was a lucrative return for moving goods essential for socioeconomic and political life, such as salt, iron, fish, and weapons, as well as luxury items marking prestige or related to religion, such as spices, precious stones, special textiles, tea, and incense (Hopkins 1973; Wang 1992; Tagliacozzo and Chang 2011). Trade tended to flourish in times of peace, but was interrupted periodically by wars across regions and times. Understandably, safety was a major concern in cross-cultural trade, and usually it was easier for the same types of polities to engage in trade. This means that, traditionally, for security and for convenience, cross-cultural trade often was mixed and intertwined with long-distance travel for other purposes, particularly political, military, religious, intellectual, or adventure (Howard 2012).

Second, private and public trade co-existed and intertwined throughout history in complicated ways, but were recorded differently. The presence, even dominance, of private trade was found in Assur (modern Iraq) in as early as the 20th to 18th centuries BC, and in Palmyra in the 1st century AD (Howard 2012: 30, 159). Even though sometimes it outstripped public trade, overall, private trade and traders were largely excluded from official history across regions and through time (e.g., Hopkins 1973: 92–98; Wang 1992: 117–129). For instance, the *Nanhai* (the South China Sea) trade between China and South and Southeast Asia started in the former Han (206 BC–9 AD) as tribute missions, or as public trade; in the subsequent ten centuries, private trade was ongoing, and at times outstripped the public trade, but was never clearly recorded (Wang 1992: 81, 117). Similarly, private European slave trade in West Africa started along with the public trade when chartered companies had exclusive rights to trade in the 17th century. Lacking capacity, chartered companies were unable to make exclusive use of their monopoly power and thus issued licenses to private traders, and they were also forced to tolerate interlopers who traded in their territories without their permission. Private trade completely outstripped charter companies in the 18th century. Between 1789 and 1791, the seven largest private firms in Liverpool alone "undertook over half the total number of slaving ventures" in Britain, which received two-thirds of all slaves to Europe (Hopkins 1973: 96, 91–99). However, only the documents of the chartered African Company was supposed to be preserved in the Public Record Office in London, and it was only by mistake that certain records of private ventures and private traders were kept (Strickrodt 2001: 294).

The exclusion of private trade from official historical records mainly had to do with the low status of private traders in various societies at different times (Meillassoux 1971; Hopkins 1973; Wang 1998: 82, 87). In ancient agricultural societies, merchants and traders were wealthier but did not derive their wealth from farming, and thus were often seen as suspicious and were accorded low social status, such as in ancient Sumer and Babylon (Howard 2012), in the Greek and Roman empires at the peaks of their respective powers (Cohen 2008; Howard 2012), and in various Chinese dynasties (Wang 1998). This was also true in West Africa for both merchants and the agents sent to various trade settlements:

> The merchant is always an alien and a cosmopolitan. . . . Since they need to be settled along the trade routes, traders are always minority groups, therefore in the need to have themselves accepted and respected. Besides, to be different is the condition of their existence as traders.
>
> *(Meillassoux 1971: 72)*

Therefore, long-distance trade as an occupation tended to be identified with particular ethnic groups or with people from particular towns or cities (Howard 2012).

Third, the marginality of private traders meant that they often had complicated and at times volatile relationships with their states of origin and states of trade – complying with or opposing state regulations, complicit in or resisting corruption, collaborating, mixing, or competing with public trade, and so on. Therefore, historically, they were encouraged some times, and banned at other times, but were more likely to hold a status anywhere in-between these two extremes. The history of Hokkein traders, in both China and in Southeast and East Asia, illustrates some of these complicated relations. Based in the southern Chinese province far from the northern political center, Fujian merchants first developed their maritime skills in China "in a relatively free, officially backed trading atmosphere. They were taxed and supervised but otherwise unrestricted" (Wang 1992: 83). In the 13th and 14th centuries, the Hokkeins developed into the most accomplished Fujian traders. However, in 1368, the founding emperor of the Ming banned private Chinese traders from maritime trade. Private trade continued outside of the law until the ban was lifted in 1567; during this sea ban, the Hokkeins established a chain of small port communities servicing a thriving trade throughout Southeast and East Asia. Their fate in the states of trade outside of China was more dramatic, if not traumatic. Spanish colonizers first recruited them to build their maritime empire in 1572, but carefully contained them in their own quarters in Manila, and then massacred them in 1603: among some 10,000 Chinese traders, only about 1,000 survived: about 500 returned to China and about 500 remained in Manila (Wang 1992: 89–91). Similarly, in 17th-century Indonesia, the Dutch in Batavia deliberately "controlled the largest Chinese communities in Southeast Asia and used them to strengthen their own maritime empires. . . . [Then] a major bloodletting occurred in 1740" (Wang 1992: 88). In Nagasaki in Japan, a center of Dutch and Portuguese influence for three centuries, the Chinese were confined to an enclosed and guarded "China town" controlled by the Japanese from the 16th to the 19th centuries (Wang 1992: 97). A prominent historian of Asia, Wang Gungwu (1992) contends that in colonial times, though deemed illegal by the Chinese government, private Chinese traders were recruited and inserted in between European colonizers and the indigenous populations, and at times became the scapegoats punished by both groups; their precarious positions forced the Chinese traders to be resilient and adaptive.

Fourth, despite or because of their marginal positions in societies, private merchants and traders have built *trade communities* and expanded them – a trade network of such interrelated communities came to be a *"trade diaspora"* (Cohen, A. 1971; Curtin 1984; Cohen, R. 2008). While there are trading posts, and trade ports, settlements, communities, and diasporas, I will use "trade communities" myself. Since the start of urban life, foreigners' quarters and trade settlements emerged in towns important for commercial life in prosperous city-states along trade routes. The earliest trade diasporas appeared in the Middle East as early as 3500 BC; detailed evidence in cuneiform inscriptions indicates there was an Assyrian trade settlement in Cappadocia in Asia Minor by 2000 BC (Curtin 1984). Trade settlements were situated in, but largely segregated from, the host societies, which often afforded traders special legal status. For instance, between 1920 and 1740 BC, Assyrian long-distance traders established merchant colonies (*karum*) and stations (*warbartum*) in Anatolia (modern Turkey); "while the Assyrian colonies were part of local Anatolian communities – Kanesh was located in the city of Nesa – they were physically separate and were afforded a special legal status (including a differential tax status)" (Howard 2012: 158). Similarly, from late antiquity to the Middle Ages, foreign traders in the Mediterranean were housed separately (Constable 2003). European slavers largely stayed in castles they built on the Golden Coast in West Africa (Hopkins 1973), while Chinese traders were segregated in China towns in Manila, Batavia, and Nagasaki respectively from the 16th to the 18th centuries (Wang 1992).

Fifth, family and kin played a crucial role in establishing and maintaining the trade diaspora, while ethnicity, religion, or a common culture seemed to be helpful too (Cohen 2008: 83). The Assyrian long-distance trade discussed earlier offers a glimpse of the structure of family firms. Usually, the head stayed at the home city-state, and a representative, usually the eldest son or some other member, was stationed in a trade settlement in a foreign state, while other family members and employees traveled between the two locales as itinerant traders (Howard 2012: 30). The family head might expand business by sending another representative to reside in another trade settlement in a different state, which would lead to the formation of a trade network. Of course, representatives of various family firms, and of public trade firms, would come into contact with each other in the trade settlement, relationships which ranged from being friendly or even collaborative, to competitive or even hostile.

Sixth, it is apparent that many players were involved in private trade, but also in public trade, and both types were hierarchical and stratified. Wealthy patrons and merchants as investors and wholesalers stayed put, while traders at the middle and lower ranks operated the trade and moved the goods, and became stationed and transient traders. Small distributors were likely to be private traders buying from private or public wholesalers. Additionally, stationed and transient traders were served by various artisans/professionals, various service providers, as well as specialized and experienced transportation and travel personnel, for example the captain and the crew on a ship, or the caravan leader along with a guide and various camel drivers, plus a dispatch of soldiers or caravan guards, and so on (Lattimore 1962; Hopkins 1973; Howard 2012).

Finally, there are different opinions regarding whether European colonialism ended the traditional trade diaspora. Historical study of cross-cultural and long-distance trade and trade diaspora generally agree that before the 14th century private trade in Asia and Africa was generally open, but it was interrupted by European colonialism, which differed significantly from earlier forms of conquests (Lattimore 1962: 510–511; Cohen 2008: 85). Curtin sees European colonies as "militarized trade diasporas" which spelled the end of traditional trade diasporas (1984: 3–4; 230–240). But I agree with Cohen, who views chartered European companies "as precursors of the transnational corporations" (Cohen 2008: 188–189, chap. 5 n. 3), or as public trade, while individual trade communities tended to be much more transient (some died out). Trade community/diaspora as an important institution for private trade has survived and persisted, albeit in different forms and sometimes have been run by different groups of people. For instance, European trade diasporas built in the European Middle Ages had largely withdrawn to their homelands by the end of the 16th century. However, the descendants of the earlier Chinese traders in Southeast Asia, and of Indian trading communities in Tanzania, Kenya, and Uganda, were transformed into "cultural minorities in foreign lands, even though these minorities no longer devoted themselves to long-distance trade" (Curtin 1984: 4). They often took up professional employment instead. But until 1926 to 1927, the commercialized nomad migrants of mostly Chinese and Mongol background, descendants of the ancient Silk Road caravan traders, were using the same route through Central Asia in almost the same way as they had for centuries (Lattimore 1962: 37–44). At the same time, new diasporas emerged, and sometimes took on new forms. For instance, the Lebanese diaspora first emerged from the 17th to the 19th centuries when wealthy merchants traded between the Middle East and Europe; and then at the turn of the 20th century, labourers started emigrating too. But both groups refused "unskilled industrial employment" and chose to "establish themselves as itinerant traders – pedlars," in countries such as Brazil, Jamaica, the United States, and Canada (Cohen 2008: 92). Lebanese merchants and labourers "coalesced in the diaspora" and became "ethnic entrepreneurs" (Cohen 2008: 189). Indeed, in newly confederated Canada, poverty and discrimination drove Jewish, Italian, and Chinese immigrants into street selling; "by 1911, over three-quarters of all the hawkers and pedlars listed in the census were foreign-born, compared to less than a third of the population as a whole" (Benson 1985: 81). In other words, trade communities as a whole persisted around the world, sometimes established by new groups of people, and took on new forms. Indeed, the 'new' Chinese traders coming to Africa in the 1990s rarely had previous experience in trading (McNamee 2012), mostly due to the discontinuity caused by wars and political movements. Many African traders in China were middle-class professionals or unemployed graduates who were trading for the first time too.

On the other hand, the world wars interrupted trade, and colonial trade enjoyed dominance. For instance, Owen Lattimore, an American and a renowned historian of Asia, worked for a British firm in China from 1920 to 1926, "a firm which imported into China everything that the West had to sell, and exported everything that the West would buy" (1962: 12). From the end of World War II to the 1950s, large-scale decolonization started in Asia, Africa and parts of Latin America, and marked the start of the post-European-colonialism era. Based on the Bretton Woods Trio – the International Monetary Bank (IMF) and the World Bank (WB) created in 1944, the General Agreement of Trade and Tariffs (GATT) in 1947, which was replaced by the WTO in 1994 (Ellwood 2010) – the post-war world order favoured Western industrialized countries. Nonetheless it provided some stability to the world economy. Newly decolonized countries made economic gains until the 1970s and fought for a fairer new economic order, but things started changing in the late 1970s and early 1980s (Ellwood 2010; Prashad 2012), when the current globalization started running in high gear.

Trade communities in globalization

By the early 1980s, most postcolonial countries saw their debts skyrocketing when the United States unilaterally devalued its currency and delinked it from gold (Ellwood 2010). The Group of Seven (G7) used the debt crisis to push through a new intellectual property and trade regime that made the transfer of technology illegal, which means that the core countries could outsource the production of commodities to the poor countries, but the bulk of the profits for their sales would stay with them as rent for intellectual property (Prashad 2012: 7). The IMF imposed strict Structural Adjustment Policies in the 1980s, which reversed the economic gains in most postcolonial countries (Ferguson 2006; Ellwood 2010). In the meantime, Western industrialized countries transitioned into information- and technology-based new economies and transferred out manufacturing, mainly to Asia, where new consumer markets emerged. Advancements in transportation and communication technology increased the rapidity of the movements of capital, information, goods, and people, and, at the same time, periodical economic crises and the increasing wealth gap pushed ever more numbers of people into private trade. Among them, African and Chinese traders stood out.

Africans have been trading on the African continent for centuries. In postcolonial Africa, many women engaged in translocal and some in transnational trade, and recently were subjected to the turmoil of the global economy (Clark 2010). But some traded beyond Africa. For instance, dismayed by the 1970's Congo and Brazzaville postcolonial economies, unemployed *Sapures* found their way to Paris to buy expensive clothes worn by the former colonizers (MacGaffey and Bazenguissa-Ganga 2000). Some African traders lost their livelihood during the 1997 financial crisis, and bought plane tickets and arrived in New York City on visitor visas, but intending to trade and make money and then to retire back at home (Stoller 2002). Lesser known were the many who went to Dubai, Indonesia, Malaysia, and Thailand; when the 1997 'Asian' economic crisis hit, they moved to China. In my fieldwork, I met some African traders, men and women, mostly West Africans from Mali, Ghana, and Guinea, who had traded in Africa first, then moved to Southeast Asia, and then to China. With China's accession to the WTO in 2001, an increasing number of African traders arrived in Guangzhou, and an African trade community emerged in the middle of the city (Li, Xue, Michael, and Brown 2008; Lyons, Brown, and Li 2013; Bodomo 2010). By 2009 when I paid my first visit, there were approximately 20,000 stationed African traders, while many more transient traders were passing through (Han, 2013).

Likewise, as early as the Song dynasty (A.D. 960–1279), traders, artisans, and miners established a trade migration pattern *within* China, which was extended abroad and became "the dominant pattern from early times in various parts of Southeast Asia," and "the only significant pattern before 1850"; Chinese coolies (indentured laborers) then dominated migration briefly before being put to an end in the Americas by the 19th century and by the 1920s in Southeast Asia (Wang 1992: 5, 6). During the two world wars and the Cold War, private trade migration was affected first and then largely shut down. But in the mid-1980s, with China becoming the world's factory, some Chinese contract workers in Eastern Europe started carrying goods from China to sell, and large open markets of Chinese goods quickly emerged in urban centers. Some successful traders later emigrated to North America or expanded their businesses to Latin America (Nyiri 2003). Similarly, in the 1990s, some Chinese contract workers and company employees working in various Afrian countries started selling China-made goods on the streets, and quickly China shops sprang up in urban centers and then spread to rural towns and villages across Africa. Most traders from China in Africa were of urban working-class or rural backgrounds, had no previous experience in trading, relied on apprenticing, family, relatives, and friends to expand their businesses, and faced tensions and conflicts with locals (e.g., McNamee 2012; Lin 2014; Han 2015). All the Chinese trader groups faced tightened visa policies over time in their countries of trade, with the earliest arrivals having the best chance to prosper, while the late arrivals had many difficulties establishing themselves (Haugen & Carling, 2005). However, since trade still represented better economic opportunities than home, most persisted and coped in different ways, with some enduring more severe consequences than others (McNamee 2012). Before arrival, most of the traders did not speak the languages they would be trading in, but they expanded their linguistic repertoires to various degrees. Next I turn to the linguistic issues.

Issues and ongoing debates

For centuries traders all over the world have traded in languages they did not know and had to learn while trading, but we have limited knowledge of how they managed to do so. Mainstream linguistics has largely focused on studying linguistic products, particularly the standard varieties. This is also the case in studying trade languages. Linguae francae, pidgins, and some trade jargons were known to be the direct linguistic products of cross-cultural trade, but each term has expanded to mean a type of language, and some have even developed into a subfield of linguistic study that has little to do with trade migration itself. Nonetheless, tracing their origins can offer us ways forward. Working in the context of China-Africa trade migration and at the intersection of applied linguistics, sociolinguistics and ethnography, I have proposed the concept of *grassroots multilingualism* as a way to focus on language practices and ideologies as constituting socioeconomic processes (Han 2013). Below I will give a brief account of these concepts and discuss several issues of and for debate.

Lingua franca, pidgins, and jargon: linguistic products of trade migration

While there must have been many other earlier linguae francae, the 'original' lingua franca was a medium of trade and commerce that emerged in the Levant as an outcome of the trading contacts in the eastern Mediterranean Sea in the medieval period. Probably based on Latin, Italian or Arabic, the term itself means 'the language of the Franks', and is said to have been coined by Arab traders who could not distinguish among various Western Europeans and referred them all as 'the Franks' (Edwards 2012). Also called Sabir, the original lingua franca was a pidgin that adopted words from Italian, Provençal, French, Spanish, Greek, Arabic, and more. Beginning as early as the 9th century, it was firmly established in the 11th century, becoming the language of commerce of all Mediterranean merchants and seamen in the later Middle Ages, and was still being used in the 19th century (Adler 1977). This lingua franca later exerted great influence on Turkish; up to the 18th century, the Turkish language was a main borrower of Italian, Greek, and other Romance languages but often via Greek. This lingua franca reached far and wide, including replacing Arabic-based nautical terms in north Africa; but when the Italians lost their commercial powers, the old Italian commercial terms were replaced by a new terminology based entirely on French (Kabane, Kabane, and Tietze 1958).

But now a lingua franca in its broadest sense refers to any medium of communication in an area where no language in common is available. A lingua franca can be any language, including a pidgin as shown earlier, but in most cases, it is a national language (Adler 1977: 101), particularly one of the "existing languages that have achieved some position of power, either regionally or globally" (Edwards 2012: 47). Historically, Aramaic, spoken in today's central Syria as early as 1100 BC, became an important early lingua franca in the Middle East in the mid-700s BC as the language for trade and diplomacy. Sanskrit was an important lingua franca in ancient South Asia, and reached into Southeast Asia, Central Asia, and East Asia, while classical Chinese served as a lingua franca throughout East Asia, and was used in parts of Southeast Asia and Central Asia. Arabic became an important lingua franca in AD

700 in Muslim territories, but also in areas where Muslim traders were active, including in some of the coastal trading ports of China, particularly Guangzhou and Quanzhou (Wang 1992; Howard 2012: 21). In Europe, after Greek and Latin, Italian, Portuguese, Spanish, French, and finally, English, took their turns to become powerful linguae francae. Needless to say, the dominance of these powerful languages lies in the military, political, social, and economic might of their original users (Edwards 2012: 49–50).

What is claimed as the original *pidgin* was also a trade language. While the etymology of the word pidgin is unclear, it is generally regarded as originating in China (likely in or around Guangzhou). Incapable of pronouncing the English word 'business', the Chinese (more precisely, the Cantonese-speaking Chinese) said 'bigeon' instead, which degenerated into 'pigeon', as recorded by Julius Berncastle in his *Voyage to China* (cited in Edwards 2012: 50). Regarded as the "mother of all pidgins," *pidgin*, commonly known as Chinese Pidgin English (CPE), functioned as a lingua franca in communities of Western traders in the Chinese coastal ports and some inland markets (Ansaldo, Mathews, and Smith 2012: 60). Recognizing earlier "illicit commerce" but focusing on public trade, Ansaldo and colleagues estimated that "micro-ecologies of informal contact" in "co-habitation societies" did not occur until the late 18th century and prior contacts between English and Cantonese "were neither frequent nor pro-longed in time" (Ansaldo et al. 2012: 63–66). Typically regarded as a "restricted pidgin" (Siegel 2010; Ansaldo et al. 2012), the most unusual aspect of CPE is that there were written records, such as booklets with single words and formulaic expressions – all in Chinese characters. Furthermore, there was a six-volume *Chinese–English Instructor* (*The Instructor* hereinafter, 英語集全 *Yingyu Jiquan*) produced by Tong King-Sing (唐景星) around 1862, which "attempted to make Standard English comprehensible to Chinese speakers." In addition to the dictionary-like main body, *The Instructor* includes extended dialogues on lawsuits, selling tea and charting ships, and other cross-cultural trade topics (Ansaldo et al. 2012: 70–75).

The term pidgin has expanded too: now pidgins, creoles and jargons are often discussed together, and in fact, pidgins and creoles have constituted a subfield of linguistic study for over a century. However, this field has focused mainly on creoles, mostly creoles with European languages as lexifiers, and has paid largely lip service to pidgins, while jargons are mostly ignored (Thomason 2003; Tryon and Charpentier 2004; Bakker and Matras 2013). There are no universally accepted definitions of jargons and pidgins (and creoles), but it is commonly accepted that jargon is the pre-pidgin stage from the first contact; pidgin is a restricted language with no 'native speakers'; and creole is a pidgin that has acquired 'native speakers'. Many see them as at different developmental stages on a continuum, or even a life cycle, even though most pidgins did not, and probably will not, develop into creoles.

Pidgins sometimes are further divided into 'restricted pidgins' (which CPE has been deemed to be) and 'expanded pidgins' (e.g., Nigerian pidgin) before becoming creoles (Siegel 2010). One attempt at more precise definition of pidgin reads:

> A pidgin is a language which (a) functions as a *lingua franca*, and which (b) is lexically and structurally *extremely limited* in its communicative possibilities.
>
> *(Parkvall and Bakker 2013: 25)*

It is interesting that a pidgin is defined as having "extremely limited" communicative possibilities here, which seems quite difficult to quantify. Likewise, a jargon or pre-pidgin "refers to intermediary contact varieties at the level of individual, with some convention (primarily a lexicon), but not enough structural norms to qualify as a pidgin" (Parkvall and Bakker 2013:

26–27). Again, it is unclear how many structural norms would be "enough" to qualify as a pidgin, where the cutting point should be set, and whether this cutting point is based on a linguistic or social criteria. Indeed, while the first contacts in cross-cultural trade theoretically should have led to jargons as linguistic products, we know little about them. On the other hand, the *Chinook Jargon*, one of the best-known and most studied "jargons," was a trade language used among indigenous peoples on the northwest coast of North America, and later was also used with French and English traders and colonizers. It was used well into the 20th century, with a literature developed in it (Thomas 1935). But despite having been called the Chinook Jargon, linguists generally regarded it as a pidgin, a poignant example of the difficult if not impossible task, to categorize these seemingly unusual, or "lesser," languages.

The study of pidgins usually includes the social-historical contexts of language contact and linguistic analysis. In most cases, the linguistic analysis seems to focus exclusively on teasing out and tracing back to the linguistic (often also ethnic, cultural, if not national) origins of the various features of the grammar, words, phonology, and the historical genesis, even when it was difficult to be certain about these sources because the languages kept mixing at various times (e.g., Kabane et al. 1958). These linguistic analyses seem to have a normative or ideal language as a reference point, mainly for the interest of categorizing languages taxonomically or testing the linguistic genesis hypotheses, when the dividing lines between categories and stages seem more *social* than *linguistic*. Indeed, treating jargons, pidgins, creoles, and pidgin-based linguae francae as 'contact languages' necessarily assumes that 'regular', 'natural' or 'normal' languages are 'pure' languages that did not get 'contaminated' by other languages.

Monica Heller argues "against the notion that languages are objectively speaking whole, bounded systems, and for the notion that speakers draw on linguistic resources which are organized in ways that makes sense under specific social conditions (or use a Foucauldian approach, within specific discursive regimes)" (2007: 1). Challenging the seemingly common-sense but in fact highly ideologized view of bilingualism as the coexistence of two bounded and separate linguistic systems (Heller 1999), Heller (2007) proposes a shift toward a more processual and materialist view of language and of bilingualism. It is under these same premises that I have conducted fieldwork on multilingualism in China-Africa trade migration, which prompted my conceptualization of *grassroots multilingualism* (Han 2013). Next I will give a brief account of what I proposed, and how I have been developing it in the past few years.

Grassroots multilingualism and trade migration: practices, discourses, ideologies, and processes

This work is informed by a Bourdieusian materialist and processual view of language as linguistic capital, and of bi/multilingualism as practices and ideologies (Heller 2007), which sees linguistic practices as constituting social processes. In my fieldwork in China, South Africa, and Namibia I have observed and documented how African and Chinese migrant traders, and those who encountered them, expanded their multilingual repertoires without formal instruction, including quite a few who never went to school. I coined the term *grassroots multilingualism* to describe practices, discourses, and ideologies that emerge from, and are associated with, socioeconomic processes of globalization from below which include but also goes beyond private trade migration. Expanding multilingual repertoires with limited to no formal instruction, for localized purposes, is often an integral dimension and process of trade migration and globalization from below, which often leads to individual- and group-level grassroots multilingualism that is often stratified, nevertheless locally necessary and useful.

Grassroots multilingualism sees multilingualism as happening at individual, group, and societal levels, and thus can be examined on these levels. So far I have focused on individual- and group-level multilingualism at the Chinese and the Namibian sites.

1   At the individual level, I examined the relations between individual trajectories and their multilingual practices and repertoires. Focusing on the cases of a male storeowner from Guinea and a female storeowner originally from Sichuan province in Africa Town in Guangzhou, I examined and demonstrated how migration meant maintaining existing and developing new transnational and translocal ties simultaneously, and how this constituted the processes of expanding multilingual repertoires without instruction. I then illustrated that these processes were shaped by material and symbolic resources, including pre-migration linguistic repertoires, intersecting with states. I further explored the role of the state in shaping individual trajectories and mobilities in globalization. I found that individual multilingual repertoires indexed life trajectories that were enabled and constrained by resources accumulated in countries and regions that were ranked differently within the world geopolitical order (Han 2013). I have done similar analysis of three 'bosses', for example China shop owners, in Oshikango, Namibia (Han 2015).
2   At the group level, I explored grassroots multilingualism and how it sounded and looked like, and explored language ideologies deciphered through analyzing relevant practices and discourses in both China and Namibia. Two lines of work are done at the group level in Africa Town in Guangzhou, First, grassroots multilingualism at the group level involves much more than learning and using a variety of English as a lingua franca. In fact, speakers use all the linguistic resources interlocutors bring to the table, be they African or Chinese varieties, such as Susu, Malinke, Fula, Nigerian Pidgin, Sichuna dialect, Mandarin, French, Arabic, and so on. And the choice of Mandarin and a lingua franca English is related to the class positions of both the Chinese and African traders (Han 2013). Pidgins are said to be 'extremely limited' in communicative possibilities, which they can be, but I have observed and documented a wide variety of interactions in grassroots multilingualism, including business negotiation, joking, flirting, couple talk, conflicts, and so on. Second, I analyzed how working-class Chinese, middle-class Africans from English-speaking countries, and Francophone Africans talked about "*Xiaobei* English" and "*Yuexiu* English," "Chinglish," and "Chinese-English," and how they themselves used it or not, to understand how class, language, race, and gender intersected (Han 2014).

Similarly, I have done two lines of work at the group level in Oshikango, Namibia. First, I sketched a community and linguistic profile and analyzed grassroots multilingualism at the group level, comprising the usage of Portuguese, Mandarin, a variety of Chinese dialects, and Oshiwambo, and the patterns of repertoire composition and functionality among members differentially positioned in the stratified community corresponding to the positions of three types of bosses, two types of shopkeepers and employees, and the so-called accompanying families. I further analyzed how, with the tightening of visas and work permits (Dobler 2009), and policing, English proficiency and literacy has become increasingly important. This contributes to further stratification among Chinese traders in the community where joint-force inspections, raids, and mass arrests happened regularly to periodically (Han 2015). Second, I have analyzed two sets of discourses that jumped out of my interviews with local Namibians: that is, their complaints that "Chinese don't speak English . . . they approach us in Portuguese as if everybody is an Angolan," and the accusations by some that the Chinese are the "colonizer" or "oppressor." I analyzed them in the local economic and racial dynamics situated in the regional, national, and global context where Chinese traders occupy the lower end of the value chain, are the most visible to the locals, and have been blamed disproportionally (Han 2015).

3   Additionally, I have also attended to changes or developments at the individual and group levels, given that trading communities are relatively transient. In rapid globalization, individual traders find themselves daily coming into contact with people and issues they have never imagined to encounter before. For instance, several focal Nigerian participants I observed in 2009 and 2011 in Guangzhou seemed to hold highly judgmental and discriminative views of 'the Chinese' underpinned by the Standard English language ideology (Han 2014). But in 2015, a couple of them had softened their attitude and became more open and accepting.

Implications

Tracing trade migration to its historical roots helps us to discover and understand the marginalization of private traders in history, a process which has intensified in the globalized economy. I hope this overview will help to bring to light the structural marginalization migrant traders face in the current visa-permit-residency regime sanctioned and implemented by governments in the periphery and semi-periphery countries. However, it is equally important to recognize the global hierarchy and geopolitics, and recognize that certain aspects of the visa policies in the periphery actually have modelled after the core countries (Han 2013). I hope that recovering some historical roots and linkages of trade migration helps to make the point that historicity is crucial in policy work. Wang Gungwu summarizes this eloquently: "It is not really possible to understand what seems to be new without reference to the past" (1992: vii).

I also hope it is clear that a shift away from focusing on linguistic products liberates us to focus on transient linguistic practices, discourses, ideologies, and processes. This shift helps to turn us away from the exclusive focus on the conquerors among languages, for example, national or official or standard languages as systems. This re-focus offers an opportunity for us to discover and actually attend to geopolitical processes that are constituted and constitutive of linguistic processes, and thus offers an opportunity to examine and understand how mundane everyday linguistic practices constitute social life. In this case, studying grassroots multilingualism offers a window to examine and understand the material and ideological reproductions and contestations that underpin processes of globalization.

Future directions

While it would be fruitful to expand research on trade migration and associated grassroots multilingualism, I also see a need to go beyond it. First, given that trading communities are transient, there is a need to pay close attention to the developmental dimension of these communities, for example, documenting the changes or development in their processes of formation, growth and decline, to explore and understand what underpinning forces interact and in what ways, such as the practices, discourses, and policies of the individual and institutional actors, particularly the states and the underpinning ideologies. While focusing on specific communities, this work has the potential to reveal processes that go beyond the pecularities of these specific cases.

As to grassroots multilingual practices, there are several lines of research that may be pursued fruitfully. First, how grassroots multi-literacy practices may help to expand multilingual repertoires and functionalities. For instance, during the last leg of my fieldwork in Oshikango, I discovered two handwritten booklets of words, expressions, and short sentences in Portuguese that are represented in mostly Chinese characters with occasional English words and Chinese phonetics. I also learned from three Chinese storeowners who used these booklets that they made phonological modifications when using them, particularly when and after interacting with Namibian shop assistants and customers as well as Angolan customers. I have been working with a Portuguese-speaking research assistant to identify and understand all items in these two booklets, and will analyze them and their usages in relation to grassroots multi-literacy practices and discourses in trade migration, which will be followed up in the next round of fieldwork.

Second, we need to study how social media constitutes an important dimension of grassroots multilingual and multi-literacy practices, including among migrant traders who never went to school and thus could not read and write in Chinese or other languages. It is worth exploring how they use social media as multi-literacy practices, and how this has contributed to expanding their multilingual repertoires and functionalities.

Third, at the interactional level, I have noticed that traders who had a very limited number of shared vocabulary managed to negotiate business deals and avoid misunderstandings. It is worth further exploration as to what interactional resources and strategies, such as the use of calculators and other artifacts, gestures and body language, as well as linguistic strategies, they mobilized to achieve comprehension and success communication.

As to discourses and ideologies, one line of inquiry might be to explore how new social media platforms, such as WeChat, serve the purpose of policing racial and gender boundaries in various communities, and what commonalities are shared across sites, and how they differ. Situating specific sites in historicized and multi-layered contexts may help to shed light on how race, class, gender, language, and religion intersect in complicated ways, which may help to shed more light on the processes of globalization.

It is also important to go beyond trade migration to examine how it intersects with other forms of migration. For instance, trade migration that is prevalent in the periphery and semi-periphery countries has become intimately linked to educational migration in those contexts, particularly with programs and schools providing language classes. It is also intimately connected to the so-called ethnic or immigrant entrepreneurs, or urban self-employment among immigrants of ethnic/racial minority backgrounds (Light and Bonacich 1988) residing in the core countries. So what are the connections, how do they connect, and with what implications and consequences for whom? And what can this tell us about globalization from below, and about mobility? Delving into these lines of research hopefully may help us to deliberately draw on, but also contribute to, social theories (Coupland 2001), in this case, to develop a social theory of trade migration in globalization.

Related topics

Slavery, indentured work, and language
Settler varieties
Rethinking (un)skilled migrants
Language in skilled migration

Further reading

Han, H. (2013). Individual grassroots multilingualism in Africa Town in Guangzhou: The role of states in globalization from below. *International Multilingual Research Journal, 7*(1), 83–97.

This is the first conceptualization of grassroots multilingualism at the individual level, based on a case study of trade migration.

McNamee, T. (2012). *Africa in Their Words: A Study of Chinese Traders in South Africa, Lesotho, Botswana, Zambia and Angola.* South Africa: The Brenthurst Foundation.

Nyiri, P. (2003). Chinese migration to Eastern Europe. *International Migration, 41*, 239–65.

Two case studies of the 'new' private Chinese trade migration to five African countries and to Eastern Europe.

MacGaffey, J. and Bazenguissa-Ganga, R. (2000). *Congo-Paris: Transnational Traders on the Margins of the Law.* Bloomington: Indiana University Press.

Stoller, P. (2002). *Money Has No Smell: The Africanization of New York City.* Chicago: University of Chicago Press.

Two case studies of new private trade migration of West Africans to Paris and New York City.

Note

1 I thank the editor Suresh Canagarajah for inviting and challenging me with this topic, and for patience and understanding when I tackled it. Historians Anshan Li, Pal Nyiri, and Tu Huynh and applied linguists Kelleen Toohey, Elizabeth Miller and Angel Lin provided invaluable feedback to earlier versions. All errors and omissions are mine.

References

Adler, M.K. (1977). *Pidgins, Creoles and Lingua Francas: A Sociolinguistic Study.* Hamburg: Buske.

Ansaldo, U., Mathews, S. and Smith, G. (2012). China coast pidgin: Texts and contexts. In U. Ansaldo (ed.), *Pidgins and Creoles in Asia* (pp. 60–90). Amsterdam and Philadelphia: John Benjamins.

Bakker, P. and Matras, Y. (2013). Introduction. In P. Bakker and Y. Matras (eds.), *Contact Languages: A Comprehensive Guide* (pp. 1–14). Berlin: Mouton de Gruyter.

Benson, J. (1985). Hawking and peddling in Canada, 1867–1914. *Histoire Sociale – Social History* XVIII(35): 75–83.

Billig, M. (1995). *Banal Nationalism.* London: Sage.

Bodomo, A. (2010). The African trading community in Guangzhou: An emerging bridge for Africa–China relations. *The China Quarterly* 203: 693–707.

Clark, G. (2010). *African Market Women: Seven Life Stories from Ghana.* Bloomington: Indiana University Press.

Cohen, A. (1971). Cultural strategies in the organization of trading diasporas. In Claude Meillassoux (ed.), *The Development of Indigenous Trade and Markets in West Africa* (pp. 266–281). Oxford: Oxford University Press.

Cohen, R. (2008). *Global Diaspora: An Introduction* (2nd ed.). London and New York: Routledge.

Constable, O.R. (2003). *Housing the Stranger in the Mediterranean World: Lodging, Trade, and Travel in Late Antiquity and the Middle Ages.* New York: Cambridge University Press, 2003.

Coupland, N. (2001). Sociolinguistic theory and social theory. In N. Coupland, S. Sarangi and C.N. Candlin, C.N. (eds.), *Sociolinguistics and Social Theory* (pp. 1–26). Harlow: Pearson Education.

Curtin, P.D. (1984). *Cross-cultural Trade in World History.* Cambridge: Cambridge University Press.

Dobler, G. (2009). Oshikango: The dynamics of growth and regulation in a northern Namibian boom town. *Journal of Southern African Studies* 35(1): 115–131.

Edwards, J. (2012). *Multilingualism: Understanding Linguistic Diversity.* London and New York: Continuum.

Ellwood, W. (2010). *The No-nonsense Guide to Globalization*. Oxford: BTL.
Ferguson, J. (2006). *Global Shadows: Africa in the Neoliberal World Order*. Durham: Duke University Press.
Green, C. (2012). "Outbound China and the Global South: New entrepreneurial immigrants in the Eastern Caribbean." *IDEAZ Journal*, Special Issue: From Unipolar to Multipolar: The Remaking of Global Hegemony 10–12(2012–2014): 24–44.
Han, H. (2013). Individual grassroots multilingualism in Africa Town in Guangzhou: The role of states in globalization from below. *International Multilingual Research Journal* 7(1): 83–97.
Han, H. (2014). *"China shops" in Oshikango: Grassroots Multilingualism at the Namibia-Angola Border in Globalization*. Invited colloquium, the University of Arizona, Tucson, AZ.
Han, H. (2015). *Understanding Race and Intersectionality in China-Africa Interactions*. Asian Studies in Africa conference, Accra, Ghana.
Haugen, H.Ø. (2012). Nigerians in China: A second state of immobility. *International Migration* 50(2): 65–80.
Haugen, H.Ø. and Carling, J. (2005). On the edge of the Chinese diaspora: The surge of Baihuo business in an African city. *Ethnic and Racial Studies* 28(4): 639–662.
Heller, M. (1999). *Linguistic Minority and Modernity: A Sociolinguistic Ethnography*. London and New York: Longman.
Heller, M. (2007). *Bilingualism: A Social Approach*. London: Palgrave.
Hopkins, A.G. (1973). *An Economic History of West Africa*. New York: Columbia University Press.
Howard, M.C. (2012). *Transnationalism in Ancient and Medieval Societies: The Role of Cross-border Trade and Travel*. Jefferson, NC: McFarland.
Hüsken, T. and Klute, G. (2010). Emerging forms of power in two African borderlands a theoretical and empirical research outline. *Journal of Borderlands Studies* 25(2): 107–121.
Kabane, H., Kabane, R. and Tietze, A. (1958). *The Lingua Franca in the Levant: Turkish Nautical Terms of Italian and Greek Origin*. Urbana: University of Illinois Press.
Lan, S. (2014). State regulation of undocumented African migrants in China: A multi-scalar analysis. *Journal of Asian and African Studies* 50(3): 289–304.
Lattimore, O. (1962). *Studies in Frontier History: Collected Papers 1928–1958*. London: Oxford University Press.
Li, Z., Xue, D., Michael, L. and Brown, A. (2008). The African enclave of Guangzhou: A case study of Xiaobeilu." *Acta Geographica Sinica* 63(2): 207–218.
Light, I. and Bonacich, E. (1988). *Immigrant Entrepreneurs: Koreans in Los Angelos 1965–1982*. Berkeley, CA: California University Press.
Lin, E. (2014). Big fish in a small pond": Chinese migrant shopkeepers in South Africa. *International Migration Review* 48(1): 181–215.
Lyons, M., Brown, A. and Li, Z. (2013). ASR forum: Engaging with African informal economies. *African Studies Review* 56(3): 77–100.
MacGaffey, J. and Bazenguissa-Ganga, R. (2000). *Congo-Paris: Transnational Traders on the Margins of the Law*. Oxford: James Currey; Bloomington: Indiana University Press.
Mathews, G. (2011). *Ghetto at the Center of the World: Chungking Mansions, Hong Kong*. Chicago: University of Chicago Press.
Mathews, G., Ribeiro, G.L. and Vega, C.A., eds. (2012). *Globalization from Below: The World's Other Economy*. London: Routledge.
McNamee, T. (2012). *Africa in Their Words: A Study of Chinese Traders in South Africa, Lesotho, Botswana, Zambia and Angola*. Johannesburg, South Africa: The Brenthurst Foundation.
Mechlinski, T. (2010). Towards an approach to borders and mobility in Africa. *Journal of Borderlands Studies* 25(2), 94–106.
Meillassoux, C. (1971). Introduction. In Claude Meillassoux (ed.), *The Development of Indigenous Trade and Markets in West Africa* (pp. 3–86). Oxford: Oxford University Press.
Nyiri, P. (2003). Chinese migration to Eastern Europe. *International Migration* 41: 239–265.

Nyíri, P. (2013). Investors, managers, brokers, and culture workers: How the "new" Chinese are changing the meaning of Chineseness in Cambodia. *Cross-Currents: East Asian History and Culture Review* 1(2): 369–397.

Parkvall, M. and Bakker, P. (2013). Pidgins. In P. Bakker and Y. Matras (eds.), *Contact Languages: A Comprehensive Guide* (pp. 15–64). Berlin: Mouton de Gruyter.

Pophiwa, N. (2010). Mobile livelihoods – The players involved in smuggling of commodities across the Zimbabwe-Mozambique border. *Journal of Borderlands Studies* 25(2): 65–76.

Prashad, V. (2012). *The Poorer Nations: A Possible History of the Global South*. New York: Verso.

Siegel, J. (2010). Pidgins and creoles. In N. Hornberger and S.L. McKay (eds.), *Sociolinguistics and Language Education* (pp. 232–262). Toronto: Multilingual Matters.

Stoller, P. (2002). *Money Has No Smell: The Africanization of New York City*. Chicago: University of Chicago Press.

Strickrodt, S. (2001). A neglected source for the history of Little Popo: The Thomas Miles papers ca. 1789–1796. *History in Africa* 28: 293–330.

Tagliacozzo, E. and Chang, W.-C. (2011). *Chinese Circulations: Capital, Commodities, and Networks in Southeast Asia*. Durham: Duke University Press.

Thomas, E. H. (1935). *Chinook: A History and Dictionary of the Northwest Coast Trade Jargon*. Portland, OR: Metropolitan Press.

Thomason, S. (2003). The journal ten years later. *Journal of Pidgin and Creole Languages* 18(2): 267–272.

Tryon, D. T. and Charpentier, J.-M. (2004). *Pacific Pidgins and Creoles: Origins, Growth and Development*. Berlin and New York: Mouton de Gruyter.

Vigouroux, C. (2013). Informal economy and language practice in the context of migrations. In A. Duchene, M. Moyer and C. Roberts (eds.), *Language, Migration and Social Inequalities: A Critical Sociolinguistic Perspective on Institutions and Work* (pp. 225–247). Bristol: Multilingual Matters.

Wang, G. (1992). *China and the Chinese Overseas*. Singapore: Times Academic Press.

Wang, G. (1998/1958). *The Nanhai Trade: The Early History of Chinese Trade in the South China Sea*. Singapore: Times Academic Press.

15
Migrations, religions, and social flux

Paul Badenhorst and Sinfree Makoni

Introduction

Identity is eternally unstable. Identities alternate, transcend, and (re)emerge. Occasionally, however, they fall into stasis. The tension inherent in identity then is a struggle between *belonging* and *becoming* (see Badenhorst 2015), and this struggle is perhaps best demonstrated through the organic phenomenon of migration and the manner it throws identities into question. Home, *the desire for rootedness and stability*, or belonging, is a notion that only the uprooted can deeply comprehend, writes Wallace Stegner (1971), and so it is for good reason that contemporary discussion on the relationship between migration, language, and religion consistently focuses on this triad as resource for the sustenance of both minority migrant identity, belonging, community, and cultural values (Warner and Wittner 1998; Hagan and Ebaugh 2003; Levitt 2003; Williams 2008; Vàsquez and Knott 2014) as well as emergent, expanded forms of social becoming. In the localized safe spaces of church, mosque, and temple, new immigrants find the support of networking relationships where life skills, stories, and existential narratives of faith are exchanged at times and reinterpreted at others. Shared social practices also come to serve as a means of *belonging* while *becoming* in the liminal space occupied by the skilled migrant worker, retiree, or economic or political refugee: those generally seeking an anticipated *good life* out of own accord (Bakewell 2008), or – as will become apparent in the ensuing case studies – both those who migrate out of free choice with an intent to serve as well as those who have been relocated by force. Yet, can the religious beliefs and practices of migrants – 'religions on the move' (Adogame, Gerloff, and Hock 2008: 1) – be demonstrated to exercise larger long-term historical effects upon the socio-political landscapes of those host territories within which migrants settle and, if so, what role does language as mobile resource (Blackledge and Creese, this volume) play in this process? This chapter asserts that the religious belief of the migrant serves as a 'host' for the transport of embedded ideologies that have historically transformed the societies into which the migrant has settled.

Furthermore, this study adopts a rhizomatic (Deleuze and Guattari 1987) lens towards engaging with the complex historical trajectories of discourse and discursive identities as these fray out relative to multiplicities inherent in discussions on the conceptual trinity of migration, language, and religion. Much like, for instance, the non-linear subterranean botanic root stem network of a bamboo plant or the complex branching structures of the Humongous Fungus in Oregon (see Schmitt and Tatum 2008), the concept of rhizomatic analysis allows for multiple non-hierarchical entry and exit points in data representation and interpretation.

Admittedly, words like *culture, language*, and *religion* that are used to describe particular instances of social phenomena as though these can be represented in static monochrome are characteristic of academic practices of categorization that often construct the very categories they claim to be studying, leading in many cases to the denigration and separation of populations over time (Brubaker 2002). Such categories are at their most basic out of odds with the fluid, molecular emphasis of rhizomatic analysis which works instead to view social phenomena outside of their bounded semiotic, representational contexts. Furthermore, this chapter argues that the history of migration is itself sine qua non to the historical social export, reproduction, and expansion of languages and religious worldviews. Migration exerts influence upon the non-binary groupings of language and religion, religion upon migration and language, and language upon religion and migration. Each of these co-constitutive conceptual units is, in turn, pregnant with political content. Here, the term *political* comprises the broad realm of decisions about our life on earth for which we are responsible (Park 2013: 3), as Žižek describes, and which we enact through particular social practices 'as carriers of routinized, over-subjective complexes of bodily movements, of forms of interpreting, knowing how and wanting and of the usage of things' (Reckwitz 2002: 259). Hence, even the statement *I am not political* becomes a political statement – apathetic perhaps, but never apolitical. The political then cannot be detached from the co-constitutive elements of religious faith, creed, and practice that are themselves hallmarks of *the stories we live by* (Van Noppen 2011). Briefly stated, the dichotomy between religious belief, on the one hand, and ideology, on the other, is misleading. The migrant imports concurrent political ideologies of economy, socialization, and identity-based organization to new territories where these, historically, have often been absorbed en masse through modes of religious coercion, proselytization, mobilization, hybridization, and commodification. This is a particularly salient point since, whereas contemporary insight rightly recognizes that the 'movement of people into societies that offer a better way of life [or perhaps the hope of an *easier* life] is a more powerful driver of cultural evolution than conflict and conquest' (Richerson and Boyd 2008), it should not go unnoticed that religion often serves as a primary accompanying ideological resource for the migrant, and such ideology relies on the application of particular hermeneutical interpretations within the socio-cultural landscape within which the migrant settles. In particular, this study will focus on two instances of the broader migratory export-cum-import of socio-political ideologies embedded in the interplay between religion and language: Christian missionary migration to Korea and its connection with the growth of an independence movement under Japanese colonialism, and coerced Malay Muslim slave migration to South Africa and its ideological role in shaping the historical socio-political landscape.

Overview

In 2011, international migration involved some 215 million people – equivalent to three percent of the world's population – so that if the international migrant population were to be counted as a whole it would constitute the fifth largest country on earth comprising Christians (forty-nine percent), Muslims (twenty-seven percent), Hindus (five percent), Buddhists (three percent), Jews (two percent), and the categories 'Other' and 'Unaffiliated' four percent and nine percent respectively (Connor and Tucker 2011: 986, 992). Here, *international migrant* refers to 'someone who is currently residing in a country other than their country of birth for a period of 1 year or longer' (Connor and Tucker 2011: 987). Interestingly, the religious destinations of migrants often match countries indirectly associated with the particular religious group: the leading destination for Christian migrants is the United States, whereas Muslim, Hindu, and Jewish migrants more often, though not exclusively, settle in Saudi Arabia, India, and Israel respectively (Connor and Tucker 2011: 995). Of course, reasons of practical efficacy aside, such broad religious categories obscure the tremendous variability among the migrant religious so that the term *Christian* not only hides the distinction between Protestant, Catholic, and Orthodox but also the distinction between, for instance, Protestants who are Pentecostal, African Initiated, Methodist, Anglican, Reformed, Restoration, Baptist, Lutheran, Seventh-Day Adventist, and Charismatic. Also missing in such broad categorization is a sense of the subjective intensity that potentially informs religion as a concrete, life-organizing framework. In this regard, then, it is important to keep in mind that while we may refer to religious groups as ideal types of approximate commonality (Weber 1978), for purposes related to descriptive efficacy they are in fact highly complex, amorphous, unstable social phenomena in which religious subjectivities exist on a continuum that ranges from nominal membership to life-transforming modes of personal devotion, as well as from having an identity ascribed through the manner in which one's origin is often read irrespective of origin. Likewise, *religion* as another moot term – especially in its relationship to language (see Darqueness and Vandenbussche 2011) – is a highly complex concept (see Punyani 2005) that is not altogether transparent, and the stigma it bears as a colonial technology of domination – a theme that will be discussed in the next section – only adds to the need of its semantic interrogation.

Critical issues and ongoing debates

The word *religion* is imbued with a plurality of ideological forces. For this very reason Chidester (2013) – referring to one such ideological effect – heeds:

> As a colonial term, the very word, "religion," must also be the focus of critical research, interrogating the term's colonial productions and deployments against the background of its imperial aspirations.
>
> *(pp. 91–92)*

Historically, language – in the form of culturally exclusive interpretations of scripture – was seized on by the colonial migrant (see Schreier, Eberle, and Perez, this volume) in the attempt to reduce the religion of the 'savage' colonized *other* to the realm of superstition (Chidester 1996). Part of the resulting 'civilizing' enterprise – especially among missionaries migrants – was to embark on linguistic research, corpus planning, and codification of the languages of the colonized in order to both translate religious text and train 'native' converts in both missionary activity and as civil servants. These practices, in turn, exercised profound influence over the resulting description of African linguistic structures and the delimitation of linguistic boundaries that were, for instance, rife with representations lacking in social deixis – stereotypes. Additionally, such reductionism led to the imposition of linguistic categories of named languages that fostered the socially constructed emergence of seemingly variegated *ethnicities* that completely obscured the vibrant fluid, multilingual practices that existed prior to colonization (Irvine 2008: 331, 338). Hence, the ethnicity of the colonized is in many instances – as the very by-product of European language ideology – a thoroughly performative identity category constructed, or invented (Ranger 1985; Mudimbe 1988), by the colonial observer through its very act of naming. This is also true, by extension, of those *language* boundaries that come to be ascribed both to and over the ethnic *other* (Makoni 2003). In other words, linguistic utterances construct the very world they appear to arise from (see Austin 1962; Butler 1990; Loxley 2007). With reference to its religious context, Van Noppen (2011) articulates this historical tendency as a mimetic fallacy in which the full conceptual, lexical, or syntactic structure of the verbal representation is projected onto the colonized subject being described, leading to inferences which foster oppressive, disparate structures of relating. Here, one need only recall the role of the Dutch Reformed Church in perpetuating utterances of white supremacy in both pre-apartheid (Elphick 2012) and apartheid South Africa (Ritner 1967) white public schools through, among others, the daily recitation of *your will be done on earth as it is in heaven* (Matt. 6:10) and the national anthem of the apartheid state – *Die Stem van Suid Afrika [The Call of South Africa]* – as well as the structures of exclusion, domination, and dehumanization these in turn affected (Goldberg 2009: 292–294). In more recent times this construction of ethnicity as a linguistically mediated variable may be implicated in the xenophobia that migrants as humans objectified often experience – as again in the example of South Africa – when their accents and language forms mark them as 'outsiders' (Hopstock and De Jager 2011: 121), and predominantly so if they are people of color elsewhere in the world (Hansen 2014: 286).

Alternatively, however, and in direct context to religious traditions as global referents, language is not only used to impose meaning *upon* – language often serves as a resource to negotiate meaning *between* (see Tovares and Kamwangamalu in this volume; *The Sociology of Language and Religion: Change, Conflict and Accommodation* edited by Tope Omoniyi; *Explorations in the Sociology of Language and Religion* by Tope Omoniyi and Joshua Fishman). For instance, Fishman (1989; see Spolsky 2003; Rosowsky 2006, 2008) draws attention to the role of religious classicals – or liturgical literacies such as the classical Arabic of the Qur'an – in preserving community identity across national and migratory shifts so that Arabic largely still maintains its intimate tie to religion (see Omoniyi 2006: 133) compared with the predominant post-1611/King James Bible secularization of English and its ascendance to becoming the language of global capitalist flows. Significantly then, language constitutes 'a living thing with built in resources enabling it to reflect various identities' (Chew 2014: 61) centered on favored practices and values, and especially so in contexts where language choice is a pliable resource from which multilingual social agents can draw. Here, the religious classical – rather than being an ancient, static text – serves as a flexible, dynamic linguistic resource for performative identity acts (Rosowsky 2012). Sikand (2003), in turn, highlights the practice whereby communities scattered across the subcontinent refuse categorization as 'Hindu' or 'Muslim' by freely borrowing from diverse oral and written traditions in order to create their own understanding of the world. Alternatively, Landau (2009) finds that migrants from inner-city religious communities in South Africa draw on rhetorical linguistic strategies based on a variegated language as a means towards tactical citizenship that makes claims to certain forms of moral superiority while also positioning them in an ephemeral, unrooted manner enabling of temporary escape from localized social and political obligations and discrimination. For instance, migrants from the Democratic Republic of Congo, Somalia, and Mozambique often brand citizens from the host nation with the same flaws levied against them – dishonesty, violence, and vectors of disease – and regularly defer to self-identifying monikers like being *African* (as a means of circumventing their exclusion from being South African) as well as being part of a larger global religious community. Such stance taking, in turn, occurs dialogically to the extent that the 'stancetaker's words derive from, and further engage with, the words of those who have spoken before' (Du Bois 2007: 140). Adogame (2007) discusses a similar phenomenon in context to members of second African diaspora churches (the first African diaspora being descendants of those who survived the Middle Passage) in the United States who self-identify as African American upon arrival but later switch religious affiliation to new African churches for reasons ranging from 'perceived cultural differences and different mentalities to accusations of arrogance, mutual suspicion, and lack of trust' (p. 28), leading to a seismic divide between African American and second African diaspora congregations. Unfortunately, in this instance, language is invoked in a manner that polarizes the black community with the circulation of slurs like 'primitive people' (in reference to second African diaspora members) and 'sugarcane people' (a reference to African Americans) (Adogame 2007: 28–29) – a phenomenon complicated no doubt by the reality that some African descendant people can make immediate connections to specific regions whereas others have no traceable connection to their African roots (Okpalaoka 2014).

Interestingly, these reactionary phenomena suggest that diaspora communities themselves over time develop particular fields of habitus as a structural means through which ongoing socialization occurs – through language and shared discourse. Drawing from Bourdieu (1990), *habitus* may be defined as:

> systems of durable, transposable dispositions, structured structures predisposed to function as structuring structures, that is, as principles which generate and organize practices and representations that can be objectively adapted to their outcomes without presupposing a conscious aiming at ends or an express mastery of the operations necessary in order to attain them.
>
> *(p. 53)*

Verter (2003), in turn, perceives cultural production in and among religious communities as operating through the exchange of spiritual capital in which 'subcultural identity shapes religious taste' (p. 169) through 'unconscious processes of socialization' (p. 159). Of course, social positioning – and the ensuing cultural and linguistic practices grounded in habitus that emanate from it – does not exclude the potential for discursive religious agents to gradually reconfigure the social status quo en masse over years or even generations by *jumping the scales* governing social mobility. Ultimately, human desire is unpredictable and multifaceted, giving rise to unpredictable lines of flight (Deleuze and Guattari 1987) – emergent historical trajectories of new becoming that correspond with the Spinozian idea of *conatus*: that productive, impulsive, and essential human striving and perseverance through which change emerges. At this point it is vital to emphasize again that religious subjectivities – as identification-based expressions of desire – exist on a continuum ranging from nominal membership to life-transforming modes of personal devotion so that qualification of being of a particular religion, in this chapter at least, has more to do with belonging to a community as identity-based resource than solely with variables such as deference to orthodoxy or piety. To assume that signifiers like Muslim, Jew, Christian, Hindu, or Buddhist, for instance, refer to fixed ideations of the signified is to neglect that intra-group disagreements and conflicts within each of these broad categories demonstrate a break in the Saussurean chain of signification that post-structuralist linguistics and philosophy has uncovered (see Deleuze and Guattari 1987). In other words, linguistic designations are as unstable as the identities they purport to represent.

In the section that follows, brief attention will be paid to two examples demonstrating the profound potential for religious migrant communities – in their interplay with language and its instability – to effect gradual historic change within host societies: the South Asian Muslim slave diaspora in colonial South Africa beginning in 1654 and American Protestant missionaries to Korea in 1884. It should be noted that such discussion is initiated due to the relative dearth of examinations centering on the particular intersection of migration, language, and religion as forms of social practice. Interestingly, these two case studies break somewhat with the aspiration-based *better life* analysis of migration hitherto tendered, further demonstrating the complexity engrained in global human movement. In the first case study, the coercive export of Malay Muslim slaves as economic commodities (see Klooster 2009) from the Dutch colonies of maritime Southeast Asia to the Cape of Good Hope (see Worden 2009) is explored. Here it should be remembered that the institution of slavery itself functioned as the dominant driver of colonizing capitalist economic growth (see Giliomee 2003: 90–94). Yet, far from being an account of victimhood void of agency, this account of forced migration uncovers the creative, vibrant emergence of new life, language, and culture (see Baderoon 2014). In the second example, a historical instance of missionaries as migrants is considered. Here, the oft-perceived secular/religious divide is collapsed through the example of Christian missionary-migrants to the Korean peninsula and the political transformation they helped facilitate under Japanese colonial occupation alongside the local Korean population. While the message of the evangelical missionaries often stressed the doctrine of salvation by grace through faith and the authority of the Bible as divine revelation, its uptake manifests the emergence of social resistance practices within Korean education circles as a precedent to a kind of liberation theology (see Havea 2013). The resultant anthropocentric emphasis upon political praxis and activism by the people on behalf of the poor and oppressed emerged at a point when the Christian language of suffering came to be accorded with the suffering of the nation itself (see Wielenga 2007: 63–64; Lee 2009).

Case study I: Islam, slave migration, and South Africa

Is the proposed synergistic formula *distance + isolation = accelerated socio-linguistic [ex]change* a historically tenable one? The Afrikaans language, for one, provides strong evidence that – in certain contexts – intra-global migratory movement brings along with it the potential for profound contact-based sociolinguistic (and ensuing sociopolitical) change (Kerswill 2006). Beginning with the arrival of the first Muslim political exiles from the Netherlands (1654), the Mardyckers – or free Malay Muslims – from Amboyna (1658), and Malay Muslim slaves from Southeast Asia (1700), and later in a second phase of immigration from the subcontinent (1860–1911), Dutch morphs into Afrikaans as slaves – some Malay Muslim and others indigenous Khoikhoi – communicate with both one another as well as with the European enslavers. Here, we find gradual language shift occurring through the intersecting variables of relocation and isolation relative to distance – the early Muslim slave and settler populations of the Cape found themselves far removed from their geographic points and communities of origin so that their respective languages underwent steady diffusion through the very discontinuity brought on by migration. Afrikaans, then, viewed historically, and in context to the sociolinguistic interplay between languages and cultures, emerges as a pidgin and – later – a creole. Interestingly, in spite of the popular colonial-period European view of the Muslim world as defined by 'the slave trade . . . polygamous practices, the complete absence of agency' and Islam threatening 'to overrun the African colonies and then all of Europe' (Habermas 2012: 132), the pervasive racial and cultural tensions that characterized the Cape did not result in the ethnolinguistic saliency of Dutch – and deference to it on the basis of prestige – that Fishman (1999) grounds in both the presence of conflict and a high degree of perceived cultural difference. Rather, in the case of Afrikaans, it was 'the dangerous physical proximity of domestic slavery as a site of cultural invention' (Baderoon 2014: 49) that led to the fluid, plurilinguistic intermingling of the Dutch of the colonial settlers, the languages of the original Khoikhoi indigenous populations, and the Malayu, Javanese, and Creole Portuguese languages of the first slaves (Stell 2007: 92), and predominantly so through biological and cultural miscegenation. It is noteworthy, for instance, that the first Afrikaans texts were written in Jawi Arabic script (Tayob 2002: 28; Jappie 2012). Hence, the perception of Afrikaans as an essentially *European* triadic product of Dutch-French-German settler heritage or Germanic language (see Hartmann and Molnárfi 2006) needs to be challenged, for as Giliomee (2003) reminds,

> During the first fifty to seventy years of the settlement, slaves and Khoikhoi servants had the greatest hand in the development of the restructured Dutch. In the course of the eighteenth century both burghers [settler inhabitants] and their servants, in interaction with each other, took the restructuring further.
>
> *(p. 53)*

Afrikaans, fundamentally, is an ethnolinguistic product of converging and alternating processes of forced and voluntary migration, or as Giliomee (2003) frames it: 'the shared cultural creation . . . of Europeans and non-Europeans, of whites and blacks, masters and slaves' (p. 53). A mere three decades ago Afrikaans was still being regarded within the apartheid state as the cultural heritage of the white European, willfully ignorant perhaps of Afrikaans' intimate roots in the interaction of settlers with Malay Muslim and indigenous populations. Such misperception likely has its roots in the construction of an Afrikaner nationalist consciousness through deference to Afrikaans as the *taal van ons volk*, or language of our people, in the two Boer republics in the mid- to late 18th century – a reaction to the increased likelihood of British colonial encroachment. As an aside, Afrikaans as a language in context to British colonial usurpation of the two Boer republics itself underwent an instance of migration when a group of white Afrikaners – unwilling to contend with the British takeover of the two Boer republics after surrender in the Anglo-Boer War (1899–1902) – left South Africa for Argentina. Today, their Afrikaner cultural and linguistic practices from a bygone era endure, albeit in a form that appears to be gradually waxing extinct in the presence of a dominant Spanish national discourse (see *The Boers at the End of the World* 2014). This being said, ultimately, it was the Malay Muslim and Khoikhoi slaves who appropriated the language of their Dutch colonial masters for their own use by mixing it with their respective linguistic repertoires as a form of translingual practice (Canagarajah 2013: 6–7), leading – much later through continued iteration – to the birth of the Afrikaans language (Wilemse and Dangor 2012). Unfortunately, with the continued development of a number of colloquial varieties of Afrikaans also came that disparity wrought by the privileging of certain varieties with greater degrees of symbolic capital and power (Bourdieu 1991). The Afrikaans of the urban white was regarded as standard, whereas the Afrikaans of the Cape Coloured – a descendent of, among others, the Malay Muslim and indigenous populations – was considered a simple and unsophisticated patois of lesser class: *kombuis Afrikaans*, or kitchen Afrikaans (Adhikari 2005: 16). During apartheid the accent of the Cape Coloured further worked to reify her as a non-white, raced subject who – along with black people – often had the violent and derogatory noun *kaffir* (implying non-white) thrust upon them. Interestingly, the word itself is an appropriation of the Arabic root form for *closed* (a heart closed off to truths valued in Islam) and is by extension linked to the ideas of *non-Muslim* and *infidel* historically used among East African Muslims (Baderoon 2014: 29–34) and popularized during the time of the Arab slave trade (Vernet 2009: 52). Such appropriation, in turn, subverted the original religious denotation of the word, imbuing it instead with a racially dehumanizing signification that served to consolidate white supremacy through allusion to its supposed inferior phenotypic opposite (see Said 1979).

Additionally, while the concept of reverse acculturation (Kim and Park 2009) – or the means whereby a minority member introduces her heritage culture to the dominant culture – can account for the absorption of, for instance, Muslim 'Cape Malay' slave cuisine and culinary vocabulary into the household culture of the Cape enslavers, much of the cultural exchange in the Cape likewise took on the form of cultural exploitation (Rogers 2006), whereby everyday aspects of non-white slave culture were harnessed due to their exoticness 'without substantive reciprocity, permission, and/or compensation' (p. 477) in a phenomenon hooks (1992) broadly refers to as *eating the other* – a phenomenon whereby Otherness 'is offered as a new delight'; a 'spice, seasoning that can liven up the dull dish that is mainstream white culture' (p. 21). For this reason, a large number of Afrikaans culinary-related terms and words originate from the Cape Malays themselves. This does not go to say that the non-white slave population did not appropriate any cultural resources from the slave owners – only that the white appropriation of slave culture takes on the form of commodity 'in which the brutal history of slavery is elided' (see Baderoon 2014: 47).

Yet, the social significance of Muslim migration to South Africa goes beyond discussion of the emergence of particular forms of language and culture (for an exhaustive bibliography on the legacy of Islam in South Africa, see Schrijver 2006), since Islam has also exercised a definitive influence over the historical political *becoming* of South Africa. Since the significance of Muslim participation on the plural South African social and political landscape has largely been occluded due to race-based ideological expediency facilitative of domination leading to its inferior recognition by the state compared to Christianity, the Muslim experience of and fight against prejudice and white domination should be avowed. And while mainstream Muslim participation in the political landscape of South Africa only began to emerge in the 20th century, this emergence should be read against the background of Asian descendent Muslims' faith not receiving equal recognition to that of Christianity, as well as the fact that while Asian descendent Muslims had made profound cultural and economic contributions to the republic, they were still not accorded the position of political equality and representation. Prior to the death of Steve Biko in 1977, for instance, Imam Abdullah Haron, prominent member of the Muslim Judicial Council, died in police custody – an event in 1969 that would further raise political consciousness among Muslims in South Africa. Further events such as the widespread Muslim condemnation of the 20th Anniversary Republic celebrations in 1981, the Muslim rejection of the Apartheid Tricameral Parliament in 1984 through deference to tenets within the Qu'ran and Sunnah, and the subsequent alliance of the Call of Islam movement to both the United Democratic Front (UDF) and the African National Congress (ANC) anti-apartheid liberation movements (Mahida 1993: 127–128, 130, 143–144) all draw attention to the eventual potency and influence of Islamic religious thought which itself germinated at the tip of Africa as a seemingly insignificant, albeit conspicuous, minority religious discourse. These resistant practices, in turn, correspond with a liberation-based means of theologizing characteristic of 'solidarity in the struggle, options for the poor, and resistance against oppressive powers' (Havea 2013: 192), and for which faith often serves as a valuable resource.

Admittedly, allusion to such instances of the Muslim South African call for 'full citizenship rights . . . extended to all' (Mahida 1993: 121) does not suggest that conservative, politically passive Muslim reactions towards apartheid – such as the latter stance adopted by the Muslim Judicial Council (Mahida 1993: 67) – were not also present (Moosa 1989). Yet, such exceptions need to be viewed in context to the fact that Muslims responded to apartheid ideology as participants in iterate forms of Islamic faith and practice and not as that monolithic whole implied by the term *Islam*. More recently, it is also through both Cape and Indian Muslim advocacy – rooted in ethical Islamic imperatives (see Quddus 2005) – that the South African government has taken a very public stance in favor of the Palestinian cause against Israeli Zionist occupation (Mandivenga 2000). Interestingly, the ongoing evolution of the South African social landscape through Muslim migration continues via the arrival of, among others, Senegalese Tijaniyya Muslims who are bringing about a platform for integrating the traditional, wealthier Asian Muslim populations with local Black Muslims who converted to Islam in the 1970s and 1980s (Literas 2009) – a phenomenon deserving deeper future analysis.

Case study II: Christianity, missionary migration, and Korea

Another example of the profound potential for diverse religious migrant communities – in their interplay with language and its instability – to effect gradual cultural and political change within host societies takes us to the Korean peninsula. The influence of various forms of migrant Christian belief and practice upon the socio-political becoming of South Korea – an anomaly in East Asia relative to other nations also once firmly rooted in Confucian orthodoxy (Yu 1996: 3) – presents a prime example of the syncretism of the Christian Gospel with local culture in a phenomenon referred to by Niebuhr as 'Christ and Culture' (2001). Here, cultural aspirations come to be mediated in accordance with the interpreted message of the Gospel, and in the case of Korea this often implied the direct correlation between the fight for liberation during the period of Japanese colonialism and the Christian message of salvation. Such appropriation of Scripture corresponds with Havea's (2013) discussion of a contextual reading and hermeneutics of Scripture in which borrowed texts are made relevant to a new context.

Since the arrival of Western Protestant Evangelical missionaries – as a type of religious migrant who was neither enslaved, nor seeking a *better life* per se – on the Korean peninsula in 1884, Christianity has become associated with nationalism through its predominant historical support of nationalists and the enlightenment campaign (Clark 1989; Yi 1996: 39–72). Here, one finds the contextualization of the Christian Gospel on the part of the missionaries, and its re-appropriation among Koreans as a material and symbolic anti-imperialist resource. Christianity has also remained relatively analogous to a national reverence for the Korean creation-of-a-nation myth, *Tangun – the grandson of heaven* – that was itself intensified through nationalist discourse during the period of liberation (Schmid 2002: 192–198). The present-day Korean national anthem, for instance, bears witness to this syncretic relationship in its second line where the word for 'God' – stemming from a shared root yet implying different nuances – can interchangeably be pronounced as either *hananim* (하나님: denoting a Christian theist concept) or *haneunim* (하느님: denoting a folkloric, pantheist concept related to foundational mythological narrative of Tangun).

Also, the Samil – or March First – Independence Movement of 1919 was one of the most enduring Korean nationalist events primarily orchestrated (though not exclusively) by Christians against Japanese colonialism, and in this regard the church played a decisive role as one of the few officially recognized organized communities possessing the ability to facilitate mobilization (Park 2003). Private Christian schools established by missionaries – such as

Osan High School, whose teachers and students played an immutable role in the Korean liberation movement (Park 2004: 521; see Kang 2001: 46, 87–98) – also served as sites of resistance towards Japanese colonialism and fostered a sense of Korean identity from the inculcation so characteristic of Japanese-run public schools (Kang 2001: 46, 87–88). Conversely, Koreans who converted to Christianity – through the activity of Protestant missionary migrants – would often migrate westward to study at American education institutions (Cha 2010: 26). An example of this trend is Yun Gil-jun – regarded as the first Korean to study in the West (Governor's Academy 2010) – who would later go on to become one of the foremost Korean independence activists and an advocate of the *Dongnip Hyeophoe* or Independence Club, which sought to 'preserve the independence of the nation through the spontaneous strengthening of the power of the Korean people' (Shin 2004a: 421). The relationship between the missionaries and Korean nationalists was therefore a symbiotic one, as each stood to benefit from the other. Additionally, many politically active foreign missionaries – like Homer Hulbert and Henry G. Appenzeller (Kale Yu 2011) – and their Korean nationalist proselytes-cum-(co)revolutionaries refused dualist separation of the spiritual from the secular, godly from the worldly, and peaceful from the militant leading to a form of resistance that co-equated spirituality, language, and materiality. Comments Clark (1989):

> There are unmistakable signs that the independence manifesto and other similar documents . . . were prepared at residences of the missionaries and in churches or hospitals . . . in collusion with these missionaries.
>
> *(p. 42)*

For this reason, the pacifist view of Korean religious leaders during the time of Japanese occupation and since needs to be challenged (Kale Yu 2011: 172). Of course, the aforementioned in no manner negates the existence of Protestant missionaries and Korean Christians (see Kang 2001: 102) who also opted to maintain a political position of supposed *apolitical* disengagement in obedience to the prescriptions of the Japanese authorities and their source country mission boards (Kale Yu 2011). At the same time, the phrase *Protestant missionary* itself needs to be made more complex relative to differences in the national (such as American, Canadian, and British) and denominational (Presbyterian, Anglican, and Pentecostal, for instance) identity affiliations and practices of the missionary migrants (Hamish Ion 1977).

Furthermore, the legacy of Christian missionary migrants in Korea, relative to the volatile socio-political local context at the time, also brought about increased calls among Koreans for the modernization, or *enlightenment*, of Korea (Lee 2004: 463–489). Later, Christian themes of victory and strength would be appropriated in the social Darwinist vision of the Korean Enlightenment thinkers who alluded to the Korean peninsula's historical *struggle* against its hostile expansionist and exploitative Japanese and Chinese neighbors. Here, the ideological assumptions of the missionaries' sending cultures undoubtedly took root, via the respective theologies of the missionaries and their hybrid uptake, in the cultural domains of the receiving culture (Lee 2006: 4). However, as a seeming paradox too, far from expressing outright rejection of foreign power, many Korean Enlightenment thinkers – especially prior to Japan's reoccupation of Korea in 1910 – stressed instead the coopting of foreign power in order to strengthen the Korean nation, and most notably so through trade (Lee 2004: 467) as well as deference to imported models of, among others, Western constitutional government and industrial development (Shin 2004a). Of course, appropriation of foreign culture does not imply its blind worship, and for this reason the Korean nationalist philosopher and independence activist Shin Chae-ho – following Japan's reoccupation of Korea – asserted that foreign culture 'should be imported with great discrimination, accepting only its merits so that national culture will continue to take the leading role' (Shin 2004b: 458).

Yet, one should not merely imagine that Christianity, as the legacy of Christian migrants, only worked towards the modernization of Korea. Rather, 'Christianity, in the course of building the enlightenment and the national spirit, also rediscovered *hangul*' (Yi 1996: 47) – the block-syllable alphabet of the Korean language. Through *Silhak*, a Korean philosophical approach that stressed the value of pragmatism, the foundational national quality of a shared Korean language was emphasized and intense research and planning of the Korean language commenced. By the late 1800s this resulted in a call for, among others, the formulation of a unified Korean grammar, compilation of a Korean dictionary, the exclusive use of *hangul*, and the horizontal transcription of *hangul* (Shin 2004a: 428). Latter thinkers, in turn, would position the Korean language itself as synonymous with the cultivation of an independent spirit (see Fishman 1999). Shin Chae-ho, for instance, pointed out 'the problem with Chinese characters lay more in the fact that they nurtured a disposition towards slavery than their difficulty to learn' (Shin 2004b: 458). Korean terms were also increasingly incorporated into the vocabulary of the church (Kim 2004), leading to the further development of a form of Christianity unique to the Korean peninsula.

Later, at a time when the Catholic clergy became especially active in the fight for political emancipation and democracy in South Korea, Korean Minjung (the masses/the people) Theology – largely a hybrid corollary of liberation theology and Millenarian Christian eschatology (Yi 1996) – would continue the anthropocentric hermeneutical association between the Gospel message and political emancipation during the military dictatorships of the 1960s, '70s, and '80s by incorporating the Korean concept of *han* (a nationally distributed emotion of grief arising from the shared burden of oppression) into Christian conscience and praxis. Significantly, it is during this Cold War period that a modernized, pro-American, anti-communist, conservative brand of Christianity also draws on the leitmotif of *han* and asserts itself alongside liberal Minjung thought in South Korea, and Christian churches experience a boom in membership. As Park (2003) ever so poignantly frames this ontological concept in a beautiful light and through allusion to migration, *han* has been

> internalized and inbred in the nature of Koreans through the tens of thousands of years of the pilgrimage in search of a new life as they advanced from the cold and gloomy mountains in Central Asia to the East, the place of sunrise, in the hopes of settling down on a bright, warm land for a bright, warm life.
>
> *(p. 525)*

As an aside, Park's (2003) ontogenetic description of migration from Central Asia to the Korean Peninsula coincides with the macro-Altaic view that understands the Korean language, along with Turkic, Mongolic, Tungusic, and Japanese, as belonging to a linguistic grouping of common origin (Norman 2009) – one believed to have taken root in the Altai mountains that run through present-day Mongolia and southern Siberia.

Back to the discussion of *han*, for one-time Osan schoolteacher and independence thinker, Ham Seok-heon, *han* – as linguistic form denoting national spirit – correlates well with *hananim* [God] and *hanul* [heaven] (Park 2003: 525). Opines Park: 'By placing *han* at the center . . . Ham could unite the national spirit and Christian faith' (2003: 526). Ultimately, for Ham, '[r]eligion causes historical change' (Park 2003: 549). It is for this reason – the preceding discussion – that the Korean churches have come to occupy such a conspicuous and dominant position across both the contemporary political field and architectural landscape of

South Korea. It is also perhaps for this reason that the association of Christianity with both the historical liberation movement and nationalism has led to its immense contemporary influence that is played out through a political split between a conservative majority who militate around the notion of nationalism and a liberal minority that calls for change (Kang 1997: 96–97), and especially so in context to the reunification of the two Koreas. In the section to follow, contemporary implications of the foregoing discussion will be discussed, while related possibilities – and questions – for future research in context to the intersection of language, migration, and religion will be explored.

Implications and future directions

The two case studies discussed in this chapter are located in radically different contexts from each other: the social positioning of the migrants (slaves/missionaries), their points of origin (East Asia/North America), and the constricting forces weighing upon them (Dutch colonial slavery/Japanese occupation), among others. Yet these case studies also present evidence that migrants exercise profound, ultimately unpredictable, highly complex/rhizomatic, and perhaps inevitable forms of social influence over those communities within which they settle. Such changes are not expressly contingent, for instance, upon the degree of influence exerted *over and against* from positions of domination, since migrant populations negotiate the political terrains they encounter through their own strategic social interactions. In this way, migrants affect profound forms of *becoming* over and in those spaces within which they struggle for *belonging*. Yet, the question needs to be posed: are we able to behold those chronotopic processes of socio-cultural shift and transformation that surround the intersection of migration, language, and religion – as discussed in the previous two historical examples of South Africa and the Korean peninsula – within the globalized confines of our contemporary day and age? Viewed rhetorically, this question certainly hints strongly in the affirmative.

Omoka (1974) insists that any study of missionaries that detaches itself from the mission-colonial continuum of domination, that is, that which does not place missionization activities into the colonial context can achieve only partial understanding. For this reason, too, Muzorewa (1990) calls for a moratorium on a Western theology of mission and the cultivation of an African theology of mission:

> Now is the time for Africans, who are a product of western missionary work, to reflect on what mission means for the church in Africa and what the church has done in Africa because of its mission.
>
> *(Muzorewa 1990: xiv)*

Havea (2013) concurrently draws attention to the need for a postcolonial hermeneutics that interrogates the working of colonialist powers within religious discourses and prescribes a contrapuntal approach in which dominant interpretations of scripture are read alongside contesting textual sources so as to bring about the undoing of contexts where dominant hermeneutics serves as the legitimizing tool of neo-colonial practice. Van Noppen (2011), in turn, introduces the concept of critical theolinguistics that works as a corollary of critical discourse analysis (Fairclough 1989; 1992) to analyze religious language as discourse that is assessed within a context of belief where its utterances are regarded as meaningful relative to unconscious assumptions and institutional practices directly or indirectly legitimizing of existing power relations (p. 28). Here, among others, religious metaphor and myth come to be reevaluated for the purposes of denouncing language that perpetuates modes of social exclusion and prejudice.

Conversely – and touching on a major outcome sprouting from rhizomatic analysis – while scholars interrogate theologies and theological languages that reify modes of domination through particular iterations of missionary migrant action, it is imperative to not only guard from interpreting all missionary activity through this lens but also to maintain respectful and sensitive attitudes towards the desires of social actors in receiving communities. For as Stambach (2010) reminds:

> The evangelical missionaries were right about one thing: the missionaries understood the value of religion for Africans while most academics (including anthropologists, they said) did not.
>
> *(p. 3)*

Likewise, and in context to the missionary-colonial continuum of domination, we would do well not to conflate the pre-colonial subject with a primitivist view of a natural human: a state of innocence and pre-enlightenment bliss ruptured at the historical moment when the *noble savage* comes into contact with the degenerate European missionary *man of culture*, and perhaps most popularly exemplified through the Tahiti-themed work of post-impressionist painter Paul Gauguin. The historical actions of mission-colonizer and subsequent means by which imported religious ideas and values have been taken up by (post)colonial social actors is one of radical discontinuity. Applied to the global colonial flow of Christianity and its uptake, Robbins (2007) articulates the need to deconstruct idealized historical continuity as follows:

> It is important to know how Christianity historically entered any given cultural setting, but in dwelling so often on the mission encounter we are in danger of making the past the whole story and thereby once again making Christianity as a lived culture in its own right disappear.
>
> *(p. 33)*

Religion as lived culture finds its expression, for instance, in the discussion tendered by Chew (2010), who elucidates the manner in which adolescent Singaporeans switch and defer to Christian – and Buddhist to a degree – metaphors associated with life and the journey towards a *better* future in English as opposed to traditional Taoist, Chinese dialect metaphors rooted in imagery of death. While the convergence of *Christianity* and *English* in this instance may be argued to strongly hint at the hegemony of Western values, the manner in which young people are drawing from these discursive resources in localized contexts for a host of personal and social reasons – accompanied by the desired outcome of benefit – should be accounted for as constituent of the process of change (aging and societal) leading to conflict (questioning of prior traditions and assumptions), morphing, in turn, to accommodation (deference to Christianity and English). Ultimately, here, we find the production of new, fluid forms of localization and global identification that transcend homogenization and imperialism (Pennycook 2007).

Merely interrogating the relationship between religion, migration, and language in context to asymmetrical structures of domination, as important as such endeavor is, only uncovers the structure of broader power relations without contending with the convoluted, often seemingly contradictory social positioning of agents who also manage to demonstrate profound levels of communal resilience (Wong 2015). Hence, future approaches would also do well to continue analyzing this phenomenon in context to those 'networks, webs, or arteries of circulation . . . in which religious discourses, practices, and associations have been both enabling and disabling' (Havea 2013: 91). Consider the history of Malay Muslim slave migrants in South Africa or the case of Korean converts of white American missionaries under Japanese occupation: enabling forms of identity often flourish in contexts of constraint and domination so that power – in line with Foucault (1979) – is everywhere; diffuse, and productive as much of resistance and life as it is of coercion and domination.

Another phenomenon that requires scrutiny is that of the international English language teaching profession and its widespread appropriation by missionaries. While foreign English language teachers often work in contexts where everyday issues of migration, religion, and language converge (see Stambach 2010; Wong, Kristjánsson, and Dörnyei 2013), it is also true that the missionary enterprise itself has – in many instances – become deeply enmeshed in the English-language teaching movement. Many missionaries – often lacking relevant language training and experience – acquire their visas by presenting themselves as language teachers within the host societies to which they relocate. Does this conflict of interests hold potential risk for the profession as a whole? Also, the fact that it is English – the first 'language of capitalism' (Holborow 1999), so to speak – as industry, and not Arabic, Chinese, or Hindi that is being taught around the globe (often in the guise of prescriptive, prestige-based Anglo-American forms) means that deeper understanding of the relationship between the spread of English and limited exposure to plural religious teacher voices among learners of English is warranted. Closely related to this concern, for instance, are the activities of the Summer Institute of Linguistics (SIL) in Mexico (see Barros 1995; Hartch 2005; Svelmoe 2008). While this missionary organization have been recognized by the likes of UNESCO for their efforts to preserve indigenous languages through study, documentation, and development, they have also been criticized for endangering the very indigenous languages they work to preserve through their missionary objective of changing the cultures within which they work. Remarks Canagarajah (2013):

> It is possible for dominant ideologies to resocialize people into monolingual practices and colonizing relationships. For this reason, critical intervention by informed scholars and committed teachers is always necessary.
>
> *(p. 202)*

Such intervention, I tender, should be an important concern of applied and socio-linguistics-related research in context to language, religion, and migration – an applied/socio-linguistics possessing a strong *ethical* edge – a position of ongoing questioning.

Additionally, there is evidence that within certain local contexts – Nigeria as a case in point – the intersection of religion and language, through the performative exercise of prayer, is bringing about a degree of peaceful social convergence through *competitive amity* (see Wicker 2015). Here, among others, a wider variety of liturgical languages (for instance, praise and thanksgiving) are being incorporated into shared prayer encounters across traditionally religious Muslim-Christian lines – a phenomenon that can be described as the intersection of multilingualism and its religious equivalent, multifaithism (Omoniyi 2006). How profuse is this phenomenon within shared migrant/host society contexts around the globe, and what potential does it hold for the utilization of language to facilitate peace (see De Matos 2005) across religious identities? Also, what can we learn from the emergence of particular languages as linguae francae – for instance, the use of a particular variety of Arabic in American mosques where Gulf Arab, North African, Indonesian, and local Muslim interlocutors are present – and the way in the phenomenon of a shared language potentially overrides ethnic and national differences in intra-religious migrant contexts?

Summary

This chapter has sought to productively challenge our approach to studying the intersections of language, migration, and religion, and asserts that the religious belief of the migrant serves as a 'host' for the transport of embedded ideologies that have historically transformed the societies into which the migrant has settled. The multiple case study approach provided discussion of the role of religion in the shaping of languages and language ideology (the case of Afrikaans) and in the crafting of political ideologies (the role of missionaries in challenging Japanese colonialism in Korea). Finally, these two case studies were employed to draw out important generalizations that can be applied to the study of the intersection of language, migration, and religion in other world contexts. Religion, rather than being separate from or void of ideology, is itself an ideological assemblage that accompanies the migrant wherever s/he moves and settles, and it is often from religious creed and practice that the future political, social, and economic shape of society begins to emerge.

Furthermore, religious identity does not exist isolated from other forms of identity-based affiliation and social practice. Rather, one's religious identity exists on a grid where the ongoing *becomings* of movement, flux, and potential (Massumi 2002) continuously collide. These collision points, in turn, form intersections where other coexisting affiliation-based identity categories such as gender, race, ethnicity, class, and sexual orientation coincide (see for instance Souza 2016) for a discussion on the intersection of religious, ethnic, and linguistic modes of identity and their relationship to migrant children's educational progress). Ultimately, 'all identities are lived and experienced as intersectional – in such a way that identity categories themselves are cut through and unstable' (Puar 2012: 52). Interestingly, though – the intersection of identities notwithstanding – social actors often appeal to religious discourse in an attempt to justify coexisting identity-based ideologies which they hold relative to, among others, gender, race, class, and nationality. Viewed in context to migratory flows, these religious discourses serve as the impetus behind ideological conflict, negotiation, and transformation in those societies within which diaspora communities settle, grow, and eventually (dis)integrate. Hence, the historical legacy of migration in this study proffers a view that extends from first-generation, primary religious diaspora immigrants to their secondary descendants in the present day, many of whom have moved to new cities or territories, thereby constituting a secondary religious diaspora (Frigerio 2004). This point is of particular salience since the larger social and political consequences of migration often only become apparent after decades, and in some cases, centuries.

At the center of such complex, rhizomatic historical transformation processes lies language as both an enacting and enacted-upon set of social practices – social practices that shape our contesting contemporary perspectives on class, race, ethnicity, gender, sexuality, species, and ethics while simultaneously shaping us. Language as an *enacting* force therefore stresses the performative (see Austin 1962; Butler 1990; Loxley 2007) dimension through which linguistic utterances construct the very world they appear to arise from. Language as *enacted upon*, on the other hand, implies the synergistic formula *distance + isolation = accelerated socio-linguistic (ex)change* whereby language itself is transformed through social and material contingencies and realignments most notably, though not exclusively, facilitated by migratory movements.

The examples of Christian missionary migration to Korea and its connection with the growth of an independence movement under Japanese colonialism as well as South Asian Muslim slave migrants to South Africa and their ideological role in co-shaping its contemporary socio-political landscape, in turn, have attempted to demonstrate how seemingly minority migrant religious values and language practices exercise profound effect upon the emergent *becoming* of receiving societies. Ultimately, it is asserted that, far from simply being a force for either good or evil, religion – and the religion of the migrant in particular – is a vibrant assemblage of ideological values and beliefs that unsettle and challenge traditional social norms and practices. Here, rather than being a matter of *heavenly or not*, religious discourses are themselves reflective of human values that are intimately related to micro-instances of human aspiration relative to the materiality of experience in broader social contexts.

Related topics

Translanguaging in mobility
Superdiversity and language
New orientations to identity in mobility
Migration trajectories
Settler migration and settler varieties
Intersections of necessity and desire in migration research: queering the migration story

Further reading

Darqueness, J. and Vandenbussche, W. (2011). Language and religion as a sociolinguistic field of study: Some introductory notes. *Sociolinguistica*, 25, 1–11.

A research article that reviews the development of discussions surrounding language and religion in sociolinguistics and provides a number of useful foundational frameworks for the study of the relationship between language and religion.

Moghissi, H., ed. (2006). *Muslim Diaspora: Gender, Culture and Identity*. London: Routledge.

In light of the apparent failure of the multicultural project and heightened public debate surrounding Islam around the globe, *Muslim Diaspora* centers the complex and contradictory experiences of migrant groups and relates these to practices grounded in both attachment to a homeland and readiness to adapt to a new country.

Omoniyi, T., ed. (2010). *The Sociology of Language and Religion: Change, Conflict and Accommodation*. London: Palgrave Macmillan.

This edited volume engages case studies involving multiple faith communities in the discussion of that *change* emerging from social forms of enablement and/or constraint, followed by the *accommodation* often sprouting from that cultural integration so characteristic of the transnational and intra-cultural flows of our contemporary globalized order.

Omoniyi, T. and Fishman, J., eds. (2006). *Explorations in the Sociology of Language and Religion*. Amsterdam: John Benjamins.

Omoniyi and Fishman's edited volume undertakes bold methodological and theoretical exploration of a field of study – religion – often relegated to the realm of the abstract, and in the process draws heightened attention to its sociological and material relevance.

References

Adhikari, M. (2005). *Not White Enough Not Black Enough: Racial Identity in the South African Coloured Community*. Athens: Center for International Studies (Ohio University).

Adogame, A. (2007). Raising champions, taking territories: African churches and the mapping of new religious landscapes in diaspora. In T. L. Trost (ed.), *The African Diaspora and the Study of Religion* (pp. 17–34). New York: Palgrave Macmillan.

Adogame, A., Gerloff, R. and Hock, K., eds.(2008). *Christianity in Africa and the African Diaspora: The Appropriation of a Scattered Heritage*. London: Continuum.

Austin, J. L. (1962). *How to Do Things with Words*. Oxford: Clarendon.

Badenhorst, P. (2015). The weathered corrugations of his face: A performative reflection on Nelson Mandela, self, and the call for racial (un)becoming. *Forum: Qualitative Sozialforschung / Qualitative Social Research* 16(2), art. 2. Retrieved 27 October 2015, from http://www.qualitativeresearch.net/index.php/fqs/article/view/2230.

Baderoon, G. (2014). *Regarding Muslims: From Slavery to Post-apartheid*. Johannesburg: Wits University.

Bakewell, O. (2008). "Keeping them in their place": The ambivalent relationship between development and migration in Africa. *Third World Quarterly* 29(7): 1341–1358.

Barros, M. C. (1995). The missionary presence in literacy campaigns in the indigenous languages of Latin America (1939–1952). *International Journal of Educational Development* 15(3): 277–287.

Bourdieu, P. (1990). *The Logic of Practice*. Stanford: Stanford University.

Bourdieu, P. (1991). *Language and Symbolic Power*. Cambridge: Polity.

Brubaker, R. (2002). Ethnicity without groups. *Archives of European Sociology* XLIII(2): 163–189.

Butler, J. (1990). *Gender Trouble*. New York: Routledge.

Canagarajah, S. (2013). *Translingual Practice: Global Englishes and Cosmopolitan Relations*. Abingdon: Routledge.

Cha, M. J. (2010). *Koreans in Central California (1903–1957): A Study of Settlement and Transnational Politics*. Lanham: University Press of America.

Chew, P.G.-L. (2010). Metaphors of change: Adolescent Singaporeans switching religion. In T. Omoniyi (ed.), *The Sociology of Language and Religion: Change, Conflict and Accommodation* (pp. 156–189). London: Palgrave Macmillan.

Chew, P.G.-L. (2014). Language choice and religious identities in three Singaporean Madrashas. *International Journal of the Sociology of Language* 229: 49–65.

Chidester, D. (1996). *Savage Systems: Colonialism and Comparative Religion in South Africa*. Charlottesville: University of Virginia.

Chidester, D. (2013). Colonialism and religion. *Critical Research on Religion* 1(1): 87–94.

Clark, D. (1989). "Surely God will work out their salvation": Protestant missionaries in the March First Movement. *Korean Studies* 13: 42–75.

Connor, P. and Tucker, C. (2011). Religion and migration around the globe: Introducing the Global Religion and Migration Database. *International Migration Review* 45(4): 985–1000.

Darqueness, J. and Vandenbussche, W. (2011). Language and religion as a sociolinguistic field of study: Some introductory notes. *Sociolinguistica* 25: 1–11.

Deleuze, G. and Guattari, F. (1987). *A Thousand Plateaus*. Minneapolis: University of Minnesota.

De Matos, G. (2005). *Using Peaceful Language: From Principles to Practices*. UNESCO-OELSS Online Encyclopedia. Retrieved 29 October 2015, from www.eolss.com

Du Bois, J. (2007). The stance triangle. In R. Englebretson, (ed.), *Stancetaking in Discourse: Subjectivity, Evaluation, Interaction* (pp. 139–182). John Benjamins: Amsterdam.

Elphick, R. (2012). *The Equality of Believers: Protestant Missionaries and the Racial Politics of South Africa*. Charlottesville: University of Virginia.

Fairclough, N. (1989). *Language and Power*. New York: Longman.Fairclough, N. (1992). *Discourse and Social Change*. Cambridge: Polity.

Fishman, J. (1989). *Language and Ethnicity in Minority Sociolinguistic Perspective*. Clevedon: Multilingual Matters.

Fishman, J. (1999). Sociolinguistics. In J. Fishman (ed.), *Handbook of Language and Ethnic Identity* (pp. 152–163). Oxford, New York.

Foucault, M. (1979). *Discipline and Punish: The Birth of the Prison*. London: Penguin.

Frigerio, A. (2004). Re-Africanization in secondary religious diasporas: Constructing a world religion. *Civilizations* 51(1/2): 39–60.

Giliomee, H. (2003). *The Afrikaners: Biography of a People*. London: C. Hurst.

Goldberg, D. T. (2009). *The Threat of Race: Reflections on Racial Neoliberalism*. Oxford: Wiley-Blackwell.

Good Work Picture Company. (2014). *The Boers at the End of the World* [Online video]. Retrieved 24 December 2014, from https://www.youtube.com/watch?v=6h39nq0KqHs.

Governor's Academy. (2010). *Governor's Boasts Strong Ties to Korea*. Retrieved 28 January 2015, from http://www.thegovernorsacademy.org/page.cfm?p=357&newsid=43.

Habermas, R. (2012). Islam debates around 1900: Colonies in Africa, Muslims in Berlin, and the role of missionaries and orientalists. In B. Becker-Cantarino (ed.), *Migration and Religion: Christian Transatlantic Missions, Islamic Migration to Germany* (pp. 123–154). Amsterdam: Rodopi.

Hagan, J. and Ebaugh, H. (2003). Calling upon the sacred: Migrants' use of religion in the migration process. *International Migration Review* 37(4): 1145–1162.

Hamish Ion, A. (1977). British and Canadian missionaries and the March 1st 1919 Movement. 北大法学論集 28(3): 152–134.

Hansen, T. (2014). Migration, religion and post-imperial formations. *Global Networks* 14(3): 273–290.

Hartch, T. (2005). *Missionaries of the State: The Summer Institute of Linguistics, State Formation, and Indigenous Mexico*. Birmingham: University of Alabama.

Hartmann, J. and Molnárfi, L. (2006). *Comparative Studies in Germanic Syntax: From Afrikaans to Zurich German*. Amsterdam: John Benjamins.

Havea, J. (2013). Diaspora contexted: Talanoa, reading, and theologising, as migrants. *Black Theology* 11(2): 185–200.

Holborow, M. (1999). *The Politics of English: A Marxist View of Language*. London: Sage.

hooks, b. (1992). *Black Looks: Race and Representation*. South End, Boston.

Hopstock, N. and De Jager, N. (2011). Locals only: Understanding xenophobia in South Africa. *Strategic Review for Southern Africa* 33(1): 120–139.

Irvine, J. (2008). Subjected words: African linguistics and the colonial encounter. *Language & Communication* 28(4): 291–408.

Jappie, S. (2012). JAWI DARI JUAH. *Indonesia and the Malay World* 40(117): 143–159.

Kale Yu, K. (2011). American missionaries and the Korean independence movement in the early 20th century, *International Journal of Korean Studies* XV(2): 171–186.

Kang, H. (2001). *Under the Black Umbrella: Voices from Colonial Korea (1910–1945)*. Ithaca: Cornell University.

Kang, W. J. (1997). *Christ and Caesar in Modern Korea: A History of Christianity and Politics*. Albany: State University of New York.

Kerswill, P. (2006). Migration and language. In K. Mattheier, U. Ammon and P. Trudgill (eds.), *Sociolinguistics/Soziolinguistik. An International Handbook of the Science of Language and Society* (Vol. 2, pp. 2271–2285). Berlin: De Gruyter.

Kim, J. H. (2004). Christianity and Korean culture: The reasons for the success of Christianity in Korea. *Exchange* 33(2): 132–152.

Kim, Y. and Park, S.-Y. (2009). Reverse acculturation: A new cultural phenomenon examined through an emerging wedding practice of Korean Americans in the United States. *Family & Consumer Sciences* 37(3): 359–375.

Klooster, W., ed. (2009). *Migration, Trade, and Slavery in an Expanding World: Essays in Honor of Pieter Emmer*. Leiden: Brill.

Landau, L. (2009). Living within and beyond Johannesburg: Exclusion, religion, and emerging forms of being. *African Studies* 68(2): 197–214.

Lee, S. H. (2004). Continuity and discontinuity of traditional and modern philosophy in Korea, in Korea National Commission for UNESCO (ed.), *Korean Philosophy: Its Tradition and Modern Transformation* (pp. 3–23). Elizabeth: Hollym.
Lee, S. H. (2006). Introduction: Korea's twentieth century transformation. In Y.-S. Chang and S. H. Lee (eds.), *Transformations in Twentieth Century Korea* (pp. 1–29). Abingdon: Routledge.
Lee, Y. W. (2009). A literature review of the history of Korean Christian education. *Theology Today Journal* 12(1): 163–173.
Levitt, P. (2003). "You know, Abraham was really the first immigrant": Religion and transnational migration. *International Migration Review* 37(3): 847–873.
Literas, S. (2009). A path to integration: Senegalese Tijanis in Cape Town. *African Studies* 68(2): 215–233.
Loxley, J. (2007). *Performativity*. London: Routledge.
Mahida, E. (1993). *History of Muslims in South Africa: A Chronology*. Durban: Arabic Study Circle.
Makoni, S. (2003). Introducing applied linguistics in Africa. In S. Makoni and U. Meinhof (eds.), *Africa and Applied Linguistics: AILA Review* (pp. 1–12, Vol. 16). Amsterdam: John Benjamins.
Mandivenga, E. (2000). The Cape Muslims and the Indian Muslims of South Africa: A comparative analysis. *Journal of Muslim Minority Affair* 20(2): 347–352.
Massumi, B. (2002). *Parables of the Virtual: Affect, Movement, Sensation*. Durham: Duke University.
Moghissi, H., ed. (2006). *Muslim Diaspora: Gender, Culture and Identity*. London: Routledge.
Moosa, E. (1989). Muslim conservatism in South Africa. *Journal of Theology for Southern Africa* 6: 73–81.
Mudimbe, V. Y. (1988). *The Invention of Africa: Gnosis, Philosophy, and the Order of Knowledge*. Bloomington: Indiana University.
Muzorewa, G. (1990). *An African Theology of Mission*. New York: Edward Mellen.
Niebuhr, H. R. (2001). *Christ and Culture*. New York: HarperCollins.
Norman, J. (2009). A new look at Altaic. *Journal of the American Oriental Society* 129(1): 83–89.
Okpalaoka, C. (2014). *(Im)migrations, Relations, and Identities: Negotiating Cultural Memory, Diaspora, and African (American) Identities*. New York: Peter Lang.
Omoka, W. (1974). *An Analysis of Some Tactics of Missionization in East Africa*. MA thesis, Kent State University, Kent.
Omoniyi, T. (2006). Societal multilingualism and multifaithism: A sociology of language and religion perspective. In T. Omoniyi and J. Fishman (eds.), *Explorations in the Sociology of Language and Religion* (pp. 121–140). Amsterdam: John Benjamins.
Omoniyi, T., ed. (2010). *The Sociology of Language and Religion: Change, Conflict and Accommodation*. London: Palgrave Macmillan.
Omoniyi, T. and Fishman, J., eds. (2006). *Explorations in the Sociology of Language and Religion*. Amsterdam: John Benjamins.
Park, C.-S. (2003). *Protestantism and Politics in Korea*. Seattle: University of Washington.
Park, J. S. (2004). Ham Seok-heon's national spirit and Christian thought. In Korean National Commision for UNESCO (ed.), *Korean Philosophy: Its Tradition and Modern Transformation* (pp. 519–554). Elizabeth: Hollym International.
Park, Y.-J. (2013). *Slavoj Žižek: Demanding the Impossible*. Cambridge: Polity.
Pennycook, A. (2007). *Global Englishes and Transcultural Flows*. Abingdon: Routledge.
Punyani, R., ed. (2005). *Religion, Power and Violence: Expressions of Politics in Contemporary Times*. New Delhi: Sage.
Puar, J. K. (2012). "I would rather be a cyborg than a goddess": Becoming-intersectional in Assemblage Theory. *philoSOPHIA* 2(1): 49–66.
Quddus, J. (2005). Islam, terrorism and the New World Order. In R. Punyani (ed.), *Religion, Power and Violence: Expression of Politics in Contemporary Times* (pp. 91–107). New Delhi: Sage.
Ranger, T. (1985). *The Invention of Tribalism in Zimbabwe*. Gweru: Mambo.
Reckwitz, A. (2002). Toward a theory of social practices: A development in culturalist theorizing. *European Journal of Social Theory* 5(2): 243–263.
Richerson, P. and Boyd, R. (2008). Migration: An engine for social change. *Nature* 456(18, p. 877.

Ritner, S. (1967). The Dutch reformed church and apartheid. *Journal of Contemporary History* 2(4): 17–37.
Robbins, J. (2007). Continuity thinking and the problem of Christian culture: Belief, time, and the anthropology of Christianity. *Current Anthropology* 48(1): 5–38.
Rogers, R. (2006). From cultural exchange to transculturation: A review and reconceptualization of cultural appropriation. *Communication Theory* 16: 474–503.
Rosowsky, A. (2006). The role of liturgical literacy in UK Muslim communities. In T. Omoniyi and J. Fishman (eds.), *Explorations in the Sociology of Language and Religion* (pp. 309–324). Amsterdam: John Benjamins.
Rosowsky, A. (2008). *Heavenly Readings: Liturgical Literacy in a Multilingual Context*. Bristol: Multilingual Matters.
Rosowsky, A. (2012). Performance and flow: The religious classical in translocal and transnational linguistic repertoires. *Journal of Sociolinguistics* 16(5): 613–637.
Said, E. (1979). *Orientalism*. New York: Vintage.
Schmid, A. (2002). *Korea between Empires: 1895–1919*. New York: Columbia University.
Schmitt, C. and Tatum, M. (2008). *The Malheur National Forest: Location of the World's Largest living Organism [The Humongous Fungus]*. United States Department of Agriculture, Washington, DC. Retrieved 28 October 2015, from http://www.fs.usda.gov/Internet/FSE_DOCUMENTS/fsbdev3_033146.pdf.
Schrijver, P. (2006). *Bibliography on Islam in Contemporary Sub-Saharan Africa*. Research Report 82, African Studies Centre, Leiden. Retrieved 12 February 2015, from https://openaccess.leidenuniv.nl/bitstream/handle/1887/12922/ASC-075287668-170-01.pdf?sequence=2.
Shin, Y.-H. (2004a). The social thought of the Independence Club. In Korean National Commission for UNESCO (ed.), *Korean Philosophy: Its Tradition and Modern Transformation* (pp. 421–439). Elizabeth: Hollym International.
Shin, Y.-H. (2004b). The philosophical world of sin Chae-ho. In Korean National Commission for UNESCO (ed.), *Korean Philosophy: Its Tradition and Modern Transformation* (pp. 441–461). Elizabeth: Hollym International.
Sikand, Y. (2003). *Sacred Spaces: Exploring Traditions of Shared Faith in India*. New Delhi: Penguin.
Souza, A. (2016). Language and faith encounters: Bridging language-ethnicity and language-religion studies. *International Journal of Multilingualism* 13(1), 134–148.
Spolsky, B. (2003). Religion as a site of language contact. *Annual Review of Applied Linguistics* 23: 81–94.
Stambach, A. (2010). *Faith in Schools: Religion, Education, and American Evangelicals in East Africa*. Stanford University, Stanford.
Stegner, W. (1971). *Angel of Repose*. New York: Doubleday.
Stell, G. (2007). From Kitaab-Hollandsch to Kitaab-Afrikaans: The evolution of a non-white literary variety of the Cape (1856–1940). *Stellenbosch Papers in Linguistics* 37: 89–127.
Svelmoe, W. L. (2008). *A New Vision for Missions: William Cameron Townsend, the Wycliffe Bible Translators, and the Culture of Early Evangelical Faith Missions, 1896-1945*. Tuscaloosa: University of Alabama.
Tayob, A. (2002). The South African Muslim communities response to September 11th. *Annual Review of Islam in South Africa* 5: 20–25.
Van Noppen, J.-P. (2011). Critical theolinguistics vs. the literalist paradigm. *Sociolinguistica* 25: 28–40.
Vàsquez, M. and Knott, K. (2014). Three dimensions of religious place making in diaspora. *Global Networks* 14(3): 1470–2266.
Vernet, T. (2009). Slave trade and slavery on the Swahili Coast, 1500–1750. In B. Mirzai, I. M. Montana and P. Lovejoy (eds.), *Slavery, Islam and Diaspora* (pp. 37–76). Trenton: Africa World.
Verter, B. (2003). Spiritual capital: Theorizing religion with Bourdieu against Bourdieu. *Sociological Theory* 21(2): 150–174.
Wielenga, B. (2007). Liberation theology in Asia. In C. Rowland (ed.), *The Cambridge companion to liberation theology* (pp. 55–78). Cambridge: Cambridge University.

Warner, S. and Wittner, J., eds. (1998). *Gatherings in Diaspora: Religious Communities and the New Immigration*. Philadelphia: Temple.

Weber, M. (1978). *Economy and Society: An Outline of Interpretative Sociology*. Berkeley: University of California.

Wicker, C. (2015). *Muslims, Christians become More Alike in an Unlikely Place: Competition Breeds Amity*. Psychology Today. Retrieved 21 January 2015, from https://www.psychologytoday.com/blog/pray-me/201501/muslims-christians-become-more-alike-in-unlikely-place.

Wilemse, H. and Dangor, S., eds. (2012). *The Afrikaans of the Cape Muslims: Achmat Davids*. Pretoria: Protea Boekhuis.

Williams, C. (2008). Female transnational migration, religion and subjectivity: The case of Indonesian domestic workers. *Asia Pacific Viewpoint* 49(3): 344–353.

Wong, F. (2015). In search for the many faces of community resilience among LGBT Individuals. *American Journal of Community Psychology* 55: 239–241.

Wong, M., Kristjánsson, C. and Dörnyei, Z., eds. (2013). *Christian Faith and English Language Teaching and Learning: Research on the Interrelationship of Religion and ELT*. New York: Routledge.

Worden, N. (2009). New approaches to VOC history in South Africa. *South African Historical Journal* 59(1): 3–18.

Yi, S.T. (1996). *Religion and Social Formation in Korea: Minjung and Millenarianism*. Berlin: Mouton de Gruyter.

Yu, C.-S. (1996). *Korea and Christianity*. Fremont: Asian Humanities.

16
Language in skilled migration

Loy Lising

Introduction/definitions

When the world witnessed the occupation of some parts of the globe by certain colonial powers such as the UK, the United States, France, Belgium, and the Netherlands, few would have expected that such would later on become one of the pivotal phenomena that would significantly pave the way for the genesis and growth of skilled migration. The story of skilled migration, to borrow Hansen's (2003) words, "is one of unforeseen development and unintended consequences" (2003: 1). Even the Spanish colonial occupation in the Philippines unexpectedly resulted in part in the earliest documented Filipino labor migration during the galleon trade between Manila and Acapulco from 1565 to 1815 (Lorente 2012). Tracing the historical development of language in skilled migration is no easy task largely because (1) of the lack of focus on and the outright lack of consideration of the language factor in earlier skilled migration studies, and (2) of the lack of consensus in the literature on the definition of skilled migration.

The rise in skilled migration can be attributed to three main causes: (1) colonization, (2) globalization, and (3) the internationalization of higher education particularly in the West, with Singapore and the People's Republic of China (PRC) aggressively positioning themselves as higher education destinations in recent years (Asian Development Bank Institute 2014). Colonization, particularly by the UK and the United States, facilitated easier movement of skilled workers to varied host colonial countries as colonial migrants, such as the 'guest-worker' schemes in Europe (Hansen 2003: 31). Globalization, on the other hand, has not only facilitated free trade and free capital flows but also a varying degree of free labor mobility (Asian Development Bank Institute 2014). Furthermore, with the development of technology, globalization has also allowed for the first time the coming together of key industry players of various ethnolinguistic backgrounds in one virtual space (Friedman 2007; Gunnarsson 2014). The third driving factor of skilled migration is the internationalization of higher education. This is seen as a logical pathway to skilled migration, as host countries are assured that if they were to hire skilled workers previously educated in their local educational institutions, they end up with a workforce that is familiar with both the workplace system and the language necessary for the successful conduct of their work (Iredale 2001).

Although language is central in carrying out one's work, especially in work that involves international collaboration, sociolinguistic research in skilled migration has shown that earlier studies have either totally ignored or relegated the study of the role of language in skilled migration to the periphery, particularly in the language policies of multinational corporations (Marschan, Welch, and Welch 1997). There is quite a rich, diverse, and complex language factor to explore in relation to language policies and language practices, particularly the question whether the two are in harmony. The language policies of different governments and international companies are varied and are often a reflection of the respective country's national language policy. On the other hand, the language practices, although ideally imagined to be consistent with such language policies, are organically more reflective of the linguistic repertoires of skilled workers, which are often varied and complex and serve as a rich tapestry of the workers' social needs and functions. As the latter section of this chapter will show, there is often a dissonance in regard to what so often is a top-down approach to language policies in skilled migration and the on-the-ground reality of language practices.

There is also a plethora of highly diverse treatment of the concept of skilled migration in the literature insofar as its label, its nature, and its typology are concerned. With regard to the label, there is a rich choice of nomenclatures in the literature insofar as 'skilled migration' is concerned. These variations include 'skilled international migration' (Findlay 1990), 'skilled international labor circulation' (Cormode 1994), 'professional transients' (Appleyard 1991), and the 'migration of expertise' (Salt and Singleton 1995), to name a few. There is also a lack of consensus with regard to the nature of skilled migration, which is consistent with the debate in the field on the distinction between "migration, movement, and mobility" (Koser and Salt 1997; Vertovec 2002). The disagreement lies in whether 'skilled migration' is something that should refer to and include both short-term and permanent movement of people in relation to work or not. Finally, divergence exists in relation to the types of 'skilled migration' as reflected in the various dichotomous terms in the literature: skilled/unskilled, white/blue collar, and high-/low-skilled. Moreover, a debate in the literature also abounds with regard to who qualifies as a 'skilled' worker – is it someone who has the appropriate higher education qualification, or one who has the necessary training and experience on the job, or both? In other words, should 'skilled migration' be about skills obtained through higher degree education or simply through (a long-term) training prior to commencement of work or on-the-job training? Purkayastha (2005), for example, in her study of Indian migrants in the United States, defines 'skilled migration, in relation to the qualifications migrants have pertinent to their tertiary education. This chapter will not belabor the distinction between skilled and unskilled workers because often studies do not make clear distinctions between the two, and government statistics are not often consistent in their account of the typology of skilled migrants in the respective country.

There are a number of factors that will be addressed in this chapter. First, it explores the historical development of skilled migration with a specific focus on selected countries in Southeast Asia, East Asia, and Oceania where some work has been done. In Southeast Asia, the focus will be on Singapore as it is the primary destination country for Asian skilled migrants, and on the Philippines as the sending nation of skilled migrants, as it is the third largest source of imported labor to OECD (Organisation for Economic Co-operation and Development) countries (Asian Development Bank Institute 2014). In East Asia, particular attention will be on South Korea, Japan, and the People's Republic of China (PRC), given that the first two are the second and third top destination countries, respectively, for Asian skilled migrants after the United States, while the PRC is the second popular destination country for higher education for Asian students and the foremost source of skilled migrants to OECD countries (Asian Development Bank Institute 2014). In Oceania, works from Australia and New Zealand will be highlighted, as these are two of the top eleven of the thirty-four OECD countries that are the main destinations for Asian migrants. Second, the chapter investigates the relevance and importance placed on language in skilled migration as reflected in the different country and company language policies. Third, the chapter reports on documented language practices in various workplaces and their relationship to existing policies, and the ideologies that underpin such policies. Finally, the chapter highlights areas of research that need further focus and attention. In doing so, this chapter will take a two-pronged approach in exploring these areas. It will first consider the history of the phenomenon of skilled migration, and then it will explore the history of research into language in skilled migration.

Overview of the topic

Skilled migration is a rich and complex phenomenon characterized by multifarious factors including but not limited to its causes and its effects. The causes are many and varied, and while it has been outlined earlier that colonization, globalization, and internationalization of higher education are the three main phenomena that undergird its existence, other push and pull factors have also contributed greatly to its continued growth. These include political unrests, economic surges in Western countries and downturns in others, shifting skilled migration laws, and continued flattening (Friedman 2007) of the world, especially in the economic sector. More recently, the expansion of the European Union (EU) in 2004 with its open market policy facilitated new possibilities for employment for both skilled and unskilled EU workers to countries that were otherwise not as easily accessible (Gunnarsson 2014).

This section of the chapter will trace the historical development of skilled migration, particularly as it was aided by colonization, globalization, and internationalization of higher education in selected countries in Southeast Asia, East Asia, and Oceania. It will then focus on the sociolinguistic research that made language relevant in skilled migration, not only in the process of seeking and securing employment, but also in regard to the kinds of language policies in place. And in relation to these policies, this section will also address the linguistic ecology in skilled migration and will report on the documented language practices in workplaces in the aforementioned countries.

Skilled migration

Skilled migration, for the purpose of this chapter, denotes the intra- and international movement of workers possessing specific skills achieved through higher education or extensive specialized work experience.

Historically, skilled migration had its early beginnings in Europe, particularly in Germany, France, and Austria. Germany introduced the guest-worker scheme, which aimed to recruit temporary workers from Southern Europe during the time of its economic boom right after the 1948 currency reform where shortage of labor ensued (Hansen 2003). In this scheme, the workers were expected to return home during a subsequent downturn in the economy.

At the same time that Germany utilized the guest-worker agreement to bring in the much-needed workforce, colonial countries such as the UK and the United States tapped on colonial labor to fill in labor shortages (Hansen 2003). In other words, colonization facilitated the use of colonial resources for labor shortages in the colonizing countries. This was particularly true for the UK when it was unable to fill in the labor gap brought about by the post-war boom (Hansen 2003).

While the late 1940s saw the birth of what would later on become the beginnings of skilled migration, globalization began to take shape. Friedman (2007) documented ten specific events that he calls 'flatteners', which ushered in and contributed to the growth of globalization that have consequently contributed to the growth of skilled migration. These include the fall of the Berlin Wall; the creation of the World Wide Web; the integration of workflow software that enabled collaboration across the world; uploading, which gave anyone a chance to author and share their work; outsourcing; offshoring; supply chaining; insourcing; in-forming; and finally what he calls 'steroids' –new technologies that enable the other flatteners to operate simultaneously and at a much faster pace (Friedman 2007). Similarly, Iredale (2001) has documented the globalization of companies and how this contributed immensely to the growth of globalization.

Another growing phenomenon that helped build skilled migration as it is today is the internationalization of higher education (Lenn and Campos 1996; Iredale 2001). In 2014, UNESCO reported that four million students were studying abroad in tertiary education. This internationalization of higher education accelerated the movement of students, particularly of Asian students, into Western countries, and more recently, into Singapore and the PRC. This development is underpinned by the belief that knowledge, especially from developed countries, holds a significant value or capital that can facilitate upward social mobility. The training of international students in a developed country has also become a source of skilled labor for these countries. Given that international students have already become familiar with the labor system of the host country and may very well possess the language proficiency necessary for workplace communication, the majority of them end up staying and taking up local jobs.

In Southeast Asia, Singapore is the major Association of Southeast Asian Nation (ASEAN) destination for skilled migration, especially for other countries in the region (Southeast Asia: ASEAN 2015). Factors of globalization, internationalization of higher education, and an aging population are the main driving forces that have catapulted this tiger economy into this position today (Alsagoff 2012; Yeoh and Lin 2012). Yeoh and Lin (2012) emphasize, in particular, the country's shortage of human capital due to its aging population. Skilled migration is so necessary for Singapore's economy, so much so that the number of skilled migrants is almost a third of its population. Another main source of skilled migration in this country is international students. In recent years, Singapore has made great strides in building a reputation for being the 'international education hub' and 'the global schoolhouse' (Yeoh and Lin 2012) in Asia to try and attract the bright students for higher education who can later on potentially vie for high-skilled work.

Within Southeast Asia, the Philippines is documented to be the third largest source of skilled migration to OECD countries behind the PRC and India. According to Tyner (2004), it is the world's primary source of government-sponsored temporary skilled labor. As alluded to earlier in this chapter, the Philippines migration history dates as far back as the 1500s in the Manila-Acapulco galleon trade during the Spanish occupation. Officially, the Philippines government's concerted effort toward labor migration began in the 1970s during the Marcos regime. Labor migration was seen as a resolution to the "deteriorating social and economic conditions in the country" (Lorente 2012: 185). Since that time, the number of the country's skilled migrant workers exponentially grew from 12,501 in 1975 to almost a million thirty years on (Kanlungan Center Foundation, Inc. as cited in Lorente 2012). The focus on export labor is primarily driven by the continued low domestic employment rate, the significant economic benefits remittances of skilled workers bring to the country's economy, and the ever-growing demand for Philippine labor.

In East Asia, South Korea and Japan are the second and third top OECD destination countries, respectively, for Asian skilled migrants, while the PRC is the primary source of skilled labor to OECD countries. The PRC is also second to the United States as the "most important destination country of Asian students" (Asian Development Bank Institute 2014: iii). South Korea was a relative newcomer in the skilled migration stage (Denny 2015). The initial driver of the growth of skilled migrant importation was its economic boom in the 1990s. Currently, there are roughly 423,481 skilled migrant workers in the country (Dong-Hoon n.d.). This constitutes almost fifty percent of the total number of foreigners in South Korea. Similarly, Japan's history of skilled migration is a very recent one, given its long-held belief in ethnic homogeneity. Although the country experienced a labor shortage at the height of the economic boom in the 1960s, the government and corporations resisted foreign labor and made concerted efforts to automate production rather than open the economy to skilled migrants (Kashiwazaki 2006). Despite this, Japan has remained as the third top destination country for Asian migrants mostly coming from South Korea, Taiwan, the PRC, Hong Kong, and the Philippines (Kashiwazaki 2006). The PRC, on the other hand, is the main country of origin for skilled migration to OECD countries accounting for more than one in ten immigrants (Asian Development Bank Institute 2014).

In Oceania, Australia and New Zealand are two of the main OECD destination countries for skilled migration (Asian Development Bank Institute 2014). Australia's skilled migration history began in the 1950s and has since steadily grown, especially with the introduction of the temporary visa scheme in 1996 (Piller and Lising 2014), which provided an alternative to an otherwise stringent requirements of the existing skilled migration program. New Zealand's skilled migration story, on the other hand, started in the late 1940s when it issued free and assisted passage schemes to bring in resources primarily from the UK, and later from other parts of Europe (Denmark, Germany, Switzerland, and Austria) to fill in domestic labor shortages (King 2003). The points system for skilled migration was introduced much later in the late 1980s.

Language policies and practices in the workplace

Although the genesis of skilled migration was well documented as it burgeoned in the early 1950s and continues to grow to this day, language and the role it played in the skilled migration stage was quite negligible and rarely a focus of sociolinguistic research. Almost twenty years ago Marschan et al. (1997) observed that language, although clearly recognized as an important aspect of workplace communication, was a "forgotten factor" (p. 591) insofar as multinational management was concerned in regard to their attitude towards multinational companies' language policies. In other words, although language was seen as crucial in the successful conduct of work especially at the multinational level, no language policy or program was ever in place to aid multilingual skilled migrants in navigating their multilingual identities. In the last decade or so, a growing interest in documenting the role of language in the successful and unsuccessful settlement of skilled migrants has led to a new body of research on the topic (see for example Clyne 1994; Marra, Holmes and Riddiford 2009; Canagarajah 2013; Angouri and Miglbauer 2014; Gunnarsson 2014; Hultgren 2014; Jansson 2014; Lønsmann 2014; Nelson 2014; Piller and Lising 2014).

McLaughlin and Salt (2002) investigated and documented the "new schemes and policy measures" (p. 2) for skilled migration in ten OECD countries including Australia, Canada, Denmark, France, Germany, Ireland, the Netherlands, Norway, UK, and the United States to understand the trends in the recruitment of skilled migrant workers. What they discovered in relation to the language requirement for skilled migrants was that, except for Australia and Canada, which stipulated "sufficient ability in English," and "working proficiency in English and French" (McLaughlin and Salt 2002: 11, 44), respectively, the other OECD countries did not specify a language requirement. This is an interesting point given that this kind of 'silent' language policy resonates in some of the countries tackled in this chapter.

In Southeast Asia, Singapore's colonial history has very much dictated the unique role of English as a lingua franca in what is otherwise a very ethnolinguistically diverse society. English is seen as a 'neutral' linguistic tool for trade, science, and commerce amid the presence of Mandarin Chinese, Bahasa Malay and Tamil (Silver 2005; Chua 2010; Alsagoff 2012). This privileged role is very much reflected in the country's bilingual education policy, which mandates the use of English and a designated mother tongue – from a choice of Mandarin Chinese, Bahasa Malay, and Tamil. In investigating the government and company websites in Singapore as they relate to skilled migration, it was found that no language policy or requirement is directly stipulated. This is consistent with what McLaughlin and Salt (2002) found in their analysis of the language requirements of the top ten OECD countries of destinations for skilled migration. What can be inferred from the available documents (for example Silver 2005; Chua 2010; Alsagoff 2012) is that English is seen as the default requirement for workplace communication. Historically, English held the position of being the language of the elite. And while such a status has shifted into a more functional economic role, nonetheless it continues to hold a privileged position and is seen as necessary capital Singaporeans have as they compete in the international economy. In regard to language practices, again, a cursory check of government and company websites indicate that applications for jobs are done in English. One can assume that there are variations in actual language practice in the workplace depending on the type of company involved, but what is clear is that as a policy and for purposes of practice, English is seen as a unifying tool in a very multilingual society. So, while the linguistic ecology is diverse, English is seen as something that brings social cohesion. This privileging of English as the lingua franca which ascribes it a dominant status over the mother tongue languages has a long history since the country's independence. This close relationship English has with the economic development of Singapore is underpinned by the ideological belief that language is a 'unifying tool' – in this case unifying Singaporeans of Mandarin, Tamil, and Malay ethnolinguistic background, and that the English language is the global economic language. As Silver (2005) puts it, "English is a means of building up national cohesion via inter-ethnic communication and of preparing a greater percentage of the population to participate in economic opportunities via international trade" (p. 51).

In the case of the Philippines, one of the main factors that have made skilled workers from this country particularly attractive to OECD countries, making it the third top source for skilled migration globally, is its reputation for English proficiency. Since the 1970s, when the government began 'managing' its labor export to alleviate domestic economic situations, the country has continued in its efforts to ensure that its language capital continues to improve and its attractiveness and competitiveness in international labor is maintained. In 2007, the Technical Education and Skills Development Authority (TESDA), an arm of the government responsible for managing and supervising technical education and skills development in the country (Lorente 2012) established the Language Skills Institute (LSI) responsible for the provision of courses in "English, Japanese, Korean, Mandarin, Arabic, and Spanish language and culture" (TESDA 2015). The institute is aimed at training potential skilled workers in the language and culture of their destination country. The establishment of LSI re-defined for the country's skilled workers what it means to have a linguistic capital. The additional language requirement is aimed at making the country's labor export language- and culture-ready. It makes English a minimum requirement and knowledge of the destination country's language an additional prerequisite for qualifying for overseas skilled labor. The success of this program, insofar as the value, prestige, and function of the skilled migrant's knowledge of the destination country's language is concerned, is yet to be documented. Like Singapore, language here is closely tied with its economic value and such valuing seems to underpin the programs offered in the LSI. The creation of LSI aimed at making Filipino export labor more competitive in the international economy.

In East Asia, the language policies and practices in South Korea, Japan, and the PRC reflect an ongoing tension between a largely monolingual practice and a strong desire to be seen as an active player in the global economy through a bilingual policy where English is positioned alongside the national language as having an official role either in the local national education policy or in multinational companies. South Korea, for instance, following the Asian Financial Crisis in the late 1990s (Piller and Cho 2013) and the publication of Geo-Il Bok's *Kwukce-e siday-ui mincok-e* (*Ethnic Languages in the Age of an International Language*), which argued that the Korean language is unsuitable for globalization, has seen an immense growth in the national discussion on 'Official English Debate' (Song 2011). Park (2009) has observed the excessive national desire for English despite a largely Korean monolingual daily existence. This obsession for English is reflected in a number of ways including but not limited to the creation of the 'English Village' dedicated to "providing the experience of the English language and the cultures of the English speaking countries" (Gyeonggi English Village 2015); short-term study abroad (Song 2011); and the fact that as of 2009, private tuition for the study of English is said to be worth KRW 1.5 trillion (Yoo, Kim and Kim as cited in Piller and Cho 2013). While the language policy in South Korea remains reflective of monolingual Korean, there is definitely a national drive to be seen as also possessing English despite the absence of a sustained social context for its use. For the skilled migrants, the success of their job application hinges on their ability to show Korean proficiency through the Test of Proficiency in Korean ('Korean Language Tests' 2015). Beyond this, there is not a lot of work documenting whether the language in the workplace is consistent with the Korean proficiency requirement. What has been documented is the fact that the majority of workers doing white-collar jobs are regularly subjected to tests of English proficiency despite its non-use in the workplace (Song 2011). In this particular case, the national desire to be seen as possessing English so as to be perceived as internationally competitive in economic terms is yet again another reflection of the ideology that Haberland (2009) calls the ideology of English as the language of globalization.

Like South Korea, Japan is largely monolingual despite the presence of some dialects (Japan National Tourism Organization 2015). Skilled migration into Japan, however, does not necessarily require a show of proficiency in Japanese, except for specific professions such as medical practitioners ('Advantages of JLPT' 2015). As of October 2013, there were 717,504 skilled foreign workers employed in Japan, most of whom come from China (Oishi 2012). Against this backdrop of a largely Japanese monolingual policy and practice, the CEO of the e-commerce giant Rakuten made one of the most controversial moves in regard to company language policy. Hiroshi Mikitani instituted and implemented what he called 'Englishnization' ('Rakuten forges ahead in English' 2015) as a company policy, where every Japanese staff member was required to learn and use English in the workplace with no exceptions. Despite having all-Japanese staff who didn't have the need to speak English for the conduct of their work, Mikitani rationalized that its staff and the company had to adopt English since it is the global language if the company is to be seen as a global company ('Rakuten forges ahead in English' 2015). Since then four other companies have followed suit: (1) Softbank, (2) Nissan, (3) Bridgestone, and (4) Fast Retailing. The incentives for (potential) employees who have or pursue English proficiency vary from assurance of a job, receipt of monetary incentives, English language training, and promotion (Olinger 2014). It is not clear, however, whether the aforementioned companies include skilled migrants. What can be inferred from this trend is that there is now a growing openness to skilled migration, particularly if skilled migrants exhibit a high proficiency in English. The sociolinguistic work that investigates the role of language, particularly English, in a multilingual community in Japan is that of Kubota and McKay (2009). However, this largely focuses on the views, attitudes, and experiences of Japanese adults learning English in a context of a small multilingual community that hosts Brazilian-Japanese or *nikkeijin*. Despite the scarcity of studies that investigate the language practices of multilingual workplaces, it is interesting to note that similar to the situation in South Korea, the large multinational companies mentioned earlier hold the same ideology of English as a global language and have gone ahead with the implementation of a language policy that does not necessarily consider and bear witness to the workers' language realities.

Compared to South Korea and Japan, the PRC has come to the skilled migration stage even later. Its closed border policy meant that it was not always easy to gain work in the country as a skilled migrant. Recent government decisions however have shifted, and the PRC now wants to attract skilled workers and open itself to foreign trade as it "sees its growth plateauing" ('China pledges wider opening-up in 2016–2020' 2015). In 2013, the country employed 269 million migrant workers, but Jiang (2014) claims it is still struggling to attract skilled migrants. Skilled migrants into the country are not necessarily required to show proficiency in Mandarin. Gao (2010) explains that a number of Chinese nationals are able to communicate in English primarily because of the College English Test introduced more than twenty years ago. The College English Test was aimed to prepare Chinese students to interact in the global society. Some discussion (Zhao 2001; Jin and Jin 2008; Gao 2010), however, indicates that there is great variability in terms of the English language proficiency among those who have undergone said test. Despite the scarcity of studies focusing on multilingual workplaces and the emerging role of English alongside Mandarin and other local dialects, discussions seem to indicate that there is a growing shift towards an increased presence of English in Chinese workplaces.

In Oceania, Australia and New Zealand have a shared language policy for skilled migration with a slight variation on language practices at work. Both countries require an evidence of variable English language proficiency for skilled migrants. The English proficiency score needed is dependent on the type of visa one is applying for. The evidence for proficiency in English is based on various internationally accredited language tests. In Australia, these include the International English Language Testing System (IELTS), and more recently, the Test of English as a Foreign Language internet-based test (TOEFL-iBT), Pearson Test of English-Academic (PTE Academic), and the Cambridge Test of English ('What English is required for skilled migration' 2015). New Zealand, similarly, requires evidence for English proficiency mainly through IELTS (Immigration New Zealand 2014). In Australia, however, there is some degree of variability with regard to the language requirement. Some companies may require evidence for English proficiency while others may not, and the actual level of proficiency required for contract renewal may vary from that required for securing permanent residency (Piller and Lising 2014). Overall, in regard to language practice in Australia, the expectation is to use English in the workplace. However, an investigation on the language practices of Filipino skilled migrants to Australia by Piller and Lising (2014) has shown that skilled workers occasionally employ their mother tongue at work especially when working alongside co-workers from the Philippines. The participants in the study used their mother tongue (Tagalog) for some and Cebuano for others to establish their relationship with co-Filipino workers on and off the job. The skilled workers also found that their mother tongue was necessary for them to discuss with other Filipino co-workers certain work-related concepts; Tagalog or Cebuano, therefore, helped them navigate their meaning-making in English. In New Zealand, the Language in the Workplace Project (LWP) headed by Janet Holmes has done significant work on workplace talk (Holmes and Vine n.d.). Insofar as language use is concerned, the diversity lies in the fact that New Zealand workplace discourse often involves Maori alongside English. The use of Maori, however, is ritualistic in form, such as a greeting or a prayer to begin a meeting (Holmes and Vine n.d.). Findings in the LWP project (for example Prebble 2007; Bres 2009; Bres, Holmes, Marra and Vine 2010) like Clyne (1994) show that much of the variation within workplace talk where skilled migrants are concerned does not necessarily involve a departure from the use of English, the lingua franca at work, but reveal more of the sociopragmatic challenges that skilled migrants have to navigate as they operate mostly in English.

What this section of the chapter has shown is that there is an overwhelming tendency to adopt a one-language policy in managing what would otherwise be a linguistically diverse workplace. This is consistent with studies in Europe that focus on companies that have implemented a similar monolingual language policy with English as a lingua franca (e.g., Firth 1995; Nickerson 2000; Poncini 2003; Louhiala-Salminen and Kankaanranta 2005; Fredriksson, Barner-Rasmussen, and Piekkari 2006; Gunnarsson 2014; Lønsmann 2014). In addition, this tendency towards English, especially for the Southeast Asian and East Asian countries, seems to be largely underpinned by dominant ideologies of English as a de facto global language. Except in Japan, where there is an attempt to provide Japanese language training to skilled migrants once they are accepted into a job, there have been very few attempts to support multilingual practices in the workplace. As Angouri and Miglbauer (2014) and Piller and Lising (2014) show in their study, multilingualism is necessary for employees and their flexible use of their mother tongue, and the local language is important for them in negotiating work and social relationships. And although in Europe there has been greater awareness among companies of the value of language as indicated by such projects as European Language Activity Network (ELAN) (Hagen 2006), Promoting, Implementing, Mapping Language and Intercultural Communication Strategies (PIMLICO) (Hagen 2011), and Assessing and Reviewing Cultural Transactions in International Companies (ARCTIC) (2014), too often the language policy of corporate companies is predominantly about putting in place a 'one language' working policy to manage multilingualism (cf. Fredriksson et al. 2006; Angouri 2013).

Issues and ongoing debates

The current issues and ongoing debates in the literature on language in skilled migration are many, but the key points largely revolve around: (1) the insistence on a monolingual policy despite an overwhelming evidence of a multilingual reality in the workforce and workplace; (2) the lack of recognition of the social functions of multilingualism due to the failure to recognize the value of language beyond its economic merit; and (3) the contentious covert use of language as a gatekeeping mechanism that serves in some cases as a tool simply to ensure a flexible labor supply.

As has been shown earlier, the dominant language policy in place in various international workplaces is a monolingual policy which in the majority of cases privileges English. This is often the obvious choice for most companies to 'manage' diversity. And although some companies have become mindful of the economic capital of language skills and have attempted to put in place some language management strategies as outlined by Hagen (2006), the overwhelming corporate language policies tend to adopt a monolingual policy (Angouri 2013). In some cases, the choice of a monolingual policy in the dominant language is often consistent with existing national language policies, like that in Oceania. In other cases, it is purely driven by a belief in English as a global language that can provide the relevant company with the competitive edge. This is certainly true for Singapore, the Philippines, South Korea, and Japan. In addition, for a number of companies, what they hope transpires with the implementation of a monolingual policy is that the skilled migrants are persuaded to minimize the use of their "other" language(s). Studies in Europe show that this is rarely the outcome (see for example Fredriksson et al. 2006). Language policies do not always shape language practices. Multilingual workplaces do not become monolingual simply because a monolingual working language policy is in place. Language(s) are not simply a commodified bundle of skills (Urciuoli and LaDousa 2013) skilled migrants have, but are a means to conduct their work, and equally importantly are tools to negotiate their social relationships and their belonging. In Canagarajah's (2013) interview-based study with African skilled migrants, it is shown that while English played an important role in securing jobs in English-dominant countries, workplace communication required multilingualism.

For the multilingual skilled migrants, there are often different functions for their many languages. The language practices documented across a number of studies demonstrate varied types of multilingualism: that is, of different languages and also of different levels of proficiency across these languages. And these diverse multilingual practices often cater to a number of social purposes of managing business relationships, managing social relationships at work, negotiating belonging, indexing identity, and nurturing mental well-being, which conversely helps the skilled migrants perform well at work. This is particularly true in the findings of Piller and Lising (2014). The current issue with multilingualism in the workplace is the failure of companies to recognize and understand that, on the one hand, multilingual practices foster and build skilled migrants' social relationships and, on the other, aid in the successful conduct of their work. Nelson (2014), for instance, drawing on findings from the KINSA project (The Communicative Situation of Immigrants at Swedish Workplace) looked into the sociopragmatics of joking and swearing. She found that in the case of her five participants, joking and swearing in Swedish played an integral part in their well-being and were used strategically to establish social relationships at work where the required corporate language is English. Piller and Lising (2014) similarly found among their participants that the use of their mother tongue, either Tagalog or Cebuano, played a significant role in alleviating homesickness through jokes that were otherwise difficult to translate to English. These and similar studies show that social interactions in the skilled migrants' own language provide the necessary salve to workers who may be missing family and home. This in turn can be argued to positively impact on the skilled migrants' attitudes and feelings towards work. Beyond the positive emotional benefit provided by social interactions in the skilled migrants' mother tongue, they also aid skilled migrants in the conduct of their work. Jansson (2014), for instance, focused on the complex reality of home care settings in her investigation of the multilingual practices of three care workers. The study showed that the immigrant care workers utilize their diverse language resource in carrying out their work not only to do their task successfully, but also to provide clients with much needed emotional support. Similar findings were shown in Angouri and Miglbauer (2014) who looked into the role of language and the demands of the global workplace and found that workers found it necessary to use their multilingual skills to cater to clients' needs. Other studies like that of Wodak and Krzyzanowski (2010) and van Mulken and Hendriks (2014), among others, show that when multilingualism is understood properly beyond the limited economic view on language, it is quite beneficial to companies as a business language policy. In addition, Canagarajah (2013) found that skilled migrants possess portable communicative dispositions that enabled them to be more tolerant of, more versatile, and more adaptable to linguistic diversity.

The third important issue that is often relegated to the periphery is the contentious covert use of language as a gatekeeping mechanism that serves in some cases as a tool simply to ensure a flexible labor supply. The practice of making language proficiency a negotiable requirement for workplace recruitment but a mandatory criterion for contract renewal and permanent residency application (Piller and Lising 2014) is subtly duplicitous. Skilled migrants are hired to ensure that labor shortage is averted but can be refused contract renewal or permanent residency because of failure to achieve the necessary language score.

Implications

One implication of the insistence on a monolingual language policy is the continued dominance of English on the international scene as an ideological construct for a global language. This consequently ignores and fails to recognize the multilingual practices and their benefits. The uncritical implementation of a monolingual policy negates the very fact that multilingualism is the dominant practice throughout the world (Myers-Scotton 2006). Moreover, it perpetuates the belief that a high level of proficiency in English alone is the only way to upward social mobility. At the same time, an insistence on the monolingual policy reinforces the devaluation of multilingualism and multilingual practices. Such a lack of recognition of the social functions of multilingualism ignores the potentially rich communicative resources it engenders, as Canagarajah (2013) has shown. Also, the covert use of language as a gatekeeping mechanism will only continue to perpetuate monolingualism unless it is recognized that multilingual practice is necessary.

Unless research and policy recognize the multilingual reality of the workplace, there will always be a dissonance between instituted language policy and workplace language reality. Moreover, lack of research into the breadth and depth of the range of policies and practices in skilled migration will be a disservice to the industry as the nuanced multilingual practices will remain undocumented.

Future directions

If we are to understand and appreciate the communicative resources skilled migrants employ in their multilingual workplaces, ethnographic research into workplace discourse across different work contexts that skilled migrants are employed in is imperative. This will provide evidence into the linguistic practices beyond instituted policy and assumed linguistic practices. It will allow documentation of various language policies in place and the ideologies that underpin them. Likewise, such research will capture the rich tapestry of multilingual workplace talk and the many social functions they achieve such as establishing social relationships, negotiating identities, and navigating potential miscommunications. Such documentation will capture the dissonance that may exist in what companies stipulate should be standard linguistic practices and on-the-ground authentic talk.

Apart from increased focus on research on multilingual workplaces in Southeast Asia, East Asia, and Oceania, a more methodological distinction of skilled migrant and unskilled migrant workplace talk is necessary. Attention also needs to be given to skilled migrants in diverse sectors, such as the education sector, because of the rise in the number of skilled migrant teachers employed in the developed world, especially in the United States.

Summary

This chapter set out to investigate the historical development of skilled migration and the role language plays in skilled migrant work. What this chapter has shown is that historically colonization, globalization, and internationalization of education ushered in the onset of skilled migration. With regard to the language factor, sociolinguistic research has shown that particularly in Southeast Asia, East Asia and Oceania, English continues to dominate language policy. While attempts have been made in establishing the relationship between policy and practice, an obvious lacunae in research on multilingual workplaces in the aforementioned countries limits a more thorough account of such a relationship. What is clear, however, is that the ideology of English as a global language continues to permeate such spaces.

Related topics

Rethinking (un)skilled migrants
Communication practices and policies in workplace mobility

Further reading

Angouri, J. (2013). The multilingual reality of the multinational workforce: Language policy and language use. *Journal of the Multilingual and Multicultural Development*, *34*(6), 584–581.

This paper explores the match between the language policies of three multinational companies and the language practices at work.

Canagarajah, S. (2013). Skilled migration and development: Portable communicative resources for transnational work. *Multilingual Education*, *3*(8), 1–19.

This was an interview-based study with African skilled migrants which showed the portable communicative dispositions they possess that is beneficial to a multilingual workplace.

Clyne, M. (1994). *Inter-cultural Communication at Work: Cultural Values in Discourse*, Cambridge: Cambridge University Press.

This research documented ethnolinguistically diverse workplaces in Australia and showed the impact of cultural values on workplace discourse.

Lønsmann, D. (2014). Linguistic diversity in the international workplace: Language ideologies and processes of exclusion. *Multilingua*, *33*(1–2), 89–116.

This article examined the positioning of English vis-à-vis other international languages and the ideology that underpins the monopoly of English.

Piller, I. and Lising, L. (2014). Language, employment, and settlement: Temporary meat workers in Australia. *Multilingua*, *33*(1–2), 35–59.

This study investigated the role of language in the employment and migration trajectories of Filipino skilled migrants in Australia.

References

Advantages of JLPT. (2015). *Japanese-Language Proficiency Test*. Retrieved 15 October, from http://www.jlpt.jp/e/about/merit.html.

Alsagoff, L. (2012). The development of English in Singapore. In H. Azira and E. L. Low (eds.), *English in Southeast Asia: Features, Policy and Language in Use* (pp. 137–154). Amsterdam: John Benjamins.

Angouri, J. (2013). The multilingual reality of the multinational workplace: Language policy and language use. *Journal of Multilingual and Multicultural Development* 34(6): 564–581.

Angouri, J. and Miglbauer, M. (2014). "And then we summarise in English for the others": The lived experience of the multilingual workplace. *Multilingua* 33(1–2): 147–171.

Appleyard, R. (1991). *International Migration: Challenge for the Nineties*. Geneva: IOM.

ARCTIC. (2014). *ARCTIC: Assessing and Reviewing Cultural Transaction in International Companies*. Retrieved 15 December 2014, www.surrey.ac.uk/arctic

Asian Development Bank Institute (ADBI). (2014). *Labor Migration, Skills & Student Mobility in Asia 2014*. Japan: ADBI.

Bres, J. (2009). Language in the Workplace Project and Workplace Communication for Skilled Migrants Course at Victoria University of Wellington, New Zealand. *Language Teaching: Surveys and Studies* 42(4): 519–524.

Bres, J., Holmes, J., Marra, M. and Vine, B. (2010). Kia ora matua: Humour and the Māori language in the workplace. *Journal of Asian Pacific Communication* 20(1): 46–68.

Canagarajah, S. (2013). Skilled migration and development: Portable communicative resources for transnational work. *Multilingual Education* 3(8): 1–19.

China pledges wider opening-up in 2016–2020. (2015). *Xinhua*, 3 November. Retrieved 15 October, from http://news.xinhuanet.com/english/2015-11/03/c_134780016.htm.

Chua, S.K.C. (2010). Singapore's language policy and its globalized concept of Bi(tri)lingualism. *Current Issues in Language Planning* 11(4): 413–429.

Clyne, M. (1994). *Inter-cultural Communication at Work: Cultural Values in Discourse*. Cambridge: Cambridge University Press.

Cormode, L. (1994). Japanese foreign direct investment and the circulation of personnel from Japan to Canada. In W.T.S. Gould and A. M. Findlay (eds.), *Population Migration and the Changing World Order* (pp. 67–90). London: John Wiley.

Denny, S. (2015). *South Korea: Migrants and Nationalism*. The Diplomat, web blog post, 19 June. Retrieved 15 October 2015, from http://thediplomat.com/2015/06/south-korea-migrants-and-nationalism/.

Department of Immigration and Citizenship. (2014). *The Continuous Survey of Australia's Migrants' Cohorts 1–5 Report 2009–2011*. Retrieved 15 December, from http://www.immi.gov.au/media/publications/research/_pdf/continuous-survey-aus-migrants.pdf.

Dong-Hoon, S. (n.d.). *"Migrants Citizenship in Korea: With a Focus on Migrant Workers and Marriage-based Migrants*. Data collected by Seoul from the Statistical Yearbook of Departures and Arrivals released by the Ministry of Justice.

Findlay, A. M. (1990). A migration channels approach to the study of high level manpower movements: A theoretical perspective. *International Migration* 28: 15–23.

Firth, A. (1995). Talking for a change: Commodity negotiating by telephone. In A. Firth (ed.), *The discourse of negotiation* (pp. 183–222). Berlin: De Gruyter.

Fredriksson, R., Barner-Rasmussen, W. and Piekkari, R. (2006). The multinational corporation as a multilingual organization: The notion of a common corporate language. *Corporate Communications: An International Journal* 11(4): 406–423.

Friedman, T. (2007). *The World Is Flat: A Brief History of the Twenty-First Century*. New York: Picador.

Gao, F. (2010). What's wrong with current Chinese College English Assessment System? Reform or not?. *International Education Studies* 3(1): 34–37.

Gunnarsson, B. (2014). Multilingualism in European workplaces. *Multilingua* 33(1–2): 11–33.

Gyeonggi English Village. (2015). Retrieved 15 October http://www.english-village.or.kr/exclude/userIndex/engIndex.do.

Haberland, H. (2009). English – The language of globalism. *Rask. Internationalt Tidsskrift for Sprog Og Kommunikation* 30: 17–45.

Hagen, S. (2006). *Effects on the European Economy of Shortages of Foreign Language Skills in Enterprise (ELAN)*. CILT & European Commission. Retrieved 15 December 2014, from http://ec.europa.eu/languages/languages-mean-business/files/elan-full-report_en.pdf.

Hagen, S. (2011). *Report on Language Management Strategies and Best Practice in European SMEs: The PIMLICO Project*. Brussels: European Commission. Retrieved 15 December 2014, from http://ec.europa.eu/languages/languages-mean-business/files/pimlico-full-report_en.pdf.

Hansen, R. (2003). Migration to Europe since 1945: Its history and its lessons. *Political Quarterly* 74(1): 25–38.

Holmes, J. and Vine, B. (n.d.). "That's just how we do things round here": Researching workplace discourse for the benefit of society. To appear in V. Viana and J. Rahilly (eds.), *Crossing Boundaries: Interdisciplinarity in Language Studies*.

Hultgren, K. (2014). Whose parallellingualism? Overt and covert ideologies in Danish university language policies. *Multilingua* 33(1–2): 61–87.

Immigration New Zealand. (2014). *English Language*. Retrieved 15 October, from http://www.immigration.govt.nz/migrant/stream/alreadyinnz/business/englishlanguagerequirements/.

Iredale, R. (2001). The migration of professionals: Theories and typologies. *International Migration* 39(5): 1–26.

Jansson, G. (2014). Bridging language barriers in multilingual care encounters. *Multilingua* 33(1–2): 201–232.

Japan National Tourism Organization. (2015). *Japan Overview*. Retrieved 15 October, from http://www.jnto.go.jp/eng/arrange/essential/overview/.

Jiang, Y. (2014). *China: Trends, foreign investment and development strategies*. Oxford: Chandos.

Jin, Y. H. and Jin, G. C. (2008). Foreign language teaching reform and improvement of college English teaching quality. *Asian Social Science* 4: 127–128.

Kashiwazaki, C. (2006). *Japanese Immigration Policy: Responding to Conflicting Pressures*. Migration Policy Institute, 1 November. Retrieved 15 October 2015, from http://www.migrationpolicy.org/article/japanese-immigration-policy-responding-conflicting-pressures.

King, M. (2003). *The Penguin History of New Zealand*. Auckland: Penguin.

Korean Language Tests. (2015). Retrieved 15 October, from http://www.korea.net/Resources/UsefulInfo/Korean-Language-Exam.

Koser, K. and Salt, J. (1997). The geography of highly skilled international migration. *International Journal of Population Geography* 3: 285–303.

Kubota, R. and McKay, S. (2009). Globalization and language learning in rural Japan: The role of English in the local linguistic ecology. *TESOL Quarterly* 43(4): 593–619.

Lenn, M. P. and Campos, L. (1996). *Globalisation of the Professions and the Quality Imperative: Professional Accreditation, Certification, and Licensure*. Madison: Magna.

Lønsmann, D. (2014). Linguistic diversity in the international workplace: Language ideologies and processes of exclusion. *Multilingua* 33(1–2): 89–116.

Lorente, B. P. (2012). The making of "Workers of the World": Language and the Labor Brokerage State. In A. Duchene and M. Heller (eds.), *Language in Late Capitalism: Pride and Profit* (pp. 183–200). London: Routledge.

Louhiala-Salminen, L. and Kankaanranta, A. (2005). "Hello Monica, kindly change your arrangements": Business genres in a state of flux. In P. Gillaerts and M. Gotti (eds.), *Genre Variation in Business Letters: Linguistic Insights* (pp. 55–84). Switzerland: Bern.

Marra, M., Holmes, J. and Riddiford, N. (2012). New Zealand's Language in the Workplace project. Workplace Communication for skilled migrants. In M. Krzanowski (ed), *Current Developments in English for Work and the Workplace: Approaches, Curricula and Materials* (pp. 91–104), Reading: Garnet.

Marschan, R., Welch, D. and Welch, L. (1997). Language: The forgotten factor in multinational Management. *European Management Journal* 15(5): 591–598.

McLaughlin, G. and Salt, J. (2002). *Migration Policies towards Highly Skilled Foreign Workers*. Report to the Home Office. London: HMSO.

Myers-Scotton, C. (2006). *Multiple voices*. Oxford: Blackwell.

Nelson, M. (2014). "You need help as usual, do you?": Joking and swearing for collegiality in a Swedish workplace. *Multilingua* 33(1–2): 173–200.

Nickerson, C. (2000). *Playing the Corporate Language Game: An Investigation of the Genres and Discourse Strategies in English Used by Dutch Writers Working in Multinational Corporations*. Amsterdam: Rodopi.

Oishi, N. (2012). The limits of immigration policies: The challenges of highly skilled migration in Japan. *American Behavioral Scientist* 56(8): 1080–1100.

Olinger, M. (2014). *Five Japanese Companies that Saw Results after Investing in Language Training*. Language Trainers USA & Canada Blog, web log post, 25 June. Retrieved 15 October 2015, from https://www.languagetrainers.com/blog/2014/06/25/five-japanese-companies-that-saw-results-after-investing-in-language-training/.

Park, J.S.Y. (2009). *The Local Construction of a Global Language: Ideologies of English in South Korea*. Berlin: Mouton de Gruyter.

Prebble, J. (2007). *Workplace Communication for Skilled Migrants: English for Professional Purposes*. VUW ELIN941. Language in the Workplace Occasional Papers 6.

Piller, I. and Cho, J. (2013). Neoliberalism as language policy. *Language in Society* 42(1): 23–44.

Piller, I. and Lising, L. (2014). Language, employment, and settlement: Temporary meat workers in Australia. *Multilingua* 33(1–2): 35–59.

Poncini, G. (2003). Multicultural business meetings and the role of languages other than English. *Journal of Intercultural Studies* 24(1): 17–32.

Purkayastha, B. (2005). Skilled migration and cumulative disadvantage: The case of highly qualified Asian Indian immigrant women in the US. *Geoforum* 36: 181–196.

Rakuten forges ahead in English. (2015). *Japan Times*, 23 May. Retrieved 15 October 2015, from http://www.japantimes.co.jp/opinion/2015/05/23/editorials/rakuten-forges-ahead-english/#.VjaO3dIrKUl.

Salt, J. and Singleton, A. (1995). The international migration of expertise: The case of the United Kingdom. *Studi Emigrazione* 117: 12–29.

Silver, R.E. (2005). The discourse of linguistic capital: Language and economic policy planning in Singapore. *Language Policy* 4: 47–66.

Song, J.J. (2011). English as an official language in South Korea: Global English or social malady?. *Language Problems and Language Planning* 35(1): 35–55.

Southeast Asia: ASEAN 2015. (2015). *Migration News*, October. Retrieved 15 August 2015, from https://migration.ucdavis.edu/mn/more.php?id=3868.

Technical Education and Skills Development Authority (TESDA). (2015). *TESDA Language Skills Institutes*. Retrieved 15 October 2015, from http://www.tesda.gov.ph/about/tesda/39.

Tyner, J.A. (2004). *Made in the Philippines: Gendered Discourses and the Making of Migrants*. London: Routledge.

Urciuoli, B. and LaDousa, C. (2013). Language management/labor. *Annual Review of Anthropology* 42(1): 175–190.

van Mulken, M. and Hendriks, B. (2014). Your language or mine? or English as a lingua franca? Comparing effectiveness in English as a lingua franca and L1-L2 interactions: Implications for corporate language policies. *Journal of Multilingual and Multicultural Development* 35: 1–22.

Vertovec, S. (2002). *Transnational Networks and Skilled Labour Migration*. University of Oxford, Transnational Communities Programme.

What English is required for skilled migration. (2015). *Australia Dream Solutions*, web log post. Retrieved 15 October, from http://australiadream.com.au/what-english-is-required-for-skilled-migration/.

Wodak, R. and Krzyżanowski, M. (2010). Hegemonic multilingualism in/of the EU institutions: An inside–outside perspective on European language policies. In C. Hülmbauer and E. Vetter (eds.), *Mehrsprachigkeit aus der Perspektive zweier EUProjekte: DYLAN meets LINEE* (pp. 115–134). Frankfurt am Main: Peter Lang.

Yeoh, B. and Lin, W. (2012). *Rapid Growth in Singapore's Immigrant Population Brings Policy Challenges*. Migration Policy Institute, 3 April. Retrieved 15 August 2015, from http://www.migrationpolicy.org/article/rapid-growth-singapores-immigrant-population-brings-policy-challenges.

Zhao, L. (2001). Current situation, consequences and responses of College English Teaching Assessment System. *Foreign Language Teaching* 1: 20–24.

17
Rethinking (un)skilled migrants
Whose skills, what skills, for what, and for whom?[1]

Cécile B. Vigouroux

Introduction

> Skills has become the global currency of the 21st century. Without proper investment in skills, people languish on the margins of society, technological progress does not translate into economic growth, and countries can no longer compete in an increasingly knowledge-based society.
>
> (OECD 2011: 1)

This comes from the foreword of the secretary general of the Organisation for Economic Co-operation and Development (OECD), Ángel Gurría, to the 2012 Skills Strategy Executive Summary. Gurría's line of argument is encapsulated in the executive summary titles *Better Skills, Better Work, Better Lives*.

The 'skills rhetoric' pervades the discourses of many supra-governmental agencies on economic growth and competitive edge in the globalized neoliberal economy. It also highlights the significance they assign to technology as a key factor in the new 'work order' (Gee, Hull, and Lankshear 1996), and therefore treat it as a potential source of inequality among workers and nations.

Regarding migrants, the skills discourse has been exploited by nationalist political parties to frame them as economic predators and 'welfare-hungry parasites'. Immigration itself has been characterized as a big threat to national economies and one of the major causes of the rise of unemployment among native workers. According to Hainmueller and Hiscox (2010), the extent to which (im)migrants are preferred over native citizens varies depending on their skill levels. The opinion survey they conducted in the United States shows a 'strong general preference for highly skilled rather than low-skilled migrants, among respondents at *all* levels of education and income' (see also Müller and Tai 2010 for similar observations).

Skills is also commonly used as a statistical category by (labor) economists working on transnational migrations, for instance, to assess how they affect the migrants' employability on the local job market, how they impact the wages of the migrants or 'local' (i.e., non-migrant) workers competing for the same positions, and whether or not the unskilled migrants draw on public services and represent a fiscal burden to welfare societies (Razin and Sadka 2000; Cohen and Razin 2008; Harell, Soroka, Iyengar, and Valentino 2012).

In this chapter, I argue that *skills* and the migrants they are used to characterize as unskilled, low-skilled, or highly skilled should be analyzed as discursive categories embedded in a web of institutional practices and multilayered ideological formations. The classification of migrants according to labor skills is not just a theoretical or methodological issue; it has implications for policies. At the ground level, it has real life-trajectory consequences for millions of people. Countless prospective migrants across the world have their lives put on hold while they wait for the 'verdict' of their immigration application, the outcome of which is often tied to the labor-skills category they have been boxed in. Indeed, migration control impinges more heavily on people qualified as 'unskilled' than on others (Global Commission on International Migration 2005).

I examine here the ways in which labor-skills classifications have been produced and used to divide and 'objectivize' transnational migrants. In particular, I deconstruct the category '(un)skilled migrants' by showing how it has become a key component of nation-states' strategies for regulating population movements across transnational boundaries.

I argue here that the division and discrimination of migrants according to labor skills rests on the following assumptions: (1) it indexes the nations' utilitarian perspective on migration (Morice 2004) and its intertwinement with the *labor market policy* (Düvell 2003: 2); (2) it re-produces and ratifies the division of labor as manufactured by capitalism and inscribes the workers/migrants into a complex web of power relations both at the micro scale of the receiving nations states and that of the larger, macro political and economic scales; (3) some migrants are considered more desirable than others, hence they should be treated differently, according to their migratory status; (4) some are more easily 'integrable' than others (e.g., the more skilled ones are more likely to assimilate economically); (5) some migrants are deemed *useful* whereas others are *useless*; and (6) migrants are an economic burden on national economies (hence the need to select the 'best' ones).

I show that the migration discourse – including that produced by scholars – has adopted uncritically the labor force segmentation, which, among other things, rationalizes the hierarchy between classes of workers and therefore of migrants (Hagan, Demonsant, and Hernández-León 2014). Among the many questions I address here are the following: Why are transnational migrants categorized into distinct groups based on labor skills? What does it tell us about the ways in which nation-states envision transnational migrations? What counts as skills? How are the migrants' skills assessed, by whom, and for what purpose?

In order to do so, I open my discussion by charting the history of the emergence of skills discourse in reference to the history of Taylorized deskilling that emerged in the late 19th century and gained steam after World War II. I argue that despite their apparent discontinuity the labor force segmentation and the regimentation of migrants belong in the same discursive formation (Foucault 1969) and therefore should be analyzed conjointly. Indeed, the genealogy of labor-skills classifications illustrates the intertwinement of national governments' and supranational and international organizations' labor and immigration policies (Düvell 2003).

Of more direct relevance to applied linguistics, I also illustrate the important role that the assessment of language skills plays in regimenting migrants' transnational mobility. I deconstruct the straightforward way in which governments have correlated language competence with the socioeconomic integration of migrants. Finally, I highlight the extent to which language skills have been commodified in corporate globalization.

Cécile B. Vigouroux

Overview

Taylorization and work management

The labor-skills regime as applied to work is historically linked to 19th-century industrialization and the rise of the capitalist mode of production. It is commonly associated with Taylorization, named after its creator Frederick Winslow Taylor, who, under the name 'scientific management of labor', synthesized ideas in circulation throughout the 19th century in Great Britain and the United States and experimented them in situ (see Braverman 1974 for a critical synthesis). Taylorization entirely reshaped the labor process, for instance by breaking down occupations into small tasks and dissociating them 'from the skills of the workers' (Braverman 1974: 78), leading to the deskilling of the latter: 'The labor process is to be rendered independent from craft, tradition, and the workers' knowledge. Henceforth it is to depend not all upon the abilities of the workers, but entirely upon the practices of management.' Such new arrangement designed primarily to increase productivity and reduce production costs enabled managers to exert control over the production process (the duration of the work day, the amount of commodities produced per hour, etc.) and, by extension, over the workers (their selection, their training, their monitoring at the workplace, etc.). This new division of labor was also shaped around 'a separation of conception from execution' (Braverman 1974: 79), qualified as 'the most decisive single step in the division of labor taken by the capitalist mode of production' (Braverman 1974: 87). Consequently, the production process was no longer controlled by and oriented toward the workers' needs but the demands of the market.

Our concise historical background on the emergence of labor-skills wouldn't be complete without mentioning how the 19th-century capitalist ideology took a new turn in the late 1970s under the influence of Austrian economist Friedrich August von Hayek, whose ideas on free-market society gained steam in the UK and the United States and profoundly impacted all sectors of society worldwide (Spring 1998). This political ideology, commonly termed 'neoliberalism', glorifies individualism, competition among institutions and people, and free enterprise; it despises states' interventionism and welfare system, which are considered too costly to governments and to be a disservice to its recipients (Harvey 2005). In the neoliberal ideology, any decision pertaining to labor, immigration, education, and health care, to cite just a few, is driven by productivity and economic growth. As illustrated later, neoliberalism has been shaping the ways in which *skills* has been discursively articulated in the workers' and migrants' selection process, training (i.e., education), and (self)evaluation.

Framing the migrant as worker

The emergence of the labor-skills regime as applied to transnational migrants shows how migrants were first and foremost envisioned as a labor force. Historically this regime is related to the migration policy mandate given to the International Labor Organization (ILO) at the end of World War I (Böhning 2008). Founded in 1919, the ILO was part of the Treaty of Versailles, which ended at World War I. Trade unions played a leading role in articulating migration policies at that time, as they worked at preventing callous employers' potential exploitation of migrant workers, especially children and women (Rogers, Lee, Swepston and Van Daele 2009).

The American and British governments initially met the ILO's immigration mission with great reservation, as they both feared losing their sovereignty over the control of immigration within their own national boundaries. As suggested by Haus (2001: 280), the ILO's immigration mandate reflected Western European governments' general position 'to view migrants solely in their role as economic actors, or manpower, and to overlook or ignore the prospective incorporation of foreigners into the society and polity'. Since its creation, the ILO has played a crucial role in shaping the discourse of nation-states over immigration and in providing them tools, expertise, and assistance to monitor population movements (Andrijasevic and Walters 2010). Supra-national agencies such as the ILO can be interpreted as instances of 'bio-politics' (Foucault 1975), in which the control of transnational populations has been achieved through ordering and counting migrants, the two being closely intertwined, as illustrated in Desrosières's (1993) history of statistics. In other words, classifying migrants was the first step toward their regimentation.

In order for the ILO to develop international standards and help produce comparative statistical data of workers across countries, initial discussions were launched about the creation of an International Standard Classification of Occupations (ISCO) at the first international conference of labor statisticians in 1921. The first version of ISCO, known as ISCO-58, was adopted much later, in 1957, at the Ninth International Conference of Labor Statisticians (ICLS). The classification aimed at providing governments a template for recruiting foreign labor and managing short- and long-term migrations of workers. While some countries have adopted the ISCO classifications, others such as Canada and South Africa have developed their own national classifications, the National Occupational Classification (NOC) and the South African Standard Classification of Occupations (SASCO), respectively.

Because these categories help produce neat calculations, they have been extensively used by experts and policy makers to write reports and scholarly articles despite their fuzziness, as acknowledged by the different parties that resort to them. Indeed, a close reading of countries' immigration regulations across the world or of global governance agencies' reports shows evidence of a lack of internationally shared definition of what counts as skills or who qualifies as (un)skilled. The International Migration Organization's authoritative *Glossary on Migration* (2011: 59) is not particularly informative in explaining the category 'low-skilled' in relation to that of 'semi-skilled' worker: an unskilled worker is 'a person who has received less training than a semi-skilled worker or, having not received any training, has still acquired his or her competence on the job'. As underscored in the 2005 report of the United Nations expert group meeting on international migration and development, the category 'highly skilled' is also far from being clear:

> It is not always clear just 'who' the highly skilled are. The most obvious starting place is to define highly skilled either by level of education or occupation. Some observers favor one over the other, depending on what one is trying to accomplish. Then again, if relevance to policy is important, most governments typically use some combination of both education and occupation to select for the highly skilled. (. . .) The most fundamental definition of highly skilled tends to be restricted to persons with a 'tertiary' education, typically meaning persons in adult age who have completed a formal two-year college degree or more. This is also the more readily available international statistics and so, by default, the most widely studied measure of highly skilled mobility.
>
> *(Lowell 2005: 2)*

Besides their denotational fuzziness, skills categories are highly problematic, as they are understood according to a plus/minus dichotomy rather than as complex continua.[2] The lack of a coherent and shared definition may seriously hinder our understanding of the impact of labor-skills categories on migrants' access to the receiving countries' labor markets, for instance; it prompts us to be critical in our use of institutional and scholarly reports based on labor stratifications. On the other hand, the lack of agreement, at the international level, on the classifications may well serve the political and economic agendas of nation-states, as it enables them to keep their prerogative over the segmentation of their labor force and, by extension, over their selection of immigrants. Nation-states or small-scale local governments (Varsanyi 2008) decide who can come in, for how long, and on which terms. Regulating immigration becomes a way for nation-states to define themselves. As Sayad (1999: 6) aptly reminds us, 'thinking immigration is thinking the state and it's the state that thinks of itself while thinking immigration' (my translation).

Issues and ongoing debates

Defining skills

The existence of categories is intrinsically linked to that of the functions they play in the social environment where they emerged and are used. They exist through and are ratified by multilayered and intertwined discourses. As shown later, they become naturalized when they are no longer seen as artificial. Regarding the latest ISCO (ISCO-08), skills 'is defined as the ability to carry out the tasks and duties of a given job' (p. 11). *Skill level* and *skill specialization* are used to divide occupations into groups. The former term denotes 'the complexity and range of tasks and duties to be performed in an occupation', while the latter designates the 'field of knowledge required, the tools and machinery used, the materials worked on or with and the kind of goods and services produced' (p. 11). The four skill levels are distinguished according to: (1) the required level of education (from primary school for level 1 to 3–6 years of higher education for level 4); (2) use of strength and endurance (level 1) vs. abstract thinking (level 4); and (3) use and level of literacy and numeracy (from peripheral use for level 1 to extended and complex use for level 4). Linguistic communication skills seem to matter only for occupations at skill levels 3 and 4, although it is not clear how the latter are assessed.

The distinction between occupations based on literacy and numeracy and those that are not tends to reproduce the ideological divide between a literate labor force deemed capable of abstract thought and a non-literate one associated with brainless mechanistic work (Farrell 2009). This institutional divide is entextualized by (prospective) migrants, as illustrated in the following exchange on a Canadian immigration discussion board under the heading: *How to find a genuine unskilled job in Canada*:

RAHULSIRF: April 24, 2012, 10:31:30 am
  (…) PLEASE GIVE ME SOME WEBSITES, EMAIL ADDRESSES, PHONE NUMBERS, COMPANY NAMES, ETC. WHERE I CAN FIND UNSKILLED JOBS
NEWTONE: April 24, 2012, 10:43:15 am
  Please define what is an unskilled job?
RAHULSIRF: April 24, 2012, 10:52:47 am
  According to me, any job that requires only the physical aspect. Uneducated usually do these jobs. Skilled jobs require certain skills and the educated do those.
    (http://www.canadavisa.com/canada-immigration-discussion-board/-t102835.0.html)

This distinction between a literate and non-literate labor force rests on at least the following two assumptions associated with Taylorization: (1) some workplaces are literacy-rich, while others are not; and (2) manual work doesn't require any literacy skills. Prinsloo and Scholtz's (2001) ethnographic work conducted in a shock absorber firm in Cape Town shows that even the silent routine work of operating machines involves writing and reading activities which are hardly recognized as such by workers. Hull's (1999) study in an electronic factory in California's Silicon Valley shows that literacy requirements of work and the evaluation of workers' literate abilities fail to capture the complex literate activities performed at the workplace. She argues that skills should be viewed as embedded in culture, knowledge, and action and not just in technical and measurable terms (see also Hull 1991; Gee et al. 1996; Belfiore, Defoe, Folinsbee, Hunter, and Jackson 2004).

The preceding distinction is also embedded in the ideologically constructed correlations between literacy and economic advancement and productivity, as illustrated by the passage from the foreword of the OECD secretary general quoted at the outset of this chapter (see also Goody 1977 for a discussion on literacy and economic development). In other words, the more skilled, the fitter the worker, and, by extension, the more economically powerful the country. Worth mentioning here is that the 2011 OECD literacy report shows also that 'on average, medium to highly skilled individuals are significantly ($p < 0.10$) more likely to engage in unpaid voluntary activities than those with low skills' (p. 101). In Canada, a society with a high level of 'volunteerism' (between fifty percent and sixty percent of the respondents of the OECD study), volunteering is framed as a key step for migrants to integrate socially and economically, by acquiring 'Canadian experience' (http://www.prepareforcanada.com/working/success-strategies/working-success-strategies-volunteering/). Needless to say, Canada's economy benefits greatly from such free labor framed in civic terms.

In institutional migration discourse and scholarly literature, the 'head and hand distinction' (Stasz 2001: 389) and the differing economic capitals it entails have been epitomized by the expression *brain drain*, initially used in Great Britain in the 1970s to describe the loss of highly educated nationals to the United States. This divide rests on the Cartesian distinction between body and mind, with the mind considered to be superior. The lack of an equivalent term to qualify low-skilled migration suggests that the origination countries do not consider the departure of their manual labor force as a loss for their national economies.

Skilling selves

Categorization is not just a technical activity that produces administrative and statistical categories; it is also a cognitive one by which social agents are perceived and identified (Desrosières and Thévenot 1988; Leigh Star and Strauss 1999; Martiniello and Simon 2005). In anti-immigration rhetoric, the conflation of *unskilled* and *illegal* migrants is often used as a discursive tool to call for stronger migratory regulations (Bhagwati 2003). Categorization also shapes the ways in which people conceive of themselves (by alignment or dis-alignment) as illustrated by the following heading written on the Canadian immigration board mentioned earlier: *How a 'unskilled' Brit goes about moving to Canada?* (http://www.canadavisa.com/canada-immigration-discussion-board/how-a-unskilled-brit-goes-about-moving-to-canada-t94224.0.html). Categorizations also shape the ways in which migrants re-examine their occupations (Hacking 2005), as institutional categories may be in sharp contrast with their own experience of their job as illustrated here:

User7866: A HUGE DISAPPOINTMENT ☹ WHAT TO DO NOW??? ☹ («**on:** January 21, 2013, 10:53:15 pm »

1 (. . .) i finally got a full time job in the bank as a teller and was so happy that i got
2 a stable job and could apply for my PR [Permanent Residence] soon. But, today

3   after my first day to work i realize that its NOC [National Occupation
4   Classification] Code 6551 which means its skill level C and its considered
5   unskilled, therefore i am not eligible to apply under CEC [Canadian Experience
6   Class] for PR ☹ OMG i waited so long (for some reason wanted to get in the
7   bank) and with a 2 year diploma i took me a year jst to get this year, i also
8   worked at as tax return prepared for 5 months full time (40 hrs a week) but that
9   job also is not considered skilled level (FML) and worked hard to get this job I
10 was so happy its good pay and full time benefits and all that n now i feel like a
11 loser ☹ what on earth im going to do now?? Damn it I had so many planssssss!!!
12 what should i do now . . . i really need a job n cant afford to quit jst this it was my
13 first day n now all ma excitement is gone knowing this job wont get me
14 anywhereee . . . is other anything i can do to appply for PR? plz advice n any sort of
15 suggestions

(http://www.canadavisa.com/canada-immigration-
discussion-board/-t132076.0.html)

User7866's narrative is constructed through multiple chronotopes: 'past' (e.g., line 1: *was, got*; line 2: *could;* line 9: *worked*), 'present' (line 3: *realize;* line 12: *need*). Each of them is associated with User7866's different categorizations of his/her newly found *job*: (1) as an economic prospect [lines 1–2: *got a stable job (. . .)*; line 10: *was so happy its good pay and full time benefits*]; and (2) as his/her immigration status perspective (line 2: *could apply for my PR*). User7866's job as experienced [lines 6–7: *i waited so long (for some reason wanted to get in the bank)*; line 9: *I worked hard to get this job*] is reframed into institutional categories: *i realize that its NOC [National Occupation Classification] Code 6551 which means its skill level C and its considered unskilled* (lines 3–5). Worth noting is how the institutional categorization of his/her professional activities (lines 8–9 *that job also is not considered skilled level*) shapes User7866's self-identification (lines 10–11: *i feel like a loser ☹*). Toward the end of the narrative his/her future as migrant in Canada is recast in light of the lack of institutional value his/her work as a bank teller carries: *this job wont get me anywhereee* (lines 13–14). User7866's self-assessment can be analyzed as an example of what Foucault calls 'governmentality' defined as the 'contact between the technologies of domination of others and those of the self' (Martin, Gutman, and Hutton 1988: 19). Individuals' subjectivity is shaped by the government's rationality, as the latter controls the ways in which people act and think of themselves as subjects, citizens, or migrants, as in the present case. (For a similar argument, see Duchêne, Moyer, and Robert 2013, particularly Allan's chapter.)

The more difficult access to a profession is (for instance, through a competitive selection process or lengthy training), the more its prestige and the economic reward increase. Labor skills classification can be analyzed as a social artifact resting on arbitrary and hierarchical distinctions whose aim is to shut people out of certain occupations (see Darrah 1994 for a highly informative and critical assessment of labor skill requirements). In the words of Parkin (1979 cited by Attewell 1990: 435), it acts as 'social closure'. As noted earlier, the latter can have very concrete life consequences for (prospective) migrants.

Although migrants don't necessarily have knowledge of governments' skill classifications – especially those who did not experience the skill requirement administrative burden – they nevertheless have 'incorporated' the stigmatization associated with institutionally defined low-skilled jobs. This is illustrated by Gaston,[3] from the Republic of Congo and a long-time and successful street cigarette seller in one of Cape Town's neighborhoods, whom I encountered in my fieldwork. Having known him for over ten years, he has shared many times how uncomfortable he feels to be 'seen' as a street corner cigarette seller, although he is grateful that his business is lucrative. During one of our many discussions, I asked him the kind of skills I would need to operate a business venture like his. His immediate answer was that no skill was required. I pointed out to him that I was impressed by his way of interacting with his customers, for instance, calling each of them by their first name (to connect personally with them), his way of anticipating their requests by pulling out the brand of cigarettes they smoke as a first interactional move (which shows how well he knows their tastes), his ability to balance a budget, his good management of his stock, his juggling with several on-the-side economic activities, and his talent to entertain a vast and resourceful network, to cite just a few. These skills are crucial in a competitive environment such as Gaston's, surrounded by stores and stalls selling almost the same products. Thanks to his highly sociable personality, he has also made himself a resourceful person for anybody who is looking for or is selling a back-door cellphone or any other electronic device. When I enumerated all his skills, Gaston looked surprised and responded: 'I thought you were talking about training.' His reaction underscores the extent to which 'skills' has been primarily internalized as 'formal training', even by those who had little exposure to higher education like Gaston.

Although skills are said to describe jobs in ISCO-08 or in NOC, people tend to take them up as metonymic characterizations of the job performer, as illustrated by Gaston's uneasiness to be identified as a street cigarette seller, an activity he said he hides from his family in the Congo. In ISCO, skills are approached from a positivist perspective, taking for granted attributes that are presented as independent of the subjectivity of the observer. For instance, years of education are used as an unchallenged index of cultural capital. The 'conversion rate' between cultural and economic capitals is assumed to be straightforward and quantifiable: the more cultural capital one has, the easier it should be for him/her to access the job market and earn more income. This way of thinking has been typical of human capital economists whose studies have found a positive correlation between years of schooling and income (see also labor economists working on migrants' income as illustrated later). Note that the notion of *human capital* does not refer to people but to the skills and assets the latter embody and, as suggest by the term *capital*, as commodities with exchange value. This logic of conversion has been informed by the neoliberal ideology according to which education's primary mission is to prepare students to fulfill the demands of the market economy (see Spring 1998, chap. 6; Urciuoli 2008); students are envisioned as 'entrepreneurial actors' in becoming (Davies and Bansel 2007) with universities as the rehearsal backroom of the workplace.

As stated earlier, the labor-skills classification has very concrete socio-economic and life consequences. On the job market, it ultimately translates into wage disparities between categories of workers and rationalizes them. When applied to migrations, labor-skills classifications produce a 'regime of mobility' (Wang 2004: 352) with unequal access to migration. The ways in which governments sort out transnational migrants by distinguishing between those deemed desirable and those deemed undesirable can be analyzed as a face of neoliberalism (Düvell 2003 and Andrijasevic and Walters 2010) that equally regiments the (locally born) labor force. As highlighted by Düvell (2003), governments are often caught between the hammer and the anvil, with, on the one hand, the need to protect their countries from the alleged invasion of hordes of poor people that would putatively destabilize their economies and, on the other hand, the need to encourage the migration of a highly flexible and cheap labor force. These competing logics have been encapsulated by the expression 'neoliberal paradox' (Varsanyi 2008: 879).

Cécile B. Vigouroux

The border-free world envisioned by some, where goods, people, and economic capitals would circulate transnationally without restrictions, has not materialized, at least when applied to populations. As noted by Bhagwati (1984: 680, cited by Haus 2001: 271), 'Immigration restrictions are virtually everywhere, making immigration the most compelling exception to liberalism in the world economy' (see also Dreher 2007).

Language skills and integration

Language skills have become a key component of the *global mobility regime* (Salter 2006). For instance, language testing has been used to regulate mobility (see Piller 2001; Extra, Spotti, and van Avermaet 2009), with states capitalizing on it to assert their sovereignty (Hogan-Brun, Mar-Molinero, and Stevenson 2009, in particular Shohamy's chapter). Worth noting is that, in institutional discourse on migration, the issue of language skills is often associated with that of migrants' integration, which has been a recurring concern for governments. Although what the different nation-states understand by 'integration' has typically remained rather elusive, there is an implicit correlation assumed between the migrants' competence in the host country's language(s) and the degree of their perceived socioeconomic integration (e.g., Esser 2006; Zimmerman et al. 2008). In other words, the migrants who speak or learn the language(s) of their new socioeconomic ecology 'well' are presumably more likely to be competitive on the local job market than those who do not. Many quantitative studies conducted by economists seem to corroborate this correlation (e.g., Chiswick 1991; Dustmann 1994; Bloom and Grenier 1996).[4]

However, the straightforward equation between economic integration and language skills rests on a number of misguided assumptions entertained by political and (some) academic discourse alike:

1   It assumes that any country is linguistically homogeneous and that a language serves primarily a referential function (e.g., Vaillancourt 2009; Grin, Sfreddo, and Vaillancourt 2010). No attention is paid to language indexicalities and therefore to 'ways of speaking' (Hymes 1989), which vary within the same polity, as an asset or a liability to speakers (Silverstein 2003; Blommaert, Collins, and Slembrouck 2005).
2   Based on the one-language-one-nation ideology inherited from the 18th century, the sharing of the same language is believed to guarantee social cohesion; therefore the migrants who do not speak the host language(s) are considered as unwilling to integrate. This position is clearly stated in the brochure given to newly granted permanent residents in Canada under the heading: *Nick Noorani's Seven Success Secrets for Canadian Immigrants*:

> Without learning the language of your adopted country, all your skills will be hidden away like a gem in a cave. If you moved to Germany or Japan, you would make a conscious decision to learn those languages. Why then do immigrants limit themselves by refusing to learn the language here? Immigrants should make a conscious effort to learn and improve their English or French.

Economic and cultural integrations are discursively articulated here as the migrant's problem and responsibility. Language acquisition is framed as a matter of effort and willingness; learning the host language(s) is implicitly treated as a sign of being a 'good immigrant'. Worth noting is also the ways in which the language classes offered to immigrants are described in the facing page: *Taxpayer-funded language classes*. While the framing of the classes emphasizes Canadian taxpayers' generosity and, by extension, Canada as a welcoming host country, it also constructs a debt-based relationship between the migrants and their adopted country. Not learning the host language(s) equates here with the immigrants not being grateful to the host population. Language acquisition is also approached from a literacy-based perspective, according to which languages are learned from formal training rather than direct and regular interactions.

3   Speaking the main language(s) of the country is likely to guarantee the migrants employment in the host country's main economy and therefore their assimilation into its social fabric (Chiswick and Miller 1995; Chiswick, Lee, and Miller 2002; Remennick 2003; Duvander 2001). Contrary to the conclusions of the above studies, Lebeau and Renaud (2002) and Godin and Renaud (2005) show how a pre-migratory knowledge of French or English in Montreal doesn't facilitate the migrants' access to their first employment. Nonetheless, competence in French plays a role within the first three years after arrival, as it helps the migrants be more mobile on the job market. Those who speak French allegedly tend to leave their first two jobs more rapidly and keep their third employment much longer than those who don't know the language. Therefore, these conclusions appear to challenge the migrants' selection process through the assessment of their language skills and education credentials, as recommended by Canada's economic action published in May 2013. In its new action plan, the Canadian federal government justifies its strengthening of migrants' language and education skills requirements as 'ensur[ing] that immigrants are ready to "hit the ground running" upon arrival' (http://actionplan.gc.ca/en/initiative/strengthening-canadas-immigration-system).

As illustrated in the preceding quote, the concern with productivity is the driving force behind Canada's selection process of migrants. It reflects more broadly the ideology of new capitalism that organizes the production and circulation of labor and capital (Gee et al. 1996; Dreher 2007). Regardless of whether they are linguistic or educational, skills become the measurable values that help assess productivity. Although skills are discursively articulated as benefiting the migrants, highly restrictive migration policies point toward the fact that what is really at stake is competitiveness between nations in the global economy.

Studies conducted by economists do not really help assess the relationship between what they identify as 'language skills' and the migrants' employment; they have documented mostly how language affects economic income rather than explaining the cause-effect relationship (Grin 1996a). Another point of contention lies also in their understanding of 'language use', which boils down to declarations made by the subjects. Indeed, data are usually collected from census returns, which are then transformed into percentages that become data for analysis and in some cases for policy development.

Grin (1996b) presents an apt discussion of methodology problems associated with this practice. It has two major shortcomings: first, it is almost impossible to provide an accurate general account, because the scope of such research is limited to countries in which reliable census data are available, while the vast majority of the countries of the world cannot provide such data and are therefore excluded. Second, hypotheses and therefore knowledge of the effect of economy on languages are grounded on a very small number of countries (typically, the United States, Canada, Australia, and Israel), which are far from being representative of worldwide economic and linguistic dynamics.

A long tradition of sociolinguistic work has also disputed the straightforward correlation between language *competence* (preferred to the notion of *skill*) and access to work, for instance; it shows how language discrimination operates during job interviews (Jupp, Robert, and Cook-Gumperz 1982; Campbell and Roberts 2007; Roberts 2012) or at the workplace (Gumperz 1982). The case of Anna, a yoga teacher in Vancouver, illustrates how language discrimination operates in the corporate world where language has increasingly been commodified:

> Last thursday [my manager] told me that however I mastered yoga I have an accent and lets see after my 6 weeks english accent reduction course what will happen. . . . I am kind of hopeless, nobody believe me that I cant teach in [Name of the yoga studio] and the reason is my accent every one is making a joke cause they don't believe that that is a cause ans not my teaching!!!
>
> *(personal email, September 8, 2015)*

Despite the highly positive reviews (including mine) she has received from the yogis who have attended her classes, Anna's application to be employed in the biggest corporate yoga studio in Canada, from which she actually received her teacher certification, has been turned down several times. After receiving several letters praising Anna's teaching, the infuriated manager of the locally managed studio told her that she will never get a job because of her (Slovakian) 'accent', advising her to take accent reduction classes, to which she refers in her email. (On the policing of accent, see Blommaert 2009.)

Communication is clearly not at issue here, as Anna's students never voiced any complaints about understanding her teaching, nor is the cultural capital to perform the job as acknowledged by the manager herself: she 'told me that however I mastered yoga'. The 'accent issue' has more to do with the social branding of the yoga studio, which every instructor is expected to embody and perform when teaching, illustrating the intrinsically indexical nature of language. In the late modernity corporate world, language performance has increasingly become what workers are recruited and therefore paid for (Cameron 2000). 'Language as neoliberal labor further presupposes the reimagining of the person of the worker as an assemblage of commodifiable elements, i.e. a bundle of skills' (Urciuoli and LaDousa 2013: 176). Because language commodification remains unnoticed to outsiders, people such as Anna feel disempowered by those who, in this particular case, call into question her own understanding of her failure (on the yoga) job market: 'the reason is my accent every one is making a joke cause they don't believe that that is a cause an[d] not my teaching!!!'

Treating the acquisition of the host language(s) as the migrants' main door-opener to employment, the studies appear to construct the host societies as race or ethnicity-free, as if access to jobs was equally available to everybody. Yet, race or ethnicity is still an axis of inequality along which societies (and job markets) operate, according to the conclusions of Oreopoulos (2009) in the Canadian context. Based on a study of 6,000 resumes he showed that the callback rate for applicants with English-sounding names was forty percent higher than for those with Chinese, Indian, or Pakistani names (even those born and educated in Canada). Moreover, the interview request rates for applicants with English-sounding names having Canadian education and experience are three times higher than for their ethnic counterparts with foreign education and experience. Curiously, British applicants with no local work experience and education have the same interview invitation rate as the locally born and educated Canadian job seekers bearing English-sounding names.

This critical assessment of the ways in which governments have instrumentalized skills in host language(s) in order to regulate population movements (Goodman 2011) does not dispute the importance of language in the migrants' access to services and resources provided in the host society. Indeed those who do not command the host language(s) or who lack a local support system that would compensate for it are likely to be more subjected to various local forms of exploitation. These observations simply underscore a non-negligible counterpoint to the widely shared assumption that the migrants' lack of competence in the main language(s) of their host economy impedes their social and economic emancipation. In the next section I argue that one needs to deconstruct the institutionalized construction of *skills* by assessing them in the sociocultural context where they are deployed and, for some of them, acquired. From a methodological point of view, this implies investigating skills ethnographically rather than by relying on proxy categories.

Implications and future directions

The institutional regimentation of migrants through skill classifications fails to account for the wide range of abilities the latter deploy on the job or to get by in their daily lives, as I am about to illustrate.

According to the institutional definition of *skills*, migrants such as Gaston, discussed earlier, are considered as unskilled, since they generally have no tertiary education and often very limited or no professional experience. However, my ethnographic examination of their modus operandi in Cape Town (South Africa) shows that they successfully deploy skills that are under the radar of economic quantitative studies, such as *boldness* and *flexibility*, which have proved useful to engaging in one activity or concurrently in several that they had no previous experience in.

Such skills belong in what Bourdieu (1986) calls 'embodied capital', which he defines as properties of the self and a social agent accumulates consciously or in practice. This form of capital cannot be measured statistically, in part because it does not consist of discrete units. In Kinshasa (DRC), where some of my subjects are from, this embodied capital is encapsulated by the notion of *la débrouille* ('fending for oneself'). It is also known as *système* D, which can be summed up as 'making whatever opportunities arise, to avoid starvation' (Lemarchand cited by Trefon 2004). Acquired sometimes at an early age, this embodied capital involves, among many things, an entrepreneurship based on a wide network of social connections, a good knowledge of alternative ways of acquiring affordable goods to be sold or exchanged, and a reliable small-scale system of *likelemba* (solidarity savings practice). The latter enables migrants to compensate for their lack of access to bank loans (Vigouroux 2013).

Thinking of *capital* makes it possible to highlight the mechanisms of convertibility (economic, symbolic, social, or cultural) – or lack of it – in a more nuanced and context-bound way than the institutional definition of skills does. From a methodological point of view this implies documenting (1) the processes that produce the different forms of capital; (2) their modes of acquisition and accumulation; (3) the field(s) in which they are mobilized; (4) the positions they enable social agents to claim or secure in this field; and (5) how they are mobilized and represented (Bourdieu 1986). For instance, an *institutionalized cultural capital* such as a tertiary education degree tends to have a very low convertibility rate in a country other than where it was acquired. Among the many reasons for this is that the 'credit' given to capital bearers is generally not based on their actual competence but on the symbolic capital the degree carries, which is itself the outcome of a series of practices such as the institution's selective recruiting process of both its students and professors.

Because the value of the institutionalized capital is measured independent of its bearer, it escapes the latter's control over or contribution to its convertibility. In a context where the institutionalized capital was acquired in a language other than the one(s) in currency in the targeted labor market, language may constitute a constraint into the convertibility of cultural capitals into economic ones. Therefore, census-based statistical studies or any quantitative studies that focus solely on the straightforward correlation between migrants' years of education and their economic integration don't help capture the complex dynamics at work regarding the convertibility of skills.

In addition, although some previously acquired skills or capitals may not be literally 'usable' in the new economy, they may help the migrants extend them to develop new functional and valued ones. According to Duleep and Regets (2002: 4), 'learning skills – the set of abilities and experiences that aid in learning new knowledge and skills – should transfer more readily than skills more specifically related to the business and production practices in the origin and destination countries.' Along these lines, Hagan, Hernández-León, and Demonsant (2015: 22) argue that migrants' skills acquisition and development should be approached 'as a lifelong process embedded in workplaces, families, and communities throughout the migrant trajectory'. By providing a thick description of migrants' skills/capital, ethnographic work makes it possible to unveil the arbitrary regimentation of transnational migrants and segmentation of the labor force.

Labor-skills classifications as applied to migrants resemble a 'black box' (Hagan et al. 2015: 11) used by policy makers, migration experts, and, more generally, governments to classify, regiment, and restrain the mobility of targeted populations. In parts of the world where up-to-date censuses are available, the appeal of measurements such as ISCO's rests on the fact that they can generate 'straightforward policy conclusions' (Attewell 1990: 425). However, one should not forget that the conclusions drawn from these kinds of studies are rather partial, as they only include a few sets of countries, primarily those in Europe, North America, and Australia as acknowledged by the World Migration Report (2013: 68): 'Migrants [in North and South receiving countries] are predominantly low-skilled, although reliable up-to-date information is largely missing, *particularly for countries of the South*' (my emphasis).

Economists who work on the economics of migration rely heavily on labor-skill classifications to produce academic articles and reports for global agencies such as the International Migration Office (IMO) or the ILO. Their work asserts and, to a certain extent, naturalizes the legitimacy of these categorizations. Worth noting is that economists (unlike linguists) have been very successful in the decision-making arena, partly 'because of their ability to participate in wide socio-political projects' (Desrosières 2008: 44). Their work and conclusions also benefit from modern democracies' fetishism of big numbers and of rational formalism that bureaucracy embraces (Porter 1995). In other words, they speak the language that policy makers understand (Vigouroux 2014). It is for these reasons that their conclusions and the premises on which they are based are important to analyze as an important part of the institutional discourse on migration and the policies that may ensue.

Labor skills categories appear to have been used as a proxy for social class, making 'the desirable ideal migrant (. . .) entirely a classed concept' (Simon-Kumar 2014: 15). Being a *good/desirable migrant* equates with that of *good worker*. In the skills hierarchy, unskilled migrants are the new proletariat. The desirability discourse is constructed along an economic axis, with *productivity* being the driving force of transnational migration policies worldwide. As illustrated by the institutional genealogy of labor skill categories, migrants have been primarily envisioned as a labor force and therefore as economic subjects. Hence, an analysis of institutional migratory categories goes hand in hand with that of labor force division and organization. The 'skilling of migrants' fits into the neoliberal project, at the local level by rationalizing the workers' hierarchy and at the global level by justifying the restructuring of international labor markets. It is therefore congruent to a concept of nationalism in tune with corporate globalization. As analysts of migration, part of our role is to denaturalize the hegemonic discourse produced by governments or any supranational agencies. I hope to have shown the extent to which the notion of *skills* deserves our critical attention and methodological savoir-faire to achieve this goal.

Further reading

Cameron, D. (2000). *Good to Talk?: Living and Working in a Communication Culture*, London: Sage.

Discusses the implications for language in service economy in the context of globalization and neoliberalism.

Duchêne, A., Moyer, M. and Robert, C. (2013). *Language, Migration and Social Inequalities: A Critical Sociolinguistic Perspective on Institutions and Work*. Bristol: Multilingual Matters.

Examines language related services and work prospects for migrants in diverse countries, situated in neoliberal conditions.

Gee, J., Hull, G. and Lankshear, C. (1996). *The New Work Order*. Boulder, CO: Westview Press.

Discusses the changes in work and communication in the post-Fordist economy.

Urciuoli, B. and LaDousa, C. (2013). Language Management/Labor. *Annual Review of Anthropology*, *42*, 175–190.

A critical and thorough review of studies on language policies and practices under neoliberalism.

Notes

1 I would like to thank Suresh Canagarajah for his extreme patience and encouragements to write this chapter. I also feel indebted to my two reviewers, especially Bonnie Urciuoli for helping me articulate the neoliberal dimension of skills more clearly. I likewise thank Alexandre Duchêne and Salikoko S. Mufwene for their very constructive and challenging comments, which this chapter has significantly benefited from. None of these scholars is responsible for any shortcomings.
2 I thank Bonnie Urciuoli for drawing my attention to this important point.
3 This name and others cited from my data are pseudonyms, used obviously to protect the actual identities of my informants.
4 In these studies, *economic integration* or *assimilation* is narrowly defined in relation to self-reported wages.

References

Allan, K. (2013). Skilling the self: The communicability of immigrants as flexible labour. In Duchêne, A. Moyer, M. and Roberts, C. (eds.), *Language, Migration and Social Inequalities* (pp. 56–78). Bristol: Multilingual Matters.

Andrijasevic, R. and Walters, W. (2010). The international organization for migration and the international government of borders. *Environment and Planning D: Society and Space* 28(6): 977–999.

Attewell, P. (1990). What is skill?. *Work and Occupations* 17(4): 422–448.

Belfiore, M.-E., Defoe, T.A., Folinsbee, S., Hunter, J. and Jackson, N.S. (2004). *Reading Work Literacies in the New Workplace*. Mahwah, NJ: Lawrence Erlbaum Associates, Inc.

Bhagwati, J. (1984) Incentives and Disincentives: International Migration. *Weltwirtschaffliches Archiv* 120(4).

Bhagwati, J. (2003). Borders beyond control. *Foreign Affairs* 82(1): 98–104.
Blommaert, J. (2009). A market of accents. *Language Policy* 8(3): 243–259.
Blommaert, J., Collins, J. and Slembrouck, S. (2005). Spaces of multilingualism. *Language and Communication* 25: 197–216.
Bloom, D.E. and Grenier, G. (1996). Language, employment, and earnings in the United States: Spanish-English differentials from 1970–1990. *International Journal of the Sociology of Language* 121: 45–68.
Böhning, R. (2008). *A Brief Account of the ILO and Policies on International Migration*. International Institute for Labor Studies. Retrieved from http://www.ilo.org/century/lang–en/index.htm [Accessed 5 May 2015].
Bourdieu, P. (1986). Forms of capital. In Richardson, J. (ed.), *Handbook of Theory and Research for the Sociology of Education* (pp. 46–58). New York: Greenwood Press.
Braverman, H. (1974). *Labor and Monopoly Capital*. New York: Monthly Review Press.
Cameron, D. (2000). *Good to Talk?: Living and Working in a Communication Culture*. London: Sage.
Campbell, S. and Roberts, C. (2007). Migration, ethnicity and competing discourses in the job interview: Synthetizing the institutional and personal. *Discourse Society* 18(3): 243–271.
Chiswick, B. (1991). Speaking, reading and earnings among low-skilled immigrants. *Journal of Labor Economics* 9: 149–170.
Chiswick, B., Lee, Y.L. and Miller, P. (2002). *Immigrants' Language Skills: The Australian Experience in a Longitudinal Survey*. Discussion Paper 502. Germany: IZA.
Chiswick, B. and Miller, P. (1995). The endogeneity between language and earnings: International analyses. *Journal of Labor Economics* 13: 246–288.
Cohen, A. and Razin, A. (2008). *The Skill Composition of Immigrants and the Generosity of the Welfare State: Free vs. Policy-controlled Migration*. National Bureau of Economic Research Working Paper No. 14459. Retrieved from http://www.nber.org/papers/w14459 [Accessed 17 June 2015].
Darrah, C. (1994). Skill requirements at work. *Work and Occupations* 21(1): 64–84.
Davies, B. and Bansel, P. (2007). Neoliberalism and education. *International Journal of Qualitative Studies in Education* 20(3): 247–259.
Desrosières, A. (1993). *La politique des grands nombres. Histoire de la raison statistique*. Paris: La Découverte.
Desrosières, A. (2008). *Gouverner par les nombres* (II). Paris: Presses de l'École des Mines.
Desrosières, A. and Thévenot, L. (1988). *Les catégories socioprofessionnelles*. Paris: La Découverte.
Dreher, S. (2007). *Neoliberalism and Migration: An Inquiry into the Politics of Globalization*. Hamburg: Lit Verlag.
Duchêne, A., Moyer, M. and Robert, C., eds. (2013). *Language, Migration and Social Inequalities: A Critical Sociolinguistic Perspective on Institutions and Work*. Bristol: Multilingual Matters.
Duleep, H.O.A. and Regets, M. (2002). *The Elusive Concept of Immigrant Quality: Evidence from 1970–1990*. IZA Discussion Paper Series No. 631. Retrieved from http://hdl.handle.net/10419/21007 [Accessed 22 May 2015].
Dustmann, C. (1994). Speaking fluency, writing fluency and earnings of migrants. *Journal of Population Economics* 7: 133–156.
Duvander, A.-Z.E. (2001). Do country-specific skills lead to improved labor market positions? *Work and Occupations* 28(2): 210–233.
Düvell, F. (2003). *The Globalization of Migration Control*. Retrieved from https://www.opendemocracy.net/people-migrationeurope/article_1274.jsp [Accessed 8 March 2015].
Esser, H. (2006). *Migration, Language and Integration*. AKI Research Review 4, Social Science Research Center Berlin.
Extra, G., Spotti, M. and van Avermaet, P., eds. (2009). *Language Testing, Migration and Citizenship*. London: Continuum Press.
Farrell, L. (2009). Texting the future: Work, literacies, and economies. In Baynham, M. and Prinsloo, M. (eds.), *The Future of Literacy Studies* (pp. 181–198). Basingstoke: Palgrave Macmillan.
Foucault, M. (1969). *Archéologie du savoir*. Paris: Gallimard.
Foucault, M. (1975). *Surveiller et punir*. Paris: Gallimard.

Gee, J.P., Hull, G. and Lankshear, C. (1996). *The New Work Order*. Boulder: Westview Press.

The Global Commission on International Migration. (2005). *Migration in an Interconnected World: New Directions for Action*. Report. www.gcim.org [Accessed 13 March 2015].

Godin, J.-F. and Renaud, J. (2005). L'intégration professionnelle des nouveaux immigrants: Effets de la connaissance pré-migratoire du français et (ou) de l'anglais. *Cahiers Québécois de Démographie* 31(1): 149–172.

Goodman, S.W. (2011). Controlling immigration through language and country knowledge requirements. *West European Politics* 34(2): 235–255.

Goody, J. (1977). *The Domestication of the Savage Mind*. Cambridge: Cambridge University Press.

Grin, F. (1996a). The economics of language: Survey, assessment, and prospects. *International Journal of the Sociology of Language* 121: 17–44.

Grin, F. (1996b). Economic approaches to language and language planning: An introduction. *International Journal of the Sociology of Language* 121: 1–16.

Grin, F., Sfreddo, C. and Vaillancourt, F. (2010). *The Economics of the Multilingual Workplace*. New York: Routledge.

Gumperz, J. (1982). *Discourse Strategy*. Cambridge: Cambridge University Press.

Hacking, I. (2005). *Neuf impératifs des sciences qui classifient les gens*. Lecture at the Collège de France, Paris. Retrieved from http://www.college-de-france.fr/site/ian-hacking/course-2005-02-22.htm [Accessed 14 April 2015].

Hagan, J.M., Demonsant, J.-L. and Hernández-León, R. (2014). Identifying and measuring the lifelong human capital of "unskilled" migrants in the Mexico-US Migratory circuit. *Journal on Migration and Human Security* 2(2): 76–100.

Hagan, J.M., Hernández-León, R. and Demonsant, J.-L. (2015). *Skills of the "Unskilled"*. Oakland: University of California Press.

Hainmueller, J. and Hiscox, M.J. (2010). Attitudes toward highly skilled and low-skilled Immigration: Evidence from a survey experiment. *American Political Science Review* 104(1): 61–84.

Harell, A., Soroka, S., Iyengar, S. and Valentino, N. (2012). The impact of economic and cultural cues on support for immigration in Canada and the United States. *Canadian Journal of Political Science* 45(3): 499–530.

Harvey, D. (2005). *A Brief History of Neoliberalism*. Oxford: Oxford University Press.

Haus, L. (2001). Migration and international economic institution. In Zolberg, A. and Benda, P. (eds.), *Global Migrants, Global Refugees: Problems and Solutions* (pp. 271–296). New York: Berghahn Books.

Hogan-Brun, G., Mar-Molinero, C. and Stevenson, P., eds. (2009). *Discourses on Language and Integration: Critical Perspective on Language Testing*. Amsterdam: John Benjamins.

Hull, G. (1991). *Hearing Other Voices: A Critical Assessment of Popular Views on Literacy and Work*. Berkeley, CA: National Center for Research in Vocational Education.

Hull, G. (1999). What's in a label? Complicating notions of the skills-poor worker. *Written Communication* 16(4): 379–411.

Hymes, D. (1989). Ways of speaking. In Bauman, R. and Sherzer, J. (eds.), *Explorations in the Ethnography of Speaking* (pp. 433–451, 2nd ed.). Cambridge: Cambridge University Press.

International Migration Organization. (2011). http://www.epim.info/wp-content/uploads/2011/01/iom.pdf.

International Organization of Migration. (2011). *Glossary on Migration*. Geneva: IOM.

Jupp, T.C., Robert, C. and Cook-Gumperz, J. (1982). Language and disadvantage: The hidden process. In Gumperz, J. (ed.), *Language and Social Identity* (pp. 232–266). Cambridge: Cambridge University Press.

Lebeau, R. and Renaud, J. (2002). Nouveaux arrivants de (1989). langue et mobilité professionnelle sur le marché du travail de Montréal: Une approche longitudinale. *Cahiers Québécois de Démographie* 31(1): 69–94.

Leigh Star, S. and Strauss, A. (1999). Layers of silence, arenas of voice: The ecology of visible and invisible work. *Computer Supported Cooperative Work* 8: 9–30.

Lowell, B.L. (2005). *Policies and Regulations for Managing Skilled International Migration for Work*. United Nations Expert Group Meeting on International Migration and Development. Retrieved from http://www.un.org/esa/population/meetings/ittmigdev2005/P03-LLowell.pdf [Accessed 19 June 2015].

Martin, L.H., Gutman, H. and Hutton, P., eds. (1988). *Technologies of the Self*. Hutton Amherst: University of Massachusetts Press.

Martiniello, M. and Simon, P. (2005). Les enjeux de la catégorisation. Rapports de domination et luttes autour de la représentation dans les sociétés post-migratoires. *Revue Européenne des Migrations Internationales* 21(2): 7–18.

Morice, A. (2004). Le travail sans le travailleur. *Plein Droit* 61: 2–7.

Müller, T. and Tai, S. (2010). *Individual Attitudes towards Migration: A Re-examination of the Evidence*. University of Genova: Mimeo. Retrieved from https://www.wto.org/english/res_e/reser_e/gtdw_e/wkshop10_e/tai_e.pdf [Accessed 23 May 2015].

Oreopoulos, P. (2009). *Why Do Skilled Immigrants Struggle in the Labor Market? A field Experiment with Six Thousand Resumes*. NBER Working Paper No. 15036. Retrieved from http://www.nber.org/papers/w15036 [Accessed 23 May 2015].

Organisation for Economic Co-operation and Development (OECD). (2011). *Literacy for Life: Further Results from the Adult Literacy and Life Skills Survey*. Statistics Canada, OECD.

Parkin, F. (1979). *Marxism and class theory: A bourgeois critique*. New York: Columbia University Press.

Piller, I. (2001). Naturalization language testing and its basis in ideologies of national identity and citizenship. *International Journal of Bilingualism* 5(3): 259–277.

Porter, T. (1995). *Trust in Numbers: The Pursuit of Objectivity in Science and Public Life*. Princeton: Princeton University Press.

Prinsloo, M. and Scholtz, S. (2001). New workplaces, new literacies, new identities. *Journal of Adolescent and Adult Literacy* 44(8): 710–713.

Razin, A. and Sadka, E. (2000). Unskilled migration: A burden or a boon for the welfare state? *Scandinavian Journal of Economics* 102(3): 463–479.

Rogers, G., Lee, E., Swepston, L. and Van Daele, J. (2009). *International Labour Organization and the Quest for Social Justice, 1919–2009*. Geneva: International Labour Office.

Remennick, L. (2003). Language acquisition as the main vehicle of social integration: Russian immigrants of the 1990s in Israel. *International Journal of the Sociology of Language* 164: 83–105.

Roberts, C. (2012). Translating global experience into institutional models of competency: Linguistic inequalities in the job interview. In Arnaut, K., Blommaert, J., Rampton, B. and Spotti, M. (eds.), *Language and Superdiversity II*, vol. 14, no. 2 (pp. 49–72). UNESCO & Max Planck Institute. http://unesdoc.unesco.org/images/0022/002223/222319e.pdf#page=50 last accessed October 24, 2016.

Salter, M. (2006). The global visa regime and the political technologies of the international self: Borders, bodies, biopolitics. *Alternatives* 31: 167–189.

Sayad, A. (1999). Immigration et "pensée d'État". *Actes de la Recherche en Sciences Sociales* 129: 5–14.

Shohamy, E. (2009). Language tests for immigrants: Why language? Why tests? Why citizenship? In Hogan-Brun, G., Mar-Molinero, C. and Stevenson, P. (eds.), *Discourses on Language and Integration: Critical Perspective on Language Testing* (pp. 45–60). Amsterdam: John Benjamins.

Silverstein, M. (2003). Indexical order and the dialectics of sociolinguistic life. *Language and Communication* 23: 193–229.

Simon-Kumar, R. (2014). Neoliberalism and the new race politics of migration policy: Changing profiles of the desirable migrant in New Zealand. *Journal of Ethnic and Migration Studies* 41(7): 1172–1191.

Spring, J. (1998). *Education and the Rise of the Global Economy*. Mahwah, NJ: Lawrence Erlbaum Associates.

Stasz, C. (2001). Assessing skills for work: Two perspectives. *Oxford Economic Papers* 53(3): 385–405.

Trefon, T. (2004). *Reinventing order in the Congo*. London: Zedbooks.

Urciuoli, B. (2008). Skills and the selves in the new workplace. *American Ethnologist* 35(2): 211–228.

Urciuoli, B. and LaDousa, C. (2013). Language management/labor. *Annual Review of Anthropology* 42: 175–190.

Vaillancourt, F. (2009). Language and poverty: Measurement, determinants and policy responses. In Harbert, W. (ed.), *Language and Poverty* (pp. 147–160). Bristol: Multilingual Matters.

Varsanyi, M. (2008). Rescaling the "Alien", rescaling personhood: Neoliberalism, immigration, and the state. *Annals of the Association of American Geographers* 98(4): 877–896.

Vigouroux, C. (2013). Informal economy and language practice in the context of migrations. In Duchêne, A. Moyer, M. and Roberts, C. (eds.), *Language, Migration and Social Inequalities* (pp. 223–245). London: Multilingual Matters.

Vigouroux, C. (2014). *Unsettling Disciplinary Boundaries: Where Do We Start, What Should We Expect, and For What Gains?* Sociolinguistic Symposium 20, Jyväskylä, Finland.

Wang, H.-L. (2004). Regulating transnational flows of people: Institutional analysis of passports and visas as a regime of mobility. *Identities: Global Studies in Culture of Power* 11(3): 351–376.

World Migration Report. (2013). http://publications.iom.int/books/world-migration-report-2013.

Zimmerman, K. F., Kahane, M., Constant, A., DeVoretz, D., Gataullina, L., and Zaiceva A. (2008). *Study on the Social and Labour Market Integration of Ethnic Minorities*. IZA Research Report 16. Bonn.

18
Diaspora and language

Jonathan Rosa and Sunny Trivedi

Introduction

This chapter illustrates how poststructuralist approaches to the analysis of language, diaspora, and migration can critically reframe understandings of linguistic practices and social identities. Rather than taking diasporas for granted as naturally occurring phenomena, we point to institutional frameworks, cultural ideologies, and politico-economic structures that organize processes of diasporization. Such an analysis of diasporization makes it possible to understand how particular languages and populations are recognized as diasporic or domestic – foreign or indigenous – in ways that often erase their histories in a given context. Thus, for example, English language use is not typically interpreted as a sign of diaspora in the United States despite its anchoring in histories of migration and displacement in this settler colonial context. In contrast, although Spanish language use predates English language use in the United States, it is often framed as a "foreign" language and its users are seen as (im)migrant, transnational, and diasporic regardless of whether they were born and raised within the fifty states or other US territories. Moreover, indigenous languages and their users occupy a precarious status vis-à-vis histories of colonialism and ongoing reconfigurations thereof that organize conceptions of the legitimacy of particular populations and practices within a given political context. These fraught dynamics illustrate the importance of carefully tracking the uneven ways in which processes of diasporization organize language hierarchies and societal inclusion and exclusion.

A focus on language ideologies and practices as they pertain to processes of diasporization shows how diasporas can be viewed not as static objects but rather as dynamic phenomena. This involves a consideration of the semiotics of sociolinguistic differentiation (Irvine and Gal 2000), namely the reproduction and transformation of boundaries demarcating linguistic forms and social identities. We deploy this semiotic approach by focusing on language ideologies in the production of signs of "elsewhere" associated with diasporic experiences. We denaturalize notions of homeland and related presumptions about authenticity by emphasizing the perspectival nature of signs of diasporic continuity and change. We interrogate ideologies of temporality associated with diasporization by showing how diasporic continuity can be produced through shifting sociolinguistic practices on the one hand, and how diasporic change can be produced through the maintenance of sociolinguistic practices on the other. Building from these insights, we propose conceptualizations of intra-diasporic relations not only in terms of emergent migration paths, technologies, and social categories, but also long-standing place-making practices, situations of linguistic and broader cultural contact, and forms of transnationalism. We analyze the ways that language ideologies and linguistic practices shape and are shaped by ethnoracial (e.g., Mexican, Chinese), religious (e.g., Muslim, Hindu), and other such cultural diasporas (e.g., hip hop, queer), as well as the potential for the emergence of linguistic diasporas in which language itself is understood as the central characteristic connecting people across time and space. Collectively, this range of diasporic phenomena illuminates the powerful role that language practices and ideologies play in shaping processes and experiences of migration and vice versa.

Overview of the topic

How have scholars approached questions about the role of language in producing diasporic populations and practices? Research on the emergence of diasporic categories often presumes upon naturalized relationships between a fixed geographical homeland, a migrant community leaving that place and ending up elsewhere, and the cultural practices associated with these populations and contexts. Diasporas were once primarily conceptualized in relation to issues of homeland and return, but as Canagarajah and Silberstein point out, it is important "to ask whether it was ever true that all diaspora subjects always held a return to their homeland as their ultimate goal" (2012: 81). Thus, work on language and returned migrants, such as Zentella's (1990) analysis of Puerto Ricans who return to Puerto Rico from the mainland United States, emphasizes the need to rethink conceptions of language based on the expectation of a singular migration path of exile or return. More recently, scholars have analyzed language and diasporic processes by focusing on migrants from a given territory who introduce linguistic and cultural difference to a new territory. For example, we see this thinking in the recent proliferation of work on language and "superdiversity," which posits increasingly "diverse" modes of linguistic practice associated with new migration patterns and settlement (Blommaert and Rampton 2011). Rather than approaching these various diasporic phenomena "as bounded, territorialized, static, and homogeneous," attention to language can reveal their dynamic, context-specific, and ideological nature (Canagarajah and Silberstein 2012: 82). Further, as Makoni, Smitherman, Ball, and Spears (2003) demonstrate in their analysis of Black language practices from a transatlantic perspective, interrogations of the historical conditions in which "diversity" is perceived and constituted can enable reconsiderations of the power relations and contestations thereof that shape the production of diasporic populations and modes of communication. These insights suggest the importance raciolinguistic ideologies (Flores and Rosa 2015), which interrogate the historical and contemporary co-naturalization of language and race, in the joint analysis of populations and language practices that might otherwise be approached separately as "diasporic," "domestic," or "foreign."

Examinations of language and the production of long-standing and emergent diasporic phenomena alike are sharpened when viewed through the theoretical lens of language ideologies (Silverstein 1979; Schieffelin, Woolard, and Kroskrity 1998). Wortham describes language ideologies as "models that link types of linguistic forms with the types of people who stereotypically use them" (Wortham 2008: 43). Dick suggests that analyses of diasporization must take into account "the influential role language ideologies and practices play in the processes of transnational people-making among migrants" (2011: 228). By bringing attention to the joint production of linguistic and social categories, language ideologies perspectives can contribute greatly to efforts toward denaturalizing assumptions about diasporic practices, places, and populations. Such assumptions are frequently anchored in what linguistic anthropologists have described as a Herderian language ideology of "one nation–one language–one people" (Bauman and Briggs 2003; Irvine 2006), which was historically tied to the emergence of modern nation-states. Studies focusing on continuity and change of language and diasporic identities are often closely related to Herderian stereotypes that associate particular linguistic practices, places, and populations with one another. Even widely embraced scholarly analyses of the creation of nation-states, such as Anderson's *Imagined Communities* (1991), position shared language practices as naturally occurring phenomena that are precursors rather than dialectic counterparts to the imagination of national identities; in fact, these language practices are every bit as imagined as the national communities to which given languages are understood to correspond (Silverstein 2000; Pennycook 2010). Thus, Herderian language ideologies reproduce and transform boundaries delimiting linguistic forms and social categories, thereby naturalizing stereotypical connections between a homeland, a particular population, and the languages they use.

Language is a crucial component of the processes through which populations, and diasporas by extension, come to be naturalized, because "language lies at the center of imagined and contested pasts and futures, mediating desire and identity" (Brown and Silberstein 2012: 2). With language at the center of imagined, ideological notions of diasporic identity formation, processes of sociolinguistic differentiation show how social and linguistic differences reproduce, transform, and maintain diasporic boundaries. These differences are rooted in institutional frameworks, cultural ideologies, and larger historical and politico-economic structures. In the discussions following in this section, we examine conceptualizations of the dynamic semiotic processes through which diasporas coalesce, as well as various populations that have come to be viewed as diasporic. We focus specifically on language as it pertains to political legitimation and recognition, and transnational practices of communication and consumption.

Legitimating, denaturalizing, and recognizing linguistic and diasporic identities

Ideologies of language and diaspora frequently focus on questions about the legitimacy of particular transnational or (im)migrant populations and practices within a given political context. These ideologies are reflected in contested conceptions of linguistic standardization, purity, authenticity, and heritage. Das's (2011) research on the Montreal Tamil diaspora examines how Sri Lankan and Indian Tamil groups engage in a diasporic and ethnolinguistic division of labor through the development of competing notions of authenticity and modernity associated with written and spoken Tamil. This division of labor differentiates Sri Lankan Tamils, who are conventionally imagined as using "classical" written Tamil, from Indian Tamils, who are often imagined as using "modern" spoken Tamil. Whereas Brahmin Tamils from India, who are of a higher caste yet stereotypically associated with a less pure form of Tamil, have difficulties proving their sociocultural and linguistic authenticity, Sri Lankan Tamils, who are less affluent yet stereotypically associated with a more classical form of Tamil, have trouble proving their caste and class legitimacy. Through their language practices and ideologies, these "groups justify their elite status on the basis of differentiated values of authenticity and modernity" (Das 2011: 779). Das argues that "these ethnonational subgroups are thus able to inhabit distinct ethnolinguistic identities by emphasizing historicized contrasts in their habitual use of colloquial and literary styles of Tamil" (2011: 779). This example illustrates the complexity of a linguistic diaspora in which not just language, but, crucially, *linguistic differentiation* (Irvine and Gal 2000) is the anchoring process connecting groups across time and space. The dynamic relationship between differentiations of language, ethnicity, caste, and class participate in the (re)production and (trans)formation of Tamil diasporic identities in Montreal.

In a related analysis of the Sri Lankan Tamil diaspora in Canada, Britain, and the United States, Canagarajah (2012) challenges ideas about ethnicity and heritage language by examining how particular youth engage in "self-styling" to assert their diasporic identities. These self-styling practices are particularly important for diasporic populations for whom "community membership has to be constructed anew all the time" (Canagarajah 2012: 134). Whereas Rampton's (1999) notion of "crossing" emphasizes out-group uses of particular linguistic tokens, Canagarajah's theorization of self-styling denaturalizes the relationship between linguistic tokens and ethnoracial identities. Thus, Canagarajah emphasizes the importance of attending to the assertion of particular identities and the recognition thereof rather than tracking the presence of forms presumed to correspond to one identity or another. For example, he shows how receptive bilingual practices constitute important components of the self-styling of diasporic Tamil repertoires consisting of familiarity with English and Tamil forms. However, the forms themselves are not the primary focus. Instead, Canagarajah persuasively suggests that "we have to consider identification practices in a more process-oriented and practice-based manner, moving self-styling beyond product-oriented considerations" (2012: 131).

In his study of the emergence of a Latino diaspora among families of Latin American labor migrants in Israel, Paz (2015) makes the complementary point that "the complex interplay between language structure, use (or practice), and ideology requires multiple methodologies to better capture what happens to language in diasporic and transnational contexts" (2015: 163). In this particular context, Paz shows how Israeli-born Latino youth reproduce the Latin American cultural value of "educacción," or politeness, while speaking Hebrew despite the popular conception that these two practices are contradictory or mutually exclusive. Paz suggests that such interactional accomplishments reflect the ways that "Latinos could perceive or produce a split between the language as denotational code and the interpersonal pragmatics" (2015: 152). For Paz, these practices reflect the diasporic deterritorialization and reterritorialization of language and identity.

Rosa (2015) also examines processes of diasporic deterritorialization and reterritorialization in his analysis of the ways that US-based Mexicans and Puerto Ricans reterritorialize spatial borders through the creation of "Mexican Chicago" and "Puerto Rican Chicago" on the one hand, and linguistic borders through the creation of hybrid Spanglish forms on the other. He draws on theories of enregisterment to track the joint creation of linguistic and social categories (Silverstein 2003a; Agha 2005). Agha defines enregisterment as "processes whereby distinct forms of speech come to be socially recognized (or enregistered) as indexical of speaker attributes by a population of language users" (Agha 2005: 38). In the case of "MexiRican" Chicago, components of the English and Spanish languages are enregistered as emblems of diasporic US Latino identities. Rosa shows how these processes of enregisterment, or "self-styling" to use Canagarajah's term, allow US Latinas/os to meet competing demands of speaking what is ideologically constructed as "unaccented" English while also signaling intimate familiarity with Spanish. Similar to the analyses of Paz and Canagarajah, these bilingual repertoires combine forms in novel ways to create emergent pragmatic effects. Such effects, as Cashman (2015) shows in her analysis of trajectories of language use and identity formation among queer US Latinas/os, challenge naturalized relationships between language and identity. Taken together, these studies demonstrate the importance of denaturalizing the relationship between linguistic forms and social identities, attending to efforts toward the linguistic legitimation of diasporic identities, and tracking the perspectival ways in which these identities are recognized (Silverstein 2003b).

Media and home-making

With the increased mobility of particular populations and forms of communication through emergent technologies, (im)migrant groups can build local diasporic identities rooted in transnational affiliations (Jacquemet 2005). To apprehend the role of technology in mediating these transformations of language and identity, we must carefully investigate "the intersection between mobile people and mobile texts – an intersection no longer located in a definable territory, but in the deterritorialized world of late modern communication" (Jacquemet 2005:5). In studies of language and diaspora, this involves reexamining assumptions about the communicative channels and practices associated with (im)migrant populations and distant homelands. Scholars have sought to do so by analyzing the role of media and mediatization in the production of diaspora and other identities (Spitulnik 1996; Shankar 2004, 2008; Eisenlohr 2007, 2011; Agha 2011). Mediatization, which Agha defines as "institutional practices that reflexively link processes of communication to processes of commoditization" (2011: 163), can both facilitate and constrain community bonds as well as relations with diasporic homelands and linked contexts. Emergent forms of media have the capacity to shape and produce sociocultural processes through platforms such as audiovisual technology, print, and digital platforms, a sentiment echoed by Eisenlohr (2011) regarding scholarly engagement with the "mediality" of language. For Eisenlohr, the interplay between media and phenomena such as diasporization can be illuminated through "the systematic comparison of language as a medium of sociocultural processes with the ways various contemporary media technologies are recognized to similarly mediate and shape such processes" (2011: 266).

In her analysis of the significance of media in contemporary processes of diasporic identity formation, Shankar notes that "topics of intertextuality, indexicality, bivalency, and more broadly, identity formation have been sociolinguistically examined in the lives of youth, but seldom with explicit attention to the pervasive role of media in shaping language practices" (2004: 317). She suggests that Bollywood, one such influential source of media consumption, functions "simultaneously as visual culture, a social institution, as well as a linguistic resource for many diasporic youth" (2004: 318). South Asian diasporic youth incorporate various aspects of Bollywood films into their communicative repertoires, such as film-specific speech genres, dialogue, and songs, indexing "how distinct voices and registers are deployed in various speech settings" (Shankar 2004: 318). Issues of voicing and intertextuality figure centrally in this analysis of the ways in which media discourses provide resources for the creation of diasporic identities (Bakhtin 1981; Bauman and Briggs 1992; Hill 1995; Agha 2005). By intertextually referencing popular media and drawing on the voices of figures in such media, diasporic populations are able to produce deterritorialized identities rooted in modern communication and technology.

In an autoethnographic account of the development of a "post-diasporic" Korean-American identity, Choi (2012) draws on related Bakhtinian themes of multivocality and dialogism to analyze her experiences of shifting language practices and modes of identification in the context of viewing Korean serial dramas. Seeking to challenge dichotomized conceptualizations of language and identity, Choi builds on Kramsch's observation that diasporic populations "tend to either idealise or demonise their country of origin" in homogenizing ways that overlook the complexity of experiences in diasporas and homelands alike (Kramsch 2006: 116). In an illustration of this point, Wortham and Rhodes (2013) show how particular language learning experiences are viewed as signs of diaspora through various forms of erasure. Their analysis involves a student whose family interprets her embrace of mainstream literacy practices as a sign of her diasporic identity as a US Mexican, thereby erasing both the affinity for similar literacy practices in Mexico and the rejection of such practices among many long-standing US-based persons. In a related study, Koven (2013) explores how the perceived influence of French on Portuguese language use among Luso-descendants in France can be simultaneously interpreted through diasporic and transnational models. Whereas the diasporic model stigmatizes such practices as the problematic abandonment of Portuguese identity, the transnational model valorizes these practices as the legitimate reflection of repertoires developed across borders. In her analysis of similar forms of diasporic and transnational simultaneity, Choi argues "that speakers of multiple languages are not different people in different languages but speakers who are complexly entangled in multiple languages and voices" (2012: 110).

Understanding the roles of language and media technologies in diasporic formations also involves a consideration of transidiomatic practices, which Jacquemet formulates as "the communicative practices of transnational groups that interact using different languages and communicative codes simultaneously present in a range of communicative channels, both local and distant" (2005: 264–265). Transidomatic practices illuminate "how new discourses and modes of representation are reterritorialized within the local environment, and as such must be taken into account in any assessment of the impact of globalization on languages" (Jacquemet 2005: 267). Such transidiomatic practices are evident in Eisenlohr's analysis of Muslims in Mauritius, for whom particular communicative channels, such as sound reproduction technologies, "have become part of devotional performances" that are central to the creation and reproduction of their religiously oriented diasporic identities (Eisenlohr 2011: 268). Eisenlohr shows how, for diasporic Mauritian Muslims, technologies such as audio cassettes, CDs, and digital MP3 files are integral to the circulation of *n'at*, a locally inflected genre of praise poetry, which involves using particular communicative practices that need to be recited by an authoritative source. Such diasporic phenomena require an examination of how particular linguistic practices, ideologies, and technologies are incorporated into local environments. These sound technologies "support what one could describe as the 'vanishing' aspects of the linguistic medium" in diasporic contexts, as part of broader "discursive regimes of authenticity" (2011: 272). Analyzing n'at as a transidiomatic practice of Mauritian Muslims demonstrates the need for a consideration of the role of media technologies and language as platforms for locally situated diasporic identity formation.

Corona (2012) is similarly concerned with the ways that media consumption and vernacular language use combine to contribute to the creation of diasporic identities among Latino youth in Barcelona. He shows how reggaeton, a musical genre with Latin American and Caribbean roots, ties to hip hop and reggae, and predominantly Spanish lyrics, becomes a template for the creation of diasporic identities among young Latin American migrant men who are racialized as non-white Latinos in the European context. Corona analyzes the ways in which these youth seek to embody Latino authenticity by adopting the language, clothing, and broader style of popular reggaeton performers. Corona's research is tied to related work on language and hip hop as a diasporic phenomenon (Alim, Ibrahim, and Pennycook 2009). This work demonstrates how the circulation of media through contemporary technologies not only participates in the reproduction of existing diasporic identities, but also creates possibilities for emergent diasporas rooted in cultural practices and geographical imaginaries that are not strictly anchored in ethnicity or relations between nations. Thus, as Eisenlohr points out, it is neither the case that "diasporic identifications . . . always stand in tension with national belonging" (2006: 395), nor that they are even primarily oriented toward nations in the conventional sense. The following section builds from these insights to analyze how scholars have been critically rethinking forms of diasporic "diversity."

Issues and ongoing debates

A central contemporary debate in research on language and diaspora involves the framing of globalization as an emergent process despite centuries of mobility among populations and practices. This section considers the ways that scholars have analyzed language, globalization, and diaspora through the development of concepts such as superdiversity. It also points to thinkers who have challenged these conceptualizations and offered alternative approaches that call into question perspectives from which particular populations and practices are positioned as diverse or superdiverse while others are left unmarked altogether.

In the last several decades, the concept of globalization, or the movement of people, commodities, culture, and knowledge across space and time, has become a prime topic of scholarly interest. To the extent that globalization is inextricably linked to relations sustained across trajectories of migration, diasporic phenomena are central to the study of such global processes. In efforts to conceptualize transformations in the range of identities and practices produced through globalization, some scholars have suggested that we must shift from thinking in terms of stable multiculturalisms associated with familiar populations in earlier eras to the contemporary condition of "super-diversity" (Vertovec 2007, 2010). For Blommaert and Rampton,

> super-diversity is characterized by a tremendous increase in the categories of migrants, not only in terms of nationality, ethnicity, language, and religion, but also in terms of motives, patterns and itineraries of migration, processes of insertion into the labour and housing markets of the host societies, and so on.
>
> *(Blommaert and Rampton 2011: 1)*

This framework is based on the premise that we are witnessing a proliferation of "categories of migrants" and distinctive linguistic repertoires dramatically superseding that of previous historical moments.

In contrast, Reyes suggests that "this speaker focus neglects a thorough conceptualization and interrogation of the listening subject: how change may not in fact begin with speaking subjects (migrants) but may be brought into being by listening subjects (those authorized to speak about migrants) and whatever anxieties and desires motivate the circulation of representations of speakers" (2014: 368). For Reyes, it is crucial to interrogate ideologies of race, ethnicity, and language that inform perceived gradations of diversity, which position some populations as unmarked and others as diverse or superdiverse. Reyes argues that we must locate the production of linguistic superdiversity in the politics of positionality that structures perceptions of "Otherness" rather than in the empirical linguistic practices of migrant populations within a globalizing world. This is related to broader critiques of the ways discourses of linguistic diversity are linked to forms of neoliberal population management (Urciuoli 2010; Gal 2012; Shankar 2015). Other scholars warn that "if we approach globalization naively . . . we overlook the fact that words like 'global' and globalization' in their most current use were first broadcast most aggressively by marketing agents and marketing schools" (Trouillot 2001: 128). Thus, in our examination of language and diaspora, we must carefully consider the commodification of linguistic and cultural difference (Dávila 2001; Comaroff and Comaroff 2009; Duchêne and Heller 2012; Cavanaugh and Shankar 2014). From this perspective, superdiversity is part of a broader set of narratives about globalization that "not only silence histories of the world but also veil our understanding of the present" (Trouillot 2001: 128).

Language is of particular concern in narratives about globalization and diaspora because of its emblematic status as a sign of identity and difference not only within the popular imagination but also in scholarly analyses. By combining homogenizing ideologies of "a people" and "a language,"

> linguistic scholarship itself played a major role in the development of the European nation-state as well as in the expansion and organization of empires . . . and the factuality of named languages continues to be taken for granted in a great deal of contemporary institutional policy and practice.
> *(Blommaert and Rampton 2011: 4)*

These paradigms become consequential for diasporic populations whose identities and practices do not correspond to hegemonic models of language and culture. Extending theorizations of diaspora by Hall (1990), Clifford (1994), and Appadurai (1996), Flores (2009) critiques hegemonic models of language and culture by suggesting that "in much thinking about diaspora, undue emphasis tends to be placed . . . either on continuity and tradition or on change and disjuncture" (2009: 17). He argues that these problematic tendencies can be avoided by "thinking diaspora from below":

> The grassroots, vernacular, "from below" approach helps to point up the many diaspora experiences that diverge from those of the relatively privileged, entrepreneurial or professional transnational connections that have tended to carry the greatest appeal in scholarly and journalistic coverage. That approach, guided by a concern for subaltern and everyday life struggles of poor and disenfranchised people, also allows for special insights into ongoing issues of racial identity and gender inequalities that are so often ignored or minimized in the grand narratives of transnational hegemony.
> *(Flores 2009: 25)*

Rosa (2014) uses this "thinking diaspora from below" approach to analyze language ideologies that inform the diasporic socialization of US-based Mexican and Puerto Rican youth. He shows how these youth learn to contest borders delimiting languages, nations, and ethnoracial categories in their production of diasporic identities. By "thinking diaspora from below," it becomes possible to track the dynamic, situated processes through which diasporic identities are constructed, enacted, and transformed. Ndhlovu (2014) demonstrates a similar approach in his examination of language and the construction of African diasporic identities in Australia, which defy conventional assumptions linking linguistic practices, populations, and territories. Such analyses of local, context-specific claims about and performances of linguistic subjectivities contribute to broader efforts toward reimagining and reconstituting boundaries that problematically circumscribe languages and identities (Canagarajah 2005; Makoni and Pennycook 2007; Pennycook 2010). The following section considers the implications of moving beyond these problematic approaches to diaspora and mobility.

Implications

Interrelations between language and diaspora are consequential not only for scholarly analyses of communication and identity in a globalized and globalizing world, but also within a range of institutional settings that profoundly impact everyday life. This section explores the implications of language and diaspora in particular institutional contexts and processes, specifically focusing on schools and language learning on the one hand, and designations of political status and access to citizenship on the other.

Language, diaspora, and education

Schools are key sites for tracking language and diasporization because they are often charged with the interrelated tasks of facilitating language socialization and reproducing national identities (Rosa 2014). Nationalist ideologies inform many educational language policies that position particular language varieties as legitimate and others as unfit for institutionally sanctioned use. In mainstream school settings, language policies are frequently informed by "monoglossic ideologies" (García and Torres-Guevara 2010) that promote socialization to the language that "ideally express[es] the spirit of [the] nation and the territory it occupies" (Gal 2006: 163). These ideologies are associated with processes of assimilation that stigmatize diasporic populations' multilingual communicative repertoires (Santa Ana 2004). This is particularly consequential for diasporic populations whose identities are specifically constructed as ethnolinguistic or raciolinguistic categories (Zentella 2007; Flores and Rosa 2015). While this marginalization through educational language policies can result in the assimilation of some diasporic populations, it can also produce diasporic sensibilities by targeting groups based on their perceived differences. Jaspers (2005) investigates the emergence of such diasporic sensibilities by analyzing how Moroccan students in Belgium engage in language styling to respond to the hegemonic structures that marginalize them. These students creatively use their supposed linguistic incompetence to disrupt classroom activities. In the US context, ideologies of linguistic incompetence stigmatize some diasporic students by perpetually designating them as "long-term English learners" regardless of whether they effectively use the English language across a range of contexts (Flores, Kleyn, and Menken 2015). Thus, it is important to analyze the ways educational language policies can stigmatize diasporic students, as well as how these students respond to and contest this stigmatization.

Schools are also central sites of language standardization and the cultivation of diasporic identities for heritage language users and learners (Das 2011). Fader (2009) analyzes the ways that heritage language learning is a central component of socializing diasporic Hasidic Jewish identities. She shows how Hasidic Jewish girls who learn English and Yiddish in school and various community settings develop complex multilingual repertoires that shift throughout the life span in relation to gender hierarchies and norms. The result is a distinction between Hasidic Yiddish and Hasidic English as "two emerging gendered varieties of Jewish languages" (2009: 32). The stigmatization of such repertoires is the focus of heritage language learning studies that interrogate and problematize the distinction between categories such as "native speaker" and "heritage learner" (Bonfiglio 2010; Flores and Rosa 2015). Kramsch (2012) analyzes the ways that such distinctions produce "feelings of imposture" among multilingual subjects whose language practices are viewed as inauthentic or illegitimate. However, Kramsch also argues that to the extent that it "forc[es] us to face the historically contingent nature of our categories and boundaries, the notion of imposture might help us understand the political promise offered by a poststructuralist approach to applied linguistics" (2012: 499).

Such a poststructuralist approach can challenge the ways in which diasporic students face linguistic marginalization in schools by contributing to the creation of educational language policies and curricula that embrace rather than stigmatize their identities.

Language, diaspora, and political status

Language requirements are often components of national policies that distinguish between and classify people as citizens and various kinds of non-citizens. This can have important consequences for diasporic populations classified as asylum seekers and refugees, whose linguistic repertoires might not correspond to expectations about the language use that indexes one's origins in a given geographical locale. Blommaert's (2009) analysis of the experiences of Joseph, a Rwandan refugee, calls attention to the institutions, cultural ideologies, and politico-economic structures that portray his sociolinguistic profile in such a way that his asylum application to the UK is denied. The Home Office in the UK questioned Joseph's Rwandan legitimacy because of his perceived sociolinguistic "abnormality," which was anchored in presumptions about linguistic authenticity and "monoglot" language ideologies (Silverstein 1996). Joseph spoke multiple of languages including Kinyarwanda, French, and English, but his sociolinguistic practices were not consistent with the imagined Rwandan repertoire. Blommaert suggests that the "repertoire displayed by Joseph is indicative of *time*, not just of *space*: it connects to the *history* of a region in the past two decades, not just to the region" (2009: 416). Reflecting on the ways that the institutionalization of monoglot language ideologies privilege particular language varieties and stigmatize others, Blommaert notes that "it is remarkable to see how powerful the nation-state is for people whose lives defy the salience of national units" (2009: 425). In a related analysis of asylum proceedings, Jacquemet is similarly concerned with the ways "national ideologies of monolingualism are increasingly difficult to be implemented as mobility (human, cultural, and semiotic) increases" (2011: 478). He points to the systematic "communicative breakdowns" that take place in asylum proceedings, which involve "the asymmetrically distributed ability to tiptoe through the different frames of an increasingly hybridized institutional talk" (2011: 494).

Scholars have also challenged the ways that language is used in citizenship tests. McNamara and Shohamy argue that applied linguists who participate in the creation of such tests must "identify and articulate the underlying assumptions and goals of the policies requiring tests" (2008: 93). They suggest that "not granting citizenship on the grounds of language is a violation of basic human/personal rights to welfare, education, and other social benefits" (2008: 93). These exclusions highlight some of the ways in which language contributes to forms of "dis-citizenship" (Ramanathan 2013). While language can play a key role in denying access to citizenship for diasporic populations, Paz (2016) shows how particular non-citizen diasporic youth are positioned as undeportable in relation to language ideologies through which they are perceived as speaking like citizens. Thus, it is important to critically examine the ways that diasporic groups can be positioned as different kinds of political subjects through a range of language policies, tests, and institutional procedures. Moreover, we must rethink the ways that language scholars are recruited to participate in and contribute to these political processes.

Future directions

Emergent directions in language and diaspora research build on existing efforts toward rethinking how populations and communicative practices come to be experienced and recognized as diasporic, as well as how these experiences and modes of recognition are (re)produced and (trans)formed. This section points to some potential paths forward in language and diaspora research, focusing specifically on perspectives that locate diasporization in relation to processes of ethnicization and racialization, and analyses linking space, time, and trajectories of diasporic identity formation.

Rethinking ethnicization, racialization, and diasporization

The ethnicization and racialization of language is a central, yet often understudied, way in which diasporic identities emerge. In her analysis of racialization and language, Urciuoli notes that "language differences are routinely attributed to origin differences and in the United States origin differences are framed as race and ethnicity" (1996: 15). Relatedly, Dick argues that "dominant U.S. indexical orders position migrants as outsiders primarily by racializing them" (Dick 2011: 229). These insights are relevant for the analysis of language and diasporic populations across nation-state contexts. Indeed, for Dick, "the exploration of racial indexicality is a primary thread that ties together language-based research on transnational migration with the broader ethnographic exploration of this subject" (2011: 229). To the extent that language and diaspora research is concerned with understanding how language practices, populations, and geographies come to be naturalized in relation to one another, it is closely linked to what Chun and Lo term "research on linguistic racialization, or the sociocultural processes through which race – as an ideological dimension of human differentiation – comes to be imagined, produced, and reified through language practices" (2016: 220). Importantly, a consideration of ethnicization and racialization is part of a broader effort toward incorporating intersectional approaches into the analysis of language and identity in general, and language and diaspora specifically (Block and Corona 2016). In their promotion of an intersectional approach, Canagarajah and Silberstein note that "as people shuttle between communities, they hold in tension their diaspora identities with other locally relevant identities" (2012: 82). Processes of ethnicization and racialization are central to constituting these various identities.

In an analysis of "raciolinguistic ideologies," Flores and Rosa (2015) show how attending to language ideologies and processes of racialization can help to draw connections between the experiences of groups that might be approached separately as racial minorities or diasporic populations. Such an analysis can help to show how particular language practices are disparately associated with transnational migrants, citizens, and various minoritized groups. These differentiations are related to processes of naturalization that are central to linguistic analyses of ethnicization and racialization. From this perspective, no group or linguistic practice is inherently diasporic or non-diasporic; they only come to be positioned as such through language ideologies and processes of naturalization. Future research on diasporic language ideologies will benefit from an analysis of the ways that ethnicization and racialization organize how particular language forms and populations come to embody a domestic "here" or a foreign "elsewhere."

Rethinking diasporic temporalities, spatialities, and teleologies

Recent analyses of the diasporic deterritorialization and reterritorialization of language have drawn on the Bakhtinian notion of "chronotope" in efforts to understand how space-time scales organize the perceived movement of populations and language forms (Eisenlohr 2007; Blommaert 2015; Paz 2015; Rosa 2016). Reiter and Rojo note that a focus on spatial and temporal frames is helpful in that it provides us with "a window from which to observe the changes in practices and ideologies in diaspora" (Reiter and Rojo 2015: 6). For Blommaert, if we are to conceptualize the configurations of power built in the processes of diasporic identity formation, "we should keep track of the strong definitional monoglot effect of the modern state – of the way in which time and space are made (literally) 'static' (i.e., a feature of the state) in relation to language – and part of any postmodern phenomenology of language and culture should be devoted to understanding the very non-postmodern ideologies and practices that shoot through postmodern, globalized realities" (Blommaert 2009: 12). Mendoza-Denton (2008) shows how diasporic actors engage and contest the power relations that are central to these spatial and temporal systems. In a process she terms "hemispheric localism," her diasporic research participants recast "Global North" and "Global South" politics onto language practices, local geographies, social groups, and expressive styles. These spatial ideologies are also tied to temporal ideologies that associate some practices with a "there" and "then" of the past or future and other practices with a "here" and "now" of the present.

Emergent work on language and diaspora interrogates these spatial and temporal scales by reconsidering diasporic teleologies that presume upon particular trajectories of movement, linguistic practice, and social identity formation. Dick's analysis of Mexican non-migrants productively redirects attention to ways that not only diasporic populations "live contrapuntally," with a focus on "lives inhabitable in some other space and time" (2013: 413). She shows how "the effort to circumnavigate barriers to socioeconomic mobility in Mexico through physical mobility to the United States only recreates diaspora at home for all but a handful of migrants and their families" (2013: 423). Thus, research on language and diaspora must focus on how diasporic experiences take shape among those who leave but also those who stay, in receiving locales and homelands alike. Similarly, teleologies of language and identity must be reconsidered, as various studies have demonstrated that language use and modes of identification among diasporic populations shift in different directions across the lifespan (Bailey 2007; Fader 2009; Choi 2012; Han 2012). Efforts towards denaturalizing diasporic spatialities, temporalities, and teleologies coincide with the insight that "diaspora has to be treated as a 'community' that embodies difference, not similarity" (Canagarajah and Silberstein 2012: 82).

Summary

This chapter has identified some of the ways that poststructural approaches to the analysis of language and diaspora can contribute powerfully to broader efforts toward denaturalizing stereotypes that equate linguistic patterns, social categories, and geographical contexts. Such poststructural approaches play a crucial role in sharpening understandings of relations among long-standing and emergent modes of migration and communication, as well as critically rethinking the conditions that structure the mobility of populations and practices. Just as language ideologies perspectives shed new light on how diasporic connections and fissures take shape, a focus on processes of diasporization illuminates the ways that linguistic practices become associated with particular people, times, and places.

As we have sought to demonstrate throughout this chapter, conceptualizations of language and diaspora have far-reaching implications within academic circles and wider publics. In these various settings, notions of belonging and signs of difference structure experiences of societal inclusion and exclusion for populations positioned as unmarked insiders and various marginalized 'others'. As these fraught dynamics unfold, analyses of the interplay between language and processes of diasporization not only document the intertwining of inequalities and diasporic identities, but also point to the everyday ways in which conceptions of homeland and displacement are contested and reconfigured.

Related topics

Translanguaging in mobility
Nation-state, transnationalism, and language
New orientations to identity in mobility
Space, place, and language
A rhizomatic account of heritage language

Further reading

Alim, H. S., Ibrahim, A. and Pennycook, A., eds. (2009). *Global Linguistic Flows: Hip Hop Cultures, Youth Identities, and the Politics of Language*. New York: Routledge.

> This volume analyzes the role of language in the production of diasporic hip hop cultures. Bringing together analyses of the linguistic mediation of diasporic identities through emergent communicative and sonic channels on a global scale, the book powerfully demonstrates the need to refine conceptualizations of diaspora by attending to the politics of contemporary popular cultural practices.

Canagarajah, S. and Silberstein, B., eds. (2012). Special Issue: Diaspora identities and language. *Journal of Language, Identity, and Education, 11*(2), 81–149.

> This special issue takes a poststructural approach to language and diasporic identities. It presents an overview of contemporary conceptualizations of diaspora, as well as a set of case studies that emphasize the often fraught, situational production of diasporic identities through language and vice versa.

Eisenlohr, P. (2007). *Little India: Diaspora, Time, and Ethnolinguistic Belonging in Hindu Mauritius*. Berkeley: University of California Press.

> Eisenlohr's semiotic approach to language and diaspora emphasizes the ideologies that organize orientations to place, time, and identity within the predominantly Indian context of Mauritius. Importantly, Eisenlohr shows how different languages can function as powerful emblems of diasporic identities regardless of the extent to which they are primary channels of everyday communication.

Mendoza-Denton, N. (2008). *Homegirls: Language and Cultural Practice among Latina Youth Gangs*. Malden: Blackwell.

> Mendoza-Denton analyzes processes of diasporic and broader social category-making among Latina youth in relation to semiotic repertoires including language use and various forms of embodiment. She shows how language use allows students to invoke, remap, and transform political dynamics within school and community contexts. For Mendoza-Denton, these practices reflect a form of "hemispheric localism" through which Latina youth enact local diasporic identities linked to "Global North" and "Global South" imaginaries.

Reiter, R. M. and Rojo, L. M. (2015). *A Sociolinguistics of Diaspora: Latino Practices, Identities, and Ideologies*. New York: Routledge.

> This volume synthesizes work on the role of language in the experiences of long-standing Latin American origin populations in North American settings and emergent Latin American (im)migrant groups in contexts such as Europe and the Middle East. By focusing on language ideologies, the various entries demonstrate that, far from a straightforward unifier among Latinos across time and space, the Spanish language functions as a cultural practice around which to simultaneously produce diasporic continuity and difference.

Shankar, S. (2006). *Desi Land: Teen Culture, Class, and Success in Silicon Valley*. Durham: Duke University Press

Shankar presents an account of diasporic language socialization among US-based South Asian youth. She explores the language ideologies and practices of consumption through which Desi youth construct diasporic identities that are differentiated along lines such as class statuses, (im)migrant generation cohorts, and ethnoracial categories. Crucially, she interrogates the socialization of diasporic Desi identities from in-group as well as out-group perspectives, attending carefully to the broader political, economic, and historical dynamics that shape notions of diasporic belonging and otherness.

References

Agha, A. (2005). Voice, footing, enregisterment. *Journal of Linguistic Anthropology* 15(1): 38–59.
Agha, A. (2011). Meet mediatization. *Language & Communication* 31(3): 163–170.
Alim, H. S., Ibrahim, A. and Pennycook, A., eds. (2009). *Global Linguistic Flows: Hip Hop Cultures, Youth Identities, and the Politics of Language*. New York: Routledge.
Anderson, B. (1991). *Imagined Communities: Reflections on the Origins and Spread of Nationalism*. New York: Verso.
Appadurai, A. (1996). *Modernity at Large: Cultural Dimensions of Globalization*. Minneapolis: University of Minnesota Press.
Bailey, B. (2007). Shifting negotiations of identity in a Dominican American community. *Latino Studies* 5(2): 157–181.
Bakhtin, M. (1981). *The Dialogic Imagination: Four Essays*. Austin: University of Texas Press.
Bauman, R. and Briggs, C. (1992). Genre, intertextuality, and social power. *Journal of Linguistic Anthropology* 2(2): 131–172.
Bauman, R. and Briggs, C. (2003). *Voices of Modernity: Language Ideologies and the Politics of Inequality*. New York: Cambridge University Press.
Block, D. and Corona, V. (2016). Intersectionality in language and identity research. In S. Preece (ed.), *The Routledge Handbook of Language and Identity* (pp. 507–522). London: Routledge.
Blommaert, J. (2009). Language, asylum, and the national order. *Current Anthropology* 50(4): 415–441.
Blommaert, J. (2015). Chronotopes, scales, and complexity in the study of language in society. *Annual Review of Anthropology* 44: 105–116.
Blommaert, J. and Rampton, B. (2011). Language and superdiversity. *Diversities* 13(2): 1–21.
Bonfiglio, T. (2010). *Mother Tongues and Nations: The Invention of the Native Speaker*. New York: De Gruyter Mouton.
Brown, M. S. and Silberstein, S. (2012). Contested diaspora: A century of Zionist and anti-zionist rhetorics in America. *Journal of Language, Identity, & Education* 11: 85–92.
Canagarajah, S., ed. (2005). *Reclaiming the Local in Language Policy and Practice*. Mahwah: Lawrence Erlbaum.
Canagarajah, S. (2012). Styling one's own in the Sri Lankan Tamil diaspora: Implication for language and ethnicity. *Journal of Language, Identity, & Education* 11: 124–135.
Canagarajah, S. and Silberstein, B. (2012). Diaspora identities and language. *Journal of Language, Identity, & Education* 11: 81–84.
Cashman, H. (2015). Queer Latin@ networks: Languages, identities, and the ties that bind. In R. M. Reiter and L. M. Rojo (eds.), *A Sociolinguistics of Diaspora: Latino Practices, Identities, and Ideologies* (pp. 66–80). New York: Routledge.
Cavanaugh, J. R. and Shankar, S. (2014). Producing authenticity in global capitalism: Language, materiality, and value. *American Anthropologist* 116(1): 51–64.
Choi, J. (2012). Multivocal post-diasporic selves: Entangled in Korean dramas. *Journal of Language, Identity, & Education* 11: 109–123.
Chun, E. W. and Lo, A. (2016). Language and racialization. In N Bonvillain (ed.), *The Routledge Handbook of Linguistic Anthropology* (pp. 220–233). New York: Routledge.

Clifford, J. (1994). Diasporas. *Cultural Anthropology* 9: 302–338.
Comaroff, J. L. and Comaroff, J (2009). *Ethnicity, Inc.* Chicago: University of Chicago Press.
Corona, V. (2012). *Globalization, Identities, and School: Latinos in Barcelona*. PhD thesis, Autonomous University of Barcelona.
Das, S. (2011). Rewriting the past and reimagining the future: The social life of a Tamil heritage language industry. *American Ethnologist* 38(4): 774–789.
Dávila, A. M. (2001). *Latinos, Inc.: The Marketing and Making of a People*. Berkeley: University of California Press.
Dick, H. (2011). Language and migration to the United States. *Annual Review of Anthropology* 40: 227–240.
Dick, H. (2013). Diaspora and discourse: The contrapuntal lives of Mexican non-migrants. In A. Quayson and G. Daswani (eds.), *A Companion to Diaspora and Transnationalism* (pp. 412–427). Malden: Blackwell.
Duchêne, A. and Heller, M., eds. (2012). *Language in Late Capitalism: Pride and Profit*. New York: Routledge.
Eisenlohr, P. (2006). The politics of diaspora and the morality of secularism: Muslim identities and Islamic authority in Mauritius. *Journal of the Royal Anthropological Institute* 12: 395–412.
Eisenlohr, P. (2007). *Little India: Diaspora, Time, and Ethnolinguistic Belonging in Hindu Mauritius*. Berkeley: University of California Press.
Eisenlohr, P. (2011). Media authenticity and authority in Mauritius: On the mediality of language in religion. *Language and Communication* 31: 266–273.
Fader, A. (2009). *Mitzvah Girls: Bringing up the Next Generation of Hasidic Jews in Brooklyn*. Princeton: Princeton University Press.
Flores, J. (2009). *The Diaspora Strikes Back: Caribeño Tales of Learning and Turning*. New York: Taylor and Frances.
Flores, N., Kleyn, T. and Menken, K. (2015). Looking holistically in a climate of partiality: Identities of students labeled "long-term English learners". *Journal of Language, Identity, & Education* 14: 113–132.
Flores, N. and Rosa, J. (2015). Undoing appropriateness: Raciolinguistic ideologies and language diversity in education. *Harvard Educational Review* 85(2): 149–171.
Gal, S. (2006). Contradictions of standard language in Europe: Implications for the study of practices and publics. *Social Anthropology* 13(2): 163–181.
Gal, S. (2012). Sociolinguistic regimes and the management of "diversity". In A. Duchêne and M. Heller (eds.), *Language in Late Capitalism: Pride and Profit* (pp. 22–42). New York: Routledge.
García, O. and Torres-Guevara, R. (2010). Monoglossic ideologies and language policies in the education of U.S. Latinas/os. In E. Murillo, S. Villeans, R. T. Galván, J. S. Muñoz, C. Martínez and M. Machado-Casas (eds.), *Handbook of Latinos and Education* (pp. 182–193). New York: Routledge.
Hall, S. (1990). Cultural identity and diaspora. In J. Rutherford (ed.), *Identity: Community, Culture, Difference* (pp. 222–237). London: Lawrence and Wishart Press.
Han, H. (2012). Being and becoming "a new immigrant" in Canada: How language matters, or not. *Journal of Language, Identity, & Education* 11(2): 136–149.
Hill, J. (1995). The voices of Don Gabriel: Responsibility and self in a modern Mexicano narrative. In D. Tedlock and B. Mannheim (eds.), *The Dialogic Emergence of Culture* (pp. 97–147). Chicago: University of Illinois Press.
Irvine, J. T. (2006). Speech and language community. In *Encyclopedia of Languages and Linguistics* (pp. 689–698, 2nd ed.). Boston: Elsevier.
Irvine, J. T. and Gal, S. (2000). Language ideology and linguistic differentiation. In P. Kroskrity (ed.), *Regimes of Language: Ideologies, Polities, Identities* (pp. 35–83). Santa Fe: School of American Research Press.
Jacquemet, M. (2005). Transidiomatic practices: Language and power in the age of globalization. *Language and Communication* 25: 257–277.
Jacquemet, M. (2011). Crosstalk 2.0: Asylum and communicative breakdowns. *Text & Talk* 31(4): 475–497.

Jaspers, J. (2005). Linguistic sabotage in a context of monolingualism and standardization. *Language & Communication* 25: 279–297.

Koven, M. (2013). Speaking French in Portugal: An analysis of contested models of emigrant personhood in narratives about return migration and language use. *Journal of Sociolinguistics* 17(3): 324–354.

Kramsch, C. (2006). Response to Alastair Pennycook and Azirah Hashim. *Asia Pacific Journal of Education* 26(1): 115–116.

Kramsch, C. (2012). Imposture: A late modern notion in poststructuralist SLA research". *Applied Linguistics* 33(5): 483–502.

Makoni, S. and Pennycook, A., eds. (2007). *Disinventing and Reconstituting Languages*. Clevedon: Multilingual Matters.

Makoni, S., Smitherman, G., Ball, A. F., and Spears, A., eds. (2003). *Black Linguistics: Language, Society, and Politics in Africa and the Americas*. London: Routledge.

McNamara, T. and Shohamy, E. (2008). Language tests and citizenship. *International Journal of Applied Linguistics* 18(1): 89–95.

Mendoza-Denton, N. (2008). *Homegirls: Language and Cultural Practice among Latina Youth Gangs*. Malden: Blackwell.

Ndhlovu, F. (2014). *Becoming an African Diaspora in Australia: Language, Culture, and Identity*. New York: Palgrave Macmillan.

Paz, A. (2015). The deterritorialization of Latino educacción: Noncitizen Latinos in Israel and the everyday diasporic subject. In R. M. Reiter and L. M. Rojo (eds.), *A Sociolinguistics of Diaspora: Latino Practices, Identities, and Ideologies* (pp. 151–165). New York: Routledge.

Paz, A. (2016). Speaking like a citizen: Biopolitics and public opinion in recognizing non-citizen children in Israel. *Language & Communication* 48: 18–27.

Pennycook, A. (2010). *Language as a Local Practice*. New York: Routledge.

Ramanathan, V. (2013). Language policies and (dis)citizenship: Who belongs? Who is a guest? Who is deported? *Journal of Language, Identity, & Education* 12: 162–166.

Rampton, B. (1999). Styling the other: Introduction. *Journal of Sociolinguistics* 3: 421–427.

Reiter, R. M. and Rojo, L. M., eds. (2015). *A Sociolinguistics of Diaspora: Latino Practices, Identities, and Ideologies*. New York: Routledge.

Reyes, A. (2014). Linguistic anthropology in 2013: Super-new-big. *American Anthropologist* 116(2): 366–378.

Rosa, J. (2014). Learning ethnolinguistic borders: Language and diaspora in the socialization of U.S. Latinas/os. In R. Rolón-Dow and J. Irizarry (eds.), *Diaspora Studies in Education: Toward a Framework for Understanding the Experiences of Transnational Communities* (pp. 39–60). New York: Peter Lang.

Rosa, J. (2015). Nuevo Chicago: Language, diaspora, and Latina/o panethnic formations. In R. M. Reiter and L. M. Rojo (eds.), *A Sociolinguistics of Diaspora: Latino Practices, Identities, and Ideologies* (pp. 31–47). New York: Routledge.

Rosa, J. (2016). Racializing language, regimenting Latinas/os: Chronotope, social tense, and American raciolinguistic futures. *Language & Communication* 46: 106–117.

Santa Ana, O., ed. (2004). *Tongue Tied: The Lives of Multilingual Children in Public Education*. Lanham: Rowman & Littlefield.

Schieffelin, B. B., Woolard, K. A. and Kroskrity, P. V., eds. (1998). *Language Ideologies: Practice and Theory*. New York: Oxford University Press.

Shankar, S. (2004). Reel to real: Desi teens' linguistic engagements with Bollywood. *Pragmatics* 14(2/3): 317–335.

Shankar, S. (2008). *Desi Land: Teen Culture, Class, and Success in Silicon Valley*. Durham: Duke University Press.

Shankar, S. (2015). *Advertising Diversity: Ad Agencies and the Creation of Asian American Consumers*. Durham: Duke University Press.

Silverstein, M. (1979). Language structure and linguistic ideology. In R. Cline, W. Hanks and C. Hofbauer (eds.), *The Elements: A Parasession on Linguistic Units and Levels* (pp. 193–247). Chicago: Chicago Linguistic Society.

Silverstein, M. (1996). Monoglot "Standard" in America. In D. Brenneis and R. Macaulay (eds.), *The Matrix of Language: Contemporary Linguistic Anthropology* (pp. 284–306). Boulder: Westview Press.

Silverstein, M. (2000). Whorfianism and the linguistic imagination of nationality. In P. Kroskrity (ed.), *Regimes of Language: Ideologies, Polities, Identities* (pp. 85–138). Santa Fe: School of American Research Press.

Silverstein, M. (2003a). Indexical order and the dialectics of sociolinguistic life. *Language & Communication* 23: 193–229.

Silverstein, M. (2003b). The whens and wheres – as well as hows – of ethnolinguistic recognition. *Public Culture* 15(3): 531–557.

Spitulnik, D. (1996). The social circulation of media discourse and the mediation of communities. *Journal of Linguistic Anthropology* 6(2): 161–187.

Trouillot, M.R. (2001). The anthropology of the state in the age of globalization: Close encounters of the deceptive kind. *Current Anthropology* 42(1): 125–138.

Urciuoli, B. (1996). *Exposing Prejudice: Puerto Rican Experiences of Language, Race, and Class*. Long Grove: Waveland Press.

Urciuoli, B. (2010). Entextualizing diversity: Semioitic incoherence in institutional discourse. *Language & Communication* 30: 48–57.

Vertovec, S. (2007). Super-diversity and its implications. *Ethnic and Racial Studies* 30(6): 1024–1054.

Vertovec, S. (2010). Towards post-multiculturalism? Changing communities, contexts, and conditions of diversity. *International Social Science Journal* 199: 83–85.

Wortham, S. (2008). Linguistic anthropology of education. *Annual Review of Anthropology* 37: 37–51.

Wortham, S. and Rhodes, C. (2013). Life as a chord: Heterogeneous resources in the social identification of one migrant girl. *Applied Linguistics* 34(5): 536–553.

Zentella, A.C. (1990). Returned migration, language, and identity: Puerto Rican bilinguals in dos worlds/two mundos. *International Journal of the Sociology of Language* 84: 81–100.

Zentella, A.C. (2007). "Dime con quién hablas, y te diré quién eres": Linguistic (in)security and Latina/o identity. In J. Flores and R. Rosaldo (eds.), *A Companion to Latina/o Studies* (pp. 25–38). Malden: Blackwell.

Part III
Methods

19
Complexity, mobility, migration

Jan Blommaert, Massimiliano Spotti, and Jef Van der Aa

Introduction and definitions

We start by taking the reader through what superdiversity means and why we believe that a research orientation on migration and mobility needs these days to keep itself occupied with superdiversity. The term superdiversity refers to the 'diversification of diversity' that occurred after the end of the Cold War, and is characterized by different and intensive flows of migration – more people moving from more places towards more places (Vertovec 2007) – combined with the generalized spread and deployment of internet-driven and long-distance information and communication technologies (ICT). More than merely capturing the recent diversification of diversity and situating its onset in global history, superdiversity has the potential to become an emerging perspective on change and unpredictability in ever more intensively encroaching social and cultural worlds (Arnaut 2012). While the first force – new migrations – caused a rapid escalation of demographic diversity in centers all over the world, the second force – mobility through ICT – has shaped new environments for communication and identity development wherever it is used. The combination of both forces leads to rapid and relatively unpredictable social and cultural change – a stage of acceleration and intensification in globalization processes raising fundamental challenges for the ways in which we imagine societies, human beings and their activities (cf. Eriksen 2001; Arnaut and Spotti 2015). In this capacity, the emergent academic discourse around superdiversity aligns itself with critical perspectives in transnational studies which reject simplifying and reifying schemes for the complex realities along national and/or ethnic lines – denounced as "methodological nationalism" (Wimmer and Glick Schiller 2003) and the "ethnic lens" (Glick Schiller 2007), respectively. Thus, superdiversity as an emerging perspective "denies the comfort of a set of easily applicable assumptions about our object, its features and its meanings," which has two profound methodological consequences: (1) we see 'complexity', 'hybridity', 'impurity', and other features of 'abnormal' sociolinguistic objects as 'normal'. (2) The uncertainty brought to bear by this emergent perspective compels us towards a (linguistic) ethnographic stance, in which "we go out to find how sociolinguistic systems operate rather than to project a priori characteristics onto them" (Blommaert 2015: 84).

Taking a lead from important predecessors in migration studies (cf. Squires 2005), superdiversity develops from a research tradition that has its solid roots in British social theory and cultural studies about 'new identities' and 'new ethnicities' (cf. Hewitt 1986; Mercer 1994; Hall 1996 and more recently revisited by Harris and Rampton 2010). Further, Blommaert and Rampton (2011) and Rampton (2013), as well as Amin (2012) and Wessendorf (2013), argue that a superdiversity perspective pushes sociolinguistics and other disciplines to move away from 'groupism' as well as from the old binary oppositions between 'host majority culture' versus 'immigrant minority culture(s)', autochthonous versus allochthones and central versus peripheral. In contradistinction, superdiversity and its emergent discourse(s) hinge heavily on the metaphor of historicized simultaneity as exemplified for instance in (1) 'multiple embeddedness' of migrants who form networks of bonding and bridging social relations across multiple social fields (see Rigoni and Saitta 2012) and (2) intersectionality, here understood as:

> the complex, irreducible, varied, and variable effects which ensue when multiple axis of differentiation economic, political, cultural, psychic, subjective and experiential intersect in historically specific contexts.
> *(Brah and Phoenix 2004: 76)*

Complexity is the keyword for superdiversity on the ground, as it involves perpetual and very rapid social and cultural change bringing under the lens of ethnographic enquiry the repositioning of groups and individuals in socio-cultural spaces that through a group-based approach were thought to be places where diversity had crystalized, for example, 'immigrant neighborhoods'. While the general vector of change may be identifiable – for instance, a tendency towards densely polycentric and multiscalar social spaces – its precise determinants and forms cannot be a priori established (Blommaert, Collins, and Slembrouck 2005; Blommaert 2013; see Waddington 1977 and Prigogyne and Stengers 1984 for inspiration). Further, in our uptake of the term 'complexity', we want to stress that it is not our intention to explicitly engage with chaos theory. Rather we wish the reader to see it as "a source of inspiration which offers us a reservoir of alternative images and metaphors" and that can "help us to reimagining sociolinguistic phenomena – not a fixed and closed doctrine which must be 'followed'" (Blommaert 2013: 15).

All this raises a number of fundamental methodological challenges, questioning a legacy of structuralism in our fields of study and dislodging several of the key notions we traditionally apply from within a fundamental imagination of the social world as stable and categorical (think of notions such as "speech community," Rampton 2000, or the notion of "language" itself, Agha 2007). This fundamental imagination has affected the tools we preferably deploy in analysis, the assumptions underlying it, and the phenomena and processes we choose to take as our object of inquiry. This chapter intends to contribute to such re-imagination, and we will seek inspiration in almost forgotten work: that of the symbolic interactionists.

In what follows, we do three things. First, we argue that a sociolinguistics of migration addressing superdiversity needs to address the real complexity of communicative situations as its object. Further, we argue that it should strive to document such complex situations in some detail, and third, we show how this sociolinguistics may produce new methodological approaches in which change, not synchronic state of events, becomes the central object of inquiry.

Overview

The neglected complexity of socio-communicative situations

In a paper written over half a century ago, Goffman (1964) suggests that the act of speaking needs always be referred to the state of the talk that is gradually unfolding and that is sustained through particular turns at talking but also through particular processes of ratification, or lack thereof, from others than the participant (cf. Blumer 1969). As we learned from the symbolic interactionist school, of which Goffman was a prominent member, interaction is a socially organized practice in which society itself is being 'made', so to speak (Blumer 1969), and this is so not only in terms of who speaks to whom in what language but as a system of mutually ratified and ritually governed actions. In order to gain a better understanding of how meaning is constructed through the mechanisms and strategies of talk in interaction, it is important to take into close examination how voices of participants in talk strive to intermingle. One way of understanding the shifting qualities of individual voices as multiple agencies or roles provided by Goffman (1981) is the concept of participation framework (based on the distinction between author, animator, and principal). At the same time, as it has been pointed out by Blommaert (2005) and Couldry (cf. 2010 for his most recent work on culture and politics after neoliberalism) voice – here understood as someone's capacity of making him/herself understood – is what really matters. That is, although we all have a voice when we talk, we all need to know that our voice matters, that our voice has legitimacy, that it is taken up by the other party involved in the communicative act and that therefore it becomes recognized as valid currency for the trading taking place in the communicative interaction at hand. Hence, following Wertsch (1991), we need to realize that in internalizing forms of social interaction, the individual takes on and interrelates with the voices of others, which accounts for the complexity of 'multi-voiced' dialogues. While joining in a dialogic polyphony of voices, each voice shares a particular experience, viewpoint, or set of attitudes to reality, all of which are instrumental in shaping actions, interactions and relationships (cf. Blumer 1969).

As a result, the situation in which dialogue takes place is also the locus where different beliefs, commitments, and ideologies come into contact and confront each other through the intersecting voices of the participants. Dialogue is also the place in which categorization takes place and where the establishment, negotiation, and rejection of categories happens. This, of course, does not imply that the meaning of categories during a dialogical situation, as that of a talk, is established afresh each time. Rather the establishment, negotiation, and possible acceptance or rejection of what a certain category means, for example who is considered to be a truthful member of a given group, are all actions that are made possible by shared structures of meaning which are established, produced, and negotiated in social interaction. Duranti and Goodwin (1994) but also Sarangi and Roberts (1999) use the notion of extra-situational context when they wish to refer to that layer of context that involves the use of social, political, and cultural discourses within which a societal encounter is taking place.

'Extra-situational', however, is a questionable term. In his 1964 paper, Goffman cautioned his generation of scholars against "the neglected situation." That is, the focus on specific parts of speech and on how they affect communicative outcomes – Goffman argued – often bypasses the complexity of the "social situation." The latter gets treated in "the most happy-go-lucky way," in an "opportunistic" fashion; "an implication is that social situations do not have properties and a structure of their own but merely mark, as it were, the geometric intersection of actors making talk and actors bearing particular social attributes" (1964: 134). Goffman underscores that "your social situation is not your country cousin" (1964: 134): familiarity with social situations does not mean that they are fully understood. Rather, specific research into the social situation is required as part and parcel of the object of analysis and not just as its 'context'. Goffman defined a social situation as "an environment of mutually monitoring possibilities anywhere within which an individual will find himself accessible to the naked senses of all others who are 'present', and similarly find them accessible to him" (1964: 135). Such meetings of humans in time and space provoke complex sets of rules for coordinating the joint social activity – of talk, but also of gaze, relative body posture, and so forth. And as we know, it is precisely such complex forms of social work where the zone in which Goffman preferred to do his work lies. Recently, another prominent member of the same symbolic interactionist movement, Howard Becker, added precision to Goffman's exhortation:

> Everything present in or connected to a situation I want to understand should be taken account of and made use of. If it is there, it is doing something, however unimportant that thing seems, no matter how unobtrusive it is. [. . .] the things I've left out could well be the center of my analysis.
>
> *(Becker 2014: 3)*

Goffman's and Becker's statements are separated by half a century of social change in which the patterns and modes of communication have dramatically changed. The tremendous complexity of face-to-face interactions described by Goffman have been complemented by the spectacular rise of online and long-distance interaction in which physical spatiotemporal co-presence is no longer a condition for creating social situations. If anything then, and keeping in mind what we said earlier about superdiversity, Becker's echo of Goffman's words is even more acutely relevant, in that social situations of human communication have acquired a bewildering variety in modes, media, scope, formats, genres, and whatnot. And yes, Goffman's complaint about the "happy-go-lucky" ways of addressing such complexities is still valid. Now even more than fifty years ago, "your social situation is not your country cousin."

All of this calls for a fresh uptake in the investigation of social situations that either involve or are a by-product of communicative interactions where complexity is the empirical outcome that we ought to study. The recipe is actually quite simple: since complexity involves a lack of presupposable features in social events and their outcomes, a meticulous ethnographic approach, following Becker's adhortation, is the research approach that guarantees best outcomes; methods in which a lot is presupposed – categories, event templates, roles for actors – run huge risks of missing the point. Mensaert (2013), for example, has shown how in times of superdiversity, using templates (here in social work) requires an enormous and time-consuming effort of the participants in order to build consensus and to come to a mutual understanding, if at all.

To shed light on this increased complexity and show how the latter cannot afford to neglect 'stuff', we present two cases, both of which highlight the presence of online events that are latently present but suddenly manifest themselves in the 'social situation' at hand. The interpenetration of online and offline interaction practices complicated the 'situation', which, as we know, Goffman saw as primarily organized around physical co-presence in a material, shared and, therefore, invokable context. The fact now is that offline, 'real' interactions are infused with online pre-supposable and invokable information and/or are blended with online interactions in ways that demand careful inspection and invite analytical and methodological reflection.

Issues and ongoing debates

A neglected socio-communicative element in an asylum seeking procedure

Asylum seeking has become one of the dominant modes of migration in the age of superdiversity. The Belgian Asylum procedure is a legal-administrative procedure in which applicants have to explain their motivation for seeking asylum in Belgium. In this procedure, the applicant has to deliver a series of facts about him/herself, explain with a certain degree of plausibility the reason why s/he has left the country of origin and, through that, he has to prove whether he really is from where he claims to be coming (Maryns 2006). As for Belgium, this procedure includes many governmental gatekeeping institutions, each of which has its specific duties and regulations to follow. Among these, the one on which we focus here is the *Commissariaat Generaal voor de Vluchtelingen en de Staatlozen* (General Commissioner's Office for Refugees and Stateless Persons, or CGRS), which is an independent asylum authority authorized by the Belgian federal state to scrutinize and examine asylum seeking applications. It follows that gatekeeping institutions – like this one – are places where the voice of the asylum seeking applicant finds itself confronted with the institutional voice of the officer(s) that is assessing his/her case. In there, the communicative situation that unfolds is expected to follow clear patterns of questioning as well as clear patterns of answering along the institutionally favored matrix of what is considered a valid proof of identity knowledge. Consequently, the applicant does not only need to understand what to speak about, it also means that the applicant – in order to fit the institutionally held frame of valid knowledge (cf. Bohmer and Shuman 2007) – should strive to match the same register used by those who are asking the questions. These registers, within social interaction, play a significant role in the processes of origin assessment in that they enable to anticipate the category to which an applicant belongs according to the attributes of his/her story. As Goffman shows us:

> we lean on anticipations that we have, transforming them into normative expectations, into righteously presented demands. [. . .] It is when an active question arises as to whether these demands will be filled] that we are likely to realize that all along we had been making certain assumptions as to what the individual before us ought to be members of a society.
>
> *(Goffman 1963: 2)*

Asylum applicants can either (re)produce, negotiate, or dodge their way through these normative expectations (Jacquemet 2015). In light of this, the question of legitimacy, performance, and responsibilities is pivotal in the examination of this social situation and of how it folds in within a specific institutional setting, like the one that is our focus here. Yet again, as Goffman, Blumer, and Becker caution us, all communicative situations constitute a reality sui generis where everything present or connected to the situation, whether online or offline and whether insignificant or unobtrusive at that time, has the potential to become central to the analysis. In what follows, we focus on two things. First, we zoom in on an unschooled young man, whom we call Bashir, who arrived as an asylum seeker in Belgium in February

2012 and who claims to be from Guinea. Second, we examine how Bashir's claims were judged as untruthful by the authorities because of a register mismatch in the process of naming things that an inhabitant of Conakry, the capital of Guinea, should know.

We focus on what the authorities have made available to us: the letter that Bashir received reporting the result of his application as well as the reasoning employed by the authorities for dismissing his asylum request. The text in question is a re-entextualization of the contents of the long interview and it works as summary of what Bashir has failed to prove during the interview (Blommaert 2001a). That the Belgian institutional agencies do take good care of guaranteeing the asylum applicant with employees who are following a precise code of conduct is a well-known fact. That the Belgian asylum agencies ask for the interview itself to be adapted to the background of the applicant is also true. On the CGRS guideline for the conduct of interviewing, it asserts that "the questions asked and the information given during the interview take into account the asylum seeker's personality, experience and cultural background (age, gender, health, education level, religion, etc.)" (CGRS 2011: 13). Bashir's officers, who also write the letter of approval or rejection including the motivation for their decision, should take into consideration this series of societal and background variables and fine-tune their questioning toward these variables. Due to his lack of literacy skills, the letter Bashir had received was read to him by his roommate whose name is Majid, a well-educated Guinean coming from a family that counted three generations of local Koranic preachers settled in the area of Télimélé. The letter, in French, indicated by the authorities as the favored language by Bashir for handling legal matters,[1] reported that after having questioned him and having taken into account Bashir's educational background, his application was rejected.

Bashir's story is a narrative that is a (more or less straightforward) representation of a segment of someone's social life in such a way as to render it according to a series of facts ordered in time and space (cf. Bauman 1986). As many other asylum seeking applicants, Bashir too had to render his life prior to coming to Belgium in a sequence of events. In his reconstruction, we understand that Bashir is the son of a Malinka-speaking father and a Peul-speaking mother. Although raised as a speaker of Peul, the mother tongue attributed to him by the Belgian authorities was Malinka. Because of inter-ethnic conflict between his family members, he had lost his father, who was beaten by his mother's brothers and died of his injuries. At this point, Bashir's mother had put him in the care of a Guinean police officer, a friend of his late father, to protect him from the internal family struggles. Shortly thereafter, this police officer had him leave for Europe. Like all asylum seekers claiming their identity, Bashir had to prove that he really was who he said he was. In other words, he had to prove that he was from the country he claimed to be from, as well as from Conakry, the city in which he claimed to have been living with his family.

An asylum interview is an administrative task that requires quite some skillful knowledge of genres from the side of the applicant (see Blommaert 2001a: 211–245; Maryns 2006). In conducting them, immigration authorities typically start from the premise that if someone claims to be from a certain country then s/he has to know facts about that country and the exact place where s/he claims to be from. It is solely by their knowledge of certain facts—whether they are political, social, urban, or relating to popular culture that asylum seekers stand a chance. Their knowledge of these facts is seen both as a confirmation of their identity and the stuff of moral judgment (i.e., their trustworthiness). The sequence of inferences goes along the line of: the applicant did not tell lies, ergo, he is who he claims to be, ergo, he is morally righteous, ergo, he can be granted permission to stay in country X. When we turn to the summary drawn up by the authorities after the long interview, Bashir has failed to prove himself on many things. He failed to provide the correct answers to a number of pertinent questions that ranged from the name of the only bottled water sold in Guinea to the name of players that were part of the Guinean national football team. Further, he was not able to name the radio channels he listened to and he was happy to limit himself to the sentence "j'écoute la musique" ("I listen to music").

What comes across as most striking is the lack of knowledge attributed to Bashir by the authorities when it comes down to name the mosque where he claimed to have gone to for Qur'anic instruction. It is true that Bashir did not know the name of this mosque; during the interview he simply stated that he went "à la grande mosquée" ("to the big mosque"). What exactly Bashir did not know about the mosque then was its official name, Mosquée du Faycal—another piece of information that the authorities obtained from the web, retrieved from holiday websites (see http://www.petitfute.com/ and http://www.aminata.com/) aimed at adventurous westerners who want to know all about the sights to see in Conakry.

In fact, the country information used in the interviewer's checklist was obtained from two major sources: information provided by other applicants and bona fide translators, and information obtained from widely accessible web sources such as Wikipedia and travel websites. The broad availability of such online information grants it the status, in the interviewers' eyes, of pre-supposable (i.e., widely shared and low-threshold) 'truth' and ends up operating in a totally different epistemology than that of the interviewee which leads to difficulties in building consensus and to the subjugation of the interviewee's frame by the interviewer. The argument runs, in fact, as follows: if you're really from place X, you should know these widely known facts. Note here how online resources change and determine the epistemic regime within which asylum interviews evolve, allowing distinctions and degrees in knowledge that become institutionally consequential – they determine the credibility of the applicant's identity claims.

What are we left with then? A register discrepancy and a lack of voice, in that the voice of Bashir did not perform the function that these websites, the neglected element in the communicative situation, made pre-supposable. The text of the letter redacted by the authorities encapsulates how the applicant repeatedly fails to speak real 'country talk' and to match the register that is expected from him, that is, the register he should draw upon in order to have his voice recognized by the authorities as indexing his essence of truthfully being from Conakry. Bashir, although illiterate and unschooled is for the authorities, a case, a file number and, as such, someone who should keep it real, someone who within the long interview had to show his knowledge. The letter, therefore, provides us with a glimpse of an omnipresent autocratically issued register, based on facts elected as true by the authorities because these authorities have espoused yet another doxa, the one that associates something on the web as something credible.

The web is the external agent neglected in the social situation at hand. Methodologically speaking, the web becomes central to the neglected situation and core element in the analysis. The web, in fact, becomes that external agent that although not synchronically co-present during the interview is still present enough to be considered as source upon which to gain yet another piece of information, possibly the biggest piece, that determines Bashir's lack of knowledge and that contributes to dismiss his identity claims and, by extension, his asylum application. Online sources here are a distant participant, so to speak, contributing 'frames' of pre-supposable and inferable knowledge to the ongoing interaction. They are very much part of the "empirical world" (Blumer 1969: vii) of asylum application procedures and demand analytic attention as such, for it is not just part of the "text trajectory" of bureaucratic procedure (Blommaert 2001b) but also appears as an immediate factor in the interaction processes – the on-the-spot ratification processes that determine a procedure outcome. The actual meaning attributed by participants in an interaction to places, people, and events mentioned and used in calibrating each other's stance and the access to such sources as well as the ability to deploy them competently shapes a structured inequality in the kinds of bureaucratic encounters we discuss here. They shape, in other words, the participants themselves as people who construct, anticipate and reconstruct each other's meanings in interaction. The next research example will take this point further.

A neglected socio-communicative element in social work

Research on the trajectories of migrant families in the Belgian welfare system has led us to Nabijah, a thirty-seven-year-old Belgian-Iraqi woman living in Antwerp North (see Van der Aa and Blommaert 2015 for a more elaborate description of this case). At the time of the research, Nabijah was living with four children in a very small apartment where irregular heating and electricity depended on what was left on the budget meter (a sort of prepaid gas/electricity system). One of the children was mentally disabled and the oldest child was not hers, but the child of her sister who lived in Germany. Having gone through a very rough and violent divorce from her Belgian/Iraqi husband, Nabijah ended up as a single mom in harsh poverty. Most bills were handled by a lawyer which immediately had to pay off the accrued debt of the (by then) imprisoned husband and various other bills, leaving Nabijah with a mere €7 a day to take care of five people. A typical dinner in the household consisted of a large can of baked beans in tomato sauce and an equally large cheap bag of salted potato chips, followed by an apple.

Nabijah and her children were monitored and followed up by Lucy, one of the care providers at the Circle, an Antwerp welfare institution dealing with children and adolescents aged six to eighteen and their families, after a transfer from court. Reasons for such transfers could be criminal activities of the youngsters; issues of violence, abuse and neglect; issues of extreme poverty, and so on. The transfer is obligatory (parents cannot refuse the help from the institution) and is often a final way to avoid the children being placed in care. At the time of the research, Lucy had weekly meetings with Nabijah in her home, often together with various other people, such as social workers, lawyers (to take care of the debt that remained after the divorce), teachers, the care provider(s) of her mentally handicapped son (who lived in a residential care institution during the week) and translators. During a period of several months one of us (Jef Van der Aa, henceforth JVDA) accompanied Lucy to Nabijah's house, taking part in at least fifteen home visits of one and a half hour each. All conversations were tape recorded and conducted in Dutch, often mediated by an Iraqi or Moroccan Arabic translator. We complemented the audio recordings with the intensive taking of field notes. It is in this context that we want to discuss the importance of 'what was left out' which in some cases may actually "be or become the center of our analysis" (Becker 2014: 3) and how we can engage with this "not-said but still-there" (Kulick 2005).

Let us have a closer look at a Goffmanian 'situation' in Nabijah's case. At one point, approximately nine weeks into JVDA's involvement with Nabijah and her family, Lucy, the translator and JVDA arrived at Nabijah's apartment for the weekly visit. There had been a traffic jam, so we came in a little late. Nabijah appeared not to be home and we thought perhaps she too had been caught up in traffic, as even trams and buses were blocked from passing through the road works. We waited for several minutes, knocked the door several times, shouted her name and so on. A little while later, someone stumbles to the door in a rush. It was Nabijah, with her laptop in hand, a very heavy object that was at least seven years old, and whose weight usually caused it to sit on an equally old folding chair next to where Nabijah was seated during our conversations. We came in, were seated across from Nabijah, as she held the laptop in her hands. She said "I was doing things on the computer, therefore I didn't hear you guys." It seemed the folding chair was destroyed, as some of the cloth was torn apart and one of its chair legs was sticking out.

The translator, being from Iraqi descent this time, and alternating with a Moroccan one for 'reasons of planning', translated in spoken Iraqi Arabic vernacular. For weeks, Nabijah had been 'stalking' Lucy about helping her with her travel passport, which seemed, for several reasons, quite hard for her to obtain. Nabijah had been married in Lebanon with her former husband, who had a double Iraqi/Belgian nationality through which Nabijah and her children had been able, eventually, to obtain Belgian nationality.

At one point, we were discussing the problem very concretely, as a negative advice regarding the passport had come in from the local authorities because of her former husband's legal trouble. The translator carefully explained the problem to Nabijah, and at the same time commenting on an appeal form Lucy had brought. Being heavily involved in the conversation, and in order to pinpoint all kinds of issues Nabijah seemed to have with the form, she had put the laptop on the floor behind her, not next to her as usual since the chair was broken. Suddenly a voice shouted something from behind Nabijah. Lucy and JVDA were both surprised, and the translator replied to the voice on the computer, telling us that it was Nabijah's brother, listening in on Skype. Nabijah confirmed this and explained that he was reacting to the information with regards to the travel passport. There had been a request from the brother to formally adopt his son, Nabijah's nephew. Nabijah then showed us the brother, we waved at him, and he disappeared from Skype as swiftly as he came once the conversation took another direction. Nabijah needed the passport in order to go and arrange things in Iraq to make the adoption possible. Also, it turned out that the brother had been listening in quite regularly in the weeks before and thus the prioritization of the travel passport and other adjacent issues was suddenly seen in a whole new light. The conversation had been regularly 'steered' for several weeks by the non-speaking but still present brother: the co-presence of online and offline interaction, sometimes manifestly present, sometimes latently lurking.

What we observed here was an extremely complex interactional situation which cannot be analyzed synchronically. We observed something like a 'total social fact' in which online and offline events merged, latent objects suddenly became manifest, and a complex interaction of linguistic, generic, cultural, and religious resources took place (Van der Aa and Blommaert 2015). Silverstein's (1985) concept of the 'total linguistic fact' can be expanded to the analysis of superdiverse settings in which the 'neglected' becomes the center of attention:

> The total linguistic fact, the datum for a science of language is irreducibly dialectic in nature. It is an unstable mutual interaction of meaningful sign forms, contextualised to situations of interested human use and mediated by the fact of cultural ideology.
> *(Silverstein 1985: 220)*

Another key point here is the co-incidental nature of the 'discovery' of the neglected element: the fact that the chair was broken by which the 'unimportant' laptop drew our attention, the brother being 'sidetracked' from the ongoing 'show' by being placed behind the chair, the suddenly intruding 'voice' of the brother, us being late causing Nabijah to have embarked in 'full conversation' with the brother, the translator being Belgian Iraqi (from the same region of Nabijah and actually vaguely knowing the family in Iraq) instead of Moroccan so that she could recognize local vocabulary, and so on. The social situation deserves analysis in its own right (Goffman 1964: 134) and all conversations contained within it are to be interpreted through many layers of fairly coincidental historicized social frames. This coincidence shouldn't worry or demoralize us, as important manifestations of these latent frames will be repeated over and over again. Therefore, sustained attention to these always slightly different manifestations will do the trick, hereby making change itself our object of analysis.

Nabijah's story, her life, her issues and her problems were necessarily reduced in the professional vision of the social worker, in order to deal with those issues the institution was professionally and legally allowed to handle. Nabijah is a 'case', has a 'file' and belongs to one or more 'problematic' social categories for which she needs 'treatment' and 'help'. Thus, the social work frames have been pre-configured and only particular elements that fitted that professional scheme were accepted as meaningful. The point we have made so far, following social interactionist sources of inspiration is that for the ethnographer, everything is potentially meaningful. Latent objects can become manifest at the blink of an eye, and this is something we cannot afford to ignore, neither as ethnographers with an academic purpose, nor as societal actors (such as social workers) with a socio-psychological, legal and human finality. The latter simply cannot afford anymore to neglect aspects of the situation that cause an entire analytical trajectory of *Hineininterpretierung* (or predisposed interpretation), lest the consequences of the neglect may be detrimental to the human beings in care, or may even become matters of life and death (see Joseph's case in Blommaert 2009). In Nabijah's case, it turned out that she did not really want to adopt the son, and that the pressure being put on her shoulders to do so anyway had been heavily impeding the attention for her other children (the key mandate of the social workers) and her own health. This resulted in severe anxiety attacks and the overusage of benzodiazepines whose nasty side effects prevented her from working on a regular basis.

But social workers have not been trained to pay attention to such analytic detail, and could benefit on such occasions from an extra pair of anthropological eyes. The exchange is mutual; as ethnographers should involve themselves in those cases deemed analytically relevant by societal actors themselves. These actors can often pinpoint things that are 'weird', 'out of routine', in other words, brief manifestations of the neglected aspects of a particular situation. Lucy had found Nabijah's communicative behavior become increasingly 'strange' over the last few weeks and had asked me along to do the case study. It is exactly there that we come in as ethnographers. Our role has changed from being a mere 'observer' who describes what he or she sees, to an 'active participant' who makes explicit the changes for which there is no vocabulary yet. In this spirit, Hymes (1980) developed a research program called 'ethnographic monitoring'. This consists of the following steps: (1) ethnographers consult social actors to identify what issues concern them most (the 'other's position); (2) observe behavior relevant to that issue in a series of contexts in which the participants are engaged (observer's position); (3) share back their findings with the participants (instant as well as more long-term feedback and uptake); (4) take stock of findings (evaluating 'effect'). We are convinced, with Hymes, that by following these steps, there is a guarantee that research plans and programs are developed organically, and in close consultation with all social actors involved. In other words, static solutions are being replaced by complex dynamics, because understanding the world involves changing it (for more on this type of 'ethnographic monitoring', see Van der Aa and Blommaert 2015).

Future directions

How not to neglect what has been so far neglected

In a celebrated text often considered the definitive statement on symbolic interactionism, Herbert Blumer mentions:

> the fact that the empirical world can 'talk back' to our pictures of it or assertions about it – talk back in the sense of challenging and resisting, or not bending to, our images or conceptions of it. This resistance gives the empirical world an obdurate character that is the mark of reality. [. . .] It is this obdurate character of the empirical world – its ability to resist and talk back – that both calls for and justifies empirical science. Fundamentally, empirical science is an enterprise that seeks to develop images and conceptions that can successfully handle and accommodate the resistance offered by the empirical world under study.
>
> *(Blumer 1969: 22–23)*

Blumer directs us toward a crucial theoretical problem for the study of language in society: to define our own 'empirical world' in an age of intense and rapid change in the empirical world in which, consequently, 'talking back' may be the rule rather than the exception, and as such we need to adopt methodologies such as 'ethnographic monitoring' (see earlier) in order to accurately capture these voices. While the field of migration may present us with the clearest and most pressing prompts for reflection, the challenge is probably general: are we sure that our constructions of objects of analysis (the "images and conceptions" referred to by Blumer) match the empirical world and successfully counter its resistance? Concretely, if we are aware of the intrinsic complexity of the social events we are observing, does our analysis bring out and explain this complexity?

The examples we have offered above involved a number of critical moves, the most crucial of which was to redefine the boundaries between what we call 'text' and 'context'. There is a tendency in our fields of study to (1) reduce the notion of 'interaction' as an object of study to the linguistically describable 'text' it involves; (2) possibly complemented by 'paralinguistic' features such as gesture, pitch and so forth, seen as secondary features of meaning; and (3) set this 'text' against a background which we call 'context' and consider relevant only to the extent to which it clarifies the 'text'; (4) where 'situational context' is narrowed down to the here-and-now of interaction. Non-immediate aspects of context, as we have seen, are seen as extra-situational (intertextual or inter-discursive, usually, in Fairclough's 1992 terminology). And finally, (5) we assume that live turn-by-turn interaction in a setting of physical co-presence ('conversation', in short) is the 'natural' object of research, often (6) using a speaker-centered framework of analyzing meaning (for the latter, see Blommaert 2014).

These assumptions, it should be clear, are problematic for several reasons. One, it is best, following several generations of scholars, to define interaction as an activity involving several practices, some of which are 'linguistic' while others have to do with the body, the objects and technologies mediating the interaction, and the space-time frame in which it develops (cf. Scollon and Scollon 2004). The description of Nabijah's case, we believe, made this abundantly clear: people make sense of each other's messages in complex arrays of things, all of which contribute to the 'meaning' produced in interaction. The 'total linguistic fact' is, in effect, the total semiotic fact in which more signs than just the 'textual' ones are being exchanged, and all of these signs are agentive in the construction of meaning outcomes (which explains, for instance, why interviews gathered at a railway station during rush hour are, as a rule, shorter than interviews gathered in a shopping area on Saturdays). Online sources and tools are inevitably included in these categories, and their dislodging effects on our standard tools of description must be addressed.

Second, a crucial agent in the production of meaning is knowledge, and sources of knowledge, or technologies of knowledge, are often dismissed without much substantive argument as mere background factors to be enacted in what really matters: the interaction itself. Paradoxically, it is the analysis of interaction itself that defies this assumption, for the work of interaction involves complex patterns of decoding and uptake of knowledge – which is the point of interaction (cf. Cicourel 1972). Furthermore, what happens in interaction can often only be explained by asymmetries in accessible knowledge; Bashir's case clearly demonstrated this. And even if such sources of knowledge and their distribution patterns are situated, strictly speaking, 'outside' of the moment of interaction (and often belong to the 'structural' scale-levels of social organization), they operate as agents of meaning in actual moments of interactional deployment. They are part, in other words, of the "participation framework," as the 'frames' on which actual people can draw in communication and, as Cicourel (1972) demonstrated, they tend to affect what we understand as 'rules' and 'norms' in social interaction. A separation between people and the knowledge they carry, consequently, makes little sense when analyzing interaction: the knowledge is a core part of the interacting person. The case of Bashir illustrated, in addition, how asymmetries in accessible knowledge clearly belong to the escalating 'diversity' in superdiversity.

Third, and as an effect of the preceding points, what is commonly understood as 'interaction' cannot be confined to the moment of interactional deployment. 'Local' and 'trans-local' are inaccurate descriptors for defining the dimensions of context in interaction, and ineffective as descriptors of interactional processes themselves. The moments of interactional deployment so favored by conversation analysts (for instance) are never autonomous, but always part of longer social activities of decision-making, opinion-forming or, in its most general sense, the emergence and reproduction of social structure (cf. Agha 2007). And, again, asymmetries in the ways in which moments of interaction are absorbed into these longer and more complex trajectories – think of the logic of bureaucracy in which one step of the process is made with a clear anticipation of the next one – account for much of what happens in moments of interactions. In fact, grasping something as elusive and unpredictable as social and cultural change demands attention, precisely, to differences in 'backgrounds' and 'futures' of people entering arenas of social engagement; a restricted notion of 'interaction' can at best yield a snapshot picture of such larger processes.

Implications

As we have discussed, the methodological challenges are probably general to all communication, but the field of migration may offer the clearest tests for the analytical frameworks we currently employ. The challenge is to arrive at a holistic mode of analysis that cancels the resistance of the empirical world of migration and interaction – one which avoids the reduction of the complexity it inevitably offers and which, given the inevitability of rapid change characterizing this empirical world, takes little for granted. What is left out, we know, might be the point of the entire thing; so let us not dismiss too many factors in advance, as irrelevant or as things that 'technically speaking' do not belong to our kinds of analysis. There is, at present, not much research that answers the challenges outlined here. This turn – a turn towards a reevaluated epistemology of realism, we would argue – now needs to be taken up in research.

Related topics

Translanguaging in mobility
Superdiversity and language
Space, place, and language

Further reading

Becker, H. (1963). *Outsiders: Studies in the Sociology of Deviance*. New York: The Free Press.

An early sociological piece documenting the interactional study of people in the margins of society.

Blumer, H. (1969). *Symbolic Interactionism: Perspective and Method*. Berkeley: University of California Press.

An overview of 'meaning' in interaction, much needed for investigating complex indexically pregnant encounters.

Cicourel, A. (1972). *Cognitive Sociology: Language and Meaning in Social Interaction*. Harmondsworth: Penguin.

This seminal book presents an array of possibilities to combine research methods in investigating complexity in social life.

Goffman, E. (1964). The neglected situation. *American Anthropologist, 66/6*, Part 2: The Ethnography of Communication: 133–136.

This article concisely comments on important aspects of social life often neglected in interactional analysis.

Kulick, D. (2005). The importance of what gets left out. *Discourse Studies*, 7(4–5), 615–624.

In this article it is argued that language, interaction and culture as indexicals cannot be reduced to actual observable performance, the 'there' in an interaction.

Note

1 Please note that there are only two languages assigned to the official *written* communication between an applicant and the CGRS's authorities, these being either French or Dutch; this is done by institutions so to replicate the ideology of stable bilingualism. In fact, the language ideological debate in Belgium is much more complex than this.

References

Agha, A. (2007). *Language and Social Structure*. Cambridge: Cambridge University Press.
Amin, A. (2012). *Land of Strangers*. Cambridge: Polity Press.
Arnaut, K. (2012). Super-diversity: Elements of an emerging perspective. *Diversities* 14(2): 1–16.
Arnaut, K. and M. Spotti (2015). Superdiversity discourse. In Tracy, K., Cornelia, I. and T. Sandel (eds.), *The International Encyclopedia of Language and Social Interaction* (pp. 1–7). Hoboken: Wiley-Blackwell.
Bauman, R. (1986). *Story, Performance and Event. Contextual Studies of Oral Narrative*. Cambridge Studies in Oral and Literate Culture 10 New York: Cambridge University Press.
Becker, H. (2014). *What About Mozart? What About Murder? Reasoning from Cases*. Chicago: University of Chicago Press.
Blommaert, J. (2001a). Investigating narrative inequality: African asylum seekers' stories in Belgium. *Discourse and Society* 12/4: 413–449.
Blommaert, J. (2001b). Context is/as critique. *Critique of Anthropology* 21/1: 13–32.
Blommaert, J. (2005). *Discourse: A Critical Introduction*. Cambridge: Cambridge University Press.
Blommaert, J. (2009). Language, Asylum and the national order. *Current Anthropology* 50(4): 415–441.

Blommaert, J. (2013). *Ethnography, Superdiversity and Linguistic Landscapes*. Bristol: Multilingual Matters.
Blommaert, J. (2014). *Meaning as a Nonlinear Effect: The Birth of Cool*. Tilburg Papers in Culture Studies, Paper 106 [Online]. Retrieved from https://www.tilburguniversity.edu/research/institutes-and-research-groups/babylon/tpcs/ [Accessed 30 October 2015]
Blommaert, J. (2015). Commentary: Superdiversity old and new. *Language & Communication* 44: 82–88.
Blommaert, J., J. Collins and Slembrouck, S. (2005). Polycentricity and interactional regimes in "global neighborhoods". *Ethnography* 6(2): 205–235.
Blommaert, J. and Rampton, B. (2011). Language and superdiversity. *Diversities* 13(2): 1–22.
Blumer, H. (1969). *Symbolic Interactionism: Perspective and Method*. Berkeley: University of California Press.
Bohmer, C. and Shuman, A. (2007). Producing epistemologies of ignorance in the political asylum application process. *Identities: Global Studies in Culture and Power*, 14(5), 603–629.
Brah, A. and Phoenix, A. (2004). 'Ain't I a Woman?' Revisiting Intersectionality. *Journal of International Women's Studies* 5(3): 75–86.
Cicourel, A. (1972). *Cognitive Sociology: Language and Meaning in Social Interaction*. Harmondsworth: Penguin.
CGRS (2011). Asylum Statistics – Overview 2011. Office of the Commissioner General for Refugees and Stateless persons. Communication and Information Office http://www.cgra.be/en/news/overview-asylum-statistics-2011
Couldry, N. (2010). *Why Voice Matters: Culture and Politics after Neo-liberalism*. London: Sage.
Duranti, A. and Goodwin, C. (1994). Rethinking context: Language as an interactive phenomenon. *American Ethnologist* 21(4): 919–920.
Eriksen, T. H. (2001). *Tyranny of the Moment*. London: Pluto Press.
Glick Schiller, N. (2007). The centrality of ethnography in the study of transnational migration. In A. Kumar Sahoo and B. Maharaj (eds.), *Sociology of Diaspora*. New Delhi, India: Rawat.
Goffman, E. (1963). *Stigma: Notes on the management of spoiled identity*. Englewood Cliffs, N.J.: Prentice-Hall.
Goffman, E. (1964). The neglected situation. *American Anthropologist*, 66/6, Part 2: The Ethnography of Communication,133–136.
Goffman, E. (1981). *Forms of Talk*. Philadelphia: UPenn Press.
Hall, S. (1996). New ethnicities. In D. Morley and K.-H. Chen (eds.), *On Postmodernism and Articulation: An Interview with Stuart Hall* (pp. 441–449). London: Routledge.
Harris, R. and B. Rampton (2010). Ethnicities without guarantees: An empirical approach. In Margareth Wetherell (ed.), *Liveable Lives: Negotiating Identities in New Times* (pp. 95–119). Basingstoke: Palgrave.
Hewitt, R. (1986). *White Talk, Black Talk: Inter-Racial Friendship and Communication amongst Adolescents*. Cambridge: Cambridge University Press.
Hymes, D. (1980). *Language in education: Ethnolinguistic essays*. Washington, DC: Center for Applied Linguistics.
Jacquemet, M. (2015). Asylum and the digitalization of evidence. Paper presented at the Symposium Political Asylum and the Politics of Suspicion, Mershon Centre for International Security, Ohio State University, 23 March 2015.
Kulick, D. (2005). The importance of what gets left out. *Discourse Studies* 7(4–5): 615–624.
Maryns, K. (2006). *The Asylum Speaker: Language in the Belgian Asylum Procedure*. Manchester: St. Jerome.
Mensaert, R. (2013). *Building and Breaking Frames in Welfare Work*. Tilburg Papers in Culture Studies, Paper 75 [Online]. Retrieved from https://www.tilburguniversity.edu/research/institutes-and-research-groups/babylon/tpcs/ [Accessed 30 October 2015].
Mercer, K. (1994). *Welcome to the Jungle: New Positions in Black Cultural Studies*. New York: Routledge.

Prigogyne, I. and I. Stengers (1984). *Order Out of Chaos: Man's New Dialogue with Nature*. New York: Bantam Books.

Rampton, B. (2000). *Speech Community*. Working Papers in Urban Language and Literacies, 15 [Online]. Retrieved from www.kcl.ac.uk/ldc [Accessed 30 October 2015].

Rampton, B. (2013). Styling in a language learn later in life. *Modern Language Journal* 97(2): 360–382.

Rigoni, I. and E. Saitta, eds. (2012). *Mediating Cultural Diversity in a Globalized Public Space*. New York: Palgrave Macmillan.

Sarangi, S. and Roberts, C. (1999). *Talk, Work and Institutional Order: Discourse in Medical Mediation and Management Settings*. Berlin: de Gruyter

Scollon, R. and S. W. Scollon (2004). *Nexus Analysis: Language and the Emerging Internet*. London: Routledge.

Silverstein, M. (1985). Language and the culture of gender. In E. Mertz and R. Parmentier (eds.), *Semiotic Mediation* (pp. 219–259). New York: Academic Press.

Squires, J. (2005). Is mainstreaming transformative? Theorizing mainstreaming in the context of diversity and deliberation. *Social Politics: International Studies in Gender, State and Society* 12(3): 366–388.

Van der Aa, J. and J. Blommaert. (2015). *Ethnographic Monitoring and the Study of Complexity*. Tilburg Papers in Culture Studies, Paper 123 [Online]. Retrieved from https://www.tilburguniversity.edu/research/institutes-and-research-groups/babylon/tpcs/ [Accessed 30 October 2015].

Vertovec, S. (2007). Super-diversity and its implications. *Ethnic and Racial Studies* 30(6): 1024–1054.

Waddington, C. (1977). *Tools for Thought*. St Albans: Paladin.

Wessendorf, S. (2013). Commonplace diversity and the "ethos of mixing": Perceptions of difference in a London neighbourhood. *Identities* 20(4): 407–422.

Wertsch, J. V. (1991). *Voices of the Mind: A Socio-Cultural Approach to Mediated Action*. Cambridge, MA: Harvard University Press.

Wimmer, A. and Glick Schiller, N. (2003). Methodological nationalism, the social sciences and the study of migration: An essay in historical epistemology. *International Migration Review* 37(3): 576–610.

20
Spatiotemporal scales and the study of mobility

Mastin Prinsloo

Introduction

The development and application of scales theory in sociolinguistics in recent years marks an important but not uncontested approach to questions of language and social inequalities, including those that affect migrants and their relationships. Scales theory suggests that language-evaluation processes – what people make of what others say and write, moment by moment – are shaped by the social effects of power, hierarchy, and status and that in contemporary globalised times these processes are ultimately effects of a capitalist world system operating across socially layered spaces on a global scale. In other words, scales theory aims to contribute to a sociolinguistics in the contemporary period of so-called globalisation by developing a set of conceptual resources and arguments for examining the way power relations on a global scale shape the use and relative prestige of varying language resources in specific contexts, as well as across geographical and social spaces. This theoretical orientation can be seen as a resource of direct relevance to researchers of language, migration, and transnational and translocal mobility because it offers an explanation and a theoretical resource for making sense of the way people's language resources get discredited or valorised as they move across continents, countries, and regions, as well as various other spaces of social activity.

Scales theory in sociolinguistics draws on social geography, and in particular on the world-systems analysis (WSA) arguments of Immanuel Wallerstein. Wallerstein's core thesis has been that there is a systemic division of the world, resulting from historical factors to do with how the global system originally expanded into core, peripheral, and semi-peripheral regions. This systemic view of structured socio-economic inequality on a global level is merged in scales theory with perspectives on language dynamics of scholars such as Pierre Bourdieu, Mikhail Bakhtin, John Gumperz, Dell Hymes, and Michael Silverstein. Scales theory in sociolinguistics, most notably in the work of Jan Blommaert and his colleagues, asks how analysis might account for the effects on language interactions of both large-scale or structural dimensions of social life, as well as those more localised social routines, habits, practices, and interactions that arise in specific contexts. Scales theory offers the argument that sociolinguistic and discursive phenomena (incidents of talk and/or writing, but including other kinds of semiosis) are "essentially *layered*, even if they appear to be one-time, purely synchronic and unique events" (Blommaert 2007: 3). This layering is a result of the fact that the immediacy of interaction and expression is performed by people by way of linguistic resources that bring a history and a socially loaded impetus to that event, and contribute to its shaping, so that unique instances of communication simultaneously point towards social and cultural norms, genres, traditions, expectations – "phenomena of a higher scale-level" (Blommaert 2007: 4). Scales theory offers an explanation of how persons can sometimes appear inarticulate, silent, deficient or powerless when they move from a space in which their linguistic resources are valued and recognised to a space where they are not. As Blommaert, Collins, and Slembrouk (2005: 198) explain this scalar perspective:

> multilingualism is not what individuals have and don't have, but what the environment, as structured determinations and interactional emergence, enables and disables. Consequently, multilingualism often occurs as truncated competence, which, depending on scalar judgments, may be declared 'valued assets' or dismissed as 'having no language'.

From the perspective of scales theory, linguistic repertoires operate in specific social and spatial domains, they are layered and stratified and they operate at scale levels, such that some are effective globally (some varieties of English); some regionally (varieties of kiSwahili across East Africa); and some only locally (including languages restricted to small numbers of speakers in local communities as well as locally specific varieties of 'bigger' languages). In this view, in multilingual settings every variety of language can be used on one or a number of scales: no language dominates all scales and there isn't a single variety that can be used in every situation with all people in that setting. What counts as appropriate, high-status, or inferior language is a situated, placed, or localised judgement, because language norms are ecological or contextual and they operate on scale levels. The structural or systemic impetus for scale-setting is an effect of global capitalism operating as a world system. Language dynamics are shaped by this structural dynamic, such that when people move across physical and social space "their language practices undergo re-evaluation at every step of the trajectory and the functions of their repertoire are redefined" (Blommaert 2002: 1).

As an example, Dong and Blommaert (2009: 9) describe how a child of migrants to Beijing from a rural location in China encountered loud, humiliating laughter from her classmates the first time she spoke at school (with marked Sichuan dialect for example "by using '*wazi*' instead of the Putonghua form 'haizi'"). The authors comment that "people with marked regional accents are positioned in spaces that rank their accents low through a scaling process: their language variety only has limited, local validity" (p. 11).

In a somewhat different illustration of scales in practice, in a European setting, Blommaert (2007: 6) describes a student discussing the outline of her essay with her tutor:

S: I'll start my dissertation with a chapter reporting on my fieldwork.

The tutor in response says:

T: We start our dissertations with a literature review chapter here.

Blommaert's analysis is that the tutor performs a scale-jump here, articulated through a shift from personal to impersonal (from 'I' and 'my' to 'we', 'our', 'here') where the student's individual plan is countered by an invocation of general rules. Blommaert sees this as a power move within a stratified, hierarchically layered system. The point here is that, whether she is an actual migrant or not, the student has nonetheless entered a centralised social space (the university) where her language resources and practices are ranked as those of a marginal outsider (or a novice), compared to those of her lecturer who is an authority in this domain of power. So, for migrants, 'unskilled' migrants in particular, as well as other less powerful people, it is more than simply accents or having access to high-status language resources, it is also about having or acquiring the know-how to use those resources in situated ways that do not mark one as an outsider or a person from or on the periphery.

As Dong and Blommaert (2009: 4) explain it,

> the notion of 'scale' introduces a *vertical* spatial metaphor: an image of a continuum on which spaces are hierarchically stratified and ordered from local to global with intermediary levels between the two poles. The vertical move from one scale to another (e.g. from local to translocal, from momentary to timeless, from specific to general) involves and presupposes access to particular resources, and such access is often subject to inequality. Thus, a move across scales is also a power move. The notion of scale is developed as a critical extension of traditional concepts of 'trajectories', 'networks' and 'flows', in the way that scale is value-laden and emphasises indexical meaning and semiotic resources, in an attempt to address sociolinguistic issues in the context of globalisation and diaspora.

This chapter goes on to critically elaborate on and examine this perspective on sociolinguistics in scales theory. It starts with an examination of the sources of these ideas in contemporary views on space as an active aspect of social organisation and complexity.

Overview of the topic

The spatial turn

In the late 20th century, social scientists began to understand space as a qualitative context, situating different behaviours and contending actions. (Lefebvre 1991; Massey 2005; Shields 2006). Moving on from preliminary understandings of space as an empty grid of mutually exclusive points, human geographers have argued that there is a spatial order to the world, this spatiality had previously been neglected in contemporary social theory and the concept of scale has been the object of sustained theoretical reflection in recent decades (Leitner and Miller 2007). The emergence of scales theory in sociolinguistics reflects this wider theoretical context, sometimes called 'the spatial turn' in social theory, or the turn to the concept of 'spacetime', that involves ideas about space and time as inextricably interconnected. Drawing on this turn in social theory, sociolinguists have started to see space not just as a neutral background but as agentive in sociolinguistic processes where "knowledge of language is rooted in situation and dynamically distributed across individuals as they engage in practices" (Blommaert et al. 2005: 205; Dong and Blommaert 2011). As Blommaert (2010: 80) describes it:

> Languages and discourses move around, but they do so between spaces that are full of rules, norms, customs and conventions, and they get adapted to the rules, norms, customs and conventions of such places before moving further on their trajectories. This dynamic of localization, delocalization and relocalization is essential for our understanding of sociolinguistic globalization processes.

A major influence from outside linguistics in the theorisation of scale in sociolinguistics has come from Immanuel Wallerstein's world-systems theory, or world-systems analysis, as it is widely known.

World-systems analysis

World-systems analysis (WSA) was originally driven by a recognition in Wallerstein's work since the 1970s that the state was not the ultimately meaningful unit of analysis, and this at a time when most social science still uncritically equated the state with society. Currently, when the idea has become established of a global economy that drives the most important social dynamics of even those regions that are peripheral to that economy, WSA arguments first made by Wallerstein in the 1970s would seem to have been prescient in their understanding of the world as the appropriate unit of analysis for understanding economics, politics and, for our purposes, language ideologies. World-systems theory (WSA) as first developed by Wallerstein (1974), drew on Gunder Frank's (1966) already available analysis of dependency relations between ex-colonial and core states. Frank's 'dependencia' theory argued that the underdevelopment of the poorer regions of the world was tied directly to the development of the core capitalist regions, in that their wealth was based on an extractive relationship with the peripheral regions. From Frank, Wallerstein developed the notion of capitalism as profit-driven economic activity, based on a division of labour at the global level (thus revising the more familiar Marxist emphasis on capital-wage labour relations at the point of production as the defining feature).

A second major influence in Wallerstein's development of WSA was the writings of the historian Fernand Braudel, most notably his study of *The Mediterranean* (1996, first published 1949) and his three volumes on *Civilization and Capitalism, 15th–18th Century* (1981–1984). Across this work, Braudel developed a perspective, first, on everyday socio-economic life; second, on market relations regarding agriculture trade and finance relations; and third on multiple "world-economies," their geographical and temporal dimensions. Braudel's construct of multiple time spans and their effects has been of considerable influence, emphasising the importance of broad social structures spanning long periods of history and their impact upon everyday life. He identified, in particular, three broad times or 'durations', that of the *longue durée* (a history of long-term, slow change with recurring cycles that represented for Wallerstein the systemic structures of long-term human history); second, the *histoire sociale* or '*histoire conjuncturelle*', a time of "slow but perceptible rhythms . . . one could call it social history, the history of groups and groupings" (Braudel 1984: 1, 20; Ethington 2007: 468); and third, the '*histoire e've'ne'mentielle*', or episodic history, the short time span or history of events in the daily lives of individuals and places. Braudel identified the first as pivotal for research because it offered a long enough time frame and a big enough spatial dimension to make large-scale transformations visible. (But while he identified these three as important, Braudel also referred to dozens more, each of them attached to a particular history – see Ethington 2007). Wallerstein (2004: 18) identified the longue durée as "the duration of a particular historical system" and drew on this concept of history and social structure to develop a perspective where social structural processes happen at this level of almost timeless rhythms of large-scale motion and change. Along these lines, Wallerstein (1974) argued that there have only been three core types of social systems in human history, (1) relatively self-contained hunting and gathering, pastoral and simple horticultural societies, operating as relatively self-contained economic units; (2) 'world-empires', maintained through military dominance and with an economy based on the extraction of surplus goods from outlying sectors; and (3) the capitalist world-system, which began in Europe in the 1500s, expanded under the spur of the accumulation of capital in Europe through expanded trade with the East from the 17th century, aided by superior means of transportation and military strength, and expanded further over the next few centuries to cover the entire globe. The processes of this expansion included the entrenchment of a division of labour with capital intensive production happening in the core Western countries while peripheral areas provided low-skill labour and raw materials. Nation-states could influence these processes through their efforts, while no state could fully dominate a world economy in which all were bound to compete. That said, particular core states have become hegemonic at specific conjunctures in the development of the world-system which has evolved through long cycles termed *hegemonic cycles* (Taylor 1982: 25), including the Netherlands in the 17th century; later, England; and then the United States in the 20th century.

WSA identifies a persisting division in the modern world-economy between core states that appropriate most of the surplus of their own as well as from elsewhere; such core states are sites of high skill and capital-intensive production, and are militarily strong or allied to strong military powers. In contrast, peripheral states and regions are characterised by low-skill, labour-intensive production and extraction of raw materials, while semi-peripheral states have more diversified economies than peripheral ones, as well as stronger national states. At the turn of the last century, the core comprised the wealthy industrialised countries, including Japan; the semi-periphery included many long-independent states outside the West while the periphery was mainly made up of relatively recently independent colonies. In the 21st century Wallerstein sees a period of transition, with growing internal contradictions, the absence of new markets to exploit, along with unameloriated and rising social inequalities within and between states (Wallerstein 2004; Featherstone 2006). In conclusion of this brief diversion into WSA, Wallerstein drew on Braudel's focus for research of a time frame and a global scale long enough and big enough to make large-scale transformations visible as well as providing an understanding of how detail was shaped by these broader dynamics. It is somewhat ironic, however, that Braudel, who described himself as "by temperament a structuralist" (quoted in Hexter 1979: 10) described WSA as stimulating but "a little too systematic, perhaps" (Braudel 1984: 70). I will return to this point when I consider critiques of WSA and scales theory.

Scales in WSA

The concept of scales in cartography refers, of course, simply to map resolution. Cartographic scale expresses the mathematical relationship between a map and the Earth or part thereof, and is usually denoted as a representative fraction. Large-scale (or large-fraction) maps show less space but typically more detail, and small-scale maps show more space, but with less detail. 'Best resolution' in terms of the choice of cartographic scale depends on the problem at hand and the focus of attention. As used in WSA, in human geography disciplinary studies influenced by WSA, and within scales approaches in sociolinguistics that rely on WSA, scale comes to relate, metaphorically, to a view that social processes are hierarchically distributed through the world along scalar lines, depending on how far they reach. Such social processes can operate at multiple scales at once and intersect with other processes operating at a different scale. In Taylor's (1982) scales of political geography, reflecting Braudel's spacetime categories and drawing on WSA, the local scale is labelled the scale of experience and is the everyday setting, reflecting the importance of place, in which events occur and where life is experienced; the nation-state scale is the scale of ideology, and the global scale is the scale of reality, to reflect the structural emphasis of world-systems theory. Gregory, Johnston, Pratt, Watts, and Whatmore (2011: 665) suggest a more detailed cascade of hierarchical levels to include the human body; households; the neighbourhood; city or district; metropolitan area or region; province or state; nation-state; continent; and globe.

The driver of social dynamics in WSA is the socio-economic and political world operating at the level of an integrated and interlinked system, thus operating at different scales of activity. These scales are both scales of time and space, or spacetime. (Because all matter is in motion, so all space is dynamic. "The only sensible term for this environment is 'spacetime'," Ethington 2007: 472). Lower-level processes operate in specific spaces in shorter time spans, by way of 'events' or episodes in the daily lives of individuals and places, whereas these in turn are shaped by the longer rhythms of particular social or institutional histories, the placed or situated dynamics of cultural practices which are in turn shaped by, respond to, and have effect on the almost timeless processes of the longue durée, the long-term cycles of human history.

Scales theory in sociolinguistics

Blommaert (2015: 11) suggests that scale in sociolinguistics was developed and presented

> as a concept that might do exactly what Braudel and Wallerstein used it for: to make fine stratigraphic distinctions between 'levels' of sociolinguistic activity, thus enabling distinctions as to power, agency, authority and validity that were hard to make without a concept that suggested vertical – hierarchical – orders in meaning making.

Scales theory in sociolinguistics follows Bourdieu (1991) in thinking about language (and other semiotic modalities) as embodying social capital in distinct ways within specific social economies, with language hierarchies that are socio-culturally shaped, spatially distributed, and systemically structured. It is offered as a response to globalization phenomena, addressing "language diversity and interaction in their situated co-occurrence as well as language hierarchy and systemic processes holding across situations and transcending localities" (Blommaert et al. 2005: 198).

Following the 'spatial turn' described earlier, people's location, or the space where they are, is seen to shape the way they connect with each other, by ascribing identities to one another in performing social and linguistic interactions. While people might maintain their linguistic (and social) competence when they move across spaces, and even add to their linguistic repertoires, they can nonetheless appear incapacitated, inarticulate and 'out of place' when they cross spaces (Dong and Blommaert 2009: 5). Scale is the term which explains such disparities as being a consequence of the way sociolinguistic and social spaces are hierarchically stratified and ordered. In scales theory, the centre-periphery model of WSA is expressed through, for example, 'central accents' such as British and American English accents being associated with status and identity, in contrast to Indian or Nigerian English, whereas peripheral accents project peripheral identities. These scaling processes operate at a world level, but also at all the other levels below that. A move from rural to urban areas, for instance, is thus also a move to a centre from the periphery, even within a peripheral region. Dong and Blommaert (2009) thus suggest that these concepts of space and scale allows us to study migration "from a fresh perspective, as migration offers an enormously rich research potential of movements across spaces and scales, both in real terms and symbolically."

The scales model suggests that each context (local, regional, national, global) has its own "orders of indexicality" which assign meanings, values, and statuses to diverse codes. These values or indexicalities are organised hierarchically at a global level in a world that is systemically organised in terms of scales that run from the global to various local contexts. Blommaert (2010: 36) argues that local scales are momentary, situated, and restricted, while the codes and literacies of dominant groupings are valued at a translocal level because they are resilient, highly mobile, and dominant groups can "jump scales," that is they can shift from using locally available ways of communicating to higher level or elite registers, that serve to put others 'in their place', to silence them, or to assert superiority over them (as happened in the case of the lecturer, described earlier, in conversation with her student).

Scales theory thus outlines a route to theorising and analysing the way language resources retain or lose social value depending on where they are placed along spatiotemporal lines within social contexts, where power relations shape the uptake of language resources. A sociolinguistics of globalisation (Blommaert 2010) working with this model of the social as a world system pays attention to language hierarchy and processes that are seen as holding across situations and transcending localities. This analysis aims to account for large-scale features of language and literacy, particularly, for example on institutional, national, and transnational levels, as well as their impact on the dynamics of face-to-face interaction (Blommaert 2010, 2007; Collins and Slembrouk 2007). Interaction between different scales is a crucial feature for understanding the socio-linguistic dimensions of such events and processes, because language and literacy practices are subject to social processes of hierarchical ordering. The importance of the term *indexicality* in scales theory as used earlier in this paragraph requires us to take a closer look at the concept and the work it does here.

Indexicality

Underlying the concept of indexicality as it is used in scales theory is the view that language, along with other communicative resources (gesture, image, etc.) is never an instrument of pure reference, because speech and writing always occur within networks of activity, in social contexts which are never neutral or ahistorical, because language is a social phenomenon – "social through its entire range and in each and every of its factors, from the sound image to the furthest reaches of abstract meaning" (Bakhtin 1981: 259). The unpredictable character of situated interactions as well as variations in the larger social patterns that provide resources for such interactions means that linguistic resources do not carry stable and context-free referential meanings from one setting to the next. As a result, it is claimed by various sociolinguists studying interaction that the meaning of any linguistic sign in use cannot be determined by decontextualized rules, whether linguistic or social (Hymes 1996; Gumperz 1982; Silverstein 2004; Wortham 2008). Language in use is shaped by the interests and intentions of situated actors who bend their meanings to suit their activities. The language people use (along with other communicative resources) is always a social language (Gee 1996) as regards its forms, its use, language ideologies that effect it and also with regard to the social domain of its use. These interlinked dimensions make up what Silverstein identified as "the total linguistic fact":

> the total linguistic fact, the datum for a science of language is irreducibly dialectic in nature. It is an unstable mutual interaction of meaningful sign forms, contextualized to situations of interested human use and mediated by the fact of cultural ideology.
>
> *(1985: 220)*

Indexicality, then, refers to this process: where language in use is invested with socio-political and cultural interests which are identifiable in the recognisable, often routinized and ritualised, ways that speakers and writers 'express themselves' as recognisably certain kinds of people engaged in identifiable socially situated actions and activities. To be understood and to communicate meaningfully, they draw on salient models for how particular kinds of meaning get made along with communicating particular identity or identification characteristics of their own, and these models for language use are always both restrictive or regimental, as well as enabling. Silverstein's (2004: 193) claim is that 'indexical order' is the concept necessary for identifying those salient models that people draw on in their communicative activities and for showing us "how to relate the micro-social to the macro-social frames of analysis of any sociolinguistic phenomenon." Blommaert (2007: 4) explains this point as follows:

> language occurs both as an individual, one-time and unique phenomenon and, simultaneously, as a collective and relatively stable phenomenon. Indexicality refers to the ways in which unique instances of communication can be seen, as 'framed', understandable communication, as pointing towards socially and culturally ordered norms, genres, traditions, expectations.

The concept of indexicality goes beyond the general idea that people draw on broad models or genres in their situated communication. It also address variability, unpredictability, and change in language pragmatics. For Silverstein, the micro-order is that of language-based interaction, while the macro-order is that of the speech community. The dialectical relationship that Silverstein identifies between these two orders indicates that the macro-order is not autonomous, in that social regularity is only always performed or enacted, dependent on the conditions of enactment, and so does not have fully predictable effects on actions and meanings. Silverstein refers to first-order, second-order and n-level construals of meaning to show that indexical order is one of ongoing interplay between specific acts and available ideologically framed resources. One example of first-order construal is that of the view of the standard register in a language community as ideologically indexing the neutral mean for all variability around it, "sweeping up people of different groups and categories into an anxiety before standard" (Silverstein 2004: 219) when hegemonic ideologies privilege language registers that are associated with powerful groups in society, with the consequence that their language use is perceived to be accentless and ideal for effective communication. Divergences from the standard – whether associated with class, ethnicity/race, or region – are considered marked and less desirable. In this case, second-order indexicality is shown by persons from outside the 'neutral centre' who attempt to approximate stylistically or phonetically to the standard in an effort to index an aspirant or high-status identity for themselves, a process which Silverstein describes as depending "on a folk- or ethno-metapragmatics of standard register and its potential gradient availability" (Silverstein 2004: 219). As one example, the normative status of English in Jamaica leads on occasion to variably unsuccessful attempts by Jamaican creole speakers to speak the standard register at particular moments, which get labelled derisively by others as 'Speaky Spoky' (Bohmann 2016). Vigouroux (2011: 62) describes a similar though contrasting dynamic regarding the advertising flyers of African migrants in Paris who work as *marabouts* (clairvoyants/spiritualists or spirit-mediums):

> Marabouts' advertisements share not only common themes (love, professional success, achievements in different domains such as sports, luck games, increase of sexual prowess,

fertility, healing of sickness etc.) but also linguistic features that can be summarized as follows: spelling mistakes, typos, lack of agreement, misuse of prepositions, cross-register transfers, misuse of diacritics, misuse of written conventions.

While French readers of their flyers comment and joke at length about the deviant literacy, language and layout of these flyers, Vigouroux argues that marabouts, indeed, choose to use such non-standard registers so as to conform to the widely held, exoticised, and stereotypical view of themselves in urban France. Not to do so would raise questions as to whether they were genuine marabouts or imposters. Their survival as practitioners depends on their 'recognisability' and this recognisability is tied up with marabouts' advertisements as a genre, or generic form, along with their syntactical, lexical, and orthographic 'errors', because these are markers that are indexical of their exoticised (racialised and 'othered') status in these settings. (Their conscious use of this marbout register, however, as Vigouroux describes it, introduces a reflexive element into these dynamics that is not always visible in analyses that draw on scales theory, as I discuss later.)

Switching (code-switching) across identifiable languages and registers by migrants or others in multilingual contexts can be seen as examples of second-order indexicality, or as forms of skilled or less skilled performance. Such switching can communicate, or be intended to communicate, specific social and pragmatic meanings, where language forms are used as culturalised resources to index particular meanings that are situated, constructed, and might be shifting, in that they arise from a history, however long or short, of usage by speakers/writers in particular social circumstances. Through recurrent connections between a context and a linguistic form, indexical meanings are constituted (Bailey 2007) and because of the interactive, reflective, or heteroglossic nature of these connections, multiple orders of indexicality are possible. As Collins and Slembrouk (2004: 9) discuss in the context of multilingual (and multimodal) shop window displays in a European town, there is a 'face-value' or first-order meaning to interpret as to what the sign says. In addition, there are, "in principle multiple 'n-level' indexical-ideological construals" available:

> Might this shop sign be taken as a joke? An indication of amicable or tense relations between autochthone and allochthone populations? As indicating the origins and low education of the migrants who use the two languages?

Collins and Slembrouk's analysis emphasises that meaning is contextual and processual, while contexts are various and yet orderable and ordered. Bailey (2007: 263) points out that indexicality can encompass a very large range of phenomena because indexical forms are highly varied. They range from phonetic features, to word choice, to visual features, to other stylistic dimensions of talk, while the distance across space and time of the indexical form and its object can also vary greatly.

Scales theory and indexicality

For Silverstein (2004: 201–202) the 'macro-social' as far as language is concerned refers to the speech community, along with its differentiating deployment of categories of "age, gender, social and socioeconomic class, profession, and other aspects of what we term institutional/positional social identity." These categories would seem to refer to class and status categories operating on a national level, though Silverstein is not specific on this point. Scales theorists, however, while drawing strongly on Silverstein's theorisation of indexicality, distance themselves from the construct of speech community, regarding it as an essentialist notion, invoking static notions of ethnolinguistic identities of peoples within unitary nation-states. While Silverstein prefers to distinguish between the concept of *language community* as designating this overbroad sense, and *speech community* as referring to a more transient, performed and less static concept, Rampton (1998) and Blommaert and Rampton (2011: 6) reject the concept of speech community outright, preferring the notion of linguistic repertoire, which they see as more appropriate in contexts of linguistic diversity, mixed language and multilingualism, because it

> refers to individuals very variable (and often rather fragmentary) grasp of a plurality of differentially shared styles, registers and genres, which are picked up (and maybe then partially forgotten) within biographical trajectories that develop in actual histories and topographies.

World-systems analysis does not feature in Silverstein's work but is a central feature of scales theory as it has developed in the work of Jan Blommaert and the various colleagues he has worked with or who draw on his work, so we need to describe some particularities that it takes on in recent theorisations of scales theory. Most notably, when the concept of language indexicalities operates at the level of the world-system, it can be used to identify language ideological dynamics that work on a transnational scale in particular ways. Blommaert (2010: 34) followed this direction to define scales according to space and time in the following way:

	Lower scale	*Higher scale*
Time	momentary	timeless
Space	local, situated	translocal, widespread

As Dong and Blommaert (2009: 6) explain,

> the notion of 'scale' introduces a *vertical* spatial metaphor: an image of a continuum on which spaces are hierarchically stratified and ordered from local to global with intermediary levels between the two poles. The vertical move from one scale to another (e.g. from local to translocal, from momentary to timeless, from specific to general) involves and presupposes access to particular resources, and such access is often subject to inequality.

We can see in this model the confluence of Braudel's time-scales or *durée* and Wallerstein's world-systems model, such that the lower scales of language use in the social periphery correspond to Braudel's notion of the momentary, situated, passing episodic events in situated daily lives, whereas the higher scale corresponds to that of the *longue durée* of slow structural time where global languages are seen to lie, along with the language resources of elite groups at any point along the various continua from periphery to core. Lower scale is associated with "diversity, variation" and higher scale with "uniformity, homogeneity" (Blommaert 2010: 35). Because scales are hierarchically stratified, there is a restricted set of universally accepted norms at the higher scale level. There is also the implication, following WSA, that these higher-scale resources are powerful because they operate at the level of 'the real', or at a systemically important level.

Issues and debates

Scales theory among geographers and sociologists is increasingly contested terrain, and it is probably appropriate that scales theory in sociolinguistics should also be subject to disputes and challenges, and that the challenges in sociolinguistics might overlap with those in other fields. Among geographers and sociologists, the status of WSA as a totalising theory of spacetime and social causation has been criticised. In particular, the systemic bird's-eye approach to situated specificity has been questioned. In one telling example, Agnew (2011) examined the debate over Braudel's view of the Mediterranean as a space of exchange, trade, diffusion, and connectivity and contrasted what he calls Braudel's "geometric or locational view" with the more "holistic, topographical and phenomenological" view of more recent work which treats the Mediterranean historically as a disorderly jumble of micro-ecologies or places separated by distinctive social practices (Agnew 2011: 317). Agnew's concern is that scalar perspectives emphasise spatial relations and de-emphasise place, along with situated specificity and complexity. Scalar perspectives in sociolinguistics might be said, in similar vein, to emphasise spatial relations in language hierarchies that are products of relations between centres and peripheries, and thus risk de-emphasising local or placed linguistic specificity and complexities. The emphasis on hierarchical scalar relations at the level of a world system that determines specificity can be seen as a view which implies that place is anachronistic and is re-placed by space and scale as the determinant spatial dynamics of globalisation. Thus, for example, in the sociolinguistic theory of scales, social and linguistic inequalities are not produced in situated and interactive or placed ways in the first instance; they are the outcomes of power working hierarchically and systemically as a function of the world system.

Blommaert, Muyllaert, Huysmans, and Dyers (2006: 399) argued, in a discussion of how scale determines language inequalities:

> Inequality occurs on the boundaries between scales, the points of transition from strict locality to translocality, from a level defined by the rules and codes of one place to a level defined by the rules and norms of different places . . . At such points of transition, the issue is the mobility offered by semiotic resources such as language skills: some skills offer a very low degree of mobility while others offer a considerably larger degree of mobility and transferability across social and spatial domains.

This argument relies on a strong notion of scalar processes, as we have discussed them, in a process of vertical differentiation where social relations are embedded in "a hierarchical scaffolding of nested territorial units stretching from the global, the supranational, and the national downwards to the regional, the metropolitan, the urban, the local, and the body" (Marston, Jones, and Woodward 2005: 416). As Marston, Jones, and Woodward point out, however, such a view of scales is countered by others, where global, national, and local scales are seen as intuitive fictions rather than existing as such; along with suggestions that scale be best used as an epistemological rather than an ontological structure which 'exists', summarised by Thrift's conclusion (quoted in Marston et al., 2005: 416) that there "is no such thing as a scale."

Disagreements with and rejections of the strong scalar perspective frequently draw on anti-systemic network theoretical perspectives from actor-network theory (Latour 1991) to talk about trans-space dynamics. That perspective stresses the contingency in networks of people and things that are constructed across space and time and rejects the systemic view of the global that is the premise of WSA. There is no system, global order or network, Law (2004: 10) argues. Instead "there are local complexities and local globalities, and the relations between them are uncertain." In this view, the global is situated, specific, and materially constructed in the practices included in each specificity. Marston (2000: 221) similarly identified a constructionist shift in theorists of scale in geography and the rejection of scale as an ontologically given category. She argued against the view that scales are unilinearly ordered and rejected the assumption that the global is theoretically and empirically superior to the local. Marston et al. (2005) take this direction of criticism of hierarchical scales in WSA further, arguing that scale as an epistemology that is tied to a global-to-local continuum diverts attention from the concrete details of people's action and interactions in the spaces where they reside and act. They proposed instead a flat ontology that resists conceptualizing processes as operating at scales that hover above these sites.

Featherstone (2006: 370) similarly questioned the model of the global as a closed system, arguing that "in the space of the 'global', heterogeneous things combine in ways that are hard to pin down with diagnostic resources which stress a global logic." He referred to such phenomena as major imbalances between cause and effect, unpredictable outcomes, and self-organizing, emergent structures as features of globalisation. He suggested that "the management of uncertainty, task predictability and orderly performances were much easier to facilitate in the 'relatively complex' organizations of modern industrial societies." A global society, on the other hand, he wrote, "entails a different form of complexity: one emanating more from microstructural arrangements that institute self-organizing principles and patterns."

Shields (2006) thought that the centre-periphery distinctions in WSA and scales theory might be Eurocentric and technocratic – just because something is happening 'over there' doesn't mean it is taking place at a different scale. Shields's point is that space and spacings are best seen as accomplishments, often contested ones, rather than systemic effects. Agnew (2011: 22), in an effort to reconfirm the specificity of place in spatial theorising, argues that places tend to have permeable rather than fixed boundaries and are internally diverse rather than homogenous with respect to their social and other attributes, even as they express a certain communality of experience and performance.

Massey (2005) offers a conceptualisation where both local and global are grounded and real, but dispersed within politics of connectivity that both construct places and connect them to other sites in a dynamic where spaces are both concrete and imagined, as well as differentiated. Massey offers a conceptualisation of the local and global that is highly pertinent to theories of scale. She insists that just as the local is grounded, concrete and real, so too is the global. She builds her argument around a reconceptualisation of the local as dispersed in its sources and repercussions. The local's relationship to the global is premised on a politics of connectivity – 'power geometries' – that recognises and exploits webs of relations and practices that construct places, but also connect them to other sites. Massey's political project is about recapturing agency so as to better address the impacts of globalisation as they affect connected places. Against the view of space as representationally fixed, Massey presents three clear counter-propositions:

> First, that we recognise space as the product of interrelations, as constituted through interactions, from the immensity of the global to the intimately tiny. Second, that we understand space as the sphere of the possibility of the existence of multiplicity in the sense of contemporaneous plurality; as the sphere in which distinct trajectories coexist; as the sphere therefore of coexisting heterogeneity. Third, that we recognise space

as always under construction. Precisely because space on this reading is a product of relations-between, relations that are necessarily embedded material practices which have to be carried out, it is always in the process of being made. It is never finished; never closed.

(Massey 2005: 9)

Implications and future directions

How does this discussion of critical aspects of scales theory relate to questions of sociolinguistic analysis and migration? I suggest that a scaled perspective can encourage a bird's-eye view on situated mediated social encounters, offering an explanation that privileges a 'top-down' view on interactive dynamics and on social history, sometimes implying that such moments automatically configure forms of social uniformity. We can sidestep this difficulty by seeing that social, linguistic, and literacy events and processes unfold through social-semiotic encounters of diverse kinds, only some of which are amenable to a scales theoretical perspective that stresses hierarchical dynamics between centres and peripheries. In our analyses we can strive to follow a context-sensitive approach to the diverse flows of engagement, knowledge, power, and desire recognising these in terms of micro-flows, as well as top-down dynamics.

This point is illustrated in the recent response by Canagarajah (2015) to Blommaert et al.'s (2006) analysis of linguistic inequalities in a schooling context in the Western Cape, South Africa. In a study carried out with students and colleagues from the University of the Western Cape at a Cape Town township school, Blommaert et al. (2006) identified students' writing as featuring grammatical, spelling, and other deviations and found the same features in teachers' writing, evidence of new, but low-status, norms that were being developed. They categorised such writing as characteristic of what Blommaert (2004; 2008) had described as 'grassroots literacy', a literacy that he saw as featuring in societies on the global periphery or in ones marked by deep inequality and identified by the use of graphic symbols in ways that defy orthographic norms: words spelled in different ways, often reflecting the way they are pronounced in spoken vernacular varieties rather than following conventional orthographic norms or prestige language forms.

Canagarajah (2015) carried out a study of his own in a similarly poorly resourced Western Cape township school setting to that of Blommaert and colleagues and he disagreed with aspects of Blommaert's analysis, specifically with Blommaert's treatment of literacy regimes as somewhat autonomous and separate, with their own logic, cut off from others. While neither study drew attention to the migrant aspects of the students they studied, it is relevant for our purposes here to point out that these students were internal migrants from the rural Eastern Cape or children of first, second, or third generations of migrants, most of whom would maintain transcontextual links with an Eastern Cape home and a heritage cultural and linguistic identity; also, that they live in an environment where the everyday language is a version of isiXhosa, for both teachers and students, whereas the prescribed language of instruction and testing was 'Standard English'. This clearly reflects a kind of language dynamic similar for migrants in many other settings, as well. Blommaert et al. (2006) emphasise the idea of 'peripheral normativity' as characterising the linguistic rules, norms, and opportunities characteristic of the peripheral context of their study. These norms appear as inferior examples of language and writing at the centre, however, pointing to the low status of these persons, on a larger stage. In contrast, Canagarajah draws attention to variability and diversity in a similar setting, rather than uniformity, arguing that while particular communities might display characteristic writing forms, they are not necessarily 'stuck' or 'locked' into using only these forms in the way Blommaert et al. suggested. Canagarajah's study found in the texts of the students he studied a *recognition* of different norms carrying more or less status across the different social contexts across which the students operated. In their writings on a school Facebook site, for example, students' use of non-standard spelling and orthography was evident in their mixing of English and isiXhosa, abbreviations and icons. He identifies their writing there as a hybrid form of literacy activity, combining diverse resources and languages. In their classroom written work, however, students didn't mix codes in the same way, and Canagarajah suggested that they had shifted to a translocal norm, approximating to 'Standard Written English' and with an emerging sense of the genre requirements of school essay writing. While student writing displayed the types of grammatical problems that Blommaert identified, Canagarajah saw teachers as selectively correcting these as they moved students towards developing their translocal English-language writing resources, albeit from a constrained starting point. He argued that it might be more productive to see social spaces as *contact zones* rather than as structurally separated ones, with diverse language and literacy resources in the same social space. Much depended, he pointed out, on how people negotiate these mobile resources. Canagarajah's argument here reflects Thrift's (1999) claim that the particularities of any situation cannot be read off from the predictions of a totalising theory. Instead, places are specific time-space configurations made up of the intersection of many encounters between people and things that reflect actual goings-on rather than the working out of a conceptual pre-given reality.

As regards migrants, Massey's reference to co-existing heterogeneity is perhaps a useful point to start in contrast to a scalar perspective which assumes that inequalities are primarily about relations between scales. As Saxena (1994, 2000) showed in relation to Punjabi speakers in the UK, migrants' attitudes to language choice and script choice and maintenance are not simply a response to where they find themselves but are also a response to where they are from, and in particular to their sometimes enduring transnational ties to the places where they are from. Warriner (2009) and Lam and Warriner (2012) make a similarly strong case for a focus on features of transnationality. Transnationalism refers to the ways that many migrants are simultaneously embedded in more than one setting, with characteristically high intensity of exchanges that often included new practices of transacting and interacting, varying language and literacy practices, identities and relationships, and activities that sometimes require cross-border travel and contacts on a sustainable basis, or translocal digital communications of various kinds. From this perspective, space and language are, as Massey described it, a product of relations-between, but relations that are necessarily embedded material practices which have to be carried out and are never finished.

Scales theory, as a methodological development in sociolinguistics and in literacy studies, in conclusion, raises key concerns for the study of language and migration. Questions of language diversity, inequalities, and change in the context of social migrations need an account of how social spaces are both interconnected and distinct under the conditions of contemporary globalisation and scales theory provides an account. It challenges researchers to address the study of language and literacy in specific contexts with an eye to the pivotal importance of wider social dynamics that lie beyond the immediately visible sphere of social interaction. It aims to provide a way to address the challenges of relating the socially macro to the locally micro dynamics of purposeful communicative interaction. It introduces for study in sociolinguistics the theme of global socio-economic, socio-cultural and socio-political processes as they impact on the movements of people and language resources across spaces. Whether scales theory, in the end, provides a satisfactory way to address both large-scale and small-scale dynamics in how linguistic inequalities are produced and perpetuated is less certain, however, as the concluding sections of this chapter have pointed out.

Related topics

Space, place, and language
Complexity, mobility, migration
Multisited ethnography and language in the study of migration

Further reading

Blommaert, J., Westinen, E. and Leppänen, S. (2015). Further notes on sociolinguistic scales. *Intercultural Pragmatics*, *12*(1), 119–127.

The authors look back at the uses of scales in Blommaert's own past work and develop a more complex orientation to scales as a semiotic resource and not enjoying ontological status.

Canagarajah, S. and de Costa, P. (2016). Introduction: Scales analysis, and its uses and prospects in educational linguistics. *Linguistics and Education*, *34*(2016), 1–10. Retrieved from http://dx.doi.org/10.1016/j.linged.2015.09.001

As an introduction to a special topic issue on scalar analysis in educational contexts, the editors argue that how scales are defined, their relationships conceived, and related to other social categories should be based on how people and institutions adopt scales in relation to their contexts and interests.

Lempert, M. (2012). Interaction rescaled: How monastic debate became a diasporic pedagogy. *Anthropology & Education Quarterly*, *43*(2), 138–156.

Seminal article that develops an orientation to scales as a category of practice rather than a category of analysis.

References

Agnew, J. (2011). Space and place. In J. Agnew and D. Livingstone (eds.), *Handbook of Geographical Knowledge* (pp. 316–330). London: Sage.
Bailey, B. (2007). Heteroglossia and boundaries. In M. Heller (ed.), *Bilingualism: A Social Approach* (pp. 257–274). Basingstoke: Palgrave Macmillan.
Bakhtin, M. (1981). *The Dialogic Imagination: Four Essays by M. M. Bakhtin* [Edited by M. Holquist], Austin: Texas University Press.
Blommaert, J. (2002). *Writing in the Margins. Notes on a Sociolinguistics of Globalization*. Unpublished written version of a lecture given at Cardiff University, April 2002, during a workshop of the Leverhulme Trust project on Language and Global Communication.
Blommaert, J. (2004). Writing as a problem: African grassroots writing, economies of literacy, and globalization. *Language in Society* 33: 643–671.
Blommaert, J. (2007). Sociolinguistic scales. *Intercultural Pragmatics* 4(1): 1–19.
Blommaert, J. (2008). *Grassroots Literacy: Writing, Identity and Voice in Central Africa*. London: Routledge.
Blommaert, J. (2010). *The Sociolinguistics of Globalization*. Cambridge: Cambridge University.
Blommaert, J. (2015). Chronotopes, scales, and complexity in the study of language in society. Draft of paper to appear in *Annual Review of Anthropology* 44. Retrieved from https://www.academia.edu/10086732/Chronotopes_scale_and_complexity_in_the_study_of_language_in_society.
Blommaert, J., Collins, J. and Slembrouk, S. (2005). Spaces of multilingualism. *Language & Communication* 25: 197–216.

Blommaert, J., Muyllaert, N., Huysmans, M. and Dyers, C. (2006). Peripheral normativity: Literacy and the production of locality in a South African township school. *Linguistics and Education* 16(4): 378–403.

Blommaert, J. and Rampton, B. (2011). Language and superdiversity. *Diversities* 13(2): 1–20.

Bohmann, A. (2016). "Nobody canna cross it": Language-ideological dimensions of hypercorrect speech in Jamaica. *English Language and Linguistics* 20(1): 129–152.

Bourdieu, P. (1991). *Language and Symbolic Power*. Cambridge, MA: Harvard University Press.

Braudel, F. (1981–84). *Civilization and Capitalism, 15th–18th Century* (Vol. 3). New York: Harper and Row, original editions in French, 1979.

Braudel, F. (1984). *Civilization and Capitalism, 15th–18th Century* (Vol. 3). *The Perspective of the World*. Berkeley: UCLA Press.

Braudel, F. (1996). *The Mediterranean and the Mediterranean World in the Age of Philip II*. Berkeley: University of California Press.

Canagarajah, S. (2015). Negotiating mobile codes and literacies at the contact zone. In C. Stroud and Mastin Prinsloo (eds.), *Language, Literacy and Diversity: Moving* Words (pp. 34–54). London: Routledge.

Collins, J., Baynham, M. and Slembrouck, S. (2011). *Globalization and Language in Contact: Scale, Migration, and Communicative Practices* (pp. 42–61). London: Continuum.

Collins, J. and Slembrouk, S. (2004). *Reading Shop Windows in Globalized Neighbourhoods*. LPI Working Papers, 21.

Collins, J. and Slembrouck, S. (2007). Reading shop windows in globalized neighborhoods: Multilingual literacy practices and indexicality. *Journal of Literacy Research* 39(3): 335–356.

Dong, J. and Blommaert, J. (2009). Space, scale and accent: Constructing migrant identity in Beijing. *Multilingua* 28(1): 1–24.

Ethington, P.J. (2007). Placing the past: "Groundwork" for a spatial theory of history. *Rethinking History* 11(4): 464–498.

Featherstone, M. (2006). Genealogies of the global. *Theory, Culture & Society* 23(2–3): 367–399.

Frank, A.G. (1966). The development of underdevelopment. *Monthly Review* 18(4): 17–31.

Gee, J. (1996). *Social Linguistics and Literacies*. London: Falmer Press.

Gregory, D., Johnston, R. Pratt, G. Watts, M. and Whatmore, S. (2011). *The Dictionary of Human Geography*. Oxford: Wiley Blackwell.

Gumperz, J. (1982). *Discourse Strategies*. Cambridge: Cambridge University Press.

Hexter, J.H. (1979). *On Historians: Reappraisals of the Masters of Modern History*. Cambridge, MA: Harvard University Press.

Hymes, D. (1996). *Ethnography, Linguistics, Narrative Inequality: Toward an Understanding of Voice*. London: Taylor & Francis.

Lam, W.S.E. and Warriner, D.S. (2012). Transnationalism and literacy: Investigating the mobility of people, languages, texts, and practices. *Reading Research Quarterly* 47(2): 191–215.

Latour, B. (1991). *We Have Never Been Modern*. Cambridge, MA: Cambridge University Press.

Law, J. (2004). And if the global were small and non-coherent? Method, complexity and the baroque. *Society and Space* 22: 13–26.

Lefebvre, H. (1991). *The Production of Space [Translated by Donald Nicholson-Smith]*. Oxford: Basil Blackwell.

Leitner, H. and Miller, B. (2007). Scale and the limitations of ontological debate: A commentary on Marston, Jones and Woodward. *Transactions of the Institute of British Geographers* 32: 116–125.

Marston, S.A. (2000). The social construction of scale. *Progress in Human Geography* 24(2): 219–242.

Marston, S., Jones, J.P. III and Woodward, K. (2005). Human geography without scale. *Transactions of the Institute of British Geographers* 30: 416–432.

Massey, D. (2005). *For Space*. London: Sage.

Rampton, B. (1998). Speech community. In J. Verschueren, J.-O Östman, J. Blommaert and C. Bulcaen (eds.), *Handbook of Pragmatics*. Amsterdam and New York: John Benjamins. Also available as WPULL 15 from http://www.kcl.ac.uk/depsta/education/ULL/wpull.html.

Saxena, M. (1994). Literacies among Punjabis in Southhall. In M. Hamilton, D. Barton and R. Ivanic (eds.), *Worlds of Literacy* (pp. 195–214). Clevedon: Multilingual Matters.

Saxena, M. (2000). Taking account of history and culture in community-based research on multilingual literacy. In M. Martin-Jones and K. Jones (eds.), *Multilingual Literacies: Reading and Writing Different Worlds* (pp. 275–298). Amsterdam: John Benjamins.

Shields, R. (2006). Knowing space. *Theory, Culture & Society* 23(2–3): 147–149.

Silverstein, M. (1985). Language and the culture of gender. In E. Mertz and R. Parmentier (eds.), *Semiotic Mediation: Sociocultural and Psychological Perspectives* (pp. 219–259). New York: Academic Press.

Silverstein, M. (2004). Indexical order and the dialectics of sociolinguistic life. *Language & Communication* 23(2003): 193–229.

Taylor, P. (1982). A materialist framework for political geography. *Transactions of the Institute of British Geographers* 7: 15–34.

Thrift, N. (1999). Steps to an ecology of place". In J. Allen, D. Massy and P. Sarre (eds.), *Human Geography Today* (pp. 295–322). Cambridge: Polity Press.

Vigouroux, C. (2011). Magic marketing: Performing grassroots literacy. *Diversities* 13(2): 53–69.

Wallerstein, I. (1974). *The Modern World-System: Capitalist Agriculture and the Origins of the European World-Economy in the Sixteenth Century*. New York: Academic Press.

Wallerstein, I. (2004). *World-Systems analysis. An Introduction*. Durham: Duke Press.

Warriner, D. (2009). Transnational literacies: Examining global flows through the lens of social practice. In M. Baynham and M. Prinsloo (eds), *The Future of Literacy Studies*. Basingstoke: Palgrave Macmillan.

Wortham, S. (2008). The objectification of identity across events. *Linguistics and Education* 19: 294–311.

21
Narrative in the study of migrants

Anna De Fina and Amelia Tseng

Introduction

Narratives are a basic mode of understanding and sharing of experience, and one of the most constitutive genres of human linguistic communication. In this chapter, we present an overview of contributions and future directions for narrative analysis in migration studies looking at different approaches, methodologies, and objects of study within sociolinguistics and other disciplines concerned with discourse in society. We begin with general definitions and considerations of the multiple roles that narratives carry in social life. We then proceed to discuss two key areas of study: (1) research on identities and representations by and about migrants, and (2) research on migrants' storytelling practices within institutions and communities. This categorization and further subdivisions within these broad areas will be discussed following the general introduction.

Telling stories is a way of sharing and making sense of experiences in the recent or remote past, and of recounting important, emotional, or traumatic events and the minutiae of everyday life. Stories are essential in conveying moral values and social norms and teaching them to children. They are central to the construction of individual and collective identities and are used to index ways of being and social identifications. Furthermore, stories carry weight in important institutional encounters such as employment and immigration processes. These many functions help explain narratives' ubiquity in everyday life and their relevance and interest for scholars.

While the terms 'story' and 'narrative' are often used synonymously, it is important to keep a terminological distinction in mind. According to William Labov, whose model of narrative analysis has dominated the field for the past fifty years (see Labov and Waletzky 1967; Labov 1981), stories are recapitulations of past events, with a structure involving complications and resolutions, told by a narrator in order to make a point. These canonical narratives recount chronologically ordered events in the past, have well-defined beginnings/middles/ends, and usually revolve around significant incidents. However, this definition does not fit all stories; for example, narrators may be seeking answers and advice rather than making a definite point. 'Narrative' thus addresses a wider gamut of less-canonical tellings, including hypothetical, habitual and generic narratives, small stories, and other genres that do not fit the classical Labovian definition. This distinction is particularly important given the contributions of data in different genres to migration studies. For example, hypothetical narratives do not recapitulate past experiences but rather describe scenarios that could have happened/could happen in the future; narratives of habitual past events and generic narratives (scenarios about protagonists carrying out actions in typical fashion) both violate Labov's principle that stories must present discrete events; and small stories address tellings of everyday, uneventful happenings rather than dramatic complications (see De Fina and Georgakopoulou 2008, chapter 2, for a discussion and references).

The field of narrative studies is wide and interdisciplinary since narratives have been a focus of attention not only for linguistics, but also for literary theorists (Herman 2010), social psychologists (Bruner 1990), sociologists (Riessman 1993), historians (White 1987), anthropologists (Hymes 1981), communication experts (Jenkins 2006), and so forth. Given these diverse research traditions, methodologies, and approaches for narrative analysis are also varied. Narrative studies of migration share this diversity as well as the unifying influence of the 'narrative turn' in the social sciences. The narrative turn represented a shift away from quantitative/experimental paradigms towards more qualitative analytic approaches to social phenomena, as theorists such as Bruner (1986) and Mishler (1986) emphasized narrative's importance as a mode of understanding. This in turn highlighted storytelling's potential for providing a voice to minorities and other underrepresented/socially isolated communities to author their own versions of their experiences. In this, work on migrants has taken prominence precisely because a primary scholarly objective has been building knowledge about processes of displacement and relocation as lived by narrators and their stories' protagonists, thus offering a counterbalance to the often-negative views about marginalized social groups circulated through political discourse and the mainstream media. Thus, research using stories both as objects and as tools is fundamentally qualitative and often ethnographically oriented.

In the following sections we will detail key questions and instruments in the field. While this discussion will demonstrate the existence of an ample diversity of perspectives and objects of study, we consider that studies can be broadly grouped into two fields: (1) studies that concentrate on the types of representations that migrants construct about their identities, experiences, values, and relations with out-groups, through storytelling; and (2) studies that concentrate on storytelling as a practice within migrant communities and institutions that deal with migrants. Although narrative is always a type of discourse and social practice (see De Fina and Georgakopoulou 2008), studies in the first category focus more on the content of stories and on the interactional dynamics through which such contents are built, while work in the second category is more concerned with the functions of stories and of storytelling within different communities and contexts. This being said, the division should not be taken as absolute.

Orientations

Identities and representations by and about migrants

Within research on identities and representations, we identify three different sub-areas: (1) work that deals with migrants as language learners, (2) work that treats migrants more in general as members of communities, and (3) work that focuses on storytelling centered on migrants but told by members of out-groups. We first discuss some general themes and approaches in this research, then we move to a discussion of each sub-area in the sections that follow.

Research on identities and representations generally addresses questions about how migrants perceive and discuss various aspects of the process of separation from their country and of relocation to new countries, how they present themselves as individuals and communities, how they define group membership, and what kind of boundaries they establish in terms of in-group and out-group belonging. Studies centered on these issues usually focus on life stories and other kinds of autobiographical narratives and narratives of personal experience usually elicited in interviews or focus groups. Some researchers (particularly in applied linguistics) use written narratives as well. Most studies within linguistics (except for research focused on literature) have an ethnographic orientation, in the sense that researchers try to get to know individuals' communities and social networks, use participant observation, and complement interview data with ethnographic notes and questionnaires. The degree to which ethnographic methods are followed varies; for example, some researchers (out of necessity or choice) only focus on narratives told in interviews.

A common conception in the study of discourse by migrants is that identity is socially constructed. Social constructionism (Berger and Luckman 1967) regards identity as a process that emerges in interaction with other human beings, therefore rejecting any essentialist view that relate identities directly to biological factors or simplistic social categorization. Researchers start from the premise that identities are not representations of essential characteristics defining individuals or particular ethnic/national groups, and inherently carried about by them, but rather that they are displayed and negotiated through 'discursive work' in interaction with others (Zimmerman and Weider 1970). This relates to the notion of 'performance' (Butler 1990) in the sense that identities are not seen as something people have, but rather something people 'do' in a process of self-presentation. Finally, identities are viewed as plural and 'heteroglossic' in that part of their construction references different 'voices' (see Bakhtin 1981), including the voices of others. These ideas are basic to research on storytelling by migrants, and, as we will see, have been operationalized through concepts such as 'self-presentation', 'positioning', and 'stance'.

Research on migrants as language learners

The study of stories told by migrants about their own language experiences has been important in reverting a tendency, common through the 1990s, of regarding migrants merely as imperfect second-language speakers, and essentially as individuals who needed to change and integrate by reaching native-speaker proficiency. Indeed, in classic SLA studies, narratives were regarded simply as texts to be analyzed in order to assess migrants' target-language competences (see for example Berman and Slobin 1994; Berman 1998), and sometimes also to detect first-language contamination and loss. With the advent of the narrative and "sociolinguistic turn" (Dörnyei and Ushioda 2011) in social sciences and applied linguistics, narrative analysis became increasingly important for understanding migrants' experiences and emotions regarding host-country language learning. In particular, studies investigate how narrators represent language learning and language learners, including themselves, in narrative; how they relate language learning to other experiences such as work; and how such representations relate to identity construction and identity categories more in general. Research in this area has focused primarily on small groups of interviewees as representatives of different categories, such as highly proficient L2 speakers (Farrell 2008), small business owners (Miller 2014), migrants further categorized by gender and or origins (Vitanova 2005; De Fina and King 2011; Relaño-Pastor 2014), and migrant writers (Pavlenko 2001). Unlike earlier studies of L2 learners' (auto)biographies, which identified recurrent topics and themes but ignored the contexts of narrative production (for a critique see Pavlenko 2007), more recent studies such as these subscribe to a dynamic view of narrative in which experiences and identities are constructed through negotiations with interlocutors, and the wider social context influences tellings. Thus, researchers resort to constructs such as 'positioning', agency and/or voice.

Following Bamberg (1997), positioning is analyzed as stemming from the kinds of positions that narrators take at three levels: vis-à-vis (1) narrative-internal ("storyworld") characters, (2) conversational interactants, or interlocutors, in the "storytelling world," and (3) general ideologies and discourses. Importantly, the second level addresses the interactional context of tellings, for example the ways in which stances are collaboratively constructed by interviewer and interviewee (see De Fina and King 2011). The Bakhtinian notion of voice is applied to the specific strategies that narrators deploy in order to represent/convey their own and other's points of view, for example reported or internal dialogues. Finally, while agency is variously defined, the construct is generally referenced to address the levels of responsibility and initiative that narrators deploy as both characters in stories and evaluators of their own narratives.

One example is Miller's (2014) research on narratives told in interviews by eighteen immigrant small business owners from a range of national backgrounds in the United States. Miller argues that instead of looking at immigrants as deficient speakers, one should consider that social context constrains agency: "situation or spaces, and the ideologies that are constructed in making such spaces recognizable, render some forms of linguistic expertise as legitimate and others as non-legitimate" (2014: 20). Miller analyzes how interviewees positioned themselves as passive or agentive when recounting their language learning experiences, focusing on subject-predicate constructions and agent-oriented modality. She found that agentive positioning was strongly influenced by language ideologies and context: migrants assumed responsibility and demonstrated agency when describing their early efforts to learn English, but did not show the same level of agentiveness when talking about workplace language learning and use.

A second example is Relaño Pastor's (2014) study of Mexican women migrants to the United States, using interviews with female participants in an after-school program that provided English and computer classes to southern California Mexican communities. Relaño Pastor examined how participants used evaluation, constructed dialogue, and emotional devices to express agency and victimization, took up moral stances, and positioned themselves vis-à-vis American and Mexican American antagonists in narratives about language learning and proficiency, and language-related conflict. Narratives further revealed a connection between language proficiency and social/parental identity, as interviewees took on agentive roles in refusing to accept language-related discrimination for their children (see also Relaño Pastor and De Fina 2005 for narrative agency on behalf of others).

Another approach is offered by Pavlenko's (2001) work on written narratives, specifically so-called cross-cultural autobiographies, by American writers whose first language was not English, Pavlenko advocates a "post-structuralist" approach to the study of identities in which prominence is given to issues of power and macro social conditions, noting that language learning is, among other things, a process of acquisition and mastering of resources that provides migrants with symbolic power. Like Miller, her analysis demonstrates how the construction of identities is profoundly influenced by language ideologies and how the process of language acquisition references and provides a terrain for the negotiation and evolution of multiple identities. A different focus is taken by Barkhuizen (2013b), who worked on social inclusion, language maintenance, and identity by South African migrants in New

Zealand. He studied narratives about language and identity in interviews with a South African businessman, Gert, at the beginning of his migrant experience in New Zealand, and at two-year intervals. Language, expressed through New Zealand English, South African English, or Afrikaans, was shown to be a salient element in his self-perception and identity construction, and related to social inclusion in different social domains. Thus, Barkhuizen illustrates how Gert's language-related identity in the South African/New Zealand migratory context was responsive to the complexities of his new migrant environment, but also to existing home-country discourses and tensions within the immigrant community.

Research on identities and representations by migrants as members of communities

Research on narratives in this category addresses migrants of diverse origins in different areas of the world. As with the research on migrants as language learners presented earlier, these studies investigate issues of identity, self-presentation, and personal experiences as depicted through narrative. Researchers in this field study identity strategies and categories of belonging, and pay particular attention to what kinds of experiences are salient in narratives and how these constructions are negotiated in interviews and other contexts. In this field, qualitative and ethnographic methodologies again predominate, and it is also common for the object of study to be represented by different types of narratives (oral/written life stories, autobiographical narratives, narratives of personal experience, habitual and generic narratives, etc.). Instruments and contexts, however, are more varied. For example, studies have employed photographs as a way of eliciting stories and accounts (Meinhof and Galasinski 2005), and have extended research to communities of practice such as online blogs (Kresova 2011) and forum discussions (Galasinska and Horolets 2012).

Agency, positioning and stance remain important constructs, but studies in this category also look at membership categorization (see Sacks 1992[1966]), or ways in which social categories are used by narrators to negotiate inclusion in and exclusion from groups. Indeed, narratives that revolve around ethnic and racial prejudice are very common in interviews with migrants Van De Mieroop 2012), and they are often a privileged object of analysis because they not only represent the kinds of social encounters that migrants are likely to have, but also their own way of labeling themselves and out-groups (see, for example, Clary-Lemon 2010 and Van De Mieroop 2012). Another important concept is indexicality. In contrast to categorization, which explicitly references socially recognized labels, indexicality (Silverstein 1976) refers to the ability of linguistic elements (for example single sounds, words, and combinations of resources such as stylistic repertoires) to evoke particular associations with identities such as groups or social personae, and related characteristics such as cultural attributions, social behavior, and values. Indexical elements in narratives are thus important in signalling implicit conceptions about people and places.

An example of early work on self-representations is De Fina's (2003a) study of fourteen first-generation Mexican economic migrants to the United States. De Fina analyzed elicited and non-elicited interview narratives of personal experience and chronicles of the border crossing to investigate different aspects of self-presentation: agency as encoded in constructed dialogue, social orientation through analysis of the use and alternation of pronouns, and membership categorization illustrated by the use of ethnic labels to introduce characters in the storyworld. The analysis showed that migrants demonstrated a marked collective orientation in their narratives and underplayed their own agency as individuals. They also demonstrated strategic and complex identifications with different communities in their negotiations with the interviewers about the meaning of stories, and a newly acquired sense of ethnicity which was a product of the migration experience.

Further studies of identity among migrants have focused on different types of narratives and social groupings. For example, Baynham (2006) underscored how generic narratives told by Moroccan migrants to the UK perpetrated gender divisions and stereotypes by making men the sole protagonists of the typical narrative of migration, while Carranza (1998) showed that habitual narratives were an important tool for Salvadoran migrants to the United States to support their self-construction as people who were forced to migrate in order to flee a violent regime. Studies in this tradition have investigated a variety of displaced populations, including migrants moving within their own countries (see McCormick 2005 and Gómez-Estern 2013) or to countries subject to redrawing of borders (Meinhof and Galasinski 2005; Liebscher and Dailey-O'Cain 2006), and refugees (Jacquemet 2005) and their descendants (Hatoss 2012). This demonstrates the significance of narratives for making sense of life-changing events and for creating social worlds in which roles and relationships are confirmed, contested, or negotiated.

Recently, research on migrants as members of communities has been influenced by sociolinguistic theorizations about globalization and mobility (see Blommaert, Collins, and Slembrouck 2005) and by a growing interest in the effect of new technologies and new ways of life on the conception and constitution of the self and the community. These new trends have brought about a heightened consciousness about the role of space and place as fundamental constructs for the narrative construction of identities and for making sense of experiences so centrally defined by mobility and dislocation.

Interest in the interdependence between space and time in narrative is not new, as scholars working on stories told by migrants realized that the traditional stress on time as a central dimension of narrative construction obscured important phenomena that came to light when migrants recounted their experiences. For example, Baynham (2003) argued that time-space orientation should not be seen simply as a backdrop for main events in a narrative, and proposed a constitutive, performative understanding of space-time relations in narrative. De Fina (2003b) demonstrated how space coordinates constitute a fundamental axis in narratives of disorientation told by migrants about their border crossing experiences and how discussions and clarifications about places can also become an important terrain for the negotiation of identities. In a similar vein, Murphy (2010) investigated how spatial identity is discursively constructed in narratives told by *sans papiers* (undocumented) migrants in France through the construals of "at-homeness" and "displacement." Another interesting reflection on time and space dimensions in migrant narratives comes from Perrino's (2005) work on the Bakhtinian notion of chronotopes. Analyzing narratives told by Senegalese migrants to Italy, she demonstrates how migrants create complex temporal and spatial configurations by exploiting the relations between present and past, the context of the telling, and the context of the told. Narrators use such configuration strategically. For example, they create empathy for their characters through 'coeval alignment', that is through and erasure of the distinction between the past of the storyworld and the present of the storytelling world.

Finally, scholars have also been revisiting traditional conceptions of time and space constraints questioning views of stories and storytelling that focus exclusively on the moment of telling, be it in interviews or in other contexts. For example, Wortham, Allard, Lee, and Mortimer (2011) who studied a neighborhood in Philadelphia followed stories circulated among neighbors, in the media, and in police reports, and analyzed their connections. In particular, they studied racialization in narratives and how the diverse ethnic groups living in the neighborhood represented each other.

Recent theorizations about mobility and insights about the role of globalization phenomena on discursive practices have also produced a greater interest in more diversified contexts of storytelling than the ones represented by interviews, for example transnational contexts and practices. Indeed, theorizations about transnationalism (see Appadurai 1996; Vertovec 2009) have been spurred precisely by new ideas on migrants and migration processes, and point to the impact of global flows of people, goods, and semiotic practices, availability of new mobile technologies, and general global economic interdependencies on the maintenance and fostering of connections between distant places, processes of identity construction, and circulation and consumption of semiotic practices.

The bulk of narrative research in this area focuses on identity construction by transnational migrants, with an emphasis on group formation and agency and on institutions and power asymmetries. For example, Sabaté i Dalmau (2016, 2015) interviewed and conducted ethnography on marginalized and unsheltered Ghanaian migrants who lived on a bench in a city in Catalonia. The interviews were 'mobile' in the sense that she traveled with her interviewees through their daily trajectories within the city. In this investigation, she explored their mobilization of homogenizing discourses about groups and individuals within their transnational experience. For example, stereotypes about 'Romanian drug dealers', 'better-off Ghanaians', and 'non-tolerant Muslim Nigerians', related to home and host-country ideologies, emerged through the interviewees' experiences within their mobile language ecologies. The salience of these categories to speakers showed that they oriented to these categories as part of translocal economies of meaning. These social organization practices showed simultaneous in-group solidarity and competition for resources and survival. Sabaté i Dalmau also shows that, rather than being agent-less victims as often presented, these marginalized narrators use storytelling itself as a form of agency, not solely in terms of self-representation and interaction with the interlocutor, but also by discursive group formation and positioning of others as particular types of people (see also Relaño Pastor and De Fina 2005; Tseng 2015).

In another study of transnational phenomena, Nyiri (2001) examined public and private narratives about national identity in the new-migrant Chinese diaspora via a comparison of online media centered in migrant communities in Japan and Hungary, with individual interviews. The analysis focuses on uniformity in circulating discourses (Gee 1996) as independent from migrants' geographic location, recursivity of media discourses and styles between the migrant diaspora and mainland China, and fluid transmission and return of people. Results show that Chinese migrants are incorporated into official PRC discourses of nationalism and success via recursive "two-way" institutionalized media. Interplay was observed between mediated discourses and individual narratives of migratory/diasporic experience.

Another point that has been stressed in research on transnational identities and practices is the centrality of hybrid versus homogenizing constructions of the self, a construct in line with postmodern understandings of identity (see Giddens 1991). An example of this can be found in Luke and Luke (1999) who investigated hybridity, dynamic identity construction, and situated racializing practices in interviews with Australian mixed-race couples. Findings indicated affirming or neutral discourses of difference pointing to a "third-space" (cf. Bhabha 2004) of identity construction, rather than lack or longing referencing dominant-culture dualistic cultural ideologies. Luke and Luke theorize that hybrid identity practices arise when links to "a priori identity discourse" (1999: 234), albeit reinforced in dominant home- and host-culture discourses, are weakened. As this example shows, identity construction relates to not just dominant-culture discourses but to local, community-specific, and home-culture discourses.

Research on identities and representations about migrants

A further area of interest has been the narrative study of discourses about migrants, particularly in the media and in institutional settings. In this area, the most influential approach is Critical Discourse Analysis (henceforth CDA), particularly the Discourse Historical Approach (Wodak, de Cillia, Reisigl, and Liebhart 2009). Researchers in this field focus on how dominant discourses construct minorities, how the ideologies of the powerful dominate social representations about minorities, and the mechanisms through which racist and anti-immigrant discourses are circulated. This research emphasizes meta-narrative, metaphors, and ideologies, with relatively less work on specific stories and on narrative understood as a conversational or interactional discourse genre. The concept of meta-narrative is in fact closer to the notion of capital-D Discourse, defined by Gee as

> a socially accepted association among ways of using language, other symbolic expressions, and artifacts, of thinking, feeling, believing, valuing and acting that can be used to identify oneself as a member of a socially meaningful group or "social network."
> *(Gee 1996: 131)*

Individual agency within the CDA model is often seen in terms of social positioning, where subjects are placed into certain social positions through power mechanisms and thus seen as possessing limited or conscripted agency. CDA's macro orientation leads to a focus on wide corpora, often in written form, coming from public and institutional contexts such as the media and governing bodies. Within these, CDA analysts look for linguistic patterns (for example, syntactic constructions and lexical/pronominal choices), but also study rhetorical moves and discursive strategies (such as inclusion, exclusion, avoidance, etc.). However, one of the first studies about narrative discourse on migrants ('foreigners') was Teun van Dijk's (1993) classic investigation of stories told by middle-class Dutch in interviews about their opinions on 'foreigners' in the Netherlands. Van Dijk looked at narrative structure and topic, or the type of complicating actions that narrators presented, and conducted a detailed analysis of the strategies they used to depict 'foreigners' and their actions. He found that the predominant topics when recounting stories of this type were aggression, violence, and threats, and that while narratives always had complicating events, they rarely had resolutions precisely because of the narrator's views of foreigners as an unsolvable issue.

The bulk of work from CDA that deals with discourses about migrants does so in the context of nationalism and national identities. It is within this tradition that narrative in conceived in terms of ideological stories or meta-narratives, tropes, and "hegemonic narratives" (Wodak and Meyer 2008: 11). See for example Ram's, definition: "nationality is a narrative, a story which people tell about themselves in order to lend meaning to their social world" (1994: 153, cf. Geertz 1983).

Research on narrative in this sense, that is of collective narratives linked with politics, history, and ideology, typically investigates the multi-modal and inter-textual creation of official and national narratives, "meta-narratives," "tropes," or "stories about groups of people," which are linked to history and time and used to construct and protect "myths" about national or group identity (Wodak and Meyer 2008: 19). These national narratives draw on collective recollection of specific historical events and are "preservative, justificatory, sanitized" (Wodak and Meyer 2008: 18–19).

For example, De Cillia et al. (1999) examined the narrative of 'real' Austrian identity in public and private discourse using data from a range of modalities, including political speeches and multimedia texts, advertisements, interviews, and discussion groups. Their study revealed ideas of an "innate nationality" (1999: 169) related to common descent, shared behaviors, and culture (expressed through markers such as food, language, and religion) to be key elements in this narrative, in addition to state-related aspects such as citizenship. The authors specifically note that these types of narrative appear in European Union countries in the context of "the propagation of a new European identity . . . accompanied by the emergence or reemergence of seemingly old, fragmented, and unstable national and ethnic identities [as] apparently firmly established national and cultural identities have become contested political terrain" (1999: 150).

Wodak's (2012, 2014) recent work on (re)inventing nationalism argues that these nationalist narratives function as a counterpoint to the othering of transnational migrants. Applying discourse-historical analysis to anti-Turkish propaganda from a right-wing Austrian political party, she shows how this narrative specifically references language as a visual emblem of conflicting group territorial claims. These exclusionary nationalist discourses typically incorporate language proficiency and testing as a gatekeeping mechanism for citizenship, a concept also noted in Blackledge's (2000) research on monolingual ideologies in Britain. Finally, another group of studies takes biographical interviewing as a method to investigate the relations between public discourses about migration and migrants' narratives (see Goldberg and Lanza 2013 and Cederberg 2014).

Research on storytelling as practice within migrant communities and institutions

Research in this area focuses on storytelling as a semiotic practice (see De Fina and Georgakopoulou 2008) within different types of contexts rather than on stories themselves. This research examines storytelling's role within institutional and community practices, different media modalities as tools for identity construction and relationships among migrants, and the global and local processes that shape and are shaped by these practices, with particular attention to power and domination. The idea is that narrative research illuminates not only identities and representations, but also the ways in which these are shaped through interactions and encounters. Methodologies are typically ethnographic, using participant observation and analysis of naturally occurring narratives and narratives within institutional encounters, sometimes complemented by interviews and elicitation.

Among the most important studies on narratives in institutional settings are those that focus on asylum seeker's stories. Examples of this work are Maryns and Blommaert (2001) and Jacquemet (2005), which show that asylum seekers' narratives are constrained and re-interpreted based on institutional needs and expectations, but that telling these stories has serious consequences for migrants since being perceived as incoherent or dishonest may lead to the rejection of their applications. Blommaert (2001) analyzed data from African asylum seekers' interviews throughout the Belgian asylum review process, finding "narrative inequality" in that "invisible power asymmetries and conflicts" (2001: 445) pervaded the process. For example, institutional demands dictate concise narratives unencumbered by "noise," and perceived veracity and consistency in asylum seekers' narratives are key to their acceptance or rejection. However, as non-native speakers of the interviewers' languages, interviewees' limited linguistic and communicative resources, including pragmatic differences, often caused their stories to be perceived as disorganized and incomprehensible.

Similarly, Lindholm, Börjesson, and Cederborg (2014) examined narratives of agency and vulnerability in police interviews of trafficked minors in Sweden, highlighting the role of institutionalized settings and expectations in narrative analysis. They also bring out the very real consequences of institutional discourse since the idealized narrative of victim/ exploiter, which interview data complicates, is required for recognition of victim status.

Recent work has focused on transnational communities and on the role of new media in the negotiation of identities and belonging, particularly among the youth. For example, Alexandra (2008) examined multimodal digital stories. She defines these as "hyper short, personally narrated multimedia fragments" (2008: 101) and noted that that storytelling allowed participants to negotiate self-representations as central or agentive vis-à-vis lived experiences, and seek a co-constructed authority shared with the investigator via a digital media project (2008: 110–111). Yi (2009) conducted an ethnography on 1.5-generation Korean teenagers in a Midwestern American city, with transnational upbringings between Korea and the United States. She examined data including interviews, feedback sessions, and analysis of online practices such as instant messaging, arguing that through these practices the teenagers created online "safe spaces" for transnational identity development and "employ[ed] a 'dual frame of reference' to explore or evaluate their life experiences and outcomes within their host country" (2009: 101). Other research has focused on families, providing insights about language, identity negotiation, cultural maintenance and home-country links. For instance, Pahl (2004) analyzed narratives as part of an ethnographic study, using multimodal data such as recorded interactions, field notes, photographs, and children's drawings, collected in schools and in family homes of multilingual immigrant families in London. She found that narratives linked with household artifacts created, referenced, and sustained cultural identity, "spanning time frames and geographical spaces . . . [to address] loss, displacement and migration" across countries and generations (2004: 356–357).

Issues and ongoing debates

As seen in this overview, orientations and approaches to narratives are rather varied, as scholars come from different traditions in sociolinguistics and applied linguistics and also use a variety of methodologies. Debates in the field reflect disagreements on the functions of narrative as a research tool, but also on the epistemological status of narrative. In terms of narrative as a research tool, a main concern has been the de-contextualization of narratives, that is, lack of attention to the discourse and semiotic practices in which narratives are embedded, most of all in the case of interviews. Narrative scholars in both applied linguistics (see, for example, Pavlenko 2007 and Barkhuizen 2013a) and sociolinguistics (see De Fina and Perrino 2011) have advocated approaches to narrative analysis that fully recognize such embedding without treating stories as unmediated windows into people's identities and experiences. They argue that the study of narrative content and topics is an important part but should not be the sole focus of analysis. However, in many interview-based studies of narrative the interviewer is erased and the analysis exclusively focuses on selected and decontextualized fragments. On the other hand, accounting for the participation of the interviewer is not always easy, as it implies painstaking attention to the details of the interaction.

Another issue that has been debated in the field is the epistemological status of narrative. While advocates of the 'narrative turn' (see McAdams 1993) talk about narrative as a fundamental mode of knowledge and a condition for the coherence of the self, others have criticized this kind of epistemology, accusing proponents of biographical approaches of reifying narrative by exaggerating its importance. For example the philosopher Strawson (2004) suggests that many narrative turn analysts seem to imply first that humans essentially understand and experience their lives as narratives and in narrative form as opposed to other modes of meaning-making, and second that these theorists seem to regard a coherent life narrative as a condition for a stable identity. Both principles represent, in Strawson's opinion, an exaggeration of the value of this form of communication and knowledge as there are many ways of experiencing and understanding reality and one's own life in particular. Strawson's critique against the emphasis on coherence is shared by many discourse analysts, who regard the corresponding devaluation of plurality and fragmentation as highly problematic for a thorough understanding of late-modern identities (for a discussion see De Fina and Georgakopoulou 2012: 17–23).

Methodology also constitutes a central concern and area of debate. Some difficulties are inherent to qualitative and ethnographic methodologies. For example, ethnographies are difficult to carry out, especially in the case of migrants. Thus, studying narrative practices, rather than simply narrative representations, is often not feasible (although digital environments present an intriguing direction in this regard). Further, context-sensitive narrative analysis can only be applied to small amounts of data and implies painstaking attention to detail and long hours of transcription. As in other qualitatively oriented areas of study, this small scale limits the generalizability of findings; however, the importance of detailed narrative analyses contextualized in the social and linguistic context of utterance should not be underestimated.

Specific methodological issues arise also in terms of identifying narratives within a given flow of talk. Debate about what constitutes a narrative or a story continues since, apart from Labov's model and story grammars (which are, however, based on cognitive perspectives), there is a lack of structural models applicable to all narratives. Researchers have studied very different texts, from life stories to biographical texts, small anecdotes to canonical stories, and often do not provide precise definitions of the genres under investigation. Thus scholars are faced with the daunting task of defining what counts as a story or a narrative, of finding the right units of analysis, and of delimiting the beginnings and ends of such texts within the flow of talk. Finally, even when analysts have chosen a model to follow and identified their units, further complications arise in connection with translation, given that many of narrative studies on immigrants are published in English, but work primarily with data in other languages.

Implications

These difficulties notwithstanding, narrative analysis has yielded a wealth of insights into the way that individuals and communities represent and talk about themselves and their experiences. On the one hand, given that storytelling is a natural and spontaneous way of reflecting on experience, it often becomes an authentic terrain of engagement for participants and interlocutors, thus allowing researchers and research subjects to create rapport. Because of this spontaneity of storytelling events, eliciting or simply analyzing stories and narratives within research events also appears as a more effective method, than other qualitative analysis tools, for offering insights into emic perspectives about the experience of migration. The use of stories has also the further advantage of leading to a more direct representation of experience. In the case of interviews, for example, while interviewees are sometimes reticent to respond to questions soliciting their opinions or feelings, they are more willing to tell stories and anecdotes because the latter allow them to offer their perspectives indirectly, by positioning themselves and others in certain ways in the storyworld, without explicitly stating their points of view. In sum, the use of narratives for eliciting the views of members of specific communities is a fundamental tool for applied and sociolinguists working on migrants. However, the issues that we have briefly described should be kept in mind when designing narrative-based studies and analyzing data, in the sense that storytelling contexts should not be erased, but rather should be used as sources of further insight and reflection.

Future directions

Narrative research is expanding and will continue to do so in terms of the range of contexts and media analyzed. In particular, scholars are becoming more interested in mediated contexts such as blogs, fora, and websites that promote storytelling and participant engagement with stories. The study of narratives in such contexts implies the development of more sophisticated tools for multimedia analysis. Scholars will also need to engage more fully with hybrid and transnational identities as the world in which migrants move becomes more and more interconnected. Research on refugees and on permanently or historically mobile populations, such as the Roma, also have yet to be fully explored (for a discussion of the importance of this research to meta-discourses or narratives of assimilation, see Vanderbeck 2009). Finally, digital storytelling also represents an important area for future research on migration studies, as practitioners and interest groups continue to develop these as tools research and for raising awareness.

Summary

In this chapter we have argued that narratives are among the most constitutive genres of human linguistic communication and are central to the construction of identities. Our main aim has been to offer an overview of how narrative analysis has contributed and can contribute to research on migrants and migration. We identified two main strands of narrative research in sociolinguistics and applied linguistics, and in disciplines concerned with the interconnections of discourse and social life: research on identities and representations by and about migrants, and research on storytelling practices among migrants within institutions and communities. Within these strands, we identified key research foci and sub-areas and described the diverse qualitative and ethnographic methodologies that scholars use to analyze narratives and narrative practices. Finally, we reviewed new directions in the field, such as hybrid identities, narratives by transnational and displaced peoples, and the role of new media and digital storytelling. Thus we have illustrated the importance of narrative analysis for a deeper understanding of language, mobility, and migration.

Related topics

> New orientations to identity in mobility
> Intersections of necessity and desire in migration research
> Complexity, mobility, migration

Further reading

Baynham, M. and De Fina, A., eds. (2005). *Dislocation/Relocations: Narratives of Displacement*. Manchester: St Jerome.
> This volume is devoted to narratives by migrants and displaced people, therefore all the chapters are relevant to those interested in migration narratives.

De Fina, A. and Georgakopoulou, A., eds. (2015). *Handbook of Narrative Analysis*. Malden, MA: Wiley.
> The handbook presents a collection of chapters on main topics in narrative analysis.

Fortier, A. M. (2000). *Migrant Belongings: Memory, Space, Identity*. Oxford: Berg.

An analysis of collective identity formation and negotiation among migrants through the study of a variety of narrative genres.

Ochs, E. and Capps, L. (2001). *Living Narrative: Creating Lives in Everyday Storytelling*. Cambridge, MA: Harvard University Press.

This book is not specifically about migration but it is useful to those who want to deepen their understanding of everyday narrative.

Piazza, R. and Fasulo, A., eds. (2015). *Marked Identities: Narrating Lives between Social Labels and Individual Biographies*. Basingstoke: Palgrave Macmillan.

This edited collection contains interesting analyses of narratives of migrant or displaced populations.

References

Alexandra, D. (2008). Digital storytelling as transformative practice: Critical analysis and creative expression in the representation of migration in Ireland. *Journal of Media Practice* 9(2): 101–112.

Appadurai, A. (1996). *Modernity at Large: Cultural Dimensions of Globalization*. Minneapolis: University of Minnesota Press.

Bakhtin, M. (1981). *The Dialogic Imagination: Four Essays by M. M. Bakhtin*, comp. M. Holquist. Austin: University of Texas Press.

Bamberg, M. (1997). Positioning between structure and performance. *Journal of Narrative and Life History* 7(1–4): 335–342.

Barkhuizen, G. (2013a). Introduction. In Barkhuizen G. (ed.), *Narrative Research in Applied Linguistics* (pp. 1–15). Cambridge: Cambridge University Press.

Barkhuizen, G. (2013b). Maintenance, identity and social inclusion narratives of an Afrikaans speaker living in New Zealand. *International Journal of the Sociology of Language* 2013(222): 77–100.

Baynham, M. (2003). Narratives in space and time: Beyond "backdrop" accounts of narrative orientation. *Narrative Inquiry* 13(2): 347–366.

Baynham, M. (2006). Performing self, family and community in Moroccan narratives of migration and settlement. In De Fina A., Schiffrin D. and Bamberg M. (eds.), *Discourse and Identity* (pp. 376–397). Cambridge: Cambridge University Press.

Berger, P. and Luckman, T. (1967). *The Social Construction of Reality*. Harmondsworth: Penguin.

Berman, R. A. (1998). Bilingual proficiency/proficient bilingualism: insights from narrative texts. In G. Extra and L. Verhoeven (eds.), *Bilingualism and Migration* (pp. 187–210). Berlin: Mouton de Gruyter.

Berman, R. A. and Slobin, D. (1994). *Relating Events in Narrative: A Cross-Linguistic Developmental Study*. Hillsdale, NJ: Lawrence Erlbaum.

Bhabha, H. (2004). *The Location of culture*. London and New York: Routledge.

Blackledge, A. (2000). Monolingual ideologies in multilingual states: Language, hegemony and social justice in Western liberal democracies. *Estudios de Sociolingüística* 1(2): 25–45.

Blommaert, J. (2001). Investigating narrative inequality: African asylum seekers' stories in Belgium. *Discourse & Society* 12: 413–449.

Blommaert, J., Collins, J. and Slembrouck, S. (2005). Spaces of multilingualism. *Language and Communication* 25(3): 197–216.

Bruner, J. 1986. Two modes of thought. In *Actual Minds Possible Worlds* (pp. 11–43). Cambridge, MA: Harvard University Press.

Bruner, J. (1990). *Acts of Meaning*. Cambridge, MA: Harvard University Press.

Butler, J. (1990). *Gender Trouble: Feminism and the Subversion of Identity*. New York: Routledge.

Carranza, I. (1998). Low narrativity narratives and argumentation. *Narrative Inquiry* 8(2): 287–317.

Cederberg, M. (2014). Public discourses and migrant stories of integration and inequality: Language and power in biographical narratives. *Sociology* 48(1): 133–149.

Clary-Lemon, J. (2010). "We're not ethnic, we're Irish!": Oral histories and the discursive construction of immigrant identity. *Discourse & Society* 21(1): 5–25.

De Cillia, R., Reisigl, M. and Wodak, R. (1999). The discursive construction of national identities. *Discourse & Society* 10(2): 149–173.

De Fina, A. (2003a). *Identity in Narrative: A Study of Immigrant Discourse*. Amsterdam: John Benjamins.

De Fina, A. (2003b). Crossing borders: Time, space and disorientation in narrative. *Narrative Inquiry* 13(2): 1–25.

De Fina, A. and Georgakopoulou, A., eds. (2008). Narrative analysis in the shift from text to practices. Special Issue *Text and Talk* 28(3): 275–281.

De Fina, A. and Georgakopoulou, A. (2012). *Analyzing Narrative. Discourse and Sociolinguistic Perspectives*. Cambridge: Cambridge University Press.

De Fina, A. and King, K. (2011). Language problem or language conflict? Narratives of immigrant women's experiences in the US. *Discourse Studies* 13: 163.

De Fina, A. and Perrino, S. (eds.) (2011). Narratives in interviews, interviews in narrative studies. Special Issue *Language in Society* 40.

Dörnyei, Z. and Ushioda, E. (2011). *Teaching and Researching Motivation* (2nd ed.). Harlow: Pearson Education.

Farrell, E. (2008). *Negotiating Identity: Discourses of Migration and Belonging*. Unpublished doctoral thesis, Macquarie University.

Galasinska, A. and Horolets, A. (2012). The (pro)long(ed) life of a "grand narrative": The case of internet forum discussions on post-2004 Polish migration to the UK. *Text and Talk* 32(2): 125–143.

Gee, J. P. (1996). *Social Linguistics and Literacies: Ideology in Discourses* (2nd ed.). London: Taylor & Francis.

Geertz, C. (1983). *Local Knowledge: Further Essays in Interpretive Anthropology*. New York: Basic Books.

Giddens, A. (1991). *Modernity and Self-Identity: Self and Society in the Late Modern Age*. Stanford: Stanford University Press.

Goldberg, A. and Lanza, E. (2013). Metaphors of culture: Identity construction in migrants' narrative discourse. *Intercultural Pragmatics* 10(2): 295–314.

Gomez-Estern, M. (2013). Narratives of migration: Emotions and the interweaving of personal and cultural identity through narrative. *Culture Psychology* 19(3): 348–368.

Hatoss, A. (2012). Where are you from? Identity construction and experiences of "othering" in the narratives of Sudanese refugee-background Australians. *Discourse & Society* 23(1): 47–68.

Herman, D. (2010). Multimodal storytelling and identity construction in graphic narratives. In Schiffrin D., De Fina A. and Nylund A. (eds.), *Telling Stories: Building Bridges among Language, Narrative, Identity, Interaction, Society and Culture* (pp. 195–208). Washington, DC: Georgetown University Press.

Hymes, D. (1981). *"In Vain I Tried to Tell You": Essays in Native American Ethnopoetics*. Philadelphia: University of Pennsylvania Press.

Jacquemet, M. (2005). The registration interview: Restricting refugees' narrative performances. In Baynham M. and De Fina A. (eds.), *Dislocations/Relocations: Narratives of Displacement* (pp. 194–216). Manchester: St. Jerome.

Jenkins, H. (2006). Blog this! In Jenkins H. (ed.), *Fans, Bloggers, and Gamers: Exploring Participatory Culture* (pp. 178–181). New York: New York University Press. [Originally published in March 2002 as Blog this: Online diarists rule an internet strewn with failed dot coms. *Technology Review*. Retrieved 6 September 2011, from http://www.technologyreview.com/energy/12768.]

Kresova, N. (2011). *Storytelling on Web 2.0: The case of migrants' personal blogs*. Paper presented at Narrative Matters 2012, UAP, Paris, May 31.

Labov, W. (1981). Speech actions and reactions in personal narrative. In Tannen D. (ed.), *Analyzing Discourse: Text and Talk* (pp. 217–247). Washington, DC: Georgetown University Press.

Labov, W. and Waletzky, J. (1967). Narrative analysis: Oral versions of personal experience. In Helm J. (ed.), *Essays on the Verbal and Visual Arts* (pp. 12–44). Seattle and London: University of Washington Press.

Liebscher, G. and Dailey-O'Cain, J. (2006). West Germans moving east: Place, political space, and positioning in conversational narratives. In Baynham M. and De Fina A. (eds.), *Dislocations/Relocations: Narratives of Displacement* (pp. 61–85). Manchester: St. Jerome.

Lindholm, J., Börjesson, M. and Cederborg, A. C. (2014). "What happened when you came to Sweden?": Attributing responsibility in police interviews with alleged adolescent human trafficking victims. *Narrative Inquiry* 24(2): 181–199.

Luke, C. and Luke, A. (1999). Theorizing interracial families and hybrid identity: An Australian perspective. *Educational Theory* 49(2): 223–249.

Maryns, K. and Blommaert, J. (2001). Stylistic and thematic shifting as a narrative resource. *Multilingual* 20(1): 61–84.

McAdams, D. P. (1993). *The Stories We Live By: Personal Myths and the Making of the Self.* New York: William C. Morrow and Co.

McCormick, K. (2005). Working with webs: Narrative constructions of forced removal and relocation. In Baynham M. and De Fina A. (eds.), *Dislocations/Relocations: Narratives of Displacement* (pp. 143–169). Manchester: St. Jerome.

Meinhof, U. and Galasinski, D. (2005). *The Language of Belonging.* London: Palgrave.

Miller, E. R. (2014). *The Language of Adult Immigrants: Agency in the Making.* Bristol: Multilingual Matters.

Mishler, E. G. (1986). *Research Interviewing: Context and Narrative.* Boston: Harvard University Press.

Murphy, M. (2010). *La mise en récit des espaces et des relation identitaires de trois femmes "sans paperFrancen France.* Unpublished doctoral thesis, Université Paris Descartes.

Nyiri, P. (2001). Expatriating is patriotic? The discourse on "new migrants" in the People's Republic of China and identity construction among recent migrants from the PRC. *Journal of Ethnic and Migration Studies* 27(4): 635–653.

Pahl, K. (2004). Narratives, artifacts and cultural identities: An ethnographic study of communicative practices in homes. *Linguistics and Education* 15(4): 339–358.

Pavlenko, A. (2001). In the world of the tradition I was unimagined: Negotiation of identities in cross-cultural autobiographies. *International Journal of Bilingualism* 5(3): 317–344.

Pavlenko, A. (2007). Autobiographical narratives as data in applied linguistics. *Applied Linguistics* 28(2): 163–188.

Perrino, S. (2005). Participant transposition in Senegalese oral narrative. *Narrative Inquiry* 15(2): 345–375.

Ram, U. (1994). Narration, Erziehung und die Erfindung des jüdischen Nationalismus. *Österreichische Zeitschrift für Geschichtswissenschaft* 5: 151–177.

Relaño Pastor, M. (2014). *Shame and Pride in Narrative: Mexican Women's Language Experiences at the U.S.-Mexico Border.* New York: Palgrave Macmillan.

Relaño Pastor, M. and De Fina, A. (2005). Contesting social place: Narratives of language conflict. In Baynham M. and De Fina A. (eds.), *Dislocations/Relocations: Narratives of Displacement* (pp. 36–60). Manchester: St. Jerome.

Riessman, C. K. (1993). *Narrative Analysis.* Thousand Oaks and London: SAGEI.

Sabaté i Dalmau, M. (2016, 2015). Migrant identities in narrative practice: In-/out-group constructions of "comrades" and "rivals" in storytelling about transnational life. *Narrative Inquiry* 25(1): 91–112.

Sacks, H. (1992[1966].) 'We'; category-bound activities. In G. Jefferson (ed.), *Harold Sacks: Lectures on Conversation* (Vol. 1, pp. 333–340). Oxford: Blackwell.

Silverstein, M. (1976). Shifters, linguistic categories, and cultural description. In Basso K. and Selby H. A. (eds.), *Meaning in Anthropology* (pp. 11–55). Albuquerque: University of New Mexico.

Strawson, G. (2004). Against narrativity. *Ratio* 17: 428–452.

Tseng, A. (2015). *Vowel Variation, Style, and Identity Construction in the English of Latinos in Washington, DC.* PhD thesis, Georgetown University.

Van De Mieroop, D. (2012). The discursive construction of gender, ethnicity and the workplace in second generation immigrants' narratives: The case of Moroccan women in Belgium. *Pragmatics* 22(2): 301–325.

Vanderbeck, R. (2009). Gypsy-traveller young people and the spaces of social welfare: A critical ethnography. *ACME: An International E-journal for Critical Geographies* 8(2): 304–339.

Van Dijk, T. A. (1993). Stories and racism. In Mumby D. (ed.), *Narrative and Social Control: Critical Perspectives* (pp. 121–142). Thousand Oaks and London: SAGE.

Vertovec, S. (2009). *Transnationalism*. London: Routledge.

Vitanova, G. (2005). Authoring the self in a nonnative language: A dialogic approach to agency and subjectivity. In Hall J. K., Vitanova G. and Marchenkova L. (eds.), *Dialogue with Bakhtin on Second and Foreign Language Learning: New Perspectives* (pp. 149–169). Mahwah, NJ: Lawrence Erlbaum.

White, H. (1987). *The Content of the Form: Narrative Discourse and Historical Representation*. Baltimore, MD: Johns Hopkins University Press.

Wodak, R. (2012). *Re/inventing Nationalism and National Identities*. Lancaster University. 30 October 2012.

Wodak, R. (2014). *Fortress Europe? – Unity in diversity. The Discursive Construction of the "The Stranger"*. Georgetown University. 27 March 2014.

Wodak, R., de Cillia, R., Reisigl, M. and Liebhart, K. (2009). *The Discursive Construction of National Identity*. Edinburgh: Edinburgh University Press.

Wodak, R. and Meyer, M. (2008). Critical discourse analysis: History, agenda, theory, and methodology. In Wodak R. and Meyer M. (eds.), *Methods for Critical Discourse Analysis* (pp. 1–33, 2nd ed.). London: SAGE.

Wortham, S., Allard, E., Lee, K. and Mortimer, K. (2011). Racialization in payday mugging narratives. *Journal of Linguistic Anthropology* 21: 56–75.

Yi, Y. (2009). Adolescent literacy and identity construction among 1.5 generation students from a transnational perspective. *Journal of Asian Pacific Communication* 19(1): 100–129.

Zimmerman, D. H. and Weider, D. L. (1970). Ethnomethodology and the problem of order: Comment on Denzin. In Douglas J. D. (ed.), *Understanding Everyday Life: Toward the Reconstruction of Sociological Knowledge* (pp. 285–298). Chicago: Aldine.

22
Multisited ethnography and language in the study of migration

Hilary Parsons Dick and Lynnette Arnold

Introduction[1]

Multisited ethnography adapts the classical tools of qualitative fieldwork in anthropology and sociology – a researcher's long-term engagement with one location that includes cultivating familiarity with local language and sociocultural life through participant observation – to the exploration of processes that unfold across multiple sites (Marcus 1995; Burawoy 2000; Burawoy et al. 2000; Hannerz 2003). This type of ethnography, then, involves research in two or more locations interconnected by a particular practice or set of practices. Multisited ethnography has been used to document a range of multiply-sited practices, from "mail-order marriages" (Constable 2003) to the global circulation of agricultural development policy (Gupta 1998). But perhaps more than any other activity, it is migration that has inspired and informed the development of multisited ethnography. Indeed, migrant communities – who influence both their home and receiving societies – mandate that researchers consider how sociocultural life is never formed in one bounded place but rather takes shape through interaction between and across different places. As work on migration shows us, to fully understand any sociocultural practice, we must account for such interaction – and multisited ethnography is uniquely well-suited for creating such accounts.

Although it had important precursors (e.g., Thomas and Znaniecki 1958[1918]), multisited ethnography took shape as a distinct method in the final decade of the 20th century. During this time, there were substantial shifts in the global economy that facilitated cross-border life. The opening of economic borders that resulted from free market capitalism, which took hold as the dominant form of economic development in the 1980s, has dramatically increased the rates of international migration over the last several decades (Marfleet 2006). Moreover, the greater availability of air travel and more widespread access to communication technologies has helped create a world where cross-border interconnections are, at least in theory, encouraged and feasible. It is not surprising that scholarly interest in multisited ethnography coincided with these shifts, which amplified cross-border practices such that scholars could no longer ignore them (Burawoy et al. 2000; Wimmer and Glick Schiller 2002: 321). This has especially been true in research on migration. Cross-border mobility, and particularly the movement of "unauthorized" populations (refugees, undocumented migrants), has become a central topic of ethnographic research since the early 1990s (Kearney 1986, 1995; De Genova 2002; Dick 2011b).

That said, technological and economic transformations cannot fully account for either the causes or contours of global processes or scholars' relatively recent interest in them. Under free market capitalism, movements between nation-states have been tightly constrained for many mobile populations, as we see reflected in the experience of migrants and refugees in diverse settings, from the Mexico-US border to the shores of New Zealand (Marfleet 2006). Rather than the movements of these people being facilitated by technological and economic change – as they are for other populations, such as tourists and high-skilled laborers, including Western academics – they are more often than not policed and detained by them (e.g., De Genova 2005; Dick 2011b; García-Sánchez 2014). Thus, while technological and economic changes help organize processes of migration, they do not determine them. The same can be said for the emergence of multisited ethnography – certainly these changes have helped make this method more possible or even more plausible, but they cannot explain how and why it took hold as it did in the 1990s, especially considering there were already scholars doing what came to be called "multisited" work many decades earlier. What is needed, therefore, is an exploration of the theoretical and conceptual transformations that made multisited ethnography irrefutable as a tool for tracking processes across sites.

As we show, multisited ethnography emerged as a distinct method in response to a broader interrogation of the creation and maintenance of geopolitical, sociocultural, and socioeconomic borders – an issue brought to the fore by migration studies in general, and work on language and migration in particular. Therefore, we organize this article around an exploration of shifting understandings of such "boundary-making" practices in ethnographic research, considering these as a subject of research and, also, as a force that shapes the aims and conduct of multisited ethnography. As we argue throughout, both *language practices* (the way humans use language in interaction) and *language ideologies* (morally loaded beliefs about the relative value of languages) play a key role in the boundary-making activities that are the subject of multisited research (Blommaert 2010; Coupland 2010; Dick 2011a; Shankar and Cavanaugh 2012). While language ideologies and practices can robustly reveal the contours and significance of global processes such as migration, many multisited ethnographies overlook the relevance of language (cf. Koven 2004). In this chapter, therefore, our discussion focuses on the intersection of multisited ethnography and studies of language and migration, especially as it has developed in anthropology and sociolinguistics – the fields that have spearheaded language-based studies of globalization, though we engage key research in sociology where relevant.

Our central aim is to show how a strategy we call *following language* provides a tool for tracking across sites some of the key issues and experiences that inform the lives of migrants, while also illuminating ways of navigating enduring methodological challenges in ethnography. By "following language" we mean attending to how language ideologies and practices – from the production of "standard national" languages to the projection of links between the present moment of interaction to places beyond the here-and-now – help constitute social spaces in ways that illuminate both the boundaries and the interconnections between people and sites. As we show, these are central themes in sociocultural studies of language more generally, and they are especially robust in studies of language and migration. We begin the article by examining the conceptual roots of contemporary multisited ethnography during the early and late 20th century, considering their links to the study of migration and language. We then address some of the ongoing debates that inform the current practice of multisited ethnography, addressing in particular the place of the nation-state in a so-called globalized world. Then we turn our attention to a systematic discussion of "following language," examining how this method allows us to document migrant identity production and skill acquisition as well as manage site selection and questions of researcher bias in ways that always hold the interests and perspectives of our research participants at the center of our work.

Overview: the conceptual roots of contemporary multisited ethnography

Whether single-sited or multisited, ethnographic research has always been constituted by the concepts of social space that order what counts as a field site (Clifford and Marcus 1986; Gupta and Ferguson 1997); thus, "the field" is always socially constructed (Hannerz 2003; Candea 2007; Falzon 2009). In the works that inaugurated ethnography as the primary methodology of anthropological research in the first part of the 20th century (e.g., Malinowski 1922 – see Stocking 1992 for discussion), the ideal field site was conceptualized as bounded off from the rest of the world, untouched by processes of historical change. This concept was part of a broader understanding of the differences between types of societies, which posited a distinction between "complex societies," marked by social, political, and economic diversity and stratification, and "simple societies," marked by an absence of such diversity and stratification. Early 20th-century anthropologists advocated for ethnography as part of their critique of 19th-century social evolutionism, which claimed that societies follow a natural progression from simple to complex. By contrast, 20th-century scholars argued that each society had an internal logic, not definable by one evolutionary standard – and they posited ethnography as a method that could document these "internal logics" from the perspectives of the people who lived them.

The classical concept of the field in ethnographic research was part of an effort to position anthropology as a science of "pure culture," untainted by boundary-crossing and cultural mixing, which researchers saw as corruptions of a true, underlying culture (Clifford and Marcus 1986; Gupta and Ferguson 1997; Irvine and Gal 2000: 52–53). Thus, while many of anthropology's putatively bounded field sites actually contained much boundary crossing and cultural mixing – often produced from the legacies of European colonialism – these were left undocumented in an effort to capture the "authentic" culture. Some of the earliest work to complexify this approach emerged from the University of Chicago school of urban ethnography (Hannerz 1980: 17). An early form of sociology, scholarship from the Chicago school is noteworthy, among other things, for its innovative work on migration. Of particular importance is Thomas and Znaniecki's *The Polish Peasant in Europe and America* (1918). This work was an early incarnation of multisited ethnography, as it investigated, first, how industrialization in Poland encouraged migration, and, second, the transformations this population underwent as they built lives in Chicago. This research also documented the cross-border practices, such as letter-writing (Stanley 2010), through which migrants maintained cross-border links, thus prefiguring contemporary scholarship on transnationalism.

That said, even within the Chicago school, scholars reproduced the boundary between "simple" and "complex" societies (Hannerz 1980: 59, 61). It was not until scholars began to interrogate underlying assumptions about so-called simple and complex societies that the groundwork for contemporary multisited ethnography was established. Central to this was a critique of the idea that "simple societies" were untouched by the outside world and had not yet been transformed by capitalism, a notion that influenced early studies of migration, which often positioned migrants as emissaries between the worlds of capitalism and pre-capitalism (Walsh 2004; Dick 2010). By the mid- to late 20th century, however, scholarship aimed to document how even the most seemingly remote fieldsites are interconnected with other sites, especially through political economic relations (e.g., Bloch 1983; Ortner 1984; Nash 1993[1979]; Marcus 1995). Interest in the *global political economy* – a phrase used to describe the mutually constitutive relationship between politics and economics across national borders – emerged in dialogue with a critique of European colonialism and its ongoing impact on global inequality between former colonizers and former colonies (e.g., Assad 1973). Examining political economy, thus, required researchers to develop methods for documenting "local-global" connections (e.g., Mintz 1985), which brought scholars to consider the processes through which social boundaries between and within social groups are formed (e.g., Barth 1969), a central focus of current qualitative studies of migration.

In sum, then, multisited ethnography took root in anthropology and sociology in the late 20th century, as scholars sought to document the production of global interconnections and the sociocultural and political economic borders that organize these processes. Similar transformations were happening in sociocultural studies of language as well. During the latter part of the 20th century, work in linguistic anthropology and sociolinguistics increasingly turned attention to the relationship between language, colonialism, and political economy (Irvine and Gal 2000) and between language and globalization (Blommaert 2010, 2013; Coupland 2010). Such work considers how language beliefs and practices mediate and generate dimensions of globalization, including migration (Dick 2011a), and also how global processes, such as the commodification of language as internationally marketable "skill sets" (Duchêne and Heller 2011), shape language, influencing – for example – linguistic change (Buchstaller 2008; Falconi 2013). Uniting this work is an interest in the historical production and interactional accomplishment of social boundaries – of the beliefs and practices that make people and places into different and often hierarchically arranged kinds, a focus that this work shares robustly with the broader anthropology and sociology of migration.

Issues and ongoing debates: transnationalism and methodological nationalism

Research on migration became a focus of sociology and anthropology in the late 1980s and early 1990s as part of the turn toward understanding global processes. At this time, scholars reconceptualized how they thought about migration, through the development of the theory of *transnationalism* (e.g., Rouse 1992; Basch, Glick Schiller, and Szanton Blanc 1994). This theory argues that migration is characterized by movements between one or more countries and by practices, such as remitting money to family in the sending country, which root migrants in more than one place. Multisited research took hold quickly in migration studies because it enabled researchers to document transnational practices. And, indeed, as we noted earlier, key precursors to contemporary multisited ethnography came from studies of migration, not only Thomas and Znaniecki's work, but also that of Manuel Gamio and Oscar Lewis, who conducted transnational, multisited research on Mexico-US migration in the early and mid-20th century (Kearney 1986; Walsh 2004). Despite these precursors, late 20th-century transnational studies produced problematic assumptions about globalization, overstating the newness and uniqueness of the interconnections being documented. In a later wave of transnational studies (Wimmer and Glick Schiller 2002: 322–324), scholars noted historical parallels to contemporary globalization, showing that migrants of the late 19th and early 20th century also lived transnational lives (Foner 1997; Stanley 2010).

But if such transnational connections are not new, then why the dramatic increase in scholarship on such connections in the late 20th century? One key factor was that free market economics forged cross-border links that challenged the centrality of the nation-state as the primary political and economic unit, opening up questions about the relevance of the nation-state in a "global world" (Wimmer and Glick Schiller 2002). The border-crossing lives of migrants suggest the possibility of social formations that are – if not entirely disconnected from nation-states – not fully encompassed or explained by membership in them either (Basch et al. 1994). Yet, contemporary scholarship on globalization often replicates the idea that the nation-state is the natural container of analysis – what is called *methodological nationalism* (Wimmer and Glick Schiller 2002: 302). Multisited research itself has reproduced methodological nationalism, tending to treat "site" as synonymous with nation-state, so that multisited research means engaging in ethnographic encounters in more than one country (e.g., Farr 2006; Smith 2006). This is, in part, because as free market capitalism has opened up economic borders, many nation-states have powerfully re-asserted their rights to defend national borders, making the nation-state a potent physical reality and frame of reference for many migrants (De Genova 2005; Marfleet 2006; Dick 2011b; Werbner 2013). But treating multisited research as synonymous with research in multiple countries can artificially situate the nation-state as the principal point of orientation because it circumscribes the kinds of social and geopolitical borders relevant to the experience of migration. Rather, the researcher should attend to the sites and contexts of practice that are salient for our research participants, remaining alive to how, when, and why the nation-state is significant, and when it is not.

The study the significance of the nation-state has drawn the attention of scholars of language and migration (e.g., Dick 2013; Eisenlohr 2006; Koven 2007; Mendoza-Denton 2008; Santa Ana 2002). For example, García-Sánchez's (2014) work on Moroccan migrant children in Spain examines how youth use multilingualism to navigate national politics of inclusion and exclusion in ways that allow them to claim national belonging in Spain while still remaining rooted in "local" Moroccan communities. This work, and also that of Mendoza-Denton and Eisenlohr discussed later, highlights the central importance of language beliefs and practices not only in constituting the boundaries that shape global processes, but also in enabling people to traverse and transform them. And yet, many studies of globalization do not consider language as a key force in globalization (Koven 2004; Blommaert 2010). Therefore, in our final section, we examine the types of processes and practices that attention to language can reveal, relating them to key methodological concerns in multisited research through the development of our concept of *following language*.

Implications: following language

As the preceding discussion suggests, multisited ethnography emerged as part of researchers' wrestling with how to adapt single-site ethnography, which aims to cultivate deep linguistic and cultural familiarity through long-term relationships with people in one location, to the study of processes that happen across multiple locations (Marcus 1995; Burawoy et al. 2000). Or, as Burawoy (2000: 1) has put it, "how can ethnography be global"? A key methodological issue underlying the movement toward multisited ethnography has been the problem of how a researcher can relate the information gathered about particular, situated events to processes unfolding across longer time periods and multiple spaces – that is, how to "scale up" detailed observations of the "micro" to the "macro" realm of global processes? This has been a central question across qualitative studies of globalization – and it is felt especially acutely in studies of language, which are often critiqued for lacking the ability to scale up. As we show in this section, however, the study of language beliefs and practices is an especially useful tool for tracking how people create links between their present lives and broader, more enduring processes. It can also help illuminate how differences between "local" and "global" or "micro" and "macro" are created, evaluated, and reproduced in the first place (Carr and Lempert 2016).

To capture how language beliefs and practices shape and are shaped by global processes, we develop the concept of *following language*. Recall that by "following language" we mean attending to how language ideologies and practices help constitute social spaces in ways that illuminate both the boundaries and the interconnections between people and sites. We develop this concept in dialogue with Marcus's influential (1995) article on multisited ethnography, in which he introduces strategies of "following" as a means for tracking processes across sites. For scholars of migration, such strategies are crucial. In these communities, which people and social processes move between sites, and which do not, are key factors in the organization of social life (De Fina and King 2011; Farr 2006; Smith 2006; Koven 2007; Dick 2010, 2013; Arnold 2015, 2016). Following language can illuminate research on migration in a number of ways. First, it can reveal how language beliefs and practices are mobilized to create social boundaries, thus helping multisited researchers manage site selection. Moreover, following language sheds light on the identities and skills of border-crossing people, contributing to a more nuanced understanding of the connection between language and geographic emplacement. In addition, following language allows researchers to grapple with long-standing methodological challenges in ethnographic research, including triangulation, bias, and researcher positionality. Finally, we suggest that following language provides a productive framework for approaching transnational communication, an understudied phenomenon that is nevertheless crucial to experiences of migration.

Defining sites and determining context

Following language allows researchers to trace the space-constituting and boundary-constructing practices through which multiply sited fields are produced. As such, this method provides an empirically grounded way to inductively select sites that are not only satisfying and sufficient to the researcher, but also to research participants (Hastrup and Olwig 1997). For example, in Norma Mendoza-Denton's ethnography *Homegirls*, she argues that Latina youth in a California high school use language and other semiotic practices to position their experiences in relationship to "larger processes of race, language, capital structures, and . . . power relations" between the Global North and the Global South (2008: 86). She demonstrates that Latina youth divide their social world into distinct sites by using language to connect the here-and-now to social worlds beyond the present. In particular, she shows that affiliation with two youth gangs, signaled by the use of marked linguistic practices, enables youth to project broader distinctions between the US and Mexico onto locally salient forms of social difference between Mexican migrants and Mexican Americans. As Mendoza-Denton follows language through multiple sites, from classroom to kitchen, she produces a multisited ethnography rooted in a single geographical location, demonstrating that the lives even of people who have never left the neighborhood can nevertheless be "transnational" (cf. Eisenlohr 2006; Dick 2010).

As this example shows, the discursive processes through which mobile populations, and people linked to them, are positioned relative to other members of sending and receiving societies can create situations in which people sharing the same physical space live in very different social worlds. This is especially evident in the lives of people, such as Latina/os in the US and Muslims in Western Europe, who occupy highly marked – often racialized and criminalized – social positionings. For people thus positioned, sites that are relatively neutral for people who are not racialized and criminalized, such as classrooms and street corners, are fraught because of the social borders that work to exclude them. Moreover, the language practices that help create those borders produce, as we see in Mendoza-Denton's work, links between the immediate "local" here-and-now and broadly circulating "global" processes of political economic inequality. This is an important point for scholars of applied linguistics, for it can have profound consequences on how people who speak in "nonstandard" ways are treated. Consider, for example, how US students tracked into "limited English proficiency" curriculum, who are often native speakers of non-standard forms of English, are treated as inherently delinquent (e.g., Mendoza-Denton 1999 – see also Dick 2011a: 229–232; Rosa and Flores 2015). Some argue this sort of diversification of social space creates contexts of "superdiversity" that constitute the newness of contemporary globalization (Blommaert 2013), while others contend that these processes are part of enduring histories of social differentiation that must be recognized (Reyes 2014).

Regardless, discussions of the diversification of social space spotlight the complexity of circumscribing the relevant contexts of our research. What is "context" and how is it created? Does it refer to the present moment or the wider frame of sociopolitical processes? How can the wider frame be related to the present interaction? These enduring problems have been the subject of extensive theorization in sociocultural studies of language (Duranti and Goodwin 1992; Gumperz 1992; Blommaert 2010, 2013). As shown in Mendoza-Denton's and García-Sánchez's ethnographies, language practices help people construct, negotiate, comment on, and traverse various contexts. One especially important set of theoretical tools to help us follow language in the production of context is work on the ways people create connections between two or more instances of discourse (Silverstein and Urban 1996; Silverstein 2005; Wortham and Reyes 2015). Analyses of such *interdiscursive* relationships are crucial to understanding how the present moment can become imbricated with multiple and sometimes conflicting ways of understanding what the relevant context is and who does and does not belong (Bonilla and Rosa 2015). For example, Dick's (2011b) analysis of anti-migrant ordinances in US municipalities shows that these ordinances gain political legitimacy and have racializing effects on Mexican migrants because of their interdiscursive links with US federal immigration law, which has marginalized Mexican migrants since the late 19th century. This work reveals that "context" is never either "micro" or "macro," never either "local" or "global," but always formed through interdiscursive webs (Wirtz 2014) that link the present to various "beyonds."

Identity and skill

As shown earlier, following language can elucidate how boundaries and interconnections between sites are constructed through communicative practices and linguistic ideologies. In traversing such boundaries, people must render and maintain identities that are intelligible in these varied sites. Mobile populations often encounter highly charged political environments organized around contestation over their identities: Do they belong here? Can they be one of "us"? Such contestation is both manifested and managed through language, as shown in the preceding examples. But similar processes can be found in quite different ethnographic settings, such as that documented in Eisenlohr's (2006) ethnography of the Indian diaspora in Mauritius, a small island nation near Madagascar. He explains how people of Indian descent use

Hindi and other signs that link their lives in Mauritius to the "beyond here" of India, creating connections with a putative Indian homeland in order to, paradoxically, lay claim to national belonging in Mauritius. Thus, such communicative practices mobilize ideologies of ancestral Hindi to construct multisited identities in Mauritius. Following both communicative practices and language ideologies, therefore, sheds light on how identities are linguistically constructed by mobile populations.

However, in tracing the construction of identities across borders, researchers must attend carefully to the multifunctionality of language. People do more than use language to create identities and manage social borders; they also use language to persuade, manipulate, obfuscate, command, and so on. Attending exclusively to the identity-making functions of language not only occludes these other functions of language, but can unintentionally skew research toward our own language ideologies, as seen in the preceding discussion of methodological nationalism. Nation-state formation often depends on language ideologies that establish links between particular languages and the "true essence" – the core identity – of a nation (Irvine and Gal 2000). While the exclusionary effects of such linkages are highly significant to many migrants, to study only this aspect of language and migration is to further the idea that the nation-state is the natural container of political economic life. Yet, free market capitalism disrupts the production of "primordial" national languages by construing language practices as marketable skill sets that theoretically could be acquired by anyone (Duchêne and Heller 2011: 4, 10). Attending to the functions of language beyond its ability to create and perform social identities is, therefore, an important part of resisting methodological nationalism, enabling us to remain open to the range of ways in which language interacts with and helps constitute globalization.

More recent research on language and migration has demonstrated that the use of language to negotiate identities also results in the development of skill sets that can both traverse and reinforce social boundaries. This is evident in scholarship on the role of bilingual migrant youth as language brokers, informally interpreting for monolingual family members in schools, hospitals, workplaces, and so on (Valenzuela 1999; Morales and Hanson 2005; Orellana 2010). For example, Reynolds and Orellana (2009) demonstrate that engaging in interpretation practices exposes children to racialized and generational surveillance. A similar finding is also emphasized in language-based research on the hearings of asylum seekers in Europe (Inghilleri 2005; Maryns 2005). For instance, Jacquemet (2009) studies how the statements made by asylum seekers are reworked in written reports that determine the validity of their asylum claims, demonstrating that these texts are shaped by assumptions about the primordial connection between language and nation that ultimately violate the human rights of asylum seekers. Thus, following the language skills employed by border-crossing populations reveals the complexity inherent in how these communicative repertoires are made meaningful in different sites. Following language can ultimately suggest productive areas of engagement for applied linguistic research to contribute to sociolinguistic justice (Bucholtz et al. 2014) for communities positioned at the margins of our multiply-sited world.

Triangulation, bias, and participation

In addition to facilitating the tracking of processes and practices, following language can also help researchers grapple with long-standing methodological challenges in ethnographic research. Most saliently, following language can contribute to the use of triangulation, a technique in which information from difference sources (for example, interviews and observation) is compared. While triangulation is sometimes represented as a means of getting to "the truth" (e.g., Fetterman 2010), this perspective does not fit with current approaches to ethnographic knowledge production which recognize that there is no unbiased, single truth (Burawoy et al. 2000). Rather, there are multiple ways of perceiving and explaining reality, and the goal of ethnography is to document, convey, and interpret those distinct realities. Of course, multisited research itself opens up a broader range of possible triangulation, facilitating comparison of sources of information across sites in ways that reveal how social spaces matter in our fieldwork contexts. Close attention to language ideologies and practices can refine the process of triangulation in multisited fieldwork, for example by allowing researchers to compare how similar language practices shift across settings. When following language is used in the process of site selection, researchers build on this perspectival way of knowing, relying on the understandings of sitedness embedded in everyday language practices to determine the range of sources from which information will be drawn and compared.

Since perspective (or "bias") in research is inescapable, the best way to manage the positionality of all information is to develop methods for bringing multiple perspectives into research design and execution. For many ethnographers, this practice involves inviting our research "subjects" to be research *participants*, including them directly in research design and implementation and in data analysis (Whyte 1991; Cameron, Frazer, Harvey, Rampton, and Richardson 1993; Reason and Bradbury 2001; Koven 2007; Chevalier and Buckles 2013). For example, in her (2016) research on cross-border communication within transnational Salvadoran families, Arnold hired and trained family research assistants at each of her fieldsites; these participant-researchers took the lead in making video and audio recordings of family interactions consistently over the course of several months, while Arnold traveled between the different sites. This participatory method allowed for the collection of continuous data that traced the cross-border negotiation of everyday concerns in the complete circuit of transnational life. For multisited research, therefore, such inclusive approaches have the added benefit of helping to manage the challenges of being in multiple places at once. This uninterrupted attention is particularly crucial for capturing the nuances of fleeting language practices. Participatory methods therefore constitute an important tool for more effectively following language in multisited studies of migration.

Participatory research models highlight the positionality of the researcher and what some call the "observer's paradox" (Labov 1972) – that our efforts to document the processes we aim to investigate necessarily change the context in which those practices are being used. Scholars of language have highlighted the importance of attending to local language practices and beliefs to understand how the social positioning of the researcher shapes the research process. For example, developing effective interviewing techniques is only possible if the researcher understands local norms about when questions can be asked and who can ask them (Briggs 1986; Mishler 1986 – see Koven 2014 for review). Thus, the positioning of the researcher matters greatly in ethnographic research, but how and why it matters cannot be determined a priori. It must be understood through close attention to linguistic practices and ideologies – the strategy of following language. This is particularly true of multisited ethnography, where facets of the researcher's social position are often taken up differently across sites. In fieldwork with marginalized migrant populations, the researcher's more privileged social position with respect to citizenship status may mean that they are the only member of the social network able to move freely between sites. Researcher mobility may be taken up by participants as a resource: researchers may be asked to carry items such as letters or photos to another site or our equipment may be used to take photos or make recordings to be sent to distant community members. Attending to this use of researcher presence, as well as the ways in which such circulating linguistic and other semiotic resources are interpreted, sheds light on the role of language within and across fieldsites. Reflexive attention to how language practices and beliefs are implicated in the ways our presence is made meaningful is thus another important tool for following language in multisited research.

Future directions

Following language has important implications for future research on language and migration. In particular, it draws attention to cross-border communication. Although digital infrastructures and literacies are not evenly distributed around the globe (Compaine 2001; Norris 2001), digital communication technologies nevertheless play a key role in facilitating communication and maintaining connections across borders (Vertovec 2004; Madianou 2012; Baldassar and Merla 2013). Digitally mediated communication allows migrant parents to make arrangements for childcare, check in on educational progress, and socialize their children, while helping adult children manage the medical care of their elderly parents, facilitating the maintenance of intimacy between separated wives and husbands, and allowing arrangements to be made to celebrate milestones of family life. Indeed, communication technologies have long played a crucial role in constituting and sustaining multisited connections (Wimmer and Glick Schiller 2002: 322). Before digital communication, other technologies – from the letter to the telegraph to the radio – carried language across space (Thomas and Znaniecki 1918; Mahler 2001; Baldassar, Baldock and Wilding 2007), helping to create and sustain cross-border connections.

Current digital technologies thus build on but also transform historical practices by which language links people across space (Hutchby 2001), and more scholarly attention is needed to understand this process. While media studies scholarship has demonstrated that technologies of communication play a crucial role in the development of close ties between different places, both for large-scale diasporic networks (Fortunati, Pertierra, and Vincent 2012) and for smaller groupings such as families (Uy-Tioco 2007; Cabanes and Acedera 2012; Madianou and Miller 2012; Chib, Malik, Aricat, and Zubeidah Kadir 2014), this work does not attend to the most pervasive form of semiosis in digitally mediated interaction: language (though see Inoue 2012; Cole 2014; Arnold 2016). Transnational communication thus presents a critical area for further multisited research that follows language. Such studies have the potential to reveal a great deal about both the boundaries and the interconnections between different sites of migrants' lives, as shown in Cole's (2014) work with Malagasy migrants in France. Tracing the language practices of these women with their transnational kin and with fellow female migrants, her analysis demonstrates that these two forms of communication are part of a single process that manages not only continued connection to the homeland, but also experiences of integration and exclusion in the host society.

The study of digitally mediated communication introduces new complexities into anthropological conversations about what a fieldsite can be (Constable 2003; Horst and Miller 2012; Bonilla and Rosa 2015). The constitution of digital spaces can be ethnographically investigated by examining how participants orient to technologies of communication, highlighting the ideologies that underlie processes of site construction. Gershon's work (2010, 2012) on media ideologies reveals that assumptions about the differences or similarities between online and offline sites have important social boundary-making functions. Similarly, in exploring the use of Twitter in the Black Lives Matter movement, Bonilla and Rosa (2015) argue that Twitter provides a space for transformative racial politics and can be investigated as a virtual fieldsite. Moreover, recent anthropological approaches to digital ethnography have called for research that explores the interconnections between digital and analog fieldsites (Akkaya 2014; Androutsopoulos and Juffermans 2014), thus seeking to understand not only the production of borders between sites but also the processes by which sites can become linked to one another. Thus, future research that follows language in digitally mediated transnational communication can contribute not only to scholarship on language and migration, but also to the very understanding of multisited ethnography, advancing the historically close relationship between these domains of work.

Summary

In this chapter, we have examined multisited ethnography, especially as it pertains to the study of language and migration. Exploring the conceptual and theoretical transformations from which multisited ethnography emerged, we have highlighted the role of shifts in scholarly understandings of social boundaries. We have suggested that studies of language and migration have a great deal to offer to ongoing debates about multisited ethnography, including a focus on transnationalism and the related challenge of methodological nationalism. We propose that close attention to language ideologies and practices, what we call following language, enriches multisited ethnographies of migration. This strategy can reveal the discursive practices through which social boundaries are constructed, assisting multisited researchers in the complex process of site definition and selection. Moreover, following language draws attention to multisited identities and the linguistic skills of border-crossing populations, providing insights into the geographic emplacement of language. This practice also allows scholars to grapple with ongoing methodological concerns in multisited ethnography, including issues of triangulation, bias, and researcher positionality. Finally, we suggest that following language constitutes a productive approach to the study of digitally mediated transnational communication, a key area for future research on language and migration. We hope to have provided insights for new multisited ethnographies of migration and language that build on past interrogations of the field and move towards a richer understanding of how the places of ethnographic fieldwork come to matter. As free market economics pushes for greater integration of global markets while nation-states work simultaneously to fortify their borders and exclude migrants, multisited ethnographies of language have an important role to play in understanding our era of increasing inequality, for they illuminate how mobile populations emplace themselves within and potentially push against that inequity.

Related topics

Nation-state, transnationalism, and language
Superdiversity and language
Space, place, and language
Complexity, mobility, migration

Further reading

Blommaert, J. (2010) *The Sociolinguistics of Globalization*. Cambridge: Cambridge University Press.
This book theorizes how linguistic and global processes influence and transform one another. It offers a way for scholars of language to adapt studies of immediate contexts to large-scale processes, reconsidering classical topics in the sociocultural study of language, especially locality, repertoires, and competence.

Burawoy, M., Blum, J., George, S., Gille, Z., Gowan, T., Haney, L., Klawiter, M., Lopéz, S., Riain, S. and Thayer, M. (2000). *Global Ethnography: Forces, Connections, and Imaginations in a Postmodern World*. Berkeley: University of California Press.

This collection of essays discusses how the methods of single-site ethnography can be adapted to research in multiple sites, providing at the same time a useful overview of the central debates around multisited ethnography in sociology.

Marcus, G. E. (1995). Ethnography in/of the world system: The emergence of multi-sited ethnography. *Annual Review of Anthropology*, *24*: 95–117.

The first work to fully theorize multisited ethnography from the perspective of anthropology, this piece is useful both for its historical perspective on the topic and also the methodological techniques it outlines, which includes several strategies for what he terms "following."

Wimmer, A. and Glick Schiller, N. (2002). Methodological nationalism and beyond: Nation-state building, migration and the social sciences. *Global Networks*, *2*(3): 301–334.

This article provides an overview of the emergence and transformation of social science scholarship on transnationalism. It provides thoughtful reflections on the place of the nation-state in a global world, discussing in detail how transnational research has reproduced methodological nationalism and offering reflections on how to avoid this methodological trap.

Wortham, S. and Reyes, A. (2015). *Discourse Analysis beyond the Speech Event*. New York: Routledge.

This book presents an approach to conducting discourse analysis of linked events, arguing that sociocultural studies of language should look beyond fixed speech events and consider the development of discourses over time and space. The authors detail many useful ways to document and analyze the production of language ideologies and practices in multiple sites.

Note

1 The authors would like to thank, above all, their research participants and friends from their fieldsites; there would be no article without you. Thanks also to Hilary's research assistants Danielle Di Verde, Camilo Lopez Delgado, and Veronica Willig for their fine editorial work. We are grateful to Suresh Canagarajah for the invitation to develop this piece, and we thank him and the external reviewer for their helpful feedback. All remaining errors are the responsibility of the authors.

References

Akkaya, A. (2014). Language, discourse. and new media: A linguistic anthropological perspective: Language and new media. *Language and Linguistics Compass* 8(7): 285–300.

Androutsopoulos, J. and Juffermans, K. (2014). Digital language practices in superdiversity: Introduction. *Discourse, Context & Media* 4–5: 1–6.

Arnold, L. (2015). The reconceptualization of agency through ambiguity and contradiction: Salvadoran women narrating unauthorized migration. *Women's Studies International Forum* 52: 10–19.

Arnold, L. (2016). *Communicative Care across Borders: Language, Materiality, and Affect in Transnational Family Life*. PhD University of California, Santa Barbara.

Assad, T. (1973). *Anthropology and the Colonial Encounter*. London: Ithaca Press.

Baldassar, L., Baldock, C. and Wilding, R. (2007). *Families Caring across Borders: Migration, Ageing and Transnational Caregiving*. Basingstoke: Palgrave Macmillan.

Baldassar, L. and Merla, L., eds. (2013). *Transnational Families, Migration and the Circulation of Care: Understanding Mobility and Absence in Family Life*. New York: Routledge.

Barth, F. (1969). *Ethnic Groups and Boundaries: The Social Organization of Culture Difference*. Boston: Little Brown.

Basch, L., Glick Schiller, N. and Szanton Blanc, C. (1994). *Nations Unbound: Transnational Projects, Postcolonial Predicaments, and Deterritorialized Nation States*. New York: Gordon and Breach.

Bloch, M. (1983). *Marxism and Anthropology: The History of a Relationship*. Oxford: Clarendon Press.
Blommaert, J. (2010). *The Sociolinguistics of Globalization*. Cambridge: Cambridge University Press.
Blommaert, J. (2013). *Ethnography, Superdiversity and Linguistic Landscapes: Chronicles of Complexity*. Bristol: Multilingual Matters.
Bonilla, Y. and Rosa, J. (2015). #Ferguson: Digital protest, hashtag ethnography, and the racial politics of social media in the United States. *American Ethnologist* 42: 4–17.
Briggs, C. L. (1986). *Learning How to Ask*. New York: Cambridge University Press.
Bucholtz, M., Lopez, A., Mojarro, A., Skapoulli, E., VanderStouwe, C. and Warner-García, S. (2014). Sociolinguistic justice in the schools: Student researchers as linguistic experts: Sociolinguistic justice in the schools. *Language and Linguistics Compass* 8(4): 144–157.
Buchstaller, I. (2008). The localization of global linguistic variants. *English World-Wide* 29(1): 15–44.
Burawoy, M. (2000). Introduction: Reaching for the global. In *Global Ethnography: Forces, Connections, and Imaginations in a Postmodern World*. Berkeley: University of California Press, pp. 1–40.
Burawoy, M., Blum, J., George, S., Gille, Z., Gowan, T., Haney, L., Klawiter, M., López, S., Riain, S. and Thayer, M. (2000). *Global Ethnography: Forces, Connections, and Imaginations in a Postmodern World*. Berkeley: University of California Press.
Cabanes, J. and Acedera, K. (2012). Of mobile phones and mother-fathers: Calls, text messages, and conjugal power relations in mother-away Filipino families. *New Media & Society* 14(6): 916–930.
Cameron, D., Frazer, E., Harvey, P., Rampton, B. and Richardson, K. (1993). Ethics, advocacy, and empowerment: Issues of method in researching language. *Language and Communication* 13: 81–94.
Candea, M. (2007). Arbitrary locations: In defense of the bounded field-site. *Journal of the Royal Anthropological Institute* 13(1): 167–184.
Carr, E.S. and Lempert, M., eds. (2016). *Scale: Discourse and Dimensions of Social Life*. Berkeley: University of California Press.
Chevalier, J. M. and Buckles, D. (2013). *Participatory Action Research: Theory and Methods for Engaged Inquiry*. New York: Routledge.
Chib, A., Malik, S., Aricat, R. G. and Zubeidah Kadir, S. (2014). Migrant mothering and mobile phones: Negotiations of transnational identity. *Mobile Media & Communication* 2(1): 73–93.
Clifford, J. and Marcus, G.E. (1986). *Writing Culture: The Poetics and Politics of Ethnography*. Berkeley: University of California Press.
Cole, J. (2014). The téléphone malgache: Transnational gossip and social transformation among Malagasy marriage migrants in France: Gossip and social transformation. *American Ethnologist* 41(2): 276–289.
Compaine, B., ed. (2001). *The Digital Divide: Facing a Crisis or Creating a Myth?* Cambridge, MA: MIT Press.
Constable, N. (2003). *Romance on a Global Stage: Pen Pals, Virtual Ethnography, and "Mail-Order" Marriages*. Berkeley: University of California Press.
Coupland, N., ed. (2010). *The Handbook of Language and Globalization*. Malden, MA: Wiley-Blackwell.
De Fina, A. and King, K. (2011). Language problem or language conflict? Narratives of immigrant women's experiences in the US. *Discourse Studies* 13(2): 163–188.
De Genova, N. (2002). Migrant "illegality" and deportability in everyday life. *Annual Review of Anthropology* 31: 419–447.
De Genova, N. (2005). *Working the Boundaries: Race, Space, and "Illegality" in Mexican Chicago*. Durham, NC: Duke University Press.
Dick, H.P. (2010). Imagined lives and modernist chronotopes in Mexican non-migrant discourse. *American Ethnologist* 37(2): 275–290.
Dick, H.P. (2011a). Language and migration to the United States. *Annual Review of Anthropology* 40: 227–240.
Dick, H.P. (2011b). Making immigrants illegal in small town USA. *Journal of Linguistic Anthropology* 21(1): e35–e55.
Dick, H.P. (2013). Diaspora and discourse: The contrapuntal lives of Mexican nonmigrants. In A. Quayson and G. Daswani, (eds.), *A Companion to Diaspora and Transnationalism Studies* (pp. 412–427). Malden, MA: Wiley Blackwell.

Duchêne, A. and Heller, M., eds. (2011). *Language in Late Capitalism: Pride and Profit*. New York: Routledge.

Duranti, A. and Goodwin, C., eds. (1992). *Rethinking Context: Language as an Interactive Phenomenon*. New York: Cambridge University Press.

Eisenlohr, P. (2006). *Little India: Diaspora, Time, and Ethnolinguistic Belonging in Hindu Mauritius*. Berkeley: University of California Press.

Falconi, E. (2013). Storytelling, language shift, and revitalization in a transborder community: "Tell It in Zapotec"! *American Anthropologist* 115(4): 622–636.

Falzon, M., ed. (2009). *Multi-Sited Ethnography: Theory, Praxis and Locality in Contemporary Research*. Burlington, VT: Ashgate.

Farr, M. (2006). *Rancheros in Chicagoacán: Language and Identity in a Transnational Community*. Austin: University of Texas Press.

Fetterman, D. M. (2010). *Ethnography: Step-by-step*. Los Angeles: Sage.

Foner, N. (1997). What is new about transnationalism?: New York immigrants today and at the turn of the century. *Diaspora* 6: 355–374.

Fortunati, L., Pertierra, R. and Vincent, J. (2012). *Migration, Diaspora, and Information Technology in Global Societies*. New York: Routledge.

García-Sánchez, I. (2014). *Language and Muslim Immigrant Childhoods: The Politics of Belonging*. Malden, MA: Wiley Blackwell.

Gershon, I. (2010). Media ideologies: An introduction. *Journal of Linguistic Anthropology* 20(2): 283–293.

Gershon, I. (2012). Fifty ways to leave your lover: Media ideologies and idioms of practice. In *The Breakup 2.0: Disconnecting over New Media*. Ithaca, NY: Cornell University Press, pp. 16–49.

Gumperz, J. J. (1992). Contextualization revisited. In P. Auer and A. Di Luzio (eds.), *The Contextualization of Language* (pp. 39–53). Amsterdam: John Benjamins.

Gupta, A. (1998). *Postcolonial Developments: Agriculture in the Making of Modern India*. Durham, NC: Duke University Press.

Gupta, A. and Ferguson, J. (1997). Discipline and practice: The "field" as site, method and location in anthropology. In *Anthropological Locations*. Berkeley: University of California Press, pp. 1–46.

Hannerz, U. (1980). *Exploring the City: Inquiries toward and Urban Anthropology*. New York: Columbia University Press.

Hannerz, U. (2003). Being there . . . and there . . . and there!: Reflections on multi-site ethnography. *Ethnography* 4(2): 201–216.

Hastrup, K. and Olwig, K. F. (1997). Introduction. In *Sitting Culture: The Shifting Anthropological Object*. New York: Routledge, pp. 1–16.

Horst, H. A. and Miller, D. (2012). *Digital Anthropology*. London: Berg.

Hutchby, I. (2001). Technologies, texts and affordances. *Sociology* 35: 441–456.

Inghilleri, M. (2005). Mediating zones of uncertainty: Interpreter agency, the interpreting habitus, and political asylum adjudication. *Translator* 11(1): 69–85.

Inoue, C. S. (2012). *Virtual "Ie" Household: Transnational Family Interactions in Japan and the United States*. PhD University of Texas at Austin.

Irvine, J. T. and Gal, S. (2000). Language ideology and linguistic differentiation. In P. Kroskrity, (ed.), *Regimes of Language: Ideologies, Polities, and Identities* (pp. 35–84). Santa Fe, NM: School of American Research Press.

Jacquemet, M. (2009). Transcribing refugees: The entextualization of asylum seekers' hearings in a transidiomatic environment. *Text & Talk* 29(5): 525–546.

Kearney, M. (1986). From the invisible hand to visible feet: Anthropological studies of migration and development. *Annual Review of Anthropology* 15: 331–361.

Kearney, M. (1995). The local and the global: The anthropology of globalization and transnationalism. *Annual Review of Anthropology* 24: 95–117.

Koven, M. (2004). Transnational perspectives on sociolinguistic capital among Luso-Descendants in France and Portugal. *American Ethnologist* 31(2): 270–290.
Koven, M. (2007). *Selves in Two Languages: Bilinguals' Verbal Enactments of Identity in French and Portuguese*. Philadelphia, PA: John Benjamins.
Koven, M. (2014). Interviewing: Practice, ideology, genre, and intertextuality. *Annual Review of Anthropology* 43: 499–520.
Labov, W. (1972). *Sociolinguistic Patterns*. Philadelphia: University of Pennsylvania Press.
Madianou, M. (2012). Migration and the accentuated ambivalence of motherhood: The role of ICTs in Filipino transnational families. *Global Networks* 12(3): 277–295.
Madianou, M. and Miller, D. (2012). *Migration and New Media: Transnational Families and Polymedia*. New York: Routledge.
Mahler, S.J. (2001). Transnational relationships: The struggle to communicate across borders. *Identities* 7: 583–619.
Malinowski, B. (1922). *Argonauts of the Western Pacific*. New York: Routledge.
Marcus, G.E. (1995). Ethnography in/of the world system: The emergence of multi-sited ethnography. *Annual Review of Anthropology* 24: 95–117.
Marfleet, P. (2006). *Refugees in a Global Era*. London: Palgrave.
Maryns, K. (2005). *The Asylum Speaker: Language in the Belgian Asylum Procedure*. Manchester: St. Jerome.
Mendoza-Denton, N. (1999). Fighting words: Latina girls, gangs, and language attitudes. In *Speaking Chicana: Voice, Power, and Identity*. Tucson, AZ: University of Arizona Press, pp. 39–56.
Mendoza-Denton, N. (2008). *Homegirls: Language and Cultural Practice among Latina Youth Gangs*. Malden, MA: Blackwell.
Mintz, S. (1985). *Sweetness and Power: The Place of Sugar in Modern History*. New York: Penguin Books.
Mishler, E.G. (1986). *Research Interviewing: Context and Narrative*. Cambridge, MA: Harvard University Press.
Morales, A. and Hanson, W.E. (2005). Language brokering: An integrative review of the literature. *Hispanic Journal of Behavioral Sciences* 27: 471–503.
Nash, J. (1993[1979]). *We Eat the Mines and the Mines Eat Us: Dependency and Exploitation in Bolivian Tin Mines*. New York: Columbia University Press.
Norris, P. (2001). *Digital Divide: Civic Engagement, Information Poverty, and the Internet Worldwide*. New York: Cambridge University Press.
Orellana, M.F. (2009). *Translating Childhoods: Immigrant Youth, Language and Culture*. New Brunswick, NJ: Rutgers University Press.
Orellana, M.F. (2010). From here to there: On the process of an ethnography of language brokering. *Mediazioni* 10. Retrieved from http://mediazioni.sitlec.unibo.it.
Ortner, S. (1984). Theory in anthropology since the sixties. *Comparative Studies in Society and History* 26: 126–166.
Reason, P. and Bradbury, H., eds. (2001). *The SAGE Handbook of Action Research: Participative Inquiry and Practice*. London: Sage.
Reyes, A. (2014). Linguistic anthropology in 2013: Super-new-big. *American Anthropologist* 116(2): 366–378.
Rosa, J. and Flores, N. (2015). Hearing language gaps and reproducing social inequality. *Journal of Linguistic Anthropology* 25(1): 77–79.
Rouse, R. (1992). Making sense of settlement: Class transformation, cultural struggle, and transnationalism among Mexican migrants in the United States. *Annuals New York Academy of Sciences* 645: 25–52.
Santa Ana, O. (2002). *Brown Tide Rising: Metaphors of Latinos in Contemporary American Discourse*. Austin: University of Texas Press.
Shankar, S. and Cavanaugh, J. (2012). Language and materiality in global capitalism. *Annual Review of Anthropology* 41(1): 355–369.

Silverstein, M. (2005). Axes of evals: Token versus type interdiscursivity. *Journal of Linguistic Anthropology* 15: 6–22.

Silverstein, M. and Urban, G., eds. (1996). *Natural Histories of Discourse*. Chicago: University of Chicago Press.

Smith, R. C. (2006). *Mexican New York: Transnational Lives of New Immigrants*. Berkeley: University of California Press.

Stanley, L. (2010). To the letter: Thomas and Znaniecki's the polish peasant and writing a life, sociologically. *Life Writing* 7(2): 139–151.

Stocking, G. (1992). The ethnographers magic: Fieldwork in British anthropology from Tyler to Malinowski. In *The Ethnographer's Magic and Other Essays in the History of Anthropology*. Madison, WI: University of Wisconsin Press, pp. 12–59.

Thomas, W. I. and Znaniecki, F. (1958 [1918]). *The Polish Peasant in Europe and America*. New York: Dover.

Uy-Tioco, C. (2007). Overseas Filipino workers and text messaging: Reinventing transnational mothering. *Continuum* 21(2): 253–265.

Valenzuela, A. (1999). Gender roles and settlement activities among children and their immigrant families. *American Behavioral Scientist* 42: 720–742.

Vertovec, S. (2004). Cheap calls: The social glue of migrant transnationalism. *Global Networks* 4(2): 219–224.

Walsh, C. (2004). Eugenic acculturation: Manuel gamio, migration studies, and the anthropology of development in Mexico, 1910–1940. *Latin American Perspectives* 31(5): 118–145.

Werbner, P. (2013). Migration and transnational studies: Between simultaneity and rupture. In *A Companion to Diaspora and Transnationalism*. Oxford: Blackwell Press, pp. 106–124.

Whyte, W. F., ed. (1991). *Participatory Action Research*. Newbury Park, CA: Sage.

Wimmer, A. and Glick Schiller, N. (2002). Methodological nationalism and beyond: Nation-state building, migration and the social sciences. *Global Networks* 2(3): 301–334.

Wirtz, K. (2014). *Performing Afro-Cuba: Image, Voice, Spectacle in the Making of Race and History*. Chicago: University of Chicago Press.

Wortham, S. and Reyes, A. (2015). *Discourse Analysis beyond the Speech Event*. New York: Routledge.

23
Traveling texts, translocal/transnational literacies, and transcontextual analysis

Catherine Kell

Introduction

The publication *A Man of Good Hope* (Steinberg 2014) is an intricately detailed, 300-page account of the life of a twenty-seven-year-old Somalian refugee, Asad Abdullahi, in which language, literacy, and texts appear as central strands in the twisted trajectory of his moves across countries and finally continents. Steinberg traces his forced and traumatic flight as a five-year-old from tribal violence in Somalia to Kenya to Ethiopia and through Eritrea and Yemen while in informal and precarious employment. A later move south takes him through Zambia, Zimbabwe, and South Africa, where he ends up in Cape Town. He finally moves on to the US after surviving horrific xenophobic attacks in South Africa. Until his arrival in South Africa in his early twenties when he finally gains official status as a refugee, Asad has no legal documents entitling him to be anywhere.[1]

The nature of Steinberg's account resonates strongly with the earlier sociological and anthropological work of Abdelmalek Sayad (1991, 1999), who, with the support of Bourdieu (outlined in Bourdieu and Wacquant 2000) and drawing on Mauss (1990), argued that migration needed to be studied as a "total social fact." By this Sayad meant that it needed to be understood ethnographically but also sociologically, anthropologically and historically – a total social fact informs and organises quite distinct practices and institutions. Silverstein (1985: 220) adopted Mauss's concept when he argued that language needed to be studied as a "total linguistic fact." This he saw as the emergent interaction between linguistic form and situated language use, mediated by culture and ideology, and as a way of understanding how societal changes are instantiated in the minutiae of language practices. A closer look reveals that many such practices are mediated through writing, even though this fact might not always be evidently visible as literacy, in situated moments.

Asad's story reveals the migrant's experience is shot through in complex ways with the possibilities and the constraints provided by the access to and practice of literacy. These are evidenced in each of the following five lenses:

1 The traveling and circulating texts of migrants and refugees;
2 Day-to-day literacy and translanguaging practices in the lives of migrants and refugees;

3 The intricate ways in which the experiences and lives of migrants and refugees are bound up with formal education and the capital that represents;
4 The mediation through written texts of the experience of migration itself;
5 The forms of surveillance by which the movements of migrants and refugees are tracked and traced.

The exponential increase in movement of people globally and the explosion in the uses of digital communication have been identified as key premises for the paradigm of "superdiversity" (as outlined first by Vertovec 2007 and then by Blommaert and Rampton 2011, among others). From the perspective of a country in the south, however, these two premises can be qualified somewhat,[2] and considered alongside a potential third premise – the increase in global social inequality and the types of polarisation related to this, discussed further later.

It is also necessary to consider the frameworks and methods available for the theoretical and empirical study of literacy as it moves across contexts. How do we theorise literacy when it takes the form of "textual projectiles" (Rampton 2000) or material objects (Budach, Kell, and Patrick 2015), or the form of texts that travel with people as they move, or in the form of the capacities, resources, and practices with which and in which migrants and refugees engage with literacy?

From its earliest origins, literacy, as communication through visually encoded inscriptions rather than auditory, gestural, or other channels offered the potential for a view of linguistic meaning-making as projected away from its human embodiment and its embedding in social situations. Writing does often involve the materialisation of language in texts that can move independently of their producers.[3] The notion of text freed from context laid the basis for theories of literacy along the lines of what Street (1984, 2003) critiqued as an "autonomous model" of literacy. In this model, literacy is seen as a universal set of skills that can be learnt and applied irrespective of context, having powerful social consequences in and of themselves. Street's critique then led to the emergence of the New Literacy Studies (NLS), and what Street (1984, 2003) called the "ideological model of literacy," in which literacy was seen to be always contextualised, and taken up in ways consistent with deep cultural and theoretical patterns in particular contexts and cultures.

From within linguistic anthropology rather than literacy studies, Bauman and Briggs (1990) and Silverstein and Urban (1996) take this idea of *projection* of texts into account, claiming that as texts are projected away from 'the situation', they are always re-contextualised and often resemiotised (Iedema 2001) into the new context – the concepts of both situatedness and of mobility are thus at the core of this view. The dilemma for literacy theory then becomes: how do we account for textual practices which are both situated/contextualised and distributed/transcontextual?

Overview

In this section a number of key moves in the theoretical frameworks for the study of literacy and for transcontextual analysis are outlined.

New literacy studies and literacies as placed resources

The development of literacy studies over the past few decades is characterised mainly by studies which led to the deconstructing of what was called the "Great Divide," a paradigm based on the idea that oral and written forms of communication were distinct modes of communication and that the development of literacy had consequences for "human development" and the "evolution" of societies. The main tenets of this approach, which became known as New Literacy Studies (NLS), were laid down in the early 1980s (Street 1984). For about two decades, first- and second-generation literacy studies (see Baynham and Prinsloo 2013) established that literacy is shaped by social context and is best viewed as a set of text-mediated practices ("literacy as social practice") within what Street (1984) called an "ideological model of literacy." Many of the studies in this period showed that people *take hold* of literacy in variable and agentic ways that are consistent with deeply rooted cultural orientations to literacy and particular contexts of practice. By not reifying the channel of communication, they demonstrated that literacy events and practices involved both spoken and written language and that these were intertwined almost inseparably in everyday events – it is the social function of the events that determines the kinds of language that are used and the form it takes, whether written or spoken.

NLS took these ideas one step further with the concept of multiple literacies – repeated configurations of literacy practices within particular domains of practice and in stratified economies of signs and symbols (Street 2003). Some literacies therefore become more dominant and institutionalised than others, with schooled and academic literacies carrying tremendous potential for social stratification and reproduction of inequalities.

Almost twenty years after the first key studies of literacy as social practice were published, two important lines of critique emerged. While accepting many of the premises of the NLS, these lines of critique identified problems, first with the pre-occupation within NLS with literacy as *situated* communication, and second, with its lack of a sufficiently explicit focus on issues of power and inequality. Another decade or so later, a third and suggestive line of critique is emerging, which relates to how we conceptualise the materiality of texts. Each of these is discussed later.

With regard to the first, Brandt and Clinton's (2002) review of the NLS raised important questions about the emphasis the NLS had placed on local events and practices. They noted that texts from outside of the local context have effects and are not necessarily absorbed into local ways of knowing and ways of taking hold of literacy. They asked:

> But can we not recognise and theorise the transcontextual aspects of literacy without calling it decontextualised? Can we not approach literacy as a technology – and even as an agent – without falling back into the autonomous model? Can we not see the ways that literacy arises out of local, particular, situated human interactions while also seeing how it regularly arrives from other places – infiltrating, disjointing and displacing local life?
>
> *(Brandt and Clinton 2002: 343)*

With regard to the second, Collins and Blot (2003) also raised problems with NLS's focus on the local, arguing that the ethnographic studies of the type produced within NLS, while valuable in their accounting for diversity and heterogeneity of literate practice, were not accounting for the persistence of literacy's role in social stratification and the reproduction of inequality.

Brandt and Clinton's critique played an important role in the emergence of studies which have paid more attention to the technologies, the media, and the different modes of communication, as well as to the materiality of texts and the artefacts (Pahl and Rowsell 2010) present in literacy events.[4] With the global explosion of digital communication, literacy studies has had to reconsider the way in which its earlier frameworks conceptualised literacy events and practices as placed resources, acknowledging that even as literacy events are always moments of instantiated communication, they can also be linked through technologies to other events which may be stretched across time and space, and are implicated in scalar practices.

The third line of critique is relatively new and has roots in a number of theoretical frameworks. Vieira's work (2016) draws on Latourian actor-network and sociomaterial theories, as does Arend's (2015) and Gourlay's (2015), which both demonstrate how people, texts, and objects are brought into engagement through assemblages that are constantly forming and reforming in order for stability in texts to be temporarily achieved. Deleuzian rhizomatic approaches are discussed by Leander and Boldt (2012), which are based on a critique of representational approaches and the disciplined rationalisation of youth's engagement in literacies. Rather the authors suggest moment-by-moment accounts revealing the emergence of literacy. Theories of the post-human (Braidotti 2013) are discussed in Budach et al. (2015) and Kell (2015b) where objects are seen as having agency.

Each of these has led to deeper analyses of the way literacy (and the texts in which it is instantiated, as well as the capacities that people have for creating and projecting texts) move across spatial and temporal contexts. Such movement can be studied at the micro scale of moment-by-moment, textually mediated interaction, across locales like neighbourhoods and institutions and across countries as nation-states.

Transcontextual analysis and translocal literacies

From within literacy studies, Brandt and Clinton's piece was a careful critique of the limitations of NLS's focus on literacy events and practices as placed and therefore contextually bounded. However, some interesting parallels can be found in earlier work in linguistic anthropology. Goffman's 1972 paper *The Neglected Situation* called for a deeper recognition of the importance of "the situation" which he saw as "an environment of mutual monitoring" and importantly, of "co-presence" (p. 63). However, Goffman's later decomposition of traditional dyadic speaker-hearer models (in his framework of principals, authors, animators) pointed at ways of transcending this "situation" and at the potential for meaning-making to be detached from and *projected* across situations that might no longer be characterised by *mutual monitoring* and *co-presence*. These two characteristics continue to be vital factors for the considerations of the relation between spoken and written encounters, especially in digitally mediated communication.

Both Silverstein's work on indexicality (1985) and Gumperz's (1977) work on moment-to-moment interaction involved groundbreaking insights about conversational inferencing, contextualisation cues and indexicality, which challenged earlier theories about language, speech communities, and variation. Instead they argued that "it is long-term exposure to similar communicative experience in institutionalized networks of relationships and not language or community membership as such that lies at the root of shared culture and shared inferential practices" (Gumperz 1977: 15).

Bauman and Briggs (1990) argued that in order to grasp more fully the dynamics of social interaction, the focus should shift to "identifying discursive practices and processes that *transcend* the face-to-face speaker-hearer dyad as the frame of reference for the elucidation of spoken interaction in the conduct and constitution of social life" (Bauman 2004: 146, my emphasis). They point out that a starting point for inquiry in relation to these concepts is a distinction between text and discourse:

> Entextualisation is the process of rendering discourse extractable, of making a stretch of linguistic production into a unit – a text – that can be lifted out of its interactional setting.
> *(Bauman and Briggs 1990, p. 61)*

The text resulting from this process may still carry elements of its history of use within it. They suggest that the task is to "discover empirically what means are available in a given social setting, to whom they may be available, under what circumstances for making discourse into text" (Bauman 2004: 65). They further argue that

> processes that anchor discourses in contexts of use may be opposed by others that potentiate its detachability. Decontextualisation from one social context involves recontextualisation in another, and this is a transformational process. We must therefore determine what the recontextualised text brings with it from its earlier context(s) and what emergent form, function and meaning it is given as it is recentered.
> *(Bauman and Briggs 1990, p. 67)*

So while we might say that Goffman and Bauman and Briggs showed how to loosen discourse from "the situation" by first entextualising it and then recontextualising it, Silverstein and Gumperz revealed how discourse is deeply contextualised, but that through the use of contextualisation cues and indexicality, frames and orders which are in a sense extra-contextual can be invoked.

These two axes of investigation are very important, and they differ in that the *entextualisation-recontextualisation* concept suggests an emic and horizontal movement of communication through spatiotemporal frames which are always separated by time (even if only milliseconds) and by shifts across participant frameworks. On the other hand the *orders of indexicality* concept can be seen as a vertical and etic one, in that it is the researcher who identifies what it is that is invoked from extra-contextual frames in the moment of contextualised discourse, and in so doing ties the analysis in to questions of power, control, and other macro categories.

Blommaert, building on this earlier work, made two key moves towards the "sociolinguistics of mobility," providing specific frameworks and tools for the study of travelling texts, translocal/transnational literacies, and transcontextual analysis. First, his earlier work (2001) on "text trajectories" (a term first coined by Silverstein and Urban 1996) examined the way in which spoken language is taken up in written language which is then recontextualised in higher levels of a bureaucracy. The breakthrough therefore was the focus on ways in which spoken language became rendered in written language in each interaction moment by moment, followed by the literal movement of the text across contexts in the bureaucracy. While others had also traced the movement of texts and of meaning-making over time and space, Blommaert examined in close detail the unequal linguistic resources that come into play at each step along the way. This was a seminal move and adds weight to the argument I made about adding a third premise to the discussion about superdiversity – the phenomenal increase in social inequality, accompanied by increased social polarisation.

Second, Blommaert's work on orders of indexicality and scale (2005, 2007) has been very influential, and it is on this basis that he claims a sociolinguistics of mobility is accomplished (2014: 4). Blommaert's claims go as follows: When people move, their "communicative resources are affected by such moves: accents, styles, modes of conversational arrangement all proved to be sensitive to mobility, and what worked well in part of the world proved to lose functional efficacy in another" (2014: 6). Blommaert argues further that the reasons for this are not linguistic but indexical, and that "mobility, sociolinguistically, is therefore a matter of determining the different orders of indexicality through which communication travels, and their effect on communicative conditions and outcomes" (2014: 8). One of the main methods he has developed for the study of communication in orders of indexicality is "layered simultaneity" (2005: 126), where multiple spatiotemporal frames come to play roles in unique moments of interaction, where "resources used have fundamentally different historicities and therefore fundamentally different indexical loads" (2014: 11).

Resonating with Collins and Blot's argument (2003) about how NLS does not account for the power of regimes of literacy all over the world, Blommaert (2010) argues further that literacies are stratified in line with these orders of indexicality and that literacy regimes specify which texts can receive uptake at which levels, bringing in the notion of scale. Powerful groups deploy and have their literacies valued at translocal scales, while the literacies of less powerful groups are restricted to deployment and value-attribution at local scales only. His central argument is that discourse forms can lose function when they are moved into different environments. Looking through a south-north lens Blommaert maps this feature of loss of function against worldwide inequalities conceptualised as centre-periphery models. He argues that as discourse forms move across spaces they are subject to changed sets of evaluative criteria, which are part of stratified economies of literacy. These different criteria position "grassroots" texts as sub-standard and convert communicative difference into communicative inequality. So while Brandt and Clinton's earlier critique focused on the ways in which the global reaches down into the local via written texts, Blommaert's work shifts the directionality so the focus falls on people's projecting of texts 'upstream' and beyond their local situations.

Canagarajah (2015) critiques Blommaert's framework for its treatment of local literacy regimes as "relatively autonomous complexes," in which people's "literacy skills are locked, so to speak, into one scale-level, the local one . . . the relocalised varieties may get 'stuck' at a local scale-level and offer little in the way of mobility potential across scales for their users" (Blommaert 2010: 96 in Canagarajah 2015: 35). Canagarajah's (2015: 37) perspective instead aims to

> encourage us to see people as not locked into only one scale level of speaking or writing. They may develop the ability to shuttle across scale levels, spanning indexical orders and literacy regimes, without necessarily being physically mobile. This is possible because all contexts are mediated by mobile resources from diverse places. People are also able to renegotiate norms and construct texts that transcend the norms of specific scale levels.

Blommaert's concepts of indexicality and orders of indexicality are almost uniformly applied in relation to vertical analysis, where the unique moment is viewed in terms of wider and bigger scales, which lead to the sense of "higher level situatedness" (Blommaert 2005: 67), and from there to claims being made about macro categories. In Kell (2015a) I have argued for a different "take" on mobility which does not consider scale as nested and value-laden in terms of power differentials, but rather simply as a measure of reach for the projection of meanings across space and time, from always placed, local contexts to other *non-local* contexts (but not necessarily higher scale or *global* contexts). I argue for the suspension of judgement on what constitutes a higher scale or even what the "global" is. I thus make an argument for a unit of analysis which literally traces the movement of text artefacts, known as a "meaning-making trajectory" which gives priority to trans-contextual analysis involving the study of recontextualising and resemiotising moves, questions of agency and intentionality and the precise ways in which semiosis materialises activity as it unfolds over time and space. Tracing trajectories focuses therefore on the distribution of meanings over space and time and the resources that come into play to configure this distribution (see Kell 2015b).

I have presented a number of different meaning-making trajectories in previous work (Kell 2009, 2011, 2015a, 2015b). Some of these showed that as vernacular texts cross contexts they do not necessarily lose function; in some cases they actually gain function. I will briefly mention two different trajectories that were discussed in Kell (2015a) in order to demonstrate the relevance of the concept for transcontextual analysis.

The first was an "Incident Report" that had to be completed by a supervisor, George (who was a migrant worker from Samoa), after a near accident on a building site in a New Zealand construction company. The report had been completed in an online template on the computer in the site office, and had been checked by the local health and safety (H&S) officer. Before "inputting" it (into the automated online system), the local H&S officer sent it to the national H&S officer, Lino, who was sitting in a traffic jam in Auckland (about 400 km away from the construction site). Lino had asked if the local H&S officers could do this, as she did not want the local "guy" writing the reports to be seen as "a bit of a wally" because he had not filled in the report appropriately, and once it was "input" it would be viewed instantaneously by management at the local, regional, national, and international levels (the company was a multinational with its head office in Australia). She said that the way the form had been filled in was not clear and that instead she wanted the "guys" to draw a sketch of the site where the near-accident happened and provide some photographs, all of which could be attached to the incident report form. I called this a scripted trajectory since the recontextualising and resemiotising moves across time and space were pre-specified. But Lino had managed to insert a detour into this scripted trajectory, whereby the effects of literacy inequalities could be mitigated through her efforts, thereby extending a sense of agency to the employees working at the local level. George's text may well have lost function as it entered into the translocal and transnational contexts, but the way Lino had worked to alter the practices around the texts would have hopefully mitigated this loss of function.

The second trajectory was drawn from a lengthy ethnography in a participatory development project in a township outside Cape Town, where 240 women who had previously lived in backyard shacks were accessing a government subsidy to build brick houses for their families. In this trajectory, a woman called Noma, as a result of her disability, had been allocated a house rather than having to build her own house. There were serious problems with the house and Noma attempted to get these addressed. She unsuccessfully raised the problems verbally numerous times in community meetings. At this point she wrote a narrative in a child's exercise book about her experiences (this was part of a writing project that I had initiated in the community). This "story" became the focus of tremendous attention in the community and much more widely, and the decision was made that she should take it and read it out aloud at a meeting of the national organisation in an adjacent area. An intervening meeting took place with a provincial level structure, and the story was read out, after which she again presented it verbally at the national meeting. An immediate decision was made that a general collection of money should be made in order to get new materials and a builder to put the house right. The process started when she moved into the problem house, and it ended when she moved back into the rebuilt house. Altogether this took about six months and shifted across organisational structures, participant structures, neighbourhoods, and buildings.

I called Noma's an "emergent" meaning-making trajectory, in contrast with George's "scripted trajectory" (Kell 2015a), since contingency was apparent in every move that unfolded along the length of the process. Noma's initial choice of mode of communication, the one that was available in the current repertoires of her immediate community, caused her attempt to make meaning to lose function. But when I introduced an alternative mode of communication to her trajectory, writing, her meaning-making rapidly and somewhat spectacularly gained function. Again, it was only by tracing the practices along the length of the trajectory that the availability of different repertoires and resources and their affordances could be revealed.

Each move in the trajectory was one in which meaning was recontextualised and/or resemiotised. As the meaning-making process shifted moment by moment and across contexts, the participant frameworks of each moment and the "mediational means" needed to be considered. The mediational means consisted of three sets of resources (each with their own affordances) needed for projecting the meaning across different participation frameworks.

Resources and repertoires in the recontextualisation of meanings

First, it is necessary to consider the *modes of communication* as resources that were available for projecting the meaning moment by moment and from context to context. The mode that was available to Noma in the first moves in her trajectory was simply that of spoken language. This did not work. It was only when she grasped the written mode and created a story in a book did her trajectory gain traction. The mode that was available to George was written language, but Lino was convinced that the visual (in the form of photos and a diagram) would have served his purpose better.

Second, it is necessary to consider *the medium/technological/infrastructural* resources that were available for projecting meaning. In Noma's case, it was the child's schoolbook which literally travelled from context to context. The affordances of the book ensured uptake of the meaning because people said that, until they saw the book, they did not realise that Noma was someone "who could say anything." In George's case it was the report form on the computer that needed to be filled in, but the affordances of the online form (initially taken up by George and the local H&S officer) which only offered space for writing of a particular type, needed to be challenged and broadened.

Third, it is necessary to consider, with regard to the mode of written language and of writing in multiple languages, the *graphic, linguistic,* and *cultural* resources for writing that were available to the actors for the projection of their meaning. Here, Freebody and Luke's (2003) very useful identification of resources for literacy is considered. These are the resources of decoding and encoding language, semantic and pragmatic resources, and critical resources. In addition to these we can add further resources for writing as specified by Blommaert (2013) – graphic resources and meta-pragmatic resources. These are brought together in registers, which is a crucial concept for examining the ways in which people deploy their resources and repertoires in the multiple communities or affinity groups through which they move. This leads me to suggest that it may be valuable to think of a new "3Rs" in the contemporary world – resources, repertoires, and registers.

Examining this a little more closely, in Noma's case, she was able to write in her own language, isiXhosa, she understood the genre of the story, she made meaning in that she constructed a powerful story of disillusionment, and she had a strong meta-pragmatic awareness of intertextuality with regard to the genre of the story (she said, "I have written my story, now I am waiting for the happy ending"). In George's case, he was able to write a very basic report in English, but the template confused him in that he followed a truncated, bullet-point style, which did not convey a clear sense of what the incident was all about. In the later sequence in the trajectory, when the report arrived on Lino's phone, she was able to draw on critical or meta-pragmatic resources to note that the report as it stood was going to create problems.

Freebody and Luke (2003) pose three valuable questions for understanding how resources work in particular contexts. They ask first, what is the breadth of an individual's or a community's repertoire of literate practices? Second, what is the depth and degree of control exercised by any given individual or community in any given literacy activity? And third, what is the extent of hybridity, novelty, and redesign at work in a literacy activity?

Freebody and Luke's set of resources and Blommaert's framework is useful for considering how these different resources travel, and give rise to what some may see as uneven and sometimes jarring texts, while others may see them as providing evidence of creativity and hybridity. The question is the extent to which the combination of resources instantiated in any particular text enables or does not enable the sharing and uptake of meaning. Kroon, Jie, and Blommaert (2015) provide a detailed exploration of how differential degrees of control of particular resources like orthographic resources, genre resources, and discursive resources each contribute to the potential (or the lack of potential) for uptake or recognition.

However, without detailed ethnographic work on the situated practices within which uptake occurs, it is difficult to make principled claims about whether or not it occurs. The point here is one of the very original and founding tenets of the New Literacy Studies, as demonstrated precisely and classically by Heath (1982) and contributors to Street's (1984) *Cross-Cultural Approaches to Literacy* – that individuals, groups and sub-cultures "take hold" of literacy in accordance with their histories and cultural orientations to literacy. Unless we study uptake ethnographically, we impute ideas about uptake to the participants in the research setting. In this way, we as researchers may well miss the depth and breadth of repertoires and resources at play in an event. More importantly, we may miss the extent of "hybridity, novelty and redesign at work in any literacy activity," and therefore the forms of individual and distributed agency within a literacy event and in the wider trajectory within which it is simply one moment.

In this claim I echo Canagarajah's call that unless we "move beyond bounded communities and consider communication at the contact zone . . . we are unable to rely on sharedness for meaning. It is practices that help people negotiate difference and achieve shared understandings" (2013: 4). And it is this claim that brings us back to the need to constantly bear in mind Silverstein's concept of the "total linguistic fact," and the way in which this echoes Sayad's invocation of Mauss's "total social fact" in the study of migration.

Issues and ongoing debates

The preceding section addressed the shift from the idea of literacy as placed resources to the conceptual tools available for the study of traveling texts and translocal literacies. It brought this round full circle to the need to study practices, and to the idea of the "total linguistic fact." In this section I move on to address transnational literacies, defined by Warriner (2007: 202) as "literacy practices that draw on funds of knowledge, identities and social relations rooted in and extending across national borders." The simplicity of this definition belies the complexity of the issues – what precisely are the "funds" that are deployed when it comes to literacy, and what is the "gaze" through which transnational literacies are studied.

Research on transnational literacies goes back to studies such as Moll, Amanti, Neff, and Gonzalez (1992) on "funds of knowledge" connecting homes and schools among Mexican migrant workers; Saxena (1994) on Punjabis' contextual and contingent use of multilingual literacies in the UK; Baynham (1993) on Moroccan migrants in the UK; and Rockhill (1993) on migrants and gender in the United States. Hornberger developed her continua of biliteracy in 1989 and has continued to develop this framework since then, and more recently Hornberger and Link (2012) address the "continua of biliteracy" in classrooms in the context of migration.

Further themes are explored with reference to the day-to-day literacy practices of migrants in negotiating their lives in the contexts of the receiving countries. There is a growing body of scholarship on the experiences of the children of migrants in schools in the United States and UK, as well as other European countries (McLean 2010; Rounsaville 2014). The relationship between classroom-based and out-of-school literacy practices is a central theme running through such studies, with a general trend in the analyses demonstrating that out-of-school literacy practices (particularly those involving social media and/or hip hop) are often enabling of students' transnational identities (Richardson Bruna 2007). A further key theme in such studies has been the importance of the role of digital technologies in enabling young people and adults to maintain links and roots, as well as draw on resources in both, or more, countries simultaneously (for example, Lam and Rosario-Ramos 2009; McLean 2010; Nogueron-Liu 2013). These studies provide insights into the first and third lenses for understanding literacy and migration – the day-to-day literacy practices of migrants and refugees and the intricate ways in which the identities of migrants and refugees are bound up with formal education and the capital that represents.

Warriner (2007, 2009) and Lam and Warriner (2012) outline more recent developments in this field, which engage with Blommaert's "sociolinguistics of mobility" (2010), discussed earlier. They argue that researchers needed to pay attention to how "historically marginalized peoples draw on existing and emerging linguistic repertoires while moving across and within contexts" (p. 3), as well as how literacy development is influenced by movement and mobility and new communicative repertoires and practices that emerge in new contexts. They point out that *simultaneity* has become an important theme for understanding the complexities of globalisation processes and the communicative practices that emerge when migrants' participation in activities and communities takes place across multiple spaces and over time. Quoting Levitt and Glick Schiller (2004), who describe this notion of simultaneity as the ways in which "people incorporate daily activities, routines and institutions located both in a destination country and transnationally into their daily practice" (p. 5), they contrast this with Blommaert's notion of layered simultaneity (as described earlier).

In finding a way to bring together the study of literacy as both a translocal and a transnational phenomenon, Leander, Phillips, and Headrick Taylor (2010) argue that one dominant discourse framing studies on learning is a "place-based" one, in which the "classroom-as-container" functions as an "imagined geography" of education, "even when research questions cross 'in school' and 'out of school' borders" (p. 332). They suggest three metaphors – learning-in-place, learning trajectories, and learning networks. Their major contribution is the argument that specific relations need to be followed, traced, and analysed, if a fully relational perspective on mobility and learning is to come into being. 'Learning-in-place' suggests an understanding of "how a particular locale is positioned in a *nexus of relations* to other such locales" (p. 334). The simultaneity of multiple locales and the contact zones between them become an expanded terrain of examination. The notion of trajectories, as the particular mobilities of people moving through locales, then becomes important. Finally, as trajectories intersect at different scales, the idea of the networking of resources across space and time then comes into play.

My own work on trajectories as outlined earlier has involved an attempt to bring the idea of situated or placed meaning together with mobility and movement of meaning-making. More recently (2015a, 2015b) I have attempted to model the ways in which trajectories intersect across different spatial and temporal scales (both translocal and transnational), thus approximating what Leander et al. (2010) conceptualise as 'networks'. In this I have tried to specify a language of description for meaning-making as *both situated*, in moments in time and space and in participant frameworks, *and mobile*, as people project their meanings across time and space, recontextualising them into new participant frameworks. The idea of the resources for writing that are brought into play in each moment along the trajectory are uncovered, in the attempt to introduce fine-grained specificity in answer to the three important questions outlined by Freebody and Luke. If we are able to consider the depth and breadth of literacy resources available and deployable, as well as the extent of hybridity, novelty, and redesign moment by moment, we may go some way further to understanding literacy inequalities.

Vieira's (2016) work is innovative in that it addresses itself directly to the fourth and fifth lenses I outlined in the introduction – the mediation through written texts of the experience of migration itself, and the forms of surveillance by which the movements of migrants and refugees are tracked and traced. In doing so, Vieira challenges the NLS's focus on the social, instead she builds a case for socio*material* approaches in the study of literacy and migration which put the emphasis on the "papers," especially the legal papers that grant and confirm status. Her work thus contributes to deeper understandings of how literacy accrues meaning by circulating through institutions and the lives of individuals.

Lam and Warriner (2012) point out that most studies on the experiences of migrant children in schooling have been carried out in the national context of the receiving country, although they suggest that this is changing, with new theoretical tools for studying cross-border connections and practices (p. 193). Of the forty-eight empirical studies they reviewed, fourteen were conducted outside the United States, and almost all of those fourteen cited are from the UK or Europe. This means that, in this case, close to zero studies were conducted from sending areas or countries. Warriner and Wyman (2013) provide some examples of exceptions, in studies of areas from which people have migrated (but these focus more on language rather than literacy) including Wyman's (2013) study of the Yup'ik in Alaska, and Han's (2013) study of African and Chinese traders who have migrated internally within China. In addition, the vast majority of these studies are synchronic in nature, in that the data collected represents a temporal slice through the day-to-day experiences of migrants, from which past practices may be reconstructed.

The challenge raised by these studies brings us back to challenges raised in the introduction – those of inequality and of the gaze the researcher brings to the research. While 'superdiversity' has provided a valuable framework for conceptualising the ways in which intensified migratory flows, combined with the uses of digital communication technologies are changing the world as we know it, I suggested earlier that a third premise is necessary. This is the idea that along with migration and digital communication there has been a concomitant increase in social inequality and polarisation. Taking account of this would add to more nuanced and precise accounts of literacy and its translocal and transnational manifestations. I introduce Friedman's (2003) work, which maintains that if we are to understand the relationship between language regimes, power and migration, we need to disaggregate types of migration, their class bases, and the polarisations that accompany intensified transnational movements of people. Furthermore, I outline key principles in Algerian anthropologist Abdelmalek Sayad's work (1991, 1997), and his disavowal of the denial of the global politics of migration and its deep roots in the experiences of conquest and exploitation under colonialism. I therefore weave together a number of the issues and debates touched on earlier and consider more explicitly Collins and Blot's critique of the literacy as social practice approach as not engaging adequately with issues of power and inequality.

Disaggregation of migration

Friedman argues that horizontal polarisations concern non-elite identity movements, as in the phenomena of diasporisation and nationalisation, and suggests that these work counter to each other. *Diasporisation* involves transnational minorities with extensive ties to their countries of origin (like Algerians in France, Turks in Germany, and new-Latinos in the United States). He defines diasporisation as the ethnicisation of migration, new patterns of segregation and the reinforcement of transnational relations which are aided by the uses of digital technologies. Diasporisation feeds the fear in the receiving countries that immigrants are not going to assimilate and such fears help fuel *nationalisation* which is an effort to claim the state for specific groups, to equate certain ethnicities with the nation.

Vertical polarisations result from a conflict between *elite cosmopolitanism* and *vernacular indigenisation*. In Collins's (2011) summary of Friedman's work:

> The former features a selective tolerance of cultural and linguistic diversity . . . the multiculturalism and multilingualism of the affluent who taste and pronounce at will, but rarely live amongst the migrants and minorities whose diversity they might find enriching . . . Counterposed to such cosmopolitanism is vernacular indigenization, a widely documented tendency to reroot identity and polarize cultural conflicts among fractions of native and immigrant working classes and poor. Such indigenization is often xenophobic and intolerant.
>
> *(p. 195)*

Friedman developed this typology in 2003. It can well be applied to the trajectories of vast numbers of migrants, with Asad Abdullahi's story as described by Steinberg providing a classic example of the Somalian diasporisation, Asad's subjection to nationalisation in some of the countries he passed through, and particularly his horrific subjection to vernacular indigenisation in the xenophobic attacks in South Africa. However since 2003, the movement of people has increased in numbers and changed in form, as witnessed in the current (September 2015) refugee crisis, from Syria, other parts of the Middle East, and Africa. Diasporisation seems an almost romantic word to use for such violent and traumatic moves. But what may be necessary to consider in adding to Friedman's disaggregation of types of migration, in the face of the growing global inequality, is an idea raised by Standing (2011) among others – that of the development of the "precariat." The precariat is a class fraction shaved off from the working class and living and working in conditions of precarity, without access to stable occupational careers, social protection, or forms of regulation. Those who form the precariat are the existing poor in neo-liberal countries, as well as refugees and migrants. Friedman's typology could well be expanded to include this group. While Friedman works through issues of language rights and practices in each of the above forms of polarisation, these would take different forms for a group such as this "precariat" who would be positioned in relation to the five lenses for studying literacy and migration in different ways.

It is in this wider context that we can consider migrants' and refugees' experiences of migration as mediated through written texts, and as forms of surveillance by which their movements are tracked and traced – the fourth and fifth lenses as listed earlier. Here much importance must be placed on the very material ways texts regulate the lives of migrants, offering little space for the ways in which these might be negotiated, circumvented, and engaged with. While the hard texts of migrants and refugees (or the absence of such texts) certainly implicate their human associates in day-by-day activities, the key NLS notions of participating in literacy events and practices around these texts seems almost voluntarist.

With this in mind, I will now turn to Sayad's work. Bourdieu and Wacquant (2000) salute Sayad's insistence on treating migration as a "total social fact." They stress that Sayad was "the phenomenon [of migration] itself . . . the brute facts of imperial oppression, chain migration, community dislocation and fractured acculturation were constantly with him because they were within him" (p. 177). Even though current literature in migration studies challenges aspects of Sayad's work, arguing that Sayad was writing under different conditions and that the intensification of migration accompanied by the explosion in digital communication has rendered aspects of his work irrelevant (for example, Diminescu 2008), I would argue that it is precisely because of the rapidly increasing inequality and social polarisation of which migration is a part, that it is important to examine the principles he outlined as central for the study of migration as a total social fact.

First, Sayad argued that "the immigrant is also an emigrant" (in Bourdieu and Wacquant 2000: 174). The implication is that any analysis of migration before examining the "concerns and cleavages of the receiving society, must start from the sending communities, their structure, history and contradictions" (p. 174). This "necessitates that one reconstitute the complete trajectory of the individuals, households and groups involved" (p. 174), which would obviously involve diachronic rather than synchronic types of studies. This is the reason I introduced Steinberg's *A Man of Good Hope* – a perfect example of such a study, where Steinberg went back to visit almost every site through which Asad migrated. Very little current work on transnational literacies adopts this principle of researching literacy practices and schooling in the place from whence the migrant or refugee came. Farr's (2006) studies of chain migration from Mexico to the US provide a notable exception, with her longitudinal study (1989 to 2006) of one social network of Mexican families and their movements between Chicago and the village in Mexico. Farr spent many periods of time living in Mexico, explaining how she became uncomfortable with the extant academic studies of Mexicans: "the people I was coming to know did not fit the descriptions of Mexicans provided by anthropologists and linguists published in the US or Mexico" (Farr 2006: 5). More recently, a special issue of *Literacy in Composition Studies* (2016) has published a number of articles by authors who did transnational ethnographies.

Up until now, many studies which focus on migrants and refugees' difficulties in participating in the literacy practices of the receiving country try to recreate, with largely synchronic forms of analysis, the history of their literacy practices from interviews, observations, examination of objects, and texts. But such studies, according to Sayad, remove the person from the context and the history, and this splitting off is a kind of collusion in which the deeply political nature of migration lies repressed. This then brings us to the second pivotal principle, which is that migration is "a product of the historical relationship of international domination, both material and symbolic." Bourdieu and Wacquant state that Sayad argues that

> every migrant carries this repressed relation of power between states within himself or herself and unwittingly recapitulates and re-enacts it in their personal strategies and

experiences. Thus the most fleeting encounter between an Algerian worker and his French boss in Lyon, or a Surinamese-born child and his schoolteacher in Rotterdam, a Jamaican mother and her social worker in London, an Ethiopian elderly man and his landlord in Naples – is fraught with the whole baggage of past intercourse between the imperial metropole and its erstwhile colony.

(Bourdieu and Wacquant 2000: 175)

This is important since it was the basis for Sayad's argument that the migrant experiences what he called a "double absence," meaning that the migrant loses her roots in the originating country, but at the same time never really establishes roots in the receiving country either. Diminescu (2008) argues that given the increase in circular migration and chain migration, as well as the affordances for digital communication to enable co-presence in multiple spaces, this "double absence" is no longer a defining feature of migration, and this argument about co-presence appears in many of the studies on transnational literacies among young people outlined earlier.

The third principle is that migration "requires collective dissimulation and social duplicity" (in Bourdieu and Wacquant 2000: 178). With this principle, Sayad was referring to earlier and organised and structured systems of migrant labour, for example, the movement of workers between Algeria and France. While such systems take different form in postcolonial societies and in conditions of the contemporary globalised world, they are not necessarily any less exploitative and damaging. This principle brings in what Sayad (1999) called a "triple lie" – that such migration was transitory and provisional, that it was determined simply by the quest for labour, and that it was politically neutral and without civic consequences (in the case he was referring to "on either side of the Mediterranean"). When arguing that migration needed to be treated as a "total social fact," Sayad was saying that migration "disrupts the whole array of institutions that make up the originating society" (in Bourdieu and Wacquant 2000: 176).

It therefore perhaps becomes important to ask, given the disaggregation of types of migration and the implications of Sayad's three principles, how should scholars of transnational literacies study their subject as a "total linguistic fact"?

Implications and future directions

Bourdieu and Wacquant (2000) argue that to study migration in the holistic way that Sayad did requires reflexivity, that it must be able to turn back on itself, and must also include the reconstruction of trajectories, as well as the lay and the scholarly discourses that "swirl" around the phenomenon. They also argue that such discourses are performative – effecting various forms of "social alchemy" (p. 177). I have suggested throughout that the "gaze" of much of the scholarship in this area is centred on migrants' and refugees' experiences in the receiving countries. Sayad's principles would suggest much more multisited and diachronic or longitudinal forms of ethnography of migration, and of networks across all kinds of translocal and transnational spaces. Given the deep and growing inequality in the real world and in the world of scholarly research, Friedman's and Sayad's work argues for a direct embracing of the political dimensions of the study of migration as refracted through the three principles he outlines.

This may involve more of a focus on the fourth and fifth lenses. In turn this would involve different theoretical approaches which are mindful of the problems with the NLS framework, yet still attuned to its foundations in ethnography. In addition, greater attention could be paid by researchers to the three Rs – resources, repertoires and registers. This then has implications for those involved in literacy education with migrants and refugees.

While the spatial turn in sociolinguistics and allied fields has been valuable, the foregoing discussion suggests that a greater focus on temporality may be the next step. My own work on trajectories draws attention to the issue of temporality and the ways in which communication unfolds moment by moment.

Related topics

Space, place, and language
Complexity, mobility, migration
Spatiotemporal scales and the study of mobility
Multisited ethnography and language in the study of migration

Further reading

Lam, W. and Warriner, D. (2012). Transnationalism and literacy: Investigating the mobility of people, languages, texts and practices in contexts of migration. *Reading Research Quarterly*, *47*(2), 191–215.

This article reviews forty-eight studies that address language and literacy practices in transnational contexts of migration. It outlines useful conceptual frames derived from these studies, including Bourdieusian concepts of capital and habitus, inter-generational processes, and the negotiation and maintenance of identities across national borders.

Lorimer Leonard, R., Vieira, K. and Young, M. (2015). A special issue on transnational literacy. *Literacy in Composition Studies*, *3*(3).

This special issue contains a number of very important articles which retheorise literacy studies in the direction of a greater focus on the materiality of writing and its consequences. The introduction states that "to do transnational work what matters most is not what researchers look at but how they look" (p. vii) and a number of the researchers conducted transnational research, visiting the sending and the receiving countries of migrants.

Stroud, C. and Prinsloo, M., eds. (2015). *Language, Literacy and Diversity: Moving Words*. London and New York: Routledge.

This collection contains a range of studies which directly address the retheorising of language and literacy in relation to social mobility and multilingualism. Stroud outlines a current of work on the issue of "entanglement" which is a useful and concrete way of conceptualising how people and objects interrelate over time. The book includes my own chapter "Ariadne's Thread: Literacy, Scale and Meaning Making across Space and Time."

Vieira, K. (2016). *American by Paper: How Documents Matter in Immigrant Literacy*. Minneapolis: University of Minnesota Press.

This book marks a shift in literacy studies towards a sociomaterial approach which takes the materiality of writing as a prime focus. It demonstrates how the experience of migration is tied up in papers, especially legal papers that confer status, and it builds a deeper understanding of the ways in which literacy accrues meaning by circulating through institutions and lives.

Notes

1 While Steinberg's book *A Man of Good Hope* is a personal biography and a social history, which has no intention of focusing on language and literacy issues, Steinberg incidentally draws attention to a number of this chapter's key themes related to language, literacy, and migration.

2 With regard to qualifying the two basic premises of superdiversity: many countries in the south have obviously experienced outflows of people, and this has led to possible reductions in diversity, and with the general principle being that the less mobile residents stay behind, the access to digital technologies also decreases. On the other hand, a country like South Africa experienced conquest by white migrants from the 1600s onwards, the importation of slaves and indentured labourers from east Asia, a brutal system of internal and forced migrant labour, continuing circular internal migration, substantial numbers of migrant workers from surrounding countries, and a recent surge of migrants and refugees from other African countries. Diversity (super or not) is thus not a particularly new nor necessarily intensified phenomenon. In addition, access to and use of digital technologies, apart from mobile phones which are the most used forms of access to the internet, are patchy and partial across southern Africa, and thus the wide range of expanded semiotic repertoires and resources that are discussed in many studies undertaken in northern countries just do not exist in large sections of society, where access to electricity cannot be taken for granted.
3 Letters, in the old-fashioned epistolary sense, exemplify such moving texts, and have been central to the experience of all types of migration for centuries, as have Bibles and Qur'ans.
4 With the work of the New London Group (1996) on "multiliteracies," the pluralisation of literacy then came to signal competence in using a range of modes of communication (like visual literacy, for example) thus losing to an extent the anthropological focus on specificity to domain of practice. This shift was echoed in the burgeoning field of work on multimodality, which raised the idea of the affordances of different modes of communication and the importance of viewing all communicative events as multimodal.

References

Arend, M. (2015). Taming tensions: Police docket production and the creation of trans-contextual stability in South Africa's criminal justice system. *Social Semiotics* 25(4): 501–516.

Bauman, R. (2004) *A World of Others' Words: Cross-cultural Perspectives on Intertextuality*. Malden and Oxford: Blackwells.

Bauman, R. and Briggs, C. (1990). Poetics and performance as critical perspectives on language and social life. *Annual Review of Anthropology* 19: 58–88.

Baynham, M. (1993). Code-switching and mode switching: Community interpreters and mediators of literacy. In Street, B. (ed) *Cross-cultural Approaches to Literacy* (pp. 294–314). Cambridge: Cambridge University Press.

Baynham, M. and Prinsloo, M., eds. (2013). *Literacy Studies*. London and New York: Sage.

Blommaert, J. (2001). Investigating narrative inequality: African asylum seekers' stories in Belgium. *Discourse and Society* 12(4): 413–449.

Blommaert, J. (2005). *Discourse*. Cambridge: Cambridge University Press.

Blommaert, J. (2007). Sociolinguistic scales. *Intercultural Pragmatics* 4(1): 1–19.

Blommaert, J. (2010). *The Sociolinguistics of Globalisation*. Cambridge: Cambridge University Press.

Blommaert, J. (2013). Writing as a sociolinguistic object. *Journal of Sociolinguistics* 17(4): 440–459.

Blommaert, J. (2014). *From Mobility to Complexity in Sociolinguistic Theory and Method*. Tilburg Papers in Culture Studies, Paper 103.

Blommaert, J. and Rampton, B. (2011). Language and superdiversity. *Diversities* 13(2): 1–21.

Bourdieu, P. and Wacquant, L. (2000). The organic ethnologist of Algerian migration. *Ethnography* 1(2): 173–182.

Braidotti, R. (2013). *The Post-human*. London: Polity Press.

Brandt, D. and Clinton, K. (2002). Limits of the local: Expanding perspectives on literacy as a social practice. *Journal of Literacy Research* 34(3): 337–356.

Budach, G., Kell, C. and Patrick, D. (2015). Objects and language in trans-contextual communication: Introduction to special issue. *Social Semiotics* 25(4): 387–400.

Canagarajah, S. (2013) *Literacy as Translingual Practice: Between Classrooms and Communities*. New York and London: Taylor and Francis.

Canagarajah, S. (2015) Negotiating mobile codes and literacies at the contact zone. In C. Stroud and M. Prinsloo (eds.), *Language, Literacy and Diversity: Moving Words*. New York and Abingdon: Routledge.

Collins, J. (2011). Literacy as social reproduction and social transformation: The challenge of diasporic communities in the contemporary period. *International Journal of Education and Development* 31(6): 614–622.

Collins, J. and Blot, R. (2003). *Literacy and Literacies*. Cambridge: Cambridge University Press.

Diminescu, D. (2008). The connected migrant: An epistemological manifesto. *Social Science Information* 47(4): 565–579.

Farr, M. (2006). *Rancheros in Chicagoacan: Language and Identity in a Transnational Community*. Austin: University of Texas Press.

Freebody, P. and Luke, A. (2003) Literacy as engaging with new forms of life: The "four roles" model. In G. Bull and M. Anstey (eds.), *The Literacy Lexicon* (pp. 52–57). Sydney: Prentice Hall.

Friedman, J. (2003). Globalizing languages. *American Anthropologist* 105: 744–752.

Goffman, E. (1972). *Relations in Public*. Harmondsworth: Penguin.

Gourlay, L. (2015). Post-human texts: Non-human actors, mediators and the digital university. *Social Semiotics* 25(4): 387–400.

Gumperz, J. (1977). Sociocultural knowledge as conversational inference. In M. Saville-Troike (ed.), *Linguistics and Anthropology, Georgetown University round Table on Languages and Linguistics 1977* (pp. 191–211). Washington, DC: Georgetown University Press.

Han, H. (2013). Individual grassroots multilingualism in Africa Town in Guangzhou: The role of states in globalization. *International Multilingualism Research Journal* 7(1): 83–97.

Heath, S. B. (1982) *Ways with Words: Language, Life and Work in Communities and Classrooms*. Cambridge: Cambridge University Press.

Hornberger, N. (1989). Continua of biliteracy. *Review of Educational Research* 59: 271–296.

Hornberger, N. and Link, H. (2012). Translanguaging and transnational literacies in multilingual classrooms: A biliteracy lens. *International Journal of Bilingual and Education and Bilingualism* 15(3): 261–278.

Iedema, R. (2001) Resemiotisation. *Semiotica* 137: 23–39.

Kell, C. (2009) Literacy practices, text/s and meaning making across time and space. In M. Prinsloo and M. Baynham (eds.), *The Future of Literacy Studies* (pp. 75–89). Basingstoke: Palgrave.

Kell, C. (2011) "Inequalities and crossings: Literacy and the spaces–in-between." *International Journal of Educational Development* 31: 301–663.

Kell, C. (2015a). Ariadne's thread: Literacy, scale and meaning making across space and time. In C. Stroud and M. Prinsloo (eds.), *Language, Literacy and Diversity: Moving Words* (pp. 72–91). London and New York: Routledge.

Kell, C. (2015b). "Making people happen": Materiality and movement in meaning making trajectories. *Social Semiotics* 25(4): 387–400.

Lam, E. and Warriner, D. (2012) Transnationalism and literacy: Investigating the mobility of people, languages, texts, and practices in contexts of migration. *Reading Research Quarterly* 47(2): 191–215.

Lam, W. and Rosario-Ramos, E. (2009). Multilingual literacies in transnational digitally mediated contexts: An exploratory study of immigrant teens in the US. *Language and Education* 23(2): 170–190.

Leander, K. and Boldt, G. (2012). Re-reading a pedagogy of multi-literacies: Bodies, texts and emergence. *Journal of Literacy Research* 41(1): 22–46.

Leander, K., Phillips, N. and Headrick Taylor, K. (2010). The changing social spaces of learning: Mapping new mobilities. *Review of Research in Education* 34, 324–394.

Levitt, P. and Glick Schiller, N. (2004) Conceptualising simultaneity: A transnational social fields perspective on society. In Alejandro Portes and Josh DeWind (eds.), *Rethinking Migration: New Theoretical and Empirical Perspectives* (pp. 181–218). New York: Centre for Migration Studies, Berghahn.

Mauss, M. (1990 [1925]) *The Gift: Form and Reason for Exchange in Archaic Societies*. London: Routledge.

McLean, C. (2010). A space called home: An immigrant adolescent's digital literacy practices. *Journal of Adult and Adolescent Literacy* 54(1): 13–22.

Moll, L., Amanti, C., Neff, D. and Gonzalez, N. (1992). Funds of knowledge for teaching: Using qualitative research to connect homes and schools. *Theory into Practice* 31: 132–141.

Nogueron-Liu, S. (2013). Access to technology in transnational social fields: Simultaneity and digital literacy socialization of adult immigrants. *International Multilingual Research Journal* 7(1): 33–48. [Special Issue on Experiences of simultaneity in complex linguistic ecologies: Implications for theory, methods and practice].

Pahl, K. and Rowsell, J. (2010). *Artefactual Literacies: Every Object Tells a Story.* New York and London: Teachers College Press.

Rampton, B. (2000). Speech community. In J. Verscheuren, O. Ostman, J. Blommaert and C. Bulcaen (eds.), *Handbook of Pragmatics* (pp. 1–34). Amsterdam: John Benjamins.

Richardson Bruna, K. (2007). Travelling tags: The informal literacies of Mexican newcomers in and out of the classroom. *Linguistics and Education* 18: 232–257.

Rockhill, K. (1993). Gender, language and the politics of literacy. In B. Street (ed) *Cross-cultural Approaches to Literacy* (pp. 294–314). Cambridge: Cambridge University Press.

Rounsaville, A. (2014). Situating transnational genre knowledge: A genre trajectory analysis of one student's personal and academic writing. *Written Communication* 31(3): 332–364.

Saxena, M. (1994). Literacies among Panjabis in Southall. In M. Hamilton, D. Barton and R. Ivanic (eds.), *Worlds of Literacy* (pp. 195–212). Clevedon and Toronto: Multilingual Matters and Ontario Institute for Studies in Education.

Sayad, A. (1991). *L'Immigration ou les Paradoxes de l'Alterite.* Brussels: Editions Universitaire-De Boeck.

Sayad, A. (1999). *La Double Absence: Des illusions de l'émigré aux souffrance de l'Immigre.* Paris: Edition du Seuil.

Silverstein, M. (1985). Language and the culture of gender. In E. Mertz and R. Parmentier (eds.), *Semiotic Mediation* (pp. 219–259). New York: Academic Press.

Silverstein, M. and Urban, G., eds. (1996) *Natural Histories of Discourse.* Chicago: University of Chicago Press.

Standing, G. (2011). *The Precariat: The New Dangerous Class.* London: Bloomsbury.

Steinberg, J. (2014). *A Man of Good Hope.* Johannesburg and Cape Town: Jonathan Ball.

Street, B. (1984). *Cross-cultural Approaches to Literacy.* Cambridge: Cambridge University Press.

Street, B. (2003) What's "new" in New Literacy Studies? Critical approaches to literacy in theory and practice. *Current Issues in Comparative Education* 5(2): 77–91.

Vertovec, S. (2007). Superdiversity and its implications. *Ethnic and Racial Studies* 30(6): 1024–1054.

Vieira, K. (2016). *American by Paper: How Documents Matter in Immigrant Literacy.* Minneapolis: University of Minnesota Press.

Warriner, D. (2007). Transnational literacies: Immigration, language learning and identity. Special Issue. *Linguistics and Education* 18.

Warriner, D. (2009). Transnational literacies: Examining global flows through the lens of literacy practice. In M. Baynham and M. Prinsloo (eds.), *The Future of Literacy Studies* (pp. 160–180). Basingstoke and New York: Palgrave Macmillan.

Warriner, D. and Leisy, W. (2013). Experiences of simultaneity in complex linguistic ecologies: Implications for theory, method and practice. *International Multilingual Research Journal* 7: 1–14.

Wyman, L. (2009). Youth, linguistic ecology, and language endangerment: A Yup'ik example. *Journal of Language, Identity and Education* 8(5), 335–349.

24
Intersections of necessity and desire in migration research
Queering the migration story

Mike Baynham

Vignette

It is late January I am in Paris, walking beside the Canal de Saint Martin with Rachid. We have just had lunch in his favourite cous cous restaurant, where I presented him with my translations of two of his books, autofictions based on his life as a boy growing up gay in Morocco. As we walk, he is searching on his iPhone for photos to show me of the Jardin Zoologique in his hometown Rabat. When at last he finds some there are some magnificent gum trees in the foreground. "Look" he says, pointing to one, "that is like the tree I used to swing on in my garden, the one I wrote about."

Rachid was born and brought up in Rabat, but moved to Paris as a young man. In this vignette, his commentary on the tree in the photo indexes simultaneously both his emotion attached to memories, regarding his home town, much loved family and early life and also the trajectory which brought him to Paris and his current life which has made him a writer. I am touched as a new friend that he is inviting me to share them.

Introduction

This chapter is both about the spatial twists and turns of such mobility and the intersecting role of necessity and desire in migration choices. It takes as a given, drawing on such work as Baynham and de Fina (2005), that migration can be understood in spatio/temporal terms as involving dislocations, re-locations, trajectories, and encounters. The basic argument of the chapter, however, is that while migration research in general and language migration research in particular have become very adept at identifying migration as necessity (and who would deny the brute economic and political facts that drive millions from their homes?), what is less well developed is the idea of migration as desire, the recognition that emotion and sexuality play a part in migration processes. Just in case that binary proves too stark, I will argue that economic and political necessity and desire are often inextricably, intersectionally caught up in each other.

There are thus three key concepts in the analysis: *necessity*, *desire*, and *intersectionality*. *Necessity* can be defined as that which is needed to sustain life, but I will shortly be arguing that this has to be defined rather broadly, to go beyond pure economic necessity and survival, to include emotional and sexual needs, the need to love and be loved, to comfort and feel comforted, to feel at home. *Desire* in relation to migration can be understood as what pulls the migrant forward in a new trajectory towards a new space but also what holds and binds him/her to what is left behind, the love of family and friends for example, love of home and homeland. This is the peculiar bind of migration. We see all these factors in the vignette which started this chapter. *Intersectionality*, a term introduced by Crenshaw (1991) and critically developed subsequently, for example in Nash (2008), considers the interconnections between dimensions of age, disability, gender, sexuality, race, and economic status in shaping and determining oppression, exclusion, unequal outcomes in social processes, and our case migration. Intersectionality has a particular commitment to bringing marginal and excluded voices into discussion (cf. Nash 2008). So in this chapter, I will be arguing that, while necessity and desire always interact intersectionally, the role of desire, particularly perhaps same-sex desire, in migration research is often the excluded or silenced other. There is now an increasing volume of research which aims to make visible and audible the role of queer desire in migration, for example Luibheid (2002), Manalansan (2006), Cantú (2009), Decena (2011), and Carrillo and Fontdevila (2014). Much of this research has a particular focus on borders, an important theme, though as this chapter will make clear, queer migrations don't stop at borders, or begin there.

Current issues and debates: migration as necessity and desire

In this chapter, I am going to conceptualize the migration process as involving on one level a series of encounters in space and time, often institutional but not always, driven by *necessity*. These start with the immigration process itself, or for refugees seeking asylum and gaining their status, then after settlement issues concerning housing, work, health, language learning, and education if they have children. Each of these encounters poses its own challenge, which can be mediated, as we see in other contributions to this volume, by professionals, volunteers, friends, and family members "on the network." These encounters, as Sabaté (2013) shows us, can extend to virtually every aspect of daily life, like getting a mobile phone contract. However I would argue that the idea of necessity should not be drawn too narrowly. The Moroccan psychiatrist and writer Tahar Ben Jelloun has written movingly in his *La Plus Haute des Solitudes*, based on cases of migrant workers from his clinic, of the sexual and emotional misery produced by their living conditions which treat them as workers, not as human beings (Ben Jelloun 1997). Emotional and sexual well-being is not an attractive add-on but a necessity for survival. This is what I mean by saying that necessity and desire intersect. Sexually driven mobility triggers or is triggered by economic needs.

Spatial trajectories of migration

> The early stages of settling for the most vulnerable migrants may mean multiple moves, perhaps through transit camps, reception centres, hostels or the streets, before arriving at a place with some security. Others, making use of family and other connections, may join earlier migrants in established areas of immigration that offer elements of familiarity, comfort and support and, for some, a microcosm of the life-world left behind.
> —Deborah Philips, *The Dynamics of Settlement*

These spatial trajectories, the absence of and search for different kinds of familiarity, support, and comfort, which Philips describes are a central construct in understanding the subjectivity of migration. I will now provide some examples of characteristic domains, spaces, and encounters of migration. I will be talking largely of cross-border migration, though there is of course within-border migration, country to city to consider. Travis Kong (2010) for example describes his research on sex workers in major cities of China. All the young men interviewed had migrated from the country to Beijing or Shanghai: "The respondents, like other rural migrants, had come to Beijing or Shanghai mainly for work, but also for independence and excitement" (Kong 2010: 22). Kong points here to this dual driver of necessity and desire, also very visible in the work of Mai and his colleagues on migration and sex work (Mai 2009, 2011; Mai and King 2009). Researchers such as de Fina have described painful and perilous journeys across borders to reach a place of settlement; in this chapter I will focus largely on the spatial trajectories of settlement, though I will start with a liminal process, that of applying for and gaining asylum, going on to consider language learning and institutional encounters as recurrent aspects of migration and settlement. Milani and Levon (forthcoming) consider issues of queer citizenship and multilingualism in the settlement process.

Asylum processes

The asylum process has been the subject of considerable research attention from sociologists, anthropologists, lawyers, and linguistic ethnographers. An example of this is *Rejecting Refugees* (Shuman and Boehmer 2004), a collaboration between a linguist and a lawyer. Maryns and Blommaert for example have looked at the process for those seeking asylum for political reasons in Belgium (Maryns 2006). In their work we see the centrality of narrative in the asylum seeking process. There is also a growing body of work on asylum based on sexual identity, as evidenced in the Stonewall report *No Going Back* (Miles 2009), the work from a legal perspective of Berg and Millbank (2009) and Millbank (2009a, 2009b). Papers in Murray (2015), for example Howe (2009) and Murray (2015) engage with the linguistic dimensions of the asylum process, its silencing and exclusions. Here A. describes his feelings of extreme isolation when he first applies for asylum as a gay man:

A: So I had my interview in Human Rights in Ankara, and that was really difficult. For me talking to you is been repeated ten times and the circumstances changed. So I'm not talking to you being scared, or thinking you're going to report me. But the first time when I talked to person talking about my problems, she said do you want an interpreter. I said no I couldn't risk to have an interpreter because he could be someone I couldn't trust to begin with. It means he has an Iranian background. Waiting in that queue, going to that . . . UNHCR I met some people in that queue. Even the criminal ones they did some stuff, they were so proud. Easily could talk about their cases. We had some people from different political groups. They could about what was their reason, but I had to hide it, what is my reason, being gay. So we had some people converted their religion to Christianity. They came with their own group, so everyone there they were talking to each other and for me it was just stay there, hang in there.
INTERVIEWER: So there were no other gay asylum seekers that you knew?
A: I didn't know that.

(Unpublished interview data)

This research is often based on an interview, however as Maryns (2006) shows, the story told in an interview is not sufficient to gain a deep understanding of the process. Participant observation and at least audio recordings of the process, meetings with lawyers and hearings, documentation relating to the process are required, which we find in the research reported in Murray (2015). This is an important methodological point to which we shall return, with reference to the study of queer Latino diasporas carried out by Cashman (2015).

Learning a new language

Language learning may be another challenging encounter for new and not so new migrants and the field has been reviewed extensively in Simpson and Whiteside (2015). Language learning for migrants is often construed in a narrow and functional way, more recently, under the influence of neoliberal policy, constrained as language for employment. As mentioned earlier Ben Jelloun is an early pointer to the dangers and distortions inherent in viewing migrants as economic ciphers. Methodologies such as Reflect (cf. Cooke and Simpson 2008) dispute the narrow functionalism of many language teaching approaches and open up a wider gamut of themes and topics. Norton (2013) and others such as Relaño Pastor (2014) have shown how identity is crucial the language learning situation of migrants and from a slightly different theoretical perspective, with an emphasis on subjectivity and subject production, so has Kramsch (2009). The approach described here is very much in line with the work on subjectivity and language learning of Kramsch and others. Recent research developments, such as the Queering ESOL seminar series (queeringesol.wordpress.com), have emphasized, following the pioneering work of Nelson (2009), the characteristic exclusion of LGBTIQ experience and voices from language classes.

Facing inequality and exclusion

Detailed linguistic ethnographies, and here I am thinking of researchers such as Vigouroux (2013) and Sabaté (2014), have pointed us to the complex negotiations of everyday life and institutional encounters in contexts of inequality and exclusion. Roberts and Campbell (2005), Campbell and Roberts (2007), and Heath and Cheung (2006) describe discrimination faced by migrants in job interviews. Sabaté (2013) describes the difficulties faced by a Romanian migrant in Barcelona in obtaining a mobile phone contract:

> Nicolae explains that he managed to get a contract by showing his passport and his European residency permit. . . . When I am about to change the topic, though, he brings it to my attention that informally and non-officially, the largest multinational operating in Spain will not accept these two proofs of legal status . . . – an idea which is repeated twice. . . . The only document that Movistar (formerly Telefónica), accepts, he states, is the Spanish ID card, the "DNI."
>
> *(p. 257)*

Perspectives on migration, institutional inequality, and exclusion can be found in Duchene, Moyer, and Roberts (2013).

Sabaté's ethnographic snippet evokes something we have found characteristic in current research on Czech Roma in Leeds (Baynham et al. 2015). Migrant workers in the precarious low-pay sector, like other low-paid workers, are operating in an uncertain employment landscape of agency work, hourly paid at minimum rates, zero-hour contracts, and are often crossing over into the zone of benefits claiming. To claim these benefits it is necessary to have the kind of document trail Nicolae describes. In our observations of advice sessions with advocates and community interpreters we observed and recorded interpreting events involving multilingual translanguaging in Czech/Slovak and English. Clients would typically come to their appointments with a bag or folder containing the necessary documentation to support their claim. If marginalization and exclusion is the commonplace of migrant experience, then arguably the LGBTIQ migrant is facing a double exclusion, their sexuality placing them on the margins of the margin. This double exclusion is something that Mole (forthcoming) has investigated in his work on queer Russian migrants in Berlin. There is also a double exclusion at work as A. waits for his asylum case to be heard in Ankara.

Current directions: researching emotion, affect, and subjectivity in the migration process

In the previous sections I have tried to outline some of the necessity driven encounters that are characteristic of the early and later stages of migration, reviewing research that has been conducted and the methodologies used. While the focus has been on necessity I have also emphasized the issues of identity, subjectivity, and desire and the need for a broader focus of attention both at the level of policy and research than the neoliberal emphasis on the purely functional and work related. Now I will move on to a more detailed review of the role of emotion, subjectivity, and desire in the migration process, picking up on an argument made by Mai (2009) and Mai and King (2009).

> We see the narratives, practices and understanding of love and sexuality as two under-researched dimensions informing people's experiences of mobility, belonging, and individual and collective identities. Love, whether it is for a partner, lover or friend, for a child, parents or other kin, is so often a key factor in the desire and the decision to move to a place where one's feelings, ambitions and expectations – emotional, sexual, political, economic, hedonistic etc. – can be lived more fully and freely. . . . Like love, and sometimes alongside it, sex can play a decisive role in the imagination and enactment of the choice to migrate.
>
> *(Mai and King 2009: 296)*

I will also consider some of the methodologies available for researching affective and emotional aspects of migration. Mai (2011) and elsewhere examines the vulnerability but also the resilience and agency of minors and young adults migrants selling sex in the cities of Western Europe. There is also relevant work in cultural geography. Ingram and others have developed the concept of queer spaces; Ingram has researched queer spaces used by migrant workers in Dubai, men on their own, far from their families for months, even years at a time:

> Dubai's Open Beach is one of the larger and more visible public sites in the Middle East for homosexual males to meet and sometimes to have sex on-site – and its social fabric was largely formed through the current period of intensifying globalization.
>
> *(Ingram 2007, p. 3)*

These men do not fit into the neat categories:

> The sexual cultures of the thousands of homosexual males who connect through the Open Beach often challenge many of the concepts that have emerged under queer theory. Few of these men identify as "queer," "gay" or "bisexual" and give little thoughts

to semantic arguments around terms such as "men who have sex with men." Most men are busy making money that they send back to often female-oriented and largely women-headed household. And the culture of the Open Beach is decidedly transnational and multicultural rather than centred on Arab experiences. Instead, the texture of the male homosexual scene in Dubai is rooted in Arab, Persian, and South Asian trading cultures with a veneer of westernization from a century and a half of British domination.

(Ingram 2007, pp. 3–4)

Ingram is here pointing to an invisible and invisibilized dimension of migration, that of sexual need. Arguably in migration studies there has been a heteronormative assumption about migration processes.

Beyond a heteronormative frame for understanding migration

One of the characteristics I identified in my own research on several migrant narratives was the heroic myth of male migration (Baynham 2006). In this extract Mustafa, who I interviewed for my doctoral research several decades ago, talks about the Moroccan migration:

> the head of the family works for a while sends the money to the family and the family arrives to london mostly to in a just a small room the husband sometimes has to go and work during the day he has got nobody to inform him the even if there was any leaflets in arabic or anything they could not read it most of them so they rely on word of mouth mostly and they try to get together it was very difficult for them but they did have a couple of cafes in the west end they were run by algerians and they used to get there and they used to get together and drink coffee and talk about various things that they can help them like for instance how do they communicate with their relatives back in morocco how do they how can they send money back home erm what immigration what the home office think about the various things what er if there is any hassle of bringing families what is the cheapest fare etc.

(Baynham and de Fina 2005, pp. 16–17)

Although I wasn't thinking along these lines at the time, this myth is also heteronormative in that it assumes the experience if the heterosexual *père de famille* as the norm and elides and erases the experiences of other migrants other migrations, single people, male and female, and children. Ingram's research is pointing to something different, to the emotional and sexual accommodations made by male single migrants far from their families.

Beyond the heteronormative, untold migration stories

I'd like therefore to introduce another kind of story. This is of a young out gay man whom I shall call Antonio, born and brought up in a village in Andalucía. When getting to know him, I asked him when he first became aware of his attraction to men. (I find this is always an interesting question because the answers are so different.) He told me how in his village in the late '80s and early '90s when he was growing up, many of the men in the village had gone to work as guest workers in Germany. For him the dads in the village divided into the exciting dads who went to Germany and came back each summer fit, their muscles toned on the building sites and in the factories, and the boring old dads who stayed at home. His own dad was a boring stay-at-home dad while his best friend Luis had an exciting dad who worked in Germany. One day he was round at Luis's house watching TV while Luis's dad was having a wash down naked in a tub in the inner patio. The young Antonio somehow found himself straying out to the doorway and he stood watching in the shadows as this handsome hunk of a man, his friend's dad, soaped himself in the sunlight. And that was when Antonio knew . . .

When he grew up Antonio himself felt that pull North and spent an Erasmus year in Denmark. Almost all his significant relationships with men had been with those from northern countries. I have lost contact with him now, but I know that once he finished university he was planning to move north and wanted his life to be in the north. And so I imagine him sometimes in Copenhagen or Amsterdam or London. And the point is that along with all the many things he is hoping for in his life, one of the things he will be looking for there is love.

So why this story? On one hand because it is a window into the elided and erased experiences of migration which I started talking about, first of a gay man who is intending to migrate, but also from the perspective of someone, a child, who was left behind or felt his family to be left behind in a migration process yet was deeply influenced and shaped by it. Second, there is an angle of migration driven by desire not simply by the necessity of economic imperatives. I don't want to underplay here the significance of the push-pull of economic factors, of sharp global inequalities, of economic and social precarity, but I also want to suggest that there is a more complex and nuanced picture and one of the strands of this may be desire. In a sense the theme of this chapter is precisely to investigate and contribute to making visible the erased and eluded experiences of migrants, LGBTIQ and others, but also to relate this to a broader theoretical agenda of how we might conceptualise migration more generally. This could be taken as a move to queer migration studies, if we understand queer as a category that affects all others including the heterosexual. As Tennessee Williams put it: "What is straight? A line can be straight or a street. But the human heart? Oh no, it's curved like a road through mountains." It is for this reason that I conceptualized the spaces of migration as involving twists and turns. Along with the push-pull of economic factors, it tugs at the heart.

This is not a one-size-fits-all approach. In the intersection between necessity and desire, sometimes it is indeed the economic imperative of necessity and precarity that drives. For José, a young gay man interviewed recently in London, his move to the UK was entirely driven by the economic crisis and work and study opportunities. He had done his coming out in Spain and migrated south to Malaga, a city he found more congenial than Madrid or London:

JOSÉ: No, to be honest I don't like this city. I was crying before I came here. My last three days in Spain I was crying. Not because of my family. For me the main reason to choose a place to live is the weather and this is not the best place. I don't like Madrid as well. I don't like these cities.
INTERVIEWER: You like the South?
JOSÉ: Yes, more like Malaga. I hate Madrid, I don't like London. I don't like big cities, because I am spending a lot of time in [unintelligible]. And if I want to visit my friends, they live one hour away or more than one hour from me. So, now I'm alone at home and this weekend I'm speaking to my friends. Now I have to work, we can meet in the town centre. And from this I feel a bit lazy maybe, but in Malaga I wasn't like that. I liked to spend every moment with my friends, to go for a walk through the promenade, many things. I lived fifteen-twenty minutes from my friends, from my work, everything. So for me this is the quality of life.

(unpublished interview data)

However once here for economic and study opportunity reasons the game changes again. He meets his boyfriend and his reasons for staying get re-sorted:

INTERVIEWER: Anyway so let's think about your reason for coming to England was to learn English.
JOSÉ: Well . . . I think so. Because my first intention was to stay here only till last June or April. But everything changed. I met my boyfriend here. I felt quite well with my friends, with my job, with my quality of life, I don't like the weather. Like I thought I don't have too many alternatives. If I lived in Malaga, I am not going to get any job, good job. And my life, the most my future was going to be was poor, without expectations . . .
INTERVIEWER: Opportunities.
JOSÉ: Opportunities. So, if I had to choose between London and Madrid, at this moment I prefer London. I have more opportunities, and well, a decision between both my boyfriend and me.

(unpublished interview data)

Life twists and turns. For both Jose and Antonio coming out and living as gay men in Spain was an option. In contrast Jose was led to migrate purely by economic factors, the crisis, while for Antonio the drive was emotional and sexual.

Migration and desire in the heterosexual life world

Of course as I suggested above such desire driven motives to migrate are also to be found in the heterosexual lifeworld (as if indeed, as I suggested earlier, the queer as a category can't encompass those who self-identify as heterosexual), particularly but not exclusively among the young and unattached. M.'s migration in the late 1960s was not, or apparently not, driven by economic necessity, but more inspired by the desire to see life and broaden his experience, a young man going out into the world with a picaresque motivation. He is driven by images, movies and TV programs, a theme that is evocatively repeated in the autobiographical accounts of Taïa and Rachid O. In his autofiction *Chocolat Chaud*, Rachid describes how as a child he is drawn to Europe by the glamour of advertisements glimpsed in shop windows, which becomes linked for him with an obsession with a French boy Noah and through him France:

> I often used to stop, glued, in front of Hitachi. There were loads of TVs on display in the window and I didn't have a single one at home. I looked at them, skipping from image to image on all the screens. The very first times I didn't dare get close, thinking you had to pay to look and I didn't have any pocket money on me. I quickly came to understand that it was free and it became a habit for me to mingle with the boys and men, slipping between their bodies to be as close as possible to the screens. My reflection in the shop window also allowed me to arrange my curly hair which my Lalla spent her time combing into a parting which was hard to guess at. It drove me crazy.
> . . .
> Those images that I spent my time looking at at the Hitachi shop during my comings and goings between home and school only provoked in me a desire which grew and linked me to Noah. France, the word and the language had a pleasant ring to me. I transferred my fixation about all that onto Noah's photo. I began to miss him to an extent that was becoming physical, all I waited for was that photo and my Lalla's stories, but

painful as it was, I preferred to live in the proximity of that lack which grew in me. It was my life and through it I learned how to grow.
(Chocolat Chaud, Rachid O., translation Mike Baynham)

M. also talks about a desire triggered by movies. "I wanted to see more of the what I have seen in the films you know sort of the high life." He contrasts this with the purely necessity driven economic migrants:

M: they were just here to make money you know
I: yeah
M: while I wanted to see more of the what I have seen in the films you know sort of the high life you know so to speak you know
I: is there a lot of high life in Buckinghamshire?

The interviewer's facetious question triggers a narrative about a girlfriend inviting him home to meet her parents, given a humorous twist being his obvious terror about meeting his girlfriend's father. The end of the narrative shows him moving on to another place and another job and the relationship coming to an end.

M: (LAUGHS) well er mm n really I did meet a girl there in in Buckinghamshire and then she was erm sixteen and that's a funny story about it
I: yeah
M: I was nineteen then and er she wanted me to take er to come with her home to meet her father and mother and I wouldn't go the I wouldn't do that noooh what do you want him to kill me or what you know that's what my reaction you know
I: yeah
M: because in Morocco that would be the same thing and eventually she persuaded me to come to the her house and they offered me tea and they tried to communicate with me well I I began by then to communicate but not really erm I would say I could get by
I: mm
M: in asking for things but not really expressing fully you know
I: yeah
M: what my feelings or anything and erm but she was young and er we stayed together and she showed me around etcetera etcetera but when I moved to Hertfordshire you know [. . .] she was young mentally and she wrote a letter like erm you know I don't love you any more and all that (LAUGHS)
I: yeah
M: you know that childish thing you know well it was erm I began to feel different you know about life er I was really maturing because I I had to work for myself
I: which I had never done before in Morocco and also mm er most of Moroccans who were with me were older than me you know

This is a narrative about change, experience and maturity. We can see here the bringing in of a kind of bildungsroman theme, working alongside the episodic, picaresque sequence of events that M. recounts. M. moves on, leaving a childish phase behind. He is maturing, having to work for himself although not for others in the pattern of the economic chain migration. M. is a free spirit ready to take a chance and go where the work is, trusting to his luck.

M. articulates clearly the picaresque structure of his life as an unattached young migrant. The structure has similarities with the young migrant sex workers in the research of Mai or

Kong. He moves up to London with little or no money, hanging out in the amusement arcades, apparently not worried till he is told in the employment agency that there is no job today:

M: that's right and I missed her and I came back to London I I mean I came back to Hertfordshire and they said you the job is gone and er so I came to London and I had virtually no money
I: yeah
M: very little money but I wasn't really concerned because I still went to the one armed bandit mm playing you know I didn't
I: yeah
M: then when I began to feel it is that when I'm went to the agency and they told me there was er no job today come back tomorrow

Another significant theme in M.'s narrative, in his self-portrayal, is his *exceptionality*. We have already seen this in the contrast he sets up between his picaresque, pleasure-seeking attitude to the high life and those of the other economically motivated Moroccan migrants, working for their families. This contrast comes out again here in relation to his initiative in challenging the employment agency ("I wasn't going to have that you know"). In an extended gloss M. contrasts his own go-getting approach to that of the other Moroccan migrants, reliant on the chain or network of contacts which is a means of introducing the newly arrived migrant to opportunities for work and accommodation.

I: yeah
M: and I wasn't going to have that you know I just er 'cos I remembered I used to work with a Spanish in Stowe School who said to me he was going to *the* London Hospital to work and I said why don't you go to *the* London Hospital now I think if there was say any Moroccan the ordinary Moroccans then he would possibly wouldn't be able to go to er go to an agency by then if he was not taken by another Moroccan who already lives in London you know
I: yeah
M: so and I had at that particular time I had nobody
M: and um so you know I was just looking for a job and I went to the London Hospital and er when I went (got) to the London hospital they accepted me and if I met Moroccans there I stayed with them
I: mm
M: for a while there

M. now goes on to gloss his story with an evaluative commentary, comparing his reliance on chance and luck as the organizing principle in his life with the planned approach which he implies is the English way of doing things. He articulates his approach to life through a series of striking phrases and similes: "whatever happened happened you know [Che sara sara].... I just let myself go it's like a leaf in the wind.... I don't say well today I'll do this and tomorrow I'll do this this money is for today that money is tomorrow." M. is here using the resources of narrative for self-disclosure, disclosing himself as the opposite as a careful planner, driven like a leaf in the wind by chance and circumstance.

M: and this is it's a chain events you know which um if a an Englishman was doing the same thing he would have planned his way
I: mm

M: well I didn't you know it just whatever happened happened you know it's you know
I: you fell into it sort of thing
M: yes I just let myself go it's like a a leaf in the wind you know yeah I don't um don't say well today I'll do this and tomorrow I'll do this this money is for today that money is for tomorrow this you know. . . .

Tugs of the heart: queer migrations

To return to the vignette with which I started this chapter, Rachid is a gay Moroccan writer who chronicled his growing up gay in Morocco in a series of autofictions which draw very closely on his life. The tree in the photo makes visible the tree in his childhood garden in the book I have just translated. Though his trajectory as a gay man and certain identifications have taken him from Morocco to Paris where he has made his life, he returns very year to spend time with his family with whom he is very close, so there is also an emotional pull back to Morocco. These are what I am calling tugs of the heart, which pull in different directions, often in conflict. When his first piece of autofiction appeared in a French magazine, for example, he brought it home proudly to show his family and his former teacher, with whom he had a protracted love affair in his early teens. Rachid is subject to all the encounters and challenges of daily life discussed above, but there is also a thread of emotional identification and affect which draws him to settle and live in Paris. It is this that I want to focus on.

The themes of Rachid's autofictions are echoed in the work of another gay Moroccan writer who has settled in France and writes in French, Abdellah Taïa. Here in his autofiction *Salvation Army,* he describes his feelings on arrival in Geneva, having left Morocco to study in Switzerland, supported and encouraged by his older Swiss lover.

> As the minutes passed, this feeling of happiness (or something just like it) started to come over me. I was in Europe! In Switzerland! And just that thought, the realization that here I was on foreign soil, someplace that wasn't Morocco, that alone was enough to sustain my upbeat mood, keep me as happy as a child on a visit to the *hammam* with his mother, as delighted and amazed as some country boy who finds himself in the city for the first time.
> *(Taïa 2009: 112)*

The freespiritedness we noted in M.'s picaresque narrative above, is echoed in *Salvation Army*, for example when the young Abdellah describes himself making impromptu love with two chance met travelling companions, from Germany and Poland, in the shared carriage of a night train crossing Spain, this leading to an unscheduled stopover in Madrid. Once in Geneva a turn in his fortunes brings him to stay in the Salvation Army hostel which gives the book its title. The picaresque trope is again alive and well here.

Back in Morocco, Taïa captures, as does Taher Ben Jelloun in his novel *Partir*, the aspiration towards migration of young Moroccans, economically driven yes, but also by something else, a pull, an attraction, a glamour. Taïa portrays Mohamed a strikingly handsome young man who provides sex services for European tourists. Mohamed's dream at first is of catching a Western woman:

Tangiers. January 1997

His name was Mohamed. And, like so many others he dreamt about leaving Morocco someday, for France, Spain, Germany, it didn't matter where, but his wildest dream was about going to the United States. He knew what he had to do, had even come up with a plan, a simple one, simple but effective: seduce a Western woman, offer himself to her, show her what a Moroccan man was capable of . . .

(Taïa 2009: 97)

Mohamed however doesn't have much luck with his dream of a Western woman, and he learns to make do with men.

Yes, it was a fact, men were nicer, less complicated, more playful, more generous they would spend money on you without counting every penny, spending more than they even had. It was that simple, really. Men came as a total surprise to him. They never interested him sexually before, but everything happens in its own good time, doesn't it? He played on their team now, had turned homosexual, but make no mistakes, only with foreigners. He'd never sleep with another Moroccan. Even the idea of being mistaken for a zamel in Tangiers filled him with horror. Besides he was no zamel, no way. It was women he found interesting, women who turned him on, and thanks to women, he still hoped to find a way out of this miserable country some day soon.

(Taïa 2009: 98–99)

In this extract, Mohamed gives voice to his adaptive sexuality, his dreams of leaving (*Partir*) while taking care not to leave go of his claim to heterosexuality and interest in women, still retained as his dreamed of passport out of Morocco into a wider world. This is a similar balancing act with their masculinity that Mai identifies in the life situation of his male migrant sex workers. While adapting to a world of sex with men, they dream of making it, closing that page of their life definitively and returning to heterosexuality. What we get in this portrait is a complex intersectional mix of aspiration and desire, desire to escape from unfavourable economic conditions combined with the excitement of the new.

Researching the affectual, emotional, and sexual dimensions of migration

So what are the methodologies available for researching the affectual, emotional and sexual dimensions of migration identified earlier? In all the studies we have examined so far the open-ended ethnographic interview has been a key methodological device. I have been doing extended ethnographic interviewing for the whole of my research career; however, interviews with a focus on sexuality are relatively new to me. Such interviews are challenging and can be charged. José for example, when I had interviewed him had been the focus of a homophobic incident in his English class the week before. A. had got over his initial humiliation around repeatedly disclosing his sexuality to strangers as part of the asylum process. What we were doing in the interview was somehow routinized, but still emotionally charged, and there were at times tears. This kind of interviewing highlights ethical issues such as protection from harm as the interview itself can bring back painful memories. The work of Mai shows the place for extended participant observation, which is vividly recreated in his ethnographic film *Samira*. But I have also shown how literary sources, for example the autofictions of Rachid O. and Abdellah Taïa, are invaluable ways of understanding the subjectivities that drive migration and the complex intersectionality between poverty, economic necessity, and desire.

There is an increasing tendency to turn to other ways of communicating this complex intersectionality: fiction, film, artworks, installations, performances. This is part of an increasing emphasis on communicating the findings of research to wider audiences than other academics through performance. Cynthia Nelson for example has turned her interview driven study of LGBTIQ teachers and students in ESOL classes (Nelson 2009) into a documentary drama, drawing on the material collected in her interviews. Here Pablo from Mexico, an ESL student in the United States, talks about the role his sexuality plays in his decision to migrate.

PABLO: I've been gay forever. Since I was (*gestures a child's height*). I never had a partner. Since I felt I was gay, I wanted good grades. To make my parents proud of me. Of course I want to meet somebody. To go to restaurant, to study together, to share, to watch TV. But what if I go out to meet somebody, and I meet the murder guy? Can you imagine what my family will feel? "Our son was gay, we never knew, and now he's dead!" They will go crazy. So I come to this country. To see what I feel, how I change.

(Nelson 2010: 37)

Mai has turned his research projects on migration and sex work into a series of ethnographic films, *Normal* and *Samira*. Based on his anthropological research, the film *Normal* examines the relationship between migration, the sex industry, and sex trafficking. The film starts with an extract from the tentative, downplayed beginning of an interview portrayed with a twenty-four-year-old Romanian sex worker:

A: How are you?
B: Ok
A: Did you have a nice week?
B: It was ok
A: How's business? How's work?
B: Normal

Normal. The normal of the title.

> *Normal* is a 65 minute creative documentary based on original anthropological research on the relationship between migration, the sex industry and sex trafficking. The film that brings the real life stories of male, female and transgender migrants working in the sex industry to the screen. It draws on original research interviews with people working in the sex industry in Albania, Italy and the UK.
> Their voices often go against the grain of popular expectations that most migrant sex workers are exploited and forced to sell sex against their will. Confronting these attitudes, *Normal* uncovers a layered, human story of migration and sex work. *Normal* is made of unexpected, disturbing, sometimes moving and often contradictory life stories. The viewer is continually challenged by the truth of their words, their dreams and the lives that they lead. All the characters are portrayed by actors, guaranteeing the anonymity and safety of the original interviewees and emphasizing the inherently performative nature of selves.
> *(http://queersexwork.net/2012/11/29/normal-a-film-by-nick-mai-4/)*

Samira tells the story of Karim, a transgender Algerian sex worker in Marseille. His/her well-developed transition leads to a successful asylum application. However a turn of fortune, following the death of Karim/Samira's father, leads her/him to transition back, having her/his breasts removed surgically, and return to Algeria to take up the role of head of the family.

All of these last examples, from Nelson's docudrama and Mai's ethnographic films, show how multidimensional issues of migration can be presented in a range of innovative media as performance, moving away from the conventional format of the research paper. All these artworks are informed by ethnographic fieldwork and interview data. I have also shown how the autofictions of Abdellah Taïa and Rachid O. resonate with many of the issues described.

Implications

This chapter has been informed by two interrelated arguments and their methodological implications. First I have argued for the intersecting relevance of both necessity and desire to understand migration processes, suggesting as have others, that while migration studies has a track record in analyzing and documenting the economic and political factors that drive migration processes, aspects of subjectivity, emotion, desire, and sexuality have, with certain distinguished exceptions such as Ben Jelloun, been less examined, airbrushed out even. I would want to argue for the complex intersectionality of these impulses. M. refers rather slightingly to the ordinary Moroccans only in London for economic reasons. I have no doubt that the "ordinary" economic migrant, the sort that might stray onto Ingram's Open Beach late one evening hoping to meet someone, is also pursuing a complex of emotional and sexual needs, searching in many spatial twists and turns for comfort that is political, economic, emotional, sexual. The lack of these and the consequent desolation that follows is the point made so tellingly by Taher Ben Jelloun so many years ago. The focus may have shifted to the single migrant workers in the Emirates, making do emotionally and sexually, or to other more recently groups rather than North Africans in France in the 1970s, but the issues remain the same. So rather than treating necessity and desire as disconnected, they must be treated holistically, intersectionally, as integral parts of the dynamic of migration.

The second argument is methodological and concerns how subjectivity, emotion, and sexuality can be investigated. I have shown in the preceding examples the power of ethnographic method, participant observation, and open-ended interviews in working with hard-to-reach groups, in precarious or illegal situations. I have also shown how literary works such as autofiction and docudrama can illuminate such issues. Ethnographic film can be a way of representing and disseminating the findings of research, going beyond the charmed circle of academic publications to reach a wider audience.

Future directions

It is clear that we are seeing a turn towards performance in the dissemination of research (Nelson 2015). However it should be noted that linguistically oriented research into subjectivity and desire in migration is itself only now emerging, evidenced for example in Murray's 2015 theme issue. Much of the research cited here has been from anthropologists, cultural geographers, sociologists. A notable exception is the work of Cashman, who has undertaken a linguistic ethnography of the queer Latina/o diaspora in Phoenix, Arizona. I have shown in this chapter that there are many valuable lessons to be learned from other social and human sciences as indeed from literary sources, but there is a need for more detailed empirical studies using methodologies such as linguistic ethnography, to discover more about the part that language plays in these processes. I hope this chapter will encourage readers involved in research on migration, to consider these areas of affect, desire, and sexuality in their research.

Related topics

Social class in migration, identity, and language research
New orientations to identity in mobility
Narrative in the study of migrants
Multisited ethnography and language in the study of migration

Further reading

Carrillo, H. and Fontdevila, J. (2014). Border crossings and shifting sexualities among Mexican gay immigrant men: Beyond monolithic conceptions. *Sexualities*, *17*(8), 919–938.

This paper, using an interview methodology, looks at shifting attitudes toward sexuality among Mexican gay men who have migrated to the United States.

Cashman, Holly R. (2015). Intersecting communities, interwoven identities: Questioning boundaries, testing bridges, and forging a Queer Latinadad in the US Southwest. *Language and Intercultural Communication*, *15*(3), 424–440.

Draws upon the author's linguistic ethnography of the queer Latina/o community in Phoenix, Arizona. The paper discusses the situation of queer, undocumented young Latinas/os, the so-called Dreamers.

Ingram, G.B. (2007). Globalizing homosexual and male guest worker identities: The strategic role of Dubai's Open Beach. Retrieved from http://gordonbrentingram.ca/scholarship/wp-content/uploads/2010/04/ingram-2007-dubais-open-beach1.pdf

A cultural geographic study of the Open Beach in Dubai as a queer public space.

Kong, T. (2010). Outcast Bodies: money, sex and desire of money boys in mainland China. In Yau Ching (ed.), *As Normal as Possible, Negotiating Sexuality and Gender in Mainland China and Hong Kong*. Hong Kong: University of Hong Kong Press.

This chapter illustrates the intersection of necessity and desire in the internal migration of young men who become sex workers in the great cities of China.

Mai, N. and King, R. (2009). Love, sexuality and migration: Mapping the issues. *Mobilities*, *4*(3)

This is a formulation of the key argument of this chapter, that the dimensions of affect and desire and sexuality are relatively underplayed in relation to economic and political drivers from migration. The discussion is illustrated with examples from the authors' research on migration and sex work.

Mole, R.C.M. (2017). *"Identity, belonging and solidarity in the Russian-speaking queer diaspora" in his Soviet and Post-Soviet Sexualities*. Abingdon: Routledge (forthcoming).

A sociological study of Russian LGBT migrants in Berlin which examines how they maintain a sense of Russian ethnic community by creating queer Russian spaces outside of the pre-existing Russian diasporic ethnoscape.

Murray, D.A.B., ed. (2015). Introduction to special issue: Queering borders language, sexuality and migration. *Journal of Language and Sexuality*, *3*(1), 1–5.

Like Cashman's work, this collection makes a focus on the language aspects of queer migrations, including asylum seekers and undocumented migrants.

References

Baynham, M. (2006). Performing self, family and community in Moroccan narratives of migration and settlement. In A. de Fina, D. Schiffrin and M. Bamberg (eds.), *Discourse and Identity* (pp. 376–397). Cambridge: Cambridge University Press.

Baynham, M. and de Fina, A. (2005). *Dislocations/Relocations: Narratives of Displacement*. Manchester: St Jerome.

Baynham, M., Bradley, J., Callaghan, J., Hanusova, J., and Simpson, J. (2015). Translanguaging business: Unpredictability and precarity in superdiverse inner city Leeds. Working Paper No. 4, Translation and Translanguaging Project (2014–2018) (AHRC).

Ben Jelloun, T. (1997). *La Plus Haute des Solitudes: Misère Affective et Sexuelle d'émigrés Nord-africains*. Paris: Editions du Seuil.

Ben Jelloun, T. (2006). *Partir*. Paris: Gallimard.

Berg, L.A. and Millbank, J. (2009). Constructing the personal narratives of lesbian, gay and bisexual asylum claimants. *Journal of Refugee Studies* 22(2): 195–223.

Campbell, S. and Roberts, C. (2007). Migration, ethnicity and competing discourses in the job interview: Synthesizing the institutional and the personal. *Discourse and Society* 18(3): 243–271.

Cantú, L. (2009). *The Sexuality of Migration: Border Crossings and Mexican Immigrant Men*. New York: New York University Press.

Carrillo, H. & Fontdevila, J. (2014). Border Crossings and Shifting Sexualities among Gay Mexican Migrant Men: beyond monolithic conceptions. *Sexualities* 17(8): 919–938.

Cashman, Holly R. (2015). Queer Latina/o networks in the city: Languages, identities and the ties that bind. In Rosina Márquez Reiter and Luisa Martín Rojo (eds.), *A Sociolinguistics of Diaspora: Latino Practices, Identities and Ideologies* (pp. 66–80). London and New York: Routledge.

Cooke, M. and Simpson, J. (2008). *ESOL: A Critical Guide*. Oxford Handbooks for Language Teachers, Oxford: Oxford University Press.

Crenshaw, K. (1991). Mapping the margins: Intersectionality, identity politics and violence against women of color. *Stanford Law Review* 43(6), 1241–1299.

Decena, C. (2011). *Tacit Subjects: Belonging and Same-sex Desire among Dominican Immigrant Men*. Durham: Duke University Press.

Duchêne, A., Moyer, M. and Roberts, C., eds. (2013). *Language, Migration and Social Inequalities*. Bristol: Multilingual Matters.

Heath, A. and Cheung, S.Y. (2006). *Ethnic Penalties in the Labour Market. Employers and Discrimination*. DWP Report No. 341 Department for Work & Pensions, Sheffield.

Howe, C. (2009) Sexual adjudications and queer transpositions. In D.A.B. Murray (ed.) (pp. 136–155).

Kong, T.S.K. (2010). Outcast Bodies: Money, sex and desire of money boys in Mainland China. In Yau Ching (ed.), *As Normal as Possible: Negotiating Sexuality and Gender in Mainland China and Hong Kong* (pp. 15–35). Hong Kong: Hong Kong University Press.

Kramsch, C. (2009). *The Multilingual Subject*. Oxford: Oxford University Press.

Luibhéid, E. (2002). *Entry Denied: Controlling Sexuality at the Border*. Minneapolis: University of Minnesota Press.

Mai, N. (2009). Between minor and errant mobility: The relation between the psychological dynamics and the migration patterns of young men selling sex in the EU. *Mobilities* 4(3): 349–366.

Mai, N. (2011). Tampering with the sex of "Angels": Migrant male minors and young adults selling sex in the EU. *Journal of Ethnic and Migration Studies* 37(8): 1237–1252.

Mai, N. and King, R. (2009). Love, sexuality and migration: Mapping the issue(s). *Mobilities* 4(3): 295–307.

Manalansan IV, M.F. (2006). Queer intersections: Sexuality and gender in migration studies. *International Migration Review* 40(1): 224–249.

Maryns, K. (2006). *The Asylum Speaker: Language in the Belgian Asylum Process*. Manchester: St Jerome.

Milani, T. and Levon, E. (forthcoming). Queering multilingualism and politics: Regimes of mobility, citizenship and (in)visibility. In R. Wodak and B. Forchtner (eds.), *The Routledge Handbook of Language and Politics*. London: Routledge.

Miles, N. (2009). *No Going Back: Lesbian and Gay People and the Asylum System*. London: Stonewall.

Millbank, J. (2009a). From discretion to disbelief: Recent trends in refugee determinations on the basis of sexual orientation in Australia and the United Kingdom. *International Journal of Human Rights* 13(2/3): 391–414.

Millbank, J. (2009b). The ring of truth: A case study of credibility assessment in particular social group refugee determinations. *International Journal of Refugee Law* 21(1): 1–33.

Murray, D.A.B. (2015a). Introduction to special issue: Queering borders language, sexuality and migration. *Journal of Language and Sexuality* 3(1): 1–5.

Murray, D.A.B. (2015b). To feel the truth: Discourse and emotion in Canadian sexual orientation refugee hearings. In D.A.B. Murray (ed.) (pp. 6–27).

Nash, J.C. (2008). Re-thinking intersectionality. *Feminist Review* 89: 1–15.

Nelson, C. (2009). *Queer as a Second Language*. Unpublished Playscript.

Nelson, C. (2010). A gay immigrant student's perspective: unspeakable acts in the language class. *TESOL Quarterly* 44(3): 441–464.

Nelson, C.D. (2015). Performed research for public engagement: Language and identity studies on stage. In D.N. Djenar, A. Mahboob and K. Cruickshank (eds.), *Language and Identity Across Modes of Communication*. The Hague: De Gruyter Mouton.

Norton, B. (2013). *Identity and Language Learning: Extending the Conversation*. Bristol: Multilingual Matters.

Phillips, D. (2014). *The Dynamics of Settlement*. Accessed 9/3/2016 <http://compasanthology.co.uk/wp-content/uploads/2014/02/Phillips_COMPASMigrationAnthology.pdf.

Rachid, O. (1998). *Chocolat Chaud*. Paris: Gallimard.

Relaño Pastor, M. (2014). *Shame and Pride in Narrative: Mexican Women's Language Experiences at the U.S.-Mexico Border*. New York: Palgrave Macmillan.

Roberts, C. and Campbell, S. (2005). Fitting stories into boxes. Rhetorical and textual constraints on candidates' performances in British Job Interviews. *Journal of Applied Linguistics* 2(1): 45–73.

Sabaté, M. (2014). *Migrant Communication Enterprises*. Bristol: Multilingual Matters.

Shuman, A. and Bohmer, C. (2004). Representing trauma: Political asylum narrative. *Journal of American Folklore* 117(466): 394–414.

Shuman, A. and Bohmer, C. (2007). *Rejecting Refugees: Political Asylum in the 21st Century*. London: Routledge.

Simpson, J. and Whiteside, A. (2015). *Adult Language Education and Migration: Challenging Agendas in Policy and Practice*. London: Routledge.

Taïa, A. (2009). *Salvation Army*. Los Angeles: Semiotext(e)Native Agents.

Vigouroux, C. (2013). Informal economy and language practice in the context of migrations. In A. Duchene, M. Moyer and C. Roberts (eds.).

Part IV
Policies

25
Citizenship, immigration laws, and language

Kamran Khan and Tim McNamara

Introduction

The challenges of immigrant mobility and settlement are a central political issue in Western societies, in Europe, North America, and Australia. One response has been the introduction of citizenship requirements (Bigo 2002; van Avermaet 2009), often framed within immigration legislation (McGhee 2008); increasingly, evidence of a certain level of language proficiency is required for naturalization. Since 2001, several countries have reinvigorated notions of language and citizenship as part of immigration and 'border control' policies. Van Avermaet (2009) and Pulinx, Van Avermaet, and Extramiana (2014) document the shift towards restricting immigration into Europe, with several countries introducing citizenship testing and/or modifying tests to make them more onerous for the migrant, in line with more stringent entry and settlement requirements. Each new legal requirement is informed by the prevalent political discourse on immigration.

The connection between immigration, law and testing is the backbone of modern-day testing regimes. These regimes are increasingly shaped by factors such as popular anti-immigration sentiment and the fervor around security (Khan 2014). Tests are linked to naturalization processes as evidence is required of a particular level of competency in the national language and/or its history, society, and institutions. With each test and assessment of language there are corresponding educational policies, preparatory materials, and pedagogic implications and the requirement of a symbolic willingness to undergo such assessments (Shohamy 2001, 2006). Shohamy (2001) says of the regulatory capacity of testing:

> Tests are capable of dictating to test takers what they need to know, what they will learn and what they will be taught . . . [They] are forced to change their behavior to suit the demands of the test.
>
> *(Shohamy 2001: 17)*

In this chapter, we first provide a discussion of the notion of citizenship, and then consider the role of language tests in citizenship procedures, underlining three dimensions: technical, ideological and symbolic. We then consider a poststructuralist, Derridean perspective on these issues. The curious lack of scholarship in applied linguistics drawing on Derrida's work is a lacuna that we seek to address. Among the breadth of Derrida's academic contributions, he placed particular emphasis on the issue of multilingualism and its relationship to citizenship rights.

Overview of the topic

Citizenship

Citizenship has been a marker of formal membership of a particular community since Greek and Roman times (Shohamy 2006). In both cases, citizens received favorable treatment, rights, and privileges through group membership. In the context of more recent transnational migratory flows, Brubaker's (1992) *Citizenship and Nationhood in France and Germany* is considered a seminal text (Joppke 2010). Brubaker notes the 'internally inclusive' and 'externally exclusive' nature of citizenship granted through membership ascribed at birth or, in the case of migrants, through a naturalization process. Citizenship offers legal affiliation and rights, yet it is also an 'instrument and object of social closure' (Brubaker 1992: 71). Citizenship defines who belongs and who is not allowed to belong, and this dual sense of inclusion/exclusion must always be considered in understanding the experiences of those potentially marginalized (and included) within this process. Examples of this, and the role of language within such processes, will be given later in this chapter. Apart from the granting of citizenship as a means of access to rights, the law in many countries also allows for the revoking of citizenship in certain cases; this possibility has been strengthened in recent UK legislation, where those holding dual nationality can have their British nationality revoked, for example on grounds of terrorist activity.

Language and language tests are now playing a crucial role in citizenship procedures. For example, the UK introduced a standardized test of knowledge of British life and institutions, conducted in English, in 2005, initially for citizenship (which gives the individual rights such as the right to vote, the right to a passport, and so on), but subsequently introduced earlier in the naturalization process for 'Indefinite Leave to Remain', the right to permanent residency but without citizenship. In Australia, the 1948 Australian Citizenship Act was updated in 2007 and a 'Knowledge of Society' citizenship test conducted in English was created. Analyses of the linguistic difficulty of the test indicated that it was at the B2 level of the Common European Framework of Reference (Council of Europe 2001), in other words a linguistically very demanding test, despite the legislation for citizenship requiring that candidates have only a basic knowledge of the language (McNamara and Ryan 2011). For many people this test had potentially troubling echoes of the White Australia Policy's Dictation Test from the early 20th century (McNamara 2009), where a language test was used to implement a discriminatory immigration policy.

Discourses of integration play a key role in justifying the management of immigration. Note that in the Netherlands the relevant test is known as the Civic Integration (*Inburgering*) Test rather than a residency or naturalization test (see later for a fuller description of this test). Bigo (2008) notes that a lack of integration is conflated with other discourses such as border control, crime, and terrorism. Particular immigrants may be seen as embodying a continuum of threats from petty crime, a lack of integration, to terrorism (Bigo 2002). These threats are often addressed through an increased commitment to citizenship and immigration legislation which is directed more at restricting immigration than developing the new citizen

(Bigo 2002, 2008). For example, in 2011 the British prime minister, in remarks on the language proficiency of immigrants, yoked together integration, elimination of terrorism, and citizenship (Cameron 2011).

The corollary of this integration discourse is that it may pathologize immigrants, including future generations of immigrant families:

> 'New citizens', whose culture and religion are perceived as different. . . . may indeed be citizens but [their] status is not the same . . . even if 'minority citizenship' has no legal existence. It is a psychological status. . . . [They] still have to integrate, to prove (often after several generations) that they can really be part of 'us'. A new citizenship has thus been created for those who are not entirely trusted . . . wherein the mere respect for the law is not sufficient.
>
> *(Ramadan 2012: 56)*

Schinkel (2010) refers to the 'virtualization' of citizenship. Using the example of Dutch citizenship, he links the 'virtues' implied within the Dutch naturalization process. He argues that the Dutch government is controlling not only the borders of the Netherlands but also society by justifying the naturalization process as a way of inculcating migrants with the 'values' or 'morals' required for life in the Netherlands.

Pitcher (2009) refers to the perceived need to 'educate' immigrants in citizenship programs as a form of 'infantilization'. In referring to the UK, only children and migrants require citizenship education. Thus, Pitcher notes that migrants require a process of learning akin to children. What is different is that the loyalty of children is not questioned.

Tests as technical instruments used to implement policy

More and more tests are fulfilling policy requirements in addition to their more conventional educational uses (Shohamy 2001; McNamara and Roever 2006; McNamara 2011). Tests create an interface between legal immigration requirements and the individual. McNamara and Roever (2006: 193) describe the test as 'the point of insertion of policy into individual lives'. Through language tests, citizenship legislation pushes legal requirements into the quotidian experiences of migrants.

The test construct is central to the test. Chapelle, Enright, and Jamieson (2008: 3) define a construct as 'a proficiency, ability, or characteristic of an individual that has been inferred from observed behavioural consistencies and that can be meaningfully interpreted'. This individualistic, cognitive interpretation, however, does not acknowledge the social values that test constructs embody (Shohamy 2001, 2006; McNamara and Roever 2006). As Messick points out, the fabric of each test contains both technical and ideological qualities (Messick 1989). Increasingly, in fact, test constructs are created through policy rather than generated by education or language experts (McNamara 2011), though the construct appears unchanged, as a form of knowledge. In contexts of immigration, test constructs are established through legislation.

In the case of the UK, the test construct as stated in legislation is a 'sufficient knowledge' of English and 'sufficient knowledge of life in the United Kingdom'; note the cognitive nature of the definition, which says nothing about the socio-political character of the construct. This definition is according to the Nationality, Immigration and Asylum Act (2002), which was introduced following the 2001 northern riots in England. This construct was already in place in the British Nationality Act (BNA) (1981), but it was rarely used

(Crick Commission 2003). In 2005, two routes to citizenship were introduced. One route was through the Life in the UK (LUK) test, which involved knowledge of British life, institutions and history, and which was administered only in English; the linguistic demands of the test were estimated as being at level B1 on the Common European Framework of Reference (Council of Europe 2001), and involved the language sub-skill of reading only (that is, there was no requirement to listen, speak, or write in English). For those who could not reach this B1 level there was an ESOL (English for Speakers of Other Languages) with Citizenship option through classes to demonstrate progress, without the need to demonstrate B1 competency. In 2013, the ESOL route was abolished and a language requirement (in addition to the Life in the UK test) was introduced for *all* applicants. The level was set at B1 on the Common European Framework of Reference. This requirement could be met by achieving the level of B1 in Speaking and Listening on approved examinations. The point here is that 'sufficient knowledge' both as a construct ('knowledge') and as a standard ('sufficient') is determined through immigration legislation. 'Sufficient' in 1981 is not the same as in 2005 nor in 2013. The construct and the standard are shaped by sociopolitical circumstances and instantiate legal requirements in the form of tests.

In the Netherlands, the Civic Integration Exam (*Inburgeringexamen*) as a requirement for settlement is the equivalent of the British Life in the UK test. In 2013, a Basic Integration Exam from Abroad was introduced, to be taken by immigrants prior to arrival in the Netherlands. Testing is now required much earlier in the process and externalizes the linguistic border into the country of origin.

If the legislation in various countries were simply reflecting the linguistic necessities of life in the country concerned, the linguistic level of the requirements could be expected to be the same. But what is required in one country is not the same as another, and often reflects the political 'heat' of the debate over immigration in each context, and the tradition of hospitality to immigrants. Van Avermaet (2009) and Pulinx et al. (2014) have traced these differences over several years in countries in Europe and shown a steady increase in the language levels required under legislation as the debate about immigration in Europe has intensified.

The 'Knowledge of Society' test is often the sole test, but as it is usually only available in a single language, the main national language, it thus constitutes a demanding de facto language test in itself, although this is often not widely acknowledged by government, or recognized by members of the general public if they are native speakers of the language concerned. They generally find the content of the test mostly falls within widely shared common knowledge of members of the society, and thus consider the test relatively easy, and therefore reasonable; its linguistic demands, which are considerable, remain completely invisible, although they constitute the main challenge of the test.

Tests as ideological mechanisms

The performance of ceremonies of power (Foucault 1977) and 'ceremonial rituals' (Shohamy 2001: 124) is part of the naturalization process. Drawing on the discussion of the social meaning and function of examinations in Foucault's *Discipline and Punish* (Foucault 1977), Shohamy (2006) notes how social conformity is achieved through judgments against the norm. The native speaker is positioned as more authentic or the 'norm' for which the other is the deviant:

> The ideology behind [language requirements] is that residents of a political entity need to be fully proficient in the national language in order to be fully accepted as part of the

nation ... It is therefore considered a very strong device for affecting language practices as it perpetuates the ideology that knowledge of the language is associated with loyalty and belonging and can be used as a device to legitimize people.

(Shohamy 2006: 66)

The ideological dimension of testing seeks to influence the language practices of the migrant population. On the one hand, it can be argued that proficiency in the national language provides a means to access rights and privileges which natives of that country already enjoy. The language requirement is however also symbolic as it conflates loyalty to the new country with language proficiency. Such assertions are premised on the notion that the unity and cohesion of the national community is based on shared characteristics which may be threatened by migrant communities (Blackledge 2005).

It must be noted that 'good' citizenship is not measured in tests, nor is passing tests necessarily a predictor for future contribution as citizens (Shohamy 2006). Rosenberg (2007) writes a comprehensive history of learning English in the UK in which she notes the contribution of migrant groups such as Jews and Poles since 1870, many of whom settled in the UK and were not subjected to the type of testing that is enforced today, yet have contributed to the country. It is clearly possible to be a fully contributing citizen without knowledge of the national language. Correspondingly, being fluent in no way guarantees good citizenship.

Citizenship legislation can be seen as a way of addressing specific social problems. In Australia the reintroduction of a citizenship test in 2007 was in response to social disturbances at home (riots on a Sydney beach) and abroad (the 7/7 terrorist attacks in London in 2005). Shohamy (2001) notes how tests are an effective way of addressing social problems. Tests become a 'method of control' (Shohamy 2001: 37), as the test restores social order in an area where control has been lost. In the case of immigration, whether through 'uncontrolled' numbers of migrants arriving or through social disturbances, tighter immigration legislation and language testing contribute to the social order. Such measures are linked to wider immigration controls.

While citizenship is a way of redesigning the national community, discourses of integration tend to focus on more local communities (Favell 2002) in which shared language is a key form of fusing social fragmentation. In traditional countries of multiculturalism, such as the UK and Australia, a more assimilationist tone has recently been adopted. Whereas multiculturalism had allowed difference to remain as a key part of social life and identity, assimilation has sought to create a more uniform approach to the 'problem' of integration. Gysen, Kuijper, and van Avermaet (2009) use the example of the Netherlands with its traditional liberal approach to multiculturalism moving to a harsher assimilationist stance. In Germany Chancellor Merkel and in the UK Prime Minister Cameron as leading political figures have dismissed multiculturalism as a failure (although Merkel's remarkable embrace of a large-scale intake into Germany of Syrian refugees, despite the opposition of many segments of German society, complicates her position somewhat). As a remedy, measures which include language testing or tougher language testing as a requirement have characterized the shift towards a more assimilationist approach.

With the accent on assimilation, language tests become a way of imposing a dominant language and therefore induce particular language behaviors that are to be at least ritually performed for the right to be in a country. These 'nationalizing practices' (Kostakopoulou 2006) conform to an ideology in which all members of the national community speak the same language.

Symbolic aspects of testing

Testing for residency and citizenship is also a highly symbolic act. The metaphor of the Shibboleth has been used in discussions of the social and political functions of testing (McNamara 2005, 2012). The Shibboleth relates to a passage in the Old Testament (Judges 12:6) in which following an inter-ethnic battle the defeated soldiers tried to mask their identity as they returned to their home territory. Those unable to correctly pronounce the word 'shibboleth' (a sociolinguistic marker of the relevant ethnic identities) revealed themselves as the defeated enemy and were put to the sword.

Today the consequences may not be as grave and the settings certainly may be less physically violent (McNamara and Roever 2006). Nevertheless, the shibboleth as a marker of identity via language proficiency remains a potent reminder of the symbolic power of tests (McNamara 2012). The shibboleth is a password, a marker of transition (Derrida 2005). Immigrants displaying their language proficiency have uttered the password and taken a step in the transition to becoming naturalized citizens. The shibboleth requires the visible display of evidence of language proficiency: the shibboleth has the character of a 'watchtower' and displays the 'vigilance of a sentinel' (Derrida 2005: 30). This visibility is clear in the form of the examination, but is also a feature of the subsequent application process. Rather than a single, defining trial, the shibboleth is proliferated in various forms of demonstration of the desire to belong. Each performance addresses the collective psyche of the national community about whether this individual really is or can be 'one of us'. Even when the legal basis of entry and settlement are satisfied, the iterations away from legal and testing contexts persist in more symbolic spheres. The passport takes over as a representation of the completed 'transition' and the visible symbol of equality, the officially endorsed form of identification used for identification purposes in a range of places, from airports through to more mundane activities such as applying for facilities (Khan 2013; Huysmans 2014).

Governments are also well aware of the symbolic qualities of language requirements. The home secretary in 2005 at the time that the Life in the UK test was introduced, Tony McNulty (2005), stated:

> This is not a test of someone's ability to be British or a test of their Britishness. It is a test of their preparedness to become citizens, in keeping with the language requirement as well. It is about looking forward, rather than an assessment of their ability to understand history.

Here the willingness to integrate becomes a precursor for being a citizen. The symbolic dimension appears as important as the technical aspect of the test.

Issues and ongoing debates

Derrida, multilingualism, and citizenship

We will frame a number of fundamental issues surrounding citizenship, immigrations laws, and language within the writings of the French poststructuralist philosopher, Jacques Derrida. Derrida's acute sensitivity towards marginality and belonging offers a compelling perspective on citizenship and its relationship to language. Derrida stresses that the manufactured demarcations dividing people through language and citizenship are political and cultural constructions: a 'border is never natural', he says (Derrida 2005: 30), and this includes linguistic borders. Similarly, citizenship 'is not natural' (Derrida 1998: 16). While law and citizenship more clearly regulate human boundaries, Derrida sees language in very much the same terms: it is less visible but equally divisive (Borradori 2008).

Where did this sensitivity come from? In *Monolingualism of the Other* (Derrida 1998), and elsewhere in the increasingly autobiographical character of his later writings, a period in Derrida's life in which he also became more explicit in dealing with wider sociopolitical issues (Cheah and Guerlac 2009), Derrida draws on his own experience of both the possession and the loss of citizenship in the course of his early life as a young member of the Algerian Jewish community in the 1940s. He states, ' I want to speak here, today as an Algerian, as an Algerian who became French at a given moment, lost his citizenship, and then recovered it' (quoted in Chérif 2008: 1). Members of the community to which Derrida belonged, the traditional, millennia-old and historically marginalized Jewish community of Algeria, were granted French citizenship via the Crémieux Decree in 1870, as part of the extension of civil rights to Jews as a fruit of the French Revolution. The safety provided by French citizenship proved illusory: seventy years after the Crémieux Decree, the same community of Algerians Jews was to suffer the loss of citizenship and its associated rights following directives from the Vichy Regime in France; a group that had experienced security and inclusion through citizenship experienced exclusion, the denial of its rights, and violence. Severe discriminatory measures were introduced against this community, whose fate would have resembled other Jewish communities in the Holocaust had it not been for the arrival in Algeria of Allied troops in 1942. This experience demonstrated for Derrida the precarity of being included and the recurrent possibility of exclusion: 'The artifice and precariousness of citizenship appear better when it is inscribed as a recent acquisition' (Derrida 1998: 16).

Although Derrida refers to his own experience as a member of the Jewish community of Algeria, the implications of his argument are more general:

> I knew that what I was saying in *The Monolingualism of the Other* was valid to a certain extent for my individual case, to wit, a generation of Algerian Jews before the Independence. But it also had the value of a universal exemplarity, even for those who are not in such historically strange and dramatic situations as . . . mine. I would venture to claim that the analysis is valid even for someone whose experience of his own mother tongue is sedentary, peaceful, and without any historical drama.
>
> *(Derrida 2005: 101)*

Frank Caputo, reflecting on Derrida's work, explains that the Jew is 'both the substance and the figure of the outsider' (Caputo 1997: 230). Derrida's reference to the Jew is both real and metaphoric and as such 'the outsider, the migrant, the exiled are represented by the figure of the Jew' (Khan 2013: 97). Stephen Frosh uses the example of the Jew as 'universal stranger' (Frosh 2005) as the permanent outsider within European societies:

> The two-thousand year history of Christian anti-Semitism has created a figure that is more than a symbol of the splits in Western society; the Jew is rather the kernel of otherness, that which is always found everywhere, but which is never allowed in . . . The Jew is the materialisation of that otherness which is most feared and least understood. . . . *All* otherness in the West is Jewish, including that inner otherness which is unconscious desire.
>
> If this is an extreme formulation, then this is because what has to be thought about is an extreme phenomenon: the recurrent, never-ending, barely even cyclical reiteration of anti-Semitic ideology and practices.
>
> *(Frosh 2005: 215)*

The historic resonance of a mistrusted minority provides a sobering reminder for the present day and the future. The figure of the Muslim threatens to become a further signifier of what Western societies are not as questions and reservations about loyalty are frequently posed (Kundnani 2014). In fact, Derrida was sympathetic to the treatment of Muslims in relation to the West. He viewed the sense of shared otherness and marginalization as a common factor, demonstrating his sense of commitment to a principle rather than the ascribed characteristics of a particular people, even though that people was his own (Chérif 2008).

The experience of Derrida's adolescence left him with a conflicted and paradoxical feeling about his membership of the community of French citizens and speakers of French: on the one hand he profoundly embraced French language and culture; on the other hand he famously claimed 'I only have one language: it is not mine' (Derrida 1998: 1).

This radical rethinking of language and belonging in Derrida invites us to consider its implications for current discussions of language and citizenship.

Law, language, and violence

Derrida's political philosophy is set out in many texts, among the most prominent of which is his essay 'Force of Law: The "Mystical Foundation of Authority" ' (Derrida 1990), a discussion of Walter Benjamin's essay 'Critique of Violence', written in 1921 (Benjamin 1978). Benjamin was a German Jewish philosopher and critical theorist who, like Derrida, was stripped of citizenship: exiled in France, as a stateless person he was imprisoned by the French authorities in 1940, following which an unsuccessful attempt to flee to the US via Spain led to his suicide. In 'Critique of Violence', Benjamin proposed that '*gewalt*' (violence) and '*recht*' (law) are inextricably related. Laws are fundamentally violent through their establishment (through law-making violence) and subsequent maintenance (law-preserving violence). The word '*gewalt*' can also mean 'force', so violence in this discussion must be understood beyond physical violence as including other kinds of coercion (imprisonment, fines, and other sanctions). For Benjamin, and for Derrida, the foundations of law are always based on violence or some form of force which establishes order: 'Law is always an authorized force, a force that justifies itself or is justified in applying itself, even if this justification may be judged from elsewhere to be unjust or unjustifiable' (Derrida 1990: 925).

Given the inevitability of violence in law, the difference between just and unjust laws is the extent to which the violence of the law is justifiable. Not all laws are just and not all laws are unjust. In other words, legal and just are not necessarily the same. Derrida argues: 'The justice of law, justice as law is not justice. Laws are not just as laws. One obeys the law not because they are just but because they have authority' (Derrida 1990: 939). Legal justice is primarily a question of the internal logic of law (Douzinas 2005). Derrida demonstrates that following the law is no guarantee of justice; it can be quite the opposite. Following the law may well perpetuate injustice because laws are followed regardless of their justice. For example, in 1641, Massachusetts used the 'Bodies of Liberties' to legalize slavery. Thus, at one time slavery was legal in the United States; an unjust practice was legal. In contrast, it might be argued that anti-discrimination laws such as the Sex Discrimination Act of 1975 and the Race Relations Act of 1976 are steps forward to create more just conditions. The point here is to not accept that what is legal is just, nor to accept that all laws are inherently good or bad. The distinction between law and justice, and the necessary violence in law, alerts us to the possible unjust uses of law, given that they will always be subject to dispute.

One key site for injustice to which Derrida was especially sensitive was in social practices involving language, especially the languages of authority, the language in which one must be heard. Derrida was a firm supporter of multilingualism and the rights of linguistic and cultural minorities. For example, he states:

> A civilization must be plural: it must ensure a respect for the multiplicity of languages, cultures, beliefs, ways of life. And it is in this plurality, this alterity . . . that a chance . . . for the future is possible.
> *(Chérif 2008: 81)*

He cites examples of the imposition of a particular language in political, academic and legal settings, including the historical examples of the Villers-Cottêret Decree of 1539 under François I which promoted French as the 'mother tongue' and the language of law and church, replacing Latin and other local dialects, and the imposed linguistic unification of France following the French Revolution. Both contexts establish a prevailing monolingual imposition that attempts to eradicate the internal diversity. Derrida eloquently describes this destruction as 'effacing the folds and flattening the text' (Derrida 1998: 40) as heterogeneity and uniqueness acquiesce to singularity enforced by the violent 'force of law'. In relation to the French Revolution, Derrida notes that 'linguistic unification sometimes took the most repressive pedagogical turns, or in any case the most authoritarian ones' and draws attention to the nexus enjoining law, language and education, still relevant 'today, where this linguistic problem is still acute and will be for a long time precisely in this place where questions of politics, education and law (*droit*) are inseparable' (Derrida 1990: 957). Derrida positions these domains as colluding in shaping the lives of individuals. The filtering effect of law, language, and education means that the multitude of identities, languages/dialects, and cultures in a polity may be devalued and in some cases eventually cast aside, a loss which Derrida characterizes in the following terms: 'They must lose their idiom in order to survive or live better. A tragic economy, an impossible counsel' (Derrida 1998: 30). Derrida describes the points of convergence of language and law in manufacturing the homogeneity of a group: 'One founding violence of the law or of the imposition of the state law has consisted in imposing a language on national or ethnic minorities regrouped by the state' (Derrida 1990: 957). This orientation towards enforcing language policies carries the weight of the law towards the marginalized minorities in the name of broader exclusive nationalistic projects. The role of law in language policies leads to paradoxes. For example:

> Try to explain to somebody who holds both force and the force of law that you want to preserve your language. You will have to learn his to convince him. Once you have appropriated the language of power, for reasons of rhetorical and political persuasion, once you master it well enough to try to convince or to defeat someone, you are in turn defeated in advance and convinced of being wrong . . . By speaking to him in his own language, you acknowledge his law and authority: you prove him right; you countersign the act that proves him right over you. A king is someone who is able to make you wait or take your time to learn his language in order to claim your rights, that is, to confirm his.
> *(Derrida 2004: 12)*

By operating within the language of the other, a power dynamic is established that subjugates the individual to the law, which Derrida likens to colonialism:

> The monolingualism imposed by the other operates by relying upon that foundation . . . through a sovereignty whose essence is always colonial, which tends, repressively and irrepressibly, to reduce language to the One, that is, to the hegemony of the homogeneous.
> *(Derrida 1998: 39–40)*

Colonialism is founded on violence in establishing the authority of the colonizer over the native. However, the reference to colonialism, which carries disturbing historical undertones, needs to be viewed beyond the literal sense:

> I would not like to make too easy use of the word 'colonialism'. All culture is originally colonial. Every culture institutes itself through the unilateral imposition of some 'politics' of language. Mastery begins, we know, through the power of naming, of imposing and legitimating appellations.
>
> *(Derrida 1998: 39)*

Iterability, law, and language

One of the arguments Derrida introduces in 'Force of Law' is that Benjamin's distinction between the violence that introduces a legal regime (for example, the political violence of a revolution) and the violence that enforces the law once it has been enacted cannot be supported. For Derrida, law reinstates its original violence in each act of enforcement of the law, by claiming as it were its right to enforce the law: 'Iterability requires the origin to repeat itself originarily, to alter itself as to have the value of the origin, that is to conserve itself' (Derrida 1990: 1006–1007). This reinscription of the original violence is played out in every moment and context in which the law acts. The crucial notion here, frequently repeated in Derrida's work, is of repetition or iterability. That is, there is no once and for all instance of the violent institution of law; instead in each instance of the operation of law the originary violence is repeated. Similarly, in the administration of justice, the routine administration of law does not automatically guarantee justice: 'Every time that something comes to pass or turns out well, every time that we placidly apply a good rule to a particular case . . . we can be sure that law (*droit*) may find itself accounted for, but certainly not justice' (Derrida 1990: 947). Each instance of the administration of justice is unique, given the unique individual circumstances in relation to which the judgment is made:

> If I were content to apply a just rule, without a spirit of justice and without in some way inventing the rule and the example for each case, I might be protected by law (*droit*), my action corresponding to objective law, but I would not be just. I would act, Kant would say, in conformity with duty, but not through duty or out of respect for the law.
>
> *(Derrida 1990: 949)*

Justice is seen in the action of 'inventing the rule and the example for each case' in each iteration: the justice or injustice of the action is not automatically determined a priori. Like language, law functions within a performative structure which 'always takes place in the shadow of the possibility of its own failure' (Dick and Wolfreys 2015: 168). What may appear to be a failure of the application of law can mitigate injustice. An unjust law may indeed repeatedly, in its implementation, perpetrate injustice, but there is always the possibility of failure; in this narrow space there is some possibility for the potential for injustice to be averted.

The notion of iterability is important for Derrida's understanding of language, too. In *Limited Inc.* (Derrida 1988), a discussion of the pragmatics of Austin and Searle, Derrida refers to iterability within language use. He sees language as necessarily involving the instability of repetition: 'The possibility of repeating and thus of identifying the marks is implicit in every code, making it into a network [*une grille*] that is communicable, transmutable, decipherable, iterable for a third' (Derrida 1988: 8). Language is both repetition (the same) and yet unique instance (different), 'repetition and alterity' (Dick and Wolfreys 2015: 167). For Derrida, 'a written sign carries with it a force that breaks with its context, that is, with the collectivity of presences organizing the moment of its inscription. This breaking force [*force de rupture*] is not an accidental predicate but the very structure of the written text' (Derrida 1998: 9). At the moment of iteration there is the force of violence, yet this force also has the capacity to turn on itself and to disrupt. This means the individual faced with such iterations is in a space of possibility for subversion, (non)compliance and (in)justice.

Thus, while using tests to influence language practices (in favor of monolingualism) may be one aim of citizenship testing, the reality raises several complexities. In an ethnographic study (Khan 2013) of the process of immigrants preparing for the UK citizenship test (see earlier in this chapter), members of a Chinese community and a Yemeni community who were facing the test were found to be relying almost entirely on Mandarin in the Chinese case and Arabic in the Yemeni case to prepare for the test, using translations of test items and test preparation materials provided by more proficient speakers. Although this approach would seem to undermine the aim of the test as a literal and symbolic test of English proficiency, it allowed lower-level learners to understand the test material on their own terms and to teach others. Thus, the test became more meaningful in the language of the candidates and converted a monolingual test into a multilingual test. The test construct of 'sufficient' knowledge of English was negated to make the test material more meaningful and to satisfy the 'sufficient knowledge of Life in the UK' construct. In a sense, the ideology promoted by the government is subverted to fulfill the legal requirements. Test-takers are making a test they perceive to be fundamentally unjust more just by using what they know rather than what they lack as a point of departure. The validity of the test is compromised as the test score no longer represents the proficiency in English that it purports to reflect. Symbolically, it could be argued that the test was negotiated by learners who have invested a great deal in taking the test. Through the multilingual and cooperative practices they employ, they overcome their perceived relative lack of proficiency; the more they engage with the test, the more they undermine yet paradoxically at the same time satisfy the requirements.

Khan (2013) refers to the highly regulated preparation materials which are published in the dominant language. The test is written in the dominant language and appears to require the test-taker to engage with this language. Crucially, there is a space in the preparation in the individual experience of engagement with the test among the test-takers in the study; in this iteration of the citizenship law the test-takers found a way of using the preparation material as they wish. Derrida states:

> Someone puts a text in front of you . . . with an intention that it is both somewhat yours and simply not yours. Each time it happens, it's a very curious, very troubling experience . . . it is never the same text . . . there are a thousand possibilities. Yet one thing is certain in all this diversity, and that is that it's never the same.
>
> *(Derrida 1988: 158)*

These spaces, both metaphoric and real, are the points where meanings can be distorted, maintained, or destabilized; such points where violence meets violence are rich for enquiry. As there is a single test, the same test, it is rich with possibilities. Some will comply in the way intended, some may comply but in ways one could not imagine. What applied linguists need to do now is to further the evidential base of such spaces and to consider the implications.

Singularity and generality in law and language

Crucially, Derrida's argument is not about particular instances of injustice, nor about the politics of the imposition of a particular language. His is a more radical argument about the generalized potential for injustice in the very nature of law and language, always considered from the point of view of the individual who is subject to them. The individual, the singular case, is always vulnerable in the face of the law, which is necessarily always about the general:

> How are we to reconcile the act of justice that must always concern singularity, individuals, irreplaceable groups and lives, the other or myself as other, in a unique situation, with rule, norm, value or the imperative of justice which necessarily have a general form, even if this generality prescribes a singular application in each case?
> *(Derrida 1990: 949)*

Derrida's concern for the vulnerability of the individual in the face of the general, the public, the social is a recurrent theme in his writing. In his discussion of some texts of Nietzsche in *The Ear of the Other* (Derrida 1988/1982), he emphasizes the problem of reception, arguing that being *heard* cannot be guaranteed by the formulation of the individual's testimony; the success or failure of communication lies in the ear of the other.

The vulnerability of the individual is also a theme in his discussion of language. Language is a shared cultural medium; as Bakhtin argues, language pre-exists us, is a coat that has been worn before, and that we have to appropriate when we attempt to express our meanings. Language is an impersonal, shared medium, which may be inimical to the expression of individual realities: this is the notion of language as shibboleth, where language allows us to participate in the actions of the culture, and thus acts to include, but may also act to inhibit the expression of our own meanings, and hence simultaneously acts to exclude (McNamara 2012). Discourses circulating in language will potentially enhance this effect of muting the expression of individual experience. Derrida gets us to imagine the permanent possibility of injustice because of the generality of law and the silencing of the individual voice through the shared medium of any language:

> To address oneself to the other in the language of the other is, it seems, the condition of all possible justice, but apparently, in all rigor, it is not only impossible (since I cannot speak the language of the other except to the extent that I appropriate it and assimilate it according to the law of an implicit third) but even excluded by justice as law (*droit*), inasmuch as justice as right seems to imply an element of universality, the appeal to a third party who suspends the unilaterality or singularity of the idiom.
> *(Derrida 1990: 949)*

This view of language is the basis for a powerful critique of the notion of the assumed protection offered by the 'mother tongue' (McNamara 2010):

> 'My mother tongue' is what they say, is what they speak; as for me, I cite and question them. I ask them in their own language . . . if they indeed know what they are saying and what they are talking about. Especially when, so lightly, they celebrate 'fraternity'. At bottom, brothers, the mother tongue, and so forth pose the same problem.

It is a bit as if I was awakening them to tell them: 'Listen, pay attention, now that is enough, you must wake up. . . . One day, you will see that what you are calling your mother tongue will no longer even respond to you.'

(Derrida 1998: 33)

There is no refuge in any language, or even in multilingualism, which pluralizes the risks he identifies.

Implications

What are we to make of such a radical vision of the potential for violence in the very structures of social order and the nature of the communicative medium? The vision has a tragic character: the involvement of violence in justice and the way language simultaneously permits expression and silences it are paradoxes, what Derrida elsewhere calls 'undecidables'. Law is both just and unjust; language is both including and excluding, expressive and silencing. And there is no place of refuge. What his analysis prompts is a vigilant attention to the potential for injustice in practices involving language and citizenship. Where, exactly, does justice lie? is the question we are required to consider. Research should be targeted to this end.

Studies in the area of law and language for immigration must include historical, legal, and pedagogic perspectives. The historical background of testing policy already informs a number of studies. For instance, we can better understand the anxiety about the introduction of citizenship tests in Australia in the early 2000s if we are aware of the historical tradition of using language tests to enforce a blatantly discriminatory immigration policy in the early years of the newly federated and independent Australia (McNamara 2009; McNamara and Ryan 2011). Blackledge (2005) adopts Wodak's discourse-historical approach to Critical Discourse Analysis (Wodak 2001) to analyze arguments for the introduction of language requirements in language testing regimes in the UK. He shows how discourses around the role of language in social dysfunction and inter-ethnic violence form an intertextual chain leading to the new requirements. Schissel (2014) outlines the history of the language testing of emergent bilinguals in policy in the United States, including the testing of adult immigrants arriving at Ellis Island from 1913; Wiley (2005) also provides useful historical background on this and earlier periods in which restrictive practices involving language were used to restrict the right of African Americans and recent immigrants to vote. It is remarkable, given this history, that the pressure to use tests restrictively in the citizenship process in the United States, while present, has never really taken hold there in the way that it has in Europe (McNamara and Roever 2006).

The legal aspects are essential to consider in the case of immigration for reasons outlined earlier. Briefer accounts of the historical context of language testing for immigration and citizenship in the Baltic countries, Sweden, Germany, Belgium, Luxembourg, the United States, Canada, Australia, and Israel can be found in Extra, Spotti, and Van Avermaet (2009); further case studies can be found in Hogan-Brun, Mar-Molinero, and Stevenson (2009). Craig (2012) represents work by a lawyer and legal researcher examining cases of the use of language analysis for the determination of origin (LADO) of refugees, a widespread and controversial practice that has attracted the attention of sociolinguists, applied linguists, and language testers internationally (Eades 2009; McNamara 2014; McNamara, van den Hazelkamp, and Verrips 2016). The pedagogic implication such as those in Shohamy (2006) offer us salient frameworks in which to situate our work.

Any work around citizenship must be tempered with a multifaceted understanding of both the benefits and drawbacks of such membership and how they impact on the individual and groups. This may tend to complicate conventional critical positions: engaging with Derrida forces us to ask uncomfortable questions. For example, his understanding of the thin line between belonging and discrimination demands that we pay attention to how citizenship can represent safety and something positive for the migrant, co-existent with the potential for discrimination (Khan 2013). Similarly, support for the rights of immigrant populations, members of whom may have deeply conservative values, may involve the need to defend the rights of other vulnerable groups, including homosexuals, ethnic minorities, and women. Empirical evidence must allow for space in comprehending how iterations of law possess within them ways of destabilizing meaning, undermining yet complying as 'there is always the potential for language to go astray' (Dick and Wolfreys 2015: 168). Viewed this way, a poststructuralist perspective allows researchers in this area to be vigilant and critically open and prepared for paradoxes and (im)possibilities in the data from research in this field.

Future directions

The situation in Europe in particular involving language, citizenship, and the law is dramatically changing. The rapid increase in the number of refugees and migrants entering Europe since 2015 is already having an impact on policy on entry, permanent residence, and citizenship. For example, the Danish government in 2015 announced its intention to change the law to require knowledge of the Danish language as a requirement for a refugee to get permanent residency in the country, and paid for advertisements announcing this and other relevant policy changes to appear in newspapers in Lebanon, where as many as one million Syrian refugees were living. The German government has announced plans to require refugees from Syria to learn German within three years of arrival in Germany or risk losing their residence permit. Norway and Sweden are also considering similarly restrictive changes. These changes are in part in response to anti-immigration sentiment and the advance of the far-right movements in countries such as France through the National Front, the UK through the United Kingdom Independence Party and in Germany through the Pegida movement and the Alternative for Germany (Alternative für Deutschland – AfD) party. One role for applied linguists is to track changes in discourse and in modifications to language requirements. The current political climate requires scholarship of the kind illustrated in Extra et al. (2009) as further legal and immigration restrictions come into operation.

In addition, Blackledge (2005), Joppke (2007), and Turner (2014) have highlighted the need for empirical research on how citizenship requirements are experienced to complement the theoretical analyses of citizenship. There remains a dearth of empirical scholarship on just how such language requirements are experienced around the world. It is in the experiences of individuals that the paradoxes, complexities, and limits of such testing regimes can be found (McNamara, Khan, and Frost 2014).

Related topics

Nation-state, transnationalism, and language
National and ethnic minorities
Language-in-education policies and mobile citizens

Further reading

Clochard, O. and Migreurop. (2013). *Atlas of Migration in Europe: A Critical Geography of Migration Policies*. Oxford: New Internationalist.

A critical assessment of the development of European policies on immigration and asylum since the 1980s.

Extra, G., Spotti, M. and van Avermaet, P., eds. (2009). *Language Testing, Citizenship and Migration: Cross-National Perspectives on Integration Regimes*. London and New York: Continuum.

A set of case studies of the policies and practices on language, immigration and citizenship in twelve countries, eight of them in Europe.

Hogan-Brun, G., Mar-Molinero, C. and Stevenson, P., eds. (2009). *Discourses of Language and Integration: Critical Perspectives on Language Testing Regimes in Europe*. Amsterdam and Philadelphia: John Benjamins.

Overview and theoretical papers on language, migration and citizenship, plus studies of the Netherlands, Britain, Luxembourg, and Austria.

Joppke, C. (2007). Transformation of citizenship: Status, rights and identity. *Citizenship Studies*, *11*(1), 37–48.

Integrated summary of state of citizenship studies, bringing together different research traditions and definitions of citizenship.

McNamara, T. and Ryan, K. (2011). Fairness vs. Justice in language testing: The place of English literacy in the Australian citizenship test. *Language Assessment Quarterly*, *8*(2), 161–178.

Discussion of new citizenship test in the light of the historical tradition of the use of language tests for purposes of discrimination in Australia. Contrasts psychometric and social approaches to thinking about the quality and function of language tests for citizenship.

References

Benjamin, W. (1978). *Reflections: Essays, Aphorisms, Autobiographical*. New York: Schrocken Books.
Bigo, D. (2002). Security and immigration: Toward a critique of the governmentality of unease. *Alternatives: Global, Local, Political* 27: 63–92.
Bigo, D. (2008). Globalized (in)security: The field and the ban-opticon. In D. Bigo and A. Tsoukala (eds.), *Terror, Insecurity Liberty: Illiberal Practices of Liberal Regimes after 9/11* (pp. 10–49). London: Routledge.
Blackledge, A. (2005). *Discourse and Power in a Multilingual World*. Amsterdam: John Benjamins.
Borradori, G. (2008). Foreword. In M. Cherif (ed.), *Islam and the West: A Conversation with Jacques Derrida* (pp. i–xxii). Chicago: University of Chicago Press.
Brubaker, R. (1992). *Citizenship and Nationhood in France and Germany*. Cambridge, MA: Harvard University Press.
Cameron, D. (2011). *Prime Minister's Speech at Munich Conference* [Online]. Retrieved from http://www.number10.gov.uk/news/pms-speech-at-munich-security-conference [Accessed 2 April 2015].
Caputo, J.D. (1997). *The Prayers and Tears of Jacques Derrida: Religion without Religion*. Bloomington, In Indiana University Press.
Chapelle, C.A., Enright, M.K. and Jamieson, J.M. (2008). Test score interpretation and use. In C.A. Chapelle, M.K. Enright and J.M. Jamieson (eds.), *Building a Validity Argument for the Test of English as a Foreign Language* (pp. 1–26). London: Routledge.
Cheah, P. and Guerlac, S., eds. (2009). *Derrida and the Time of the Political*. Durham, NC: Duke University Press.
Chérif, M. (2008). *Islam and the West: A Conversation with Jacques Derrida*. Chicago: University of Chicago Press.
Council of Europe (2001). *Common European Framework of Reference for Languages*. Cambridge: Cambridge University Press.

Craig, S. (2012). The use of language analysis in asylum decision making in the UK: A discussion. *Journal of Immigration, Asylum and Nationality Law* 26(3): 255–268.

Crick Commission (2003). *The New and the Old: The Report of the "Life in the United Kingdom' Advisory Group"*. London: HMSO.

Derrida, J. (1988/1982). *The Ear of the Other* [Edited by C. McDonald; a translation by P. Kamuf of the French edition edited by C. Levesque and C. McDonald]. Lincoln: University of Nebraska Press.

Derrida, J. (1988). *Limited Inc*. Evanston, IL: Northwestern University Press.

Derrida, J. (1990). Force of law: The "mystical foundation of authority". *Cardozo Law Review* 11(5–6): 919–1046.

Derrida, J. (1998). *Monolingualism of the Other: Or, the Prosthesis of Origin* [Translated by P. Mensah]. Stanford, CA: Stanford University Press.

Derrida, J. (2004). *Eyes of the University: Right to Philosophy 2* [Translated by J. Plug and Others]. Stanford, CA: Stanford University Press.

Derrida, J. (2005). *Sovereignties in Question: The Poetics of Paul Celan* [Edited by T. Dutoit and O. Pasanen]. New York: Fordham University Press.

Dick, M. and Wolfreys, J. (2015). *The Derrida Wordbook*. Edinburgh: Edinburgh University Press.

Douzinas, C. (2005). Violence, justice, deconstruction. *German Law Journal* 6(1): 171–178.

Eades, D. (2009). Testing the claims of asylum seekers: The role of language analysis. *Language Assessment Quarterly* 6(1): 30–40.

Extra, G., Spotti, M. and van Avermaet, P. (2009). Testing regimes for newcomers. In G. Extra, M. Spotti and P. Avermaert (eds.), *Language Testing, Migration and Citizenship* (pp. 1–34). London and New York: Continuum.

Favell, A. (2002). *Philosophies of Integration: Immigration and the Idea of Citizenship* (2nd ed.). Basingstoke: Macmillan.

Foucault, M. (1977). *Discipline and Punish* [Translated by A. Sheridan]. Harmondsworth: Penguin Books.

Frosh, S. (2005). *Hate and the Jewish Science*. Basingstoke: Palgrave Macmillan.

Gysen, S., Kuijper, H. and van Avermaet, P. (2009). Language testing in the context of immigration and citizenship: The case of the Netherlands and Flanders (Belgium). *Language Assessment Quarterly* 6(1): 98–105.

Hogan-Brun, G., Mar-Molinero, C. and Stevenson, P. (2009). Testing regimes: Introducing cross-national perspectives in language, migration and citizenship. In G. Hogan-Brun, C. Mar-Molinero and P. Stevenson (eds), *Discourse on Language and Integration* (pp. 1–14). Amsterdam: John Benjamins.

Huysmans, J. (2014). *Security Unbound: Enacting Democratic Limits*. London: Routledge.

Joppke, C. (2007). Transformation of citizenship: Status, rights, identity. *Citizenship Studies* 11(1): 37–48.

Joppke, C. (2010). *Citizenship and Immigration*. Cambridge: Polity Press.

Khan, K. (2013). *Becoming British: A Migrant's Journey*. Unpublished PhD thesis, University of Birmingham and University of Melbourne.

Khan, K. (2014). *Citizenship, Securitization and "Suspicion" in UK ESOL Policy*. Working Papers in Urban Language and Literacies, Working Paper 130. London: Kings College.

Kostakopoulou, D. (2006). Thick, thin and thinner patriotisms: Is this all there is? *Oxford Journal of Legal Studies* 26(1): 73–106.

Kundnani, A. (2014). *The Muslims Are Coming! Islam, Extremism and the Domestic War on Terror*. London: Verso.

McGhee, D. (2008). *Intolerant Britain?* Maidenhead: Open University Press.

McNamara, T. (2005). 21st century shibboleth: Language tests, identity and intergroup conflict. *Language Policy* 4(4): 351–370.

McNamara, T. (2009). Australia: The dictation test redux. *Language Assessment Quarterly* 6(1): 106–111.

McNamara, T. (2010). Reading Derrida: Language, identity and violence. *Applied Linguistics Review* 2: 23–43.

McNamara, T. (2011). Managing learning: Authority and language assessment. *Language Teaching* 44(4): 500–515.

McNamara, T. (2012). Language assessments as shibboleths: A poststructuralist perspective. *Applied Linguistics* 33(5): 564–581.
McNamara, T. (2014). The promise and threat of the shibboleth: Linguistic representations of asylum seekers. In D.H. Rellstab and C. Schlote (eds.), *Representations of War, Migration and Refugeehood: Interdisciplinary Perspectives* (pp. 93–108). London: Routledge.
McNamara, T., Khan, K. and Frost, K. (2014). Language tests for residency and citizenship and the conferring of individuality. In B. Splosky, O. Inbar-Lourie and M. Tannenbaum (eds.), *Challenges for Language Education and Policy* (pp. 11–22). Abingdon: Routledge.
McNamara, T. and Roever, C. (2006). *Language Testing: The Social Dimension*. Oxford: Blackwell.
McNamara, T. and Ryan, K. (2011). Fairness versus justice in language testing: The place of English literacy in the Australian citizenship test. *Language Assessment Quarterly* 8(2): 161–178.
McNamara, T., van den Hazelkamp, C. and Verrips, M. (2016). LADO as a language test: Issues of validity. *Applied Linguistics* 37(2): 262–283.
McNulty, T. (2005). *New UK Citizenship Testing Starts* [Online]. Retrieved from http://news.bbc.co.uk/1/hi/uk_politics/4391710.stm [Accessed 20th February 2012].
Messick, S. (1989). Validity. In R. L. Linn (ed.), *Educational Measurement. Third Edition* (pp. 13–105). New York and London: Macmillan.
Nationality, Immigration and Asylum Act (2002). [Online] Available from: http://www.legislation.gov.uk/ukpga/2002/41/pdfs/ukpga_20020041_en.pdf [Date Accessed: 3 November 2016].
Pitcher, B. (2009). *The Politics of Multiculturalism*. Basingstoke: Palgrave Macmillan.
Pulinx, R., Van Avermaet, P. and Extramiana, C. (2014). *Linguistic Integration of Adult Migrants: Policy and Practice. Final Report of the 3rd Council of Europe Survey*. Strasbourg: Council of Europe.
Ramadan, T. (2012). *On Super-diversity, Reflections 02*. Berlin: Sternberg Press.
Rosenberg, S. K. (2007). *A Critical History of ESOL in the UK, 1870–2007*. Leicester: NIACE.
Schinkel, W. (2010). The virtualization of citizenship. *Critical Sociology* 36(2): 265–283.
Schissel, J. (2014). Classroom use of test accommodations: Issues of access, equity and conflation. *Current Issues in Language Planning* 15(3): 282–295.
Shohamy, E. (2001). *The Power of Tests*. Harlow: Pearson Education.
Shohamy, E. (2006). *Language Policy: Hidden Agendas and New Approaches*. London and New York: Routledge.
Turner, J. (2014). Testing the liberal subject: (In)security, responsibility and "self-improvement" in the UK citizenship test. *Citizenship Studies* 18(3–4): 332–348.
Van Avermaet, P. (2009). Fortress Europe. In G. Hogan-Brun, C. Mar-Molinero and P. Stevenson (eds.), *Discourses on Language and Integration* (pp. 15–44). Amsterdam: John Benjamins.
Wiley, T. (2005). *Literacy and Language Diversity in the United States* (2nd ed.). Washington, DC: Center for Applied Linguistics.
Wodak, R. (2001). The discourse-historical approach. In R. Wodak and M. Meyer (eds.), *Methods of Critical Discourse Analysis* (pp. 63–94). London: Sage.

26
A rhizomatic account of heritage language

E. K. Tan

Introduction

"Heritage language" is sometimes referred to as ancestral language, native language, ethnic language, minority language, *langue d'origine*, mother tongue and community language, and so forth (Baker 1995: 129; He 2010: 66). The fact that heritage language can be defined as synonymous with these terms points to, first, heritage language as potentially an umbrella term referring to a language that is inherited. This is regardless of the social and cultural specificity of the given language and the community that acknowledges the language as their own. Second, it highlights heritage language as defined differently with respect to the social and cultural makeup of a society and migratory pattern. *Native language* often refers to the language of those who are historically the earliest occupants of the land. In this case, native language is understood as existing prior to the migration of people in history to the land that is being discussed. *Ancestral language* indexes a connection between language and place marked by distance, usually as a result of migration. Similarly, the French term *langue d'origine* underscores the dispersal of people as a consequence of colonialism when former colonial subjects navigate toward the metropoles of European colonial powers such as France (Aissaoui 2009). For example, the term marks French as distinct from Arabic, the *langue d'origine* of a Maghrebi diasporic subject living in France (Derrida 1998). *Ethnic language* refers to the language of ethnic minority, often in the context of multi-ethnic societies, such as the United States. This is sometimes conflated with minority language. *Community language*, though place-bound like the native language, seems to be focused more on the adoption, not inheritance, of a place to building communal identification alongside language usage. In fact, the convenient interchange between these terms and heritage language urges us to examine, specifically, what some of these terms mean or represent individually. In short, there is a lack of consensus among academics in terms of what a common definition of heritage language is. For example, in North America, the term heritage language is used concurrently to mean immigrant, indigenous, and ancestral language according to specific contexts, while in Australia the term is interchangeably used with community language (Wiley and Valdés 2000; Fishman 2001; Wiley 2001; Cummins 2005; He 2010).

To address the difficulties in defining heritage language (HL) and its complexities, Joshua Fishman (2001) categorizes heritage language into three subgroups, namely immigrant, indigenous, and colonial heritage. Basing his research in the US context, Fishman describes immigrant heritage language as languages spoken by immigrants who have migrated to the United States, while indigenous heritage language as languages of the Native Americans. These are two distinct versions of HLs that are equally seen as "other" languages vis-à-vis English, the dominant language in the United States since the nation's independence. Guadalupe Valdés (2001: 39) notes that HLs in the United States are "all non-English languages, including those spoken by Native American peoples." Colonial heritage language, on the other hand, refers to the language of settler communities in the United States, such as the pockets of German and Dutch communities spread out across the country. Echoing Fishman, Terrence Wiley (2005) further expands these categories to subgroups of refugee and former colonial languages. These efforts in exploring the complexities of heritage language encourage scholars to move beyond the dominant discourse and limiting approach of treating heritage language as a privilege field synonymous to immigrant heritage language. With the broadening of our understanding of heritage language as a field of study, we grow in awareness to the diverse social and political nature of heritage language in an increasingly globalized and multilingual world (Fishman 2001).

Issues and ongoing debates

Theoretical developments

As a noun, "heritage" denotes an element of identity belonging to the past. Simultaneously, it connotes an origin of a fixed essence. Both Wiley (2001) and Ofelia García (2005) question the utility of "heritage" as a theoretical and conceptual framework for the study of ethnic languages and cultures by pointing out that, even though the term "heritage" was first introduced in Canada to frame the concept of shared heritage among ethnic communities, the term, paradoxically, locks these communities in cultural and linguistic representations of the distant past. As an adjective, the word complements the actual subject in discussion, in the case of this chapter, heritage language. As the main subject, the term "language" conditions "heritage," not the other way round since "heritage" is an add-on to "language." If most people understood the fact that languages change over time, why, then when a language is tied to the notion of heritage, many tend to conveniently locate it within an essentially stable and unchanging framework? To see heritage as fixed and unchanging is to see it as a mere descriptor; to see it as fluid and always in flux with respect to social and cultural factors is to acknowledge its potential as a critical tool to facilitate our understanding of its relationship with the movement of people and the dispersal of cultures in the phenomenon of diaspora. To García (2005), heritage language is not just "rear-viewing" but also lacks the mobility and currency to be "projected into the future" (p. 601). Regardless, it is important to note that the term "heritage" has earned significant currency as a critical concept in the study of global cultures and languages during the second half of the 20th century.

Neriko Musha Doerr (2011) points out that even though it is inspiring to see scholars engaging in such study of language and migration by privileging the status of heritage cultures, many have neglected the need to understand the politics of heritage language both in theory and practice. Without examining important questions such as "what heritage is, who decides what it is, and for whom is the decision made," heritage appears as a general concept that can be conveniently adopted and appropriated out of context (2011: 1). Heritage is not simply another word for culture or traditions; the complexities it embodies, especially for immigrant communities, can be empowering, for "claiming which language is their heritage language can also be a political statement" (2011: 2). Simultaneously, this political agenda can also take on a different and wider dimension, for example, in the context of the United States with the growing awareness of the lack of support for non-English-speaking children in US schools due to educational policies that privilege monolingual norms (English language education). It is in this context that heritage language embodies positive and generative political power to promote the preservation of ethnic languages at home and in school (García 2005), even though the state's investment in heritage language education is lacking and is in need of evaluation.

García (2011) and García, Zakharua, and Otcu (2013) argue that, in order to address the disabling effect of the monolingual paradigm in the US educational system on heritage language teaching, scholars and educators should first and foremost acknowledge the heteroglossic nature of both individual and community linguistic practices. Only in doing so can they adopt a diverse and fluid pedagogy, such as García's (2011: 7) concept of "sustainable languaging," which focuses on language shifts and transformation of the heritage language through interaction with other languages in specific social and political context. Instead of treating heritage language as a cultural tradition to be inherited, we should see it as "an ongoing process" that evolves over time. Languaging, as theory and practice, challenges the notion of standard language and reified notions of language and identity by deconstructing the politics of difference embodied in a paradigm of linguistic binary of heritage versus national language.

With respect to the promotion of heritage education in the United States, Thomas Ricento (2005) cautions us against the state's appropriation of language learning programs to facilitate its political and economic interests. Ricento claims that the growing interest among scholars and researchers in the promotion of heritage language learning in the United States, by treating language as resource alongside the missions of the state, compromises the actual interests of individuals in their attempts to preserve their heritage languages. In other words, the "language-as-resource" (see Ruiz 1984; for origin of the term) discourse in the promotion of heritage languages while supporting state-funded language policies on language education fails to directly consider the needs and the benefits of the linguistic communities of which these languages belong to. Ricento arrives at this conclusion after analyzing the content of mission statements and position papers on the promotion of language programs in the United States with regards to state policies. What seems missing in these documents and papers is an investment in the study of the historical context of each respective heritage language. It is precisely this neglect in the study and promotion of heritage languages that renders the discourse of language-as-resource possible; hence, by focusing on state discourse of the economic and political utility of heritage languages, the needs of individuals and their linguistic communities are often displaced (Ricento 2005: 362). Languages regarded as not having values and assets in participating in the global market will eventually dissipate in time. To dislodge this threat to the preservation of heritage languages in the United States, Ricento suggests that local linguistic communities be given a central voice in participating in language policy and program planning to better promote their heritage languages and cultural significance. Such collaborations between program developers and local communities will cater simultaneously to the needs of both the state and the linguistic communities involved.

The evolution of heritage language is a result of colonialism and a condition of postcolonial and postmodern reality. It presupposes the movement of people to metropolises where their home languages are reduced to heritage languages while they are interpellated into adopting the languages of their host countries, such as English and other European languages, as their working language. The inevitable language rivalry between the heritage language and host language is the outcome of social conditions framed by a hierarchy of language in the age of globalization. In addition, heritage language also takes on different meaning for ethnic groups of different social statuses (Edwards 2001; de Fina 2007; Blommaert 2010; Pennycook 2010; Canagarajah 2013). The mapping of one language to one culture leads to the problematic assumption of the promotion of heritage as synonymous to language preservation. This assumption of heritage language embodying a singular meaning for everyone in the same community undermines the difference in experience among individuals from less privileged background such as those from the working class. Heritage language functions differently for different people, to achieve different goals among various groups that subscribe to the common understanding of an ethnic culture. The emphasis on preserving cultural heritage often hinders the less privileged from achieving social and economic mobility. This is especially so when privileged languages, such as English in postcolonial and/or multiethnic societies, are taken for granted as tools to achieve success, demotivating those who prefer to preserve the heritage language for ethnic traditions.

Expounding on earlier research in ethnography of communications (Hymes 1974, 1996) and interactional sociolinguistics (Gumperz 1982), Jan Blommaert engages with a sociolinguistics of mobility (2010) to examine the impact of globalization on traditional sociolinguistic discourse and methodology. Mobility, in various forms of globalization, forces sociolinguists to adopt an ecological perspective in revising the study of language by considering linguistic variation and change based on mobile language resources such as accents, dialects, and narrative techniques. The focus on concrete socio-cultural, political, and historical contexts grounds the sociolinguistics of mobility in ethnographic concerns of locality, diaspora, inequality, poverty, and so forth, to excavate postmodern social realities of the discrepancy between the local and the global. This discrepancy is a problematic of globalization often overlooked due to a myopic view of the phenomenon. Blommaert stresses that the loosening of border due to global phenomena, such as the movement of people and the rapid growth in global media, has brought about the challenge to sociolinguists' treatment and study of language from a village or community perspective to a mobile approach that is structured in the form of a network of language flow, movement, and exchange; in Blommaert words, it is an approach that examines "a complex world of villages, towns, neighborhoods, settlements connected by material and symbolic ties in often unpredictable ways" (2010: 1). Blommaert's proposal of the sociolinguistics of globalization to a great extent helps us counter the problems with language-as-resources in the United States raised by Ricento (2005). Similar to Ricento's proposal, it emphasizes the importance of historical contexts, and treats heritage language as mobile and in constant interaction with its environment, including dominant and other ethnic languages. These new approaches in sociolinguistics point to a changing field in the study of heritage language; they also reveal that language hierarchy is the product of a network of relations among languages, not a simplistic binary of language rivalry between a dominant and minority language. Only by thinking of languages as always in progress and in motion (García 2011) can we deconstruct the myth of heritage language as constant and unchanging.

Hierarchy between languages in postcolonial or multiethnic societies such as Singapore and the United States is often the root of ethnic communities' anxiety of losing their heritage languages. Scholars working on heritage language and ethnic identity often ask questions such as those Suresh Canagarajah raises in his examination of Tamil identity in North America (California and Toronto) and England (East London): "[Is] the heritage language dying?

And is ethnic identity lost with the heritage language?" (2013: 148). Canagarajah's examination of Tamil as a heritage language among the Sri Lankan diaspora embarks on an interesting detour, as most of his interviewees point out that even though they might not perceive and practice their ethnic identity in its essentialized forms, their hybrid identity, a product of migratory history and assimilation into the host society, is indexed by their Tamil, regardless of how it deviates from the initial form which their ancestors brought with them when they migrated to the host countries (2013: 138). The fact that they speak a hybrid Tamil and are not regarded as proficient Tamil speakers did not stop these interviewees from believing that their heritage language is still intact; they believe that it has gone through transformation due to contact and exchange between languages. This detour leads Canagarajah to conclude that heritage languages among diasporic communities go through redefinition as ethnic identities negotiate their place in the host societies and among cultures: "Mobility of the community [results] in the reconstruction of heritage language for diaspora contexts with new indexicality" (2013: 149). Because language indexes culture and identity, as culture and identity acquire newer forms, language also transforms in order to acquire new indexicality, hence, creating new values. It is necessary to acknowledge that ethnic identity undergoes transformation along with heritage language; this relationship is complementary and mutually transformative. Because of the contextual evolution of both heritage language and ethnic identity, the study of heritage language, culture, and ethnic identity should be examined in social, cultural, and political contexts. No single experience can be conveniently mapped onto another, regardless of origin. Similarly, when examining various branches of Chinese migrant routes with respect to their maintenance of heritage language, we would end up with a web or network of heritage language practices that delineates a rhizomatic dispersal of migratory development of language and cultures. Due to social and cultural differences, there can be no uniform pattern of heritage language maintenance.

Canagarajah's article leads us back to Agnes He's essay on heritage language (2010). In this essay, He proposes the following: because the common perception of heritage language assumes that it is an essential entity located in ethnic culture, applied linguistic scholars take to task the examination of heritage language by destabilizing this essentialized notion (2013: 149). He asks, "How do the political history, geography, demography, and social status of the [Heritage Language] impact its maintenance or attrition?" (2010: 67–68) in the introduction section of her essay. She arrives at the following conclusion:

> HL is not static but dynamic; it is constantly undergoing transformation by its learners and users, so that at the same time it serves as a resource for the transformation of learner identities, it is also transformed itself as result of learners' and users' language ideologies and practices.
>
> *(2010: 77)*

To gradually propose her thesis, He begins by pointing out the limitations and problematics of studying heritage language via the correlational approach in psycholinguistics and sociolinguistics. This approach is not only limiting but it also restricts any potential breakthrough in the study of heritage language in the age of globalization, where the movement of people of different backgrounds and statuses repeatedly challenge and reconstruct the stability of heritage language and its counterpart, heritage culture. This is especially so in a correlational approach because the approach takes for granted that sociocultural factors are always stable, for they embody a sociocultural history that sets these factors apart from language practices (2010: 68). As a result, by regarding language patterns and practices as independent of sociohistorical reality, a structuralist orientation is adopted, and an empirical approach, which is crucial to the understanding of transforming heritage language, is conveniently downplayed. The convenient mapping of sociocultural variables onto heritage language variations consequently neglects the importance of actual interactions between heritage language users who are active agents of heritage language construction.

Linguistic rhizome: an approach to the examination of heritage language

We have to caution ourselves not to focus on the reproduction or endorsement of heritage language and culture as a set of essentialized practices and concepts. Instead, we should be focusing on the study of how heritage languages establish connections, relate, identify, and recreate new identification based on a familiar/familial set of ethnolinguistic indexicalities. In this chapter, along with our advocacy to regard and understand heritage language as a product of interactions between users and their environments, we propose to examine the development of heritage language as a rhizomatic system, an imagery that resembles Atkinson's "rainforest" and "lush ecology" imagery (2002: 526). The *Oxford English Dictionary* defines *rhizome* as "[an] elongated, usually horizontal, subterranean stem which sends out roots and leafy shoots at intervals along its length." In layman's term, a rhizome is an underground horizontal stem that reproduces by sending out shoots and roots at its nodes. Gilles Deleuze and Félix Guattari appropriate this biological concept of the rhizome as metaphor to emphasize the principles of relationality, connectivity, and heterogeneity in the study of language, culture, and identity (2004: 7). The rhizome, which resists a vertical hierarchical structure to promote lateral relations, is more distinct and potent compared to Atkinson's imagery. It allows for a lateral comparison, not the perpetuation of hierarchical language rivalries held in place by binary opposites that consist of ideological differences such as politics of exclusion, which unfortunately proliferate discrimination and inequalities.

Unlike the imagery of the tree, which is centralized and hierarchical, the rhizome is a system of multiplicity that spreads multidirectionally. It does not obsess over the myth of an origin or the principle of a foundation, which would constitute an organic whole that the figure of a tree embodies. Thought, for Deleuze and Guattari, is a rhizome. It is an underground stem that is neither an origin nor an end (2004: 12). It is the middle piece that sends out roots and shoots that gradually break off from the source to produce new rhizomes, which lead to a system of proliferations. It is in this sense that Deleuze and Guattari appropriates rhizome as a figure for thought: a thought does not have a beginning or ending; it is always in the middle and can be connected to other thoughts to generate new thoughts. Because the rhizome is always "in the middle" and spreads in multiple directions and forms a network of communications, it violates any systematic mapping of memory and hierarchical structures of knowledge.

Language, according to Deleuze and Guattari, is a typical example of the rhizome. To them, language as a means of communication to connect people, communities, and societies is not pure, original, or fixed. It involves multiple sets of heterogeneous elements that are interconnected with other heterogeneous entities. "Language stabilizes around a parish, a bishopric, a capital. It forms a bulb. It evolves by subterranean stems and flows, along river valleys or train tracks; it spreads like a patch of oil" (2004: 2). If language does not have a fixed center, and it evolves and spreads in multiple directions, then it cannot be conceptualized in terms of a linear and stable semiotic chain. Its impurity is a characteristic, not a problematic that points to the significance of its interaction with multiple linguistic and non-linguistic connections. Hence, it is important for us to acknowledge that no linguistic community is homogeneous if we were to appropriately study heritage language in terms of its maintenance and evolution with the global movement of people.

Following this approach of the rhizomatic structure, identification, network building, and communication are keywords to the examination of heritage language. If we understood heritage identity and culture as rooted in the kind of discourse of ethnic studies in multicultural societies such as the United States and Singapore, which always involves a political dimension, then heritage languages by default "have a sociocultural function, both as a means of communication and as a way of identifying and transforming sociocultural groups" (He 2010: 68). It is within the same discourse of ethnic studies that He defines heritage culture: "The heritage culture is by definition a complex, developing, transnational, intercultural, cross-linguistic, and hybrid one" (2010: 73). By characterizing heritage language as a reality in multicultural environment vis-à-vis the mother tongue[1] in a monolingual environment, He emphasizes the very nature of heritage language as a process that is always deconstructing and reconstructing itself through language acquisition and groups' socialization with their environment (2010: 72).

In following He's conception of heritage language, we can trace a constructivist development of heritage language in a specific context (such as multilingual, multicultural, immigrant, refugee) integral to the actual experience and environment of each ethnic group. Even as an academic paradigm in the field of applied linguistic, the trajectory of this constructivist approach can be located in works by scholar such as Ochs, Blommaert from the 1990s, and the more recent works of He and Pennycook. We believe that the study of heritage language and its maintenance have to be contextualized within its migratory history and its interaction with the host environment. In a sense, even though not many scholars focus on making the distinction between language preservation and maintenance, the former connotes the need to preserve and perpetuate a linguistic essence that precedes one's identity. Conversely, the latter can be argued as keeping track or taking stock of cultural or ethnic identifiers (in this case, linguistically) as they negotiate new values and indexicalities, to borrow Canagarajah's words. By acknowledging heritage language maintenance as a negotiating process of balancing old and new within context, we are endorsing the role of heritage language users as their own agents to manage the mobility and potential transformation of their language. This, in a sense, corresponds to García's (2011) concept of "sustainable languaging" mentioned earlier in the chapter and Ricento's (2005) advocacy for community participation in language programming and planning. In practice, heritage language proves to be more flexible than the way it is theorized; it allows us to understand how heritage language users reconstruct their situational relationships with identity and community across spatiotemporal contexts. It is in this sense, we propose, that heritage languages not only transform each other over time, they also influence and are influenced by the host or other community languages and cultures in the same environment (Blommaert 2010; Canagarajah 2013).

Case study

Heritage language(s) and the Sinophone Singapore community

Chinese migration in the late 19th century and early 20th century created a global network of overseas Chinese communities (Wang 1991, 1997, 2000; Tu 1994; Kuhn 2009). These include Southeast Asia where most of these overseas Chinese communities aggregated, the Americas, South Africa, Europe, and the South Pacific. Most of these Chinese migrants were sojourners who believed that their travels away from home were temporary and they would eventually return home. Hence, they did not invest in assimilating into the host societies; instead, the maintenance of their heritage and languages were more urgent to them when in diaspora. Because of the various migratory patterns of Chinese people migrating at different times and to different places across the globe, the concept of the Chinese diaspora can easily lead to the myopic view of the these patterns and experience generated by the migrants as the same across the globe. Due to the differences between the Chinese histories of migration, conditioned by disparate motivations of the migrants, their class and economic backgrounds, and the social and political structure of the host countries, each diaspora community forms its own distinct features and relations with their heritage culture and language(s). We propose in this chapter that the nature of Chinese migrations throughout history constitutes a rhizomatic pattern of diasporas that share certain similar cultural traditions but are rooted in diverse routes in different environments.

To suggest that Chinese diaspora consists of a rhizomatic network of migratory patterns, Ronald Skeldon (2003) raises three important questions concerning the characteristics of Chinese diaspora:

> first, whether there is a truly Chinese diaspora or whether there are a series of separate diasporas based on specific place of origin of the groups concerned; second, whether any juxtaposing of the various Chinese groups with non-Chinese peoples in overseas destinations has forged a new composite sense of Chineseness; and third, whether the diaspora experience of the Chinese has forged new identities and, if so, whether these have expression in the structure and function of the diaspora communities.
>
> *(p. 54)*

These questions seem obvious to scholars working on Chinese diaspora; however, a reevaluation of these critical questions reminds us of the importance of not treating the Chinese diasporas and their experience as a homogenous entity. We ought to acknowledge that the dispersal of Chinese people across the globe over centuries has created a network of Sinophone communities with distinct local features. By raising these questions, Skeldon has seemingly initiated a conception of a network of Sinophone communities within the rhizomatic pattern of linguistic and cultural multiplicity. For example, heritage language carries a very different meaning to the Chinese people in Singapore in contrast to those living in the US precisely because the sociopolitical status and environment between the two groups are distinctly different. In addition, the promotion and maintenance of heritage language in both places are distinct because of the difference in agenda and motivation in the official policies in each respective state. Unlike the status of Chinese American, the Sinophone Singapore community in Singapore is not the minority; despite the similarity in both governments' approaches to heritage-language-as-resource in a globalizing world, the status of Chinese as one of the official mother tongues in the case of Singapore and as an ethnic/immigrant language in the case of the United States sets the two distinctively apart, like two rhizomatic branches developing in different ways and directions after breaking from the root. The rest of the chapter will focus on this particular branch of the Chinese diaspora in order to discuss how heritage language is redefined among the Sinophone Singapore community with the nation's independence.

Despite the fact that the major wave of Chinese people migrating to different parts of the world in the modern era consisted of mainly contract laborers and coolies, the different social class makeup of those who migrated to Singapore, which was then a part of Malaya, casts a different trajectory of what heritage culture and language mean for the Chinese community there in the 20th and 21st centuries. Because the Chinese in Singapore have constituted the majority population for more than a century and have run the government since the country's independence in 1965, Singapore today is no doubt a settler country by definition, with its multicultural population consisting of immigrants from different parts of the world. Yet, it is very different from the typical settler nations such as the United States, Australia, and New Zealand where the settlers are predominantly descendants of white colonialists, not Chinese immigrants (Chua 1998; Holden 2008; Shih 2011).

The first major wave of Chinese immigrants who migrated to Southeast Asia during the 19th century consisted of trade diasporas, port managers, custom collectors, tax farmers, contract laborers, and coolies (Wang 1998; Kong and Yeoh 2003). Most of them flourished in the region, especially Malaya, during the period when European colonial powers began establishing important trading posts in their respective colonies. These colonial projects facilitated the migration of Chinese merchants who came to seek resources and trade opportunities, and coolies who were brought over to the area to serve as labor forces for the colonizers. Despite the fact that these trade diasporas benefited from the colonial system facilitated by the Europeans, they never subscribed to the colonial powers or attempted at fully integrating into the local society or colonial system. They regarded their stay in Malaya as temporary for economic reasons, forming an *imperium imperio* (Kong and Yeoh 2003: 196); the merchants believed that they would eventually return to China. It was because of this mentality of the Chinese in diaspora in Malaya that there was not much sentiment of a Chinese consciousness or urgency to preserve the Chinese heritage in the form of culture or language. This is because, first, it was thought of as essential to all Chinese; second, it did not conflict with their status in Malaya due to their political autonomy in the colony. Ironically, this status of the Chinese in diaspora in Malaya was temporary in a different sense. As China underwent civil wars and foreign invasions from the second half of the 19th century onwards, the Chinese in Malaya and their stay in the region became more permanent. Yet, conversely, this sense of security of a stable identity gave rise to the threat of permanent displacement from home. The rise of a Chinese consciousness among them was further strengthened by the mobilization of a Chinese nationalism among the overseas Chinese to support the Chinese government's effort in suppressing civil wars and end foreign exploitation—an indirect impact of the May Fourth Movement in 1919 in China.

This national consciousness heightened during World War II when the Japanese invaded China, and later conquered Malaya and occupied Singapore. Overseas Chinese had actively boycotted the Japanese to support their homeland at the dawn of the war in East Asia and collaborated with the British to fight the Japanese troops when the latter ravaged Southeast Asia through Thailand. The sharing of a common trauma of war in the hands of the same enemy brought the overseas Chinese closer to their fellow people in China, despite the physical distance separating them. However, in the 1950s, with the departure of the British from Malaya after the war, this Chinese national consciousness began to fade. The introduction of the Singapore Citizenship Ordinance in 1957 acknowledged the rights to Singapore citizenship for anyone who had lived on the island for eight years or more, regardless of his or her place of birth. This policy began to encourage immigrants to rethink about their sentiments of allegiance to their host societies. As China began to close its door to the rest of the world with the formation of socialist China under the rule of the Chinese Communist Party, ties between overseas Chinese and their homeland, China, were cut or suspended. This resulted in the urgency among Chinese overseas to assimilate into their host societies in order to provide stability for themselves and their families. This is the point where the eventual return to "home" became less realizable for them. The independence of Singapore from the Federation of Malaya in 1965 further dissolved the Chinese national consciousness among the Chinese in Singapore. The burgeoning nation provided the Chinese with a different sense of identity, a national identity that is inclusive and multiracial. The change in attitude in national allegiance and identification with the host society gradually transformed the host society into a new home for Chinese Singaporeans. As China transformed from homeland into ancestral homeland for the Chinese diaspora in Singapore, the Chinese national consciousness evolved into a heritage consciousness vis-à-vis the multicultural makeup of the island city. In addition, as the Chinese national consciousness subsided among Singaporeans, one sentiment remains – the nostalgia for the homeland. Yet, due to the lack of a concept of a modern nation among the Chinese until the modernization of China, this nostalgia for the homeland for most Chinese in diaspora is a longing for the home village (*qiaoxiang*), not the Chinese nation per se (Pan 1990; Kuah-Pearce and Hu-Dehart 2006). It is, after all, this nostalgia for the home village which constituted the basis of a heritage narrative for the Chinese community in the postcolonial and post-independence Singapore. In this way, the Chinese heritage is always already a network of rhizomes. Every region or village has its distinct dialect and customs, though it overlaps with other groups to some degree.

Heritage language and the bilingual policy

Once we understand that the heritage culture and its preservation has to do more with the rhizomatic traditions of the home village rather than the national ideology of the homeland for the Chinese diaspora, we can then claim that what is most central to the experience of the Chinese diasporic communities is their ambivalent relationship with their heritage language(s). But what is the heritage language of the Chinese diaspora. Is Mandarin the de facto heritage language for Chinese diasporic communities around the world? What about the dialects?

During the past decades, immigrants from Taiwan, Hong Kong, and all around Mainland China have diversified the Chinese population in diaspora. However, prior to the mid-1960s, Chinese immigrants around the world mostly originated from the southern coastal regions such as the provinces of Guangdong and Fujian. They are descendants of five major dialect groups (*bang*): Hokkien, Teochew, Cantonese, Hakka, and Hainanese (Yen 1986; Li, Saravanan, and Ng 1997; Kong and Yeoh 2003; Skeldon 2003). Prior to the building of a modern China in the 20th century, Mandarin was merely a northern dialect sharing similar status as any other regional dialects. Even though some form of Mandarin dialect was adopted as the official language in the 14th century in China, the Mandarin commonly used today is a standard form based on the Beijing dialect. The lack of understanding of this minute detail in history often leads to the myopic claim of Mandarin as the official language of Chinese people for centuries. In the early 20th century, as China embarked on the journey to modern nationhood, a vote was cast to decide on the official Chinese language.

In 1913, a year after the founding of the Chinese Republic, the Ministry of Education proposed the establishing of a standard pronunciation for an official national language for modern China. The delegates from the north advocated for the Mandarin dialect, arguing that Mandarin has always served as the lingua franca for Chinese people, while the delegates from the south insisted that the adoption of Mandarin as the official Chinese language over a southern dialect such as Cantonese would undermine the fact that southerners were not necessarily familiar with northern dialects. After much deliberation, Mandarin was voted the official language of China (DeFrancis 1984; Ramsey 1987). As a result, Mandarin became the de facto national/ethnic language that unifies Chinese people in China and overseas. The official acknowledgment of Mandarin as the Chinese language naturally prioritizes Mandarin as the heritage language for Chinese in diaspora, downplaying the role of dialects when it comes to ethnic representation and unity, despite the fact that many diasporic Chinese communities still rely on dialects in their everyday communication within their communities. For example, Cantonese is still a dominant spoken language in some Chinatowns in the United States. In a sense, even though language is an important aspect of identity formation, the prioritizing of certain regional dialects over others can create a hierarchy of language, which will eventually end up oppressing and marginalizing the ones lower in the hierarchy. Mandarin, which has become the official Chinese language and de facto language of the Chinese diaspora since the turn of the 20th century, is one such example. Here, the concept of the rhizome is useful in helping us think beyond such hierarchy and language rivalry by focusing on the multiplicity of language within a linguistic network. By acknowledging the plurality of Sinitic languages, we are questioning the stability of Chinese identity based on an official language and dominant culture (the Han culture), simply because there is an array of dialect groups and also ethnic minorities throughout China that speak a variety of languages other than Mandarin and practice ethnic traditions disparate from the Han Chinese. So, by discussing Chinese language within the purview of Mandarin when we examine the heritage language of the Chinese diaspora, we are engaging with a misnomer, especially among those who neither identify with nor speak Mandarin.

Returning to the case of Singapore, the building of a multiracial and multicultural nation requires careful planning of government policies. One important area of such planning with the independence of Singapore in 1965 is that of the language policies. Independence, while ushering the settler nation to embark on a journey to the future, simultaneously forced it to engage with the migratory histories of its multiethnic population that constituted the majority. With the writing of multiracialism as a policy into the constitution in 1966, the nation invested in promoting a uniform national identity conducive to the acceptance and coexistence of its various ethnic groups. Yet, this uniform national identity has to accommodate the maintenance of various heritage cultures in order to sustain the openness and inclusiveness of a multiethnic society at large. Language as the most relevant expression of heritage culture became the most important ideological tool for the government to construct a multicultural society. Language policies are needed to balance the building of a common culture and the maintenance of heritage cultures.

The implementation of the bilingual education policy in 1966 was not unproblematic to the newly formed democratic nation. The policy, unfortunately, ended up creating a hierarchy of languages in Singapore, with English – the language of the British colonizers – prevailing as the common language among all racial communities, and Mandarin as the most prominent among the mother tongues. The efforts involved in promoting Malay and Tamil were far less than that invested in Mandarin education and the promotion of the language via a nationwide campaign in the late seventies. Phyllis Chew reminds us that one important implications of the "Speak Mandarin" campaign is its impact on the compartmentalization of racial groups in Singapore. Instead of unifying racial communities, the campaign contributed to a certain level of division among racial groups due to this reason (Chew 2013). To make Mandarin learning more accessible to the English-educated Chinese and the Chinese-educated ones, and also to encourage non-Chinese to pick up Mandarin as a third or fourth language, the romanized Chinese phonetic system (or the *pinyin* system) was adopted to replace the old phonetic system, and to facilitate the speaking of Mandarin with the "proper" accent and accurate tones (*Straits Times*, May 1, 1973).

A decade after its implementation, the government began to see the bilingual policy as the solution to "reconciling different cultural values and attitudes" (*Straits Times*, April 19, 1977). But the ideology of the nation-state with regards to its language policies advocated a reproduction of the colonial rhetoric of the mother tongues as the embodiment of "traditional values, culture and languages," while English maintained its role as the "key to the advanced technology of the West" (*Straits Times*, April 19, 1977). The focus on the functionality of bilingualism is the government's way of claiming its promotion of fairness and equality for everyone in the burgeoning nation, regardless of race, class, ethnicity, and religion. In this sense, the bilingual education policy was a policy to ease the tension derived from the rivalry among languages of various ethnic groups, including dialects (Bokhorst-Heng 1998, 1999; Wee 2006). However, the government's attitude towards dialects was not a favorable one. Prime Minister Lee Kuan Yew encouraged Chinese Singaporeans to consider Mandarin as their lingua franca instead of the dialects they spoke at home. He urged parents to support the bilingual policy by reminding their children to use English and Mandarin in their daily conversation. For Lee, the continuing use of dialects in Singapore household would end up creating a "fractured multilingual society" because he understood that, to be literate, one should master Mandarin in order "to read the books, the proverbs, the parables, the stories of heroes and villains, so that [one knows] what a good upright man should do and be" (*Straits Times*, March 13, 1978). Not only was Mandarin seen as the only Sinitic language that could educate, it was also the language in which traditional and moral values lie. Lee called the decision to privilege Mandarin over other dialects a conscious choice the nation had to make (*Straits Times*, March 13, 1978).

Because English is after all a working language for Singaporeans while ushering the country toward modernity, Western technology, and commerce, the Singapore government was concerned about the fact that its citizens would end up having no connections to their own cultures. To prevent Singaporeans from falling into a state of anomie, the government adopted the discourse of the mother tongue/heritage language to link three out of the four official languages (Malay, Mandarin, and Tamil) conveniently to their respective ancestral cultures (Bokhorst-Heng 1998, 1999). It is partly because of this concern among Singaporeans, especially Chinese parents who were afraid that their bilingual children would lose their roots, that the government adopted the narrative of preserving heritage culture to promote Mandarin. The conflation of a localized Chinese identity with that of the ancestral Chinese identity through a dominant Sinitic language, Mandarin, presented a skewed perspective on what it meant to be an ethnic Chinese subject in Singapore at the dawn of the nation's independence. This myopic view contributed to the state-endorsed discourse of reclamation and reconstruction of the mother tongues for its three main racial groups. Ironically, it also downplayed the significance of the Chinese diasporic community as a rhizomatic branch with its unique characteristics, not a mere copy of an essentialized Chinese heritage based on one's imagination of the past.

Heritage language and "Speak Mandarin" campaign

The suppression of Sinitic dialects became official with the launch of the "Speak Mandarin" campaign on September 7, 1979. In the name of preserving "the fine cultural tradition of the Chinese and [aiding] in promoting the bilingual educational policy," Mandarin-speaking became the uniform representation of a Chinese identity and experience, despite the fact that most Chinese Singaporeans came from dialect-speaking households other than Mandarin (*Straits Times*, August 17, 1979; *Straits Times*, September 7, 1979). In fact, the slogan of this campaign – "Speak More Mandarin, Less Dialects" – was much more telling than it sounded. The purpose of the campaign was to wean Singaporeans off their dialect-speaking habits and to adopt Mandarin as a common language among the larger Chinese community. It is futile to claim any real purpose to the promotion of the "Speak Mandarin" campaign, because the campaign is the product of a set of government ideologies including the management of the Chinese communities by way of a common language and the choice of Mandarin as the vehicle to preserve the rich Chinese cultural tradition in order to ward off the lure of Western decadent values, according to Peter Teo (2005).

Before the official introduction of the "Speak Mandarin" campaign, Chinese dialects were considered mother tongues of the various clans and dialect groups. They were also used as language of instructions in most Chinese schools in the 1960s. In 1966, Soon Peng Yam, president of the Chinese Chamber of Commerce, inaugurated the "Promote the Mother Tongue" education month campaign with the support of representatives from 250 Chinese schools and 300 Chinese guilds and associations (*Straits Times*, May 3, 1966). In a sense, dialects were the legitimate mother tongue since they were everyday languages of most Sinophone households. However, with the government's effort in promoting Mandarin as a common language among the Sinophone community, Mandarin eventually became the mother tongue of the community over time (Stroud and Wee 2012: 33–34). The government's call to promote Mandarin-speaking over dialects among ethnic Chinese began as early as 1978 (*Straits Times*, April 29, 1978). Two months before the official launch of the campaign in July, twelve schools collaborated to launch a "Speak Our School Languages" campaign. This campaign stressed that if students continued to speak in dialects, the effectiveness of their English and Mandarin learning in school would be affected (*Straits Times*, July 6, 1979). In this sense, dialects became the scapegoat of Mandarin's lack of popularity among the Sinophone community. This agenda to eliminate dialects, or to "de-link dialects of local identities" (Stroud and Wee 2010: 187) became clearer at the launch of the "Speak Mandarin" campaign.

So, why was the learning of Mandarin significant to Sinophone Singaporeans? As *Straits Times* columnist Tong Hai Ngiam bluntly put it, with the increased importance of Mandarin in the political and economic environment in Asia, the promotion of Mandarin-speaking would facilitate the communication among Sinophone Singaporeans and other Mandarin-speaking people in the region, especially China (*Straits Times*, August 13, 1979). As China's modernization program matures, it seemed relevant for the Chinese in Singapore to equip themselves with Mandarin to facilitate their communication with China, especially in the field of business as China reopened its doors to the world (*Straits Times*, October 24, 1979; *Straits Times*, December 2, 1979). As a result of the bilingual education policy and the "Speak Mandarin" campaign, Sinitic dialects, though the "first language" for many students from Chinese households, were deemed a burden to the students due to the fact that dialects lack the instrumentality of Mandarin as a language of commercial exchange (*Straits Times*, October 2, 1979).

Even though the campaign's objective was to promote better communication among the Sinophone community through Mandarin in order to facilitate bilingual education in schools, most dialect speakers who participated in the campaign felt that dialects carry sentimental values that were connected to their ethnic cultures (*Straits Times*, September 9, 1979). Dialects to those who spoke them were not just a matter of speaking; they represented an entire aspect of life. Dialects, in other words, were deeply rooted in the cultures and traditions of the local Chinese (Stroud and Wee 2012: 42–43). To persuade dialect-speaking Chinese to switch to Mandarin, Lee proposed a slight modification to the campaign slogan, to drop the second part of the couplet: "Use Less Dialect" (*Straits Times*, October 3, 1979).

To drive home the importance of the "Speak Mandarin" Campaign, the Ministry of Culture published a twenty-four-page bilingual booklet, *Speak More Mandarin and Less Dialect* to explain the scope and purpose of the campaign, and to provide examples of Mandarin conversations. This booklet, while promoting the campaign, reinforced the fact that the campaign complemented the Bilingual Education policy (*Straits Times*, November 19, 1979). To facilitate the learning of both Chinese writing and Mandarin-speaking, simplified Chinese characters were adopted to replace traditional characters,[2] and *pinyin* romanization was introduced to facilitate the learning of Mandarin tones.[3]

As we suggested earlier, Chinese heritage culture among the diasporic communities is pluralistic in nature and can be defined by an array of characteristics such as clan associations, dialect groups, kinship affiliations, and regional traditions. This plurality is often conflated within the larger representation and discourse of Mandarin as the de facto heritage language for the Chinese; in the case of Singapore, the dialects were suppressed in order to promote Mandarin as the community language among the Chinese. Despite the fact that Chinese Singaporeans spoke different dialects, the government argued that the choice of Mandarin as the "mother tongue" for Chinese Singaporeans is "a sensible compromise" (*Straits Times*, September 22, 1979).

The ethnolinguistic framework of Singapore's language policies and campaigns are products of modernity of which issues of ethnicity and class are weaved into new forms of linguistic hierarchy in the post-independence nation. On the one hand, the urgency to preserve heritage cultures and languages was important to a postcolonial society like Singapore; on the other, the tension and rivalry for resources among and within ethnic groups were challenging for a government that was seeking a common culture to promote a sense of belonging among the groups. This tension was an outcome of the ambivalence of a postcolonial society balancing both modernity and tradition. In the unique case of Singapore, due to its multiethnic population, a restructuring of heritage languages, in the form of mother tongues, was needed. The unfortunate outcome of such a political move is the decontextualization of the historical characteristics of language shift through migration. Language shift due to the migration of people is always rhizomatic in structure; it is never a linear process. By excavating the history of language shift in the case of Sinophone Singapore, we historicize one such rhizomatic pattern of heritage language in migration in order to assess the usefulness of heritage language education and maintenance as assets to individuals and local communities of whom these languages belong to, not simply as resource for the state.

Implications and future directions

Our purpose of unveiling this complexity of what heritage language and culture mean to the Chinese diaspora is not to cast an easy criticism on the hierarchy of language but to expand our understanding of heritage language as an area of study that is highly politicized and ideological. In so doing, we hope to have illustrated that the promotion and maintenance of heritage language is situational and contextual for each diasporic community from the same place of origin. For example, what an ethnic Chinese in Singapore understands as her heritage language and what constitutes it can be very different from that of an ethnic Chinese living in New York City's Chinatown. Furthermore, what condition the meanings, scope, and utility of the heritage language in these two locales are products of each social and political environment such as educational policies, and community efforts. The trajectory of a diverse network of Chinese community and their relations to a heritage culture and language leads us to the conclusion that migration does not simply produce a linear inheritance of heritage language but a network of heritage language and culture that is multi-directional, like the dispersal of people in the phenomenon of diaspora.

To conclude, we return to the larger question of heritage language and migration. Only when we begin to acknowledge that heritage language is situational and non-essential can we begin to understand that heritage language as an indexical system of heritage identity and culture is also a social, cultural, and economic product that reflects the everyday experience and reality of each ethnic community contextually. And only by acknowledging the acquisition and utilization of heritage language as part of an ethnic community's socialization process can we understand the complementary relationship between language and identity as mutually transformative. In a similar fashion, building on theories by scholars such as Ochs (1993) and Ochs and Schieffelin (1995), we see this relationship as exemplified by heritage language users who "actively [(re)construct] themselves as members of a particular ethnicity, nationality, speech community, social rank, and profession . . . on the open-ended, negotiated, contested character of the interactional routine as a resource for language growth, maintenance, and change" (He 2010: 72–73). In other words, the performativity of language in everyday scenarios becomes part and parcel of how a subject constructs his or her own identity through language and other cultural properties. This, in turn, contributes to the mapping of a larger network of languages diversity that truly embraces difference in the interaction and transformation between language through linguistic theories such as "sociolinguistics of mobility," "sustainable languaging," and "translanguaging."

Related topics

Superdiversity and language
New orientations to identity in mobility
Migration trajectories
Diaspora and language

Further reading

Cho, G. (2000). The role of heritage language in social interactions and relationships: Reflections from a language minority group. *Bilingual Research Journal, 24*, 369–384.

This article examines the effects of one's competency with her heritage language on social interactions, relationships with other heritage language speakers from the same ethnic group, and the individual herself to propose that heritage language development, while providing personal gains to the individual, offers positive contributions to the society as a whole.

Cummins, J. (2005). A proposal for action: Strategies for recognizing heritage language competence as a learning resource within the mainstream classroom. *Modern Language Journal, 89*, 585–592.

This article suggests some approaches to contest and overcome the monolingual instructional assumptions in the form of bilingual instructional strategies such as incorporating heritage language teaching in after-school programs.

Polinsky, M. (2008). Heritage language narratives. In *Heritage Language Education: A New Field Emerging*. New York: Routledge, 149–164.

This preliminary study of the structure of heritage speakers' narratives attempts to deduce a methodology that will enable a better understanding of the main characteristics of such narratives and how they differ from those of fully competent speakers in order to contribute to the development of heritage language teaching.

Scontras, G., Fuchs, Z. and Polinsky, M. (2015). Heritage language and linguistic theory. *Frontiers in Psychology*, 6(1545), 1–20.

This article examines heritage linguistics by focusing on the typical features of heritage language speakers in order to theorize the practice and development of heritage language in the broader field of linguistic theory.

Notes

1 Even though He makes a clear distinction in her essay between heritage language and mother tongue, the latter is often used interchangeably with the former in some multilingual society. One such example is Sinophone Singapore, which we will examine in the second half of this chapter.
2 Research conducted by Loo Shaw Chang, the acting director of Nanyang University's Chinese Language and Research Center to standardize the Chinese language in Singapore reported: "Simplified characters, numbering 502, were first introduced here in 1969. They were increased to 2,248 characters in 1976. These simplified characters are identical to those introduced in China" (*Straits Times*, October 29, 1979).
3 *Straits Times* (October 29, 1979). The research also noted "Pinyin romanization was introduced in education here in 1971. The Pinyin system has greatly enhanced the standard pronunciation of Mandarin."

References

Aissaoui, R. (2009). *Immigration and National Identity: North African Political Movements in Colonial and Postcolonial France*. New York: Tauris Academic Studies.
Atkinson, D. (2002). Toward a sociocognitive approach to SLA. *Modern Language Journal* 86: 525–545.
Baker, C. (1995) *Foundations of Bilingual Education and Bilingualism*. Buffalo, NY: Multilingual Matters.
Blommaert, J. (2010). *The Sociolinguistics of Globalization*. Cambridge: Cambridge University Press.
Bokhorst-Heng, W. (1998). Language planning and management in Singapore. In J.A. Foley, T. Kandiah, A.E. Gupta, L. Alsagoff, C.L. Ho, I.S. Talib and W. Bokhorst-Heng (eds.), *English in New Cultural Contexts: Reflections from Singapore* (pp. 287–319). Singapore: Oxford University Press.
Bokhorst-Heng, W. (1999). Singapore's speak mandarin campaign: Language ideological debates in the imagining of the nation. In J. Blommaert (ed.), *Language Ideological Debates* (pp. 235–266). Berlin: Mouton de Gruyter.
Canagarajah, S. (2013). Reconstructing heritage language: Resolving dilemmas in language maintenance for Sri Lankan Tamil migrants. *International Journal of the Sociology of Language* 222: 131–155.
Chew, P.G.-L. (2013). *A Sociolinguistic History of Early Identities in Singapore: From Colonialism to Nationalism*. New York: Palgrave Macmillan.
Chua, B.H. (1998). Southeast Asia in Postcolonial Studies: An introduction. *Postcolonial Studies* 11(3): 231–240.
Cummins, J. (2005). A proposal for action: Strategies for recognizing HL competence as a learning resource within the mainstream classroom. *Modern Language Journal* 89: 585–592.
De Fina, A. (2007). Code-switching and the construction of ethnic identity in a community of practice. *Language in Society* 36: 371–392.
DeFrancis, J. (1984). *The Chinese Language: Fact and Fantasy*. Honolulu: University of Hawaii Press.
Deleuze, G. and Guattari, F. (2004). *A Thousand Plateaus* [Translated by B. Massumi]. New York: Continuum.
Derrida, J. (1998). *Monolingualism of the Other: Or, the Prosthesis of Origin* [Translated by P. Mensah]. California: Stanford University Press.
Doerr, N.M. (2011). Introduction to heritage, nationhood, and language: Migrants with Japan connections. In N.M. Doerr (ed.), *Heritage, Nationhood and Language: Migrants with Japan Connections* (pp. 1–6). New York: Routledge.

Edwards, J. (2001). The ecology of language revival. *Current Issues in Language Planning* 2: 231–241.
Fishman, J.A. (2001). 300-plus years of heritage language education in the United States. In J.K. Peyton, D.A. Ranard and S. McGinnis (eds.), *Heritage Languages in America: Preserving a National Resource*. McHenry, IL: Center for Applied Linguistics.
García, O. (2005). Positioning heritage languages in the United States. *Modern Language Journal* 89(4): 601–605.
García, O. (2011). From language garden to sustainable languaging: Bilingual education in a global world. *Perspective: A Publication of the National Association for Bilingual Education*, Sept/Oct: 5–10.
García, O., Zakharua, X. and Otcu, X. (2013). *Bilingual Community Education for American Children: Beyond Heritage Languages in a Global City*. Bristol: Multilingual Matters.
Gumperz, J.J. (1982). *Discourse Strategies*. Cambridge: Cambridge University Press.
He, A. (2010). The heart of heritage: Sociocultural dimensions of heritage language learning. *Annual Review of Applied Linguistics* 30: 66–82.
Holden, P. (2008). Postcolonial desire: Placing Singapore. *Postcolonial Studies* 11(3): 345–361.
Hymes, D. (1974). *Foundations in Sociolinguistics: An Ethnographic Approach*. Philadelphia: University of Pennsylvania Press.
Hymes, D. (1996). *Ethnography, Linguistics, Narrative Inequality: Toward an Understanding of Voice*. London: Taylor & Francis.
Kong, L. and Yeoh, B. (2003). Nation, ethnicity, and identity: Singapore and the dynamics and discourses of Chinese migration. In L.J.C. Ma and C. Cartier (eds.), *The Chinese Diaspora: Space, Place, Mobility, and Identity* (pp. 193–219). Lanham, MD: Rowman & Littlefield.
Kuah-Pearce, K.E. and Hu-DeHart, E. (2006). *Voluntary Organizations in the Chinese Diaspora*. Hong Kong: Hong Kong University Press.
Kuhn, P.A. (2009). *Chinese among Others: Emigration in Modern Times*. Lanham, MD: Rowman & Littlefield.
Li, W., Saravanan, V. and Ng, J. (1997). Language shift in the Teochew community in Singapore: A family domain analysis. *Journal of Multilingual and Multicultural Development* 18(5): 364–384.
Ngiam, T.H. (1979). Chamber in favour of emphasis on Mandarin. *Straits Times*, April 8.
Ngiam, T.H. (1979). Goal for common language among Chinese. *Straits Times*, August 13.
Ochs, E. (1993). Constructing social identity. *Research on Language and Social Interaction* 26: 287–306.
Ochs, E. and Schieffelin, B. (1995). The impact of language socialization on grammatical development. In P. Fletcher and B. MacWhinney (eds.), *The Handbook of Child Language* (pp. 73–94). Malden, MA: Blackwell.
Pan, L. (1990). *Sons of the Yellow Emperor: A History of the Chinese Diaspora*. Lanham, MD: Rowman & Littlefield.
Pennycook, A. (2010). *Language as a Local Practice*. New York: Routledge.
Ramsey, S.R. (1987). *The Language of China*. Princeton, NJ: Princeton University Press.
Ricento, T. (2005). Problems with the "language-as-resource" discourse in the promotion of heritage languages in the U.S.A. *Journal of Sociolinguistics* 9(3): 348–368.
Ruiz, R. (1984). Orientations in language planning. *Bilingual Research Journal* 8(2): 15–34.
Shih, S.M. (2011). The concept of the Sinophone. *PMLA* 126(3): 709–718.
Skeldon, R. (2003). The Chinese diaspora or the migration of Chinese peoples? In L.J.C. Ma and C. Cartier (eds.), *The Chinese Diaspora: Space, Place, Mobility, and Identity* (pp. 51–66). Lanham, MD: Rowman & Littlefield.
Straits Times. (1966). "Promote Mother Tongue" campaign by Chinese in Singapore. May 3.
Straits Times. (1973). Mandarin misconceptions and how to get rid of that stumbling block. May 1.
Straits Times. (1977). Bilingualism will unify our society. April 19.
Straits Times. (1978). Lee explains need to use mandarin. March 13.
Straits Times. (1979). Drive to discourage dialect speaking. July 6.
Straits Times. (1979). Panel set up to promote Mandarin. August 17.
Straits Times. (1979). Lee to launch "Use Mandarin" campaign. September 7.

Straits Times. (1979). Heads say "yes" but hearts. . . . September 9.
Straits Times. (1979). Gently now. September 22.
Straits Times. (1979). Dialects are extra burden for our school children. October 2.
Straits Times. (1979). Hearts must be won over not only minds. October 3.
Straits Times. (1979). Mandarin drive linked to past efforts. October 29.
Straits Times. (1979). English group to air views over TV. November 19.
Straits Times. (1979). Mandarin an asset for future, says professor on high blood. December 2.
Stroud, C. and Wee, S. (2012). *Style, Identity and Literacy*. New York: Multilingual Matters.
Tan, B. H. (1979). Chinese language widely used at the United Nations. *Straits Times*, October 24.
Teo, P. (2005). Mandarinising Singapore: A critical analysis of slogans in Singapore's "Speak Mandarin" campaign. *Critical Discourse Studies* 2(2): 121–142.
Tu, W. (1994). Cultural China: The periphery as the center. In *The Living Tree: The Changing Meaning of Being Chinese Today* (pp. 1–34). Stanford, CA: Stanford University Press.
Valdés, G. (2001). *Learning and Not Learning English: Latino Students in American Schools*. New York: Teachers College Press.
Wang, G. W. (1991). *China and the Chinese Overseas*. Singapore: Times Academic Press.
Wang, G. W. (1997). *Global History and Migration*. Boulder, CO: Westview Press.
Wang, G. W. (1998). The status of Overseas Chinese Studies. In L. C. Wang and G. W. Wang (eds.), *The Chinese Diasporas: Selected Essays* (pp. 1–13). Singapore: Times Academic Press.
Wang, G. W. (2000). *The Chinese Overseas: From Earthbound China to the Quest for Autonomy*. Massachusetts: Harvard University Press.
Wee, L. (2006). The semiotics of language ideologies in Singapore. *Journal of Sociolinguistics* 10(3): 344–361.
Wiley, T. G. (2001). On defining heritage languages and their speakers. In J. K. Peyton, D. A. Ranard and S. McGinnis (eds.), *Heritage Languages in America: Preserving a National Resource*. McHenry, IL: Center for Applied Linguistics.
Wiley, T. G. (2005). *Literacy and Language Diversity in the United States* (2nd ed.). McHenry, IL: Center for Applied Linguistics.
Wiley, T. G. and Valdés, G. (2000). Heritage languages instruction in the United States: A time for renewal. *Bilingual Research Journal* 24: i–v.
Yen, C. H. (1986). *A Social History of the Chinese in Singapore and Malaya, 1800–1911*. Singapore: Oxford University Press.

27
Language-in-education policies and mobile citizens

Beatriz P. Lorente

Introduction

In a world that has become "more open to flows of goods and capital but more closed to the circulation of human bodies" (Mezzadra and Neilson 2013: 19) even as migration is increasingly characterized by multiple chains of movement and transnational interconnections, language-in-education policies have become powerful mechanisms by which states govern, manage, and calibrate increasing and ever more diverse global flows of people to and from their borders. Current articulations of language-in-education policies are underpinned by the tensions between two distinct and overlapping forces: the fixity engendered by the endurance of the monolingual and monocultural nation-state as the ideal model of political organization where recognition as a legitimate speaker (Heller 2010) of a standard national language is a gatekeeper to citizenship; and the fluidity espoused by neo-liberalization where the individual and self-dependent learning of commodifiable language skills – whether these be the standard variety of a national language, English, and/or a 'foreign language' – is considered to be a desirable quality of a globally competitive, flexible and mobile citizen (Bernstein et al. 2015; Perez-Milans 2015a). These tensions between fixity and fluidity and the discursive processes that brings the two together have produced language-in-education policies that maintain the monolingual habitus of nation-states while at the same time promoting particular forms of multilingualism. In effect, such inconsistent policies spatialize linguistic diversity by zoning off the national territory as monolingual while locating multilingualism in the individual (as skills) or in international communication (Jaspers 2015: 110).

This chapter begins with an overview of what language-in-education policy is and how it is connected to citizenship. This provides the background for the survey of language-in-education policies and how they shape and are shaped by migration. The chapter then examines how the tensions between fixity and fluidity produce disjunctures and contradictions in language-in-education policy. The inclination for fixity can be seen in language-in-education policies that are shaped by discourses around the integration of migrants, especially in their host countries. In such contexts, knowledge of an official or de facto national language or mother tongue is seen as essential for the performance of various kinds of citizenship, from carrying out one's rights and obligations to fitting into particular constructions of national identity. The tendency for fluidity can be seen in language-in-education policies that reflect the (re)alignment of relations between state and capital. These aim to capitalize on globalization by producing citizens who are globally competitive and mobile. Here, knowledge of English is unquestionably considered to be a basic skill and the promotion of the learning of "foreign languages" is seen as essential for accessing the promises of mobility such as a cosmopolitan identity, a common supra-national sense of belonging and economic betterment. The final part of the chapter considers the implications for applied linguistics, in particular to language teaching, and points to future possibilities for research on multilingual policies that might serve inclusive and empowering objectives.

Overview

It is first necessary to define what language-in-education policy is. Apart from the term "language-in-education" policy, which is the term that will be used in this chapter, researchers have also used "language education policy," "language policy in education," or "educational language policy" interchangeably or deliberately in order to emphasize distinctions in how language-in-education policies are understood and analytically approached (see Johnson 2013 for an overview of how these different terms are used). No matter what they are called, research on such policies focus on de facto language practices in educational institutions, the mechanisms that create them (Shohamy 2006: 76) and their consequences or effects. Language-in-education policies address issues such as:

> which language(s) to teach and learn in schools? When (at what age) to begin teaching these languages? For how long (number of years and hours of study) should they be taught? By whom, for whom (who is qualified to teach and who is entitled or obligated to learn) and how (which methods, materials, tests, etc.)?
>
> *(Shohamy 2006: 76)*

Research on language-in-education policy has expanded to include not just top-down, overt and de jure policies expressed through official documents establishing the rationale and the mechanics of language programs or expressing mission statements or curricula, but also bottom-up policies that are not explicit or not established by authority but are derived or inferred from what people do and what people believe in (Spolsky 2004). In educational contexts, this would refer to the language ideologies and practices of administrators, teachers, and students in classrooms and schools, as reflected in their choice and use of textbooks and testing instruments, as well as their everyday, in situ interactions in schools. In this light, 'policy' in general and 'language-in-education policy' in particular can be seen as "a practice of power that operates at multiple, intersecting levels: that is, the micro level of individuals in face-to-face interaction, the meso level of local communities of practice, and the macro-level of nation-states and larger global forces" (McCarty 2011: 3). This expanded, processual, and multi-layered view of policy is fundamental to critically understanding how the infrastructures and processes by which regimes of language are (re)produced and linguistic capital is distributed and established in educational systems, schools, and classrooms (Tollefson 1991, 2002; Tollefson and Tsui 2004; Lin and Martin 2005). As importantly, this view makes visible the potentially agentive roles played by local educators and students as they create, interpret, resist, and appropriate language-in-education policies (Ricento and Hornberger 1996; Hornberger and Johnson 2007; McCarty 2011). Not losing sight of human agency is crucial to "insist(ing) against the odds that language policies may be the site of both transit and difference" (Ramanathan 2013: 165).

Language-in-education policies are rooted in nation-states and are an essential means of socializing people into the nation and constructing citizenship as a central category of identity. Nation-building often comes hand in hand with a linguistic nationalism that is founded on the ideology of one nation, one language, one culture. This monoglot nation is not just an imagined community, "whereby people come to imagine a shared experience of identification with an extended community, but also exclusionary historical and institutional practices to which access is restricted via citizenship" (Piller 2001: 259). The ways in which language is used as an exclusionary instrument have been documented in work on language and integration, and language testing regimes and naturalization (cf. Hogan-Brun, Mar-Molinero, and Stevenson 2009). The most recent work on language and citizenship emphasizes how citizenship is not an end product or a goal to be attained (Ramanathan 2013, 2015) and how citizenship includes but is not reducible to rights and responsibilities (Milani 2015). Ramanathan (2013: 162) defines citizenship as "being able to participate fully," with such participation being locally defined and viewed "as a process amidst tensions, fluid contexts and diverse meanings." Milani (2015: 319) emphasizes the enactment of citizenship and how "it is also a set of norms and (linguistic) behaviours that individuals are socialized into, as well as a series of practices that social actors perform through an array of semiotic means". These process- and practice-oriented definitions of citizenship highlight all the more the importance of particular forms and performances of language, and the role of language-in-education policies as a gatekeeper regulating access to the legitimate language and to recognition as a legitimate speaker.

As an infrastructure of the nation, national education systems in general and compulsory education in particular are instrumentalized in nation-building projects (Wright 2012). As García, Skutnabb-Kangas, and Torres-Guzmán (2006: 12) point out: "regardless of more or less flexibility, all state schools participate in functioning as agents of imagined nationhood . . . This often promotes the semblance of, or the idealized image of one identity, one culture, and one standard language and literacy". As such, in models for the different stages of language planning, schools are considered to be the most important institutions for promoting and implementing national language policies and for propagating the use of the standard, as it is through schools that citizens can be socialized into the linguistic and cultural practices by which the nation defines itself. As an infrastructure of the state, the education system plays a key role in organizing linguistic resources, behaviors, and meanings (Heller 2007) that lead to "particular forms of stratification in value attribution to linguistic varieties and forms of usage" (Blommaert 2005: 219). In education systems, it is the standard variety of a national or official language that is valuable and that, at least in theory, is used as the medium of instruction. Language-in-education policies are the concrete manifestations of how such valuable linguistic resources, behaviors, and meanings are organized by the state, and they provide a template for how they will be distributed.

Migration puts a spotlight on language-in-education policies, especially on the role of states as conduits between the local and the global (Blommaert 2005). This is because the sovereignty of nation-states depends on the construction and maintenance of an indexical order that naturalizes the categories 'citizens' and 'immigrant' (Dick 2011: 228). In such an indexical order, cultural belonging coincides with residing within the nation's territory and speaking a standard national language. In this light, language-in-education policies can be viewed as sites where the authentic and legitimate citizen is constructed and differentiated from the inauthentic and the illegitimate, thus determining the differential inclusion and exclusion of people from the rights and the obligations of full participation in nation-states. This territorialized citizenship is being fragmented by neoliberalism which is changing how citizenship is viewed. Within neoliberalism, the rationale of national belonging is being supplemented and, at times, supplanted by the view of citizens as human capital (Ong 2006). Selection, inclusion, and exclusion are predicated on the extent to which a body can be self-governing and productive, that is, able to join the formal labor market and able to contribute to the economy. This layering of pride and profit (Duchêne and Heller 2012), where national belonging and citizenship are rationalized by economic arguments – for example, proficiency in the national standard language as a prerequisite for participation in the labor market – has led to the tensions between fixity and fluidity that characterize current language-in-education policies.

Issues and ongoing debates

Language-in-education policies and fixity

The friction between the monolingual and monocultural ideology of nation-states and the transnational movements of people is evident in how language-in-education policies generally privilege national languages and marginalize the languages of students from migration backgrounds. This entails a "reductive re-ordering and re-evaluation of (migrants') linguistic repertoires which serve both to index and be partly constitutive of their unequal social status" (Orman 2012: 301) and results in migrant children experiencing educational disadvantage vis-à-vis their native-born peers. Migrants are often not given the choice of learning and using a new language, while keeping and maintaining their 'old' languages; the new countries where migrants are in often seek to force a choice between one or the other (Hornberger 1998: 446). Thus, migration entails cultural and linguistic integration, and eventually assimilation into the receiving country. This monolingual norm is increasingly framed in the emancipatory language of social inclusion (Piller and Takahashi 2011) where "in a society which claims an identity which is tolerant, even proud, of its diversity, the underlying, dominant ideology is one which erases difference in favor of homogeneity" (Blackledge 2009: 84).

Historically, multilingualism has been considered to be antithetical to nation-building processes (Wright 2012). It must be noted though that it is not multilingualism per se that is considered to be a threat to social cohesion; it is multilingualism in languages that are not circumscribed as part of the nation that is considered undesirable or not valuable. The multilingualism that is often treated as a problem rather than as a resource is the 'natural' or vernacular multilingualism of ethnic minorities and migrants (Luchtenberg 2011). As such, the default mode of language-in-education policies seems to be that of fixity, of implicitly or explicitly requiring migrants to know a national language in order to reap the benefits of inclusion in the state. These policies not only put pressure on social groups to give up their affiliations to better assimilate; they also reproduce and exacerbate inequalities between 'citizens' who speak the medium of instruction and migrants who don't.

That language-in-education policies seek first and foremost to 'fix' migrants in place is evident in research on explicit and implicit language-in-education policies in migrant-receiving countries such as Canada (Darvin and Norton 2014), France (Helot and Young 2002), Germany (Luchtenberg 2002; Duarte 2011; Stevenson 2015), Greece (Gkaintartzi, Killiari, and Tsokalidou 2015), Spain (Martín Rojo 2010; see Pujolar 2010 for the case of Catalonia), the UK (Safford and Drury 2013), and the United States (Stritikus 2002; Johnson 2012; Warriner

2015; Wiley and García 2016; see Pavlenko 2002 and McCarty 2004 for a history). One can also assume that this is the default mode in countries where there are significant flows of people but where very little is known about migration and language policies-in-education. Very little research has been done as to how language-in-education policies in the South address the mostly South-South migratory flows that characterize migration to the South. This is despite the fact that South-South migration is as common as South-North migration (United Nations Population Division 2014). If migrants can and do access the public education system in these countries, they would be subject to a monolingual and monocultural ideology. In Southeast Asia, for example, there is a general tendency towards monolingualism, with a clear trend towards assimilation (Sercombe and Tupas 2014). It can be assumed that like in the case of minority ethnic groups, the main kinds of language education open to migrants (that is, if they are permitted by the state to attend public schools) who do not speak the medium of instruction are "largely forms of transitional bilingualism which (intentionally or not) aim at language shift" (Sercombe and Tupas 2014: 8). In Thailand, where Thai is the medium of instruction and where there are significant numbers of migrant children and children of migrants from Cambodia, the Lao People's Republic Democratic Republic, and Myanmar, children who are registered with the Ministry of the Interior are, in principle, permitted to attend Thai schools. However, only a small percentage do attend school and "many local schools do not accept migrants, partially owing to language difficulties" (Huguet and Punpuing 2005: 127).

Perhaps the friction between the monolingual ideology of nation-states and the transnational circulation of people is most evident in the case of transnational Mexican migrant students who face difficulties in the education systems of the United States (when they migrate) and Mexico (when they return home). Bazán-Ramírez and Galván-Zariñana (2013: 5) highlight how schools in both the United States and Mexico lack the strategies to help these transnational students adapt and thrive. Both systems emphasize monolingual norms (English in the United States and Spanish in Mexico) and have curricula and systems of evaluation that do not reflect the prior knowledge, skills, and abilities which the students have acquired. As such, these Mexican American students are faced with "rigid mono-national educational systems, homogenously structured, and not adapted to the needs of these students who are erroneously perceived and stereotyped" (Bazán-Ramírez and Galván-Zariñana 2013: 5).

In order to be given access to important economic and symbolic capital, it is necessary that migrants learn not just a language that is recognized and legitimized by the nation-state, they must also learn and know the standard variety (Lippi-Green 2012). This can be seen not only in the studies that have been described in the previous section but also in studies that have examined how speakers of non-standard varieties and stigmatized varieties of a national language are confronted with disjunctures in school when they learn that the 'dialects' they speak are no longer valuable for academic learning (Martín Rojo 2010), as for example in the Spanish spoken by Ecuadorians living in Madrid and English-creole speakers of Caribbean descent in Toronto (Schecter et al. 2014). A similar pattern can be seen in China, where massive rural to urban migration is taking place and where the monoglot ideologies focused on Putonghua produce obstacles for the children of migrant workers who attend school in urban areas and whose Putonghua proficiency is limited (Dong and Blommaert 2009; Dong and Dong 2013). These shape the trajectories of the children of migrant workers with many of them stereotyped as "bad students" and channeled into secondary vocational schools where they are trained to provide the cheap labor needed for manufacturing and 'low-skilled' service industries (Ling 2015).

The level of support for migrant students who do not speak the medium of instruction is a highly contentious and politicized issue. Bilingual education programs can be divided into two categories: programs that promote bilingualism (L2 + the native language) and programs that promote only the acquisition of the L2. Bilingual education programs fall between the extremes of these two categories. In the United States, programs that fall in the first category include two-way bilingual education, dual language immersion, late-exit bilingual education or developmental bilingual education, and early exit bilingual education or transitional bilingual education. Programs that fall in the second category include sheltered content, structured immersion, content-based English as a Second Language (ESL) and pull-out ESL (see Menken 2008). In Europe, similarly diverse bilingual education programs are offered ranging from maintenance bilingual education to 'immersion' where students with limited proficiency in the medium of instruction are taught in a mainstream classroom (Martín Rojo 2010).

While there are exceptions (cf. Duarte 2011; Möllering, Benholz, and Mavruk 2014), across migrant-receiving countries the current level of support for migrant children is that of transitional bilingual education. In the United States, weak forms of bilingual education are the norm and additive forms of bilingual language education programs are far less common. As such, bilingual education programs for children with migrant backgrounds are overwhelmingly conceived as transitory; they are temporary and are aimed at quickly developing the children's language skills in at least one of the host country's national languages. Thus, "ELLs most often find themselves in classrooms where English is the only language of instruction, as in the prevalent . . . ESL programs" (Menken 2008: 24). In Europe, the most prominent approach is immersion (or to be more accurate, submersion) in the L2 with students receiving additional classes in specified periods of instruction aimed at developing their language skills in the L2 with variations to the extent in which such compensatory programs are integrated into the school curricula (Martín Rojo 2010: 33–34).

This current trend in language-in-education policies is contrary to research findings that show that dual-immersion programs can mitigate, if not erase, the educational disadvantage of migrant children. For example, in Duarte's study (2011) of Portuguese bilingual migrant students who were part of the dual-immersion programs in Italian, Portuguese, Spanish, and Turkish being offered in Hamburg, the Portuguese bilingual migrant students performed significantly better in assessments of academic language proficiency and subject or content mastery than their Portuguese peers in a mainstream German primary school; they also had proficiency levels in Portuguese that were comparable to those of monolingual Portuguese children in Portugal.

Weak forms of bilingual education have been shown to reproduce the invisibility of the multilingualism of migrants and the framing of the multilingualism of migrants as a problem. They reinforce the border between the migrants' linguistic resources and the linguistic resources of the school. Furthermore, they contribute to the racialization of migrants (Schmidt 2002; Dick 2011; Fleming 2015) and the class distinctions not just between migrant students and the native-born but also between migrant students coming from economically advantageous backgrounds and those who do not (Darvin and Norton 2014). In the United States, the problems of so-called English language learners (ELLs), the majority of whom have Spanish as their first language, have been exacerbated by the use of wide-scale testing as the main means by which schools and school districts demonstrate they are meeting the mandates of the standards-based movement and No Child Left Behind (Escamilla 2006: 186). Under the No Child Left Behind program, which was introduced in 2002, funding for bridging and other strong forms of bilingual education was cut down. Under the program, wide-scale tests are only conducted in English, and only a few states and federal governments are creating special testing policies with regard to ELL students (Menken 2008). ELL students do not perform well in these tests. This highlights how testing policies can shape language-in-education policies and how tests are often about language uniformity (Shohamy 2013). It has also been argued that the poor performance of Latinos in these tests contributes to and reinforces the racialization of Spanish speakers in the US where the term " 'bilingual' has ceased referring simply to someone who can speak two or more languages, but is used to refer to Latinos specifically, who are cast as unable and unwilling to speak English at all" (Nieto in Fuller and Hoseman 2015: 172). In the case of the Compensatory and Welcome programs implemented in the Madrid region, Martín Rojo (2010: 137) shows how, through pedagogical practices, a compensatory logic emerges where "students' inclusion and content selection are handled in such a way that indicates that not much is expected of the students in groups where significant numbers are from a migrant background." Codo and Patiño-Santos (2014) made similar observations in a multilingual secondary school in the Barcelona metropolitan area, where the majority of the students came from a migrant background and were unable to use Catalan, the language of the school. Through its practices and especially through the teachers' behaviors, the school oriented students from migrant backgrounds to a non-academic trajectory, and towards the non- or low-skilled labor market.

Language-in-education policies and fluidity

While the one-nation, one-language, one-culture model remains a dominant model and driving force behind language-in-education policies, language is no longer viewed solely in terms of its link to national identity. Knowledge and proficiency in a language is also viewed as commodifiable skill (Heller 2010), one that can be used to differentiate workers and to maintain or increase their competitiveness. Underpinning the shift to a view of language as a commodifiable skill are neoliberal regimes of self, which shifts responsibility from the state to the individual (Urciuoli 2008; Urciuoli and La Dousa 2013; Kubota 2014). Within these regimes, education is seen as a means of providing citizens and would-be citizens with the necessary linguistic and other skills for them to be competitive and mobile in and across local and global labor markets. Language-in-education policies could be considered to have an orientation towards fluidity, that is, to the potential mobility of its citizens when such policies are framed within discourses of 'globalization', 'internationalization', 'competitiveness', or 'cosmopolitanism'. In terms of language-in-education policies, these key words are associated with, first, the commodification of English as a basic skill (Ricento 2000; Lo Bianco 2014) which reinforces and consolidates the dominance of English, and second, the valuing of 'elite' forms of bilingualism, especially of English-knowing bilingualism (Pakir 1999) as indexical of cosmopolitan, competitive, and globally mobile citizens.

The fact that countries can send emigrants and receive immigrants may partly account for the paradox in language-in-education policies where value is placed on foreign and, increasingly, English language instruction for citizens even as there is a reluctance to acknowledge and capitalize on the 'foreign' languages of migrants (and languages other than the national or official ones). Stevenson's (2015: 77) analysis of language education in Germany aptly captures this disjuncture in language-in-education policies: "the state education system is still characterized by an implicit distinction between elite and vernacular multilingualism, the former widely perceived as a mark of cultivation and *Weltoffenheit* (cosmopolitanism), the latter as an impediment to cohesion".

The commodification of English as a basic skill means that if there is bilingual or foreign language education in countries, the chances are that the L2 or first foreign language that is being learned is English. This means that in non-English-speaking countries, there is a narrowing of foreign language choices with English being given priority over other foreign languages. In English-speaking countries, there are 'widened' foreign language choices with a tendency to institutionalize European languages (e.g., French, German), or what are now called 'languages of wider communication' (e.g., Chinese) that are considered to be globally important (Lo Bianco 2014). It must be noted that the choice of English as the second language or first foreign language in language-in-education policies is framed in a discourse that positions English as a *basic* skill and therefore, as part of compulsory education. The rationale for such policies is framed in terms of 'modernization' and 'internationalization' and hence should be understood as part of the response to align education curricula and programs with neoliberal policies (Sayer 2015). In this framing, English is positioned as a neutral and useful language for international mobility; it ignores the reality of "unequal Englishes" (Tupas 2015a), that is, that the political legitimacies of different Englishes are uneven and that the value of one's English is determined by the "unequal ways and situations in which in which Englishes are arranged, configured, and contested" (Tupas and Rubdy 2015: 3).

In developing countries, the view that English is a basic and necessary language skill has led to expanded English instruction in public schools that are implementing primary English language teaching programs. In Southeast Asia and Latin America, national Ministries of Education in Southeast Asia and Latin America are taking a 'more and earlier' approach of integrating English into the public primary school curriculum (Sayer 2015). In East Asia, foreign language learning has practically become synonymous with studying English as a Foreign Language (EFL) (Guangwei and McKay 2012; Butler 2015).

The link between language-in-education policies, English, and mobile citizens is perhaps most explicit in the Philippines, the world's leading source of government-sponsored migrant labor. The language skills of overseas Filipino workers (OFWs) in English and more recently, in the languages of their destination countries, have been a central part of the discourse of Filipino competitiveness in global labor markets and of sustaining the OFW 'brand' (Lorente 2012). Gonzalez (1998) considers the Philippines' position as a labor-sending state to have significantly influenced Philippine language policy, especially the maintenance of English as a medium of instruction. This "grip of English" (Lorente 2013) on language-in-education policy has remained and has been reinforced further by the rise of outsourcing and more specifically, of call centers (Salonga 2010). More recently though, English seems to be increasingly recognized as a basic language skill, one that Filipinos are expected to have as a 'minimum requirement'. To ensure and increase competitiveness, Filipinos, especially those who may leave as OFWs, are being encouraged to learn 'foreign' languages, an indication that from the perspective of the Philippines as a labor-sending country, English is no longer enough to distinguish and add value to its citizens in the global labor market. This continued emphasis on English and the emerging discourse regarding the importance of 'foreign languages' is happening alongside the implementation of Mother-Tongue Based Multilingual Education (MTBMLE), where the mother tongues are used as the primary medium of instruction in all subjects from preschool up to the end of elementary school. Supporters of MTBMLE have been careful to point out that using the mother tongue in the lower grades would help children learn English better once they are in the upper grades, thus sustaining the dominance of English in Philippine language-in-education policy (Tupas and Lorente 2014).

The case of the Philippines captures the neo-liberal discourses used to rationalize the promotion of English as a language of mobility, as well as the consequences of language-in-education policies that are shaped by such discourses. In postcolonial countries such as the Philippines, the promotion of English as a language of internationalization and mobility often occurs side by side with national language and/or mother tongue projects promoting national languages or mother tongues as part of nation-building efforts. The continued dominance of English in such cases may lead to the marginalization of mother tongues and national languages vis-à-vis English (Tupas 2015b). It also challenges decolonization projects where the development of "authentic" national languages has been subsumed or subverted by globalization, even before the former process was complete (Canagarajah 2005a: 419). In Europe, the spread of the view that English is a basic skill has contributed to the continued marginalization of migrants' languages. In the case of the Madrid region, the implementation of content and language integrated learning (CLIL) through the medium of Spanish and English constructs Madrid as a bilingual Spanish-English community at the cost of erasing the languages that immigrant students who do not speak languages other than Spanish and English. It must be noted here that the Spanish/English CLIL program in public primary and secondary schools was promoted as an inclusive educational measure aimed at giving working-class students from ethnically diverse backgrounds access to the valuable linguistic resources more privileged schools had (Relaño Pastor 2015: 135). It seems to have had the opposite result.

The promotion of English and of commodifiable foreign languages seems to have been reinforced by supra-national groupings. In Southeast Asia, where the choice of an intra-regional language seems to be driven by instrumental and economic concerns, the role of English in the region has been strengthened with the launch of the ASEAN Economic Community, where the official language of business will be English. This has led to a renewed emphasis on the teaching of English in ASEAN member countries (Kirkpatrick 2012). In the European Union, language learning is "being framed in direct relationship with employability and mobility, as well as with ideas of European cultural heritage" (Perez-Milans 2015a: 154). Officially, the European Union promotes proficiency in several EU languages as a precondition for EU citizens to benefit from a border-free single market and as a means of building the feeling of being European with all its cultural wealth and diversity. In practice, this impetus for foreign language learning in the EU has led to the consolidation of the dominance of English in the EU (Phillipson 2003; Perez-Milans 2015a), the teaching of 'useful' European standard languages such as French or German over migrant or minority languages (García 2015), and the introduction of what are characterized as languages of the wider world such as Mandarin Chinese in English-speaking countries, for example the UK (Perez-Milans 2015b).

This teaching and emphasis on English and on marketable or 'useful' foreign languages employ the framework of inclusivity where access to such valuable languages is supposedly made available to all students, thus leveling the playing field. This framework is based on neoliberal notions of competitiveness and is aimed at producing "a neoliberal subject that fits the political and economic context of our current sociohistorical period – in particular, the desire for flexible workers and lifelong learners to perform service oriented and technological jobs as part of a post-Fordist political economy" (Flores 2013: 501). It masks the already huge structural gaps that students already face, in the first place. This discourse of inclusivity conceals policies that are, in effect, exclusionary (Blackledge 2009).

Implications

The previous discussion shows that language-in-education policies have been slow to adapt to the transnational reality of mobile citizens. Language-in-education policies tend to reproduce existing inequalities by sustaining and reinforcing the monolingual habitus of nation-states and marginalizing the multilingualism of students from migration backgrounds even as they promote the learning of English and valuable 'foreign' languages among citizens. The tensions between fixity and fluidity in language-in-education policies have implications on language education and especially on the role of local educators and local communities in the design, implementation, appropriation, and transformation of language-in-education policies.

Disjunctures in language-in-education policies mean that it is all the more important to carve out spaces for multilingual education where language-in-education policies may be negotiated, changed, or even subverted (see García et al. 2006). This is especially so, as it is in these spaces that inequalities between migrant students and local students may be mitigated, to the advantage of both the migrant students and those who are native-born. The acknowledgement of the needs of migrant students may also have the effect of making visible the needs of long-existing ethnic minorities who are also marginalized from and by mainstream education, as was the case for ethnic Koreans in Japan (Okano 2006). As was shown earlier, language-in-education policy is both a top-down and bottom-up process, and so the fate of multilingual or bilingual education depends on the many layers between the national level and the classroom. In these spaces – where the multilingualism of students with migration backgrounds is seen as a resource instead of a problem – teachers play a central role (Menken and García 2010; Johnson 2012) in initiating and sustaining bottom-up processes that may wedge open ideological spaces that are being closed by top-down processes (Hornberger in Johnson 2012: 58). However, this must be tempered by a nuanced understanding of the often difficult contexts teachers are in and the tough decisions they have to make. In Jaspers's (2015) study of a Dutch-medium secondary school in Brussels where most of the pupils spoke a language other than Dutch at home, he traces how teachers constructed an informal multilingual space in order to overcome daily limitations even as this did not diminish their belief in the good that may come of the school's monolingual policy. While these multilingual interstices were important, they were also relatively marginal, "zoned off to the margins of official business" (Jaspers 2015: 126), indexing that such multilingual behavior is only acceptable at marginal moments and socializing students into the predominant sociolinguistic hierarchy that would alienate and devalue the linguistic resources they had. Given the very limited options the teachers were faced with, however, Jaspers (2015) notes that such decisions, while problematic, were probably the best that could be made.

In carving out and sustaining such multilingual spaces where migrants' languages are considered to be resources, it seems that successful, long-term bilingual programs grow out of the sustained, grassroots involvement between the stakeholders (i.e., the students, the educators and the communities to which the students belong). In the case of Germany, Möllering et al. (2014) describe the Förderunterricht program in Essen which grew out of a small-scale research project that studied the bilingualism of immigrant children. The program aims to diminish the educational gap between monolingual German students and bi- or multilingual students with a migration background. In this program, migrant children who are attending secondary school are mentored by trainee teachers, many of whom come from migrant backgrounds themselves; the mentors help orient students towards education goals such as having a German university entrance qualification. They work with each student and bring in the students' languages as well as their own in the teaching of content, thus valuing the students' multilingual resources. The program has also focused on improving teacher training and it has introduced 'German as a second language' as a compulsory component of all teacher training degrees at the university. What is distinctive about the program is the way in which it has involved local schools, local politicians, the local community, funding bodies, and migrant communities. The program has been considered a success and has been emulated in thirty-five cities in Germany; it is a model for how micro-level activities can, in time, impact language policy at the regional and even national levels.

The role of applied linguistics research in influencing and shaping the design and implementation of language-in-education policies for migrant students cannot be underestimated. Johnson (2010), for example, shows the complex ways in which beliefs about applied linguistics research influenced the interpretation and implementation of federal language policy, in one US school district. He argues that because applied linguistics researchers are positioned as experts, researchers can team up with local educators and especially administrators in order to foster ideological spaces where developmental bilingual education may be championed (Johnson 2010: 90).

Finally, Kubota (2014) points out the continued importance of noting which languages are part of multilingual practices that are celebrated and taught; "it is important to ask whether all language users regardless of their racial, gender, socioeconomic and other background equally transgress linguistic boundaries and engage in hybrid and fluid linguistic practices" (Kubota 2014: 10).There is a need to continue examining the bases and rationale for such multi/plurilingual programs. She highlights how the multi/plurilingual turn has become integrated into the canon of neoliberal capitalist academic culture and argues for the need to shift attention from individual plurality to inequality. This is especially so as there is a "close conceptual alignment between the constructs of neoliberal multiculturalism (e.g., flexibility, diversity, mobility) and critical approaches to applied linguistics" (Kubota 2014: 18). Kubota suggests that "one strategy might be to appropriate the discourse of neoliberalism to promote critical awareness of diversity without endorsing capitalist domination" (Kubota 2014: 18).

Future directions

Applied linguistics is well placed to contribute to ethnographic research of language-in-education policies (Canagarajah 2005b, 2006; McCarty 2011) and migration in both sending and receiving countries in the Global South and the Global North. Current research is mostly done from the point of view of receiving countries in the Global North. Research in applied linguistics could also look beyond language-in-education policies as they are implemented in compulsory education. While the state is still a central actor in the education system, increasingly other non-state actors are filling in gaps in the education system or extending what the education system provides. These range from non-governmental organizations who provide some form of schooling for those who do not or are not given access to mainstream schools (e.g., refugees, children of seasonal workers) to private, profit-driven enterprises who control their curricula, independently determine their medium of instruction, and provide 'quality' education at a price. With the state's increasing relegation of education to the market, it is especially important to trace the trajectories of language-in-education policies in these relatively 'unregulated' institutions and to closely examine how such non-state actors are shaping their own spheres of influence and/or influencing the language-in-education policies of the state.

Sociolinguistics has the tools for understanding the complexity of language use in an age of migration. Concepts such as translingualism (Canagarajah 2013) and metrolingualism (Pennycook and Otsuji 2015) have gone a long way in broadening understandings of language practices in contexts of mobility and articulating policy implications for more inclusive communities. For as long as bilingualism and multilingualism are understood as separate monolingualisms (Heller 2007), the linguistic resources of migrant (and non-migrant) citizens will not be recognized and will contribute to the reproduction of inequalities. Sociolinguistics has the tools for understanding the complexity with which language is used and belonging is imagined – and this knowledge must find its way into mainstream applied linguistics and policy circles.

Finally, applied linguistics could continue contributing to new understandings of how citizenship is conceived and how the notion of citizenship can be widened. Applied linguistics has already contributed to showing the tenuous links between language testing and naturalization and to questioning and deconstructing the seemingly foundational triad of language-nation-culture. Recent work has emphasized the processual and performative nature of citizenship and the central role language plays in such processes and performances (Milani 2015; Ramanathan 2015). More work needs to be done on this.

Summary

Language-in-education policies are sites where the tensions of fixity and fluidity are negotiated. The tendency for fixity is engendered by the enduring monoglot ideology of nation-states where recognition as a speaker of a standard national language is valued. The tendency for fluidity is driven by neo-liberalization where the individual, self-motivated and self-dependent learning of commodifiable language skills – whether these skills be English, a 'foreign language', or a standard variety of a national language – is considered to be a desirable quality of a modern and mobile citizen. It is important to continue interrogating the bases and the consequences of language-in-education policies as they establish the infrastructures by which regimes of inclusion and exclusion are (re)produced. Given ever-increasing and ever more diverse migration flows, the lives of mobile citizens can no longer be understood by looking only at what happens within the boundaries of the nation, language-in-education policies need to be critically re-framed as transnational subject-making processes.

Related topics

Nation-state, transnationalism, and language
Neoliberalism, language, and migration
National and ethnic minorities
Citizenship, immigration laws, and language

Further reading

García, O., Skutnabb-Kangas, T. and Torres-Guzmán, M. E., eds. (2006). *Imagining Multilingual Schools: Languages in Education and Glocalization*. Clevedon: Multilingual Matters.

An edited collection that shows how schools, local languages, and cultures resist homogenizing tendencies. It also presents ways of imagining how schools may build on and support multilingualism and diversity.

Perez-Milans, M., ed. (2015). Language education policy in late modernity: (socio)linguistic ethnographies in the European Union. *Language Policy, 14*.

A special issue on language-in-education policy in the European Union in relation to transnational mobility and economic neo-liberalization. The papers are about specific cases in Madrid, London, and Brussels; all of them are based on ethnographic and critical sociolinguistic approaches.

Martin-Rojo, L. M. (2010). *Constructing Inequality in Multilingual Classrooms*. Berlin and New York: Mouton de Gruyter.

A comprehensive and in-depth ethnographic study of how schools in Madrid perceive and respond to the challenges of integrating migrant children. Martin-Rojo introduces the notion of 'decapitalization' and identifies the processes which produce it.

References

Bazán-Ramírez, A. and Galván-Zariñana, G. (2013). Incorporation of migrant students returning from the United States to high schools in Mexico. *International Migration* 53(1): 3–14.

Bernstein, K. A., Hellmich, E. A., Katznelson, N., Shin, J. and Vinall, K. (2015). Introduction to special issue: Critical perspectives on neoliberalism in second/foreign language education. *L2 Journal* 7(3): 3–14.

Blackledge, A. (2009). Being English, speaking English: Extension to English language testing legislation and the future of multicultural Britain. In G. Hogan-Brun, C. Mar-Molinero and P. Stevenson (eds.), *Discourses on Language and Integration: Critical Perspectives on Language Testing Regimes in Europe* (pp. 84–107). Amsterdam: John Benjamins.

Blommaert, J. (2005). *Discourse: A Critical Introduction*. Cambridge: Cambridge University Press.

Butler, Y. G. (2015). English language education among young learners in East Asia: A review of current research (2002–2014). *Language Teaching* 48(3): 303–342.

Canagarajah, A. S. (2005a). Dilemmas in planning English/vernacular relations in post-colonial communities. *Journal of Sociolinguistics* 4(1): 418–447.

Canagarajah, A. S., ed. (2005b). *Reclaiming the Local in Language Policy and Practice*. Mahwah, NJ: Lawrence Erlbaum Associates.

Canagarajah, S. (2006). Ethnographic methods in language policy. In T. Ricento (ed.), *An Introduction to Language Policy: Theory and Method* (pp. 153–169). Malden, MA: Blackwell.

Canagarajah, S. (2013). *Translingual Practice: Global Englishes and Cosmopolitan Relations*. London and New York: Routledge.

Codo, E. and Patiño-Santos, A. (2014). Beyond language: Class, social categorization and academic achievement in a Catalan high school. *Linguistics and Education* 25: 51–63.

Darvin, R. and Norton, B. (2014). Social class, identity and migrant students. *Journal of Language, Identity and Education* 13(2): 111–117.

Dick, H. P. (2011). Language and migration to the United States. *Annual Review of Anthropology* 40: 227–240.

Dong, J. and Blommaert, J. (2009). Space, scale and accents: Constructing migrant identity in Beijing. *Multilingua* 28: 1–24.

Dong, J. and Dong, Y. (2013). Voicing as an essential problem of communication: Language and education of Chinese immigrant children in globalization. *Anthropology and Education Quarterly* 44(2): 161–176.

Duarte, J. (2011). "Migrants" educational success through innovation: The case of the Hamburg bilingual schools. *International Review of Education* 57: 631–649.

Duchêne, A. and Heller, M., eds. (2012). *Language in Late Capitalism: Pride and Profit*. New York and London: Routledge.

Escamilla, K. (2006). Monolingual assessment and emerging bilinguals: A case study in the US. In O. García, T. Skutnabb-Kangas and M. E. Torres-Guzmán (eds.), *Imagining Multilingual Schools: Languages in Education and Glocalization* (pp. 184–199). Clevedon: Multilingual Matters.

Fleming, D. (2015). Citizenship and race in second-language education. *Journal of Multilingual and Multicultural Development* 36(1): 42–52.

Flores, N. (2013). The unexamined relationship between neoliberalism and plurilingualism: A cautionary tale. *TESOL Quarterly* 47(3): 500–520.

Fuller, J. and Hosemann, A. (2015). Latino education. *Language and Linguistics Compass* 9(4): 168–180.

García, N. (2015). Tensions between cultural and utilitarian dimensions of language: A comparative analysis of "multilingual" education policies in France and Germany. *Current Issues in Language Planning* 16(1–2): 43–59.

García, O., Skutnabb-Kangas, T. and Torres-Guzmán, M., eds. (2006). *Imagining Multilingual Schools: Languages in Education and Glocalization*. Clevedon: Multilingual Matters.

Gkaintartzi, A., Killiari, A. and Tsokalidou, A. (2015). "Invisible" bilingualism – "invisible" language ideologies: Greek teachers' attitudes towards immigrant pupils' heritage languages. *International Journal of Bilingual Education and Bilingualism* 18(1): 60–72.

Gonzalez, A. (1998). The language planning situation in the Philippines. *Journal of Multilingual and Multicultural Development* 19(5/6): 481–525.

Guangwei, H. and McKay, S. L. (2012). English language education in East Asia: Some recent developments. *Journal of Multilingual and Multicultural Development* 33(4): 345–362.

Heller, M., ed. (2007). *Bilingualism: A Social Approach*. Houndmills: Palgrave Macmillan.

Heller, M. (2010). The commodification of language. *Annual Review of Anthropology* 39: 101–114.

Helot, C. and Young, A. (2002). Bilingualism and language education in French primary schools: Why and how should migrant languages be valued?' *International Journal of Bilingual Education and Bilingualism* 5(2): 96–112.

Hogan-Brun, G., Mar-Molinero, C. and Stevenson, P., eds. (2009). *Discourses on Language and Integration: Critical Perspectives on Language Testing Regimes in Europe*. Amsterdam: John Benjamins.

Hornberger, N. H. (1998). Language policy, language education, language rights: Indigenous, immigrant, and international perspectives. *Language in Society* 27: 439–458.

Hornberger, N.H. and Johnson, D. C. (2007). Slicing the onion ethnographically: Layers and spaces in multilingual language education and practice. *TESOL Quarterly* 41(3): 509–532.

Huguet, J.W. and Punpuing, S. (2005). Child migrants and children of migrants in Thailand. *Asia-Pacific Population Journal* 20(3): 123–142.

Jaspers, J. (2015). Modelling linguistic diversity at school: The excluding impact of inclusive multilingualism. *Language Policy* 14: 109–129.

Johnson, D.C. (2010). The relationship between applied linguistic research and language policy for bilingual education. *Applied Linguistics* 31(1): 72–93.

Johnson, D.C. (2013). *Language Policy*. Houndmills: Palgrave Macmillan.

Johnson, E.J. (2012). Arbitrating repression: Language policy and education in Arizona. *Language and Education* 26(1): 53–76.

Kirkpatrick, A. (2012). English in ASEAN: Implications for regional multilingualism. *Journal of Multilingual and Multicultural Development* 33(4): 331–344.

Kubota, R. (2014). The multi/plural turn, postcolonial theory, and neoliberal multiculturalism: Complicities and implications for applied linguistics. *Applied Linguistics*, doi:10.1093/applin/amu045

Lin, A.M.Y. and Martin, P.W., eds. (2005). *Decolonisation, Globalization: Language-in-education Policy and Practice*. Clevedon: Multilingual Matters.

Ling, M. (2015). "Bad students go to vocational schools": Vocational education for migrant youth in urban China. *China Journal* 73: 108–131.

Lippi-Green, R. (2012). *English with an Accent: Language, Ideology, and Discrimination in the United States*. London and New York: Routledge.

Lo Bianco, J. (2014). Domesticating the foreign: Globalization's effects on the place/s of languages. *Modern Language Journal* 98(1): 312–325.

Lorente, B.P. (2012). The making of workers of the world: Language and the labor brokerage state. In A. Duchêne and M. Heller (eds.), *Pride and Profit: Language in Late Capitalism* (pp. 183–206). London and New York: Routledge.

Lorente, B. P. (2013). The grip of English and Philippine language policy. In L. H. A. Wee, L. Lim and R. B. H. Goh (eds.), *The Politics of English in Asia: Language Policy and Cultural Expression in South and Southeast Asia* (pp. 187–203). Amsterdam: John Benjamins.

Luchtenberg, S. (2002). Bilingualism and bilingual education and their relationship to citizenship from a comparative German-Australian perspective. *Intercultural Education* 13(1): 49–61.

Martín Rojo, L. (2010). *Constructing Inequality in Multilingual Classrooms*. Berlin and New York: Mouton De Gruyter.

McCarty, T. L., ed. (2011). *Ethnography and Language Policy*. New York and London: Routledge.

McCarty, T. L. (2004). Dangerous difference: A critical-historical analysis of language education policies in the United States. In J. W. Tollefson and A. B. M. Tsui (eds.), *Medium of Instruction Policies: Which Agenda? Whose Agenda?* (pp. 71–93). Mahwah, NJ: Lawrence Erlbaum Associates.

Menken, K. (2008). *English Learners Left behind: Standardized Testing as Language Policy*. Clevedon: Multilingual Matters.

Menken, K. and García, O., eds. (2010). *Negotiating Language Policies in Schools: Educators as Policymakers*. New York: Routledge.

Mezzadra, S. and Neilson, B. (2013). *Border as Method, or, the Multiplication of Labor*. Durham and London: Duke University Press.

Milani, T. (Ed.). Language and citizenship: Broadening the agenda [Special issue]. *Journal of Language and Politics* 14(3).

Möllering, M., Benholz, C. and Mavruk, G. (2014). Reconstructing language policy in urban education: The Essen model of Förderunterricht. *Current Issues in Language Planning* 15(3): 296–311.

Okano, K. (2006). The impact of immigrants on long-lasting ethnic minorities in Japanese schools: Globalization from below. *Language and Education* 20(4): 338–354.

Ong, A. (2006). *Neoliberalism as Exception: Mutations in Citizenship and Sovereignty*. Durham and London: Duke University Press.

Orman, J. (2012). Language and "new" African migration to South Africa: An overview and some reflections on theoretical implications for policy and planning. *Language Policy* 11(4): 301–322.

Pakir, A. (1999). Connecting with English in the context of internationalisation. *TESOL Quarterly* 33(1): 103–113.

Pavlenko, A. (2002). "We have room for but one language here": Language and national identity in the US at the turn of the 20th century. *Multilingua* 21: 163–196.

Pennycook, A. and Otsuji, E. (2015). *Metrolingualism: Language in the City*. London and New York: Routledge.

Perez-Milans, M. (2015a). Language education policy in late modernity: (Socio)linguistic ethnographies in the European Union. *Language Policy* 14: 99–107.

Perez-Milans, M. (2015b). Mandarin Chinese in London education: Language aspirations in a working-class secondary school. *Language Policy* 14: 153–181.

Phillipson, R. (2003). *English-only Europe? Challenging Language Policy*. London and New York: Routledge.

Piller, I. (2001). Naturalization, language testing and its basis in ideologies of national identity and citizenship. *International Journal of Bilingualism* 5(3): 259–277.

Piller, I. and Takahashi, K. (2011). Linguistic diversity and social inclusion. *International Journal of Bilingual Education and Bilingualism* 14(4): 371–381.

Pujolar, J. (2010). Immigration and language education in Catalonia: Between national and social agendas. *Linguistics and Education* 21: 229–243.

Ramanathan, V. (2013). Language policies and (dis)citizenship: Who belongs? Who is a guest? Who is deported?' *Journal of Language, Identity and Education* 12: 162–166.

Ramanathan, V., ed. (2015). *Language Policies and (dis)Citizenship: Rights, Access and Pedagogies*. Bristol: Multilingual Matters.

Relaño Pastor, A. M. (2015). The commodification of English in "Madrid: Comunidad bilingue": Insights from the CLIL classroom. *Language Policy* 14: 131–152.

Ricento, T. (2000). *Ideology, Politics and Language Policies: Focus on English*. Amsterdam and Philadelphia: John Benjamins.

Ricento, T. and Hornberger, N. H. (1996). Unpeeling the onion: Language planning and policy and the ELT professional. *TESOL Quarterly* 30(3): 401–427.

Safford, K. and Drury, R. (2013). The "problem" of bilingual children in educational settings: Policy and research in England. *Language and Education* 27(1): 70–81.

Salonga, A. O. (2010). *Language and Situated Agency: An Exploration of the Dominant Linguistic and Communication Practices in the Philippine Offshore Call Centers*. PhD thesis, National University of Singapore.

Sayer, P. (2015). More and earlier: Neoliberalism and primary English education in Mexican public schools. *L2 Journal* 7(3): 40–56.

Schecter, S. R. Parejo, I. G., Ambadiang, T. and James, C. E. (2014). Schooling transnational speakers of the societal language: Language variation policy-making in Madrid and Toronto. *Language Policy* 13: 121–144.

Schmidt, Sr., R. (2002). Racialization and language policy: The case of the U.S.A. *Multilingua* 21: 141–161.

Sercombe, P. and Tupas, R., eds. (2014). *Language, Education and Nation-building: Assimilation and Shift in Southeast Asia*. Houndmills: Palgrave Macmillan.

Shohamy, E. (2006). *Language Policy: Hidden Agendas and New Approaches*. London and New York: Routledge.

Shohamy, E. (2013). The discourse of language testing as a tool for shaping national, global, and transnational identities. *Language and Intercultural Communication* 13(2): 225–236.

Spolsky, B. (2004). *Language Policy*. Cambridge: Cambridge University Press.

Stevenson, P. (2015). The language question in contemporary Germany: The challenges of multilingualism. *German Politics and Society* 33(1/2): 69–83.

Stritikus, T. (2002). *Immigrant Children and the Politics of English-only: Views from the Classroom*. New York: LFB Scholarly.

Tollefson, J. W. (1991). *Planning Language, Planning Inequality: Language Policy in the Community*. London: Longman.

Tollefson, J. W. (2002). *Language Policies in Education: Critical Issues*. Mahwah, NJ: Lawrence Erlbaum Associates.

Tollefson, J. W. and Tsui, A. B. M., eds. (2004). *Medium of Instruction Policies: Which Agenda? Whose Agenda?* Mahwah, NJ: Lawrence Erlbaum Associates.

Tupas, R., ed. (2015a). *Unequal Englishes: The Politics of English Today*. Houndmills: Palgrave Macmillan.

Tupas, R. (2015b). Inequalities of multilingualism: Challenges to mother tongue-based multilingual education. *Language and Education* 29(2): 112–124.

Tupas, R. and Lorente, B. P. (2014). A "new" politics of language in the Philippines: Bilingual education and the challenge of the mother tongues. In P. Sercombe and R. Tupas (eds.), *Language, Education and Nation-building: Assimilation and Shift in Southeast Asia* (pp. 165–180). Basingstoke and New York: Palgrave Macmillan.

Tupas, R. and Rubdy, R. (2015). Introduction: From world Englishes to unequal Englishes. In R. Tupas (ed.), *Unequal Englishes: The Politics of English Today* (pp. 1–17). Houndmills: Palgrave Macmillan.

United Nations Population Division. (2014). *International Migration 2013: Migrants by Origin and Destination*. Population Facts No. 2013/3 Rev.1.

Urciuoli, B. (2008). Skills and selves in the new workplace. *American Ethnologist* 35(2): 211–228.

Urciuoli, B. and LaDousa, C. (2013). Language management/labour. *Annual Review of Anthropology* 42: 175–190.

Warriner, D. (2015). "Here, without English, you are dead": Ideologies of language and discourses of neoliberalism in adult English language learning. *Journal of Multilingual and Multicultural Development*. doi:10.1080/01434632.2015.1071827

Wiley, T. G. and García, O. (2016). Language policy and planning in language education: Legacies, consequences and possibilities. *Modern Language Journal* 100: 48–63.

Wright, S. (2012). Language policy, the nation and nationalism. In B. Spolsky (ed.), *The Cambridge Handbook of Language Policy* (pp. 59–78). Cambridge: Cambridge University Press.

28
Mobility and English language policies and practices in higher education

Jennifer Jenkins

Introduction/definitions

Higher education is arguably one of the domains most affected by globalisation and, hence, by mobility. And since, as Van Parijs observes, "it is English and English alone that can reasonably claim to have become a global lingua franca" (2011: 11), it is not surprising that the globalisation of higher education, that is, the dissemination of knowledge in post-secondary education on a global scale, is taking place principally in English. Thus, 'the globalisation of higher education' is generally understood to mean 'the globalisation of higher education *in English*'. As a direct result, a fast-growing amount of university content teaching is being conducted in English medium in countries where English is not the first, or even official, language. And while English medium teaching in such countries is often designed to attract students from elsewhere, a substantial proportion of those being taught in English may comprise non-mobile local students such as Chinese and Japanese students studying academic subjects in English medium in, respectively, Chinese and Japanese universities. In global higher education, perhaps more than any other domain, we can therefore talk of mobility in two senses: those of both mobile *people* and mobile *language*. For although we tend to think of the two as going hand in hand, and language travelling with people, where higher education is concerned it is increasingly the case that the language, English, 'travels' while many people remain in situ either in locally run English medium instruction (EMI) universities or in 'branches' (also known as 'offshore campuses') of other, predominantly Anglophone-led institutions.

The 'mobile English/non-mobile student' situation also results from a third phenomenon, that is, the rapidly increasing amount of study taking place virtually through English, especially on distance masters programmes and more recently on massive open online courses (MOOCs). Both involve student participants in many countries within the non-Anglophone as well as Anglophone world. A recent MOOC, 'Understanding Language', run by my own university department on the *Futurelearn* platform, for example, had over 60,000 participants, of whom the majority were non-native English speakers living in a wide range of countries spread across Asia, Africa, Australasia, Europe, Latin America, and North America (see http://www.futurelearn.com/). For the purposes of this chapter, however, I am focusing exclusively on face-to-face rather than virtual higher education. This is because the language related issues involved in the latter are as yet under-researched whereas those of the former have, by contrast, already formed the subject of a substantial and ongoing body of research and extensive debate.

This chapter therefore explores language policy issues on the one hand in university settings where English is the dominant language (i.e., in the Anglophone world), and on the other hand in non-Anglophone settings where English is the medium of instruction but not the dominant/local language. In both cases, I also consider the role given (or not) to the languages of those students who are not native English speakers, regardless of whether they have travelled from elsewhere to study in English medium or are studying through English medium within an institution in their native country. The chapter begins with a discussion of globalisation and internationalisation within the higher education context. It then turns to the role that English currently plays in international/global education and explores the communicative needs of mobile (so-called international) students. Following that, it examines the kinds of language policies employed both overtly and covertly (or unwittingly) by universities that present themselves as 'international' or 'global'. And finally, it looks ahead to how the tensions, difficulties, and contradictions that have been identified in research into the globalisation of higher education might be resolved.

The concepts/terms 'globalisation' and 'internationalisation' are often used interchangeably as they were, in fact, in the previous section of this chapter. However, as Maringe and Foskett (2010: 1) point out, there are differences between the two, and these differences are particularly evident in respect of higher education (HE). The concept of globalisation, Maringe and Foskett observe, is widely understood to refer to "the creation of world relations based on the operation of free markets." Meanwhile, internationalisation with respect to universities, they note, tends to mean "the integration of an international or intercultural dimension into the tripartite mission of teaching, research and service functions of Higher Education" (Maringe and Foskett 2010). In other words, internationalisation is the key strategy by which universities are responding to globalisation.

The most obvious way in which universities have been adding an international dimension to their profile has been by recruiting students – and to a lesser extent, staff – from other countries. Indeed, it is sometimes argued in the research literature that the internationalisation of HE amounts to little more than an expansion in international student numbers, and that the main motivation for this is financial gain (a point that is not lost on international students themselves, as I will discuss later). Ferguson (2007), for example, considers international student recruitment to be a key feature of the internationalisation of HE. He argues that the goal is not internationalisation per se, but that English medium instruction has been introduced primarily "to attract fee-paying international students" as well as "to enhance the university's international prestige and contacts" and "develop the English language skills of their staff and students" (p. 13). Coleman, likewise, considers the motivation to be "to attract fee-paying international students, gifted teachers and researchers, and the most talented postgraduates to enhance the university's reputation" (2013: xv). Such objectives all relate either directly or indirectly to the financial imperative, and therefore may help explain why the *intercultural* dimension, which relates more to international students' needs than to university profits, tends to be lagging far behind the international dimension. The financial objectives may, in turn, also contribute to, if not account solely for, the finding of the International Association of Universities' 4th Global Survey on the Internationalization of Higher Education that the internationalisation of HE is not developing within institutions in an integrated or comprehensive manner (on this finding, see also De Wit 2015).

Jennifer Jenkins

Regardless of the motivations that underlie the pursuit of student mobility and promotion of the English language, both are central to the internationalisation of HE. However, while English is a common factor across most of international HE regardless of individual universities' national settings, the distribution of international students currently varies dramatically. That is, Anglophone countries do by far the largest amount of recruiting, while Asian countries are by far the most heavily recruited from. Statistics from the Organisation for Economic Co-operation and Development (OECD) for the year 2012 (OECD 2014a: 34) include the following facts:

- More than 4.5 million students are enrolled in university-level education outside their home country.
- Australia, Austria, Luxembourg, New Zealand, Switzerland, and the UK have the highest proportion of international students as a percentage of their total tertiary enrolments. In terms of broad geographical area, Europe (forty-eight percent) is the top destination, followed by North America (twenty-one percent) and Asia (eighteen percent).
- Students from Asia represent fifty-three percent of foreign students enrolled worldwide. The largest numbers of foreign students are from China, India, and Korea.

With regard to the number of students studying outside their home country, Bordia, Bordia, and Restubog (2015: 213) observe, citing Marklein (2007), that "the international student diaspora is expected to reach 7.2 million by 2025." Where this diaspora will ultimately be located is nevertheless as yet unclear. While Anglophone countries, particularly the United States, followed by the UK, are currently by far the highest recruiters of international students, the East Asian proportion has started to grow, with a number of Asian governments, particularly in Japan and China, actively engaging in initiatives to increase their share of the international student market. In this respect, Leonard (2015) reports that the number of Korean university students studying at home or in China has already increased, and argues that the decline in their numbers travelling further afield is likely to continue. This, in turn, has implications both for the amount of academic teaching that will done in English medium in their own universities for their home students, and for international student recruitment in Anglophone universities.

Even the percentage of international students currently studying within the Anglophone countries is not straightforward. As the breakdown in Table 28.1 demonstrates, four Anglophone recruiters between them shared just over forty percent of international students in 2010, and the figure was only marginally lower in 2012 (OECD 2014b). But while the US had the largest number of international students of any country, this nevertheless amounted to a very modest share of its total university student population. By contrast, the UK and

Table 28.1 Top ten destinations for international students

Country	% market share 2010	International students as % overall student population 2010
US	16.6	3.4
UK	13	16
Australia	6.6	21.2
Canada	4.7	6.6

Source: Adapted from *Times Higher Education* (January 31, 2013: 39).

Australia recruited a smaller percentage of the international student market, but their respective shares constituted a much higher proportion of their overall student populations. Indeed, at the postgraduate level in both countries, as the literature and my own experience testify, it is not uncommon to find large numbers of masters and doctoral programmes across a range of disciplines in which international students vastly outnumber home students. In the academic year 2012–2013, for example, forty-nine percent of full-time research postgraduates and seventy-one percent of full-time taught postgraduates in UK universities came from international backgrounds (UKCISA 2015; see also Jenkins and Wingate 2015).

We turn now to the implications of these developments in relation to the English language and its relationship with other languages spoken by those studying in English dominant and EMI universities.

Overview

Bare statistics such as those cited earlier invariably reveal little about what happens in real life – in this instance, students' lived lingua-cultural experience on campus. Our focus therefore shifts now to the role that language, and particularly English, plays for mobile students. In this section we will explore some prominent language-related issues that have arisen as a result of the spread of English as the main language of HE in both English-dominant and EMI settings. In addition, we will consider the role played by native English-speaking 'home' students in English-dominant settings, and the ways in which intercultural communication takes place (or does not) between them and their non-native English-speaking international student peers.

The phenomenon of English as a lingua franca

When we talk of English serving as the language of intercultural communication, we are referring to the phenomenon usually known as English as a lingua franca, or ELF for short. Space does not permit me to discuss ELF at length, and readers who would like to know more about the ELF research paradigm are therefore referred to works such as Jenkins, Cogo, and Dewey (2011) and Seidlhofer (2011) for, respectively, journal and book-length coverage of the entire field, as well as Mauranen (2012), Björkman (2013), and Jenkins (2014) for book-length treatments of ELF in academic settings, and Baker (2015) for the first book to explore the synergies between ELF and intercultural communication theory in detail.

For present purposes, a few key points will suffice. First, a definition: ELF refers, in a nutshell, to communication in English among people from different first language backgrounds or, more precisely, to "any use of English among speakers of different first languages for whom English is the communicative medium of choice, and often the only option" (Seidlhofer 2011: 7; her italics). Like all current definitions of ELF, the latter includes native English speakers (NES). Nevertheless, given the world's small number of NES by contrast with the massive and still-growing number of non-native English speakers (NNES), the presence of NES in ELF interactions tends to be much less frequent. And when they are present, from an ELF perspective, their English does not serve as a model of correctness for their NNES interlocutors. Although the point is implied rather than stated in the above definition (but discussed at length in all the works cited above), ELF is very different from traditional EFL (English as a Foreign Language), where 'near-native' production is, indeed, the ultimate goal. In ELF, by contrast, the goal is successful intercultural communication, in which correctness according to native English is not a priority and may even be a hindrance. But as we will see later on, it is still the kind of English required for entry to, and often in order to achieve good grades in, international HE, especially, but not exclusively, in Anglophone settings.

A further point about ELF that has major relevance to the role of English in HE is that ELF differs from all conventional language varieties, including postcolonial English varieties, on account of its highly variable, contingent nature. This is dependent on both a speaker's own L1 (first language) background and the L1s of the other participants in any specific conversation and in any individual's English-using trajectory. Given the diverse range of the L1s of potential interlocutors in ELF communication, it makes far better sense to talk of ELF in terms of 'similects' (Mauranen 2012) than of varieties. That is, from a similect perspective, speakers from the same L1 background retain among themselves a shared element in their use of English as a result of same-L1 influence. But this similarity does not develop into a variety of English as would happen if they spoke English with each other. Instead, speakers for whom English serves little or no intra-national function develop their English in parallel with, and not among, speakers from their own L1. Their English thus develops not through, for example, a Japanese person speaking English with other Japanese people, but through a Japanese person speaking English with L1 speakers of Korean, Thai, Spanish, and the like. There can, then, be no such thing as a 'Japanese English' variety. There can only be English with a greater or lesser degree of Japanese L1 influence, alongside influences from the L1s of the Japanese person's English-using interlocutors in their primary communities of English-using practice. And when it comes to HE, as was pointed out earlier, such communities of practice are found by definition in international universities, and in Anglophone universities more than any others, with large numbers of international students from different L1s habitually communicating with each other in English as their chosen lingua franca.

The final key point about ELF communication concerns the essential role played by ELF users' accommodation skills. The phenomenon of accommodation was identified in my own early ELF research (Jenkins 2000), in which the analysis of my empirical data demonstrated how speakers adjusted their English pronunciation for the benefit of interlocutors from different L1s, particularly in situations where it was crucial for them to be mutually intelligible. From that time, research has shown accommodation to be a defining feature of ELF communication at a range of linguistic levels including lexis, grammar, and pragmatics (see e.g., Cogo and Dewey 2012 for many examples from their own research and that of others). Accommodation thus has much in common with what Canagarajah (2005: xxvi) describes as the ability to "shuttle between communities by deploying relevant codes." Other research has demonstrated that in intercultural communication, the accommodation skills of NES tend to be less developed than those of NNES (see e.g., Sweeney and Zhu Hua 2010). At present, there is insufficient data for us to be able to determine why this might be so. On the one hand, it could be more of an attitude issue (an assumption that NNES of English should fit in with NES's ways of speaking 'their' language, English). On the other hand, it could simply be caused by a lack of awareness of what it is in native English that needs adjusting for the benefit of those from different lingua-cultural backgrounds, and how to make the necessary adjustments. Either way, it presents a potential problem for successful communication in ELF contexts whenever NES are present, and therefore to communication in international universities. It is to such university settings that we now turn.

Student mobility and non-mobility

Mobility, as was pointed out earlier, is to some extent a feature of all universities that claim international status. It also affects all of us in international universities, even those who consider themselves to be non-mobile, by virtue of their contact with incoming staff and students. As was also observed, outward mobility, for now at least, mostly involves students from non-Anglophone countries, particularly East Asia, travelling to Western (especially Anglophone, but also mainland European) universities. Meanwhile, relatively few Western students are currently mobile (less than twenty percent in the case of European students, according to De Wit 2014). The many Western non-mobile students are thus losing the opportunity to increase their international/cultural awareness, knowledge and skills by the prime means available, that is, study abroad. De Wit (2014) argues, therefore, that to enable non-mobile home students to become sufficiently international, it is crucial to internationalise the university curriculum in their home universities, a phenomenon known as 'internationalisation at home', or IaH for short (see the European Association of International Education's IaH website at http://www.eaie.org/home/about-EAIE/expert-communities/overview/iah.html).

IaH would nevertheless be of benefit of incoming mobile students as well as to non-mobile home students, in that it would provide the former with a more international environment rather than one whose emphasis was on their willingness and ability to assimilate to local (national) practices. In this respect, occasional examples of good practice are reported in which home and international students are, for example, encouraged to participate together in "on-campus global/international coursework" (Soria and Troisi 2014: 261), or in which the university "engages [international students] as cultural resources" (Urban and Palmer 2014: 305). However, such instances are the exception rather than the rule in the HE literature, and to my knowledge, even where they occur, there is little if any consideration of language-related issues. Thus, with its focus on the narrow remit of the curriculum on the one hand, and on vague notions of 'global citizenship' on the other, instead of on the lingua-cultural (and multilingua-cultural) skills involved in successful intercultural communication, important opportunities are being lost 'at home'. And this seems to be especially true when 'home' is in the UK and United States, the two largest importers but among the smallest exporters of mobile students, and where for the majority of NES academics, there still appears to be both a deep-rooted sense of their ownership of the (academic) English language, their right to determine what kinds of English are acceptable, and a belief that (native or near-native) English should be the only language used on campus, and other languages not at all.

Because the United States and UK are the highest recruiters of international students, because international students form a far larger proportion of total student numbers in the UK (although an even larger proportion, though from a much smaller intake, in Australia), and because I am able to draw on my own empirical evidence in respect of the UK, this geographical setting will form the main focus of the discussion in respect of intercultural communication on campus in this part of the chapter. However, I will also draw on evidence from other sources/settings where this has the potential to cast further light on the subject.

Intercultural communication practices on the international campus

In this section, we will consider in particular the communicative needs of international students (by which, as just pointed out, I am referring to NNES international students in UK university settings). The discussion will relate to their interactions both with each other, and with home students and staff. It is often said that many and perhaps most NNES international students arrive on an Anglophone university campus assuming that most of their communication will be with NES (see, for example, Adolphs 2005/2009). That is, they anticipate that the majority of both their student peer group and their lecturers will be NES.

However, once international students commence their studies in the Anglophone setting, and especially if these studies are at postgraduate level and the university is in the UK (or Australia, though with lower total numbers involved), international students often discover that the situation is not quite as they had predicted. This is because their peer group is likely to be linguistically and culturally diverse, with the majority of students in their programmes coming from a range of non-Anglophone countries other than their own, though sometimes also from the same country, particularly if it is China. They also tend to find, if to a lesser extent, that some of their lecturers and supervisors are also NNES.

Intercultural communication on campus is thus not of the conventional 'EFL' kind that international students expect, in which their principal need is to understand and be understood by NES students and staff. Instead, it is rather more complex. For on the one hand, much of their communication in English involves the use of ELF rather than EFL. But on the other hand, as will become clear later in the chapter, university language policies and (required) practices are still predicated on international students' EFL knowledge and skills. That is, UK universities are still "monolingual, normative," and "largely unchanged despite the diversification and internationalisation of higher education" (Jenkins and Wingate 2015). And while home students may be a small minority on any programme, it is their English and that of the (mostly NES) lecturers that is regarded as the norm, and with which international students are expected to fit in. Thus, their sociolinguistic reality involves a central contradiction: that they study in an ELF setting but are required to communicate in both speech and writing as if it was an ENL one. And although I cannot generalise from the small number of participants with experience of HE in the US among the international students in my UK study (Jenkins 2014), it was interesting that those who had previously studied in US universities described the same "monolingual normative" ethos. For example, one participant, a Saudi Arabian student, described to me how even on a sociolinguistics module, the lecturer, who might be expected to have a better understanding of linguistic diversity than those in certain other disciplines, told her that her English was "strange" and that she should try to sound more "American."

The marginalising of linguistic diversity in Anglophone HE does not only affect the kinds of *English* that are considered acceptable. For languages other than English are even more marginalised on campus than 'non-standard' (i.e., non-native) English. Whereas another language (or, less often, languages) than English is usually the principal native language of home students in non-Anglophone universities, particularly in non-postcolonial countries, this obviously is not so in the Anglophone HE world. Perhaps it is for this reason that the outdated belief in the need for international students to 'acculturate' or 'assimilate' prevails to such an extent among US and UK university staff, who tend to take it for granted not only that NNES students should become more 'native-like' in their English, but also that they should avoid using their own native languages, or any other languages than English that they speak. In my experience, it is not at all uncommon to hear colleagues complaining that, for example, their Chinese students speak Chinese together in group work, or for home students to complain that international students keep to themselves outside class and only speak their own languages (although research including my own provides counter evidence demonstrating that it may in fact be the home students who are the 'guiltier' parties in terms of keeping themselves apart). These same points can even be found in the HE research literature, sometimes with advice on how to ensure that (particularly) Chinese students integrate in class. And yet, for a university to be 'international' language-wise, the implication is that it is multilingual, not in the simplistic sense that its members come from a diverse range of first languages (although this is of course true), but that their languages are *built into the ethos* of the university, that these languages are part of what a university means when it presents itself as 'international'.

The same goes for international universities in the non-Anglophone world of HE. That is, to be international, it is not sufficient for another language to be present merely because it is a country's mother tongue (although this is certainly an improvement on the 'English-only' of Anglophone universities). Other languages than the local one and English would need to have an intrinsic role in a university's "tripartite mission of teaching, research and service functions" (Maringe and Foskett 2010: 1) for it to be international in respect of linguistic diversity. However, as Wilkins and Urbanovič (2014) point out, the current trend is moving in the opposite direction, with an increasing number of HE institutions especially in mainland Europe and East/Southeast Asia not only teaching in English medium, but also establishing EMI branch campuses in other non-Anglophone countries than their own. One example that the latter authors cite is a top Chinese university, Xiamen, which is opening a branch in Malaysia in 2015. Again, for such a university to be international, it is not sufficient for the host (e.g., Chinese) and home (e.g., Malay) languages to merely exist in the background against an English medium foreground. But this appears to be what is happening apart from a few exceptions where non-Anglophone universities have established small campuses abroad teaching in languages other than English. For example, Soochow University of Laos is teaching in Chinese, Paris-Sorbonne University Abu Dhabi in French, and Stockholm School of Economics Russia in Swedish (see Wilkins and Urbanovič 2014). Despite all that we know from research into translanguaging in education (e.g., Creese and Blackledge 2010, 2015; Canagarajah 2011; García and Wei 2014), it seems that a time when the notion of 'international HE' will mean 'multilingual HE' in any genuine sense is even more distant than that when it will mean diversity within the English language.

We return now to the subject of international students. To date there has been little research exploring the lived experiences and views of international students, let alone any in-depth research on this subject. Most published work on the subject of intercultural communication in HE, wherever in the world, has been conceptual and/or has focused on curriculum or global citizenship issues rather than language (e.g., most of the contributions to Sovič and Blythman 2013), or has been interested in how to 'help' NNES international students 'improve' their English. Other research, such as Smit (2010), Mauranen (2012), and Björkman (2013), while undoubtedly large-scale, in-depth, ELF-oriented, and essential in providing empirical linguistic evidence, focuses more on matters of English language contact and change in ELF settings. There are a number of smaller scale empirical studies focusing international students in respect of EMI practices. These include several of the chapters in Doiz et al. (2013), as well as House (2016) on a German university, Iino and Murata (2016) on a Japanese university, and Wang (2015) on a Chinese one. The interview research of my own to which I referred earlier (Jenkins 2014) is nevertheless unusual in being a more in-depth empirical study focusing exclusively on language issues, and from an ELF rather than native-English-normative perspective. For these reasons, I now briefly discuss the study's key findings.

The participants were almost unanimous, across their various first languages, degree types, and disciplines, in their criticisms of NES staff and students. A point repeated by many of them was that their NES lecturers habitually used local idiomatic language and slang that was not familiar to people from other countries. A Chilean participant, for example, talked of their use of "street language." Another frequently mentioned point was the use of local jokes. A Chinese student described how she and her Chinese peers could not understand their lecturers' jokes, but laughed because others were laughing. Likewise, a Korean student said that "everyone laugh, but I can't understand that, but I just follow the laughter." He went on to point out what many of the NES staff had apparently not appreciated – that joking is culture-specific: "the laughing point is different." Others criticised lecturers for speaking too fast, too quietly, mumbling, and refusing to let students record their lectures. A Mexican student observed that even in the rare event that a lecturer adjusts his or her speech for the benefit of NNES students, s/he seems unable to carry the adjustment through to spontaneous parts of the session such as questions and answers. He described the lecture itself as coming through a kind of "filter," but the unprepared interaction as being "a loop of bad communication." In general, the participants felt that lecturers did not understand the situation of international students and needed training in intercultural communication.

NES students fared just as badly in the participants' eyes, particularly in seminar situations, where they were considered to show little willingness to engage with international students. A Thai student, for instance, reported that "the British students discuss together" and "talk very fast," making it difficult for the NNES students to "catch what they say." This meant, she said, that by the time any of the international students were ready to contribute to the discussion, the focus had moved to another topic. Many other participants in the study reported likewise that the home students dominated seminars, spoke very fast, and used a lot of slang and jokes, all of which served to exclude the international students. By contrast, the majority found it far easier to communicate with NNES students from other first languages than with home students. They also noted that they were aware from first-hand experience of the need to adjust the way they spoke so as to communicate more effectively in intercultural interactions. In other words, without knowing the term, they were describing how they used accommodation strategies to enhance their intercultural communications. But despite their criticisms of home students' behaviour, most said they did not believe that the latter deliberately excluded them, but that they lacked intercultural awareness and like the NES lecturers needed training in intercultural communication skills. The effect, nevertheless, was to lower international students' confidence in settings when NES students (and staff) were present. Some talked of being made to feel that their English was "bad" and that they were being "judged." What the students described in these respects seemed to me to have an element of old-fashioned colonialism about it on the part of the NES staff and students, a kind of 'colonialism at home'. One student even used the word "colonialism" himself. It also demonstrated a degree of irresponsibility (if unwitting) on the part of a university that claims to be international but makes its NNES members feel uncomfortable for the very fact of not being NES.

Issues and ongoing debates

Having explored some international university language practices more broadly, and the experiences of international students in a single university in more detail, we will next consider what international universities' stated and implicit English language policies have to say (if anything) about the issues covered so far in this chapter.

International university language policy

Spolsky argues that it is an institution's practices that are its de facto policies "to the extent that they are regular and predictable" (2009: 4). Nevertheless, he conceptualises language policy as consisting of three interrelated components: practices, beliefs, and management. The 'belief' component refers to language ideology, "the values or statuses that are assigned to named languages, varieties, and features" (2009), and the 'management' component to "the explicit and observable effort by someone or some group that has or claims authority over the participants in the domain to modify their practices or beliefs" (2009). In the following discussion of international university language policies, I will explore the ideologies (whether overt or, more often, covert) that appear to underpin the language-related choices made by management by their most public means, that is, on their websites. Much of my focus will be on issues relating to English language entry testing as well as to orientations to the written English of NNES, both of which have implications for fairness in the treatment of NNES students in general, and international NNES students in Anglophone settings in particular.

Before we turn to language testing, let us first consider what other kinds of language policy evidence universities present on their websites and related documents. As already mentioned, there is very little, if any, reference to language policy, so this has mostly to be inferred from what they say indirectly and from their practices. Over the past two years, I have closely scrutinised the websites of all universities at which I have given plenary talks, along with those of the other plenary speakers. Without exception, I have found statements, often illustrated with photographs, in which they refer proudly to their diverse student intake. Here, for example, is a quotation I took from the University of Vienna website in June 2013:

> From 363 European partner universities, the University of Vienna has entered into an ERASMUS-Partnership with 350 universities. Students from approximately 130 countries attend more than 10,000 lectures at the University of Vienna every year.

This was illustrated with a photograph of an East Asian-looking student sitting at a desk. Similarly, I found this (in November 2013) on the website of the University of Hamburg:

> Universität Hamburg is international and cosmopolitan, qualities integral to being what we call the "gateway to the world of science." Universität Hamburg explicitly sees itself as part of Hamburg, a harbor city which in turn sees itself, both politically and culturally, as a "gateway to the world." In all of its scientific and scholarly pursuits, the University upholds the city's long-standing tradition of openness, tolerance and international cooperation and universality. For this reason, the University cooperates with numerous international universities and welcomes international students and academics to Hamburg.

As well as proclaiming their welcoming of students and staff from around the world, universities are often keen to emphasise their goal as preparing their students to become more international in their outlook. Here, for example, is a quotation from the website of the School of International Liberal Studies at Waseda University, Tokyo (accessed February 2014):

> **International environment draws a multicultural student body**
>
> International students comprise nearly a third of SILS enrollment, representing some 50 nations worldwide. At SILS, cross-cultural/multicultural communication is an everyday experience, serving to sharpen the international sensibilities of Japanese and overseas students alike.

So far, so international. However, this is generally where the international ethos ends. From here on, we are instead back with Ferguson's (2007) point that I quoted earlier, in which he argues that universities introduce EMI not in order to promote internationalisation as such, but to attract higher fee paying students and talented teachers and researchers, and so improve their global reputation. For once we turn to diversity in respect of language, we find little other than a focus on one or both of two native English varieties: 'standard' American and British English. This can be found in orientations to students' writing, where any reference is purely to remedial help to bring their English into line with native academic English. There is no sense of any awareness of the findings of research by scholars of critical academic writing such as Canagarajah (2002), of the notion of 'codemeshing' (e.g., Canagarajah 2013), or of the relevance of ELF research to academic writing for an international audience (e.g., Mauranen 2012; Flowerdew and Wang 2015). This is even the case when such scholars are, themselves, connected to an institution (e.g., Wen Qiufang in China; James D'Angelo and Kumiko Murata in Japan; and Rakesh Bhatt, Suresh Canagarajah, and Braj Kachru in the United States, to name but a few).

But it is above all when it comes to English language entry testing that the most serious contradictions emerge between the underlying situation and the surface level presentation of diversity. In this respect, Shohamy's (2006) notion of 'mechanisms' is particularly useful. Shohamy draws on Spolsky's tripartite framework to provide an expanded view of language policy that has stronger focus on ideology. Her mechanisms are "overt and covert devices that are used as the means for affecting, creating, and perpetuating de facto language policies" and "lie at the heart of the battle between ideology and practice" (Shohamy 2006: 54). There are, she argues, six 'mechanisms', and of these it is that of 'language tests' that has the main relevance in the context of university language policy. This is because, as we will see later, universities produce very little in the way of overt language policy, and so their language tests provide one of the strongest covert clues as to the ideology that informs their 'policy'.

Almost without exception, the websites that I have explored stipulate in their entry requirements that students must achieve a certain score in one of a small number of 'international' English language tests. These are principally IELTS and TOEFL, although some others of a very similar nature are also accepted (see McNamara 2011 and Jenkins and Leung 2014 for a fuller discussion and examples of descriptors). And to illustrate what these examination boards mean by 'international', here is what IELTS has to say in the *IELTS Guide for Teachers* (2013: 11; my italics):

International English

IELTS recognises both *British and American English in terms of spelling, grammar and choice of words*. It also incorporates a mix of *native speaker accents from Australia, Canada, New Zealand, the UK and US* in the Listening component.

International content

The IELTS approach is recognised by academics and admissions professionals as being fair, reliable and valid to all candidates, whatever their nationality, cultural background, gender or specific needs. *The test questions are developed by item writers in Australia, Canada, New Zealand, the UK and the US.*

In other words, there is nothing international about IELTS or, indeed, any of the other supposedly 'international' tests. In terms of English, they are national, pure and simple. In respect of Shohamy's (2006) 'Language tests' mechanism, they serve as "a powerful device . . . to affect language practices and criteria of correctness often leading to inclusions and exclusions and to perpetuate ideologies" (p. 93). Or, in Spolsky's (2004) terms, they are a means of forcing people (in this case, NNES students who want to gain university entry) to "modify their practices," that is, to use more 'nativelike' English.

I referred earlier to the fact that the international students in my 2014 study had a lot to say about issues of fairness. The participants in that study found much to criticise in terms of what they saw as unfair practices in their UK university. One major target of their criticisms was the assimilation approach, according to which they were expected to fit in, while the home students and staff were allowed to continue with (national) business as usual, using the ways they habitually spoke with each other, with no regard for the needs of international students. They also complained about the unfairness of no allowances being made for those who were studying in a language other than their mother tongue. Although some of them estimated that to produce work of equivalent standard to that of a home student took them four times as long, this was disregarded in respect of all deadlines and milestones. Meanwhile the presence of large numbers of NES served to undermine their confidence in their own abilities, as if not speaking native English somehow implied that they were less intelligent and knowledgeable in their subject of study.

By contrast, outside of Anglophone HE, where there are few if any NES studying alongside NNES students, and where most staff are also NNES, from the evidence available to date, it seems that there is more of an "all in the same (NNES) boat together" outlook, not to mention that any deadlines and milestones are fairer as they apply equally to everyone, instead of advantaging one (NES) group and disadvantaging another (NNES) one. The lack of NES to provide benchmarks of 'good' English is another benefit to boost confidence, while lectures are likely to be more comprehensible to NNES students, and seminar discussions more accessible. However, there is likely to be dissatisfaction among students and staff in universities that switch from teaching home students in the local language to EMI, not only because of the added difficulties of studying in another language, but because of a perceived threat to the local language and identity. An extreme example occurred in France in 2013 when the law changed to permit teaching in languages other than French, which in practice meant English. A British newspaper reported the response to this decision as follows:

> a row has ensued as a number of academics have vented their rage. The Académie Française, guardian of the French language, appealed to French MPs to oppose the plan, claiming the new law "favours a marginalisation of the French language." Academics opposed to the plan have launched a petition, with Claude Hagège, a professor at the Collège de France, warning in the newspaper Le Monde of "an act of sabotage" of the French language.
> (Guardian Newspaper, *May 11, 2013, online at http://www.guardian.co.uk/world/2013/may/10/ French-universities-english-language)*

At present, there is insufficient evidence to be sure of the extent to which any of these things are true of non-Anglophone HE, and to an extent this must remain an empirical question.

Implications for language policy and practice

As Stier pointed out some years ago in respect of education, "discussions tend to be fairly idealistic and founded in taken-for-granted assumptions, rarely questioned or investigated more closely. . . . The spirit of internationalisation does not let itself easily be transformed into educational practice" (2004: 88). Likewise, Hélot observes, "paradoxically, although schools everywhere . . . have seen a growing change in their populations, the increased visibility of linguistic diversity is not reflected in classroom practices" (2012: 214). Both comments are overwhelmingly relevant to language issues in international HE, where anachronistic "taken-for-granted assumptions" about the appropriateness of native English still prevail, and where "linguistic diversity" continues to be marginalised in the seminar room and lecture theatre.

The research discussed in this chapter has revealed the following failures of international HE's approach to language:

- Positive orientations to diversity on campus rarely extended to English.
- University managements claim to prepare students for life in a multicultural world, but lack awareness of what this means in terms of English or other languages.
- Instead, internationalisation is seen as going hand in hand with English only, and only native English (mainly American and British).
- Problematising of English language use is almost always in relation to NNES.
- There is little awareness that NES students and staff often lack intercultural communication skills.
- NES management and staff show little awareness of the difficulties for NNES of operating in another language, and have no sense of linguistic unfairness.
- The situation nevertheless seems to be worse in Anglophone than non-Anglophone settings. For while native English discourses may be stronger in non-Anglophone settings, there is a tension between policy and practice, that is, a tendency for non-Anglophone communities to profess adherence to native English in principle while using ELF in practice.

The implications of these points for language policy in HE can be summed up very briefly as follows. The global language situation has changed, and continues to change. English may (currently) be the primary lingua franca of international HE, but for most people in HE, it is not their first language, nor is it a foreign language, but a lingua franca, a tool of communication. On the one hand, therefore, NNES students may wish (and have the right) to use languages other than English during their studies, while on the other hand, their English is not that of NES, and nor should it be expected to be. Universities that wish to proclaim themselves as international need to take note of these two key developments and build them into their stated policies and mission statements. In other words, they need to orient to (and not merely condone) diverse NNES uses of English, and to conduct their teaching, research, and administration in languages other than English. This applies as much to universities in Anglophone as in non-Anglophone countries, and perhaps even more, given the far larger numbers of mobile students that they recruit. It will involve a degree of critical thinking about language that university management, staff, and students (often NNES as well as NES) have so far not demonstrated. The alternative is for universities to declare themselves 'national', use only the local national native language, whatever it is, and stop recruiting international students.

Future directions

In order to resolve the tensions, difficulties, and contradictions around language in international HE that have been described and discussed in this chapter, far more research is needed, in particular, the kind of research that Doiz et al. (2013) describe as follows:

Every context has its own characteristics and, therefore, studies rooted in each specific context will be much welcomed. Results from other contexts may always be helpful and enlightening, but every institution should carry out its own research, which ideally will lay the foundations of the most appropriate language policy for them.

(p. 219)

Their point is that while "diversity does not prevent the emergence of many commonalities between the different case studies presented (i.e., the case studies in Doiz et al. 2013), namely the way EMI affects multilingualism, policy planning concerns, and the university community" (p. 213), the local context is paramount. To this end, an ethnographically informed case study project is currently underway, led by Anna Mauranen and myself, and involving one university in each of nine countries (Australia, China, Finland, Italy, Japan, Malaysia, Netherlands, Spain, and the UK). In each case, the researchers are composed of teams of people who work in that institution on a daily basis, rather than flying in for a few days or accessing it online. Smaller-scale, in-depth studies of this kind will enable researchers to identify nuances and to understand similarities and differences in local and mobile student needs that are likely to escape attention in other kinds of projects. It is to be hoped that many other studies of this smaller-scale, locally researched kind will be conducted over the next few years.

Summary

This chapter has examined current English language policies and practices in international HE in the context of mobility. It has explored international students' experiences and needs in the context of intercultural communication along with responses to the internationalisation of HE by university management, staff, and non-mobile home students.

Despite calling for more empirical research, the chapter amply demonstrates that existing research has already exposed the need for a reconsideration of what it means to be an *international* university: how it involves an understanding that international university English is not the language of NES, but a lingua franca in a multilingual setting, and therefore not only is it *not native English*, but *not English only* either. When many people in a university setting are multilingual, it is unnatural to expect monolingual (English) use. This in turn implies an urgent need to modernise English language entry testing so as not to exclude potential students merely because their English is not sufficiently 'near-native' or they practise translanguaging. Research has also demonstrated the need for everyone, but particularly NES students and staff, to improve their intercultural communication skills. In this respect, it is nonsense that the term 'international student' has hitherto been reserved for those students who come from overseas and pay high fees. As I have asked repeatedly in conference talks over the past few years, do NES students (and staff) not want to be 'international' too?

Related topics

Translanguaging in mobility
Neoliberalism, language, and migration
Traveling texts, translocal/transnational literacies, and transcontextual analysis
Language in skilled migration
Mobility, language, and schooling

Further reading

Björkman, B. (2013). *English as an Academic Lingua Franca. An Investigation of Form and Communicative Effectiveness*. Berlin: De Gruyter Mouton.

A study of ELF communication in a Swedish international university setting, based on authentic spoken data, and focusing on form and pragmatic issues.

Jenkins, J. (2014). *English as a Lingua Franca in the International University. The Politics of Academic English Language Policy*. London and New York: Routledge.

An exploration of international universities' language policies and practices on the basis of three empirical datasets: a web survey, a qualitative questionnaire, and an interview study.

Mauranen, A. (2012). *Exploring ELF. Academic English Shaped by Non-native Speakers*. Cambridge: Cambridge University Press.

A study of the use of English as an academic lingua franca in a Finnish university, drawing on the corpus of ELF in academic settings, and focusing on both social and cognitive perspectives.

Smit, U. (2010). *English as a Lingua Franca in Higher Education*. Berlin: De Gruyter Mouton.

An ethnographic analysis of the use of English as a lingua franca among a student group studying tourism in an English medium university setting in Vienna.

Sovič, S. and Blythman, M., eds. (2013). *International Students Negotiating Higher Education*. London and New York: Routledge.

Focusing on Anglophone settings, the authors take a critical stance on current orientations to international students, demonstrating both the difficulties that they face and the advantages that they bring to their institutions.

References

Adolphs, S. (2005/2009). "I don't think I should learn all this" – A longitudinal view of attitudes towards "native speaker" English. In C. Gnutzmann and F. Intemann (eds.), *The Globalisation of English and the English Language Classroom* (pp. 119–131). Tübingen: Narr Verlag.

Baker, W. (2015). *Culture and Identity through English as a Lingua Franca Rethinking Concepts and Goals in Intercultural Communication*. Berlin: De Gruyter Mouton.

Bordia, S., Bordia, P. and Restubog, S.L.D. (2015). Promises from afar: A model of international student psychological contract in business education. *Studies in Higher Education* 40(2): 212–232.

Canagarajah, A. S. (2002). *Critical Academic Writing and Multilingual Students*. Michigan: University of Michigan Press.

Canagarajah, A. S. (2005). Introduction. In A. S. Canagarajah (ed.), *Reclaiming the Local in Language Policy and Practice* (pp. xiii–xxx). Mahwah, NJ: Lawrence Erlbaum.

Canagarajah, A. S. (2011). Translanguaging in the classroom: Emerging issues for research and pedagogy. *Applied Linguistics Review* 2: 1–28.

Canagarajah, A. S. (2013). *Translingual Practice: Global Englishes and Cosmopolitan Relations*. London and New York: Routledge.

Cogo, A. and Dewey, M. (2012). *Analysing English as a Lingua Franca: A Corpus-driven Investigation*. London: Continuum.

Coleman, J. (2013). Foreword. In A. Doiz, D. Lasagabaster and J.M. Sierra (eds.), *English-Medium Instruction at Universities Worldwide* (pp. xiii–xv). Bristol: Multilingual Matters.

Creese, A. and Blackledge, A. (2010). Translanguaging in the bilingual classroom: A pedagogy for learning and teaching. *Modern Language Journal* 94: 103–115.

Creese, A. and Blackledge, A. (2015). Translanguaging in educational settings. *Annual Review of Linguistics* 35: 20–35.

De Wit, H. (2014). Erasmus report fuels internationalisation debate. *University World News Global Edition* 338. Retrieved from http://www.universityworldnews.com/article.php?story=20141008142207417 [accessed 2 March 2015].

De Wit, H. (2015). Who owns internationalisation? *University World News Global Edition* 350. Retrieved from http://www.universityworldnews.com/index.php?page=UW_Main [accessed 18 January 2015].

Doiz, A., Lasagabaster, D. and Sierra, J.M. (2013). *English-Medium Instruction at Universities Worldwide*. Bristol: Multilingual Matters.

Ferguson, G. (2007). The global spread of English, scientific communication and ESP: Questions of equity, access and domain loss. *Ibérica* 13: 7–38.

Flowerdew, J. and Wang, S. (2015). Identity in academic writing. *Annual Review of Applied Linguistics* 35: 81–99.

García, O. and Li Wei (2014). *Translanguaging: Language, Bilingualism and Education*. Basingstoke: Palgrave Macmillan.

Hélot, C. (2012). Linguistic diversity and education. In M. Martin-Jones, A. Blackledge and A. Creese (eds.), *The Routledge Handbook of Multilingualism* (pp. 214–231). London and New York: Routledge.

House, J. (2016). Own-language use in academic discourse in English as a lingua franca. In Murata (ed.), *Exploring ELF in Japanese Academic and Business Contexts: Conceptualizations, Research and Pedagogic Implications* (pp. 59–69). London and New York: Routledge.

Iino, M. and Murata, K. (2016). Dynamics of ELF communication in an English-medium academic context in Japan: From EFL learners to ELF users. In K. Murata (ed.), *Exploring ELF in Japanese Academic and Business Contexts: Conceptualizations, Research and Pedagogic Implications* (pp. 111–131). London and New York: Routledge.

International Association of Universities. *4th Global Survey on the Internationalization of Higher Education*. Retrieved from http://www.eaie.org/blog/iau-global-survey/ [accessed 19 January 2015].

Jenkins, J. (2000). *The Phonology of English as an International Language: New Models, New Norms, New Goals*. Oxford: Oxford University Press.

Jenkins, J. (2014). *English as a Lingua Franca in the International University: The Politics of Academic English Language Policy*. Abingdon: Routledge.

Jenkins J., Cogo, A. and Dewey, M. (2011). Review of developments in research into English as a lingua franca. *Language Teaching* 44(3): 281–315.

Jenkins, J. and Leung, C. (2014). English as a Lingua Franca. In A. Kunnan (ed.), *The Companion to Language Assessment* (pp. 1605–1616). Oxford: Wiley-Blackwell.

Jenkins, J. and Wingate, U. (2015). Staff and students' perceptions of English language policies and practices in "international" universities: A case study from the UK. *Higher Education Review* 47(2): 47–73.

Leonard, P.L. (2015). Price and rise of China behind decline in mobility. *University World News Global Edition* 356. Retrieved from http://www.universityworldnews.com/article.php?story=20150225085720931 [accessed 1 March 2015].

Maringe, F. and Foskett, N. (2010). Introduction: Globalization and universities. In F. Maringe and N. Foskett (eds.), *Globalization and Internationalization in Higher Education* (pp. 1–13). London: Continuum.

Marklein, M.B. (2007). USA sees first increase in foreign students since 9/11. *USA Today*, December 11.

Mauranen, A. (2012). *Exploring ELF: Academic English Shaped by Non-native Speakers*. Cambridge: Cambridge University Press.

McNamara, T. (2011). Managing learning: Authority and language assessment. *Language Teaching* 44(4): 500–515.

OECD. (2014a). *Education at a Glance 2014: OECD Highlights*. OECD. Retrieved from http://dx.doi.org/10.1787/eag-2014-en [accessed December 2016].

OECD. (2014b). *Chart C4.3*. Retrieved from http://dx.doi.org/10.1787/888933118827 [accessed December 2016].

Seidlhofer, B. (2011). *Understanding English as a Lingua Franca*. Oxford: Oxford University Press.

Shohamy, E. (2006). *Language Policy: Hidden Agendas and New Approaches*. London: Routledge.

Soria, K. M. and Troisi, J. (2014). Internationalization at home alternatives to study abroad: Implications for students' development of global, international, and intercultural competencies. *Journal of Studies in International Education* 18(3): 261–280.

Spolsky, B. (2004). *Language Policy*. Cambridge: Cambridge University Press.

Spolsky, B. (2009). *Language Management*. Cambridge: Cambridge University Press.

Stier, J. (2004). Taking a critical stance toward internationalization ideologies in higher education: Idealism, instrumentalism and educationalism. *Globalisation, Societies and Education* 2(1): 1–28.

Sweeney, E. and Zhu Hua (2010). Accommodating to your audience. Do native speakers of English know how to accommodate their communication strategies toward non-native speakers of English? *Journal of Business Communication* 47(4): 477–504.

Times Higher Education. (2013). *Top 10 Destinations for International Students*. 31 January 2013: 39.

UK Council for International Students Affairs (UKCISA). (2015). *International Students Statistics: UK Higher Education*. Retrieved from http://www.ukcisa.org.uk/Info-for-universities-colleges – schools/ Policy-research – statistics/Research – statistics/International-students-in-UK-HE/#International-(non-UK)-students-in-UK-HE-in-2013–14 [Accessed 28 February 2015].

Urban, E. L. and Palmer, L. B. (2014). International students as a resource for internationalization of higher education. *Journal of Studies in International Education* 18(4): 305–324.

Van Parijs, P. (2011). *Linguistic Justice for Europe and for the World*. Oxford: Oxford University Press.

Wang, Y. (2015). A case study of the role of English in a Chinese university. Waseda University *English as a Lingua Franca Working Papers* 4: 209–218.

Wilkins, S. and Urbanovič, J. (2014). English as the lingua franca in transnational higher education: Motives and prospects of institutions that teach in languages other than English. *Journal of Studies in International Education* 18(5): 405–425.

29
Mobility, language, and schooling

Margaret R. Hawkins and Anneliese Cannon

Introduction

Mobility has, with good reason, become a key theme in considerations of modernity. With ever-increasing global movement, virtually every aspect of societal and individual functioning is impacted, from families, households and communities to "the constellation of countries linked by migration flows" (King and Skeldon as quoted in Glick Schiller and Salazar 2013: 183). Our interest in this chapter is on one particular institutional phenomenon: schooling. Here we focus on the intersection of global movement, language, and schooling at the early childhood, primary and secondary levels.

There is ample evidence that people are ever-increasingly mobile. As one example, the United Nations (2014: 5) claims that "International migration is overall increasing; the number has grown from 154 million in 1990 . . . [to] 232 million in 2013." They also claim that, as of 2013, 23.4 million of these migrants were fourteen years of age or younger, and 28.2 million were between fifteen and twenty-four years of age. Of particular importance to this chapter is their claim that, while the majority of international migrants are hosted by developed countries, growth figures show that young migrant populations are increasing in direct reverse correlation with the level of development of the receiving countries. Put another way, the growth rates remain flat in developed countries, but are increasing rapidly in less developed nations. In 2013, there were 83 million immigrant children and youth in developed countries, 107 million in developing countries, 18.9 million in the least developed countries, and 98 million in other developing countries.

As mobility increases, there are few places where all youth are being schooled in the language they speak at home. Here we use the term mobility not only to describe global movements of people – with a particular focus on school-aged children and youth – but also the migration of goods, resources, languages, knowledge, ideologies, and ideas. In this we follow Glick Schiller and Salazar, who claim:

> Mobility studies emerged from a postmodern moment in which global 'flows' of capital, people and objects were increasingly noted and celebrated. Within this new scholarship, categories of migrancy are all seen through the same analytical lens.
>
> *(2013: 183)*

One direct result is that, in looking at language and schooling, we recognize that youth are being schooled in languages other than their home languages not only because youth (and families) migrate, but also because languages migrate (often but not always as a legacy of colonialism), ideologies migrate (such as the value and status of certain languages and speakers of those languages over others), and knowledge, resources, and goods migrate (including curriculum, pedagogies, and educational materials that reflect particular languages and language ideologies). Thus, we can point to many instances of immigrants being schooled in the language of the new place in which they live. We can also point to places where students live in communities where the language spoken is their mother tongue, but are schooled in languages set by national language-in-education policies. In some places there are multiple local languages being spoken in the same geographical region, yet one is privileged for schooling. In others, the language of schooling may be a 'foreign' language – one that is not spoken in the community by anyone (as is often the case in many postcolonial settings). Therefore, the language of schooling may be a particular local language that holds precedence over others, or may be an imported language that has value/prestige.

Drawing on sociocultural educational and language theory, we pay attention to an array of scholarly perspectives, and to the terrain of specific places, citing specific empirical examples from various international contexts to understand the factors and phenomena at play at the intersection of mobility, language, and education. We particularly acknowledge that students who live in poverty, who may have had interrupted/disrupted schooling trajectories, whose families may have limited formal education or may not speak the language of schooling, and/or whose language and culture are not highly valued in their academic or societal environments, are at high risk of academic failure, as attested to in a multitude of literature from all over the globe (as will be seen throughout this chapter). And, while this chapter is about schooling, we wish to acknowledge that, despite the United Nations claim that, as of 2012, "90 percent of children in developing regions are attending primary school," (United Nations 2014: 5), there remain many children in all regions of the globe who do not complete primary school, or are not in school at all. For example, Sancheti and Sudhir (2009) claim that in India, only 219 million of the 361 million children of school age attend schools. At heart, the question that drives us is, how do we ensure that all students, wherever they may be – from all national, racial, ethnic, linguistic, cultural and socioeconomic backgrounds – have equal educational access and opportunity?

Overview

Research on the education of students who do not speak the language of school has burgeoned in the last decade or so. In reviewing this literature, we have identified specific themes that have been taken up in multiple geographic locations. In this chapter, we will draw on the notion of 'ecologies' (Hawkins 2004; Van Lier 2008; Creese and Blackledge 2010) to not only address these themes, but to point to ways in which individual factors and components mutually affect and influence one another (in ever-shifting constellations) to shape the landscape of schooling for linguistically diverse learners.

Sociocultural and social justice perspectives

Foundational to our work, as well as to many of the researchers writing about schooling for students who speak non-school-dominant languages, are sociocultural and social justice perspectives. Understandings of schooling, and school achievement and effectiveness, are rooted in beliefs about the nature of knowledge and learning. Sociocultural perspectives take knowledge and learning to be both situated and social. By this we mean that knowledge is constructed among people engaged in meaning-making; it is co-constructed among members of specific communities in specific places (Lave and Wenger 1991; Rogoff 1994), then propelled on a trajectory through time and space, shifting as it is taken up, re-negotiated and re-voiced along its trajectory (Bakhtin 1981; Blommaert, Collins, and Slembrouck 2005; Compton-Lilly 2014). Learning occurs as people jointly negotiate meanings of ideas, concepts, and language that they encounter (always in specific places, at specific times, and among specific people), and come to new understandings.

Thus, as may be apparent, attention must be paid to the site of learning, the broader environment and geography of spaces of learning, the actors involved in the learning process, the ways in which meaning is constructed among all participants (and the tools that mediate this, including language processes and use), what counts as knowledge, and trajectories of ideas and meaning.

Social justice adds another layer of complexity to socially situated perspectives of learning. According to social justice in education scholars (e.g., Freire 2000; Ayers, Quinn, and Stovall 2009), youth have unequal access to schooling and educational achievement primarily because there are differences in status and power represented in every dimension of schooling, including policy, resources, and practices. Social justice perspectives mandate our attention to these issues as they play out in ecologies of schooling and learning, and, for our purposes here, particularly as they play out in relation to languages and language use.

The ecology of schooling

In the diagram in Figure 29.1, Hawkins (2005) illustrates the dynamics at play as students learn in different situated environments. This diagram offers a visual representation of the notion of ecologies and the socially situated nature of learning outlined earlier.

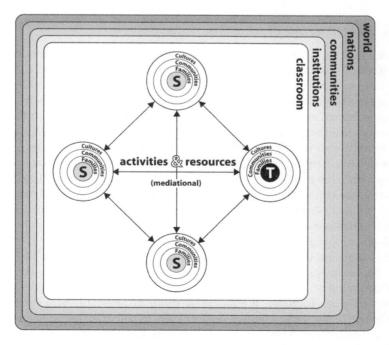

Figure 29.1 The ecology of schooling (taken from Hawkins 2005). Reproduced by permission of Taylor and Francis Group Ltd.

As represented, "T" represents teacher and "S" represents student. The significance is that each student comes to school embedded in and socialized into specific cultural and linguistic ways of knowing, thinking, and learning, and into practices, from their families, communities, and cultures, as do teachers and all other actors in each learning environment. Learning occurs as these actors negotiate meanings of concepts and ideas together, mediated through the learning materials, resources, and language available and in use, and the activities and pedagogies in which they engage (Hawkins 2004, 2005). However, cultures, families, and communities do not hold equal status in any given environment, nor do the languages in use. And what happens in the classroom, including what languages, resources, and activities are present, is shaped by policies, beliefs, and practices of the larger institution, which in turn reflect those of communities, nations, and worlds. Thus much of the current research on schooling, language, and mobile youth looks at how ideologies, interactions, and practices play out in and shape the lives of diverse global youth – including but not limited to those specific to language – and impact their emerging identities and their access to and ability to achieve in school.

While it is difficult to consider components discretely, given the complex interplay among them, we have categorized issues from current research and literature into the following clusters, which will organize our discussion about mobility, youth and schooling:

- Place (the situated nature of schooling);
- In and out of school languages and literacies;
- Program models and curricular designs;
- Standards and assessments.

Issues and ongoing debates

Place: the situated nature of schooling

Much of the work on schooling for youth who speak languages other than that used for school instruction is done in communities where an immigrant population is fairly established. In fact, as Purcell-Gates (2013) discusses, referring to her work with children of Mexican-origin migrant farm workers in the United States, there is a paucity of research outside of government research reports on the children of agricultural workers (who migrate regularly across nation-state borders), particularly in regards to their language and literacy practices. Further, also writing about Mexico and the United States, Zuñiga and Hamann (2009) report that few studies consider the experiences of so-called sojourner students' educational experiences as they traverse borders – also often multiple times. They demonstrate how "enduring geographic mobility affects the complicated work of identify formation and affiliation." While these studies point to differences in immigration patterns and longevity of residence of newcomers, we concern ourselves not only with schooling for youth who are not indigenous to the communities in which they are living, but also for youth who may live in their indigenous communities, but are being schooled in a language that is not their own, and, importantly, does not reflect their heritage or culture. We maintain, following our earlier definition of mobility, that mobility affects schooling for all students not being schooled in their home language. Whether these youth are physically traversing borders, or facing challenges to linguistic, cultural, or family ties to real or imagined homelands, there are important educational issues and implications to be considered.

Implicit in schooling, and all societal institutions, are ideologies – messages conveyed through the organization of the space, activities, policies, programs, pedagogies, and interactions – about the values and beliefs that are represented and perpetuated (Apple 2004). Schools, tasked with the responsibility of educating those who will contribute to their society, are guided by implicit views of what that society is and should be, what valued forms of participation and contributions are, and who is positioned to make them. Kanno (2003), for example, through a lens of *imagined communities* (Anderson 1991), explores the education of bilingual students in schools in Japan, and "argue(s) that schools envision imagined communities for the students they serve, and that these visions have a large impact on their current policies and practices, thereby ultimately affecting the identities of the students." (Kanno 2003: 286). Perhaps not surprisingly, she found that "the least privileged bilingual students . . . are socialized into the least privileged imagined communities" (Kanno 2003: 298).

In a second, and powerful, example from Belgium, Jaspers details how societal ideologies lead to a discourse of "the intrinsic inferiority and dangerousness of Islam" (2005: 283). This ultimately positions Moroccan boys as having " 'deviant' cultural backgrounds [and] unwillingness to integrate into Flemish society, [and as] proof of the impossibility of this integration" (p. 283). Through a close linguistic analysis of the communications and interactions of Moroccan boys in a Flemish school, Jaspers portrays their integration into "an unequal society that reproduces itself partially via language use and linguistic evaluation" (p. 296), thus pointing to the power of societal views and beliefs to shape identities of immigrant youth, and to determine what happens to them in (and ultimately beyond) school.

In yet another example, Canessa (2007) explores a school, situated in a complex Bolivian environment, where the majority of students and teachers are Indian (Aymaran) and share culture and ethnicity, but they are a low status and subordinate group in their larger region. What are mobile in this account are ideologies, formed and carried through time, via public institutions, policies and discourses (such as 'assimilationist policies' and 'education reform'). Canessa claims, "The term [Indian] has always referred to an unequal power relation; be it between conqueror and conquered, the ruler and the ruled, urban and rural, Spanish-speakers and speakers of indigenous languages, and generally all of these" (p. 188). Further, the language this community speaks is low status in relation to Spanish, and also to other indigenous languages. Currently in Bolivia bilingual education is mandated, and students are schooled in their mother tongue in early years of schooling, yet Canessa offers numerous examples of messages that children receive throughout every aspect of schooling about the inferior status of their language and ethnicity. Place-based ideologies – views and beliefs about what 'society' is, who students are, what they might have to contribute (or be reasonably expected to contribute), the value of their language, religion, and ethnicity – shape all aspects of students' schooling experience. As shown in Figure 29.1, the politics and relations of the world and nations filter through those of communities, into schools and ultimately classrooms, playing out in situated local interactions that, in turn, reify and reproduce existing ideologies.

There is now a solid body of work from many disciplines juxtaposing the global and the local in *place* (see Hawkins 2014 for a fuller discussion). On the one hand, educational sites are always local and situated. Each community and institution is distinctive, and the array of components and resources that shape and mediate learning in each are unique. On the other hand (as noted earlier), there are societal, national, and global discourses and practices that permeate every aspect of learning and interaction. In the fields of literacy and applied linguistics, much attention is now being paid to notions of space, time, and scale (e.g., Blommaert et al. 2005; Compton-Lilly 2014; Rowsell and Sefton-Greene 2014). This work accounts for movements and trajectories of language and literacy practices and engagements across time and space, and their intersections with the lives and identities of people who move through them. This, too, is a necessary component of considering mobility, language, and schooling, as languages and literacies are themselves social practices, and shape and are shaped by those who engage in them. In the remainder of the chapter we will address aspects of schooling and learning through a lens of mobility, and consider implications for youth being schooled in languages other than their heritage language.

In and out of school languages and literacies

Many accounts and investigations of schooling for children who are not fluent in the language of schooling focus on what happens in classrooms. As we move more deeply into a neoliberal era of schooling (Clark and Morgan 2011), standards and assessments proliferate, and drive educational policies and curricula worldwide (Kibler, Valdes, and Walqui 2014). The move, it seems, is toward standardization, and there is an underlying belief in a one-size-fits-all educational approach.

One result is that definitions of what count as 'language' and as 'literacy' become increasingly narrow and circumscribed, given that schools must teach them, and that students' mastery of them must be measured and compared (e.g., Shohamy 2011; Laursen 2013; Bunch, Walqui and Pearson 2014). Yet there is a robust body of work that explores uses of languages and literacies across the domains of students' lives and argues that learning happens most effectively when policies, curricula, and pedagogies are culturally and linguistically responsive to learners, value the everyday literacies of learners' lives, and take into account what learners know and bring to the classroom (Knobel 1999; Gonzalez, Moll, and Amanti 2005; Hawkins 2010; Erickson 2014). This also counters practices that are deficit-based, as it makes visible the assets that all learners, families, and communities have, and the language and literacy practices they engage in, rather than focusing on what they do not have and do.

Spaces of learning

Spaces of learning are typically taken to be school classrooms. Although these are certainly primary sites of formal learning, and serve as gatekeepers in the lives of youth, learning (including language learning) occurs in formal and informal spaces, in and out of schools. Research on school learning for students who do not speak the language of schooling (whom we will from here forward call 'emergent bilinguals', following Creese and Blackledge 2010 and García and Kleifgen 2010),[1] has pointed to the importance of distinguishing 'academic' or 'school-based' language from vernacular, or everyday, language (e.g., Hawkins 2004; Bunch 2006; Richardson-Bruna, Vann, and Perales Escudero 2007). In policy and assessment internationally, the belief is that if we can teach the particular genre(s) of language that are tied to the disciplinary content of school, all students will succeed. However, it is not so simple.

Importantly, there is no real agreement on what 'academic language' is. Much research has shown that school teachers and administrators believe that the reason that emergent bilinguals don't succeed in school is because they don't have the requisite vocabulary and grammatical structures (Kanno 2003; Milans 2006; Lee and Hawkins 2015). Although we know that academic language encompasses more than just vocabulary, there is little agreement on just what it comprises (Gutiérrez 1995; Valdés 1997; Richardson-Bruna et al. 2007). There is also little agreement on successful program models and/or approaches to their implementation, or on effective pedagogies. To provide one example, Richardson-Bruna et al. (2007), in their study of academic language instruction and science in a US secondary school, demonstrate how, when teachers too narrowly focus on teaching emergent bilinguals vocabulary, they ignore the other critical components of language required to be proficient in a given academic subject. The authors argue that this narrow focus on words ultimately serves to "reduce instructional expectations" (p. 51) and to diminish "students' opportunities to demonstrate achievement and meet identified academic criteria" (p. 52).

These issues contribute to the overwhelming lack of educational success of mobile and emergent bilingual students who live in poverty, and those whose languages and cultures are not valued in the educational spaces they inhabit. Milans, considering Chinese immigrant students in Spain, claims

> students from other systems and cultures, with different languages and background knowledge, are not valued and legitimated in classrooms, so that they are not allowed to reach minimum educational objectives. Indeed, the fact that they do not reach these objectives is considered by the Spanish teachers as the students' failures.
>
> *(2006: 61)*

While these examples highlight some of the challenges that emergent bilinguals face in meeting educational goals in school settings, there are also multiple, often contrasting, examples of how students learn language and literacy outside of official school spaces. For example, there is a body of research, conducted primarily in immigrant and diasporic communities, which identifies structured spaces within (and sponsored by) the community, where languages and literacies are taught and learned. Often, the motivation for such programs is a desire on the part of the community to offer formal tuition to their children about their languages, cultures, and practices that are absent in schools (e.g., Hélot and Young 2006; Creese and Blackledge 2010; García-Sanchez 2010). Where indigenous/native languages and cultures may be invisible and/or subordinated in schools, they can be maintained, valued, and sustained in community learning settings.

Many communities provide heritage- and language-based education in outside-of-school time and spaces. As Creese and Blackledge (2010) explain:

> we describe one particular model common in many nations with linguistic and cultural diversity, that of complementary schools, also known as heritage language schools, supplementary schools, and community language schools. These schools are invariably established by community members and focus on language, culture, and heritage teaching.
>
> *(p. 103)*

A smaller set of studies focus on faith-based instruction in religious sites (e.g., Han 2009; García-Sanchez 2010; Lytra 2010). Studies done in complementary schools and other community-centered sites focusing on instructional models, pedagogies, language use, identity work, and other aspects of teaching and learning point to what is possible when we take away the constraints and ideologies of formal schooling and supplant them with educational spaces that reflect the ethnicities, languages, cultures, and even religions of communities. In stressing the importance of community-based sites of learning, Han argues:

> The issue of supporting minority learners in and beyond classrooms leads us right back to the issue that mainstream institutions must systematically recognize, value, and incorporate the multilingual and multicultural realities minority immigrants and their

children live on a daily basis. Monolingual bias toward minority groups in the form of devaluing their multilingual resources permeates public policies and everyday practices in the domain of immigration, settlement, education, and employment.

(Han 2009: 664)

Local/indigenous languages and literacies

In concert with the discussion above regarding the current tendency toward uniformity in education, *literacy*, while undergoing a conceptual shift within the last two decades, is still predominantly conceptualized through a Western, and relatively narrowly defined, lens, as the ability to encode and decode print. This definition shapes current global aid programs in literacy and education, offering another example of how *mobility* – in this case mobile ideologies, programs and materials regarding literacy and literacy instruction – impacts learning for emergent bilinguals worldwide.

While literature in the field of literacy studies addresses global and/versus local literacies (e.g., Brandt and Clinton 2002; Prinsloo and Baynham 2008), and includes technologically mediated forms of communication as literacies (Lam and Warriner 2012; Hawkins 2014; Stornaiuolo and LeBlanc 2014), there remains the historical divide between 'oracy' and 'literacy' (Ong 1982), with 'literacy' focusing on the visual and an assumption that alphabetic codes are foundational to its definition. McCarty (2013), however, claims:

> I argue that alphabetic or print literacy is only one facet of what "counts" as literacy; in Indigenous sociolinguistic ecologies, literacy is more broadly construed as "the ability to interpret the complex system of cultural symbols" that enable community members to participate actively and appropriately in communicative events.
>
> *(Benjamin, Pecos, and Romero 1996: 116, as cited in McCarty 2013: 170)*

In a detailed analysis of geometric figures used in communication by Amerindian cultures of Brazil, de Souza (2008) illuminates the how these symbols represent 'perspective', 'ethic', and 'interconnectivity', and are rooted in the 'cosmovisions' of their cultural community. Lopez-Gopar (2007), in an analysis of messages found in a Triqui *huipil* (indigenously woven article of clothing) in Oaxaca, Mexico, convincingly demonstrates that the huipil serves as a 'walking text'. These are powerful examples of the importance of distinguishing between visual and alphabetic texts. McCarty (2013), too, calls for conceptualizing a literacy continuum that "illuminates the potential for harmonizing alphabetic and non-alphabetic literacies and Indigenous and non-Indigenous knowledge systems" (p. 171). Importantly, de Souza points out that the decontextualization and bounded definition of literacy serve to strengthen the 'asymmetry of power' (p. 197) between colonizers and colonized in colonial empires. Thus 'literacy', as perceived of by schools, delegitimates and devalues indigenous communication systems and ways of knowing.

McCarty (2013) connects indigenous literacies to work on multiliteracies (Cope and Kalantzis 2013) and multimodal literacies (Kress and Van Leeuwen 2001), arguing that a broader definition of literacy as multi-modal meaning-making not only sheds light on indigenous literacies, but can ultimately serve to empower indigenous groups. Hornberger (2009), too, urges us to move beyond narrow definitions of literacy as "communicative modalities encompass more than written and spoken language" (p. 9), and suggests that "multilingual education activates voices for reclaiming the local" (p. 12; speaking of indigenous communities). McCarty also highlights connections between indigenous literacies and language loss/revitalization, offering evidence that introducing systems of orthography into indigenous languages supports language maintenance and revitalization efforts. In the current U.S. landscape, where only 20 of the 175 surviving indigenous languages are being transmitted intergenerationally in the home (McCarty 2013: 169), this is significant. However, Lopez-Gopar (2007) offers a caution: "Alphabetic literacy for indigenous languages should be developed by indigenous people to serve their own purposes." (p. 170). Otherwise orthographies are developed by outsiders and imposed (another example of mobility), thus transmitting their ideologies and agendas.

There are now many countries worldwide that have policies providing indigenous-language education to youth, especially at younger ages. There are challenges to implementation, including ideologies that privilege the status language of the region, inadequate preparation of indigenous teachers, lack of orthographic systems for indigenous languages, and access to curriculum in indigenous languages (Nyhati-Ramahobo 2006; Szulc 2009; Altinyelken, Moorcroft and van der Draai 2014; Terra 2014). Nonetheless, there is a concerted attempt in many places to valorize indigenous languages, and to recruit them to support student learning.

There are many accounts of indigenous youth coming to school with indigenous/local languages and literacies, and struggling in the face of the differential status endowed to languages in the curriculum and instruction. This de-valorization of indigenous languages and culture results in deficit ideologies surrounding indigenous youth (e.g., Canessa 2004; Nyhati-Ramahobo 2006). However, there is a body of literature addressing the efforts of indigenous communities to provide instruction in their own languages. These accounts illustrate the power of bilingual/bicultural schools to: affirm, empower, and connect families (Dick and McCarty 1996); link languages to cultural heritages to sustain/revitalize at-risk groups (Hill and May 2011); bridge indigenous ways of knowing and communicating to schooling to support school achievement for indigenous students (de la Piedra 2006; Szulc 2009); and utilize the language and cultural knowledge students bring as meditational tools for accessing texts and curriculum in the status language (de la Piedra 2006; Nyhati-Ramahobo 2006; Hornberger 2009; Szulc 2009).

Although there are clearly many potential benefits to indigenous education, many questions and concerns surrounding curriculum, pedagogies, and teacher preparation, and especially around ideologies and identity work as they play out through these programs, remain unexplored and/or unanswered. Szulc (2009), for example, points to the conflicting identities as Mapuche children being schooled (in their indigenous language) in Argentina are forced to 'swear their loyalty to the Argentine flag or wear the uniform white jacket required by all Argentine public school students" (p. 143). He claims that, "by fossilizing Mapuche culture and limiting it to the rural sphere, the (government) subordinates that culture, incorporating it in the program's redoubled efforts to make Mapuche children loyal citizens of Argentina" (p. 144).

It is clear that, despite many advantages, bilingual/bicultural schooling as a situated social phenomenon reflects the ecological model portrayed earlier; while it is local and situated, and may reflect aspects of the lives and languages of those in its classrooms, it is nonetheless shaped and mediated by internal and external forces that carry (mobile) dominant ideologies, thus positioning indigenous children inequitably.

Program models and curricular design

The preceding discussion focused on the mobility of languages, resources, and ideologies for students who may not, themselves, be mobile, but who are nonetheless subject to deficit ideologies surrounding non-dominant languages and cultures. But what of mobile youth being schooled in the language of their new environments, where the dominant language and culture of that environment reflects those of many of their teachers and peers, but not of them or their families?

For both groups, it is important to note that choices of program designs and models reflect ideologies about the role of L1 and L2 in teaching and learning, and in learners' lives. Research offers insights into the varieties of program models and instructional designs in use across the globe. Program models can be categorized based on whether the medium of instruction is the students' native language or the primary language of schooling, and on the ways in which, and the degree to which, the languages are utilized in schooling in relation to each other. Many programs, as described later, are based on monolingual ideologies; that is, learners use either one language or the other, and the faster they learn the dominant language the better. More recently, as the field of language learning and teaching has undergone a multilingual turn (e.g., May 2014), theorizations of multilingualism include concepts such as translanguaging (García and Li Wei 2013) and translingualism (Canagarajah 2013), pointing to the ways that language users move fluidly between codes in meaning-making, and, by implication, bringing into focus the ways in which program designs mandate language separation or integration.

Programs that offer instruction in the students' home languages (L1), or bilingual programs, have been termed early exit, late exit, developmental bilingual, transitional bilingual, and dual language immersion. Models vary in terms of the ultimate goal (transitional has rapid learning of the dominant language as its goal, developmental the maintenance of the heritage language and the learning of the dominant language), when and how much native language is used (there is separation by classes, and often by subject, between L1 and L2), and the amount of time students are expected to remain in the program (early exit is typically two to three years; late exit varies). While there is general agreement that instruction in the primary language supports children to learn academic content, and to use their L1 to support acquisition of their L2, all but the last model mentioned (two-way, or dual language, immersion) have been critiqued for (1) separating the two languages as two distinct and separate codes for meaning-making, (2) physically separating emergent bilinguals from their native-speaking peers, and (3) offering less access to rigorous and high-quality academic content than monolingual programs.

The two-way immersion model has been touted as the preferred model of bilingual education, but, as it requires a classroom consisting of one-half native speakers of the dominant language and one-half native speakers of another targeted language, it is not feasible and/or available for all newcomers in given communities. Further, even in two-way programs there is often strict language separation, which prevents students from using their full semiotic repertoires for meaning-making and learning.

More commonly, schools do not offer instruction for newcomers in languages other than the one that is dominant in the community. There is often, however, support offered for second language learning. This may be through newcomer programs (usually providing introductory dominant language and social service information for new arrivals), sheltered programs (where emergent bilinguals have separate tracks and classes with reduced language demands), having second language teachers provide either pull-out or push-in support for language instruction, or the provision of instructional aides who may be fluent in the students' L1s (for a fuller discussion of program models see Ovando and Combs 2012; also see García 2005; Genesee and Christian 2008; García and Kleifgen 2010).

Kanno (2004), in a study of Japanese as a second language (JSL) in a Tokyo primary school, describes two programs run simultaneously in the school. One, where students not yet fluent in Japanese were pulled out of their classrooms for Japanese instruction, she calls a 'monolingual' JSL classroom; all instruction was in Japanese. Reflecting the traditional rationale for pull-out classes, she reports that teachers and students regard this as "a safe haven where students can be themselves" (p. 324). Yet, while students reported feeling comfortable because they could understand their instruction, she demonstrates reductive teaching, heavily reliant on decontextualized drills, with little intellectual challenge. The other classroom, for newcomers, was bilingual (Cambodian/Japanese), and had markedly lower status in the school, including a remote, dark classroom that was significantly distanced from homeroom classrooms. It, too, had the same reductive instructional techniques. In this example we see the debilitating effects of well-intentioned educational interventions.

Similarly Milans (2006), investigating Chinese immigrants in Spain, focuses on how deficit views of immigrant youth lead to compensatory programs based on 'assimilation principles', and become embedded in school discourses and activities. He demonstrates that a 'discourse of deficit' and a 'paternalistic view' toward immigrants shaped reductive and non-challenging academic practices in a 'Welcome Classroom' for new immigrants. "Spanish language is taught for daily life rather than focusing on academic purposes," he claims; students are not taught academic language and struggle once they are transitioned into mainstream classrooms (which occurs after six months). Importantly, he points to cultural differences in understandings of teaching and learning, and in interaction patterns, as leading to communication breakdowns between teachers and students, leading to teachers' negative evaluation of students, and thus central to students' lack of success.

Gogolin (2002), in Germany, also points to cultural differences as central to students' access to the curriculum. She discusses the 'monolingual habitus' (drawing from Bourdieu's notion of linguistic *habitus* [1991] or a set of unquestioned beliefs about the status/use of a language) of teachers as they draw on their assumptions about what is known and normalized in students' lives in their teaching methods and routines, showing how curriculum based on monolingual habitus effectively shuts down participation for immigrant students.

It is clear that ideologies, once again, play a significant role in the design and implementation of programs and instruction. Hélot and Young (2006), for example, address bilingual education in France, stating, "Bilingual education in France is viewed mainly as a way to improve foreign language learning for monolingual pupils and not as a means to support bilingual children to cope with the curriculum in their second language" (p. 75). They provide examples of a bilingual instructional model that offers L2 instruction (in European languages) for French children, while schoolchildren who do not have French as their mother tongue effectively become invisible. Put simply, ideologies not only determine who gets what (and what types of) instruction, but whether or not students' lives are represented in classroom curriculum and instruction.

Through the preceding discussion, we are able to pinpoint issues attendant to mobility in the education of youth who are not fluent in the dominant language of schooling regarding program models and curricular design in schools. They are:

- Ways in which ideologies about languages and speakers of those languages are reflected/reinscribed by programs;
- Maintenance of L1 in addition to (or versus) learning L2;
- Value assigned to various programs, classrooms, and languages;
- Separation of L1 and L2 speakers;
- Opportunities for students to draw on and utilize their full repertoires for (language and content) learning;

- Utilization of discourse and interaction patterns, learning approaches, resources, and materials that reflect students' L1s and C1s (home languages and cultures).

Choices of program models and curriculum may be made at the government, local (district), school, and/or classroom level. In line with our ecological framework, it is the interplay among specificities of families and communities, local and national policies around education, ideologies infused throughout systems and institutions, and affordances and constraints of particular program models and instructional designs that determine emergent bilinguals' opportunities for school achievement.

Standards and assessments

Throughout the world, researchers, policy makers and educators look to standardized reforms, and their concomitant assessments, to improve educational outcomes, and to benchmark student progress on an individual, national, and international scale. Wagner (2011) reminds us that standards and assessments, while always controversial, are seen by many as useful for informing policy, creating public awareness, measuring learning, and fostering greater accountability.

There is ample evidence that "emergent bilinguals are found to underperform in comparison to their peers on language and content assessments" (Menken, Hudson, and Leung 2014: 586). Menken et al. claim, "any English-medium test is actually a language proficiency exam for a (language) learner, because proficiency mediates test performance" (Menken et al. 2014: 604). One of the many challenges to creating fair and equitable assessments is the language experience of test takers; as we will discuss, critics of common tests illustrate how "monolingual ideology[ies]" (Shohamy 2011) that underlie both large and small scale assessment instruments often serve to frame multilingual pupils solely in terms of their deficits (e.g., Laursen 2013).

When emergent bilingual students fail to meet standards and perform poorly on tests, interventions intended as remedies often ignore and even erode students' linguistic and cultural resources, and their *funds of knowledge* (Gonzalez et al. 2005), leading to yet more reductive programs and practices (e.g., Valenzuela 1999; Menken 2008). Of critical importance, standards and assessments, once adopted, almost always drive curriculum design (and often pedagogy). We now turn to two large-scale curricular reforms to exemplify these claims.

Across the developing world, a growing number of international bodies and non-governmental organizations (NGOs) have rallied support for the Early Grades Reading Assessment (EGRA). While this is nominally a reading test, in reality it is an entire packaged curriculum, including materials, pedagogies, benchmarks, and continuous assessments. Developed by the Research Triangle Institute (RTI), it is aimed at early grade classrooms (through grade 3), with the goal of ensuring that all children learn basic reading skills (Gove and Cvelich 2010). According to Gove and Cvelich (2010), while the United Nations Millennium Goals promote access to universal primary education, schools in developing countries suffer in the face of burgeoning classroom sizes, ineffective pedagogical practices, and most importantly, a knowledge gap caused by students' failure to learn to read in the first three years of their primary education. In most cases, children in the regions EGRA targets are poor, and are being schooled in a language that is not that of their homes and communities.

Administered in seventy-four indigenous and colonial languages in Africa, Asia, and South America (Gove and Cvelich 2011), EGRA is based on research (primarily from the

United States) about the strongest predictors of reading: alphabetic awareness, phonemic awareness, phonics, oral reading fluency, and comprehension. Here, again, is an example of mobile Western ideologies imposing educational design and practice across the globe. The goal is to help administrators and teachers pinpoint students' deficiencies in reading so that they can implement effective interventions (contributing to deficit ideologies of emergent bilinguals). Proponents of EGRA celebrate the curriculum/test as an example of a Smaller Quicker Cheaper (SQC) Assessment that accurately and quickly identifies students' deficits for remediation (Wagner 2011) and simultaneously "pay[s] close attention to a variety of factors such as: population diversity, linguistic and orthographic diversity, individual differences in learning, and timeliness of analysis" (Wagner 2011: 11).

Despite Wagner's contention that SQCs like EGRA can provide a wealth of information to local stakeholders inexpensively and expediently, he acknowledges this particular assessment's limitations for emergent bilingual students. One is that these kinds of assessments are based on ideas generated from research and theories from the United States and other OECD countries that may not always "take into account the varieties of cultures, languages, orthographies, experiences, family situations, and local school contexts" (p. 71). Benson (2013) expands on this critique, contending that EGRA relies too heavily on American and English research on learning to read that often does not take into account orthographic or linguistic features, particularly of non-alphabetic languages. She identifies several problems inherent in the EGRA/SQC model; namely, that it perpetuates an autonomous model of literacy that ignores the multiple literate and linguistic resources students bring. This narrow focus on discrete skills, she argues, perpetuates an orientation to monolingual (or transitional bilingual) instruction rather than to supportive bilingual or multilingual instruction.

Thus EGRA, although having the use of indigenous languages as a starting point, through its curriculum that embeds policy around language use, ideologies around languages and users of those languages, circumscribed reductive curricular and literacy practices, and rote pedagogies, exemplifies uniformity and a one-size-fits-all system that is not inclusive of nor responsive to local communities and stakeholders. In this case, it is the curriculum, materials, and assessments that are mobile (as well as some of the students for whom it is mandated), and it firmly embeds Western and deficit perspectives and ideologies into schooling worldwide.

While Smaller Quicker Cheaper Assessments aim to assess as many students as possible in diverse communities large and small across the developing world, Large-Scale Educational Assessments (LSEAs) like PISA aim to gather a representative sample of a population's educational progress in order to make cross-national comparisons or measure large-scale educational progress. The examination was developed by the OECD and is administered every three years to students in up to seventy "Economies" [nations], (http://www.oecd.org/pisa/aboutpisa/2015), primarily from the industrialized world. PISA assesses abilities in reading comprehension, math, and science when students reach the age of fifteen (with the rationale that most students at this age are approaching the ends of their secondary or compulsory education).[2]

Despite the obvious differences between EGRA and PISA, both tests are critiqued for their monolingual (primarily English focused) and/or acultural orientation. Sjøberg (2012) describes PISA as a decontextualized "IQ test of schools"; this neutral approach is problematic according to the author because this approach to testing goes against educational recommendations for "context-based teaching and localized curricula" (p. 6). Sjøberg (2012) further notes that while psychometricians and content experts make coordinated and extensive efforts in creating and revamping the PISA, it is also notable that the creators of the test are often from the English-speaking world or are required to have fluency in English. While PISA, like EGRA, is given in multiple languages, the fundamental guidance about learning is monolingual.

Particularly germane to the topic of the education of emergent bilinguals, including immigrants, is how PISA results are politicized to show that an individual country may be winning or, more often than not, losing status when it comes to the successful educational integration of linguistically diverse pupils. These worrying scores have been documented and discussed widely, particularly in Europe, where in several countries (Germany, Austria, New Zealand, and Belgium) second-generation immigrants who have spent their educations and lives in the country score more poorly on PISA than their first-generation counterparts (see Schnepf 2007; Song and Róbert 2010). Song and Róbert provide a nuanced, thought-provoking analysis of how these scores are often superficially analyzed and therefore misinterpreted. PISA results often have dramatic consequences, driving politicians and policy makers to make rash decisions to remedy what they see as gaps in their educational systems (see Sjøberg 2012 for a discussion of Norwegian politics and international competitiveness in relation to PISA scores).

For example, Pfaff (2011) demonstrates how German policy makers, in their rush to remedy the achievement gap, have instituted policies that are detrimental to linguistically diverse students. Specifically, she writes:

> the findings that immigrants' use of languages other than German at home was correlated with low reading proficiency scores . . . reinforced the ideology that minority languages are detrimental, and supported emphasis on German-only policies in preschool.
> *(p. 6)*

Laursen (2013), writing about the Danish context, demonstrates how the lower PISA scores of bilingual students (who speak a language other than Danish at home) disregard their bilingual skills, render them as "functionally illiterate" (p. 690), and also contribute to racist ideologies that promulgate the notion that bilingual immigrants (often from a non-European background) do not have the requisite abilities for social integration or upward mobility.

While EGRA and PISA provide two distinct examples of assessments – one is used primarily in local settings and lauded for its grass roots approach and expeditiousness, the other is tied to industrialized nations' notions of progress and future success – both assessments aim to capture universal knowledge about literacy and language. As discussed earlier, the definitions of 'language and literacy' used in this sense are both mobile and reductive, and have consequences for curriculum and instruction that ultimately serve to marginalize emergent bilinguals.

These policies/standards/assessments have political and social consequences and put several key issues into focus, including:

- Can a monolingual approach to standards and assessment truly measure the abilities of linguistically diverse pupils?
- How are results interpreted and to what effects on linguistically diverse students and their teachers in often challenging environments?

Implications

In this chapter, we have used sociocultural and social justice–oriented perspectives to explore the ecologies of schooling for emergent bilinguals across the globe within a context of mobility. We have explored how emergent bilinguals often must learn, and demonstrate learning, in unfamiliar languages and in contexts where their languages, literacies, and cultures are not recognized and/or valued. We also see how nationalistic and deficit-based ideologies infuse and shape language policies, curriculum, and interactions among students and teachers. When multilingual educational spaces and approaches have monolingual habituses, students are effectively stripped of the forms of knowledge and multiple literacies they bring to school. The issues and research discussed demonstrate that when students feel stigma or pressure to assimilate into one dominant language, they often lose a critical sense of investment in their schooling (Valenzuela 1999), leading to high rates of dropout and school failure.

At the same time, in the literature reviewed we also find stories/cases of learning environments that engender greater learning and investment while celebrating students' ties to their communities, languages, and faiths. Often, as we noted, students seem to thrive in these community-based spaces where they have been able to use, as Lytra (2010) writes describing a Turkish complementary school in Britain, "rich linguistic, cultural and other semiotic resources . . . to negotiate and transform texts and the talk and action around them in classroom interactions" (p. 36). Similarly, we see how effective indigenous language education can build bridges between home, culture, and family, increasing school achievement and individual student agency. Implicit in community-based or indigenous literacy education is an expansive and celebratory view of the translingual and transcultural repertoires students bring to their learning. These cases demonstrate that indigenous or community-based learning environments deserve to be more than a footnote or minor counter-narrative to the "bad news" of emergent bilinguals' educational challenges and/or failures. Instead, we argue that these kinds of educational ecologies give students opportunities to negotiate their multiple ways of knowing, being, and communicating that are critical to their success.

To quote Erickson (2014), "a teacher does not teach children in general, but particular children in particular circumstances of learning and teaching in classrooms and in community life." (p. 3). We maintain that the current move toward standardization in policy, curriculum, and instruction, with its underlying monolingual habitus, inhibits successful schooling for emergent bilinguals. We urge educators to look to these indigenous and community-based models to guide educational decisions worldwide so that emergent bilinguals may thrive in schools and beyond.

Future directions

The preceding discussion has implications for educational policy and practice. One clear message is that education globally, by and large, does not pay sufficient attention to the contexts and trajectories of the lives of youth outside of schools. While there is abundant literature from around the globe on the importance of culturally and linguistically responsive educational practices and pedagogies, and on the effects of privilege and power in attaining equitable educational outcomes, there is little evidence of these discourses permeating into school policies, programs, and practices. In fact, as we have pointed out, the educational realm in general seems to be moving in the opposite direction, such that assessment and accountability – measurements of discrete learning outcomes – are becoming ever more prevalent. Thus we suggest that educators and policy makers (1) design policy and practice from asset-based perspectives, rather than deficit, which mandates the need for school staff and policy makers to better know and understand the lives and communities of their diverse constituencies; (2) attend to issues of power, positioning, status, and equity in all decision-making; and (3) balance the focus on "language," or "academic language," with a focus on sociocultural issues and ecologies. Lastly we recommend that schools incorporate translanguaging into educational policies and practices in innovative ways, affording students opportunities to make and negotiate meanings using their full repertoires, such that heritage languages are fully visible and valued. This increased attention to the integrated use of learners' full linguistic repertoires will support heritage language maintenance (with full proficiency), help protect endangered languages, offer students a range of resources for learning, and provide them with the multiple languages that can afford them access to school and life opportunities.

Future research is greatly needed to more fully understand the dimensions and consequences of schooling and mobility. In the midst of debates about language choice, program design, effective pedagogies, and assessment for youth being schooled in a language other than their home language, we have little evidence on which to base decisions. What is the impact of heritage language education, or various program models, on language proficiency and academic achievement, and what are long-term effects of language-of-instruction on the futures of youth, communities and societies? How can we determine how best to integrate plurilingualism/multilingualism into curriculum and classrooms in specific place-based instantiations of schooling, and how to assess appropriately? And importantly, how might we rethink relationships between families, schools, and communities to ensure that they are interdependent, enabling them to pool resources and expertise in order to forge equitable partnerships in supporting the learning of youth?

The ecological framing that we promote suggests that aspects of schooling for emergent bilinguals cannot be considered or addressed discretely. Rather, education must be considered as fully contextualized: as actions and interactions embedded in and mediated through overlapping spheres of relationships, activities, spaces, mobilities, ideologies, and trajectories. Only through this approach can we acknowledge, connect, and represent the multiple, interconnected domains of learners' lives, such that all youth may be visible, and able to locate themselves, within schooling environments, pedagogies, and practices. And only in this way can educational policies, initiatives, and assessments be designed and implemented to offer equitable educational opportunities for all.

Related topics

>Nation-state, transnationalism, and language
>Language-in-education policies and mobile citizens
>Mobility and English-language policies and practices in higher education

Further reading

Benson, C. and Kosensen, K., eds. (2013). *Language Issues in Comparative Education: Inclusive Teaching and Learning in Non-dominant Languages and Cultures.* Rotterdam, NL: Sense.

>This edited volume provides a collection of articles about multilingualism in diverse international contexts, paying specific attention to issues of power and the interactions between non-dominant languages (NDLs) and the "official" languages in educational institutions.

Creese, A. and Blackledge, A. (2010). Translanguaging in the bilingual classroom: A pedagogy for learning and teaching? *Modern Language Journal, 94,* 103–115.

>In this article, the authors employ an ecological framework to discuss the positive cultural and linguistic affordances of flexible bilingual educational practices in British complementary schools.

García, O. (2009). *Bilingual Education in the 21st Century: A Global Perspective.* Sussex: Wiley-Blackwell.

This book offers a thorough examination of bilingualism, providing cases of multilingual pedagogical practices, program models, and policies across various international contexts.

Hawkins, M. R., ed. (2013). *Framing Languages and Literacies: Socially Situated Views and Perspectives*. New York: Routledge.

This edited volume provides a grounding in key theories regarding social and cultural dimensions of languages and literacies, including the genesis and trajectories of the theories, and ways in which they have been taken up and applied.

Kibler, A., Valdés, G. and Walqui, A., eds. (2014). Special topic issue: K-12 standards-based educational reform: Implications for English language learner populations, *TESOL Quarterly*, *48*(3), 433–453.

In this special topic issue, various dimensions of standards and assessment in the field of language teaching and learning are discussed, with a particular focus on how 21st-century monolingual, top-down standards and assessments affect multilingual children and youth in English medium schools in various international contexts.

Notes

1 We choose to use 'emergent bilinguals' as the term to describe students who are in the process of using and learning multiple languages in lieu of other terms in the field because it (1) represents the trajectory of learning; (2) ascribes equal importance and value to learners' multiple languages, thus negating deficit views; and (3) points to the fluid and dynamic potentials for moving between languages for meaning-making.
2 Significantly, PISA is not administered as frequently in the developing world, where the basic fact is that students may not still be in school at age fifteen (Wagner 2011)

References

Altinyelken, H. K., Moorcroft, S. and van der Draai, H. (2014). The dilemmas and complexities of implementing language-in-education policies: Perspectives from urban and rural contexts in Uganda. *International Journal of Educational Development* 36: 90–99. Retrieved 11 March 2015, from http://linkinghub.elsevier.com/retrieve/pii/S0738059313000837.

Anderson, B. (1991). *Imagined Communities: Reflections on the Origin and Spread of Nationalism* (Rev. ed.). London: Verso.

Apple, M. (2004). *Ideology and Curriculum* (3rd ed.). New York and London: Routledge Falmer.

Ayers, W., Quinn, T. and Stovall, D., eds. (2009). *Handbook of Social Justice in Education*. New York: Routledge.

Bakhtin, M. M. (1981). The dialogic imagination: Four essays. In M. Holquist (ed.), *Four Essays by M. M. Bakhtin* [Translated by C. Emerson and M. Holquist] (pp. 84–258). Austin, TX: University of Texas Press.

Benjamin, R., Pecos, R. and Romero, M. E. (1996). Language revitalization efforts in the Pueblo de Cochiti: Becoming "literate" in an oral society. In N. H. Hornberger (ed.), *Indigenous Literacies in the Americas: Language Planning from the Bottom up* (pp. 115–136). Berlin: Mouton de Gruyter.

Benson, C. (2013). *L1-based Multilingual Education and EGRA: Where Do They Meet?* PRAESA Occasional Papers, No. 40, University of Cape Town, Cape Town, South Africa.

Blommaert, J., Collins, A. and Slembrouck, S. (2005). Spaces of multilingualism. *Language and Communication* 25: 197–216. Retrieved 1 March 2015, from www.elsevier.com/locate/langcom

Bourdieu, P. (1991). *Language and Symbolic Power*. Cambridge: Polity Press.

Brandt, D. and Clinton, K. (2002). Limits of the local: Expanding perspectives on literacy as a social practice. *Journal of Literacy Research* 34: 337–356.

Bunch, G. (2006). "Academic English" in the 7th grade: Broadening the lens, expanding access. *Journal of English for Academic Purposes* 5(4): 284–301. Retrieved 6 April 2015, from EBSCO Database.

Bunch, G.C., Walqui, A. and Pearson, P.D. (2014). Complex text and new common standards in the United States: Pedagogical implications for English learners. *TESOL Quarterly* 48(3): 533–559.

Canagarajah, A.S. (2013). *Translingual Practice: Global Englishes and Cosmopolitan Relations*. New York: Routledge.

Canessa, A. (2004). Reproducing racism: Schooling and race in highland Bolivia. *Race Ethnicity and Education* 7(2): 185–204. Retrieved 11 March 2015, from http://www.tandfonline.com/doi/abs/10.1080/1361332042000234295.

Canessa, A. (2007). Reproducing racism: Schooling and race in highland Bolivia. *Race Ethnicity and Education* 7(2): 185–204. Retrieved 1 December 2014, from http://dx.doi.org/10.1080/1361332042000234295.

Clark, M. and Morgan, B. (2011). Education and social justice in neoliberal times: Historical and pedagogical perspectives from two postcolonial contexts. In M.R. Hawkins (ed.), *Social Justice Language Teacher Education* (pp. 57–79). Bristol: Multilingual Matters.

Compton-Lilly, C. (2014). The development of writing habitus: A ten-year case study of a young writer. *Written Communication* 31: 371–403.

Cope, B. and Kalantzis, M. (2013). "Multiliteracies": New literacies, new learning. In M.R. Hawkins (ed.), *Framing Languages and Literacies: Socially Situated Views and Perspectives* (pp. 105–135). New York: Routledge.

Creese, A. and Blackledge, A. (2010). Translanguaging in the bilingual classroom: A pedagogy for learning and teaching? *Modern Language Journal* 94: 103–115.

De la Piedra, M.T. (2006). Literacies and Quechua oral language: Connecting sociocultural worlds and linguistic resources for biliteracy development. *Journal of Early Childhood Literacy* 6(3): 383–406.

De Souza, L.M.M. (2008). Beyond "here's a culture, here's a literacy": Vision in Amerindian literacies. In M. Prinsloo and M. Baynham (eds.), *Literacies, Global and Local* (pp. 193–214). John Benjamins, Amsterdam.

Dick, G.S. and McCarty, T. (1996). Reclaiming Navajo: Language renewal in a Navajo community school. In N.H. Hornberger (ed.), *Indigenous Literacies in the Americas: Language Planning from the Bottom Up* (pp. 69–94). Berlin: Mouton de Gruyter.

Erickson, F. (2014). Scaling down: A modest proposal for practice-based policy research in teaching. *Education Policy Analysis Archives* 22(9): 1–9.

Freire, P. (2000). *Pedagogy of the Oppressed* (30th Anniversary ed.) [Translated by M.B. Ramos]. New York: Bloomsbury Press.

García, E.E. (2005). *Teaching and Learning in Two Languages: Bilingualism and Schooling in the United States*. New York: Teachers College Press.

García, O. and Kleifgen, J. (2010). *Educating Emergent Bilinguals: Policies, Programs and Practices for English Language Learners*. New York: Teachers College Press.

García, O. and Li Wei (2013). *Translanguaging: Language, Bilingualism and Education*. New York: Palgrave Pivot.

García-Sanchez, I.M. (2010). The policies of Arabic language education: Moroccan immigrant children's language socialization into ethnic and religious identities. *Linguistics and Education* 21. Retrieved 8 April 2015, from www.eslevier.com/locate/linged

Genesee, F. and Christian, D. (2008). Essay: Programs for teaching English language learners. In chap. 16 A.S. Rosebery and B. Warren (eds.), *Teaching Science to English Language Learners: Building on Students' Strengths* (pp. 129–146). Arlington, VA: NSTA Press.

Glick Schiller, N. and Salazar, N.B. (2013). Regimes of mobility across the globe. *Journal of Ethnic and Migration Studies* 39(2): 183–200.

Gogolin, I. (2002). Linguistic and cultural diversity in Europe: A challenge for educational research and practice. *European Educational Research Journal* 1(1): 123–138. Retrieved 10 March 2015, from http://eer.sagepub.com/lookup/doi/10.2304/eerj.2002.1.1.3.

Gonzalez, N., Moll, L.C. and Amanti, C. (2005). *Funds of Knowledge: Theorizing Practices in Households, Communities, and Classrooms*. Mahwah, NJ: Erlbaum.

Gove, A. and Cvelich, P. (2011). *Early Reading: Igniting Education for All*. A report by the Early Grade Reading community of practice, Research Triangle Institute, Research Triangle Park, NC.

Gutierrez, K. D. (1995). Developing a sociocritical literacy in the third space. *Reading Research Quarterly* 43(2): 148–164.
Han, H. (2009). Institutionalized inclusion: A case study on support for immigrants in English learning. *TESOL Quarterly* 43(4): 643–668.
Hawkins, M. R. (2004). Researching English language and literacy development in schools. *Educational Researcher* 33(3): 14–25.
Hawkins, M. R. (2005). ESL in elementary education. In E. Hinkel (ed.), *Handbook of Research in Second Language Teaching and Learning* (pp. 25–44). Mahwah, NJ: Lawrence Erlbaum Associates.
Hawkins, M. (2010). Sociocultural approaches to language teaching and learning. In A. Creese and C. Leung (eds.), *English as an Additional Language: Approaches to Teaching Language Minority Students* (pp. 97–107). London: Sage Press.
Hawkins, M. R. (2014). Ontologies of place, creative meaning making and cosmopolitan education. *Curriculum Inquiry* 44(1): 90–113.
Hélot, C. and Young, A. (2006). Imagining multilingual schools in France: A language and cultural awareness project at a primary level. In O. García, T. Skutnab-Kangas and M. E. Torres-Guzmán (eds.), *Imagining Multilingual Schools: Languages in Education and Glocalization* (pp. 66–90). Bristol: Multilingual Matters.
Hill, R. and May, S. (2011). Exploring biliteracy in Mâori-medium education: An ethnographic perspective. In T. L. McCarty (ed.), *Ethnography and Language Policy* (pp. 163–183). New York: Routledge.
Hornberger, N. H. (2009). Multilingual education policy and practice: Ten certainties (grounded in Indigenous experience), *Working Papers in Educational Linguistics* 24(2): 1–8.
Jaspers, J. (2005). Linguistic sabotage in a context of monolingualism and standardization. *Language & Communication* 25(3): 279–297.
Kanno, Y. (2003). Imagined communities, school visions, and the education of bilingual students in Japan. *Journal of Language, Identity and Education* 2(4): 285–300.
Kanno, Y. (2004). Sending mixed messages: Language minority education at a Japanese public elementary school. In A. Pavlenko and A. Blackledge (eds.), *Negotiation of Identities in Multilingual Contexts* (pp. 285–300). Clevedon: Multilingual Matters.
Kibler, A., Valdés, G. and Walqui, A. (eds). (2014). What does standards-based educational reform mean for English language learner populations in primary and secondary schools? *TESOL Quarterly* 48(3): 433–453.
King, R. and Skeldon, R. (2010) Mind the gap! Integrating approaches to internal and international migration, *Journal of Ethnic and Migration Studies* 36(10): 1619–1646.
Knobel, M. (1999). *Everyday Literacies: Students, Discourses, and Social Practice*. New York: Peter Lang.
Kress, G. and van Leeuwen, T. (2001). *Multimodal Discourse: The Modes and Media of Contemporary Communication*. Oxford: Oxford University Press.
Lam, E. and Warriner, D. S. (2012). Transnationalism and literacy: Investigating the mobility of people, languages, texts, and practices in contexts of migration. *Reading Research Quarterly* 47(2): 191–215.
Laursen, E. P. (2013). Umbrellas and angels standing straight – a social semiotic perspective on multilingual children's literacy. *International Journal of Bilingual Education and Bilingualism* 16(6): 690–706. Retrieved 11 March 2015, from http://www.tandfonline.com/doi/abs/10.1080/13670050.2012.709818.
Lave, J. and Wenger, E. (1991). *Situated Learning: Legitimate Peripheral Participation*. Cambridge: Cambridge University Press.
Lee, S. J. and Hawkins, M. R. (2015). Policy, context and schooling: The education of English learners in rural new destinations. *Global Education Review* 2(4): 40–59.
López-Gopar, M. E. (2007). Beyond the alienating alphabetic literacy: Multiliteracies in indigenous education in Mexico. *Diaspora, Indigenous, and Minority Education* 1(3): 159–174.
Lytra, V. (2010). Negotiating language, culture and pupil agency in complementary school classrooms. *Linguistics and Education* 22: 23–36. Retrieved 9 April 2015, www.sciencedirect.com

May, S., ed. (2014). *The Multilingual Turn: Implications for SLA, TESOL and Bilingual Education.* New York: Routledge.

McCarty, T. L. (2013). Indigenous literacies: Continuum or divide? In M. R. Hawkins (ed.), *Framing Languages and Literacies: Socially Situated Views and Perspectives* (pp. 169–191). New York: Routledge.

Menken, K. (2008). *English Learners Left behind: Standardized Testing as Language Policy.* Bristol: Multilingual Matters.

Menken, K., Hudson, T. and Leung, C. (2014). Symposium: Language assessment in standards-based education reform. *TESOL Quarterly* 48(3): 586–614.

Milans, P. M. (2006). Spanish education and Chinese immigrants in a new multicultural context: Cross-cultural and interactive perspectives in the study of language teaching methods. *Journal of Multicultural Discourses* 1(1): 60–85.

Nyhati-Ramahobo, L. (2006). The long road to multilingual schools in Botswana. In O. García, T. Skutnab-Kangas and M. E. Torres-Guzmán (eds.), *Imagining Multilingual Schools: Languages in Education and Glocalization* (pp. 200–223). Bristol: Multilingual Matters.

Ong, W. (1982). *Orality and Literacy: The Technologizing of the Word.* London: Methuen Press.

Ovando, C. J. and Combs, M. C. (2012). *Bilingual and ESL Classrooms: Teaching in Multicultural Contexts* (5th ed.). New York: McGraw-Hill.

Pfaff, C. W. (2011). Multilingual development in Germany in the crossfire of ideology and politics: Monolingual and multilingual expectations, polylingual practices. *Transit* 7. Retrieved 1 April 2015, from http://escholarship.org/uc/item/9gp0f163.

Prinsloo, M. & Baynham, M. (eds.). (2008). *Literacies, Global and Local.* Amsterdam: John Benjamins.

Purcell-Gates, V. (2013). Literacy worlds of children of migrant farmworker communities participating in a migrant head start program. *Research in the Teaching of English* 48(1): 68–97.

Richardson-Bruna, K., Vann, R. and Perales Escudero, M. (2007). What's language got to do with it?: A case study of academic language instruction in a high school "English Learner Science" class. *Journal of English for Academic Purposes* 6: 36–54.

Rogoff, B. (1994). Developing understanding of the idea of a community of learners. *Mind, Culture and Activity* 1(4): 209–229. Retrieved 30 March 2015, from http://www.tandfonline.com/loi/hmca20#.UhTYMqXetU0.

Rowsell, J. and Sefton-Greene, J., eds. (2014). *Revisiting Learning Lives: Longitudinal Perspectives on Literacy in Educational Research.* New York: Routledge.

Sancheti, S. and Sudhir, K. (2009). Education consumption in an emerging market. Retrieved 9 April 2015, from http://www.som.yale.edu/Faculty/sk389/MS-Final-April%2022%202009.pdf.

Schnepf, S. V. (2007). Immigrants' educational disadvantage: An examination across ten countries and three surveys. *Journal of Popular Economics* 20(3): 527–545. doi:10.1007/s00148-006-0102-y

Shohamy, E. (2011). Assessing multilingual competencies: Adopting construct valid assessment policies. *Modern Language Journal* 95(3): 418–429. Retrieved 15 March 2015, from http://doi.wiley.com/10.1111/j.1540-4781.2011.01210.x.

Sjøberg, S. (2012). PISA: Politics, fundamental problems and intriguing results *La Revue. Recherches en Education* 14: 1–21. Retrieved 27 February 2015, from http://folk.uio.no/sveinsj/.

Song, S. and Róbert, P. (2010). Immigrant student investigation in PISA 2006: A call for a more nuanced examination, Untersuchungen zu Schülern mit Migrationshintergrund bei PISA 2006: Eine Aufforderung zu nuancierteren. *Journal for Educational Research Online* 2: 32–52. Retrieved 27 February 2015, from urn:nbn:de:0111-opus-45664

Stornaiuolo, A. and LeBlanc, R. J. (2014). Local literacies, global scales: The labor of global connectivity. *Journal of Adolescent & Adult Literacy* 58(3): 192–196.

Szulc, A. (2009). Becoming Neuquino in Mapuzugun: Teaching Mapuche language and culture in the Neuquén, Argentina. *Anthropology and Education Quarterly* 40(2): 129–149.

Terra, S. E. (2014). *Language and Educational Trajectories in Mozambique: Policies, Perspectives and Practices.* Unpublished doctoral dissertation.

United Nations (2014). *The Millennium Development Goals Report.* New York: United Nations.

Valdés, G. (1997). Dual-language immersion programs: A cautionary note concerning the education of language-minority students. *Harvard Educational Review* 67(3): 391–429.

Valenzuela, A. (1999). *Subtractive Schooling*. Albany: State University of New York Press.

Van Lier, L. (2008). The ecology of language learning and sociocultural theory. In A. Creese, P. Martin and N. H. Hornberger (eds.), *Encyclopedia of Language and Education*, Ecology of language (pp. 53–65, 2nd ed., Vol. 9). Boston, MA: Springer Press.

Wagner, D. A. (2011). *Smaller, Quicker, Cheaper: Improving Learning Assessments for Developing Countries*. Paris: International Institute for Educational Planning.

Zúñiga, V. and Hamann, E. T. (2009). *Sojourners in Mexico with U.S. School Experience: A New Taxonomy for Transnational Students*. Faculty Publications: Department of Teaching, Learning and Teacher Education, Paper 91. Retrieved 17 June 2015, from http://digitalcommons.unl.edu/teachlearnfacpub/91.

30
Communication practices and policies in workplace mobility

Marta Kirilova and Jo Angouri

Introduction and overview

This chapter addresses the issue of communication policy in the workplace. Modern workplaces are multinational and multilingual, and employees interact in languages other than their L1 as part of their daily reality at work. At the same time, a number of workplaces have introduced a 'one-language policy' as a strategy to manage linguistic diversity as well as to encourage integration and, allegedly, shared decision making. Research has repeatedly shown, however, that this is a political and ideological decision rather than a purely linguistic one. Languages have different symbolic power and this is reflected in the linguistic ecosystem of the various work settings. In this chapter, we discuss issues around language use, language policy, and language ideology in the workplace as well as gatekeeping. We draw on our recently completed and ongoing work as well as illustrative studies from sociolinguistics and applied linguistics research. Special attention is paid to the notions of symbolic capital and power as well as to language attitudes particularly in relation to linguistic evaluation and 'common-sense' perceptions of language practice. We explore the relationship between language policy and access to the workplace and we discuss examples from various workplaces. We close the chapter with some terminological considerations and we identify areas for future research.

A language policy can be defined in a number of ways. Most commonly, a language policy is what institutions and states do officially to determine and alter language choice and language use in public contexts. A language policy enacts the 'policy genre' by mobilizing specific institutional discourses on how the policy should be implemented as well as what the repercussions of non-adherence might be. In some cases, a language policy might take the form of a text that includes explicit guidelines on how to facilitate communication, produce written and oral documents, or recruit personnel. In other cases, in businesses or multilingual communities, for example, a language policy can be less explicit and only exist in hidden norms or unwritten rules. At a national level, language policies, especially in Europe, have promoted the use of national varieties and have associated common language with the homogeneity of the population; a politically vital argument in relation to claiming a distinct national identity for the many historically recent, European nation-states. At a supranational level, discourses on multilingualism by the European Union are also of interest. In this context, multilingualism, seen as an asset for European citizens to benefit from free movement and understood as the knowledge of a 'foreign language', acquires a clear economic value. These discourses equate language to dominant national standardized varieties which are again portrayed as the norm. Although this is a political and a socioeconomic matter and not a linguistic one, it has serious implications concerning the requested 'skills' of those entering the country and attempting to access the job market. Majority members, including central political figures often take for granted that immigrants and refugees should assimilate to a majority language and culture. In many countries schools, universities, and workplaces are overly concerned with teaching the "appropriate" usage of the majority language and culture (e.g., Kristiansen 2010 on linguistic purism in the Nordic countries).

As a consequence, one of the outcomes of a language policy is a discursively constructed standard ideology. This ideology presupposes other language varieties to be considered as 'inappropriate' or 'wrong'. Hence 'common-sense' evaluations of competence and performance are ratified on the basis of the preferred language or languages. Language ideologies are also associated with acceptance of 'foreign' accents which bring different capital. For example, in a matched-guise test, Ritzau, Kirilova, and Jørgensen (2009) showed that Danes showed positive attitudes towards foreign accents in Danish associated with Northern Europe compared to the Middle and Far East. The presumed speakers of Germanic languages were favoured as intelligent, friendly, and highly educated, while the Middle Eastern accents were associated with very low social status and very low levels of education.

Clearly, ideas of language and culture as homogeneous entities endow policies that stand for purism and allow prescriptivism as they consider linguistic and cultural diversity a social and a political threat (Jaffe 2007). The notion of 'one national language' as a result of nation-state ideology has been popular in most countries in the process of building national founding myths, although a number of studies (Blommaert, Collins, and Slembrouck 2005; Rampton 2006) have shown that monolingual communities are the exception rather than the rule. Language policy can certainly be a powerful instrument of regulation by representing the voice of those in power and occupying the role of the privileged. Although this has been discussed widely in relation to linguistic human rights (Skutnabb-Kangas, Phillipson, and Rannut 1995) and postcolonial language policies (Phillipson 1992, 2003) in a number of countries around the world, it is still less common to discuss language policy in relation to the white- and blue-collar workplaces. Further to this, language policy in blue- and white-collar settings tends to be studied separately. This is often necessary for research management, but it can result in a fragmented picture.

Accordingly, this chapter is concerned with language use in the multilingual and multinational workplace, and the relationship between policy and practice. We use the term language policy broadly to include the actual text but also the discourses surrounding and being enacted by it. From this perspective the label communication policies is also used in the chapter to indicate our broader reading. Given the space of a chapter, the discussion that follows is necessarily simplified, but we pay special attention to the concept of ideology and the relationship between language choice and language use. In order to illustrate the issues we raise, we draw on data from job interviews for different jobs, a prototypical gatekeeping event where policy and practice are negotiated between the interactants. We compare and contrast this data with excerpts from narratives on language policy and language practice and pay special attention to the ways in which ideology is enacted in discourse. We aim to provide a holistic account on the issues raised in the chapter and close the discussion with areas future research can address.

Issues and ongoing debates

Ideology and language choice in the multilingual workplace

Already in 1985, Silverstein argues for the existence of a "total linguistic fact." To understand how linguistic signs have meaning in practice, he suggests that we consider the following four aspects of language: *form, use, ideology*, and *domain*. Silverstein acknowledges the importance of linguistic ideology, on a par with the formal aspects of language. He defines language ideologies as "sets of beliefs about language articulated by users as a rationalization or justification of perceived language structure and use" (Silverstein 1979: 193). Similarly, Rumsey (1990: 346) argues that ideologies are "shared bodies of commonsense notions about the nature of language in the world," while Irvine (1989: 255) sees them as "the cultural system of ideas about social and linguistic relationships, together with their loading with moral and political interests." Irvine (2001: 25) makes an important point suggesting that "some of the most important and interesting aspects of ideology lie behind the scenes, in assumptions that are taken for granted – that are never explicitly stated in any format that would permit them also to be explicitly denied." Silverstein (1979) suggests also that the best place to look at linguistic ideology is the metapragmatic discourse and what lies in its presuppositions. What these definitions have in common is that *beliefs, common sense* and *interests* are important components of ideology. These components function as subjective interpretative filters (Woolard and Schieffelin 1994) used to shape the interaction through the processes of interpretation and manage the relationship of language and society. Discourses, such as those enacted in a language policy, bring to the fore powerful beliefs and values that influence expectations of language use. Ideology, however, can also be invisible to the outsider (including the researcher), which raises important theoretical and methodological issues when studying ideology in the workplace in relation to language use.

The term common sense (*sensus communis* or a sense shared by both speaker and audience) is particularly relevant here. It was originally introduced by Aristotle (384–322 BC) who believed that speakers should make appeal to the *sensus communis* in order to maximize their speech impact. The appeal to common sense is particularly important in classic rhetoric too with reference to *logos* which has been widely discussed over the centuries. Appeal to *logos* presupposes common ground between the interlocutors which is negotiated in situ. Common sense with regard to attitudes and ideologies has been discussed by Billig (1991, 1996), Wetherell and Potter (1992), and Van Dijk (1998). To Van Dijk, common-sense beliefs are accepted by the members of a community and hence they are understood as *true* (1998: chap. 10). This does not mean however that common-sense beliefs are founded upon epistemic criteria; they may be contradictory to evidence and stances accepted as scientific *facts* at different moments in human history. Common sense is typically tacit and understood as given and hence it does not necessarily explicitly manifest itself in interaction. Members of a community can enact common-sense beliefs through a process of explication which is evidently subject to the individual construction processes and the context where this is taking place. The power of shared norms is particularly relevant to language choice and perceptions of appropriateness in any workplace context. Everyday thinking and shared belief systems underpin the enactment of abstract policies in relation to individual practices in general and language use in particular.

To elaborate further, Billig (1991) argues that the contents of everyday thinking (e.g., values, opinions) are ideological cultural products. He suggests that ideology is presented as dually expressed arguments, meaning that when we argue *for* a certain position, we are at the same time justifying our negative attitudes. For example, an utterance like "I am not prejudiced but . . ." represents an advance justification (or *prolepsis*) against the criticism of being prejudiced. Using this utterance structure, the speaker attempts to deflect possible criticism and lays claim to being a member of the moral community of the unprejudiced (see also Billig 1987 for further discussion). Van Dijk (1987) points out that prejudices are complex concepts, because when people want to express negative experiences or evaluations, they also try to stick to social norms which force them to make a 'good' socially accepted impression. The juxtaposition of ideologically contradictory statements is also used to create an *us and them* ideology, very common in political discourse (Wodak and Angouri 2014). The speaker creates an in-group 'us' which has directly or indirectly associated with a certain set of characteristics, at the same time to provide value to the claims the speaker needs to create the right 'persona' for themselves. However, such dual positionings reveal a new form of a discursive discrimination coined "new racism" (Van Dijk 2000). In new racism, people try to resist being labeled as extremists or rightists. They distance themselves from the idea of minorities as biologically inferior but instead, they talk about 'difficulties' and 'problems' with 'foreign' language or culture. These ideologies do not exist only in a societal macro context. They form part of the nexus of ideologies and the negotiation process in any workplace as well as a way to regulate the system has implications for who is allowed 'in' and who stays out.

The following example illustrates the dual argument described above in a workplace context. It is a part of a wash-up session, recorded after a set of job interviews in which a manager explains who is the preferred candidate for the job as a front desk secretary at a municipal office (see also Kirilova 2013 for extended analysis).

Example 1

English translation	Danish original
. . . the one with the Asian background where they have this complaisance, yeah, they are deeply service minded. I love travelling in those countries; I myself think they are wonderful people [. . .] but I am concerned that she may not be able to put her foot down, she won't be able to say no, and things may fall apart. Well she did this [bows, hands on chest], she was very eager to get the job. And then I could be really concerned that this complaisance would affect her integration in this house in a negative way	. . . hende der havde asiatisk baggrund, hvor de har den ydmyghed, altså de har servicegen ud over alle grænser. Jeg elsker at rejse i de lande, jeg synes selv de er nogle fantastiske mennesker [. . .] men jeg kan være bekymret for at hun ikke kan sige fra, kan ikke sige nej, og at tingene på den måde kan smuldre. Altså, hun lavede selv den der [bøjer hovedet med samlede hænder ved brystet], altså hun var så opsat på at få det her arbejde. Så det kunne jeg være rigtig bekymret for at den ydmyghed kom til at få en forkert afsmitning på hendes integration her i huset

The manager equals Asian background to showing extreme deference bordering on servility and lack of critical thinking as well as independent voice. Danish working culture is contrasted as a non-hierarchical structure, praising independent thinking and a casual working atmosphere. The prolepsis "I love travelling in those countries but I am concerned" is a step-back and a justification of the manager's actual attitude. Distinguishing between the travel and the work contexts usefully separates what is represented as needed for the 'task at hand'. What she in fact expresses is a reductionist view, saying that the candidate is not going to fit in because of certain ethnic characteristics. These abstract characteristics are projected upon the candidate and are made relevant to decisions of recruitment. In what is commonly considered the blue-collar workplace, 'diversity' is often represented as a set of challenges and anticipation of poor performance or 'non-fit'.

To take this further, in a study of categorization processes in internship interviews between Danish employers and minority background adolescents and refugees, Tranekjaer (2015) demonstrates how the evaluations made by the representatives of the majority national group define and justify the actions of the candidates trying to access that context. Tranekjaer examines the broader structures of power and ideology related to social issues of controversy and debate such as migration, integration, and second-language learning, arguing that the participants' orientation towards nationality, religion, and language in the interview results in an uneven distribution of power, rights, knowledge, and status. In this context language, culture, and religion are mobilized as arguments for non-recruitment (see also the next sections).

Turning to narratives collected in the context of research addressing language policy issues in the multinational workplace, a different set of discourses is observed – often following a similar reductionist process. Diversity, in the form of ethnicity, sex, role, professional background, and organizational affiliation (see e.g., Cummings 2004) has been represented as an 'asset' related to greater productivity and team performance. Recruiting employees from different national backgrounds provides employers with access to the 'global' talent and a way to address local skill shortage (e.g., Burke and Ng 2006). The quote below represents a frequent discourse that is enacted by white-collar employees.

> **Example 2**
>
> I am kind of catching myself not asking where you come from anymore (. . .) it's kind of an irrelevant question as everybody comes from somewhere and sometimes there is a majority sometimes there isn't.

The neoliberal workplace (Gee, Hull, and Lankshear 1996) has been criticized for reducing the employees to a set of skills and for assessing value against performance-related and financial criteria. Professional and self-identities (Giddens 1991) become commodities with a specific market value. Turning a demographic characteristic (such as the ethnic background of an employee) to a problem or a resource follows the reductionist process described earlier.

Moving to language use, the same process applies as a multinational workforce is by definition a multilingual one. This has been seen as an asset – a rich linguistic landscape means for example easier access to local markets, *more contacts and contracts* (Angouri and Miglbauer 2014) – but it has also been associated with accountability and transparency.

In this context, a number of organizations have introduced a one-language policy, typically English or other linguae francae. English is one of the key languages of international business with a number of employers requesting that policy documents and written communication is done in the company language (Angouri 2013; Lønsmann 2014). The modern workplace, however, does not operate on one language only – far from it actually. A number of languages are used as part of the daily reality at work and this has become unmarked for a number of employees in different industries. In recent work on email interaction (e.g., Mahili 2014) diversity in language practices was noted. The speakers mobilize a range of languages to achieve different goals, to include or exclude others from the message but also to restrain circulation beyond specific teams marked through the ability to access the information. Linguistic diversity, evidently, does not mean that there is no power imbalance between dominant and peripheral languages. But these power hierarchies are dynamic and negotiated in situ. Companies often portray the use of one language as a commitment to an 'egalitarian' workplace; this is clearly not achieved through a monolingual language policy (Hultgren 2011). Not all employees share the same levels of proficiency to the company language and hence groups are (dis)advantaged in terms of accessing decision making centres in the workplace. And evidently in contexts where there is a majority local language or languages, these are equally important for 'fitting in'.

Overall what a monolingual policy means for the different teams and departments in a workplace is typically left usefully ambiguous (Fredriksson, Barner-Rasmussen, and Piekkari 2006). This strategic ambiguity (Angouri 2013) allows members of the workplace community (different departments or teams or senior managers in this context) to represent, enact, and enforce the policy according to the dominant ideologies. A senior manager succinctly represents a 'what works best' ideology that recurrently emerges in the data as underpinning language choice.

Example 3

I want [refers to his team] to achieve our deadlines. If uh Italian helps them fine with me [laughter] I don't see why it [the communication between colleagues] should be in English (.) well uhh the [refers to types of documents] need to be in English but [name] well that's a different matter (. . .).

In the same corpus, language choice is related, among others, to *the task at hand*, the *structure of the team*, and the *individuals' agendas* for including or excluding others from decision making. The language policy seems to have clearer visibility and enforcement in written communication though genres such as the business email present interesting cases affording ad hoc decisions of language choice (Mahili 2014). Research repeatedly shows that employees in the modern workplace operate at the interface of linguistic boundaries, which has implications for access to centres of power and gatekeeping, as we discuss in the next section.

Power, policy, and fitting in

We already defined language policy as (formal) course of action that contributes to determine and alter language choice and language use at companies and institutions. One of the first instantiations of workplace communication policies is the job interview. While language choice and language use are often well described and made available to those interested in applying for a job, the reality of the job interview is much less explicit and much more intricate. Candidates are judged on the basis of tacit social, cultural, and linguistic norms, where interviewers' individual preferences and gut feeling are just as valid as a good CV. In this sense job interviews contain an inherent paradox – on the one hand, they present an assumption that everyone has equal chances for getting a job by following explicit policies (communication and other); on the other hand, they are an instrument of power in which candidates need to 'play the game' in the company language, infallibly and convincingly to be offered a job. In other words, job candidates need to demonstrate that they fit in for a particular (yet hypothetic) situation. The concept of fitting in is an interesting one in many ways. To conceptualize *habitus*, Bourdieu and Wacquant (1992) talk about 'being out of place' or 'being a fish out of water'. Although they do not use the phrasing 'fitting in', they argue that individuals, who are not in the comfort zone of the fish in water, will perform less well because they will be in an outsider position. In workplace contexts, as well as in many other new settings, individuals try to live up to certain social and cultural norms in order to fit in. If newcomers experience that they do not fit in, they will either try to adapt to the norm or resist it.

Fitting in is closely related to the concept of performances (Goffman 1959). Goffman argues that when individuals present themselves before others (i.e., in all communicative events) their performance incorporates the officially accredited values of the society rather than their personal behavior. He uses the notion of 'idealization' to explain how people's 'ideas' of performance in a given situation are influenced by 'outside' societal norms. In his later work *Presentation of Self in Everyday Life*, Goffman (1963) introduces the term 'passing', which can also be interpreted as a performance through which one aims at avoiding negative categorizations (stigmata). "Passing" helps individuals to conceal a disability – a mental or physical misfitting – to avoid stigmatization and gain social acceptance from others, who, they believe, are better positioned than them. We provide an example of passing in the next section.

Negotiating fitting in the workplace does not only involve showing competence to the dominant language but also showing competence in the sociocultural norms shared by the speakers of the language. Employers perceive fitting in to be the responsibility of the employee alone and tend to show lack of awareness to the complexity of the process (Roberts and Campbell 2006; Kirilova 2013). Further to this, recent work shows that dominant groups tend to position newcomers as those in 'need' to adapt and this expectation goes with either a requirement to pick a language (see e.g., Hultgren 2014 on language policy in higher education) or to perform according to tacit norms and knowledge . This is particularly pronounced in the modern workplace where employees need to work closely in teams and on specific projects, more often than not under time pressure. In the data we analyzed, we found language, ethnicity, religion, and ways of 'doing' work to be inextricably linked and mobilized as resources to do inclusion or exclusion in both the white- and blue-collar settings.

Yet another important dimension of workplace communication is that it is shaped and determined by norms and hierarchical structures that sustain an uneven distribution of power. Explicit or implicit language policies play a key role in this matrix. Power is constructed through interaction and involves both processes of domination and subordination. Foucault (1982: 788) points out that "the exercise of power is not simply a relationship between partners, individual or collective; it is a way in which certain actions modify others." Various interactional events at the workplace, such as recruitment and staff development interviews as well as salary reviews, are per definition asymmetrical. In a study of the role of the interview in social science research, Briggs (1986) discusses the process of hegemonic power in conversations and argues for their multiple footings that are 'simultaneously rooted in the dynamics of the interview' and 'the social spheres constructed by the responses' (see also Briggs 2003). He illustrates how interviewers control the content of the interview as well as the length of questions and turns, suggesting that power asymmetries and difference in the sets of norms will lead to problems such as misunderstanding, resistance or conflict. This is further complexified by the use of a non L1 for the interviewee. Power asymmetries may construct a "minority voice" for marginalized populations to sustain their hegemonic status as Example 4 reveals. Briggs (2003: 249) points out that "whereas native-born, middle-class whites just naturally seem to be part of the dialogue, people of color and working-class persons can be portrayed as needing the mediation of the researchers, journalists, or other professionals to make their voices heard on public stages." He argues that by classifying respondents as members of different ethnic or religious groups, interviewers may create a logic that will feed into generalizations about other representatives of the same ethnic or religious groups. When a candidate fails to correctly interpret subtle cues, although not explicitly part of the language skills expected, this results in being constructed as the unwanted 'other' who does not have the skills to fit in a particular workplace. Given that productivity and effectiveness of teams are dominant values in the neoliberal workplace, anticipation of non-performance results in non-recruitment. We discuss this further in relation to linguistic, cultural, and institutional requirements.

A term that captures well the asymmetrical mechanisms through which language exercises power in professional settings is institutional gatekeeping. The term gatekeeping is a metaphor of achieving social status. It relates to the physical and social passage from *outside* to *inside* which often requires a possibility or permission to access resources on offer. When people communicate with each other in institutional settings (i.e., at the office, at school, at the hospital), they use the right and authority to make decisions of inclusion or exclusion. These decisions have direct consequences to other people. For example, they may negatively affect socially marginalized individuals, especially those applying for asylum, citizenship, or a job (McNamara and Shohamy 2008; Blommaert 2009; Spotti 2011; Fosgerau 2013), and can also 'block' access to decision making.

As an ideological construction, gatekeeping is both overt and covert. It is overt, as it is mutually accepted and practiced by the parties in workplace communication, and covert, as it deals with individual communicative practices and the way they become basis for social evaluation. However, as Tranekjaer (2015: 54) points out, it is important to understand that "gatekeeping is found in any process of categorization that involves the establishment of an asymmetric and hierarchical relation between categories and thereby between the members of such categories." In particular, she argues that "the notion of gatekeeping should not be limited to describe the aspect of discrimination related to differential treatment and unequal evaluation in institutional processes."

We illustrate the complexity of negotiating gatekeeping, power, and fitting in with an example from a job interview for an IT (information technology) support position. The applicant Hamid (HAM) tries to fit it and make a good impression on the interviewing employee (CEM) and the manager (MAN).

Example 4

English translation	Danish original
1. CEM: hh we are very much	1. MED: hh vi søger jo meget
2. looking for someone	2. en med øh der har den
3. that erm that is good	3. tekniske kunnen
4. at the technical stuff	4. men som også har den
5. but has also (.) the	5. (.) pædagogiske (.)
6. pedagogic (.)	6. HAM: ja
7. HAM: yes	7. MED: hvad skal man sige
8. CEM: what should we say	8. mellemmenneskelig
9. mutual	9. HAM: [ja
10. HAM: [yeah	10. MED: [øh forståelse (.) hh
11. CEM: [erm understanding (.)	11. (.) øh (.) så øh
12. hh (.) erhm (.) so erhm	12. så det gør
13. so it is not that	13. ingenting at du er
14. important that you are	14. knald dygtig
15. pretty skillful on the	15. hh på den
16. technical t- side but	16. tekniske t- side
17. it is also important to	17. men det er også
18. be able to reach (.)	18. vigtigt at kunne nå
19. this employee	19. (.) den medarbejder]
20. HAM: [xxx	20. HAM: [xxx
21. CEM: [who-	21. MED: [som-
22. HAM: [yeah you mean-	22. HAM: [ja du mener-
23. CEM: [-is not quite	23. MED: [-bare ikke er det
24. HAM: [-wo- women- why is	24. HAM: [-kv- kvinder- hvorfor
25. technical ye:ah↑ ma-	25. er teknisk j:a↑ det må-
26. maybe women can also	26. måske kan kvinder også
27. good at technical stuff	27. god til teknik
28. ha ha ha]	28. ha ha ha]
29. MAN: [yes!	29. LED: [ja!
30. ITM: of course they can	30. ITM: det kan de sagtens
31. CEM: sure they can	31. MED: det kan de helt sikkert
32. h°yeah	32. h°ja
33. HAM: erm yes er:m it is not a	33. HAM: øh ja ø:h det er ingen
34. problem for me	34. problem for mig
35. CEM: mm	35. ITM: mm
36. HAM: for example because erm	36. HAM: for eksempel fordi øh
37. CEM: mm	37. MED: mm
38. I from a family that (.)	38. HAM: jeg fra en familie som
39. with a man and a woman	39. (.) med kvinde og mand
40. there is equality there	40. der er lighed det er
41. is no problem (.) for	41. ingen problem (.) for

42. example
43. MAN: mm
44. HAM: {we are also} although my
45. xxx wife or she erm a
46. party or something (.)
47. er:m we (.)we celebrate
48. a party for example
49. a birthday we put in
50. front of an (.) an erm
51. hh an erm glass of wine
52. or something else xxx
53. but although I drink
54. vodka or something else
55. (.) but it is not a
56. problem for us (.)
57. MAN: no no no no
58. HAM: no or
59. MAN: xxx
60. HAM: do you mean this or
61. what
62. MAN: [no hh
63. ITM: [no
64. CEM: no I meant
65. HAM: or technical
66. CEM: I I mean erm that erhm
67. (.) that we erm (.) w-
68. (.) that we of course we
69. are looking for someone
70. good at IT h
71. HAM: mm
72. CEM: but erhm m- erhm and also
73. m- technically
74. technically skilled hh
75. HAM: yes

42. eksempel
43. LED: mm
44. HAM: {vi er også} selv om min
45. xxx kone eller hun øh
46. nogen fest eller nogen
47. (.) ø:h vi (.) vi fejrer
48. nogen fest for eksempel
49. fødselsdag vi sætter for
50. en (.) en øh hh en øh
51. glas vin eller noget
52. andet xxx
53. men selvom jeg
54. drikker vodka eller noget
55. andet(.)med det er ingen
56. problemer for os (.)
57. LED: nej nej nej nej
58. HAM: nej eller
59. LED: xxx
60. HAM: mener du den der eller
61. hvad
62. LED: [nej hh
63. ITM: [nej
64. MED: nej jeg mente
65. HAM: eller teknisk
66. MED: jeg jeg mener øh at øh
67. (.) at vi øh (.) v- (.)
68. at vi selvfølgelig
69. søger en der er dygtig
70. til i_t hh
71. HAM: mm
72. MED: men øh m- øh og så også
73. m- teknisk teknisk
74. dygtig hh
75. HAM: ja

The example is emblematic in many ways. In the first part of conversation Hamid seems confident about answering the hypothetical question of how to assist colleagues with IT problems. In the second part of the conversation, however, a misunderstanding takes place putting Hamid into a difficult situation. He ends up defending himself by bringing up several Muslim taboo issues such as alcohol intake and repression of women (see Kirilova 2013 for further analysis). The episode starts as a product of a linguistic misunderstanding but results in cultural mismatch that culminates in stereotyping. In this particular case, Hamid tries to *pass* for a westernized person with a modern liberal view on family. He strives to negotiate an identity that he perceives the employers would appreciate in a language that is not his L1. However, trying too hard on an identity candidates believe leads them to a job, also enhances stereotyping (see also Erickson and Shultz 1982; Roberts and Campbell 2006; Kirilova 2013). Overall, the challenges candidates are faced with are multifaceted: they need to be able to negotiate macro policies indicating an abstract set of (linguistic and other) skills future employees need to demonstrate but they can also negotiate strong ideologies that underpin workplace events. Carrying out an interview in the target language is not in itself enough for communicating the stances and expected positions. The candidates need to have the skills to show alignment with the in-group and resist being constructed as the 'other' in order to be allowed 'in'.

Commodification of language skills in communication policies

Assessing an employee's skills in a dominant language has direct implications for recruitment, promotion, and overall development in the workplace. This however becomes again an ideological matter. Labels such as 'poor' or 'good' (language skills) are assigned by the speakers themselves and can indicate perceptions of similarity/difference to native speaker varieties of the language. The native speaker as a 'benchmark' of performance has a long history in applied linguistics and has been challenged in relation to language use in general and language in the globalized workplace in particular (for English lingua franca debates see Mortensen and Haberland 2012; Angouri and Miglbauer 2014). At the same time, speakers in the white-collar workplaces we have analyzed have also enacted the counter-narrative of having 'enough' of the language for their own purposes. From this point of view, 'good' or 'bad' becomes irrelevant and the speakers assess their competence in relation to what is needed for them to carry out specific tasks. Canagarajah's work on translingual practices (Canagarajah 2013) has also shown how speakers mobilize communicative resources that go beyond single languages. The language skills one has are assessed against the gain for, primarily, the company and then for the individual. In most cases however, what these narratives enact is a reduced multilingualism, an approach where language is another commodity to bring to the mix. Heller (2010: 107) points out that "the commodification of language confronts monolingualism with multilingualism, standardization with variability, and prestige with authenticity in a market where linguistic resources have gained salience and value." She argues that the recent interest in language as a commodity requires explanation on at least two levels. One level relates to standardized language and the way it is seen as a matter of good education, taste, intellectual competence, or rational thought (for example when applying for a job). The other level concerns the circulation of goods that used to depend on various manual resources (e.g., physical strength) now depends on linguistic resources (e.g., communicative skills).

In the context of the knowledge economy, the gain is economic and symbolic. We use these terms in relation to Bourdieu's notion of capital. Bourdieu refers to four forms of capital – economic, cultural, social, and symbolic (Bourdieu 2011[1986]). While economic capital typically denotes financial and material assets, cultural, social, and symbolic capital are seen as sources of influence through knowledge, skills, networks, prestige, and social acceptance. Cultural capital is the most complex among the forms of capital Bourdieu describes, as it refers to both culture and language at the same time. In the context of the global workplace, access to the local cultural capital and the way it is negotiated in specific events include or exclude employees from either accessing the job market altogether or progressing if already 'in'.

Although Bourdieu was not a linguist, his framing of cultural capital reveals a highly complex understanding of the conceptual relationship between language and culture. According to Bourdieu, cultural capital requires eloquence in those ways of speaking which are valued as powerful in the society in general and those in power in specific contexts. Displaying cultural capital singles out speakers as part of the dominant group within a particular social structure. Migrant speakers, for example, might be denied a good job or an opportunity for an education because they will be perceived as not possessing adequate cultural capital in order to be part of the society.

Drawing on the concept of cultural capital, in an extensive study of job interviews, Roberts and Campbell (2006) show how job candidates born outside the UK suffer exclusion from the job market. These candidates are given a *linguistic penalty*. However, this penalty does not necessarily arise from the lack of linguistic knowledge but, rather, from the hidden (cultural) requirements of institutional communication. They argue that the communicative demands of job interviews, for instance, are often greater than those of the job itself. They conclude that non-native speakers of English have bigger difficulties in getting a job than white British speakers not because they lack fluency in English, but because they are expected to talk in institutionally credible ways. For example, interviewers might judge candidates negatively if their communicative style is too personal and does not include institutional discourse. In such cases, candidates are regarded as poor users of English. "Poor English" becomes a legitimate catch-all term encompassing misunderstandings, interactional difficulties, and individual communicative styles but is nevertheless an ideological statement because the listener is relieved of any responsibility in the communication and the full burden is put on the speaker (see also Lippi-Green 1997 on English with an accent, and Bremer, Roberts, Vasseur, Simonot and Broeder 2013 on ways of achieving understanding).

Let us now consider the following example from a job interview for a consultant in an unemployment office (MAN: manager, EMP: interviewing employee, ALI: candidate Alice).

In Example 5 language policy is enforced through performance. The manager applies the institution's policy to assess Alice's linguistic proficiency in Danish. She is not trained in

Example 5

Alice, Unemployment Office Consultant, unsuccessful

	Danish
MAN: =today (.) we will assess whether you are good enough at [your] <ALI: well I'll try> Danish {smiling voice} <EMP: yes> {laughs}	LED: =i dag (.) da skal vi vurdere om du er god nok med dit <ALI: vel jeg prøver> dansk {smilende stemme} <MED: ja> {griner}

assessing candidates' linguistic performance, but as a 'native' speaker of Danish, she makes decisions about who is 'good enough' and who is not. A closer look at the interaction reveals a certain degree of embarrassment in the manager's act of exercising power. To minimize the effect of power and to distance herself from the role as a gatekeeper, she uses a smiling voice, pauses, and an institutional "we."

Practices of linguistic evaluation by 'natives' are so common in multilingual workplaces that they are not even questioned. Nevertheless they are highly problematic as they disclose the intricate relationship between policy, ideology, and power. By assessing linguistic skills alongside professional qualifications, many L2 candidates are doubly subordinated: first, they need to address the institutional requirements of the company (very often implicit); and second, they need to pass an unofficial language test, the criteria of which are highly subjective. As a result language policies become grounds for social inclusion and exclusion long before employees enter the job market. Once 'in' a process of hurdles in negotiating belonging also affects the move from the periphery (or the status of the novice) to the core of the team or department. Hence irrespective of whether it is a white- or blue-collar context or job, the relationship between language policy and ideology needs to be understood as intertwined and political. Although the one corporate language policy has often been portrayed as 'neutral', research on either blue- or white-collar settings shows that language use and language choice is multifaceted and co-constructed. Employees are assessed on language competence, which often becomes a 'broad brush' account of performance as we have discussed in this chapter. Although this has been primarily associated with blue-collar environments, the same applies to all workplace contexts. Discourses such as the one in Example 6 legitimize assessment processes where language skills become a proxy for all other areas of performance and fitting in. The quote is from a senior manager commenting on his team (see Angouri and Miglbauer 2014).

Example 6

They [non L1 speakers] come with basic skills on language but they can't use the language. The key is pure communication. (. . .) They don't have the awareness to understand (. . .)

The complex relationship between language policy and language practice has been addressed through a comparison of blue- and white-collar settings. Although this is often a necessity for research designs – we argued here that approaching the workplace holistically and looking the same phenomena at both entry jobs and higher up in the hierarchy ladder is beneficial for achieving a more nuanced understanding of the ways in which language, ideology and power interconnect.

Although in this chapter we cautiously use the terms white and blue collar, we also argue that they are limited in their descriptive and analytical value. The terms have served the field as analytical metaphors in order to study different workplace settings. And this is, evidently, very important for research design purposes. However in the modern workplace the boundaries and distinctions between blue/white are difficult to maintain. This does not mean that there are no divisions; there are low and high(er) paid jobs as well as jobs often seen as 'entry' jobs to a new country. The terms used to describe them though will need to capture that those who occupy these positions (more or less) temporarily would not be a homogenous group of manual labour and the like.

Implications

This chapter has shown that language communication practices and policies cannot be studied through a one-size-fits all-approach. The various case studies discussed in this chapter have shown that language policy and language use are negotiated in situ and the terms mean different things in the different settings. Hence more work is needed in order for patterns to emerge. Further to this, the complexity and fluidity of the global workplace needs new methodological and theoretical tools for further exploring multilingualism at work. Finally, the research on language communication practices and policies needs to be made relevant to language teaching and training. Language educators and trainers, mainly those who teach language for specific purposes, are asked to prepare the (future) employees for a very complex linguistic ecosystem. The transition from the classroom to the workplace, however, needs to be more holistically addressed, and this is an area open to further research.

Future directions

Although the chapter has argued for going beyond a static binary of blue/white collar, because of access issues, anonymity and practical concerns, 'white-collar' environments have attracted and are still attracting increasing attention by scholars. At the same time more research is necessary at entry positions to understand the processes of negotiating access and integration in contexts where power (im)balance may be more marked. Similarly, although spoken discourse is relatively widely covered in the literature, the phenomena in question are still under-researched if one considers the diversity of workplaces, the pace of change, and the influence of technology and mobility to the way 'activity' is carried out in different industries. Going beyond the spoken, further research is needed on written discourse. This applies to all employees as well as written texts produced by and for skilled migrants to find out what role written interaction plays in their fitting in or not fitting in in the workplace. Thus, more research is necessary on the relationship between language taught for business and the language used in different workplace. Finally, it is important to expand the research outside the boundaries of the 'Western world'. Currently, most of the studies are conducted in English-speaking countries, with some exceptions from Southern Europe and Scandinavia. We still know very little about workplace communication in East Asia, Eastern Europe, and the Middle East, and what we know is likely to be influenced by Anglo-Saxon research practices and points of view.

Summary

The chapter provides an overview of workplace communication practices and policies in multilingual and multinational workplaces. It discusses issues around language ideology and language choice. Special attention is paid to the notions of language attitudes, particularly in relation to linguistic evaluation and 'common-sense' perceptions of language practice. We touch briefly upon the concept of 'fitting in' to link up power, identity theory, and language policy. We draw on different datasets (from high-flying executives to asylum seekers) to illustrate that different participants experience difference realities. One of the important contributions of the chapter is that it draws on both blue- and white-collar contexts and makes a case for going beyond static binaries in understanding workplace practice. Although the datasets discussed here are different, they disclose similar processes of reducing employees to a set of skills and narrow the understandings of the employees' various competences. One of the main arguments in the chapter is that communication policies are invariably related to issues of power and gatekeeping. The ambiguity built in many corporate and institutional systems allows those in power to interpret a policy in whatever way best suits the interests of the dominant group. The chapter closes with identifying areas open to further research.

Related topics

> Language in skilled migration
> Rethinking (un)skilled migrants
> Citizenship, immigration laws, and language

Further reading

Angouri, J. (2014). Multilingualism in the Workplace: Language Practices in Multilingual Contexts. *Multilingua, 33*(1–2), 1–9.

> A recent double special issue which provides an overview of current research in different multilingual contexts. The articles discuss cases from different workplace settings and geographical contexts and draw on both white- and blue-collar environments. The double issue includes nine contributions which provide a state of the art and indicate areas open for further research.

Campbell, S. and Roberts, C. (2007). Migration, ethnicity and competing discourses in the job interview: Synthesizing the institutional and personal. *Discourse & Society, 18*(3), 243–271.

> The article is based on a unique data set of video-recorded job interviews in UK. It demonstrates convincingly how the interview's requirement for the synthesis of work-based and personal identities is particularly disadvantaging to foreign-born minority ethnic candidates. They are judged by interviewers as 'inconsistent', 'untrustworthy', and non-belongers to the organization.

Duchêne, A, Moyer, M. and Roberts, C., eds. (2013). *Language, Migration and Social Inequalities: A Critical Sociolinguistic Perspective on Institutions and Work* (vol. 2) Bristol: Multilingual Matters.

> A collection of articles that brings together ethnographic research from around the world to explore linguistic inequality and its (re)production in different workplace contexts. Most importantly, it re-examines 'migration' as a social process of workforce mobility, proposing a wider and more global political and socio-economic understanding of the concept.

Gee, J.P., Hull, G.A. and Lankshear, C. (1996). *The New Work Order: Behind the Language of the New Capitalism*. Westview Press.

> A landmark publication on the modern workplace and the changes in the way activity is organized and perceived. The reader will find a guided discussion and analysis of the language of the new (or fast) capitalism and the implications for the individual. The book shows the power of tacit policies and beliefs and the ways in which they are manifested in the world of work.

Holmes, J. and Stubbe, M. (2014). *Power and Politeness in the Workplace*. London: Routledge.

> A key publication on workplace discourse. The book provides the reader with an overview of priority areas for workplace discourse analysts and the ways in which data can be captured and analyzed.

Roberts, C. (2012). Translating global experience into institutional models of competency: Linguistic inequalities in the job interview. *Diversities, 14*(2), 49–71, UNESCO (http://www.unesco.org/shs/diversities/vol14/issue2/art4)

The paper elaborates on concepts previously introduced by Roberts and shows how discursive regimes position migrant applicants as less capable within the competence-based interview. It reveals the implicit dimensions of linguistic and interactional work required from non-native job candidates to manage the extra contextual and equivalences burden.

References

Angouri, J. (2013). The multilingual reality of the multinational workplace: Language policy and language use. *Journal of Multilingual and Multicultural Development* 34(6): 564–581.

Angouri, J. and Miglbauer, M. (2014). "And then we summarise in English for the others": The lived experience of the multilingual workplace. *Multilingua-Journal of Cross-Cultural and Interlanguage Communication* 33(1–2): 147–172.

Billig, M. (1987). *Arguing and Thinking: A Rhetorical Approach to Social Psychology*. Cambridge: Cambridge University Press

Billig, M. (1991). *Ideology and Opinions*. London: Sage.

Billig, M. (1996). *Arguing and Thinking: A Rhetorical Approach to Social Psychology*. Cambridge: Cambridge University Press.

Blommaert, J. (2009). Language, asylum, and the national order. *Current Anthropology* 50(4): 415–441.

Blommaert, J., Collins, J. and Slembrouck, S. (2005). Spaces of multilingualism. *Language & Communication* 25(3): 197–216.

Bourdieu, P. (2011). The forms of capital. In I. Szeman and T. Kaposy (eds.), *Cultural Theory: An Anthology* (pp. 81–93). Chichester: Wiley Blackwell. Original work published 1986.

Bourdieu, P. and Wacquant, L. (1992). The purpose of reflexive sociology (The Chicago Workshop). In P. Bourdieu and L. Wacquant (eds.), *An Invitation to Reflexive Sociology* (pp. 61–216). Cambridge: Polity.

Bremer, K. and Roberts, C., Vasseur, T., Simonot, M. and Broeder, P. eds. (2014). *Achieving Understanding: Discourse in Intercultural Encounters*. London: Routledge.

Briggs, C.L. (1986). *Learning How to Ask: A sociolinguistic Appraisal of the Role of the Interview in Social Science Research*. Cambridge: Cambridge University Press.

Briggs, C.L. (2003). *Stories in the Time of Cholera: Racial Profiling During a Medical Nightmare*. Berkeley, CA: University of California Press.

Burke, R.J. and Ng, E. (2006). The changing nature of work and organizations: Implications for human resource management. *Human Resource Management Review* 16(2): 86–94.

Canagarajah, A.S. (2013). *Translingual Practice: Global Englishes and Cosmopolitan Relations*. New York and Abingdon: Routledge.

Cummings, J.N. (2004). Work groups, structural diversity, and knowledge sharing in a global organization. *Management Science* 50(3): 352–364.

Erickson, F. and Shultz, J. (1982). *The Counselor as Gatekeeper: Social Interaction in Interviews*. New York: Academic Press.

Fosgerau, C.F. (2013). The co-construction of understanding in Danish naturalization interviews. *International Journal of Bilingualism* 17(2): 221–236.

Foucault, M. (1982). The subject and power. *Critical Inquiry* 8(4): 777–795.

Fredriksson, R., Barner-Rasmussen, W. and Piekkari, R. (2006). The multinational corporation as a multilingual organization: The notion of a common corporate language. *Corporate Communications: An International Journal* 11(4): 406–423.

Gee, J.P., Hull, G.A. and Lankshear, C. (1996). *The New Work Order: Behind the Language of the New Capitalism*. Boulder, CO: Westview Press.

Giddens, A. (1991). *Modernity and Self-identity: Self and Society in the Late Modern Age*. Stanford, CA: Stanford University Press.

Goffman, E. (1959). *Stigma*. London: Penguin.

Goffman, E. (1963). *Presentation of Self in Everyday Life*. New York: Anchor Books.

Heller, M. (2010). The commodification of language. *Annual Review of Anthropology* 39: 101–114.

Hultgren, A.K. (2011). "Building rapport" with customers across the world: The global diffusion of a call centre speech style. *Journal of Sociolinguistics* 15(1): 36–64.

Hultgren, A.K. (2014). Whose parallellingualism? Overt and covert ideologies in Danish university language policies. *Multilingua* 33(1–2): 61–87.

Irvine, J. (1989). When talk isn't cheap: Language and political economy. *American Ethnologist* 16(2): 248–267.

Irvine, J. (2001). "Style" as distinctiveness In Eckert, P., & Rickford, J. R. (eds). *Style and sociolinguistic variation* (pp. 9–43). Cambridge: Cambridge University Press.

Jaffe, A. (2007). Discourses of endangerment: Contexts and consequences of essentializing discourses. In A. Duchêne and M. Heller (eds.), *Discourses of Endangerment: Ideology and Interest in the Defence of Languages* (pp. 57–75). London: Continuum.

Kirilova, M. (2013). *All Dressed Up and Nowhere to Go: Linguistic, Cultural and Ideological Aspects of Job Interviews with Second Language Speakers of Danish*. Doctoral dissertation, University of Copenhagen, Faculty of Humanities.

Kirilova, M. (2017). Oh it's a DANISH boyfriend you've got' – co-membership and cultural fluency in job interviews with minority background applicants in Denmark. In J. Angouri, M. Marra and J. Holmes (eds.), *Negotiating Boundaries at Work*. Edinburgh: Edinburgh University Press.

Kristiansen, T. (2010). The potency and impotence of official language policy. In L-G. Andersson, O. Josephson, I. Lindberg and M. Thelander (eds.), *Språkvård och språkpolitik: Svenska språknämndens forskningskonferens i Saltsjöbaden 2008* (pp. 163–179). Stockholm: Norstedts.

Lippi-Green, R. (1997). *English with an Accent: Language, Ideology, and Discrimination in the United States*. London and New York: Routledge.

Lønsmann, D. (2014). Linguistic diversity in the international workplace: Language ideologies and processes of exclusion. *Multilingua* 33(1–2): 89–116.

Mahili, I. (2014). "It's pretty simple and in Greek . . .": Global and local languages in the Greek corporate setting. *Multilingua-Journal of Cross-Cultural and Interlanguage Communication* 33(1–2): 117–146.

McNamara, T. and Shohamy, E. (2008). Language tests and human rights. *International Journal of Applied Linguistics* 18(1): 89–95.

Mortensen, J. and Haberland, H. (2012). English – The new Latin of academia? Danish universities as a case. *International Journal of the Sociology of Language* 216: 175–197.

Phillipson, R. (1992). *Linguistic Imperialism*. Oxford: Oxford University Press.

Phillipson, R. (2003). *English-Only Europe? Challenging Language Policy*. London: Routledge.

Rampton, B. (2006). *Language in Late Modernity: Interaction in an Urban School*. Cambridge: Cambridge University Press.

Reisigl, M. and Wodak, R. (2005). *Discourse and Discrimination: Rhetorics of Racism and Antisemitism*. London: Routledge.

Ritzau, U, Kirilova, M. and Jørgensen, J.N. (2009). Danish as a second language: Attitudes, accents, and variation. In M. Maegaard, F. Gregersen, P. Quist and J.N. Jørgensen (eds.), *Language Attitudes, Standardization and Language Change: Perspectives on Themes Raised by Tore Kristiansen on the Occasion of His 60th Birthday* (pp. 255–271). Oslo: Novus forlag.

Roberts, C. and Campbell, S. (2006). *Talk on Trial: Job Interviews, Language and Ethnicity*. No. 344, Corporate Document Services. Retrieved from http://www.researchonline.org.uk/sds/search/download.do?ref=B1568, 1.4.2015.

Rumsey, A. (1990). Wording, meaning, and linguistic ideology. *American Anthropologist* 92(2): 346–361.

Silverstein, M. (1979). Language structure and linguistic ideology. In R. Cline, W. Hanks and C. Hofbauer (eds.), *The Elements: A Parasession on Linguistic Units and Levels* (pp. 193–247). Chicago: Chicago Linguistic Society.

Silverstein, M. (1985). Language and the culture of gender: At the intersection of structure, usage, and ideology. In E. Mertz and R. Parmentier (eds.), *Semiotic Mediation: Sociocultural and Psychological Perspectives* (pp. 219–259). Orlando: Academic Press.

Skutnabb-Kangas, T., Phillipson, R. and Rannut, M. (1995). *Linguistic Human Rights: Overcoming Linguistic Discrimination*. Berlin and New York: Mouton De Gruyter.
Spotti, M. (2011). Ideologies of success for superdiverse citizens: The Dutch testing regime for integration and the online private sector. *Diversities* 13(2): 38–52.
Tranekjaer, L. (2015). *Interactional Categorisation and Gatekeeping: Institutional Encounters with Otherness*. Bristol: Multilingual Matters.
Van Dijk, T.A. (1987). *Communicating Racism*. Thousand Oaks, CA: Sage.
Van Dijk, T.A. (1998). *Ideology: A Multidisciplinary Approach*. London: Sage.
Van Dijk, T.A. (2000). New(s) racism: A discourse analytical approach. In S. Cottle (ed.), *Ethnic Minorities and the Media* (pp. 33–49). Buckingham and Philadelphia: Open University Press.
Wetherell, M. and Potter, J. (1992). *Mapping the Language of Racism: Discourse and the Legitimation of Exploitation*. Brighton: Harvester/Wheatsheaf, New York: Columbia University Press.
Wodak, R. and Angouri, J. (2014). From Grexit to Grecovery: Euro/crisis discourses. *Discourse & Society* 25(4): 417–423.
Woolard, K.A. and Schieffelin, B.B. (1994). Language ideology. *Annual Review of Anthropology* 23: 55–82.

31
Language-mediated services for migrants
Monolingualist institutional regimes and translinguistic user practices

Maria Sabaté Dalmau, Maria Rosa Garrido Sardà, and Eva Codó

Introduction[1]

The life trajectories of migrant populations and mobile citizens are dependent upon their opportunities of accessing a number of services which are key for transnational survival, including, among others, advice on legality and settlement issues, assistance for job search, health provision or entry into professional (re)training programs. In all these cases, migrant accessibility hinges upon the mobilization of "appropriate" linguistic and communicative resources. Some services, as for example, housing, education, employment, or welfare, may not be migrant specific, but rather, aimed at the general population; in that case, as Roberts (2013: 82) points out, "for the great majority of migrants establishing their legitimacy is only the entry point in the more general societal competition for scarce resources." The institutional challenge becomes how to serve all service users in ways that ensure rationality of decision, fairness, and equality. For a long time, the concern of sociolinguists and interaction analysts (Gumperz and Roberts 1991; Campbell and Roberts 2007) has been precisely to show the multiple ways in which discrimination and inequality is built into the strict gatekeeping mechanisms that regulate entry into institutions and access to the resources distributed therein. More recently, the focus has shifted towards the scrutinization of service provision in migrant-specific institutional spaces. A fair amount of studies have examined citizenship procedures (Codó 2008; Gómez Díez 2010; Jacquemet 2011; Maryns 2013), though not exclusively (see e.g., the work of Sabaté i Dalmau 2014, on migrant-owned, migrant-oriented telecommunication shops in Barcelona; Allan 2013, on professional language programs in Canada; or Kirilova 2013, on job interviews for newcomers to Denmark who experience difficulties entering the labor market). This chapter focuses on the second type of services, that is, those constituted by the migrant experience, and it adopts a general perspective on them linked to the analysis of language ideologies and practices. This has two consequences.

First, it does not focus exclusively on language services, that is, on the institutional provision of translation, mediation, or interpreting in migrant languages, but on how these services (or lack thereof) shape access to resources key for survival such as residence visas, shelter, or technology. Second, it reaches beyond the examination of language-focused services, such as local language training schemes, and into various other types of key institutional contexts.

Although traditionally provided by the nation-state, over the last decades migrant-focused services have been strategically outsourced to its ancillary agencies, including non-governmental organizations (NGOs) and multinationals, which participate, whether directly or indirectly, in late capitalist forms of governmentality and citizenship regimentation akin to those of the nation-state (Inda 2006), that is, linked to (national) identity performance and concerned with issues of legitimacy and judgment (Moyer and Martín Rojo 2007). The aim of this chapter is, therefore, not just to provide an overview of critical issues in this research area and lines for further investigation, as is customary in a publication of this type, but also, quite originally, to present detailed ethnographic data from different types of service-providing organizations situated in the same geographical space to reveal differences but also striking ideological similarities among state, nonprofit, and private agencies in the delivery of services to migrants. We do this from a socially engaged, critical sociolinguistic perspective to language in institutions and workplaces (Duchêne, Moyer, and Roberts 2013).

This chapter is organized as follows. It begins by introducing readers to the key issues that have emerged in sociolinguistic research on language, migration and access to resources over the last two decades. Then we zoom in on ethnographic research conducted in three distinct research spaces which are central to migrants' emplacement processes: (1) a government agency handling work permit applications; (2) an NGO-regulated residential project for homeless migrants offering settlement and shelter services; and (3) a selection of multinationals and "ethnic" ventures; that is, operators selling information and communication technology specifically to the "immigrant" market niche. In that section, we discuss how public, nonprofit (NGO) and private institutions manage linguistic diversity and how current transnational populations react to this management as service users. The data comes from Catalonia, an autonomous community of over 7.5 million inhabitants in northeastern Spain (Generalitat de Catalunya 2014), where a majority and a minority language, Spanish and Catalan, coexist, although in a complex manner.[2] Though Catalonia is officially bilingual, the specific ideological dynamics of Spanish and Catalan in migrant-oriented services in the community, where Catalan is still constructed as an authentic, in-group language and Spanish as an anonymous language for everyone (Woolard 2008), entail that the institutional language regimes framing service provision are still largely monolingualist and monoglossic, inspired by modernist ideologies of the (Spanish) nation-state, and comparable to those found in officially monolingual countries of the world. Yet, as a society which has experienced incoming mass migration as a relatively new (yet intense) social phenomenon, the focus on Catalonia serves to shed light onto the linguistic organization of service provision in the neoliberalizing economies of the 21st century. We draw on extensive fieldwork and participant observation in each of the three spaces, in-depth interviews with both service providers and service users, audio-recorded naturally occurring interactions among them, and visual materials. Finally, we provide some recommendations for further research on migration, language, and service provision.

Overview

Some key aspects of sociolinguistic research on mobility, migration, and language

The intensified globalization processes of the late 20th century brought about an influential body of literature which, from different but mutually informing disciplines (sociology, geography, demography, anthropology, education, cultural and communication studies, etc.), focused on the analysis of the mobilities of people and all sorts of material and symbolic resources across the globe (see e.g., Appadurai 1996; Urry 2007). In general terms, attention was first paid to "fluidism" (Wimmer and Glick Schiller 2002), that is, to the flows and interconnections of heterogeneous networks of people who organized their life trajectories with the help of the new information and communication technologies (Castells 2000 [1996]), the "social glue" of transnationally oriented populations (Vertovec 2009: 54). Research in this field then centered on less explored, but concomitant, spatial immobilities (Cresswell 2005; Hannam, Sheller, and Urry 2006), which included forms of socioeconomic stagnation, legal and financial insecurity, and technological disconnection, particularly at the onset of a global economic crisis. In the 21st century, it became apparent that the increased (but by no means new) diversification of practices and transnational imaginations was mobilized by an also intensified multiplicity of transnational social actors and networks of people (Faist 2013). These held various citizenship statuses and had different family projects, work prospects, and socioeconomic resources, religious affiliations, cultural experiences, and language backgrounds, which made it very difficult to classify them into "fixed" categories of migrants. Overall, this transnational mobility called into question the use of the classic nation-state framework as the "natural" unity of analysis in social-scientific analysis interested in (im)mobilities phenomena (see Glick Schiller 2010) – without assuming, however, that nation-state power has disappeared with globalization (Fairclough 2006).

Despite being traditionally overshadowed in migration studies, language is at the core of people's unequal opportunities for organizing transnational social life (see Canagarajah, in the introduction to this volume). The communicative lives of migrant populations (whether literate or not) have been approached from structuralist perspectives which share prescriptivist notions of linguistic codes as whole bounded "static" units (Heller 2001; Pennycook 2012). These studies have tended to focus on the analysis of the extent to which migrants' communicative comportments fit into the hegemonic linguistic regimes of the discursive spaces that they inhabit. Their socialization into the prevailing sociolinguistic orders has been taken as a "barometer" for legitimizing or delegitimizing their insertion processes into the host societies. At times, their multilingual resources have been acknowledged and celebrated as an emblem of global democratic harmony and citizenship, but this rhetoric, in fact, has naturalized or backgrounded the concrete forms of linguistic differentiation and marginalization to which they are exposed (see e.g., Heller 2006 [1999]; Baaij 2012). By contrast, ethnographic approaches to migrants' linguistic diversity have generally focused on the inherently translinguistic[3] nature of migrants' linguistic capitals and literacy repertoires (see Canagarajah 2013 for an overview of these foci). They have shown that situated practices often transcend neat language boundaries (Martín-Rojo and Molina 2012; Corona, Nussbaum, and Unamuno 2013), and thus challenge what counts as "doing language" (Piller 2011; Makoni and Pennycook 2012). They also transgress the ideological foundations of the "native speaker" (Pennycook 2007: 36), and in fact "propose and embody alternate models of the social world" (Gal 2001: 425). Several of these studies have sought to problematize the pro-linguistic diversity discourses that prevail in many European nation-states, arguing that these, "although nowadays *de facto* multicultural and multilingual, nonetheless still see themselves as essentially and indisputably monolingual" (Hogan-Brun, Mar-Molinero, and Stevenson 2009: 5), and that they value forms of elite multilingualism while dismissing migration-produced multilingual practices (Weichselbraun 2014), particularly in service provision. Others have tried to highlight the empowering potential that the multimodal and fluid multilingual practices of migrants, frequently categorized as "not-quite-languages" (Gal 2006: 15), may have for those who need access to services such as advice on legality issues, shelter, or technology for transnational survival. In the following section, we shall illustrate some of these contemporary language practices through the analysis of data from three case studies focusing on migrants' experiences with key language-mediated services in their host societies.

Issues and ongoing debates

Monolingualist regimes and translinguistic multilingual user practices in service provision[4]

In this section, we examine how three institutional fields in the public, nonprofit, and private arenas deliver service provision to current transnational populations at the beginning of the 21st century, and deal with the multiple language issues that emerge. The three spaces are (1) a state bureaucratic agency dealing with migrant legalization issues, (2) an NGO-regulated residential project for homeless migrants providing settlement and shelter, and (3) a selection of multinational and "ethnic" ventures selling information and technology, all located in Catalonia. We believe that the analysis of the examples taken from these different migrant-oriented research spaces provide a nuanced, comprehensive picture concerning language use in migrant services with regard to (1) how the migrants' multilingualism is institutionally addressed on the ground via established monolingualist and monoglossic practices and ideologies, and (2) how migrant language service users interact with this management in a bottom-up manner, in situated translinguistic language practices (the full ethnographic projects upon which we draw are available in Codó 2008; Garrido 2010; Sabaté i Dalmau 2014).

Service provision in a public administration office

The first service space presented here is a bureaucratic agency of key symbolic and material significance for migrants' insertion into a host society, that is, a state immigration office. Research was conducted in Barcelona in 2000, a turning point in Spanish immigration policy, because this was the year when the first mass legalization campaign or amnesty of a number that were to follow was organized. The beginning of the 21st century was marked in Catalonia and Spain at large by an unprecedented economic boom which required the immediate availability of a low-skilled workforce, especially in the construction, tourism, and domestic service sectors. This attracted many workers, mostly from outside the EU, who either entered the country illegally or overstayed their tourist visas. Unregistered migrant work insertion was facilitated by the traditionally large informal sector in the Spanish economy. The data collected included (1) five months of intensive fieldwork in the Barcelona agency responsible for processing migrants' applications, (2) twenty hours of audio-recorded frontline service interactions, (3) institutional documents, and (4) semi-structured interviews with key social actors. The largest client groups were North Africans (forty percent of applicants observed) and South Asians (over thirty percent). Data analysis departed from (but did not stop at) the in-depth examination of face-to-face service talk at the agency's information desk, which was the communicative interface between applicants and the Spanish state during the legalization process. The full comprehension of frontline talk required a clear understanding of how the institutional logics and the broader moral, linguistic, interactional, and social orders intersected in its constitution (Heller 2007).

The institutional agents' management of service provision

This agency was a highly regimented space socially, linguistically, interactionally, and morally. In fact, despite it being an information service, meaningful and accurate information was difficult to obtain. Officers' practices of service provision were routinized and contained extremely simplified information (often reduced to single key words, like *falta* – "missing"). Officers appeared to be extremely uncooperative and even disrespectful at times. The structuring of service interactions was rigid, with certain episodes like the handing in of all petition forms being required to occur first, thus contravening expectations of practice in service contexts where inquiries are made one at a time (Ventola 1987). Migrant enquirers were expected to know these idiosyncratic norms of behavior and were reprimanded and even not served if they did not follow them. This takes us to moral evaluation, another key feature of communication in this agency. Entrenched feelings of suspicion towards the eligibility of most applicants, a hegemonic discourse that circulated in media and political circles at the time, legitimized unfair institutional decisions (such as withholding certain key pieces of information from clients) and regimenting service practices on the ground. These practices aimed to discipline, judge and hierarchize the agency's clientele in an attempt to (re)assert employees' power and authority through symbolic gatekeeping. Though decisions were not made face-to-face, officers acted as if the selection of (morally) deserving from undeserving candidates had been entrusted upon them. One of the technologies of control in this regime of (symbolic) inclusion and exclusion was language. Spanish was constructed as the only legitimate language of frontline communication. Failure by clients to know the language was taken to index their unwillingness to "integrate" into Spanish society (Catalan was constructed as an in-group language, and thus totally absent from frontline service talk) and/or their lack of eligibility, as familiarity with Spanish was used to measure migrants' fulfilment of the requirement to have been in the country for at least one year. Other languages, mostly English, were employed in actual communication, but they were categorized as exceptional linguistic resources. Institutionally, only Arabic and Russian were officially supported through the hiring of "specialist" staff members who were referred to as "interpreters" but whose language expertise was never made known to migrants, and therefore, only occasionally resorted to. Russian speakers were in any case a minority and Arabic was not helpful, as the only available interpreter did not speak Moroccan Arabic, the variety that would have been most needed given the geographical origin of many applicants. This reveals the institution's lack of investment in relevant and useful multilingualism. Officers' competence in English was the product of chance rather than institutional planning. Only one of four staff members was somewhat fluent in that language, yet he had been employed as an interpreter of Arabic, and thus, did not consider communicating in English as part of his work duties. No language requirements had been specified for the other two officers (apart from the interpreter of Russian, who did not master English). When absolutely necessary, they would utter isolated words while voicing their unhappiness at having to do so, and switch back to Spanish at their earliest convenience. This restricted migrants' possibilities of comprehending the progress/fate of their applications and sent clear messages to them about the practical and symbolic value of Spanish in the state administration.

The migrants' management of service provision

Migrant applicants devised creative ways of circumventing the regulatory regime of the agency. For example, they would inquire more often than told in the hope of obtaining less routinized, illuminating responses, or employ their social networks to figure out the meaning of whatever keyword or abbreviation that was handwritten on their application slips by officers to then go back to the agency and challenge institutional agents. On the linguistic level, most often, they would require ad hoc interpreting from relatives or fellow countrymen, or simply ask someone to inquire on their behalf. While North Africans spoke mostly Spanish (which bore, of course, linguistic traces of their migration trajectories), South Asians communicated largely in English (again, with various translinguistic marks). Their English was barely comprehensible for officers, unacquainted with outer circle varieties, but whose mistrust of South Asians' English was profoundly ideological in various ways. English was conceived of as a language migrants did not (and could not possibly) "own" and whose prestigious status globally and middle-class indexicalities locally clashed with the socially marginal position migrants were ascribed to. Despite their limited linguistic competence, officers would systematically construe themselves as better at English than migrants. Quite significantly, South Asians' variety of English was understood as a (further) attempt to deceive institutional representatives. On occasion, competence in English became the symbolic terrain over which issues of linguistic and professional legitimacy were fought. The following encounter (Example 1) illustrates how an instance of communication asynchrony due to interlocutors' differential access to insider knowledge of administrative procedures is attributed by the migrant enquirer to the officer's faulty English (line 8). The latter retorts angrily using the migrant's translinguistic turn (line 11) as evidence to dismiss not just the migrant's (claimed) competence in English but also, crucially, his legitimacy to evaluate the officer's proficiency.

Example 1[5]

MIQ: Miquel, officer; ENQ: Migrant enquirer

1 *ENQ: but look look this falta.
  %tra: but look look this missing.
2 *MIQ: <falta sí> [>].
  %tra: missing yes.
3 *ENQ: <understand> [<] ?
4 *ENQ: falta hm okay <no> [>] falta no okay # you understand ? but this my name # finito # finish.
5 %tra: missing hm okay no missing no okay # you understand ? but this my name finished # finish.
6 *MIQ: <oka::y> [<] ?
7 *MIQ: I don't understand.

```
 8   *ENQ:   you what is the English you speak xxx ?
 9   *MIQ:   I speak English you don't speak English!
10   *ENQ:   yes.
11   *MIQ:   my name no finito!
12   *ENQ:   +^ yes finish.
13   *MIQ:   finish what ? # finish ?
14   *ENQ:   yes this immigration #0_2 <finish> [>] but you understand?
15   *MIQ     <no> [<].
```

This example shows how multiple ideologies of language and clienthood were interwoven in these interactions, where evaluative moves were constant and where possibilities of resisting or subverting the strictly regulated institutional order via, among others, translinguistic practices were few, and for the most part, unsuccessful for migrants. While it is true that somewhat similar practices can be found in regular services addressed to the general population in Catalonia, the intensity of the surveillance of migrants and the uncivility with which they were treated set this service atmosphere apart from similar settings. To a large extent, this was possible because of migrants' lack of legitimate language resources to be able to challenge service providers on their own terms.

Service provision in a nongovernmental residential project (shelter and settlement services)

The data in this section come from a two-year ethnography (2007–2009) of a nongovernmental residential project for homeless migrants in the outskirts of Barcelona. The institutional space investigated was a three-month residential and settlement project for eight newly arrived, homeless and undocumented migrants run by a faith-based, voluntary association with the collaboration of a local migrant-support NGO and mostly financed by the city hall. The data gathered included (1) field narratives of everyday activities, (2) NGO documents, (3) recordings of service interactions as well as of Catalan and Spanish language classes, and (4) interviews with employees, volunteers, and users. Most participants were young men in their twenties and thirties from Morocco and Senegambia. They spoke between two and six languages each, the most represented being Wolof, Mandinka, Tamazight, Arabic, Hausa, Djola, and Fula. Generally, institutional agents were Catalan/Spanish-speaking NGO representatives ranging from their early twenties to their eighties, who had restricted competences in French and English, with few exceptions.

The institutional agents' management of service provision

The findings show that the institutions that ran the residential project (re)produced the established local and global sociolinguistic orders in a top-down fashion without any input from their users. The NGO justified its restricted construction of multilingualism with official integration-through-language discourses. First, this residential project (re)produced the contradictions between the commonsensical sociolinguistic comportment to address "non-Catalans" in Spanish (Pujolar 2007) as observed in service encounters with social workers in this project, on the one hand, and the Catalan autonomous government's integration-through-Catalan discourses, on the other (see Generalitat de Catalunya 2010). The latter justified the decision to switch from compulsory Spanish to Catalan lessons in this residential project in late 2008. According to the project manager, "El fet que un immigrant parli català per mi canvia totalment perquè hi ha com una voluntat gran d'integració" [The fact that an immigrant speaks Catalan for me totally changes [object missing, in the original] because there is like a greater willingness to integrate].

In keeping with these official integration discourses, the majority of NGO agents, including voluntary teachers, concurred in the ideology of bilingualism as two separate monolingualisms. Consequently, participants were strongly discouraged to "mix languages" in spite of the translinguistic practices that they were exposed to in the shelter. In the following service encounter (Example 2), the participant, John, mobilizes his knowledge of Italian, Spanish, English, and Catalan to recount past events. The social worker Alex consistently recasts John's hybrid productions – a mixture of Italian and Spanish resources with some Catalan and English resources – into institutionally sanctioned monolingual Spanish (lines 3, 5, and 7), which shows that the social worker perfectly understands John's narrative but polices its non-standard Spanish linguistic form.

Example 2

ALE: Alex, social worker; JOH: John, migrant user

1	*ALE:	cuántos días estuviste en Plaza Catalunya? # más o menos.
	%tra:	how many days were you in Plaza Catalunya? # more or less.
2	*JOH:	+^ yo: # cuase: # cuase tre: # tre settimane.
	%tra:	+^ I: # almost # almost three: # three weeks.
3	*ALE:	tres semanas.
	%tra:	three weeks.
4	*JOH:	tres tre: casi semana.
	%tra:	three three: almost week.
5	*ALE:	+^ casi tres semanas.
	%tra:	+^ almost three weeks.
6	*JOH:	yeah yeah # cose: qua # io ehh venito qua # veinti:<cinco> [<].
	%tra:	yeah yeah # thing here # I ehh come here # twenty-<fifth> [<].
7	*ALE:	<venir> [>] aquí.
	%tra:	<come> [>] here.
8	*JOH:	xxx from the veinti:sette o ventisette venito qua ehh dormir a fora.
	%tra:	xxx from the twenty seventh or twenty seventh come here ehh sleep outside.

Second, official integration discourses nominally recognized linguistic diversity, but multilingualism was actually restricted to English and French as temporary concessions (i.e., as legitimate communication facilitating devices), and African languages were silenced, both in service provision and in the language classroom. This elite, restrictive construction of multilingualism placed an expectation on migrants to at least speak one of these two languages and they were then categorized as Anglophones or Francophones. Nevertheless, participants could only use English or French with few institutional actors and its use was limited to initial and negotiation sequences if the migrant user was not accompanied by an ad hoc interpreter. For example, one of the social workers replied to a user who opened a service encounter in English "cariño, aquí hablamos castellano" [sweetie, we speak Spanish here] and insisted that he had to practice Spanish. Ideologically, the participants that spoke global languages were constructed as more "linguistically manageable" and, thus, as better equipped to "integrate" and learn Spanish/Catalan. By contrast, those who did not were problematized as uneducated, rural people whose "local" African languages were not considered potential vehicles for "integration." Despite the low prestige that African languages such as Wolof or Tamazight carry in the global sociolinguistic order, the migrant participants' African linguae francae could play a greater facilitating and communicative role in service encounters at this NGO. As has been the case in local migrant-created associations, this could take the form of the hiring of employees or the welcoming of volunteers (social workers, receptionists, and teachers) with (interpreting) competences in these widely spoken languages in the city. A first step would be to ensure both visibility and legitimate use of these languages in frontstage institutional communication rather than as invisible practices in the peripheral and backstage spaces, as we shall see next.

The migrants' management of service provision

The top-down management approach described earlier (re)created power relations, since NGO actors symbolically owned legitimate linguistic capitals, whereas highly multilingual, newly arrived migrants occupying peripheral social spaces faced difficulties to access institutionally sanctioned Spanish and Catalan. Because of their limited access to legitimate languages, they engaged in hybrid practices to communicate in institutional spaces – as in Example 2 – and in backstage spaces, which emerged as spaces for alternative multilingual practices. Simultaneously, these service users tended to appropriate, voice, and invest in NGO discourses of integration within and beyond the institutional space.

Participants distinguished between two clear periods in their narrated biographies, the "before" and the "after" participation in the residential project, in connection to their everyday language practices. For instance, Kalilu – a Gambian man who spoke English, Mandinka, and Wolof – stated that "ahora yo vive a aquí, en España, Sarrona [city], quiero hablar castellano" [now I live here, in Spain, Sarrona [city], I want to speak Spanish]. Another participant, Duwa, who spoke Wolof, Pula, Mandinka, and Sonike, claimed that he used to use English in Catalonia, "sí, antes, ahora sólo hablo en castellano" [yes, before, now I only speak in Spanish] after a few months. A significant fact is that both participants chose to have their interviews in Spanish instead of English despite their difficulties in answering the questions posed by the researcher in both languages, which triggered some occasional code-switching to ensure communication.

On the other hand, backstage practices, such as private conversations in the language classroom, were characterized by hybridity involving African languages and English or French as linguae francae. They might have constituted a form of contestation of institutional ideologies in the residential project, albeit coexisting with integration discourses and Spanish/Catalan learning in the institutional frontstage. Migrants used languages belonging to other social groups and even mocked Catalan and Spanish speakers around them (like the researcher's intonation). The fieldnotes in Example 3 are from a football match between the project participants and "African"[6] men in a working-class neighborhood (organized by

Language-mediated services for migrants

the social worker). This ethnographic vignette shows that participants subverted linguistic norms at the shelter in a different (but related) space. In particular, it demonstrates that migrants socialized in the transnational networks in the city via grassroots French lingua franca translinguistic practices.

Example 3

Dia talks to the players in a variety of French which is clearly distinct from the way he talks to me, closer to standard Parisian French. [...] What strikes me the most is that he keeps saying things in French to Duwa G., who reported speaking some English but not French. [...] Where has Duwa learnt French? Here in Sarrona [city] or in the streets of Gambia? "Pan-African" French is the lingua franca among these African guys playing football. The variety used among individuals who speak different languages (like between Dia and Emmanuel) sounds more "standard" than the varieties between Dia and Abdoulaye (Côte d'Ivoire) and Dia and Duwa (who share Mandinka). Players use some Spanish expressions like "muy bien" [very well], "mira mira" [look, look], "tío" [dude] or football terms like "falta" [foul], but the presence of Spanish is just tokenistic and communication is conducted mainly in French, with some code-switching into African languages. French competence proves to be essential to communicate and actively participate in the match (e.g., to contest a foul), since those who lack it, like Rostilav and Mustafa, do not speak at all and are rarely spoken to.

This football match brings to the fore that these transnational migrants engaged in different linguistic practices for in-group communication among African people with mobile trajectories. This institutionally marginal space allows for a transgression of institutional rules concerning service provision for out-group communication in the NGO which, as we saw earlier, legitimizes non-translinguistic varieties of European languages. We could argue that service users displayed more agency in their linguistic practices here than in more language-policed spaces, like the social office in Example 2.

Service provision in the telecommunications world (ICT services)

The data in this research space consists of an ethnographic analysis of the management of migrants' linguistic diversity by the thirty multinational information and communication technologies (ICT) ventures and "ethnic" mobile phone businesses that operated in Catalonia between 2007 and 2009. More specifically, the study focused on the languages that these companies employed in (1) call centers, (2) official websites, and (3) advertising campaigns (this included six interviews with mobile phone entrepreneurs and automatic translation specialists). A second set of data was gathered, simultaneously, by means of a two-year ethnography of an "ethnic" call shop located in a Spanish-speaking neighborhood near Barcelona, run by a twenty-six-year-old Pakistani man, which we understand as an alternative "shelter" institution of transnationalism organized by and for (pauperized) migrants at the margins of their host society. This second set of data consisted of (1) participant observation (i.e., shadowing) of the heterogeneous network of twenty undocumented and unemployed migrants, men and women aged between twenty-seven and fifty-two, born in Pakistan, Morocco, Romania, and various countries of Latin America, who networked there on a daily basis; (2) informal interviews with these informants; (3) naturally occurring interactions among themselves; and (4) a range of visual materials illustrating the multimodal iconography of the place.

The institutional agents' management of service provision

The findings show that the telecommunications industry mobilizes a "pro-multiculturalism neoliberal rhetoric" (Krzyzanowski and Wodak 2011) based on welcoming discourses that revolve around inclusiveness and respect for the linguistic diversity of their migrant clients. With commercial statements such as "A cada cual en su idioma. Esta es la clave para llegar a la comunidad extranjera en España" [Everyone in their own language. This is the key to reaching the foreign community in Spain] (Metro 2008: 15) or "Somos multilingües" [We are multilingual] (Telefónica's consultant; personal communication), the thirty companies analyzed all claimed to offer services in their clients' languages. On the ground, though, this emergent lucrative market niche was catered for basically in Spanish. Only three multinationals and eleven phone operators offered some information in English, very unsystematically, and only for some online services, following the communicative practices of global advertising (see Piller 2011). That is, it transmitted symbolic, rather that content, information, frequently with the use of non-functional (and fetish-like) word-for-word automatic translation (Kelly-Holmes 2005). A case in point was the company Mundimóvil, which presented its international phone call card for migrants with the logo "Calling yours never was so easy" (Mundimóvil 2009). The presence and use of Catalan was by no means normalized, since this co-official local language was only used by three multinationals and by five Catalonia-based ICT ventures whose clientele were mainly Catalan-born. Finally, the migrants' languages were almost completely absent. Only about ten percent of all companies (in fact, the newest "ethnic operators" specifically launched to target the migrant sector), offered some (but not all) services in them, notably, in Romanian and Modern Standard Arabic. For example, the company Digi Mobile, launched in 2009 and "specially designed for Romanians living in Spain," addressed its clients in Spanish and Romanian.

Overall, this management of linguistic diversity reproduces the monolingualist and monoglossic language hierarchies of the Spanish nation-state. Despite being de facto "multilingual" and making adjustments to better suit their particular target markets (by offering some Romanian to "Romanian" clients or Catalan to "Catalans"), the telecommunications sector ultimately fosters the use of Spanish as the main functional language for all its services and products, reproducing the integration-through-the-nation-state-language ideology simultaneously tied to legitimate citizenship. This management is exclusionary in the sense that it leaves those who are non-literate or non-familiarized with the dominant Western alphanumeric ICT systems and/or non-competent in Spanish (or English) unattended. They are positioned outside the established local telecommunication sector's regimes and sociolinguistic norms of clienthood.

The migrants' management of service provision

Despite this institutional (non)management of linguistic diversity in ICT service provision, migrant populations in Barcelona found alternative ways to gain access to communication technology and circumvent the language barriers that have been detailed earlier. Such practices were demonstrated mainly in local "*locutoris*" (call shops) regulated by and for migrant populations, as illustrated with the following ethnographic snapshots taken from fieldwork notes (Example 4).

Language-mediated services for migrants

Example 4

1. Informant Rachid from Pakistan complained that his mobile phone company did not give him the English language option to conduct top-ups via SMS, and decided to buy this service in the call shop, where he was catered for in Urdu and Panjabi.
2. Similarly, Jawara from Senegal tried to send remittances from a regular post office, without much success. He did not fully understand the information required in Spanish or the steps he was supposed to follow there, and was simply given a plasticized card called "translator" containing the same written information in other dominant languages, which he could not read. In the call shop, the remittances form was filled in, and sent, by the worker, who acted as a linguistic broker and cultural mediator of the place (without being paid for his multilingual repertoires).
3. Rachid needed to check his labor situation but could not figure out how to do this online, for the local administration office had simply given him a number and had told him to check it on the internet. At the call shop, he was informally provided with these sorts of technoliteracy capitals which are needed to surf the internet system (described in Area Moreira, Gros Salvat, and Marzal García-Quismondo 2008), when the worker there showed him how to use the Google search engine for this type of bureaucratic matters.
4. Sheema from Pakistan found information about a multinational's discount for calling services, but this was available only in Spanish. He decided to translate the information into Urdu and to type and photocopy it in the call shop, so that other Urdu users in his social network could make use of it, showing that language services were also provided among migrant clients themselves, as shown in Figure 31.1.

Figure 31.1 Written translinguistic user practices (Sabaté i Dalmau, 2014: 79)

In general, call shops try to emulate the service provision of multinationals and other ICT business, in the sense that the public floor tends to be unified in Spanish, too (for instance, the computer programs, invoices, and so on tend to be provided to migrants only in Peninsular Spanish). However, this "Spanish" is truly translinguistic and functions as the hybrid multimodal in-group code of the place. It contains traces of xenoglossy, which is the ability to appropriate and use a code without having fully understood or learned it (Jacquemet 2005), multiple literacies (digraphia) and heterography, or the deployment of unorthodox graphic symbols (Blommaert 2008), to mention but a few of its linguistic features. This is epitomized by the routinized circulation of translinguistic expressions both in the oral and the written mode. In the call shop that was observed, for instance, the person in charge of the computer programs was systematically called *el technición* (which is an amalgamation of "the technician," in English, and *el técnico*, in Spanish), both by the migrant users and the Pakistani service providers. Similarly, the word *habitación* (for "room") was used in writing in various non-standard forms, including *abtacion* (which may index multiple literacies in Arabic and in Spanish) and *habitasion* (with orality traits of many Latin American Spanishes). All in all, this shows that migrants circumvent linguistic marginalization by establishing discursive spaces which, in fact, do the real (informal) multilingual service provision that the telecommunications sector has left unattended. These bottom-up initiatives have been so successful that migrant-regulated call shops now attract more clients than most multinationals (Ros and Boso 2010).

The three research spaces compared: linguistic regimentation and resistance in service provision

The findings presented for each of the research spaces investigated show that, in late capitalist European societies like Catalonia, explicit institutional linguistic regimentation now coexists with other technologies of citizenship based on the capillary governmentality of migrants; that is, on neoliberal citizenship governance and surveillance practices that are increasingly regulated in decentralized, outsourced, or privatized sites of language-based services provision which are dependent on, but no longer exclusively monopolized, by the nation-state. They also show that the public, NGO, and private arenas all tend to follow unproblematized, and unidirectional, integration-through-language ideologies and to address these transnational populations through naturalized language-regulated social orders where linguae francae like English and French fulfill a practical and symbolic subsidiary role to the state's language, Spanish, and to a much lesser extent, to Catalan as a co-official language. These linguistic regimes censor and exclude the migrants' linguistic resources, on the one hand, and dismiss multilingual migrant personas with pejorative moralistic overtones on speakerhood and on personhood, on the other. The findings also demonstrate that current language policies concerning language service provision have not been successful in regimenting foreign populations into established institutional sociolinguistic hierarchies. This is so because, regardless of their linguistic backgrounds, migrant populations manage to gain access to these services and to incorporate into their host societies via ad hoc interpreting and informal mediation and socialization among themselves in a bottom-up manner. Their myriad translinguistic repertoires are delegitimized by society at large, but these ultimately become the multilingual capital whereby they ultimately manage to gain some access to the services that we have analyzed.

Implications

In this section, we identify transnational spaces and processes which would deserve further exploration within the field of migration and language in the service-based economy, and we discuss emergent trends for sociolinguistic research on migration from a transnational, historicizing, and integrative perspective.

First, our ethnographic research in informally regulated "ethnic" businesses and nonprofit agencies has shown the relative lack of sociolinguistic studies in the types of institutions which have emerged as part and parcel of the globalized new economy, with remarkable exceptions (e.g., Widin 2010). Both research spaces (i.e., "ethnic" businesses and nonprofit agencies) are key for the transnational survival of vulnerable populations, since they provide services through largely unchartered "ecumenical" forms of nation-state languages to ensure comprehension, thereby licensing some translinguistic communicative practices which would be deemed inappropriate outside multiethnic urban spaces (Eley 2015).

Our second recommendation for further research concerns places of transnational movement and passage, departing from the current (im)mobilities turn in migration studies. These places, which include airports, immigration reception centers, borders and border zones, as well as vehicles like long-distance planes, boats, and trains (see e.g., Maryns 2006; Duchêne 2011), have been underexplored from a critical sociolinguistic perspective, despite the fact that they constitute in-between/liminal multilingual spaces where linguistic norms are not clear-cut and allow us to see how service provision gets mobilized beyond, above, and in tension with multiple nation-state ideologies and linguistic regimes of citizenship.

Third, we should foreground the particular sociohistorical junctures of (im)mobilities in our studies on language and migration. Research spaces such as (informally regulated) migrant ethnic businesses in Barcelona or a Spanish state government office need to be historicized within wider social, economic, political, and cultural processes (i.e., the opportunities and constraints) that shape the mobility of actors over time, including the current global recession, humanitarian emergencies, or self-determination political movements. The analysis of the wide array of motivations behind migrants' mobilities from South to North, but also within the South (Vigouroux 2008; Han 2013), which include economic improvement, job transfer, lifestyle choice, or social activism, is equally relevant.

Finally, ethnographic studies of migration should adopt an approach to institutional communication that places specific service encounters in the context of other backstage and simultaneous interactions, institutional documents and practices, and state policies. This means that sociolinguistic ethnographies shall necessarily draw on critical discourse analysis, interactional sociolinguistics, and political theory tools to elucidate the role of language in services for migrant populations, growing increasingly inter- and transdisciplinary (see Burawoy 2009).

Future directions

In this contribution many issues which concern language in service provision to mobile citizens were only partially addressed due to space constraints, though they point to the following future lines of investigation and comparatively less researched social domains relevant within the field:

- Transnational identity management: the role of translocal (i.e., simultaneously local and global) migrant linguistic identities and ethnolinguistic presentations of the self, and the

ways in which these get individually and collectively enacted; that is, framed, embodied, inhabited, negotiated or resisted, in situated service encounters in transnational or liminal discursive spaces.
- Late-capitalist language policies: the study of the policy changes and strategies adopted by host-society states in their attempts to fulfil new supra-national (i.e., EU) governmental requirements, in connection to the (frequently hidden) language testing regimes of citizenship instituted by non-public transnational institutions which today participate in the governmentality of migrants (e.g., multinationals or financial institutions managing remittances).
- Mobile research methodologies: the role of multisited and network ethnographic research methods in the provision of a comprehensive picture of language-based service provision in transnational discursive spaces that get shaped in, and are mutually constituted by, complex dialogic forms, in disparate geographical areas of the globe, across and beyond institutional spaces and nation-state borders.

Related topics

Translanguaging in mobility
Citizenship, immigration laws, and language
Neoliberalism, language, and migration
Traveling texts, translocal/transnational literacies, and transcontextual analysis

Further reading

Codó, E. (2008). *Immigration and Bureaucratic Control: Language Practices in Public Administration*. Berlin: Mouton de Gruyter.

This monograph analyzes routinized practices of service provision in a state immigration office in Barcelona. It focuses on how officers exert interactional, linguistic, physical, and moral regimentation over migrant petitioners and shows how multiple social and institutional orders intersect in the shaping of practical and symbolic citizenship gatekeeping.

Duchêne, A., Moyer, M.G. and Roberts, C., eds. (2013). *Language, Migration and Social Inequalities: A Critical Sociolinguistic Perspective of Institutions and Work*. Bristol: Multilingual Matters.

With a focus on the (re)production of linguistic inequality in a range of geographical areas, this collection analyzes the place of migrants and the role of language in various institutional (healthcare, school, etc.) and workplace settings whose sociolinguistic orders and citizenship regimes are now challenged by the socioeconomic and mobility dynamics of late capitalism.

Márquez Reiter, R. and Martín-Rojo, L., eds. (2010). Service provision in a globalised world. Special Issue of *Sociolinguistic Studies*, 4(2), 259–504.

From interactional, discursive, and ethnographic perspectives, this special issue explores service encounters in highly multilingual transnational environments (such as call centers or refugee offices) in which Spanish plays a major role. By examining public, private, nonprofit institutions and public-private partnerships in the Spanish state and in Latin America, the compilation shows that the institutions investigated do not adapt to their multilingual clientele, and naturalize the Castilian Spanish standard as a homogenizing state and postcolonial language.

Sabaté i Dalmau, M. (2014). *Migrant Communication Enterprise: Regimentation and Resistance*, Bristol: Multilingual Matters.

This ethnography analyzes how states and telecommunications industries attempt to control migrants in how they use language to access mobile communications. It also provides an account of how these populations develop ways of mobilizing their translinguistic communicative practices to circumvent this linguistic regimentation in their own alternative discursive spaces, more specifically, in "ethnic" call shops.

Notes

1 Data used in this chapter come from studies funded by the following research grants: 2007ARAFI00018, 2009SGR1340, 2014SGR1508 and 2014SGR1061 (Catalan Government); HUM2007–61864 and FFI2011–26964 (Spanish Government) and 2008UAB2015 (Autonomous University of Barcelona).
2 Catalan, which has a long historical trajectory of prosecution and subordination, and which is not recognized as an official language by the European Union, is regarded as the co-official minority national language or *llengua pròpia* (literally, "own language") of Catalonia, whereas Spanish has a secured status both as the dominant official majority language of the entire Spanish nation-state and as a global lingua franca, too. The Catalan sociolinguistic context and the debates around the roles of these two languages are summarized in Pujolar and Gonzàlez (2013) and Woolard and Frekko (2013).
3 In this chapter, we use the term *translinguistic* to make reference to the hybrid linguistic repertoires which constitute the truncated amalgamations of simultaneously local and transnational communicative codes mobilized by transnational mobile populations (Jacquemet 2005; Corona et al. 2013).
4 The various data presented here was gathered with oral and written informed consent. All names used are pseudonyms in order to preserve the anonymity of the informants, following the guidelines for academic research established by the UAB Ethics Committee.
5 These are the transcription conventions for the spoken data presented in this chapter:

+^	quick uptake or latching
xxx	unintelligible material
#	pause
#figure	length of pause in seconds (minimum 1 sec)
[>]	overlap follows
[<]	overlap precedes
< >	scope symbols
:	lengthened vowel
::	longer lengthening of vowel
%tra:	free English translation of the turn

6 Inverted commas are used to denote emic ethnolinguistic identities and social categorizations (including naming practices), such as "African," "Catalan," "immigrant," or "ethnic."

References

Allan, K. (2013). Skilling the self: The communicability of immigrants as flexible labour. In A. Duchêne, M. Moyer and C. Roberts (eds.), *Language, Migration and Social Inequalities: A Critical Perspective on Institutions and Work* (pp. 56–78). Bristol: Multilingual Matters.
Appadurai, A. (1996). *Modernity at Large: Cultural Dimensions of Globalization*. Minneapolis: University of Minnesota Press.
Area Moreira, M., Gros Salvat, B. and Marzal García-Quismondo, M.A. (2008). *Alfabetizaciones y tecnologías de la información y la comunicación*. Madrid: Síntesis.
Baaij, C.J. (2012). The EU policy on institutional multilingualism: Between principles and practicality. *Language & Law* 1 [Online]. Retrieved from https://www.languageandlaw.de/volume-1/3338 [Accessed October 26, 2015].
Blommaert, J. (2008). *Grassroots Literacy: Writing, Identity and Voice in Central Africa*. London: Routledge.
Burawoy, M. (2009). *The Extended Case Method: Four Countries, Four Decades, Four Great Transformations and One Theoretical Tradition*. Berkeley, Los Angeles and London: University of California Press.

Campbell, S. and Roberts, C. (2007). Migration, ethnicity and competing discourses in the job interview: Synthesizing the institutional and the personal. *Discourse & Society* 18(3): 243–271.

Canagarajah, A.S. (2013). *Translingual Practice: Global Englishes and Cosmopolitan Relations.* Abingdon: Routledge.

Castells, M. (2000 [1996]). *The Rise of the Network Society.* Oxford: Blackwell.

Codó, E. (2008). *Immigration and Bureaucratic Control: Language Practices in Public Administration.* Berlin: Mouton de Gruyter.

Corona, V., Nussbaum, L. and Unamuno, V. (2013). The emergence of new linguistic repertoires among Barcelona's youth of Latin American origin. *International Journal of Bilingual Education and Bilingualism* 16(2): 182–194.

Cresswell, T. (2005). *Place: A Short Introduction.* Oxford: Blackwell.

Duchêne, A. (2011). Néolibéralisme, inégalités sociales et plurilinguisme: L'exploitation des ressources langagières et des locuteurs. *Langage et Société* 136: 81–108.

Duchêne, A., Moyer, M.G. and Roberts, C., eds. (2013). *Language, Migration and Social Inequalities: A Critical Sociolinguistic Perspective of Institutions and Work.* Bristol: Multilingual Matters.

Eley, L. (2015). *A Micro-ecology of Language in Multi-Ethnic Frankfurt: The Linguistic Ethnography of a Barbershop.* Urban Language and Literacies WP155 [Online]. Retrieved from https://www.academia.edu/11365690/WP155 [Accessed 20 June 2015].

Fairclough, N. (2006). *Language and Globalisation.* London: Routledge.

Faist, T. (2013). The mobility turn: A new paradigm for the social sciences? *Ethnic and Racial Studies* 36(11): 1637–1646.

Gal, S. (2001). Language, gender, and power: An anthropological review. In A. Duranti (ed.), *Linguistic Anthropology: A Reader* (pp. 420–430). Oxford: Blackwell.

Gal, S. (2006). Migration, minorities and multilingualism: Language ideologies in Europe. In C. Mar-Molinero and P. Stevenson (eds.), *Language Ideologies, Policies and Practices* (pp. 13–27). Basingstoke: Palgrave.

Garrido, M.R. (2010). *"If You Slept in Catalunya You Know That Here It's a Paradise": Multilingual Practices and Ideologies in a Residential Project for Migrants.* Unpublished MA thesis, Universitat Autònoma de Barcelona.

Generalitat de Catalunya. Departament d'Acció Social i Ciutadania, Secretaria per a la Immigració. (2010). *Llei d'acollida de les persones immigrades i retornades a Catalunya* [Online]. Retrieved from http://www.gencat.cat/drep/dgri/sumaris/revista_activitat_22.pdf [Accessed 27 April 2015].

Generalitat de Catalunya. Institut d'Estadística de Catalunya. (2014). *Padró municipal d'habitants per sexe* [Online]. Retrieved from http://www.idescat.cat/territ/basicterr?TC=8&V3=669&V4=446&ALLINFO=TRUE&PARENT=1&V0=3&V1=0&CTX=B&VN=3&VOK=Confirmar [Accessed 16 February 2015].

Glick Schiller, N. (2010). A global perspective on transnational migration: Theorising migration without methodological nationalism. In R. Bauböck and T. Faist (eds.), *Diaspora and Transnationalism: Concepts, Theories and Methods* (pp. 109–129). Amsterdam: Amsterdam University Press.

Gómez Díez, I. (2010). The role of the interpreter in constructing asylum seeker's credibility: A hearing at the Spanish asylum and refugee office. *Sociolinguistic Studies* 4(2): 333–370.

Gumperz, J.J. and Roberts, C. (1991). Understanding in intercultural encounters. In J. Blommaert and J. Verschueren (eds.), *The Pragmatics of International and Intercultural Communication: Selected Papers from the International Pragmatics Conference, Antwerp, August 1987* (pp. 51–90). Amsterdam: John Benjamins.

Han, H. (2013). Individual grassroots multilingualism in Africa Town in Guangzhou: The role of states in globalization. *International Multilingual Research Journal* 7: 83–97.

Hannam, K., Sheller, M. and Urry, J. (2006). Editorial: Mobilities, immobilities and moorings. *Mobilities* 1(1): 1–22.

Heller, M. (2001). Undoing the macro/micro dichotomy: Ideology and categorization in a linguistic minority school. In N. Coupland, S. Sarangi and C.N. Candlin (eds.), *Sociolinguistics and Social Theory* (pp. 212–234). London: Longman.

Heller, M. (2006 [1999]). *Linguistic Minorities and Modernity: A Sociolinguistic Ethnography*. London: Continuum.

Heller, M. (2007). Distributed knowledge, distributed power: A sociolinguistics of structuration. *Text & Talk* 27(5–6): 633–653.

Hogan-Brun, G., Mar-Molinero, C. and Stevenson, P. (2009). Testing regimes: Introducing cross-national perspectives on language, migration and citizenship. In G. Hogan-Brun, C. Mar-Molinero and P. Stevenson (eds.), *Discourses on Language and Integration: Critical Perspectives on Language Testing Regimes in Europe* (pp. 1–14). Amsterdam: John Benjamins.

Inda, J.X. (2006). *Targeting Immigrants: Government, Technology and Ethics*. Malden, MA: Blackwell.

Jacquemet, M. (2005). Transidiomatic practices: Language and power in the age of globalization. *Language and Communication* 25(3): 257–277.

Jacquemet, M. (2011). Crosstalk 2.0. Asylum and communicative breakdowns. *Text and Talk* 31(4): 475–498.

Kelly-Holmes, H. (2005). *Advertising as Multilingual Communication*. London: Palgrave Macmillan.

Kirilova, M. (2013). *All Dressed up and Nowhere to Go: Linguistic, Cultural and Ideological Aspects of Job Interviews with Second Language Speakers of Danish*. Unpublished PhD dissertation, Københavns Universitet, Copenhagen.

Krzyzanowski, M. and Wodak, R. (2011). Political strategies and language policies: The European Union Lisbon strategy and its implications for the EU's language and multilingualism policy. *Language Policy* 10(2): 115–136.

Makoni, S. and Pennycook, A. (2012). Disinventing multilingualism: From monological multilingualism to multilingual franca. In M. Martin-Jones, A. Blackledge and A. Creese (eds.), *The Routledge Handbook of Multilingualism* (pp. 439–453). Abingdon: Routledge.

Martín-Rojo, L. and Molina, C. (2012). *Madrid multilingüe: Lengua pa' la citi* [Online]. Retrieved from http://web.uam.es/ss/Satellite/es/1242652961025/1242664605633/articulo/articu lo/Madrid_multilingue:_Lenguas_pa%E2%80%99_la_city.htm [Accessed 23 September 2015].

Maryns, K. (2006). *The Asylum Seeker: Language in the Belgian Asylum Procedure*. Abingdon: Routledge.

Maryns, K. (2013). Disclosure and (re)performance of gender-based evidence in an interpreter-mediated asylum interview. *Journal of Sociolinguistics* 17(5): 661–686.

Metro. (2008). El éxito es móvil. *Metro*. 29 April. p. 15. Barcelona: Metro News S.L.

Moyer, M. and Martín-Rojo, L. (2007). Language, migration and citizenship: New challenges in the regulation of bilingualism. In M. Heller (ed.), *Bilingualism: A Social Approach* (pp. 137–160). London: Palgrave.

Mundimóvil. (2009). *The World in Your Hands* [Online]. Retrieved from http://www.mundimovil.es [Accessed 23 June 2010].

Pennycook, A. (2007). *Global Englishes and Transcultural Flows*. London and New York: Routledge.

Pennycook, A. (2012). *Language and Mobility: Unexpected Places*. Bristol: Multilingual Matters.

Piller, I. (2003). Advertising as a site of language contact. *Annual Review of Applied Linguistics* 23: 170–183.

Piller, I. (2011). *Intercultural Communication: A Critical Introduction*. Edinburgh: Edinburgh University Press.

Pujolar, J. (2007). African women in Catalan language courses: Struggles over class, gender and ethnicity in advanced liberalism. In B. McElhinny (ed.), *Words, Worlds and Material Girls: Language, Gender, Globalization* (pp. 305–348). Berlin: Mouton de Gruyter.

Pujolar, J. and Gonzàlez, I. (2013). Linguistic "*mudes*" and the de-ethnicization of language choice in Catalonia. *International Journal of Bilingual Education and Bilingualism* 16(2): 138–152.

Roberts, C. (2013). The gatekeeping of Babel: Job interviews and the linguistic penalty. In A. Duchêne, M. Moyer and C. Roberts (eds.), *Language, Migration and Social Inequalities: A Critical Perspective on Institutions and Work* (pp. 81–94). Bristol: Multilingual Matters.

Ros, A. and Boso, A. (2010). La población inmigrante en la nueva era digital. In M. Gimeno (ed.), *2010 e-España Informe anual sobre el desarrollo de la sociedad de la información en España* (pp. 142–148). Madrid: Fundación Orange.

Sabaté i Dalmau, M. (2014). *Migrant Communication Enterprise: Regimentation and Resistance.* Bristol: Multilingual Matters.

Urry, J. (2007). *Mobilities.* Cambridge: Polity Press.

Ventola, E. (1987). *The Structure of Social Interaction.* London: Pinter.

Vertovec, S. (2009). *Transnationalism.* London: Routledge.

Vigouroux, C.B. (2008). From Africa to Africa: Globalization, migration and language vitality. In C.B. Vigouroux and S. Mufwene (eds.), *Globalization and Language Vitality: Perspectives from Africa* (pp. 229–254). London: Continuum.

Weichselbraun, A. (2014). "People here speak five languages!": The reindexicalization of minority language practice among Carinthian Solvenes in Vienna, Austria. *Language in Society* 43: 421–444.

Widin, J. (2010). *Illegitimate Practices: Global English Language Education.* Bristol: Multilingual Matters.

Wimmer, A. and Glick Schiller, N. (2002). Methodological nationalism and beyond: Nation-state building, migration and the social sciences. *Global Networks* 2(4): 301–334.

Woolard, K.A. (2008). Language and identity choice in Catalonia: The interplay of contrasting ideologies of linguistic authority. In K. Süselbeck, U. Mühlschlegel and P. Masson (eds.), *Lengua, nación e identidad. La regulación del plurilingüismo en España y América Latina* (pp. 303–324). Frankfurt am Main: Vervuert, Madrid: Iberoamericana.

Woolard, K.A. and Frekko, S.E. (2013). Catalan in the twenty-first century: Romantic publics and cosmopolitan communities. *International Journal of Bilingual Education and Bilingualism* 16(2): 29–137.

Index

Note: figures and tables are denoted with italicized page numbers; end note information is denoted with an n and note number following the page number.

Afghanistan, displacement in 192
agency: displacement impacting 191; identity and 126, 127; language-in-education policies reflecting 487–8; narrative analysis consideration of 384, 385, 387, 388; scalar analysis of 16
Angola, displacement in 193, 194
anti-exceptionalism vs. exceptionalism 233–4
Argentina: identities in mobility in 123; schooling and indigenous language in 527; settler migration and settler varieties in 244
assimilation process: English language policies and practices encouraging 508, 513; immigration policies encouraging 455; language-in-education policies supporting 489, 490; with migration trajectories 218–19; for translanguaging in mobility 37
asylum seekers: diasporic populations as 339; multisited ethnography on 404; narrative analysis of stories of 389; nation-state vs. transnational ties of 51–2; neccessity-desire intersection for 433–4; socio-communicative complexity for 353–6; superdiversity and interviews with 68–9
Australia: diasporization in 337; English language in education in 303–4; heritage language in 468; higher education internationalization in 504, 504–5, 508, 509; immigration policies and citizenship in 452, 455, 463; migration trajectories in 217, 218, 219–20, 221; settler migration and settler varieties in 245, 246, 254; skilled migration in 298, 300, 301, 303–4, 305; space and language in 109
Austria: higher education internationalization in 504, 511; narrative analysis of migrants in 388–9; skilled migration in 298

Bangladesh, regional flows to/from 177
Belgium: Belgian Asylum procedure in 353–6, 389, 433–4; complexity of socio-communicative interactions in 353–8; diasporization in 338; language-in-education policies in 495; narrative analysis of migrants in 389; schooling in 523; superdiversity in 70
Benjamin, Walter 458
bioprogramme theory 231–2
bisexual individuals see LGBTIQ individuals
Bolivia, schooling in 523
Botswana, displacement in 193, 194, 196, 201
Bourdieu, Pierre: on cultural capital and workplace communication 550–1; on grassroots multilingualism 268; on literacy 413, 425–6; scales theory following 369; on skills as embodied capital 323; on social class 136, 138; on value of language within regional flows 171, 172
Brazil: schooling and indigenous language in 526; settler migration and settler varieties in 246; trade migration from/to 264

Cameroon, languages in 177
Canada: call centres in 83; diasporization in 332–3; heritage language in 52–3, 152, 469, 471–2; higher education internationalization in 504, 504; identities in mobility in 121, 124, 127; immigration policies in 88–90; labor-skills classification in 315, 316, 317–18, 320–2; language-in-education policies in 489, 490; minority populations in 154, 157, 158, 159–60; National Language Training Program in 89; neoliberal influences in 83, 86, 88–90; regional flows to/from 175, 177; settler migration and settler varieties in 247; skilled migration in 58, 301; social class in 140; space and language in 110; trade migration from/to 259, 264; volunteerism in 317
Catalonia, language-mediated services in 559, 561–70
Central African Republic (CAR), displacement in 192, 198

577

Index

chain migration 216–17
China, People's Republic of: economy of 80; English language in education in 303, 502, 509; heritage language of migrants from 474–81; higher education in 296, 297, 299, 504, 509; language-in-education policies in 490; language policy in 74, 477–8; literacy events in 423; migration trajectories in 211, 490; skilled migration in 297–8, 299, 300, 302, 303; trade migration from/to 258–9, 261–3, 264, 265–71; *see also* Hong Kong; Taiwan
chronotopes 34–5, 340–1, 386
circular migration 213, 214, 215
citizenship: Derrida on 456–63, 464; diasporization in relation to 339; displacement and dis-citizenship 187, 188; flexible 50; immigration policies and 451–65; integration and 85–6, 452–3, 455; language and 53–4, 68, 86, 90, 112–13, 149–53, 339, 451–64, 486–7, 488–9, 497; language-in-education policy connection to 486–7, 488–9, 497; language testing for 54, 68, 86, 90, 150, 339, 451, 452, 453–6, 461, 463, 464; law-justice divide in relation to 458–63; minority populations's 149–53; nation-state *vs.* transnationalism influences on 50, 53–4, 56–7, 68, 110, 149–53, 339, 486–7, 488–9; neoliberalism and 85–8, 90; overview and introduction to 452–3; religion in relation to 457–8; revocation of 452; skilled migration and 56; symbolic aspects of testing for 456, 461
code-switching 32, 33, 173, 372
Colombia, displacement in 190, 192
colonialism: diasporization and 330; displacement and 187–8; heritage language impacted by 468, 469, 470–1, 476; law and violence with 459–60; regional and language flows due to 175, 177; religious beliefs and practices with 277–8, 280–7; settler migration and settler varieties with 243–55; skilled migration ties to 296, 298–9; slavery and indenture in relation to 229, 234; superdiversity and 72–3; trade migration with 262–4, 476
communication practices and policies in workplace 540–55; in blue- *vs.* white-collar jobs 541, 544, 546, 552–3 (*see also* skilled migration *sub-entry*); commodification of language skills in 550–3; common sense beliefs underlying 542; cultural capital and 550–1; dually expressed arguments in 542–4, *543*; English usage as 20, 545, 551; fitting in or passing with 546, 550, 552; further reading on 554–5; future research on 553; gatekeeping via 547, 552; ideology and language choice in 541, 542–5, 552; implications of 553; issues and ongoing debates on 542–53; in job interviews 546, 547–50, *548–9, 551,* 551–2; overview and introduction to 540–1, 553–4; power access and exercise in 545–50, 552; reductionist process in 544, *544*; related topics to 554; skilled migration affected by 298, 300–7
communication technologies *see* information and communication technologies
communicative repertoires *see* repertoires
community: imagined, schools envisioning 523; narrative analysis of migrants as members of 385–7; schooling supported or sponsored by 525, 533; superdiversity in relation to 2, 67–8, 74
complexity 349–61; in asylum seeking procedure 353–6; chaos theory and 350; further reading on 361; future research in 359–60; of identities 118–21, 126; implications of 360; information and communication technologies adding to 349, 352–3, 355–60; issues and ongoing debates on 353–8; knowledge of 360; of multi-voiced dialogues 351, 353, 357–8; neglected complexity of socio-communicative situations 351–8; overview and introduction to 349–53; related topics to 361; of religious beliefs and practices 277; remedying neglect of 359–60; in social work interactions 356–8; superdiversity and 67, 68, 73, 74, 349–50, 352, 360; symbolic interactionists on 350, 351–3, 359; text and context boundaries in 359–60
conviviality, superdiversity and 70, 106, 108
cosmopolitanism 2–3
Critical Discourse Analysis 388, 463

Democratic Republic of Congo, displacement in 190, 192, 198–9, 211
Denmark: communication practices and policies in workplace in 541, *543,* 544, *548–9,* 550, *551,* 551–2; identities in mobility in 126; immigration policies and citizenship in 464; neccessity-desire intersection for migrants in 437; regional flows to/from 176; schooling in 532; skilled migration in 301
Derrida, Jacques, on immigration policies and citizenship 456–63, 464
diasporization 330–43; definition and description of 252, 424; deterritorialization and reterritorialization with 333, 334, 340; education in relation to 338–9; ethnicization, racialization and 340; further reading on 342–3; future research on 339–41; globalization and 336–7; heritage language impacted by 333, 338, 471–2, 475–82;

578

identities and 330, 332–6, 337, 338–9, 340–1; implications of 338–9; indenture as basis for 234–9; information and communication technologies impacting 334; issues and ongoing debates on 336–7; language and 110, 252–3, 330–43, 387, 424, 471–2, 475–82; literacy and polarization with 424; media impacting 334–6; narrative analysis related to 387; overview and introduction to 330–6, 341–2; political status in relation to 339; related topics to 342; religious beliefs and practices with 279–80, 289, 335; settler migration and settler varieties with 252–3; space and language with 110, 339, 340–1; superdiversity and 70–1, 331, 336–7; temporal frame for 339, 340–1; trade migration as 263–4; transidiomatic language reflecting 335

digital technologies *see* information and communication technologies

disciplinary space for language-migration interface 1–24; cautions and qualifications for development of 22–3; context-text distinction in 11–12; future methodological developments in 15–18; implications for 18–21; migration and language in 2–4; migration and mobility in 4–5; mixed research methods in 18; mobile research methods in 17; multimodal analysis in 13–14; multisited ethnography in 17; organization of book on 23–4; overview of 1; participatory research methods in 17–18; research and analytical methods in 10–18; scalar analysis in 15–17, 21; spatial orientation in 8–9, 13–15; theoretical shifts in 5–10

displacement 187–204; causes of 189, 190–1; colonialism and 187–8; conflict and 187, 189, 190–1, 192–3, 194, 196, 198–200; definition and description of 187, 211; dis-citizenship with 187, 188; double divide with 188; educational impacts of 196, 197–8, 199–200, 201–2; further reading on 203–4; future research on 201–2; *Guiding Principles on Internal Displacement* on 189; implications of 200–1; internally displaced persons *vs.* refugees 188–9, 191, 202–3; issues and ongoing debates on 191–200; language and 187–204, 211; marginalization and 187–8, 191, 196, 200–1; number of people impacted by 189, 191–2; overview and introduction to 187–91, 202–3; of pastoral peoples of Eastern Africa 190, 196–8, 201–2; 'Protecting Internally Displaced Persons: A Manual for Law and Policymakers' on 193; related topics to 203; resettlement following 192, 199, 200, 201; of San and Khoe peoples of Southern Africa 190, 193–6, 201; shame associated with 195–6; statistics and forecasts on 191–2; superdiversity and 73; vulnerability due to 189, 190, 191

Durkheim, Emile, on social class 136

Early Grade Reading Assessment (EGRA) 530–2

economy: employment issues impacting (*see* employment issues); globalization impacting 55–6, 63 (*see also* globalization); Keynesian theory on 80; language as resource in relation to 171–2, 176, 182, 320–3; migration trajectories seeking improved 209, 210; nation-state *vs.* transnational issues with 55–7, 135, 400–1; neoliberal (*see* neoliberalism); regional flows in search of improved 174; social class and economic resources 136; superdiversity and global 63; trade as element of 229, 258–72, 476; world-systems analysis on 367–9

education: diasporization in relation to 338–9; displacement impacting 196, 197–8, 199–200, 201–2; educational resources for regional flows 178, 180, 181–2, 183; heritage language in 52–3, 54–5, 111–13, 152, 470, 478–9, 480, 481, 525, 526–7, 533, 534; labor-skills classification in relation to 316, 319, 323–4; literacy practices in 422–3; migration for 81, 87–8, 296, 299, 502, 503–4, 507–15; migration trajectories and level of 209; minority population languages in 150, 153, 154, 155–7, 158–9; policies for (*see* educational policies); religion and 197, 200, 202, 283–4, 288, 525; scales theory on linguistic inequality in 376–7; settler migration and settler varieties impacting 251; social class in relation to 137, 141, 145; spatial turn in context of 111–13; superdiversity in 69–70; translanguaging in 33, 112, 497, 528, 534

educational policies: English language 87–8, 90–2, 301–4, 479, 487, 492–4, 502–16; on heritage language 52–3, 54–5, 111–13, 152, 470, 478–9, 480, 481, 525, 526–7, 533, 534; in higher education 296, 299, 502–16; language-in-education 52–3, 54–5, 111–13, 152, 197–8, 199–200, 202, 338–9, 470, 478–9, 480, 481, 486–98, 525, 526–7, 533, 534; neoliberal influences on 81, 86–8, 90–2, 486, 489, 492–4, 496, 497, 524; schooling and 111–13, 376–7, 519–35

employment issues: in call centres 83, 91; communication practices and policies in workplace as 20, 298, 300–7, 540–55; in domestic work 83, 91, 138; flexible workers as 83–4; labor-skills classification as 312–25; language as 19–20, 57–9, 89–90, 91–2, 296–307, 313, 316–17, 320–3, 540–55;

579

low-skilled migration as 56, 57–9, 312–25; migration trajectories based on 210; nation-state *vs.* transnational considerations for 56, 57–9; neoliberal impacts on 81, 83–5, 88–92; skilled migration as 19–20, 56, 57–9, 89–90, 296–307, 312–25, 403–4; social class in relation to 136, 138–9, 140; visas and work permits as 258, 260, 270, 300, 303; workplace mobility as (*see* workplace mobility)

English language policies and practices 502–16; accommodation in 506, 510; communication deficits in 509–10, 514; communication practices and policies in workplace using 20, 545, 551; diasporization and 330, 338; English as lingua franca 12–13, 502, 505–6, 508, 509, 514; entry testing for universities in 512–13; further reading on 516; future research on 514–15; globalization and use of 59, 171–2, 302–3, 502, 503–4; heritage language in relation to 479; higher education internationalization and 502, 503–4, 507–15; implications for 513–14; intercultural communication practices with 507–10; international university language policy impacting 510–13; issues and ongoing debates on 510–13; language-in-education policies on 487, 492–4; language-mediated services including 562, 563, *563–4,* 565–6, 568; language value associated with 171–2, 177–9, 180, 181–3, 212, 218, 219; local context importance for 515; migration trajectories and value of 212, 218, 219; nation-state *vs.* transnational views of 59; neoliberal views on 84, 85, 86–7, 90–2; overview and introduction to 502–10, 515; related topics to 515; religious ties to 287, 288; scales theory on linguistic inequality and 376–7; settler migration and settler varieties influencing 247–8, 249–50, 251, 252, 254; skilled migration and 301–4, 305, 306; social class in relation to 140; space views influencing 108, 110, 112–13; standardized language tests in 84, 86, 303, 512–13; student mobility and non-mobility impacting 506–7; trade migration and use of 267, 269–70

enregisterment 105, 124

Ethiopia, displacement in 190, 196–8, 201–2

ethnolinguistic vitality 217, 219, 249–50, 251–2

European Union: Bologna Process in 87; European Charter for Regional or Minority Languages in 155, 156; Framework Convention for the Protection of National Minorities in 155–6; language-in-education policies in 494; language policy in 541; migration trajectories in 215, 216; neoliberalism in 86, 87; skilled migration in 298, 304; *see also specific countries*

Fiji: indenture in 235, 238; settler migration and settler varieties in 243

Finland, minority populations in 158

flexible citizenship 50

flexible workers 83–4

Foucauldian approach to neoliberalism 81–2, 83, 90

Framework Convention for the Protection of National Minorities 155–6

France: diasporization in 335; English language in education in 513; immigration policies and citizenship in 457–8, 459, 464; language-in-education policies in 489; literacy events in 426; migration trajectories in 213–14; minority populations in 154; narrative analysis of migrants in 386; national language in 48; neccessity-desire intersection for migrants in 441; scales theory and indexicality of context in 371–2; schooling in 529; skilled migration in 298, 301; social class in 138

Friedman, Milton 79

gay individuals *see* LGBTIQ individuals

gender: identities in relation to 125, 126, 145; migration trajectories influenced by 210–11, 217; social class and 145

General Agreement of Trade and Tariffs (GATT) 264

Georgia, displacement in 190

Germany: higher education internationalization in 511; immigration policies and citizenship in 464; language-in-education policies in 489, 491, 492, 495–6; migration trajectories in 216; nationalism in 6, 48; schooling in 529, 532; skilled migration in 298, 301; social class in 138

Ghana, trade migration from/to 265

globalization: diasporization and 336–7; economic impacts of 55–6, 63; English as global language with 59, 171–2, 302–3, 502, 503–4; global diaspora and 70–1; heritage language in relation to 471; language-in-education policies influenced by 487, 492, 494; migration trajectories and 211–13, 220; multisited ethnography influenced by 400–1, 403; narrative analysis influenced by 386, 387; neoliberalism conflation with 80, 87; regional flows and language resources in 171–2; scale-setting as effect of 364, 365, 369, 375; settler migration and settler varieties impacted by 250–1, 253–4; skilled migration impacted by 296, 299; trade migration impacted by 259–60, 264–6; translanguaging in mobility with 31, 32, 36; transnationalism and 47, 49, 51, 53, 55–6, 59–60

governmentality, superdiversity challenges to 67

gradualism 232–3, *233*

Greece: language-in-education policies in 489; migration trajectories in 216, 218; neoliberalism response in 81; social class and migration in 135
Grierson, George 236
groupism 159–60, 350
Guiding Principles on Internal Displacement 189
Guinea: asylum seeker from 354–6; trade migration from/to 265, 269
Guyana, indenture in 235

Haiti, regional flows to/from 177
Haron, Abdullah 282
Hayek, Friedrich von 79, 314
Herder, Johann Gottfried 48
Herderian triad 6, 48, 332
heritage language 468–83; bilingual policy and 477–81; colonialism impacting 468, 469, 470–1, 476; definition and description of 468–9; diasporization and use of 333, 338, 471–2, 475–82; dynamic nature and transformation of 469, 470, 471, 472–4; educational policies on 52–3, 54–5, 111–13, 152, 470, 478–9, 480, 481, 525, 526–7, 533, 534; further reading on 482–3; future research on 481–2; globalization in relation to 471; identity ties to 152, 482; implications of 481–2; indexicality of 52, 54–5, 482; issues and ongoing debates on 469–81; migration trajectories and loss of 219; overview and introduction to 468–9; related topics to 482; rhizomatic analysis of 473–4, 475–81; schooling in relation to 525, 526–7, 533, 534; settler varieties detached from 249, 250; Singapore as context for case study of 471, 474–81; social class impacts of 471; spatial turn in relation to 111–13; "Speak Mandarin" campaign and 478, 479–81; theoretical developments in study of 469–73; trade migration impacts on 476; transnationalism affecting 52–3, 54–5
higher education: English language policies and practices in 502–16; intercultural communication practices in 507–10; internationalization of 296, 299, 502, 503–4, 507–15; skilled migration and 296, 299; *see also* education
homosexuality *see* LGBTIQ individuals
Hong Kong: English language in education in 87; settler migration and settler varieties in 244, 245–6; skilled migration in 300
Hungary, narrative analysis of migrants in 387

identities 117–28; agency and 126, 127; asylum seekers proving 353–6; authenticity of 119–20, 126; being (fixed) to becoming and doing (emerging) 121–4, 125–6; bias associated with 127; binary dichotomies of 120; complexity of 118–21, 126; definition and description of 117; diasporization and 330, 332–6, 337, 338–9, 340–1; displacement impacting 194; enregisterment for analysis of 124; further reading on 128; future research on 127; generational differences in 122; heritage language ties to 152, 482; heritaging or traditionalization of 119; hybridity of 118–19, 126; identities in mobility 117–28, 387, 390; imagination role in shaping 121–2; implications of 126–7; indexical cues to 123–4; inequality considerations with 127; intersectionality of 124–5, 139–40, 142, 144–5; issues and ongoing debates on 125–6; liminality of 118; marginality of 118, 119; membership categorisation device for analysis of 123; migration trajectories's implications for 207–21; multisited ethnography on 403–4; narratives for reflecting and constructing 381, 382–9; national 6, 47, 50, 51, 53, 56, 110, 151–2, 388–9, 487, 488; negotiation for alignment of 122–3, 126; neoliberal views of personhood and 84–5; overview and introduction to 117–25, 127; positioning in relation to 124; related topics to 128; religious beliefs and practices in relation to 275, 278, 279, 284, 288, 289–90; settler migration and settler varieties influencing 248; sexual 125, 432, 433–5; social class in relation to 125, 133–4, 139–40, 142, 144–5; space and ethnolinguistic 108–13; stance in relation to 123–4; strategic emphasis on 122; superdiversity impacting 121, 122, 127
immigration policies 451–65; citizenship and 451–65; Derrida on 456–63, 464; further reading on 465; future research on 464; ideologies associated with 454–5; implementation of, tests for 453–4; implications of 463–4; integration considerations in 452–3, 455; issues and ongoing debates on 456–63; iterability in enforcement of 460–1, 464; labor-skills classification considered in 312, 313, 314–16, 319–20, 324–5; language and 451–64, 561–4; language-mediated services to navigate 561–4; law-justice divide in 458–63; neoliberal influences on 88–92; overview and introduction to 451–6; related topics to 464; religion in relation to 457–8; singularity *vs.* generality of experience under 462–3; symbolic aspects of testing in 456, 461; testing requirements in 451, 452, 453–6, 461, 463, 464; violence imposed by 458–61, 463
indenture *see* slavery and indenture
indexicality: first order 371; heritage language 52, 54–5, 482; identity analysis using 123–4;

581

language resource 179–80; literacy in relation to 417–18; narrative analysis consideration of 385; repertoires as indexical biographies 35–6, 58, 65; of scales theory context 370–3; second order 65, 70, 74, 371–2; superdiversity and 65, 70, 74; translanguaging in mobility and 32, 35–6, 372

India: call centres in 83; diasporization in 234–9, 240, 332–3; displacement in 188; English language in education in 87; higher education internationalization in 504; indenture in 234–9, 240; minority populations in 158; regional flows to/from 175, 177; religious beliefs of migrants in 277; schooling in 520; superdiversity in 72; trade migration from/to 264

Indonesia, trade migration from/to 262, 265

information and communication technologies: complexity of communication including 349, 352–3, 355–60; diasporization impacted by 334; English language use in 502–3; global diaspora and use of 70–1; higher education use of 502–3; identities impacted by 119, 390; language-mediated services in industry of 567–70; literacy events via 415–16, 422, 423; migration trajectories influenced by 220; multisited ethnography on 406–7; narrative analysis via 385, 386, 387, 390, 392; skilled migration and 296, 299; space and language navigated via 111; superdiversity influenced by 63, 67, 70–1, 349; trade migration impacted by 265, 271; transnationalism via 49, 51, 119, 390; *see also* social media

internal displacement *see* displacement

International Labor Organization (ILO) 314–15

International Monetary Fund (IMF): General Agreement of Trade and Tariffs by 264; neoliberalism and 80, 81, 91; trade policies of 264, 265

International Standard Classification of Occupations (ISCO) 315, 316, 319, 324

intersectionality: of identities 124–5, 139–40, 142, 144–5; of necessity and desire 431–45

Iran, English language in education in 87

Iraq, displacement in 190, 192

Ireland, skilled migration in 301

Israel: diasporization in 333; religious beliefs of migrants in 277

Italy: narrative analysis of migrants in 386; neoliberalism in 82; social class and migration in 135

Jamaica: scales theory and indexicality of context in 371; trade migration from/to 264

Japan: English language in education in 302–3, 502; higher education internationalization in 504, 511; identities in mobility in 124; language-in-education policies in 495; narrative analysis of migrants in 387; nationalism in 48; neoliberal views in 84, 87; schooling in 523, 528–9; skilled migration in 297, 300, 302–3, 304, 305; trade migration from/to 262

Jordan: migration trajectories in 217–18; regional flows to/from 177

Kenya: migration trajectories in 212–13; trade migration from/to 264

koine 236–9, *237, 238, 239,* 240, 243–4, 247–9

labor-skills classification 312–25; assumptions based on 313; convertibility of capital or skills for 323–4; defining skills for 316–17; education in relation to 316, 319, 323–4; embodied capital not credited in 323–4; framing migrant as worker through 314–16; further reading on 325; future research on 323–5; immigration policy consideration of 312, 313, 314–16, 319–20, 324–5; implications of 323–5; integration of migrants and 313, 317, 320–3; issues and ongoing debates on 316–23; language and literacy skills assessment in 313, 316–17, 320–3; neoliberal influences on 314, 319–20, 325; overview and introduction to 312–16; self-assessment of skills for 317–20; as social class proxy 324; Taylorization and work management ideas for 313, 314, 316

language-in-education policies 486–98; agency reflected in 487–8; bilingual 491–2, 495–6; bottom-up approach to 487, 495; citizenship connection to 486–7, 488–9, 497; definition and description of 487; diasporic identities and 338–9; displaced persons's concerns with 197–8, 199–200, 202; English language in 487, 492–4 (*see also* English language policies and practices); fixity and 486, 489–92, 497; fluidity and 486, 492–4, 497; further reading on 497–8; future research on 496–7; globalization influencing 487, 492, 494; heritage language in 52–3, 54–5, 111–13, 152, 470, 478–9, 480, 481, 525, 526–7, 533, 534; implications of 495–6; issues and ongoing debates on 489–94; marginalization via 489, 494, 495; nation-state influences on 486–7, 488–92, 497; neoliberal influences on 486, 489, 492–4, 496, 497; non-state actors influencing 496; overview and introduction to 486–9, 497; related topics to 497; testing policies shaping 491–2; transnationalism reflected in 486, 489, 490, 495, 497

language-mediated services 558–73; further reading on 572–3; future research on 571–2; implications of 571; institutional agents's management of 562–3, 564–6, *565,* 568; issues and ongoing debates on 561–70; linguistic regimentation and resistance in 570; migrants's management of 563–4, 566–7, *567,* 568, *569,* 570; monolingualist regimes and translinguistic multilingual users of 561–70; in nongovernmental residential project 564–7; overview and introduction to 558–61; in public administration office 561–4; related topics to 572; in telecommunications world 567–70

language-migration interface: citizenship in (*see* citizenship); complexity in (*see* complexity); diasporization in (*see* diasporization); disciplinary space for (*see* disciplinary space for language-migration interface); displacement in (*see* displacement); educational policies in (*see* educational policies); employment issues in (*see* employment issues); heritage language in (*see* heritage language); identities in (*see* identities); immigration policies in (*see* immigration policies); labor-skills classification in (*see* labor-skills classification); language-mediated services in (*see* language-mediated services); literacy in (*see* literacy); migration trajectories in (*see* migration trajectories); minority populations in (*see* minority populations); mobility in (*see* mobility); multisited ethnography in (*see* multisited ethnography); narrative analysis in (*see* narrative analysis); nation-states in (*see* nation-states); necessity-desire intersection in (*see* neccessity-desire intersection); neoliberalism in (*see* neoliberalism); regional flows in (*see* regional flows); religions in (*see* religious beliefs and practices); research on (*see* research); settler migration and settler varieties in (*see* settler migration and settler varieties); skilled migration in (*see* skilled migration); slavery and indenture in (*see* slavery and indenture); social class in (*see* social class); space in (*see* space); spatiotemporal scales in (*see* scales theory; spatiotemporal scales); superdiversity in (*see* superdiversity); trade migration in (*see* trade migration); translanguaging in mobility in (*see* translanguaging in mobility); transnationalism in (*see* transnationalism); workplace mobility in (*see* workplace mobility)

Lattimore, Owen 264
Lebanon, trade migration from/to 264
LGBTIQ individuals: asylum processes for 433–4; inequality and exclusion issues for 435; language learning by 434; neccessity-desire intersection for 432–8, 441–4
Liberia, displacement in 192

life-cycle theory 231
Linguistic Landscape approaches 106–8
literacy 413–28; disaggregation of migration and 424–6; displaced persons's concerns with 199–200, 202; educational practices of 422–3; entextualisation-recontextualisation for 417; further reading on 427; future research on 426–7; implications of 426–7; in- and out-of-school languages and literacies 524–7; indexicality of 417–18; information and communication technologies and 415–16, 422, 423; issues and ongoing debates on 421–6; labor-skills classification in relation to 316–17; local context of 415; meaning-making trajectories of 418–20, 423; multimodal 428n4; nation-state and rise of 151; New Literacy Studies on 414–16, 418, 421, 423, 425; overview and introduction to 413–21; as placed resource 415–16, 422–3; related topics to 427; resources and repertoires for 420–1, 422; scales theory on linguistic inequality and 376–7, 418–19, 423; sending communities's influences on 425–6; simultaneity in relation to 422; superdiversity and 417, 423, 428n2; trade migration and multi-literacy practices 271; transcontextual analysis of 416–20; translocal/transnational 417–26

low-skilled migration: labor-skills classification for 312–25; language considerations with 57–9; nation-state *vs.* transnational considerations for 56, 57–9

Luxembourg: higher education internationalization in 504; superdiversity in 71

Malawi, regional flows to/from 175
Malaysia: English language in education in 87; trade migration from/to 265
Mali, trade migration from/to 265
A Man of Good Hope (Steinberg) 413, 424, 425, 427n1
marginalization: displacement and 187–8, 191, 196, 200–1; of identities 118, 119; trade migration and 262–3, 270; via language-in-education policies 489, 494, 495
Marxist approach: to neoliberalism 81–3, 90; to social class 135–6, 137, 138
Mauritius: diasporization in 335; indenture in 235, 238; multisited ethnography in 403–4
media, diasporization impacted by 334–6; *see also* information and communication technologies
membership categorisation device (MCD) 123, 385
metrolingualism: language-in-education policies broadened via 497; minority population

multilingual repertoires as 161; regional flows and language resources with 176–7; space intertwined in 106, 108

Mexico: diasporization in 333, 335, 337, 341; displacement in 190, 192; economy of 80; English language in education in 87; language-in-education policies in 490; religious beliefs and language in 288; schooling and indigenous language in 526

migration-language interface *see* language-migration interface

migration trajectories 207–22; assimilation with 218–19; chain migration 216–17; circular migration 213, 214, 215; definition and description of 207–8; ethnolinguistic vitality with 217, 219; family reunification prompting 216–17; further reading on 222; future research in 220–1; gender influences on 210–11, 217; globalization and 211–13, 220; identities impacted by 207–21; implications of 219–20; information and communication technologies influencing 220; issues and ongoing debates on 217–19; language-in-education policies shaping 490; language issues with 207–22, 490; language maintenance with 217–20, 221; neccessity-desire intersection in 432–5; north-north 208–9; north-south 208, 210; number of migrants in 209; overview and introduction to 207–17, 221; people-making with 212; place-making with 212; related topics to 221; religious ties in 218; return migration 213–14; rural-urban 174, 177, 180–2, 208–13, 215, 217, 433, 490; south-north 208–13, 214, 217, 219; south-south 208–10, 215; step migration 215–16, 220; superdiversity and 220; *see also* regional flows

minority populations 149–64; citizenship issues for 149–53; displacement of 73, 187–204; education in native languages of 150, 153, 154, 155–7, 158–9; ethnic minorities in 149, 152, 156–9; external protections for 160; further reading on 163–4; future research on 160–3; "groupism" problem for 159–60; human rights *vs.* language rights of 153–4; ideology of contempt for languages of 152–3; implications for 163; indigenous peoples in 149, 154, 155, 158; internal restrictions in 160; international law on language rights of 153–9; issues and ongoing debates on 153–60; language issues for 149–64; linguistic homogeneity and 151–3; multilingual repertoires of 161–3; national minorities in 149, 154–6, 157, 158; overview and introduction to 149–53; polyethnic rights of 157; reasonableness requirements for rights of 157–8; related topics to 163; self-government rights of 157; significant and sufficient criteria for 157–8; superdiversity considerations for 149, 159, 160–3

mobility: identities in 117–28, 387, 390; migration distinction from 4–5; schooling, language and 519–35; superdiversity impacted by 66–7; translanguaging in (*see* translanguaging in mobility); workplace (*see* workplace mobility)

Morocco, diasporization in 338

multisited ethnography 17, 397–408; bias management in 405; boundary-making practices in 398; contemporary roots of 399–400; definition and description of 17, 397; following language strategy in 398–9, 401–7; further reading on 407–8; future research on 406–7; globalization influencing 400–1, 403; identity and skill considered in 403–4; implications of 401–6; information and communication technologies considered in 406–7; issues and ongoing debates on 400–1; overview and introduction to 397–400, 407; participatory method of 405–6; related topics to 407; sites and context defined and determined for 402–3; superdiversity considered in 403; transnational and methodological nationalism in 400–1; triangulation technique in 404–5

Namibia: displacement in 193, 194; trade migration from/to 258, 268–71

narrative analysis 381–93; agency considered in 384, 385, 387, 388; Critical Discourse Analysis as 388; further reading on 392–3; future research on 392; globalization influencing 386, 387; identities and representations in 381, 382–9; implications of 391–2; indexical elements in 385; information and communication technologies in 385, 386, 387, 390, 392; issues and ongoing debates on 390–1; migrants as community members in 385–7; migrants as language learners in 383–5; migrants as subject of narrative in 388–9; nationalism and national identity as context for 388–9; overview and introduction to 381–90, 392; positioning in 384; related topics to 392; stories distinction from narrative in 381–2; storytelling as practice in 389–90; time-space orientation of narratives 386; transnationalism considered in 387, 390

Natal, indenture in 235

nationalism: language-in-education policies supporting 488; literacy and polarization with 424; methodological 10, 349, 401; multisited ethnography on 401; narrative analysis in context of 388–9; nation-state promotion of 6, 48–9, 151–2; religious beliefs and practices ties to 283–4 nation-states 47–61; citizenship in 50, 53–4, 56–7, 68, 110, 149–53, 339, 486–7, 488–9; definition and description of 48; deterritorialized culture not specific to 49–50, 51–2; diasporization and ties to 332, 338, 339; displacement within 73, 187–204; economic considerations for 55–7, 401; education controlled by (*see* education); further reading on 60–1; future research on 57–9; governmentality challenges for 67; heritage language education in 52–3, 54–5; immigration policies of (*see* immigration policies); implications of transnationalism for 53–7; issues and ongoing debates on 51–3; language and 47–9, 50, 51–7, 59, 68, 149–64, 338–9, 486–7, 488–92, 497, 559, 561–4; language-in-education policies of 486–7, 488–92, 497; language-mediated services by 559, 561–4; language testing for citizenship in 54, 68, 150, 339; linguistic homogeneity and 151–3; minority populations in 149–64; multisited ethnography on 401, 404; national identity tied to 6, 47, 50, 51, 53, 56, 110, 151–2, 388–9, 487, 488; nationalism in 6, 10, 48–9, 151–2, 283–4, 349, 388–9, 401, 424, 488; national or official language of 6, 48, 49, 52, 53–4, 59, 149–53, 158, 338, 404, 486–7, 488–92, 497, 540, 541; overview of issues facing 47–50, 59–60; premodern *vs.* modern 151–2; regional flows to/from 171–84; related topics to 60; skilled *vs.* low-skilled migration to 56, 57–8; social class considerations in 57–9; superdiversity considerations for 54, 67, 68–70; trade migration crossing borders of 259; transidiomatic *vs.* national language in 51–3, 55; transnationalism and challenges to 6, 47, 49–50; world-systems analysis on 368, 369

neccessity-desire intersection 431–45; asylum processes and 433–4; beyond heteronormative frame for understanding 436–8; definition and description of 431–2; emotion in 431–2, 435–44; exceptionality perspective in 440; films documenting 443–4; further reading on 445; future research on 444; heterosexual migrants's 438–42; implications of 444; inequality and exclusion consideration in 434–5; issues and ongoing debates on 435; language learning in 434; LGBTIQ migrants's 432–8, 441–4; overview and introduction to 431–2; related topics to 445; research methodologies for 442–4; sexuality in 431–44; spatial trajectories of migration in 432–5

neighborhoods: conviviality and superdiversity in 70; social class and types of 137

neoliberalism 79–94; Canada's policy influenced by 83, 86, 88–90; citizenship and 85–8, 90; consumerism and 85; educational policy influenced by 81, 86–8, 90–2, 486, 489, 492–4, 496, 497, 524; employment issues impacted by 81, 83–5, 88–92; Foucauldian approach to 81–3, 90; further reading on 94; future research on 92–3; globalization, late capitalism and 80, 87; immigration policies influenced by 88–92; implications of 88–92; integration goals in 85–6; issues and ongoing debates on 81–8; labor-skills classification influenced by 314, 319–20, 325; labour and personhood in 83–5; language, migration, and 3, 23, 79–94; language-in-education policies influenced by 486, 489, 492–4, 496, 497; legitimation of inequity in 82; Marxist approach to 81–3, 90; materiality considerations with 82–3; overview of 79–81, 93–4; Philippines's policy influenced by 83, 88, 90–2; related topics to 94; roll-out 81; in sociolinguistics and applied linguistics 79–80, 82–8, 93; value of language in 83

Netherlands, the: immigration policies and citizenship in 452, 453, 454; narrative analysis of migrants in 388; skilled migration in 301; superdiversity in 74

New Zealand: English language in education in 303–4; higher education internationalization in 504; literacy events in 419, 420–1; minority populations in 158–9, 164n4; narrative analysis of migrants in 384–5; neoliberal views in 84; settler migration and settler varieties in 243, 245, 246; skilled migration in 298, 300, 303–4, 305

Nigeria: displacement in 192; religious beliefs and language in 288; trade migration from/to 270

Normal (film) 443

Norway: identities in mobility in 122; immigration policies and citizenship in 464; skilled migration in 301; space and language in 111

online communication *see* information and communication technologies

Pakistan, displacement in 192

Paraguay, settler migration and settler varieties in 246, 249–50, 252

Philippines: call centres in 83, 91; English language in education in 88, 90–2, 493–4; immigration policies in 88, 90–2; language-in-education policies in 493–4; neoliberal influences in 83, 88, 90–2; regional flows to/from 177; skilled migration in 297, 299–300, 301–2, 304, 305

pidgins, creoles and jargon 230–4, 239, 240, 266–8

place: deterritorialization of 109–11; Linguistic Landscape approaches to 106–8; literacies as placed resource 415–16, 422–3; migration trajectories and place-making 212; nexus analysis of 106; regional dialectology focus on 104; reterritorialization of 111; scales theory deemphasizing 374; scapes *vs.* 107–8, 111; schooling situated in 522–4; space *vs.* 6–7, 35, 103; territorialization of 108–9; variationist sociolinguistic frameworks for 104–5

policies: educational (*see* educational policies); heritage language (*see* heritage language); immigration (*see* immigration policies); language-mediated service 558–73; superdiversity focus influencing 74–5; workplace communication 20, 298, 300–7, 540–55

Portugal: migration trajectories in 213–14; slavery and language in 239–40; social class and migration in 135

positioning 124, 384

Programme for International Student Assessment (PISA) 531–2

'Protecting Internally Displaced Persons: A Manual for Law and Policymakers' 193

Puerto Rico: diasporization in 332, 333, 337; migration trajectories in 214

queer individuals *see* LGBTIQ individuals

race: ethnicization, racialization and diasporization 340; identities in relation to 125, 126, 127, 145; narrative representations of 386, 387, 388; new racism 543; social class and 145

regional dialectology 104

regional flows 171–84; continental 179–80; definition and description of 173–5; educational resources for 178, 180, 181–2, 183; further reading on 184; future research on 183; implications for 182–3; international 178–9; issues and ongoing debates on 178–82; language loss due to 179, 182, 183; language resources within 171–3, 175–84; metrolingualism and 176–7; national 180–2; North-North migration as 174; North-South migration as 174–5, 178; overview and introduction to 171–8, 183–4; related topics to 184; rural-urban migration as 174, 177, 180–2; South-North migration as 174, 177, 180–2; South-South migration as 174, 179–83; superdiversity and 176–7; value of language within 171, 176–84; *see also* migration trajectories

religious beliefs and practices 275–90; colonialism impacts on 277–8, 280–7; complexity of 277; demographics of 276–7; diasporization and 279–80, 289, 335; displacement due to conflict over 191; education and 197, 200, 202, 283–4, 288, 525; further reading on 290; future research on 286–9; historic change in host societies due to 280–6, 289–90; identities in relation to 275, 278, 279, 284, 288, 289–90; immigration policies and citizenship in relation to 457–8; implications of 286–9; issues and ongoing debates on 277–86; migration, language and 275–90; migration trajectories and ties to 218; missionaries espousing 280, 283–7, 288; overview and introduction to 275–7, 289–90; related topics to 290; rhizomatic analysis of 275–6, 287; slavery and migration of 280–3; socio-political ideologies and 276–90

repertoires: displaced persons's 188, 191, 198–9, 200–1, 202; language resources including 172–3; literacy using 420–1, 422; migration trajectories and value of 207–8, 210, 214, 219; multilingual 161–3, 268–70, 271; nation-state *vs.* transnational views of 58; polyglot 173; scales theory on value of 365, 373; spatial 9, 36, 107–8, 109; superdiversity and 65, 66, 69, 70, 72; in translanguaging in mobility 35–6, 41, 172–3; truncated 173

research: on complexity 349–61; disciplinary methodologies for 10–18; future (*see under specific topics*); on literacy 413–28; multisited ethnography as 397–408; narrative analysis as 381–93; on neccessity-desire intersection 431–45; on spatiotemporal scales 364–78

return migration 213–14

rhizomatic analysis: of heritage language 473–4, 475–81; of religious beliefs and practices 275–6, 287

Russia, neoliberal views in 84

Rwanda: diasporization in 339; displacement in 192

same-sex relationships *see* LGBTIQ individuals

Samira (film) 443–4

Saudi Arabia, religious beliefs of migrants in 277

scales theory: disciplinary applications for 15–17, 21; further reading on 378; future research on 376–8; globalization effects in 364, 365, 369, 375; implications of 376–8; indexicality of context in 370–3; issues and ongoing debates on 374–6; layering of sociolinguistic and discursive phenomena in 364–5; literacy in terms of 376–7, 418–19, 423; overview and introduction to 364–73; related topics to 378; in sociolinguistics 369–70; spatial turn in 366–7, 369; spatiotemporal scales in 15–17, 364–78, 418–19, 423; transnational perspective *vs.*

377; value of linguistic resources in 365, 370, 373; world-systems analysis and 364, 367–9, 373, 374–5

schooling 519–35; ecology of *521,* 521–2; further reading on 534–5; future research on 533–4; implications of 532–3; in- and out-of-school languages and literacies 524–7; issues and ongoing debates on 522–32; local/indigenous languages and literacy in relation to 525, 526–7, 533, 534; mobility, language and 519–35; neoliberal influences on 524; overview and introduction to 519–22; place and situated nature of 522–4; program models and curricular design for 527–30; related topics to 534; religious- or faith-based 525; scales theory on linguistic inequality in 376–7; sociocultural and social justice perspectives on 520–1; spaces of learning including 524–6; spatial turn in context of 111–13; standards and assessments in 530–2; translanguaging in 528, 534; *see also* education

services, language-mediated *see* language-mediated services

settler migration and settler varieties 243–55; contact-derived dialects or koine developed from 243–4, 247–9; definition and description of 243–4; degree of contact with other populations impacting 246, 247, 249; demographic influences on 249–50, 252; diasporization and 252–3; directionality of voyages impacting 245–6, 252–3; Dynamic Model on 247–9; educational issues with 251; ethnolinguistic vitality influencing 249–50, 251–2; forced *vs.* voluntary migration as 245; formation and maintenance of 246–7; further reading on 255; future research on 253–4; globalization impacting 250–1, 253–4; identities influenced by 248; implications of 250–3; institutional support for 249, 252; issues and ongoing debates on 246–50; language islands in 246, 249, 252; multiethnolectalization of 251–2, 253–4; overview and introduction to 243–6, 254–5; relocation-diffusion with 244; status of 249, 250, 252; timing or waves of 247

sexuality: identities in relation to 125, 432, 433–5; neccessity-desire intersection in relation to 431–44; *see also* LGBTIQ individuals

Sierra Leone, displacement in 192

simultaneity 2, 67, 74, 422

Singapore: citizenship in 476; English language in education in 87, 88, 301, 479; heritage language in 471, 474–81; higher education in 296, 299; identities in mobility in 125; language policies in 478–81; migration trajectories in 212; religious beliefs and language in 287; skilled migration in 297, 299, 301, 305; "Speak Mandarin" campaign in 478, 479–81

skilled migration 296–307; brain drain from 317; causes of 296, 298; citizenship and 56; colonialism ties to 296, 298–9; definition of 298; English as lingua franca for 301–4, 305, 306; further reading on 307; future research on 306–7; globalization impacting 296, 299; historical development of 297–300; implications of monolingual policy for 306; internationalization of higher education impacting 296, 299; issues and ongoing debates on 304–6; labor-skills classification for 312–25; language considerations with 19–20, 57–9, 89–90, 296–307; low-skilled migration *vs.* (*see* low-skilled migration); multilingualism benefits for 305–7; multisited ethnography on 403–4; nation-state *vs.* transnational considerations for 56, 57–9; neoliberal influences on 89–90; overview and introduction to 296–304, 307; related topics to 307; terminology related to 297; visas and work permits for 300, 303; workplace language policies and practices affecting 298, 300–7

slavery and indenture 228–41; anti-exceptionalism *vs.* exceptionalism on language with 233–4; bioprogramme theory on language with 231–2; further reading on 241; future research on 240; gradualism on language with 232–3, *233*; implications of 239–40; indenture, specifically 228, 234–9; issues and ongoing debates on 230–4, 235–9; koine or high contact languages arising from 236–9, *237, 238, 239,* 240; language and 228–41; life-cycle theory on language with 231; overview and introduction to 228–30, 234–5; pidgins and creoles arising from 230–4, 239, 240; related topics to 240; religious beliefs and practices migrating with 280–3; slavery, specifically 228–34; slave trade for 229, 261–2

Slovak Republic, neoliberal views in 84

social class 133–46; behaviour in 137; constellation of interrelated dimensions model of 136–7, 141–2; critical realist perspective on 143–4; declassing from 134, 140; economic resources in 136; education in relation to 137, 141, 145; employment in relation to 136, 138–9, 140; further reading on 146; future research on 144–5; heritage language impacts on 471; identity in relation to 125, 133–4, 139–40, 142, 144–5; implications of 143–4; inequality recognition and redistribution with 142–3; issues and ongoing debates on 141–3;

labor-skills classification as proxy for 324; language and 133, 139–41; life conditions in 137; in migration, identity, and language research 133, 139–45; in migration research 137–9, 141–3; nation-state *vs.* transnational considerations of 57–9, 134–5, 141; overview and introduction to 133–41, 145; political economy perspective on 135, 137–8, 139, 143, 144, 145; reclassing to 134, 140; related topics to 146; scholarly conceptualizations of 135–6, 137, 138; sociocultural resources in 136–7; spatial conditions in 137; traders's 262; vertical mobility via 5

social media: scales theory on language choices on 377; trade migration and use of 271; transnationalism via 49; *see also* information and communication technologies

social network theory 104–5, 111

Somalia, displacement in 192

South Africa: displacement in 193, 194–6, 201; English language in education in 87, 164n2, 183; indenture and language in 234–9, 240; labor-skills classification in 315, 316–17; literacy events in 419–20; migration trajectories in 209, 212, 215; minority populations in 160, 164nn1–2; regional flows and language resources in 178–83; religious beliefs and language in 278, 280–3; scales theory on educational linguistic inequality in 376–7; settler migration and settler varieties in 243, 244, 254; trade migration from/to 258, 268

South Korea: diasporization in 334; English language in education in 87, 88, 110, 302; *han* in 285; higher education internationalization in 504; nationalism in 48, 283–4; religious beliefs and language in 280, 283–6; skilled migration in 297, 300, 302, 305; space and language in 110–11

South Sudan, displacement in 190, 192, 198–200

space 102–14; associational view of 107; chronotopes as timespace 34–5, 340–1, 386; deterritorialization of 109–11; diasporization spatial frame 110, 339, 340–1; disciplinary, for language-migration interface 1–24; ethnolinguistic identities and 108–13; fixity-fluidity spectrum in 108–9; further reading on 114; future research in 113; implications of 111–13; issues and ongoing debates on 108–11; language and 8–9, 13–15, 102–14, 208; Linguistic Landscape approaches to 106–8; metrolingualism in 106, 108; migration trajectories through 208, 432–5; narrative time-space orientation 386; nexus analysis of 106; overview and introduction to 102–8, 113–14; place *vs.* 6–7, 35, 103; regional dialectology focus on 104; related topics to 114; reterritorialization of 111; scapes in 107–8, 111; schooling as context for 111–13, 524–6; social construction of 102–3, 106; social network theory on 104–5, 111; spaces of learning 524–6; spatial conditions in social class 137; spatial repertoires 9, 36, 107–8, 109; spatial trajectories of migration 208, 432–5; spatial turn 102–14, 366–7, 369; spatiotemporal scales 15–17, 364–78, 418–19, 423; superdiversity of 65, 106, 108; territorialization of 108–9; Thirdspace concept 103, 387; triadic views of 102, 103; urban 36, 65, 102–3, 174, 177, 180–2, 208–13, 215, 217, 433, 490; variationist sociolinguistic frameworks for 104–5

Spain: diasporization in 335; identities in mobility in 125; language-in-education policies in 489, 490, 492, 494; language-mediated services in 559, 561–70; minority populations in 154, 157; multisited ethnography in 401; narrative analysis of migrants in 387; neccessity-desire intersection for migrants in 437; neoliberalism in 86; regional flows to/from 177–8; schooling in 525, 529; slavery and language in 239; social class and migration in 135, 139, 144–5

spatiotemporal scales 15–17, 364–78, 418–19, 423

Sri Lanka: diasporization in 332–3; space and language in 110

stance 123–4

step migration 215–16, 220

Sudan: displacement in 192; migration trajectories in 218–19

superdiversity 63–76; asylum seeker interviews and issues of 68–9; colonialism and indigenous contexts for 72–3; community concept with 2, 74; complexity and 67, 68, 73, 74, 349–50, 352, 360; controversies over term 71–3; convivial 70, 106, 108; definition and description of 63–4, 349; diasporization and 70–1, 331, 336–7; displacement and 73; further reading on 76; future research on 74, 75; governmentality challenges of 67; identities impacted by 121, 122, 127; implications of 73–5; indexicality (second order) and 65, 70, 74; individual *vs.* community patterns of 67–8; information and communication technologies impacting 63, 67, 70–1, 349; issues and ongoing debates on 68–73; language and 63–76; literacy and 417, 423, 428n2; migration trajectories and 220; minority population considerations of 149, 159, 160–3; mobility impacting 66–7; multisited ethnography on 403; nation-state *vs.* transnational issues with 54, 67, 68–70; in neighborhoods 70; overview of 64–8,

75; regional flows and language resources with 176–7; related topics to 75; repertoires and 65, 66, 69, 70, 72; in schools 69–70; of shared social space 65, 106, 108; simultaneity lens for 67, 74; state-controlled practices impacting 68–70; translanguaging in mobility and 32, 65; unpredictability impacting 67, 68–9

Suriname, indenture in 235

Sweden: identities in mobility in 121; immigration policies and citizenship in 464; language in 52, 54; migration trajectories in 216; narrative analysis of migrants in 389–90

Switzerland: higher education internationalization in 504; neccessity-desire intersection for migrants in 441; social class in 138

Syria, displacement in 190, 192

Taiwan, skilled migration in 300

Tanzania: space and language in 109; trade migration from/to 264

Taylor, Frederick Winslow 314

Taylorization 313, 314, 316

technology *see* information and communication technologies

Thailand: language-in-education policies in 490; trade migration from/to 265

Thirdspace concept 103, 387

time: chronotopes as timespace 34–5, 340–1, 386; diasporization temporal frame 339, 340–1; narrative time-space orientation 386; spatiotemporal scales of 15–17, 364–78, 418–19, 423; time scales for migration trajectories 208; timing of settler migration 247

trade migration 258–72; definition and description of 259; familial roles in 263; further reading on 272; future research on 270–1; General Agreement of Trade and Tariffs on 264; globalization impacting 259–60, 264–6; grassroots multilingualism with 258, 260, 268–70, 271; heritage language impacted by 476; hierarchy of players in 263; historical patterns of 261–4, 265, 266, 270; implications of 270; intellectual property laws impacting 264–5; issues and ongoing debates on 266–70; language and 258, 260, 266–70, 271; lingua franca, pidgins, and jargon with 266–8; marginalization and 262–3, 270; overview and introduction to 258–66; private *vs.* public 261–4, 265; related topics to 271; risk-reward trade-off with 261; slave trade in 229, 261–2; stationed *vs.* transient traders in 258, 260, 263; terminology related to 259; trade communities and 263–4, 264–6, 270–1; visas, work permits and residency permits for 258, 260, 270

transgender individuals *see* LGBTIQ individuals

transidiomatic language 51–3, 55, 335

translanguaging in mobility 31–44; assimilation process for 37; case illustration of 37–42; chronotopes and 34–5; code-switching and 32, 33, 173, 372; communicative repertoires in 35–6, 41, 172–3; definition and description of 33–4; educational contexts for 33, 112, 497, 528, 534; further reading on 43–4; future research on 42–3; ideological becoming, emergence and 36–7, 40, 41–2; implications of 41–2; issues and ongoing debates on 36–40; language-in-education policies broadened via 497; language resources for 7–8, 172–3; minority population multilingual repertoires as 161; overview of 31–6, 43; place *vs.* space in 35; related topics to 43; superdiversity and 32, 65; terminology related to 32–3; voice and 36, 37, 40

transnationalism 47–61; citizenship impacted by 50, 53–4, 56–7; definition and description of 49, 134–5; deterritorialized culture with 49–50, 51–2; diasporization and 330, 331, 335; economic considerations with 55–7, 135, 400–1; further reading on 60–1; future research on 57–9; globalization and 47, 49, 51, 53, 55–6, 59–60; heritage language education impacted by 52–3, 54–5; identities in mobility due to 117–28, 387, 390; implications of, for nation-states 53–7; issues and ongoing debates on 51–3; language affected by 50, 51–7; language-in-education policies reflecting 486, 489, 490, 495, 497; multisited ethnography on 400–1; nation-state challenges from 6, 47, 49–50; overview of impacts of 47–50, 59–60; related topics to 60; scales theory *vs.* transnational perspective 377; skilled *vs.* low-skilled migration with 56, 57–8; social class considerations with 57–9, 134–5, 141; transidiomatic language reflecting 51–3, 55, 335; transnational literacies 417–26

Trinidad, indenture in 235

Turkey: English language in education in 87; migration trajectories in 216

Uganda: displacement in 190, 192, 198–200, 201, 202; settler migration and settler varieties in 252; trade migration from/to 264

Ukraine: displacement in 211; migration trajectories in 210–11, 212, 213

United Arab Emirates: neccessity-desire intersection for migrants in 435–6; trade migration from/to 265

United Kingdom: call centres in 83; diasporization in 333, 339; English language in education in 507, 508, 513; heritage

589

language in 54–5, 471–2; higher education internationalization in *504,* 504–5, 507, 508; identities in mobility in 122, 123–4, 127; immigration policies and citizenship in 452, 453–4, 455, 456, 461, 463, 464; labor-skills classification in 314; language-in-education policies in 489, 494; literacy events in 422, 423; migration trajectories in 209, 213, 220; minority populations in 154; narrative analysis of migrants in 386, 390; neccessity-desire intersection for migrants in 437–8; neoliberalism in 83, 86; regional flows to/from 175, 176, 177; settler migration and settler varieties in 246, 251, 252–4; skilled migration in 298–9, 301, 317; social class in 138–9, 140; space and language in 104–5, 109–10, 111–13; superdiversity in 63, 69–70; translanguaging case illustration from 37–42

United Nations Declaration on the Rights of Indigenous Peoples (UNDRIP) 155

United Nations Declaration on the Rights of Persons Belonging to National or Ethnic or Religious Minorities 154–5

United Nations High Commissioner for Refugees (UNHCR) 189

United Nations Universal Declaration of Human Rights (UDHR) 153–4

United States: diasporization in 330, 333–4, 335, 337, 338, 340, 341, 475; economy of 80; English language in education in 507, 508; heritage language in 469, 470, 471–2, 474, 475; higher education internationalization in 504, *504,* 507, 508; identities in mobility in 119–20, 124, 125, 126, 127; immigration policies and citizenship in 90, 463; labor-skills classification in 314, 317; language-in-education policies in 489, 490–1, 496; literacy events in 422, 423, 425; migration trajectories in 214, 219; minority populations in 150, 154; multisited ethnography in 402–3; narrative analysis of migrants in 384, 385–6, 390; neccessity-desire intersection for migrants in 443; regional flows to/from 175; religious beliefs and language in 277, 279, 289; schooling in 522, 524–5, 531; settler migration and settler varieties in 245, 249, 252; skilled migration in 58, 298, 301, 317; social class in 133; space and language in 105, 108, 109, 110, 111, 112; superdiversity in 73; trade migration from/to 264, 265

university education *see* higher education

unpredictability, superdiversity impacted by 67, 68–9

urban space: rural-urban migration to 174, 177, 180–2, 208–13, 215, 217, 433, 490; social construction of 102–3; spatial repertoires in 36; superdiversity in 65

Uruguay: English language in education in 87, 92; neoliberalism response in 81, 87, 92

visas and work permits 258, 260, 270, 300, 303

voice: complexity of multi-voiced dialogues 351, 353, 357–8; displacement impacting 191; narrative analysis of 383; translanguaging in mobility and 36, 37, 40

Weber, Max, on social class 136, 137, 138

workplace mobility: communication practices and policies in 20, 298, 300–7, 540–55; labor-skills classification in 312–25; language issues in 19–20, 57–9, 89–90, 91–2, 296–307, 313, 316–17, 320–3, 540–55; low-skilled migration as 56, 57–9, 312–25; nation-state *vs.* transnational considerations for 56, 57–9; neoliberal impacts on 81, 83–5, 88–92; skilled migration as 19–20, 56, 57–9, 89–90, 296–307, 312–25, 403–4; visas and work permits for 258, 260, 270, 300, 303; *see also* employment issues

World Bank 80, 91, 264

world-systems analysis (WSA) 364, 367–9, 373, 374–5

World Trade Organization (WTO) 258, 264, 265

Yun Gil-jun 284

Zambia, regional flows to/from 175

Zimbabwe: migration trajectories in 209, 215; regional flows to/from 175, 179–80